Volume 2 Chapters 12–25

19 edition

Fundamental Accounting Principles

John J. Wild
University of Wisconsin at Madison

Ken W. Shaw
University of Missouri at Columbia

Barbara Chiappetta
Nassau Community College

Boston Burr Ridge, IL Dubuque, IA New York
San Francisco St. Louis Bangkok Bogotá Caracas Kuala Lumpur
Lisbon London Madrid Mexico City Milan Montreal New Delhi
Santiago Seoul Singapore Sydney Taipei Toronto

To my wife **Gail** and children, **Kimberly, Jonathan, Stephanie,** and **Trevor.**
To my wife **Linda** and children, **Erin, Emily,** and **Jacob.**
To my husband **Bob,** my sons **Michael** and **David,** and my **mother.**

McGraw-Hill Irwin

FUNDAMENTAL ACCOUNTING PRINCIPLES
Published by McGraw-Hill/Irwin, a business unit of The McGraw-Hill Companies, Inc., 1221 Avenue of the Americas, New York, NY, 10020.

This book is printed on acid-free paper.

1 2 3 4 5 6 7 8 9 0 DOW/DOW 0 9 8

ISBN-13: 978-0-07-337954-8 (combined edition)
ISBN-10: 0-07-337954-9 (combined edition)
ISBN-13: 978-0-07-336629-6 (volume 1, chapters 1–12)
ISBN-10: 0-07-336629-3 (volume 1, chapters 1–12)
ISBN-13: 978-0-07-336628-9 (volume 2, chapters 12–25)
ISBN-10: 0-07-336628-5 (volume 2, chapters 12–25)
ISBN-13: 978-0-07-336630-2 (with working papers volume 1, chapters 1–12)
ISBN-10: 0-07-336630-7 (with working papers volume 1, chapters 1–12)
ISBN-13: 978-0-07-336631-9 (with working papers volume 2, chapters 12–25)
ISBN-10: 0-07-336631-5 (with working papers volume 2, chapters 12–25)
ISBN-13: 978-0-07-336627-2 (principles, chapters 1–17)
ISBN-10: 0-07-336627-7 (principles, chapters 1–17)

Vice president and editor-in-chief: *Brent Gordon*
Editorial director: *Stewart Mattson*
Publisher: *Tim Vertovec*
Executive editor: *Steve Schuetz*
Senior developmental editor: *Christina A. Sanders*
Executive marketing manager: *Sankha Basu*
Managing editor: *Lori Koetters*
Full service project manager: *Sharon Monday®, Aptara, Inc.*
Lead production supervisor: *Carol A. Bielski*
Lead designer: *Matthew Baldwin*
Senior photo research coordinator: *Lori Kramer*
Photo researcher: *Sarah Evertson*
Lead media project manager: *Brian Nacik*
Cover and interior design: *Matthew Baldwin*
Cover photo: *© Photolibrary*
Typeface: *10.5/12 Times Roman*
Compositor: *Aptara®, Inc.*
Printer: *R. R. Donnelley*

The Library of Congress has cataloged the single volume edition of this work as follows

Wild, John J.
Fundamental accounting principles / John J. Wild, Ken W. Shaw, Barbara Chiappetta.—19 ed.
p. cm.
Includes index.
ISBN-13: 978-0-07-337954-8 (combined edition : alk. paper)
ISBN-10: 0-07-337954-9 (combined edition : alk. paper)
ISBN-13: 978-0-07-336629-6 (volume 1 ch. 1–12 : alk. paper)
ISBN-10: 0-07-336629-3 (volume 1 ch. 1–12 : alk. paper)
[etc.]
1. Accounting. I. Shaw, Ken W. II. Chiappetta, Barbara. III. Title.
HF5635.P975 2009
657—dc22

2008035921

www.mhhe.com

Dear Colleagues/Friends,

As we roll out the new edition of *Fundamental Accounting Principles*, we thank each of you who provided suggestions to enrich this textbook. As teachers, we know how important it is to select the right book for our course. This new edition reflects the advice and wisdom of many dedicated reviewers, focus group participants, students, and instructors. Our book consistently rates number one in customer loyalty because of you. Together, we have created the most readable, concise, current, accurate, and innovative accounting book available today.

We are thrilled to welcome Ken Shaw to the *Fundamental Accounting Principles* team with this edition. Ken's teaching and work experience, along with his enthusiasm and dedication to students, fit nicely with our continuing commitment to develop cutting–edge classroom materials for instructors and students.

Throughout the writing process, we steered this book in the manner you directed. This path of development enhanced this book's technology and content, and guided its clear and concise writing.

Reviewers, instructors, and students say this book's enhanced technology caters to different learning styles and helps students better understand accounting. *Homework Manager Plus* offers new features to improve student learning and to assist instructor grading. Our *iPod* content lets students study on the go, while our *Algorithmic Test Bank* provides an infinite variety of exam problems. You and your students will find all these tools easy to apply.

We owe the success of this book to our colleagues who graciously took time to help us focus on the changing needs of today's instructors and students. We feel fortunate to have witnessed our profession's extraordinary devotion to teaching. Your feedback and suggestions are reflected in everything we write. Please accept our heartfelt thanks for your dedication in helping today's students understand and appreciate accounting.

With kindest regards,

John J. Wild   *Ken W. Shaw*   *Barbara Chiappetta*

#1 with Customers

Fundamental Accounting Principles rates #1 in Instructor and Student satisfaction over the prior three editions, and we are now proud to report that both independent research and development reviews show that *Fundamental Accounting Principles* is now #1 in customer loyalty!

#1 CUSTOMER LOYALTY

#1 in Accuracy

#1 in Assignments

#1 in Topic Coverage

#1 in Supplements

#1 in Readability

#1 in Organization

#1 in Overall Textbook Satisfaction

With ratings such as these, it is no surprise that *Fundamental Accounting Principles* is the fastest growing textbook in the accounting principles market. Take a look at **what instructors are saying** about *Fundamental Accounting Principles.*

Ken Coffey, Johnson County Community College
"There is nothing about this text that I do not like. We have been using it since I started teaching the course in 1971. We switched texts three times, but always went back to this one and I do not think we will try anything else."

Linda Rose, Westwood College
"Very thorough, readable, and graphically pleasant! Engages students in a variety of activities that create learning opportunities and [...link] materials to real-work scenarios and situations. End-of-chapter materials are engaging learning tools and broaden the learner's opportunity to practice and enhance retention of the chapter content."

Shafi Ullah, Broward CC
"The book contains detailed information with alternative exercises, problems, and cases with 'Beyond the Numbers'."

Marilyn Cilolino, Delgado CC
"I have always been a big fan of this book and praise it every chance I get. The authors are great people and are really concerned with their product. They listened to the instructors and take our comments and suggestions seriously. And they are always ready to help or answer any questions one might have."

Gloria Worthy, Southwest Tennessee CC
"FAP is a very good text and it is also good for our students because it addresses a variety of learning styles"

Phillip Lee, Nashville State Tech CC
"The Wild text packs more useful material into fewer pages than other principles of accounting textbooks."

John J. Wild is a distinguished professor of accounting at the University of Wisconsin at Madison. He previously held appointments at Michigan State University and the University of Manchester in England. He received his BBA, MS, and PhD from the University of Wisconsin.

Professor Wild teaches accounting courses at both the undergraduate and graduate levels. He has received numerous teaching honors, including the Mabel W. Chipman Excellence-in-Teaching Award, the departmental Excellence-in-Teaching Award, and the Teaching Excellence Award from the 2003 and 2005 business graduates at the University of Wisconsin. He also received the Beta Alpha Psi and Roland F. Salmonson Excellence-in-Teaching Award from Michigan State University. Professor Wild has received several research honors and is a past KPMG Peat Marwick National Fellow and is a recipient of fellowships from the American Accounting Association and the Ernst and Young Foundation.

Professor Wild is an active member of the American Accounting Association and its sections. He has served on several committees of these organizations, including the Outstanding Accounting Educator Award, Wildman Award, National Program Advisory, Publications, and Research Committees. Professor Wild is author of *Financial Accounting, Managerial Accounting,* and *College Accounting*, each published by McGraw-Hill/Irwin. His research articles on accounting and analysis appear in The Accounting Review, Journal of Accounting Research, Journal of Accounting and Economics, Contemporary Accounting Research, Journal of Accounting, Auditing and Finance, Journal of Accounting and Public Policy, and other journals. He is past associate editor of Contemporary Accounting Research and has served on several editorial boards including The Accounting Review.

Professor Wild, his wife, and four children enjoy travel, music, sports, and community activities.

Ken W. Shaw is an associate professor of accounting and the CBIZ/MHM Scholar at the University of Missouri. He previously was on the faculty at the University of Maryland at College Park. He received an accounting degree from Bradley University and an MBA and PhD from the University of Wisconsin. He is a Certified Public Accountant with work experience in public accounting.

Professor Shaw teaches financial accounting at the undergraduate and graduate levels. He received the Wiliams Keepers LLC Teaching Excellence award in 2007, was voted the "Most Influential Professor" by the 2005 and 2006 School of Accountancy graduating classes, and is a two-time recipient of the O'Brien Excellence in Teaching Award. He is the advisor to his School's chapter of Beta Alpha Psi, a national accounting fraternity.

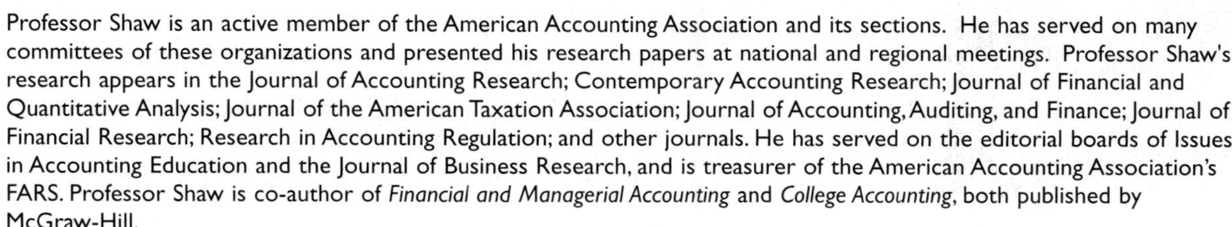

Professor Shaw is an active member of the American Accounting Association and its sections. He has served on many committees of these organizations and presented his research papers at national and regional meetings. Professor Shaw's research appears in the Journal of Accounting Research; Contemporary Accounting Research; Journal of Financial and Quantitative Analysis; Journal of the American Taxation Association; Journal of Accounting, Auditing, and Finance; Journal of Financial Research; Research in Accounting Regulation; and other journals. He has served on the editorial boards of Issues in Accounting Education and the Journal of Business Research, and is treasurer of the American Accounting Association's FARS. Professor Shaw is co-author of *Financial and Managerial Accounting* and *College Accounting*, both published by McGraw-Hill.

In his leisure time, Professor Shaw enjoys tennis, cycling, music, and coaching his children's sports teams.

Barbara Chiappetta received her BBA in Accountancy and MS in Education from Hofstra University and is a tenured full professor at Nassau Community College. For the past two decades, she has been an active executive board member of the Teachers of Accounting at Two-Year Colleges (TACTYC), serving 10 years as vice president and as president from 1993 through 1999. As an active member of the American Accounting Association, she has served on the Northeast Regional Steering Committee, chaired the Curriculum Revision Committee of the Two-Year Section, and participated in numerous national committees.

Professor Chiappetta has been inducted into the American Accounting Association Hall of Fame for the Northeast Region. She had also received the Nassau Community College dean of instruction's Faculty Distinguished Achievement Award. Professor Chiappetta was honored with the State University of New York Chancellor's Award for Teaching Excellence in 1997. As a confirmed believer in the benefits of the active learning pedagogy, Professor Chiappetta has authored *Student Learning Tools*, an active learning workbook for a first-year accounting course, published by McGraw-Hill/Irwin.

In her leisure time, Professor Chiappetta enjoys tennis and participates on a U.S.T.A. team. She also enjoys the challenge of bridge. Her husband, Robert, is an entrepreneur in the leisure sport industry. She has two sons—Michael, a lawyer, specializing in intellectual property law in New York, and David, a composer, pursuing a career in music for film in Los Angeles.

Helping students achieve their goal!

Fundamental Accounting Principles 19e

Assist your students in achieving their goals by giving them what they need to succeed in today's accounting principles course.

Whether the goal is to become an accountant or a businessperson, or even just gain an understanding of the principles of accounting, *Fundamental Accounting Principles* (FAP) has helped generations of students succeed by giving them the support in the form of leading-edge accounting content that engages students, with state-of-the-art technology.

With FAP on your team, you'll be passed **engaging content** and a **motivating style** to help students see the relevance of accounting. Students are motivated when reading materials that are clear and relevant. FAP runs ahead of the field in engaging students. Its chapter-opening vignettes showcase dynamic, successful entrepreneurial individuals and companies guaranteed **to interest and excite students**. This edition's featured companies–Best Buy, Circuit City, RadioShack, and Apple–engage students with their annual reports, which are a pathway for learning financial statements. Further, this book's coverage of the accounting cycle fundamentals is widely praised for its clarity and effectiveness.

FAP also delivers innovative technology to help students succeed. **Homework Manager** provides students with instant grading and feedback for assignments that are completed online. **Homework Manager Plus** integrates an online version of the textbook with Homework Manager. Our algorithmic test bank in Homework Manager offers infinite variations of numerical test bank questions. FAP also offers students portable **iPod-ready content** to help students study and raise their scores.

We're confident you'll agree that **FAP will help your students achieve their goal**.

Engaging Content

FAP content continues to set the standard in the principles course. Take a look at Chapters 1, 2 and 3 and you'll see how *FAP* leads with the best coverage of the accounting cycle. We are the first book to cover equity transactions the way most instructors teach it and students learn it–by introducing the separate equity accounts upfront and not waiting until a chapter or two later. Chapter 2 has the time-tested 4-step approach to analyzing transactions: [1] Identify, [2] Analyze, [3] Record, and [4] Post. And Chapter 3 offers a new 3-step process to simplify adjusting accounts. *FAP* also motivates students with engaging chapter openers. Students identify with them and can even picture themselves as future entrepreneurs. Each book includes the financial statements of Best Buy, Circuit City, RadioShack, and Apple to further engage students.

State-of-the-Art Technology

FAP offers the most advanced and comprehensive technology on the market in a seamless, easy-to-use platform. As students learn in different ways, *FAP* provides a technology smorgasbord that helps students learn more effectively and efficiently. Homework Manager, eBook options, and iPod content are some of the options. Homework Manager Plus takes learning to another level by integrating an online version of the book with all the power of Homework Manager. Technology offerings follow:

- Homework Manager
- Homework Manager Plus
- iPod content
- Algorithmic Test Bank
- Online Learning Center
- Carol Yacht's General Ledger
- ALEKS for the Accounting Cycle
- ALEKS for Financial Accounting

Premier Support

McGraw-Hill/Irwin has mobilized a new force of specialists committed to training and supporting the technology we offer. Our commitment to instructor service and support is top notch and leads the industry. Our new "McGraw-Hill Cares" program provides you with the fastest answers to your questions or solutions to your training needs. Ask your McGraw-Hill sales rep about our Key Media Support Plan and the McGraw-Hill Cares Program.

Through contemporary and engaging content, state-of-the-art technology, and committed service and support, **FAP** provides yo and your students everything you need to achieve your g

How Technology helps

What Can McGraw-Hill Technology Offer You?

Whether you are just getting started with technology in your course, or you are ready to embrace the latest advances in electronic content delivery and course management, McGraw-Hill/Irwin has the technology you need, and provides training and support that will help you every step of the way.

Our most popular technologies, Homework Manager and Homework Manager Plus, are optional online Homework Management systems that will allow you to assign problems and exercises from the text for your students to work out in an online format. Student results are automatically graded, and the students receive instant feedback on their work. Homework Manager Plus adds an online version of the book.

Students can also use the Online Learning Center associated with this book to enhance their knowledge of accounting. Plus we now offer iPod content for students who want to study on the go.

For instructors, we provide all of the crucial instructor supplements on one easy to use Instructor CD-ROM; we can help build a custom class Website for your course using PageOut; we can deliver an online course cartridge for you to use in Blackboard, WebCT, or eCollege; and we have a technical support team that will provide training and support for our key technology products.

How Can Students Study on the Go Using Their iPod?

iPod Content

Harness the power of one of the most popular technology tools students use today–the Apple iPod. Our innovative approach allows students to download audio and video presentations right into their iPod and take learning materials with them wherever they go. Students just need to visit the Online Learning Center at **www.mhhe.com/wildFAP19e** to download our iPod content. For each chapter of the book they will be able to download audio narrated lecture presentations and financial accounting videos for use on various versions of iPods. iPod Touch users can even access self-quizzes.

…akes review and study time as easy as putting in headphones.

How Can My Students Use the Web to Complete Their Homework?

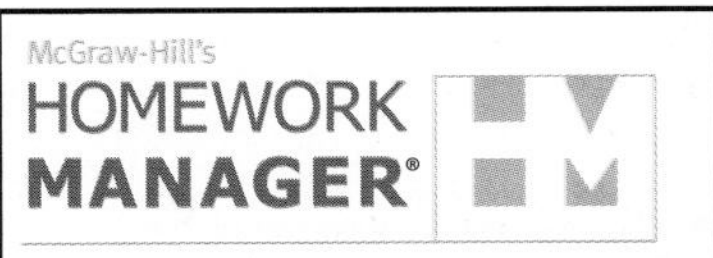

McGraw-Hill's Homework Manager®
is a Web-based supplement that duplicates problem structures directly from the end-of-chapter material in your textbook, using algorithms to provide a limitless supply of online self-graded assignments that can be used for student practice, homework, or testing. Each assignment has a unique solution. Say goodbye to cheating in your classroom; say hello to the power and flexibility you've been waiting for in creating assignments. Most Quick Studies, Exercises, and Problems are available with Homework Manager.

McGraw-Hill's Homework Manager is also a useful grading tool. All assignments can be delivered over the Web and are graded automatically, with the results stored in your private grade book. Detailed results let you see at a glance how each student does on an assignment or an individual problem—you can even see how many tries it took them to solve it.

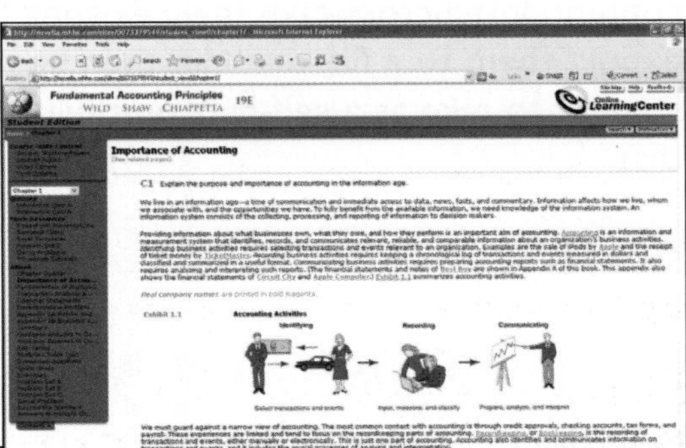

Barbara Gershowitz, Nashville State Technical Community College
"Very thorough . . . and there is a wide variety of supplemental materials that can be used by students. Homework Manager is a real time saver for instructors . . . as it provides immediate feedback to the students and gives them the opportunity to rework problems so that if they did not understand the concept the first time, they can repeat several times until they get it. Homework Manager Plus has worked very well for us. The instructors like it and I have lots of positive feedback from students."

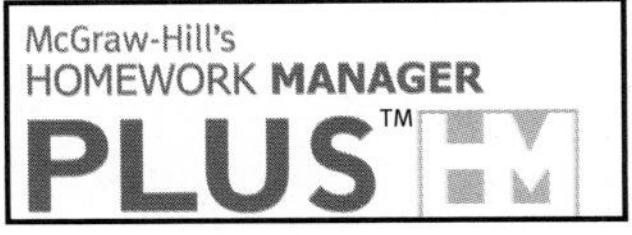

Homework Manager Plus
is an extension of McGraw-Hill's popular Homework Manager System. With Homework Manager Plus you get all of the power of Homework Manager plus an integrated online version of the book. Students simply receive one single access code which provides access to all of the resources available through Homework Manager Plus.

Paula Ratliff, Arkansas State University
"I like the idea that there are online assignments that change algorithmically so that students can practice with them."

When students find themselves needing to reference the textbook to complet[...] now simply click on hints and link directly to the most relevant ma[...] problem or exercise they are working on.

Use EZ Test Online with Apple iPod® iQuiz to help students succeed.

Using our EZ Test Online you can make test and quiz content available for a student's Apple iPod®.

Students must purchase the iQuiz game application from Apple for 99¢ to use the iQuiz content. It works on the iPod fifth generation iPods and better.

Instructors only need EZ Test Online to produce iQuiz-ready content. Instructors take their existing tests and quizzes and export them to a file that can then be made available to the student to take as a self-quiz on their iPods. It's as simple as that.

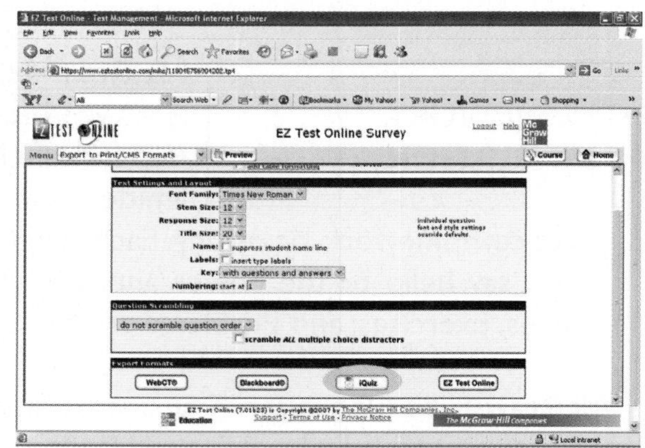

How Can Text-Related Web Resources Enhance My Course?

Online Learning Center (OLC)

We offer an Online Learning Center (OLC) that follows *Fundamental Accounting Principles* chapter by chapter. It doesn't require any building or maintenance on your part. It's ready to go the moment you and your students type in the URL: **www.mhhe.com/wildFAP19e**.
As students study and learn from *Fundamental Accounting Principles*, they can visit the Student Edition of the OLC Website to work with a multitude of helpful tools:

- Generic Template Working Papers
- Chapter Learning Objectives
- Interactive Chapter Quizzes
- PowerPoint® Presentations
- Problem Set C
- Narrated PowerPoint® Presentations
- Video Library
- Excel Template Assignments
- Animated Demonstration Problems
- iPod Content
- Peachtree Templates

A secured Instructor Edition stores essential course materials to save you prep time before class. Everything you need to run a lively classroom and an efficient course is included. All resources available to students, plus . . .

- General Ledger and Peachtree Solution Files
- Problem Set C Solutions
- Instructor's Manual
- Solutions Manual
- Solutions to Excel Template Assignments
- Test Bank

The OLC Website also serves as a doorway to other technology solutions, like course management systems.

Lillian Grose, Delgado CC
"Logical, concise, comprehensive with excellent publisher support material."

McGraw-Hill/Irwin CARES

At McGraw-Hill/Irwin, we understand that getting the most from new technology can be challengir That's why our services don't stop after you purchase our book. You can e-mail our Product S 24 hours a day, get product training online, or search our knowledge bank of Frequently Questions on our support Website.

McGraw-Hill/Irwin Customer Care Contact Information

For all Customer Support call **(800) 331-5094**
Email **be_support@mcgraw-hill.com**
Or visit **www.mhhe.com/support**
One of our Technical Support Analysts will be able to assist you in a timely fashion.

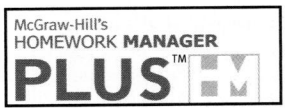

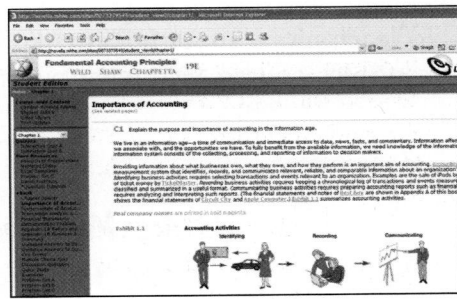

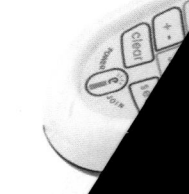

How Can McGraw-Hill Help Me Teach My Course Online?

ALEKS®

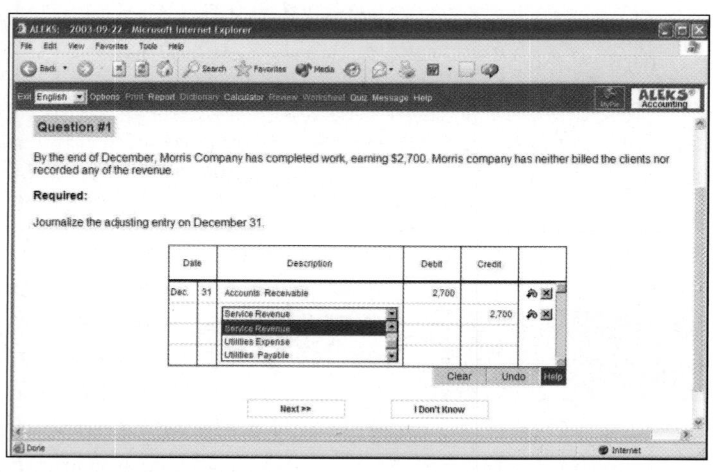

ALEKS® for the Accounting Cycle and ALEKS® for Financial Accounting

Available from McGraw-Hill over the World Wide Web, ALEKS (Assessment and LEarning in Knowledge Spaces) provides precise assessment and individualized instruction in the fundamental skills your students need to succeed in accounting.

ALEKS motivates your students because ALEKS can tell what a student knows, doesn't know, and is most ready to learn next. ALEKS does this using the ALEKS Assessment and Knowledge Space Theory as an artificial intelligence engine to exactly identify a student's knowledge of accounting. When students focus on precisely what they are ready to learn, they build the confidence and learning momentum that fuel success.

To learn more about adding ALEKS to your principles course, visit www.business.aleks.com.

Janice Stoudemire, Midlands Technical College
"The supplemental material that this principles accounting text provides is impressive: homework manager, the extensive online learning center, general ledger application software, as well as ALEKS."

How Can I Make My Classroom Discussions More Interactive?

CPS Classroom Performance System

This is a revolutionary system that brings ultimate interactivity to the classroom. CPS is a wireless response system that gives you immediate feedback from every student in the class. CPS units include easy-to-use software for creating and delivering questions and assessments to your class. With CPS you can ask subjective and objective questions. Then every student simply responds with their individual, wireless response pad, providing instant results. CPS is the perfect tool for engaging students while gathering important assessment data.

eInstruction

Liz Ott, Casper College
"I originally adopted the book because of the tools that accompanied it: Homework Manager, ALEKS, CPS."

Online Course Management

No matter what online course management system you use (WebCT, BlackBoard, or eCollege), we have a course content ePack available for *FAP* 19e. Our new ePacks are specifically designed to make it easy for students to navigate and access content online. They are easier than ever to install on the latest version of the course management system available today.

Don't forget that you can count on the highest level of service from McGraw-Hill. Our online course management specialists are ready to assist you with your online course needs. They provide training and will answer any questions you have throughout the life of your adoption. So try our new ePack for *FAP* 19e and make online course content delivery easy and fun.

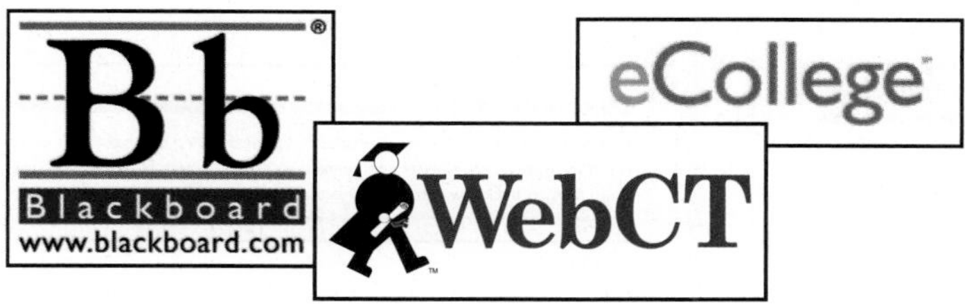

PageOut: McGraw-Hill's Course Management System

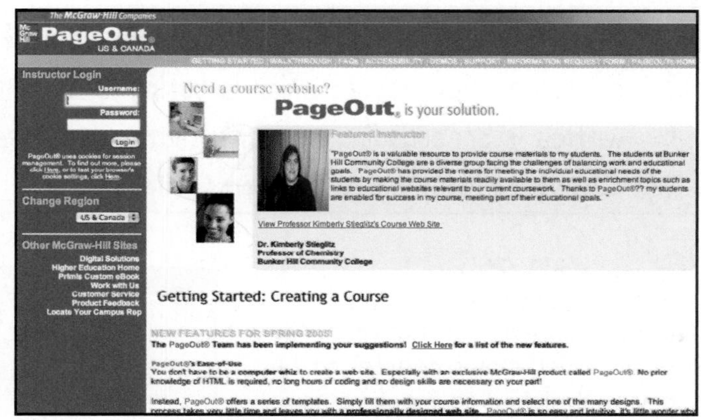

PageOut is the easiest way to create a Website for your accounting course. There is no need for HTML coding, graphic design, or a thick how-to book. Just fill in a series of boxes with simple English and click on one of our professional designs. In no time, your course is online with a Website that contains your syllabus!

Should you need assistance in preparing your Website, we can help. Our team of product specialists is ready to take your course materials and build a custom Website to your specifications. You simply need to call a McGraw-Hill/Irwin PageOut specialist to start the process. To learn more, please visit www.pageout.net and see "PageOut & Service" below.

Best of all, PageOut is free when you adopt *Fundamental Accounting Principles*!

PageOut Service

Our team of product specialists is happy to help you design your own course Website. Just call 1-800-634-3963, press 0, and ask to speak with a PageOut specialist. You will be asked to send in your course materials and then participate in a brief telephone consultation. Once we have your information, we build your Website for you, from scratch.

What tools bring Accounting to life

Decision Center

Whether we prepare, analyze, or apply accounting information, one skill remains essential: decision-making. To help develop good decision-making habits and to illustrate the relevance of accounting, *Fundamental Accounting Principles* 19e uses a unique pedagogical framework called the Decision Center. This framework is comprised of a variety of approaches and subject areas, giving students insight into every aspect of business decision-making. Answers to Decision Maker and Ethics boxes are at the end of each chapter.

Decision Insight

IFRSs IFRSs require that companies report the following four financial statements with explanatory notes:
—Balance sheet —Statement of changes in equity (or statement of recognized revenue and expense)
—Income statement —Statement of cash flows
IFRSs do not prescribe specific formats; and comparative information is required for the preceding period only.

Decision Analysis

A2 Compute the debt ratio and describe its use in analyzing financial condition.

An important business objective is gathering information to pay its debts. Companies finance their assets with either lia a relatively large portion of its assets with liabilities is sai *age*. Higher financial leverage involves greater risk because

Decision Ethics

Credit Manager As a new credit manager, you are being trained by the outgoing manager. She explains that the system prepares checks for amounts net of favorable cash discounts, and the checks are dated the last day of the discount period. She also tells you that checks are not mailed until five days later, adding that "the company gets free use of cash for an extra five days, and our department looks better. When a supplier complains, we blame the computer system and the mailroom." Do you continue this payment policy? [Answer—p. 203]

Decision Maker

Entrepreneur You open a wholesale business selling entertainment equipment to retail outlets. You find that most of your customers demand to buy on credit. How can you use the balance sheets of these customers to decide which ones to extend credit to? [Answer—p. 71]

"This text has the best introductions of any text that I have reviewed or used. Some texts simply summarize the chapter, which is boring to students. Research indicates that material needs to be written in an 'engaging manner.' That's what these vignettes do—they get the students interested."
Clarice McCoy, Brookhaven College

CAP Model

The Conceptual/Analytical/Procedural (CAP) Model allows courses to be specially designed to meet your teaching needs or those of a diverse faculty. This model identifies learning objectives, textual materials, assignments, and test items by C, A, or P, allowing different instructors to teach from the same materials, yet easily customize their courses toward a conceptual, analytical, or procedural approach (or a combination thereof) based on personal preferences.

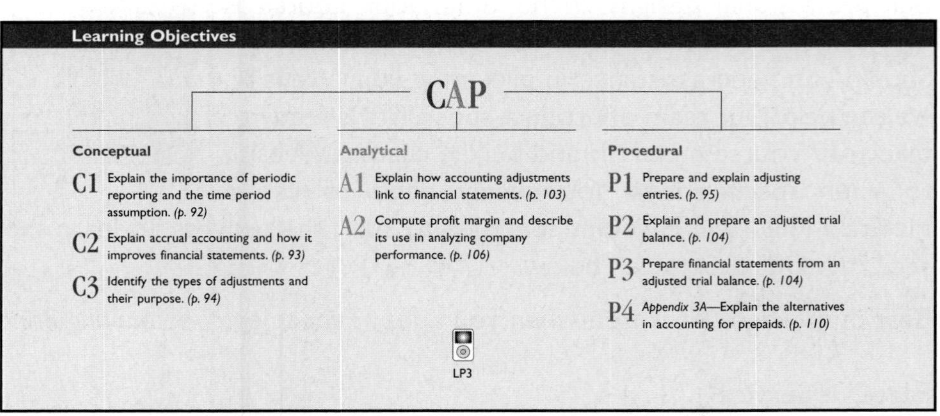

Learning Objectives

CAP

Conceptual

C1 Explain the importance of periodic reporting and the time period assumption. *(p. 92)*

C2 Explain accrual accounting and how it improves financial statements. *(p. 93)*

C3 Identify the types of adjustments and their purpose. *(p. 94)*

Analytical

A1 Explain how accounting adjustments link to financial statements. *(p. 103)*

A2 Compute profit margin and describe its use in analyzing company performance. *(p. 106)*

Procedural

P1 Prepare and explain adjusting entries. *(p. 95)*

P2 Explain and prepare an adjusted trial balance. *(p. 104)*

P3 Prepare financial statements from an adjusted trial balance. *(p. 104)*

P4 *Appendix 3A*—Explain the alternatives in accounting for prepaids. *(p. 110)*

LP3

Chapter Preview with Flow Chart

This feature provides a handy textual/visual guide at the start of every chapter. Students can now begin their reading with a clear understanding of what they will learn and when, allowing them to stay more focused and organized along the way.

Buyers of merchandise expect many products, discount prices, inventory on demand, and high quality. This chapter introduces the accounting practices used by companies engaged in merchandising. We show how financial statements reflect merchandising activities and explain the new financial statement items created by merchandising activities. We also analyze and record merchandise purchases and sales, and explain the adjustments and the closing process for these companies.

Accounting for Merchandising Operations
Merchandising Activities
• Reporting income
• Reporting inventory
• Operating cycles
• Inventory systems
Merchandising Purchases
• Purchase discounts
• Purchase returns and allowances
• Transportation costs
Merchandising Sales
• Sales of merchandise
• Sales discounts
• Sales returns and allowances
Accounting Cycle
• Adjusting entries
• Preparing financial statements
• Closing entries
Financial Statement Formats
• Multiple-step income statement
• Single-step income statement
• Classified balance sheet

Quick Check

These short question/answer features reinforce the material immediately preceding them. They allow the reader to pause and reflect on the topics described, then receive immediate feedback before going on to new topics. Answers are provided at the end of each chapter.

Quick Check — Answers—p. 204

4. How long are the credit and discount periods when credit terms are 2/10, n/60?
5. Identify which items are subtracted from the *list* amount and not recorded when computing purchase price: (*a*) freight-in; (*b*) trade discount; (*c*) purchase discount; (*d*) purchase return.
6. What does *FOB* mean? What does *FOB destination* mean?

"(This book is) visually friendly with many illustrations. Good balance sheet presentation in margin."
Joan Cook, Milwaukee Area Technical College

Marginal Student Annotations

These annotations provide students with additional hints, tips, and examples to help them more fully understand the concepts and retain what they have learned. The annotations also include notes on global implications of accounting and further examples.

ransactions is to post journal entries to dger is up-to-date, entries are posted as ime permits. All entries must be posted o ensure that account balances are up- ts in journal entries are transferred into

Point: Computerized systems often provide a code beside a balance such as *dr.* or *cr.* to identify its balance. Posting is automatic and immediate with accounting software.

FastForward

FastForward is a case that takes students through the Accounting Cycle, chapters 1-4. The FastForward icon is placed in the margin when this case is discussed.

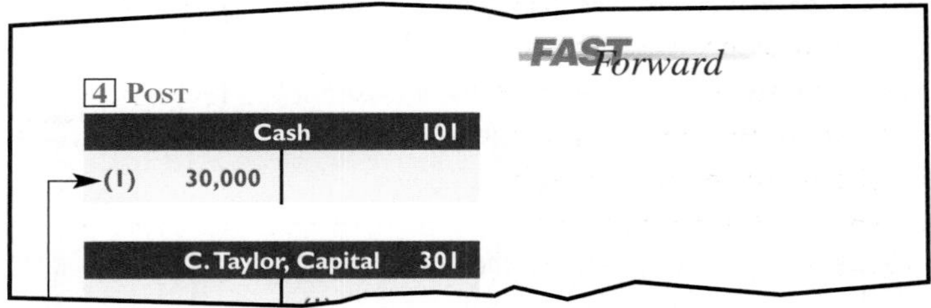

How are chapter concepts

Once a student has finished reading the chapter, how well he or she retains the material can depend greatly on the questions, exercises, and problems that reinforce it. This book leads the way in comprehensive, accurate assignments.

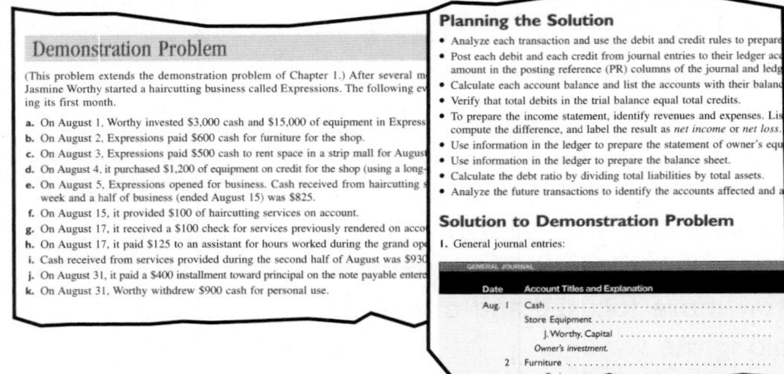

Demonstration Problem

(This problem extends the demonstration problem of Chapter 1.) After several m
Jasmine Worthy started a haircutting business called Expressions. The following ev
ing its first month.

a. On August 1, Worthy invested $3,000 cash and $15,000 of equipment in Express
b. On August 2, Expressions paid $600 cash for furniture for the shop.
c. On August 3, Expressions paid $500 cash to rent space in a strip mall for August
d. On August 4, it purchased $1,200 of equipment on credit for the shop (using a long-
e. On August 5, Expressions opened for business. Cash received from haircutting s week and a half of business (ended August 15) was $825.
f. On August 15, it provided $100 of haircutting services on account.
g. On August 17, it received a $100 check for services previously rendered on acco
h. On August 17, it paid $125 to an assistant for hours worked during the grand op
i. Cash received from services provided during the second half of August was $930
j. On August 31, it paid a $400 installment toward principal on the note payable entere
k. On August 31, Worthy withdrew $900 cash for personal use.

Planning the Solution

- Analyze each transaction and use the debit and credit rules to prepare
- Post each debit and each credit from journal entries to their ledger acc amount in the posting reference (PR) columns of the journal and ledg
- Calculate each account balance and list the accounts with their balanc
- Verify that total debits in the trial balance equal total credits.
- To prepare the income statement, identify revenues and expenses. Lis compute the difference, and label the result as *net income* or *net loss*.
- Use information in the ledger to prepare the statement of owner's equ
- Use information in the ledger to prepare the balance sheet.
- Calculate the debt ratio by dividing total liabilities by total assets.
- Analyze the future transactions to identify the accounts affected and a

Solution to Demonstration Problem

1. General journal entries:

GENERAL JOURNAL

Date	Account Titles and Explanation
Aug. 1	Cash
	Store Equipment
	J. Worthy, Capital
	Owner's investment.
2	Furniture
	Cash

Demonstration Problems present both a problem and a complete solution, allowing students to review the entire problem-solving process and achieve success.

Chapter Summaries provide students with a review organized by learning objectives. Chapter Summaries are a component of the CAP model (see page xiv), which recaps each conceptual, analytical, and procedural objective.

Key Terms are bolded in the text and repeated at the end of the chapter with page numbers indicating their location. The book also includes a complete Glossary of Key Terms.

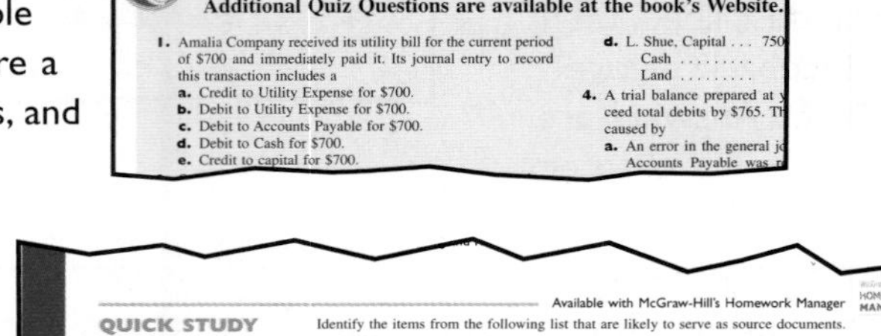

Multiple Choice Quiz — Answers on p. 89

Additional Quiz Questions are available at the book's Website.

1. Amalia Company received its utility bill for the current period of $700 and immediately paid it. Its journal entry to record this transaction includes a
   a. Credit to Utility Expense for $700.
   b. Debit to Utility Expense for $700.
   c. Debit to Accounts Payable for $700.
   d. Debit to Cash for $700.
   e. Credit to capital for $700.

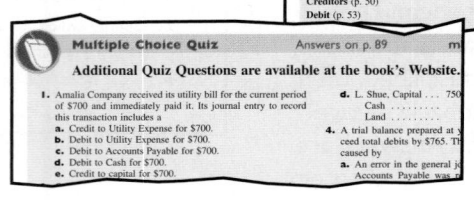

Multiple Choice Questions Multiple Choice Questions quickly test chapter knowledge before a student moves on to complete Quick Studies, Exercises, and Problems.

Quick Study assignments are short exercises that often focus on one learning objective. All are included in Homework Manager. There are usually 8-10 Quick Study assignments per chapter.

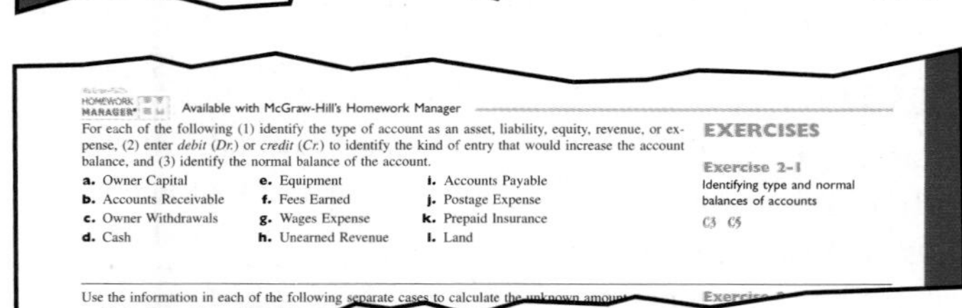

Available with McGraw-Hill's Homework Manager

EXERCISES

Exercise 2-1 — Identifying type and normal balances of accounts — C3 C5

For each of the following (1) identify the type of account as an asset, liability, equity, revenue, or expense, (2) enter *debit (Dr.)* or *credit (Cr.)* to identify the kind of entry that would increase the account balance, and (3) identify the normal balance of the account.

a. Owner Capital e. Equipment i. Accounts Payable
b. Accounts Receivable f. Fees Earned j. Postage Expense
c. Owner Withdrawals g. Wages Expense k. Prepaid Insurance
d. Cash h. Unearned Revenue l. Land

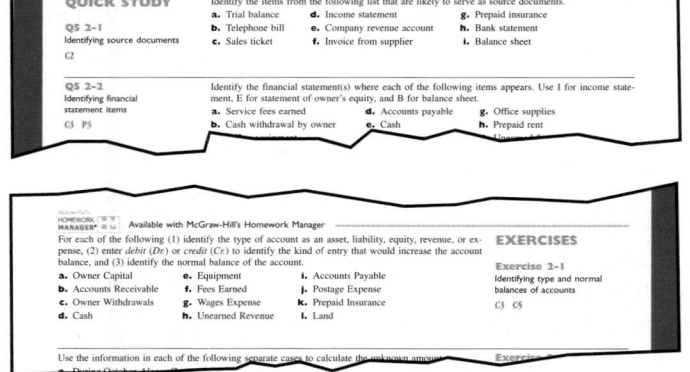

Exercises are one of this book's many strengths and a competitive advantage. There are about 10-15 per chapter and all are included in Homework Manager.

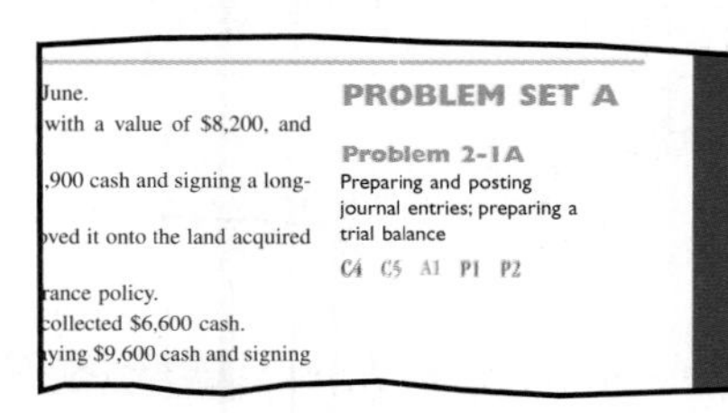

PROBLEM SET A

Problem 2-1A — Preparing and posting journal entries; preparing a trial balance — C4 C5 A1 P1 P2

Problem Sets A & B are proven problems that can be assigned as homework or for in-class projects. Problem Set C is available on the book's Website. All problems are coded according to the CAP model (see page xiv), and Set A is included in Homework Manager.

"One of the best features in FAP is the Serial Problem. I find the continuation of a company from a service to a merchandiser, to a manufacturing, and from a sole proprietorship form or business to a corporation, provides the student a real picture of a company's development. It also provides a consistency from one lesson to another."

Barbara Marotta, Northern Virginia Community College, Woodbridge

Beyond the Numbers exercises ask students to use accounting figures and understand their meaning. Students also learn how accounting applies to a variety of business situations. These creative and fun exercises are all new or updated, and are divided into sections:

- Reporting in Action
- Comparative Analysis
- Ethics Challenge
- Communicating in Practice
- Taking It To The Net
- Teamwork in Action
- Hitting the Road
- Entrepreneurial Decision
- Global Decision

BEYOND THE NUMBERS

REPORTING IN ACTION

A1 A2

BTN 2-1 Refer to Best Buy's financial statements in Appendix

Required

1. What amount of total liabilities does it report for each of the fisc and March 3, 2007?
2. What amount of total assets does it report for each of the fiscal ye March 3, 2007?
3. Compute its debt ratio for each of the fiscal years ended February
4. In which fiscal year did it employ more financial leverage (Febru Explain.

Serial Problem uses a continuous running case study to illustrate chapter concepts in a familiar context. The Serial Problem can be followed continuously from the first chapter or picked up at any later point in the book; enough information is provided to ensure students can get right to work.

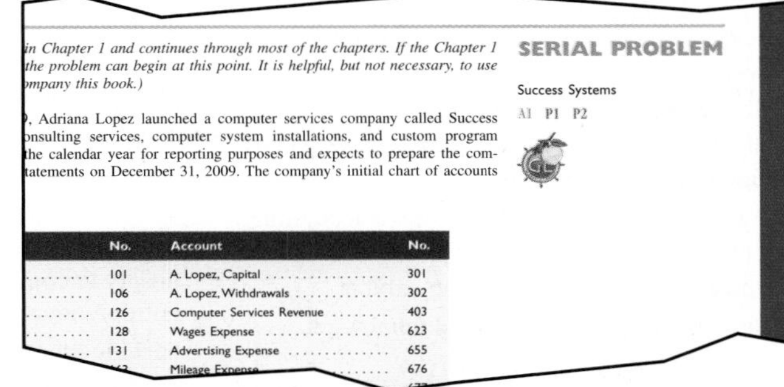

in Chapter 1 and continues through most of the chapters. If the Chapter 1 the problem can begin at this point. It is helpful, but not necessary, to use mpany this book.)

), Adriana Lopez launched a computer services company called Success onsulting services, computer system installations, and custom program he calendar year for reporting purposes and expects to prepare the com- tatements on December 31, 2009. The company's initial chart of accounts

SERIAL PROBLEM

Success Systems

A1 P1 P2

	No.	Account	No.
....	101	A. Lopez, Capital	301
....	106	A. Lopez, Withdrawals	302
....	126	Computer Services Revenue	403
....	128	Wages Expense	623
....	131	Advertising Expense	655
		Mileage Expense	676

"The best feature of this book is the use of real (financial) information in the Beyond the Numbers section. This is something that I do on my own, which can be very time consuming. I also like the Entrepreneurial questions, which are not even addressed in most textbooks."

Cindy Navaroli, Chaffey Community College

The End of the Chapter Is Only the Beginning

Our valuable and proven assignments aren't just confined to the book. From problems that require technological solutions to materials found exclusively online, this book's end-of-chapter material is fully integrated with its technology package.

- Quick Studies, Exercises, and Problems available on Homework Manager (see page ix) are marked with an icon.

- Problems supported by the General Ledger Application Software or Peachtree are marked with an icon.

- Online Learning Center (OLC) includes Interactive Quizzes, Excel template assignments, and more.

- Problems supported with Microsoft Excel template assignments are marked with an icon.

- Material that receives additional coverage (slide shows, videos, audio, etc.) available in iPod ready format are marked with an icon.

Put Away Your Red Pen

We pride ourselves on the accuracy of this book's assignment materials. Independent research reports that instructors and reviewers point to the accuracy of this book's assignment materials as one of its key competitive advantages.

The authors extend a special thanks to accuracy checkers Barbara Schnathorst, The Write Solution, Inc.; Helen Roybark, Radford University; Beth Woods, CPA, Accuracy Counts; David Krug, Johnson Community College; ANSR Source; David Burba, Bowling Green State University; and Marilyn Sagrillo, University of Wisconsin - Green Bay.

Enhancements for FAP 19e

This edition's revisions are driven by feedback from instructors and students. Many of the revisions are summarized here. Feedback suggests that this is the book instructors want to teach from and students want to learn from. General revisions include:

- Revised and updated assignments throughout
- Updated ratio analyses for each chapter
- New material on International Financial Reporting Standards (IFRSs) in most chapters
- New and revised entrepreneurial elements
- Revised serial problem through nearly all chapters
- New art program, visual graphics, and text layout
- New Best Buy Annual Report with comparisons to Circuit City, RadioShack, Apple, and DSG (UK) with new assignments
- New graphics added to each chapter's analysis section
- New iPod content integrated and referenced in book

Chapter 1

Life is Good NEW opener with new entrepreneurial assignment

Revised section on accounting principles and assumptions

New visual layout on building blocks for GAAP

New graphic listing recent publicized accounting scandals

Transaction analysis with expanded accounting equation

Updated compensation data in exhibit

New discussion of conceptual framework linked to IFRSs

Chapter 2

SPANX NEW opener with new entrepreneurial assignment

New 4-step process to learn accounting for transactions: Identify, Analyze, Record, and Post

New sequential art layout for visualizing transaction accounting

New arrow lines link journal entries to the ledger

New material on financial statements related to IFRSs

Chapter 3

PopCap Games NEW opener with new entrepreneurial assignment

New 3-step process for accounting adjustments: (1) Determine what is, (2) Determine what should be, (3) Record adjustment

New summary tables show the accounting adjustment AND account balances before and after adjustment

New adjustment tables for prepaid expenses, including insurance, supplies, and depreciation

New adjustment tables for unearned revenue, accrued expenses, and accrued revenues

Chapter 4

Kathryn Kerrigan NEW opener with new entrepreneurial assignment

New graphic for learning the 4-step closing process

New graphic to aid learning of accounting cycle

Streamlined presentation of classified balance sheet

Chapter 5

BigBadToyStore NEW opener with new entrepreneurial assignment

Enhanced discussions on purchase allowances and purchase returns

Revised discussions on sales returns and sales allowances

Streamlined 4-step process for merchandisers' closing entries

New material on income statement formats for U.S. GAAP vis-à-vis IFRSs

Chapter 6

Beauty Encounter NEW opener with new entrepreneurial assignment

Specific Identification explanation revised for additional clarity

New explanation added to First-in, First-Out

Enhanced explanation to Last-in, First-Out

New description of weighted average

Enhanced explanations for LCM

New material on inventory methods for U.S. GAAP vis-à-vis IFRSs

Illustration of inventory errors is revised and enhanced

Revised exhibit on inventory errors for balance sheet

Appendix 6A, enhanced discussion of periodic inventory

Appendix 6A, expanded explanations of periodic FIFO, LIFO, and weighted average

Chapter 7

TerraCycle NEW opener with new entrepreneurial assignment

Enhanced exhibits for special journals and ledgers

New explanations for controlling and subsidiary ledgers

Updated discussion of enterprise resource planning

Chapter 8

Dylan's Candy Bar NEW opener with new entrepreneurial assignment

New material added on Sarbanes-Oxley and internal controls required

New section on cash management

Additional description of electronic funds transfer

Enhanced explanation of bank reconciliation with new assignments

New discussion of internal controls for IFRSs conversion

Chapter 9

Under Armor NEW opener with new entrepreneurial assignment

Reorganized sections on valuing accounts receivable

Enhanced explanation of recovering a bad debt

New material on assessing the direct write-off method

Reorganized section on estimating bad debts using percent of receivables

New enhanced summary Exhibit 9.13 on methods to estimate bad debts

Added new exercises on bad debts estimation

Chapter 10

Sambazon NEW opener with new entrepreneurial assignment

Updated all real world examples and graphics

Enhanced explanations on declining-balance and impairments

New description of ordinary repairs and its journal entry

Reorganized discussion of betterments and extraordinary repairs

New material on depreciation estimates for U.S. GAAP vis-à-vis IFRSs

Enhanced illustration for depletion including journal entry

Reorganized section on types of intangibles

Enhanced material related to franchises, licenses, trademarks and other intangibles

Enhanced explanation of exchanging plant assets

Chapter 11

Feed Granola Company NEW opener with new entrepreneurial assignment

Updated real world examples including those for Univision, Six Flags, AMF, and K2

New material on contingent liabilities for U.S. GAAP vis-à-vis IFRSs

Updated tax illustrations and assignments using the most recent rates

New section on "Who Pays What Payroll Taxes and Benefits"

Chapter 12

Samanta Shoes NEW opener with new entrepreneurial assignment

Updated real world examples including those for Macadamia Orchards and Big River

Productions

New example of partnership accounting using Trump Entertainment Resorts

Streamlined explanation of partnership liquidation

Chapter 13

Inogen NEW opener with new entrepreneurial assignment

New info graphic on subcategories of authorized stock

Updated many real world examples

New info graphic on stock splits

New material on preferred stock classification for U.S. GAAP vis-à-vis IFRSs

Additional explanation on closing process for corporations

Updated statement of stockholders' equity using Apple

Chapter 14

Rap Snacks NEW opener with new entrepreneurial assignment

Enhanced graphic and explanation of determining bond discount and premium

Revised bond illustration to use a 4-period bond

Streamlined bond illustration to show entire amortization process from issuance to maturity

Streamlined bond illustration for effective interest amortization

New material on bond interest computation for U.S. GAAP vis-à-vis IFRSs

Added new assignments that require accounting for bonds given an amortization table

Chapter 15

Tibi NEW opener with new entrepreneurial assignment

Updated real world examples and graphics including those for Gap, Pfizer, Starbucks, and Brunswick

Enhanced summary graphic on accounting for securities

Updated discussion related to FAS 157 and 159

New material on consolidation per U.S. GAAP vis-à-vis IFRSs

Chapter 16

Jungle Jim's NEW opener with new entrepreneurial assignment

Updated graphics for operating, investing and financing cash flows

Enhanced steps 1 through 5 for preparing the statement of cash flows

Simplified summary Exhibit 16.12 for indirect adjustments

Updated real world examples and graphics including that for Harley, Starbucks, and Nike

New info on indirect vs direct method for U.S. GAAP vis-à-vis IFRSs

Chapter 17

The Motley Fool REVISED opener with new entrepreneurial assignment

New Best Buy, Circuit City and RadioShack data throughout chapter, exhibits, and illustrations with comparative analysis

Enhanced presentation on comparative financial statements

Chapter 18

Kernel Season's NEW opener with new entrepreneurial assignment

New section on fraud and the role of ethics in managerial accounting

Added discussion on Institute of Management Accountants and its road-map for resolving ethical dilemmas

Updated real-world examples including that for Apple

Added balance sheet to exhibits that show cost flows across accounting reports

New discussion on role of nonfinancial information

Chapter 19

Sprinturf NEW opener with new entrepreneurial assignment

New info on custom design involving Nike

Enhanced exhibit on job order production activities

Added discussion linking accurate overhead application for jobs to both product pricing and performance evaluation

Streamlined explanation of closing over- and underapplied overhead

New discussion of employee payroll fraud schemes

Chapter 20

Hood River Juice Company NEW opener with new entrepreneurial assignment

New discussion on impact of automation for quality control and overhead application

Added explanation for use of a process cost summary in product pricing

Chapter 21

RockBottomGolf.com NEW opener with new entrepreneurial assignment

Enhanced explanation of evaluating investment center performance with financial measures

New discussion of residual income

Added explanation of economic value added

New section on evaluating investment center performance with nonfinancial measures including balanced scorecard

New Appendix 21A on transfer pricing

Decision Analysis: new explanation of investment center profit margin and investment turnover with new assignments

Chapter 22

Moe's Southwest Grill NEW opener with new entrepreneurial assignment

New section on working with changes in estimates for CVP analysis

New graphics illustrating how changes in estimates impact break-even analysis

New discussion on weighted average contribution margin in multiple product CVP analysis

New Appendix 22A on using Excel to estimate least squares regression

New assignments on break-even and changes in estimates

Chapter 23

Jibbitz NEW opener with new entrepreneurial assignment

Enhanced discussion of master budgets

New assignments on preparing budgets and budgeted financial statements

Chapter 24

Martin Guitar NEW opener with new entrepreneurial assignment

Reorganized discussion of overhead variance analysis

Revised graphics on framework for understanding overhead variances

New discussion of increased automation for overhead application

Revised explanation of journal entries for standard costing

Simplified discussion of closing variance accounts

New assignments on variance analysis

Added journal entries to chapter demonstration problem

Chapter 25

Prairie Sticks Bat Company NEW opener with new entrepreneurial assignment

New info graphic on cost of capital estimates across industries

Added discussion and example on use of profitability index to compare projects

New discussion on incorporating inflation in net present value calculations

Added explanation on conflicts between meeting analysts' forecasts and choosing profitable long-term projects

New Appendix 25A on using Excel to compute net present value and internal rate of return

New assignments on profitability index

Instructor Supplements

Assurance of Learning Ready

Assurance of learning is an important element of many accreditation standards. *Fundamental Accounting Principles* 19e is designed specifically to support your assurance of learning initiatives.

Each chapter in the book begins with a list of numbered learning objectives which appear throughout the chapter, as well as in the end-of-chapter problems and exercises. Every test bank question is also linked to one of these objectives, in addition to level of difficulty, AICPA skill area, and AACSB skill area. EZ Test, McGraw-Hill's easy-to-use test bank software, can search the test bank by these and other categories, providing an engine for targeted Assurance of Learning analysis and assessment.

AACSB Statement

The McGraw-Hill Companies is a proud corporate member of AACSB International. Understanding the importance and value of AACSB accreditation, *Fundamental Accounting Principles* 19e has sought to recognize the curricula guidelines detailed in the AACSB standards for business accreditation by connecting selected questions in the test bank to the general knowledge and skill guidelines found in the AACSB standards.

The statements contained in *Fundamental Accounting Principles* 19e are provided only as a guide for the users of this text. The AACSB leaves content coverage and assessment within the purview of individual schools, the mission of the school, and the faculty. While *Fundamental Accounting Principles* 19e and the teaching package make no claim of any specific AACSB qualification or evaluation, we have, within the *Fundamental Accounting Principles* 19e test bank labeled questions according to the six general knowledge and skills areas.

Instructor's Resource CD-ROM

FAP 19e, Chapters 1-25
ISBN13: 9780073366456
ISBN10: 0073366455

This is your all-in-one resource. It allows you to create custom presentations from your own materials or from the following text-specific materials provided in the CD's asset library:

- Instructor's Resource Manual
  Written by Barbara Chiappetta, Nassau Community College, and Patricia Walczak, Lansing Community College.
  This manual contains (for each chapter) a Lecture Outline, a chart linking all assignment materials to Learning Objectives, a list of relevant active learning activities, and additional visuals with transparency masters.
- Solutions Manual
- Test Bank, Computerized Test Bank
- PowerPoint® Presentations
  Prepared by Jon Booker, Charles Caldwell, and Susan Galbreth.
  Presentations allow for revision of lecture slides, and includes a viewer, allowing screens to be shown with or without the software.
- Link to PageOut

Test Bank

Vol. 1, Chapters 1-12
ISBN13: 9780073366524
ISBN10: 0073366528

Vol. 2, Chapters 13-25
ISBN13: 9780073366487
ISBN10: 007336648X

Revised by Barbara Gershowitz and Laurie Swanson of Nashville State Technical Community College.

Algorithmic Test Bank

ISBN13: 9780073366395
ISBN10: 0073366390

Solutions Manual

Vol. 1, Chapters 1-12
ISBN13: 9780073366517
ISBN10: 007336651X

Vol. 2, Chapters 13-25
ISBN13: 9780073366470
ISBN10: 0073366471

Written by John J. Wild, Ken W. Shaw, and Marilyn Sagrillo.

Geoffrey Heriot, Greenville Technical College
"The text is well presented and has excellent materials for both students and instructors. It is certainly one of the top texts in an entry level principles of accounting marketplace."

Excel Working Papers CD *(Chapters 1-25)*

ISBN13: 9780073366371
ISBN10: 0073366374

Written by John J. Wild.

Working Papers delivered in Excel spreadsheets. These Excel Working Papers are available on CD-ROM and can be bundled with the printed Working Papers; see your representative for information.

Working Papers

Vol. 1, Chapters 1-12
ISBN13: 9780077289515
ISBN10: 007728951X

Vol. 2, Chapters 12-25
ISBN13: 9780073366364
ISBN10: 0073366366

PFA, Chapters 1-17
ISBN13: 9780073366340
ISBN10: 007336634X

Written by John J. Wild.

Study Guide

Vol. 1, Chapters 1-12
ISBN13: 9780073366388
ISBN10: 0073366382

Vol. 2, Chapters 12-25
ISBN13: 9780073366357
ISBN10: 0073366358

Written by Barbara Chiappetta, Nassau Community College, and Patricia Walczak, Lansing Community College.

Covers each chapter and appendix with reviews of the learning objectives, outlines of the chapters, summaries of chapter materials, and additional problems with solutions.

Carol Yacht's General Ledger CD-ROM

ISBN13: 9780073366401
ISBN10: 0073366404

The CD-ROM includes fully functioning versions of McGraw-Hill's own General Ledger Application software. Problem templates prepared by Carol Yacht and student user guides are included that allow you to assign text problems for working in Yacht's General Ledger or Peachtree.

Contributing Author

The authors and book team wish to thank Marilyn Sagrillo for her excellent contributions.

Marilyn Sagrillo is an associate professor at the University of Wisconsin at Green Bay. She received her BA and MS from Northern Illinois University and her PhD from the University of Wisconsin at Madison. Her scholarly articles are published in *Accounting Enquiries*, *Journal of Accounting Case Research*, and the *Missouri Society of CPAs Casebook*. She is a member of the American Accounting Association and the Institute of Management Accountants. She previously received the UWGB Founder's Association Faculty Award for Excellence in Teaching. Professor Sagrillo is an active volunteer for the Midwest Renewable Energy Association. She also enjoys reading, traveling, and hiking.

Acknowledgments

John J. Wild, Ken W. Shaw, Barbara Chiappetta, and McGraw-Hill/Irwin would like to recognize the following instructors for their valuable feedback and involvement in the development of *Fundamental Accounting Principles* 19e. We are thankful for their suggestions, counsel, and encouragement.

Janet Adeyiga, Hampton University

Audrey Agnello, Niagara County Community College

John Ahmad, Northern Virginia Community College

Sylvia Allen, Los Angeles Valley College

Donna Altepeter, University of North Dakota

Juanita Ardavany, Los Angeles Valley College

Charles Baird, University of Wisconsin-Stout

Scott Barhight, Northampton Community College

Richard Barnhart, Grand Rapids Community College

Mary Barnum, Grand Rapids Community College

Allen Bealle, Delgado Community College

Susan Beasley, Community College of Baltimore County-Catonsville

Beverly Beatty, Anne Arundel Community College

Irene Bembenista, Davenport University

Laurel Berry, Bryant and Stratton College

Jaswinder Bhangal, Chabot College

Rick Bowden, Oakland Community College-Auburn Hills

Deborah Boyce, Mohawk Valley Community College

Nancy Boyd, Middle Tennessee State University

Debbie Branch, Surry Community College

Karen Brayden, Front Range Community College-Fort Collins

Nat Briscoe, Northwestern State University

Linda Bruff, Strayer University

Scott Butterfield, University of Colorado-Colorado Springs

James Capone, Kean University

Roy Carson, Anne Arundel Community College

Trudy Chiaravelli, Lansing Community College

Siu Chung, Los Angeles Valley College

Marilyn Ciolino, Delgado Community College

Ken Coffey, Johnson County Community College

Edwin Cohen, DePaul University

Kerry Colton, Aims Community College-Main Campus

James Cosby, John Tyler Community College

Kenneth Couvillion, San Joaquin Delta College

Ana Cruz, Miami-Dade College-Wolfson

Walter DeAguero, Saddleback College

Suryekaent Desai, Cedar Valley College-Lancaster

Mike Deschamps, Chaffey College

Susan Dickey, Motlow State Community College

Beth Dietz, South Texas College

Andy Dressler, Walla Walla College

Betty Driver, Murray State University

Michael Farina, Cerritos College

Jeannie Folk, College of DuPage

Jim Formosa, Nashville State Technical College

Ron Dustin, Fresno City College

Anthony Espisito, Community College of Baltimore County-Essex

Steve Fabian, Hudson County Community College

Patricia Feller, Nashville State Technical Community College

Anna Fitzpatrick, Gloucester City College

John Gabelman, Columbus State Community College

Dan Galvin, Diablo Valley College

Barbara Gershowitz, Nashville State Technical Community College

Lillian Grose, Delgado Community College

Betty Habershon, Prince George's Community College

Patricia Halliday, Santa Monica College

Jeff Hamm, University of Arkansas-Little Rock

John Hancock, University of California Davis

Jeannie Harrington, Middle Tennessee State University

Sara Harris, Arapahoe Community College

Laurie Hays, Western Michigan University-Kalamazoo

Kathy Hill, Leeward Community College

Patricia Holmes, Des Moines Area Community College

Constance Hylton, George Mason University

Vincent Huygen, North Greenville University

Bill Johnstone, Montgomery College

Jeffery Jones, Community College of Southern Nevada

Richard Irvine, Pensacola Jr. College

Irv Jason, Southwest Tennessee Community College-Macon Campus

Frank Jordan, Erie Community College South Campus-Orchard Park

Thomas Kam, Hawaii Pacific University

John Karbens, Hawaii Pacific University

George Katzt, Phillips College

Charles Kee, Kingsborough Community College

Howard Keller, Indiana University/Purdue University Indiana

Monique Kelly (Byrd), Fresno City College

Chula King, University of West Florida

Debra Kiss, Davenport University

Shirley Kleiner, Johnson County Community College

Robert Koch, St. Peter's College

Jerry Kreuze, Western Michigan University

David Krug, Johnson County Community College

Tara Laken, Joliet Junior College

Michael Landers, Middlesex County Community College

Sherman Layell, Surry Community College

Philip Lee, Nashville State Technical Community College

Paul Lee, Cleveland State University

Natasha Librizzi, Milwaukee Area Technical College

Danny Litt, University of California-Los Angeles

Steve Ludwig, Northwest Missouri State University

Maria Mari, Miami Dade College

Diane Marker, University of Toledo-Scott Park

Barbara Marotta, Northern Virginia Community College-Woodbridge

Brenda Mattison, Tri-County Technical College

Lynn Mazzola, Nassau County Community College

Cynthia McCall, Des Moines Area Community College

Patricia McClure, Springfield Technical Community College

Robert Mcwhorter, Northwest Vista College

Audrey Morrison, Pensacola Junior College

Andrea Murowski, Brookdale Community College

Tim Murphy, Diablo Valley College

Joe Nicassio, Westmoreland County Community College

Jamie O'Brien, South Dakota State University

Kathleen O'Donnell, Onondaga Community College

Ralph Ostrowski, Illinois Central College

Shelley Ota, Lee Ward Community College

Susan Pallas, Southeast Community College

Thomas Parker, Surry Community College

Ash Patel, Normandale Community College

Anahid Petrosian, South Texas College

Yvonne Phang, Boro of Manhattan Community College

Mary Phillips, Middle Tennessee State University

Gary Pieroni, Diablo Valley College

Greg Prescott, University of Southern Alabama

Paula Ratliff, Arkansas State University-State University

David Ravetch, University of California-Los Angeles

Jenny Resnick, Santa Monica College

Jim Riley, Palo Alto College

Richard Roding, Red Rocks Community College

Linda Rose, Westwood College

Al Ruggiero, Suffolk County Community College-Selden

Roger Sands, Milwaukee Area Tech-Milwaukee

Marilyn Sagrillo, University of Wisconsin-Green Bay

Richard Sarkisian, Camden County College

Wallace Satchell, St. Phillips College

Christine Schalow, University of Wisconsin-Stevens Point

William Schmalz, Sanford Brown College

Brad Smith, Des Moines Area Community College

Nancy Snow, University of Toledo

Laura Solano, Pueblo Community College

Charles Spector, State University of New York-Oswego

Gene Sullivan, Liberty University

Laurie Swanson, Nashville State Technical Community College

Larry Swisher, Muskegon County Community College

Margaret Tanner, University of Arkansas-Fort Smith

Domenico Tavella, Pittsburgh Technical Institute

Thomas G. Thompson, Madison Area Technical College

Debra Tyson, Bryant & Stratton College

Shafi Ullah, Broward Community College

Bob Urell, Irvine Valley College

Patricia Walczak, Lansing Community College

Valerie Walmsley, South Texas College

Keith Weidkamp, Sierra College

Dale Westfall, Midland College

Gloria Worthy, Southwest Tennessee Community College

Ray Wurzburger, New River Community College

Lynnette Yerbury, St. Louis Community College

Judith Zander, Grossmont College

In addition to the helpful and generous colleagues listed above, we thank the entire McGraw-Hill/Irwin *Fundamental Accounting Principles* 19e team, including Stewart Mattson, Tim Vertovec, Steve Schuetz, Christina Sanders, Sharon Monday of Aptara, Lori Koetters, Matthew Baldwin, Carol Bielski, and Brian Nacik. We also thank the great marketing and sales support staff, including Krista Bettino, Sankha Basu, and Randy Sealy. Many talented educators and professionals worked hard to create the supplements for this book, and for their efforts we're grateful. Finally, many more people we either did not meet or whose efforts we did not personally witness nevertheless helped to make this book everything that it is, and we thank them all.

John J. Wild   Ken W. Shaw   Barbara Chiappetta

Brief Contents

Contents

15 Investments and International Operations 590

16 Reporting the Statement of Cash Flows 626

17 Analysis of Financial Statements 678

18 Managerial Accounting Concepts and Principles 724

19 Job Order Cost Accounting 768

20 Process Cost Accounting 806

21 Cost Allocation and Performance Measurement 850

22 Cost-Volume-Profit Analysis 900

23 Master Budgets and Planning 938

24 Flexible Budgets and Standard Costs 978

25 Capital Budgeting and Managerial Decisions 1022

A Look Back

Chapter 11 focused on how current liabilities are identified, computed, recorded, and reported. Attention was directed at notes, payroll, sales taxes, warranties, employee benefits, and contingencies.

A Look at This Chapter

This chapter explains the partnership form of organization. Important partnership characteristics are described along with the accounting concepts and procedures for its most fundamental transactions.

A Look Ahead

Chapter 13 extends our discussion to the corporate form of organization. We describe the accounting and reporting for stock issuances, dividends, and other equity transactions.

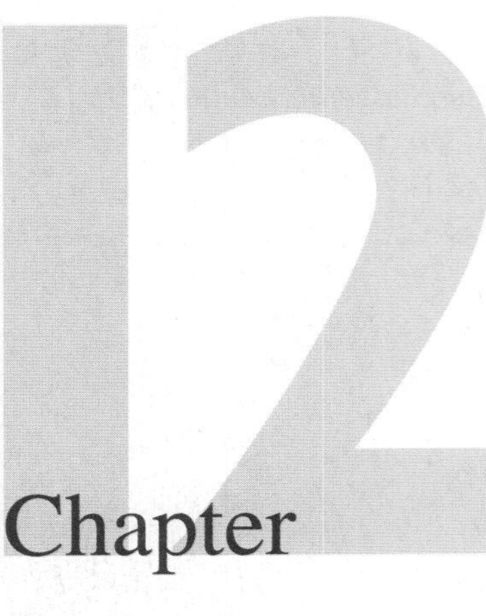

Chapter 12

Accounting for Partnerships

Learning Objectives

CAP

Conceptual

C1 Identify characteristics of partnerships and similar organizations. *(p. 478)*

Analytical

A1 Compute partner return on equity and use it to evaluate partnership performance. *(p. 490)*

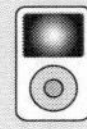

LP12

Procedural

P1 Prepare entries for partnership formation. *(p. 481)*

P2 Allocate and record income and loss among partners. *(p. 481)*

P3 Account for the admission and withdrawal of partners. *(p. 484)*

P4 Prepare entries for partnership liquidation. *(p. 488)*

Decision Feature

A Fitting Pair

"Be your best, make a difference, and live with passion"—Samanta and Kelvin Joseph

NEW YORK—Business recipe: Take one information systems graduate, mix a bit of international flair, add an accountant, and stir. The result is **Samanta Shoes (SamantaShoes.com),** a start-up shoe manufacturer. Founded by Samanta and Kelvin Joseph, their partnership is aimed at providing "stylish, comfortable, and affordable" shoes, explains Samanta. "I design every shoe, and nothing less than the best material is used."

Kelvin's focus is on the accounting and financial side of Samanta Shoes. "The knowledge gained from my years at Ernst & Young LLP [a major accounting firm]," explains Kelvin, "has enabled me to be more helpful." Kelvin's knowledge of partnerships and their financial implications are important to Samanta's success. Both partners stress the importance of attending to partnership formation, partnership agreements, and financial reports to stay afloat. They refer to the partners' return on equity and the organizational form as key inputs to partnership success.

Success is causing their partnership to evolve, but the partners adhere to a quality first mentality. "It's all in the design," insists Samanta. "[A quality design] allows for more comfort and support." But quality also extends to style and uniqueness. "Women don't like other women having their shoe," explains Samanta. "We don't want to dilute our brand by being too mass market." Kelvin explains that the smallest manufacturing run they can have is 18 pairs of a special line. In a world of 6 billion people, that is unique.

The partners also continue to apply strict accounting fundamentals. "The partnership cannot survive," says Kelvin, "unless our business is profitable." They regularly review the accounting results and assess the partnership's costs and revenues. Although he adds, "money does not equal happiness." Samanta explains, "Live your dreams . . . make a difference . . . give back to your community"—advice that we can all live by. "If you're not enjoying it," continues Samanta, "there's no point to doing it."

[Sources: *Samanta Shoes Website,* January 2009; *New York Resident,* August 2004; *Caribbean Vibe,* August 2004; *Black Enterprise,* June 2006; *Regine Magazine,* Spring 2004; *Inc.com,* July 2007]

Chapter Preview

The three basic types of business organizations are proprietorships, partnerships, and corporations. Partnerships are similar to proprietorships, except they have more than one owner. This chapter explains partnerships and looks at several variations of them such as limited partnerships, limited liability partnerships, S corporations, and limited liability companies. Understanding the advantages and disadvantages of the partnership form of business organization is important for making informed business decisions.

Accounting for Partnerships

Partnership Organization
- Characteristics
- Organizations with partnership characteristics
- Choice of business form

Basic Partnership Accounting
- Organizing a partnership
- Dividing income or loss
- Partnership financial statements

Partner Admission and Withdrawal
- Admission of partner
- Withdrawal of partner
- Death of partner

Partnership Liquidation
- No capital deficiency
- Capital deficiency

Partnership Form of Organization

C1 Identify characteristics of partnerships and similar organizations.

A **partnership** is an unincorporated association of two or more people to pursue a business for profit as co-owners. Many businesses are organized as partnerships. They are especially common in small retail and service businesses. Many professional practitioners, including physicians, lawyers, investors, and accountants, also organize their practices as partnerships.

Characteristics of Partnerships

Partnerships are an important type of organization because they offer certain advantages with their unique characteristics. We describe these characteristics in this section.

Voluntary Association A partnership is a voluntary association between partners. Joining a partnership increases the risk to one's personal financial position. Some courts have ruled that partnerships are created by the actions of individuals even when there is no *express agreement* to form one.

Partnership Agreement Forming a partnership requires that two or more legally competent people (who are of age and of sound mental capacity) agree to be partners. Their agreement becomes a **partnership contract,** also called *articles of copartnership.* Although it should be in writing, the contract is binding even if it is only expressed verbally. Partnership agreements normally include details of the partners' (1) names and contributions, (2) rights and duties, (3) sharing of income and losses, (4) withdrawal arrangement, (5) dispute procedures, (6) admission and withdrawal of partners, and (7) rights and duties in the event a partner dies.

Point: When a new partner is admitted, all parties usually must agree to the admission.

Limited Life The life of a partnership is limited. Death, bankruptcy, or any event taking away the ability of a partner to enter into or fulfill a contract ends a partnership. Any one of the partners can also terminate a partnership at will.

Point: The end of a partnership is referred to as its *dissolution.*

Taxation A partnership is not subject to taxes on its income. The income or loss of a partnership is allocated to the partners according to the partnership agreement, and it is included in determining the taxable income for each partner's tax return. Partnership income or loss is allocated each year whether or not cash is distributed to partners.

Point: Partners are taxed on their share of partnership income, not on their withdrawals.

Mutual Agency **Mutual agency** implies that each partner is a fully authorized agent of the partnership. As its agent, a partner can commit or bind the partnership to any contract within the scope of the partnership business. For instance, a partner in a merchandising business can sign contracts binding the partnership to buy merchandise, lease a store building, borrow money, or hire employees. These activities are all within the scope of a merchandising firm. A partner in a law firm, acting alone, however, cannot bind the other partners to a contract to buy snowboards for resale or rent an apartment for parties. These actions are outside the normal scope of a law firm's business. Partners also can agree to limit the power of any one or more of the partners to negotiate contracts for the partnership. This agreement is binding on the partners and on outsiders who know it exists. It is not binding on outsiders who do not know it exists. Outsiders unaware of the agreement have the right to assume each partner has normal agency powers for the partnership. Mutual agency exposes partners to the risk of unwise actions by any one partner.

Point: The majority of states adhere to the Uniform Partnership Act for the basic rules of partnership formation, operation, and dissolution.

Unlimited Liability **Unlimited liability** implies that each partner can be called on to pay a partnership's debts. When a partnership cannot pay its debts, creditors usually can apply their claims to partners' *personal* assets. If a partner does not have enough assets to meet his or her share of the partnership debt, the creditors can apply their claims to the assets of the other partners. A partnership in which all partners have *mutual agency* and *unlimited liability* is called a **general partnership.** Mutual agency and unlimited liability are two main reasons that most general partnerships have only a few members.

Point: Limited life, mutual agency, and unlimited liability are disadvantages of a partnership.

Co-Ownership of Property Partnership assets are owned jointly by all partners. Any investment by a partner becomes the joint property of all partners. Partners have a claim on partnership assets based on their capital account and the partnership contract.

Organizations with Partnership Characteristics

Organizations exist that combine certain characteristics of partnerships with other forms of organizations. We discuss several of these forms in this section.

Limited Partnerships Some individuals who want to invest in a partnership are unwilling to accept the risk of unlimited liability. Their needs can be met with a **limited partnership.** This type of organization is identified in its name with the words "Limited Partnership" or "Ltd." or "LP." A limited partnership has two classes of partners, general and limited. At least one partner must be a **general partner,** who assumes management duties and unlimited liability for the debts of the partnership. The **limited partners** have no personal liability beyond the amounts they invest in the partnership. Limited partners have no active role except as specified in the partnership agreement. A limited partnership agreement often specifies unique procedures for allocating income and losses between general and limited partners. The accounting procedures are similar for both limited and general partnerships.

Decision Insight

Nutty Partners The Hawaii-based **ML Macadamia Orchards LP** is one of the world's largest growers of macadamia nuts. It reported the following partners' capital balances ($ 000s) in its balance sheet:

General Partner	$ 81
Limited Partners	$43,297

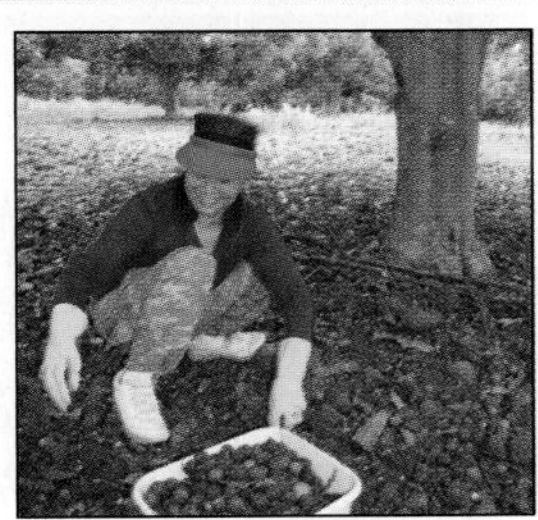

Limited Liability Partnerships Most states allow individuals to form a **limited liability partnership.** This is identified in its name with the words "Limited Liability Partnership" or by "LLP." This type of partnership is designed to protect innocent partners from malpractice or negligence claims resulting from the acts of another partner. When a partner provides service resulting in a malpractice claim, that partner has personal liability for the claim. The remaining partners who were not responsible for the actions resulting in the claim are not personally liable for it. However, most states hold all partners personally liable for other partnership debts. Accounting for a limited liability partnership is the same as for a general partnership.

Point: Many accounting services firms are set up as LLPs.

S Corporations Certain corporations with 75 or fewer stockholders can elect to be treated as a partnership for income tax purposes. These corporations are called *Sub-Chapter S* or simply **S corporations.** This distinguishes them from other corporations, called *Sub-Chapter C* or simply **C corporations.** S corporations provide stockholders the same limited liability feature that C corporations do. The advantage of an S corporation is that it does not pay income taxes. If stockholders work for an S corporation, their salaries are treated as expenses of the corporation. The remaining income or loss of the corporation is allocated to stockholders for inclusion on their personal tax returns. Except for C corporations having to account for income tax expenses and liabilities, the accounting procedures are the same for both S and C corporations.

Point: The majority of proprietorships and partnerships that are organized today are set up as LLCs.

Limited Liability Companies A relatively new form of business organization is the **limited liability company.** The names of these businesses usually include the words "Limited Liability Company" or an abbreviation such as "LLC" or "LC." This form of business has certain features similar to a corporation and others similar to a limited partnership. The owners, who are called *members,* are protected with the same limited liability feature as owners of corporations. While limited partners cannot actively participate in the management of a limited partnership, the members of a limited liability company can assume an active management role. A limited liability company usually has a limited life. For income tax purposes, a limited liability company is typically treated as a partnership. This treatment depends on factors such as whether the members' equity interests are freely transferable and whether the company has continuity of life. A limited liability company's accounting system is designed to help management comply with the dictates of the articles of organization and company regulations adopted by its members. The accounting system also must provide information to support the company's compliance with state and federal laws, including taxation.

Point: Accounting for LLCs is similar to that for partnerships (and proprietorships). One difference is that Owner (Partner), Capital is usually called *Members, Capital* for LLCs.

Choosing a Business Form

Choosing the proper business form is crucial. Many factors should be considered, including taxes, liability risk, tax and fiscal year-end, ownership structure, estate planning, business risks, and earnings and property distributions. The following table summarizes several important characteristics of business organizations:

	Proprietorship	Partnership	LLP	LLC	S Corp.	Corporation
Business entity	Yes	Yes	Yes	Yes	Yes	Yes
Legal entity	No	No	No	Yes	Yes	Yes
Limited liability	No	No	Limited*	Yes	Yes	Yes
Business taxed	No	No	No	No	No	Yes
One owner allowed	Yes	No	No	Yes	Yes	Yes

* A partner's personal liability for LLP debts is limited. Most LLPs carry insurance to protect against malpractice.

Point: The Small Business Administration provides suggestions and information on setting up the proper form for your organization—see SBA.gov.

We must remember that this table is a summary, not a detailed list. Many details underlie each of these business forms, and several details differ across states. Also, state and federal laws change, and a body of law is still developing around LLCs. Business owners should look at these details and consider unique business arrangements such as organizing various parts of their businesses in different forms.

Quick Check

Answers—p. 493

1. A partnership is terminated in the event (*a*) a partnership agreement is not in writing, (*b*) a partner dies, (*c*) a partner exercises mutual agency.
2. What does the term *unlimited liability* mean when applied to a general partnership?
3. Which of the following forms of organization do not provide limited liability to *all* of its owners? (*a*) S corporation, (*b*) limited liability company, (*c*) limited partnership.

Basic Partnership Accounting

Since ownership rights in a partnership are divided among partners, partnership accounting

- Uses a capital account for each partner.
- Uses a withdrawals account for each partner.
- Allocates net income or loss to partners according to the partnership agreement.

This section describes partnership accounting for organizing a partnership, distributing income and loss, and preparing financial statements.

Organizing a Partnership

P1 Prepare entries for partnership formation.

When partners invest in a partnership, their capital accounts are credited for the invested amounts. Partners can invest both assets and liabilities. Each partner's investment is recorded at an agreed-on value, normally the market values of the contributed assets and liabilities at the date of contribution. To illustrate, Kayla Zayn and Hector Perez organize a partnership on January 11 called BOARDS that offers year-round facilities for skateboarding and snowboarding. Zayn's initial net investment in BOARDS is $30,000, made up of cash ($7,000), boarding facilities ($33,000), and a note payable reflecting a bank loan for the new business ($10,000). Perez's initial investment is cash of $10,000. These amounts are the values agreed on by both partners. The entries to record these investments follow.

Zayn's Investment

Jan. 11	Cash	7,000	
	Boarding facilities	33,000	
	Note payable		10,000
	K. Zayn, Capital		30,000
	To record the investment of Zayn.		

Assets	= Liabilities +	Equity
+7,000	+10,000	+30,000
+33,000		

Perez's Investment

Jan. 11	Cash	10,000	
	H. Perez, Capital		10,000
	To record the investment of Perez.		

Assets	= Liabilities +	Equity
+10,000		+10,000

In accounting for a partnership, the following additional relations hold true: (1) Partners' withdrawals are debited to their own separate withdrawals accounts. (2) Partners' capital accounts are credited (or debited) for their shares of net income (or net loss) when closing the accounts at the end of a period. (3) Each partner's withdrawals account is closed to that partner's capital account. Separate capital and withdrawals accounts are kept for each partner.

Point: Both equity and cash are reduced when a partner withdraws cash from a partnership.

Decision Insight

Broadway Partners Big River Productions is a partnership that owns the rights to the play *Big River*. The play is performed on tour and periodically on Broadway. For 2006, its Partners' Capital was $288,640, and it was distributed in its entirety to the partners.

Dividing Income or Loss

P2 Allocate and record income and loss among partners.

Partners are not employees of the partnership but are its owners. If partners devote their time and services to their partnership, they are understood to do so for profit, not for salary. This means there are no salaries to partners that are reported as expenses on the partnership income statement. However, when net income or loss of a partnership is allocated among partners, the partners can agree to allocate "salary allowances" reflecting the relative value of services provided. Partners also can agree to allocate "interest allowances" based on the amount invested. For instance, since Zayn contributes three times the investment of Perez, it is only fair that this be considered when allocating income between them. Like salary allowances, these interest allowances are not expenses on the income statement.

Partners can agree to any method of dividing income or loss. In the absence of an agreement, the law says that the partners share income or loss of a partnership equally. If partners agree on how to share income but say nothing about losses, they share losses the same way they share income. Three common methods to divide income or loss use (1) a stated ratio basis, (2) the ratio of capital balances, or (3) salary and interest allowances and any remainder according to a fixed ratio. We explain each of these methods in this section.

Point: Partners can agree on a ratio to divide income and another ratio to divide a loss.

Allocation on Stated Ratios The *stated ratio* (also called the *income-and-loss-sharing ratio,* the *profit and loss ratio,* or the *P&L ratio*) method of allocating partnership income or loss gives each partner a fraction of the total. Partners must agree on the fractional share each receives. To illustrate, assume the partnership agreement of K. Zayn and H. Perez says Zayn receives two-thirds and Perez one-third of partnership income and loss. If their partnership's net income is $60,000, it is allocated to the partners when the Income Summary account is closed as follows.

Point: The fractional basis can be stated as a proportion, ratio, or percent. For example, a 3:2 basis is the same as ⅗ and ⅖, or 60% and 40%.

Assets	=	Liabilities	+	Equity
				−60,000
				+40,000
				+20,000

Dec. 31	Income Summary	60,000	
	K. Zayn, Capital		40,000
	H. Perez, Capital		20,000
	To allocate income and close Income Summary.		

Allocation on Capital Balances The *capital balances* method of allocating partnership income or loss assigns an amount based on the ratio of each partner's relative capital balance. If Zayn and Perez agree to share income and loss on the ratio of their beginning capital balances—Zayn's $30,000 and Perez's $10,000—Zayn receives three-fourths of any income or loss ($30,000/$40,000) and Perez receives one-fourth ($10,000/$40,000). The journal entry follows the same format as that using stated ratios (see the preceding entries).

Point: To determine the percent of income received by each partner, divide an individual partner's share by total net income.

Allocation on Services, Capital, and Stated Ratios The *services, capital, and stated ratio* method of allocating partnership income or loss recognizes that service and capital contributions of partners often are not equal. Salary allowances can make up for differences in service contributions. Interest allowances can make up for unequal capital contributions. Also, the allocation of income and loss can include *both* salary and interest allowances. To illustrate, assume that the partnership agreement of K. Zayn and H. Perez reflects differences in service and capital contributions as follows: (1) annual salary allowances of $36,000 to Zayn and $24,000 to Perez, (2) annual interest allowances of 10% of a partner's beginning-year capital balance, and (3) equal share of any remaining balance of income or loss. These salaries and interest allowances are *not* reported as expenses on the income statement. They are simply a means of dividing partnership income or loss. The remainder of this section provides two illustrations using this three-point allocation agreement.

Illustration when income exceeds allowance. If BOARDS has first-year net income of $70,000, and Zayn and Perez apply the three-point partnership agreement described in the prior paragraph, income is allocated as shown in Exhibit 12.1. Zayn gets $42,000 and Perez gets $28,000 of the $70,000 total.

Illustration when allowances exceed income. The sharing agreement between Zayn and Perez must be followed even if net income is less than the total of the allowances. For example, if BOARDS' first-year net income is $50,000 instead of $70,000, it is allocated to the partners as shown in Exhibit 12.2. Computations for salaries and interest are identical to those in Exhibit 12.1. However, when we apply the total allowances against income, the balance of income is negative. This $(14,000) negative balance is allocated equally to the partners per their sharing agreement. This means that a negative $(7,000) is allocated to each partner. In this case, Zayn ends up with $32,000 and Perez with $18,000. If BOARDS had experienced a net loss, Zayn and Perez would share it in the same manner as the $50,000 income. The only difference is that they would have begun with a negative amount because of the loss. Specifically, the partners

Point: When allowances exceed income, the amount of this negative balance often is referred to as a *sharing agreement loss or deficit.*

Point: Check to make sure the sum of the dollar amounts allocated to each partner equals net income or loss.

EXHIBIT 12.1

Dividing Income When Income Exceeds Allowances

	Zayn	Perez	Total
Net income			$70,000
Salary allowances			
Zayn	$ 36,000		
Perez		$ 24,000	
Interest allowances			
Zayn (10% × $30,000)	3,000		
Perez (10% × $10,000)		1,000	
Total salaries and interest	39,000	25,000	64,000
Balance of income			6,000
Balance allocated equally			
Zayn	3,000		
Perez		3,000	
Total allocated			6,000
Balance of income			$ 0
Income of each partner	$42,000	$28,000	

EXHIBIT 12.2

Dividing Income When Allowances Exceed Income

	Zayn	Perez	Total
Net income			$50,000
Salary allowances			
Zayn	$ 36,000		
Perez		$ 24,000	
Interest allowances			
Zayn (10% × $30,000)	3,000		
Perez (10% × $10,000)		1,000	
Total salaries and interest	39,000	25,000	64,000
Balance of income			(14,000)
Balance allocated equally			
Zayn	(7,000)		
Perez		(7,000)	
Total allocated			(14,000)
Balance of income			$ 0
Income of each partner	$32,000	$18,000	

would still have been allocated their salary and interest allowances, further adding to the negative balance of the loss. This *total* negative balance *after* salary and interest allowances would have been allocated equally between the partners. These allocations would have been applied against the positive numbers from any allowances to determine each partner's share of the loss.

Point: When a loss occurs, it is possible for a specific partner's capital to increase (when closing income summary) if that partner's allowance is in excess of his or her share of the negative balance. This implies that decreases to the capital balances of other partners exceed the partnership's loss amount.

Quick Check Answers—p. 493

4. Denzel and Shantell form a partnership by contributing $70,000 and $35,000, respectively. They agree to an interest allowance equal to 10% of each partner's capital balance at the beginning of the year, with the remaining income shared equally. Allocate first-year income of $40,000 to each partner.

Partnership Financial Statements

Partnership financial statements are similar to those of other organizations. The **statement of partners' equity,** also called *statement of partners' capital,* is one exception. It shows *each* partner's beginning capital balance, additional investments, allocated income or loss, withdrawals, and ending capital balance. To illustrate, Exhibit 12.3 shows the statement of partners' equity for BOARDS prepared using the sharing agreement of Exhibit 12.1. Recall that BOARDS' income was $70,000; also, assume that Zayn withdrew $20,000 and Perez $12,000 at year-end.

EXHIBIT 12.3

Statement of Partners' Equity

BOARDS
Statement of Partners' Equity
For Year Ended December 31, 2009

	Zayn		Perez		Total
Beginning capital balances		$ 0		$ 0	$ 0
Plus					
Investments by owners		30,000		10,000	40,000
Net income					
Salary allowances	$36,000		$24,000		
Interest allowances	3,000		1,000		
Balance allocated	3,000		3,000		
Total net income		42,000		28,000	70,000
		72,000		38,000	110,000
Less partners' withdrawals		(20,000)		(12,000)	(32,000)
Ending capital balances		**$52,000**		**$26,000**	**$78,000**

The equity section of the balance sheet of a partnership usually shows the separate capital account balance of each partner. In the case of BOARDS, both K. Zayn, Capital, and H. Perez, Capital, are listed in the equity section along with their balances of $52,000 and $26,000, respectively.

Decision Insight

Gambling Partners **Trump Entertainment Resorts LP** and subsidiaries operate three casino hotel properties in Atlantic City: Trump Taj Mahal Casino Resort ("Trump Taj Mahal"), Trump Plaza Hotel and Casino ("Trump Plaza"), and Trump Marina Hotel Casino ("Trump Marina"). Its recent statement of partners' equity reports $979,000 in partners' withdrawals, leaving $594,230,000 in partners' capital balances.

Admission and Withdrawal of Partners

P3 Account for the admission and withdrawal of partners.

A partnership is based on a contract between individuals. When a partner is admitted or withdraws, the present partnership ends. Still, the business can continue to operate as a new partnership consisting of the remaining partners. This section considers how to account for the admission and withdrawal of partners.

Admission of a Partner

A new partner is admitted in one of two ways: by purchasing an interest from one or more current partners or by investing cash or other assets in the partnership.

Purchase of Partnership Interest The purchase of partnership interest is a *personal transaction between one or more current partners and the new partner.* To become a partner, the current partners must accept the purchaser. Accounting for the purchase of partnership interest involves reallocating current partners' capital to reflect the transaction. To illustrate, at the end of BOARDS' first year, H. Perez sells one-half of his partnership interest to Tyrell Rasheed for $18,000. This means that Perez gives up a $13,000 recorded interest ($26,000 × 1/2) in the partnership (see the ending capital balance in Exhibit 12.3). The partnership records this January 4 transaction as follows.

Assets = Liabilities + Equity
−13,000
+13,000

Jan. 4	H. Perez, Capital	13,000	
	T. Rasheed, Capital		13,000
	To record admission of Rasheed by purchase.		

After this entry is posted, BOARDS' equity shows K. Zayn, Capital; H. Perez, Capital; and T. Rasheed, Capital, and their respective balances of $52,000, $13,000, and $13,000.

Two aspects of this transaction are important. First, the partnership does *not* record the $18,000 Rasheed paid Perez. The partnership's assets, liabilities, and *total equity* are unaffected by this transaction among partners. Second, Zayn and Perez must agree that Rasheed is to become a partner. If they agree to accept Rasheed, a new partnership is formed and a new contract with a new income-and-loss-sharing agreement is prepared. If Zayn or Perez refuses to accept Rasheed as a partner, then (under the Uniform Partnership Act) Rasheed gets Perez's sold share of partnership income and loss. If the partnership is liquidated, Rasheed gets Perez's sold share of partnership assets. Rasheed gets no voice in managing the company unless Rasheed is admitted as a partner.

Point: Partners' withdrawals are not constrained by the partnership's annual income or loss.

Investing Assets in a Partnership Admitting a partner by accepting assets is a *transaction between the new partner and the partnership.* The invested assets become partnership property. To illustrate, if Zayn (with a $52,000 interest) and Perez (with a $26,000 interest) agree to accept Rasheed as a partner in BOARDS after an investment of $22,000 cash, this is recorded as follows.

Jan. 4	Cash	22,000	
	T. Rasheed, Capital.		22,000
	To record admission of Rasheed by investment.		

Assets	= Liabilities +	Equity
+22,000		+22,000

After this entry is posted, both assets (cash) and equity (T. Rasheed, Capital) increase by $22,000. Rasheed now has a 22% equity in the assets of the business, computed as $22,000 divided by the entire partnership equity ($52,000 + $26,000 + $22,000). Rasheed does not necessarily have a right to 22% of income. Dividing income and loss is a separate matter on which partners must agree.

Bonus to old partners. When the current value of a partnership is greater than the recorded amounts of equity, the partners usually require a new partner to pay a bonus for the privilege of joining. To illustrate, assume that Zayn and Perez agree to accept Rasheed as a partner with a 25% interest in BOARDS if Rasheed invests $42,000. Recall that the partnership's accounting records show that Zayn's recorded equity in the business is $52,000 and Perez's recorded equity is $26,000 (see Exhibit 12.3). Rasheed's equity is determined as follows.

Equities of existing partners ($52,000 + $26,000)	$ 78,000
Investment of new partner	42,000
Total partnership equity	$120,000
Equity of Rasheed (25% × $120,000)	$ 30,000

Although Rasheed invests $42,000, the equity attributed to Rasheed in the new partnership is only $30,000. The $12,000 difference is called a *bonus* and is allocated to existing partners (Zayn and Perez) according to their income-and-loss-sharing agreement. A bonus is shared in this way because it is viewed as reflecting a higher value of the partnership that is not yet reflected in income. The entry to record this transaction follows.

Jan. 4	Cash	42,000	
	T. Rasheed, Capital.		30,000
	K. Zayn, Capital ($12,000 × ½).		6,000
	H. Perez, Capital ($12,000 × ½)		6,000
	To record admission of Rasheed and bonus.		

Assets	= Liabilities +	Equity
+42,000		+30,000
		+6,000
		+6,000

Bonus to new partner. Alternatively, existing partners can grant a bonus to a new partner. This usually occurs when they need additional cash or the new partner has exceptional talents. The bonus to the new partner is in the form of a larger share of equity than the amount invested. To illustrate, assume that Zayn and Perez agree to accept Rasheed as a partner with a 25%

interest in the partnership, but they require Rasheed to invest only $18,000. Rasheed's equity is determined as follows.

Equities of existing partners ($52,000 + $26,000)	$78,000
Investment of new partner	18,000
Total partnership equity	$96,000
Equity of Rasheed (25% × $96,000)	$24,000

The old partners contribute the $6,000 bonus (computed as $24,000 minus $18,000) to Rasheed according to their income-and-loss-sharing ratio. Moreover, Rasheed's 25% equity does not necessarily entitle Rasheed to 25% of future income or loss. This is a separate matter for agreement by the partners. The entry to record the admission and investment of Rasheed is

Assets	= Liabilities +	Equity
+18,000		−3,000
		−3,000
		+24,000

Jan. 4	Cash	18,000	
	K. Zayn, Capital ($6,000 × ½)	3,000	
	H. Perez, Capital ($6,000 × ½)	3,000	
	T. Rasheed, Capital.........................		24,000
	To record Rasheed's admission and bonus.		

Withdrawal of a Partner

A partner generally withdraws from a partnership in one of two ways. (1) First, the withdrawing partner can sell his or her interest to another person who pays for it in cash or other assets. For this, we need only debit the withdrawing partner's capital account and credit the new partner's capital account. (2) The second case is when cash or other assets of the partnership are distributed to the withdrawing partner in settlement of his or her interest. To illustrate these cases, assume that Perez withdraws from the partnership of BOARDS in some future period. The partnership shows the following capital balances at the date of Perez's withdrawal: K. Zayn, $84,000; H. Perez, $38,000; and T. Rasheed, $38,000. The partners (Zayn, Perez, and Rasheed) share income and loss equally. Accounting for Perez's withdrawal depends on whether a bonus is paid. We describe three possibilities.

No Bonus If Perez withdraws and takes cash equal to Perez's capital balance, the entry is

Assets	= Liabilities +	Equity
−38,000		−38,000

Oct. 31	H. Perez, Capital...........................	38,000	
	Cash		38,000
	To record withdrawal of Perez from partnership with no bonus.		

Perez can take any combination of assets to which the partners agree to settle Perez's equity. Perez's withdrawal creates a new partnership between the remaining partners. A new partnership contract and a new income-and-loss-sharing agreement are required.

Bonus to Remaining Partners A withdrawing partner is sometimes willing to take less than the recorded value of his or her equity to get out of the partnership or because the recorded value is overstated. Whatever the reason, when this occurs, the withdrawing partner in effect gives the remaining partners a bonus equal to the equity left behind. The remaining partners share this unwithdrawn equity according to their income-and-loss-sharing ratio. To illustrate, if Perez withdraws and agrees to take $34,000 cash in settlement of Perez's capital balance, the entry is

Assets	= Liabilities +	Equity
−34,000		−38,000
		+2,000
		+2,000

Oct. 31	H. Perez, Capital...........................	38,000	
	Cash		34,000
	K. Zayn, Capital.........................		2,000
	T. Rasheed, Capital.......................		2,000
	To record withdrawal of Perez and bonus to remaining partners.		

Perez withdrew $4,000 less than Perez's recorded equity of $38,000. This $4,000 is divided between Zayn and Rasheed according to their income-and-loss-sharing ratio.

Bonus to Withdrawing Partner A withdrawing partner may be able to receive more than his or her recorded equity for at least two reasons. First, the recorded equity may be understated. Second, the remaining partners may agree to remove this partner by giving assets of greater value than this partner's recorded equity. In either case, the withdrawing partner receives a bonus. The remaining partners reduce their equity by the amount of this bonus according to their income-and-loss-sharing ratio. To illustrate, if Perez withdraws and receives $40,000 cash in settlement of Perez's capital balance, the entry is

Oct. 31	H. Perez, Capital	38,000	
	K. Zayn, Capital	1,000	
	T. Rasheed, Capital	1,000	
	Cash		40,000
	To record Perez's withdrawal from partnership with a bonus to Perez.		

Assets	= Liabilities +	Equity
−40,000		−38,000
		−1,000
		−1,000

Falcon Cable Communications LLC set up a partnership withdrawal agreement. Falcon owns and operates cable television systems and had two managing general partners. The partnership agreement stated that either partner "can offer to sell to the other partner the offering partner's entire partnership interest . . . for a negotiated price. If the partner receiving such an offer rejects it, the offering partner may elect to cause [the partnership] . . . to be liquidated and dissolved."

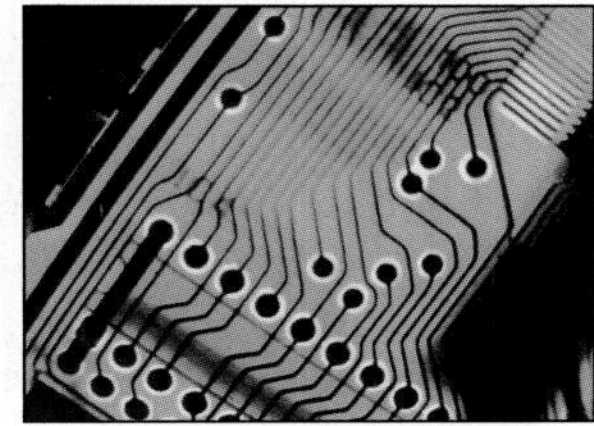

Death of a Partner

A partner's death dissolves a partnership. A deceased partner's estate is entitled to receive his or her equity. The partnership contract should contain provisions for settlement in this case. These provisions usually require (1) closing the books to determine income or loss since the end of the previous period and (2) determining and recording current market values for both assets and liabilities. The remaining partners and the deceased partner's estate then must agree to a settlement of the deceased partner's equity. This can involve selling the equity to remaining partners or to an outsider, or it can involve withdrawing assets.

Decision Ethics

Financial Planner You are hired by the two remaining partners of a three-member partnership after the third partner's death. The partnership agreement states that a deceased partner's estate is entitled to a "share of partnership assets equal to the partner's relative equity balance" (partners' equity balances are equal). The estate argues that it is entitled to one-third of the current value of partnership assets. The remaining partners say the distribution should use asset book values, which are 75% of current value. They also point to partnership liabilities, which equal 40% of total asset book value and 30% of current value. How would you resolve this situation? [Answer—p. 493]

Liquidation of a Partnership

When a partnership is liquidated, its business ends and four concluding steps are required.

1. Record the sale of noncash assets for cash and any gain or loss from their liquidation.
2. Allocate any gain or loss from liquidation of the assets in step 1 to the partners using their income-and-loss-sharing ratio.

3. Pay or settle all partner liabilities.
4. Distribute any remaining cash to partners based on their capital balances.

Partnership liquidation usually falls into one of two cases, as described in this section.

No Capital Deficiency

P4 Prepare entries for partnership liquidation.

No capital deficiency means that all partners have a zero or credit balance in their capital accounts for final distribution of cash. To illustrate, assume that Zayn, Perez, and Rasheed operate their partnership in BOARDS for several years, sharing income and loss equally. The partners then decide to liquidate. On the liquidation date, the current period's income or loss is transferred to the partners' capital accounts according to the sharing agreement. After that transfer, assume the partners' recorded equity balances (immediately prior to liquidation) are Zayn, $70,000; Perez, $66,000; and Rasheed, $62,000.

Next, assume that BOARDS sells its noncash assets for a net gain of $6,000. In a liquidation, gains or losses usually result from the sale of noncash assets, which are called *losses and gains from liquidation.* Partners share losses and gains from liquidation according to their income-and-loss-sharing agreement (equal for these partners) yielding the partners' revised equity balances of Zayn, $72,000; Perez, $68,000; and Rasheed, $64,000.[1] Then, after partnership assets are sold and any gain or loss is allocated, the liabilities must be paid. After creditors are paid, any remaining cash is divided among the partners according to their capital account balances. BOARDS' only liability at liquidation is $20,000 in accounts payable. The entries to record the payment to creditors and the final distribution of cash to partners follow.

Assets	= Liabilities	+ Equity
−20,000	−20,000	

Assets	= Liabilities	+ Equity
−204,000		−72,000
		−68,000
		−64,000

Date	Account	Debit	Credit
Jan. 15	Accounts Payable	20,000	
	Cash		20,000
	To pay claims of creditors.		
Jan. 15	K. Zayn, Capital	72,000	
	H. Perez, Capital	68,000	
	T. Rasheed, Capital	64,000	
	Cash		204,000
	To distribute remaining cash to partners.		

It is important to remember that the final cash payment is distributed to partners according to their capital account balances, whereas gains and losses from liquidation are allocated according to the income-and-loss-sharing ratio.

[1] The concepts behind these entries are not new. For example, assume that BOARDS has two noncash assets recorded as boarding facilities, $15,000, and land, $25,000. The entry to sell these assets for $46,000 is

Date	Account	Debit	Credit
Jan. 15	Cash	46,000	
	Boarding facilities		15,000
	Land		25,000
	Gain from liquidation		6,000
	Sold noncash assets at a gain.		

We then record the allocation of any loss or gain (a gain in this case) from liquidation according to the partners' income-and-loss-sharing agreement as follows.

Date	Account	Debit	Credit
Jan. 15	Gain from liquidation	6,000	
	K. Zayn, Capital		2,000
	H. Perez, Capital		2,000
	T. Rasheed, Capital		2,000
	To allocate liquidation gain to partners.		

Capital Deficiency

Capital deficiency means that at least one partner has a debit balance in his or her capital account at the point of final cash distribution. This can arise from liquidation losses, excessive withdrawals before liquidation, or recurring losses in prior periods. A partner with a capital deficiency must, if possible, cover the deficit by paying cash into the partnership.

To illustrate, assume that Zayn, Perez, and Rasheed operate their partnership in BOARDS for several years, sharing income and losses equally. The partners then decide to liquidate. Immediately prior to the final distribution of cash, the partners' recorded capital balances are Zayn, $19,000; Perez, $8,000; and Rasheed, $(3,000). Rasheed's capital deficiency means that Rasheed owes the partnership $3,000. Both Zayn and Perez have a legal claim against Rasheed's personal assets. The final distribution of cash in this case depends on how this capital deficiency is handled. Two possibilities exist.

Partner Pays Deficiency Rasheed is obligated to pay $3,000 into the partnership to cover the deficiency. If Rasheed is willing and able to pay, the entry to record receipt of payment from Rasheed follows.

Jan. 15	Cash	3,000	
	T. Rasheed, Capital		3,000
	To record payment of deficiency by Rasheed.		

Assets	= Liabilities +	Equity
+3,000		+3,000

After the $3,000 payment, the partners' capital balances are Zayn, $19,000; Perez, $8,000; and Rasheed, $0. The entry to record the final cash distributions to partners is

Jan. 15	K. Zayn, Capital	19,000	
	H. Perez, Capital	8,000	
	Cash		27,000
	To distribute remaining cash to partners.		

Assets	= Liabilities +	Equity
−27,000		−19,000
		−8,000

Partner Cannot Pay Deficiency The remaining partners with credit balances absorb any partner's unpaid deficiency according to their income-and-loss-sharing ratio. To illustrate, if Rasheed is unable to pay the $3,000 deficiency, Zayn and Perez absorb it. Since they share income and loss equally, Zayn and Perez each absorb $1,500 of the deficiency. This is recorded as follows.

Jan. 15	K. Zayn, Capital	1,500	
	H. Perez, Capital	1,500	
	T. Rasheed, Capital		3,000
	To transfer Rasheed deficiency to Zayn and Perez.		

Assets	= Liabilities +	Equity
		−1,500
		−1,500
		+3,000

After Zayn and Perez absorb Rasheed's deficiency, the capital accounts of the partners are Zayn, $17,500; Perez, $6,500; and Rasheed, $0. The entry to record the final cash distribution to the partners is

Jan. 15	K. Zayn, Capital	17,500	
	H. Perez, Capital	6,500	
	Cash		24,000
	To distribute remaining cash to partners.		

Assets	= Liabilities +	Equity
−24,000		−17,500
		−6,500

Rasheed's inability to cover this deficiency does not relieve Rasheed of the liability. If Rasheed becomes able to pay at a future date, Zayn and Perez can each collect $1,500 from Rasheed.

Decision Analysis — Partner Return on Equity

A1 Compute partner return on equity and use it to evaluate partnership performance.

An important role of partnership financial statements is to aid current and potential partners in evaluating partnership success compared with other opportunities. One measure of this success is the **partner return on equity** ratio:

$$\textbf{Partner return on equity} = \frac{\textbf{Partner net income}}{\textbf{Average partner equity}}$$

This measure is separately computed for each partner. To illustrate, Exhibit 12.4 reports selected data from the **Boston Celtics LP**. The return on equity for the *total* partnership is computed as $216/[($84 + $252)/2] = 128.6%. However, return on equity is quite different across the partners. For example, the **Boston Celtics LP I** partner return on equity is computed as $44/[($122 + $166)/2] = 30.6%, whereas the **Celtics LP** partner return on equity is computed as $111/[($270 + $333)/2] = 36.8%. Partner return on equity provides *each* partner an assessment of its return on its equity invested in the partnership. A specific partner often uses this return to decide whether additional investment or withdrawal of resources is best for that partner. Exhibit 12.4 reveals that the year shown produced good returns for all partners (the Boston Celtics LP II return is not computed because its average equity is negative due to an unusual and large distribution in the prior year).

EXHIBIT 12.4

Selected Data from Boston Celtics LP

($ thousands)	Total*	Boston Celtics LP I	Boston Celtics LP II	Celtics LP
Beginning-year balance	$ 84	$122	$(307)	$270
Net income (loss) for year	216	44	61	111
Cash distribution	(48)	—	—	(48)
Ending-year balance	$252	$166	$(246)	$333
Partner return on equity	**128.6%**	**30.6%**	**n.a.**	**36.8%**

* Totals may not add up due to rounding.

Demonstration Problem

DP12

The following transactions and events affect the partners' capital accounts in several successive partnerships. Prepare a table with six columns, one for each of the five partners along with a total column to show the effects of the following events on the five partners' capital accounts.

Part 1

4/13/2007 Ries and Bax create R&B Company. Each invests $10,000, and they agree to share income and losses equally.

12/31/2007 R&B Co. earns $15,000 in income for its first year. Ries withdraws $4,000 from the partnership, and Bax withdraws $7,000.

1/1/2008 Royce is made a partner in RB&R Company after contributing $12,000 cash. The partners agree that a 10% interest allowance will be given on each partner's beginning-year capital balance. In addition, Bax and Royce are to receive $5,000 salary allowances. The remainder of the income or loss is to be divided evenly.

12/31/2008 The partnership's income for the year is $40,000, and withdrawals at year-end are Ries, $5,000; Bax, $12,500; and Royce, $11,000.

1/1/2009 Ries sells her interest for $20,000 to Murdock, whom Bax and Royce accept as a partner in the new BR&M Co. Income or loss is to be shared equally after Bax and Royce receive $25,000 salary allowances.

12/31/2009 The partnership's income for the year is $35,000, and year-end withdrawals are Bax, $2,500, and Royce, $2,000.

1/1/2010 Elway is admitted as a partner after investing $60,000 cash in the new Elway & Associates partnership. He is given a 50% interest in capital after the other partners transfer $3,000 to his account from each of theirs. A 20% interest allowance (on the beginning-year capital balances) will be used in sharing any income or loss, there will be no salary allowances, and Elway will receive 40% of the remaining balance—the other three partners will each get 20%.

12/31/2010 Elway & Associates earns $127,600 in income for the year, and year-end withdrawals are Bax, $25,000; Royce, $27,000; Murdock, $15,000; and Elway, $40,000.

1/1/2011 Elway buys out Bax and Royce for the balances of their capital accounts after a revaluation of the partnership assets. The revaluation gain is $50,000, which is divided in using a 1:1:1:2 ratio (Bax:Royce:Murdock:Elway). Elway pays the others from personal funds. Murdock and Elway will share income on a 1:9 ratio.

2/28/2011 The partnership earns $10,000 of income since the beginning of the year. Murdock retires and receives partnership cash equal to her capital balance. Elway takes possession of the partnership assets in his own name, and the partnership is dissolved.

Part 2

Journalize the events affecting the partnership for the year ended December 31, 2008.

Planning the Solution

- Evaluate each transaction's effects on the capital accounts of the partners.
- Each time a new partner is admitted or a partner withdraws, allocate any bonus based on the income-or-loss-sharing agreement.
- Each time a new partner is admitted or a partner withdraws, allocate subsequent net income or loss in accordance with the new partnership agreement.
- Prepare entries to (1) record Royce's initial investment; (2) record the allocation of interest, salaries, and remainder; (3) show the cash withdrawals from the partnership; and (4) close the withdrawal accounts on December 31, 2008.

Solution to Demonstration Problem

Part 1

Event	Ries	Bax	Royce	Murdock	Elway	Total
4/13/2007						
Initial investment	$10,000	$10,000				$ 20,000
12/31/2007						
Income (equal)	7,500	7,500				15,000
Withdrawals	(4,000)	(7,000)				(11,000)
Ending balance	$13,500	$10,500				$ 24,000
1/1/2008						
New investment			$12,000			$ 12,000
12/31/2008						
10% interest	1,350	1,050	1,200			3,600
Salaries		5,000	5,000			10,000
Remainder (equal)	8,800	8,800	8,800			26,400
Withdrawals	(5,000)	(12,500)	(11,000)			(28,500)
Ending balance	$18,650	$12,850	$16,000			$ 47,500
1/1/2009						
Transfer interest	(18,650)			$18,650		$ 0
12/31/2009						
Salaries		25,000	25,000			50,000
Remainder (equal)		(5,000)	(5,000)	(5,000)		(15,000)
Withdrawals		(2,500)	(2,000)			(4,500)
Ending balance	$ 0	$30,350	$34,000	$13,650		$ 78,000
1/1/2010						
New investment					$ 60,000	60,000
Bonuses to Elway		(3,000)	(3,000)	(3,000)	9,000	0
Adjusted balance		$27,350	$31,000	$10,650	$ 69,000	$138,000

[continued on next page]

[continued from previous page]

Event	Ries	Bax	Royce	Murdock	Elway	Total
12/31/2010						
20% interest		5,470	6,200	2,130	13,800	27,600
Remainder (1:1:1:2)		20,000	20,000	20,000	40,000	100,000
Withdrawals		(25,000)	(27,000)	(15,000)	(40,000)	(107,000)
Ending balance		$27,820	$30,200	$17,780	$ 82,800	$158,600
1/1/2011						
Gain (1:1:1:2)		10,000	10,000	10,000	20,000	50,000
Adjusted balance		$37,820	$40,200	$27,780	$102,800	$208,600
Transfer interests		(37,820)	(40,200)		78,020	0
Adjusted balance		$ 0	$ 0	$27,780	$180,820	$208,600
2/28/2011						
Income (1:9)				1,000	9,000	10,000
Adjusted balance				$28,780	$189,820	$218,600
Settlements				(28,780)	(189,820)	(218,600)
Final balance				$ 0	$ 0	$ 0

Part 2

Date	Account	Debit	Credit
2008			
Jan. 1	Cash	12,000	
	Royce, Capital		12,000
	To record investment of Royce.		
Dec. 31	Income Summary	40,000	
	Ries, Capital		10,150
	Bax, Capital		14,850
	Royce, Capital		15,000
	To allocate interest, salaries, and remainders.		
Dec. 31	Ries, Withdrawals	5,000	
	Bax, Withdrawals	12,500	
	Royce, Withdrawals	11,000	
	Cash		28,500
	To record cash withdrawals by partners.		
Dec. 31	Ries, Capital	5,000	
	Bax, Capital	12,500	
	Royce, Capital	11,000	
	Ries, Withdrawals		5,000
	Bax, Withdrawals		12,500
	Royce, Withdrawals		11,000
	To close withdrawal accounts.		

Summary

C1 **Identify characteristics of partnerships and similar organizations.** Partnerships are voluntary associations, involve partnership agreements, have limited life, are not subject to income tax, include mutual agency, and have unlimited liability. Organizations that combine selected characteristics of partnerships and corporations include limited partnerships, limited liability partnerships, S corporations, and limited liability companies.

A1 **Compute partner return on equity and use it to evaluate partnership performance.** Partner return on equity provides each partner an assessment of his or her return on equity invested in the partnership.

P1 **Prepare entries for partnership formation.** A partner's initial investment is recorded at the market value of the assets contributed to the partnership.

P2 **Allocate and record income and loss among partners.** A partnership agreement should specify how to allocate partnership income or loss among partners. Allocation can be based on a stated ratio, capital balances, or salary and interest allowances to compensate partners for differences in their service and capital contributions.

P3 **Account for the admission and withdrawal of partners.** When a new partner buys a partnership interest directly from one or more existing partners, the amount of cash paid from one partner to another does not affect the partnership total recorded equity. When a new partner purchases equity by investing additional assets in the partnership, the new partner's investment can yield a bonus either to existing partners or to the new partner. The entry to record a withdrawal can involve payment from either (1) the existing partners' personal assets or (2) partnership assets. The latter can yield a bonus to either the withdrawing or remaining partners.

P4 **Prepare entries for partnership liquidation.** When a partnership is liquidated, losses and gains from selling partnership assets are allocated to the partners according to their income-and-loss-sharing ratio. If a partner's capital account has a deficiency that the partner cannot pay, the other partners share the deficit according to their relative income-and-loss-sharing ratio.

Guidance Answers to **Decision Ethics**

Financial Planner The partnership agreement apparently fails to mention liabilities or use the term *net assets.* To give the estate one-third of total assets is not fair to the remaining partners because if the partner had lived and the partners had decided to liquidate, the liabilities would need to be paid out of assets before any liquidation. Also, a settlement based on the deceased partner's recorded equity would fail to recognize excess of current value over book value. This value increase would be realized if the partnership were liquidated. A fair settlement would seem to be a payment to the estate for the balance of the deceased partner's equity based on the *current value of net assets.*

Guidance Answers to **Quick Checks**

1. (*b*)
2. *Unlimited liability* means that the creditors of a partnership require each partner to be personally responsible for all partnership debts.
3. (*c*)
4.

	Denzel	Shantell	Total
Net income			$40,000
Interest allowance (10%)	$ 7,000	$ 3,500	10,500
Balance of income	↓	↓	**$29,500**
Balance allocated equally	14,750	14,750	29,500
Balance of income			$ 0
Income of partners	**$21,750**	**$18,250**	

Key Terms

mhhe.com/wildFAP19e

Key Terms are available at the book's Website for learning and testing in an online Flashcard Format.

C corporation (p. 480)
General partner (p. 479)
General partnership (p. 479)
Limited liability company (LLC) (p. 480)
Limited liability partnership (p. 479)
Limited partners (p. 479)
Limited partnership (p. 479)
Mutual agency (p. 478)
Partner return on equity (p. 490)
Partnership (p. 478)
Partnership contract (p. 478)
Partnership liquidation (p. 488)
S corporation (p. 480)
Statement of partners' equity (p. 483)
Unlimited liability (p. 479)

Multiple Choice Quiz

Answers on p. 503

mhhe.com/wildFAP19e

Additional Quiz Questions are available at the book's Website.

1. Stokely and Leder are forming a partnership. Stokely invests a building that has a market value of $250,000; and the partnership assumes responsibility for a $50,000 note secured by a mortgage on that building. Leder invests $100,000 cash. For the partnership, the amounts recorded for the building and for Stokely's Capital account are these:
   a. Building, $250,000; Stokely, Capital, $250,000.
   b. Building, $200,000; Stokely, Capital, $200,000.
   c. Building, $200,000; Stokely, Capital, $100,000.
   d. Building, $200,000; Stokely, Capital, $250,000.
   e. Building, $250,000; Stokely, Capital, $200,000.

2. Katherine, Alliah, and Paulina form a partnership. Katherine contributes $150,000, Alliah contributes $150,000, and Paulina contributes $100,000. Their partnership agreement calls for the income or loss division to be based on the ratio of capital invested. If the partnership reports income of $90,000 for its first year of operations, what amount of income is credited to Paulina's capital account?
a. $22,500
b. $25,000
c. $45,000
d. $30,000
e. $90,000

3. Jamison and Blue form a partnership with capital contributions of $600,000 and $800,000, respectively. Their partnership agreement calls for Jamison to receive $120,000 per year in salary. Also, each partner is to receive an interest allowance equal to 10% of the partner's beginning capital contributions, with any remaining income or loss divided equally. If net income for its initial year is $270,000, then Jamison's and Blue's respective shares are
a. $135,000; $135,000.
b. $154,286; $115,714.
c. $120,000; $150,000.
d. $185,000; $85,000.
e. $85,000; $185,000.

4. Hansen and Fleming are partners and share equally in income or loss. Hansen's current capital balance in the partnership is $125,000 and Fleming's is $124,000. Hansen and Fleming agree to accept Black with a 20% interest. Black invests $75,000 in the partnership. The bonus granted to Hansen and Fleming equals
a. $13,000 each.
b. $5,100 each.
c. $4,000 each.
d. $5,285 to Hansen; $4,915 to Fleming.
e. $0; Hansen and Fleming grant a bonus to Black.

5. Mee Su is a partner in Hartford Partners, LLC. Her partnership capital balance at the beginning of the current year was $110,000, and her ending balance was $124,000. Her share of the partnership income is $10,500. What is her partner return on equity?
a. 8.97%
b. 1060.00%
c. 9.54%
d. 1047.00%
e. 8.47%

Discussion Questions

1. ♝ If a partnership contract does not state the period of time the partnership is to exist, when does the partnership end?

2. What does the term *mutual agency* mean when applied to a partnership?

3. ♝ Can partners limit the right of a partner to commit their partnership to contracts? Would such an agreement be binding (*a*) on the partners and (*b*) on outsiders?

4. ♝ Assume that Amey and Lacey are partners. Lacey dies, and her son claims the right to take his mother's place in the partnership. Does he have this right? Why or why not?

5. ♝ Assume that the Barnes and Ardmore partnership agreement provides for a two-third/one-third sharing of income but says nothing about losses. The first year of partnership operation resulted in a loss, and Barnes argues that the loss should be shared equally because the partnership agreement said nothing about sharing losses. Is Barnes correct? Explain.

6. Allocation of partnership income among the partners appears on what financial statement?

7. What does the term *unlimited liability* mean when it is applied to partnership members?

8. How does a general partnership differ from a limited partnership?

9. ♝ George, Burton, and Dillman have been partners for three years. The partnership is being dissolved. George is leaving the firm, but Burton and Dillman plan to carry on the business. In the final settlement, George places a $75,000 salary claim against the partnership. He contends that he has a claim for a salary of $25,000 for each year because he devoted all of his time for three years to the affairs of the partnership. Is his claim valid? Why or why not?

10. ♝ Kay, Kat, and Kim are partners. In a liquidation, Kay's share of partnership losses exceeds her capital account balance. Moreover, she is unable to meet the deficit from her personal assets, and her partners shared the excess losses. Does this relieve Kay of liability?

11. After all partnership assets have been converted to cash and all liabilities paid, the remaining cash should equal the sum of the balances of the partners' capital accounts. Why?

12. Assume a partner withdraws from a partnership and receives assets of greater value than the book value of his equity. Should the remaining partners share the resulting reduction in their equities in the ratio of their relative capital balances or according to their income-and-loss-sharing ratio?

♝ ***Denotes Discussion Questions that involve decision making.***

McGraw-Hill's HOMEWORK MANAGER® Available with McGraw-Hill's Homework Manager

QUICK STUDY

QS 12-1
Partnership liability
C1 

Otis and Hunan are partners in operating a store. Without consulting Otis, Hunan enters into a contract to purchase merchandise for the store. Otis contends that he did not authorize the order and refuses to pay for it. The vendor sues the partners for the contract price of the merchandise. (*a*) Must the partnership pay for the merchandise? Why? (*b*) Does your answer differ if Otis and Hunan are partners in a public accounting firm? Explain.

QS 12-2
Partnership income allocation
P2

Ramona Stolton and Jerry Bright are partners in a business they started two years ago. The partnership agreement states that Stolton should receive a salary allowance of $30,000 and that Bright should receive a $40,000 salary allowance. Any remaining income or loss is to be shared equally. Determine each partner's share of the current year's net income of $104,000.

QS 12-3
Partnership income allocation
P2 

Hiram and Tyrone are partners who agree that Hiram will receive a $50,000 salary allowance and that any remaining income or loss will be shared equally. If Tyrone's capital account is credited for $1,000 as her share of the net income in a given period, how much net income did the partnership earn in that period?

QS 12-4
Liability in limited partnerships
P1

Vernon organized a limited partnership and is the only general partner. Xavier invested $40,000 in the partnership and was admitted as a limited partner with the understanding that he would receive 10% of the profits. After two unprofitable years, the partnership ceased doing business. At that point, partnership liabilities were $170,000 larger than partnership assets. How much money can the partnership's creditors obtain from Xavier's personal assets to satisfy the unpaid partnership debts?

QS 12-5
Partner admission through purchase of interest P3

Dresden agrees to pay Choi and Amal $20,000 each for a one-third (33⅓%) interest in the Choi and Amal partnership. Immediately prior to Dresden's admission, each partner had a $60,000 capital balance. Make the journal entry to record Dresden's purchase of the partners' interest.

QS 12-6
Admission of a partner P3

Neal and Vanier are partners, each with $80,000 in their partnership capital accounts. Brantford is admitted to the partnership by investing $80,000 cash. Make the entry to show Brantford's admission to the partnership.

QS 12-7
Partner return on equity
A1 

Paulson and Fleming's company is organized as a partnership. At the prior year-end, partnership equity totaled $300,000 ($200,000 from Paulson and $100,000 from Fleming). For the current year, partnership net income is $49,000 ($38,400 allocated to Paulson and $10,600 allocated to Fleming), and year-end total partnership equity is $400,000 ($280,000 from Paulson and $120,000 from Fleming). Compute the total partnership return on equity *and* the individual partner return on equity ratios.

McGraw-Hill's HOMEWORK MANAGER® Available with McGraw-Hill's Homework Manager

EXERCISES

Exercise 12-1
Characteristics of partnerships
C1

Next to the following list of eight characteristics of business organizations, enter a brief description of how each characteristic applies to general partnerships.

Characteristic	Application to General Partnerships
1. Life	
2. Owners' liability	
3. Legal status	
4. Tax status of income	
5. Owners' authority	
6. Ease of formation	
7. Transferability of ownership	
8. Ability to raise large amounts of capital	

Exercise 12-2
Forms of organization
C1 

For each of the following separate cases, recommend a form of business organization. With each recommendation, explain how business income would be taxed if the owners adopt the form of organization recommended. Also list several advantages that the owners will enjoy from the form of business organization that you recommend.

a. Sharif, Henry, and Saanen are recent college graduates in computer science. They want to start a Website development company. They all have college debts and currently do not own any substantial computer equipment needed to get the company started.

b. Dr. LeBlanc and Dr. Liu are recent graduates from medical residency programs. Both are family practice physicians and would like to open a clinic in an underserved rural area. Although neither has any funds to bring to the new venture, a banker has expressed interest in making a loan to provide start-up funds for their practice.

c. Novato has been out of school for about five years and has become quite knowledgeable about the commercial real estate market. He would like to organize a company that buys and sells real estate. Novato believes he has the expertise to manage the company but needs funds to invest in commercial property.

Exercise 12-3
Journalizing partnership transactions
P2

On March 1, 2009, Eckert and Kelley formed a partnership. Eckert contributed $83,000 cash and Kelley contributed land valued at $66,400 and a building valued at $96,400. The partnership also assumed responsibility for Kelley's $77,800 long-term note payable associated with the land and building. The partners agreed to share income as follows: Eckert is to receive an annual salary allowance of $30,500, both are to receive an annual interest allowance of 11% of their beginning-year capital investment, and any remaining income or loss is to be shared equally. On October 20, 2009, Eckert withdrew $32,000 cash and Kelley withdrew $25,000 cash. After the adjusting and closing entries are made to the revenue and expense accounts at December 31, 2009, the Income Summary account had a credit balance of $86,000.

1. Prepare journal entries to record (*a*) the partners' initial capital investments, (*b*) their cash withdrawals, and (*c*) the December 31 closing of both the Withdrawals and Income Summary accounts.

Check (2) Kelley, $87,860

2. Determine the balances of the partners' capital accounts as of December 31, 2009.

Exercise 12-4
Income allocation in a partnership
P2

Daria and Farrah began a partnership by investing $64,000 and $58,000, respectively. During its first year, the partnership earned $175,000. Prepare calculations showing how the $175,000 income should be allocated to the partners under each of the following three separate plans for sharing income and loss: (1) the partners failed to agree on a method to share income; (2) the partners agreed to share income and loss in proportion to their initial investments (round amounts to the nearest dollar); and (3) the partners agreed to share income by granting a $52,000 per year salary allowance to Daria, a $42,000 per year salary allowance to Farrah, 8% interest on their initial capital investments, and the remaining balance shared equally.

Check Plan 3, Daria, $92,740

Exercise 12-5
Income allocation in a partnership
P2

Assume that the partners of Exercise 12-4 agreed to share net income and loss by granting annual salary allowances of $52,000 to Daria and $42,000 to Farrah, 8% interest allowances on their investments, and any remaining balance shared equally.

1. Determine the partners' shares of Daria and Farrah given a first-year net income of $98,800.

Check (2) Daria, $(3,160)

2. Determine the partners' shares of Daria and Farrah given a first-year net loss of $16,800.

Exercise 12-6
Sale of partnership interest P3

The partners in the Biz Partnership have agreed that partner Estella may sell her $111,000 equity in the partnership to Sean, for which Sean will pay Estella $88,800. Present the partnership's journal entry to record the sale of Estella's interest to Sean on September 30.

Exercise 12-7
Admission of new partner
P3

The Josetti Partnership has total partners' equity of $558,000, which is made up of Dopke, Capital, $392,000, and Hughes, Capital, $166,000. The partners share net income and loss in a ratio of 85% to Dopke and 15% to Hughes. On November 1, Nillsen is admitted to the partnership and given a 10% interest in equity and a 10% share in any income and loss. Prepare the journal entry to record the admission of Nillsen under each of the following separate assumptions: Nillsen invests cash of (1) $62,000; (2) $97,000; and (3) $32,000.

Exercise 12-8
Retirement of partner
P3

Edison, Delray, and West have been partners while sharing net income and loss in a 5:4:1 ratio. On January 31, the date West retires from the partnership, the equities of the partners are Edison, $330,000; Delray, $231,000; and West, $165,000. Present journal entries to record West's retirement under each of the following separate assumptions: West is paid for her equity using partnership cash of (1) $165,000; (2) $192,000; and (3) $129,000.

Exercise 12-9
Liquidation of partnership
P4

The Red, White & Blue partnership was begun with investments by the partners as follows: Red, $153,000; White, $183,000; and Blue, $180,000. The operations did not go well, and the partners eventually decided to liquidate the partnership, sharing all losses equally. On August 31, after all assets were converted to cash and all creditors were paid, only $39,000 in partnership cash remained.

Check (1) Red, $(6,000)

1. Compute the capital account balance of each partner after the liquidation of assets and the payment of creditors.
2. Assume that any partner with a deficit agrees to pay cash to the partnership to cover the deficit. Present the journal entries on August 31 to record (*a*) the cash receipt from the deficient partner(s) and (*b*) the final disbursement of cash to the partners.
3. Assume that any partner with a deficit is not able to reimburse the partnership. Present journal entries (*a*) to transfer the deficit of any deficient partners to the other partners and (*b*) to record the final disbursement of cash to the partners.

Exercise 12-10
Liquidation of partnership P4

Brewster, Conway, and Ogden are partners who share income and loss in a 1:5:4 ratio. After lengthy disagreements among the partners and several unprofitable periods, the partners decide to liquidate the partnership. Immediately before liquidation, the partnership balance sheet shows total assets, $117,000; total liabilities, $87,750; Brewster, Capital, $1,600; Conway, Capital, $11,600; and Ogden, Capital, $16,050. The cash proceeds from selling the assets were sufficient to repay all but $20,500 to the creditors. (*a*) Calculate the loss from selling the assets. (*b*) Allocate the loss to the partners. (*c*) Determine how much of the remaining liability should be paid by each partner.

Check (b) Ogden, Capital after allocation, $(3,850)

Exercise 12-11
Liquidation of limited partnership
P4

Assume that the Brewster, Conway, and Ogden partnership of Exercise 12-10 is a limited partnership. Brewster and Conway are general partners and Ogden is a limited partner. How much of the remaining $20,500 liability should be paid by each partner? (Round amounts to the nearest dollar.)

Exercise 12-12
Partner return on equity
A1 

Hunt Sports Enterprises LP is organized as a limited partnership consisting of two individual partners: Soccer LP and Football LP. Both partners separately operate a minor league soccer team and a semipro football team. Compute partner return on equity for each limited partnership (and the total) for the year ended June 30, 2009, using the following selected data on partner capital balances from Hunt Sports Enterprises LP.

	Soccer LP	Football LP	Total
Balance at 6/30/2008	$331,000	$1,357,100	$1,688,100
Annual net income	35,405	725,803	761,208
Cash distribution	—	(65,000)	(65,000)
Balance at 6/30/2009	$366,405	$2,017,903	$2,384,308

McGraw-Hill's HOMEWORK MANAGER® Available with McGraw-Hill's Homework Manager

PROBLEM SET A

Problem 12-1A
Allocating partnership income
P2

Alex Jeffers, Jo Ford, and Rose Verne invested $32,500, $45,500, and $52,000, respectively, in a partnership. During its first calendar year, the firm earned $391,200.

Check (3) Verne, Capital, $136,760

Required

Prepare the entry to close the firm's Income Summary account as of its December 31 year-end and to allocate the $391,200 net income to the partners under each of the following separate assumptions: The partners (1) have no agreement on the method of sharing income and loss; (2) agreed to share income and loss in the ratio of their beginning capital investments; and (3) agreed to share income and loss by providing annual salary allowances of $40,000 to Jeffers, $35,000 to Ford, and $46,000 to Verne; granting 8% interest on the partners' beginning capital investments; and sharing the remainder equally.

Problem 12-2A
Allocating partnership income and loss; sequential years
P2

mhhe.com/wildFAP19e

Jasmine Watts and Liz Thomas are forming a partnership to which Watts will devote one-half time and Thomas will devote full time. They have discussed the following alternative plans for sharing income and loss: (*a*) in the ratio of their initial capital investments, which they have agreed will be $30,000 for Watts and $45,000 for Thomas; (*b*) in proportion to the time devoted to the business; (*c*) a salary allowance of $3,000 per month to Thomas and the balance in accordance with the ratio of their initial capital investments; or (*d*) a salary allowance of $3,000 per month to Thomas, 10% interest on their initial capital investments, and the balance shared equally. The partners expect the business to perform as follows: year 1, $18,000 net loss; year 2, $45,000 net income; and year 3, $75,000 net income.

Required

Prepare three tables with the following column headings.

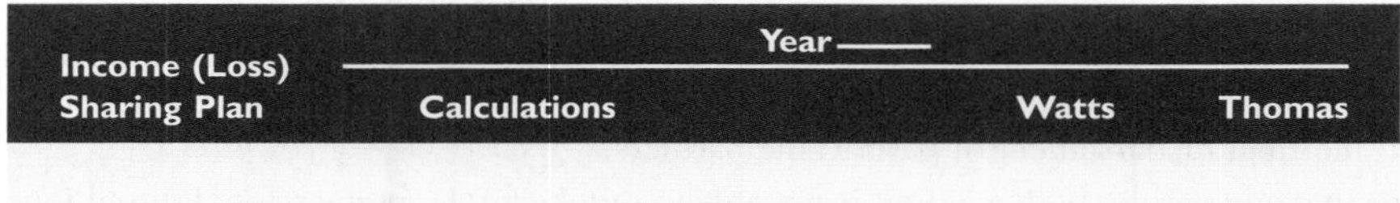

Income (Loss) Sharing Plan	Calculations	Year ___ Watts	Thomas

Complete the tables, one for each of the first three years, by showing how to allocate partnership income or loss to the partners under each of the four plans being considered. (Round answers to the nearest whole dollar.)

Check Plan d, year 1, Thomas's share, $9,750

Problem 12-3A
Partnership income allocation, statement of partners' equity, and closing entries
P2

mhhe.com/wildFAP19e

Will Beck, Trevor Beck, and Barb Beck formed the BBB Partnership by making capital contributions of $142,500, $118,750, and $213,750, respectively. They predict annual partnership net income of $210,000 and are considering the following alternative plans of sharing income and loss: (*a*) equally; (*b*) in the ratio of their initial capital investments; or (*c*) salary allowances of $38,000 to Will, $28,000 to Trevor, and $43,000 to Barb; interest allowances of 10% on their initial capital investments; and the balance shared equally.

Required

1. Prepare a table with the following column headings.

Income (Loss) Sharing Plan	Calculations	Will	Trevor	Barb	Total

   Use the table to show how to distribute net income of $210,000 for the calendar year under each of the alternative plans being considered. (Round answers to the nearest whole dollar.)
2. Prepare a statement of partners' equity showing the allocation of income to the partners assuming they agree to use plan (*c*), that income earned is $87,500, and that Will, Trevor, and Barb withdraw $18,000, $25,000, and $34,000, respectively, at year-end.
3. Prepare the December 31 journal entry to close Income Summary assuming they agree to use plan (*c*) and that net income is $87,500. Also close the withdrawals accounts.

Check (2) Barb, Ending Capital, $221,125

Problem 12-4A
Partner withdrawal and admission
P3

Part 1. Meir, Zarcus, and Ross are partners and share income and loss in a 1:4:5 ratio. The partnership's capital balances are as follows: Meir, $43,000; Zarcus, $179,000; and Ross, $228,000. Zarcus decides to withdraw from the partnership, and the partners agree to not have the assets revalued upon Zarcus's retirement. Prepare journal entries to record Zarcus's February 1 withdrawal from the partnership under each of the following separate assumptions: Zarcus (*a*) sells her interest to Garcia for $160,000 after Meir and Ross approve the entry of Garcia as a partner; (*b*) gives her interest to a son-in-law, Fields, and thereafter Meir and Ross accept Fields as a partner; (*c*) is paid $179,000 in partnership cash for her equity; (*d*) is paid $215,000 in partnership cash for her equity; and (*e*) is paid $20,000 in partnership cash plus equipment recorded on the partnership books at $70,000 less its accumulated depreciation of $23,200.

Check (1e) Cr. Ross, Capital, $93,500

Part 2. Assume that Zarcus does not retire from the partnership described in Part 1. Instead, Potter is admitted to the partnership on February 1 with a 25% equity. Prepare journal entries to record Potter's entry into the partnership under each of the following separate assumptions: Potter invests (*a*) $150,000; (*b*) $110,000; and (*c*) $196,000.

(2c) Cr. Zarcus, Capital, $13,800

Problem 12-5A
Liquidation of a partnership
P4

Kendra, Cogley, and Mei share income and loss in a 3:2:1 ratio. The partners have decided to liquidate their partnership. On the day of liquidation their balance sheet appears as follows.

KENDRA, COGLEY, AND MEI
Balance Sheet
May 31

Assets		Liabilities and Equity	
Cash	$199,100	Accounts payable	$258,000
Inventory	548,400	Kendra, Capital	97,900
		Cogley, Capital	220,275
		Mei, Capital	171,325
Total assets	$747,500	Total liabilities and equity	$747,500

Required

Prepare journal entries for (*a*) the sale of inventory, (*b*) the allocation of its gain or loss, (*c*) the payment of liabilities at book value, and (*d*) the distribution of cash in each of the following separate cases: Inventory is sold for (1) $625,200; (2) $452,400; (3) $321,000 and any partners with capital deficits pay in the amount of their deficits; and (4) $249,000 and the partners have no assets other than those invested in the partnership. (Round to the nearest dollar.)

Check (4) Cash distribution: Mei, $104,158

PROBLEM SET B

Problem 12-1B
Allocating partnership income
P2

Erin Rock, Sal Arthur, and Chloe Binder invested $47,840, $64,400, and $71,760, respectively, in a partnership. During its first calendar year, the firm earned $361,800.

Required

Prepare the entry to close the firm's Income Summary account as of its December 31 year-end and to allocate the $361,800 net income to the partners under each of the following separate assumptions. (Round answers to whole dollars.) The partners (1) have no agreement on the method of sharing income and loss; (2) agreed to share income and loss in the ratio of their beginning capital investments; and (3) agreed to share income and loss by providing annual salary allowances of $33,000 to Rock, $28,000 to Arthur, and $40,000 to Binder; granting 10% interest on the partners' beginning capital investments; and sharing the remainder equally.

Check (3) Binder, Capital, $127,976

Problem 12-2B
Allocating partnership income and loss; sequential years
P2

Maria Selk and David Green are forming a partnership to which Selk will devote one-third time and Green will devote full time. They have discussed the following alternative plans for sharing income and loss: (*a*) in the ratio of their initial capital investments, which they have agreed will be $208,000 for Selk and $312,000 for Green; (*b*) in proportion to the time devoted to the business; (*c*) a salary allowance of $8,000 per month to Green and the balance in accordance with the ratio of their initial capital investments; or (*d*) a salary allowance of $8,000 per month to Green, 10% interest on their initial capital investments, and the balance shared equally. The partners expect the business to perform as follows: year 1, $72,000 net loss; year 2, $152,000 net income; and year 3, $376,000 net income.

Required

Prepare three tables with the following column headings.

Income (Loss) Sharing Plan	Year____		
	Calculations	Selk	Green

Check Plan d, year 1, Green's share, $17,200

Complete the tables, one for each of the first three years, by showing how to allocate partnership income or loss to the partners under each of the four plans being considered. (Round answers to the nearest whole dollar.)

Problem 12-3B
Partnership income allocation, statement of partners' equity, and closing entries
P2

Sally Cook, Lin Xi, and Sami Bruce formed the CXB Partnership by making capital contributions of $169,750, $121,250, and $194,000, respectively. They predict annual partnership net income of $270,000 and are considering the following alternative plans of sharing income and loss: (*a*) equally; (*b*) in the ratio of their initial capital investments; or (*c*) salary allowances of $40,000 to Cook, $29,000 to Xi, and $42,000 to Bruce; interest allowances of 12% on their initial capital investments; and the balance shared equally.

Required

1. Prepare a table with the following column headings.

Income (Loss) Sharing Plan	Calculations	Cook	Xi	Bruce	Total

Use the table to show how to distribute net income of $270,000 for the calendar year under each of the alternative plans being considered. (Round answers to the nearest whole dollar.)

Check (2) Bruce, Ending Capital, $208,380

2. Prepare a statement of partners' equity showing the allocation of income to the partners assuming they agree to use plan (*c*), that income earned is $124,500, and that Cook, Xi, and Bruce withdraw $19,000, $26,000, and $36,000, respectively, at year-end.

3. Prepare the December 31 journal entry to close Income Summary assuming they agree to use plan (*c*) and that net income is $124,500. Also close the withdrawals accounts.

Problem 12-4B
Partner withdrawal and admission
P3

Part 1. Davis, Brown, and Nell are partners and share income and loss in a 5:1:4 ratio. The partnership's capital balances are as follows: Davis, $303,000; Brown, $74,000; and Nell, $223,000. Davis decides to withdraw from the partnership, and the partners agree not to have the assets revalued upon Davis's retirement. Prepare journal entries to record Davis's April 30 withdrawal from the partnership under each of the following separate assumptions: Davis (*a*) sells her interest to Leer for $125,000 after Brown and Nell approve the entry of Leer as a partner; (*b*) gives her interest to a daughter-in-law, Gibson, and thereafter Brown and Nell accept Gibson as a partner; (*c*) is paid $303,000 in partnership cash for her equity; (*d*) is paid $175,000 in partnership cash for her equity; and (*e*) is paid $100,000 in partnership cash plus manufacturing equipment recorded on the partnership books at $269,000 less its accumulated depreciation of $168,000.

Check (1e) Cr. Nell, Capital, $81,600

Part 2. Assume that Davis does not retire from the partnership described in Part 1. Instead, McCann is admitted to the partnership on April 30 with a 20% equity. Prepare journal entries to record the entry of McCann under each of the following separate assumptions: McCann invests (*a*) $150,000; (*b*) $98,000; and (*c*) $213,000.

Check (2c) Cr. Brown, Capital, $5,040

Problem 12-5B
Liquidation of a partnership
P4

London, Ramirez, and Toney, who share income and loss in a 3:2:1 ratio, plan to liquidate their partnership. At liquidation, their balance sheet appears as follows.

LONDON, RAMIREZ, AND TONEY
Balance Sheet
January 18

Assets		Liabilities and Equity	
Cash	$179,500	Accounts payable	$241,500
Equipment	552,000	London, Capital	98,000
		Ramirez, Capital	220,500
		Toney, Capital	171,500
Total assets	$731,500	Total liabilities and equity	$731,500

Required

Prepare journal entries for (*a*) the sale of equipment, (*b*) the allocation of its gain or loss, (*c*) the payment of liabilities at book value, and (*d*) the distribution of cash in each of the following separate cases: Equipment is sold for (1) $605,400; (2) $474,000; (3) $301,200 and any partners with capital deficits pay in the amount of their deficits; and (4) $271,200 and the partners have no assets other than those invested in the partnership. (Round amounts to the nearest dollar.)

Check (4) Cash distribution: Ramirez, $98,633

SERIAL PROBLEM

Success Systems

(This serial problem began in Chapter 1 and continues through most of the book. If previous chapter segments were not completed, the serial problem can begin at this point. It is helpful, but not necessary, to use the Working Papers that accompany the book.)

SP 12 At the start of 2010, Adriana Lopez is considering adding a partner to her business. She envisions the new partner taking the lead in generating sales of both services and merchandise for Success Systems. Lopez's equity in Success Systems as of January 1, 2010, is reflected in the following capital balance.

A. Lopez, Capital	$90,148

Required

1. Lopez is evaluating whether the prospective partner should be an equal partner with respect to capital investment and profit sharing (1:1) or whether the agreement should be 4:1 with Lopez retaining four-fifths interest with rights to four-fifths of the net income or loss. What factors should she consider in deciding which partnership agreement to offer?

2. Prepare the January 1, 2010, journal entry(ies) necessary to admit a new partner to Success Systems through the purchase of a partnership interest for each of the following two separate cases: (*a*) 1:1 sharing agreement and (*b*) 4:1 sharing agreement.

3. Prepare the January 1, 2010, journal entry(ies) required to admit a new partner if the new partner invests cash of $22,537.

4. After posting the entry in part 3, what would be the new partner's equity percentage?

BEYOND THE NUMBERS

REPORTING IN ACTION

C1 

BTN 12-1 Take a step back in time and imagine **Best Buy** in its infancy as a company. The year is 1966.

Required

1. Read the history of Best Buy at BestBuymedia.tekgroup.com. Can you determine from the history whether Best Buy was originally organized as a sole proprietorship, partnership, or corporation?

2. Assume that Best Buy was originally organized as a partnership. Best Buy's income statement in Appendix A varies in several key ways from what it would look like for a partnership. Identify at least two ways in which a corporate income statement differs from a partnership income statement.

3. Compare the Best Buy balance sheet in Appendix A to what a partnership balance sheet would have shown. Identify and explain any account differences you would anticipate.

COMPARATIVE ANALYSIS

C1 

BTN 12-2 Over the years **Best Buy** and **Circuit City** have evolved into large corporations. Today it is difficult to imagine them as fledgling start-ups. Research each company's history online.

Required

1. Which company is older?

2. Which company started as a partnership?

3. In what years did each company first achieve $1,000,000 in sales?

4. In what years did each company have its first public offering of stock?

ETHICS CHALLENGE

P2 

BTN 12-3 Doctors Maben, Orlando, and Clark have been in a group practice for several years. Maben and Orlando are family practice physicians, and Clark is a general surgeon. Clark receives many referrals for surgery from his family practice partners. Upon the partnership's original formation, the three doctors agreed to a two-part formula to share income. Every month each doctor receives a salary allowance of $3,000. Additional income is divided according to a percent of patient charges the doctors generate for the month. In the current month, Maben generated 10% of the billings, Orlando 30%, and Clark 60%. The group's income for this month is $50,000. Clark has expressed dissatisfaction with the income-sharing formula and asks that income be split entirely on patient charge percents.

Required

1. Compute the income allocation for the current month using the original agreement.
2. Compute the income allocation for the current month using Clark's proposed agreement.
3. Identify the ethical components of this partnership decision for the doctors.

COMMUNICATING IN PRACTICE

C1

BTN 12-4 Assume that you are studying for an upcoming accounting exam with a good friend. Your friend says that she has a solid understanding of general partnerships but is less sure that she understands organizations that combine certain characteristics of partnerships with other forms of business organization. You offer to make some study notes for your friend to help her learn about limited partnerships, limited liability partnerships, S corporations, and limited liability companies. Prepare a one-page set of well-organized, complete study notes on these four forms of business organization.

TAKING IT TO THE NET

P1 P2 

BTN 12-5 Access the March 6, 2007, filing of the December 31, 2006, 10-K of **America First Tax Exempt Investors LP**. This company deals with tax-exempt mortgage revenue bonds that, among other things, finance student housing properties.

1. Locate its December 31, 2006, balance sheet and list the account titles reported in the equity section of the balance sheet.
2. Locate its statement of partners' capital and comprehensive income (loss). How many units of limited partnership (known as "beneficial unit certificate holders") are outstanding at December 31, 2006?
3. What is the partnership's largest asset and its amount at December 31, 2006?

TEAMWORK IN ACTION

P2

BTN 12-6 This activity requires teamwork to reinforce understanding of accounting for partnerships.

Required

1. Assume that Baker, Warner, and Rice form the BWR Partnership by making capital contributions of $200,000, $300,000, and $500,000, respectively. BWR predicts annual partnership net income of $600,000. The partners are considering various plans for sharing income and loss. Assign a different team member to compute how the projected $600,000 income would be shared under each of the following separate plans:
   - **a.** Shared equally.
   - **b.** In the ratio of the partners' initial capital investments.
   - **c.** Salary allowances of $50,000 to Baker, $60,000 to Warner, and $70,000 to Rice, with the remaining balance shared equally.
   - **d.** Interest allowances of 10% on the partners' initial capital investments, with the remaining balance shared equally.
2. In sequence, each member is to present his or her income-sharing calculations with the team.
3. As a team, identify and discuss at least one other possible way that income could be shared.

BTN 12-7 Recall the chapter's opening feature involving Samanta and Kelvin Joseph, and their company, Samanta Shoes. Assume that Samanta and Kelvin, partners in Samanta Shoes, decide to expand their business with the help of general partners.

ENTREPRENEURIAL DECISION

C1 

Required

1. What details should Samanta, Kelvin, and their future partners specify in the general partnership agreements?
2. What advantages should Samanta, Kelvin, and their future partners be aware of with respect to organizing as a general partnership?
3. What disadvantages should Samanta, Kelvin, and their future partners be aware of with respect to organizing as a general partnership?

BTN 12-8 Access DSG international's Website (www.DSGiplc.com) and research the company's history.

GLOBAL DECISION

C1 

DSG

1. When was the company founded, and what was its original form of ownership?
2. Why did the company change its name from Dixons to DSG international?
3. What are some of the companies that are part of DSG international?

ANSWERS TO MULTIPLE CHOICE QUIZ

1. e; Capital = $250,000 − $50,000
2. a; $90,000 × [$100,000/($150,000 + $150,000 + $100,000)] = $22,500
3. d;

	Jamison	Blue	Total
Net income			$ 270,000
Salary allowance	$120,000		(120,000)
Interest allowance	60,000	$80,000	(140,000)
Balance of income			10,000
Balance divided equally	5,000	5,000	(10,000)
Totals	$185,000	$85,000	$ 0

4. b; Total partnership equity = $125,000 + $124,000 + $75,000 = $324,000
   Equity of Black = $324,000 × 20% = $64,800
   Bonus to old partners = $75,000 − $64,800 = $10,200, split equally
5. a; $10,500/[($110,000 + $124,000)/2] = 8.97%

A Look Back

Chapter 12 focused on the partnership form of organization. We described crucial characteristics of partnerships and the accounting and reporting of their important transactions.

A Look at This Chapter

This chapter emphasizes details of the corporate form of organization. The accounting concepts and procedures for equity transactions are explained. We also describe how to report and analyze income, earnings per share, and retained earnings.

A Look Ahead

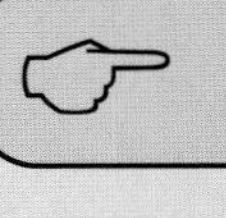

Chapter 14 focuses on long-term liabilities. We explain how to value, record, amortize, and report these liabilities in financial statements.

Chapter 13 Accounting for Corporations

Learning Objectives

CAP

Conceptual

C1 Identify characteristics of corporations and their organization. *(p. 506)*

C2 Describe the components of stockholders' equity. *(p. 509)*

C3 Explain characteristics of common and preferred stock. *(p. 517)*

C4 Explain the items reported in retained earnings. *(p. 522)*

Analytical

A1 Compute earnings per share and describe its use. *(p. 524)*

A2 Compute price-earnings ratio and describe its use in analysis. *(p. 525)*

A3 Compute dividend yield and explain its use in analysis. *(p. 525)*

A4 Compute book value and explain its use in analysis. *(p. 526)*

Procedural

P1 Record the issuance of corporate stock. *(p. 510)*

P2 Record transactions involving cash dividends. *(p. 513)*

P3 Account for stock dividends and stock splits. *(p. 514)*

P4 Distribute dividends between common stock and preferred stock. *(p. 517)*

P5 Record purchases and sales of treasury stock and the retirement of stock. *(p. 520)*

LP13

Decision Feature

Breathing New Life

"We weren't planning on starting a company"
—Ali Perry

SANTA BARBARA, CA—"My grandma has COPD [chronic obstructive pulmonary disease] and she got put on oxygen," explains Ali Perry. "Her quality of life got destroyed because she couldn't go anywhere, she couldn't do anything. Everything was limited by how much she had in her bottles of compressed oxygen." Ali dreamed to help her grandma. She explains that COPD is the fourth leading cause of death, and is predicted to soon be third on that list. COPD is a disease where the airways of the lungs narrow, which limits the flow of air and causes shortness of breath.

To make her dream a reality, Ali enlisted the aid of two college classmates, Byron Myers and Brenton Taylor. The three of them designed a portable oxygen system, wrote a business plan, and set off to secure financing. Their company, named **Inogen**, which is a combination of the words innovation and oxygen **(Inogen.net),** soon had a portable oxygen supply unit whose sales exceed 10,000 units to date. "We worked really hard at the technology," explains Ali. "We saw the value of the company was in creating technology that was thought impossible in the marketplace."

The three founders insist that proper financing was a key to their success. To make it happen, says Ali, they needed equity (stock) financing. With their business plan and prototype, the three raised a whopping $4 million from a venture capital firm. Still, explains Ali, the focus is on helping folks, including her grandma. Adds Byron, "Oxygen users can now take off on a moment's notice, without having to watch the clock or guess at how long their oxygen will last."

Their equity financing "brings both opportunities and challenges," explains Byron. "New patients do not know anything about oxygen therapy. All they know is that their life has changed and they now need to have a supply of oxygen with them whenever and wherever." Inogen answers that call. Their focus on people continues to reap rewards as they recently secured another $22 million in equity financing. As Byron put it: "[Inogen] makes old ways of thinking and operating inadequate."

[Sources: *Inogen Website,* January 2009; *HME Business,* January 2006; *Daily Nexus,* January 2004; *Goleta Valley Voice,* December 2003; *Inc.com,* July 2007]

Chapter Preview

This chapter focuses on equity transactions. The first part of the chapter describes the basics of the corporate form of organization and explains the accounting for common and preferred stock. We then focus on several special financing transactions, including cash and stock dividends, stock splits, and treasury stock. The final section considers accounting for retained earnings, including prior period adjustments, retained earnings restrictions, and reporting guidelines.

Accounting for Corporations

Corporations
- Characteristics
- Organization and management
- Stockholders
- Stock basics

Common Stock
- Par value
- No-par value
- Stated value
- Stock for noncash assets

Dividends
- Cash dividends
- Stock dividends
- Stock splits

Preferred Stock
- Issuance
- Dividend preferences
- Convertible preferred
- Callable preferred

Treasury Stock
- Purchasing treasury stock
- Reissuing treasury stock
- Retiring stock

Reporting on Equity
- Statement of retained earnings
- Statement of stockholders' equity
- Stock options

Corporate Form of Organization

Video13.1

A **corporation** is an entity created by law that is separate from its owners. It has most of the rights and privileges granted to individuals. Owners of corporations are called *stockholders* or *shareholders*. Corporations can be separated into two types. A *privately held* (or *closely held*) corporation does not offer its stock for public sale and usually has few stockholders. A *publicly held* corporation offers its stock for public sale and can have thousands of stockholders. *Public sale* usually refers to issuance and trading on an organized stock market.

Characteristics of Corporations

C1 Identify characteristics of corporations and their organization.

Corporations represent an important type of organization. Their unique characteristics offer advantages and disadvantages.

Advantages of Corporate Characteristics

- **Separate legal entity:** A corporation conducts its affairs with the same rights, duties, and responsibilities of a person. It takes actions through its agents, who are its officers and managers.
- **Limited liability of stockholders:** Stockholders are neither liable for corporate acts nor corporate debt.
- **Transferable ownership rights:** The transfer of shares from one stockholder to another usually has no effect on the corporation or its operations except when this causes a change in the directors who control or manage the corporation.
- **Continuous life:** A corporation's life continues indefinitely because it is not tied to the physical lives of its owners.
- **Lack of mutual agency for stockholders:** A corporation acts through its agents, who are its officers and managers. Stockholders, who are not its officers and managers, do not have the power to bind the corporation to contracts—referred to as *lack of mutual agency.*
- **Ease of capital accumulation:** Buying stock is attractive to investors because (1) stockholders are not liable for the corporation's acts and debts, (2) stocks usually are transferred easily, (3) the life of the corporation is unlimited, and (4) stockholders are not corporate agents. These advantages enable corporations to accumulate large amounts of capital from the combined investments of many stockholders.

Point: The *business entity assumption* requires a corporation to be accounted for separately from its owners (shareholders).

Global: U.S., U.K., and Canadian corporations finance much of their operations with stock issuances, but companies in countries such as France, Germany, and Japan finance mainly with note and bond issuances.

Disadvantages of Corporate Characteristics

- **Government regulation:** A corporation must meet requirements of a state's incorporation laws, which subject the corporation to state regulation and control. Proprietorships and partnerships avoid many of these regulations and governmental reports.
- **Corporate taxation:** Corporations are subject to the same property and payroll taxes as proprietorships and partnerships plus *additional* taxes. The most burdensome of these are federal and state income taxes that together can take 40% or more of corporate pretax income. Moreover, corporate income is usually taxed a second time as part of stockholders' personal income when they receive cash distributed as dividends. This is called *double taxation.* (The usual dividend tax is 15%; however, it is less than 15% for lower income taxpayers, and in some cases zero.)

Point: Proprietorships and partnerships are not subject to income taxes. Their income is taxed as the personal income of their owners.

Point: Double taxation is less severe when a corporation's owner-manager collects a salary that is taxed only once as part of his or her personal income.

Decision Insight

Stock Financing Marc Andreessen cofounded **Netscape** at age 22, only four months after earning his degree. One year later, he and friends issued Netscape shares to the public. The stock soared, making Andreessen a multimillionaire.

Corporate Organization and Management

This section describes the incorporation, costs, and management of corporate organizations.

Point: A corporation is not required to have an office in its state of incorporation.

Incorporation A corporation is created by obtaining a charter from a state government. A charter application usually must be signed by the prospective stockholders called *incorporators* or *promoters* and then filed with the proper state official. When the application process is complete and fees paid, the charter is issued and the corporation is formed. Investors then purchase the corporation's stock, meet as stockholders, and elect a board of directors. Directors oversee a corporation's affairs.

Organization Expenses **Organization expenses** (also called *organization costs*) are the costs to organize a corporation; they include legal fees, promoters' fees, and amounts paid to obtain a charter. The corporation records (debits) these costs to an expense account called *Organization Expenses*. Organization costs are expensed as incurred because it is difficult to determine the amount and timing of their future benefits.

Management of a Corporation The ultimate control of a corporation rests with stockholders who control a corporation by electing its *board of directors,* or simply, *directors.* Each stockholder usually has one vote for each share of stock owned. This control relation is shown in Exhibit 13.1. Directors are responsible for and have final authority for managing corporate activities. A board can act only as a collective body and usually limits its actions to setting general policy.

EXHIBIT 13.1

Corporate Structure

Stockholders
↓
Board of Directors
↓
President, Vice President, and Other Officers
↓
Employees of the Corporation

A corporation usually holds a stockholder meeting at least once a year to elect directors and transact business as its bylaws require. A group of stockholders owning or controlling votes of more than a 50% share of a corporation's stock can elect the board and control the corporation. Stockholders who do not attend stockholders' meetings must have an opportunity to delegate their voting rights to an agent by signing a **proxy,** a document that gives a designated agent the right to vote the stock.

Point: *Bylaws* are guidelines that govern the behavior of individuals employed by and managing the corporation.

Day-to-day direction of corporate business is delegated to executive officers appointed by the board. A corporation's chief executive officer (CEO) is often its president. Several vice

Global: Some corporate labels are:

Country	Label
United States	Inc.
France	SA
United Kingdom	
Public	PLC
Private	LTD
Germany	
Public	AG
Private	GmbH
Sweden	AB
Italy	SpA

presidents, who report to the president, are commonly assigned specific areas of management responsibility such as finance, production, and marketing. One person often has the dual role of chairperson of the board of directors and CEO. In this case, the president is usually designated the chief operating officer (COO).

Decision Insight

Seed Money Sources for start-up money include (1) "angel" investors such as family, friends, or anyone who believes in a company, (2) employees, investors, and even suppliers who can be paid with stock, and (3) venture capitalists (investors) who have a record of entrepreneurial success. See the National Venture Capital Association (**NVCA.org**) for information.

Stockholders of Corporations

This section explains stockholder rights, stock purchases and sales, and the role of registrar and transfer agents.

Rights of Stockholders When investors buy stock, they acquire all *specific* rights the corporation's charter grants to stockholders. They also acquire *general* rights granted stockholders by the laws of the state in which the company is incorporated. When a corporation has only one class of stock, it is identified as **common stock.** State laws vary, but common stockholders usually have the general right to

1. Vote at stockholders' meetings.
2. Sell or otherwise dispose of their stock.
3. Purchase their proportional share of any common stock later issued by the corporation. This **preemptive right** protects stockholders' proportionate interest in the corporation. For example, a stockholder who owns 25% of a corporation's common stock has the first opportunity to buy 25% of any new common stock issued.
4. Receive the same dividend, if any, on each common share of the corporation.
5. Share in any assets remaining after creditors and preferred stockholders are paid when, and if, the corporation is liquidated. Each common share receives the same amount.

Stockholders also have the right to receive timely financial reports.

Stock Certificates and Transfer Investors who buy a corporation's stock, sometimes receive a *stock certificate* as proof of share ownership. Many corporations issue only one certificate for each block of stock purchased. A certificate can be for any number of shares. Exhibit 13.2 shows a stock certificate of the **Green Bay Packers**. A certificate shows the company name, stockholder name, number of shares, and other crucial information. Issuance of certificates is becoming less common. Instead, many stockholders maintain accounts with the corporation or their stockbrokers and never receive actual certificates.

EXHIBIT 13.2

Stock Certificate

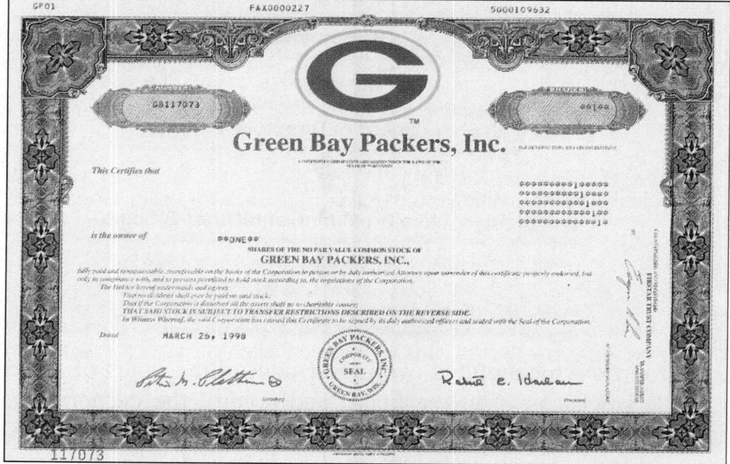

Registrar and Transfer Agents If a corporation's stock is traded on a major stock exchange, the corporation must have a registrar and a transfer agent. A *registrar* keeps stockholder records and prepares official lists of stockholders for stockholder meetings and dividend payments. A *transfer agent* assists with purchases and sales of shares by receiving and issuing certificates as necessary. Registrars and transfer agents are usually large banks or trust companies with computer facilities and staff to do this work.

Decision Insight

Pricing Stock A prospectus accompanies a stock's initial public offering (IPO), giving financial information about the company issuing the stock. A prospectus should help answer these questions to price an IPO: (1) Is the underwriter reliable? (2) Is there growth in revenues, profits, and cash flows? (3) What is management's view of operations? (4) Are current owners selling? (5) What are the risks?

Basics of Capital Stock

C2 Describe the components of stockholders' equity.

Capital stock is a general term that refers to any shares issued to obtain capital (owner financing). This section introduces terminology and accounting for capital stock.

Authorized Stock **Authorized stock** is the number of shares that a corporation's charter allows it to sell. The number of authorized shares usually exceeds the number of shares issued (and outstanding), often by a large amount. (*Outstanding stock* refers to issued stock held by stockholders.) No formal journal entry is required for stock authorization. A corporation must apply to the state for a change in its charter if it wishes to issue more shares than previously authorized. A corporation discloses the number of shares authorized in the equity section of its balance sheet or notes. Best Buy's balance sheet in Appendix A reports 1 billion shares authorized as of the start of its 2008 fiscal year.

Subcategories of Authorized Stock

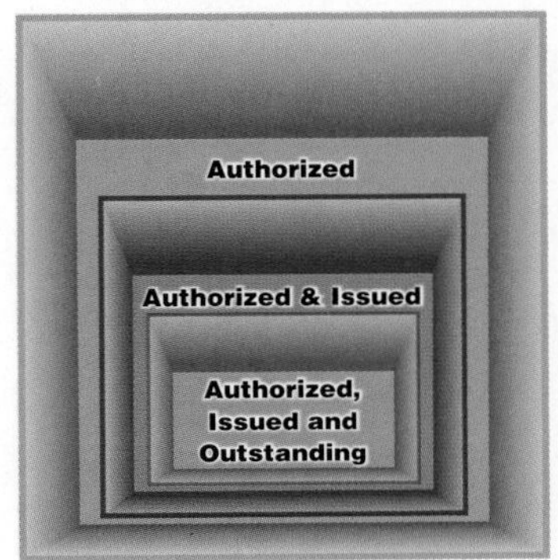

Selling (Issuing) Stock A corporation can sell stock directly or indirectly. To *sell directly,* it advertises its stock issuance to potential buyers. This type of issuance is most common with privately held corporations. To *sell indirectly,* a corporation pays a brokerage house (investment banker) to issue its stock. Some brokerage houses *underwrite* an indirect issuance of stock; that is, they buy the stock from the corporation and take all gains or losses from its resale.

Market Value of Stock **Market value per share** is the price at which a stock is bought and sold. Expected future earnings, dividends, growth, and other company and economic factors influence market value. Traded stocks' market values are available daily in newspapers such as *The Wall Street Journal* and online. The current market value of previously issued shares (for example, the price of stock in trades between investors) does not impact the issuing corporation's stockholders' equity.

Classes of Stock When all authorized shares have the same rights and characteristics, the stock is called *common stock.* A corporation is sometimes authorized to issue more than one class of stock, including preferred stock and different classes of common stock. American Greetings, for instance, has two types of common stock: Class A stock has 1 vote per share and Class B stock has 10 votes per share.

Par Value Stock **Par value stock** is stock that is assigned a **par value,** which is an amount assigned per share by the corporation in its charter. For example, Best Buy's common stock has a par value of $0.10. Other commonly assigned par values are $10, $5, $1 and $0.01. There is no restriction on the assigned par value. In many states, the par value of a stock establishes **minimum legal capital,** which refers to the least amount that the buyers of stock must contribute to the corporation or be subject to paying at a future date. For example, if a corporation issues 1,000 shares of $10 par value stock, the corporation's minimum legal capital in these states would be $10,000. Minimum legal capital is intended to protect a corporation's creditors. Since creditors cannot demand payment from stockholders' personal assets, their claims are limited to the corporation's assets and any minimum legal capital. At liquidation, creditor claims are paid before any amounts are distributed to stockholders.

Point: Managers are motivated to set a low par value when minimum legal capital or state issuance taxes are based on par value.

Point: Minimum legal capital was intended to protect creditors by requiring a minimum level of net assets.

No-Par Value Stock **No-par value stock,** or simply *no-par stock,* is stock *not* assigned a value per share by the corporate charter. Its advantage is that it can be issued at any price without the possibility of a minimum legal capital deficiency.

Point: Par, no-par, and stated value do *not* set the stock's market value.

EXHIBIT 13.3
Equity Composition

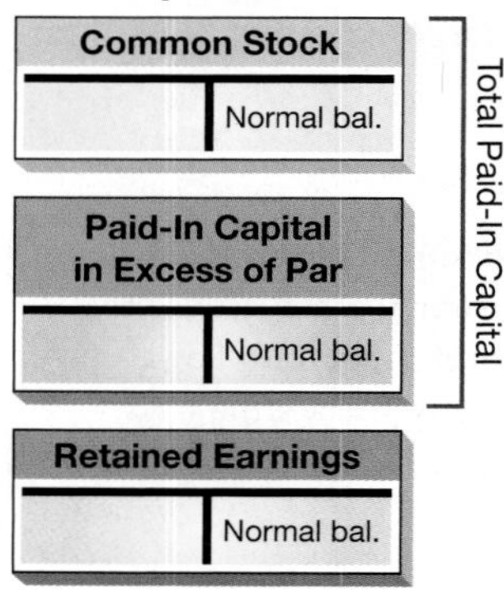

Point: Paid-in capital comes from stock-related transactions, whereas retained earnings comes from operations.

Stated Value Stock **Stated value stock** is no-par stock to which the directors assign a "stated" value per share. Stated value per share becomes the minimum legal capital per share in this case.

Stockholders' Equity A corporation's equity is known as **stockholders' equity,** also called *shareholders' equity* or *corporate capital.* Stockholders' equity consists of (1) paid-in (or contributed) capital and (2) retained earnings; see Exhibit 13.3. **Paid-in capital** is the total amount of cash and other assets the corporation receives from its stockholders in exchange for its stock. **Retained earnings** is the cumulative net income (and loss) not distributed as dividends to its stockholders.

Decision Insight

Stock Quote The **Best Buy** stock quote is interpreted as (left to right): **Hi,** highest price in past 52 weeks; **Lo,** lowest price in past 52 weeks; **Sym,** company exchange symbol; **Div,** dividends paid per share in past year; **Yld %,** dividend divided by closing price; **PE,** stock price per share divided by earnings per share; **Vol mil.,** number (in millions) of shares traded; **Hi,** highest price for the day; **Lo,** lowest price for the day; **Close,** closing price for the day; **Net Chg,** change in closing price from prior day.

52 Weeks				Yld		Vol				Net
Hi	Lo	Sym	Div	%	PE	mil.	Hi	Lo	Close	Chg
54.15	41.85	BBY	0.13	0.98	19	7.2	53.14	52.36	52.91	+0.20

Quick Check

Answers—p. 531

1. Which of the following is *not* a characteristic of the corporate form of business? (*a*) Ease of capital accumulation, (*b*) Stockholder responsibility for corporate debts, (*c*) Ease in transferability of ownership rights, or (*d*) Double taxation.
2. Why is a corporation's income said to be taxed twice?
3. What is a proxy?

Common Stock

P1 Record the issuance of corporate stock.

Accounting for the issuance of common stock affects only paid-in (contributed) capital accounts; no retained earnings accounts are affected.

Video13.2

Issuing Par Value Stock

Par value stock can be issued at par, at a premium (above par), or at a discount (below par). In each case, stock can be exchanged for either cash or noncash assets.

Issuing Par Value Stock at Par When common stock is issued at par value, we record amounts for both the asset(s) received and the par value stock issued. To illustrate, the entry to record Dillon Snowboards' issuance of 30,000 shares of $10 par value stock for $300,000 cash on June 5, 2009, follows.

Assets	=	Liabilities	+	Equity
+300,000				+300,000

June 5	Cash	300,000	
	Common Stock, $10 Par Value		300,000
	Issued 30,000 shares of $10 par value common stock at par.		

Exhibit 13.4 shows the stockholders' equity of Dillon Snowboards at year-end 2009 (its first year of operations) after income of $65,000 and no dividend payments.

EXHIBIT 13.4

Stockholders' Equity for Stock Issued at Par

Stockholders' Equity	
Common Stock—$10 par value; 50,000 shares authorized; 30,000 shares issued and outstanding	$300,000
Retained earnings	65,000
Total stockholders' equity	$365,000

Issuing Par Value Stock at a Premium A **premium on stock** occurs when a corporation sells its stock for more than par (or stated) value. To illustrate, if Dillon Snowboards issues its $10 par value common stock at $12 per share, its stock is sold at a $2 per share premium. The premium, known as **paid-in capital in excess of par value,** is reported as part of equity; it is not revenue and is not listed on the income statement. The entry to record Dillon Snowboards' issuance of 30,000 shares of $10 par value stock for $12 per share on June 5, 2009, follows

Point: A *premium* is the amount by which issue price exceeds par (or stated) value. It is recorded in the "Paid-In Capital in Excess of Par Value, Common Stock" account; also called "Additional Paid-In Capital, Common Stock."

June 5	Cash	360,000	
	Common Stock, $10 Par Value		300,000
	Paid-In Capital in Excess of Par Value, Common Stock		**60,000**
	Sold and issued 30,000 shares of $10 par value common stock at $12 per share.		

Assets	= Liabilities +	Equity
+360,000		+300,000
		+60,000

The Paid-In Capital in Excess of Par Value account is added to the par value of the stock in the equity section of the balance sheet as shown in Exhibit 13.5.

Point: The *Paid-In Capital* terminology is interchangeable with *Contributed Capital.*

EXHIBIT 13.5

Stockholders' Equity for Stock Issued at a Premium

Stockholders' Equity	
Common Stock—$10 par value; 50,000 shares authorized; 30,000 shares issued and outstanding	$300,000
Paid-in capital in excess of par value, common stock	**60,000**
Retained earnings	65,000
Total stockholders' equity	$425,000

Issuing Par Value Stock at a Discount A **discount on stock** occurs when a corporation sells its stock for less than par (or stated) value. Most states prohibit the issuance of stock at a discount. In states that allow stock to be issued at a discount, its buyers usually become contingently liable to creditors for the discount. If stock is issued at a discount, the amount by which issue price is less than par is debited to a *Discount on Common Stock* account, a contra to the common stock account, and its balance is subtracted from the par value of stock in the equity section of the balance sheet. This discount is not an expense and does not appear on the income statement.

Point: Retained earnings can be negative, reflecting accumulated losses. Amazon.com had an accumulated deficit of $1.8 billion at the start of 2007.

Issuing No-Par Value Stock

When no-par stock is issued and is not assigned a stated value, the amount the corporation receives becomes legal capital and is recorded as Common Stock. This means that the entire proceeds are credited to a no-par stock account. To illustrate, a corporation records its October 20 issuance of 1,000 shares of no-par stock for $40 cash per share as follows.

Oct. 20	Cash	40,000	
	Common Stock, No-Par Value		40,000
	Issued 1,000 shares of no-par value common stock at $40 per share.		

Assets	= Liabilities +	Equity
+40,000		+40,000

Frequency of Stock Types

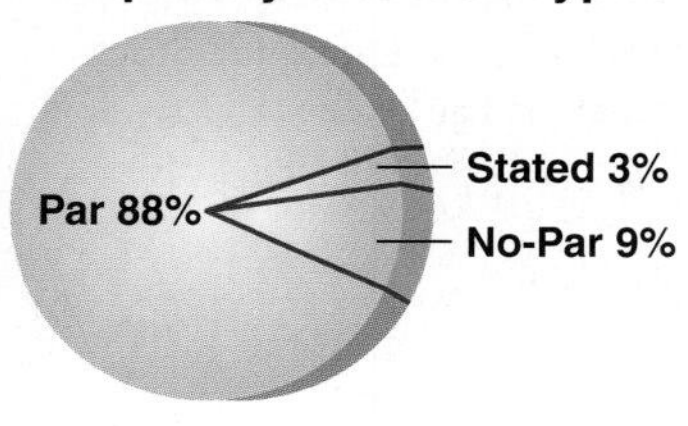

Issuing Stated Value Stock

When no-par stock is issued and assigned a stated value, its stated value becomes legal capital and is credited to a stated value stock account. Assuming that stated value stock is issued at an amount in excess of stated value (the usual case), the excess is credited to Paid-In Capital in Excess of Stated Value, Common Stock, which is reported in the stockholders' equity section. To illustrate, a corporation that issues 1,000 shares of no-par common stock having a stated value of $40 per share in return for $50 cash per share records this as follows.

Assets	= Liabilities	+ Equity
+50,000		+40,000
		+10,000

Oct. 20	Cash	50,000	
	Common Stock, $40 Stated Value		40,000
	Paid-In Capital in Excess of Stated Value, Common Stock		10,000
	Issued 1,000 shares of $40 per share stated value stock at $50 per share.		

Issuing Stock for Noncash Assets

Point: Stock issued for noncash assets should be recorded at the market value of either the stock or the noncash asset, whichever is more clearly determinable.

A corporation can receive assets other than cash in exchange for its stock. (It can also assume liabilities on the assets received such as a mortgage on property received.) The corporation records the assets received at their market values as of the date of the transaction. The stock given in exchange is recorded at its par (or stated) value with any excess recorded in the Paid-In Capital in Excess of Par (or Stated) Value account. (If no-par stock is issued, the stock is recorded at the assets' market value.) To illustrate, the entry to record receipt of land valued at $105,000 in return for issuance of 4,000 shares of $20 par value common stock on June 10 is

Assets	= Liabilities	+ Equity
+105,000		+80,000
		+25,000

June 10	Land	105,000	
	Common Stock, $20 Par Value		80,000
	Paid-In Capital in Excess of Par Value, Common Stock		25,000
	Exchanged 4,000 shares of $20 par value common stock for land.		

Point: Any type of stock can be issued for noncash assets.

A corporation sometimes gives shares of its stock to promoters in exchange for their services in organizing the corporation, which the corporation records as **Organization Expenses.** The entry to record receipt of services valued at $12,000 in organizing the corporation in return for 600 shares of $15 par value common stock on June 5 is

Assets	= Liabilities	+ Equity
		−12,000
		+9,000
		+3,000

June 5	Organization Expenses	12,000	
	Common Stock, $15 Par Value		9,000
	Paid-In Capital in Excess of Par Value, Common Stock		3,000
	Gave promoters 600 shares of $15 par value common stock in exchange for their services.		

Quick Check

Answers—p. 531

4. A company issues 7,000 shares of its $10 par value common stock in exchange for equipment valued at $105,000. The entry to record this transaction includes a credit to (*a*) Paid-In Capital in Excess of Par Value, Common Stock, for $35,000. (*b*) Retained Earnings for $35,000. (*c*) Common Stock, $10 Par Value, for $105,000.
5. What is a premium on stock issuance?
6. Who is intended to be protected by minimum legal capital?

Dividends

This section describes both cash and stock dividend transactions.

P2 Record transactions involving cash dividends.

Cash Dividends

The decision to pay cash dividends rests with the board of directors and involves more than evaluating the amounts of retained earnings and cash. The directors, for instance, may decide to keep the cash to invest in the corporation's growth, to meet emergencies, to take advantage of unexpected opportunities, or to pay off debt. Alternatively, many corporations pay cash dividends to their stockholders at regular dates. These cash flows provide a return to investors and almost always affect the stock's market value.

Video13.2

Accounting for Cash Dividends Dividend payment involves three important dates: declaration, record, and payment. **Date of declaration** is the date the directors vote to declare and pay a dividend. This creates a legal liability of the corporation to its stockholders. **Date of record** is the future date specified by the directors for identifying those stockholders listed in the corporation's records to receive dividends. The date of record usually follows the date of declaration by at least two weeks. Persons who own stock on the date of record receive dividends. **Date of payment** is the date when the corporation makes payment; it follows the date of record by enough time to allow the corporation to arrange checks, money transfers, or other means to pay dividends.

Percent of Corporations Paying Dividends

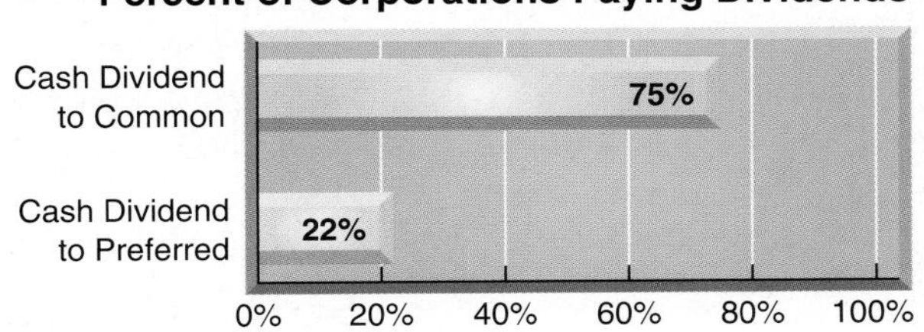

To illustrate, the entry to record a January 9 declaration of a $1 per share cash dividend by the directors of Z-Tech, Inc., with 5,000 outstanding shares is

Date of Declaration

Jan. 9	Retained Earnings	5,000	
	Common Dividend Payable		5,000
	Declared $1 per common share cash dividend.[1]		

Assets = Liabilities + Equity
+5,000 −5,000

Common Dividend Payable is a current liability. The date of record for the Z-Tech dividend is January 22. *No formal journal entry is needed on the date of record.* The February 1 date of payment requires an entry to record both the settlement of the liability and the reduction of the cash balance, as follows:

Date of Payment

Feb. 1	Common Dividend Payable	5,000	
	Cash		5,000
	Paid $1 per common share cash dividend.		

Assets = Liabilities + Equity
−5,000 −5,000

Deficits and Cash Dividends A corporation with a debit (abnormal) balance for retained earnings is said to have a **retained earnings deficit,** which arises when a company incurs cumulative losses and/or pays more dividends than total earnings from current and prior years. A deficit is reported as a deduction on the balance sheet, as shown in Exhibit 13.6. Most states prohibit a corporation with a deficit from paying a cash dividend to its stockholders. This legal restriction is designed to protect creditors by preventing distribution of assets to stockholders when the company may be in financial difficulty.

Point: It is often said a dividend is a distribution of retained earnings, but it is more precise to describe a dividend as a distribution of assets to satisfy stockholder claims.

Point: The Retained Earnings Deficit account is also called *Accumulated Deficit.*

[1] An alternative entry is to debit Dividends instead of Retained Earnings. The balance in Dividends is then closed to Retained Earnings at the end of the reporting period. The effect is the same: Retained Earnings is decreased and a Dividend Payable is increased. For simplicity, all assignments in this chapter use the Retained Earnings account to record dividend declarations.

EXHIBIT 13.6

Stockholders' Equity with a Deficit

Common stock—$10 par value, 5,000 shares authorized, issued, and outstanding	$50,000
Retained earnings deficit	(6,000)
Total stockholders' equity	$44,000

Some state laws allow cash dividends to be paid by returning a portion of the capital contributed by stockholders. This type of dividend is called a **liquidating cash dividend,** or simply *liquidating dividend,* because it returns a part of the original investment back to the stockholders. This requires a debit entry to one of the contributed capital accounts instead of Retained Earnings at the declaration date.

Point: Amazon.com has never declared a cash dividend.

Quick Check Answers—p. 531

7. What type of an account is the Common Dividend Payable account?
8. What three crucial dates are involved in the process of paying a cash dividend?
9. When does a dividend become a company's legal obligation?

Stock Dividends

P3 Account for stock dividends and stock splits.

A **stock dividend,** declared by a corporation's directors, is a distribution of additional shares of the corporation's own stock to its stockholders without the receipt of any payment in return. Stock dividends and cash dividends are different. A stock dividend does not reduce assets and equity but instead transfers a portion of equity from retained earnings to contributed capital.

Reasons for Stock Dividends Stock dividends exist for at least two reasons. First, directors are said to use stock dividends to keep the market price of the stock affordable. For example, if a corporation continues to earn income but does not issue cash dividends, the price of its common stock likely increases. The price of such a stock may become so high that it discourages some investors from buying the stock (especially in lots of 100 and 1,000). When a corporation has a stock dividend, it increases the number of outstanding shares and lowers the per share stock price. Another reason for a stock dividend is to provide evidence of management's confidence that the company is doing well and will continue to do well.

Accounting for Stock Dividends A stock dividend affects the components of equity by transferring part of retained earnings to contributed capital accounts, sometimes described as *capitalizing* retained earnings. Accounting for a stock dividend depends on whether it is a small or large stock dividend. A **small stock dividend** is a distribution of 25% or less of previously outstanding shares. It is recorded by capitalizing retained earnings for an amount equal to the market value of the shares to be distributed. A **large stock dividend** is a distribution of more than 25% of previously outstanding shares. A large stock dividend is recorded by capitalizing retained earnings for the minimum amount required by state law governing the corporation. Most states require capitalizing retained earnings equal to the par or stated value of the stock.

To illustrate stock dividends, we use the equity section of Quest's balance sheet shown in Exhibit 13.7 just *before* its declaration of a stock dividend on December 31.

EXHIBIT 13.7

Stockholders' Equity *before* Declaring a Stock Dividend

Stockholders' Equity (before dividend)	
Common stock—$10 par value, 15,000 shares authorized, 10,000 shares issued and outstanding	$100,000
Paid-in capital in excess of par value, common stock	8,000
Retained earnings	35,000
Total stockholders' equity	$143,000

Recording a small stock dividend. Assume that Quest's directors declare a 10% stock dividend on December 31. This stock dividend of 1,000 shares, computed as 10% of its 10,000 issued and outstanding shares, is to be distributed on January 20 to the stockholders of record on January 15. Since the market price of Quest's stock on December 31 is $15 per share, this small stock dividend declaration is recorded as follows:

Point: Small stock dividends are recorded at market value.

Date of Declaration

Dec. 31	Retained Earnings	15,000	
	Common Stock Dividend Distributable.		10,000
	Paid-In Capital in Excess of Par Value, Common Stock		5,000
	Declared a 1,000-share (10%) stock dividend.		

Assets = Liabilities + Equity
−15,000
+10,000
+5,000

The $10,000 credit in the declaration entry equals the par value of the shares and is recorded in *Common Stock Dividend Distributable,* an equity account. Its balance exists only until the shares are issued. The $5,000 credit equals the amount by which market value exceeds par value. This amount increases the Paid-In Capital in Excess of Par Value account in anticipation of the issuance of shares. In general, the balance sheet changes in three ways when a stock dividend is declared. First, the amount of equity attributed to common stock increases; for Quest, from $100,000 to $110,000 for 1,000 additional declared shares. Second, paid-in capital in excess of par increases by the excess of market value over par value for the declared shares. Third, retained earnings decreases, reflecting the transfer of amounts to both common stock and paid-in capital in excess of par. The stockholders' equity of Quest is shown in Exhibit 13.8 *after* its 10% stock dividend is declared on December 31—the items impacted are in bold.

Point: The term *Distributable* (not *Payable*) is used for stock dividends. A stock dividend is never a liability because it never reduces assets.

Point: The credit to Paid-In Capital in Excess of Par Value is recorded when the stock dividend is declared. This account is not affected when stock is later distributed.

EXHIBIT 13.8

Stockholders' Equity *after* Declaring a Stock Dividend

Stockholders' Equity (after dividend)	
Common stock—$10 par value, 15,000 shares authorized, 10,000 shares issued and outstanding	$100,000
Common stock dividend distributable—1,000 shares	**10,000**
Paid-in capital in excess of par value, common stock	**13,000**
Retained earnings	**20,000**
Total stockholders' equity	$143,000

No entry is made on the date of record for a stock dividend. On January 20, the date of payment, Quest distributes the new shares to stockholders and records this entry:

Date of Payment

Jan. 20	Common Stock Dividend Distributable	10,000	
	Common Stock, $10 Par Value		10,000
	To record issuance of common stock dividend.		

Assets = Liabilities + Equity
−10,000
+10,000

The combined effect of these stock dividend entries is to transfer (or capitalize) $15,000 of retained earnings to paid-in capital accounts. The amount of capitalized retained earnings equals the market value of the 1,000 issued shares ($15 × 1,000 shares). A stock dividend has no effect on the ownership percent of individual stockholders.

Point: A stock dividend does not affect assets.

Recording a large stock dividend. A corporation capitalizes retained earnings equal to the minimum amount required by state law for a large stock dividend. For most states, this amount is the par or stated value of the newly issued shares. To illustrate, suppose Quest's board declares a stock dividend of 30% instead of 10% on December 31. Since this dividend is more

Point: Large stock dividends are recorded at par or stated value.

than 25%, it is treated as a large stock dividend. Thus, the par value of the 3,000 dividend shares is capitalized at the date of declaration with this entry:

Assets = Liabilities + Equity
−30,000
+30,000

Date of Declaration

Dec. 31	Retained Earnings	30,000	
	Common Stock Dividend Distributable		30,000
	Declared a 3,000-share (30%) stock dividend.		

This transaction decreases retained earnings and increases contributed capital by $30,000. On the date of payment the company debits Common Stock Dividend Distributable and credits Common Stock for $30,000. The effects from a large stock dividend on balance sheet accounts are similar to those for a small stock dividend except for the absence of any effect on paid-in capital in excess of par.

Before 5:1 Split: 1 share, $50 par

After 5:1 Split: 5 shares, $10 par

Point: Berkshire Hathaway has resisted a stock split. Its recent stock price was $150,000 per share.

Point: A **reverse stock split** is the opposite of a stock split. It increases both the market value per share and the par or stated value per share with a split ratio less than 1-for-1, such as 1-for-2. A reverse split results in fewer shares.

Stock Splits

A **stock split** is the distribution of additional shares to stockholders according to their percent ownership. When a stock split occurs, the corporation "calls in" its outstanding shares and issues more than one new share in exchange for each old share. Splits can be done in any ratio, including 2-for-1, 3-for-1, or higher. Stock splits reduce the par or stated value per share. The reasons for stock splits are similar to those for stock dividends.

To illustrate, CompTec has 100,000 outstanding shares of $20 par value common stock with a current market value of $88 per share. A 2-for-1 stock split cuts par value in half as it replaces 100,000 shares of $20 par value stock with 200,000 shares of $10 par value stock. Market value is reduced from $88 per share to about $44 per share. The split does not affect any equity amounts reported on the balance sheet or any individual stockholder's percent ownership. Both the Paid-In Capital and Retained Earnings accounts are unchanged by a split, and *no journal entry is made.* The only effect on the accounts is a change in the stock account description. CompTec's 2-for-1 split on its $20 par value stock means that after the split, it changes its stock account title to Common Stock, $10 Par Value. This stock's description on the balance sheet also changes to reflect the additional authorized, issued, and outstanding shares and the new par value.

The difference between stock splits and large stock dividends is often blurred. Many companies report stock splits in their financial statements without calling in the original shares by simply changing their par value. This type of "split" is really a large stock dividend and results in additional shares issued to stockholders by capitalizing retained earnings or transferring other paid-in capital to Common Stock. This approach avoids administrative costs of splitting the stock. **Harley-Davidson** recently declared a 2-for-1 stock split executed in the form of a 100% stock dividend.

Decision Maker

Entrepreneur A company you cofounded and own stock in announces a 50% stock dividend. Has the value of your stock investment increased, decreased, or remained the same? Would it make a difference if it was a 3-for-2 stock split executed in the form of a dividend? [Answer—p. 531]

Quick Check

Answers—p. 531

10. How does a stock dividend impact assets and retained earnings?

11. What distinguishes a large stock dividend from a small stock dividend?

12. What amount of retained earnings is capitalized for a small stock dividend?

Preferred Stock

A corporation can issue two basic kinds of stock, common and preferred. **Preferred stock** has special rights that give it priority (or senior status) over common stock in one or more areas. Special rights typically include a preference for receiving dividends and for the distribution of assets if the corporation is liquidated. Preferred stock carries all rights of common stock unless the corporate charter nullifies them. Most preferred stock, for instance, does not confer the right to vote. Exhibit 13.9 shows that preferred stock is issued by about one-fourth of large corporations. All corporations issue common stock.

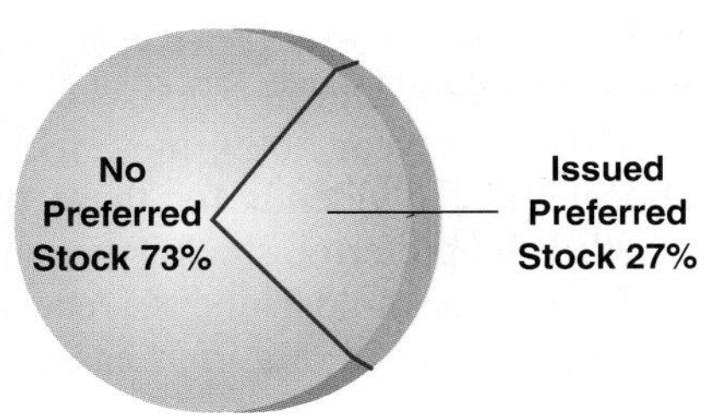

EXHIBIT 13.9

Corporations and Preferred Stock

Issuance of Preferred Stock

C3 Explain characteristics of common and preferred stock.

Preferred stock usually has a par value. Like common stock, it can be sold at a price different from par. Preferred stock is recorded in its own separate capital accounts. To illustrate, if Dillon Snowboards issues 50 shares of $100 par value preferred stock for $6,000 cash on July 1, 2009, the entry is

July 1	Cash	6,000	
	Preferred Stock, $100 Par Value		5,000
	Paid-In Capital in Excess of Par Value, Preferred Stock		1,000
	Issued preferred stock for cash.		

Assets	=	Liabilities	+	Equity
+6,000				+5,000
				+1,000

The equity section of the year-end balance sheet for Dillon Snowboards, including preferred stock, is shown in Exhibit 13.10. (This exhibit assumes that common stock was issued at par.) Issuing no-par preferred stock is similar to issuing no-par common stock. Also, the entries for issuing preferred stock for noncash assets are similar to those for common stock.

EXHIBIT 13.10

Stockholders' Equity with Common and Preferred Stock

Stockholders' Equity	
Common stock—$10 par value; 50,000 shares authorized; 30,000 shares issued and outstanding	$300,000
Preferred stock—$100 par value; 1,000 shares authorized; 50 shares issued and outstanding	5,000
Paid-in capital in excess of par value, preferred stock	1,000
Retained earnings	65,000
Total stockholders' equity	$371,000

Dividend Preference of Preferred Stock

P4 Distribute dividends between common stock and preferred stock.

Preferred stock usually carries a preference for dividends, meaning that preferred stockholders are allocated their dividends before any dividends are allocated to common stockholders. The dividends allocated to preferred stockholders are usually expressed as a dollar amount per share or a percent applied to par value. A preference for dividends does *not* ensure dividends. If the directors do not declare a dividend, neither the preferred nor the common stockholders receive one.

Cumulative or Noncumulative Dividend Most preferred stocks carry a cumulative dividend right. **Cumulative preferred stock** has a right to be paid both the current and all prior periods' unpaid dividends before any dividend is paid to common stockholders. When preferred stock is cumulative and the directors either do not declare a dividend to preferred stockholders or declare one that does not cover the total amount of cumulative dividend, the unpaid dividend amount is called **dividend in arrears.** Accumulation of dividends in arrears on cumulative preferred stock does not guarantee they will be paid. **Noncumulative preferred stock** confers no right to prior periods' unpaid dividends if they were not declared in those prior periods.

Point: Dividend preference does not imply that preferred stockholders receive more dividends than common stockholders, nor does it guarantee a dividend.

To illustrate the difference between cumulative and noncumulative preferred stock, assume that a corporation's outstanding stock includes (1) 1,000 shares of $100 par, 9% preferred

Video13.2

stock—yielding $9,000 per year in potential dividends, and (2) 4,000 shares of $50 par value common stock. During 2008, the first year of operations, the directors declare cash dividends of $5,000. In year 2009, they declare cash dividends of $42,000. See Exhibit 13.11 for the allocation of dividends for these two years. Allocation of year 2009 dividends depends on whether the preferred stock is noncumulative or cumulative. With noncumulative preferred, the preferred stockholders never receive the $4,000 skipped in 2008. If the preferred stock is cumulative, the $4,000 in arrears is paid in 2009 before any other dividends are paid.

EXHIBIT 13.11

Allocation of Dividends (noncumulative vs. cumulative preferred stock)

	Preferred	Common
Preferred Stock Is Noncumulative		
Year 2008	$ 5,000	$ 0
Year 2009		
Step 1: Current year's preferred dividend	$ 9,000	
Step 2: Remainder to common		$33,000
Preferred Stock Is Cumulative		
Year 2008	$ 5,000	$ 0
Year 2009		
Step 1: Dividend in arrears	$ 4,000	
Step 2: Current year's preferred dividend	9,000	
Step 3: Remainder to common		$29,000
Totals for year 2009	$13,000	$29,000

Example: What dividends do cumulative preferred stockholders receive in 2009 if the corporation paid only $2,000 of dividends in 2008? How does this affect dividends to common stockholders in 2009? *Answers:* $16,000 ($7,000 dividends in arrears, plus $9,000 current preferred dividends). Dividends to common stockholders decrease to $26,000.

A liability for a dividend does not exist until the directors declare a dividend. If a preferred dividend date passes and the corporation's board fails to declare the dividend on its cumulative preferred stock, the dividend in arrears is not a liability. The *full-disclosure principle* requires a corporation to report (usually in a note) the amount of preferred dividends in arrears as of the balance sheet date.

Participating or Nonparticipating Dividend **Nonparticipating preferred stock** has a feature that limits dividends to a maximum amount each year. This maximum is often stated as a percent of the stock's par value or as a specific dollar amount per share. Once preferred stockholders receive this amount, the common stockholders receive any and all additional dividends. **Participating preferred stock** has a feature allowing preferred stockholders to share with common stockholders in any dividends paid in excess of the percent or dollar amount stated on the preferred stock. This participation feature does not apply until common stockholders receive dividends equal to the preferred stock's dividend percent. Many corporations are authorized to issue participating preferred stock but rarely do, and most managers never expect to issue it.[2]

Convertible Preferred Stock

Preferred stock is more attractive to investors if it carries a right to exchange preferred shares for a fixed number of common shares. **Convertible preferred stock** gives holders the option to

[2] Participating preferred stock is usually authorized as a defense against a possible corporate *takeover* by an "unfriendly" investor (or a group of investors) who intends to buy enough voting common stock to gain control. Taking a term from spy novels, the financial world refers to this type of plan as a *poison pill* that a company swallows if enemy investors threaten its capture. A poison pill usually works as follows: A corporation's common stockholders on a given date are granted the right to purchase a large amount of participating preferred stock at a very low price. This right to purchase preferred shares is *not* transferable. If an unfriendly investor buys a large block of common shares (whose right to purchase participating preferred shares does *not* transfer to this buyer), the board can issue preferred shares at a low price to the remaining common shareholders who retained the right to purchase. Future dividends are then divided between the newly issued participating preferred shares and the common shares. This usually transfers value from common shares to preferred shares, causing the unfriendly investor's common stock to lose much of its value and reduces the potential benefit of a hostile takeover.

exchange their preferred shares for common shares at a specified rate. When a company prospers and its common stock increases in value, convertible preferred stockholders can share in this success by converting their preferred stock into more valuable common stock.

Callable Preferred Stock

Callable preferred stock gives the issuing corporation the right to purchase (retire) this stock from its holders at specified future prices and dates. The amount paid to call and retire a preferred share is its **call price,** or *redemption value,* and is set when the stock is issued. The call price normally includes the stock's par value plus a premium giving holders additional return on their investment. When the issuing corporation calls and retires a preferred stock, the terms of the agreement often require it to pay the call price *and* any dividends in arrears.

Point: The issuing corporation has the right, or option, to retire its callable preferred stock.

Decision Insight

IFRSs Like U.S. GAAP, IFRSs require that preferred stock be classified as debt or equity based on analysis of the stock's contractual terms. However, IFRSs use different criteria for such classification.

Reasons for Issuing Preferred Stock

Corporations issue preferred stock for several reasons. One is to raise capital without sacrificing control. For example, suppose a company's organizers have $100,000 cash to invest and organize a corporation that needs $200,000 of capital to start. If they sell $200,000 worth of common stock (with $100,000 to the organizers), they would have only 50% control and would need to negotiate extensively with other stockholders in making policy. However, if they issue $100,000 worth of common stock to themselves and sell outsiders $100,000 of 8%, cumulative preferred stock with no voting rights, they retain control.

A second reason to issue preferred stock is to boost the return earned by common stockholders. To illustrate, suppose a corporation's organizers expect to earn an annual after-tax income of $24,000 on an investment of $200,000. If they sell and issue $200,000 worth of common stock, the $24,000 income produces a 12% return on the $200,000 of common stockholders' equity. However, if they issue $100,000 of 8% preferred stock to outsiders and $100,000 of common stock to themselves, their own return increases to 16% per year, as shown in Exhibit 13.12.

EXHIBIT 13.12

Return to Common Stockholders When Preferred Stock Is Issued

Net (after-tax) income	$24,000
Less preferred dividends at 8%	(8,000)
Balance to common stockholders	$16,000
Return to common stockholders ($16,000/$100,000)	16%

Common stockholders earn 16% instead of 12% because assets contributed by preferred stockholders are invested to earn $12,000 while the preferred dividend is only $8,000. Use of preferred stock to increase return to common stockholders is an example of **financial leverage** (also called *trading on the equity*). As a general rule, when the dividend rate on preferred stock is less than the rate the corporation earns on its assets, the effect of issuing preferred stock is to increase (or *lever)* the rate earned by common stockholders.

Point: Financial leverage also occurs when debt is issued and the interest rate paid on it is less than the rate earned from using the assets the creditors lend the company.

Other reasons for issuing preferred stock include its appeal to some investors who believe that the corporation's common stock is too risky or that the expected return on common stock is too low.

Decision Maker

Concert Organizer Assume that you alter your business strategy from organizing concerts targeted at under 1,000 people to those targeted at between 5,000 to 20,000 people. You also incorporate because of increased risk of lawsuits and a desire to issue stock for financing. It is important that you control the company for decisions on whom to schedule. What types of stock do you offer? [Answer—p. 531]

Quick Check Answers—p. 531

13. In what ways does preferred stock often have priority over common stock?

14. Increasing the return to common stockholders by issuing preferred stock is an example of (*a*) Financial leverage. (*b*) Cumulative earnings. (*c*) Dividend in arrears.

15. A corporation has issued and outstanding (i) 9,000 shares of $50 par value, 10% cumulative, nonparticipating preferred stock and (ii) 27,000 shares of $10 par value common stock. No dividends have been declared for the two prior years. During the current year, the corporation declares $288,000 in dividends. The amount paid to common shareholders is (*a*) $243,000. (*b*) $153,000. (*c*) $135,000.

Treasury Stock

P5 Record purchases and sales of treasury stock and the retirement of stock.

Corporations acquire shares of their own stock for several reasons: (1) to use their shares to acquire another corporation, (2) to purchase shares to avoid a hostile takeover of the company, (3) to reissue them to employees as compensation, and (4) to maintain a strong market for their stock or to show management confidence in the current price.

Corporations and Treasury Stock

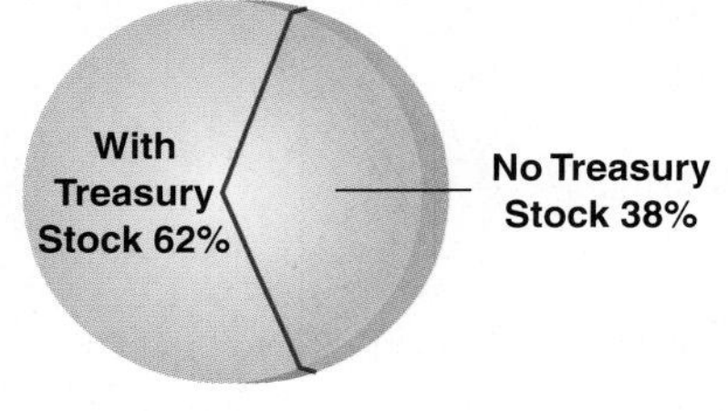

A corporation's reacquired shares are called **treasury stock,** which is similar to unissued stock in several ways: (1) neither treasury stock nor unissued stock is an asset, (2) neither receives cash dividends or stock dividends, and (3) neither allows the exercise of voting rights. However, treasury stock does differ from unissued stock in one major way: The corporation can resell treasury stock at less than par without having the buyers incur a liability, provided it was originally issued at par value or higher. Treasury stock purchases also require management to exercise ethical sensitivity because funds are being paid to specific stockholders instead of all stockholders. Managers must be sure the purchase is in the best interest of all stockholders. These concerns cause companies to fully disclose treasury stock transactions.

Purchasing Treasury Stock

Purchasing treasury stock reduces the corporation's assets and equity by equal amounts. (We describe the *cost method* of accounting for treasury stock, which is the most widely used method. The *par value* method is another method explained in advanced courses.) To illustrate, Exhibit 13.13 shows Cyber Corporation's account balances *before* any treasury stock purchase (Cyber has no liabilities).

EXHIBIT 13.13

Account Balances *before* Purchasing Treasury Stock

Assets		Stockholders' Equity	
Cash	$ 30,000	Common stock—$10 par; 10,000 shares authorized, issued, and outstanding	$100,000
Other assets	95,000	Retained earnings	25,000
Total assets	$125,000	Total stockholders' equity	$125,000

Cyber then purchases 1,000 of its own shares for $11,500 on May 1, which is recorded as follows.

Assets	= Liabilities +	Equity
−11,500		−11,500

May 1	Treasury Stock, Common	11,500	
	Cash		11,500
	Purchased 1,000 treasury shares at $11.50 per share.		

This entry reduces equity through the debit to the Treasury Stock account, which is a contra equity account. Exhibit 13.14 shows account balances *after* this transaction.

Assets		Stockholders' Equity	
Cash	$ 18,500	Common stock—$10 par; 10,000 shares authorized and issued; 1,000 shares in treasury	$100,000
Other assets	95,000	Retained earnings, $11,500 restricted by treasury stock purchase	25,000
		Less cost of treasury stock	**(11,500)**
Total assets	$113,500	Total stockholders' equity	$113,500

EXHIBIT 13.14

Account Balances *after* Purchasing Treasury Stock

The treasury stock purchase reduces Cyber's cash, total assets, and total equity by $11,500 but does not reduce the balance of either the Common Stock or the Retained Earnings account. The equity reduction is reported by deducting the cost of treasury stock in the equity section. Also, two disclosures are evident. First, the stock description reveals that 1,000 issued shares are in treasury, leaving only 9,000 shares still outstanding. Second, the description for retained earnings reveals that it is partly restricted.

Point: The Treasury Stock account is *not* an asset. Treasury stock does not carry voting or dividend rights.

Point: A treasury stock purchase is also called a *stock buyback*.

Reissuing Treasury Stock

Treasury stock can be reissued by selling it at cost, above cost, or below cost.

Selling Treasury Stock at Cost If treasury stock is reissued at cost, the entry is the reverse of the one made to record the purchase. For instance, if on May 21 Cyber reissues 100 of the treasury shares purchased on May 1 at the same $11.50 per share cost, the entry is

May 21	Cash	1,150	
	Treasury Stock, Common.		1,150
	Received $11.50 per share for 100 treasury shares costing $11.50 per share.		

Assets = Liabilities + Equity
+1,150 +1,150

Selling Treasury Stock *above* Cost If treasury stock is sold for more than cost, the amount received in excess of cost is credited to the Paid-In Capital, Treasury Stock account. This account is reported as a separate item in the stockholders' equity section. No gain is ever reported from the sale of treasury stock. To illustrate, if Cyber receives $12 cash per share for 400 treasury shares costing $11.50 per share on June 3, the entry is

Point: Treasury stock does not represent ownership. A company cannot own a part of itself.

June 3	Cash	4,800	
	Treasury Stock, Common.		4,600
	Paid-In Capital, Treasury Stock.		**200**
	Received $12 per share for 400 treasury shares costing $11.50 per share.		

Assets = Liabilities + Equity
+4,800 +4,600
+200

Selling Treasury Stock *below* Cost When treasury stock is sold below cost, the entry to record the sale depends on whether the Paid-In Capital, Treasury Stock account has a credit balance. If it has a zero balance, the excess of cost over the sales price is debited to Retained Earnings. If the Paid-In Capital, Treasury Stock account has a credit balance, it is debited for the excess of the cost over the selling price but not to exceed the balance in this account. When the credit balance in this paid-in capital account is eliminated, any remaining difference between the cost and selling price is debited to Retained Earnings. To illustrate, if Cyber sells its remaining 500 shares of treasury stock at $10 per share on July 10,

Point: The phrase *treasury stock* is believed to arise from the fact that reacquired stock is held in a corporation's treasury.

Point: The Paid-In Capital, Treasury Stock account can have a zero or credit balance but never a debit balance.

equity is reduced by $750 (500 shares × $1.50 per share excess of cost over selling price), as shown in this entry:

Assets	=	Liabilities	+	Equity
+5,000				−200
				−550
				+5,750

July 10	Cash	5,000	
	Paid-In Capital, Treasury Stock	**200**	
	Retained Earnings	**550**	
	Treasury Stock, Common		5,750
	Received $10 per share for 500 treasury shares costing $11.50 per share.		

This entry eliminates the $200 credit balance in the paid-in capital account created on June 3 and then reduces the Retained Earnings balance by the remaining $550 excess of cost over selling price. A company never reports a loss (or gain) from the sale of treasury stock.

Retiring Stock

Point: Recording stock retirement results in canceling the equity from the original issuance of the shares.

A corporation can purchase its own stock and retire it. Retiring stock reduces the number of issued shares. Retired stock is the same as authorized and unissued shares. Purchases and retirements of stock are permissible under state law only if they do not jeopardize the interests of creditors and stockholders. When stock is purchased for retirement, we remove all capital amounts related to the retired shares. If the purchase price exceeds the net amount removed, this excess is debited to Retained Earnings. If the net amount removed from all capital accounts exceeds the purchase price, this excess is credited to the Paid-In Capital from Retirement of Stock account. A company's assets and equity are always reduced by the amount paid for the retiring stock.

Quick Check

Answers—p. 531

16. Purchase of treasury stock (*a*) has no effect on assets; (*b*) reduces total assets and total equity by equal amounts; or (*c*) is recorded with a debit to Retained Earnings.

17. Southern Co. purchases shares of Northern Corp. Should either company classify these shares as treasury stock?

18. How does treasury stock affect the authorized, issued, and outstanding shares?

19. When a company purchases treasury stock, (*a*) retained earnings are restricted by the amount paid; (*b*) Retained Earnings is credited; or (*c*) it is retired.

Reporting of Equity

Statement of Retained Earnings

C4 Explain the items reported in retained earnings.

Retained earnings generally consist of a company's cumulative net income less any net losses and dividends declared since its inception. Retained earnings are part of stockholders' claims on the company's net assets, but this does *not* imply that a certain amount of cash or other assets is available to pay stockholders. For example, **Circuit City** has $1,336 million in retained earnings, but only $141 million in cash. This section describes events and transactions affecting retained earnings and how retained earnings are reported.

Video13.1

Restrictions and Appropriations The term **restricted retained earnings** refers to both statutory and contractual restrictions. A common *statutory* (or *legal*) *restriction* is to limit treasury stock purchases to the amount of retained earnings. The balance sheet in Exhibit 13.14 provides an example. A common *contractual restriction* involves loan agreements that restrict paying dividends beyond a specified amount or percent of retained earnings. Restrictions are usually described in the notes. The term **appropriated retained earnings** refers to a voluntary transfer of amounts from the Retained Earnings account to the Appropriated Retained Earnings account to inform users of special activities that require funds.

Prior Period Adjustments **Prior period adjustments** are corrections of material errors in prior period financial statements. These errors include arithmetic mistakes, unacceptable accounting, and missed facts. Prior period adjustments are reported in the *statement of retained earnings* (or the statement of stockholders' equity), net of any income tax effects. Prior period adjustments result in changing the beginning balance of retained earnings for events occurring prior to the earliest period reported in the current set of financial statements. To illustrate, assume that ComUS makes an error in a 2007 journal entry for the purchase of land by incorrectly debiting an expense account. When this is discovered in 2009, the statement of retained earnings includes a prior period adjustment, as shown in Exhibit 13.15. This exhibit also shows the usual format of the statement of retained earnings.

Point: If a year 2007 error is discovered in 2008, the company records the adjustment in 2008. But if the financial statements include 2007 and 2008 figures, the statements report the correct amounts for 2007, and a note describes the correction.

EXHIBIT 13.15

Statement of Retained Earnings with a Prior Period Adjustment

ComUS Statement of Retained Earnings For Year Ended December 31, 2009	
Retained earnings, Dec. 31, 2008, as previously reported	$4,745,000
Prior period adjustment	
Cost of land incorrectly expensed (net of $63,000 income taxes)	**147,000**
Retained earnings, Dec. 31, 2008, as adjusted	4,892,000
Plus net income	1,224,300
Less cash dividends declared	(301,800)
Retained earnings, Dec. 31, 2009	$5,814,500

Many items reported in financial statements are based on estimates. Future events are certain to reveal that some of these estimates were inaccurate even when based on the best data available at the time. These inaccuracies are *not* considered errors and are *not* reported as prior period adjustments. Instead, they are identified as **changes in accounting estimates** and are accounted for in current and future periods. To illustrate, we know that depreciation is based on estimated useful lives and salvage values. As time passes and new information becomes available, managers may need to change these estimates and the resulting depreciation expense for current and future periods.

Point: Accounting for changes in estimates is sometimes criticized as two wrongs to make a right. Consider a change in an asset's life. Depreciation neither before nor after the change is the amount computed if the revised estimate were originally selected. Regulators chose this approach to avoid restating prior period numbers.

Closing Process The closing process was explained earlier in the book as: (1) Close credit balances in revenue accounts to Income Summary, (2) Close debit balances in expense accounts to Income Summary, and (3) Close Income Summary to Retained Earnings. If dividends are recorded in a Dividends account, and not as an immediate reduction to Retained Earnings (as shown in this chapter), a fourth step is necessary to close the Dividends account to Retained Earnings.

Statement of Stockholders' Equity

Instead of a separate statement of retained earnings, companies commonly report a statement of stockholders' equity that includes changes in retained earnings. A **statement of stockholders' equity** lists the beginning and ending balances of key equity accounts and describes the changes that occur during the period. The companies in Appendix A report such a statement. The usual format is to provide a column for each component of equity and use the rows to describe events occurring in the period. Exhibit 13.16 shows a condensed statement for Apple.

Reporting Stock Options

The majority of corporations whose shares are publicly traded issue **stock options,** which are rights to purchase common stock at a fixed price over a specified period. As the stock's price rises, the option's value increases. Starbucks and Home Depot offer stock options to both full- and part-time employees. Stock options are said to motivate managers and employees to (1) focus on company performance, (2) take a long-run perspective, and (3) remain with

EXHIBIT 13.16

Statement of Stockholders' Equity

APPLE Statement of Stockholders' Equity					
($ millions, shares in thousands)	Common Stock Shares	Common Stock Amount	Retained Earnings	Other	Total Equity
Balance, Sept. 30, 2006	**855,263**	**$4,355**	**$5,607**	**$22**	**$9,984**
Net income	—	—	3,496	—	3,496
Issuance of Common Stock	17,066	364	(2)	—	362
Other	—	649	—	41	690
Cash Dividends ($0.00 per share)	—	—	—	—	—
Balance, Sept. 29, 2007	**872,329**	**$5,368**	**$9,101**	**$63**	**$14,532**

the company. A stock option is like having an investment with no risk ("a carrot with no stick").

To illustrate, Quantum grants each of its employees the option to purchase 100 shares of its $1 par value common stock at its current market price of $50 per share anytime within the next 10 years. If the stock price rises to $70 per share, an employee can exercise the option at a gain of $20 per share (acquire a $70 stock at the $50 option price). With 100 shares, a single employee would have a total gain of $2,000, computed as $20 × 100 shares. Companies report the cost of stock options in the income statement. Measurement of this cost is explained in advanced courses.

Video13.1

Decision Analysis — Earnings per Share, Price-Earnings Ratio, Dividend Yield, and Book Value per Share

Earnings per Share

A1 Compute earnings per share and describe its use.

The income statement reports **earnings per share,** also called *EPS* or *net income per share,* which is the amount of income earned per each share of a company's outstanding common stock. The **basic earnings per share** formula is shown in Exhibit 13.17. When a company has no preferred stock, then preferred dividends are zero. The weighted-average common shares outstanding is measured over the income reporting period; its computation is explained in advanced courses.

EXHIBIT 13.17

Basic Earnings per Share

$$\textbf{Basic earnings per share} = \frac{\textbf{Net income} - \textbf{Preferred dividends}}{\textbf{Weighted-average common shares outstanding}}$$

To illustrate, assume that Quantum Co. earns $40,000 net income in 2009 and declares dividends of $7,500 on its noncumulative preferred stock. (If preferred stock is *non*cumulative, the income available [numerator] is the current period net income less any preferred dividends *declared* in that same period. If preferred stock is cumulative, the income available [numerator] is the current period net income less the preferred dividends whether declared or not.) Quantum has 5,000 weighted-average common shares outstanding during 2009. Its basic EPS[3] is

$$\text{Basic earnings per share} = \frac{\$40{,}000 - \$7{,}500}{5{,}000 \text{ shares}} = \$6.50$$

[3] A corporation can be classified as having either a simple or complex capital structure. The term **simple capital structure** refers to a company with only common stock and nonconvertible preferred stock outstanding. The term **complex capital structure** refers to companies with dilutive securities. **Dilutive securities** include options, rights to purchase common stock, and any bonds or preferred stock that are convertible into common stock. A company with a complex capital structure must often report two EPS figures: basic and diluted. **Diluted earnings per share** is computed by adding all dilutive securities to the denominator of the basic EPS computation. It reflects the decrease in basic EPS *assuming* that all dilutive securities are converted into common shares.

Price-Earnings Ratio

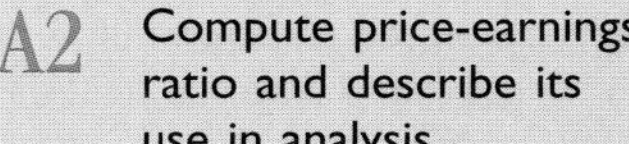
A2 Compute price-earnings ratio and describe its use in analysis.

A stock's market value is determined by its *expected* future cash flows. A comparison of a company's EPS and its market value per share reveals information about market expectations. This comparison is traditionally made using a **price-earnings** (or **PE**) **ratio,** expressed also as *price earnings, price to earnings,* or *PE.* Some analysts interpret this ratio as what price the market is willing to pay for a company's current earnings stream. Price-earnings ratios can differ across companies that have similar earnings because of either higher or lower expectations of future earnings. The price-earnings ratio is defined in Exhibit 13.18.

Point: The average PE ratio of stocks in the 1950–2008 period is about 14.

EXHIBIT 13.18

Price-Earnings Ratio

$$\textbf{Price-earnings ratio} = \frac{\textbf{Market value (price) per share}}{\textbf{Earnings per share}}$$

This ratio is often computed using EPS from the most recent period (for Amazon, its PE is 31; for Altria, its PE is 13). However, many users compute this ratio using *expected* EPS for the next period.

Some analysts view stocks with high PE ratios (higher than 20 to 25) as more likely to be overpriced and stocks with low PE ratios (less than 5 to 8) as more likely to be underpriced. These investors prefer to sell or avoid buying stocks with high PE ratios and to buy or hold stocks with low PE ratios. However, investment decision making is rarely so simple as to rely on a single ratio. For instance, a stock with a high PE ratio can prove to be a good investment if its earnings continue to increase beyond current expectations. Similarly, a stock with a low PE ratio can prove to be a poor investment if its earnings decline below expectations.

Point: Average PE ratios for U.S. stocks increased over the past two decades. Some analysts interpret this as a signal the market is overpriced. But higher ratios can at least partly reflect accounting changes that have reduced reported earnings.

Decision Maker

Money Manager You plan to invest in one of two companies identified as having identical future prospects. One has a PE of 19 and the other a PE of 25. Which do you invest in? Does it matter if your *estimate* of PE for these two companies is 29 as opposed to 22? [Answer—p. 531]

Dividend Yield

A3 Compute dividend yield and explain its use in analysis.

Investors buy shares of a company's stock in anticipation of receiving a return from either or both cash dividends and stock price increases. Stocks that pay large dividends on a regular basis, called *income stocks,* are attractive to investors who want recurring cash flows from their investments. In contrast, some stocks pay little or no dividends but are still attractive to investors because of their expected stock price increases. The stocks of companies that distribute little or no cash but use their cash to finance expansion are called *growth stocks*. One way to help identify whether a stock is an income stock or a growth stock is to analyze its dividend yield. **Dividend yield,** defined in Exhibit 13.19, shows the annual amount of cash dividends distributed to common shares relative to their market value.

EXHIBIT 13.19

Dividend Yield

$$\textbf{Dividend yield} = \frac{\textbf{Annual cash dividends per share}}{\textbf{Market value per share}}$$

Dividend yield can be computed for current and prior periods using actual dividends and stock prices and for future periods using expected values. Exhibit 13.20 shows recent dividend and stock price data for Amazon and Altria Group to compute dividend yield.

EXHIBIT 13.20

Dividend and Stock Price Information

Company	Cash Dividends per Share	Market Value per Share	Dividend Yield
Amazon	$0.00	$90	0.0%
Altria Group	3.32	70	4.7

Dividend yield is zero for Amazon, implying it is a growth stock. An investor in Amazon would look for increases in stock prices (and eventual cash from the sale of stock). Altria has a dividend yield of 4.7%, implying it is an income stock for which dividends are important in assessing its value.

Point: The *payout ratio* equals cash dividends declared on common stock divided by net income. A low payout ratio suggests that a company is retaining earnings for future growth.

Book Value per Share

A4 Compute book value and explain its use in analysis.

Case 1: Common Stock (Only) Outstanding. **Book value per common share,** defined in Exhibit 13.21, reflects the amount of equity applicable to *common* shares on a per share basis. To illustrate, we use Dillon Snowboards' data from Exhibit 13.4. Dillon has 30,000 outstanding common shares, and the stockholders' equity applicable to common shares is $365,000. Dillon's book value per common share is $12.17, computed as $365,000 divided by 30,000 shares.

EXHIBIT 13.21

Book Value per Common Share

$$\textbf{Book value per common share} = \frac{\textbf{Stockholders' equity applicable to common shares}}{\textbf{Number of common shares outstanding}}$$

Point: Book value per share is also referred to as *stockholders' claim to assets on a per share basis.*

Case 2: Common and Preferred Stock Outstanding. To compute book value when both common and preferred shares are outstanding, we allocate total equity between the two types of shares. The **book value per preferred share** is computed first; its computation is shown in Exhibit 13.22.

EXHIBIT 13.22

Book Value per Preferred Share

$$\textbf{Book value per preferred share} = \frac{\textbf{Stockholders' equity applicable to preferred shares}}{\textbf{Number of preferred shares outstanding}}$$

The equity applicable to preferred shares equals the preferred share's call price (or par value if the preferred is not callable) plus any cumulative dividends in arrears. The remaining equity is the portion applicable to common shares. To illustrate, consider LTD's equity in Exhibit 13.23. Its preferred stock is callable at $108 per share, and two years of cumulative preferred dividends are in arrears.

EXHIBIT 13.23

Stockholders' Equity with Preferred and Common Stock

Stockholders' Equity	
Preferred stock—$100 par value, 7% cumulative, 2,000 shares authorized, 1,000 shares issued and outstanding	$100,000
Common stock—$25 par value, 12,000 shares authorized, 10,000 shares issued and outstanding	250,000
Paid-in capital in excess of par value, common stock	15,000
Retained earnings	82,000
Total stockholders' equity	$447,000

The book value computations are in Exhibit 13.24. Equity is first allocated to preferred shares before the book value of common shares is computed.

EXHIBIT 13.24

Computing Book Value per Preferred and Common Share

Total stockholders' equity		$447,000
Less equity applicable to preferred shares		
Call price (1,000 shares × $108)	$108,000	
Dividends in arrears ($100,000 × 7% × 2 years)	14,000	(122,000)
Equity applicable to common shares		$325,000
Book value per preferred share ($122,000/1,000 shares)		**$ 122.00**
Book value per common share ($325,000/10,000 shares)		**$ 32.50**

Book value per share reflects the value per share if a company is liquidated at balance sheet amounts. Book value is also the starting point in many stock valuation models, merger negotiations, price setting for public utilities, and loan contracts. The main limitation in using book value is the potential difference between recorded value and market value for assets and liabilities. Investors often adjust their analysis for estimates of these differences.

Decision Maker

Investor You are considering investing in **BMX**, whose book value per common share is $4 and price per common share on the stock exchange is $7. From this information, are BMX's net assets priced higher or lower than its recorded values? [Answer—p. 531]

Demonstration Problem 1

Barton Corporation began operations on January 1, 2008. The following transactions relating to stockholders' equity occurred in the first two years of the company's operations.

DP13

2008

Jan. 1 Authorized the issuance of 2 million shares of $5 par value common stock and 100,000 shares of $100 par value, 10% cumulative, preferred stock.
Jan. 2 Issued 200,000 shares of common stock for $12 cash per share.
Jan. 3 Issued 100,000 shares of common stock in exchange for a building valued at $820,000 and merchandise inventory valued at $380,000.
Jan. 4 Paid $10,000 cash to the company's founders for organization activities.
Jan. 5 Issued 12,000 shares of preferred stock for $110 cash per share.

2009

June 4 Issued 100,000 shares of common stock for $15 cash per share.

Required

1. Prepare journal entries to record these transactions.
2. Prepare the stockholders' equity section of the balance sheet as of December 31, 2008, and December 31, 2009, based on these transactions.
3. Prepare a table showing dividend allocations and dividends per share for 2008 and 2009 assuming Barton declares the following cash dividends: 2008, $50,000, and 2009, $300,000.
4. Prepare the January 2, 2008, journal entry for Barton's issuance of 200,000 shares of common stock for $12 cash per share assuming
   a. Common stock is no-par stock without a stated value.
   b. Common stock is no-par stock with a stated value of $10 per share.

Planning the Solution

- Record journal entries for the transactions for 2008 and 2009.
- Determine the balances for the 2008 and 2009 equity accounts for the balance sheet.
- Prepare the contributed capital portion of the 2008 and 2009 balance sheets.
- Prepare a table similar to Exhibit 13.11 showing dividend allocations for 2008 and 2009.
- Record the issuance of common stock under both specifications of no-par stock.

Solution to Demonstration Problem 1

1. Journal entries.

Date	Account	Debit	Credit
2008			
Jan. 2	Cash	2,400,000	
	Common Stock, $5 Par Value		1,000,000
	Paid-In Capital in Excess of Par Value, Common Stock		1,400,000
	Issued 200,000 shares of common stock.		
Jan. 3	Building	820,000	
	Merchandise Inventory	380,000	
	Common Stock, $5 Par Value		500,000
	Paid-In Capital in Excess of Par Value, Common Stock		700,000
	Issued 100,000 shares of common stock.		
Jan. 4	Organization Expenses	10,000	
	Cash		10,000
	Paid founders for organization costs.		

[continued on next page]

[continued from previous page]

		Debit	Credit
Jan. 5	Cash	1,320,000	
	Preferred Stock, $100 Par Value		1,200,000
	Paid-In Capital in Excess of Par Value, Preferred Stock		120,000
	Issued 12,000 shares of preferred stock.		
2009			
June 4	Cash	1,500,000	
	Common Stock, $5 Par Value		500,000
	Paid-In Capital in Excess of Par Value, Common Stock		1,000,000
	Issued 100,000 shares of common stock.		

2. Balance sheet presentations (at December 31 year-end).

	2009	2008
Stockholders' Equity		
Preferred stock—$100 par value, 10% cumulative, 100,000 shares authorized, 12,000 shares issued and outstanding	$1,200,000	$1,200,000
Paid-in capital in excess of par value, preferred stock	120,000	120,000
Total paid-in capital by preferred stockholders	1,320,000	1,320,000
Common stock—$5 par value, 2,000,000 shares authorized, 300,000 shares issued and outstanding in 2008, and 400,000 shares issued and outstanding in 2009	2,000,000	1,500,000
Paid-in capital in excess of par value, common stock	3,100,000	2,100,000
Total paid-in capital by common stockholders	5,100,000	3,600,000
Total paid-in capital	$6,420,000	$4,920,000

3. Dividend allocation table.

	Common	Preferred
2008 ($50,000)		
Preferred—current year (12,000 shares × $10 = $120,000)	$ 0	$ 50,000
Common—remainder (300,000 shares outstanding)	0	0
Total for the year	$ 0	$ 50,000
2009 ($300,000)		
Preferred—dividend in arrears from 2008 ($120,000 − $50,000)	$ 0	$ 70,000
Preferred—current year	0	120,000
Common—remainder (400,000 shares outstanding)	110,000	0
Total for the year	$110,000	$190,000
Dividends per share		
2008	$ 0.00	$ 4.17
2009	$ 0.28	$ 15.83

4. Journal entries.

a. For 2008 (no-par stock without a stated value):

		Debit	Credit
Jan. 2	Cash	2,400,000	
	Common Stock, No-Par Value		2,400,000
	Issued 200,000 shares of no-par common stock at $12 per share.		

b. For 2008 (no-par stock with a stated value):

Jan. 2	Cash	2,400,000	
	Common Stock, $10 Stated Value		2,000,000
	Paid-In Capital in Excess of Stated Value, Common Stock		400,000
	Issued 200,000 shares of $10 stated value common stock at $12 per share.		

Demonstration Problem 2

Precision Company began year 2008 with the following balances in its stockholders' equity accounts.

Common stock—$10 par, 500,000 shares authorized, 200,000 shares issued and outstanding	$2,000,000
Paid-in capital in excess of par, common stock	1,000,000
Retained earnings	5,000,000
Total	$8,000,000

All outstanding common stock was issued for $15 per share when the company was created. Prepare journal entries to account for the following transactions during year 2008.

Jan. 10	The board declared a $0.10 cash dividend per share to shareholders of record Jan. 28.
Feb. 15	Paid the cash dividend declared on January 10.
Mar. 31	Declared a 20% stock dividend. The market value of the stock is $18 per share.
May 1	Distributed the stock dividend declared on March 31.
July 1	Purchased 30,000 shares of treasury stock at $20 per share.
Sept. 1	Sold 20,000 treasury shares at $26 cash per share.
Dec. 1	Sold the remaining 10,000 shares of treasury stock at $7 cash per share.

Planning the Solution

- Calculate the total cash dividend to record by multiplying the cash dividend declared by the number of shares as of the date of record.
- Decide whether the stock dividend is a small or large dividend. Then analyze each event to determine the accounts affected and the appropriate amounts to be recorded.

Solution to Demonstration Problem 2

Jan. 10	Retained Earnings	20,000	
	Common Dividend Payable		20,000
	Declared a $0.10 per share cash dividend.		
Feb. 15	Common Dividend Payable	20,000	
	Cash		20,000
	Paid $0.10 per share cash dividend.		
Mar. 31	Retained Earnings	720,000	
	Common Stock Dividend Distributable		400,000
	Paid-In Capital in Excess of Par Value, Common Stock		320,000
	Declared a small stock dividend of 20% or 40,000 shares; market value is $18 per share.		

[continued on next page]

[continued from previous page]

Date	Account	Debit	Credit
May 1	Common Stock Dividend Distributable	400,000	
	Common Stock		400,000
	Distributed 40,000 shares of common stock.		
July 1	Treasury Stock, Common	600,000	
	Cash		600,000
	Purchased 30,000 common shares at $20 per share.		
Sept. 1	Cash	520,000	
	Treasury Stock, Common		400,000
	Paid-In Capital, Treasury Stock		120,000
	Sold 20,000 treasury shares at $26 per share.		
Dec. 1	Cash	70,000	
	Paid-In Capital, Treasury Stock	120,000	
	Retained Earnings	10,000	
	Treasury Stock, Common		200,000
	Sold 10,000 treasury shares at $7 per share.		

Summary

C1 Identify characteristics of corporations and their organization. Corporations are legal entities whose stockholders are not liable for its debts. Stock is easily transferred, and the life of a corporation does not end with the incapacity of a stock holder. A corporation acts through its agents, who are its officers and managers. Corporations are regulated and subject to income taxes.

C2 Describe the components of stockholders' equity. Authorized stock is the stock that a corporation's charter authorizes it to sell. Issued stock is the portion of authorized shares sold. Par value stock is a value per share assigned by the charter. No-par value stock is stock *not* assigned a value per share by the charter. Stated value stock is no-par stock to which the directors assign a value per share. Stockholders' equity is made up of (1) paid-in capital and (2) retained earnings. Paid-in capital consists of funds raised by stock issuances. Retained earnings consists of cumulative net income (losses) not distributed.

C3 Explain characteristics of common and preferred stock. Preferred stock has a priority (or senior status) relative to common stock in one or more areas, usually (1) dividends and (2) assets in case of liquidation. Preferred stock usually does not carry voting rights and can be convertible or callable. Convertibility permits the holder to convert preferred to common. Callability permits the issuer to buy back preferred stock under specified conditions.

C4 Explain the items reported in retained earnings. Many companies face statutory and contractual restrictions on retained earnings. Corporations can voluntarily appropriate retained earnings to inform others about their disposition. Prior period adjustments are corrections of errors in prior financial statements.

A1 Compute earnings per share and describe its use. A company with a simple capital structure computes basic EPS by dividing net income less any preferred dividends by the weighted-average number of outstanding common shares. A company with a complex capital structure must usually report both basic and diluted EPS.

A2 Compute price-earnings ratio and describe its use in analysis. A common stock's price-earnings (PE) ratio is computed by dividing the stock's market value (price) per share by its EPS. A stock's PE is based on expectations that can prove to be better or worse than eventual performance.

A3 Compute dividend yield and explain its use in analysis. Dividend yield is the ratio of a stock's annual cash dividends per share to its market value (price) per share. Dividend yield can be compared with the yield of other companies to determine whether the stock is expected to be an income or growth stock.

A4 Compute book value and explain its use in analysis. Book value per common share is equity applicable to common shares divided by the number of outstanding common shares. Book value per preferred share is equity applicable to preferred shares divided by the number of outstanding preferred shares.

P1 Record the issuance of corporate stock. When stock is issued, its par or stated value is credited to the stock account and any excess is credited to a separate contributed capital account. If a stock has neither par nor stated value, the entire proceeds are credited to the stock account. Stockholders must contribute assets equal to minimum legal capital or be potentially liable for the deficiency.

P2 Record transactions involving cash dividends. Cash dividends involve three events. On the date of declaration, the directors bind the company to pay the dividend. A dividend declaration reduces retained earnings and creates a current liability. On the date of record, recipients of the dividend are identified. On the date of payment, cash is paid to stockholders and the current liability is removed.

P3 Account for stock dividends and stock splits. Neither a stock dividend nor a stock split alters the value of the company. However, the value of each share is less due to the distribution of additional shares. The distribution of additional shares is according to individual stockholders' ownership percent. Small stock dividends ($\leq$25%) are recorded by capitalizing retained earnings equal to the market value of distributed shares. Large stock dividends (>25%) are recorded by capitalizing retained earnings equal to the par or stated value of distributed shares. Stock splits do not yield journal entries but do yield changes in the description of stock.

P4 **Distribute dividends between common stock and preferred stock.** Preferred stockholders usually hold the right to dividend distributions before common stockholders. When preferred stock is cumulative and in arrears, the amount in arrears must be distributed to preferred before any dividends are distributed to common.

P5 **Record purchases and sales of treasury stock and the retirement of stock.** When a corporation purchases its own previously issued stock, it debits the cost of these shares to Treasury Stock. Treasury stock is subtracted from equity in the balance sheet. If treasury stock is reissued, any proceeds in excess of cost are credited to Paid-In Capital, Treasury Stock. If the proceeds are less than cost, they are debited to Paid-In Capital, Treasury Stock to the extent a credit balance exists. Any remaining amount is debited to Retained Earnings. When stock is retired, all accounts related to the stock are removed.

Guidance Answers to **Decision Maker** and **Decision Ethics**

Entrepreneur The 50% stock dividend provides you no direct income. A stock dividend often reveals management's optimistic expectations about the future and can improve a stock's marketability by making it affordable to more investors. Accordingly, a stock dividend usually reveals "good news" and because of this, it likely increases (slightly) the market value for your stock. The same conclusions apply to the 3-for-2 stock split.

Concert Organizer You have two basic options: (1) different classes of common stock or (2) common and preferred stock. Your objective is to issue to yourself stock that has all or a majority of the voting power. The other class of stock would carry limited or no voting rights. In this way, you maintain control and are able to raise the necessary funds.

Money Manager Since one company requires a payment of $19 for each $1 of earnings, and the other requires $25, you would prefer the stock with the PE of 19; it is a better deal given identical prospects. You should make sure these companies' earnings computations are roughly the same, for example, no extraordinary items, unusual events, and so forth. Also, your PE estimates for these companies do matter. If you are willing to pay $29 for each $1 of earnings for these companies, you obviously expect both to exceed current market expectations.

Investor Book value reflects recorded values. BMX's book value is $4 per common share. Stock price reflects the market's expectation of net asset value (both tangible and intangible items). BMX's market value is $7 per common share. Comparing these figures suggests BMX's market value of net assets is higher than its recorded values (by an amount of $7 versus $4 per share).

Guidance Answers to **Quick Checks**

1. (*b*)
2. A corporation pays taxes on its income, and its stockholders normally pay personal income taxes (at the 15% rate or lower) on any cash dividends received from the corporation.
3. A proxy is a legal document used to transfer a stockholder's right to vote to another person.
4. (*a*)
5. A stock premium is an amount in excess of par (or stated) value paid by purchasers of newly issued stock.
6. Minimum legal capital intends to protect creditors of a corporation by obligating stockholders to some minimum level of equity financing and by constraining a corporation from excessive payments to stockholders.
7. Common Dividend Payable is a current liability account.
8. The date of declaration, date of record, and date of payment.
9. A dividend is a legal liability at the date of declaration, on which date it is recorded as a liability.
10. A stock dividend does not transfer assets to stockholders, but it does require an amount of retained earnings to be transferred to a contributed capital account(s).
11. A small stock dividend is 25% or less of the previous outstanding shares. A large stock dividend is more than 25%.
12. Retained earnings equal to the distributable shares' market value should be capitalized for a small stock dividend.
13. Typically, preferred stock has a preference in receipt of dividends and in distribution of assets.
14. (*a*)
15. (*b*)

Total cash dividend	$288,000
To preferred shareholders	135,000*
Remainder to common shareholders	$153,000

* 9,000 × $50 × 10% × 3 years = $135,000.

16. (*b*)
17. No. The shares are an investment for Southern Co. and are issued and outstanding shares for Northern Corp.
18. Treasury stock does not affect the number of authorized or issued shares, but it reduces the outstanding shares.
19. (*a*)

Key Terms

mhhe.com/wildFAP19e

Key Terms are available at the book's Website for learning and testing in an online Flashcard Format.

Appropriated retained earnings (p. 523)
Authorized stock (p. 509)
Basic earnings per share (p. 524)
Book value per common share (p. 526)
Book value per preferred share (p. 526)
Call price (p. 519)
Callable preferred stock (p. 519)
Capital stock (p. 509)
Changes in accounting estimates (p. 523)
Common stock (p. 508)
Complex capital structure (p. 524)
Convertible preferred stock (p. 518)
Corporation (p. 506)
Cumulative preferred stock (p. 517)
Date of declaration (p. 513)
Date of payment (p. 513)
Date of record (p. 513)
Diluted earnings per share (p. 524)
Dilutive securities (p. 524)
Discount on stock (p. 511)
Dividend in arrears (p. 517)
Dividend yield (p. 525)
Earnings per share (EPS) (p. 524)
Financial leverage (p. 519)
Large stock dividend (p. 514)
Liquidating cash dividend (p. 514)
Market value per share (p. 509)
Minimum legal capital (p. 509)
Noncumulative preferred stock (p. 517)
Nonparticipating preferred stock (p. 518)
No-par value stock (p. 509)
Organization expenses (pp. 507, 512)
Paid-in capital (p. 510)
Paid-in capital in excess of par value (p. 511)
Participating preferred stock (p. 518)
Par value (p. 509)
Par value stock (p. 509)
Preemptive right (p. 508)
Preferred stock (p. 516)
Premium on stock (p. 511)
Price-earnings (PE) ratio (p. 525)
Prior period adjustments (p. 523)
Proxy (p. 507)
Restricted retained earnings (p. 522)
Retained earnings (p. 510)
Retained earnings deficit (p. 513)
Reverse stock split (p. 516)
Simple capital structure (p. 524)
Small stock dividend (p. 514)
Stated value stock (p. 510)
Statement of stockholders' equity (p. 523)
Stock dividend (p. 514)
Stock options (p. 523)
Stock split (p. 516)
Stockholders' equity (p. 510)
Treasury stock (p. 520)

Multiple Choice Quiz

Answers on p. 547

mhhe.com/wildFAP19e

Additional Quiz Questions are available at the book's Website.

Quiz13

1. A corporation issues 6,000 shares of $5 par value common stock for $8 cash per share. The entry to record this transaction includes:
a. A debit to Paid-In Capital in Excess of Par Value for $18,000.
b. A credit to Common Stock for $48,000.
c. A credit to Paid-In Capital in Excess of Par Value for $30,000.
d. A credit to Cash for $48,000.
e. A credit to Common Stock for $30,000.

2. A company reports net income of $75,000. Its weighted-average common shares outstanding is 19,000. It has no other stock outstanding. Its earnings per share is:
a. $4.69
b. $3.95
c. $3.75
d. $2.08
e. $4.41

3. A company has 5,000 shares of $100 par preferred stock and 50,000 shares of $10 par common stock outstanding. Its total stockholders' equity is $2,000,000. Its book value per common share is:
a. $100.00
b. $ 10.00
c. $ 40.00
d. $ 30.00
e. $ 36.36

4. A company paid cash dividends of $0.81 per share. Its earnings per share is $6.95 and its market price per share is $45.00. Its dividend yield is:
a. 1.8%
b. 11.7%
c. 15.4%
d. 55.6%
e. 8.6%

5. A company's shares have a market value of $85 per share. Its net income is $3,500,000, and its weighted-average common shares outstanding is 700,000. Its price-earnings ratio is:
a. 5.9
b. 425.0
c. 17.0
d. 10.4
e. 41.2

Discussion Questions

1. What are organization expenses? Provide examples.
2. How are organization expenses reported?
3. Who is responsible for directing a corporation's affairs?
4. What is the preemptive right of common stockholders?
5. List the general rights of common stockholders.
6. What is the difference between authorized shares and outstanding shares?
7. Why would an investor find convertible preferred stock attractive?
8. What is the difference between the market value per share and the par value per share?
9. What is the difference between the par value and the call price of a share of preferred stock?
10. Identify and explain the importance of the three dates relevant to corporate dividends.
11. Why is the term *liquidating dividend* used to describe cash dividends debited against paid-in capital accounts?
12. How does declaring a stock dividend affect the corporation's assets, liabilities, and total equity? What are the effects of the eventual distribution of that stock?
13. What is the difference between a stock dividend and a stock split?
14. Courts have ruled that a stock dividend is not taxable income to stockholders. What justifies this decision?
15. How does the purchase of treasury stock affect the purchaser's assets and total equity?
16. Why do laws place limits on treasury stock purchases?
17. How are EPS results computed for a corporation with a simple capital structure?
18. What is a stock option?
19. How is book value per share computed for a corporation with no preferred stock? What is the main limitation of using book value per share to value a corporation?
20. Review the balance sheet for Best Buy in Appendix A and list the classes of stock that it has issued.

21. Refer to the balance sheet for Circuit City in Appendix A. What is the par value per share of its common stock? Suggest a rationale for the amount of par value it assigned.

22. Refer to RadioShack's balance sheet in Appendix A. How many shares of common stock are authorized? How many shares of common stock are issued?
23. Refer to the financial statements for Apple in Appendix A. What are its cash proceeds from issuance of common stock and its cash repurchases of common stock for the year ended September 30, 2006? Explain.

Denotes Discussion Questions that involve decision making.

McGraw-Hill's HOMEWORK MANAGER® Available with McGraw-Hill's Homework Manager

QUICK STUDY

QS 13-1
Characteristics of corporations
C1

Of the following statements, which are true for the corporate form of organization?

1. Capital is more easily accumulated than with most other forms of organization.
2. Corporate income that is distributed to shareholders is usually taxed twice.
3. Owners have unlimited liability for corporate debts.
4. Ownership rights cannot be easily transferred.
5. Owners are not agents of the corporation.
6. It is a separate legal entity.
7. It has a limited life.

QS 13-2
Issuance of common stock
P1

Prepare the journal entry to record Miltone Company's issuance of 50,000 shares of $1 par value common stock assuming the shares sell for:

a. $1 cash per share.
b. $3 cash per share.

QS 13-3
Issuance of par and stated value common stock
P1

Prepare the journal entry to record Katrick Company's issuance of 75,000 shares of its common stock assuming the shares have a:

a. $5 par value and sell for $12 cash per share.
b. $5 stated value and sell for $12 cash per share.

QS 13-4
Issuance of no-par common stock
P1

Prepare the journal entry to record Gaylord Company's issuance of 52,000 shares of no-par value common stock assuming the shares:

a. Sell for $30 cash per share.

b. Are exchanged for land valued at $1,560,000.

QS 13-5
Issuance of common stock
P1

Prepare the issuer's journal entry for each separate transaction. (*a*) On March 1, Atlantic Co. issues 37,500 shares of $5 par value common stock for $300,000 cash. (*b*) On April 1, BP Co. issues no-par value common stock for $90,000 cash. (*c*) On April 6, MPG issues 3,500 shares of $10 par value common stock for $20,000 of inventory, $130,000 of machinery, and acceptance of a $75,000 note payable.

QS 13-6
Issuance of preferred stock
C3

a. Prepare the journal entry to record Tamar Company's issuance of 6,000 shares of $100 par value 6% cumulative preferred stock for $102 cash per share.

b. Assuming the facts in part 1, if Tamar declares a year-end cash dividend, what is the amount of dividend paid to preferred shareholders? (Assume no dividends in arrears.)

QS 13-7
Accounting for cash dividends
P2

Prepare journal entries to record the following transactions for Forrest Corporation.

May 15 Declared a $32,000 cash dividend payable to common stockholders.
June 30 Paid the dividend declared on May 15.

QS 13-8
Accounting for small stock dividend
C2 P3

The stockholders' equity section of Atari Company's balance sheet as of April 1 follows. On April 2, Atari declares and distributes a 10% stock dividend. The stock's per share market value on April 2 is $18 (prior to the dividend). Prepare the stockholders' equity section immediately after the stock dividend.

Common stock—$5 par value, 375,000 shares authorized, 200,000 shares issued and outstanding	$1,000,000
Paid-in capital in excess of par value, common stock	600,000
Retained earnings	833,000
Total stockholders' equity	$2,433,000

QS 13-9
Dividend allocation between classes of shareholders
P4 

Stockholders' equity of Marwick Company consists of 10,000 shares of $20 par value, 8% cumulative preferred stock and 400,000 shares of $1 par value common stock. Both classes of stock have been outstanding since the company's inception. Marwick did not declare any dividends in the prior year, but it now declares and pays a $92,000 cash dividend at the current year-end. Determine the amount distributed to each class of stockholders for this two-year-old company.

QS 13-10
Purchase and sale of treasury stock P5

On May 3, Winmac Corporation purchased 3,000 shares of its own stock for $45,000 cash. On November 4, Winmac reissued 850 shares of this treasury stock for $14,450. Prepare the May 3 and November 4 journal entries to record Winmac's purchase and reissuance of treasury stock.

QS 13-11
Accounting for changes in estimates; error adjustments
C4 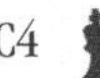

Answer the following questions related to a company's activities for the current year:

1. A review of the notes payable files discovers that three years ago the company reported the entire amount of a payment (principal and interest) on an installment note payable as interest expense. This mistake had a material effect on the amount of income in that year. How should the correction be reported in the current year financial statements?

2. After using an expected useful life of seven years and no salvage value to depreciate its office equipment over the preceding three years, the company decided early this year that the equipment will last only two more years. How should the effects of this decision be reported in the current year financial statements?

QS 13-12
Basic earnings per share A1

Campbell Company reports net income of $840,000 for the year. It has no preferred stock, and its weighted-average common shares outstanding is 300,000 shares. Compute its basic earnings per share.

QS 13-13
Basic earnings per share A1

Epic Company earned net income of $950,000 this year. The number of common shares outstanding during the entire year was 400,000, and preferred shareholders received a $40,000 cash dividend. Compute Epic Company's basic earnings per share.

QS 13-14
Price-earnings ratio A2

Compute Tripp Company's price-earnings ratio if its common stock has a market value of $31.50 per share and its EPS is $3.75. Would an analyst likely consider this stock potentially over- or underpriced? Explain.

QS 13-15
Dividend yield
A3

Payne Company expects to pay a $1.62 per share cash dividend this year on its common stock. The current market value of Payne stock is $22.50 per share. Compute the expected dividend yield on the Payne stock. Would you classify the Payne stock as a growth or an income stock? Explain.

QS 13-16
Book value per common share
A4

The stockholders' equity section of Klaus Company's balance sheet follows. The preferred stock's call price is $25. Determine the book value per share of the common stock.

Preferred stock—5% cumulative, $10 par value, 20,000 shares authorized, issued and outstanding	$ 200,000
Common stock—$5 par value, 200,000 shares authorized, 150,000 shares issued and outstanding	750,000
Retained earnings	889,500
Total stockholders' equity	$1,839,500

McGraw-Hill's HOMEWORK MANAGER® Available with McGraw-Hill's Homework Manager

EXERCISES

Exercise 13-1
Characteristics of corporations
C1

Describe how each of the following characteristics of organizations applies to corporations.

1. Owner authority and control	5. Duration of life
2. Ease of formation	6. Owner liability
3. Transferability of ownership	7. Legal status
4. Ability to raise large capital amounts	8. Tax status of income

Exercise 13-2
Accounting for par, stated, and no-par stock issuances
P1

Rodriguez Corporation issues 12,000 shares of its common stock for $182,700 cash on February 20. Prepare journal entries to record this event under each of the following separate situations.

1. The stock has neither par nor stated value.
2. The stock has a $12 par value.
3. The stock has a $6 stated value.

Exercise 13-3
Recording stock issuances
P1

Prepare journal entries to record the following four separate issuances of stock.

1. A corporation issued 2,500 shares of no-par common stock to its promoters in exchange for their efforts, estimated to be worth $43,500. The stock has no stated value.
2. A corporation issued 2,500 shares of no-par common stock to its promoters in exchange for their efforts, estimated to be worth $43,500. The stock has a $2 per share stated value.
3. A corporation issued 5,000 shares of $30 par value common stock for $180,000 cash.
4. A corporation issued 1,250 shares of $100 par value preferred stock for $168,500 cash.

Exercise 13-4
Stock issuance for noncash assets
P1

Soku Company issues 12,000 shares of $9 par value common stock in exchange for land and a building. The land is valued at $75,000 and the building at $120,000. Prepare the journal entry to record issuance of the stock in exchange for the land and building.

Exercise 13-5
Identifying characteristics of preferred stock
C2 C3

Match each description 1 through 6 with the characteristic of preferred stock that it best describes by writing the letter of that characteristic in the blank next to each description.

A. Convertible **B.** Cumulative **C.** Noncumulative
D. Nonparticipating **E.** Participating **F.** Callable

_____ **1.** Holders of the stock are entitled to receive current and all past dividends before common stockholders receive any dividends.
_____ **2.** The issuing corporation can retire the stock by paying a prespecified price.
_____ **3.** Holders of the stock can receive dividends exceeding the stated rate under certain conditions.
_____ **4.** Holders of the stock are not entitled to receive dividends in excess of the stated rate.
_____ **5.** Holders of this stock can exchange it for shares of common stock.
_____ **6.** Holders of the stock lose any dividends that are not declared in the current year.

Exercise 13-6
Stock dividends and splits
P3

On June 30, 2009, Samson Corporation's common stock is priced at $30.50 per share before any stock dividend or split, and the stockholders' equity section of its balance sheet appears as follows.

Common stock—$8 par value, 80,000 shares authorized, 32,000 shares issued and outstanding	$256,000
Paid-in capital in excess of par value, common stock	100,000
Retained earnings	356,000
Total stockholders' equity	$712,000

1. Assume that the company declares and immediately distributes a 100% stock dividend. This event is recorded by capitalizing retained earnings equal to the stock's par value. Answer these questions about stockholders' equity as it exists *after* issuing the new shares.
   a. What is the retained earnings balance?
   b. What is the amount of total stockholders' equity?
   c. How many shares are outstanding?

Check (1*b*) $712,000

2. Assume that the company implements a 2-for-1 stock split instead of the stock dividend in part 1. Answer these questions about stockholders' equity as it exists *after* issuing the new shares.
   a. What is the retained earnings balance?
   b. What is the amount of total stockholders' equity?
   c. How many shares are outstanding?

(2*a*) $356,000

3. Explain the difference, if any, to a stockholder from receiving new shares distributed under a large stock dividend versus a stock split.

Exercise 13-7
Stock dividends and per share book values
P3

The stockholders' equity of Tyron Company at the beginning of the day on February 5 follows.

Common stock—$25 par value, 150,000 shares authorized, 64,000 shares issued and outstanding	$1,600,000
Paid-in capital in excess of par value, common stock	525,000
Retained earnings	671,800
Total stockholders' equity	$2,796,800

On February 5, the directors declare a 15% stock dividend distributable on February 28 to the February 15 stockholders of record. The stock's market value is $50 per share on February 5 before the stock dividend. The stock's market value is $43.60 per share on February 28.

1. Prepare entries to record both the dividend declaration and its distribution.
2. One stockholder owned 900 shares on February 5 before the dividend. Compute the book value per share and total book value of this stockholder's shares immediately before *and* after the stock dividend of February 5.

Check (2) Book value per share: before, $43.70; after, $38.00

3. Compute the total market value of the investor's shares in part 2 as of February 5 and February 28.

Exercise 13-8
Dividends on common and noncumulative preferred stock
P4

Norton's outstanding stock consists of (*a*) 13,000 shares of noncumulative 8% preferred stock with a $10 par value and (*b*) 32,500 shares of common stock with a $1 par value. During its first four years of operation, the corporation declared and paid the following total cash dividends.

2009	$ 8,000
2010	24,000
2011	120,000
2012	197,000

Determine the amount of dividends paid each year to each of the two classes of stockholders. Also compute the total dividends paid to each class for the four years combined.

Check Total paid to preferred, $39,200

Exercise 13-9
Dividends on common and cumulative preferred stock P4

Use the data in Exercise 13-8 to determine the amount of dividends paid each year to each of the two classes of stockholders assuming that the preferred stock is cumulative. Also determine the total dividends paid to each class for the four years combined.

Exercise 13-10
Recording and reporting treasury stock transactions
P5

On October 10, the stockholders' equity of Syntax Systems appears as follows.

Common stock—$10 par value, 72,000 shares authorized, issued, and outstanding	$ 720,000
Paid-in capital in excess of par value, common stock	216,000
Retained earnings	864,000
Total stockholders' equity	$1,800,000

1. Prepare journal entries to record the following transactions for Syntax Systems.
   a. Purchased 5,000 shares of its own common stock at $22 per share on October 11.
   b. Sold 1,000 treasury shares on November 1 for $28 cash per share.
   c. Sold all remaining treasury shares on November 25 for $17 cash per share.

2. Explain how the company's equity section changes after the October 11 treasury stock purchase, and prepare the revised equity section of its balance sheet at that date.

Check (1c) Dr. Retained Earnings, $14,000

Exercise 13-11
Preparing a statement of retained earnings
C4

The following information is available for Arturo Company for the year ended December 31, 2009.

a. Balance of retained earnings, December 31, 2008, prior to discovery of error, $1,375,000.
b. Cash dividends declared and paid during 2009, $43,000.
c. It neglected to record 2007 depreciation expense of $55,500, which is net of $4,500 in income taxes.
d. The company earned $126,000 in 2009 net income.

Prepare a 2009 statement of retained earnings for Arturo Company.

Exercise 13-12
Earnings per share
A1

Grossmont Company reports $1,375,500 of net income for 2009 and declares $192,500 of cash dividends on its preferred stock for 2009. At the end of 2009, the company had 350,000 weighted-average shares of common stock.

1. What amount of net income is available to common stockholders for 2009?
2. What is the company's basic EPS for 2009?

Check (2) $3.38

Exercise 13-13
Earnings per share
A1

Franklin Company reports $1,875,000 of net income for 2009 and declares $262,500 of cash dividends on its preferred stock for 2009. At the end of 2009, the company had 250,000 weighted-average shares of common stock.

1. What amount of net income is available to common stockholders for 2009?
2. What is the company's basic EPS for 2009?

Check (2) $6.45

Exercise 13-14
Price-earnings ratio computation and interpretation
A2

Compute the price-earnings ratio for each of these four separate companies. Which stock might an analyst likely investigate as being potentially undervalued by the market? Explain.

Company	Earnings per Share	Market Value per Share
1	$12.00	$145.20
2	11.00	116.60
3	7.80	74.10
4	43.20	60.48

Exercise 13-15
Dividend yield computation and interpretation
A3 

Compute the dividend yield for each of these four separate companies. Which company's stock would probably *not* be classified as an income stock? Explain.

Company	Annual Cash Dividend per Share	Market Value per Share
1	$14.00	$229.51
2	11.00	110.00
3	5.52	60.00
4	1.90	118.75

Exercise 13-16
Book value per share
A4 

The equity section of Westchester Corporation's balance sheet shows the following.

Preferred stock—6% cumulative, $30 par value, $35 call price, 10,000 shares issued and outstanding	$300,000
Common stock—$10 par value, 35,000 shares issued and outstanding	350,000
Retained earnings	267,500
Total stockholders' equity	$917,500

Determine the book value per share of the preferred and common stock under two separate situations.

1. No preferred dividends are in arrears.

2. Three years of preferred dividends are in arrears.

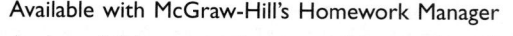

Check (1) Book value of common, $16.21

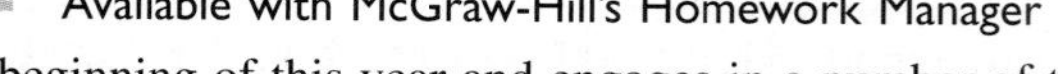

Available with McGraw-Hill's Homework Manager
McGraw-Hill's
HOMEWORK MANAGER®

PROBLEM SET A

Problem 13-1A
Stockholders' equity transactions and analysis
C2 C3 P1

Keshena Co. is incorporated at the beginning of this year and engages in a number of transactions. The following journal entries impacted its stockholders' equity during its first year of operations.

a.	Cash	320,000	
	Common Stock, $25 Par Value		250,000
	Paid-In Capital in Excess of Par Value, Common Stock		70,000
b.	Organization Expenses	160,000	
	Common Stock, $25 Par Value		125,000
	Paid-In Capital in Excess of Par Value, Common Stock		35,000

[continued on next page]

[continued from previous page]

c.	Cash	45,500	
	Accounts Receivable	16,000	
	Building	82,000	
	Notes Payable		59,500
	Common Stock, $25 Par Value		50,000
	Paid-In Capital in Excess of Par Value, Common Stock		34,000
d.	Cash	123,000	
	Common Stock, $25 Par Value		75,000
	Paid-In Capital in Excess of Par Value, Common Stock		48,000

Required

1. Explain the transaction(s) underlying each journal entry (*a*) through (*d*).
2. How many shares of common stock are outstanding at year-end?
3. What is the amount of minimum legal capital (based on par value) at year-end?
4. What is the total paid-in capital at year-end?
5. What is the book value per share of the common stock at year-end if total paid-in capital plus retained earnings equals $785,000?

Check (2) 20,000 shares
(3) $500,000
(4) $687,000

Problem 13-2A
Cash dividends, treasury stock, and statement of retained earnings
C2 C4 P2 P5

Rocklin Corporation reports the following components of stockholders' equity on December 31, 2009.

Common stock—$25 par value, 100,000 shares authorized, 45,000 shares issued and outstanding	$1,125,000
Paid-in capital in excess of par value, common stock	60,000
Retained earnings	460,000
Total stockholders' equity	$1,645,000

In year 2010, the following transactions affected its stockholders' equity accounts.

Jan. 1 Purchased 4,500 shares of its own stock at $25 cash per share.
Jan. 5 Directors declared a $3 per share cash dividend payable on Feb. 28 to the Feb. 5 stockholders of record.
Feb. 28 Paid the dividend declared on January 5.
July 6 Sold 1,688 of its treasury shares at $29 cash per share.
Aug. 22 Sold 2,812 of its treasury shares at $22 cash per share.
Sept. 5 Directors declared a $3 per share cash dividend payable on October 28 to the September 25 stockholders of record.
Oct. 28 Paid the dividend declared on September 5.
Dec. 31 Closed the $388,000 credit balance (from net income) in the Income Summary account to Retained Earnings.

Required

1. Prepare journal entries to record each of these transactions for 2010.
2. Prepare a statement of retained earnings for the year ended December 31, 2010.
3. Prepare the stockholders' equity section of the company's balance sheet as of December 31, 2010.

Check (2) Retained earnings, Dec. 31, 2010, $589,816.

Problem 13-3A
Equity analysis—journal entries and account balances
P2 P3

At September 30, the end of Chan Company's third quarter, the following stockholders' equity accounts are reported.

Common stock, $10 par value	$420,000
Paid-in capital in excess of par value, common stock	100,000
Retained earnings	400,000

In the fourth quarter, the following entries related to its equity are recorded.

Oct. 2	Retained Earnings	63,000	
	Common Dividend Payable		63,000
Oct. 25	Common Dividend Payable	63,000	
	Cash		63,000
Oct. 31	Retained Earnings	92,400	
	Common Stock Dividend Distributable		42,000
	Paid-In Capital in Excess of Par Value, Common Stock		50,400
Nov. 5	Common Stock Dividend Distributable	42,000	
	Common Stock, $10 Par Value		42,000
Dec. 1	Memo—Change the title of the common stock account to reflect the new par value of $5.		
Dec. 31	Income Summary	230,000	
	Retained Earnings		230,000

Required

1. Explain the transaction(s) underlying each journal entry.

2. Complete the following table showing the equity account balances at each indicated date (include the balances from September 30).

	Oct. 2	Oct. 25	Oct. 31	Nov. 5	Dec. 1	Dec. 31
Common stock	$____	$____	$____	$____	$____	$____
Common stock dividend distributable	____	____	____	____	____	____
Paid-in capital in excess of par, common stock	____	____	____	____	____	____
Retained earnings	____	____	____	____	____	____
Total equity	$____	$____	$____	$____	$____	$____

Check Total equity: Oct. 2, $857,000; Dec. 31, $1,087,000

Problem 13-4A
Analysis of changes in stockholders' equity accounts
C4 P2 P3 P5 

The equity sections from Sierra Group's 2009 and 2010 year-end balance sheets follow.

Stockholders' Equity (December 31, 2009)	
Common stock—$6 par value, 100,000 shares authorized, 45,000 shares issued and outstanding	$270,000
Paid-in capital in excess of par value, common stock	230,000
Retained earnings	340,000
Total stockholders' equity	$840,000

Stockholders' Equity (December 31, 2010)	
Common stock—$6 par value, 100,000 shares authorized, 53,200 shares issued, 4,000 shares in treasury	$319,200
Paid-in capital in excess of par value, common stock	262,800
Retained earnings ($60,000 restricted by treasury stock)	400,000
	982,000
Less cost of treasury stock	(60,000)
Total stockholders' equity	$922,000

The following transactions and events affected its equity during year 2010.

Jan. 5 Declared a $0.50 per share cash dividend, date of record January 10.
Mar. 20 Purchased treasury stock for cash.
Apr. 5 Declared a $0.50 per share cash dividend, date of record April 10.
July 5 Declared a $0.50 per share cash dividend, date of record July 10.
July 31 Declared a 20% stock dividend when the stock's market value is $10 per share.

Aug. 14 Issued the stock dividend that was declared on July 31.
Oct. 5 Declared a $0.50 per share cash dividend, date of record October 10.

Required

1. How many common shares are outstanding on each cash dividend date?
2. What is the total dollar amount for each of the four cash dividends?
3. What is the amount of the capitalization of retained earnings for the stock dividend?
4. What is the per share cost of the treasury stock purchased?
5. How much net income did the company earn during year 2010?

Check (3) $82,000
(4) $15
(5) $230,100

Problem 13-5A
Computation of book values and dividend allocations
C3 A4 P4 

Folsom Corporation's common stock is currently selling on a stock exchange at $183 per share, and its current balance sheet shows the following stockholders' equity section.

Preferred stock—5% cumulative, $___ par value, 1,000 shares authorized, issued, and outstanding	$ 85,000
Common stock—$___ par value, 4,000 shares authorized, issued, and outstanding	200,000
Retained earnings	350,000
Total stockholders' equity	$635,000

Required

1. What is the current market value (price) of this corporation's common stock?
2. What are the par values of the corporation's preferred stock and its common stock?
3. If no dividends are in arrears, what are the book values per share of the preferred stock and the common stock?
4. If two years' preferred dividends are in arrears, what are the book values per share of the preferred stock and the common stock?
5. If two years' preferred dividends are in arrears and the preferred stock is callable at $95 per share, what are the book values per share of the preferred stock and the common stock?
6. If two years' preferred dividends are in arrears and the board of directors declares cash dividends of $24,750, what total amount will be paid to the preferred and to the common shareholders? What is the amount of dividends per share for the common stock?

Check (4) Book value of common, $135.38
(5) Book value of common, $132.88
(6) Dividends per common share, $3.00

Analysis Component

7. What are some factors that can contribute to a difference between the book value of common stock and its market value (price)?

PROBLEM SET B

Problem 13-1B
Stockholders' equity transactions and analysis
C2 C3 P1 

Mayport Company is incorporated at the beginning of this year and engages in a number of transactions. The following journal entries impacted its stockholders' equity during its first year of operations.

a.	Cash	60,000	
	Common Stock, $1 Par Value		1,500
	Paid-In Capital in Excess of Par Value, Common Stock		58,500
b.	Organization Expenses	20,000	
	Common Stock, $1 Par Value		500
	Paid-In Capital in Excess of Par Value, Common Stock		19,500
c.	Cash	6,650	
	Accounts Receivable	4,000	
	Building	18,500	
	Notes Payable		9,150
	Common Stock, $1 Par Value		400
	Paid-In Capital in Excess of Par Value, Common Stock		19,600

[continued on next page]

[continued from previous page]

d.	Cash	30,000	
	Common Stock, $1 Par Value		600
	Paid-In Capital in Excess of Par Value, Common Stock		29,400

Required

1. Explain the transaction(s) underlying each journal entry (*a*) through (*d*).
2. How many shares of common stock are outstanding at year-end?
3. What is the amount of minimum legal capital (based on par value) at year-end?
4. What is the total paid-in capital at year-end?
5. What is the book value per share of the common stock at year-end if total paid-in capital plus retained earnings equals $141,500?

Check (2) 3,000 shares
(3) $3,000
(4) $130,000

Problem 13-2B
Cash dividends, treasury stock, and statement of retained earnings
C2 C4 P2 P5

San Marco Corp. reports the following components of stockholders' equity on December 31, 2009.

Common stock—$1 par value, 160,000 shares authorized, 100,000 shares issued and outstanding	$ 100,000
Paid-in capital in excess of par value, common stock	700,000
Retained earnings	1,080,000
Total stockholders' equity	$1,880,000

It completed the following transactions related to stockholders' equity in year 2010.

Jan. 10 Purchased 20,000 shares of its own stock at $12 cash per share.
Mar. 2 Directors declared a $1.50 per share cash dividend payable on March 31 to the March 15 stockholders of record.
Mar. 31 Paid the dividend declared on March 2.
Nov. 11 Sold 12,000 of its treasury shares at $13 cash per share.
Nov. 25 Sold 8,000 of its treasury shares at $9.50 cash per share.
Dec. 1 Directors declared a $2.50 per share cash dividend payable on January 2 to the December 10 stockholders of record.
Dec. 31 Closed the $536,000 credit balance (from net income) in the Income Summary account to Retained Earnings.

Required

1. Prepare journal entries to record each of these transactions for 2010.
2. Prepare a statement of retained earnings for the year ended December 31, 2010.
3. Prepare the stockholders' equity section of the company's balance sheet as of December 31, 2010.

Check (2) Retained earnings, Dec. 31, 2010, $1,238,000

Problem 13-3B
Equity analysis—journal entries and account balances
P2 P3

At December 31, the end of Santee Communication's third quarter, the following stockholders' equity accounts are reported.

Common stock, $10 par value	$480,000
Paid-in capital in excess of par value, common stock	192,000
Retained earnings	800,000

In the fourth quarter, the following entries related to its equity are recorded.

Jan. 17	Retained Earnings	48,000	
	Common Dividend Payable		48,000
Feb. 5	Common Dividend Payable	48,000	
	Cash		48,000

[continued on next page]

[continued from previous page]

Feb. 28	Retained Earnings	126,000	
	Common Stock Dividend Distributable		60,000
	Paid-In Capital in Excess of Par Value, Common Stock		66,000
Mar. 14	Common Stock Dividend Distributable	60,000	
	Common Stock, $10 Par Value		60,000
Mar. 25	Memo—Change the title of the common stock account to reflect the new par value of $5.		
Mar. 31	Income Summary	360,000	
	Retained Earnings		360,000

Required

1. Explain the transaction(s) underlying each journal entry.

2. Complete the following table showing the equity account balances at each indicated date (include the balances from December 31).

	Jan. 17	Feb. 5	Feb. 28	Mar. 14	Mar. 25	Mar. 31
Common stock	$____	$____	$____	$____	$____	$____
Common stock dividend distributable	____	____	____	____	____	____
Paid-in capital in excess of par, common stock	____	____	____	____	____	____
Retained earnings	____	____	____	____	____	____
Total equity	$____	$____	$____	$____	$____	$____

Check Total equity: Jan. 17, $1,424,000; Mar. 31, $1,784,000

Problem 13-4B
Analysis of changes in stockholders' equity accounts
C4 P2 P3 P5 

The equity sections from Kiwa Corporation's 2009 and 2010 balance sheets follow.

Stockholders' Equity (December 31, 2009)	
Common stock—$20 par value, 15,000 shares authorized, 8,500 shares issued and outstanding	$170,000
Paid-in capital in excess of par value, common stock	30,000
Retained earnings	135,000
Total stockholders' equity	$335,000

Stockholders' Equity (December 31, 2010)	
Common stock—$20 par value, 15,000 shares authorized, 9,500 shares issued, 500 shares in treasury	$190,000
Paid-in capital in excess of par value, common stock	52,000
Retained earnings ($20,000 restricted by treasury stock)	147,600
	389,600
Less cost of treasury stock	(20,000)
Total stockholders' equity	$369,600

The following transactions and events affected its equity during year 2010.

Feb. 15 Declared a $0.40 per share cash dividend, date of record five days later.
Mar. 2 Purchased treasury stock for cash.
May 15 Declared a $0.40 per share cash dividend, date of record five days later.
Aug. 15 Declared a $0.40 per share cash dividend, date of record five days later.
Oct. 4 Declared a 12.5% stock dividend when the stock's market value is $42 per share.
Oct. 20 Issued the stock dividend that was declared on October 4.
Nov. 15 Declared a $0.40 per share cash dividend, date of record five days later.

Required

Check (3) $42,000
(4) $40
(5) $68,000

1. How many common shares are outstanding on each cash dividend date?
2. What is the total dollar amount for each of the four cash dividends?
3. What is the amount of the capitalization of retained earnings for the stock dividend?
4. What is the per share cost of the treasury stock purchased?
5. How much net income did the company earn during year 2010?

Problem 13-5B
Computation of book values and dividend allocations
C3 A4 P4 

Hansen Company's common stock is currently selling on a stock exchange at $90 per share, and its current balance sheet shows the following stockholders' equity section.

Preferred stock—8% cumulative, $___ par value, 1,500 shares authorized, issued, and outstanding	$ 187,500
Common stock—$___ par value, 18,000 shares authorized, issued, and outstanding	450,000
Retained earnings	562,500
Total stockholders' equity	$1,200,000

Required

1. What is the current market value (price) of this corporation's common stock?
2. What are the par values of the corporation's preferred stock and its common stock?
3. If no dividends are in arrears, what are the book values per share of the preferred stock and the common stock?
4. If two years' preferred dividends are in arrears, what are the book values per share of the preferred stock and the common stock?
5. If two years' preferred dividends are in arrears and the preferred stock is callable at $140 per share, what are the book values per share of the preferred stock and the common stock?
6. If two years' preferred dividends are in arrears and the board of directors declares cash dividends of $50,000, what total amount will be paid to the preferred and to the common shareholders? What is the amount of dividends per share for the common stock?

Check (4) Book value of common, $54.58
(5) Book value of common, $53.33
(6) Dividends per common share, $0.28

Analysis Component

7. Discuss why the book value of common stock is not always a good estimate of its market value.

SERIAL PROBLEM

Success Systems

(This serial problem began in Chapter 1 and continues through most of the book. If previous chapter segments were not completed, the serial problem can begin at this point. It is helpful, but not necessary, to use the Working Papers that accompany the book.)

SP 13 Adriana Lopez created Success Systems on October 1, 2009. The company has been successful, and Adriana plans to expand her business. She believes that an additional $86,000 is needed and is investigating three funding sources.

a. Adriana's sister Cicely is willing to invest $86,000 in the business as a common shareholder. Since Adriana currently has about $129,000 invested in the business, Cicely's investment will mean that Adriana will maintain about 60% ownership, and Cicely will have 40% ownership of Success Systems.
b. Adriana's uncle Marcello is willing to invest $86,000 in the business as a preferred shareholder. Marcello would purchase 860 shares of $100 par value, 7% preferred stock.
c. Adriana's banker is willing to lend her $86,000 on a 7%, 10-year note payable. Adriana would make monthly payments of $1,000 per month for 10 years.

Required

1. Prepare the journal entry to reflect the initial $86,000 investment under each of the options (a), (b), and (c).

2. Evaluate the three proposals for expansion, providing the pros and cons of each option.

3. Which option do you recommend Adriana adopt? Explain.

BEYOND THE NUMBERS

REPORTING IN ACTION

C2 C3 A1 A4

BTN 13-1 Refer to Best Buy's financial statements in Appendix A to answer the following.

1. How many shares of common stock are issued and outstanding at March 3, 2007, and February 25, 2006? How do these numbers compare with the basic weighted-average common shares outstanding at March 3, 2007, and February 25, 2006?

2. What is the book value of its entire common stock at March 3, 2007?

3. What is the total amount of cash dividends paid to common stockholders for the years ended March 3, 2007, and February 25, 2006?

4. Identify and compare basic EPS amounts across fiscal years 2007, 2006, and 2005. Identify and comment on any marked changes.

5. Does Best Buy hold any treasury stock as of March 3, 2007? As of February 25, 2006?

Fast Forward

6. Access Best Buy's financial statements for fiscal years ending after March 3, 2007, from its Website (BestBuy.com) or the SEC's EDGAR database (www.SEC.gov). Has the number of common shares outstanding increased since March 3, 2007? Has Best Buy increased the total amount of cash dividends paid compared to the total amount for fiscal year 2007?

COMPARATIVE ANALYSIS

A1 A2 A3 A4

BTN 13-2 Key comparative figures for Best Buy, Circuit City, and RadioShack follow.

Key Figures	Best Buy	Circuit City	RadioShack
Net income (in millions)	$1,377	$ (8)	$ 73
Cash dividends declared per common share	$ 0.36	$ 0.12	$ 0.25
Common shares outstanding (in millions)	481	171	136
Weighted-average common shares outstanding (in mil.)	482	170	136
Market value (price) per share	$46.35	$19.00	$16.78
Equity applicable to common shares (in millions)	$6,201	$1,791	$ 654

Required

1. Compute the book value per common share for each company using these data.

2. Compute the basic EPS for each company using these data.

3. Compute the dividend yield for each company using these data. Does the dividend yield of any of the companies characterize it as an income or growth stock? Explain.

4. Compute, compare, and interpret the price-earnings ratio for each company using these data.

ETHICS CHALLENGE

C4

BTN 13-3 Brianna Moore is an accountant for New World Pharmaceuticals. Her duties include tracking research and development spending in the new product development division. Over the course of the past six months, Brianna notices that a great deal of funds have been spent on a particular project for a new drug. She hears "through the grapevine" that the company is about to patent the drug and expects it to be a major advance in antibiotics. Brianna believes that this new drug will greatly improve company performance and will cause the company's stock to increase in value. Brianna decides to purchase shares of New World in order to benefit from this expected increase.

Required

What are Brianna's ethical responsibilities, if any, with respect to the information she has learned through her duties as an accountant for New World Pharmaceuticals? What are the implications to her planned purchase of New World shares?

COMMUNICATING IN PRACTICE

A1 A2

BTN 13-4 Teams are to select an industry, and each team member is to select a different company in that industry. Each team member then is to acquire the selected company's financial statements (or Form 10-K) from the SEC EDGAR site (www.sec.gov). Use these data to identify basic EPS. Use the financial press (or finance.yahoo.com) to determine the market price of this stock, and then compute the price-earnings ratio. Communicate with teammates via a meeting, e-mail, or telephone to discuss the meaning of this ratio, how companies compare, and the industry norm. The team must prepare a single memorandum reporting the ratio for each company and identifying the team conclusions or consensus of opinion. The memorandum is to be duplicated and distributed to the instructor and teammates.

Hint: Make a transparency of each team's memo for a class discussion.

TAKING IT TO THE NET

C2

BTN 13-5 Access the February 26, 2007, filing of the 2006 calendar-year 10-K report of **McDonald's**, (ticker MCD) from www.sec.gov.

Required

1. Review McDonald's balance sheet and identify how many classes of stock it has issued.
2. What are the par values, number of authorized shares, and issued shares of the classes of stock you identified in part 1?
3. Review its statement of cash flows and identify what total amount of cash it paid in 2006 to purchase treasury stock.
4. What amount did McDonald's pay out in common stock cash dividends for 2006?

TEAMWORK IN ACTION

P5

BTN 13-6 This activity requires teamwork to reinforce understanding of accounting for treasury stock.

1. Write a brief team statement (*a*) generalizing what happens to a corporation's financial position when it engages in a stock "buyback" and (*b*) identifying reasons that a corporation would engage in this activity.
2. Assume that an entity acquires 100 shares of its $100 par value common stock at a cost of $134 cash per share. Discuss the entry to record this acquisition. Next, assign *each* team member to prepare *one* of the following entries (assume each entry applies to all shares):
   a. Reissue treasury shares at cost.
   b. Reissue treasury shares at $150 per share.
   c. Reissue treasury shares at $120 per share; assume the paid-in capital account from treasury shares has a $1,500 balance.
   d. Reissue treasury shares at $120 per share; assume the paid-in capital account from treasury shares has a $1,000 balance.
   e. Reissue treasury shares at $120 per share; assume the paid-in capital account from treasury shares has a zero balance.
3. In sequence, each member is to present his/her entry to the team and explain the *similarities* and *differences* between that entry and the previous entry.

Hint: Instructor should be sure each team accurately completes part 1 before proceeding.

ENTREPRENEURIAL DECISION

C2 C3 P2 

BTN 13-7 Assume that Ali Perry, Byron Myers, and Brenton Taylor of **Inogen** decide to launch a new retail chain to market their portable oxygen systems. This chain, named O-to-Go, requires $500,000 of start-up capital. The three contribute $375,000 of personal assets in return for 15,000 shares of common stock, but they need to raise another $125,000 in cash. There are two alternative plans for raising the additional cash. Plan A is to sell 3,750 shares of common stock to one or more investors for $125,000 cash. Plan B is to sell 1,250 shares of cumulative preferred stock to one or more investors for $125,000 cash (this preferred stock would have a $100 par value, an annual 8% dividend rate, and be issued at par).

1. If the new business is expected to earn $72,000 of after-tax net income in the first year, what rate of return on beginning equity will the three (as a group) earn under each alternative? Which plan will provide the higher expected return to them?
2. If the new business is expected to earn $16,800 of after-tax net income in the first year, what rate of return on beginning equity will the three (as a group) earn under each alternative? Which plan will provide the higher expected return to them?
3. Analyze and interpret the differences between the results for parts 1 and 2.

BTN 13-8 Watch 30 to 60 minutes of financial news programming on television. Take notes on companies that are catching analysts' attention. You might hear reference to over- and undervaluation of firms and to reports about PE ratios, dividend yields, and earnings per share. Be prepared to give a brief description to the class of your observations.

HITTING THE ROAD
A1 A2 A3

BTN 13-9 Financial information for **DSG international plc** (www.DSGiplc.com) follows.

GLOBAL DECISION
A1 C4
DSG

Net income (in millions)	£ 207
Cash dividends declared per share	£ 0.07
Number of shares outstanding (in millions)*	1,843
Equity applicable to shares (in millions)	£1,304

* Assume that the year-end number of shares outstanding approximates the weighted-average shares outstanding.

Required

1. Compute book value per share for DSG.
2. Compute earnings per share (EPS) for DSG.
3. Compare DSG's dividends per share with its EPS. Is DSG paying out a large or small amount of its income as dividends? Explain.

ANSWERS TO MULTIPLE CHOICE QUIZ

1. e; Entry to record this stock issuance is:

Cash (6,000 × $8)	48,000	
Common Stock (6,000 × $5)		30,000
Paid-In Capital in Excess of Par Value, Common Stock		18,000

2. b; $75,000/19,000 shares = $3.95 per share
3. d; Preferred stock = 5,000 × $100 = $500,000
   Book value per share = ($2,000,000 − $500,000)/50,000 shares = $30 per common share
4. a; $0.81/$45.00 = 1.8%
5. c; Earnings per share = $3,500,000/700,000 shares = $5 per share
   PE ratio = $85/$5 = 17.0

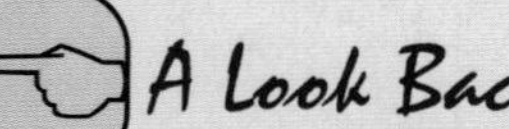

A Look Back

Chapter 13 focused on corporate equity transactions, including stock issuances and dividends. We also explained how to report and analyze income, earnings per share, and retained earnings.

A Look at This Chapter

This chapter describes the accounting for and analysis of bonds and notes. We explain their characteristics, payment patterns, interest computations, retirement, and reporting requirements. An appendix to this chapter introduces leases and pensions.

A Look Ahead

Chapter 15 focuses on how to classify, account for, and report investments in both debt and equity securities. We also describe accounting for transactions listed in a foreign currency.

Chapter 14 Long-Term Liabilities

Learning Objectives

CAP

Conceptual

C1 Explain the types and payment patterns of notes. *(p. 560)*

C2 *Appendix 14A*—Explain and compute the present value of an amount(s) to be paid at a future date(s). *(p. 567)*

C3 *Appendix 14C*—Describe the accrual of bond interest when bond payments do not align with accounting periods. *(p. 571)*

C4 *Appendix 14D*—Describe accounting for leases and pensions. *(p. 573)*

Analytical

A1 Compare bond financing with stock financing. *(p. 550)*

A2 Assess debt features and their implications. *(p. 563)*

A3 Compute the debt-to-equity ratio and explain its use. *(p. 563)*

LP14

Procedural

P1 Prepare entries to record bond issuance and bond interest expense. *(p. 552)*

P2 Compute and record amortization of bond discount. *(p. 553)*

P3 Compute and record amortization of bond premium. *(p. 556)*

P4 Record the retirement of bonds. *(p. 559)*

P5 Prepare entries to account for notes. *(p. 562)*

Decision Feature

Hip-Hop Financing

PHILADELPHIA—James "Fly" Lindsay and his three sisters were raised by their mother in North Philadelphia. "We were poor," explains Lindsay, "but we were rich in the values that she [mother] set forth." One of those values was education—Lindsay was the first in his family to attend college—and another was the commitment to community. "You have everyone taking away, but you have to give back," insists Lindsay.

Lindsay decided to give back by launching his own business. "I wanted to have a chip company that kids from the hood could relate to," he explains. But Lindsay knew that success depended on securing financing and then planning for long-term liabilities. "Between family and friends," explains Lindsay, "we put our dollars together and made it happen." With $40,000 in financing, he launched **Rap Snacks** **[RapSnacks.com]**, a maker of snack foods with a twist: Lindsay would sell his snacks with rappers on the wrappers. The snacks would be targeted to urban youth immersed in hip-hop culture. The snack wrappers, importantly, would include positive messages to the kids such as "Stay in School," "Respect Yourself," and "Money equals Education." Lindsay hopes they instill a craving for success, commitment, and entrepreneurship.

"I wanted to create a product that inner-city kids would relate to" — James Lindsay

Lindsay insists that urban youth need to learn about business and how it can help a community. Basic accounting principles and financing concepts such as bonds and notes are like another language to urban youth, he explains. Lindsay struggles to change that and more. "You can make money," says Lindsay, "but also have a social responsibility to where you came from." Actor and rapper Lil' Romeo has recently taken a lead in funding Rap Snacks.

Making investments in urban youth is a priority, says Lindsay. He continually works to convey knowledge of business financing, with the belief that urban youth can be successful. He manages his own company's long-term liabilities, interest payments, and collateral agreements, and is confident that urban youth can do the same. Understanding liabilities is not easy, says Lindsay, but the costs of not understanding are more severe—and more of the same—for the kids. "It feels good to make a difference," says Lindsay, "and set an example for the kids."

[Sources: *Rap Snacks Website,* January 2009; *Entrepreneur,* July 2003; *Philadelphia Inquirer,* October 2002; *Source Magazine,* June 2001; *Maxim,* March 2002; *Business Review,* September 2007; *PR Newswire,* September 2007]

Chapter Preview

Individuals, companies, and governments issue bonds to finance their activities. In return for financing, bonds promise to repay the lender with interest. This chapter explains the basics of bonds and the accounting for their issuance and retirement. The chapter also describes long-term notes as another financing source. We explain how present value concepts impact both the accounting for and reporting of bonds and notes. Appendixes to this chapter discuss present value concepts applicable to liabilities, effective interest amortization, and the accounting for leases and pensions.

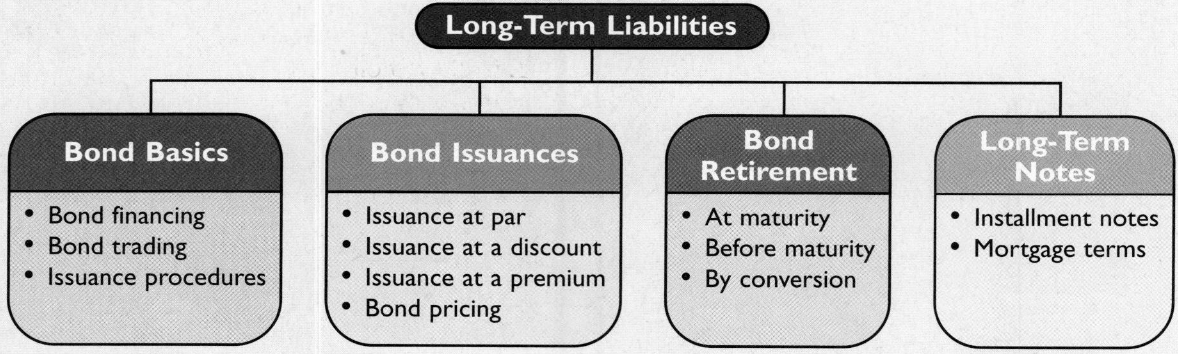

Basics of Bonds

Video14.2

This section explains the basics of bonds and a company's motivation for issuing them.

Bond Financing

A1 Compare bond financing with stock financing.

Projects that demand large amounts of money often are funded from bond issuances. (Both for-profit and nonprofit companies, as well as governmental units, such as nations, states, cities, and school districts, issue bonds.) A **bond** is its issuer's written promise to pay an amount identified as the par value of the bond with interest. The **par value of a bond,** also called the *face amount* or *face value,* is paid at a specified future date known as the bond's *maturity date.* Most bonds also require the issuer to make semiannual interest payments. The amount of interest paid each period is determined by multiplying the par value of the bond by the bond's contract rate of interest. This section explains both advantages and disadvantages of bond financing.

Advantages of Bonds There are three main advantages of bond financing:

1. *Bonds do not affect owner control.* Equity financing reflects ownership in a company, whereas bond financing does not. A person who contributes $1,000 of a company's $10,000 equity financing typically controls one-tenth of all owner decisions. A person who owns a $1,000, 11%, 20-year bond has no ownership right. This person, or bondholder, is to receive from the bond issuer 11% interest, or $110, each year the bond is outstanding and $1,000 when it matures in 20 years.

2. *Interest on bonds is tax deductible.* Bond interest payments are tax deductible for the issuer, but equity payments (distributions) to owners are not. To illustrate, assume that a corporation with no bond financing earns $15,000 in income *before* paying taxes at a 40% tax rate, which amounts to $6,000 ($15,000 × 40%) in taxes. If a portion of its financing is in bonds, however, the resulting bond interest is deducted in computing taxable income. That is, if bond interest expense is $10,000, the taxes owed would be $2,000 ([$15,000 − $10,000] × 40%), which is less than the $6,000 owed with no bond financing.

3. *Bonds can increase return on equity.* A company that earns a higher return with borrowed funds than it pays in interest on those funds increases its return on equity. This process is called *financial leverage* or *trading on the equity.*

Point: Financial leverage reflects issuance of bonds, notes, or preferred stock.

To illustrate the third point, consider Magnum Co., which has $1 million in equity and is planning a $500,000 expansion to meet increasing demand for its product. Magnum predicts the

$500,000 expansion will yield $125,000 in additional income before paying any interest. It currently earns $100,000 per year and has no interest expense. Magnum is considering three plans. Plan A is to not expand. Plan B is to expand and raise $500,000 from equity financing. Plan C is to expand and issue $500,000 of bonds that pay 10% annual interest ($50,000). Exhibit 14.1 shows how these three plans affect Magnum's net income, equity, and return on equity (net income/equity). The owner(s) will earn a higher return on equity if expansion occurs. Moreover, the preferred expansion plan is to issue bonds. Projected net income under Plan C ($175,000) is smaller than under Plan B ($225,000), but the return on equity is larger because of less equity investment. Plan C has another advantage if income is taxable. This illustration reflects a general rule: *Return on equity increases when the expected rate of return from the new assets is higher than the rate of interest expense on the debt financing.*

Example: Compute return on equity for all three plans if Magnum currently earns $150,000 instead of $100,000.
Answer ($ 000s):
Plan A = 15% ($150/$1,000)
Plan B = 18.3% ($275/$1,500)
Plan C = 22.5% ($225/$1,000)

EXHIBIT 14.1

Financing with Bonds versus Equity

	Plan A: Do Not Expand	Plan B: Equity Financing	Plan C: Bond Financing
Income before interest expense	$ 100,000	$ 225,000	$ 225,000
Interest expense	—	—	(50,000)
Net income	**$ 100,000**	**$ 225,000**	**$ 175,000**
Equity	$1,000,000	$1,500,000	$1,000,000
Return on equity	**10.0%**	**15.0%**	**17.5%**

Disadvantages of Bonds The two main disadvantages of bond financing are these:

1. *Bonds can decrease return on equity.* When a company earns a lower return with the borrowed funds than it pays in interest, it decreases its return on equity. This downside risk of financial leverage is more likely to arise when a company has periods of low income or net losses.
2. *Bonds require payment of both periodic interest and the par value at maturity.* Bond payments can be especially burdensome when income and cash flow are low. Equity financing, in contrast, does not require any payments because cash withdrawals (dividends) are paid at the discretion of the owner (or board).

Point: Debt financing is desirable when interest is tax deductible, when owner control is preferred, and when return on equity exceeds the debt's interest rate.

A company must weigh the risks and returns of the disadvantages and advantages of bond financing when deciding whether to issue bonds to finance operations.

Bond Trading

Bonds are securities that can be readily bought and sold. A large number of bonds trade on both the New York Exchange and the American Exchange. A bond *issue* consists of a number of bonds, usually in denominations of $1,000 or $5,000, and is sold to many different lenders. After bonds are issued, they often are bought and sold by investors, meaning that any particular bond probably has a number of owners before it matures. Since bonds are exchanged (bought and sold) in the market, they have a market value (price). For convenience, bond market values are expressed as a percent of their par (face) value. For example, a company's bonds might be trading at 103½, meaning they can be bought or sold for 103.5% of their par value. Bonds can also trade below par value. For instance, if a company's bonds are trading at 95, they can be bought or sold at 95% of their par value.

Decision Insight

Bonds	Rate	Mat	Yld	Vol	Close	Chg
IBM	7	25	5.9	130	119¼	+1¼

Quotes The **IBM** bond quote here is interpreted (left to right) as **Bonds,** issuer name; **Rate,** contract interest rate (7%); **Mat,** matures in year 2025 when principal is paid; **Yld,** yield rate (5.9%) of bond at current price; **Vol,** daily dollar worth ($130,000) of trades (in 1,000s); **Close,** closing price (119.25) for the day as percentage of par value; **Chg,** change (+1.25) in closing price from prior day's close.

Bond-Issuing Procedures

State and federal laws govern bond issuances. Bond issuers also want to ensure that they do not violate any of their existing contractual agreements when issuing bonds. Authorization of bond issuances includes the number of bonds authorized, their par value, and the contract interest rate.

EXHIBIT 14.2

Bond Certificate

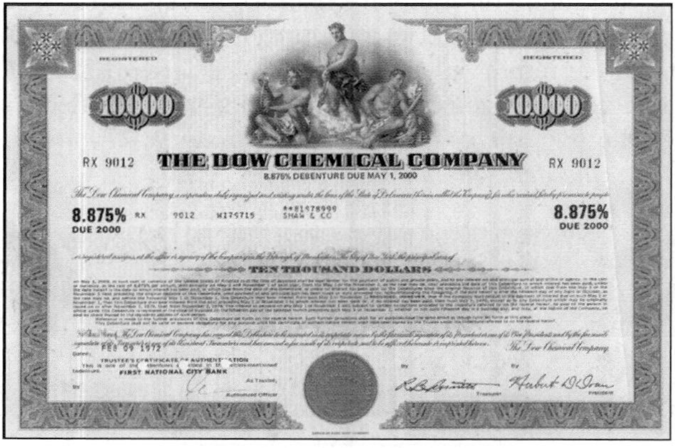

The legal document identifying the rights and obligations of both the bondholders and the issuer is called the **bond indenture,** which is the legal contract between the issuer and the bondholders. A bondholder may also receive a bond certificate as evidence of the company's debt. A **bond certificate,** such as that shown in Exhibit 14.2, includes specifics such as the issuer's name, the par value, the contract interest rate, and the maturity date. Many companies reduce costs by not issuing paper certificates to bondholders.[1]

Point: *Indenture* refers to a bond's legal contract; *debenture* refers to an unsecured bond.

Bond Issuances

Video14.2

This section explains accounting for bond issuances at par, below par (discount), and above par (premium). It also describes how to amortize a discount or premium and record bonds issued between interest payment dates.

Issuing Bonds at Par

P1 Prepare entries to record bond issuance and bond interest expense.

To illustrate an issuance of bonds at par value, suppose a company receives authorization to issue $800,000 of 9%, 20-year bonds dated January 1, 2009, that mature on December 31, 2028, and pay interest semiannually on each June 30 and December 31. After accepting the bond indenture on behalf of the bondholders, the trustee can sell all or a portion of the bonds to an underwriter. If all bonds are sold at par value, the issuer records the sale as follows.

Assets	= Liabilities	+ Equity
+800,000	+800,000	

2009			
Jan. 1	Cash	800,000	
	Bonds Payable		800,000
	Sold bonds at par.		

This entry reflects increases in the issuer's cash *and* long-term liabilities.

The issuer records the first semiannual interest payment as follows.

Assets	= Liabilities	+ Equity
−36,000		−36,000

2009			
June 30	Bond Interest Expense	36,000	
	Cash		36,000
	Paid semiannual interest (9% × $800,000 × ½ year).		

Point: The *spread* between the dealer's cost and what buyers pay can be huge. Dealers earn more than $25 billion in annual spread revenue.

Global: In the United Kingdom, government bonds are called *gilts*—short for gilt-edged investments.

[1] The issuing company normally sells its bonds to an investment firm called an *underwriter,* which resells them to the public. An issuing company can also sell bonds directly to investors. When an underwriter sells bonds to a large number of investors, a *trustee* represents and protects the bondholders' interests. The trustee monitors the issuer to ensure that it complies with the obligations in the bond indenture. Most trustees are large banks or trust companies. The trustee writes and accepts the terms of a bond indenture before it is issued. When bonds are offered to the public, called *floating an issue,* they must be registered with the Securities and Exchange Commission (SEC). SEC registration requires the issuer to file certain financial information. Most company bonds are issued in par value units of $1,000 or $5,000. *A baby bond* has a par value of less than $1,000, such as $100.

The issuer pays and records its semiannual interest obligation every six months until the bonds mature. When they mature, the issuer records its payment of principal as follows.

2028			
Dec. 31	Bonds Payable	800,000	
	Cash		800,000
	Paid bond principal at maturity.		

Assets	=	Liabilities	+	Equity
−800,000		−800,000		

Bond Discount or Premium

The bond issuer pays the interest rate specified in the indenture, the **contract rate,** also referred to as the *coupon rate, stated rate,* or *nominal rate*. The annual interest paid is determined by multiplying the bond par value by the contract rate. The contract rate is usually stated on an annual basis, even if interest is paid semiannually. For example, if a company issues a $1,000, 8% bond paying interest semiannually, it pays annual interest of $80 (8% × $1,000) in two semiannual payments of $40 each.

The contract rate sets the amount of interest the issuer pays in *cash,* which is not necessarily the *bond interest expense* actually incurred by the issuer. Bond interest expense depends on the bond's market value at issuance, which is determined by market expectations of the risk of lending to the issuer. The bond's **market rate** of interest is the rate that borrowers are willing to pay and lenders are willing to accept for a particular bond and its risk level. As the risk level increases, the rate increases to compensate purchasers for the bonds' increased risk. Also, the market rate is generally higher when the time period until the bond matures is longer due to the risk of adverse events occurring over a longer time period.

Many bond issuers try to set a contract rate of interest equal to the market rate they expect as of the bond issuance date. When the contract rate and market rate are equal, a bond sells at par value, but when they are not equal, a bond does not sell at par value. Instead, it is sold at a *premium* above par value or at a *discount* below par value. Exhibit 14.3 shows the relation between the contract rate, market rate, and a bond's issue price.

EXHIBIT 14.3

Relation between Bond Issue Price, Contract Rate, and Market Rate

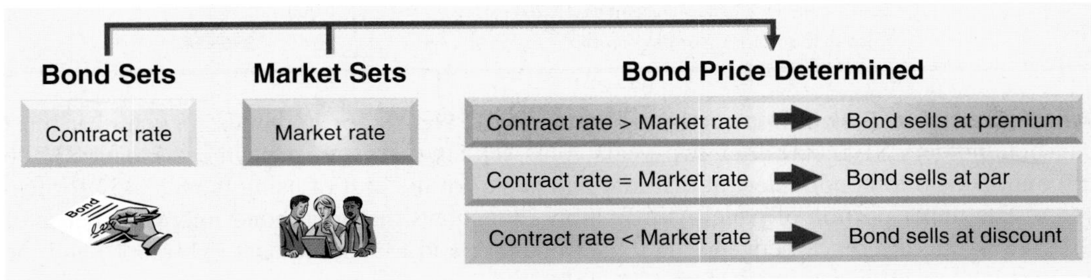

Quick Check Answers—p. 576

1. Unsecured bonds backed only by the issuer's general credit standing are called (*a*) serial bonds, (*b*) debentures, (*c*) registered bonds, or (*d*) convertible bonds.
2. How do you compute the amount of interest a bond issuer pays in cash each year?
3. When the contract rate is above the market rate, do bonds sell at a premium or a discount? Do purchasers pay more or less than the par value of the bonds?

Issuing Bonds at a Discount

P2 Compute and record amortization of bond discount.

A **discount on bonds payable** occurs when a company issues bonds with a contract rate less than the market rate. This means that the issue price is less than par value. To illustrate, assume that **Fila** announces an offer to issue bonds with a $100,000 par value, an 8% annual contract rate (paid semiannually), and a two-year life. Also assume that the market rate for Fila

Point: The difference between the contract rate and the market rate of interest on a new bond issue is usually a fraction of a percent. We use a difference of 2% to emphasize the effects.

bonds is 10%. These bonds then will sell at a discount since the contract rate is less than the market rate. The exact issue price for these bonds is stated as 96.454 (implying 96.454% of par value, or $96,454); we show how to compute this issue price later in the chapter. These bonds obligate the issuer to pay two separate types of future cash flows:

1. Par value of $100,000 cash at the end of the bonds' two-year life.
2. Cash interest payments of $4,000 (4% × $100,000) at the end of each semiannual period during the bonds' two-year life.

The exact pattern of cash flows for the Fila bonds is shown in Exhibit 14.4.

EXHIBIT 14.4

Cash Flows for Fila Bonds

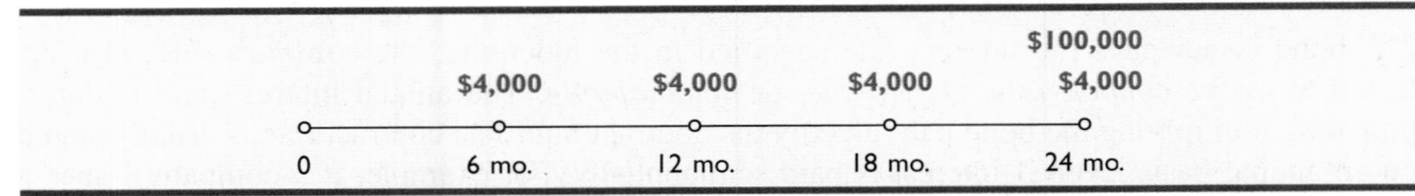

When Fila accepts $96,454 cash for its bonds on the issue date of December 31, 2009, it records the sale as follows.

Assets = Liabilities + Equity
+96,454 +100,000
−3,546

Dec. 31	Cash	96,454	
	Discount on Bonds Payable	3,546	
	Bonds Payable		100,000
	Sold bonds at a discount on their issue date.		

Point: Book value at issuance always equals the issuer's cash borrowed.

These bonds are reported in the long-term liability section of the issuer's December 31, 2009, balance sheet as shown in Exhibit 14.5. A discount is deducted from the par value of bonds to yield the **carrying (book) value of bonds.** Discount on Bonds Payable is a contra liability account.

EXHIBIT 14.5

Balance Sheet Presentation of Bond Discount

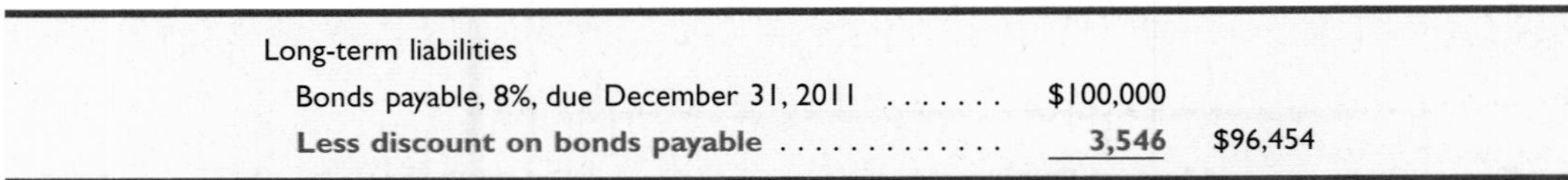

Long-term liabilities		
Bonds payable, 8%, due December 31, 2011	$100,000	
Less discount on bonds payable	3,546	$96,454

Amortizing a Bond Discount Fila receives $96,454 for its bonds; in return it must pay bondholders $100,000 after two years (plus semiannual interest payments). The $3,546 discount is paid to bondholders at maturity and is part of the cost of using the $96,454 for two years. The upper portion of panel A in Exhibit 14.6 shows that total bond interest expense of $19,546 is the difference between the total amount repaid to bondholders ($116,000) and the amount borrowed from bondholders ($96,454). Alternatively, we can compute total bond interest expense as the sum of the four interest payments and the bond discount. This alternative computation is shown in the lower portion of panel A.

Point: *Zero-coupon bonds* do not pay periodic interest (contract rate is zero). These bonds always sell at a discount because their 0% contract rate is always below the market rate.

The total $19,546 bond interest expense must be allocated across the four semiannual periods in the bonds' life, and the bonds' carrying value must be updated at each balance sheet date. This is accomplished using the straight-line method (or the effective interest method in Appendix 14B). Both methods systematically reduce the bond discount to zero over the two-year life. This process is called *amortizing a bond discount.*

Video14.2

Straight-Line Method The **straight-line bond amortization** method allocates an equal portion of the total bond interest expense to each interest period. To apply the straight-line method to Fila's bonds, we divide the total bond interest expense of $19,546 by 4 (the number of semiannual periods in the bonds' life). This gives a bond interest expense of $4,887 per period, which is $4,886.5 rounded to the nearest dollar per period (all computations, including those for assignments, are rounded to the nearest whole dollar). Alternatively, we can find this number by first dividing the $3,546 discount by 4, which yields the $887 amount of discount to be amortized each interest period. When the $887 is added to the $4,000 cash payment, the

EXHIBIT 14.6

Interest Computation and Entry for Bonds Issued at a Discount

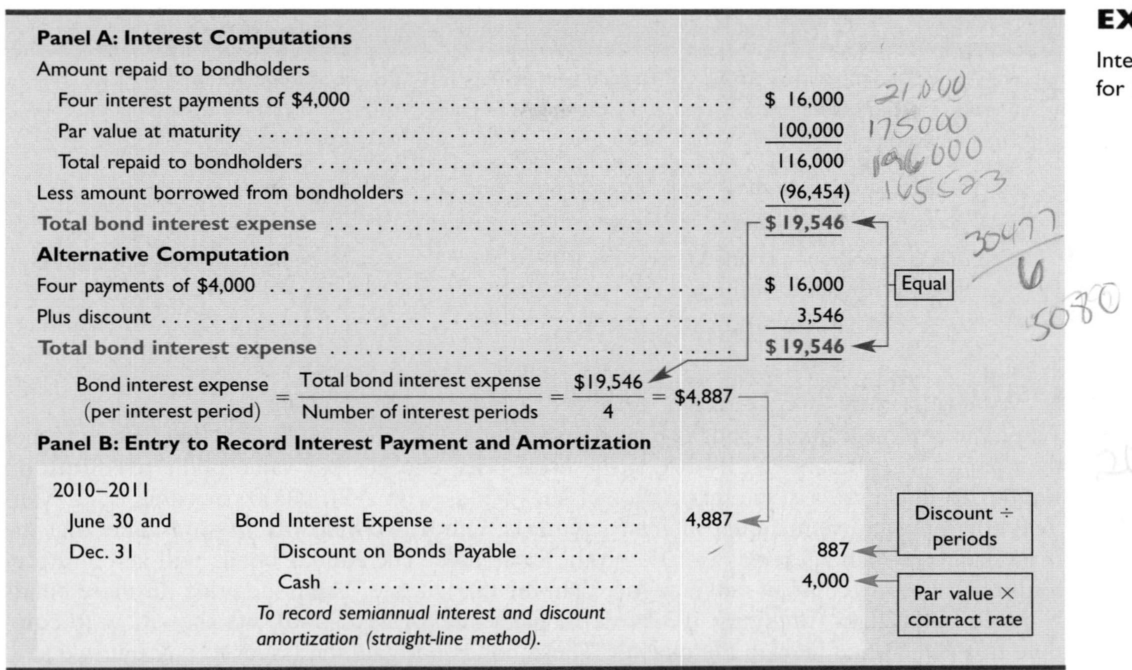

Panel A: Interest Computations

Amount repaid to bondholders	
Four interest payments of $4,000	$ 16,000
Par value at maturity	100,000
Total repaid to bondholders	116,000
Less amount borrowed from bondholders	(96,454)
Total bond interest expense	**$ 19,546**
Alternative Computation	
Four payments of $4,000	$ 16,000
Plus discount	3,546
Total bond interest expense	**$ 19,546**

(The two totals are marked "Equal".)

$$\frac{\text{Bond interest expense}}{\text{(per interest period)}} = \frac{\text{Total bond interest expense}}{\text{Number of interest periods}} = \frac{\$19{,}546}{4} = \$4{,}887$$

Panel B: Entry to Record Interest Payment and Amortization

2010–2011			
June 30 and Dec. 31	Bond Interest Expense	4,887	
	Discount on Bonds Payable		887 (Discount ÷ periods)
	Cash		4,000 (Par value × contract rate)
	To record semiannual interest and discount amortization (straight-line method).		

bond interest expense for each period is $4,887. Panel B of Exhibit 14.6 shows how the issuer records bond interest expense and updates the balance of the bond liability account at the end of *each* of the four semiannual interest periods (June 30, 2010, through December 31, 2011).

Exhibit 14.7 shows the pattern of decreases in the Discount on Bonds Payable account and the pattern of increases in the bonds' carrying value. The following points summarize the discount bonds' straight-line amortization:

EXHIBIT 14.7

Straight-Line Amortization of Bond Discount

Semiannual Period-End	Unamortized Discount*	Carrying Value†
(0) 12/31/2009	$3,546	$ 96,454
(1) 6/30/2010	2,659	97,341
(2) 12/31/2010	1,772	98,228
(3) 6/30/2011	885	99,115
(4) **12/31/2011**	**0‡**	**100,000**

* Total bond discount (of $3,546) less accumulated periodic amortization ($887 per semiannual interest period).

† Bond par value (of $100,000) less unamortized discount.

‡ Adjusted for rounding.

The two columns always sum to par value for a discount bond.

1. At issuance, the $100,000 par value consists of the $96,454 cash received by the issuer plus the $3,546 discount.
2. During the bonds' life, the (unamortized) discount decreases each period by the $887 amortization ($3,546/4), and the carrying value (par value less unamortized discount) increases each period by $887.
3. At maturity, the unamortized discount equals zero, and the carrying value equals the $100,000 par value that the issuer pays the holder.

We see that the issuer incurs a $4,887 bond interest expense each period but pays only $4,000 cash. The $887 unpaid portion of this expense is added to the bonds' carrying value. (The total $3,546 unamortized discount is "paid" when the bonds mature; $100,000 is paid at maturity but only $96,454 was received at issuance.)

Decision Insight

Ratings Game Many bond buyers rely on rating services to assess bond risk. The best known are **Standard & Poor's** and **Moody's**. These services focus on the issuer's financial statements and other factors in setting ratings. Standard & Poor's ratings, from best quality to default, are AAA, AA, A, BBB, BB, B, CCC, CC, C, and D. Ratings can include a plus (+) or minus (−) to show relative standing within a category.

Quick Check Answers—p. 576

Five-year, 6% bonds with a $100,000 par value are issued at a price of $91,893. Interest is paid semiannually, and the bonds' market rate is 8% on the issue date. Use this information to answer the following questions:

4. Are these bonds issued at a discount or a premium? Explain your answer.
5. What is the issuer's journal entry to record the issuance of these bonds?
6. What is the amount of bond interest expense recorded at the first semiannual period using the straight-line method?

Issuing Bonds at a Premium

P3 Compute and record amortization of bond premium.

When the contract rate of bonds is higher than the market rate, the bonds sell at a price higher than par value. The amount by which the bond price exceeds par value is the **premium on bonds.** To illustrate, assume that **Adidas** issues bonds with a $100,000 par value, a 12% annual contract rate, semiannual interest payments, and a two-year life. Also assume that the market rate for Adidas bonds is 10% on the issue date. The Adidas bonds will sell at a premium because the contract rate is higher than the market rate. The issue price for these bonds is stated as 103.546 (implying 103.546% of par value, or $103,546); we show how to compute this issue price later in the chapter. These bonds obligate the issuer to pay out two separate future cash flows:

1. Par value of $100,000 cash at the end of the bonds' two-year life.
2. Cash interest payments of $6,000 (6% × $100,000) at the end of each semiannual period during the bonds' two-year life.

The exact pattern of cash flows for the Adidas bonds is shown in Exhibit 14.8.

EXHIBIT 14.8

Cash Flows for Adidas Bonds

0	6 mo.	12 mo.	18 mo.	24 mo.
	$6,000	$6,000	$6,000	$100,000 $6,000

When Adidas accepts $103,546 cash for its bonds on the issue date of December 31, 2009, it records this transaction as follows.

Assets = Liabilities + Equity
+103,546 +100,000
+3,546

Dec. 31	Cash	103,546	
	Premium on Bonds Payable		3,546
	Bonds Payable		100,000
	Sold bonds at a premium on their issue date.		

These bonds are reported in the long-term liability section of the issuer's December 31, 2009, balance sheet as shown in Exhibit 14.9. A premium is added to par value to yield the carrying (book) value of bonds. Premium on Bonds Payable is an adjunct (also called *accretion*) liability account.

EXHIBIT 14.9

Balance Sheet Presentation of Bond Premium

Long-term liabilities		
Bonds payable, 12%, due December 31, 2011	$100,000	
Plus premium on bonds payable	3,546	$103,546

Amortizing a Bond Premium Adidas receives $103,546 for its bonds; in return, it pays bondholders $100,000 after two years (plus semiannual interest payments). The $3,546 premium not repaid to issuer's bondholders at maturity goes to reduce the issuer's expense of using the $103,546 for two years. The upper portion of panel A of Exhibit 14.10 shows that total bond interest expense of $20,454 is the difference between the total amount repaid to bondholders ($124,000) and the amount borrowed from bondholders ($103,546). Alternatively, we can compute

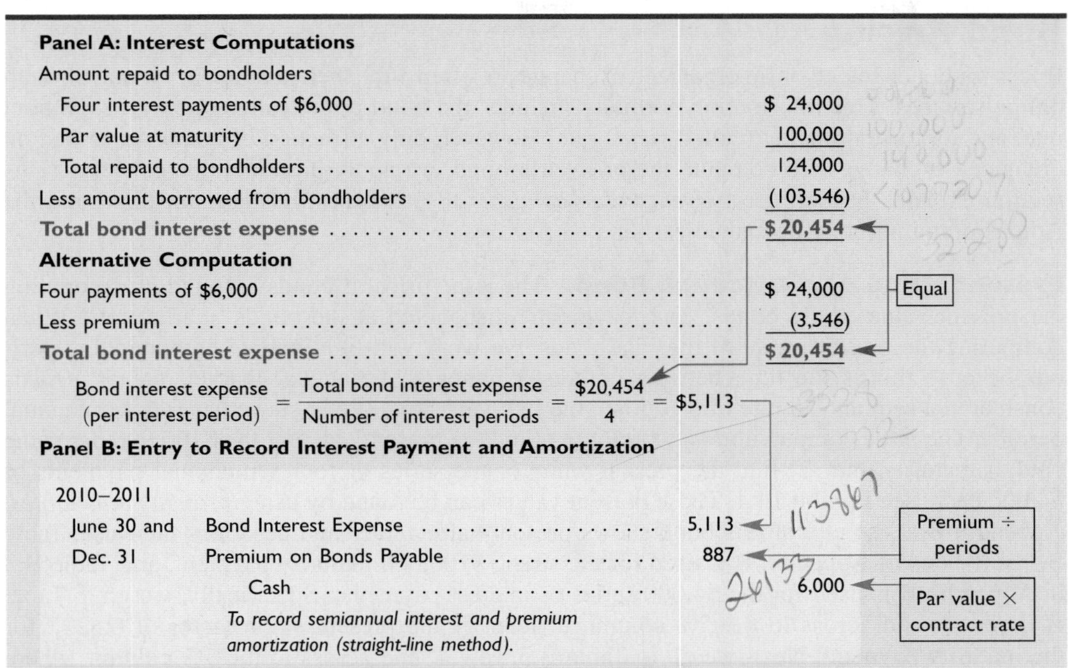

Panel A: Interest Computations

Amount repaid to bondholders	
Four interest payments of $6,000	$ 24,000
Par value at maturity	100,000
Total repaid to bondholders	124,000
Less amount borrowed from bondholders	(103,546)
Total bond interest expense	**$ 20,454**
Alternative Computation	
Four payments of $6,000	$ 24,000
Less premium	(3,546)
Total bond interest expense	**$ 20,454**

Equal

$$\text{Bond interest expense (per interest period)} = \frac{\text{Total bond interest expense}}{\text{Number of interest periods}} = \frac{\$20{,}454}{4} = \$5{,}113$$

Panel B: Entry to Record Interest Payment and Amortization

2010–2011			
June 30 and Dec. 31	Bond Interest Expense	5,113	
	Premium on Bonds Payable	887	
	Cash		6,000
	To record semiannual interest and premium amortization (straight-line method).		

Premium ÷ periods

Par value × contract rate

EXHIBIT 14.10

Interest Computation and Entry for Bonds Issued at a Premium

total bond interest expense as the sum of the four interest payments less the bond premium. The premium is subtracted because it will not be paid to bondholders when the bonds mature; see the lower portion of panel A. Total bond interest expense must be allocated over the four semiannual periods using the straight-line method (or the effective interest method in Appendix 14B).

Straight-Line Method The straight-line method allocates an equal portion of total bond interest expense to each of the bonds' semiannual interest periods. To apply this method to Adidas bonds, we divide the two years' total bond interest expense of $20,454 by 4 (the number of semiannual periods in the bonds' life). This gives a total bond interest expense of $5,113 per period, which is $5,113.5 rounded down so that the journal entry balances and for simplicity in presentation (alternatively, one could carry cents). Panel B of Exhibit 14.10 shows how the issuer records bond interest expense and updates the balance of the bond liability account for *each* semiannual period (June 30, 2010, through December 31, 2011).

Point: A premium decreases Bond Interest Expense; a discount increases it.

EXHIBIT 14.11

Straight-Line Amortization of Bond Premium

Semiannual Period-End	Unamortized Premium*	Carrying Value†
(0) 12/31/2009	$3,546	$103,546
(1) 6/30/2010	2,659	102,659
(2) 12/31/2010	1,772	101,772
(3) 6/30/2011	885	100,885
(4) 12/31/2011	0‡	**100,000**

* Total bond premium (of $3,546) less accumulated periodic amortization ($887 per semiannual interest period).

† Bond par value (of $100,000) plus unamortized premium.

‡ Adjusted for rounding.

During the bond life, carrying value is adjusted to par and the amortized premium to zero.

Exhibit 14.11 shows the pattern of decreases in the unamortized Premium on Bonds Payable account and in the bonds' carrying value. The following points summarize straight-line amortization of the premium bonds:

1. At issuance, the $100,000 par value plus the $3,546 premium equals the $103,546 cash received by the issuer.
2. During the bonds' life, the (unamortized) premium decreases each period by the $887 amortization ($3,546/4), and the carrying value decreases each period by the same $887.
3. At maturity, the unamortized premium equals zero, and the carrying value equals the $100,000 par value that the issuer pays the holder.

The next section describes bond pricing. An instructor can choose to cover bond pricing or not. Assignments requiring the next section are Quick Study 14-4, Exercises 14-9 & 14-10, and Problems 14-1A & 14-1B and 14-4A & 14-4B.

Bond Pricing

Prices for bonds traded on an organized exchange are often published in newspapers and through online services. This information normally includes the bond price (called *quote*), its contract rate, and its current market (called *yield*) rate. However, only a fraction of bonds are traded on organized exchanges. To compute the price of a bond, we apply present value concepts. This section explains how to use *present value concepts* to price the Fila discount bond and the Adidas premium bond described earlier.

Point: InvestingInBonds.com is a bond research and learning source.

Present Value of a Discount Bond The issue price of bonds is found by computing the present value of the bonds' cash payments, discounted at the bonds' market rate. When computing the present value of the Fila bonds, we work with *semiannual* compounding periods because this is the time between interest payments; the annual market rate of 10% is considered a semiannual rate of 5%. Also, the two-year bond life is viewed as four semiannual periods. The price computation is twofold: (1) Find the present value of the $100,000 par value paid at maturity and (2) find the present value of the series of four semiannual payments of $4,000 each; see Exhibit 14.4. These present values can be found by using *present value tables*. Appendix B at the end of this book shows present value tables and describes their use. Table B.1 at the end of Appendix B is used for the single $100,000 maturity payment, and Table B.3 in Appendix B is used for the $4,000 series of interest payments. Specifically, we go to Table B.1, row 4, and across to the 5% column to identify the present value factor of 0.8227 for the maturity payment. Next, we go to Table B.3, row 4, and across to the 5% column, where the present value factor is 3.5460 for the series of interest payments. We compute bond price by multiplying the cash flow payments by their corresponding present value factors and adding them together; see Exhibit 14.12.

Point: A bond's market value (price) at issuance equals the present value of its future cash payments, where the interest (discount) rate used is the bond's market rate.

Point: Many calculators have present value functions for computing bond prices.

EXHIBIT 14.12

Computing Issue Price for the Fila Discount Bonds

Cash Flow	Table	Present Value Factor	Amount	Present Value
$100,000 par (maturity) value	B.1	0.8227	× $100,000 =	$ 82,270
$4,000 interest payments	B.3	3.5460	× 4,000 =	14,184
Price of bond				$96,454

Present Value of a Premium Bond We find the issue price of the Adidas bonds by using the market rate to compute the present value of the bonds' future cash flows. When computing the present value of these bonds, we again work with *semiannual* compounding periods because this is the time between interest payments. The annual 10% market rate is applied as a semiannual rate of 5%, and the two-year bond life is viewed as four semiannual periods. The computation is twofold: (1) Find the present value of the $100,000 par value paid at maturity and (2) find the present value of the series of four payments of $6,000 each; see Exhibit 14.8. These present values can be found by using present value tables. First, go to Table B.1, row 4, and across to the 5% column where the present value factor is 0.8227 for the maturity payment. Second, go to Table B.3, row 4, and across to the 5% column, where the present value factor is 3.5460 for the series of interest payments. The bonds' price is computed by multiplying the cash flow payments by their corresponding present value factors and adding them together; see Exhibit 14.13.

Point: There are nearly 5 million individual U.S. bond issues, ranging from huge treasuries to tiny municipalities. This compares to about 12,000 individual U.S. stocks that are traded.

EXHIBIT 14.13

Computing Issue Price for the Adidas Premium Bonds

Cash Flow	Table	Present Value Factor	Amount	Present Value
$100,000 par (maturity) value	B.1	0.8227	× $100,000 =	$ 82,270
$6,000 interest payments	B.3	3.5460	× 6,000 =	21,276
Price of bond				$103,546

Quick Check Answers—p. 576

On December 31, 2008, a company issues 16%, 10-year bonds with a par value of $100,000. Interest is paid on June 30 and December 31. The bonds are sold to yield a 14% annual market rate at an issue price of $110,592. Use this information to answer questions 7 through 9:

7. Are these bonds issued at a discount or a premium? Explain your answer.
8. Using the straight-line method to allocate bond interest expense, the issuer records the second interest payment (on December 31, 2009) with a debit to Premium on Bonds Payable in the amount of (*a*) $7,470, (*b*) $530, (*c*) $8,000, or (*d*) $400.
9. How are these bonds reported in the long-term liability section of the issuer's balance sheet as of December 31, 2009?

Bond Retirement

This section describes the retirement of bonds (1) at maturity, (2) before maturity, and (3) by conversion to stock.

Bond Retirement at Maturity

P4 Record the retirement of bonds.

The carrying value of bonds at maturity always equals par value. For example, both Exhibits 14.7 (a discount) and 14.11 (a premium) show that the carrying value of bonds at the end of their lives equals par value ($100,000). The retirement of these bonds at maturity, assuming interest is already paid and entered, is recorded as follows:

2011			
Dec. 31	Bonds Payable	100,000	
	Cash		100,000
	To record retirement of bonds at maturity.		

Assets	= Liabilities	+ Equity
−100,000	−100,000	

Bond Retirement before Maturity

Issuers sometimes wish to retire some or all of their bonds prior to maturity. For instance, if interest rates decline greatly, an issuer may wish to replace high-interest-paying bonds with new low-interest bonds. Two common ways to retire bonds before maturity are to (1) exercise a call option or (2) purchase them on the open market. In the first instance, an issuer can reserve the right to retire bonds early by issuing callable bonds. The bond indenture can give the issuer an option to *call* the bonds before they mature by paying the par value plus a *call premium* to bondholders. In the second case, the issuer retires bonds by repurchasing them on the open market at their current price. Whether bonds are called or repurchased, the issuer is unlikely to pay a price that exactly equals their carrying value. When a difference exists between the bonds' carrying value and the amount paid, the issuer records a gain or loss equal to the difference.

Point: Bond retirement is also referred to as *bond redemption.*

Point: Gains and losses from retiring bonds were *previously* reported as extraordinary items. New standards require that they now be judged by the "unusual and infrequent" criteria for reporting purposes.

To illustrate the accounting for retiring callable bonds, assume that a company issued callable bonds with a par value of $100,000. The call option requires the issuer to pay a call premium of $3,000 to bondholders in addition to the par value. Next, assume that after the June 30, 2009, interest payment, the bonds have a carrying value of $104,500. Then on July 1, 2009, the issuer calls these bonds and pays $103,000 to bondholders. The issuer recognizes a $1,500 gain from the difference between the bonds' carrying value of $104,500 and the retirement price of $103,000. The issuer records this bond retirement as follows.

July 1	Bonds Payable	100,000	
	Premium on Bonds Payable	4,500	
	Gain on Bond Retirement		1,500
	Cash		103,000
	To record retirement of bonds before maturity.		

Assets	= Liabilities	+ Equity
−103,000	−100,000	+1,500
	−4,500	

An issuer usually must call all bonds when it exercises a call option. However, to retire as many or as few bonds as it desires, an issuer can purchase them on the open market. If it retires less than the entire class of bonds, it recognizes a gain or loss for the difference between the carrying value of those bonds retired and the amount paid to acquire them.

Bond Retirement by Conversion

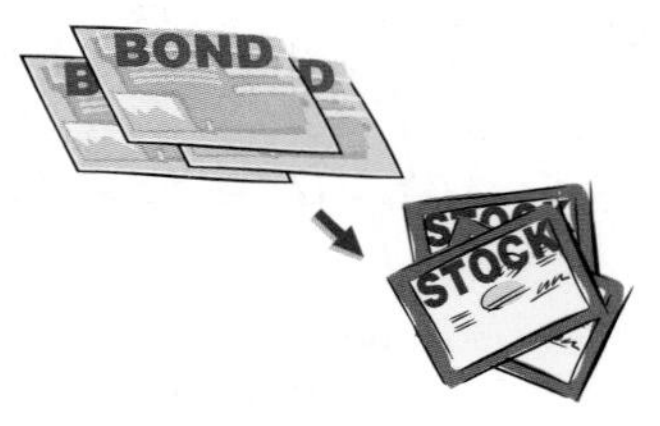

Convertible Bond

Holders of convertible bonds have the right to convert their bonds to stock. When conversion occurs, the bonds' carrying value is transferred to equity accounts and no gain or loss is recorded. (We further describe convertible bonds in the Decision Analysis section of this chapter.)

To illustrate, assume that on January 1 the $100,000 par value bonds of **Converse**, with a carrying value of $100,000, are converted to 15,000 shares of $2 par value common stock. The entry to record this conversion follows (the market prices of the bonds and stock are *not* relevant to this entry; the material in Chapter 13 is helpful in understanding this transaction):

Assets	= Liabilities	+ Equity
	−100,000	+30,000
		+70,000

Jan. 1	Bonds Payable	100,000	
	Common Stock		30,000
	Paid-In Capital in Excess of Par Value		70,000
	To record retirement of bonds by conversion.		

Decision Insight

Junk Bonds Junk bonds are company bonds with low credit ratings due to a higher than average likelihood of default. On the upside, the high risk of junk bonds can yield high returns if the issuer survives and repays its debt.

Quick Check

Answer—p. 576

10. Six years ago, a company issued $500,000 of 6%, eight-year bonds at a price of 95. The current carrying value is $493,750. The company decides to retire 50% of these bonds by buying them on the open market at a price of 102½. What is the amount of gain or loss on the retirement of these bonds?

Long-Term Notes Payable

Video14.1

Like bonds, notes are issued to obtain assets such as cash. Unlike bonds, notes are typically transacted with a *single* lender such as a bank. An issuer initially records a note at its selling price—that is, the note's face value minus any discount or plus any premium. Over the note's life, the amount of interest expense allocated to each period is computed by multiplying the market rate (at issuance of the note) by the beginning-of-period note balance. The note's carrying (book) value at any time equals its face value minus any unamortized discount or plus any unamortized premium; carrying value is also computed as the present value of all remaining payments, discounted using the market rate at issuance.

Installment Notes

C1 Explain the types and payment patterns of notes.

An **installment note** is an obligation requiring a series of payments to the lender. Installment notes are common for franchises and other businesses when lenders and borrowers agree to spread payments over several periods. To illustrate, assume that Foghog borrows $60,000 from a bank to purchase equipment. It signs an 8% installment note requiring six annual payments of principal plus interest and it records the note's issuance at January 1, 2009, as follows.

Assets	= Liabilities	+ Equity
+60,000	+60,000	

Jan. 1	Cash	60,000	
	Notes Payable		60,000
	Borrowed $60,000 by signing an 8%, six-year installment note.		

Payments on an installment note normally include the accrued interest expense plus a portion of the amount borrowed (the *principal*). This section describes an installment note with equal payments.

The equal total payments pattern consists of changing amounts of both interest and principal. To illustrate, assume that Foghog borrows $60,000 by signing a $60,000 note that requires six *equal payments* of $12,979 at the end of each year. (The present value of an annuity of six annual payments of $12,979, discounted at 8%, equals $60,000; we show this computation in footnote 2 on the next page.) The $12,979 includes both interest and principal, the amounts of which change with each payment. Exhibit 14.14 shows the pattern of equal total payments and its two parts, interest and principal. Column A shows the note's beginning balance. Column B shows accrued interest for each year at 8% of the beginning note balance. Column C shows the impact on the note's principal, which equals the difference between the total payment in column D and the interest expense in column B. Column E shows the note's year-end balance.

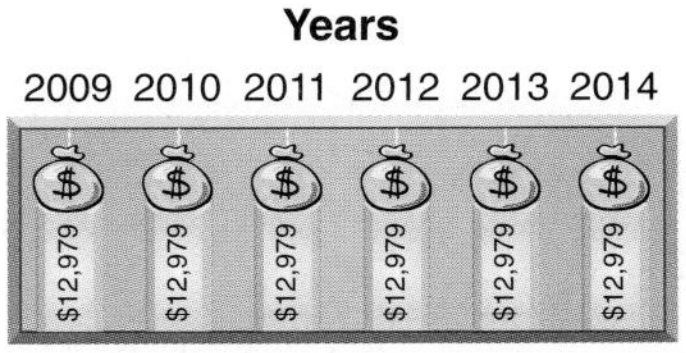

Point: Most consumer notes are installment notes that require equal total payments.

EXHIBIT 14.14

Installment Note: Equal Total Payments

		Payments					
Period Ending Date	(A) Beginning Balance	(B) *Debit* Interest Expense 8% × (A)	+	(C) *Debit* Notes Payable (D) − (B)	=	(D) *Credit* Cash (computed)	(E) Ending Balance (A) − (C)
(1) **12/31/2009**	**$60,000**	**$ 4,800**		**$ 8,179**		**$12,979**	**$51,821**
(2) 12/31/2010	51,821	4,146		8,833		12,979	42,988
(3) 12/31/2011	42,988	3,439		9,540		12,979	33,448
(4) 12/31/2012	33,448	2,676		10,303		12,979	23,145
(5) 12/31/2013	23,145	1,852		11,127		12,979	12,018
(6) 12/31/2014	12,018	961		12,018		12,979	0
		$17,874		**$60,000**		**$77,874**	

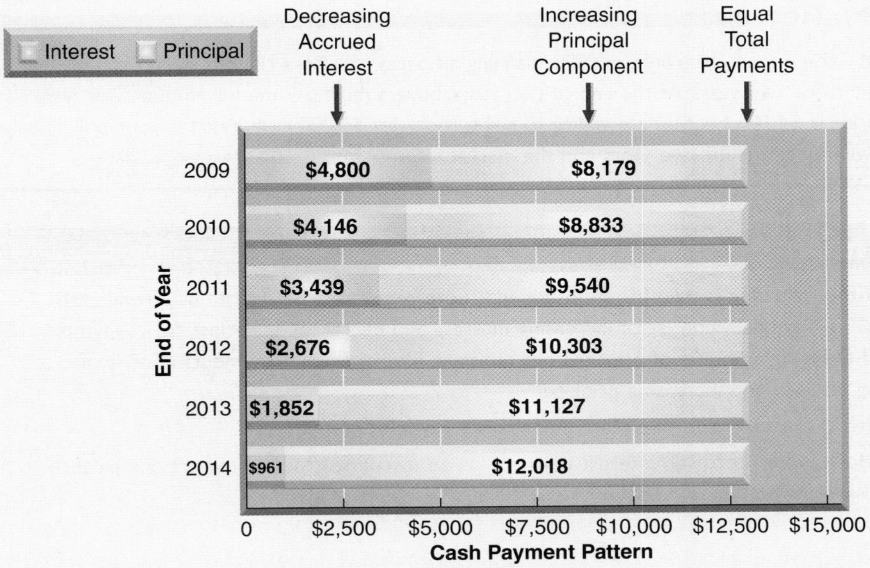

Although the six cash payments are equal, accrued interest decreases each year because the principal balance of the note declines. As the amount of interest decreases each year, the portion of each payment applied to principal increases. This pattern is graphed in the lower part

Point: The Truth-in-Lending Act requires lenders to provide information about loan costs including finance charges and interest rate.

P5 Prepare entries to account for notes.

of Exhibit 14.14. Foghog uses the amounts in Exhibit 14.14 to record its first two payments (for years 2009 and 2010) as follows:

Assets = Liabilities + Equity
−12,979 −8,179 −4,800

2009			
Dec. 31	Interest Expense	4,800	
	Notes Payable	8,179	
	Cash		12,979
	To record first installment payment.		

Assets = Liabilities + Equity
−12,979 −8,833 −4,146

2010			
Dec. 31	Interest Expense	4,146	
	Notes Payable	8,833	
	Cash		12,979
	To record second installment payment.		

Foghog records similar entries but with different amounts for each of the remaining four payments. After six years, the Notes Payable account balance is zero.[2]

Mortgage Notes and Bonds

A **mortgage** is a legal agreement that helps protect a lender if a borrower fails to make required payments on notes or bonds. A mortgage gives the lender a right to be paid from the cash proceeds of the sale of a borrower's assets identified in the mortgage. A legal document, called a *mortgage contract,* describes the mortgage terms.

Mortgage notes carry a mortgage contract pledging title to specific assets as security for the note. Mortgage notes are especially popular in the purchase of homes and the acquisition of plant assets. Less common *mortgage bonds* are backed by the issuer's assets. Accounting for mortgage notes and bonds is similar to that for unsecured notes and bonds, except that the mortgage agreement must be disclosed. For example, **Musicland** reports that its "mortgage note payable is collateralized by land, buildings and certain fixtures."

Global: Countries vary in the preference given to debtholders vs. stockholders when a company is in financial distress. Some countries such as Germany, France, and Japan give preference to stockholders over debtholders.

Decision Maker

Entrepreneur You are an electronics retailer planning a holiday sale on a custom stereo system that requires no payments for two years. At the end of two years, buyers must pay the full amount. The system's suggested retail price is $4,100, but you are willing to sell it today for $3,000 cash. What is your holiday sale price if payment will not occur for two years and the market interest rate is 10%? [Answer—p. 576]

Quick Check

Answers—p. 576

11. Which of the following is true for an installment note requiring a series of equal total cash payments? (*a*) Payments consist of increasing interest and decreasing principal; (*b*) payments consist of changing amounts of principal but constant interest; or (*c*) payments consist of decreasing interest and increasing principal.

12. How is the interest portion of an installment note payment computed?

13. When a borrower records an interest payment on an installment note, how are the balance sheet and income statement affected?

[2] Table B.3 in Appendix B is used to compute the dollar amount of the six payments that equal the initial note balance of $60,000 at 8% interest. We go to Table B.3, row 6, and across to the 8% column, where the present value factor is 4.6229. The dollar amount is then computed by solving this relation:

Table	Present Value Factor		Dollar Amount		Present Value
B.3	4.6229	×	?	=	$60,000

The dollar amount is computed by dividing $60,000 by 4.6229, yielding $12,979.

Example: Suppose the $60,000 installment loan has an 8% interest rate with eight equal annual payments. What is the annual payment? *Answer* (using Table B.3): $60,000/5.7466 = $10,441

Debt Features and the Debt-to-Equity Ratio

Decision Analysis

Collateral agreements can reduce the risk of loss for both bonds and notes. Unsecured bonds and notes are riskier because the issuer's obligation to pay interest and principal has the same priority as all other unsecured liabilities in the event of bankruptcy. If a company is unable to pay its debts in full, the unsecured creditors (including the holders of debentures) lose all or a portion of their balances. These types of legal agreements and other characteristics of long-term liabilities are crucial for effective business decisions. The first part of this section describes the different types of features sometimes included with bonds and notes. The second part explains and applies the debt-to-equity ratio.

Features of Bonds and Notes

A2 Assess debt features and their implications.

This section describes common features of debt securities.

Secured or Unsecured **Secured bonds** (and notes) have specific assets of the issuer pledged (or *mortgaged*) as collateral. This arrangement gives holders added protection against the issuer's default. If the issuer fails to pay interest or par value, the secured holders can demand that the collateral be sold and the proceeds used to pay the obligation. **Unsecured bonds** (and notes), also called *debentures,* are backed by the issuer's general credit standing. Unsecured debt is riskier than secured debt. *Subordinated debentures* are liabilities that are not repaid until the claims of the more senior, unsecured (and secured) liabilities are settled.

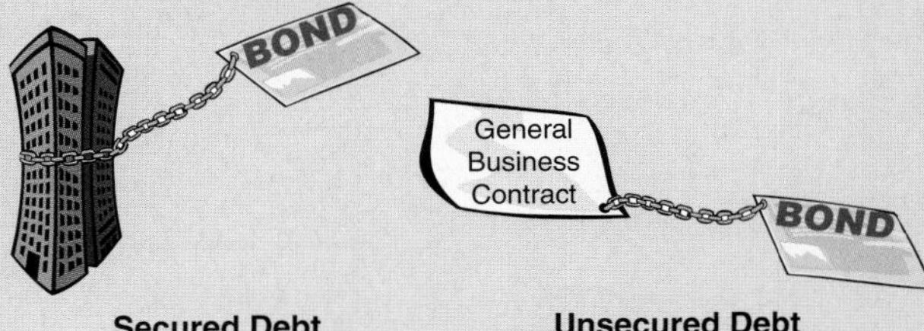

Secured Debt   Unsecured Debt

Term or Serial **Term bonds** (and notes) are scheduled for maturity on one specified date. **Serial bonds** (and notes) mature at more than one date (often in series) and thus are usually repaid over a number of periods. For instance, $100,000 of serial bonds might mature at the rate of $10,000 each year from 6 to 15 years after they are issued. Many bonds are **sinking fund bonds,** which to reduce the holder's risk require the issuer to create a *sinking fund* of assets set aside at specified amounts and dates to repay the bonds.

Registered or Bearer Bonds issued in the names and addresses of their holders are **registered bonds.** The issuer makes bond payments by sending checks (or cash transfers) to registered holders. A registered holder must notify the issuer of any ownership change. Registered bonds offer the issuer the practical advantage of not having to actually issue bond certificates. Bonds payable to whoever holds them (the *bearer*) are called **bearer bonds** or *unregistered bonds*. Sales or exchanges might not be recorded, so the holder of a bearer bond is presumed to be its rightful owner. As a result, lost bearer bonds are difficult to replace. Many bearer bonds are also **coupon bonds.** This term reflects interest coupons that are attached to the bonds. When each coupon matures, the holder presents it to a bank or broker for collection. At maturity, the holder follows the same process and presents the bond certificate for collection. Issuers of coupon bonds cannot deduct the related interest expense for taxable income. This is to prevent abuse by taxpayers who own coupon bonds but fail to report interest income on their tax returns.

Convertible and/or Callable **Convertible bonds** (and notes) can be exchanged for a fixed number of shares of the issuing corporation's common stock. Convertible debt offers holders the potential to participate in future increases in stock price. Holders still receive periodic interest while the debt is held and the par value if they hold the debt to maturity. In most cases, the holders decide whether and when to convert debt to stock. **Callable bonds** (and notes) have an option exercisable by the issuer to retire them at a stated dollar amount before maturity.

Convertible Debt

Callable Debt

Decision Insight

Munis More than a million municipal bonds, or "munis," exist, and many are tax exempt. Munis are issued by state, city, town, and county governments to pay for public projects including schools, libraries, roads, bridges, and stadiums.

Debt-to-Equity Ratio

A3 Compute the debt-to-equity ratio and explain its use.

Beyond assessing different characteristics of debt as just described, we want to know the level of debt, especially in relation to total equity. Such knowledge helps us assess the risk of a company's financing structure. A company financed mainly with debt is more risky because liabilities must be repaid—usually with periodic interest—whereas equity financing does not. A measure to assess the risk of a company's financing structure is the **debt-to-equity ratio** (see Exhibit 14.15).

EXHIBIT 14.15
Debt-to-Equity Ratio

$$\textbf{Debt-to-equity} = \frac{\textbf{Total liabilities}}{\textbf{Total equity}}$$

The debt-to-equity ratio varies across companies and industries. Industries that are more variable tend to have lower ratios, while more stable industries are less risky and tend to have higher ratios. To apply the debt-to-equity ratio, let's look at this measure for Six Flags in Exhibit 14.16.

EXHIBIT 14.16
Six Flags' Debt-to-Equity Ratio

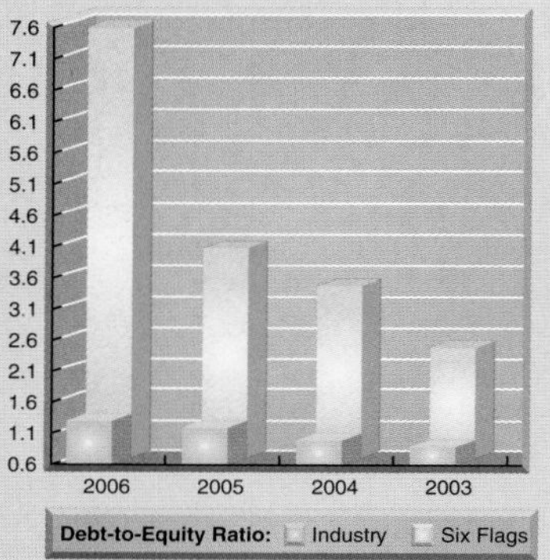

($ millions)	2006	2005	2004	2003
Total liabilities	$2,811	$2,799	$2,816	$3,321
Total equity	$ 376	$ 694	$ 826	$1,362
Debt-to-equity	7.5	4.0	3.4	2.4
Industry debt-to-equity	1.2	1.1	0.9	0.8

Six Flags' 2006 debt-to-equity ratio was 7.5, meaning that debtholders contributed $7.5 for each $1 contributed by equityholders. This implies a fairly risky financing structure for Six Flags. A similar concern is drawn from a comparison of Six Flags with its competitors, where the 2006 industry ratio was 1.2. Analysis across the years shows that Six Flags' financing structure has grown increasingly risky in recent years. Given its sluggish revenues and increasing operating expenses in recent years (see its annual report), Six Flags is increasingly at risk of financial distress.

Decision Maker

Bond Investor You plan to purchase debenture bonds from one of two companies in the same industry that are similar in size and performance. The first company has $350,000 in total liabilities, and $1,750,000 in equity. The second company has $1,200,000 in total liabilities, and $1,000,000 in equity. Which company's debenture bonds are less risky based on the debt-to-equity ratio? [Answer—p. 576]

Demonstration Problem

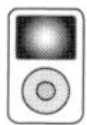
DP14

Water Sports Company (WSC) patented and successfully test-marketed a new product. To expand its ability to produce and market the new product, WSC needs to raise $800,000 of financing. On January 1, 2009, the company obtained the money in two ways:

a. WSC signed a $400,000, 10% installment note to be repaid with five equal annual installments to be made on December 31 of 2009 through 2013.

b. WSC issued five-year bonds with a par value of $400,000. The bonds have a 12% annual contract rate and pay interest on June 30 and December 31. The bonds' annual market rate is 10% as of January 1, 2009.

Required

1. For the installment note, (*a*) compute the size of each annual payment, (*b*) prepare an amortization table such as Exhibit 14.14, and (*c*) prepare the journal entry for the first payment.

2. For the bonds, (*a*) compute their issue price; (*b*) prepare the January 1, 2009, journal entry to record their issuance; (*c*) prepare an amortization table using the straight-line method; (*d*) prepare the June 30, 2009, journal entry to record the first interest payment; and (*e*) prepare a journal entry to record retiring the bonds at a $416,000 call price on January 1, 2011.

3.[B] Redo parts 2(*c*), 2(*d*), and 2(*e*) assuming the bonds are amortized using the effective interest method.

Planning the Solution

- For the installment note, divide the borrowed amount by the annuity factor (from Table B.3) using the 10% rate and five payments to compute the amount of each payment. Prepare a table similar to Exhibit 14.14 and use the numbers in the table's first line for the journal entry.
- Compute the bonds' issue price by using the market rate to find the present value of their cash flows (use tables found in Appendix B). Then use this result to record the bonds' issuance. Next, prepare an amortization table like Exhibit 14.11 (and Exhibit 14B.2) and use it to get the numbers needed for the journal entry. Also use the table to find the carrying value as of the date of the bonds' retirement that you need for the journal entry.

Solution to Demonstration Problem

Part 1: Installment Note

a. Annual payment = Note balance/Annuity factor = \$400,000/3.7908 = \$105,519 (The annuity factor is for five payments and a rate of 10%.)

b. An amortization table follows.

		Payments				
Annual Period Ending	(a) Beginning Balance	(b) Debit Interest Expense	+	(c) Debit Notes Payable	=	(d) Credit Cash	(e) Ending Balance
(1) 12/31/2009	\$400,000	\$ 40,000		\$ 65,519		\$105,519	\$334,481
(2) 12/31/2010	334,481	33,448		72,071		105,519	262,410
(3) 12/31/2011	262,410	26,241		79,278		105,519	183,132
(4) 12/31/2012	183,132	18,313		87,206		105,519	95,926
(5) 12/31/2013	95,926	9,593		95,926		105,519	0
		\$127,595		\$400,000		\$527,595	

c. Journal entry for December 31, 2009, payment.

Dec. 31	Interest Expense	40,000	
	Notes Payable	65,519	
	Cash		105,519
	To record first installment payment.		

Part 2: Bonds (Straight-Line Amortization)

a. Compute the bonds' issue price.

Cash Flow	Table	Present Value Factor*	Amount	Present Value
Par (maturity) value	B.1 in App. B (PV of 1)	0.6139	× 400,000	= \$245,560
Interest payments	B.3 in App. B (PV of annuity)	7.7217	× 24,000	= 185,321
Price of bond				\$430,881

* Present value factors are for 10 payments using a semiannual market rate of 5%.

b. Journal entry for January 1, 2009, issuance.

Jan. 1	Cash	430,881	
	Premium on Bonds Payable		30,881
	Bonds Payable		400,000
	Sold bonds at a premium.		

c. Straight-line amortization table for premium bonds.

Semiannual Period-End	Unamortized Premium	Carrying Value
(0) 1/1/2009	$30,881	$430,881
(1) 6/30/2009	27,793	427,793
(2) 12/31/2009	24,705	424,705
(3) 6/30/2010	21,617	421,617
(4) 12/31/2010	18,529	418,529
(5) 6/30/2011	15,441	415,441
(6) 12/31/2011	12,353	412,353
(7) 6/30/2012	9,265	409,265
(8) 12/31/2012	6,177	406,177
(9) 6/30/2013	3,089	403,089
(10) 12/31/2013	0*	400,000

* Adjusted for rounding.

d. Journal entry for June 30, 2009, bond payment.

June 30	Bond Interest Expense	20,912	
	Premium on Bonds Payable	3,088	
	Cash		24,000
	Paid semiannual interest on bonds.		

e. Journal entry for January 1, 2011, bond retirement.

Jan. 1	Bonds Payable	400,000	
	Premium on Bonds Payable	18,529	
	Cash		416,000
	Gain on Retirement of Bonds		2,529
	To record bond retirement (carrying value as of Dec. 31, 2010).		

Part 3: Bonds (Effective Interest Amortization)[B]

c. The effective interest amortization table for premium bonds.

Semiannual Interest Period	(A) Cash Interest Paid 6% × $400,000	(B) Interest Expense 5% × Prior (E)	(C) Premium Amortization (A) − (B)	(D) Unamortized Premium Prior (D) − (C)	(E) Carrying Value $400,000 + (D)
(0) 1/1/2009				$30,881	$430,881
(1) 6/30/2009	$ 24,000	$ 21,544	$ 2,456	28,425	428,425
(2) 12/31/2009	24,000	21,421	2,579	25,846	425,846
(3) 6/30/2010	24,000	21,292	2,708	23,138	423,138
(4) 12/31/2010	24,000	21,157	2,843	20,295	420,295
(5) 6/30/2011	24,000	21,015	2,985	17,310	417,310
(6) 12/31/2011	24,000	20,866	3,134	14,176	414,176
(7) 6/30/2012	24,000	20,709	3,291	10,885	410,885
(8) 12/31/2012	24,000	20,544	3,456	7,429	407,429
(9) 6/30/2013	24,000	20,371	3,629	3,800	403,800
(10) 12/31/2013	24,000	20,200*	3,800	0	400,000
	$240,000	$209,119	$30,881		

* Adjusted for rounding

d. Journal entry for June 30, 2009, bond payment.

June 30	Bond Interest Expense	21,544	
	Premium on Bonds Payable	2,456	
	Cash		24,000
	Paid semiannual interest on bonds.		

e. Journal entry for January 1, 2011, bond retirement.

Jan. 1	Bonds Payable	400,000	
	Premium on Bonds Payable	20,295	
	Cash		416,000
	Gain on Retirement of Bonds		4,295
	To record bond retirement (carrying value as of December 31, 2010).		

APPENDIX

Present Values of Bonds and Notes

14A

This appendix explains how to apply present value techniques to measure a long-term liability when it is created and to assign interest expense to the periods until it is settled. Appendix B at the end of the book provides additional discussion of present value concepts.

Present Value Concepts

C2 Explain and compute the present value of an amount(s) to be paid at a future date(s).

The basic present value concept is that cash paid (or received) in the future has less value now than the same amount of cash paid (or received) today. To illustrate, if we must pay $1 one year from now, its present value is less than $1. To see this, assume that we borrow $0.9259 today that must be paid back in one year with 8% interest. Our interest expense for this loan is computed as $0.9259 × 8%, or $0.0741. When the $0.0741 interest is added to the $0.9259 borrowed, we get the $1 payment necessary to repay our loan with interest. This is formally computed in Exhibit 14A.1. The $0.9259 borrowed is the present value of the $1 future payment. More generally, an amount borrowed equals the present value of the future payment. (This same interpretation applies to an investment. If $0.9259 is invested at 8%, it yields $0.0741 in revenue after one year. This amounts to $1, made up of principal and interest.)

EXHIBIT 14A.1

Components of a One-Year Loan

Amount borrowed	**$0.9259**
Interest for one year at 8%	0.0741
Amount owed after 1 year	$ 1.0000

To extend this example, assume that we owe $1 two years from now instead of one year, and the 8% interest is compounded annually. *Compounded* means that interest during the second period is based on the total of the amount borrowed plus the interest accrued from the first period. The second period's interest is then computed as 8% multiplied by the sum of the amount borrowed plus interest earned in the first period. Exhibit 14A.2 shows how we compute the present value of $1 to be paid in two years. This amount is $0.8573. The first year's interest of $0.0686 is added to the principal so that the second year's interest is based on $0.9259. Total interest for this two-year period is $0.1427, computed as $0.0686 plus $0.0741.

Point: Benjamin Franklin is said to have described compounding as "the money, money makes, makes more money."

EXHIBIT 14A.2

Components of a Two-Year Loan

Amount borrowed	**$0.8573**
Interest for first year ($0.8573 × 8%)	0.0686
Amount owed after 1 year	0.9259
Interest for second year ($0.9259 × 8%)	0.0741
Amount owed after 2 years	$ 1.0000

Present Value Tables

The present value of $1 that we must repay at some future date can be computed by using this formula: $1/(1 + i)^n$. The symbol i is the interest rate per period and n is the number of periods until the future payment must be made. Applying this formula to our two-year loan, we get $\$1/(1.08)^2$, or $0.8573. This is the same value shown in Exhibit 14A.2. We can use this formula to find any present value. However, a simpler method is to use a *present value table,* which lists present values computed with this formula for various interest rates and time periods. Many people find it helpful in learning present value concepts to first work with the table and then move to using a calculator.

EXHIBIT 14A.3

Present Value of 1

	Rate		
Periods	6%	8%	10%
1	0.9434	**0.9259**	0.9091
2	0.8900	**0.8573**	0.8264
3	0.8396	0.7938	0.7513
4	0.7921	0.7350	0.6830
5	0.7473	0.6806	0.6209
6	0.7050	0.6302	0.5645
7	0.6651	0.5835	0.5132
8	0.6274	0.5403	0.4665
9	0.5919	0.5002	0.4241
10	0.5584	0.4632	0.3855

Exhibit 14A.3 shows a present value table for a future payment of 1 for up to 10 periods at three different interest rates. Present values in this table are rounded to four decimal places. This table is drawn from the larger and more complete Table B.1 in Appendix B at the end of the book. Notice that the first value in the 8% column is 0.9259, the value we computed earlier for the present value of a $1 loan for one year at 8% (see Exhibit 14A.1). Go to the second row in the same 8% column and find the present value of 1 discounted at 8% for two years, or 0.8573. This $0.8573 is the present value of our obligation to repay $1 after two periods at 8% interest (see Exhibit 14A.2).

Example: Use Exhibit 14A.3 to find the present value of $1 discounted for 2 years at 6%. *Answer:* $0.8900

Applying a Present Value Table

To illustrate how to measure a liability using a present value table, assume that a company plans to borrow cash and repay it as follows: $2,000 after one year, $3,000 after two years, and $5,000 after three years. How much does this company receive today if the interest rate on this loan is 10%? To answer, we need to compute the present value of the three future payments, discounted at 10%. This computation is shown in Exhibit 14A.4 using present values from Exhibit 14A.3. The company can borrow $8,054 today at 10% interest in exchange for its promise to make these three payments at the scheduled dates.

EXHIBIT 14A.4

Present Value of a Series of Unequal Payments

Periods	Payments	Present Value of 1 at 10%	Present Value of Payments
1	$2,000	0.9091	$ 1,818
2	3,000	0.8264	2,479
3	5,000	0.7513	3,757
Present value of all payments			**$8,054**

Present Value of an Annuity

The $8,054 present value for the loan in Exhibit 14A.4 equals the sum of the present values of the three payments. When payments are not equal, their combined present value is best computed by adding the individual present values as shown in Exhibit 14A.4. Sometimes payments follow an **annuity,** which is a series of *equal* payments at equal time intervals. The present value of an annuity is readily computed.

To illustrate, assume that a company must repay a 6% loan with a $5,000 payment at each year-end for the next four years. This loan amount equals the present value of the four payments discounted at 6%. Exhibit 14A.5 shows how to compute this loan's present value of $17,326 by multiplying each payment by its matching present value factor taken from Exhibit 14A.3.

EXHIBIT 14A.5

Present Value of a Series of Equal Payments (Annuity) by Discounting Each Payment

Periods	Payments	Present Value of 1 at 6%	Present Value of Payments
1	$5,000	0.9434	$ 4,717
2	5,000	0.8900	4,450
3	5,000	0.8396	4,198
4	5,000	0.7921	3,961
Present value of all payments		**3.4651**	**$17,326**

However, the series of $5,000 payments is an annuity, so we can compute its present value with either of two shortcuts. First, the third column of Exhibit 14A.5 shows that the sum of the present values of 1 at 6% for periods 1 through 4 equals 3.4651. One shortcut is to multiply this total of 3.4651 by the $5,000 annual payment to get the combined present value of $17,326. It requires one multiplication instead of four.

The second shortcut uses an *annuity table* such as the one shown in Exhibit 14A.6, which is drawn from the more complete Table B.3 in Appendix B. We go directly to the annuity table to get the present value factor for a specific number of payments and interest rate. We then multiply this factor by the amount of the payment to find the present value of the annuity. Specifically, find the row for four periods and go across to the 6% column, where the factor is 3.4651. This factor equals the present value of an annuity with four payments of 1, discounted at 6%. We then multiply 3.4651 by $5,000 to get the $17,326 present value of the annuity.

EXHIBIT 14A.6

Present Value of an Annuity of 1

	Rate		
Periods	**6%**	**8%**	**10%**
1	0.9434	0.9259	0.9091
2	1.8334	1.7833	1.7355
3	2.6730	2.5771	2.4869
4	**3.4651**	3.3121	3.1699
5	4.2124	3.9927	3.7908
6	4.9173	4.6229	4.3553
7	5.5824	5.2064	4.8684
8	6.2098	5.7466	5.3349
9	6.8017	6.2469	5.7590
10	7.3601	6.7101	6.1446

Example: Use Exhibit 14A.6 to find the present value of an annuity of eight $15,000 payments with an 8% interest rate. *Answer:* $15,000 × 5.7466 = $86,199

Compounding Periods Shorter Than a Year

The present value examples all involved periods of one year. In many situations, however, interest is compounded over shorter periods. For example, the interest rate on bonds is usually stated as an annual rate but interest is often paid every six months (semiannually). This means that the present value of interest payments from such bonds must be computed using interest periods of six months.

Assume that a borrower wants to know the present value of a series of 10 *semiannual payments* of $4,000 made over five years at an *annual interest rate* of 12%. The interest rate is stated as an annual rate of 12%, but it is actually a rate of 6% per semiannual interest period. To compute the present value of this series of $4,000 payments, go to row 10 of Exhibit 14A.6 and across to the 6% column to find the factor 7.3601. The present value of this annuity is $29,440 (7.3601 × $4,000).

Appendix B further describes present value concepts and includes more complete present value tables and assignments.

Example: If this borrower makes five semiannual payments of $8,000, what is the present value of this annuity at a 12% rate? *Answer:* 4.2124 × $8,000 = $33,699

Quick Check Answers—p. 576

14. A company enters into an agreement to make four annual year-end payments of $1,000 each, starting one year from now. The annual interest rate is 8%. The present value of these four payments is (*a*) $2,923, (*b*) $2,940, or (*c*) $3,312.

15. Suppose a company has an option to pay either (*a*) $10,000 after one year or (*b*) $5,000 after six months and another $5,000 after one year. Which choice has the lower present value?

APPENDIX 14B

Effective Interest Amortization

Effective Interest Amortization of a Discount Bond

The straight-line method yields changes in the bonds' carrying value while the amount for bond interest expense remains constant. This gives the impression of a changing interest rate when users divide a constant bond interest expense over a changing carrying value. As a result, accounting standards allow use of the straight-line method only when its results do not differ materially from those obtained using the effective interest method. The **effective interest method,** or simply *interest method,* allocates total bond interest expense over the bonds' life in a way that yields a constant rate of interest. This constant rate of interest is the market rate at the issue date. Thus, bond interest expense for a period equals the carrying value of the bond at the beginning of that period multiplied by the market rate when issued.

Point: The effective interest method computes bond interest expense using the market rate at issuance. This rate is applied to a changing carrying value.

Exhibit 14B.1 shows an effective interest amortization table for the Fila bonds (as described in Exhibit 14.4). The key difference between the effective interest and straight-line methods lies in computing bond interest expense. Instead of assigning an equal amount of bond interest expense to each period, the effective interest method assigns a bond interest expense amount that increases over the life of a discount bond. **Both methods allocate the *same* $19,546 of total bond interest expense to the bonds' life, but in different patterns.** Specifically, the amortization table in Exhibit 14B.1 shows that the balance of the discount (column D) is amortized until it reaches zero. Also, the bonds' carrying value (column E) changes each period until it equals par value at maturity. Compare columns D and E to the corresponding columns in Exhibit 14.7 to see the amortization patterns. Total bond interest expense is $19,546, consisting of $16,000 of semiannual cash payments and $3,546 of the original bond discount, the same for both methods.

EXHIBIT 14B.1

Effective Interest Amortization of Bond Discount

Bonds: $100,000 Par Value, Semiannual Interest Payments, Two-Year Life, 4% Semiannual Contract Rate, 5% Semiannual Market Rate

Semiannual Interest Period-End	(A) Cash Interest Paid	(B) Bond Interest Expense	(C) Discount Amortization	(D) Unamortized Discount	(E) Carrying Value
(0) **12/31/2009**				**$3,546**	**$ 96,454**
(1) **6/30/2010**	**$4,000**	**$4,823**	**$ 823**	**2,723**	**97,277**
(2) 12/31/2010	4,000	4,864	864	1,859	98,141
(3) 6/30/2011	4,000	4,907	907	952	99,048
(4) 12/31/2011	4,000	4,952	952	**0**	**100,000**
	$16,000	$19,546	$3,546		

Column (**A**) is the par value ($100,000) multiplied by the semiannual contract rate (4%).
Column (**B**) is the prior period's carrying value multiplied by the semiannual market rate (5%).
Column (**C**) is the difference between interest paid and bond interest expense, or [(B) − (A)].
Column (**D**) is the prior period's unamortized discount less the current period's discount amortization.
Column (**E**) is the par value less unamortized discount, or [$100,000 − (D)].

Except for differences in amounts, journal entries recording the expense and updating the liability balance are the same under the effective interest method and the straight-line method. We can use the numbers in Exhibit 14B.1 to record each semiannual entry during the bonds' two-year life (June 30, 2010, through December 31, 2011). For instance, we record the interest payment at the end of the first semiannual period as follows:

Assets	=	Liabilities	+	Equity
−4,000		+823		−4,823

2010			
June 30	Bond Interest Expense	4,823	
	Discount on Bonds Payable		823
	Cash		4,000
	To record semiannual interest and discount amortization (effective interest method).		

Effective Interest Amortization of a Premium Bond

Exhibit 14B.2 shows the amortization table using the effective interest method for the Adidas bonds (as described in Exhibit 14.8). Column A lists the semiannual cash payments. Column B shows the amount of bond interest expense, computed as the 5% semiannual market rate at issuance multiplied by the beginning-of-period carrying value. The amount of cash paid in column A is larger than the bond interest expense because the cash payment is based on the higher 6% semiannual contract rate. The excess cash payment over the interest expense reduces the principal. These amounts are shown in column C. Column E

EXHIBIT 14B.2

Effective Interest Amortization of Bond Premium

Bonds: $100,000 Par Value, Semiannual Interest Payments, Two-Year Life, 6% Semiannual Contract Rate, 5% Semiannual Market Rate					
Semiannual Interest Period-End	(A) Cash Interest Paid	(B) Bond Interest Expense	(C) Premium Amortization	(D) Unamortized Premium	(E) Carrying Value
(0) **12/31/2009**				**$3,546**	**$103,546**
(1) **6/30/2010**	**$6,000**	**$5,177**	**$ 823**	**2,723**	**102,723**
(2) 12/31/2010	6,000	5,136	864	1,859	101,859
(3) 6/30/2011	6,000	5,093	907	952	100,952
(4) 12/31/2011	6,000	5,048	952	**0**	**100,000**
	$24,000	$20,454	$3,546		

Column (**A**) is the par value ($100,000) multiplied by the semiannual contract rate (6%).
Column (**B**) is the prior period's carrying value multiplied by the semiannual market rate (5%).
Column (**C**) is the difference between interest paid and bond interest expense, or [(A) − (B)].
Column (**D**) is the prior period's unamortized premium less the current period's premium amortization.
Column (**E**) is the par value plus unamortized premium, or [$100,000 + (D)].

shows the carrying value after deducting the amortized premium in column C from the prior period's carrying value. Column D shows the premium's reduction by periodic amortization. When the issuer makes the first semiannual interest payment, the effect of premium amortization on bond interest expense and bond liability is recorded as follows:

2010			
June 30	Bond Interest Expense	5,177	
	Premium on Bonds Payable.	823	
	Cash		6,000
	To record semiannual interest and premium amortization (effective interest method).		

Assets	=	Liabilities	+	Equity
−6,000		−823		−5,177

Similar entries with different amounts are recorded at each payment date until the bond matures at the end of 2011. The effective interest method yields decreasing amounts of bond interest expense and increasing amounts of premium amortization over the bonds' life.

Decision Insight

IFRSs Unlike U.S. GAAP, IFRSs require that interest expense be computed using the effective interest method with *no exemptions.*

APPENDIX

Issuing Bonds between Interest Dates

14C

C3 Describe the accrual of bond interest when bond payments do not align with accounting periods.

An issuer can sell bonds at a date other than an interest payment date. When this occurs, the buyers normally pay the issuer the purchase price plus any interest accrued since the prior interest payment date. This accrued interest is then repaid to these buyers on the next interest payment date. To illustrate, suppose **Avia** sells $100,000 of its 9% bonds at par on March 1, 2009, 60 days after the stated issue date. The interest on Avia bonds is payable semiannually on each June 30 and December 31. Since 60 days have passed, the issuer collects accrued interest from the buyers at the time of issuance. This amount is $1,500 ($100,000 × 9% × 60/360 year). This case is reflected in Exhibit 14C.1.

EXHIBIT 14C.1

Accruing Interest between Interest Payment Dates

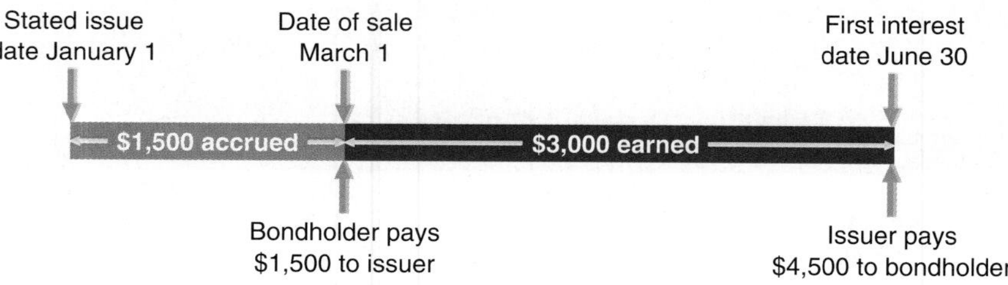

Avia records the issuance of these bonds on March 1, 2009, as follows:

Assets	= Liabilities	+ Equity
+101,500	+100,000	
	+1,500	

Mar. 1	Cash	101,500	
	Interest Payable		1,500
	Bonds Payable		100,000
	Sold bonds at par with accrued interest.		

Example: How much interest is collected from a buyer of $50,000 of Avia bonds sold at par 150 days after the contract issue date? *Answer:* $1,875 (computed as $50,000 × 9% × 150/360 year)

Liabilities for interest payable and bonds payable are recorded in separate accounts. When the June 30, 2009, semiannual interest date arrives, Avia pays the full semiannual interest of $4,500 ($100,000 × 9% × ½ year) to the bondholders. This payment includes the four months' interest of $3,000 earned by the bondholders from March 1 to June 30 *plus* the repayment of the 60 days' accrued interest collected by Avia when the bonds were sold. Avia records this first semiannual interest payment as follows:

Assets	= Liabilities	+ Equity
−4,500	−1,500	−3,000

June 30	Interest Payable	1,500	
	Bond Interest Expense	3,000	
	Cash		4,500
	Paid semiannual interest on the bonds.		

The practice of collecting and then repaying accrued interest with the next interest payment is to simplify the issuer's administrative efforts. To explain, suppose an issuer sells bonds on 15 or 20 different dates between the stated issue date and the first interest payment date. If the issuer does not collect accrued interest from buyers, it needs to pay different amounts of cash to each of them according to the time that passed after purchasing the bonds. The issuer needs to keep detailed records of buyers and the dates they bought bonds. Issuers avoid this recordkeeping by having each buyer pay accrued interest at purchase. Issuers then pay the full semiannual interest to all buyers, regardless of when they bought bonds.

Accruing Bond Interest Expense

If a bond's interest period does not coincide with the issuer's accounting period, an adjusting entry is needed to recognize bond interest expense accrued since the most recent interest payment. To illustrate, assume that the stated issue date for Adidas bonds described in Exhibit 14.10 is September 1, 2009, instead of December 31, 2009, and that the bonds are sold on September 1, 2009. As a result, four months' interest (and premium amortization) accrue before the end of the 2009 calendar year. Interest for this period equals $3,409, or 4/6 of the first six months' interest of $5,113. Also, the premium amortization is $591, or 4/6 of the first six months' amortization of $887. The sum of the bond interest expense and the amortization is $4,000 ($3,409 + $591), which equals 4/6 of the $6,000 cash payment due on February 28, 2010. Adidas records these effects with an adjusting entry at December 31, 2009.

Point: Computation of accrued bond interest may use months instead of days for simplicity purposes. For example, the accrued interest computation for the Adidas bonds is based on months.

Assets	= Liabilities	+ Equity
	−591	−3,409
	+4,000	

Dec. 31	Bond Interest Expense	3,409	
	Premium on Bonds Payable	591	
	Interest Payable		4,000
	To record four months' accrued interest and premium amortization.		

Similar entries are made on each December 31 throughout the bonds' two-year life. When the $6,000 cash payment occurs on each February 28 interest payment date, Adidas must recognize bond interest expense and amortization for January and February. It must also eliminate the interest payable liability created by the December 31 adjusting entry. For example, Adidas records its payment on February 28, 2010, as follows:

Feb. 28	Interest Payable	4,000	
	Bond Interest Expense ($5,113 × 2/6)	1,705	
	Premium on Bonds Payable ($887 × 2/6)	295*	
	Cash		6,000
	To record 2 months' interest and amortization, and eliminate accrued interest liability.		

Assets	=	Liabilities	+	Equity
−6,000		−4,000		−1,705
		−295		

*Adjusted for rounding.

The interest payments made each August 31 are recorded as usual because the entire six-month interest period is included within this company's calendar-year reporting period.

Decision Maker

Bond Rater You must assign a rating to a bond that reflects its risk to bondholders. Identify factors you consider in assessing bond risk. Indicate the likely levels (relative to the norm) for the factors you identify for a bond that sells at a discount. [Answer—p. 576]

Quick Check

Answer—p. 576

16. On May 1, a company sells 9% bonds with a $500,000 par value that pay semiannual interest on each January 1 and July 1. The bonds are sold at par plus interest accrued since January 1. The issuer records the first semiannual interest payment on July 1 with (*a*) a debit to Interest Payable for $15,000, (*b*) a debit to Bond Interest Expense for $22,500, or (*c*) a credit to Interest Payable for $7,500.

APPENDIX

Leases and Pensions 14D

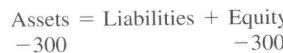

This appendix briefly explains the accounting and analysis for both leases and pensions.

Lease Liabilities

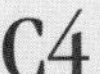

C4 Describe accounting for leases and pensions.

A **lease** is a contractual agreement between a *lessor* (asset owner) and a *lessee* (asset renter or tenant) that grants the lessee the right to use the asset for a period of time in return for cash (rent) payments. Nearly one-fourth of all equipment purchases are financed with leases. The advantages of lease financing include the lack of an immediate large cash payment and the potential to deduct rental payments in computing taxable income. From an accounting perspective, leases can be classified as either operating or capital leases.

Operating Leases **Operating leases** are short-term (or cancelable) leases in which the lessor retains the risks and rewards of ownership. Examples include most car and apartment rental agreements. The lessee records such lease payments as expenses; the lessor records them as revenue. The lessee does not report the leased item as an asset or a liability (it is the lessor's asset). To illustrate, if an employee of Amazon leases a car for $300 at an airport while on company business, Amazon (lessee) records this cost as follows:

Point: Home Depot reports that its rental expenses from operating leases total more than $900 million.

July 4	Rental Expense	300	
	Cash		300
	To record lease rental payment.		

Assets	=	Liabilities	+	Equity
−300				−300

Capital Leases **Capital leases** are long-term (or noncancelable) leases by which the lessor transfers substantially all risks and rewards of ownership to the lessee.[3] Examples include most leases of airplanes and department store buildings. The lessee records the leased item as its own asset along with a lease liability at the start of the lease term; the amount recorded equals the present value of all lease payments. To illustrate, assume that K2 Co. enters into a six-year lease of a building in which it will sell sporting equipment. The lease transfers all building ownership risks and rewards to K2 (the present value of its $12,979 annual lease payments is $60,000). K2 records this transaction as follows:

Assets = Liabilities + Equity
+60,000 +60,000

2009			
Jan. 1	Leased Asset—Building.	60,000	
	Lease Liability		60,000
	To record leased asset and lease liability.		

Point: Home Depot reports *"certain locations . . . are leased under capital leases."* The net present value of this Lease Liability is about $400 million.

K2 reports the leased asset as a plant asset and the lease liability as a long-term liability. The portion of the lease liability expected to be paid in the next year is reported as a current liability.[4] At each year-end, K2 records depreciation on the leased asset (assume straight-line depreciation, six-year lease term, and no salvage value) as follows:

Assets = Liabilities + Equity
−10,000 −10,000

Dec. 31	Depreciation Expense—Building	10,000	
	Accumulated Depreciation—Building		10,000
	To record depreciation on leased asset.		

K2 also accrues interest on the lease liability at each year-end. Interest expense is computed by multiplying the remaining lease liability by the interest rate on the lease. Specifically, K2 records its annual interest expense as part of its annual lease payment ($12,979) as follows (for its first year):

Assets = Liabilities + Equity
−12,979 −8,179 −4,800

2009			
Dec. 31	Interest Expense	4,800	
	Lease Liability.	8,179	
	Cash		12,979
	*To record first annual lease payment.**		

* These numbers are computed from a *lease payment schedule.* For simplicity, we use the same numbers from Exhibit 14.14 for this lease payment schedule—with different headings as follows:

		Payments			
	(A)	(B) *Debit*	(C) *Debit*	(D) *Credit*	(E)
Period Ending Date	Beginning Balance of Lease Liability	Interest on Lease Liability 8% × (A) +	Lease Liability (D) − (B) =	Cash Lease Payment	Ending Balance of Lease Liability (A) − (C)
12/31/2009	**$60,000**	**$ 4,800**	**$ 8,179**	**$12,979**	**$51,821**
12/31/2010	51,821	4,146	8,833	12,979	42,988
12/31/2011	42,988	3,439	9,540	12,979	33,448
12/31/2012	33,448	2,676	10,303	12,979	23,145
12/31/2013	23,145	1,852	11,127	12,979	12,018
12/31/2014	12,018	961	12,018	12,979	0
		$17,874	**$60,000**	**$77,874**	

[3] A *capital lease* meets any one or more of four criteria: (1) transfers title of leased asset to lessee, (2) contains a bargain purchase option, (3) has a lease term that is 75% or more of the leased asset's useful life, or (4) has a present value of lease payments that is 90% or more of the leased asset's market value.

[4] Most lessees try to keep leased assets and lease liabilities off their balance sheets by failing to meet any one of the four criteria of a capital lease. This is because a lease liability increases a company's total liabilities, making it more difficult to obtain additional financing. The acquisition of assets without reporting any related liabilities (or other asset outflows) on the balance sheet is called **off-balance-sheet financing.**

Pension Liabilities

A **pension plan** is a contractual agreement between an employer and its employees for the employer to provide benefits (payments) to employees after they retire. Most employers pay the full cost of the pension, but sometimes employees pay part of the cost. An employer records its payment into a pension plan with a debit to Pension Expense and a credit to Cash. A *plan administrator* receives payments from the employer, invests them in pension assets, and makes benefit payments to *pension recipients* (retired employees). Insurance and trust companies often serve as pension plan administrators.

Point: Fringe benefits are often 40% or more of salaries and wages, and pension benefits make up nearly 15% of fringe benefits.

Many pensions are known as *defined benefit plans* that define future benefits; the employer's contributions vary, depending on assumptions about future pension assets and liabilities. Several disclosures are necessary in this case. Specifically, a pension liability is reported when the accumulated benefit obligation is *more than* the plan assets, a so-called *underfunded plan.* The accumulated benefit obligation is the present value of promised future pension payments to retirees. *Plan assets* refer to the market value of assets the plan administrator holds. A pension asset is reported when the accumulated benefit obligation is *less than* the plan assets, a so-called *overfunded plan.* An employer reports pension expense when it receives the benefits from the employees' services, which is sometimes decades before it pays pension benefits to employees. (*Other Postretirement Benefits* refer to nonpension benefits such as health care and life insurance benefits. Similar to a pension, costs of these benefits are estimated and liabilities accrued when the employees earn them.)

Point: Two types of pension plans are (1) *defined benefit plan*—the retirement benefit is defined and the employer estimates the contribution necessary to pay these benefits—and (2) *defined contribution plan*—the pension contribution is defined and the employer and/or employee contributes amounts specified in the pension agreement.

Summary

C1 Explain the types and payment patterns of notes. Notes repaid over a period of time are called *installment notes* and usually follow one of two payment patterns: (1) decreasing payments of interest plus equal amounts of principal or (2) equal total payments. Mortgage notes also are common.

C2^A Explain and compute the present value of an amount(s) to be paid at a future date(s). The basic concept of present value is that an amount of cash to be paid or received in the future is worth less than the same amount of cash to be paid or received today. Another important present value concept is that interest is compounded, meaning interest is added to the balance and used to determine interest for succeeding periods. An annuity is a series of equal payments occurring at equal time intervals. An annuity's present value can be computed using the present value table for an annuity (or a calculator).

C3^C Describe the accrual of bond interest when bond payments do not align with accounting periods. Issuers and buyers of debt record the interest accrued when issue dates or accounting periods do not coincide with debt payment dates.

C4^D Describe accounting for leases and pensions. A lease is a rental agreement between the lessor and the lessee. When the lessor retains the risks and rewards of asset ownership (an *operating lease*), the lessee debits Rent Expense and credits Cash for its lease payments. When the lessor substantially transfers the risks and rewards of asset ownership to the lessee (a *capital lease*), the lessee capitalizes the leased asset and records a lease liability. Pension agreements can result in either pension assets or pension liabilities.

A1 Compare bond financing with stock financing. Bond financing is used to fund business activities. Advantages of bond financing versus stock include (1) no effect on owner control, (2) tax savings, and (3) increased earnings due to financial leverage. Disadvantages include (1) interest and principal payments and (2) amplification of poor performance.

A2 Assess debt features and their implications. Certain bonds are secured by the issuer's assets; other bonds, called *debentures,* are unsecured. Serial bonds mature at different points in time; term bonds mature at one time. Registered bonds have each bondholder's name recorded by the issuer; bearer bonds are payable to the holder. Convertible bonds are exchangeable for shares of the issuer's stock. Callable bonds can be retired by the issuer at a set price. Debt features alter the risk of loss for creditors.

A3 Compute the debt-to-equity ratio and explain its use. Both creditors and equity holders are concerned about the relation between the amount of liabilities and the amount of equity. A company's financing structure is at less risk when the debt-to-equity ratio is lower, as liabilities must be paid and usually with periodic interest.

P1 Prepare entries to record bond issuance and bond interest expense. When bonds are issued at par, Cash is debited and Bonds Payable is credited for the bonds' par value. At bond interest payment dates (usually semiannual), Bond Interest Expense is debited and Cash credited—the latter for an amount equal to the bond par value multiplied by the bond contract rate.

P2 Compute and record amortization of bond discount. Bonds are issued at a discount when the contract rate is less than the market rate, making the issue (selling) price less than par. When this occurs, the issuer records a credit to Bonds Payable (at par) and debits both Discount on Bonds Payable and Cash. The amount of bond interest expense assigned to each period is computed using either the straight-line or effective interest method.

P3 Compute and record amortization of bond premium. Bonds are issued at a premium when the contract rate is higher than the market rate, making the issue (selling) price greater than par. When this occurs, the issuer records a debit to Cash and credits both Premium on Bonds Payable and Bonds Payable (at par). The amount of bond interest expense assigned to each period is computed using either the straight-line or effective interest method. The Premium on Bonds Payable is allocated to reduce bond interest expense over the life of the bonds.

P4 Record the retirement of bonds. Bonds are retired at maturity with a debit to Bonds Payable and a credit to Cash at par value. The issuer can retire the bonds early by exercising a call option or purchasing them in the market. Bondholders can also retire bonds early by exercising a conversion feature on convertible bonds. The issuer recognizes a gain or loss for the difference between the amount paid and the bond carrying value.

P5 **Prepare entries to account for notes.** Interest is allocated to each period in a note's life by multiplying its beginning-period carrying value by its market rate at issuance. If a note is repaid with equal payments, the payment amount is computed by dividing the borrowed amount by the present value of an annuity factor (taken from a present value table) using the market rate and the number of payments.

Guidance Answers to **Decision Maker**

Entrepreneur This is a "present value" question. The market interest rate (10%) and present value ($3,000) are known, but the payment required two years later is unknown. This amount ($3,630) can be computed as $3,000 × 1.10 × 1.10. Thus, the sale price is $3,630 when no payments are received for two years. The $3,630 received two years from today is equivalent to $3,000 cash today.

Bond Investor The debt-to-equity ratio for the first company is 0.2 ($350,000/$1,750,000) and for the second company is 1.2 ($1,200,000/$1,000,000), suggesting that the financing structure of the second company is more risky than that of the first company. Consequently, as a buyer of unsecured debenture bonds, you prefer the first company (all else equal).

Bond Rater Bonds with longer repayment periods (life) have higher risk. Also, bonds issued by companies in financial difficulties or facing higher than normal uncertainties have higher risk. Moreover, companies with higher than normal debt and large fluctuations in earnings are considered of higher risk. Discount bonds are more risky on one or more of these factors.

Guidance Answers to **Quick Checks**

1. (*b*)

2. Multiply the bond's par value by its contract rate of interest.

3. Bonds sell at a premium when the contract rate exceeds the market rate and the purchasers pay more than their par value.

4. The bonds are issued at a discount, meaning that issue price is less than par value. A discount occurs because the bond contract rate (6%) is less than the market rate (8%).

5.

Cash	91,893	
Discount on Bonds Payable	8,107	
Bonds Payable		100,000

6. $3,811 (total bond interest expense of $38,107 divided by 10 periods; or the $3,000 semiannual cash payment plus the $8,107 discount divided by 10 periods).

7. The bonds are issued at a premium, meaning issue price is higher than par value. A premium occurs because the bonds' contract rate (16%) is higher than the market rate (14%).

8. (*b*) For each semiannual period: $10,592/20 periods = $530 premium amortization.

9.

Bonds payable, 16%, due 12/31/2018	$100,000	
Plus premium on bonds payable	9,532*	$109,532

* Original premium balance of $10,592 less $530 and $530 amortized on 6/30/2009 and 12/31/2009, respectively.

10. $9,375 loss, computed as the difference between the repurchase price of $256,250 [50% of ($500,000 × 102.5%)] and the carrying value of $246,875 (50% of $493,750).

11. (*c*)

12. The interest portion of an installment payment equals the period's beginning loan balance multiplied by the market interest rate at the time of the note's issuance.

13. On the balance sheet, the account balances of the related liability (note payable) and asset (cash) accounts are decreased. On the income statement, interest expense is recorded.

14. (*c*), computed as 3.3121 × $1,000 = $3,312.

15. The option of paying $10,000 after one year has a lower present value. It postpones paying the first $5,000 by six months. More generally, the present value of a further delayed payment is always lower than a less delayed payment.

16. (*a*) Reflects payment of accrued interest recorded back on May 1; $500,000 × 9% × 4/12 = $15,000.

Key Terms

mhhe.com/wildFAP19e

Key Terms are available at the book's Website for learning and testing in an online Flashcard Format.

Pension plan (p. 575)	**Secured bonds** (p. 563)	**Straight-line bond amortization** (p. 554)
Premium on bonds (p. 556)	**Serial bonds** (p. 563)	**Term bonds** (p. 563)
Registered bonds (p. 563)	**Sinking fund bonds** (p. 563)	**Unsecured bonds** (p. 563)

Multiple Choice Quiz

Answers on p. 589 mhhe.com/wildFAP19e

Additional Quiz Questions are available at the book's Website.

Quiz14

1. A bond traded at 97½ means that
- **a.** The bond pays 97½% interest.
- **b.** The bond trades at $975 per $1,000 bond.
- **c.** The market rate of interest is below the contract rate of interest for the bond.
- **d.** The bonds can be retired at $975 each.
- **e.** The bond's interest rate is 2½%.

2. A bondholder that owns a $1,000, 6%, 15-year bond has
- **a.** The right to receive $1,000 at maturity.
- **b.** Ownership rights in the bond issuing entity.
- **c.** The right to receive $60 per month until maturity.
- **d.** The right to receive $1,900 at maturity.
- **e.** The right to receive $600 per year until maturity.

3. A company issues 8%, 20-year bonds with a par value of $500,000. The current market rate for the bonds is 8%. The amount of interest owed to the bondholders for each semiannual interest payment is
- **a.** $40,000.
- **b.** $0.
- **c.** $20,000.
- **d.** $800,000.
- **e.** $400,000.

4. A company issued 5-year, 5% bonds with a par value of $100,000. The company received $95,735 for the bonds. Using the straight-line method, the company's interest expense for the first semiannual interest period is
- **a.** $2,926.50.
- **b.** $5,853.00.
- **c.** $2,500.00.
- **d.** $5,000.00.
- **e.** $9,573.50.

5. A company issued 8-year, 5% bonds with a par value of $350,000. The company received proceeds of $373,745. Interest is payable semiannually. The amount of premium amortized for the first semiannual interest period, assuming straight-line bond amortization, is
- **a.** $2,698.
- **b.** $23,745.
- **c.** $8,750.
- **d.** $9,344.
- **e.** $1,484.

Superscript letter B (C, D) denotes assignments based on Appendix 14B (14C, 14D).

Discussion Questions

1. What is the main difference between a bond and a share of stock?

2. What is the main difference between notes payable and bonds payable?

3. ♝ What is the advantage of issuing bonds instead of obtaining financing from the company's owners?

4. What are the duties of a trustee for bondholders?

5. What is a bond indenture? What provisions are usually included in it?

6. What are the *contract* rate and the *market* rate for bonds?

7. ♝ What factors affect the market rates for bonds?

8.[B] ♝ Does the straight-line or effective interest method produce an interest expense allocation that yields a constant rate of interest over a bond's life? Explain.

9.[C] Why does a company that issues bonds between interest dates collect accrued interest from the bonds' purchasers?

10. ♝ If you know the par value of bonds, the contract rate, and the market rate, how do you compute the bonds' price?

11. What is the issue price of a $2,000 bond sold at 98¼? What is the issue price of a $6,000 bond sold at 101½?

12. Describe the debt-to-equity ratio and explain how creditors and owners would use this ratio to evaluate a company's risk.

13. ♝ What obligation does an entrepreneur (owner) have to investors that purchase bonds to finance the business?

14. Refer to **Best Buy**'s annual report in Appendix A. Is there any indication that Best Buy has issued bonds?

15. Refer to the statement of cash flows for **Circuit City** in Appendix A. For the year ended February 28, 2007, what was the amount of principal payments on long-term debt?

16. Did **RadioShack**'s long-term debt increase or decrease during 2006?

RadioShack.

17. Refer to the annual report for **Apple** in Appendix A. For the year ended September 30, 2006, did it raise more cash by issuing stock or debt?

18.[D] When can a lease create both an asset and a liability for the lessee?

19.[D] Compare and contrast an operating lease with a capital lease.

20.[D] Describe the two basic types of pension plans.

♝ *Denotes Discussion Questions that involve decision making.*

Available with McGraw-Hill's Homework Manager McGraw-Hill's HOMEWORK MANAGER®

QUICK STUDY

Round dollar amounts to the nearest whole dollar.

QS 14-1
Bond computations—straight-line P1 P2

Randell Company issues 7%, 10-year bonds with a par value of $150,000 and semiannual interest payments. On the issue date, the annual market rate for these bonds is 8%, which implies a selling price of 93¼. The straight-line method is used to allocate interest expense.

1. What are the issuer's cash proceeds from issuance of these bonds?
2. What total amount of bond interest expense will be recognized over the life of these bonds?
3. What is the amount of bond interest expense recorded on the first interest payment date?

QS 14-2[B]
Bond computations—effective interest
P1 P3

Elton Company issues 7%, 15-year bonds with a par value of $350,000 and semiannual interest payments. On the issue date, the annual market rate for these bonds is 6%, which implies a selling price of 109¾. The effective interest method is used to allocate interest expense.

1. What are the issuer's cash proceeds from issuance of these bonds?
2. What total amount of bond interest expense will be recognized over the life of these bonds?
3. What amount of bond interest expense is recorded on the first interest payment date?

QS 14-3
Journalize bond issuance P1

Prepare the journal entries for the issuance of the bonds in both QS 14-1 and QS 14-2. Assume that both bonds are issued for cash on January 1, 2009.

QS 14-4
Computing bond price P2 P3

Using the bond details in both QS 14-1 and QS 14-2, confirm that the bonds' selling prices given in each problem are approximately correct. Use the present value tables B.1 and B.3 in Appendix B.

QS 14-5
Recording bond issuance and discount amortization P1 P2

Boulware Company issues 8%, five-year bonds, on December 31, 2008, with a par value of $100,000 and semiannual interest payments. Use the following straight-line bond amortization table and prepare journal entries to record (*a*) the issuance of bonds on December 31, 2008; (*b*) the first interest payment on June 30, 2009; and (*c*) the second interest payment on December 31, 2009.

Semiannual Period-End	Unamortized Discount	Carrying Value
(0) 12/31/2008	$7,723	$92,277
(1) 6/30/2009	6,951	93,049
(2) 12/31/2009	6,179	93,821

QS 14-6
Bond retirement by call option
P4

On July 1, 2009, Teller Company exercises a $4,000 call option (plus par value) on its outstanding bonds that have a carrying value of $208,000 and par value of $200,000. The company exercises the call option after the semiannual interest is paid on June 30, 2009. Record the entry to retire the bonds.

QS 14-7
Bond retirement by stock conversion P4

On January 1, 2009, the $1,000,000 par value bonds of Staten Company with a carrying value of $1,000,000 are converted to 500,000 shares of $1.00 par value common stock. Record the entry for the conversion of the bonds.

QS 14-8
Computing payments for an installment note C1

Jordyn Company borrows $600,000 cash from a bank and in return signs an installment note for five annual payments of equal amount, with the first payment due one year after the note is signed. Use Table B.3 in Appendix B to compute the amount of the annual payment for each of the following annual market rates: (*a*) 4%, (*b*) 6%, and (*c*) 8%.

QS 14-9
Bond features and terminology
A2

Enter the letter of the description *A* through *H* that best fits each term or phrase 1 through 8.

A. Records and tracks the bondholders' names.
B. Is unsecured; backed only by the issuer's credit standing.
C. Has varying maturity dates for amounts owed.
D. Identifies rights and responsibilities of the issuer and the bondholders.
E. Can be exchanged for shares of the issuer's stock.
F. Is unregistered; interest is paid to whoever possesses them.
G. Maintains a separate asset account from which bondholders are paid at maturity.

H. Pledges specific assets of the issuer as collateral.

1. ______ Convertible bond		**5.** ______ Registered bond	
2. ______ Bond indenture		**6.** ______ Serial bond	
3. ______ Sinking fund bond		**7.** ______ Secured bond	
4. ______ Debenture		**8.** ______ Bearer bond	

QS 14-10
Debt-to-equity ratio
A2

Compute the debt-to-equity ratio for each of the following companies. Which company appears to have a riskier financing structure? Explain.

	NLF Company	ABL Company
Total liabilities	$615,000	$ 480,000
Total equity	820,000	1,500,000

QS 14-11[C]
Issuing bonds between interest dates
P1

Knapp Company plans to issue 6% bonds on January 1, 2009, with a par value of $2,000,000. The company sells $1,800,000 of the bonds on January 1, 2009. The remaining $200,000 sells at par on March 1, 2009. The bonds pay interest semiannually as of June 30 and December 31. Record the entry for the March 1 cash sale of bonds.

QS 14-12[D]
Recording operating leases C4

Lu Villena, an employee of ETrain.com, leases a car at O'Hare airport for a three-day business trip. The rental cost is $400. Prepare the entry by ETrain.com to record Lu Villena's short-term car lease cost.

QS 14-13[D]
Recording capital leases C4

Artel, Inc., signs a five-year lease for office equipment with Office Solutions. The present value of the lease payments is $13,500. Prepare the journal entry that Artel records at the inception of this capital lease.

McGraw-Hill's HOMEWORK MANAGER® Available with McGraw-Hill's Homework Manager

Round dollar amounts to the nearest whole dollar. Assume no reversing entries are used.

EXERCISES

Exercise 14-1
Recording bond issuance and interest
P1

On January 1, 2009, Bartel Enterprises issues bonds that have a $3,650,000 par value, mature in 20 years, and pay 10% interest semiannually on June 30 and December 31. The bonds are sold at par.

1. How much interest will Bartel pay (in cash) to the bondholders every six months?

2. Prepare journal entries to record (*a*) the issuance of bonds on January 1, 2009; (*b*) the first interest payment on June 30, 2009; and (*c*) the second interest payment on December 31, 2009.

3. Prepare the journal entry for issuance assuming the bonds are issued at (*a*) 98 and (*b*) 105.

Exercise 14-2
Straight-line amortization of bond discount
P2

Sears issues bonds with a par value of $175,000 on January 1, 2009. The bonds' annual contract rate is 4%, and interest is paid semiannually on June 30 and December 31. The bonds mature in three years. The annual market rate at the date of issuance is 6%, and the bonds are sold for $165,523.

1. What is the amount of the discount on these bonds at issuance?

2. How much total bond interest expense will be recognized over the life of these bonds?

3. Prepare an amortization table like the one in Exhibit 14.7 for these bonds; use the straight-line method to amortize the discount.

Exercise 14-3[B]
Effective interest amortization of bond discount
P2

Ritter issues bonds dated January 1, 2009, with a par value of $300,000. The bonds' annual contract rate is 9%, and interest is paid semiannually on June 30 and December 31. The bonds mature in three years. The annual market rate at the date of issuance is 12%, and the bonds are sold for $277,872.

1. What is the amount of the discount on these bonds at issuance?

2. How much total bond interest expense will be recognized over the life of these bonds?

3. Prepare an amortization table like the one in Exhibit 14B.1 for these bonds; use the effective interest method to amortize the discount.

Exercise 14-4
Straight-line amortization of bond premium P3

Dell Co. issues bonds dated January 1, 2009, with a par value of $450,000. The bonds' annual contract rate is 9%, and interest is paid semiannually on June 30 and December 31. The bonds mature in three years. The annual market rate at the date of issuance is 8%, and the bonds are sold for $461,795.

1. What is the amount of the premium on these bonds at issuance?
2. How much total bond interest expense will be recognized over the life of these bonds?
3. Prepare an amortization table like the one in Exhibit 14.11 for these bonds; use the straight-line method to amortize the premium.

Exercise 14-5[B]
Effective interest amortization of bond premium P3

Refer to the bond details in Exercise 14-4 and prepare an amortization table like the one in Exhibit 14B.2 for these bonds using the effective interest method to amortize the premium.

Exercise 14-6
Recording bond issuance and premium amortization
P1 P3

Anna Company issues 8%, five-year bonds, on December 31, 2008, with a par value of $100,000 and semiannual interest payments. Use the following straight-line bond amortization table and prepare journal entries to record (*a*) the issuance of bonds on December 31, 2008; (*b*) the first interest payment on June 30, 2009; and (*c*) the second interest payment on December 31, 2009.

Semiannual Period-End	Unamortized Premium	Carrying Value
(0) 12/31/2008	$7,720	$107,720
(1) 6/30/2009	6,948	106,948
(2) 12/31/2009	6,176	106,176

Exercise 14-7
Recording bond issuance and discount amortization
P1 P2

St. Charles Company issues 10%, four-year bonds, on December 31, 2009, with a par value of $100,000 and semiannual interest payments. Use the following straight-line bond amortization table and prepare journal entries to record (*a*) the issuance of bonds on December 31, 2009; (*b*) the first interest payment on June 30, 2010; and (*c*) the second interest payment on December 31, 2010.

Semiannual Period-End	Unamortized Discount	Carrying Value
(0) 12/31/2009	$8,000	$92,000
(1) 6/30/2010	7,000	93,000
(2) 12/31/2010	6,000	94,000

Exercise 14-8
Recording bond issuance and discount amortization
P1 P2

Zander Company issues 6%, two-year bonds, on December 31, 2009, with a par value of $100,000 and semiannual interest payments. Use the following straight-line bond amortization table and prepare journal entries to record (*a*) the issuance of bonds on December 31, 2009; (*b*) the first through fourth interest payments on each June 30 and December 31; and (*c*) the maturity of the bond on December 31, 2011.

Semiannual Period-End	Unamortized Discount	Carrying Value
(0) 12/31/2009	$4,000	$ 96,000
(1) 6/30/2010	3,000	97,000
(2) 12/31/2010	2,000	98,000
(3) 6/30/2011	1,000	99,000
(4) 12/31/2011	0	100,000

Exercise 14-9
Computing bond interest and price; recording bond issuance
P2

Target Company issues bonds with a par value of $950,000 on their stated issue date. The bonds mature in 15 years and pay 10% annual interest in semiannual payments. On the issue date, the annual market rate for the bonds is 12%.

1. What is the amount of each semiannual interest payment for these bonds?
2. How many semiannual interest payments will be made on these bonds over their life?
3. Use the interest rates given to determine whether the bonds are issued at par, at a discount, or at a premium.
4. Compute the price of the bonds as of their issue date.
5. Prepare the journal entry to record the bonds' issuance.

Check (4) $819,223

Exercise 14-10
Computing bond interest and price; recording bond issuance
P3

Boston Company issues bonds with a par value of $160,000 on their stated issue date. The bonds mature in six years and pay 8% annual interest in semiannual payments. On the issue date, the annual market rate for the bonds is 6%.

1. What is the amount of each semiannual interest payment for these bonds?
2. How many semiannual interest payments will be made on these bonds over their life?
3. Use the interest rates given to determine whether the bonds are issued at par, at a discount, or at a premium.
4. Compute the price of the bonds as of their issue date.
5. Prepare the journal entry to record the bonds' issuance.

Check (4) $175,930

Exercise 14-11
Bond computations, straight-line amortization, and bond retirement
P2 P4

On January 1, 2009, Seldon issues $450,000 of 10%, 15-year bonds at a price of 93¼. Six years later, on January 1, 2015, Seldon retires 20% of these bonds by buying them on the open market at 109¾. All interest is accounted for and paid through December 31, 2014, the day before the purchase. The straight-line method is used to amortize any bond discount.

1. How much does the company receive when it issues the bonds on January 1, 2009?
2. What is the amount of the discount on the bonds at January 1, 2009?
3. How much amortization of the discount is recorded on the bonds for the entire period from January 1, 2009, through December 31, 2014?
4. What is the carrying (book) value of the bonds as of the close of business on December 31, 2014? What is the carrying value of the 20% soon-to-be-retired bonds on this same date?
5. How much did the company pay on January 1, 2015, to purchase the bonds that it retired?
6. What is the amount of the recorded gain or loss from retiring the bonds?
7. Prepare the journal entry to record the bond retirement at January 1, 2015.

Check (6) $12,420 loss

Exercise 14-12^C
Recording bond issuance with accrued interest
C4 P1

On May 1, 2009, Bradley Enterprises issues bonds dated January 1, 2009, that have a $1,950,000 par value, mature in 20 years, and pay 8% interest semiannually on June 30 and December 31. The bonds are sold at par plus four months' accrued interest.

1. How much accrued interest do the bond purchasers pay Bradley on May 1, 2009?
2. Prepare Bradley's journal entries to record (*a*) the issuance of bonds on May 1, 2009; (*b*) the first interest payment on June 30, 2009; and (*c*) the second interest payment on December 31, 2009.

Check (1) $52,000

Exercise 14-13
Straight-line amortization and accrued bond interest expense
P1 P2

Stockton Co. issues four-year bonds with a $50,000 par value on June 1, 2009, at a price of $47,850. The annual contract rate is 8%, and interest is paid semiannually on November 30 and May 31.

1. Prepare an amortization table like the one in Exhibit 14.7 for these bonds. Use the straight-line method of interest amortization.
2. Prepare journal entries to record the first two interest payments and to accrue interest as of December 31, 2009.

Exercise 14-14
Installment note with equal total payments C1 P5

On January 1, 2009, American Eagle borrows $90,000 cash by signing a four-year, 5% installment note. The note requires four equal total payments of accrued interest and principal on December 31 of each year from 2009 through 2012.

1. Compute the amount of each of the four equal total payments.
2. Prepare an amortization table for this installment note like the one in Exhibit 14.14.

Check (1) $25,381

Exercise 14-15
Installment note entries P5

Use the information in Exercise 14-14 to prepare the journal entries for American Eagle to record the loan on January 1, 2009, and the four payments from December 31, 2009, through December 31, 2012.

Exercise 14-16
Applying debt-to-equity ratio
A3

Motin Company is considering a project that will require a $250,000 loan. It presently has total liabilities of $110,000, and total assets of $310,000.

1. Compute Motin's (*a*) present debt-to-equity ratio and (*b*) the debt-to-equity ratio assuming it borrows $250,000 to fund the project.
2. Evaluate and discuss the level of risk involved if Motin borrows the funds to pursue the project.

Exercise 14-17[D]
Identifying capital and operating leases
C4

Indicate whether the company in each separate case 1 through 3 has entered into an operating lease or a capital lease.

1. The lessor retains title to the asset, and the lease term is three years on an asset that has a five-year useful life.
2. The title is transferred to the lessee, the lessee can purchase the asset for $1 at the end of the lease, and the lease term is five years. The leased asset has an expected useful life of six years.
3. The present value of the lease payments is 95% of the leased asset's market value, and the lease term is 70% of the leased asset's useful life.

Exercise 14-18[D]
Accounting for capital lease
C4

Hartel (lessee) signs a five-year capital lease for office equipment with a $21,000 annual lease payment. The present value of the five annual lease payments is $88,460, based on a 6% interest rate.

1. Prepare the journal entry Hartel will record at inception of the lease.
2. If the leased asset has a five-year useful life with no salvage value, prepare the journal entry Hartel will record each year to recognize depreciation expense related to the leased asset.

Exercise 14-19[D]
Analyzing lease options
C2 C3 C4

General Motors advertised three alternatives for a 25-month lease on a new Blazer: (1) zero dollars down and a lease payment of $2,522 per month for 25 months, (2) $5,000 down and $2,240 per month for 25 months, or (3) $55,000 down and no payments for 25 months. Use the present value Table B.3 in Appendix B to determine which is the best alternative (assume you have enough cash to accept any alternative and the annual interest rate is 12% compounded monthly).

Available with McGraw-Hill's Homework Manager McGraw-Hill's HOMEWORK MANAGER®

PROBLEM SET A

Round dollar amounts to the nearest whole dollar. Assume no reversing entries are used.

Problem 14-1A
Computing bond price and recording issuance
P1 P2 P3

Check (1) Premium, $4,760

(3) Discount, $4,223

Harvard Research issues bonds dated January 1, 2009, that pay interest semiannually on June 30 and December 31. The bonds have a $45,000 par value and an annual contract rate of 6%, and they mature in six years.

Required

For each of the following three separate situations, (*a*) determine the bonds' issue price on January 1, 2009, and (*b*) prepare the journal entry to record their issuance.

1. The market rate at the date of issuance is 4%.
2. The market rate at the date of issuance is 6%.
3. The market rate at the date of issuance is 8%.

Problem 14-2A
Straight-line amortization of bond discount and bond premium
P1 P2 P3

mhhe.com/wildFAP19e

Check (3) $4,676,000

(4) 12/31/2010 carrying value, $3,087,468

Braeburn issues $3,500,000 of 8%, 15-year bonds dated January 1, 2009, that pay interest semiannually on June 30 and December 31. The bonds are issued at a price of $3,024,000.

Required

1. Prepare the January 1, 2009, journal entry to record the bonds' issuance.
2. For each semiannual period, compute (*a*) the cash payment, (*b*) the straight-line discount amortization, and (*c*) the bond interest expense.
3. Determine the total bond interest expense to be recognized over the bonds' life.
4. Prepare the first two years of an amortization table like Exhibit 14.7 using the straight-line method.
5. Prepare the journal entries to record the first two interest payments.
6. Assume that the bonds are issued at a price of $4,284,000. Repeat parts 1 through 5.

Problem 14-3A
Straight-line amortization of bond premium
P1 P3

mhhe.com/wildFAP19e

Check (2) 6/30/2009 carrying value, $234,644

Jules issues 4.5%, five-year bonds dated January 1, 2009, with a $230,000 par value. The bonds pay interest on June 30 and December 31 and are issued at a price of $235,160. The annual market rate is 4% on the issue date.

Required

1. Calculate the total bond interest expense over the bonds' life.
2. Prepare a straight-line amortization table like Exhibit 14.11 for the bonds' life.
3. Prepare the journal entries to record the first two interest payments.

Problem 14-4A[B]
Effective interest amortization of bond premium; computing bond price P1 P3

Check (2) 6/30/2011 carrying value, $232,704
(4) $232,179

Refer to the bond details in Problem 14-3A.

Required

1. Compute the total bond interest expense over the bonds' life.
2. Prepare an effective interest amortization table like the one in Exhibit 14B.2 for the bonds' life.
3. Prepare the journal entries to record the first two interest payments.
4. Use the market rate at issuance to compute the present value of the remaining cash flows for these bonds as of December 31, 2011. Compare your answer with the amount shown on the amortization table as the balance for that date (from part 2) and explain your findings.

Problem 14-5A
Straight-line amortization of bond discount
P1 P2

Check (2) $81,112
(3) 12/31/2010 carrying value, $338,944

Legacy issues $345,000 of 5%, four-year bonds dated January 1, 2009, that pay interest semiannually on June 30 and December 31. They are issued at $332,888 and their market rate is 6% at the issue date.

Required

1. Prepare the January 1, 2009, journal entry to record the bonds' issuance.
2. Determine the total bond interest expense to be recognized over the bonds' life.
3. Prepare a straight-line amortization table like the one in Exhibit 14.7 for the bonds' first two years.
4. Prepare the journal entries to record the first two interest payments.

Analysis Component

5. Assume the market rate on January 1, 2009, is 4% instead of 6%. Without providing numbers, describe how this change affects the amounts reported on Legacy's financial statements.

Problem 14-6A[B]
Effective interest amortization of bond discount P1 P2

Check (2) $81,112
(3) 12/31/2010 carrying value, $338,586

mhhe.com/wildFAP19e

Refer to the bond details in Problem 14-5A.

Required

1. Prepare the January 1, 2009, journal entry to record the bonds' issuance.
2. Determine the total bond interest expense to be recognized over the bonds' life.
3. Prepare an effective interest amortization table like the one in Exhibit 14B.1 for the bonds' first two years.
4. Prepare the journal entries to record the first two interest payments.

Problem 14-7A[B]
Effective interest amortization of bond premium; retiring bonds
P1 P3 P4 

Check (3) 6/30/2010 carrying value, $187,494
(5) $7,256 gain

eXcel
mhhe.com/wildFAP19e

Shopko issues $185,000 of 12%, three-year bonds dated January 1, 2009, that pay interest semiannually on June 30 and December 31. They are issued at $189,620. Their market rate is 11% at the issue date.

Required

1. Prepare the January 1, 2009, journal entry to record the bonds' issuance.
2. Determine the total bond interest expense to be recognized over the bonds' life.
3. Prepare an effective interest amortization table like Exhibit 14B.2 for the bonds' first two years.
4. Prepare the journal entries to record the first two interest payments.
5. Prepare the journal entry to record the bonds' retirement on January 1, 2011, at 97.

Analysis Component

6. Assume that the market rate on January 1, 2009, is 13% instead of 11%. Without presenting numbers, describe how this change affects the amounts reported on Shopko's financial statements.

Problem 14-8A
Installment notes
C1 P5

Check (2) 10/31/2013 ending balance, $159,556

On November 1, 2009, Norwood borrows $700,000 cash from a bank by signing a five-year installment note bearing 7% interest. The note requires equal total payments each year on October 31.

Required

1. Compute the total amount of each installment payment.
2. Complete an amortization table for this installment note similar to the one in Exhibit 14.14.
3. Prepare the journal entries in which Norwood records (*a*) accrued interest as of December 31, 2009 (the end of its annual reporting period), and (*b*) the first annual payment on the note.

Problem 14-9A
Applying the debt-to-equity ratio
A3

At the end of the current year, the following information is available for both the Pulaski Company and the Scott Company.

	Pulaski Company	Scott Company
Total assets	$1,800,000	$900,000
Total liabilities	723,600	478,800
Total equity	1,080,000	420,000

Required

1. Compute the debt-to-equity ratios for both companies.

2. Comment on your results and discuss the riskiness of each company's financing structure.

Problem 14-10A[D]
Capital lease accounting
C4

Thomas Company signs a five-year capital lease with Universal Company for office equipment. The annual lease payment is $14,000, and the interest rate is 8%.

Required

Check (1) $55,898

(3) Year 3 ending balance, $24,966

1. Compute the present value of Thomas's five-year lease payments.

2. Prepare the journal entry to record Thomas's capital lease at its inception.

3. Complete a lease payment schedule for the five years of the lease with the following headings. Assume that the beginning balance of the lease liability (present value of lease payments) is $55,898. (*Hint:* To find the amount allocated to interest in year 1, multiply the interest rate by the beginning-of-year lease liability. The amount of the annual lease payment not allocated to interest is allocated to principal. Reduce the lease liability by the amount allocated to principal to update the lease liability at each year-end.)

Period Ending Date	Beginning Balance of Lease Liability	Interest on Lease Liability	Reduction of Lease Liability	Cash Lease Payment	Ending Balance of Lease Liability

4. Use straight-line depreciation and prepare the journal entry to depreciate the leased asset at the end of year 1. Assume zero salvage value and a five-year life for the office equipment.

PROBLEM SET B

Round dollar amounts to the nearest whole dollar. Assume no reversing entries are used.

Problem 14-1B
Computing bond price and recording issuance
P1 P2 P3

Fortune Systems issues bonds dated January 1, 2009, that pay interest semiannually on June 30 and December 31. The bonds have a $35,000 par value and an annual contract rate of 4%, and they mature in four years.

Required

For each of the following three separate situations, (*a*) determine the bonds' issue price on January 1, 2009, and (*b*) prepare the journal entry to record their issuance.

Check (1) Premium, $2,679

(3) Discount, $2,457

1. The market rate at the date of issuance is 2%.

2. The market rate at the date of issuance is 4%.

3. The market rate at the date of issuance is 6%.

Problem 14-2B
Straight-line amortization of bond discount and bond premium
P1 P2 P3

Long Beach issues $4,500,000 of 8%, 15-year bonds dated January 1, 2009, that pay interest semiannually on June 30 and December 31. The bonds are issued at a price of $3,888,000.

Required

1. Prepare the January 1, 2009, journal entry to record the bonds' issuance.

2. For each semiannual period, compute (*a*) the cash payment, (*b*) the straight-line discount amortization, and (*c*) the bond interest expense.

Check (3) $6,012,000

(4) 6/30/2010 carrying value, $3,949,200

3. Determine the total bond interest expense to be recognized over the bonds' life.

4. Prepare the first two years of an amortization table like Exhibit 14.7 using the straight-line method.

5. Prepare the journal entries to record the first two interest payments.

6. Assume that the bonds are issued at a price of $5,508,000. Repeat parts 1 through 5.

Problem 14-3B
Straight-line amortization of bond premium
P1 P3

San Mateo Company issues 7%, five-year bonds dated January 1, 2009, with a $220,000 par value. The bonds pay interest on June 30 and December 31 and are issued at a price of $229,385. Their annual market rate is 6% on the issue date.

Required

1. Calculate the total bond interest expense over the bonds' life.
2. Prepare a straight-line amortization table like Exhibit 14.11 for the bonds' life.
3. Prepare the journal entries to record the first two interest payments.

Check (2) 12/31/2011 carrying value, $223,751

Problem 14-4B[B]
Effective interest amortization of bond premium; computing bond price P1 P3

Refer to the bond details in Problem 14-3B.

Required

1. Compute the total bond interest expense over the bonds' life.
2. Prepare an effective interest amortization table like the one in Exhibit 14B.2 for the bonds' life.
3. Prepare the journal entries to record the first two interest payments.
4. Use the market rate at issuance to compute the present value of the remaining cash flows for these bonds as of December 31, 2011. Compare your answer with the amount shown on the amortization table as the balance for that date (from part 2) and explain your findings.

Check (2) 6/30/2011 carrying value, $225,041

(4) $224,092

Problem 14-5B
Straight-line amortization of bond discount
P1 P2

Kelly issues $315,000 of 4%, 15-year bonds dated January 1, 2009, that pay interest semiannually on June 30 and December 31. They are issued at $253,263, and their market rate is 6% at the issue date.

Required

1. Prepare the January 1, 2009, journal entry to record the bonds' issuance.
2. Determine the total bond interest expense to be recognized over the life of the bonds.
3. Prepare a straight-line amortization table like the one in Exhibit 14.7 for the bonds' first two years.
4. Prepare the journal entries to record the first two interest payments.

Check (2) $250,737

(3) 6/30/2010 carrying value, $259,437

Problem 14-6B[B]
Effective interest amortization of bond discount
P1 P2 

Refer to the bond details in Problem 14-5B.

Required

1. Prepare the January 1, 2009, journal entry to record the bonds' issuance.
2. Determine the total bond interest expense to be recognized over the bonds' life.
3. Prepare an effective interest amortization table like the one in Exhibit 14B.1 for the bonds' first two years.
4. Prepare the journal entries to record the first two interest payments.

Check (2) $250,737;
(3) 6/30/2010 carrying value, $257,275

Problem 14-7B[B]
Effective interest amortization of bond premium; retiring bonds
P1 P3 P4 

Kendall issues $175,000 of 11%, three-year bonds dated January 1, 2009, that pay interest semiannually on June 30 and December 31. They are issued at $179,439, and their market rate is 10% at the issue date.

Required

1. Prepare the January 1, 2009, journal entry to record the bonds' issuance.
2. Determine the total bond interest expense to be recognized over the bonds' life.
3. Prepare an effective interest amortization table like the one in Exhibit 14B.2 for the bonds' first two years.
4. Prepare the journal entries to record the first two interest payments.
5. Prepare the journal entry to record the bonds' retirement on January 1, 2011, at 105.

Check (3) 6/30/2010 carrying value, $177,380

(5) $7,126 loss

Analysis Component

6. Assume that the market rate on January 1, 2009, is 12% instead of 10%. Without presenting numbers, describe how this change affects the amounts reported on Kendall's financial statements.

Problem 14-8B
Installment notes
C1 P5

Check (2) 9/30/2011 ending balance, $71,223

On October 1, 2009, Miami Enterprises borrows $200,000 cash from a bank by signing a three-year installment note bearing 7% interest. The note requires equal total payments each year on September 30.

Required

1. Compute the total amount of each installment payment.
2. Complete an amortization table for this installment note similar to the one in Exhibit 14.14.
3. Prepare the journal entries to record (*a*) accrued interest as of December 31, 2009 (the end of its annual reporting period) and (*b*) the first annual payment on the note.

Problem 14-9B
Applying the debt-to-equity ratio
A3

At the end of the current year, the following information is available for both Caesar Company and Delta Company.

	Caesar Company	Delta Company
Total assets	$360,000	$1,500,000
Total liabilities	162,360	1,125,000
Total equity	198,000	375,000

Required

1. Compute the debt-to-equity ratios for both companies.
2. Comment on your results and discuss what they imply about the relative riskiness of these companies.

Problem 14-10B[D]
Capital lease accounting
C4

Check (1) $51,905

(3) Year 3 ending balance, $23,182

Allan Company signs a five-year capital lease with Vortal Company for office equipment. The annual lease payment is $13,000, and the interest rate is 8%.

Required

1. Compute the present value of Allan's lease payments.
2. Prepare the journal entry to record Allan's capital lease at its inception.
3. Complete a lease payment schedule for the five years of the lease with the following headings. Assume that the beginning balance of the lease liability (present value of lease payments) is $51,905. (*Hint:* To find the amount allocated to interest in year 1, multiply the interest rate by the beginning-of-year lease liability. The amount of the annual lease payment not allocated to interest is allocated to principal. Reduce the lease liability by the amount allocated to principal to update the lease liability at each year-end.)

Period Ending Date	Beginning Balance of Lease Liability	Interest on Lease Liability	Reduction of Lease Liability	Cash Lease Payment	Ending Balance of Lease Liability

4. Use straight-line depreciation and prepare the journal entry to depreciate the leased asset at the end of year 1. Assume zero salvage value and a five-year life for the office equipment.

SERIAL PROBLEM

Success Systems

(This serial problem began in Chapter 1 and continues through most of the book. If previous chapter segments were not completed, the serial problem can begin at this point. It is helpful, but not necessary, to use the Working Papers that accompany the book.)

SP 14 Adriana Lopez has consulted with her local banker and is considering financing an expansion of her business by obtaining a long-term bank loan. Selected account balances at March 31, 2010, for Success Systems follow.

Total assets	$129,909	Total liabilities	$875	Total equity	$129,034

Required

1. The bank has offered a long-term secured note to Success Systems. The bank's loan procedures require that a client's debt-to-equity ratio not exceed 0.8. As of March 31, 2010, what is the maximum amount that Success Systems could borrow from this bank (rounded to nearest dollar)?
2. If Success Systems borrows the maximum amount allowed from the bank, what percentage of assets would be financed (*a*) by debt and (*b*) by equity?
3. What are some factors Lopez should consider before borrowing the funds?

Check (1) $102,352

BEYOND THE NUMBERS

REPORTING IN ACTION

A1 A2

BTN 14-1 Refer to **Best Buy**'s financial statements in Appendix A to answer the following.

1. Identify the items that make up Best Buy's long-term debt at March 3, 2007. (*Hint:* See note 5.)
2. How much annual cash interest must Best Buy pay on its 2.25% convertible subordinated debt?
3. Did it have any additions to long-term debt that provided cash for the year ending March 3, 2007?

Fast Forward

4. Access Best Buy's financial statements for the years ending after March 3, 2007, from its Website (BestBuy.com) or the SEC's EDGAR database (www.SEC.gov). Has it issued additional long-term debt since the year-end March 3, 2007? If yes, identify the amount(s).

COMPARATIVE ANALYSIS

A3

BTN 14-2 Key figures for **Best Buy**, **Circuit City**, and **RadioShack** follow.

($ millions)	Best Buy Current Year	Best Buy Prior Year	Circuit City Current Year	Circuit City Prior Year	RadioShack Current Year	RadioShack Prior Year
Total assets	$13,570	$11,864	$4,007	$4,069	$2,070	$2,205
Total liabilities	7,369	6,607	2,216	2,114	1,416	1,616
Total equity	6,201	5,257	1,791	1,955	654	589

Required

1. Compute the debt-to-equity ratios for Best Buy, Circuit City, and RadioShack for both the current year and the prior year.
2. Use the ratios you computed in part 1 to determine which company's financing structure is least risky. Assume an industry average of 0.24 for debt-to-equity.

ETHICS CHALLENGE

C4 A1

BTN 14-3 Brevard County needs a new county government building that would cost $24 million. The politicians feel that voters will not approve a municipal bond issue to fund the building since it would increase taxes. They opt to have a state bank issue $24 million of tax-exempt securities to pay for the building construction. The county then will make yearly lease payments (of principal and interest) to repay the obligation. Unlike conventional municipal bonds, the lease payments are not binding obligations on the county and, therefore, require no voter approval.

Required

1. Do you think the actions of the politicians and the bankers in this situation are ethical?
2. How do the tax-exempt securities used to pay for the building compare in risk to a conventional municipal bond issued by Brevard County?

COMMUNICATING IN PRACTICE

P3

BTN 14-4 Your business associate mentions that she is considering investing in corporate bonds currently selling at a premium. She says that since the bonds are selling at a premium, they are highly valued and her investment will yield more than the going rate of return for the risk involved. Reply with a memorandum to confirm or correct your associate's interpretation of premium bonds.

TAKING IT TO THE NET

A2

BTN 14-5 Access the March 29, 2007, filing of the 10-K report of **Home Depot** for the year ended January 28, 2007, from www.sec.gov (Ticker: HD). Refer to Home Depot's balance sheet, including its note 4 (on debt).

Required

1. Identify Home Depot's long-term liabilities and the amounts for those liabilities from Home Depot's balance sheet at January 28, 2007.

2. Review Home Depot's note 4. The note reports that it "issued $3.0 billion of 5.875% senior notes due December 16, 2036, at a discount of $42 million with interest payable semiannually on June 16 and December 16 each year."

- **a.** Why would Home Depot issue $3.0 billion of its notes for only $2.958 billion?
- **b.** How much cash interest must Home Depot pay each June 16 and December 16 on these notes?

TEAMWORK IN ACTION

P2 P3

BTN 14-6[B] Break into teams and complete the following requirements related to effective interest amortization for a premium bond.

1. Each team member is to independently prepare a blank table with proper headings for amortization of a bond premium. When all have finished, compare tables and ensure that all are in agreement.

Parts 2 and 3 require use of these facts: On January 1, 2008, BC issues $100,000, 9%, five-year bonds at 104.1. The market rate at issuance is 8%. BC pays interest semiannually on June 30 and December 31.

2. In rotation, *each* team member must explain how to complete *one* line of the bond amortization table, including all computations for his or her line. (Round amounts to the nearest dollar.) All members are to fill in their tables during this process. You need not finish the table; stop after all members have explained a line.

3. In rotation, *each* team member is to identify a separate column of the table and indicate what the final number in that column will be and explain the reasoning.

Hint: Rotate teams to report on parts 4 and 5. Consider requiring entries for issuance and interest payments.

4. Reach a team consensus as to what the total bond interest expense on this bond issue will be if the bond is not retired before maturity.

5. As a team, prepare a list of similarities and differences between the amortization table just prepared and the amortization table if the bond had been issued at a discount.

ENTREPRENEURIAL DECISION

A1 

BTN 14-7 James Lindsay is the founder of **Rap Snacks**. Assume that his company currently has $250,000 in equity, and he is considering a $100,000 expansion to meet increased demand. The $100,000 expansion would yield $16,000 in additional annual income before interest expense. Assume that the business currently earns $40,000 annual income before interest expense of $10,000, yielding a return on equity of 12% ($30,000/$250,000). To fund the expansion, he is considering the issuance of a 10-year, $100,000 note with annual interest payments (the principal due at the end of 10 years).

Required

1. Using return on equity as the decision criterion, show computations to support or reject the expansion if interest on the $100,000 note is (*a*) 10%, (*b*) 15%, (*c*) 16%, (*d*) 17%, and (*e*) 20%.

2. What general rule do the results in part 1 illustrate?

HITTING THE ROAD

A1

BTN 14-8 Visit your city or county library. Ask the librarian to help you locate the recent financial records of your city or county government. Examine those records.

Required

1. Determine the amount of long-term bonds and notes currently outstanding.

2. Read the supporting information to your municipality's financial statements and record

- **a.** The market interest rate(s) when the bonds and/or notes were issued.
- **b.** The date(s) when the bonds and/or notes will mature.
- **c.** Any rating(s) on the bonds and/or notes received from **Moody's**, **Standard & Poor's**, or another rating agency.

GLOBAL DECISION

A3 

DSG

BTN 14-9 DSG international plc (www.DSGiplc.com), Best Buy, Circuit City, and RadioShack are competitors in the global marketplace. Selected results from these companies follow.

	DSG (£ millions)		Best Buy ($ millions)		Circuit City ($ millions)		RadioShack ($ millions)	
Key Figures	Current Year	Prior Year	Current Year	Prior Year	Current Year	Prior Year	Current Year	Prior Year
Total assets	£3,977	£4,120	$13,570	$11,864	$4,007	$4,069	$2,070	$2,205
Total liabilities	2,673	2,696	7,369	6,607	2,216	2,114	1,416	1,616
Total equity	1,304	1,424	6,201	5,257	1,791	1,955	654	589
Debt-to-equity ratio	?	?	1.2	1.3	1.2	1.1	2.2	2.7

Required

1. Compute DSG's debt-to-equity ratios for the current year and the prior year.

2. Use the data provided and the ratios you computed in part 1 to determine which company's financing structure is least risky.

ANSWERS TO MULTIPLE CHOICE QUIZ

1. b

2. a

3. c; $500,000 × 0.08 × ½ year = $20,000

4. a; Cash interest paid = $100,000 × 5% × ½ year = $2,500
Discount amortization = ($100,000 − $95,735)/10 periods = $426.50
Interest expense = $2,500.00 + $426.50 = $2,926.50

5. e; ($373,745 − $350,000)/16 periods = $1,484

A Look Back

Chapter 14 focused on long-term liabilities—a main part of most companies' financing. We explained how to value, record, amortize, and report these liabilities in financial statements.

A Look at This Chapter

This chapter focuses on investments in securities. We explain how to identify, account for, and report investments in both debt and equity securities. We also explain accounting for transactions listed in a foreign currency.

A Look Ahead

Chapter 16 focuses on reporting and analyzing a company's cash flows. Special emphasis is directed at the statement of cash flows reported under the indirect method.

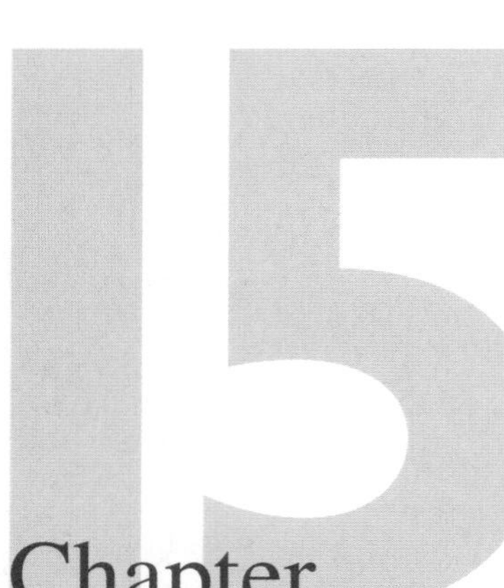

Chapter 15 Investments and International Operations

Learning Objectives

CAP

Conceptual

C1 Distinguish between debt and equity securities and between short-term and long-term investments. *(p. 592)*

C2 Identify and describe the different classes of investments in securities. *(p. 593)*

C3 Describe how to report equity securities with controlling influence. *(p. 599)*

C4 *Appendix 15A*—Explain foreign exchange rates between currencies. *(p. 605)*

Analytical

A1 Compute and analyze the components of return on total assets. *(p. 600)*

LP15

Procedural

P1 Account for trading securities. *(p. 595)*

P2 Account for held-to-maturity securities. *(p. 596)*

P3 Account for available-for-sale securities. *(p. 596)*

P4 Account for equity securities with significant influence. *(p. 598)*

P5 *Appendix 15A*—Record transactions listed in a foreign currency. *(p. 606)*

Decision Feature

Designing Business

"It's a wonderful insanity"—Amy Smilovic

NEW YORK—Amy Smilovic loves business. But after a job transfer by her husband to Hong Kong, she quit her job and looked for her next inspiration. Within weeks, and inspired by the colorful and comfortable clothing she saw, Amy jumped into the designing business of clothes. Her company, **Tibi (Tibi.com),** experienced quick success. "I really kind of just did it," explains Amy. "I tried not to over-think it."

What Amy did was design a clothing line that appeals to the masses. "Just design for yourself, someone will identify with it," insists Amy. "You'll find a group of people who want to dress like you." Amy has been so successful that this group of people extends to many countries. She now has showrooms in Milan and London, and locations in Australia, Hong Kong, Indonesia, Japan, Korea, Malaysia, New Zealand, and Singapore.

This broad reach became what she calls her biggest challenge: investments and international operations. "I didn't know what custom regulations were," explains Amy. "I didn't know how to set up a U.S. base and distribute . . . I was buying books on customs and international shipping laws." Her investments in international operations require Amy to translate their performance into U.S. dollars for financial reports. It also requires conducting international transactions and doing currency translations. Those tasks require knowledge of accounting and reporting requirements for investments, including investments in securities of other companies.

Amy's continued success is sure to include more investments and further international operations. She views her business background and focus as key to that success. "People always ask me, 'How are you a designer without a design background,'" laughs Amy. "I always wonder, 'How are you a designer without a business background?' It's really a business at the end of the day."

[Sources: *Tibi Website,* January 2009, *Entrepreneur,* October 2007; *Fashion Week,* 2008; *Ladies Who Launch,* 2008; *New York Social Diary,* April 2007]

Chapter Preview

This chapter's main focus is investments in securities. Many companies have investments, and many of these are in the form of debt and equity securities issued by other companies. We describe investments in these securities and how to account for them. An increasing number of companies also invest in international operations. We explain how to account for and report international transactions listed in foreign currencies.

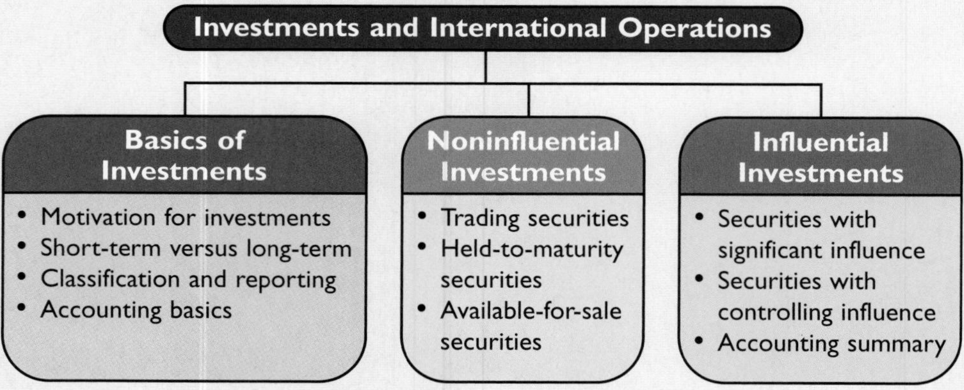

Basics of Investments

C1 Distinguish between debt and equity securities and between short-term and long-term investments.

This section describes the motivation for investments, the distinction between short- and long-term investments, and the different classes of investments.

Motivation for Investments

Companies make investments for at least three reasons. First, companies transfer *excess cash* into investments to produce higher income. Second, some entities, such as mutual funds and pension funds, are set up to produce income from investments. Third, companies make investments for strategic reasons. Examples are investments in competitors, suppliers, and even customers. Exhibit 15.1 shows short-term (S-T) and long-term (L-T) investments as a percent of total assets for several companies.

EXHIBIT 15.1

Investments of Selected Companies

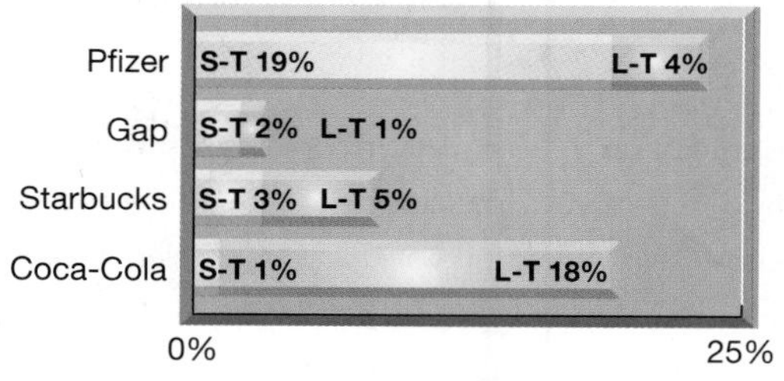

Short-Term versus Long-Term

Cash equivalents are investments that are both readily converted to known amounts of cash and mature within three months. Many investments, however, mature between 3 and 12 months. These investments are **short-term investments,** also called *temporary investments* and *marketable securities*. Specifically, short-term investments are securities that (1) management intends to convert to cash within one year or the operating cycle, whichever is longer, and (2) are readily convertible to cash. Short-term investments are reported under current assets and serve a purpose similar to cash equivalents.

Long-term investments in securities are defined as those securities that are not readily convertible to cash or are not intended to be converted into cash in the short term. Long-term investments can also include funds earmarked for a special purpose, such as bond sinking funds and investments in land or other assets not used in the company's operations. Long-term investments are reported in the noncurrent section of the balance sheet, often in its own separate line titled *Long-Term Investments*.

Investments in securities can include both debt and equity securities. *Debt securities* reflect a creditor relationship such as investments in notes, bonds, and certificates of deposit; they are issued by governments, companies, and individuals. *Equity securities* reflect an owner relationship such as shares of stock issued by companies.

Classification and Reporting

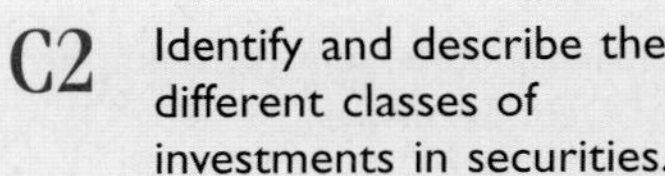
C2 Identify and describe the different classes of investments in securities.

Accounting for investments in securities depends on three factors: (1) security type, either debt or equity, (2) the company's intent to hold the security either short term or long term, and (3) the company's (investor's) percent ownership in the other company's (investee's) equity securities. Exhibit 15.2 identifies five classes of securities using these three factors. It describes each of these five classes of securities and the standard reporting required under each class.

EXHIBIT 15.2

Investments in Securities

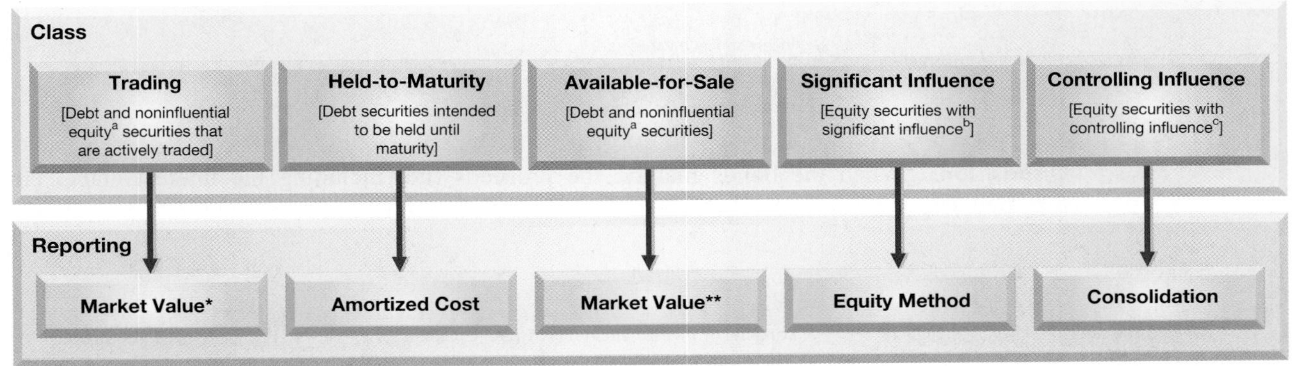

[a] Holding less than 20% of voting stock (equity securities only). [b] Holding 20% or more, but not more than 50%, of voting stock.
[c] Holding more than 50% of voting stock.
* Unrealized gains and losses reported on the income statement.
** Unrealized gains and losses reported in the equity section of the balance sheet and in comprehensive income.

Accounting Basics for Debt Securities

This section explains the accounting basics for *debt securities,* including that for acquisition, disposition, and any interest.

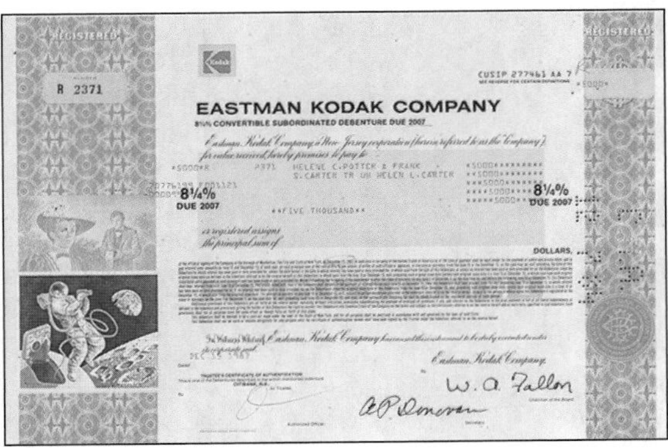

Acquisition. Debt securities are recorded at cost when purchased. To illustrate, assume that Music City paid $29,500 plus a $500 brokerage fee on September 1, 2008, to buy Dell's 7%, two-year bonds payable with a $30,000 par value. The bonds pay interest semiannually on August 31 and February 28. Music City intends to hold the bonds until they mature on August 31, 2010; consequently, they are classified as held-to-maturity (HTM) securities. The entry to record this purchase follows. (If the maturity of the securities was short term, and management's intent was to hold them until they mature, then they would be classified as Short-Term Investments—HTM.)

2008			
Sept. 1	Long-Term Investments—HTM (Dell)	30,000	
	Cash		30,000
	Purchased bonds to be held to maturity.		

Assets = Liabilities + Equity
+30,000
−30,000

Interest earned. Interest revenue for investments in debt securities is recorded when earned. To illustrate, on December 31, 2008, at the end of its accounting period, Music City accrues interest receivable as follows.

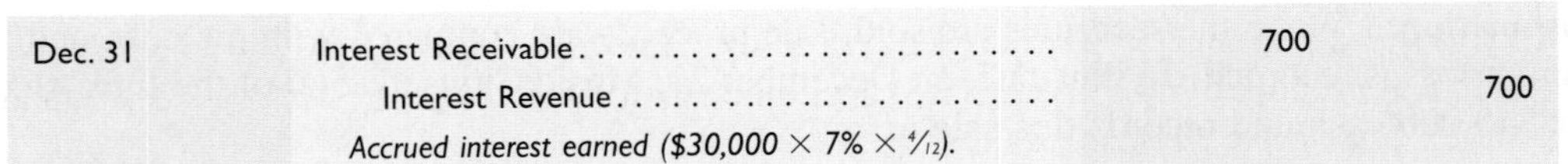

Dec. 31	Interest Receivable	700	
	Interest Revenue		700
	Accrued interest earned ($30,000 × 7% × 4/12).		

Assets = Liabilities + Equity
+700 +700

The $700 reflects 4/6 of the semiannual cash receipt of interest—the portion Music City earned as of December 31. Relevant sections of Music City's financial statements at December 31, 2008, are shown in Exhibit 15.3.

EXHIBIT 15.3

Financial Statement Presentation of Debt Securities

On the income statement for year 2008:	
Interest revenue	**$ 700**
On the December 31, 2008, balance sheet:	
Long-term investments—Held-to-maturity securities (at amortized cost)	**$30,000**

On February 28, 2009, Music City records receipt of semiannual interest.

Assets = Liabilities + Equity
+1,050 +350
−700

Feb. 28	Cash	1,050	
	Interest Receivable		700
	Interest Revenue		350
	Received six months' interest on Dell bonds.		

Disposition. When the bonds mature, the proceeds (not including the interest entry) are recorded as:

Assets = Liabilities + Equity
+30,000
−30,000

2010			
Aug. 31	Cash	30,000	
	Long-Term Investments—HTM (Dell)		30,000
	Received cash from matured bonds.		

Example: What is cost per share? *Answer:* Cost per share is the total cost of acquisition, including broker fees, divided by number of shares acquired.

The cost of a debt security can be either higher or lower than its maturity value. When the investment is long term, the difference between cost and maturity value is amortized over the remaining life of the security. We assume for ease of computations that the cost of a long-term debt security equals its maturity value.

Accounting Basics for Equity Securities

This section explains the accounting basics for *equity securities,* including that for acquisition, dividends, and disposition.

Acquisition. Equity securities are recorded at cost when acquired, including commissions or brokerage fees paid. To illustrate, assume that Music City purchases 1,000 shares of Intex common stock at par value for $86,000 on October 10, 2008. It records this purchase of available-for-sale (AFS) securities as follows.

Assets = Liabilities + Equity
+86,000
−86,000

Oct. 10	Long-Term Investments—AFS (Intex)	86,000	
	Cash		86,000
	Purchased 1,000 shares of Intex.		

Dividend earned. Any cash dividends received are credited to Dividend Revenue and reported in the income statement. To illustrate, on November 2, Music City receives a $1,720 quarterly cash dividend on the Intex shares, which it records as:

Assets = Liabilities + Equity
+1,720 +1,720

Nov. 2	Cash	1,720	
	Dividend Revenue		1,720
	Received dividend of $1.72 per share.		

Disposition. When the securities are sold, sale proceeds are compared with the cost, and any gain or loss is recorded. To illustrate, on December 20, Music City sells 500 of the Intex shares for $45,000 cash and records this sale as:

Assets = Liabilities + Equity
+45,000 +2,000
−43,000

Dec. 20	Cash	45,000	
	Long-Term Investments—AFS (Intex)		43,000
	Gain on Sale of Long-Term Investments		2,000
	Sold 500 Intex shares ($86,000 × 500/1,000).		

Reporting of *Non*influential Investments

Companies must value and report most noninfluential investments at *fair market value,* or simply *market value.* The exact reporting requirements depend on whether the investments are classified as (1) trading, (2) held-to-maturity, or (3) available-for-sale.

P1 Account for trading securities.

Trading Securities

Trading securities are *debt and equity securities* that the company intends to actively manage and trade for profit. Frequent purchases and sales are expected and are made to earn profits on short-term price changes. Trading securities are *always* reported as current assets.

Valuing and reporting trading securities. The entire portfolio of trading securities is reported at its market value; this requires a "market adjustment" from the cost of the portfolio. The term *portfolio* refers to a group of securities. Any **unrealized gain (or loss)** from a change in the market value of the portfolio of trading securities is reported on the income statement. Most users believe accounting reports are more useful when changes in market value for trading securities are reported in income.

To illustrate, TechCom's portfolio of trading securities had a total cost of $11,500 and a market value of $13,000 on December 31, 2008, the first year it held trading securities. The difference between the $11,500 cost and the $13,000 market value reflects a $1,500 gain. It is an unrealized gain because it is not yet confirmed by actual sales. The market adjustment for trading securities is recorded with an adjusting entry at the end of each period to equal the difference between the portfolio's cost and its market value. TechCom records this gain as follows.

Point: '*Unrealized gain (or loss)*' refers to a change in market value that is not yet realized through actual sale.

Point: 'Market Adjustment—Trading' is a *permanent account*, shown as a deduction or addition to 'Short-Term Investments—Trading.'

Dec. 31	Market Adjustment—Trading.	1,500	
	Unrealized Gain—Income		1,500
	To reflect an unrealized gain in market values of trading securities.		

Assets	=	Liabilities	+	Equity
+1,500				+1,500

The Unrealized Gain (or Loss) is reported in the Other Revenues and Gains (or Expenses and Losses) section on the income statement. Unrealized Gain (or Loss)—Income is a *temporary* account that is closed to Income Summary at the end of each period. Market Adjustment—Trading is a *permanent* account, which adjusts the reported value of the trading securities portfolio from its prior period market value to the current period market value. The total cost of the trading securities portfolio is maintained in one account, and the market adjustment is recorded in a separate account. For example, TechCom's investment in trading securities is reported in the current assets section of its balance sheet as follows.

Example: If TechCom's trading securities have a cost of $14,800 and a market of $16,100 at Dec. 31, 2009, its adjusting entry is
Unrealized Loss—Income 200
Market Adj.—Trading 200
This is computed as: $1,500 Beg. Dr. bal. + $200 Cr. = $1,300 End. Dr. bal.

Current Assets		
Short-term investments—Trading (at cost)	$11,500	
Market adjustment—Trading	1,500	
Short-term investments—Trading (at market)		$13,000
or simply		
Short-term investments—Trading (at market; cost is $11,500)		$13,000

Selling trading securities. When individual trading securities are sold, the difference between the net proceeds (sale price less fees) and the cost of the individual trading securities that are sold is recognized as a gain or a loss. Any prior period market adjustment to the portfolio is *not* used to compute the gain or loss from sale of individual trading securities. For example, if TechCom sold some of its trading securities that had cost $1,000 for $1,200 cash on January 9, 2009, it would record the following.

Point: Reporting securities at market value is referred to as *mark-to-market* accounting.

Assets = Liabilities + Equity
+1,200 +200
−1,000

Jan. 9	Cash	1,200	
	Short-Term Investments—Trading		1,000
	Gain on Sale of Short-Term Investments		200
	Sold trading securities costing $1,000 for $1,200 cash.		

A gain is reported in the Other Revenues and Gains section on the income statement, whereas a loss is shown in Other Expenses and Losses. When the period-end market adjustment for the portfolio of trading securities is computed, it excludes the cost and market value of any securities sold.

Held-to-Maturity Securities

P2 Account for held-to-maturity securities.

Held-to-maturity (HTM) securities are *debt* securities a company intends and is able to hold until maturity. They are reported in current assets if their maturity dates are within one year or the operating cycle, whichever is longer. HTM securities are reported in long-term assets when the maturity dates extend beyond one year or the operating cycle, whichever is longer. All HTM securities are recorded at cost when purchased, and interest revenue is recorded when earned.

The portfolio of HTM securities is usually reported at (amortized) cost, which is explained in advanced courses. There is no market adjustment to the portfolio of HTM securities—neither to the short-term nor long-term portfolios. The basics of accounting for HTM securities were described earlier in this chapter.

Point: Only debt securities can be classified as *held-to-maturity;* equity securities have no maturity date.

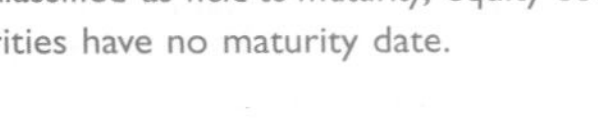

Decision Maker

Money Manager You expect interest rates to sharply fall within a few weeks and remain at this lower rate. What is your strategy for holding investments in fixed-rate bonds and notes? [Answer—p. 608]

Available-for-Sale Securities

P3 Account for available-for-sale securities.

Available-for-sale (AFS) securities are *debt and equity securities* not classified as trading or held-to-maturity securities. AFS securities are purchased to yield interest, dividends, or increases in market value. They are not actively managed like trading securities. If the intent is to sell AFS securities within the longer of one year or operating cycle, they are classified as short-term investments. Otherwise, they are classified as long-term.

Valuing and reporting available-for-sale securities. As with trading securities, companies adjust the cost of the portfolio of AFS securities to reflect changes in market value. This is done with a market adjustment to its total portfolio cost. However, any unrealized gain or loss for the portfolio of AFS securities is *not* reported on the income statement. Instead, it is reported in the equity section of the balance sheet (and is part of *comprehensive income,* explained later). To illustrate, assume that Music City had no prior period investments in available-for-sale securities other than those purchased in the current period. Exhibit 15.4 shows both the cost and market value of those investments on December 31, 2008, the end of its reporting period.

Example: If market value in Exhibit 15.4 is $70,000 (instead of $74,550), what entry is made? *Answer:*
Unreal. Loss—Equity . . . 3,000
Market Adj.—AFS 3,000

EXHIBIT 15.4
Cost and Market Value of Available-for-Sale Securities

	Cost	Market Value	Unrealized Gain (Loss)
Improv bonds	$30,000	$29,050	$ (950)
Intex common stock, 500 shares	43,000	45,500	2,500
Total	$73,000	$74,550	**$1,550**

The year-end adjusting entry to record the market value of these investments follows.

Assets = Liabilities + Equity
+1,550 +1,550

Dec. 31	Market Adjustment—Available-for-Sale (LT)	1,550	
	Unrealized Gain—Equity		1,550
	To record adjustment to market value of available-for-sale securities.		

Exhibit 15.5 shows the December 31, 2008, balance sheet presentation—it assumes these investments are long term, but they can also be short term. It is also common to combine the cost of investments with the balance in the Market Adjustment account and report the net as a single amount.

Point: 'Unrealized Loss—Equity' and 'Unrealized Gain—Equity' are *permanent* (balance sheet) equity *accounts.*

EXHIBIT 15.5

Balance Sheet Presentation of Available-for-Sale Securities

Assets		
Long-term investments—Available-for-sale (at cost)	$73,000	
Market adjustment— Available-for-sale	1,550	
Long-term investments—Available-for-sale (at market)		$74,550
or simply		
Long-term investments—Available-for-sale (at market; cost is $73,000)		$74,550
Equity		
. . . consists of usual equity accounts . . .		
Add unrealized gain on available-for-sale securities*		$ 1,550

Reconciled

* Often included under the caption Accumulated Other Comprehensive Income.

Let's extend this illustration and assume that at the end of its next calendar year (December 31, 2009), Music City's portfolio of long-term AFS securities has an $81,000 cost and an $82,000 market value. It records the adjustment to market value as follows.

Point: Income can be window-dressed upward by selling AFS securities with unrealized gains; income is reduced by selling those with unrealized losses.

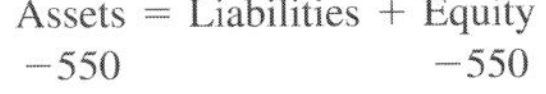

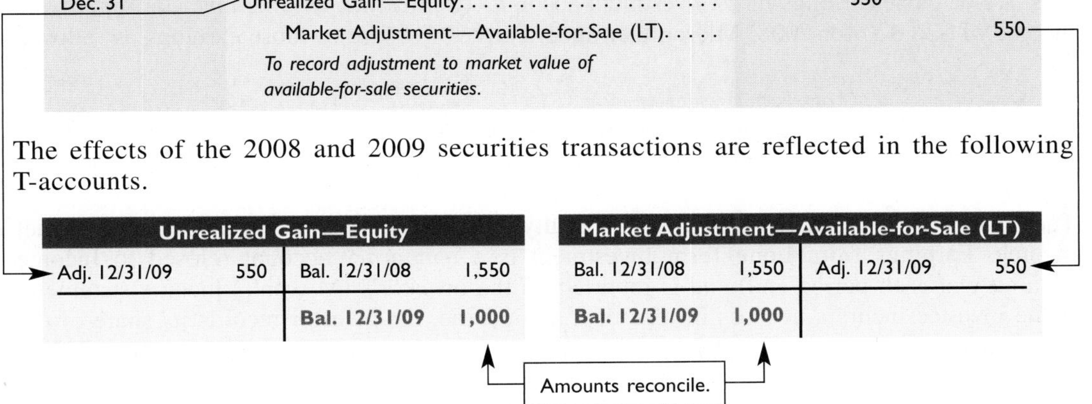

Dec. 31	Unrealized Gain—Equity	550	
	Market Adjustment—Available-for-Sale (LT)		550
	To record adjustment to market value of available-for-sale securities.		

The effects of the 2008 and 2009 securities transactions are reflected in the following T-accounts.

Example: If cost is $83,000 and market is $82,000 at Dec. 31, 2009, it records the following adjustment:
Unreal. Gain—Equity . . . 1,550
Unreal. Loss—Equity . . . 1,000
Mkt. Adj.—AFS 2,550

Unrealized Gain—Equity			
Adj. 12/31/09	550	Bal. 12/31/08	1,550
		Bal. 12/31/09	**1,000**

Market Adjustment—Available-for-Sale (LT)			
Bal. 12/31/08	1,550	Adj. 12/31/09	550
Bal. 12/31/09	**1,000**		

Amounts reconcile.

Selling available-for-sale securities. Accounting for the sale of individual AFS securities is identical to that described for the sale of trading securities. When individual AFS securities are sold, the difference between the cost of the individual securities sold and the net proceeds (sale price less fees) is recognized as a gain or loss.

Point: 'Market Adjustment—Available-for-Sale' is a permanent account, shown as a deduction or addition to the Investment account.

Quick Check

Answers—p. 608

1. How are short-term held-to-maturity securities reported (valued) on the balance sheet?
2. How are trading securities reported (valued) on the balance sheet?
3. Where are unrealized gains and losses on available-for-sale securities reported?
4. Where are unrealized gains and losses on trading securities reported?

Alert *The FASB released* FAS 157 *and* FAS 159 *that permit companies to use market value in reporting financial assets (referred to as the fair value option). This option allows companies to report any financial asset at fair market value and recognize value changes in income. This method was previously reserved only for trading securities, but would now be an option for available-for-sale and held-to-maturity securities (and other 'financial assets and liabilities' such as accounts and notes receivable, accounts and notes payable, and bonds). These standards also set a 3-level system to determine fair value:*
—Level 1: Use quoted market values
—Level 2: Use observable values from related assets or liabilities
—Level 3: Use unobservable values from estimates or assumptions
To date, a fairly small set of companies has chosen to broadly apply the fair value option—but, we continue to monitor its use...

Reporting of Influential Investments

Investment in Securities with Significant Influence

P4 Account for equity securities with significant influence.

A long-term investment classified as **equity securities with significant influence** implies that the investor can exert significant influence over the investee. An investor that owns 20% or more (but not more than 50%) of a company's voting stock is usually presumed to have a significant influence over the investee. In some cases, however, the 20% test of significant influence is overruled by other, more persuasive, evidence. This evidence can either lower the 20% requirement or increase it. The **equity method** of accounting and reporting is used for long-term investments in equity securities with significant influence, which is explained in this section.

Long-term investments in equity securities with significant influence are recorded at cost when acquired. To illustrate, Micron Co. records the purchase of 3,000 shares (30%) of Star Co. common stock at a total cost of $70,650 on January 1, 2008, as follows.

Assets = Liabilities + Equity
+70,650
−70,650

Jan. 1	Long-Term Investments—Star	70,650	
	Cash		70,650
	To record purchase of 3,000 Star shares.		

The investee's (Star) earnings increase both its net assets and the claim of the investor (Micron) on the investee's net assets. Thus, when the investee reports its earnings, the investor records its share of those earnings in its investment account. To illustrate, assume that Star reports net income of $20,000 for 2008. Micron then records its 30% share of those earnings as follows.

Assets = Liabilities + Equity
+6,000 +6,000

Dec. 31	Long-Term Investments—Star	6,000	
	Earnings from Long-Term Investment		6,000
	To record 30% equity in investee earnings.		

The debit reflects the increase in Micron's equity in Star. The credit reflects 30% of Star's net income. Earnings from Long-Term Investment is a *temporary* account (closed to Income Summary at each period-end) and is reported on the investor's (Micron's) income statement. If the investee incurs a net loss instead of a net income, the investor records its share of the loss and reduces (credits) its investment account. The investor closes this earnings or loss account to Income Summary.

The receipt of cash dividends is not revenue under the equity method because the investor has already recorded its share of the investee's earnings. Instead, cash dividends received by an investor from an investee are viewed as a conversion of one asset to another; that is, dividends reduce the balance of the investment account. To illustrate, Star declares and pays $10,000 in cash dividends on its common stock. Micron records its 30% share of these dividends received on January 9, 2009, as:

Assets = Liabilities + Equity
+3,000
−3,000

Jan. 9	Cash	3,000	
	Long-Term Investments—Star.		3,000
	To record share of dividend paid by Star.		

The book value of an investment under the equity method equals the cost of the investment plus (minus) the investor's equity in the *undistributed* (*distributed*) earnings of the investee. Once Micron records these transactions, its Long-Term Investments account appears as in Exhibit 15.6.

EXHIBIT 15.6

Investment in Star Common Stock (Ledger Account)

Date	Explanation	Debit	Credit	Balance
2008				
Jan. 1	Investment acquisition	70,650		70,650
Dec. 31	Share of earnings	6,000		76,650
2009				
Jan. 9	Share of dividend		3,000	73,650

Micron's account balance on January 9, 2009, for its investment in Star is $73,650. This is the investment's cost *plus* Micron's equity in Star's earnings since its purchase *less* Micron's equity in Star's cash dividends since its purchase. When an investment in equity securities is sold, the gain or loss is computed by comparing proceeds from the sale with the book value of the investment on the date of sale. If Micron sells its Star stock for $80,000 on January 10, 2009, it records the sale as:

Point: Security prices are sometimes listed in fractions. For example, a debt security with a price of $22\frac{1}{4}$, is the same as $22.25.

Jan. 10	Cash	80,000	
	Long-Term Investments—Star		73,650
	Gain on Sale of Investment		6,350
	Sold 3,000 shares of stock for $80,000.		

Assets	= Liabilities +	Equity
+80,000		+6,350
−73,650		

Investment in Securities with Controlling Influence

C3 Describe how to report equity securities with controlling influence.

A long-term investment classified as **equity securities with controlling influence** implies that the investor can exert a controlling influence over the investee. An investor who owns more than 50% of a company's voting stock has control over the investee. This investor can dominate all other shareholders in electing the corporation's board of directors and has control over the investee's management. In some cases, controlling influence can extend to situations of less than 50% ownership. Exhibit 15.7 summarizes the accounting for investments in equity securities based on an investor's ownership in the stock.

EXHIBIT 15.7

Accounting for Equity Investments by Percent of Ownership

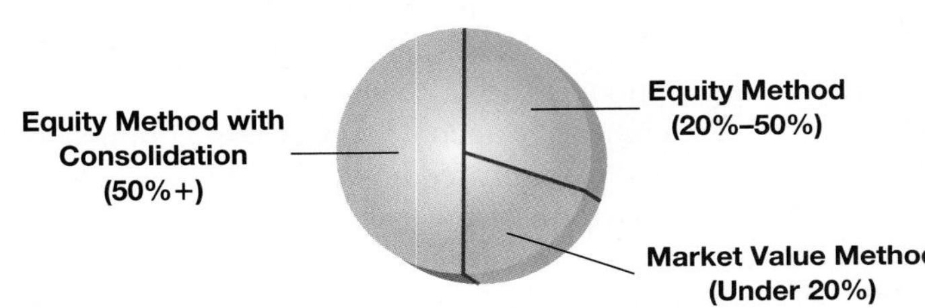

The *equity method with consolidation* is used to account for long-term investments in equity securities with controlling influence. The investor reports *consolidated financial statements* when owning such securities. The controlling investor is called the **parent,** and the investee is called the **subsidiary.** Many companies are parents with subsidiaries. Examples are (1) **McGraw-Hill**, the parent of *BusinessWeek,* Standard & Poor's, and Compustat; (2) **Gap, Inc.**, the parent of Gap, Old Navy, and Banana Republic; and (3) **Brunswick**, the parent of Mercury Marine, Sea Ray, and U.S. Marine. A company owning all the outstanding stock of a subsidiary can, if it desires, take over the subsidiary's assets, retire the subsidiary's stock, and merge the subsidiary into the parent. However, there often are financial, legal, and tax advantages if a business operates as a parent controlling one or more subsidiaries. When a company operates as a parent with subsidiaries, each entity maintains separate accounting records. From a legal viewpoint, the parent and each subsidiary are separate entities with all rights, duties, and responsibilities of individual companies.

Consolidated financial statements show the financial position, results of operations, and cash flows of all entities under the parent's control, including all subsidiaries. These statements are prepared as if the business were organized as one entity. The parent uses the equity method in its accounts, but the investment account is *not* reported on the parent's financial statements. Instead, the individual assets and liabilities of the parent and its subsidiaries are combined on one balance sheet. Their revenues and expenses also are combined on one income statement, and their cash flows are combined on one statement of cash flows. The procedures for preparing consolidated financial statements are in advanced courses.

Decision Insight

IFRSs Unlike U.S. GAAP, IFRSs require uniform accounting policies be used throughout the group of consolidated subsidiaries. Also, unlike U.S. GAAP, IFRSs offer no detailed guidance on valuation procedures.

Accounting Summary for Investments in Securities

Exhibit 15.8 summarizes the standard accounting for investments in securities. Recall that many investment securities are classified as either short term or long term depending on management's

EXHIBIT 15.8

Accounting for Investments in Securities

Classification	Accounting
Short-Term Investment in Securities	
Held-to-maturity (debt) securities	**Cost** (without any discount or premium amortization)
Trading (debt and equity) securities	**Market value** (with market adjustment to income)
Available-for-sale (debt and equity) securities	**Market value** (with market adjustment to equity)
Long-Term Investment in Securities	
Held-to-maturity (debt) securities	**Cost** (with any discount or premium amortization)
Available-for-sale (debt and equity) securities	**Market value** (with market adjustment to equity)
Equity securities with significant influence	Equity method
Equity securities with controlling influence	Equity method (with consolidation)

intent and ability to convert them in the future. Understanding the accounting for these investments enables us to draw better conclusions from financial statements in making business decisions.

Comprehensive Income The term **comprehensive income** refers to all changes in equity for a period except those due to investments and distributions to owners. This means that it includes (1) the revenues, gains, expenses, and losses reported in net income *and* (2) the gains and losses that bypass net income but affect equity. An example of an item that bypasses net income is unrealized gains and losses on available-for-sale securities. These items make up *other comprehensive income* and are usually reported as a part of the statement of stockholders' equity. (Two other options are as a second separate income statement or as a combined income statement of comprehensive income; these less common options are described in advanced courses.) Most often this simply requires one additional column for Other Comprehensive Income in the usual columnar form of the statement of stockholders' equity (the details of this are left for advanced courses). The FASB encourages, but does *not* require, other comprehensive income items to be grouped under the caption *Accumulated Other Comprehensive Income* in the equity section of the balance sheet, which would include unrealized gains and losses on available-for-sale securities. For instructional benefits, we use actual account titles for these items in the equity section instead of this general, less precise caption.

Point: Some users believe that since AFS securities are not actively traded, reporting market value changes in income would unnecessarily increase income variability and decrease usefulness.

Quick Check

Answers—p. 608

5. Give at least two examples of assets classified as long-term investments.
6. What are the requirements for an equity security to be listed as a long-term investment?
7. Identify similarities and differences in accounting for long-term investments in debt securities that are held-to-maturity versus those available-for-sale.
8. What are the three possible classifications of long-term equity investments? Describe the criteria for each class and the method used to account for each.

Decision Analysis — Components of Return on Total Assets

A1 Compute and analyze the components of return on total assets.

A company's **return on total assets** (or simply *return on assets*) is important in assessing financial performance. The return on total assets can be separated into two components, profit margin and total asset turnover, for additional analyses. Exhibit 15.9 shows how these two components determine return on total assets.

EXHIBIT 15.9

Components of Return on Total Assets

Return on total assets = Profit margin × Total asset turnover

$$\frac{\text{Net income}}{\text{Average total assets}} = \frac{\text{Net income}}{\text{Net sales}} \times \frac{\text{Net sales}}{\text{Average total assets}}$$

Profit margin reflects the percent of net income in each dollar of net sales. Total asset turnover reflects a company's ability to produce net sales from total assets. All companies desire a high return on total assets.

By considering these two components, we can often discover strengths and weaknesses not revealed by return on total assets alone. This improves our ability to assess future performance and company strategy.

To illustrate, consider return on total assets and its components for **Gap Inc.** in Exhibit 15.10.

Fiscal Year	Return on Total Assets	=	Profit Margin	×	Total Asset Turnover
2007	9.0%	=	4.9%	×	1.84
2006	11.8	=	6.9	×	1.70
2005	11.1	=	7.1	×	1.57

EXHIBIT 15.10

Gap's Components of Return on Total Assets

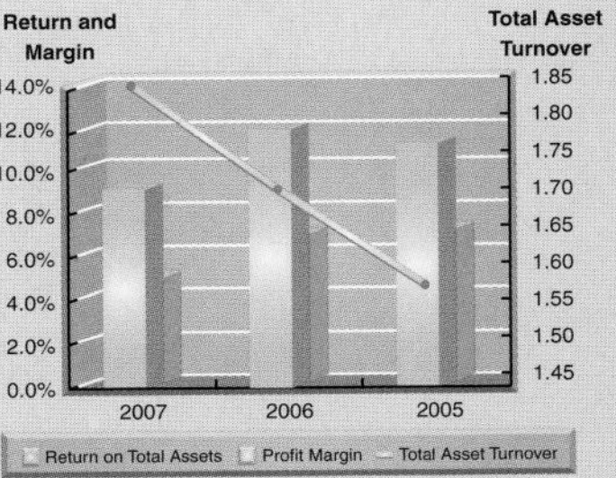

At least three findings emerge. First, Gap's return on total assets improved from 11.1% in 2005 to 11.8% in 2006, but then declined to 9.0% in 2007. Second, total asset turnover has markedly improved from 1.57 to 1.70 to 1.84 over this period. Third, Gap's profit margin steadily declined from 7.1% to 6.9%, and then to 4.9% over this period. These components reveal the dual role of profit margin and total asset turnover in determining return on total assets. They also reveal that the driver of Gap's recent decline is not total asset turnover but profit margin.

Generally, if a company is to maintain or improve its return on total assets, it must meet any decline in either profit margin or total asset turnover with an increase in the other. If not, return on assets will decline. Companies consider these components in planning strategies. A component analysis can also reveal where a company is weak and where changes are needed, especially in a competitor analysis. If asset turnover is lower than the industry norm, for instance, a company should focus on raising asset turnover at least to the norm. The same applies to profit margin.

Decision Maker

Retailer You are an entrepreneur and owner of a retail sporting goods store. The store's recent annual performance reveals (industry norms in parentheses): return on total assets = 11% (11.2%); profit margin = 4.4% (3.5%); and total asset turnover = 2.5 (3.2). What does your analysis of these figures reveal? [Answer—p. 608]

Demonstration Problem—1

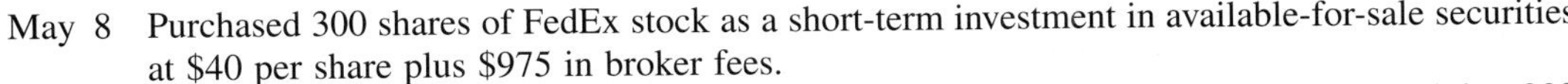

Garden Company completes the following selected transactions related to its short-term investments during 2008.

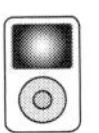

DP15

May 8 Purchased 300 shares of FedEx stock as a short-term investment in available-for-sale securities at $40 per share plus $975 in broker fees.

Sept. 2 Sold 100 shares of its investment in FedEx stock at $47 per share and held the remaining 200 shares; broker's commission was $225.

Oct. 2 Purchased 400 shares of Ajay stock for $60 per share plus $1,600 in commissions. The stock is held as a short-term investment in available-for-sale securities.

Required

1. Prepare journal entries for the above transactions of Garden Company for 2008.
2. Prepare an adjusting journal entry as of December 31, 2008, if the market prices of the equity securities held by Garden Company are $48 per share for FedEx and $55 per share for Ajay. (Year 2008 is the first year Garden Company acquired short-term investments.)

Solution to Demonstration Problem—1

1.

Date	Account	Debit	Credit
May 8	Short-Term Investments—AFS (FedEx)	12,975	
	Cash		12,975
	Purchased 300 shares of FedEx stock (300 × $40) + $975.		

[continued on next page]

[continued from previous page]

Sept. 2	Cash	4,475	
	Gain on Sale of Short-Term Investment		150
	Short-Term Investments—AFS (FedEx)		4,325
	Sold 100 shares of FedEx for $47 per share less a $225 commission. The original cost is ($12,975 × 100/300).		
Oct. 2	Short-Term Investments—AFS (Ajay).	25,600	
	Cash		25,600
	Purchased 400 shares of Ajay for $60 per share plus $1,600 in commissions.		

2. Computation of unrealized gain or loss follows.

Short-Term Investments in Available-for-Sale Securities	Shares	Cost per Share	Total Cost	Market Value per Share	Total Market Value	Unrealized Gain (Loss)
FedEx	200	$43.25	$ 8,650	$48.00	$ 9,600	
Ajay	400	64.00	25,600	55.00	22,000	
Totals			$34,250		$31,600	$(2,650)

The adjusting entry follows.

Dec. 31	Unrealized Loss—Equity.	2,650	
	Market Adjustment—Available-for-Sale (ST)		2,650
	To reflect an unrealized loss in market values of available-for-sale securities.		

Demonstration Problem—2

The following transactions relate to Brown Company's long-term investments during 2008 and 2009. Brown did not own any long-term investments prior to 2008. Show (1) the appropriate journal entries and (2) the relevant portions of each year's balance sheet and income statement that reflect these transactions for both 2008 and 2009.

2008

Sept. 9	Purchased 1,000 shares of Packard, Inc., common stock for $80,000 cash. These shares represent 30% of Packard's outstanding shares.
Oct. 2	Purchased 2,000 shares of AT&T common stock for $60,000 cash. These shares represent less than a 1% ownership in AT&T.
17	Purchased as a long-term investment 1,000 shares of Apple Computer common stock for $40,000 cash. These shares are less than 1% of Apple's outstanding shares.
Nov. 1	Received $5,000 cash dividend from Packard.
30	Received $3,000 cash dividend from AT&T.
Dec. 15	Received $1,400 cash dividend from Apple.
31	Packard's net income for this year is $70,000.
31	Market values for the investments in equity securities are Packard, $84,000; AT&T, $48,000; and Apple Computer, $45,000.
31	For preparing financial statements, note the following post-closing account balances: Common Stock, $500,000, and Retained Earnings, $350,000.

2009

Jan. 1	Sold Packard, Inc., shares for $108,000 cash.
May 30	Received $3,100 cash dividend from AT&T.
June 15	Received $1,600 cash dividend from Apple.

Aug. 17 Sold the AT&T stock for $52,000 cash.

19 Purchased 2,000 shares of Coca-Cola common stock for $50,000 cash as a long-term investment. The stock represents less than a 5% ownership in Coca-Cola.

Dec. 15 Received $1,800 cash dividend from Apple.

31 Market values of the investments in equity securities are Apple, $39,000, and Coca-Cola, $48,000.

31 For preparing financial statements, note the following post-closing account balances: Common Stock, $500,000, and Retained Earnings, $410,000.

Planning the Solution

- Account for the investment in Packard under the equity method.
- Account for the investments in AT&T, Apple, and Coca-Cola as long-term investments in available-for-sale securities.
- Prepare the information for the two years' balance sheets by including the appropriate asset and equity accounts.

Solution to Demonstration Problem—2

1. Journal entries for 2008.

Date	Account	Debit	Credit
Sept. 9	Long-Term Investments—Packard	80,000	
	Cash		80,000
	Acquired 1,000 shares, representing a 30% equity in Packard.		
Oct. 2	Long-Term Investments—AFS (AT&T)	60,000	
	Cash		60,000
	Acquired 2,000 shares as a long-term investment in available-for-sale securities.		
Oct. 17	Long-Term Investments—AFS (Apple)	40,000	
	Cash		40,000
	Acquired 1,000 shares as a long-term investment in available-for-sale securities.		
Nov. 1	Cash	5,000	
	Long-Term Investments—Packard.		5,000
	Received dividend from Packard.		
Nov. 30	Cash	3,000	
	Dividend Revenue		3,000
	Received dividend from AT&T.		
Dec. 15	Cash	1,400	
	Dividend Revenue		1,400
	Received dividend from Apple.		
Dec. 31	Long-Term Investments—Packard	21,000	
	Earnings from Investment (Packard)		21,000
	To record 30% share of Packard's annual earnings of $70,000.		
Dec. 31	Unrealized Loss—Equity.	7,000	
	Market Adjustment—Available-for-Sale (LT)*		7,000
	To record change in market value of long-term available-for-sale securities.		

* Market adjustment computations:

	Cost	Market Value	Unrealized Gain (Loss)
AT&T	$ 60,000	$48,000	$(12,000)
Apple	40,000	45,000	5,000
Total	$100,000	$93,000	$ (7,000)

Required balance of the Market Adjustment—Available-for-Sale (LT) account (credit)	$(7,000)
Existing balance	0
Necessary adjustment (credit)	$(7,000)

2. The December 31, 2008, selected balance sheet items appear as follows.

Assets	
Long-term investments	
Available-for-sale securities (at market; cost is $100,000)	$ 93,000
Investment in equity securities	96,000
Total long-term investments	189,000
Stockholders' Equity	
Common stock	500,000
Retained earnings	350,000
Unrealized loss—Equity	(7,000)

The relevant income statement items for the year ended December 31, 2008, follow.

Dividend revenue	$ 4,400
Earnings from investment	21,000

1. Journal entries for 2009.

Date	Account	Debit	Credit
Jan. 1	Cash	108,000	
	Long-Term Investments—Packard		96,000
	Gain on Sale of Long-Term Investments		12,000
	Sold 1,000 shares for cash.		
May 30	Cash	3,100	
	Dividend Revenue		3,100
	Received dividend from AT&T.		
June 15	Cash	1,600	
	Dividend Revenue		1,600
	Received dividend from Apple.		
Aug. 17	Cash	52,000	
	Loss on Sale of Long-Term Investments	8,000	
	Long-Term Investments—AFS (AT&T)		60,000
	Sold 2,000 shares for cash.		
Aug. 19	Long-Term Investments—AFS (Coca-Cola)	50,000	
	Cash		50,000
	Acquired 2,000 shares as a long-term investment in available-for-sale securities.		
Dec. 15	Cash	1,800	
	Dividend Revenue		1,800
	Received dividend from Apple.		
Dec. 31	Market Adjustment—Available-for-Sale (LT)*	4,000	
	Unrealized Loss—Equity		4,000
	To record change in market value of long-term available-for-sale securities.		

* Market adjustment computations:

	Cost	Market Value	Unrealized Gain (Loss)
Apple	$40,000	$39,000	$(1,000)
Coca-Cola	50,000	48,000	(2,000)
Total	$90,000	$87,000	$(3,000)

Required balance of the Market Adjustment—Available-for-Sale (LT) account (credit)	$(3,000)
Existing balance (credit)	(7,000)
Necessary adjustment (debit)	$ 4,000

2. The December 31, 2009, balance sheet items appear as follows.

Assets	
Long-term investments	
Available-for-sale securities (at market; cost is $90,000)	$ 87,000
Stockholders' Equity	
Common stock	500,000
Retained earnings	410,000
Unrealized loss—Equity	(3,000)

The relevant income statement items for the year ended December 31, 2009, follow.

Dividend revenue	$ 6,500
Gain on sale of long-term investments	12,000
Loss on sale of long-term investments	(8,000)

APPENDIX

Investments in International Operations

15A

Many entities from small entrepreneurs to large corporations conduct business internationally. Some entities' operations occur in so many different countries that the companies are called **multinationals.** Many of us think of Coca-Cola and McDonald's, for example, as primarily U.S. companies, but most of their sales occur outside the United States. Exhibit 15A.1 shows the percent of international sales and income for selected U.S. companies. Managing and accounting for multinationals present challenges. This section describes some of these challenges and how to account for and report these activities.

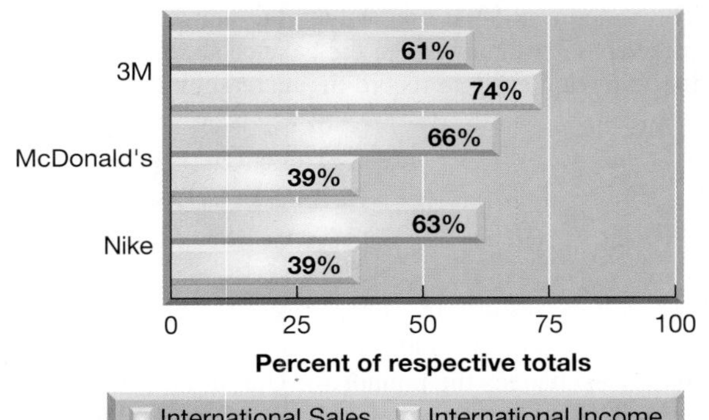

EXHIBIT 15A.1

International Sales and Income as a Percent of Their Totals

Two major accounting challenges that arise when companies have international operations relate to transactions that involve more than one currency. The first is to account for sales and purchases listed in a foreign currency. The second is to prepare consolidated financial statements with international subsidiaries. For ease in this discussion, we use companies with a U.S. base of operations and assume the need to prepare financial statements in U.S. dollars. This means the *reporting currency* of these companies is the U.S. dollar.

Point: Transactions *listed* or *stated* in a foreign currency are said to be *denominated* in that currency.

Exchange Rates between Currencies

C4 Explain foreign exchange rates between currencies.

Markets for the purchase and sale of foreign currencies exist all over the world. In these markets, U.S. dollars can be exchanged for Canadian dollars, British pounds, Japanese yen, Euros, or any other legal currencies. The price of one currency stated in terms of another currency is called a **foreign exchange rate.** Exhibit 15A.2 lists recent exchange rates for selected currencies. The exchange rate for British pounds and U.S. dollars is $1.8054, meaning 1 British pound could be purchased for $1.8054. On that same day, the exchange rate between Mexican pesos and U.S. dollars is $0.0925, or 1 Mexican peso can be purchased for $0.0925. Exchange rates fluctuate due to changing economic and political conditions, including the supply and demand for currencies and expectations about future events.

Point: To convert currency, see XE.com

Decision Insight

Rush to Russia Investors are still eager to buy Russian equities even in the face of rampant crime, corruption, and slow economic growth. Why? Many argue Russia remains a bargain-priced, if risky, bet on future growth. Some analysts argue that natural-resource-rich Russia is one of the least expensive emerging markets.

EXHIBIT 15A.2

Foreign Exchange Rates for Selected Currencies*

Source (unit)	Price in $U.S.	Source (unit)	Price in $U.S.
Britain (pound)	$1.8980	Canada (dollar)	$0.9793
Mexico (peso)	0.0925	Japan (yen)	0.0090
Taiwan (dollar)	0.0305	Europe (Euro)	1.2920

* Rates will vary over time based on economic, political, and other changes.

Sales and Purchases Listed in a Foreign Currency

P5 Record transactions listed in a foreign currency.

When a U.S. company makes a credit sale to an international customer, accounting for the sale and the account receivable is straightforward if sales terms require the international customer's payment in U.S. dollars. If sale terms require (or allow) payment in a foreign currency, however, the U.S. company must account for the sale and the account receivable in a different manner.

Sales in a Foreign Currency To illustrate, consider the case of the U.S.-based manufacturer Boston Company, which makes credit sales to London Outfitters, a British retail company. A sale occurs on December 12, 2008, for a price of £10,000 with payment due on February 10, 2009. Boston Company keeps its accounting records in U.S. dollars. To record the sale, Boston Company must translate the sales price from pounds to dollars. This is done using the exchange rate on the date of the sale. Assuming the exchange rate on December 12, 2008, is $1.80, Boston records this sale as follows.

Assets	= Liabilities +	Equity
+18,000		+18,000

Dec. 12	Accounts Receivable—London Outfitters	18,000	
	Sales*		18,000
	To record a sale at £10,000, when the exchange rate equals $1.80. * (£10,000 × $1.80)		

When Boston Company prepares its annual financial statements on December 31, 2008, the current exchange rate is $1.84. Thus, the current dollar value of Boston Company's receivable is $18,400 (10,000 × $1.84). This amount is $400 higher than the amount recorded on December 12. Accounting principles require a receivable to be reported in the balance sheet at its current dollar value. Thus, Boston Company must make the following entry to record the increase in the dollar value of this receivable at year-end.

Assets	= Liabilities +	Equity
+400		+400

Dec. 31	Accounts Receivable—London Outfitters	400	
	Foreign Exchange Gain		400
	To record the increased value of the British pound for the receivable.		

Point: Foreign exchange gains are credits, and foreign exchange losses are debits.

On February 10, 2009, Boston Company receives London Outfitters' payment of £10,000. It immediately exchanges the pounds for U.S. dollars. On this date, the exchange rate for pounds is $1.78. Thus, Boston Company receives only $17,800 (£10,000 × $1.78). It records the cash receipt and the loss associated with the decline in the exchange rate as follows.

Assets	= Liabilities +	Equity
+17,800		−600
−18,400		

Feb. 10	Cash	17,800	
	Foreign Exchange Loss	600	
	Accounts Receivable—London Outfitters		18,400
	Received foreign currency payment of an account and converted it into dollars.		

Gains and losses from foreign exchange transactions are accumulated in the Foreign Exchange Gain (or Loss) account. After year-end adjustments, the balance in the Foreign Exchange Gain (or Loss) account is reported on the income statement and closed to the Income Summary account.

Purchases in a Foreign Currency Accounting for credit purchases from an international seller is similar to the case of a credit sale to an international customer. In particular, if the U.S. company is required to make payment in a foreign currency, the account payable must be translated into dollars before the U.S. company can record it. If the exchange rate is different when preparing financial statements and when paying for the purchase, the U.S. company must recognize a foreign exchange gain or loss at those dates. To illustrate, assume NC Imports, a U.S. company, purchases products costing

Example: Assume that a U.S. company makes a credit purchase from a British company for £10,000 when the exchange rate is $1.62. At the balance sheet date, this rate is $1.72. Does this imply a gain or loss for the U.S. company? *Answer:* A loss.

€20,000 (euros) from Hamburg Brewing on January 15, when the exchange rate is $1.20 per euro. NC records this transaction as follows.

Jan. 15	Inventory.	24,000	
	Accounts Payable—Hamburg Brewing.		24,000
	To record a €20,000 purchase when exchange rate is $1.20 (€20,000 × $1.20)		

Assets	=	Liabilities	+	Equity
+24,000		+24,000		

NC Imports makes payment in full on February 14 when the exchange rate is $1.25 per euro, which is recorded as follows.

Feb. 14	Accounts Payable—Hamburg Brewing	24,000	
	Foreign Exchange Loss	1,000	
	Cash		25,000
	To record cash payment towards €20,000 account when exchange rate is $1.25 (€20.000 × $1.25).		

Assets	=	Liabilities	+	Equity
−25,000		−24,000		−1,000

Decision Insight

Global Greenback What do changes in foreign exchange rates mean? A decline in the price of the U.S. dollar against other currencies usually yields increased international sales for U.S. companies, without hiking prices or cutting costs, and puts them on a stronger competitive footing abroad. At home, they can raise prices without fear that foreign rivals will undercut them.

Consolidated Statements with International Subsidiaries

A second challenge in accounting for international operations involves preparing consolidated financial statements when the parent company has one or more international subsidiaries. Consider a U.S.-based company that owns a controlling interest in a French subsidiary. The reporting currency of the U.S. parent is the dollar. The French subsidiary maintains its financial records in euros. Before preparing consolidated statements, the parent must translate financial statements of the French company into U.S. dollars. After this translation is complete (including that for accounting differences), it prepares consolidated statements the same as for domestic subsidiaries. Procedures for translating an international subsidiary's account balances depend on the nature of the subsidiary's operations. The process requires the parent company to select appropriate foreign exchange rates and to apply those rates to the foreign subsidiary's account balances. This is described in advanced courses.

Global: A weaker U.S. dollar often increases global sales for U.S. companies.

Decision Maker

Entrepreneur You are a U.S. home builder that purchases lumber from mills in both the U.S. and Canada. The price of the Canadian dollar in terms of the U.S. dollar jumps from US$0.70 to US$0.80. Are you now more or less likely to buy lumber from Canadian or U.S. mills? [Answer—p. 608]

Summary

C1 Distinguish between debt and equity securities and between short-term and long-term investments. *Debt securities* reflect a creditor relationship and include investments in notes, bonds, and certificates of deposit. *Equity securities* reflect an owner relationship and include shares of stock issued by other companies. Short-term investments in securities are current assets that meet two criteria: (1) They are expected to be converted into cash within one year or the current operating cycle of the business, whichever is longer and (2) they are readily convertible to cash, or *marketable*. All other investments in securities are long-term. Long-term investments also include assets not used in operations and those held for special purposes, such as land for expansion.

C2 Identify and describe the different classes of investments in securities. Investments in securities are classified into one of five groups: (1) trading securities, which are always short-term, (2) debt securities held-to-maturity, (3) debt and equity securities available-for-sale, (4) equity securities in which an investor has a significant influence over the investee, and (5) equity securities in which an investor has a controlling influence over the investee.

C3 Describe how to report equity securities with controlling influence. If an investor owns more than 50% of another company's voting stock and controls the investee, the investor's financial reports are prepared on a consolidated basis. These reports are prepared as if the company were organized as one entity.

C4[A] Explain foreign exchange rates between currencies. A foreign exchange rate is the price of one currency stated in terms of another. An entity with transactions in a foreign currency when the exchange rate changes between the transaction dates and their settlement will experience exchange gains or losses.

A1 Compute and analyze the components of return on total assets. Return on total assets has two components: profit margin and total asset turnover. A decline in one component must be met with an increase in another if return on assets is to be maintained. Component analysis is helpful in assessing company performance compared to that of competitors and its own past.

P1 Account for trading securities. Investments are initially recorded at cost, and any dividend or interest from these investments is recorded in the income statement. Investments classified as trading securities are reported at market value. Unrealized gains and losses on trading securities are reported in income. When investments are sold, the difference between the net proceeds from the sale and the cost of the securities is recognized as a gain or loss.

P2 Account for held-to-maturity securities. Debt securities held-to-maturity are reported at cost when purchased. Interest revenue is recorded as it accrues. The cost of long-term held-to-maturity securities is adjusted for the amortization of any difference between cost and maturity value.

P3 Account for available-for-sale securities. Debt and equity securities available-for-sale are recorded at cost when purchased. Available-for-sale securities are reported at their market values on the balance sheet with unrealized gains or losses shown in the equity section. Gains and losses realized on the sale of these investments are reported in the income statement.

P4 Account for equity securities with significant influence. The equity method is used when an investor has a significant influence over an investee. This usually exists when an investor owns 20% or more of the investee's voting stock but not more than 50%. The equity method means an investor records its share of investee earnings with a debit to the investment account and a credit to a revenue account. Dividends received reduce the investment account balance.

P5[A] Record transactions listed in a foreign currency. When a company makes a credit sale to a foreign customer and sales terms call for payment in a foreign currency, the company must translate the foreign currency into dollars to record the receivable. If the exchange rate changes before payment is received, exchange gains or losses are recognized in the year they occur. The same treatment is used when a company makes a credit purchase from a foreign supplier and is required to make payment in a foreign currency.

Guidance Answers to **Decision Maker**

Money Manager If you have investments in fixed-rate bonds and notes when interest rates fall, the value of your investments increases. This is so because the bonds and notes you hold continue to pay the same (high) rate while the market is demanding a new lower interest rate. Your strategy is to continue holding your investments in bonds and notes, and, potentially, to increase these holdings through additional purchases.

Retailer Your store's return on assets is 11%, which is similar to the industry norm of 11.2%. However, disaggregation of return on assets reveals that your store's profit margin of 4.4% is much higher than the norm of 3.5%, but your total asset turnover of 2.5 is much lower than the norm of 3.2. These results suggest that, as compared with competitors, you are less efficient in using assets. You need to focus on increasing sales or reducing assets. You might consider reducing prices to increase sales, provided such a strategy does not reduce your return on assets. For instance, you could reduce your profit margin to 4% to increase sales. If total asset turnover increases to more than 2.75 when profit margin is lowered to 4%, your overall return on assets is improved.

Entrepreneur You are now less likely to buy Canadian lumber because it takes more U.S. money to buy a Canadian dollar (and lumber). For instance, the purchase of lumber from a Canadian mill with a $1,000 (Canadian dollars) price would have cost the U.S. builder $700 (U.S. dollars, computed as C$1,000 × US$0.70) before the rate change, and $800 (US dollars, computed as C$1,000 × US$0.80) after the rate change.

Guidance Answers to **Quick Checks**

1. Short-term held-to-maturity securities are reported at cost.
2. Trading securities are reported at market value.
3. The equity section of the balance sheet (and in comprehensive income).
4. The income statement.
5. Long-term investments include (1) long-term funds earmarked for a special purpose, (2) debt and equity securities that do not meet current asset requirements, and (3) long-term assets not used in the regular operations of the business.
6. An equity investment is classified as long term if it is not marketable or, if marketable, it is not held as an available source of cash to meet the needs of current operations.
7. Debt securities held-to-maturity and debt securities available-for-sale are both recorded at cost. Also, interest on both is accrued as earned. However, only long-term securities held-to-maturity require amortization of the difference between cost and maturity value. In addition, only securities available-for-sale require a period-end adjustment to market value.
8. Long-term equity investments are placed in one of three categories and accounted for as follows: (a) **available-for-sale** (noninfluential, less than 20% of outstanding stock)—market value; (b) **significant influence** (20% to 50% of outstanding stock)—equity method; and (c) **controlling influence** (holding more than 50% of outstanding stock)—equity method with consolidation.

Key Terms

mhhe.com/wildFAP19e

Key Terms are available at the book's Website for learning and testing in an online Flashcard Format.

Available-for-sale (AFS) securities (p. 596)
Comprehensive income (p. 600)
Consolidated financial statements (p. 599)
Equity method (p. 598)
Equity securities with controlling influence (p. 599)
Equity securities with significant influence (p. 598)
Foreign exchange rate (p. 605)
Held-to-maturity (HTM) securities (p. 596)
Long-term investments (p. 592)
Multinational (p. 605)
Parent (p. 599)
Return on total assets (p. 600)
Short-term investments (p. 592)
Subsidiary (p. 599)
Trading securities (p. 595)
Unrealized gain (loss) (p. 595)

Multiple Choice Quiz

Answers on p. 625 mhhe.com/wildFAP19e

Additional Quiz Questions are available at the book's Website.

1. A company purchased $30,000 of 5% bonds for investment purposes on May 1. The bonds pay interest on February 1 and August 1. The amount of interest revenue accrued at December 31 (the company's year-end) is:
   a. $1,500
   b. $1,375
   c. $1,000
   d. $625
   e. $300
2. Earlier this period, Amadeus Co. purchased its only available-for-sale investment in the stock of Bach Co. for $83,000. The period-end market value of this stock is $84,500. Amadeus records a:
   a. Credit to Unrealized Gain—Equity for $1,500
   b. Debit to Unrealized Loss—Equity for $1,500
   c. Debit to Investment Revenue for $1,500
   d. Credit to Market Adjustment—Available-for-Sale for $3,500
   e. Credit to Cash for $1,500
3. Mozart Co. owns 35% of Melody Inc. Melody pays $50,000 in cash dividends to its shareholders for the period. Mozart's entry to record the Melody dividend includes a:
   a. Credit to Investment Revenue for $50,000.
   b. Credit to Long-Term Investments for $17,500.
   c. Credit to Cash for $17,500.
   d. Debit to Long-Term Investments for $17,500.
   e. Debit to Cash for $50,000.
4. A company has net income of $300,000, net sales of $2,500,000, and total assets of $2,000,000. Its return on total assets equals:
   a. 6.7%
   b. 12.0%
   c. 8.3%
   d. 80.0%
   e. 15.0%
5. A company had net income of $80,000, net sales of $600,000, and total assets of $400,000. Its profit margin and total asset turnover are:

	Profit Margin	Total Asset Turnover
a.	1.5%	13.3
b.	13.3%	1.5
c.	13.3%	0.7
d.	7.0%	13.3
e.	10.0%	26.7

Superscript A denotes assignments based on Appendix 15A.

Discussion Questions

1. Under what two conditions should investments be classified as current assets?
2. On a balance sheet, what valuation must be reported for short-term investments in trading securities?
3. If a short-term investment in available-for-sale securities costs $6,780 and is sold for $7,500, how should the difference between these two amounts be recorded?
4. Identify the three classes of noninfluential and two classes of influential investments in securities.
5. Under what conditions should investments be classified as current assets? As long-term assets?
6. If a company purchases its only long-term investments in available-for-sale debt securities this period and their market value is below cost at the balance sheet date, what entry is required to recognize this unrealized loss?
7. On a balance sheet, what valuation must be reported for debt securities classified as available-for-sale?

8. Under what circumstances are long-term investments in debt securities reported at cost and adjusted for amortization of any difference between cost and maturity value?

9. For investments in available-for-sale securities, how are unrealized (holding) gains and losses reported?

10. In accounting for investments in equity securities, when should the equity method be used?

11. Under what circumstances does a company prepare consolidated financial statements?

12.[A] What are two major challenges in accounting for international operations?

13.[A] Assume a U.S. company makes a credit sale to a foreign customer that is required to make payment in its foreign currency. In the current period, the exchange rate is $1.40 on the date of the sale and is $1.30 on the date the customer pays the receivable. Will the U.S. company record an exchange gain or loss?

14.[A] If a U.S. company makes a credit sale to a foreign customer required to make payment in U.S. dollars, can the U.S. company have an exchange gain or loss on this sale?

15. Refer to **Best Buy**'s statement of changes in shareholders' equity in Appendix A. What is the amount of foreign currency translation adjustment for the year ended March 3, 2007? Is this adjustment an unrealized gain or an unrealized loss?

16. Refer to the balance sheet of **Circuit City** in Appendix A. How can you tell that Circuit City uses the consolidated method of accounting?

17. Refer to **RadioShack**'s statement of stockholders' equity. What was the amount of its 2006 unrealized gain or loss on securities?

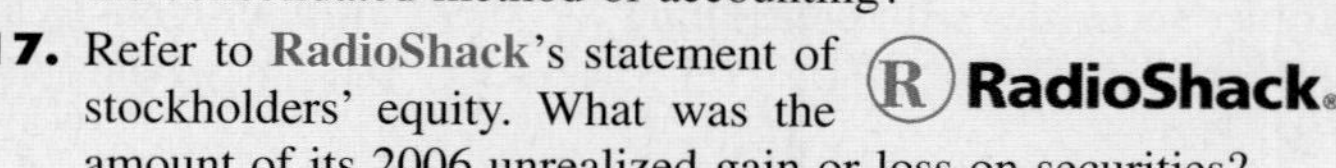

18. Refer to the financial statements of **Apple** in Appendix A. Compute its return on total assets for the year ended September 30, 2006.

Denotes Discussion Questions that involve decision making.

Available with McGraw-Hill's Homework Manager

QUICK STUDY

QS 15-1
Short-term equity investments C2 P1

On April 18, Rollo Co. made a short-term investment in 600 common shares of TXT Co. The purchase price is $84 per share and the broker's fee is $500. The intent is to actively manage these shares for profit. On May 30, Rollo Co. receives $0.75 per share from TXT in dividends. Prepare the April 18 and May 30 journal entries to record these transactions.

QS 15-2
Available-for-sale securities C2 P3

Malox Co. purchased short-term investments in available-for-sale securities at a cost of $100,000 on November 25, 2009. At December 31, 2009, these securities had a market value of $94,000. This is the first and only time the company has purchased such securities.

1. Prepare the December 31, 2009, year-end adjusting entry for the securities' portfolio.
2. For each account in the entry for part 1, explain how it is reported in financial statements.
3. Prepare the April 6, 2010, entry when Malox sells one-fourth of these securities for $27,000.

QS 15-3
Available-for-sale securities C2 P3

Prepare Vikon Company's journal entries to reflect the following transactions for the current year.

May 7 Purchases 200 shares of Felton stock as a short-term investment in available-for-sale securities at a cost of $100 per share plus $400 in broker fees.
June 6 Sells 200 shares of its investment in Felton stock at $112 per share. The broker's commission on this sale is $250.

QS 15-4
Available-for-sale securities C2 P3

Texar Company completes the following transactions during the current year.

May 9 Purchases 400 shares of Crayton stock as a short-term investment in available-for-sale securities at a cost of $30 per share plus $200 in broker fees.
June 2 Sells 200 shares of its investment in Crayton stock at $32 per share. The broker's commission on this sale is $120.
Dec. 31 The closing market price of the Crayton stock is $28 per share.

Prepare the May 9 and June 2 journal entries and the December 31 adjusting entry. This is the first and only time the company purchased such securities.

QS 15-5
Identifying long-term investments C1

Which of the following statements are true of long-term investments?

a. They are held as an investment of cash available for current operations.
b. They can include funds earmarked for a special purpose, such as bond sinking funds.

c. They can include investments in trading securities.
d. They can include debt securities held-to-maturity.
e. They are always easily sold and therefore qualify as being marketable.
f. They can include debt and equity securities available-for-sale.
g. They can include bonds and stocks not intended to serve as a ready source of cash.

QS 15-6
Describing investments in securities
C1 C2 C3

Complete the following descriptions by filling in the blanks.

1. Equity securities giving an investor significant influence are accounted for using the ____ ____.
2. Trading securities are classified as ____ assets.
3. Accrual of interest on bonds held as long-term investments requires a credit to ____ ____.
4. The controlling investor (more than 50% ownership) is called the ____, and the investee company is called the ____.
5. Available-for-sale debt securities are reported on the balance sheet at ____ ____.

QS 15-7
Debt securities transactions
C2 P2

On February 1, 2009, Garzon purchased 6% bonds issued by Integal Utilities at a cost of $80,000, which is their par value. The bonds pay interest semiannually on July 31 and January 31. For 2009, prepare entries to record Garzon's July 31 receipt of interest and its December 31 year-end interest accrual.

QS 15-8
Recording equity securities
C2 P3

On May 20, 2009, Chiu Co. paid $1,500,000 to acquire 25,000 common shares (10%) of BBE Corp. as a long-term investment. On August 5, 2010, Chiu sold one-half of these shares for $937,500. What valuation method should be used to account for this stock investment? Prepare entries to record both the acquisition and the sale of these shares.

QS 15-9
Equity method transactions
C2 P4

Assume the same facts as in QS 15-8 except that the stock acquired represents 40% of BBE Corp.'s outstanding stock. Also assume that BBE Corp. paid a $150,000 dividend on November 1, 2009, and reported a net income of $1,050,000 for 2009. Prepare the entries to record (*a*) the receipt of the dividend and (*b*) the December 31, 2009, year-end adjustment required for the investment account.

QS 15-10
Recording market adjustment for securities
P3

During the current year, Marketplace Consulting Group acquired long-term available-for-sale securities at an $85,000 cost. At its December 31 year-end, these securities had a market value of $62,000. This is the first and only time the company purchased such securities.

1. Prepare the necessary year-end adjusting entry related to these securities.
2. Explain how each account used in part 1 is reported in the financial statements.

QS 15-11
Return on total assets A1

The return on total assets is the focus of analysts, creditors, and other users of financial statements.

1. How is the return on total assets computed?
2. What does this important ratio reflect?

QS 15-12
Component return on total assets A1

Return on total assets can be separated into two important components.

1. Write the formula to separate the return on total assets into its two basic components.
2. Explain how these components of the return on total assets are helpful to financial statement users for business decisions.

QS 15-13[A]
Foreign currency transactions
P5

A U.S. company sells a product to a British company with the transaction listed in British pounds. On the date of the sale, the transaction total of $40,600 is billed as £20,000, reflecting an exchange rate of 2.03 (that is, $2.03 per pound). Prepare the entry to record (1) the sale and (2) the receipt of payment in pounds when the exchange rate is 1.95.

QS 15-14[A]
Foreign currency transactions
P5

On March 1, 2009, a U.S. company made a credit sale requiring payment in 30 days from a Malaysian company, Hamac Sdn. Bhd., in 20,000 Malaysian ringgits. Assuming the exchange rate between Malaysian ringgits and U.S. dollars is $0.2963 on March 1 and $0.3005 on March 31, prepare the entries to record the sale on March 1 and the cash receipt on March 31.

EXERCISES

Exercise 15-1

Accounting for transactions in short-term securities

C2 P1 P2 P3

Check (c) Dr. Cash $173,400

(f) Dr. Cash $13,025

Prepare journal entries to record the following transactions involving the short-term securities investments of Bolton Co., all of which occurred during year 2009.

a. On February 15, paid $170,000 cash to purchase ACC's 90-day short-term debt securities ($170,000 principal), dated February 15, that pay 8% interest (categorized as held-to-maturity securities).

b. On March 22, purchased 850 shares of Ross Company stock at $21 per share plus a $100 brokerage fee. These shares are categorized as trading securities.

c. On May 16, received a check from ACC in payment of the principal and 90 days' interest on the debt securities purchased in transaction *a*.

d. On August 1, paid $70,000 cash to purchase Nita Co.'s 11% debt securities ($70,000 principal), dated July 30, 2009, and maturing January 30, 2010 (categorized as available-for-sale securities).

e. On September 1, received a $1.10 per share cash dividend on the Ross Company stock purchased in transaction *b*.

f. On October 8, sold 425 shares of Ross Co. stock for $31 per share, less a $150 brokerage fee.

g. On October 30, received a check from Nita Co. for 90 days' interest on the debt securities purchased in transaction *d*.

Exercise 15-2

Accounting for trading securities

C1 P1 

Check (3) Gain, $2,250

Borchert Co. purchases various investments in trading securities at a cost of $76,000 on December 27, 2009. (This is its first and only purchase of such securities.) At December 31, 2009, these securities had a market value of $85,000.

1. Prepare the December 31, 2009, year-end adjusting entry for the trading securities' portfolio.

2. Explain how each account in the entry of part 1 is reported in financial statements.

3. Prepare the January 3, 2010, entry when Borchert sells a portion of its trading securities (that had originally cost $38,000) for $40,250.

Exercise 15-3

Adjusting available-for-sale securities to market

C2 P3 

Check Unrealized loss, $392

On December 31, 2009, Tagert Company held the following short-term investments in its portfolio of available-for-sale securities. Tagert had no short-term investments in its prior accounting periods. Prepare the December 31, 2009, adjusting entry to report these investments at market value.

	Cost	Market Value
Verrizano Corporation bonds payable	$ 81,400	$92,000
Porter Corporation notes payable	54,900	47,928
Laverne Company common stock	100,500	96,480

Exercise 15-4

Transactions in short-term and long-term investments

C1 C2

Prepare journal entries to record the following transactions involving both the short-term and long-term investments of Corveau Corp., all of which occurred during calendar year 2009. Use the account Short-Term Investments for any transactions that you determine are short term.

a. On February 15, paid $100,000 cash to purchase Anthem's 90-day short-term notes at par, which are dated February 15 and pay 6% interest (classified as held-to-maturity).

b. On March 22, bought 600 shares of Frain Industries common stock at $43 cash per share plus a $140 brokerage fee (classified as long-term available-for-sale securities).

c. On May 15, received a check from Anthem in payment of the principal and 90 days' interest on the notes purchased in transaction *a*.

d. On July 30, paid $30,000 cash to purchase Moto Electronics' 5% notes at par, dated July 30, 2009, and maturing on January 30, 2010 (classified as trading securities).

e. On September 1, received a $0.40 per share cash dividend on the Frain Industries common stock purchased in transaction *b*.

f. On October 8, sold 300 shares of Frain Industries common stock for $49 cash per share, less a $120 brokerage fee.

g. On October 30, received a check from Moto Electronics for three months' interest on the notes purchased in transaction *d*.

Exercise 15-5
Market adjustment to available-for-sale securities
P3

On December 31, 2009, Loren Co. held the following short-term available-for-sale securities.

	Cost	Market Value
Nintendo Co. common stock	$64,500	$70,305
Unilever bonds payable	25,800	23,994
Kellogg Co. notes payable	46,440	43,654
McDonald's Corp. common stock	87,075	82,721

Loren had no short-term investments prior to the current period. Prepare the December 31, 2009, year-end adjusting entry to record the market adjustment for these securities.

Exercise 15-6
Market adjustment to available-for-sale securities
P3

Patica Co. began operations in 2008. The cost and market values for its long-term investments portfolio in available-for-sale securities are shown below. Prepare Patica's December 31, 2009, adjusting entry to reflect any necessary market adjustment for these investments.

	Cost	Market Value
December 31, 2008	$67,842	$61,736
December 31, 2009	73,479	77,888

Exercise 15-7
Multi-year market adjustments to available-for-sale securities
P3

Basil Services began operations in 2007 and maintains long-term investments in available-for-sale securities. The year-end cost and market values for its portfolio of these investments follow. Prepare journal entries to record each year-end market adjustment for these securities.

	Cost	Market Value
December 31, 2007	$392,900	$381,113
December 31, 2008	447,906	474,780
December 31, 2009	609,152	720,627
December 31, 2010	919,820	818,640

Exercise 15-8
Classifying investments in securities; recording market values
C1 C2 P2 P3 P4 

Information regarding Seaton Company's individual investments in securities during its calendar-year 2009, along with the December 31, 2009, market values, follows.

a. Investment in Beeman Company bonds: $443,150 cost, $481,704 market value. Seaton intends to hold these bonds until they mature in 2014.

b. Investment in Baybridge common stock: 29,500 shares; $352,304 cost; $382,954 market value. Seaton owns 32% of Baybridge's voting stock and has a significant influence over Baybridge.

c. Investment in Carroll common stock: 12,000 shares; $181,692 cost; $195,864 market value. This investment amounts to 3% of Carroll's outstanding shares, and Seaton's goal with this investment is to earn dividends over the next few years.

d. Investment in Newtech common stock: 3,500 shares; $101,038 cost; $99,320 market value. Seaton's goal with this investment is to reap an increase in market value of the stock over the next three to five years. Newtech has 30,000 common shares outstanding.

e. Investment in Flock common stock: 16,300 shares; $110,788 cost; $117,657 market value. This stock is marketable and is held as an investment of cash available for operations.

Required

1. Identify whether each investment should be classified as a short-term or long-term investment. For each long-term investment, indicate in which of the long-term investment classifications it should be placed.

2. Prepare a journal entry dated December 31, 2009, to record the market value adjustment of the long-term investments in available-for-sale securities. Seaton had no long-term investments prior to year 2009.

Check (2) Unrealized gain, $12,454

Exercise 15-9
Securities transactions; equity method
P4 C2

Prepare journal entries to record the following transactions and events of Kareen Company.

2009

Jan. 2	Purchased 55,000 shares of Altus Co. common stock for $374,000 cash plus a broker's fee of $2,650 cash. Altus has 137,500 shares of common stock outstanding and its policies will be significantly influenced by Kareen.
Sept. 1	Altus declared and paid a cash dividend of $3.05 per share.
Dec. 31	Altus announced that net income for the year is $1,106,900.

2010

June 1	Altus declared and paid a cash dividend of $3.30 per share.
Dec. 31	Altus announced that net income for the year is $1,240,900.
Dec. 31	Kareen sold 11,000 shares of Altus for $294,250 cash.

Exercise 15-10
Return on total assets
A1

The following information is available from the financial statements of Interstate Industries. Compute Interstate's return on total assets for 2009 and 2010. (Round returns to one-tenth of a percent.) Comment on the company's efficiency in using its assets in 2009 and 2010.

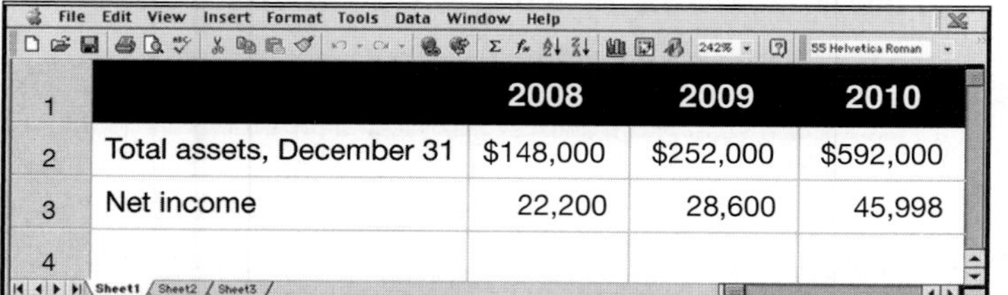

	2008	2009	2010
Total assets, December 31	$148,000	$252,000	$592,000
Net income	22,200	28,600	45,998

Exercise 15-11[A]
Foreign currency transactions
P5

Leigh of New York sells its products to customers in the United States and the United Kingdom. On December 16, 2009, Leigh sold merchandise on credit to Berton Ltd. of London at a price of 20,000 pounds. The exchange rate on that day for £1 was $2.0325. On December 31, 2009, when Leigh prepared its financial statements, the rate was £1 for $2.0292. Berton paid its bill in full on January 15, 2010, at which time the exchange rate was £1 for $2.0340. Leigh immediately exchanged the 20,000 pounds for U.S. dollars. Prepare Leigh's journal entries on December 16, December 31, and January 15 (round to the nearest dollar).

Exercise 15-12[A]
Computing foreign exchange gains and losses on receivables
C4 P5

On May 8, 2009, Jett Company (a U.S. company) made a credit sale to Munoz (a Mexican company). The terms of the sale required Munoz to pay 850,000 pesos on February 10, 2010. Jett prepares quarterly financial statements on March 31, June 30, September 30, and December 31. The exchange rates for pesos during the time the receivable is outstanding follow.

May 8, 2009	$0.0932
June 30, 2009	0.0941
September 30, 2009	0.0952
December 31, 2009	0.0935
February 10, 2010	0.0974

Compute the foreign exchange gain or loss that Jett should report on each of its quarterly income statements for the last three quarters of 2009 and the first quarter of 2010. Also compute the amount reported on Jett's balance sheets at the end of each of its last three quarters of 2009.

Available with McGraw-Hill's Homework Manager — McGraw-Hill's HOMEWORK MANAGER®

PROBLEM SET A

Problem 15-1A
Recording transactions and market adjustments for trading securities
C2 P1

Protom Company, which began operations in 2009, invests its idle cash in trading securities. The following transactions are from its short-term investments in its trading securities.

2009

Jan. 20	Purchased 800 shares of Ford Motor Co. at $26 per share plus a $120 commission.
Feb. 9	Purchased 2,600 shares of Lucent at $39 per share plus a $578 commission.
Oct. 12	Purchased 800 shares of Z-Seven at $7.50 per share plus a $200 commission.

2010

Apr. 15 Sold 800 shares of Ford Motor Co. at $30 per share less a $300 commission.
July 5 Sold 800 shares of Z-Seven at $11 per share less a $103 commission.
July 22 Purchased 2,000 shares of Hunt Corp. at $39 per share plus a $444 commission.
Aug. 19 Purchased 1,600 shares of Donna Karan at $19.50 per share plus a $290 commission.

2011

Feb. 27 Purchased 3,500 shares of HCA at $31 per share plus a $420 commission.
Mar. 3 Sold 2,000 shares of Hunt at $35 per share less a $250 commission.
June 21 Sold 2,600 shares of Lucent at $36.75 per share less a $420 commission.
June 30 Purchased 1,300 shares of Black & Decker at $47.50 per share plus a $595 commission.
Nov. 1 Sold 1,600 shares of Donna Karan at $19.50 per share less a $309 commission.

Required

1. Prepare journal entries to record these short-term investment activities for the years shown. (Ignore any year-end adjusting entries.)

2. On December 31, 2011, prepare the adjusting entry to record any necessary market adjustment for the portfolio of trading securities when HCA's share price is $33 and Black & Decker's share price is $43.50. (Assume the Market Adjustment—Trading account had an unadjusted balance of zero.)

Check (2) Dr. Market Adjustment—Trading $785

Problem 15-2A
Recording, adjusting, and reporting short-term available-for-sale securities
C2 P3

Freema Company had no short-term investments prior to year 2009. It had the following transactions involving short-term investments in available-for-sale securities during 2009.

Apr. 16 Purchased 8,000 shares of Gem Co. stock at $29.75 per share plus a $440 brokerage fee.
May 1 Paid $125,000 to buy 90-day U.S. Treasury bills (debt securities): $125,000 principal amount, 4% interest, securities dated May 1.
July 7 Purchased 4,000 shares of PepsiCo stock at $47.75 per share plus a $410 brokerage fee.
20 Purchased 2,000 shares of Xerox stock at $19.75 per share plus a $490 brokerage fee.
Aug. 3 Received a check for principal and accrued interest on the U.S. Treasury bills that matured on July 29.
15 Received a $0.90 per share cash dividend on the Gem Co. stock.
28 Sold 4,000 shares of Gem Co. stock at $36.50 per share less a $250 brokerage fee.
Oct. 1 Received a $1.75 per share cash dividend on the PepsiCo shares.
Dec. 15 Received a $1.05 per share cash dividend on the remaining Gem Co. shares.
31 Received a $1.30 per share cash dividend on the PepsiCo shares.

Required

1. Prepare journal entries to record the preceding transactions and events.

2. Prepare a table to compare the year-end cost and market values of Freema's short-term investments in available-for-sale securities. The year-end market values per share are: Gem Co., $32.00; PepsiCo, $45.00; and Xerox, $16.75.

Check (2) Cost = $350,620

3. Prepare an adjusting entry, if necessary, to record the year-end market adjustment for the portfolio of short-term investments in available-for-sale securities.

(3) Dr. Unrealized Loss—Equity $9,120

Analysis Component

4. Explain the balance sheet presentation of the market adjustment for Freema's short-term investments.

5. How do these short-term investments affect Freema's (*a*) income statement for year 2009 and (*b*) the equity section of its balance sheet at year-end 2009?

Problem 15-3A
Recording, adjusting, and reporting long-term available-for-sale securities
C2 P3

Tennant Security, which began operations in 2009, invests in long-term available-for-sale securities. Following is a series of transactions and events determining its long-term investment activity.

2009

Jan. 20 Purchased 1,200 shares of Johnson & Johnson at $20.50 per share plus a $240 commission.
Feb. 9 Purchased 1,000 shares of Sony at $46.20 per share plus a $220 commission.
June 12 Purchased 1,700 shares of Mattel at $28 per share plus a $195 commission.
Dec. 31 Per share market values for stocks in the portfolio are Johnson & Johnson, $21.50; Mattel, $26.50; Sony, $38.

2010

Apr. 15 Sold 1,200 shares of Johnson & Johnson at $23.50 per share less a $525 commission.
July 5 Sold 1,700 shares of Mattel at $26.50 per share less a $235 commission.
July 22 Purchased 500 shares of Sara Lee at $22.50 per share plus a $420 commission.
Aug. 19 Purchased 900 shares of Eastman Kodak at $14 per share plus a $198 commission.
Dec. 31 Per share market values for stocks in the portfolio are: Kodak, $16.25; Sara Lee, $20.00; Sony, $35.00.

2011

Feb. 27 Purchased 3,000 shares of Microsoft at $65 per share plus a $520 commission.
June 21 Sold 1,000 shares of Sony at $48.00 per share less an $880 commission.
June 30 Purchased 1,500 shares of Black & Decker at $38 per share plus a $435 commission.
Aug. 3 Sold 500 shares of Sara Lee at $16.25 per share less a $435 commission.
Nov. 1 Sold 900 shares of Eastman Kodak at $19.75 per share less a $625 commission.
Dec. 31 Per share market values for stocks in the portfolio are: Black & Decker, $41; Microsoft, $67.

Required

1. Prepare journal entries to record these transactions and events and any year-end market adjustments to the portfolio of long-term available-for-sale securities.

Check (2b) Market adjustment bal.: 12/31/09, $(10,205); 12/31/10; $(11,263)

2. Prepare a table that summarizes the (*a*) total cost, (*b*) total market adjustment, and (*c*) total market value of the portfolio of long-term available-for-sale securities at each year-end.

(3b) Unrealized Gain at 12/31/2011, $9,545

3. Prepare a table that summarizes (*a*) the realized gains and losses and (*b*) the unrealized gains or losses for the portfolio of long-term available-for-sale securities at each year-end.

Problem 15-4A
Long-term investment transactions; unrealized and realized gains and losses
C2 C3 P3 P4

Elevant Co.'s long-term available-for-sale portfolio at December 31, 2008, consists of the following.

Available-for-Sale Securities	Cost	Market Value
40,000 shares of Company A common stock	$535,300	$500,000
7,000 shares of Company B common stock	159,380	151,000
17,500 shares of Company C common stock	662,600	640,938

Elevant enters into the following long-term investment transactions during year 2009.

Jan. 29 Sold 3,500 shares of Company B common stock for $79,100 less a brokerage fee of $1,400.
Apr. 17 Purchased 9,900 shares of Company W common stock for $197,500 plus a brokerage fee of $2,300. The shares represent a 30% ownership in Company W.
July 6 Purchased 4,200 shares of Company X common stock for $118,125 plus a brokerage fee of $1,650. The shares represent a 10% ownership in Company X.
Aug. 22 Purchased 50,000 shares of Company Y common stock for $375,000 plus a brokerage fee of $1,100. The shares represent a 51% ownership in Company Y.
Nov. 13 Purchased 8,300 shares of Company Z common stock for $261,596 plus a brokerage fee of $2,350. The shares represent a 5% ownership in Company Z.
Dec. 9 Sold 40,000 shares of Company A common stock for $515,000 less a brokerage fee of $4,000.

The market values of its investments at December 31, 2009, are: B, $81,375; C, $610,312; W, $191,250; X, $110,250; Y, $531,250; and Z, $272,240.

Required

1. Determine the amount Elevant should report on its December 31, 2009, balance sheet for its long-term investments in available-for-sale securities.

Check (2) Cr. Unrealized Loss—Equity, $13,508

2. Prepare any necessary December 31, 2009, adjusting entry to record the market value adjustment for the long-term investments in available-for-sale securities.

3. What amount of gains or losses on transactions relating to long-term investments in available-for-sale securities should Elevant report on its December 31, 2009, income statement?

Problem 15-5A
Accounting for long-term investments in securities; with and without significant influence
C2 P3 P4

Selk Steel Co., which began operations on January 4, 2009, had the following subsequent transactions and events in its long-term investments.

2009

Jan. 5 Selk purchased 50,000 shares (20% of total) of Wulf's common stock for $1,567,000.
Oct. 23 Wulf declared and paid a cash dividend of $3.20 per share.
Dec. 31 Wulf's net income for 2009 is $1,164,000, and the market value of its stock at December 31 is $34 per share.

2010

Oct. 15 Wulf declared and paid a cash dividend of $2.50 per share.
Dec. 31 Wulf's net income for 2010 is $1,476,000, and the market value of its stock at December 31 is $36.00 per share.

2011

Jan. 2 Selk sold all of its investment in Wulf for $1,895,500 cash.

Part 1

Assume that Selk has a significant influence over Wulf with its 20% share of stock.

Required

1. Prepare journal entries to record these transactions and events for Selk.
2. Compute the carrying (book) value per share of Selk's investment in Wulf common stock as reflected in the investment account on January 1, 2011.
3. Compute the net increase or decrease in Selk's equity from January 5, 2009, through January 2, 2011, resulting from its investment in Wulf.

Check (2) Carrying value per share, $36.20

Part 2

Assume that although Selk owns 20% of Wulf's outstanding stock, circumstances indicate that it does not have a significant influence over the investee and that it is classified as an available-for-sale security investment.

Required

1. Prepare journal entries to record the preceding transactions and events for Selk. Also prepare an entry dated January 2, 2011, to remove any balance related to the market adjustment.
2. Compute the cost per share of Selk's investment in Wulf common stock as reflected in the investment account on January 1, 2011.
3. Compute the net increase or decrease in Selk's equity from January 5, 2009, through January 2, 2011, resulting from its investment in Wulf.

(1) 1/2/2011 Dr. Unrealized Gain—Equity $233,000

(3) Net increase, $613,500

Problem 15-6A[A]
Foreign currency transactions
C4 P5

Patriot Company, a U.S. corporation with customers in several foreign countries, had the following selected transactions for 2009 and 2010.

2009

Apr. 8 Sold merchandise to Salinas & Sons of Mexico for $27,456 cash. The exchange rate for pesos is $0.0932 on this day.
July 21 Sold merchandise on credit to Sumito Corp. in Japan. The price of 2.7 million yen is to be paid 120 days from the date of sale. The exchange rate for yen is $0.0082 on this day.
Oct. 14 Sold merchandise for 18,000 pounds to Smithers Ltd. of Great Britain, payment in full to be received in 90 days. The exchange rate for pounds is $2.0330 on this day.
Nov. 18 Received Sumito's payment in yen for its July 21 purchase and immediately exchanged the yen for dollars. The exchange rate for yen is $0.0079 on this day.
Dec. 20 Sold merchandise for 20,000 ringgits to Hamid Albar of Malaysia, payment in full to be received in 30 days. On this day, the exchange rate for ringgits is $0.2963.

Dec. 31 Recorded adjusting entries to recognize exchange gains or losses on Patriot's annual financial statements. Rates for exchanging foreign currencies on this day follow.

Pesos (Mexico)	$0.0937
Yen (Japan)	0.0075
Pounds (Britain)	2.0345
Ringgits (Malaysia)	0.2949

2010

Jan. 12 Received full payment in pounds from Smithers for the October 14 sale and immediately exchanged the pounds for dollars. The exchange rate for pounds is $2.0355 on this day.

Jan. 19 Received Hamid Albar's full payment in ringgits for the December 20 sale and immediately exchanged the ringgits for dollars. The exchange rate for ringgits is $0.2936 on this day.

Required

1. Prepare journal entries for the Patriot transactions and adjusting entries (round amounts to the nearest dollar).

Check (2) 2009 total foreign exchange loss, $811

2. Compute the foreign exchange gain or loss to be reported on Patriot's 2009 income statement.

Analysis Component

3. What actions might Patriot consider to reduce its risk of foreign exchange gains or losses?

PROBLEM SET B

Problem 15-1B
Recording transactions and market adjustments for trading securities

C2 P1

Harter Company, which began operations in 2009, invests its idle cash in trading securities. The following transactions relate to its short-term investments in its trading securities.

2009

Mar. 10 Purchased 900 shares of Timex at $28.00 per share plus a $125 commission.
May 7 Purchased 2,500 shares of MTV at $37.00 per share plus a $578 commission.
Sept. 1 Purchased 780 shares of UPS at $7.00 per share plus a $200 commission.

2010

Apr. 26 Sold 2,500 shares of MTV at $35.50 per share less a $295 commission.
Apr. 27 Sold 780 shares of UPS at $10.50 per share less a $103 commission.
June 2 Purchased 1,600 shares of SPW at $34.00 per share plus a $444 commission.
June 14 Purchased 1,600 shares of Wal-Mart at $20.00 per share plus a $290 commission.

2011

Jan. 28 Purchased 3,400 shares of PepsiCo at $38.00 per share plus a $400 commission.
Jan. 31 Sold 1,600 shares of SPW at $29.00 per share less a $250 commission.
Aug. 22 Sold 900 shares of Timex at $26.25 per share less a $420 commission.
Sept. 3 Purchased 1,500 shares of Vodaphone at $47.50 per share plus a $600 commission.
Oct. 9 Sold 1,600 shares of Wal-Mart at $22.50 per share less a $309 commission.

Required

1. Prepare journal entries to record these short-term investment activities for the years shown. (Ignore any year-end adjusting entries.)

Check (2) Cr. Market Adjustment—Trading $13,050

2. On December 31, 2011, prepare the adjusting entry to record any necessary market adjustment for the portfolio of trading securities when PepsiCo's share price is $36.00 and Vodaphone's share price is $44.00. (Assume the Market Adjustment—Trading account had an unadjusted balance of zero.)

Problem 15-2B
Recording, adjusting, and reporting short-term available-for-sale securities
C2 P3

SP Systems had no short-term investments prior to 2009. It had the following transactions involving short-term investments in available-for-sale securities during 2009.

Feb.	6	Purchased 6,000 shares of Nokia stock at $24.75 per share plus a $400 brokerage fee.
	15	Paid $250,000 to buy six-month U.S. Treasury bills (debt securities): $250,000 principal amount, 4% interest, securities dated February 15.
Apr.	7	Purchased 3,000 shares of Dell Co. stock at $49.25 per share plus a $370 brokerage fee.
June	2	Purchased 1,500 shares of Merck stock at $18.25 per share plus a $450 brokerage fee.
	30	Received a $0.19 per share cash dividend on the Nokia shares.
Aug.	11	Sold 1,500 shares of Nokia stock at $29.50 per share less a $490 brokerage fee.
	16	Received a check for principal and accrued interest on the U.S. Treasury bills purchased February 15.
	24	Received a $0.16 per share cash dividend on the Dell shares.
Nov.	9	Received a $0.20 per share cash dividend on the remaining Nokia shares.
Dec.	18	Received a $0.21 per share cash dividend on the Dell shares.

Required

1. Prepare journal entries to record the preceding transactions and events.

2. Prepare a table to compare the year-end cost and market values of the short-term investments in available-for-sale securities. The year-end market values per share are: Nokia, $23.50; Dell, $55.50; and Merck, $15.25.

Check (2) Cost = $287,620

3. Prepare an adjusting entry, if necessary, to record the year-end market adjustment for the portfolio of short-term investments in available-for-sale securities.

(3) Cr. Unrealized Gain—Equity, $7,505

Analysis Component

4. Explain the balance sheet presentation of the market adjustment to SP's short-term investments.

5. How do these short-term investments affect (*a*) its income statement for year 2009 and (*b*) the equity section of its balance sheet at the 2009 year-end?

Problem 15-3B
Recording, adjusting, and reporting long-term available-for-sale securities
C2 P3

Bleeker Enterprises, which began operations in 2009, invests in long-term available-for-sale securities. Following is a series of transactions and events involving its long-term investment activity.

2009

Mar. 10	Purchased 1,000 shares of Apple at $23.00 per share plus $240 commission.
Apr. 7	Purchased 1,300 shares of Ford at $46.20 per share plus $225 commission.
Sept. 1	Purchased 1,500 shares of Polaroid at $25.00 per share plus $195 commission.
Dec. 31	Per share market values for stocks in the portfolio are: Apple, $24.00; Ford, $42.00; Polaroid, $27.00.

2010

Apr. 26	Sold 1,300 shares of Ford at $44.00 per share less a $250 commission.
June 2	Purchased 1,800 shares of Duracell at $19.25 per share plus a $235 commission.
June 14	Purchased 600 shares of Sears at $22.50 per share plus a $470 commission.
Nov. 27	Sold 1,500 shares of Polaroid at $29 per share less a $198 commission.
Dec. 31	Per share market values for stocks in the portfolio are: Apple, $26.00; Duracell, $18.00; Sears, $25.00.

2011

Jan. 28	Purchased 2,000 shares of Coca-Cola Co. at $69 per share plus a $530 commission.
Aug. 22	Sold 1,000 shares of Apple at $20.00 per share less a $280 commission.
Sept. 3	Purchased 2,000 shares of Motorola at $36 per share plus a $435 commission.
Oct. 9	Sold 600 shares of Sears at $26.25 per share less a $435 commission.
Oct. 31	Sold 1,800 shares of Duracell at $15.00 per share less a $425 commission.
Dec. 31	Per share market values for stocks in the portfolio are: Coca-Cola, $75.00; Motorola, $32.00.

Required

1. Prepare journal entries to record these transactions and events and any year-end market adjustments to the portfolio of long-term available-for-sale securities.

2. Prepare a table that summarizes the (*a*) total cost, (*b*) total market adjustment, and (*c*) total market value for the portfolio of long-term available-for-sale securities at each year-end.

3. Prepare a table that summarizes (*a*) the realized gains and losses and (*b*) the unrealized gains or losses for the portfolio of long-term available-for-sale securities at each year-end.

Check (2b) Market adjustment bal.: 12/31/09, $(2,120); 12/31/10, $1,305

(3b) Unrealized Gain at 12/31/2011, $3,035

Problem 15-4B

Long-term investment transactions; unrealized and realized gains and losses

C2 C3 P3 P4

Chavez's long-term available-for-sale portfolio at December 31, 2008, consists of the following.

Available-for-Sale Securities	Cost	Market Value
55,000 shares of Company R common stock	$1,118,250	$1,198,000
17,000 shares of Company S common stock	600,600	586,500
22,000 shares of Company T common stock	294,590	303,600

Chavez enters into the following long-term investment transactions during year 2009.

Jan. 13 Sold 4,250 shares of Company S stock for $145,500 less a brokerage fee of $650.

Mar. 24 Purchased 31,000 shares of Company U common stock for $565,750 plus a brokerage fee of $1,980. The shares represent a 62% ownership interest in Company U.

Apr. 5 Purchased 85,000 shares of Company V common stock for $267,750 plus a brokerage fee of $1,125. The shares represent a 10% ownership in Company V.

Sept. 2 Sold 22,000 shares of Company T common stock for $313,500 less a brokerage fee of $2,700.

Sept. 27 Purchased 5,000 shares of Company W common stock for $101,000 plus a brokerage fee of $350. The shares represent a 25% ownership interest in Company W.

Oct. 30 Purchased 10,000 shares of Company X common stock for $97,500 plus a brokerage fee of $300. The shares represent a 13% ownership interest in Company X.

The market values of its investments at December 31, 2009, are: R, $1,136,250; S, $420,750; U, $545,600; V, $269,876; W, $109,378; and X, $91,250.

Required

1. Determine the amount Chavez should report on its December 31, 2009, balance sheet for its long-term investments in available-for-sale securities.

2. Prepare any necessary December 31, 2009, adjusting entry to record the market value adjustment of the long-term investments in available-for-sale securities.

3. What amount of gains or losses on transactions relating to long-term investments in available-for-sale securities should Chavez report on its December 31, 2009, income statement?

Check (2) Dr. Unrealized Gain—Equity, $74,660; Cr. Market Adjustment, $91,909

Problem 15-5B

Accounting for long-term investments in securities; with and without significant influence

C2 P3 P4

Devin Company, which began operations on January 3, 2009, had the following subsequent transactions and events in its long-term investments.

2009

Jan. 5 Devin purchased 25,000 shares (25% of total) of Bloch's common stock for $401,000.

Aug. 1 Bloch declared and paid a cash dividend of $1.10 per share.

Dec. 31 Bloch's net income for 2009 is $164,000, and the market value of its stock is $17.50 per share.

2010

Aug. 1 Bloch declared and paid a cash dividend of $1.30 per share.

Dec. 31 Bloch's net income for 2010 is $156,000, and the market value of its stock is $19.25 per share.

2011

Jan. 8 Devin sold all of its investment in Bloch for $550,000 cash.

Part 1

Assume that Devin has a significant influence over Bloch with its 25% share.

Required

1. Prepare journal entries to record these transactions and events for Devin.
2. Compute the carrying (book) value per share of Devin's investment in Bloch common stock as reflected in the investment account on January 7, 2011.
3. Compute the net increase or decrease in Devin's equity from January 5, 2009, through January 8, 2011, resulting from its investment in Bloch.

Check (2) Carrying value per share, $16.84

Part 2

Assume that although Devin owns 25% of Bloch's outstanding stock, circumstances indicate that it does not have a significant influence over the investee and that it is classified as an available-for-sale security investment.

Required

1. Prepare journal entries to record these transactions and events for Devin. Also prepare an entry dated January 8, 2011, to remove any balance related to the market adjustment.
2. Compute the cost per share of Devin's investment in Bloch common stock as reflected in the investment account on January 7, 2011.
3. Compute the net increase or decrease in Devin's equity from January 5, 2009, through January 8, 2011, resulting from its investment in Bloch.

(1) 1/8/2011 Dr. Unrealized Gain—Equity $80,250

(3) Net increase, $209,000

Problem 15-6B[A]
Foreign currency transactions
C4 P5

Kitna, a U.S. corporation with customers in several foreign countries, had the following selected transactions for 2009 and 2010.

2009

May 26 Sold merchandise for 5.5 million yen to Fuji Company of Japan, payment in full to be received in 60 days. On this day, the exchange rate for yen is $0.0088.

June 1 Sold merchandise to Fordham Ltd. of Great Britain for $73,500 cash. The exchange rate for pounds is $2.0331 on this day.

July 25 Received Fuji's payment in yen for its May 26 purchase and immediately exchanged the yen for dollars. The exchange rate for yen is $0.0087 on this day.

Oct. 15 Sold merchandise on credit to Martinez Brothers of Mexico. The price of 425,000 pesos is to be paid 90 days from the date of sale. On this day, the exchange rate for pesos is $0.0932.

Dec. 6 Sold merchandise for 300,000 yuans to Chi-Ying Company of China, payment in full to be received in 30 days. The exchange rate for yuans is $0.1335 on this day.

Dec. 31 Recorded adjusting entries to recognize exchange gains or losses on Kitna's annual financial statements. Rates of exchanging foreign currencies on this day follow.

Yen (Japan)	$0.0089
Pounds (Britain)	2.0402
Pesos (Mexico)	0.0994
Yuans (China)	0.1351

2010

Jan. 5 Received Chi-Ying's full payment in yuans for the December 6 sale and immediately exchanged the yuans for dollars. The exchange rate for yuans is $0.1372 on this day.

Jan. 13 Received full payment in pesos from Martinez for the October 15 sale and immediately exchanged the pesos for dollars. The exchange rate for pesos is $0.0960 on this day.

Required

1. Prepare journal entries for the Kitna transactions and adjusting entries.
2. Compute the foreign exchange gain or loss to be reported on Kitna's 2009 income statement.

Check 2009 total foreign exchange gain, $2,565

Analysis Component

3. What actions might Kitna consider to reduce its risk of foreign exchange gains or losses?

SERIAL PROBLEM

Success Systems

(This serial problem began in Chapter 1 and continues through most of the book. If previous chapter segments were not completed, the serial problem can begin at this point. It is helpful, but not necessary, to use the Working Papers that accompany the book.)

SP 15 While reviewing the March 31, 2010, balance sheet of Success Systems, Adriana Lopez notes that the business has built a large cash balance of $77,845. Its most recent bank money market statement shows that the funds are earning an annualized return of 0.75%. Lopez decides to make several investments with the desire to earn a higher return on the idle cash balance. Accordingly, in April 2010, Success Systems makes the following investments in trading securities:

April 16 Purchases 400 shares of Johnson & Johnson stock at $50 per share plus $300 commission.
April 30 Purchases 200 shares of Starbucks Corporation at $22 per share plus $250 commission.

On June 30, 2010, the per share market price of the Johnson & Johnson shares is $55 and the Starbucks shares is $19.

Required

1. Prepare journal entries to record the April purchases of trading securities by Success Systems.
2. On June 30, 2010, prepare the adjusting entry to record any necessary market adjustment to its portfolio of trading securities.

BEYOND THE NUMBERS

REPORTING IN ACTION

C3 C4 A1 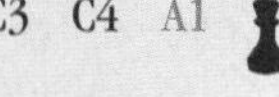

BTN 15-1 Refer to **Best Buy**'s financial statements in Appendix A to answer the following.

1. Are Best Buy's financial statements consolidated? How can you tell?
2. What is Best Buy's *comprehensive income* for the year ended March 3, 2007?
3. Does Best Buy have any foreign operations? How can you tell?
4. Compute Best Buy's return on total assets for the year ended March 3, 2007.

Fast Forward

5. Access Best Buy's annual report for a fiscal year ending after March 3, 2007, from either its Website (BestBuy.com) or the SEC's EDGAR database (www.sec.gov). Recompute Best Buy's return on total assets for the years subsequent to March 3, 2007.

COMPARATIVE ANALYSIS

A1 

BTN 15-2 Key figures for **Best Buy**, **Circuit City**, and **RadioShack** follow.

($ millions)	Best Buy			Circuit City			RadioShack		
	Current Year	1 Year Prior	2 Years Prior	Current Year	1 Year Prior	2 Years Prior	Current Year	1 Year Prior	2 Years Prior
Net income	$ 1,377	$ 1,140	$ 984	$ (8)	$ 140	$ 62	$ 73	$ 267	$ 337
Net sales	35,934	30,848	27,433	12,430	11,514	10,414	4,778	5,082	4,841
Total assets	13,570	11,864	10,294	4,007	4,069	3,840	2,070	2,205	2,517

Required

1. Compute return on total assets for Best Buy, Circuit City, and RadioShack for the two most recent years.
2. Separate the return on total assets computed in part 1 into its components for all three companies and both years according to the formula in Exhibit 15.9.
3. Which company has the highest total return on assets? The highest profit margin? The highest total asset turnover? What does this comparative analysis reveal? (Assume an industry average of 8.2% for return on assets.)

BTN 15-3 Kaylee Wecker is the controller for Wildcat Company, which has numerous long-term investments in debt securities. Wildcat's investments are mainly in 10-year bonds. Wecker is preparing its year-end financial statements. In accounting for long-term debt securities, she knows that each long-term investment must be designated as a held-to-maturity or an available-for-sale security. Interest rates rose sharply this past year causing the portfolio's market value to substantially decline. The company does not intend to hold the bonds for the entire 10 years. Wecker also earns a bonus each year, which is computed as a percent of net income.

ETHICS CHALLENGE

C2 P2 P3

Required

1. Will Wecker's bonus depend in any way on the classification of the debt securities? Explain.
2. What criteria must Wecker use to classify the securities as held-to-maturity or available-for-sale?
3. Is there likely any company oversight of Wecker's classification of the securities? Explain.

BTN 15-4 Assume that you are Jackson Company's accountant. Company owner Abel Terrio has reviewed the 2009 financial statements you prepared and questions the $6,000 loss reported on the sale of its investment in Blackhawk Co. common stock. Jackson acquired 50,000 shares of Blackhawk's common stock on December 31, 2007, at a cost of $500,000. This stock purchase represented a 40% interest in Blackhawk. The 2008 income statement reported that earnings from all investments were $126,000. On January 3, 2009, Jackson Company sold the Blackhawk stock for $575,000. Blackhawk did not pay any dividends during 2008 but reported a net income of $202,500 for that year. Terrio believes that because the Blackhawk stock purchase price was $500,000 and was sold for $575,000, the 2009 income statement should report a $75,000 gain on the sale.

COMMUNICATING IN PRACTICE

C2 P4 

Required

Draft a one-half page memorandum to Terrio explaining why the $6,000 loss on sale of Blackhawk stock is correctly reported.

BTN 15-5 Access the August 3, 2007, 10-K filing (for year-end June 30, 2007) of Microsoft (MSFT) at www.SEC.gov. Review its note 3, "Investments."

TAKING IT TO THE NET

C1 C2 

Required

1. How does the cost-basis total for its investments as of June 30, 2007, compare to the prior year-end amount?
2. Identify at least eight types of short-term investments held by Microsoft as of June 30, 2007.
3. What were Microsoft's unrealized gains and its unrealized losses from its investments for 2007?
4. Was the cost or market ("recorded") value of the investments higher as of June 30, 2007?

BTN 15-6 Each team member is to become an expert on a specific classification of long-term investments. This expertise will be used to facilitate other teammates' understanding of the concepts and procedures relevent to the classification chosen.

TEAMWORK IN ACTION

C1 C2 C3 P1 P2 P3 P4

1. Each team member must select an area for expertise by choosing one of the following classifications of long-term investments.
   a. Held-to-maturity debt securities
   b. Available-for-sale debt and equity securities
   c. Equity securities with significant influence
   d. Equity securities with controlling influence
2. Learning teams are to disburse and expert teams are to be formed. Expert teams are made up of those who select the same area of expertise. The instructor will identify the location where each expert team will meet.
3. Expert teams will collaborate to develop a presentation based on the following requirements. Students must write the presentation in a format they can show to their learning teams in part (4).

Requirements for Expert Presentation

a. Write a transaction for the acquisition of this type of investment security. The transaction description is to include all necessary data to reflect the chosen classification.

b. Prepare the journal entry to record the acquisition.

[*Note:* The expert team on equity securities with controlling influence will substitute requirements (*d*) and (*e*) with a discussion of the reporting of these investments.]

c. Identify information necessary to complete the end-of-period adjustment for this investment.

d. Assuming that this is the only investment owned, prepare any necessary year-end entries.

e. Present the relevant balance sheet section(s).

4. Re-form learning teams. In rotation, experts are to present to their teams the presentations they developed in part 3. Experts are to encourage and respond to questions.

ENTREPRENEURIAL DECISION

C4 P5 

BTN 15-7[A] Refer to the opening feature in this chapter about Amy Smilovic and her company, Tibi. Assume that Amy must acquire the Japanese rights to certain clothing designs that will then be produced for sale to U.S. consumers. Amy acquires those rights on January 1, 2008, from a Japanese distributor and agrees to pay 12,000,000 yen per year for those rights. Quarterly payments are due March 31, June 30, September 30, and December 31 each year. On January 1, 2008, the yen is worth $0.00891.

Required

1. Prepare the journal entry to record the rights purchased on January 1, 2008.

2. Prepare the journal entries to record the payments on March 31, June 30, September 30, and December 31, 2008. The value of the yen on those dates follows.

March 31	$0.00893
June 30	0.00901
September 30	0.00902
December 31	0.00897

3. How can Amy protect herself from unanticipated gains and losses from currency translation if all of her payments are specified to be paid in yen?

HITTING THE ROAD

C4

BTN 15-8[A] Assume that you are planning a spring break trip to Europe. Identify three locations where you can find exchange rates for the dollar relative to the Euro or other currencies.

GLOBAL DECISION

A1

BTN 15-9 DSG international, Best Buy, Circuit City, and RadioShack are competitors in the global marketplace. Following are selected data from each company.

	DSG (£ millions)			Best Buy		Circuit City		RadioShack	
Key Figure	Current Year	One Year Prior	Two Years Prior	Current Year	Prior Year	Current Year	Prior Year	Current Year	Prior Year
Net income . . .	£ 18	£ 256	£ 212	—	—	—	—	—	—
Total assets . . .	3,977	4,120	4,104	—	—	—	—	—	—
Net sales	7,930	6,984	7,072	—	—	—	—	—	—
Profit margin . .	?	?	—	3.8%	3.7%	(0.1)%	1.2%	1.5%	5.3%
Total asset turnover	?	?	—	2.8	2.8	3.1	2.9	2.2	2.2

Required

1. Compute DSG's return on total assets for the most recent two years using the data provided.
2. Which of these four companies has the highest return on total assets? Highest profit margin? Highest total asset turnover?

ANSWERS TO MULTIPLE CHOICE QUIZ

1. d; $30,000 × 5% × 5/12 = $625
2. a; Unrealized gain = $84,500 − $83,000 = $1,500
3. b; $50,000 × 35% = $17,500
4. e; $300,000/$2,000,000 = 15%
5. b; Profit margin = $80,000/$600,000 = 13.3%
   Total asset turnover = $600,000/$400,000 = 1.5

A Look Back

Chapter 15 focused on how to identify, account for, and report investments in securities. We also accounted for transactions listed in a foreign currency.

A Look at This Chapter

This chapter focuses on reporting and analyzing cash inflows and cash outflows. We emphasize how to prepare and interpret the statement of cash flows.

A Look Ahead

Chapter 17 focuses on tools to help us analyze financial statements. We also describe comparative analysis and the application of ratios for financial analysis.

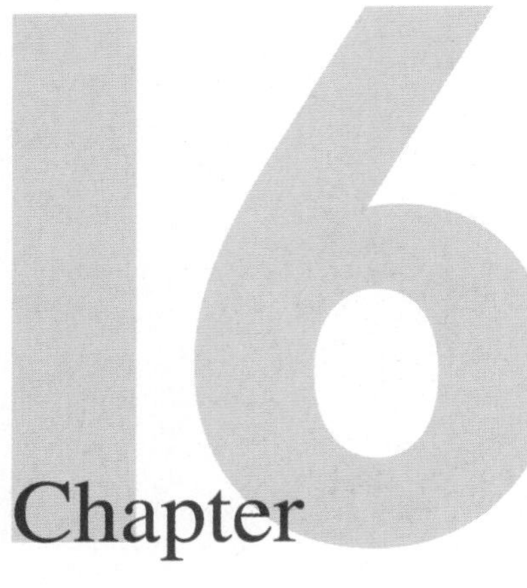

Chapter 16

Reporting the Statement of Cash Flows

Learning Objectives

CAP

Conceptual

C1 Explain the purpose and importance of cash flow information. *(p. 628)*

C2 Distinguish between operating, investing, and financing activities. *(p. 629)*

C3 Identify and disclose noncash investing and financing activities. *(p. 631)*

C4 Describe the format of the statement of cash flows. *(p. 631)*

Analytical

A1 Analyze the statement of cash flows. *(p. 645)*

A2 Compute and apply the cash flow on total assets ratio. *(p. 646)*

Procedural

P1 Prepare a statement of cash flows. *(p. 632)*

P2 Compute cash flows from operating activities using the indirect method. *(p. 635)*

P3 Determine cash flows from both investing and financing activities. *(p. 641)*

P4 *Appendix 16A*—Illustrate use of a spreadsheet to prepare a statement of cash flows. *(p. 649)*

P5 *Appendix 16B*—Compute cash flows from operating activities using the direct method. *(p. 652)*

LP16

Decision Feature

Wizard of Odd

"If you put enough energy into your dream, you can make anything happen" —Jim Bonaminio

FAIRFIELD, OH—Jim Bonaminio built his roadside produce stand while living in an abandoned gas station. "I would get up and leave at 4 in the morning to buy everything fresh [and] my wife opened the market at 8 a.m.," recalls Jim. "By 10 o'clock at night, we'd be sitting on the bed balancing the register receipts . . . we worked seven days a week." The fruit of those early efforts is **Jungle Jim's International Market (JungleJims.com).**

Jungle Jim's is no Wal-Mart wannabe, but it is arguably America's wackiest supermarket. Instead of trying to beat the big chains at the price-squeezing game, Jim's is a funhouse maze of a store. A seven-foot Elvis lion sings "Jailhouse Rock," an antique fire engine rests atop cases of hot sauce, port-a-potties lead to fancy restrooms, and Robin Hood greets customers with English food set within a 30-foot-tall Sherwood Forest. This is just a sampling.

"If you don't go out on a limb, then you're just like everybody else," insists Jim. "The stuff I've collected—all sorts of weird stuff—gets reused." Despite the wackiness, Jim is first and foremost a businessman. He learned firsthand about the importance of monitoring cash inflows and cash outflows. In the early days, recalls Jim, it was all about sales and profits. Then inventory and asset growth yielded negative cash flows, and Jim was in a pinch. That's when he realized that tracking cash flows was important, explains Jim.

Jim eventually learned how to monitor and control cash flows for each of his operating, investing, and financing activities. Today, says Jim, "I hire professional people to [help me monitor cash] . . . and to look for ways to make money." Yet Jim explains that he always reviews the statement of cash flows and the individual cash inflows and outflows.

Cash management has not curtailed Jim's fun-loving approach to business. "I'm trying to create something that has never been done," laughs Jim. "I just want to see if I can do it and have fun."

[Sources: *Jungle Jim's Website,* January 2009; *BusinessWeek,* April 2005; *Country Living,* November 2004; *Miamian,* Summer 2004; *Plain Dealer,* November 2004; *Supermarket News,* September 2006; *Cintas,* August 2007]

Chapter Preview

A company cannot achieve or maintain profits without carefully managing cash. Managers and other users of information pay attention to a company's cash position and the events and transactions affecting cash. This chapter explains how we prepare, analyze, and interpret a statement of cash flows. It also discusses the importance of cash flow information for predicting future performance and making managerial decisions. More generally, effectively using the statement of cash flows is crucial for managing and analyzing the operating, investing, and financing activities of businesses.

Reporting the Statement of Cash Flows

Basics of Cash Flow Reporting
- Purpose
- Importance
- Measurement
- Classification
- Noncash activities
- Format and preparation

Cash Flows from Operating
- Indirect and direct methods of reporting
- Application of indirect method of reporting
- Summary of indirect method adjustments

Cash Flows from Investing
- Three-stage process of analysis
- Analysis of noncurrent assets
- Analysis of other assets

Cash Flows from Financing
- Three-stage process of analysis
- Analysis of noncurrent liabilities
- Analysis of equity

Basics of Cash Flow Reporting

This section describes the basics of cash flow reporting, including its purpose, measurement, classification, format, and preparation.

Purpose of the Statement of Cash Flows

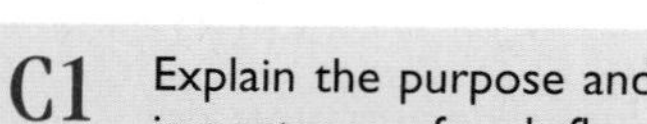

C1 Explain the purpose and importance of cash flow information.

The purpose of the **statement of cash flows** is to report cash receipts (inflows) and cash payments (outflows) during a period. This includes separately identifying the cash flows related to operating, investing, and financing activities. The statement of cash flows does more than simply report changes in cash. It is the detailed disclosure of individual cash flows that makes this statement useful to users. Information in this statement helps users answer questions such as these:

- How does a company obtain its cash?
- Where does a company spend its cash?
- What explains the change in the cash balance?

Point: Internal users rely on the statement of cash flows to make investing and financing decisions. External users rely on this statement to assess the amount and timing of a company's cash flows.

The statement of cash flows addresses important questions such as these by summarizing, classifying, and reporting a company's cash inflows and cash outflows for each period.

Importance of Cash Flows

Information about cash flows can influence decision makers in important ways. For instance, we look more favorably at a company that is financing its expenditures with cash from operations than one that does it by selling its assets. Information about cash flows helps users decide whether a company has enough cash to pay its existing debts as they mature. It is also relied upon to evaluate a company's ability to meet unexpected obligations and pursue unexpected opportunities. External information users especially want to assess a company's ability to take advantage of new business opportunities. Internal users such as managers use cash flow information to plan day-to-day operating activities and make long-term investment decisions.

Macy's striking turnaround is an example of how analysis and management of cash flows can lead to improved financial stability. Several years ago Macy's obtained temporary protection from bankruptcy, at which time it desperately needed to improve its cash flows. It did so by engaging in aggressive cost-cutting measures. As a result, Macy's annual cash flow rose to $210 million, up from a negative cash flow of $38.9 million in the prior year. Macy's eventually met its financial obligations and then successfully merged with **Federated Department Stores**.

The case of W. T. Grant Co. is a classic example of the importance of cash flow information in predicting a company's future performance and financial strength. Grant reported net income of more than $40 million per year for three consecutive years. At that same time, it was experiencing an alarming decrease in cash provided by operations. For instance, net cash outflow was more than $90 million by the end of that three-year period. Grant soon went bankrupt. Users who relied solely on Grant's income numbers were unpleasantly surprised. This reminds us that cash flows as well as income statement and balance sheet information are crucial in making business decisions.

Video16.1

Decision Insight

Cash Savvy "A lender must have a complete understanding of a borrower's cash flows to assess both the borrowing needs and repayment sources. This requires information about the major types of cash inflows and outflows. I have seen many companies, whose financial statements indicate good profitability, experience severe financial problems because the owners or managers lacked a good understanding of cash flows."—Mary E. Garza, Bank of America

Measurement of Cash Flows

Cash flows are defined to include both *cash* and *cash equivalents*. The statement of cash flows explains the difference between the beginning and ending balances of cash and cash equivalents. We continue to use the phrases *cash flows* and the *statement of cash flows,* but we must remember that both phrases refer to cash and cash equivalents. Recall that a cash equivalent must satisfy two criteria: (1) be readily convertible to a known amount of cash and (2) be sufficiently close to its maturity so its market value is unaffected by interest rate changes. In most cases, a debt security must be within three months of its maturity to satisfy these criteria. Companies must disclose and follow a clear policy for determining cash and cash equivalents and apply it consistently from period to period. American Express, for example, defines its cash equivalents as "time deposits and other highly liquid investments with original maturities of 90 days or less."

Classification of Cash Flows

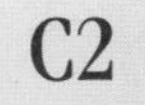

C2 Distinguish between operating, investing, and financing activities.

Since cash and cash equivalents are combined, the statement of cash flows does not report transactions between cash and cash equivalents such as cash paid to purchase cash equivalents and cash received from selling cash equivalents. However, all other cash receipts and cash payments are classified and reported on the statement as operating, investing, or financing activities. Individual cash receipts and payments for each of these three categories are labeled to identify their originating transactions or events. A net cash inflow (source) occurs when the receipts in a category exceed the payments. A net cash outflow (use) occurs when the payments in a category exceed the receipts.

Operating Activities **Operating activities** include those transactions and events that determine net income. Examples are the production and purchase of merchandise, the sale of goods and services to customers, and the expenditures to administer the business. Not all items in income, such as unusual gains and losses, are operating activities (we discuss these exceptions later in the chapter). Exhibit 16.1 lists the more common cash inflows and outflows from operating activities. (Although cash receipts and cash payments from buying and selling trading

EXHIBIT 16.1

Cash Flows from Operating Activities

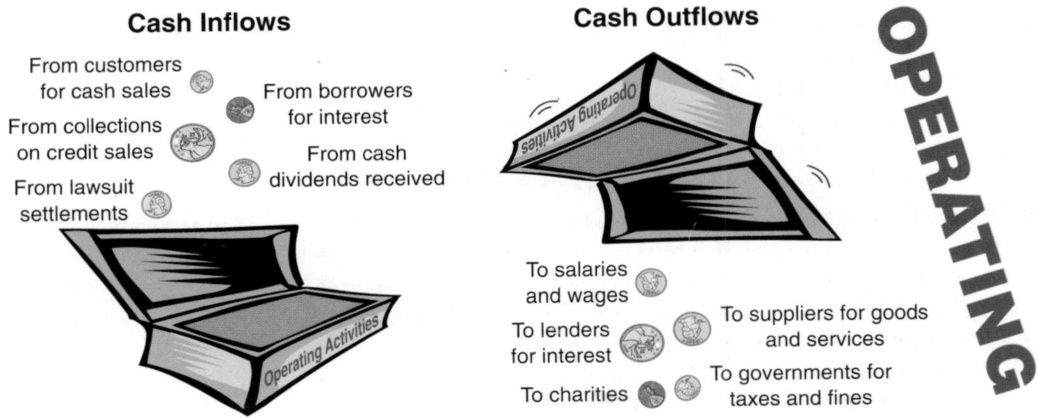

securities are often reported under operating activities, new standards require that these receipts and payments be classified based on the nature and purpose of those securities.)

Investing Activities **Investing activities** generally include those transactions and events that affect long-term assets—namely, the purchase and sale of long-term assets. They also include (1) the purchase and sale of short-term investments in the securities of other entities, other than cash equivalents and trading securities and (2) lending and collecting money for notes receivable. Exhibit 16.2 lists examples of cash flows from investing activities. Proceeds from collecting the principal amounts of notes deserve special mention. If the note results from sales to customers, its cash receipts are classed as operating activities whether short-term or long-term. If the note results from a loan to another party apart from sales, however, the cash receipts from collecting the note principal are classed as an investing activity. The FASB requires that the collection of interest on loans be reported as an operating activity.

Point: The FASB requires that *cash dividends received* and *cash interest received* be reported as operating activities.

EXHIBIT 16.2

Cash Flows from Investing Activities

Cash Inflows
From selling investments in securities
From collecting principal on loans
From selling (discounting) of notes
From selling long-term productive assets
Investing Activities

Cash Outflows
Investing Activities
To make loans to others
To purchase long-term productive assets
To purchase investments in securities
INVESTING

Financing Activities **Financing activities** include those transactions and events that affect long-term liabilities and equity. Examples are (1) obtaining cash from issuing debt and repaying the amounts borrowed and (2) receiving cash from or distributing cash to owners. These activities involve transactions with a company's owners and creditors. They also often involve borrowing and repaying principal amounts relating to both short- and long-term debt. GAAP requires that payments of interest expense be classified as operating activities. Also, cash payments to settle credit purchases of merchandise, whether on account or by note, are operating activities. Exhibit 16.3 lists examples of cash flows from financing activities.

EXHIBIT 16.3

Cash Flows from Financing Activities

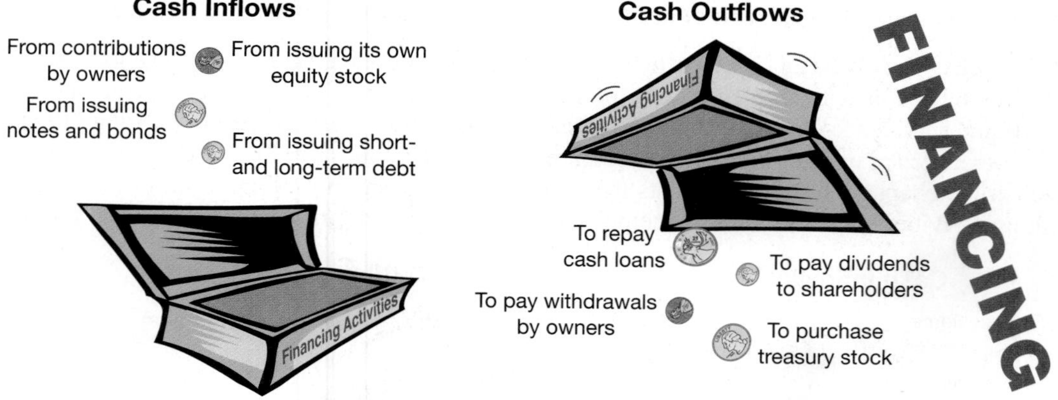

Point: Interest payments on a loan are classified as operating activities, but payments of loan principal are financing activities.

Decision Insight

Cash Reporting Cash flows can be delayed or accelerated at the end of a period to improve or reduce current period cash flows. Also, cash flows can be misclassified. Cash outflows reported under operations are interpreted as expense payments. However, cash outflows reported under investing activities are interpreted as a positive sign of growth potential. Thus, managers face incentives to misclassify cash flows. For these reasons, cash flow reporting warrants our scrutiny.

Noncash Investing and Financing

C3 Identify and disclose noncash investing and financing activities.

When important investing and financing activities do not affect cash receipts or payments, they are still disclosed at the bottom of the statement of cash flows or in a note to the statement because of their importance and the *full-disclosure principle*. One example of such a transaction is the purchase of long-term assets using a long-term note payable (loan). This transaction involves both investing and financing activities but does not affect any cash inflow or outflow and is not reported in any of the three sections of the statement of cash flows. This disclosure rule also extends to transactions with partial cash receipts or payments.

To illustrate, assume that Goorin purchases land for $12,000 by paying $5,000 cash and trading in used equipment worth $7,000. The investing section of the statement of cash flows reports only the $5,000 cash outflow for the land purchase. The $12,000 investing transaction is only partially described in the body of the statement of cash flows, yet this information is potentially important to users because it changes the makeup of assets. Goorin could either describe the transaction in a footnote or include information at the bottom of its statement that lists the $12,000 land purchase along with the cash financing of $5,000 and a $7,000 trade-in of equipment. As another example, Borg Co. acquired $900,000 of assets in exchange for $200,000 cash and a $700,000 long-term note, which should be reported as follows:

Point: A stock dividend transaction involving a transfer from retained earnings to common stock or a credit to contributed capital is *not* considered a noncash investing and financing activity because the company receives no consideration for shares issued.

Fair value of assets acquired	$900,000
Less cash paid	200,000
Liabilities incurred or assumed	$700,000

Exhibit 16.4 lists transactions commonly disclosed as noncash investing and financing activities.

EXHIBIT 16.4

Examples of Noncash Investing and Financing Activities

- Retirement of debt by issuing equity stock.
- Conversion of preferred stock to common stock.
- Lease of assets in a capital lease transaction.
- Purchase of long-term assets by issuing a note or bond.
- Exchange of noncash assets for other noncash assets.
- Purchase of noncash assets by issuing equity or debt.

Format of the Statement of Cash Flows

C4 Describe the format of the statement of cash flows.

Accounting standards require companies to include a statement of cash flows in a complete set of financial statements. This statement must report information about a company's cash receipts and cash payments during the period. Exhibit 16.5 shows the usual format. A company must report cash flows from three activities: operating, investing, and financing. The statement explains how transactions and events impact the prior period-end cash (and cash equivalents) balance to produce its current period-end balance.

EXHIBIT 16.5

Format of the Statement of Cash Flows

COMPANY NAME
Statement of Cash Flows
For *period* Ended *date*

Cash flows from operating activities	
[List of individual inflows and outflows]	
Net cash provided (used) by operating activities	$ #
Cash flows from investing activities	
[List of individual inflows and outflows]	
Net cash provided (used) by investing activities	#
Cash flows from financing activities	
[List of individual inflows and outflows]	
Net cash provided (used) by financing activities	#
Net increase (decrease) in cash	$ #
Cash (and equivalents) balance at prior period-end	#
Cash (and equivalents) balance at current period-end	$ #

Separate schedule or note disclosure of any "noncash investing and financing transactions" is required.

Decision Maker

Entrepreneur You are considering purchasing a start-up business that recently reported a $110,000 annual net loss and a $225,000 annual net cash inflow. How are these results possible? [Answer—p. 658]

Quick Check

Answers—p. 658

1. Does a statement of cash flows report the cash payments to purchase cash equivalents? Does it report the cash receipts from selling cash equivalents?
2. Identify the three categories of cash flows reported separately on the statement of cash flows.
3. Identify the cash activity category for each transaction: (*a*) purchase equipment for cash, (*b*) cash payment of wages, (*c*) sale of common stock for cash, (*d*) receipt of cash dividends from stock investment, (*e*) cash collection from customers, (*f*) notes issued for cash.

Preparing the Statement of Cash Flows

P1 Prepare a statement of cash flows.

Preparing a statement of cash flows involves five steps: (1) compute the net increase or decrease in cash; (2) compute and report the net cash provided or used by operating activities (using either the direct or indirect method; both are explained); (3) compute and report the net cash provided or used by investing activities; (4) compute and report the net cash provided or used by financing activities; and (5) compute the net cash flow by combining net cash provided or used by operating, investing, and financing activities and then *prove it* by adding it to the beginning cash balance to show that it equals the ending cash balance.

Step 1: Compute net increase or decrease in cash

Step 2: Compute net cash from operating activities

Step 3: Compute net cash from investing activities

Step 4: Compute net cash from financing activities

Step 5: Prove and report beginning and ending cash balances

Computing the net increase or net decrease in cash is a simple but crucial computation. It equals the current period's cash balance minus the prior period's cash balance. This is the *bottom-line* figure for the statement of cash flows and is a check on accuracy. The information we need to prepare a statement of cash flows comes from various sources including comparative balance sheets at the beginning and end of the period, and an income statement for the period. There are two alternative approaches to preparing the statement: (1) analyzing the Cash account and (2) analyzing noncash accounts.

Analyzing the Cash Account A company's cash receipts and cash payments are recorded in the Cash account in its general ledger. The Cash account is therefore a natural place to look for information about cash flows from operating, investing, and financing activities. To illustrate, review the summarized Cash T-account of Genesis, Inc., in Exhibit 16.6. Individual cash transactions are summarized in this Cash account according to the major types of cash receipts and cash payments. For instance, only the total of cash receipts from all customers is listed. Individual cash transactions underlying these totals can number in the thousands. Accounting software is available to provide summarized cash accounts.

Preparing a statement of cash flows from Exhibit 16.6 requires determining whether an individual cash inflow or outflow is an operating, investing, or financing activity, and then listing each by

EXHIBIT 16.6

Summarized Cash Account

Accounting System:

File Edit Maintain Tasks Analysis Options Reports Window Help

Cash			
Balance, Dec. 31, 2008	12,000		
Receipts from customers	570,000	Payments for merchandise	319,000
Receipts from asset sales	12,000	Payments for wages and operating expenses	218,000
Receipts from stock issuance	15,000	Payments for interest	8,000
		Payments for taxes	5,000
		Payments for assets	10,000
		Payments for notes retirement	18,000
		Payments for dividends	14,000
Balance, Dec. 31, 2009	17,000		

Sales Purchases General Ledger Payroll Inventory Company Analysis

activity. This yields the statement shown in Exhibit 16.7. However, preparing the statement of cash flows from an analysis of the summarized Cash account has two limitations. First, most companies have many individual cash receipts and payments, making it difficult to review them all. Accounting software minimizes this burden, but it is still a task requiring professional judgment for many transactions. Second, the Cash account does not usually carry an adequate description of each cash transaction, making assignment of all cash transactions according to activity difficult.

Point: View the change in cash as a *target* number that we will fully explain and prove in the statement of cash flows.

EXHIBIT 16.7

Statement of Cash Flows—Direct Method

GENESIS
Statement of Cash Flows
For Year Ended December 31, 2009

Cash flows from operating activities		
Cash received from customers	$570,000	
Cash paid for merchandise	(319,000)	
Cash paid for wages and other operating expenses	(218,000)	
Cash paid for interest	(8,000)	
Cash paid for taxes	(5,000)	
Net cash provided by operating activities		$20,000
Cash flows from investing activities		
Cash received from sale of plant assets	12,000	
Cash paid for purchase of plant assets	(10,000)	
Net cash provided by investing activities		2,000
Cash flows from financing activities		
Cash received from issuing stock	15,000	
Cash paid to retire notes	(18,000)	
Cash paid for dividends	(14,000)	
Net cash used in financing activities		(17,000)
Net increase in cash		$ 5,000
Cash balance at prior year-end		12,000
Cash balance at current year-end		$17,000

Analyzing Noncash Accounts A second approach to preparing the statement of cash flows is analyzing noncash accounts. This approach uses the fact that when a company records cash inflows and outflows with debits and credits to the Cash account (see Exhibit 16.6), it also records credits and debits in noncash accounts (reflecting double-entry accounting). Many of these noncash accounts are balance sheet accounts—for instance, from the sale of land for cash. Others are revenue and expense accounts that are closed to equity. For instance, the sale of services for cash yields a credit to Services Revenue that is closed to Retained Earnings for a corporation. In sum, *all cash transactions eventually affect noncash balance sheet accounts*. Thus, we can determine cash inflows and outflows by analyzing changes in noncash balance sheet accounts.

Exhibit 16.8 uses the accounting equation to show the relation between the Cash account and the noncash balance sheet accounts. This exhibit starts with the accounting equation at the top. It is then expanded in line (2) to separate cash from noncash asset accounts. Line (3) moves noncash asset accounts to the right-hand side of the equality where they are subtracted. This shows that cash equals the sum of the liability and equity accounts *minus* the noncash asset accounts. Line (4) points

EXHIBIT 16.8

Relation between Cash and Noncash Accounts

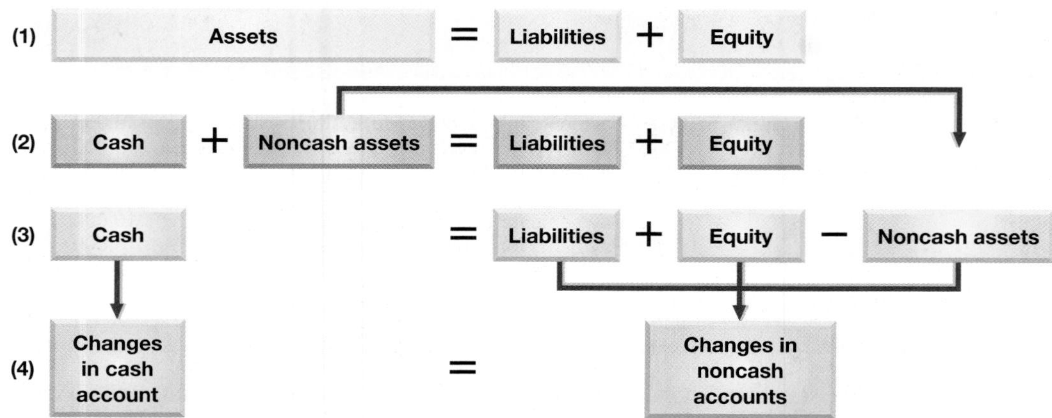

out that *changes* on one side of the accounting equation equal *changes* on the other side. It shows that we can explain changes in cash by analyzing changes in the noncash accounts consisting of liability accounts, equity accounts, and noncash asset accounts. By analyzing noncash balance sheet accounts and any related income statement accounts, we can prepare a statement of cash flows.

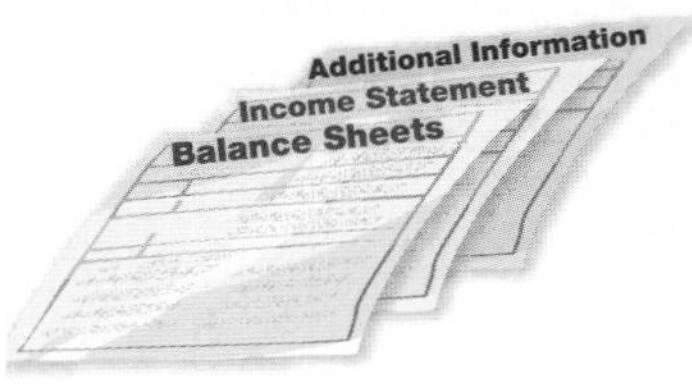

Information to Prepare the Statement Information to prepare the statement of cash flows usually comes from three sources: (1) comparative balance sheets, (2) the current income statement, and (3) additional information. Comparative balance sheets are used to compute changes in noncash accounts from the beginning to the end of the period. The current income statement is used to help compute cash flows from operating activities. Additional information often includes details on transactions and events that help explain both the cash flows and noncash investing and financing activities.

Decision Insight

e-Cash Every credit transaction on the Net leaves a trail that a hacker or a marketer can pick up. Enter e-cash—or digital money. The encryption of e-cash protects your money from snoops and thieves and cannot be traced, even by the issuing bank.

Cash Flows from Operating

Indirect and Direct Methods of Reporting

Cash flows provided (used) by operating activities are reported in one of two ways: the *direct method* or the *indirect method.* **These two different methods apply only to the operating activities section.**

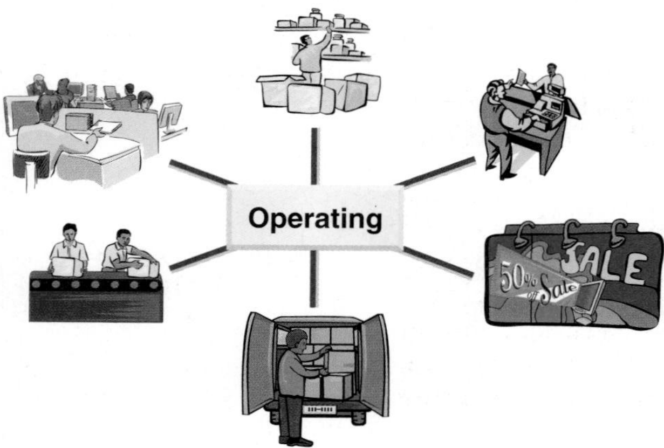

The **direct method** separately lists each major item of operating cash receipts (such as cash received from customers) and each major item of operating cash payments (such as cash paid for merchandise). The cash payments are subtracted from cash receipts to determine the net cash provided (used) by operating activities. The operating activities section of Exhibit 16.7 reflects the direct method of reporting operating cash flows.

The **indirect method** reports net income and then adjusts it for items necessary to obtain net cash provided or used by operating activities. It does *not* report individual items of cash inflows and cash outflows from operating activities. Instead, the indirect method reports the necessary adjustments to reconcile net income to net cash provided or used by operating activities. The operating activities section for Genesis prepared under the indirect method is shown in Exhibit 16.9.

EXHIBIT 16.9

Operating Activities Section—Indirect Method

Cash flows from operating activities		
Net income	$ 38,000	
Adjustments to reconcile net income to net cash provided by operating activities		
Increase in accounts receivable	(20,000)	
Increase in merchandise inventory	(14,000)	
Increase in prepaid expenses	(2,000)	
Decrease in accounts payable	(5,000)	
Decrease in interest payable	(1,000)	
Increase in income taxes payable	10,000	
Depreciation expense	24,000	
Loss on sale of plant assets	6,000	
Gain on retirement of notes	(16,000)	
Net cash provided by operating activities		**$20,000**

The net cash amount provided by operating activities is *identical* under both the direct and indirect methods. This equality always exists. The difference in these methods is with the computation and presentation of this amount. The FASB recommends the direct method, but because it is not required and the indirect method is arguably easier to compute, nearly all companies report operating cash flows using the indirect method.

Point: To better understand the direct and indirect methods of reporting operating cash flows, identify similarities and differences between Exhibits 16.7 and 16.11.

To illustrate, we prepare the operating activities section of the statement of cash flows for Genesis. Exhibit 16.10 shows the December 31, 2008 and 2009, balance sheets of Genesis along with its 2009 income statement. We use this information to prepare a statement of cash flows that explains the $5,000 increase in cash for 2009 as reflected in its balance sheets. This $5,000 is computed as Cash of $17,000 at the end of 2009 minus Cash of $12,000 at the end of 2008. Genesis discloses additional information on its 2009 transactions:

Video16.1

a. The accounts payable balances result from merchandise inventory purchases.

b. Purchased $70,000 in plant assets by paying $10,000 cash and issuing $60,000 of notes payable.

c. Sold plant assets with an original cost of $30,000 and accumulated depreciation of $12,000 for $12,000 cash, yielding a $6,000 loss.

d. Received $15,000 cash from issuing 3,000 shares of common stock.

e. Paid $18,000 cash to retire notes with a $34,000 book value, yielding a $16,000 gain.

f. Declared and paid cash dividends of $14,000.

The next section describes the indirect method. Appendix 16B describes the direct method. An instructor can choose to cover either one or both methods. Neither section depends on the other.

Application of the Indirect Method of Reporting

P2 Compute cash flows from operating activities using the indirect method.

Net income is computed using accrual accounting, which recognizes revenues when earned and expenses when incurred. Revenues and expenses do not necessarily reflect the receipt and payment of cash. The indirect method of computing and reporting net cash flows from operating activities involves adjusting the net income figure to obtain the net cash provided or used by operating activities. This includes subtracting noncash increases (credits) from net income and adding noncash charges (debits) back to net income.

To illustrate, the indirect method begins with Genesis's net income of $38,000 and adjusts it to obtain net cash provided by operating activities of $20,000. Exhibit 16.11 shows the results of the indirect method of reporting operating cash flows, which adjusts net income for three types of adjustments. There are adjustments ① to reflect changes in noncash current assets and current liabilities related to operating activities, ② to income statement items involving operating activities that do not affect cash inflows or outflows, and ③ to eliminate gains and losses resulting from investing and financing activities (not part of operating activities). This section describes each of these adjustments.

Point: *Noncash credits* refer to *revenue* amounts reported on the income statement that are *not collected in cash* this period. *Noncash charges* refer to *expense* amounts reported on the income statement that are *not paid* this period.

EXHIBIT 16.10

Financial Statements

GENESIS
Income Statement
For Year Ended December 31, 2009

Sales		$590,000
Cost of goods sold	$300,000	
Wages and other operating expenses	216,000	
Interest expense	7,000	
Depreciation expense	24,000	(547,000)
		43,000
Other gains (losses)		
Gain on retirement of notes	16,000	
Loss on sale of plant assets	(6,000)	10,000
Income before taxes		53,000
Income taxes expense		(15,000)
Net income		$ 38,000

GENESIS
Balance Sheets
December 31, 2009 and 2008

	2009	2008
Assets		
Current assets		
Cash	$ 17,000	$ 12,000
Accounts receivable	60,000	40,000
Merchandise inventory	84,000	70,000
Prepaid expenses	6,000	4,000
Total current assets	167,000	126,000
Long-term assets		
Plant assets	250,000	210,000
Accumulated depreciation	(60,000)	(48,000)
Total assets	$357,000	$288,000
Liabilities		
Current liabilities		
Accounts payable	$ 35,000	$ 40,000
Interest payable	3,000	4,000
Income taxes payable	22,000	12,000
Total current liabilities	60,000	56,000
Long-term notes payable	90,000	64,000
Total liabilities	150,000	120,000
Equity		
Common stock, $5 par	95,000	80,000
Retained earnings	112,000	88,000
Total equity	207,000	168,000
Total liabilities and equity	$357,000	$288,000

① **Adjustments for Changes in Current Assets and Current Liabilities** This section describes adjustments for changes in noncash current assets and current liabilities.

Point: Operating activities are typically those that determine income, which are often reflected in changes in current assets and current liabilities.

Adjustments for changes in noncash current assets. Changes in noncash current assets normally result from operating activities. Examples are sales affecting accounts receivable and building usage affecting prepaid rent. Decreases in noncash current assets yield the following adjustment:

Decreases in noncash current assets are added to net income.

To see the logic for this adjustment, consider that a decrease in a noncash current asset such as accounts receivable suggests more available cash at the end of the period compared to the beginning. This is so because a decrease in accounts receivable implies higher cash receipts than reflected in sales. We add these higher cash receipts (from decreases in noncash current assets) to net income when computing cash flow from operations.

In contrast, an increase in noncash current assets such as accounts receivable implies less cash receipts than reflected in sales. As another example, an increase in prepaid rent indicates that more cash is paid for rent than is deducted as rent expense. Increases in noncash current assets yield the following adjustment:

Increases in noncash current assets are subtracted from net income.

To illustrate, these adjustments are applied to the noncash current assets in Exhibit 16.10.

Accounts receivable. Accounts receivable *increase* $20,000, from a beginning balance of $40,000 to an ending balance of $60,000. This increase implies that Genesis collects less cash than is reported in sales. That is, some of these sales were in the form of accounts receivable and that amount increased during the period. To see this it is helpful to use *account analysis.* This usually involves setting up a T-account and reconstructing its major entries to compute cash receipts or payments. The following reconstructed Accounts Receivable T-account reveals that cash receipts are less than sales:

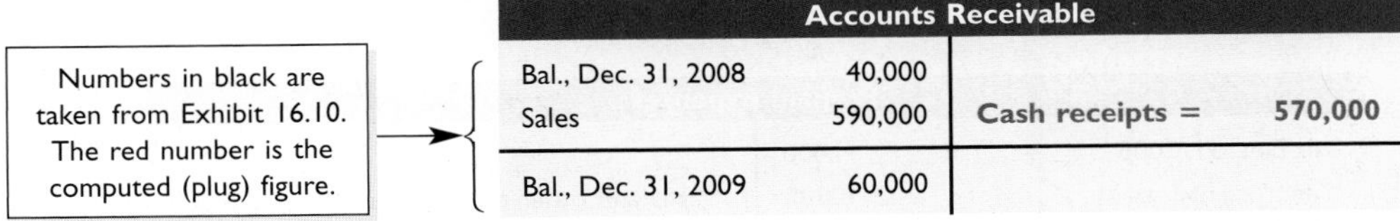
Numbers in black are taken from Exhibit 16.10. The red number is the computed (plug) figure.

Accounts Receivable			
Bal., Dec. 31, 2008	40,000		
Sales	590,000	**Cash receipts =**	**570,000**
Bal., Dec. 31, 2009	60,000		

We see that sales are $20,000 greater than cash receipts. This $20,000—as reflected in the $20,000 increase in Accounts Receivable—is subtracted from net income when computing cash provided by operating activities (see Exhibit 16.11).

Merchandise inventory. Merchandise inventory *increases* by $14,000, from a $70,000 beginning balance to an $84,000 ending balance. This increase implies that Genesis had greater cash purchases than cost of goods sold. This larger amount of cash purchases is in the form of inventory, as reflected in the following account analysis:

Merchandise Inventory			
Bal., Dec. 31, 2008	70,000		
Purchases =	**314,000**	Cost of goods sold	300,000
Bal., Dec. 31, 2009	84,000		

EXHIBIT 16.11

Statement of Cash Flows—Indirect Method

GENESIS Statement of Cash Flows For Year Ended December 31, 2009			
Cash flows from operating activities			
Net income		$ 38,000	
Adjustments to reconcile net income to net cash provided by operating activities			
①	Increase in accounts receivable	(20,000)	
①	Increase in merchandise inventory	(14,000)	
①	Increase in prepaid expenses	(2,000)	
①	Decrease in accounts payable	(5,000)	
①	Decrease in interest payable	(1,000)	
①	Increase in income taxes payable	10,000	
②	Depreciation expense	24,000	
③	Loss on sale of plant assets	6,000	
③	Gain on retirement of notes	(16,000)	
Net cash provided by operating activities			$20,000
Cash flows from investing activities			
Cash received from sale of plant assets		12,000	
Cash paid for purchase of plant assets		(10,000)	
Net cash provided by investing activities			2,000
Cash flows from financing activities			
Cash received from issuing stock		15,000	
Cash paid to retire notes		(18,000)	
Cash paid for dividends		(14,000)	
Net cash used in financing activities			(17,000)
Net increase in cash			$ 5,000
Cash balance at prior year-end			12,000
Cash balance at current year-end			$17,000

Point: Refer to Exhibit 16.10 and identify the $5,000 change in cash. This change is what the statement of cash flows explains; it serves as a check.

The amount by which purchases exceed cost of goods sold—as reflected in the $14,000 increase in inventory—is subtracted from net income when computing cash provided by operating activities (see Exhibit 16.11).

Prepaid expenses. Prepaid expenses *increase* $2,000, from a $4,000 beginning balance to a $6,000 ending balance, implying that Genesis's cash payments exceed its recorded prepaid expenses. These higher cash payments increase the amount of Prepaid Expenses, as reflected in its reconstructed T-account:

Prepaid Expenses			
Bal., Dec. 31, 2008	4,000		
Cash payments =	**218,000**	Wages and other operating exp.	216,000
Bal., Dec. 31, 2009	6,000		

The amount by which cash payments exceed the recorded operating expenses—as reflected in the $2,000 increase in Prepaid Expenses—is subtracted from net income when computing cash provided by operating activities (see Exhibit 16.11).

Adjustments for changes in current liabilities. Changes in current liabilities normally result from operating activities. An example is a purchase that affects accounts payable. Increases in current liabilities yield the following adjustment to net income when computing operating cash flows:

Increases in current liabilities are added to net income.

To see the logic for this adjustment, consider that an increase in the Accounts Payable account suggests that cash payments are less than the related (cost of goods sold) expense. As another example, an increase in wages payable implies that cash paid for wages is less than the recorded wages expense. Since the recorded expense is greater than the cash paid, we add the increase in wages payable to net income to compute net cash flow from operations.

Conversely, when current liabilities decrease, the following adjustment is required:

Decreases in current liabilities are subtracted from net income.

To illustrate, these adjustments are applied to the current liabilities in Exhibit 16.10.

Accounts payable. Accounts payable *decrease* $5,000, from a beginning balance of $40,000 to an ending balance of $35,000. This decrease implies that cash payments to suppliers exceed purchases by $5,000 for the period, which is reflected in the reconstructed Accounts Payable T-account:

Accounts Payable			
		Bal., Dec. 31, 2008	40,000
Cash payments =	**319,000**	Purchases	314,000
		Bal., Dec. 31, 2009	35,000

The amount by which cash payments exceed purchases—as reflected in the $5,000 decrease in Accounts Payable—is subtracted from net income when computing cash provided by operating activities (see Exhibit 16.11).

Interest payable. Interest payable *decreases* $1,000, from a $4,000 beginning balance to a $3,000 ending balance. This decrease indicates that cash paid for interest exceeds interest expense by $1,000, which is reflected in the Interest Payable T-account:

Interest Payable			
		Bal., Dec. 31, 2008	4,000
Cash paid for interest =	**8,000**	Interest expense	7,000
		Bal., Dec. 31, 2009	3,000

The amount by which cash paid exceeds recorded expense—as reflected in the $1,000 decrease in Interest Payable—is subtracted from net income (see Exhibit 16.11).

Income taxes payable. Income taxes payable *increase* $10,000, from a $12,000 beginning balance to a $22,000 ending balance. This increase implies that reported income taxes exceed the cash paid for taxes, which is reflected in the Income Taxes Payable T-account:

Income Taxes Payable			
		Bal., Dec. 31, 2008	12,000
Cash paid for taxes =	5,000	Income taxes expense	15,000
		Bal., Dec. 31, 2009	22,000

The amount by which cash paid falls short of the reported taxes expense—as reflected in the $10,000 increase in Income Taxes Payable—is added to net income when computing cash provided by operating activities (see Exhibit 16.11).

Summary Adjustments for Changes in Current Assets and Current Liabilities		
Account	Increases	Decreases
Noncash current assets	Deduct from NI	Add to NI
Current liabilities	Add to NI	Deduct from NI

② Adjustments for Operating Items Not Providing or Using Cash The income statement usually includes some expenses that do not reflect cash outflows in the period. Examples are depreciation, amortization, depletion, and bad debts expense. The indirect method for reporting operating cash flows requires that

Expenses with no cash outflows are added back to net income.

To see the logic of this adjustment, recall that items such as depreciation, amortization, depletion, and bad debts originate from debits to expense accounts and credits to noncash accounts. These entries have *no* cash effect, and we add them back to net income when computing net cash flows from operations. Adding them back cancels their deductions.

Similarly, when net income includes revenues that do not reflect cash inflows in the period, the indirect method for reporting operating cash flows requires that

Revenues with no cash inflows are subtracted from net income.

We apply these adjustments to the Genesis operating items that do not provide or use cash.

Depreciation. Depreciation expense is the only Genesis operating item that has no effect on cash flows in the period. We must add back the $24,000 depreciation expense to net income when computing cash provided by operating activities. (We later explain that any cash outflow to acquire a plant asset is reported as an investing activity.)

③ Adjustments for Nonoperating Items Net income often includes losses that are not part of operating activities but are part of either investing or financing activities. Examples are a loss from the sale of a plant asset and a loss from retirement of notes payable. The indirect method for reporting operating cash flows requires that

Nonoperating losses are added back to net income.

To see the logic, consider that items such as a plant asset sale and a notes retirement are normally recorded by recognizing the cash, removing all plant asset or notes accounts, and recognizing any loss or gain. The cash received or paid is not part of operating activities but is part of either investing or financing activities. *No* operating cash flow effect occurs. However, because the nonoperating loss is a deduction in computing net income, we need to add it back to net income when computing cash flow from operations. Adding it back cancels the deduction.

Point: An income statement reports revenues, gains, expenses, and losses on an accrual basis. The statement of cash flows reports cash received and cash paid for operating, financing, and investing activities.

Similarly, when net income includes gains not part of operating activities, the indirect method for reporting operating cash flows requires that

Nonoperating gains are subtracted from net income.

To illustrate these adjustments, we consider the nonoperating items of Genesis.

Loss on sale of plant assets. Genesis reports a $6,000 loss on sale of plant assets as part of net income. This loss is a proper deduction in computing income, but it is *not part of operating activities*. Instead, a sale of plant assets is part of investing activities. Thus, the $6,000 nonoperating loss is added back to net income (see Exhibit 16.11). Adding it back cancels the loss. We later explain how to report the cash inflow from the asset sale in investing activities.

Gain on retirement of debt. A $16,000 gain on retirement of debt is properly included in net income, but it is *not part of operating activities*. This means the $16,000 nonoperating gain must be subtracted from net income to obtain net cash provided by operating activities (see Exhibit 16.11). Subtracting it cancels the recorded gain. We later describe how to report the cash outflow to retire debt.

Summary of Adjustments for Indirect Method

Exhibit 16.12 summarizes the most common adjustments to net income when computing net cash provided or used by operating activities under the indirect method.

EXHIBIT 16.12

Summary of Selected Adjustments for Indirect Method

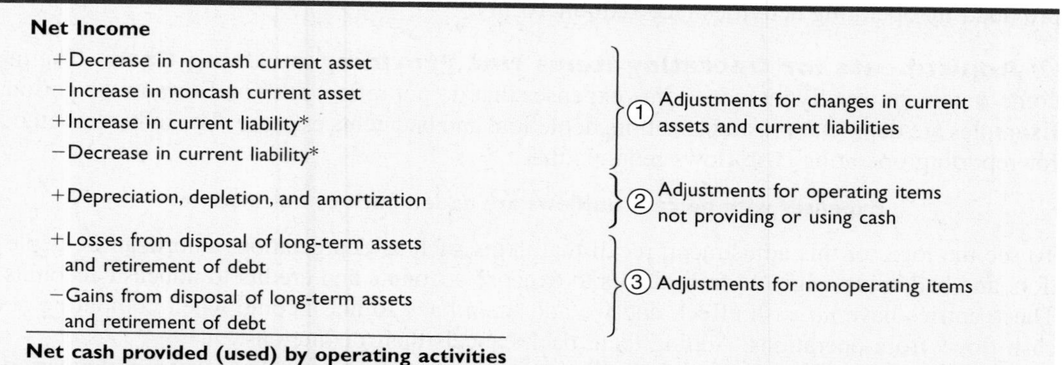

Net Income

+Decrease in noncash current asset	① Adjustments for changes in current assets and current liabilities
−Increase in noncash current asset	
+Increase in current liability*	
−Decrease in current liability*	
+Depreciation, depletion, and amortization	② Adjustments for operating items not providing or using cash
+Losses from disposal of long-term assets and retirement of debt	③ Adjustments for nonoperating items
−Gains from disposal of long-term assets and retirement of debt	

Net cash provided (used) by operating activities

* Excludes current portion of long-term debt and any (nonsales-related) short-term notes payable—both are financing activities.

The computations in determining cash provided or used by operating activities are different for the indirect and direct methods, but the result is identical. Both methods yield the same $20,000 figure for cash from operating activities for Genesis; see Exhibits 16.7 and 16.11.

Decision Insight

Cash or Income The difference between net income and operating cash flows can be large and sometimes reflects on the quality of earnings. This bar chart shows the net income and operating cash flows of three companies. Operating cash flows can be either higher or lower than net income.

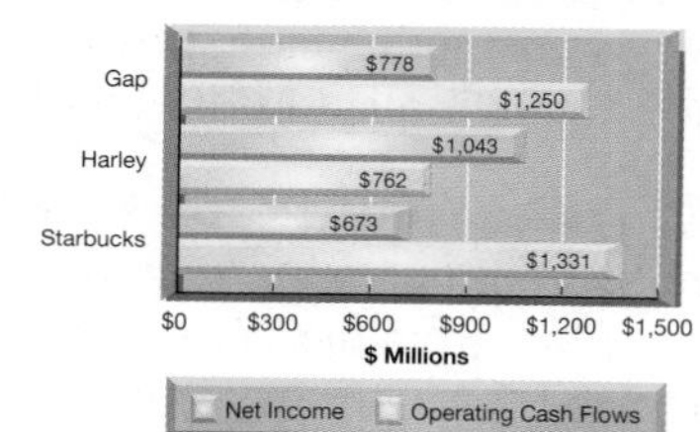

Quick Check

Answers—p. 658

4. Determine the net cash provided or used by operating activities using the following data: net income, $74,900; decrease in accounts receivable, $4,600; increase in inventory, $11,700; decrease in accounts payable, $1,000; loss on sale of equipment, $3,400; payment of cash dividends, $21,500.
5. Why are expenses such as depreciation and amortization added to net income when cash flow from operating activities is computed by the indirect method?
6. A company reports net income of $15,000 that includes a $3,000 gain on the sale of plant assets. Why is this gain subtracted from net income in computing cash flow from operating activities using the indirect method?

Cash Flows from Investing

The third major step in preparing the statement of cash flows is to compute and report cash flows from investing activities. We normally do this by identifying changes in (1) all noncurrent asset accounts and (2) the current accounts for both notes receivable and investments in securities (excluding trading securities). We then analyze changes in these accounts to determine their effect, if any, on cash and report the cash flow effects in the investing activities section of the statement of cash flows. **Reporting of investing activities is identical under the direct method and indirect method.**

Three-Stage Process of Analysis

Video16.1

Information to compute cash flows from investing activities is usually taken from beginning and ending balance sheets and the income statement. We use a three-stage process to determine cash provided or used by investing activities: (1) identify changes in investing-related accounts, (2) explain these changes using reconstruction analysis, and (3) report their cash flow effects.

Analysis of Noncurrent Assets

P3 Determine cash flows from both investing and financing activities.

Information about the Genesis transactions provided earlier reveals that the company both purchased and sold plant assets during the period. Both transactions are investing activities and are analyzed for their cash flow effects in this section.

Plant Asset Transactions The first stage in analyzing the Plant Assets account and its related Accumulated Depreciation is to identify any changes in these accounts from comparative balance sheets in Exhibit 16.10. This analysis reveals a $40,000 increase in plant assets from $210,000 to $250,000 and a $12,000 increase in accumulated depreciation from $48,000 to $60,000.

The second stage is to explain these changes. Items *b* and *c* of the additional information for Genesis (page 635) are relevant in this case. Recall that the Plant Assets account is affected by both asset purchases and sales, while its Accumulated Depreciation account is normally increased from depreciation and decreased from the removal of accumulated depreciation in asset sales. To explain changes in these accounts and to identify their cash flow effects, we prepare *reconstructed entries* from prior transactions; *they are not the actual entries by the preparer.*

Point: Investing activities include (1) purchasing and selling long-term assets, (2) lending and collecting on notes receivable, and (3) purchasing and selling short-term investments other than cash equivalents and trading securities.

Point: Financing and investing info is available in ledger accounts to help explain changes in comparative balance sheets. Post references lead to relevant entries and explanations.

To illustrate, item *b* reports that Genesis purchased plant assets of $70,000 by issuing $60,000 in notes payable to the seller and paying $10,000 in cash. The reconstructed entry for analysis of item *b* follows:

Reconstruction	Plant Assets	70,000	
	Notes Payable		60,000
	Cash		**10,000**

This entry reveals a $10,000 cash outflow for plant assets and a $60,000 noncash investing and financing transaction involving notes exchanged for plant assets.

Next, item *c* reports that Genesis sold plant assets costing $30,000 (with $12,000 of accumulated depreciation) for $12,000 cash, resulting in a $6,000 loss. The reconstructed entry for analysis of item *c* follows:

Reconstruction	**Cash**	**12,000**	
	Accumulated Depreciation	12,000	
	Loss on Sale of Plant Assets	6,000	
	Plant Assets		30,000

This entry reveals a $12,000 cash inflow from assets sold. The $6,000 loss is computed by comparing the asset book value to the cash received and does not reflect any cash inflow or outflow. We also reconstruct the entry for Depreciation Expense using information from the income statement.

Reconstruction	Depreciation Expense	24,000	
	Accumulated Depreciation		24,000

This entry shows that Depreciation Expense results in no cash flow effect. These three reconstructed entries are reflected in the following plant asset and related T-accounts.

Plant Assets			
Bal., Dec. 31, 2008	210,000		
Purchase	**70,000**	**Sale**	**30,000**
Bal., Dec. 31, 2009	250,000		

Accumulated Depreciation—Plant Assets			
		Bal., Dec. 31, 2008	48,000
Sale	**12,000**	**Depr. expense**	**24,000**
		Bal., Dec. 31, 2009	60,000

Example: If a plant asset costing $40,000 with $37,000 of accumulated depreciation is sold at a $1,000 loss, what is the cash flow? What is the cash flow if this asset is sold at a gain of $3,000? *Answers:* +$2,000; +$6,000.

This reconstruction analysis is complete in that the change in plant assets from $210,000 to $250,000 is fully explained by the $70,000 purchase and the $30,000 sale. Also, the change in accumulated depreciation from $48,000 to $60,000 is fully explained by depreciation expense of $24,000 and the removal of $12,000 in accumulated depreciation from an asset sale. (Preparers of the statement of cash flows have the entire ledger and additional information at their disposal, but for brevity reasons only the information needed for reconstructing accounts is given.)

The third stage looks at the reconstructed entries for identification of cash flows. The two identified cash flow effects are reported in the investing section of the statement as follows (also see Exhibit 16.7 or 16.11):

Cash flows from investing activities	
Cash received from sale of plant assets	$12,000
Cash paid for purchase of plant assets	(10,000)

The $60,000 portion of the purchase described in item *b* and financed by issuing notes is a noncash investing and financing activity. It is reported in a note or in a separate schedule to the statement as follows:

Noncash investing and financing activity	
Purchased plant assets with issuance of notes	$60,000

Analysis of Other Assets

Many other asset transactions (including those involving current notes receivable and investments in certain securities) are considered investing activities and can affect a company's cash flows. Since Genesis did not enter into other investing activities impacting assets, we do not need to extend our analysis to these other assets. If such transactions did exist, we would analyze them using the same three-stage process illustrated for plant assets.

Quick Check

Answer—p. 658

7. Equipment costing $80,000 with accumulated depreciation of $30,000 is sold at a loss of $10,000. What is the cash receipt from this sale? In what section of the statement of cash flows is this transaction reported?

Cash Flows from Financing

The fourth major step in preparing the statement of cash flows is to compute and report cash flows from financing activities. We normally do this by identifying changes in all noncurrent liability accounts (including the current portion of any notes and bonds) and the equity accounts. These accounts include long-term debt, notes payable, bonds payable, common stock, and retained earnings. Changes in these accounts are then analyzed using available information to determine their effect, if any, on cash. Results are reported in the financing activities section of the statement. **Reporting of financing activities is identical under the direct method and indirect method.**

Three-Stage Process of Analysis

Video16.1

We again use a three-stage process to determine cash provided or used by financing activities: (1) identify changes in financing-related accounts, (2) explain these changes using reconstruction analysis, and (3) report their cash flow effects.

Analysis of Noncurrent Liabilities

Information about Genesis provided earlier reveals two transactions involving noncurrent liabilities. We analyzed one of those, the $60,000 issuance of notes payable to purchase plant assets. This transaction is reported as a significant noncash investing and financing activity in a footnote or a separate schedule to the statement of cash flows. The other remaining transaction involving noncurrent liabilities is the cash retirement of notes payable.

Point: Financing activities generally refer to changes in the noncurrent liability and the equity accounts. Examples are (1) receiving cash from issuing debt or repaying amounts borrowed and (2) receiving cash from or distributing cash to owners.

Notes Payable Transactions The first stage in analysis of notes is to review the comparative balance sheets from Exhibit 16.10. This analysis reveals an increase in notes payable from $64,000 to $90,000.

The second stage explains this change. Item *e* of the additional information for Genesis (page 635) reports that notes with a carrying value of $34,000 are retired for $18,000 cash, resulting in a $16,000 gain. The reconstructed entry for analysis of item *e* follows:

Reconstruction	Notes Payable	34,000	
	Gain on retirement of debt		16,000
	Cash		**18,000**

This entry reveals an $18,000 cash outflow for retirement of notes and a $16,000 gain from comparing the notes payable carrying value to the cash received. This gain does not reflect any cash inflow or outflow. Also, item *b* of the additional information reports that Genesis purchased plant assets costing $70,000 by issuing $60,000 in notes payable to the seller and paying $10,000 in cash. We reconstructed this entry when analyzing investing activities: It showed a $60,000 increase to notes payable that is reported as a noncash investing and financing transaction. The Notes Payable account reflects (and is fully explained by) these reconstructed entries as follows:

Notes Payable			
		Bal., Dec. 31, 2008	64,000
Retired notes	**34,000**	**Issued notes**	**60,000**
		Bal., Dec. 31, 2009	90,000

The third stage is to report the cash flow effect of the notes retirement in the financing section of the statement as follows (also see Exhibit 16.7 or 16.11):

Cash flows from financing activities	
Cash paid to retire notes	$(18,000)

Analysis of Equity

The Genesis information reveals two transactions involving equity accounts. The first is the issuance of common stock for cash. The second is the declaration and payment of cash dividends. We analyze both.

Common Stock Transactions The first stage in analyzing common stock is to review the comparative balance sheets from Exhibit 16.10, which reveals an increase in common stock from $80,000 to $95,000.

The second stage explains this change. Item *d* of the additional information (page 635) reports that 3,000 shares of common stock are issued at par for $5 per share. The reconstructed entry for analysis of item *d* follows:

Reconstruction	**Cash**	**15,000**	
	Common Stock		15,000

This entry reveals a $15,000 cash inflow from stock issuance and is reflected in (and explains) the Common Stock account as follows:

Common Stock			
		Bal., Dec. 31, 2008	80,000
		Issued stock	**15,000**
		Bal., Dec. 31, 2009	95,000

The third stage discloses the cash flow effect from stock issuance in the financing section of the statement as follows (also see Exhibit 16.7 or 16.11):

Cash flows from financing activities	
Cash received from issuing stock	$15,000

Retained Earnings Transactions The first stage in analyzing the Retained Earnings account is to review the comparative balance sheets from Exhibit 16.10. This reveals an increase in retained earnings from $88,000 to $112,000.

The second stage explains this change. Item *f* of the additional information (page 635) reports that cash dividends of $14,000 are paid. The reconstructed entry follows:

Reconstruction	Retained Earnings.	14,000	
	Cash		**14,000**

This entry reveals a $14,000 cash outflow for cash dividends. Also see that the Retained Earnings account is impacted by net income of $38,000. (Net income was analyzed under the operating section of the statement of cash flows.) The reconstructed Retained Earnings account follows:

Retained Earnings			
		Bal., Dec. 31, 2008	88,000
Cash dividend	**14,000**	**Net income**	**38,000**
		Bal., Dec. 31, 2009	112,000

Point: Financing activities not affecting cash flow include *declaration* of a cash dividend, *declaration* of a stock dividend, payment of a stock dividend, and a stock split.

The third stage reports the cash flow effect from the cash dividend in the financing section of the statement as follows (also see Exhibit 16.7 or 16.11):

Cash flows from financing activities	
Cash paid for dividends	$(14,000)

Global: There are no requirements to separate domestic and international cash flows, leading some users to ask, "Where in the world is cash flow?"

We now have identified and explained all of the Genesis cash inflows and cash outflows and one noncash investing and financing transaction. Specifically, our analysis has reconciled changes in all noncash balance sheet accounts.

Proving Cash Balances

The fifth and final step in preparing the statement is to report the beginning and ending cash balances and prove that the *net change in cash* is explained by operating, investing, and financing cash flows. This step is shown here for Genesis.

Net cash provided by operating activities	$20,000
Net cash provided by investing activities	2,000
Net cash used in financing activities	(17,000)
Net increase in cash	**$ 5,000**
Cash balance at 2008 year-end	12,000
Cash balance at 2009 year-end	$ 17,000

The preceding table shows that the $5,000 net increase in cash, from $12,000 at the beginning of the period to $17,000 at the end, is reconciled by net cash flows from operating ($20,000 inflow), investing ($2,000 inflow), and financing ($17,000 outflow) activities. This is formally reported at the bottom of the statement of cash flows as shown in both Exhibits 16.7 and 16.11.

Decision Maker

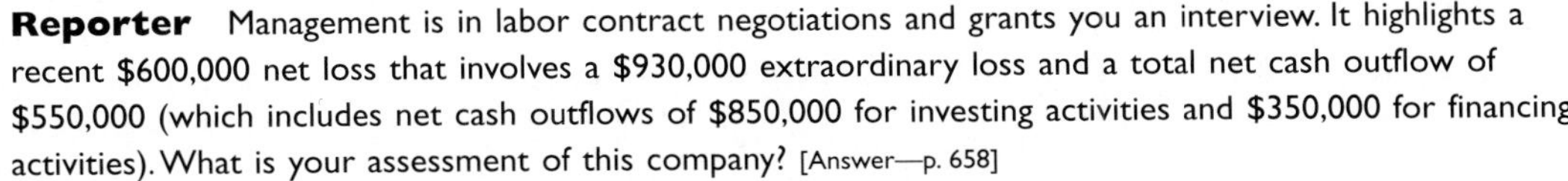

Reporter Management is in labor contract negotiations and grants you an interview. It highlights a recent $600,000 net loss that involves a $930,000 extraordinary loss and a total net cash outflow of $550,000 (which includes net cash outflows of $850,000 for investing activities and $350,000 for financing activities). What is your assessment of this company? [Answer—p. 658]

Cash Flow Analysis

Decision Analysis

Analyzing Cash Sources and Uses

A1 Analyze the statement of cash flows.

Most managers stress the importance of understanding and predicting cash flows for business decisions. Creditors evaluate a company's ability to generate cash before deciding whether to lend money. Investors also assess cash inflows and outflows before buying and selling stock. Information in the statement of cash flows helps address these and other questions such as (1) How much cash is generated from or used in operations? (2) What expenditures are made with cash from operations? (3) What is the source of cash for debt payments? (4) What is the source of cash for distributions to owners? (5) How is the increase in investing activities financed? (6) What is the source of cash for new plant assets? (7) Why is cash flow from operations different from income? (8) How is cash from financing used?

To effectively answer these questions, it is important to separately analyze investing, financing, and operating activities. To illustrate, consider data from three different companies in Exhibit 16.13. These companies operate in the same industry and have been in business for several years.

EXHIBIT 16.13

Cash Flows of Competing Companies

($ thousands)	BMX	ATV	Trex
Cash provided (used) by operating activities	$90,000	$40,000	$(24,000)
Cash provided (used) by investing activities			
Proceeds from sale of plant assets			26,000
Purchase of plant assets	(48,000)	(25,000)	
Cash provided (used) by financing activities			
Proceeds from issuance of debt			13,000
Repayment of debt	(27,000)		
Net increase (decrease) in cash	$15,000	$15,000	$ 15,000

Each company generates an identical $15,000 net increase in cash, but its sources and uses of cash flows are very different. BMX's operating activities provide net cash flows of $90,000, allowing it to purchase plant assets of $48,000 and repay $27,000 of its debt. ATV's operating activities provide $40,000 of cash flows, limiting its purchase of plant assets to $25,000. Trex's $15,000 net cash increase is due to selling plant assets and incurring additional debt. Its operating activities yield a net cash outflow of $24,000.

Overall, analysis of these cash flows reveals that BMX is more capable of generating future cash flows than is ATV or Trex.

Decision Insight

Free Cash Flows Many investors use cash flows to value company stock. However, cash-based valuation models often yield different stock values due to differences in measurement of cash flows. Most models require cash flows that are "free" for distribution to shareholders. These *free cash flows* are defined as cash flows available to shareholders after operating asset reinvestments and debt payments. Knowledge of the statement of cash flows is key to proper computation of free cash flows. A company's growth and financial flexibility depend on adequate free cash flows.

Cash Flow on Total Assets

A2 Compute and apply the cash flow on total assets ratio.

Cash flow information has limitations, but it can help measure a company's ability to meet its obligations, pay dividends, expand operations, and obtain financing. Users often compute and analyze a cash-based ratio similar to return on total assets except that its numerator is net cash flows from operating activities. The **cash flow on total assets** ratio is in Exhibit 16.14.

EXHIBIT 16.14

Cash Flow on Total Assets

$$\textbf{Cash flow on total assets} = \frac{\textbf{Cash flow from operations}}{\textbf{Average total assets}}$$

This ratio reflects actual cash flows and is not affected by accounting income recognition and measurement. It can help business decision makers estimate the amount and timing of cash flows when planning and analyzing operating activities.

To illustrate, the 2007 cash flow on total assets ratio for Nike is 18.3%—see Exhibit 16.15. Is an 18.3% ratio good or bad? To answer this question, we compare this ratio with the ratios of prior years (we could also compare its ratio with those of its competitors and the market). Nike's cash flow on total assets ratio for several prior years is in the second column of Exhibit 16.15. Results show that its 18.3% return is the median of the prior years' returns.

EXHIBIT 16.15

Nike's Cash Flow on Total Assets

Year	Cash Flow on Total Assets	Return on Total Assets
2007	18.3%	14.5%
2006	17.9	14.9
2005	18.8	14.5
2004	20.6	12.8
2003	13.9	7.1

As an indicator of *earnings quality,* some analysts compare the cash flow on total assets ratio to the return on total assets ratio. Nike's return on total assets is provided in the third column of Exhibit 16.15. Nike's cash flow on total assets ratio exceeds its return on total assets in each of the five years, leading some analysts to infer that Nike's earnings quality is high for that period because more earnings are realized in the form of cash.

Decision Insight

Cash Flow Ratios Analysts use various other cash-based ratios, including the following two:

(1) $$\textbf{Cash coverage of growth} = \frac{\textbf{Operating cash flow}}{\textbf{Cash outflow for plant assets}}$$

where a low ratio (less than 1) implies cash inadequacy to meet asset growth, whereas a high ratio implies cash adequacy for asset growth.

(2) $$\textbf{Operating cash flow to sales} = \frac{\textbf{Operating cash flow}}{\textbf{Net sales}}$$

When this ratio substantially and consistently differs from the operating income to net sales ratio, the risk of accounting improprieties increases.

Point: The following ratio helps assess whether operating cash flow is adequate to meet long-term obligations:
Cash coverage of debt = Cash flow from operations ÷ Noncurrent liabilities. A low ratio suggests a higher risk of insolvency; a high ratio suggests a greater ability to meet long-term obligations.

Demonstration Problem

Umlauf's comparative balance sheets, income statement, and additional information follow.

DP16

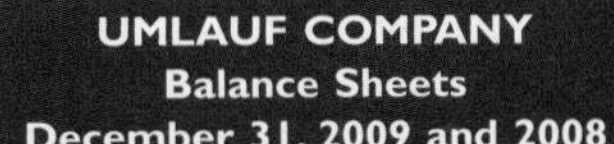

UMLAUF COMPANY
Balance Sheets
December 31, 2009 and 2008

	2009	2008
Assets		
Cash	$ 43,050	$ 23,925
Accounts receivable	34,125	39,825
Merchandise inventory	156,000	146,475
Prepaid expenses	3,600	1,650
Equipment	135,825	146,700
Accum. depreciation—Equipment	(61,950)	(47,550)
Total assets	$310,650	$311,025
Liabilities and Equity		
Accounts payable	$ 28,800	$ 33,750
Income taxes payable	5,100	4,425
Dividends payable	0	4,500
Bonds payable	0	37,500
Common stock, $10 par	168,750	168,750
Retained earnings	108,000	62,100
Total liabilities and equity	$310,650	$311,025

UMLAUF COMPANY
Income Statement
For Year Ended December 31, 2009

Sales		$446,100
Cost of goods sold	$222,300	
Other operating expenses	120,300	
Depreciation expense	25,500	(368,100)
		78,000
Other gains (losses)		
Loss on sale of equipment	3,300	
Loss on retirement of bonds	825	(4,125)
Income before taxes		73,875
Income taxes expense		(13,725)
Net income		$ 60,150

Additional Information

a. Equipment costing $21,375 with accumulated depreciation of $11,100 is sold for cash.

b. Equipment purchases are for cash.

c. Accumulated Depreciation is affected by depreciation expense and the sale of equipment.

d. The balance of Retained Earnings is affected by dividend declarations and net income.

e. All sales are made on credit.

f. All merchandise inventory purchases are on credit.

g. Accounts Payable balances result from merchandise inventory purchases.

h. Prepaid expenses relate to "other operating expenses."

Required

1. Prepare a statement of cash flows using the indirect method for year 2009.

2.[B] Prepare a statement of cash flows using the direct method for year 2009.

Planning the Solution

- Prepare two blank statements of cash flows with sections for operating, investing, and financing activities using the (1) indirect method format and (2) direct method format.
- Compute the cash paid for equipment and the cash received from the sale of equipment using the additional information provided along with the amount for depreciation expense and the change in the balances of equipment and accumulated depreciation. Use T-accounts to help chart the effects of the sale and purchase of equipment on the balances of the Equipment account and the Accumulated Depreciation account.
- Compute the effect of net income on the change in the Retained Earnings account balance. Assign the difference between the change in retained earnings and the amount of net income to dividends declared. Adjust the dividends declared amount for the change in the Dividends Payable balance.
- Compute cash received from customers, cash paid for merchandise, cash paid for other operating expenses, and cash paid for taxes as illustrated in the chapter.
- Enter the cash effects of reconstruction entries to the appropriate section(s) of the statement.
- Total each section of the statement, determine the total net change in cash, and add it to the beginning balance to get the ending balance of cash.

Solution to Demonstration Problem

Supporting computations for cash receipts and cash payments.

(1)	*Cost of equipment sold	$ 21,375
	Accumulated depreciation of equipment sold	(11,100)
	Book value of equipment sold	10,275
	Loss on sale of equipment	(3,300)
	Cash received from sale of equipment	$ 6,975
	Cost of equipment sold	$ 21,375
	Less decrease in the equipment account balance	(10,875)
	Cash paid for new equipment	$ 10,500
(2)	Loss on retirement of bonds	$ 825
	Carrying value of bonds retired	37,500
	Cash paid to retire bonds	$ 38,325
(3)	Net income	$ 60,150
	Less increase in retained earnings	45,900
	Dividends declared	14,250
	Plus decrease in dividends payable	4,500
	Cash paid for dividends	$ 18,750
(4)[B]	Sales	$ 446,100
	Add decrease in accounts receivable	5,700
	Cash received from customers	$451,800
(5)[B]	Cost of goods sold	$ 222,300
	Plus increase in merchandise inventory	9,525
	Purchases	231,825
	Plus decrease in accounts payable	4,950
	Cash paid for merchandise	$236,775
(6)[B]	Other operating expenses	$ 120,300
	Plus increase in prepaid expenses	1,950
	Cash paid for other operating expenses	$122,250
(7)[B]	Income taxes expense	$ 13,725
	Less increase in income taxes payable	(675)
	Cash paid for income taxes	$ 13,050

* Supporting T-account analysis for part 1 follows:

Equipment			
Bal., Dec. 31, 2008	146,700		
Cash purchase	10,500	Sale	21,375
Bal., Dec. 31, 2009	135,825		

Accumulated Depreciation—Equipment			
		Bal., Dec. 31, 2008	47,550
Sale	11,100	Depr. expense	25,500
		Bal., Dec. 31, 2009	61,950

UMLAUF COMPANY
Statement of Cash Flows (Indirect Method)
For Year Ended December 31, 2009

Cash flows from operating activities		
Net income	$60,150	
Adjustments to reconcile net income to net cash provided by operating activities		
Decrease in accounts receivable	5,700	
Increase in merchandise inventory	(9,525)	
Increase in prepaid expenses	(1,950)	
Decrease in accounts payable	(4,950)	
Increase in income taxes payable	675	
Depreciation expense	25,500	
Loss on sale of plant assets	3,300	
Loss on retirement of bonds	825	
Net cash provided by operating activities		$79,725

[continued on next page]

[continued from previous page]

Cash flows from investing activities		
Cash received from sale of equipment	6,975	
Cash paid for equipment	(10,500)	
Net cash used in investing activities		(3,525)
Cash flows from financing activities		
Cash paid to retire bonds payable	(38,325)	
Cash paid for dividends	(18,750)	
Net cash used in financing activities		(57,075)
Net increase in cash		$19,125
Cash balance at prior year-end		23,925
Cash balance at current year-end		$43,050

UMLAUF COMPANY
Statement of Cash Flows (Direct Method)
For Year Ended December 31, 2009

Cash flows from operating activities		
Cash received from customers	$451,800	
Cash paid for merchandise	(236,775)	
Cash paid for other operating expenses	(122,250)	
Cash paid for income taxes	(13,050)	
Net cash provided by operating activities		$79,725
Cash flows from investing activities		
Cash received from sale of equipment	6,975	
Cash paid for equipment	(10,500)	
Net cash used in investing activities		(3,525)
Cash flows from financing activities		
Cash paid to retire bonds payable	(38,325)	
Cash paid for dividends	(18,750)	
Net cash used in financing activities		(57,075)
Net increase in cash		$19,125
Cash balance at prior year-end		23,925
Cash balance at current year-end		$43,050

APPENDIX

Spreadsheet Preparation of the Statement of Cash Flows

16A

This appendix explains how to use a spreadsheet to prepare the statement of cash flows under the indirect method.

Preparing the Indirect Method Spreadsheet

P4 Illustrate use of a spreadsheet to prepare a statement of cash flows.

Analyzing noncash accounts can be challenging when a company has a large number of accounts and many operating, investing, and financing transactions. A *spreadsheet,* also called *work sheet* or *working paper,* can help us organize the information needed to prepare a statement of cash flows. A spreadsheet also makes it easier to check the accuracy of our work. To illustrate, we return to the comparative balance sheets and income statement shown in Exhibit 16.10. We use the following identifying letters *a* through *g* to code changes in accounts, and letters *h* through *m* for additional information, to prepare the statement of cash flows:

a. Net income is $38,000.
b. Accounts receivable increase by $20,000.
c. Merchandise inventory increases by $14,000.
d. Prepaid expenses increase by $2,000.
e. Accounts payable decrease by $5,000.
f. Interest payable decreases by $1,000.
g. Income taxes payable increase by $10,000.
h. Depreciation expense is $24,000.
i. Plant assets costing $30,000 with accumulated depreciation of $12,000 are sold for $12,000 cash. This yields a loss on sale of assets of $6,000.
j. Notes with a book value of $34,000 are retired with a cash payment of $18,000, yielding a $16,000 gain on retirement.
k. Plant assets costing $70,000 are purchased with a cash payment of $10,000 and an issuance of notes payable for $60,000.
l. Issued 3,000 shares of common stock for $15,000 cash.
m. Paid cash dividends of $14,000.

Exhibit 16A.1 shows the indirect method spreadsheet for Genesis. We enter both beginning and ending balance sheet amounts on the spreadsheet. We also enter information in the Analysis of Changes columns (keyed to the additional information items *a* through *m*) to explain changes in the accounts and determine the cash flows for operating, investing, and financing activities. Information about noncash investing and financing activities is reported near the bottom.

Entering the Analysis of Changes on the Spreadsheet

The following sequence of procedures is used to complete the spreadsheet after the beginning and ending balances of the balance sheet accounts are entered:

① Enter net income as the first item in the Statement of Cash Flows section for computing operating cash inflow (debit) and as a credit to Retained Earnings.

② In the Statement of Cash Flows section, adjustments to net income are entered as debits if they increase cash flows and as credits if they decrease cash flows. Applying this same rule, adjust net income for the change in each noncash current asset and current liability account related to operating activities. For each adjustment to net income, the offsetting debit or credit must help reconcile the beginning and ending balances of a current asset or current liability account.

③ Enter adjustments to net income for income statement items not providing or using cash in the period. For each adjustment, the offsetting debit or credit must help reconcile a noncash balance sheet account.

④ Adjust net income to eliminate any gains or losses from investing and financing activities. Because the cash from a gain must be excluded from operating activities, the gain is entered as a credit in the operating activities section. Losses are entered as debits. For each adjustment, the related debit and/or credit must help reconcile balance sheet accounts and involve reconstructed entries to show the cash flow from investing or financing activities.

⑤ After reviewing any unreconciled balance sheet accounts and related information, enter the remaining reconciling entries for investing and financing activities. Examples are purchases of plant assets, issuances of long-term debt, stock issuances, and dividend payments. Some of these may require entries in the noncash investing and financing section of the spreadsheet (reconciled).

⑥ Check accuracy by totaling the Analysis of Changes columns and by determining that the change in each balance sheet account has been explained (reconciled).

Point: Analysis of the changes on the spreadsheet are summarized here:

1. Cash flows from operating activities generally affect net income, current assets, and current liabilities.
2. Cash flows from investing activities generally affect noncurrent asset accounts.
3. Cash flows from financing activities generally affect noncurrent liability and equity accounts.

We illustrate these steps in Exhibit 16A.1 for Genesis:

Step	Entries
①	(*a*)
②	(*b*) through (*g*)
③	(*h*)
④	(*i*) through (*j*)
⑤	(*k*) through (*m*)

EXHIBIT 16A.1

Spreadsheet for Preparing Statement of Cash Flows—Indirect Method

GENESIS
Spreadsheet for Statement of Cash Flows—Indirect Method
For Year Ended December 31, 2009

	Dec. 31, 2008		Analysis of Changes Debit		Analysis of Changes Credit	Dec. 31, 2009
Balance Sheet—Debits						
Cash	$ 12,000					$ 17,000
Accounts receivable	40,000	(b)	$ 20,000			60,000
Merchandise inventory	70,000	(c)	14,000			84,000
Prepaid expenses	4,000	(d)	2,000			6,000
Plant assets	210,000	(k1)	70,000	(i)	$ 30,000	250,000
	$336,000					$417,000
Balance Sheet—Credits						
Accumulated depreciation	$ 48,000	(i)	12,000	(h)	24,000	$ 60,000
Accounts payable	40,000	(e)	5,000			35,000
Interest payable	4,000	(f)	1,000			3,000
Income taxes payable	12,000			(g)	10,000	22,000
Notes payable	64,000	(j)	34,000	(k2)	60,000	90,000
Common stock, $5 par value	80,000			(l)	15,000	95,000
Retained earnings	88,000	(m)	14,000	(a)	38,000	112,000
	$336,000					$417,000
Statement of Cash Flows						
Operating activities						
Net income		(a)	38,000			
Increase in accounts receivable				(b)	20,000	
Increase in merchandise inventory				(c)	14,000	
Increase in prepaid expenses				(d)	2,000	
Decrease in accounts payable				(e)	5,000	
Decrease in interest payable				(f)	1,000	
Increase in income taxes payable		(g)	10,000			
Depreciation expense		(h)	24,000			
Loss on sale of plant assets		(i)	6,000			
Gain on retirement of notes				(j)	16,000	
Investing activities						
Receipts from sale of plant assets		(i)	12,000			
Payment for purchase of plant assets				(k1)	10,000	
Financing activities						
Payment to retire notes				(j)	18,000	
Receipts from issuing stock		(l)	15,000			
Payment of cash dividends				(m)	14,000	
Noncash Investing and Financing Activities						
Purchase of plant assets with notes		(k2)	60,000	(k1)	60,000	
			$337,000		$337,000	

Since adjustments *i*, *j*, and *k* are more challenging, we show them in the following debit and credit format. These entries are for purposes of our understanding; they are *not* the entries actually made in the journals. Changes in the Cash account are identified as sources or uses of cash.

		Debit	Credit
i.	Loss from sale of plant assets	6,000	
	Accumulated depreciation	12,000	
	Receipt from sale of plant assets **(source of cash)**	12,000	
	Plant assets		30,000
	To describe sale of plant assets.		

[continued on next page]

[continued from previous page]

j.	Notes payable	34,000	
	Payments to retire notes **(use of cash)**		18,000
	Gain on retirement of notes		16,000
	To describe retirement of notes.		
k1.	Plant assets	70,000	
	Payment to purchase plant assets **(use of cash)**		10,000
	Purchase of plant assets financed by notes		60,000
	To describe purchase of plant assets.		
k2.	Purchase of plant assets financed by notes	60,000	
	Notes payable		60,000
	To issue notes for purchase of assets.		

APPENDIX

16B Direct Method of Reporting Operating Cash Flows

P5 Compute cash flows from operating activities using the direct method.

We compute cash flows from operating activities under the direct method by adjusting accrual-based income statement items to the cash basis. The usual approach is to adjust income statement accounts related to operating activities for changes in their related balance sheet accounts as follows:

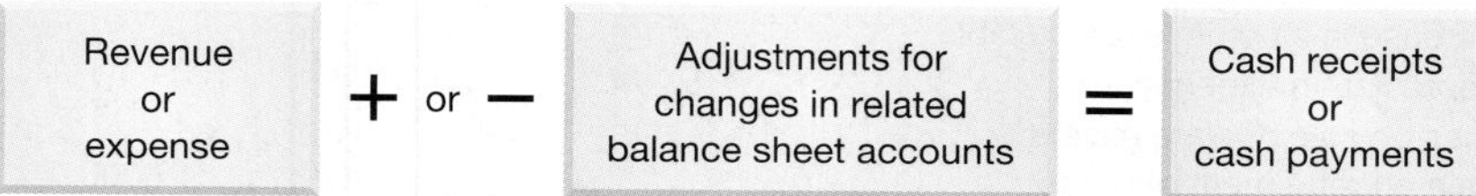

Revenue or expense
+ or −
Adjustments for changes in related balance sheet accounts
=
Cash receipts or cash payments

The framework for reporting cash receipts and cash payments for the operating section of the cash flow statement under the direct method is shown in Exhibit 16B.1. We consider cash receipts first and then cash payments.

EXHIBIT 16B.1

Major Classes of Operating Cash Flows

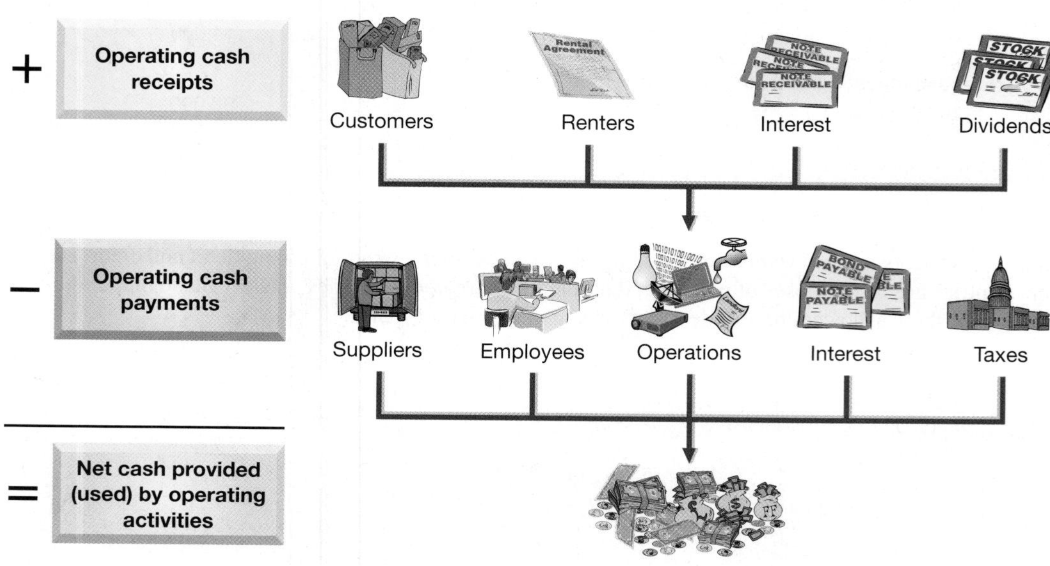

Operating Cash Receipts

A review of Exhibit 16.10 and the additional information reported by Genesis suggests only one potential cash receipt: sales to customers. This section, therefore, starts with sales to customers as reported on the income statement and then adjusts it as necessary to obtain cash received from customers to report on the statement of cash flows.

Cash Received from Customers If all sales are for cash, the amount received from customers equals the sales reported on the income statement. When some or all sales are on account, however, we must adjust the amount of sales for the change in Accounts Receivable. It is often helpful to use *account analysis* to do this. This usually involves setting up a T-account and reconstructing its major entries, with emphasis on cash receipts and payments. To illustrate, we use a T-account that includes accounts receivable balances for Genesis on December 31, 2008 and 2009. The beginning balance is $40,000 and the ending balance is $60,000. Next, the income statement shows sales of $590,000, which we enter on the debit side of this account. We now can reconstruct the Accounts Receivable account to determine the amount of cash received from customers as follows:

Point: An accounts receivable increase implies that cash received from customers is less than sales (the converse is also true).

Accounts Receivable			
Bal., Dec. 31, 2008	40,000		
Sales	590,000	**Cash receipts =**	**570,000**
Bal., Dec. 31, 2009	60,000		

This T-account shows that the Accounts Receivable balance begins at $40,000 and increases to $630,000 from sales of $590,000, yet its ending balance is only $60,000. This implies that cash receipts from customers are $570,000, computed as $40,000 + $590,000 − [?] = $60,000. This computation can be rearranged to express cash received as equal to sales of $590,000 minus a $20,000 increase in accounts receivable. This computation is summarized as a general rule in Exhibit 16B.2. The statement of cash flows in Exhibit 16.7 reports the $570,000 cash received from customers as a cash inflow from operating activities.

Example: If the ending balance of accounts receivable is $20,000 (instead of $60,000), what is cash received from customers? *Answer:* $610,000

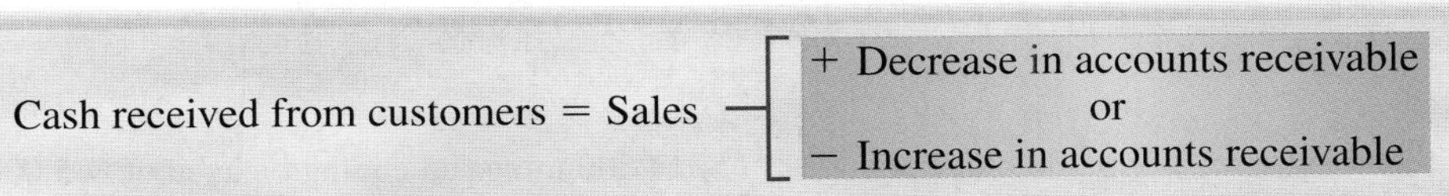

EXHIBIT 16B.2

Formula to Compute Cash Received from Customers—Direct Method

Other Cash Receipts While Genesis's cash receipts are limited to collections from customers, we often see other types of cash receipts, most commonly cash receipts involving rent, interest, and dividends. We compute cash received from these items by subtracting an increase in their respective receivable or adding a decrease. For instance, if rent receivable increases in the period, cash received from renters is less than rent revenue reported on the income statement. If rent receivable decreases, cash received is more than reported rent revenue. The same logic applies to interest and dividends. The formulas for these computations are summarized later in this appendix.

Point: Net income is measured using accrual accounting. Cash flows from operations are measured using cash basis accounting.

Operating Cash Payments

A review of Exhibit 16.10 and the additional Genesis information shows four operating expenses: cost of goods sold; wages and other operating expenses; interest expense; and taxes expense. We analyze each expense to compute its cash amounts for the statement of cash flows. (We then examine depreciation and the other losses and gains.)

Cash Paid for Merchandise We compute cash paid for merchandise by analyzing both cost of goods sold and merchandise inventory. If all merchandise purchases are for cash and the ending balance of Merchandise Inventory is unchanged from the beginning balance, the amount of cash paid for merchandise equals cost of goods sold—an uncommon situation. Instead, there normally is some change in the Merchandise Inventory balance. Also, some or all merchandise purchases are often made on credit, and this yields changes in the Accounts Payable balance. When the balances of both Merchandise Inventory and Accounts Payable change, we must adjust the cost of goods sold for changes in both accounts to compute cash paid for merchandise. This is a two-step adjustment.

First, we use the change in the account balance of Merchandise Inventory, along with the cost of goods sold amount, to compute cost of purchases for the period. An increase in merchandise inventory implies that we bought more than we sold, and we add this inventory increase to cost of goods sold to compute cost of purchases. A decrease in merchandise inventory implies that we bought less than we sold, and we subtract the inventory decrease from cost of goods sold to compute purchases. We illustrate the *first step* by reconstructing the Merchandise Inventory account of Genesis:

Merchandise Inventory			
Bal., Dec. 31, 2008	70,000		
Purchases =	**314,000**	Cost of goods sold	300,000
Bal., Dec. 31, 2009	84,000		

The beginning balance is $70,000, and the ending balance is $84,000. The income statement shows that cost of goods sold is $300,000, which we enter on the credit side of this account. With this information, we determine the amount for cost of purchases to be $314,000. This computation can be rearranged to express cost of purchases as equal to cost of goods sold of $300,000 plus the $14,000 increase in inventory.

The second step uses the change in the balance of Accounts Payable, and the amount of cost of purchases, to compute cash paid for merchandise. A decrease in accounts payable implies that we paid for more goods than we acquired this period, and we would then add the accounts payable decrease to cost of purchases to compute cash paid for merchandise. An increase in accounts payable implies that we paid for less than the amount of goods acquired, and we would subtract the accounts payable increase from purchases to compute cash paid for merchandise. The *second step* is applied to Genesis by reconstructing its Accounts Payable account:

Accounts Payable			
		Bal., Dec. 31, 2008	40,000
Cash payments =	**319,000**	Purchases	314,000
		Bal., Dec. 31, 2009	35,000

Example: If the ending balances of Inventory and Accounts Payable are $60,000 and $50,000, respectively (instead of $84,000 and $35,000), what is cash paid for merchandise? *Answer:* $280,000

Its beginning balance of $40,000 plus purchases of $314,000 minus an ending balance of $35,000 yields cash paid of $319,000 (or $40,000 + $314,000 − [?] = $35,000). Alternatively, we can express cash paid for merchandise as equal to purchases of $314,000 plus the $5,000 decrease in accounts payable. The $319,000 cash paid for merchandise is reported on the statement of cash flows in Exhibit 16.7 as a cash outflow under operating activities.

We summarize this two-step adjustment to cost of goods sold to compute cash paid for merchandise inventory in Exhibit 16B.3.

EXHIBIT 16B.3

Two Steps to Compute Cash Paid for Merchandise—Direct Method

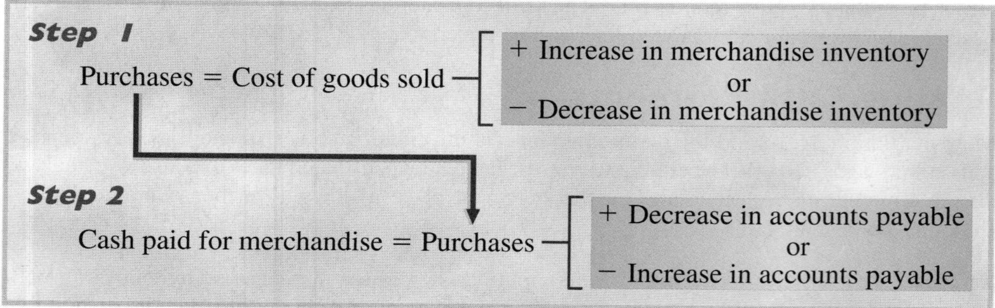

Cash Paid for Wages and Operating Expenses (Excluding Depreciation)

The income statement of Genesis shows wages and other operating expenses of $216,000 (see Exhibit 16.10). To compute cash paid for wages and other operating expenses, we adjust this amount for any changes in their related balance sheet accounts. We begin by looking for any prepaid expenses and accrued liabilities related to wages and other operating expenses in the balance sheets of Genesis in

Exhibit 16.10. The balance sheets show prepaid expenses but no accrued liabilities. Thus, the adjustment is limited to the change in prepaid expenses. The amount of adjustment is computed by assuming that all cash paid for wages and other operating expenses is initially debited to Prepaid Expenses. This assumption allows us to reconstruct the Prepaid Expenses account:

Prepaid Expenses			
Bal., Dec. 31, 2008	4,000		
Cash payments =	**218,000**	Wages and other operating exp.	216,000
Bal., Dec. 31, 2009	6,000		

Prepaid Expenses increase by $2,000 in the period, meaning that cash paid for wages and other operating expenses exceeds the reported expense by $2,000. Alternatively, we can express cash paid for wages and other operating expenses as equal to its reported expenses of $216,000 plus the $2,000 increase in prepaid expenses.[1]

Point: A decrease in prepaid expenses implies that reported expenses include an amount(s) that did not require a cash outflow in the period.

Exhibit 16B.4 summarizes the adjustments to wages (including salaries) and other operating expenses. The Genesis balance sheet did not report accrued liabilities, but we include them in the formula to explain the adjustment to cash when they do exist. A decrease in accrued liabilities implies that we paid cash for more goods or services than received this period, so we add the decrease in accrued liabilities to the expense amount to obtain cash paid for these goods or services. An increase in accrued liabilities implies that we paid cash for less than what was acquired, so we subtract this increase in accrued liabilities from the expense amount to get cash paid.

EXHIBIT 16B.4

Formula to Compute Cash Paid for Wages and Operating Expenses—Direct Method

Cash paid for wages and other operating expenses	=	Wages and other operating expenses	+ Increase in prepaid expenses or − Decrease in prepaid expenses	+ Decrease in accrued liabilities or − Increase in accrued liabilities

Cash Paid for Interest and Income Taxes Computing operating cash flows for interest and taxes is similar to that for operating expenses. Both require adjustments to their amounts reported on the income statement for changes in their related balance sheet accounts. We begin with the Genesis income statement showing interest expense of $7,000 and income taxes expense of $15,000. To compute the cash paid, we adjust interest expense for the change in interest payable and then the income taxes expense for the change in income taxes payable. These computations involve reconstructing both liability accounts:

Interest Payable			
		Bal., Dec. 31, 2008	4,000
Cash paid for interest =	**8,000**	Interest expense	7,000
		Bal., Dec. 31, 2009	3,000

Income Taxes Payable			
		Bal., Dec. 31, 2008	12,000
Cash paid for taxes =	**5,000**	Income taxes expense	15,000
		Bal., Dec. 31, 2009	22,000

These accounts reveal cash paid for interest of $8,000 and cash paid for income taxes of $5,000. The formulas to compute these amounts are in Exhibit 16B.5. Both of these cash payments are reported as operating cash outflows on the statement of cash flows in Exhibit 16.7.

[1] The assumption that all cash payments for wages and operating expenses are initially debited to Prepaid Expenses is not necessary for our analysis to hold. If cash payments are debited directly to the expense account, the total amount of cash paid for wages and other operating expenses still equals the $216,000 expense plus the $2,000 increase in Prepaid Expenses (which arise from end-of-period adjusting entries).

EXHIBIT 16B.5

Formulas to Compute Cash Paid for Both Interest and Taxes—Direct Method

Cash paid for interest	=	Interest expense	+ Decrease in interest payable or − Increase in interest payable
Cash paid for taxes	=	Income taxes expenses	+ Decrease in income taxes payable or − Increase in income taxes payable

Analysis of Additional Expenses, Gains, and Losses Genesis has three additional items reported on its income statement: depreciation, loss on sale of assets, and gain on retirement of debt. We must consider each for its potential cash effects.

Depreciation Expense Depreciation expense is $24,000. It is often called a *noncash expense* because depreciation has no cash flows. Depreciation expense is an allocation of an asset's depreciable cost. The cash outflow with a plant asset is reported as part of investing activities when it is paid for. Thus, depreciation expense is *never* reported on a statement of cash flows using the direct method; nor is depletion or amortization expense.

Loss on Sale of Assets Sales of assets frequently result in gains and losses reported as part of net income, but the amount of recorded gain or loss does *not* reflect any cash flows in these transactions. Asset sales result in cash inflow equal to the cash amount received, regardless of whether the asset was sold at a gain or a loss. This cash inflow is reported under investing activities. Thus, the loss or gain on a sale of assets is *never* reported on a statement of cash flows using the direct method.

Gain on Retirement of Debt Retirement of debt usually yields a gain or loss reported as part of net income, but that gain or loss does *not* reflect cash flow in this transaction. Debt retirement results in cash outflow equal to the cash paid to settle the debt, regardless of whether the debt is retired at a gain or loss. This cash outflow is reported under financing activities; the loss or gain from retirement of debt is *never* reported on a statement of cash flows using the direct method.

Point: The direct method is usually viewed as *user friendly* because less accounting knowledge is required to understand and use it.

Summary of Adjustments for Direct Method

Exhibit 16B.6 summarizes common adjustments for net income to yield net cash provided (used) by operating activities under the direct method.

EXHIBIT 16B.6

Summary of Selected Adjustments for Direct Method

Item	From Income Statement	Adjustments to Obtain Cash Flow Numbers	
Receipts			
From sales	Sales Revenue	+Decrease in Accounts Receivable −Increase in Accounts Receivable	
From rent	Rent Revenue	+Decrease in Rent Receivable −Increase in Rent Receivable	
From interest	Interest Revenue	+Decrease in Interest Receivable −Increase in Interest Receivable	
From dividends	Dividend Revenue	+Decrease in Dividends Receivable −Increase in Dividends Receivable	
Payments			
To suppliers	Cost of Goods Sold	+Increase in Inventory −Decrease in Inventory	+Decrease in Accounts Payable −Increase in Accounts Payable
For operations	Operating Expense	+Increase in Prepaids −Decrease in Prepaids	+Decrease in Accrued Liabilities −Increase in Accrued Liabilities
To employees	Wages (Salaries) Expense	+Decrease in Wages (Salaries) Payable −Increase in Wages (Salaries) Payable	
For interest	Interest Expense	+Decrease in Interest Payable −Increase in Interest Payable	
For taxes	Income Tax Expense	+Decrease in Income Tax Payable −Increase in Income Tax Payable	

Direct Method Format of Operating Activities Section

Exhibit 16.7 shows the Genesis statement of cash flows using the direct method. Major items of cash inflows and cash outflows are listed separately in the operating activities section. The format requires that operating cash outflows be subtracted from operating cash inflows to get net cash provided (used) by operating activities. The FASB recommends that the operating activities section of the statement of cash flows be reported using the direct method, which is considered more useful to financial statement users. *However, the FASB requires a reconciliation of net income to net cash provided (used) by operating activities when the direct method is used* (which can be reported in the notes). This reconciliation is similar to preparation of the operating activities section of the statement of cash flows using the indirect method.

Point: Some preparers argue that it is easier to prepare a statement of cash flows using the indirect method. This likely explains its greater frequency in financial statements.

Decision Insight

IFRSs Like U.S. GAAP, IFRSs allow cash flows from operating activities to be reported using either the indirect method or the direct method.

Quick Check

Answers—p. 658

8. Net sales in a period are $590,000, beginning accounts receivable are $120,000, and ending accounts receivable are $90,000. What cash amount is collected from customers in the period?
9. The Merchandise Inventory account balance decreases in the period from a beginning balance of $32,000 to an ending balance of $28,000. Cost of goods sold for the period is $168,000. If the Accounts Payable balance increases $2,400 in the period, what is the cash amount paid for merchandise inventory?
10. This period's wages and other operating expenses total $112,000. Beginning-of-period prepaid expenses totaled $1,200, and its ending balance is $4,200. There were no beginning-of-period accrued liabilities, but end-of-period wages payable equal $5,600. How much cash is paid for wages and other operating expenses?

Summary

C1 Explain the purpose and importance of cash flow information. The main purpose of the statement of cash flows is to report the major cash receipts and cash payments for a period. This includes identifying cash flows as relating to operating, investing, or financing activities. Most business decisions involve evaluating activities that provide or use cash.

C2 Distinguish between operating, investing, and financing activities. Operating activities include transactions and events that determine net income. Investing activities include transactions and events that mainly affect long-term assets. Financing activities include transactions and events that mainly affect long-term liabilities and equity.

C3 Identify and disclose noncash investing and financing activities. Noncash investing and financing activities must be disclosed in either a note or a separate schedule to the statement of cash flows. Examples are the retirement of debt by issuing equity and the exchange of a note payable for plant assets.

C4 Describe the format of the statement of cash flows. The statement of cash flows separates cash receipts and cash payments into operating, investing, or financing activities.

A1 Analyze the statement of cash flows. To understand and predict cash flows, users stress identification of the sources and uses of cash flows by operating, investing, and financing activities. Emphasis is on operating cash flows since they derive from continuing operations.

A2 Compute and apply the cash flow on total assets ratio. The cash flow on total assets ratio is defined as operating cash flows divided by average total assets. Analysis of current and past values for this ratio can reflect a company's ability to yield regular and positive cash flows. It is also viewed as a measure of earnings quality.

P1 Prepare a statement of cash flows. Preparation of a statement of cash flows involves five steps: (1) Compute the net increase or decrease in cash; (2) compute net cash provided or used by operating activities (*using either the direct or indirect method*); (3) compute net cash provided or used by investing activities; (4) compute net cash provided or used by financing activities; and (5) report the beginning and ending cash balance and prove that it is explained by net cash flows. Noncash investing and financing activities are also disclosed.

P2 Compute cash flows from operating activities using the indirect method. The indirect method for reporting net cash provided or used by operating activities starts with net income and then adjusts it for three items: (1) changes in noncash current assets and current liabilities related to operating activities, (2) revenues and expenses not providing or using cash, and (3) gains and losses from investing and financing activities.

P3 Determine cash flows from both investing and financing activities. Cash flows from both investing and financing activities are determined by identifying the cash flow effects of transactions and events affecting each balance sheet account related to these activities. All cash flows from these activities are identified when we can explain changes in these accounts from the beginning to the end of the period.

P4[A] **Illustrate use of a spreadsheet to prepare a statement of cash flows.** A spreadsheet is a useful tool in preparing a statement of cash flows. Six key steps (see Appendix 16A) are applied when using the spreadsheet to prepare the statement.

P5[B] **Compute cash flows from operating activities using the direct method.** The direct method for reporting net cash provided or used by operating activities lists major operating cash inflows less cash outflows to yield net cash inflow or outflow from operations.

Guidance Answers to **Decision Maker**

Entrepreneur Several factors might explain an increase in net cash flows when a net loss is reported, including (1) early recognition of expenses relative to revenues generated (such as research and development), (2) cash advances on long-term sales contracts not yet recognized in income, (3) issuances of debt or equity for cash to finance expansion, (4) cash sale of assets, (5) delay of cash payments, and (6) cash prepayment on sales. Analysis needs to focus on the components of both the net loss and the net cash flows and their implications for future performance.

Reporter Your initial reaction based on the company's \$600,000 loss with a \$550,000 decrease in net cash flows is not positive. However, closer scrutiny reveals a more positive picture of this company's performance. Cash flow from operating activities is \$650,000, computed as [?] − \$850,000 − \$350,000 = \$(550,000). You also note that net income *before* the extraordinary loss is \$330,000, computed as [?] − \$930,000 = \$(600,000).

Guidance Answers to **Quick Checks**

1. No to both. The statement of cash flows reports changes in the sum of cash plus cash equivalents. It does not report transfers between cash and cash equivalents.

2. The three categories of cash inflows and outflows are operating activities, investing activities, and financing activities.

3. **a.** Investing **b.** Operating **c.** Financing **d.** Operating **e.** Operating **f.** Financing

4. \$74,900 + \$4,600 − \$11,700 − \$1,000 + \$3,400 = \$70,200

5. Expenses such as depreciation and amortization do not require current cash outflows. Therefore, adding these expenses back to net income eliminates these noncash items from the net income number, converting it to a cash basis.

6. A gain on the sale of plant assets is subtracted from net income because a sale of plant assets is not an operating activity; it is an investing activity for the amount of cash received from its sale. Also, such a gain yields no cash effects.

7. \$80,000 − \$30,000 − \$10,000 = \$40,000 cash receipt. The \$40,000 cash receipt is reported as an investing activity.

8. \$590,000 + (\$120,000 − \$90,000) = \$620,000

9. \$168,000 − (\$32,000 − \$28,000) − \$2,400 = \$161,600

10. \$112,000 + (\$4,200 − \$1,200) − \$5,600 = \$109,400

Key Terms

mhhe.com/wildFAP19e

Key Terms are available at the book's Website for learning and testing in an online Flashcard Format.

Cash flow on total assets (p. 646)
Direct method (p. 634)
Financing activities (p. 630)
Indirect method (p. 634)
Investing activities (p. 630)
Operating activities (p. 629)
Statement of cash flows (p. 628)

Multiple Choice Quiz

Answers on p. 677 mhhe.com/wildFAP19e

Additional Quiz Questions are available at the book's Website.

Quiz16

1. A company uses the indirect method to determine its cash flows from operating activities. Use the following information to determine its net cash provided or used by operating activities.

Net income	\$15,200
Depreciation expense	10,000
Cash payment on note payable	8,000
Gain on sale of land	3,000
Increase in inventory	1,500
Increase in accounts payable	2,850

a. $23,550 used by operating activities
b. $23,550 provided by operating activities
c. $15,550 provided by operating activities
d. $42,400 provided by operating activities
e. $20,850 provided by operating activities

2. A machine with a cost of $175,000 and accumulated depreciation of $94,000 is sold for $87,000 cash. The amount reported as a source of cash under cash flows from investing activities is
a. $81,000.
b. $6,000.
c. $87,000.
d. Zero; this is a financing activity.
e. Zero; this is an operating activity.

3. A company settles a long-term note payable plus interest by paying $68,000 cash toward the principal amount and $5,440 cash for interest. The amount reported as a use of cash under cash flows from financing activities is
a. Zero; this is an investing activity.
b. Zero; this is an operating activity.
c. $73,440.
d. $68,000.
e. $5,440.

4. The following information is available regarding a company's annual salaries and wages. What amount of cash is paid for salaries and wages?

Salaries and wages expense	$255,000
Salaries and wages payable, prior year-end	8,200
Salaries and wages payable, current year-end	10,900

a. $252,300
b. $257,700
c. $255,000
d. $274,100
e. $235,900

5. The following information is available for a company. What amount of cash is paid for merchandise for the current year?

Cost of goods sold	$545,000
Merchandise inventory, prior year-end	105,000
Merchandise inventory, current year-end	112,000
Accounts payable, prior year-end	98,500
Accounts payable, current year-end	101,300

a. $545,000
b. $554,800
c. $540,800
d. $535,200
e. $549,200

Superscript letter A(B) denotes assignments based on Appendix 16A (16B).

Discussion Questions

1. What is the reporting purpose of the statement of cash flows? Identify at least two questions that this statement can answer.

2. Describe the direct method of reporting cash flows from operating activities.

3. When a statement of cash flows is prepared using the direct method, what are some of the operating cash flows?

4. Describe the indirect method of reporting cash flows from operating activities.

5. What are some investing activities reported on the statement of cash flows?

6. What are some financing activities reported on the statement of cash flows?

7. Where on the statement of cash flows is the payment of cash dividends reported?

8. Assume that a company purchases land for $100,000, paying $20,000 cash and borrowing the remainder with a long-term note payable. How should this transaction be reported on a statement of cash flows?

9. On June 3, a company borrows $50,000 cash by giving its bank a 160-day, interest-bearing note. On the statement of cash flows, where should this be reported?

10. If a company reports positive net income for the year, can it also show a net cash outflow from operating activities? Explain.

11. Is depreciation a source of cash flow?

12. Refer to **Best Buy**'s statement of cash flows in Appendix A. (*a*) Which method is used to compute its net cash provided by operating activities? (*b*) While its balance sheet shows an increase in receivables from fiscal years 2006 to 2007, why is this increase in receivables subtracted when computing net cash provided by operating activities for the year ended March 3, 2007?

13. Refer to **Circuit City**'s statement of cash flows in Appendix A. What are its cash flows from financing activities for the year ended February 28, 2007? List items and amounts.

14. Refer to **RadioShack**'s statement of cash flows in Appendix A. List its cash flows from operating activities, investing activities, and financing activities.

15. Refer to **Apple**'s statement of cash flows in Appendix A. What investing activities result in cash outflows for the year ended September 30, 2006? List items and amounts.

Denotes Discussion Questions that involve decision making.

Available with McGraw-Hill's Homework Manager

McGraw-Hill's HOMEWORK MANAGER®

QUICK STUDY

QS 16-1
Statement of cash flows
C1 C2 C3

The statement of cash flows is one of the four primary financial statements.

1. Describe the content and layout of a statement of cash flows, including its three sections.
2. List at least three transactions classified as investing activities in a statement of cash flows.
3. List at least three transactions classified as financing activities in a statement of cash flows.
4. List at least three transactions classified as significant noncash financing and investing activities in the statement of cash flows.

QS 16-2
Transaction classification by activity
C2

Classify the following cash flows as operating, investing, or financing activities.

1. Sold long-term investments for cash.
2. Received cash payments from customers.
3. Paid cash for wages and salaries.
4. Purchased inventories for cash.
5. Paid cash dividends.
6. Issued common stock for cash.
7. Received cash interest on a note.
8. Paid cash interest on outstanding notes.
9. Received cash from sale of land at a loss.
10. Paid cash for property taxes on building.

QS 16-3
Computing cash from operations (indirect)
P2

Use the following information to determine this company's cash flows from operating activities using the indirect method.

LOLLAND COMPANY
Selected Balance Sheet Information
December 31, 2009 and 2008

	2009	2008
Current assets		
Cash	$169,300	$ 53,600
Accounts receivable	50,000	64,000
Inventory	120,000	108,200
Current liabilities		
Accounts payable	60,800	51,400
Income taxes payable	4,100	4,400

LOLLAND COMPANY
Income Statement
For Year Ended December 31, 2009

Sales		$1,030,000
Cost of goods sold		663,200
Gross profit		366,800
Operating expenses		
Depreciation expense	$ 72,000	
Other expenses	243,000	315,000
Income before taxes		51,800
Income taxes expense		15,400
Net income		$ 36,400

QS 16-4
Computing cash from asset sales
P3

The following selected information is from Manning Company's comparative balance sheets.

At December 31	2009	2008
Furniture	$ 264,000	$ 369,000
Accumulated depreciation—Furniture	(174,400)	(221,400)

The income statement reports depreciation expense for the year of $36,000. Also, furniture costing $105,000 was sold for its book value. Compute the cash received from the sale of furniture.

QS 16-5
Computing financing cash flows
P3

The following selected information is from the Tanner Company's comparative balance sheets.

At December 31	2009	2008
Common stock, $10 par value	$ 210,000	$200,000
Paid-in capital in excess of par	1,134,000	684,000
Retained earnings	627,000	575,000

The company's net income for the year ended December 31, 2009, was $96,000.

1. Compute the cash received from the sale of its common stock during 2009.
2. Compute the cash paid for dividends during 2009.

QS 16-6
Computing cash from operations (indirect) P2 

Use the following balance sheets and income statement to answer QS 16-6 through QS 16-11.

Use the indirect method to prepare the cash provided or used from operating activities section only of the statement of cash flows for this company.

AMMONS, INC.
Comparative Balance Sheets
December 31, 2009

	2009	2008
Assets		
Cash	$189,600	$ 48,000
Accounts receivable, net	82,000	102,000
Inventory	171,600	191,600
Prepaid expenses	10,800	8,400
Furniture	218,000	238,000
Accum. depreciation—Furniture	(34,000)	(18,000)
Total assets	$638,000	$570,000
Liabilities and Equity		
Accounts payable	$ 30,000	$ 42,000
Wages payable	18,000	10,000
Income taxes payable	2,800	5,200
Notes payable (long-term)	58,000	138,000
Common stock, $5 par value	458,000	358,000
Retained earnings	71,200	16,800
Total liabilities and equity	$638,000	$570,000

AMMONS, INC.
Income Statement
For Year Ended December 31, 2009

Sales		$976,000
Cost of goods sold		628,000
Gross profit		348,000
Operating expenses		
Depreciation expense	$ 75,200	
Other expenses	178,200	253,400
Income before taxes		94,600
Income taxes expense		34,600
Net income		$ 60,000

QS 16-7
Computing cash from asset sales P3 

Refer to the data in QS 16-6.
Furniture costing $110,000 is sold at its book value in 2009. Acquisitions of furniture total $90,000 cash, on which no depreciation is necessary because it is acquired at year-end. What is the cash inflow related to the sale of furniture?

QS 16-8
Computing financing cash outflows P3

Refer to the data in QS 16-6.

1. Assume that all common stock is issued for cash. What amount of cash dividends is paid during 2009?
2. Assume that no additional notes payable are issued in 2009. What cash amount is paid to reduce the notes payable balance in 2009?

QS 16-9[B]
Computing cash received from customers P5

Refer to the data in QS 16-6.

1. How much cash is received from sales to customers for year 2009?
2. What is the net increase or decrease in cash for year 2009?

QS 16-10[B]
Computing operating cash outflows P5

Refer to the data in QS 16-6.

1. How much cash is paid to acquire merchandise inventory during year 2009?
2. How much cash is paid for operating expenses during year 2009?

QS 16-11[B]
Computing cash from operations (direct) P5 

Refer to the data in QS 16-6.
Use the direct method to prepare the cash provided or used from operating activities section only of the statement of cash flows for this company.

QS 16-12
Analyses of sources and uses of cash A1 A2 

Financial data from three competitors in the same industry follow.

1. Which of the three competitors is in the strongest position as shown by its statement of cash flows?
2. Analyze and compare the strength of Peña's cash flow on total assets ratio to that of Garcia.

($ thousands)	Peña	Garcia	Piniella
Cash provided (used) by operating activities	$ 140,000	$ 120,000	$ (48,000)
Cash provided (used) by investing activities			
Proceeds from sale of operating assets			52,000
Purchase of operating assets	(56,000)	(68,000)	
Cash provided (used) by financing activities			
Proceeds from issuance of debt			46,000
Repayment of debt	(12,000)		
Net increase (decrease) in cash	$ 72,000	$ 52,000	$ 50,000
Average total assets	$ 1,580,000	$ 1,250,000	$ 600,000

QS 16-13ᴬ
Noncash accounts on a spreadsheet P4

When a spreadsheet for a statement of cash flows is prepared, all changes in noncash balance sheet accounts are fully explained on the spreadsheet. Explain how these noncash balance sheet accounts are used to fully account for cash flows on a spreadsheet.

QS 16-14
Computing cash flows from operations (indirect)
P2

For each of the following separate cases, compute cash flows from operations. The list includes all balance sheet accounts related to operating activities.

	Case A	Case B	Case C
Net income	$ 8,000	$200,000	$144,000
Depreciation expense	60,000	16,000	48,000
Accounts receivable increase (decrease)	80,000	40,000	(8,000)
Inventory increase (decrease)	(40,000)	(20,000)	21,000
Accounts payable increase (decrease)	48,000	(44,000)	28,000
Accrued liabilities increase (decrease)	(88,000)	24,000	(16,000)

QS 16-15
Computing cash flows from investing
P3

Compute cash flows from investing activities using the following company information.

Sale of short-term investments	$12,000
Cash collections from customers	32,000
Purchase of used equipment	10,000
Depreciation expense	4,000

QS 16-16
Computing cash flows from financing
P3

Compute cash flows from financing activities using the following company information.

Additional short-term borrowings	$40,000
Purchase of short-term investments	10,000
Cash dividends paid	32,000
Interest paid	16,000

EXERCISES

Exercise 16-1
Cash flow from operations (indirect)
P2

Hehman Company reports net income of $530,000 for the year ended December 31, 2009. It also reports $95,400 depreciation expense and a $4,000 gain on the sale of machinery. Its comparative balance sheets reveal a $42,400 increase in accounts receivable, $21,730 increase in accounts payable, $11,660 decrease in prepaid expenses, and $16,430 decrease in wages payable.

Required

Prepare only the operating activities section of the statement of cash flows for 2009 using the *indirect method.*

The following transactions and events occurred during the year. Assuming that this company uses the *indirect method* to report cash provided by operating activities, indicate where each item would appear on its statement of cash flows by placing an *x* in the appropriate column.

Exercise 16-2
Cash flow classification (indirect) C2 C3 P2 

	Statement of Cash Flows			Noncash Investing and Financing Activities	Not Reported on Statement or in Notes
	Operating Activities	Investing Activities	Financing Activities		
a. Paid cash to purchase inventory.	____	____	____	____	____
b. Purchased land by issuing common stock.	____	____	____	____	____
c. Accounts receivable decreased in the year.	____	____	____	____	____
d. Sold equipment for cash, yielding a loss.	____	____	____	____	____
e. Recorded depreciation expense.	____	____	____	____	____
f. Income taxes payable increased in the year.	____	____	____	____	____
g. Declared and paid a cash dividend.	____	____	____	____	____
h. Accounts payable decreased in the year	____	____	____	____	____
i. Paid cash to settle notes payable	____	____	____	____	____
j. Prepaid expenses increased in the year	____	____	____	____	____

The following transactions and events occurred during the year. Assuming that this company uses the *direct method* to report cash provided by operating activities, indicate where each item would appear on the statement of cash flows by placing an *x* in the appropriate column.

Exercise 16-3[B]
Cash flow classification (direct) C2 C3 P5

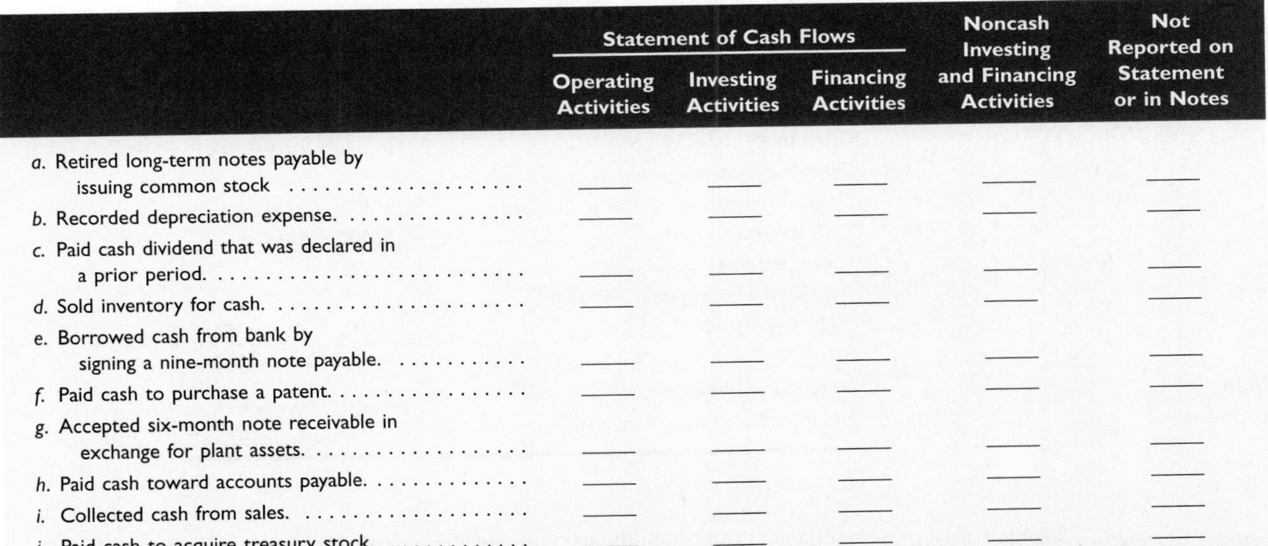

	Statement of Cash Flows			Noncash Investing and Financing Activities	Not Reported on Statement or in Notes
	Operating Activities	Investing Activities	Financing Activities		
a. Retired long-term notes payable by issuing common stock	____	____	____	____	____
b. Recorded depreciation expense.	____	____	____	____	____
c. Paid cash dividend that was declared in a prior period.	____	____	____	____	____
d. Sold inventory for cash.	____	____	____	____	____
e. Borrowed cash from bank by signing a nine-month note payable.	____	____	____	____	____
f. Paid cash to purchase a patent.	____	____	____	____	____
g. Accepted six-month note receivable in exchange for plant assets.	____	____	____	____	____
h. Paid cash toward accounts payable.	____	____	____	____	____
i. Collected cash from sales.	____	____	____	____	____
j. Paid cash to acquire treasury stock.	____	____	____	____	____

Zander Company's calendar-year 2009 income statement shows the following: Net Income, $395,000; Depreciation Expense, $48,980; Amortization Expense, $9,875; Gain on Sale of Plant Assets, $4,900. An examination of the company's current assets and current liabilities reveals the following changes (all from operating activities): Accounts Receivable decrease, $7,600; Merchandise Inventory decrease, $22,040; Prepaid Expenses increase, $2,000; Accounts Payable decrease, $5,000; Other Payables increase, $760. Use the *indirect method* to compute cash flow from operating activities.

Exercise 16-4
Cash flows from operating activities (indirect)
P2

Exercise 16-5[B]
Computation of cash flows (direct)
P5

For each of the following three separate cases, use the information provided about the calendar-year 2010 operations of Kowa Company to compute the required cash flow information.

Case A: Compute cash received from customers:	
Sales	$590,000
Accounts receivable, December 31, 2009	38,000
Accounts receivable, December 31, 2010	52,440
Case B: Compute cash paid for rent:	
Rent expense	$117,400
Rent payable, December 31, 2009	6,700
Rent payable, December 31, 2010	5,561
Case C: Compute cash paid for merchandise:	
Cost of goods sold	$651,000
Merchandise inventory, December 31, 2009	201,810
Accounts payable, December 31, 2009	84,760
Merchandise inventory, December 31, 2010	165,484
Accounts payable, December 31, 2010	105,102

Exercise 16-6
Cash flows from operating activities (indirect)
P2

Use the following income statement and information about changes in noncash current assets and current liabilities to prepare only the cash flows from operating activities section of the statement of cash flows using the *indirect* method.

SEYMOUR COMPANY
Income Statement
For Year Ended December 31, 2009

Sales		$2,175,000
Cost of goods sold		1,065,750
Gross profit		1,109,250
Operating expenses		
Salaries expense	$297,975	
Depreciation expense	52,200	
Rent expense	58,725	
Amortization expenses—Patents	6,525	
Utilities expense	23,925	439,350
		669,900
Gain on sale of equipment		8,700
Net income		$ 678,600

Changes in current asset and current liability accounts for the year that relate to operations follow.

Accounts receivable	$45,300 increase	Accounts payable	$10,075 decrease
Merchandise inventory	35,150 increase	Salaries payable	4,750 decrease

Exercise 16-7[B]
Cash flows from operating activities (direct) P5

Refer to the information about Seymour Company in Exercise 16-6.
Use the *direct method* to prepare only the cash provided or used by operating activities section of the statement of cash flows for this company.

Exercise 16-8
Cash flows from investing activities
P3

Use the following information to determine this company's cash flows from investing activities.

a. Equipment with a book value of $72,500 and an original cost of $158,000 was sold at a loss of $22,000.
b. Paid $95,000 cash for a new truck.
c. Sold land costing $315,000 for $400,000 cash, yielding a gain of $15,000.
d. Long-term investments in stock were sold for $94,700 cash, yielding a gain of $5,750.

Exercise 16-9
Cash flows from financing activities
P3

Use the following information to determine this company's cash flows from financing activities.

a. Net income was $53,000.
b. Issued common stock for $75,000 cash.
c. Paid cash dividend of $13,000.
d. Paid $90,000 cash to settle a note payable at its $90,000 maturity value.
e. Paid $18,000 cash to acquire its treasury stock.
f. Purchased equipment for $67,000 cash.

Exercise 16-10
Preparation of statement of cash flows (indirect)
C2 A2 P1 P2 P3 

Use the following financial statements and additional information to (1) prepare a statement of cash flows for the year ended June 30, 2009, using the *indirect method,* and (2) compute the company's cash flow on total assets ratio for its fiscal year 2009.

BOULWARE INC.
Comparative Balance Sheets
June 30, 2009 and 2008

	2009	2008
Assets		
Cash	$ 84,663	$ 49,494
Accounts receivable, net	65,720	56,952
Inventory	62,620	106,107
Prepaid expenses	4,960	5,763
Equipment	118,387	131,532
Accum. depreciation—Equipment	(26,350)	(10,848)
Total assets	$310,000	$339,000
Liabilities and Equity		
Accounts payable	$ 24,490	$ 35,256
Wages payable	6,510	17,628
Income taxes payable	2,170	4,068
Notes payable (long term)	31,953	76,953
Common stock, $5 par value	208,000	158,000
Retained earnings	36,877	47,095
Total liabilities and equity	$310,000	$339,000

BOULWARE INC.
Income Statement
For Year Ended June 30, 2009

Sales		$976,600
Cost of goods sold		625,024
Gross profit		351,576
Operating expenses		
Depreciation expense	$ 88,753	
Other expenses	101,879	
Total operating expenses		190,632
		160,944
Other gains (losses)		
Gain on sale of equipment		3,125
Income before taxes		164,069
Income taxes expense		56,604
Net income		$107,465

Additional Information

a. A $45,000 note payable is retired at its carrying (book) value in exchange for cash.
b. The only changes affecting retained earnings are net income and cash dividends paid.
c. New equipment is acquired for $85,000 cash.
d. Received cash for the sale of equipment that had cost $98,145, yielding a $3,125 gain.
e. Prepaid Expenses and Wages Payable relate to Other Expenses on the income statement.
f. All purchases and sales of merchandise inventory are on credit.

Exercise 16-11[B]
Preparation of statement of cash flows (direct) C2 P1 P3 P5

Refer to the data in Exercise 16-10.
Using the *direct method,* prepare the statement of cash flows for the year ended June 30, 2009.

Exercise 16-12[B]
Preparation of statement of cash flows (direct) and supporting note
C2 C3 C4 P1

Use the following information about the cash flows of Valencia Company to prepare a complete statement of cash flows (*direct method*) for the year ended December 31, 2009. Use a note disclosure for any noncash investing and financing activities.

Cash and cash equivalents balance, December 31, 2008	$ 43,000
Cash and cash equivalents balance, December 31, 2009	120,916
Cash received as interest	4,300
Cash paid for salaries	124,700
Bonds payable retired by issuing common stock (no gain or loss on retirement)	180,000
Cash paid to retire long-term notes payable	215,000
Cash received from sale of equipment	105,350
Cash received in exchange for six-month note payable	43,000
Land purchased by issuing long-term note payable	104,400
Cash paid for store equipment	40,850
Cash dividends paid	25,800
Cash paid for other expenses	68,800
Cash received from customers	834,200
Cash paid for merchandise	433,784

Exercise 16-13[B]
Preparation of statement of cash flows (direct) from Cash T-account
C2 A1 P1 P3 P5 

The following summarized Cash T-account reflects the total debits and total credits to the Cash account of Clarett Corporation for calendar year 2009.

(1) Use this information to prepare a complete statement of cash flows for year 2009. The cash provided or used by operating activities should be reported using the *direct method.*

(2) Refer to the statement of cash flows prepared for part 1 to answer the following questions *a* through *d*: (*a*) Which section—operating, investing, or financing—shows the largest cash (i) inflow and (ii) outflow? (*b*) What is the largest individual item among the investing cash outflows? (*c*) Are the cash proceeds larger from issuing notes or issuing stock? (*d*) Does the company have a net cash inflow or outflow from borrowing activities?

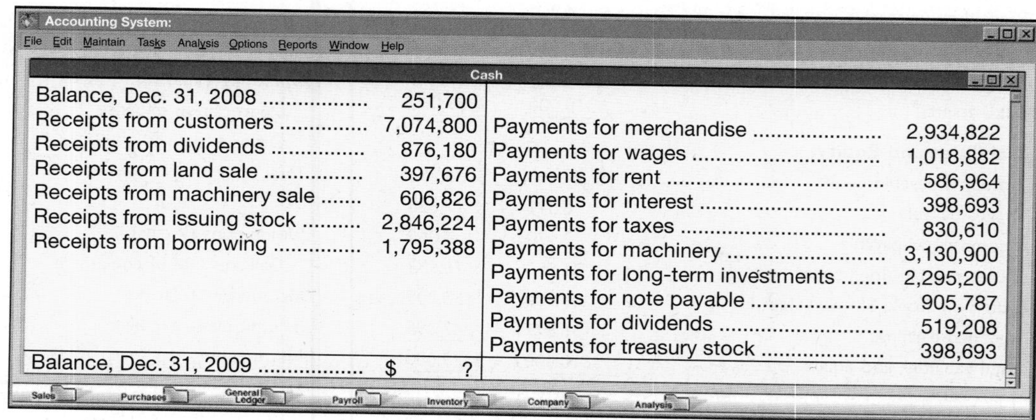

Cash			
Balance, Dec. 31, 2008	251,700		
Receipts from customers	7,074,800	Payments for merchandise	2,934,822
Receipts from dividends	876,180	Payments for wages	1,018,882
Receipts from land sale	397,676	Payments for rent	586,964
Receipts from machinery sale	606,826	Payments for interest	398,693
Receipts from issuing stock	2,846,224	Payments for taxes	830,610
Receipts from borrowing	1,795,388	Payments for machinery	3,130,900
		Payments for long-term investments	2,295,200
		Payments for note payable	905,787
		Payments for dividends	519,208
		Payments for treasury stock	398,693
Balance, Dec. 31, 2009	$?		

Exercise 16-14
Reporting cash flows from operations (indirect)
C4 P2

Woodlock Company reports the following information for its recent calendar year.

Sales	$80,000
Expenses	
Cost of goods sold	50,000
Salaries expense	12,000
Depreciation expense	6,000
Net income	$12,000
Accounts receivable increase	$ 5,000
Inventory decrease	8,000
Salaries payable increase	500

Required

Prepare the operating activities section of the statement of cash flows for Woodlock Company using the indirect method.

Exercise 16-15
Reporting and interpreting cash flows from operations (indirect)
C4 P2

Portland Company disclosed the following information for its recent calendar year.

Revenues	$200,000
Expenses	
Salaries expense	168,000
Utilities expense	28,000
Depreciation expense	29,200
Other expenses	6,800
Net loss	$ (32,000)
Accounts receivable decrease	$ 48,000
Purchased a machine	20,000
Salaries payable increase	36,000
Other accrued liabilities decrease	16,000

Required

1. Prepare the operating activities section of the statement of cash flows using the indirect method.
2. What were the major reasons that this company was able to report a net loss but positive cash flow from operations?
3. Of the potential causes of differences between cash flow from operations and net income, which are the most important to investors?

McGraw-Hill's HOMEWORK MANAGER® Available with McGraw-Hill's Homework Manager

PROBLEM SET A

Problem 16-1A
Statement of cash flows (indirect method)
C2 C3 A1 P1 P2 P3

Georgia Company, a merchandiser, recently completed its calendar-year 2009 operations. For the year, (1) all sales are credit sales, (2) all credits to Accounts Receivable reflect cash receipts from customers, (3) all purchases of inventory are on credit, (4) all debits to Accounts Payable reflect cash payments for inventory, and (5) Other Expenses are paid in advance and are initially debited to Prepaid Expenses. The company's balance sheets and income statement follow.

GEORGIA COMPANY
Comparative Balance Sheets
December 31, 2009 and 2008

	2009	2008
Assets		
Cash	$ 49,800	$ 73,500
Accounts receivable	65,840	56,000
Merchandise inventory	277,000	252,000
Prepaid expenses	1,000	1,500
Equipment	158,500	107,500
Accum. depreciation—Equipment	(43,000)	(52,000)
Total assets	$509,140	$438,500
Liabilities and Equity		
Accounts payable	$ 42,965	$113,000
Short-term notes payable	10,000	7,000
Long-term notes payable	70,000	48,000
Common stock, $5 par value	162,750	151,000
Paid-in capital in excess of par, common stock	35,250	0
Retained earnings	188,175	119,500
Total liabilities and equity	$509,140	$438,500

GEORGIA COMPANY
Income Statement
For Year Ended December 31, 2009

Sales		$584,500
Cost of goods sold		281,000
Gross profit		303,500
Operating expenses		
Depreciation expense	$ 20,000	
Other expenses	132,800	152,800
Other gains (losses)		
Loss on sale of equipment		5,875
Income before taxes		144,825
Income taxes expense		24,250
Net income		$120,575

Additional Information on Year 2009 Transactions

a. The loss on the cash sale of equipment was $5,875 (details in *b*).
b. Sold equipment costing $46,500, with accumulated depreciation of $29,000, for $11,625 cash.
c. Purchased equipment costing $97,500 by paying $35,000 cash and signing a long-term note payable for the balance.
d. Borrowed $3,000 cash by signing a short-term note payable.
e. Paid $40,500 cash to reduce the long-term notes payable.
f. Issued 2,350 shares of common stock for $20 cash per share.
g. Declared and paid cash dividends of $51,900.

Required

Check Cash from operating activities, $42,075

1. Prepare a complete statement of cash flows; report its operating activities using the *indirect method*. Disclose any noncash investing and financing activities in a note.

Analysis Component

2. Analyze and discuss the statement of cash flows prepared in part 1, giving special attention to the wisdom of the cash dividend payment.

Problem 16-2A[A]
Cash flows spreadsheet (indirect method)
P1 P2 P3 P4

Refer to the information reported about Georgia Company in Problem 16-1A.

Required

Prepare a complete statement of cash flows using a spreadsheet as in Exhibit 16A.1; report its operating activities using the indirect method. Identify the debits and credits in the Analysis of Changes columns with letters that correspond to the following list of transactions and events.

a. Net income was $120,575.
b. Accounts receivable increased.
c. Merchandise inventory increased.
d. Prepaid expenses decreased.
e. Accounts payable decreased.
f. Depreciation expense was $20,000.
g. Sold equipment costing $46,500, with accumulated depreciation of $29,000, for $11,625 cash. This yielded a loss of $5,875.
h. Purchased equipment costing $97,500 by paying $35,000 cash and **(i.)** by signing a long-term note payable for the balance.
j. Borrowed $3,000 cash by signing a short-term note payable.
k. Paid $40,500 cash to reduce the long-term notes payable.
l. Issued 2,350 shares of common stock for $20 cash per share.
m. Declared and paid cash dividends of $51,900.

Check Analysis of Changes column totals, $594,850

Problem 16-3A[B]
Statement of cash flows (direct method) C3 P1 P3 P5

Check Cash used in financing activities, $(42,400)

Refer to Georgia Company's financial statements and related information in Problem 16-1A.

Required

Prepare a complete statement of cash flows; report its operating activities according to the *direct method*. Disclose any noncash investing and financing activities in a note.

Problem 16-4A
Statement of cash flows (indirect method) C3 P1 P2 P3

mhhe.com/wildFAP19e

Memphis Corp., a merchandiser, recently completed its 2009 operations. For the year, (1) all sales are credit sales, (2) all credits to Accounts Receivable reflect cash receipts from customers, (3) all purchases of inventory are on credit, (4) all debits to Accounts Payable reflect cash payments for inventory, (5) Other Expenses are all cash expenses, and (6) any change in Income Taxes Payable reflects the accrual and cash payment of taxes. The company's balance sheets and income statement follow.

MEMPHIS CORPORATION Comparative Balance Sheets December 31, 2009 and 2008	2009	2008
Assets		
Cash	$ 165,000	$137,000
Accounts receivable	82,000	74,000
Merchandise inventory	620,000	525,000
Equipment	345,000	240,000
Accum. depreciation—Equipment	(159,000)	(102,000)
Total assets	$1,053,000	$874,000
Liabilities and Equity		
Accounts payable	$ 160,000	$ 96,000
Income taxes payable	22,000	19,000
Common stock, $2 par value	588,000	560,000
Paid-in capital in excess of par value, common stock	201,000	159,000
Retained earnings	82,000	40,000
Total liabilities and equity	$1,053,000	$874,000

MEMPHIS CORPORATION Income Statement For Year Ended December 31, 2009		
Sales		$1,794,000
Cost of goods sold		1,088,000
Gross profit		706,000
Operating expenses		
Depreciation expense	$ 57,000	
Other expenses	500,000	557,000
Income before taxes		149,000
Income taxes expense		22,000
Net income		$ 127,000

Additional Information on Year 2009 Transactions

a. Purchased equipment for $105,000 cash.
b. Issued 14,000 shares of common stock for $5 cash per share.
c. Declared and paid $85,000 in cash dividends.

Required

Prepare a complete statement of cash flows; report its cash inflows and cash outflows from operating activities according to the *indirect method*.

Check Cash from operating activities, $148,000

Problem 16-5A[A]
Cash flows spreadsheet (indirect method)
P1 P2 P3 P4

mhhe.com/wildFAP19e

Refer to the information reported about Memphis Corporation in Problem 16-4A.

Required

Prepare a complete statement of cash flows using a spreadsheet as in Exhibit 16A.1; report operating activities under the indirect method. Identify the debits and credits in the Analysis of Changes columns with letters that correspond to the following list of transactions and events.

a. Net income was $127,000.
b. Accounts receivable increased.
c. Merchandise inventory increased.
d. Accounts payable increased.
e. Income taxes payable increased.
f. Depreciation expense was $57,000.
g. Purchased equipment for $105,000 cash.
h. Issued 14,000 shares at $5 cash per share.
i. Declared and paid $85,000 of cash dividends.

Check Analysis of Changes column totals, $614,000

Problem 16-6A[B]
Statement of cash flows (direct method) P1 P3 P5

mhhe.com/wildFAP19e

Refer to Memphis Corporation's financial statements and related information in Problem 16-4A.

Required

Prepare a complete statement of cash flows; report its cash flows from operating activities according to the *direct method*.

Check Cash used in financing activities, $(15,000)

Problem 16-7A
Computing cash flows from operations (indirect)
C4 P2

Rawling Company's 2009 income statement and selected balance sheet data at December 31, 2008 and 2009, follow ($ thousands).

RAWLING COMPANY
Income Statement

Sales revenue		$48,600
Expenses		
Cost of goods sold		21,000
Depreciation expense		6,000
Salaries expense		9,000
Rent expense		4,500
Insurance expense		1,900
Interest expense		1,800
Utilities expense		1,400
Net income		$ 3,000

RAWLING COMPANY
Selected Balance Sheet Accounts

At December 31	2009	2008
Accounts receivable	$280	$290
Inventory	99	77
Accounts payable	220	230
Salaries payable	44	35
Utilities payable	11	8
Prepaid insurance	13	14
Prepaid rent	11	9

Required

Prepare the cash flows from operating activities section only of the company's 2009 statement of cash flows using the indirect method.

Check Cash from operating activities, $8,989

Problem 16-8A[B]
Computing cash flows from operations (direct)
C4 P5

Refer to the information in Problem 16-7A.

Required

Prepare the cash flows from operating activities section only of the company's 2009 statement of cash flows using the direct method.

PROBLEM SET B

Problem 16-1B
Statement of cash flows (indirect method)
C2 C3 A1 P1 P2 P3

Wilson Corporation, a merchandiser, recently completed its calendar-year 2009 operations. For the year, (1) all sales are credit sales, (2) all credits to Accounts Receivable reflect cash receipts from customers, (3) all purchases of inventory are on credit, (4) all debits to Accounts Payable reflect cash payments for inventory, and (5) Other Expenses are paid in advance and are initially debited to Prepaid Expenses. The company's balance sheets and income statement follow.

WILSON CORPORATION
Comparative Balance Sheets
December 31, 2009 and 2008

	2009	2008
Assets		
Cash	$ 49,400	$ 74,000
Accounts receivable	65,830	55,000
Merchandise inventory	277,000	252,000
Prepaid expenses	1,250	1,600
Equipment	158,500	107,500
Accum. depreciation—Equipment	(36,625)	(46,000)
Total assets	$515,355	$444,100
Liabilities and Equity		
Accounts payable	$ 55,380	$112,000
Short-term notes payable	9,000	7,000
Long-term notes payable	70,000	48,250
Common stock, $5 par	162,500	150,750
Paid-in capital in excess of par, common stock	35,250	0
Retained earnings	183,225	126,100
Total liabilities and equity	$515,355	$444,100

WILSON CORPORATION
Income Statement
For Year Ended December 31, 2009

Sales		$585,000
Cost of goods sold		285,000
Gross profit		300,000
Operating expenses		
Depreciation expense	$ 20,000	
Other expenses	134,000	
Total operating expenses		154,000
		146,000
Other gains (losses)		
Loss on sale of equipment		5,625
Income before taxes		140,375
Income taxes expense		24,250
Net income		$116,125

Additional Information on Year 2009 Transactions

a. The loss on the cash sale of equipment was $5,625 (details in *b*).

b. Sold equipment costing $46,500, with accumulated depreciation of $29,375, for $11,500 cash.

c. Purchased equipment costing $97,500 by paying $25,000 cash and signing a long-term note payable for the balance.

d. Borrowed $2,000 cash by signing a short-term note payable.

e. Paid $50,750 cash to reduce the long-term notes payable.

f. Issued 2,350 shares of common stock for $20 cash per share.

g. Declared and paid cash dividends of $59,000.

Required

1. Prepare a complete statement of cash flows; report its operating activities using the *indirect method.* Disclose any noncash investing and financing activities in a note.

Check Cash from operating activities, $49,650

Analysis Component

2. Analyze and discuss the statement of cash flows prepared in part 1, giving special attention to the wisdom of the cash dividend payment.

Problem 16-2B[A]
Cash flows spreadsheet (indirect method)
P1 P2 P3 P4

Refer to the information reported about Wilson Corporation in Problem 16-1B.

Required

Prepare a complete statement of cash flows using a spreadsheet as in Exhibit 16A.1; report its operating activities using the *indirect method.* Identify the debits and credits in the Analysis of Changes columns with letters that correspond to the following list of transactions and events.

a. Net income was $116,125.

b. Accounts receivable increased.

c. Merchandise inventory increased.

d. Prepaid expenses decreased.

e. Accounts payable decreased.

f. Depreciation expense was $20,000.

g. Sold equipment costing $46,500, with accumulated depreciation of $29,375, for $11,500 cash. This yielded a loss of $5,625.

h. Purchased equipment costing $97,500 by paying $25,000 cash and **(i.)** by signing a long-term note payable for the balance.

j. Borrowed $2,000 cash by signing a short-term note payable.

k. Paid $50,750 cash to reduce the long-term notes payable.

l. Issued 2,350 shares of common stock for $20 cash per share.

m. Declared and paid cash dividends of $59,000.

Check Analysis of Changes column totals, $604,175

Problem 16-3B[B]
Statement of cash flows (direct method) C3 P1 P3 P5

Refer to Wilson Corporation's financial statements and related information in Problem 16-1B.

Required

Prepare a complete statement of cash flows; report its operating activities according to the *direct method.* Disclose any noncash investing and financing activities in a note.

Check Cash used in financing activities, $(60,750)

Problem 16-4B
Statement of cash flows (indirect method)
C3 P1 P2 P3

Prius Company, a merchandiser, recently completed its 2009 operations. For the year, (1) all sales are credit sales, (2) all credits to Accounts Receivable reflect cash receipts from customers, (3) all purchases of inventory are on credit, (4) all debits to Accounts Payable reflect cash payments for inventory, (5) Other Expenses are cash expenses, and (6) any change in Income Taxes Payable reflects the accrual and cash payment of taxes. The company's balance sheets and income statement follow.

PRIUS COMPANY
Comparative Balance Sheets
December 31, 2009 and 2008

	2009	2008
Assets		
Cash	$ 164,000	$ 131,000
Accounts receivable	82,000	70,000
Merchandise inventory	605,000	515,000
Equipment	350,000	276,000
Accum. depreciation—Equipment	(157,000)	(102,000)
Total assets	$1,044,000	$ 890,000
Liabilities and Equity		
Accounts payable	$ 173,000	$ 119,000
Income taxes payable	20,000	17,000
Common stock, $2 par value	580,000	560,000
Paid-in capital in excess of par, common stock	193,000	163,000
Retained earnings	78,000	31,000
Total liabilities and equity	$1,044,000	$ 890,000

PRIUS COMPANY
Income Statement
For Year Ended December 31, 2009

Sales		$1,792,000
Cost of goods sold		1,087,000
Gross profit		705,000
Operating expenses		
Depreciation expense	$ 55,000	
Other expenses	494,000	549,000
Income before taxes		156,000
Income taxes expense		24,000
Net income		$ 132,000

Additional Information on Year 2009 Transactions

a. Purchased equipment for $74,000 cash.
b. Issued 10,000 shares of common stock for $5 cash per share.
c. Declared and paid $85,000 of cash dividends.

Required

Check Cash from operating activities, $142,000

Prepare a complete statement of cash flows; report its cash inflows and cash outflows from operating activities according to the *indirect method.*

Problem 16-5B^A
Cash flows spreadsheet (indirect method)
P1 P2 P3 P4

Refer to the information reported about Prius Company in Problem 16-4B.

Required

Prepare a complete statement of cash flows using a spreadsheet as in Exhibit 16A.1; report operating activities under the *indirect method.* Identify the debits and credits in the Analysis of Changes columns with letters that correspond to the following list of transactions and events.

a. Net income was $132,000.
b. Accounts receivable increased.
c. Merchandise inventory increased.
d. Accounts payable increased.
e. Income taxes payable increased.
f. Depreciation expense was $55,000.
g. Purchased equipment for $74,000 cash.
h. Issued 10,000 shares at $5 cash per share.
i. Declared and paid $85,000 of cash dividends.

Check Analysis of Changes column totals, $555,000

Problem 16-6B[B]
Statement of cash flows (direct method) P1 P3 P5

Refer to Prius Company's financial statements and related information in Problem 16-4B.

Required

Prepare a complete statement of cash flows; report its cash flows from operating activities according to the *direct method.*

Check Cash used by financing activities, $(35,000)

Problem 16-7B
Computing cash flows from operations (indirect)
C4 P2

Kodak Company's 2009 income statement and selected balance sheet data at December 31, 2008 and 2009, follow ($ thousands).

KODAK COMPANY Income Statement	
Sales revenue	$312,000
Expenses	
Cost of goods sold	144,000
Depreciation expense	64,000
Salaries expense	40,000
Rent expense	10,000
Insurance expense	5,200
Interest expense	4,800
Utilities expense	4,000
Net income	$ 40,000

KODAK COMPANY Selected Balance Sheet Accounts		
At December 31	**2009**	**2008**
Accounts receivable	$720	$600
Inventory	172	196
Accounts payable	480	520
Salaries payable	180	120
Utilities payable	40	0
Prepaid insurance	28	36
Prepaid rent	20	40

Required

Prepare the cash flows from operating activities section only of the company's 2009 statement of cash flows using the indirect method.

Check Cash from operating activities, $103,992

Problem 16-8B[B]
Computing cash flows from operations (direct)
C4 P5

Refer to the information in Problem 16-7B.

Required

Prepare the cash flows from operating activities section only of the company's 2009 statement of cash flows using the direct method.

SERIAL PROBLEM

Success Systems

(This serial problem began in Chapter 1 and continues through most of the book. If previous chapter segments were not completed, the serial problem can begin at this point. It is helpful, but not necessary, to use the Working Papers that accompany the book.)

SP 16 Adriana Lopez, owner of Success Systems, decides to prepare a statement of cash flows for her business. (Although the serial problem allowed for various ownership changes in earlier chapters, we will prepare the statement of cash flows using the following financial data.)

SUCCESS SYSTEMS Income Statement For Three Months Ended March 31, 2010		
Computer services revenue		$25,160
Net sales		18,693
Total revenue		43,853
Cost of goods sold	$14,052	
Depreciation expense—Office equipment	400	
Depreciation expense—Computer equipment	1,250	
Wages expense	3,250	
Insurance expense	555	
Rent expense	2,475	
Computer supplies expense	1,305	
Advertising expense	600	
Mileage expense	320	
Repairs expense—Computer	960	
Total expenses		25,167
Net income		$18,686

SUCCESS SYSTEMS Comparative Balance Sheets December 31, 2009, and March 31, 2010	2010	2009
Assets		
Cash	$ 77,845	$58,160
Accounts receivable	22,720	5,668
Merchandise inventory	704	0
Computer supplies	2,005	580
Prepaid insurance	1,110	1,665
Prepaid rent	825	825
Office equipment	8,000	8,000
Accumulated depreciation—Office equipment	(800)	(400)
Computer equipment	20,000	20,000
Accumulated depreciation—Computer equipment	(2,500)	(1,250)
Total assets	$129,909	$93,248
Liabilities and Equity		
Accounts payable	$ 0	$ 1,100
Wages payable	875	500
Unearned computer service revenue	0	1,500
Common stock	108,000	83,000
Retained earnings	21,034	7,148
Total liabilities and equity	$129,909	$93,248

Required

Prepare a statement of cash flows for Success Systems using the *indirect method* for the three months ended March 31, 2010. Recall that the owner Adriana Lopez contributed $25,000 to the business in exchange for additional stock in the first quarter of 2010 and has received $4,800 in cash dividends.

Check Cash flows used by operations: $(515)

BEYOND THE NUMBERS

REPORTING IN ACTION

C4 A1 

BTN 16-1 Refer to **Best Buy**'s financial statements in Appendix A to answer the following.

1. Is Best Buy's statement of cash flows prepared under the direct method or the indirect method? How do you know?
2. For each fiscal year 2007, 2006, and 2005, is the amount of cash provided by operating activities more or less than the cash paid for dividends?
3. What is the largest amount in reconciling the difference between net income and cash flow from operating activities in 2007? In 2006? In 2005?
4. Identify the largest cash flows for investing and for financing activities in 2007 and in 2006.

Fast Forward

5. Obtain Best Buy's financial statements for a fiscal year ending after March 3, 2007, from either its Website (BestBuy.com) or the SEC's EDGAR database (www.SEC.gov). Since March 3, 2007, what are Best Buy's largest cash outflows and cash inflows in the investing and in the financing sections of its statement of cash flow?

COMPARATIVE ANALYSIS

A1 A2

BTN 16-2 Key figures for **Best Buy**, **Circuit City**, and **RadioShack** follow.

($ millions)	Best Buy			Circuit City			RadioShack		
	Current Year	1 Year Prior	2 Years Prior	Current Year	1 Year Prior	2 Years Prior	Current Year	1 Year Prior	2 Years Prior
Operating cash flows	$ 1,762	$ 1,740	$ 1,981	$ 316	$ 365	$ 389	$ 315	$ 363	$ 353
Total assets	13,570	11,864	10,294	4,007	4,069	3,840	2,070	2,205	2,517

Required

1. Compute the recent two years' cash flow on total assets ratios for Best Buy, Circuit City, and RadioShack.
2. What does the cash flow on total assets ratio measure?
3. Which company has the highest cash flow on total assets ratio for the periods shown?
4. Does the cash flow on total assets ratio reflect on the quality of earnings? Explain.

ETHICS CHALLENGE

C1 C2 A1

BTN 16-3 Kaelyn Gish is preparing for a meeting with her banker. Her business is finishing its fourth year of operations. In the first year, it had negative cash flows from operations. In the second and third years, cash flows from operations were positive. However, inventory costs rose significantly in year 4, and cash flows from operations will probably be down 25%. Gish wants to secure a line of credit from her banker as a financing buffer. From experience, she knows the banker will scrutinize operating cash flows for years 1 through 4 and will want a projected number for year 5. Gish knows that a steady progression upward in operating cash flows for years 1 through 4 will help her case. She decides to use her discretion as owner and considers several business actions that will turn her operating cash flow in year 4 from a decrease to an increase.

Required

1. Identify two business actions Gish might take to improve cash flows from operations.
2. Comment on the ethics and possible consequences of Gish's decision to pursue these actions.

COMMUNICATING IN PRACTICE

C1 C4

BTN 16-4 Your friend, Hanna Willard, recently completed the second year of her business and just received annual financial statements from her accountant. Willard finds the income statement and balance sheet informative but does not understand the statement of cash flows. She says the first section is especially confusing because it contains a lot of additions and subtractions that do not make sense to her. Willard adds, "The income statement tells me the business is more profitable than last year and that's most important. If I want to know how cash changes, I can look at comparative balance sheets."

Required

Write a half-page memorandum to your friend explaining the purpose of the statement of cash flows. Speculate as to why the first section is so confusing and how it might be rectified.

TAKING IT TO THE NET

A1

BTN 16-5 Access the April 19, 2007, filing of the 10-K report (for fiscal year ending February 3, 2007) of **J. Crew Group, Inc.**, at www.sec.gov.

Required

1. Does J. Crew use the direct or indirect method to construct its consolidated statement of cash flows?
2. For the fiscal year ended February 3, 2007, what is the largest item in reconciling the net income to net cash provided by operating activities?
3. In the recent three years, has the company been more successful in generating operating cash flows or in generating net income? Identify the figures to support the answer.
4. In the year ended February 3, 2007, what was the largest cash outflow for investing activities and for financing activities?
5. What item(s) does J. Crew report as supplementary cash flow information?
6. Does J. Crew report any noncash financing activities for fiscal year 2007? Identify them, if any.

TEAMWORK IN ACTION

C1 C4 A1 P2 P5

BTN 16-6 Team members are to coordinate and independently answer one question within each of the following three sections. Team members should then report to the team and confirm or correct teammates' answers.

1. Answer *one* of the following questions about the statement of cash flows.
   a. What are this statement's reporting objectives?
   b. What two methods are used to prepare it? Identify similarities and differences between them.
   c. What steps are followed to prepare the statement?
   d. What types of analyses are often made from this statement's information?

2. Identify and explain the adjustment from net income to obtain cash flows from operating activities using the indirect method for *one* of the following items.
   a. Noncash operating revenues and expenses.
   b. Nonoperating gains and losses.
   c. Increases and decreases in noncash current assets.
   d. Increases and decreases in current liabilities.

3.[B] Identify and explain the formula for computing cash flows from operating activities using the direct method for *one* of the following items.
   a. Cash receipts from sales to customers.
   b. Cash paid for merchandise inventory.
   c. Cash paid for wages and operating expenses.
   d. Cash paid for interest and taxes.

Note: For teams of more than four, some pairing within teams is necessary. Use as an in-class activity or as an assignment. If used in class, specify a time limit on each part. Conclude with reports to the entire class, using team rotation. Each team can prepare responses on a transparency.

ENTREPRENEURIAL DECISION

C1 A1 

BTN 16-7 Review the chapter's opener involving **Jungle Jim's International Market**.

Required

1. In a business such as Jungle Jim's, monitoring cash flow is always a priority. Even though Jungle Jim's now has thousands in annual sales and earns a positive net income, explain how cash flow can lag behind earnings.

2. Jungle Jim's is a closely held corporation. What are potential sources of financing for its future expansion?

C2 A1 

BTN 16-8 Jenna and Matt Wilder are completing their second year operating Mountain High, a downhill ski area and resort. Mountain High reports a net loss of $(10,000) for its second year, which includes an $85,000 extraordinary loss from fire. This past year also involved major purchases of plant assets for renovation and expansion, yielding a year-end total asset amount of $800,000. Mountain High's net cash outflow for its second year is $(5,000); a summarized version of its statement of cash flows follows:

Net cash flow provided by operating activities	$295,000
Net cash flow used by investing activities	(310,000)
Net cash flow provided by financing activities	10,000

Required

Write a one-page memorandum to the Wilders evaluating Mountain High's current performance and assessing its future. Give special emphasis to cash flow data and their interpretation.

HITTING THE ROAD

C1

BTN 16-9 Visit **The Motley Fool**'s Website (Fool.com). Click on the sidebar link titled *Fool's School* (or *Fool.com/School*). Identify and select the link *How to Value Stocks*.

Required

1. Click on *Introduction to Valuation,* and then *Cash-Flow-Based Valuations.* How does the Fool's school define cash flow? What is the school's reasoning for this definition?

2. Per the school's instruction, why do analysts focus on earnings before interest and taxes (EBIT)?

3. Visit other links at this Website that interest you such as "How to Read a Balance Sheet," or find out what the "Fool's Ratio" is. Write a half-page report on what you find.

BTN 16-10 Key comparative information for **DSG international plc** (DSGiplc.com) follows.

GLOBAL DECISION

C1 C2 C4

DSG

RadioShack.

(£ millions)	Current Year	1 Year Prior	2 Years Prior
Operating cash flows	£ 207	£ 338	£ 375
Total assets	3,977	4,120	4,104

Required

1. Compute the recent two years' cash flow on total assets ratio for DSG.

2. How does DSG's ratio compare to Best Buy's, Circuit City's, and RadioShack's ratios from BTN 16-2?

ANSWERS TO MULTIPLE CHOICE QUIZ

1. b;

Net income	$15,200
Depreciation expense	10,000
Gain on sale of land	(3,000)
Increase in inventory	(1,500)
Increase in accounts payable	2,850
Net cash provided by operations	$23,550

2. c; cash received from sale of machine is reported as an investing activity.

3. d; FASB requires cash interest paid to be reported under operating.

4. a; Cash paid for salaries and wages = $255,000 + $8,200 − $10,900 = $252,300

5. e; Increase in inventory = $112,000 − $105,000 = $7,000
Increase in accounts payable = $101,300 − $98,500 = $2,800
Cash paid for merchandise = $545,000 + $7,000 − $2,800 = $549,200

A Look Back

Chapter 16 focused on reporting and analyzing cash inflows and cash outflows. We explained how to prepare, analyze, and interpret the statement of cash flows.

A Look at This Chapter

This chapter emphasizes the analysis and interpretation of financial statement information. We learn to apply horizontal, vertical, and ratio analyses to better understand company performance and financial condition.

A Look Ahead

Chapter 18 introduces us to managerial accounting. We discuss its purposes, concepts, and roles in helping managers gather and organize information for decisions. We also explain basic management principles.

Chapter 17 Analysis of Financial Statements

Learning Objectives

CAP

Conceptual

C1 Explain the purpose of analysis. *(p. 680)*

C2 Identify the building blocks of analysis. *(p. 681)*

C3 Describe standards for comparisons in analysis. *(p. 682)*

C4 Identify the tools of analysis. *(p. 682)*

Analytical

A1 Summarize and report results of analysis. *(p. 700)*

A2 *Appendix 17A*—Explain the form and assess the content of a complete income statement. *(p. 703)*

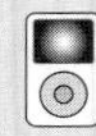

LP17

Procedural

P1 Explain and apply methods of horizontal analysis. *(p. 682)*

P2 Describe and apply methods of vertical analysis. *(p. 687)*

P3 Define and apply ratio analysis. *(p. 690)*

Decision Feature

Motley Fool

"What goes on at The Motley Fool . . . is similar to what goes on in a library"
—Tom Gardner (David Gardner on left)

ALEXANDRIA, VA—In Shakespeare's Elizabethan comedy *As You Like It,* only the fool could speak truthfully to the King without getting his head lopped off. Inspired by Shakespeare's stage character, Tom and David Gardner vowed to become modern-day fools who tell it like it is. With under $10,000 in start-up money, the brothers launched **The Motley Fool (Fool.com).** And befitting of a Shakespearean play, the two say they are "dedicated to educating, amusing, and enriching individuals in search of the truth."

The Gardners do not fear the wrath of any King, real or fictional. They are intent on exposing the truth, as they see it, "that the financial world preys on ignorance and fear." As Tom explains, "There is such a great need in the general populace for financial information." Who can argue, given their brilliant success through practically every medium; including their Website, radio shows, newspaper columns, online store, investment newsletters, and global expansion.

Despite the brothers' best efforts, however, ordinary people still do not fully use information contained in financial statements. For instance, discussions keep appearing on The Motley Fool's online bulletin board that can be easily resolved using reliable and available accounting data. So, it would seem that the Fools must continue their work of "educating and enriching" individuals.

Resembling The Motley Fools' objectives, this chapter introduces horizontal and vertical analyses—tools used to reveal crucial trends and insights from financial information. It also expands on ratio analysis, which gives insight into a company's financial condition and performance. By arming ourselves with the information contained in this chapter and the investment advice of The Motley Fool, *we* can be sure to not play the fool in today's financial world.

[Sources: *Motley Fool Website,* January 2009; *Entrepreneur,* July 1997; *What to Do with Your Money Now,* June 2002; *USA Weekend,* July 2004; *Washington Post,* November 2007; *Money after 40,* April 2007]

Chapter Preview

This chapter shows how we use financial statements to evaluate a company's financial performance and condition. We explain financial statement analysis, its basic building blocks, the information available, standards for comparisons, and tools of analysis. Three major analysis tools are presented: horizontal analysis, vertical analysis, and ratio analysis. We apply each of these tools using **Best Buy**'s financial statements, and we introduce comparative analysis using **Circuit City** and **RadioShack**. This chapter expands and organizes the ratio analyses introduced at the end of each chapter.

Analysis of Financial Statements

Basics of Analysis
- Purpose
- Building blocks
- Information
- Standards for comparisons
- Tools

Horizontal Analysis
- Comparative balance sheets
- Comparative income statements
- Trend analysis

Vertical Analysis
- Common-size balance sheet
- Common-size income statement
- Common-size graphics

Ratio Analysis
- Liquidity and efficiency
- Solvency
- Profitability
- Market prospects
- Ratio summary

Basics of Analysis

Video17.1

Financial statement analysis applies analytical tools to general-purpose financial statements and related data for making business decisions. It involves transforming accounting data into more useful information. Financial statement analysis reduces our reliance on hunches, guesses, and intuition as well as our uncertainty in decision making. It does not lessen the need for expert judgment; instead, it provides us an effective and systematic basis for making business decisions. This section describes the purpose of financial statement analysis, its information sources, the use of comparisons, and some issues in computations.

Purpose of Analysis

C1 Explain the purpose of analysis.

Internal users of accounting information are those involved in strategically managing and operating the company. They include managers, officers, internal auditors, consultants, budget directors, and market researchers. The purpose of financial statement analysis for these users is to provide strategic information to improve company efficiency and effectiveness in providing products and services.

Point: Financial statement analysis tools are also used for personal financial investment decisions.

External users of accounting information are *not* directly involved in running the company. They include shareholders, lenders, directors, customers, suppliers, regulators, lawyers, brokers, and the press. External users rely on financial statement analysis to make better and more informed decisions in pursuing their own goals.

Point: Financial statement analysis is a topic on the CPA, CMA, CIA, and CFA exams.

We can identify other uses of financial statement analysis. Shareholders and creditors assess company prospects to make investing and lending decisions. A board of directors analyzes financial statements in monitoring management's decisions. Employees and unions use financial statements in labor negotiations. Suppliers use financial statement information in establishing credit terms. Customers analyze financial statements in deciding whether to establish supply relationships. Public utilities set customer rates by analyzing financial statements. Auditors use financial statements in assessing the "fair presentation" of their clients' financial results. Analyst services such as **Dun & Bradstreet**, **Moody's**, and **Standard & Poor's** use financial statements in making buy-sell recommendations and in setting credit ratings. The common goal of these users is to evaluate company performance and financial condition. This includes evaluating (1) past and current performance, (2) current financial position, and (3) future performance and risk.

Building Blocks of Analysis

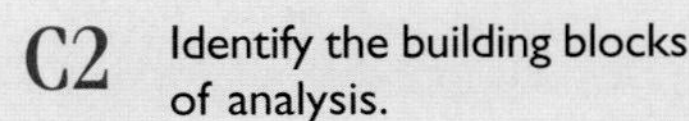

Financial statement analysis focuses on one or more elements of a company's financial condition or performance. Our analysis emphasizes four areas of inquiry—with varying degrees of importance. These four areas are described and illustrated in this chapter and are considered the *building blocks* of financial statement analysis:

- **Liquidity** and **efficiency**—ability to meet short-term obligations and to efficiently generate revenues.
- **Solvency**—ability to generate future revenues and meet long-term obligations.
- **Profitability**—ability to provide financial rewards sufficient to attract and retain financing.
- **Market prospects**—ability to generate positive market expectations.

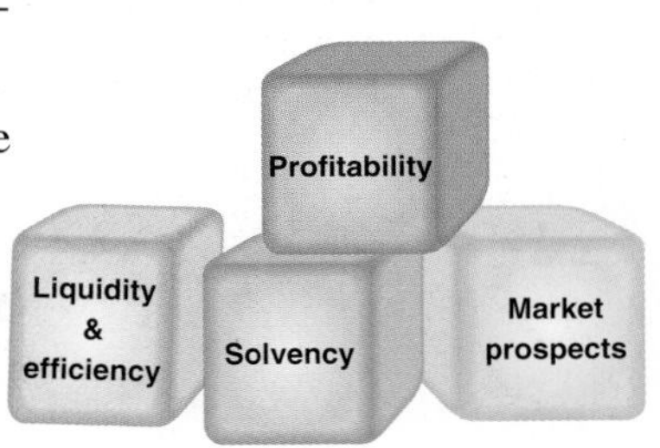

Applying the building blocks of financial statement analysis involves determining (1) the objectives of analysis and (2) the relative emphasis among the building blocks. We distinguish among these four building blocks to emphasize the different aspects of a company's financial condition or performance, yet we must remember that these areas of analysis are interrelated. For instance, a company's operating performance is affected by the availability of financing and short-term liquidity conditions. Similarly, a company's credit standing is not limited to satisfactory short-term liquidity but depends also on its profitability and efficiency in using assets. Early in our analysis, we need to determine the relative emphasis of each building block. Emphasis and analysis can later change as a result of evidence collected.

Decision Insight

Chips and Brokers The phrase *blue chips* refers to stock of big, profitable companies. The phrase comes from poker; where the most valuable chips are blue. The term *brokers* refers to those who execute orders to buy or sell stock. The term comes from wine retailers—individuals who broach (break) wine casks.

Information for Analysis

Some users, such as managers and regulatory authorities, are able to receive special financial reports prepared to meet their analysis needs. However, most users must rely on **general-purpose financial statements** that include the (1) income statement, (2) balance sheet, (3) statement of stockholders' equity (or statement of retained earnings), (4) statement of cash flows, and (5) notes to these statements.

Financial reporting refers to the communication of financial information useful for making investment, credit, and other business decisions. Financial reporting includes not only general-purpose financial statements but also information from SEC 10-K or other filings, press releases, shareholders' meetings, forecasts, management letters, auditors' reports, and Webcasts.

Management's Discussion and Analysis (MD&A) is one example of useful information outside traditional financial statements. **Best Buy**'s MD&A (available at BestBuy.com), for example, begins with an overview and strategic initiatives. It then discusses operating results followed by liquidity and capital resources—roughly equivalent to investing and financing. The final few parts discuss special financing arrangements, key accounting policies, interim results, and the next year's outlook. The MD&A is an excellent starting point in understanding a company's business activities.

Decision Insight

Analysis Online Many Websites offer free access and screening of companies by key numbers such as earnings, sales, and book value. For instance, **Standard & Poor's** has information for more than 10,000 stocks (StandardPoor.com).

Standards for Comparisons

C3 Describe standards for comparisons in analysis.

When interpreting measures from financial statement analysis, we need to decide whether the measures indicate good, bad, or average performance. To make such judgments, we need standards (benchmarks) for comparisons that include the following:

- *Intracompany*—The company under analysis can provide standards for comparisons based on its own prior performance and relations between its financial items. **Best Buy**'s current net income, for instance, can be compared with its prior years' net income and in relation to its revenues or total assets.
- *Competitor*—One or more direct competitors of the company being analyzed can provide standards for comparisons. **Coca-Cola**'s profit margin, for instance, can be compared with **PepsiCo**'s profit margin.
- *Industry*—Industry statistics can provide standards of comparisons. Such statistics are available from services such as **Dun & Bradstreet**, **Standard & Poor's**, and **Moody's**.
- *Guidelines (rules of thumb)*—General standards of comparisons can develop from experience. Examples are the 2:1 level for the current ratio or 1:1 level for the acid-test ratio. Guidelines, or rules of thumb, must be carefully applied because context is crucial.

Point: Each chapter's *Reporting in Action* problems engage students in *intracompany* analysis, whereas *Comparative Analysis* problems require competitor analysis (Best Buy vs. Circuit City).

All of these comparison standards are useful when properly applied, yet measures taken from a selected competitor or group of competitors are often best. Intracompany and industry measures are also important. Guidelines or rules of thumb should be applied with care, and then only if they seem reasonable given past experience and industry norms.

Tools of Analysis

C4 Identify the tools of analysis.

Three of the most common tools of financial statement analysis are

1. **Horizontal analysis**—Comparison of a company's financial condition and performance across time.
2. **Vertical analysis**—Comparison of a company's financial condition and performance to a base amount.
3. **Ratio analysis**—Measurement of key relations between financial statement items.

The remainder of this chapter describes these analysis tools and how to apply them.

Quick Check

Answers—p. 706

1. Who are the intended users of general-purpose financial statements?
2. General-purpose financial statements consist of what information?
3. Which of the following is *least* useful as a basis for comparison when analyzing ratios? (*a*) Company results from a different economic setting. (*b*) Standards from past experience. (*c*) Rule-of-thumb standards. (*d*) Industry averages.
4. What is the preferred basis of comparison for ratio analysis?

Horizontal Analysis

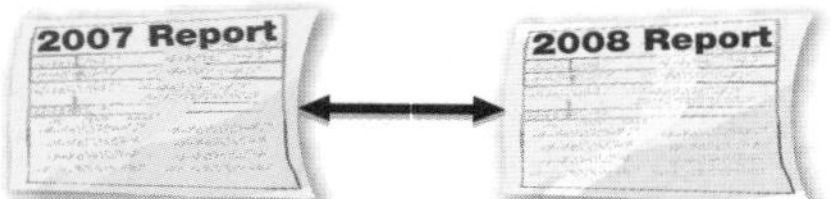

Analysis of any single financial number is of limited value. Instead, much of financial statement analysis involves identifying and describing relations between numbers, groups of numbers, and changes in those numbers. Horizontal analysis refers to examination of financial statement data *across time*. [The term *horizontal analysis* arises from the left-to-right (or right-to-left) movement of our eyes as we review comparative financial statements across time.]

Comparative Statements

P1 Explain and apply methods of horizontal analysis.

Comparing amounts for two or more successive periods often helps in analyzing financial statements. **Comparative financial statements** facilitate this comparison by showing financial amounts in side-by-side columns on a single statement, called a *comparative format*. Using figures from **Best Buy**'s financial statements, this section explains how to compute dollar changes and percent changes for comparative statements.

Video17.1

Computation of Dollar Changes and Percent Changes Comparing financial statements over relatively short time periods—two to three years—is often done by analyzing changes in line items. A change analysis usually includes analyzing absolute dollar amount changes and percent changes. Both analyses are relevant because dollar changes can yield large percent changes inconsistent with their importance. For instance, a 50% change from a base figure of $100 is less important than the same percent change from a base amount of $100,000 in the same statement. Reference to dollar amounts is necessary to retain a proper perspective and to assess the importance of changes. We compute the *dollar change* for a financial statement item as follows:

Example: What is a more significant change, a 70% increase on a $1,000 expense or a 30% increase on a $400,000 expense? *Answer:* The 30% increase.

Dollar change = Analysis period amount − Base period amount

Analysis period is the point or period of time for the financial statements under analysis, and *base period* is the point or period of time for the financial statements used for comparison purposes. The prior year is commonly used as a base period. We compute the *percent change* by dividing the dollar change by the base period amount and then multiplying this quantity by 100 as follows:

$$\textbf{Percent change (\%)} = \frac{\textbf{Analysis period amount} - \textbf{Base period amount}}{\textbf{Base period amount}} \times 100$$

We can always compute a dollar change, but we must be aware of a few rules in working with percent changes. To illustrate, look at four separate cases in this chart:

			Change Analysis	
Case	Analysis Period	Base Period	Dollar	Percent
A	$ 1,500	$(4,500)	$ 6,000	—
B	(1,000)	2,000	(3,000)	—
C	8,000	—	8,000	—
D	0	10,000	(10,000)	(100%)

When a negative amount appears in the base period and a positive amount in the analysis period (or vice versa), we cannot compute a meaningful percent change; see cases A and B. Also, when no value is in the base period, no percent change is computable; see case C. Finally, when an item has a value in the base period and zero in the analysis period, the decrease is 100 percent; see case D.

Example: When there is a value in the base period and zero in the analysis period, the decrease is 100%. Why isn't the reverse situation an increase of 100%? *Answer:* A 100% increase of zero is still zero.

It is common when using horizontal analysis to compare amounts to either average or median values from prior periods (average and median values smooth out erratic or unusual fluctuations).[1] We also commonly round percents and ratios to one or two decimal places, but practice on this matter is not uniform. Computations are as detailed as necessary, which is judged by whether rounding potentially affects users' decisions. Computations should not be excessively detailed so that important relations are lost among a mountain of decimal points and digits.

Comparative Balance Sheets Comparative balance sheets consist of balance sheet amounts from two or more balance sheet dates arranged side by side. Its usefulness is often improved by showing each item's dollar change and percent change to highlight large changes.

[1] *Median* is the middle value in a group of numbers. For instance, if five prior years' incomes are (in 000s) $15, $19, $18, $20, and $22, the median value is $19. When there are two middle numbers, we can take their average. For instance, if four prior years' sales are (in 000s) $84, $91, $96, and $93, the median is $92 (computed as the average of $91 and $93).

Point: Spreadsheet programs can help with horizontal, vertical, and ratio analyses, including graphical depictions of financial relations.

Point: Business consultants use comparative statement analysis to provide management advice.

Analysis of comparative financial statements begins by focusing on items that show large dollar or percent changes. We then try to identify the reasons for these changes and, if possible, determine whether they are favorable or unfavorable. We also follow up on items with small changes when we expected the changes to be large.

Exhibit 17.1 shows comparative balance sheets for **Best Buy**. A few items stand out. Many asset categories substantially increase, which is probably not surprising because Best Buy is a growth company. Much of the increase in current assets is from the 20.7% increase in merchandise inventories. The long-term assets of property, equipment, and goodwill also increased. Of course, its sizeable total asset growth of 14.4% must be accompanied by future income to validate Best Buy's growth strategy.

We likewise see substantial increases on the financing side, the most notable ones being accounts payable and long-term debt totaling about $1,112 million. The increase in payables is related to the increase in cash levels, and the increase in debt is partly explained by the increase in long-term assets. Best Buy also reinvested much of its income as reflected in the $1,203 million increase in retained earnings. Again, we must monitor these increases in

EXHIBIT 17.1

Comparative Balance Sheets

BEST BUY
Comparative Balance Sheets
March 3, 2007, and February 25, 2006

(in millions)	2007	2006	Dollar Change	Percent Change
Assets				
Cash and cash equivalents	$ 1,205	$ 748	$ 457	61.1%
Short-term investments	2,588	3,041	(453)	(14.9)
Receivables, net	548	449	99	22.0
Merchandise inventories	4,028	3,338	690	20.7
Other current assets	712	409	303	74.1
Total current assets	9,081	7,985	1,096	13.7
Property and equipment	4,904	4,836	68	1.4
Less accumulated depreciation	1,966	2,124	(158)	(7.4)
Net property and equipment	2,938	2,712	226	8.3
Goodwill	919	557	362	65.0
Tradenames	81	44	37	84.1
Long-term investments	318	218	100	45.9
Other long-term assets	233	348	(115)	(33.0)
Total assets	$13,570	$11,864	$1,706	14.4
Liabilities				
Accounts payable	$ 3,934	$ 3,234	$ 700	21.6%
Unredeemed gift card liabilities	496	469	27	5.8
Accrued compensation and related expenses	332	354	(22)	(6.2)
Accrued liabilities	990	878	112	12.8
Accrued income taxes	489	703	(214)	(30.4)
Short-term debt	41	0	41	—
Current portion of long-term debt	19	418	(399)	(95.5)
Total current liabilities	6,301	6,056	245	4.0
Long-term liabilities	443	373	70	18.8
Long-term debt	590	178	412	231.5
Minority interests	35	0	35	—
Stockholders' Equity				
Common stock	48	49	(1)	(2.0)
Additional paid-in capital	430	643	(213)	(33.1)
Retained earnings	5,507	4,304	1,203	28.0
Accumulated other comprehensive income	216	261	(45)	(17.2)
Total stockholders' equity	6,201	5,257	944	18.0
Total liabilities and stockholders' equity	$13,570	$11,864	$1,706	14.4

investing and financing activities to be sure they are reflected in increased operating performance.

Comparative Income Statements Comparative income statements are prepared similarly to comparative balance sheets. Amounts for two or more periods are placed side by side, with additional columns for dollar and percent changes. Exhibit 17.2 shows Best Buy's comparative income statements.

EXHIBIT 17.2

Comparative Income Statements

BEST BUY
Comparative Income Statements
For Years Ended March 3, 2007, and February 25, 2006

(in millions, except per share data)	2007	2006	Dollar Change	Percent Change
Revenues	$35,934	$30,848	$5,086	16.5%
Cost of goods sold	27,165	23,122	4,043	17.5
Gross profit	8,769	7,726	1,043	13.5
Selling, general, and administrative expenses	6,770	6,082	688	11.3
Operating income	1,999	1,644	355	21.6
Net interest income (expense)	111	77	34	44.2
Gain on investments	20	0	20	—
Earnings from continuing operations before income taxes	2,130	1,721	409	23.8
Income tax expense	752	581	171	29.4
Minority interest in earnings	1	0	1	—
Net earnings	$ 1,377	$ 1,140	$ 237	20.8
Basic earnings per share	$ 2.86	$ 2.33	$ 0.53	22.7
Diluted earnings per share	$ 2.79	$ 2.27	$ 0.52	22.9

Best Buy has substantial revenue growth of 16.5% in 2007. This finding helps support management's growth strategy as reflected in the comparative balance sheets. Best Buy also reveals some ability to control cost of sales and general and administrative expenses, which increased 17.5% and 11.3%, respectively. Best Buy's net income growth of 20.8% on revenue growth of 16.5% is impressive.

Point: Percent change can also be computed by dividing the current period by the prior period and subtracting 1.0. For example, the 16.5% revenue increase of Exhibit 17.2 is computed as: ($35,934/$30,848) − 1.

Trend Analysis

Trend analysis, also called *trend percent analysis* or *index number trend analysis,* is a form of horizontal analysis that can reveal patterns in data across successive periods. It involves computing trend percents for a series of financial numbers and is a variation on the use of percent changes. The difference is that trend analysis does not subtract the base period amount in the numerator. To compute trend percents, we do the following:

1. Select a *base period* and assign each item in the base period a weight of 100%.
2. Express financial numbers as a percent of their base period number.

Point: *Index* refers to the comparison of the analysis period to the base period. Percents determined for each period are called *index numbers.*

Specifically, a *trend percent,* also called an *index number,* is computed as follows:

$$\textbf{Trend percent (\%)} = \frac{\textbf{Analysis period amount}}{\textbf{Base period amount}} \times 100$$

To illustrate trend analysis, we use the **Best Buy** data shown in Exhibit 17.3.

EXHIBIT 17.3

Revenues and Expenses

(in millions)	2007	2006	2005	2004	2003
Revenues	$35,934	$30,848	$27,433	$24,548	$20,943
Cost of goods sold	27,165	23,122	20,938	18,677	15,998
Selling, general & administrative expenses	6,770	6,082	5,053	4,567	3,935

These data are from Best Buy's *Selected Financial Data* section. The base period is 2003 and the trend percent is computed in each subsequent year by dividing that year's amount by its 2003 amount. For instance, the revenue trend percent for 2007 is 171.6%, computed as $35,934/$20,943. The trend percents—using the data from Exhibit 17.3—are shown in Exhibit 17.4.

EXHIBIT 17.4

Trend Percents for Revenues and Expenses

	2007	2006	2005	2004	2003
Revenues	171.6%	147.3%	131.0%	117.2%	100.0%
Cost of goods sold	169.8	144.5	130.9	116.7	100.0
Selling, general & administrative expenses	172.0	154.6	128.4	116.1	100.0

Point: Trend analysis expresses a percent of base, not a percent of change.

Graphical depictions often aid analysis of trend percents. Exhibit 17.5 shows the trend percents from Exhibit 17.4 in a *line graph,* which can help us identify trends and detect changes in direction or magnitude. It reveals that the trend line for revenues consistently exceeds that for cost of goods sold. Moreover, the magnitude of that difference has slightly grown. This result bodes well for Best Buy because its cost of goods sold are by far its largest cost, and the company shows an ability to control these expenses as it expands. The line graph also reveals a consistent increase in each of these accounts, which is typical of growth companies. The trend line for selling, general and administrative expenses is less encouraging because it exceeds the revenue trend line in 2006–2007. The good news is that nearly all of that upward shift in costs occured in one year (2006). In other years, management appears to have limited those costs to not exceed revenue growth.

EXHIBIT 17.5

Trend Percent Lines for Revenues and Expenses of Best Buy

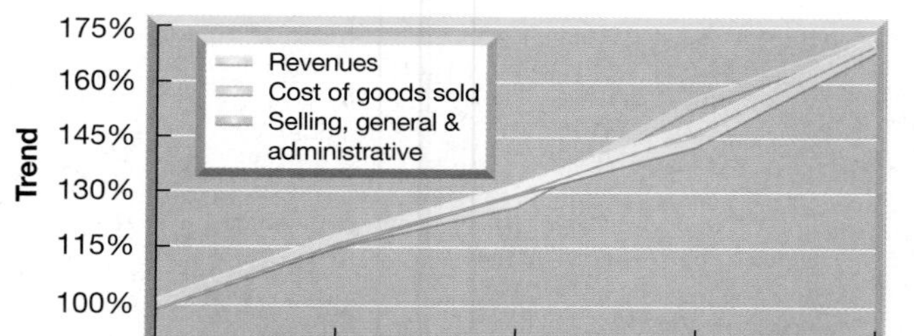

Exhibit 17.6 compares Best Buy's revenue trend line to that of Circuit City and RadioShack for this same period. Best Buy's revenues sharply increased over this time period while those of Circuit City exhibited less growth, and those for RadioShack were flat. These data indicate that Best Buy's products and services have met with considerable consumer acceptance.

EXHIBIT 17.6

Trend Percent Lines—Best Buy, Circuit City, and RadioShack

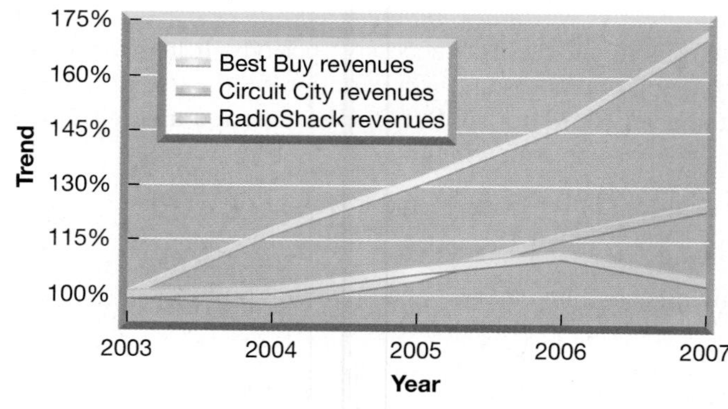

Trend analysis of financial statement items can include comparisons of relations between items on different financial statements. For instance, Exhibit 17.7 compares Best Buy's revenues and total assets. The rate of increase in total assets (176.4%) is greater than the increase in revenues (171.6%) since 2003. Is this result favorable or not? It suggests that Best Buy was slightly less efficient in using its assets in 2007. Management apparently is expecting future years' revenues to compensate for this asset growth.

Overall we must remember that an important role of financial statement analysis is identifying questions and areas of interest, which often direct us to important factors bearing

EXHIBIT 17.7

Revenue and Asset Data for Best Buy

($ millions)	2007	2003	Trend Percent (2007 vs. 2003)
Revenues	$35,934	$20,943	171.6%
Total assets	13,570	7,694	176.4

on a company's future. Accordingly, financial statement analysis should be seen as a continuous process of refining our understanding and expectations of company performance and financial condition.

Decision Maker

Auditor Your tests reveal a 3% increase in sales from $200,000 to $206,000 and a 4% decrease in expenses from $190,000 to $182,400. Both changes are within your "reasonableness" criterion of ±5%, and thus you don't pursue additional tests. The audit partner in charge questions your lack of follow-up and mentions the *joint relation* between sales and expenses. To what is the partner referring? [Answer—p. 706]

Vertical Analysis

Vertical analysis is a tool to evaluate individual financial statement items or a group of items in terms of a specific base amount. We usually define a key aggregate figure as the base, which for an income statement is usually revenue and for a balance sheet is usually total assets. This section explains vertical analysis and applies it to Best Buy. [The term *vertical analysis* arises from the up-down (or down-up) movement of our eyes as we review common-size financial statements. Vertical analysis is also called *common-size analysis*.]

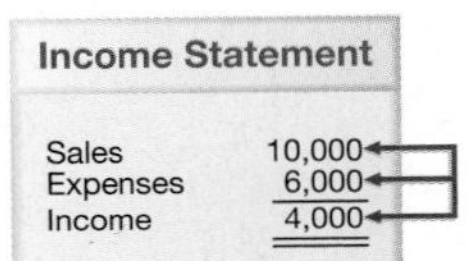

Common-Size Statements

P2 Describe and apply methods of vertical analysis.

The comparative statements in Exhibits 17.1 and 17.2 show the change in each item over time, but they do not emphasize the relative importance of each item. We use **common-size financial statements** to reveal changes in the relative importance of each financial statement item. All individual amounts in common-size statements are redefined in terms of common-size percents. A *common-size percent* is measured by dividing each individual financial statement amount under analysis by its base amount:

$$\textbf{Common-size percent (\%)} = \frac{\textbf{Analysis amount}}{\textbf{Base amount}} \times \textbf{100}$$

Common-Size Balance Sheets Common-size statements express each item as a percent of a *base amount,* which for a common-size balance sheet is usually total assets. The base amount is assigned a value of 100%. (This implies that the total amount of liabilities plus equity equals 100% since this amount equals total assets.) We then compute a common-size percent for each asset, liability, and equity item using total assets as the base amount. When we present a company's successive balance sheets in this way, changes in the mixture of assets, liabilities, and equity are apparent.

Point: The *base* amount in common-size analysis is an *aggregate* amount from that period's financial statement.

Exhibit 17.8 shows common-size comparative balance sheets for Best Buy. Some relations that stand out on both a magnitude and percentage basis include (1) a 41% increase in cash and equivalents, (2) a 6.5% decline in short-term investments as a percentage of assets, (3) a 1.2% decrease in net property and equipment as a percentage of assets, (4) a 1.7% increase in the percentage of accounts payable, (5) a 3.4% decline in the current portion of long-term debt, and (6) a marked increase in retained earnings. Most of these changes are characteristic of a successful growth/stable company. The concern, if any, is whether Best Buy can continue to generate sufficient revenues and income to support its asset buildup within a very competitive industry.

Point: Common-size statements often are used to compare two or more companies in the same industry.

Point: Common-size statements are also useful in comparing firms that report in different currencies.

EXHIBIT 17.8

Common-Size Comparative Balance Sheets

BEST BUY
Common-Size Comparative Balance Sheets
March 3, 2007, and February 25, 2006

(in millions)	2007	2006	Common-Size Percents* 2007	Common-Size Percents* 2006
Assets				
Cash and cash equivalents	$ 1,205	$ 748	8.9%	6.3%
Short-term investments	2,588	3,041	19.1	25.6
Receivables, net	548	449	4.0	3.8
Merchandise inventories	4,028	3,338	29.7	28.1
Other current assets	712	409	5.2	3.4
Total current assets	9,081	7,985	66.9	67.3
Property and equipment	4,904	4,836	36.1	40.8
Less accumulated depreciation	1,966	2,124	14.5	17.9
Net property and equipment	2,938	2,712	21.7	22.9
Goodwill	919	557	6.8	4.7
Tradenames	81	44	0.6	0.4
Long-term investments	318	218	2.3	1.8
Other long-term assets	233	348	1.7	2.9
Total assets	$13,570	$11,864	100.0%	100.0%
Liabilities				
Accounts payable	$ 3,934	$ 3,234	29.0%	27.3%
Unredeemed gift card liabilities	496	469	3.7	4.0
Accrued compensation and related expenses	332	354	2.4	3.0
Accrued liabilities	990	878	7.3	7.4
Accrued income taxes	489	703	3.6	5.9
Short-term debt	41	0	0.3	0.0
Current portion of long-term debt	19	418	0.1	3.5
Total current liabilities	6,301	6,056	46.4	51.0
Long-term liabilities	443	373	3.3	3.1
Long-term debt	590	178	4.3	1.5
Minority interests	35	0	0.3	0.0
Stockholders' Equity				
Common stock	48	49	0.4	0.4
Additional paid-in capital	430	643	3.2	5.4
Retained earnings	5,507	4,304	40.6	36.3
Accumulated other comprehensive income	216	261	1.6	2.2
Total stockholders' equity	6,201	5,257	45.7	44.3
Total liabilities and stockholders' equity	$13,570	$11,864	100.0%	100.0%

* Percents are rounded to tenths and thus may not exactly sum to totals and subtotals.

Global: International companies sometimes disclose "convenience" financial statements, which are statements translated in other languages and currencies. However, these statements rarely adjust for differences in accounting principles across countries.

Common-Size Income Statements Analysis also benefits from use of a common-size income statement. Revenues is usually the base amount, which is assigned a value of 100%. Each common-size income statement item appears as a percent of revenues. If we think of the 100% revenues amount as representing one sales dollar, the remaining items show how each revenue dollar is distributed among costs, expenses, and income.

Exhibit 17.9 shows common-size comparative income statements for each dollar of Best Buy's revenues. The past two years' common-size numbers are similar. The good news is that Best Buy has been able to squeeze an extra 0.1 cent in earnings per revenue dollar—evidenced by the 3.7% to 3.8% rise in earnings as a percentage of revenues. This implies that management is effectively controlling costs and/or the company is reaping growth benefits, so-called *economies of scale*. The bad news is that gross profit lost 0.6 cent per revenue dollar—evidenced by the 25.0% to 24.4% decline in gross profit as a percentage of revenues. This is a concern given the price-competitive

EXHIBIT 17.9

Common-Size Comparative Income Statements

BEST BUY Common-Size Comparative Income Statements For Years Ended March 3, 2007, and February 25, 2006			Common-Size Percents*	
($ millions)	2007	2006	2007	2006
Revenues	$35,934	$30,848	100.0%	100.0%
Cost of goods sold	27,165	23,122	75.6	75.0
Gross profit	8,769	7,726	24.4	25.0
Selling, general, and administrative expenses	6,770	6,082	18.8	19.7
Operating income	1,999	1,644	5.6	5.3
Net interest income (expense)	111	77	0.3	0.2
Gain on investments	20	0	0.1	0.0
Earnings from continuing operations before income taxes	2,130	1,721	5.9	5.6
Income tax expense	752	581	2.1	1.9
Minority interest in earnings	1	0	0.0	0.0
Net earnings	$ 1,377	$ 1,140	3.8%	3.7%

* Percents are rounded to tenths and thus may not exactly sum to totals and subtotals.

electronics market. Analysis here shows that common-size percents for successive income statements can uncover potentially important changes in a company's expenses. Evidence of no changes, especially when changes are expected, is also informative.

Common-Size Graphics

Two of the most common tools of common-size analysis are trend analysis of common-size statements and graphical analysis. The trend analysis of common-size statements is similar to that of comparative statements discussed under vertical analysis. It is not illustrated here because the only difference is the substitution of common-size percents for trend percents. Instead, this section discusses graphical analysis of common-size statements.

An income statement readily lends itself to common-size graphical analysis. This is so because revenues affect nearly every item in an income statement. Exhibit 17.10 shows Best Buy's 2007 common-size income statement in graphical form. This pie chart highlights the contribution of each component of revenues for net earnings.

EXHIBIT 17.10

Common-Size Graphic of Income Statement

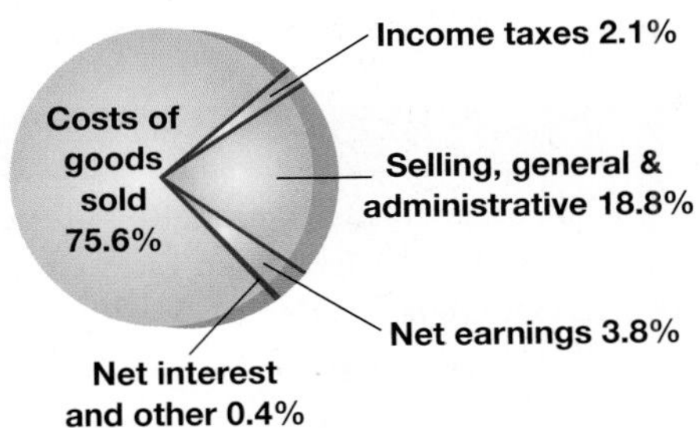

Exhibit 17.11 previews more complex graphical analyses available and the insights they provide. The data for this exhibit are taken from Best Buy's *Segments* footnote. Best Buy has two reportable segments: domestic and international.

EXHIBIT 17.11

Revenue and Operating Income Breakdown by Segment

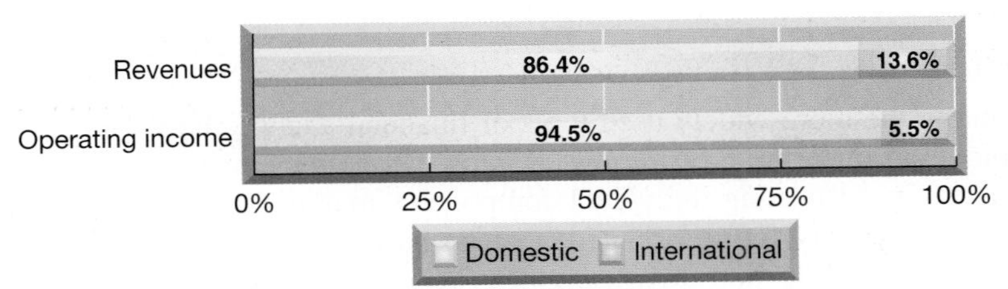

EXHIBIT 17.12

Common-Size Graphic of Asset Components

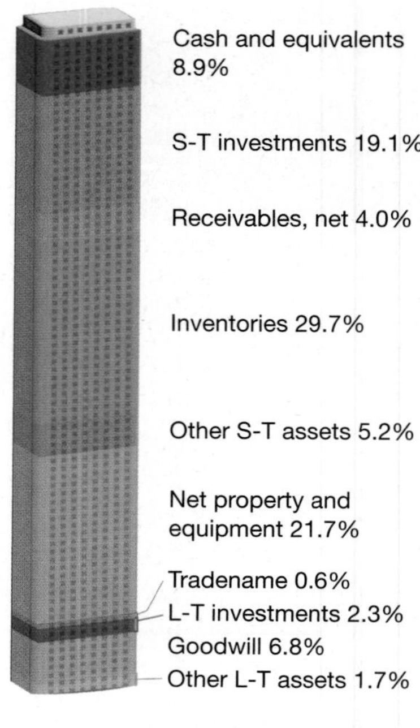

The upper bar in Exhibit 17.11 shows the percent of revenues from each segment. The major revenue source is Domestic (86.4%). The lower bar shows the percent of operating income from each segment. Although International provides 13.6% of revenues, it provides only 5.5% of operating income. This type of information can help users in determining strategic analyses and actions.

Graphical analysis is also useful in identifying (1) sources of financing including the distribution among current liabilities, noncurrent liabilities, and equity capital and (2) focuses of investing activities, including the distribution among current and noncurrent assets. As illustrative, Exhibit 17.12 shows a common-size graphical display of Best Buy's assets. Common-size balance sheet analysis can be extended to examine the composition of these subgroups. For instance, in assessing liquidity of current assets, knowing what proportion of current assets consists of inventories is usually important, and not simply what proportion inventories are of total assets.

Common-size financial statements are also useful in comparing different companies. Exhibit 17.13 shows common-size graphics of Best Buy, Circuit City, and RadioShack on financing sources. This graphic highlights the larger percent of equity financing for Best Buy and Circuit City than for RadioShack. It also highlights the much larger noncurrent (debt) financing of RadioShack. Comparison of a company's common-size statements with competitors' or industry common-size statistics alerts us to differences in the structure or distribution of its financial statements but not to their dollar magnitude.

EXHIBIT 17.13

Common-Size Graphic of Financing Sources—Competitor Analysis

	Best Buy	Circuit City	RadioShack
Current liabilities	46.4%	42.8%	47.5%
Noncurrent liabilities	7.9%	12.5%	20.9%
Equity	45.7%	44.7%	31.6%

Quick Check

Answers—p. 706

5. Which of the following is true for common-size comparative statements? (*a*) Each item is expressed as a percent of a base amount. (*b*) Total assets often are assigned a value of 100%. (*c*) Amounts from successive periods are placed side by side. (*d*) All are true. (*e*) None is true.
6. What is the difference between the percents shown on a comparative income statement and those shown on a common-size comparative income statement?
7. Trend percents are (*a*) shown on comparative income statements and balance sheets, (*b*) shown on common-size comparative statements, or (*c*) also called *index numbers.*

Ratio Analysis

P3 Define and apply ratio analysis.

Ratios are among the more widely used tools of financial analysis because they provide clues to and symptoms of underlying conditions. A ratio can help us uncover conditions and trends difficult to detect by inspecting individual components making up the ratio. Ratios, like other analysis tools, are usually future oriented; that is, they are often adjusted for their probable future trend and magnitude, and their usefulness depends on skillful interpretation.

A ratio expresses a mathematical relation between two quantities. It can be expressed as a percent, rate, or proportion. For instance, a change in an account balance from \$100 to \$250 can be expressed as (1) 150%, (2) 2.5 times, or (3) 2.5 to 1 (or 2.5:1). Computation of a ratio is a simple arithmetic operation, but its interpretation is not. To be meaningful, a ratio must refer to an economically important relation. For example, a direct and crucial relation exists between an item's sales price and its cost. Accordingly, the ratio of cost of goods sold to sales is meaningful. In contrast, no obvious relation exists between freight costs and the balance of long-term investments.

This section describes an important set of financial ratios and its application. The selected ratios are organized into the four building blocks of financial statement analysis: (1) liquidity and efficiency, (2) solvency, (3) profitability, and (4) market prospects. All of these ratios were explained at relevant points in prior chapters. The purpose here is to organize and apply them under a summary framework. We use four common standards, in varying degrees, for comparisons: intracompany, competitor, industry, and guidelines.

Point: Some sources for industry norms are *Annual Statement Studies* by Robert Morris Associates, *Industry Norms & Key Business Ratios* by Dun & Bradstreet, *Standard & Poor's Industry Surveys,* and Reuters.com/finance.

Liquidity and Efficiency

Liquidity refers to the availability of resources to meet short-term cash requirements. It is affected by the timing of cash inflows and outflows along with prospects for future performance. Analysis of liquidity is aimed at a company's funding requirements. *Efficiency* refers to how productive a company is in using its assets. Efficiency is usually measured relative to how much revenue is generated from a certain level of assets.

Both liquidity and efficiency are important and complementary. If a company fails to meet its current obligations, its continued existence is doubtful. Viewed in this light, all other measures of analysis are of secondary importance. Although accounting measurements assume the company's continued existence, our analysis must always assess the validity of this assumption using liquidity measures. Moreover, inefficient use of assets can cause liquidity problems. A lack of liquidity often precedes lower profitability and fewer opportunities. It can foretell a loss of owner control. To a company's creditors, lack of liquidity can yield delays in collecting interest and principal payments or the loss of amounts due them. A company's customers and suppliers of goods and services also are affected by short-term liquidity problems. Implications include a company's inability to execute contracts and potential damage to important customer and supplier relationships. This section describes and illustrates key ratios relevant to assessing liquidity and efficiency.

Working Capital and Current Ratio The amount of current assets less current liabilities is called **working capital,** or *net working capital.* A company needs adequate working capital to meet current debts, to carry sufficient inventories, and to take advantage of cash discounts. A company that runs low on working capital is less likely to meet current obligations or to continue operating. When evaluating a company's working capital, we must not only look at the dollar amount of current assets less current liabilities, but also at their ratio. The *current ratio* is defined as follows (see Chapter 3 for additional explanation):

$$\textbf{Current ratio} = \frac{\textbf{Current assets}}{\textbf{Current liabilities}}$$

Drawing on information in Exhibit 17.1, Best Buy's working capital and current ratio for both 2007 and 2006 are shown in Exhibit 17.14. Circuit City (1.68), RadioShack (1.63), and the Industry's current ratio of 1.6 is shown in the margin. Best Buy's 2007 ratio (1.44) is lower than any of the comparison ratios, but it does not appear in danger of defaulting on loan payments. A high current ratio suggests a strong liquidity position and an ability to meet current obligations. A company can, however, have a current ratio that is too high. An excessively high current ratio means that the company has invested too much in current assets compared to its current obligations. An

EXHIBIT 17.14

Best Buy's Working Capital and Current Ratio

(\$ millions)	2007	2006
Current assets	\$ 9,081	\$ 7,985
Current liabilities	6,301	6,056
Working capital	**\$2,780**	**\$1,929**
Current ratio		
\$9,081/\$6,301	**1.44 to 1**	
\$7,985/\$6,056		**1.32 to 1**

Current ratio
Circuit City = 1.68
RadioShack = 1.63
Industry = 1.6

excessive investment in current assets is not an efficient use of funds because current assets normally generate a low return on investment (compared with long-term assets).

Many users apply a guideline of 2:1 (or 1.5:1) for the current ratio in helping evaluate a company's debt-paying ability. A company with a 2:1 or higher current ratio is generally thought to be a good credit risk in the short run. Such a guideline or any analysis of the current ratio must recognize at least three additional factors: (1) type of business, (2) composition of current assets, and (3) turnover rate of current asset components.

Type of business. A service company that grants little or no credit and carries few inventories can probably operate on a current ratio of less than 1:1 if its revenues generate enough cash to pay its current liabilities. On the other hand, a company selling high-priced clothing or furniture requires a higher ratio because of difficulties in judging customer demand and cash receipts. For instance, if demand falls, inventory may not generate as much cash as expected. Accordingly, analysis of the current ratio should include a comparison with ratios from successful companies in the same industry and from prior periods. We must also recognize that a company's accounting methods, especially choice of inventory method, affect the current ratio. For instance, when costs are rising, a company using LIFO tends to report a smaller amount of current assets than when using FIFO.

Point: When a firm uses LIFO in a period of rising costs, the standard for an adequate current ratio usually is lower than if it used FIFO.

Composition of current assets. The composition of a company's current assets is important to an evaluation of short-term liquidity. For instance, cash, cash equivalents, and short-term investments are more liquid than accounts and notes receivable. Also, short-term receivables normally are more liquid than inventory. Cash, of course, can be used to immediately pay current debts. Items such as accounts receivable and inventory, however, normally must be converted into cash before payment is made. An excessive amount of receivables and inventory weakens a company's ability to pay current liabilities. The acid-test ratio (see below) can help with this assessment.

Turnover rate of assets. Asset turnover measures a company's efficiency in using its assets. One relevant measure of asset efficiency is the revenue generated. A measure of total asset turnover is revenues divided by total assets, but evaluation of turnover for individual assets is also useful. We discuss both receivables turnover and inventory turnover on the next page.

Decision Maker

Banker A company requests a one-year, $200,000 loan for expansion. This company's current ratio is 4:1, with current assets of $160,000. Key competitors carry a current ratio of about 1.9:1. Using this information, do you approve the loan application? Does your decision change if the application is for a 10-year loan? [Answer—p. 706]

Acid-Test Ratio Quick assets are cash, short-term investments, and current receivables. These are the most liquid types of current assets. The *acid-test ratio,* also called *quick ratio,* and introduced in Chapter 5, reflects on a company's short-term liquidity.

$$\textbf{Acid-test ratio} = \frac{\textbf{Cash + Short-term investments + Current receivables}}{\textbf{Current liabilities}}$$

Best Buy's acid-test ratio is computed in Exhibit 17.15. Best Buy's 2007 acid-test ratio (0.69) is between that for Circuit City (0.65) and RadioShack (0.73), and less than the 1:1 common

EXHIBIT 17.15

Acid-Test Ratio

($ millions)	2007	2006
Cash and equivalents	$1,205	$ 748
Short-term investments	2,588	3,041
Current receivables	548	449
Total quick assets	$4,341	$4,238
Current liabilities	$6,301	$6,056
Acid-test ratio		
$4,341/$6,301	**0.69 to 1**	
$4,238/$6,056		**0.70 to 1**

Acid-test ratio
Circuit City = 0.65
RadioShack = 0.73
Industry = 0.7

guideline for an acceptable acid-test ratio; each of these ratios is similar to the 0.7 industry ratio. As with analysis of the current ratio, we need to consider other factors. For instance, the frequency with which a company converts its current assets into cash affects its working capital requirements. This implies that analysis of short-term liquidity should also include an analysis of receivables and inventories, which we consider next.

Global: Ratio analysis helps overcome currency translation problems, but it does *not* overcome differences in accounting principles.

Accounts Receivable Turnover We can measure how frequently a company converts its receivables into cash by computing the *accounts receivable turnover*. This ratio is defined as follows (see Chapter 9 for additional explanation):

$$\textbf{Accounts receivable turnover} = \frac{\textbf{Net sales}}{\textbf{Average accounts receivable, net}}$$

Short-term receivables from customers are often included in the denominator along with accounts receivable. Also, accounts receivable turnover is more precise if credit sales are used for the numerator, but external users generally use net sales (or net revenues) because information about credit sales is typically not reported. Best Buy's 2007 accounts receivable turnover is computed as follows ($ millions).

Point: Some users prefer using gross accounts receivable (before subtracting the allowance for doubtful accounts) to avoid the influence of a manager's bad debts estimate.

$$\frac{\$35{,}934}{(\$548 + \$449)/2} = 72.1 \text{ times}$$

Accounts receivable turnover
Circuit City = 41.2
RadioShack = 17.1

Best Buy's value of 72.1 is larger than Circuit City's 41.2 and RadioShack's 17.1. Accounts receivable turnover is high when accounts receivable are quickly collected. A high turnover is favorable because it means the company need not commit large amounts of funds to accounts receivable. However, an accounts receivable turnover can be too high; this can occur when credit terms are so restrictive that they negatively affect sales volume.

Point: Ending accounts receivable can be substituted for the average balance in computing accounts receivable turnover if the difference between ending and average receivables is small.

Inventory Turnover How long a company holds inventory before selling it will affect working capital requirements. One measure of this effect is *inventory turnover,* also called *merchandise turnover* or *merchandise inventory turnover,* which is defined as follows (see Chapter 6 for additional explanation):

$$\textbf{Inventory turnover} = \frac{\textbf{Cost of goods sold}}{\textbf{Average inventory}}$$

Using Best Buy's cost of goods sold and inventories information, we compute its inventory turnover for 2007 as follows (if the beginning and ending inventories for the year do not represent the usual inventory amount, an average of quarterly or monthly inventories can be used).

$$\frac{\$27{,}165}{(\$4{,}028 + \$3{,}338)/2} = 7.38 \text{ times}$$

Inventory turnover
Circuit City = 5.70
RadioShack = 2.96
Industry = 4.5

Best Buy's inventory turnover of 7.38 is higher than Circuit City's 5.70, RadioShack's 2.96, and the industry's 4.5. A company with a high turnover requires a smaller investment in inventory than one producing the same sales with a lower turnover. Inventory turnover can be too high, however, if the inventory a company keeps is so small that it restricts sales volume.

Days' Sales Uncollected Accounts receivable turnover provides insight into how frequently a company collects its accounts. Days' sales uncollected is one measure of this activity, which is defined as follows (Chapter 8 provides additional explanation):

$$\textbf{Days' sales uncollected} = \frac{\textbf{Accounts receivable, net}}{\textbf{Net sales}} \times 365$$

Any short-term notes receivable from customers are normally included in the numerator.

Best Buy's 2007 days' sales uncollected follows.

Day's sales uncollected
Circuit City = 11.23
RadioShack = 18.94

$$\frac{\$548}{\$35{,}934} \times 365 = 5.57 \text{ days}$$

Both Circuit City's days' sales uncollected of 11.23 days and RadioShack's 18.94 days are longer than the 5.57 days for Best Buy. Days' sales uncollected is more meaningful if we know company credit terms. A rough guideline states that days' sales uncollected should not exceed 1⅓ times the days in its (1) credit period, *if* discounts are not offered or (2) discount period, *if* favorable discounts are offered.

Days' Sales in Inventory *Days' sales in inventory* is a useful measure in evaluating inventory liquidity. Days' sales in inventory is linked to inventory in a way that days' sales uncollected is linked to receivables. We compute days' sales in inventory as follows (Chapter 6 provides additional explanation).

$$\textbf{Days' sales in inventory} = \frac{\textbf{Ending inventory}}{\textbf{Cost of goods sold}} \times \textbf{365}$$

Best Buy's days' sales in inventory for 2007 follows.

Days' sales in inventory
Circuit City = 62.9
RadioShack = 107.9

$$\frac{\$4{,}028}{\$27{,}165} \times 365 = 54.1 \text{ days}$$

Point: *Average collection period* is estimated by dividing 365 by the accounts receivable turnover ratio. For example, 365 divided by an accounts receivable turnover of 6.1 indicates a 60-day average collection period.

If the products in Best Buy's inventory are in demand by customers, this formula estimates that its inventory will be converted into receivables (or cash) in 54.1 days. If all of Best Buy's sales were credit sales, the conversion of inventory to receivables in 54.1 days *plus* the conversion of receivables to cash in 5.57 days implies that inventory will be converted to cash in about 59.67 days (54.1 + 5.57).

Total Asset Turnover *Total asset turnover* reflects a company's ability to use its assets to generate sales and is an important indication of operating efficiency. The definition of this ratio follows (Chapter 10 offers additional explanation).

$$\textbf{Total asset turnover} = \frac{\textbf{Net sales}}{\textbf{Average total assets}}$$

Best Buy's total asset turnover for 2007 follows and is less than Circuit City's, but greater than that for RadioShack.

Total asset turnover
Circuit City = 3.08
RadioShack = 2.24

$$\frac{\$35{,}934}{(\$13{,}570 + \$11{,}864)/2} = 2.83 \text{ times}$$

Quick Check

Answers—p. 706

8. Information from Paff Co. at Dec. 31, 2008, follows: cash, $820,000; accounts receivable, $240,000; inventories, $470,000; plant assets, $910,000; accounts payable, $350,000; and income taxes payable, $180,000. Compute its (*a*) current ratio and (*b*) acid-test ratio.
9. On Dec. 31, 2009, Paff Company (see question 8) had accounts receivable of $290,000 and inventories of $530,000. During 2009, net sales amounted to $2,500,000 and cost of goods sold was $750,000. Compute (*a*) accounts receivable turnover, (*b*) days' sales uncollected, (*c*) inventory turnover, and (*d*) days' sales in inventory.

Solvency

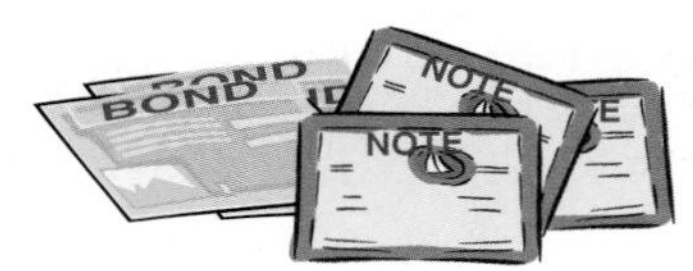

Solvency refers to a company's long-run financial viability and its ability to cover long-term obligations. All of a company's business activities—financing, investing, and operating—affect its solvency. Analysis of solvency is long term and uses less precise but more encompassing measures than liquidity. One of the most important components of solvency analysis is the composition of a company's capital structure. *Capital structure* refers to a company's financing sources. It ranges from relatively permanent equity financing to riskier or more temporary short-term financing. Assets represent security for financiers, ranging from loans secured by specific assets to the assets available as general security to unsecured creditors. This section describes the tools of solvency analysis. Our analysis focuses on a company's ability to both meet its obligations and provide security to its creditors *over the long run*. Indicators of this ability include *debt* and *equity* ratios, the relation between *pledged assets and secured liabilities*, and the company's capacity to earn sufficient income to *pay fixed interest charges*.

Debt and Equity Ratios One element of solvency analysis is to assess the portion of a company's assets contributed by its owners and the portion contributed by creditors. This relation is reflected in the debt ratio (also described in Chapter 2). The *debt ratio* expresses total liabilities as a percent of total assets. The **equity ratio** provides complementary information by expressing total equity as a percent of total assets. Best Buy's debt and equity ratios follow.

Point: For analysis purposes, Minority Interest is usually included in equity.

($ millions)	2007	Ratios	
Total liabilities	$ 7,369	54.3%	[Debt ratio]
Total equity	6,201	45.7	[Equity ratio]
Total liabilities and equity	$13,570	100.0%	

Debt ratio :: Equity ratio
Circuit City = 55.3% :: 44.7%
RadioShack = 68.4% :: 31.6%

Best Buy's financial statements reveal more debt than equity. A company is considered less risky if its capital structure (equity and long-term debt) contains more equity. One risk factor is the required payment for interest and principal when debt is outstanding. Another factor is the greater the stockholder financing, the more losses a company can absorb through equity before the assets become inadequate to satisfy creditors' claims. From the stockholders' point of view, if a company earns a return on borrowed capital that is higher than the cost of borrowing, the difference represents increased income to stockholders. The inclusion of debt is described as *financial leverage* because debt can have the effect of increasing the return to stockholders. Companies are said to be highly leveraged if a large portion of their assets is financed by debt.

Point: Bank examiners from the FDIC and other regulatory agencies use debt and equity ratios to monitor compliance with regulatory capital requirements imposed on banks and S&Ls.

Debt-to-Equity Ratio The ratio of total liabilities to equity is another measure of solvency. We compute the ratio as follows (Chapter 14 offers additional explanation).

$$\textbf{Debt-to-equity ratio} = \frac{\textbf{Total liabilities}}{\textbf{Total equity}}$$

Best Buy's debt-to-equity ratio for 2007 is

$$\$7,369/\$6,201 = 1.19$$

Debt-to-equity
Circuit City = 1.24
RadioShack = 2.17
Industry = 0.99

Best Buy's 1.19 debt-to-equity ratio is less than the 1.24 ratio for Circuit City and the 2.17 for RadioShack, but greater than the industry ratio of 0.99. Consistent with our inferences from the debt ratio, Best Buy's capital structure has more debt than equity, which increases risk. Recall that debt must be repaid with interest, while equity does not. These debt requirements can be burdensome when the industry and/or the economy experience a downturn. A larger debt-to-equity ratio also implies less opportunity to expand through use of debt financing.

Times Interest Earned The amount of income before deductions for interest expense and income taxes is the amount available to pay interest expense. The following

Point: The times interest earned ratio and the debt and equity ratios are of special interest to bank lending officers.

times interest earned ratio reflects the creditors' risk of loan repayments with interest (see Chapter 11 for additional explanation).

$$\textbf{Times interest earned} = \frac{\textbf{Income before interest expense and income taxes}}{\textbf{Interest expense}}$$

The larger this ratio, the less risky is the company for creditors. One guideline says that creditors are reasonably safe if the company earns its fixed interest expense two or more times each year. Best Buy's times interest earned ratio follows; its value suggests that its creditors have little risk of nonrepayment.

Times interest earned
Circuit City = 12.5
RadioShack = 3.5

$$\frac{\$1{,}377 + \$31 \text{ (see Best Buy note \#7)} + \$752}{\$31} = 69.7$$

Decision Insight

Bears and Bulls A *bear market* is a declining market. The phrase comes from bear-skin jobbers who often sold the skins before the bears were caught. The term *bear* was then used to describe investors who sold shares they did not own in anticipation of a price decline. A *bull market* is a rising market. This phrase comes from the once popular sport of bear and bull baiting. The term *bull* came to mean the opposite of *bear.*

Profitability

We are especially interested in a company's ability to use its assets efficiently to produce profits (and positive cash flows). *Profitability* refers to a company's ability to generate an adequate return on invested capital. Return is judged by assessing earnings relative to the level and sources of financing. Profitability is also relevant to solvency. This section describes key profitability measures and their importance to financial statement analysis.

Profit Margin A company's operating efficiency and profitability can be expressed by two components. The first is *profit margin,* which reflects a company's ability to earn net income from sales (Chapter 3 offers additional explanation). It is measured by expressing net income as a percent of sales (*sales* and *revenues* are similar terms). Best Buy's profit margin follows.

Profit margin
Circuit City = −0.1%
RadioShack = 1.5%

$$\textbf{Profit margin} = \frac{\textbf{Net income}}{\textbf{Net sales}} = \frac{\$1{,}377}{\$35{,}934} = 3.8\%$$

To evaluate profit margin, we must consider the industry. For instance, an appliance company might require a profit margin between 10% and 15%; whereas a retail supermarket might require a profit margin of 1% or 2%. Both profit margin and *total asset turnover* make up the two basic components of operating efficiency. These ratios reflect on management because managers are ultimately responsible for operating efficiency. The next section explains how we use both measures to analyze return on total assets.

Return on Total Assets *Return on total assets* is defined as follows.

$$\textbf{Return on total assets} = \frac{\textbf{Net income}}{\textbf{Average total assets}}$$

Best Buy's 2007 return on total assets is

Return on total assets
Circuit City = −0.2%
RadioShack = 3.4%
Industry = 3.0

$$\frac{\$1{,}377}{(\$13{,}570 + \$11{,}864)/2} = 10.8\%$$

Best Buy's 10.8% return on total assets is lower than that for many businesses but is higher than RadioShack's return of 3.4% and the industry's 3.0% return. We also should evaluate any trend in the rate of return.

Point: Many analysts add back *Interest expense* × *(1 − Tax rate)* to net income in computing return on total assets.

The following equation shows the important relation between profit margin, total asset turnover, and return on total assets.

Profit margin × Total asset turnover = Return on total assets

or

$$\frac{\textbf{Net income}}{\textbf{Net sales}} \times \frac{\textbf{Net sales}}{\textbf{Average total assets}} = \frac{\textbf{Net income}}{\textbf{Average total assets}}$$

Both profit margin and total asset turnover contribute to overall operating efficiency, as measured by return on total assets. If we apply this formula to Best Buy, we get

$$3.8\% \times 2.83 = 10.8\%$$

Circuit City: −0.1% × 3.08 = −0.2%
RadioShack: 1.5% × 2.24 = 3.4%
(with rounding)

This analysis shows that Best Buy's superior return on assets versus that of Circuit City and RadioShack is driven mainly by its higher profit margin.

Return on Common Stockholders' Equity Perhaps the most important goal in operating a company is to earn net income for its owner(s). *Return on common stockholders' equity* measures a company's success in reaching this goal and is defined as follows.

$$\textbf{Return on common stockholders' equity} = \frac{\textbf{Net income} - \textbf{Preferred dividends}}{\textbf{Average common stockholders' equity}}$$

Best Buy's 2007 return on common stockholders' equity is computed as follows:

$$\frac{\$1{,}377 - \$0}{(\$6{,}236 + \$5{,}257)/2} = 24.0\%$$

Return on common equity
Circuit City = −0.4%
RadioShack = 11.8%

The denominator in this computation is the book value of common equity (including minority interest). In the numerator, the dividends on cumulative preferred stock are subtracted whether they are declared or are in arrears. If preferred stock is noncumulative, its dividends are subtracted only if declared.

Decision Insight

Wall Street *Wall Street* is synonymous with financial markets, but its name comes from the street location of the original New York Stock Exchange. The street's name derives from stockades built by early settlers to protect New York from pirate attacks.

Market Prospects

Market measures are useful for analyzing corporations with publicly traded stock. These market measures use stock price, which reflects the market's (public's) expectations for the company. This includes expectations of both company return and risk—as the market perceives it.

Price-Earnings Ratio Computation of the *price-earnings ratio* follows (Chapter 13 provides additional explanation).

$$\textbf{Price-earnings ratio} = \frac{\textbf{Market price per common share}}{\textbf{Earnings per share}}$$

Point: PE ratio can be viewed as an indicator of the market's expected growth and risk for a stock. High expected risk suggests a low PE ratio. High expected growth suggests a high PE ratio.

Predicted earnings per share for the next period is often used in the denominator of this computation. Reported earnings per share for the most recent period is also commonly used. In both cases, the ratio is used as an indicator of the future growth and risk of a company's earnings as perceived by the stock's buyers and sellers.

The market price of Best Buy's common stock at the start of fiscal year 2008 was $46.35. Using Best Buy's $2.86 basic earnings per share, we compute its price-earnings ratio as follows (some analysts compute this ratio using the median of the low and high stock price).

PE (year-end)
Circuit City = −380.0
RadioShack = 31.1

$$\frac{\$46.35}{\$2.86} = 16.2$$

Point: Some investors avoid stocks with high PE ratios under the belief they are "overpriced." Alternatively, some investors *sell these stocks short*—hoping for price declines.

Best Buy's price-earnings ratio is less than that for RadioShack, but is slightly higher than the norm. (Circuit City's ratio is negative due to its abnormally low earnings.) Best Buy's middle-of-the-pack ratio likely reflects investors' expectations of continued growth but normal earnings.

Dividend Yield *Dividend yield* is used to compare the dividend-paying performance of different investment alternatives. We compute dividend yield as follows (Chapter 13 offers additional explanation).

$$\textbf{Dividend yield} = \frac{\textbf{Annual cash dividends per share}}{\textbf{Market price per share}}$$

Best Buy's dividend yield, based on its fiscal year-end market price per share of $46.35 and its policy of $0.36 cash dividends per share, is computed as follows.

Dividend yield
Circuit City = 0.6%
RadioShack = 1.5%

$$\frac{\$0.36}{\$46.35} = 0.8\%$$

Some companies do not declare and pay dividends because they wish to reinvest the cash.

Summary of Ratios

Point: Corporate PE ratios and dividend yields are found in daily stock market quotations listed in *The Wall Street Journal, Investor's Business Daily,* or other publications and Web services.

Exhibit 17.16 summarizes the major financial statement analysis ratios illustrated in this chapter and throughout the book. This summary includes each ratio's title, its formula, and the purpose for which it is commonly used.

Decision Insight

Ticker Prices *Ticker prices* refer to a band of moving data on a monitor carrying up-to-the-minute stock prices. The phrase comes from *ticker tape*, a 1-inch-wide strip of paper spewing stock prices from a printer that ticked as it ran. Most of today's investors have never seen actual ticker tape, but the phrase survives.

Quick Check

Answers—p. 706

10. Which ratio best reflects a company's ability to meet immediate interest payments? (*a*) Debt ratio. (*b*) Equity ratio. (*c*) Times interest earned.

11. Which ratio best measures a company's success in earning net income for its owner(s)? (*a*) Profit margin. (*b*) Return on common stockholders' equity. (*c*) Price-earnings ratio. (*d*) Dividend yield.

12. If a company has net sales of $8,500,000, net income of $945,000, and total asset turnover of 1.8 times, what is its return on total assets?

EXHIBIT 17.16

Financial Statement Analysis Ratios*

Ratio	Formula	Measure of
Liquidity and Efficiency		
Current ratio	$= \frac{\text{Current assets}}{\text{Current liabilities}}$	Short-term debt-paying ability
Acid-test ratio	$= \frac{\text{Cash + Short-term investments + Current receivables}}{\text{Current liabilities}}$	Immediate short-term debt-paying ability
Accounts receivable turnover	$= \frac{\text{Net sales}}{\text{Average accounts receivable, net}}$	Efficiency of collection
Inventory turnover	$= \frac{\text{Cost of goods sold}}{\text{Average inventory}}$	Efficiency of inventory management
Days' sales uncollected	$= \frac{\text{Accounts receivable, net}}{\text{Net sales}} \times 365$	Liquidity of receivables
Days' sales in inventory	$= \frac{\text{Ending inventory}}{\text{Cost of goods sold}} \times 365$	Liquidity of inventory
Total asset turnover	$= \frac{\text{Net sales}}{\text{Average total assets}}$	Efficiency of assets in producing sales
Solvency		
Debt ratio	$= \frac{\text{Total liabilities}}{\text{Total assets}}$	Creditor financing and leverage
Equity ratio	$= \frac{\text{Total equity}}{\text{Total assets}}$	Owner financing
Debt-to-equity ratio	$= \frac{\text{Total liabilities}}{\text{Total equity}}$	Debt versus equity financing
Times interest earned	$= \frac{\text{Income before interest expense and income taxes}}{\text{Interest expense}}$	Protection in meeting interest payments
Profitability		
Profit margin ratio	$= \frac{\text{Net income}}{\text{Net sales}}$	Net income in each sales dollar
Gross margin ratio	$= \frac{\text{Net sales} - \text{Cost of goods sold}}{\text{Net sales}}$	Gross margin in each sales dollar
Return on total assets	$= \frac{\text{Net income}}{\text{Average total assets}}$	Overall profitability of assets
Return on common stockholders' equity	$= \frac{\text{Net income} - \text{Preferred dividends}}{\text{Average common stockholders' equity}}$	Profitability of owner investment
Book value per common share	$= \frac{\text{Shareholders' equity applicable to common shares}}{\text{Number of common shares outstanding}}$	Liquidation at reported amounts
Basic earnings per share	$= \frac{\text{Net income} - \text{Preferred dividends}}{\text{Weighted-average common shares outstanding}}$	Net income per common share
Market Prospects		
Price-earnings ratio	$= \frac{\text{Market price per common share}}{\text{Earnings per share}}$	Market value relative to earnings
Dividend yield	$= \frac{\text{Annual cash dividends per share}}{\text{Market price per share}}$	Cash return per common share

* Additional ratios also examined in previous chapters included credit risk ratio; plant asset useful life; plant asset age; days' cash expense coverage; cash coverage of growth; cash coverage of debt; free cash flow; cash flow on total assets; and payout ratio.

Decision Analysis

Analysis Reporting

A1 Summarize and report results of analysis.

Understanding the purpose of financial statement analysis is crucial to the usefulness of any analysis. This understanding leads to efficiency of effort, effectiveness in application, and relevance in focus. The purpose of most financial statement analyses is to reduce uncertainty in business decisions through a rigorous and sound evaluation. A *financial statement analysis report* helps by directly addressing the building blocks of analysis and by identifying weaknesses in inference by requiring explanation: It forces us to organize our reasoning and to verify its flow and logic. A report also serves as a communication link with readers, and the writing process reinforces our judgments and vice versa. Finally, the report helps us (re)evaluate evidence and refine conclusions on key building blocks. A good analysis report usually consists of six sections:

1. **Executive summary**—brief focus on important analysis results and conclusions.
2. **Analysis overview**—background on the company, its industry, and its economic setting.
3. **Evidential matter**—financial statements and information used in the analysis, including ratios, trends, comparisons, statistics, and all analytical measures assembled; often organized under the building blocks of analysis.
4. **Assumptions**—identification of important assumptions regarding a company's industry and economic environment, and other important assumptions for estimates.
5. **Key factors**—list of important favorable and unfavorable factors, both quantitative and qualitative, for company performance; usually organized by areas of analysis.
6. **Inferences**—forecasts, estimates, interpretations, and conclusions drawing on all sections of the report.

We must remember that the user dictates relevance, meaning that the analysis report should include a brief table of contents to help readers focus on those areas most relevant to their decisions. All irrelevant matter must be eliminated. For example, decades-old details of obscure transactions and detailed miscues of the analysis are irrelevant. Ambiguities and qualifications to avoid responsibility or hedging inferences must be eliminated. Finally, writing is important. Mistakes in grammar and errors of fact compromise the report's credibility.

Decision Insight

Short Selling *Short selling* refers to selling stock before you buy it. Here's an example: You borrow 100 shares of Nike stock, sell them at $40 each, and receive money from their sale. You then wait. You hope that Nike's stock price falls to, say, $35 each and you can replace the borrowed stock for less than you sold it for, reaping a profit of $5 each less any transaction costs.

Demonstration Problem

DP17

Use the following financial statements of Precision Co. to complete these requirements.

1. Prepare comparative income statements showing the percent increase or decrease for year 2009 in comparison to year 2008.

2. Prepare common-size comparative balance sheets for years 2009 and 2008.

3. Compute the following ratios as of December 31, 2009, or for the year ended December 31, 2009, and identify its building block category for financial statement analysis.

a. Current ratio
b. Acid-test ratio
c. Accounts receivable turnover
d. Days' sales uncollected
e. Inventory turnover
f. Debt ratio
g. Debt-to-equity ratio
h. Times interest earned
i. Profit margin ratio
j. Total asset turnover
k. Return on total assets
l. Return on common stockholders' equity

PRECISION COMPANY Comparative Balance Sheets December 31, 2009 and 2008	2009	2008
Assets		
Current assets		
Cash	$ 79,000	$ 42,000
Short-term investments	65,000	96,000
Accounts receivable, net	120,000	100,000
Merchandise inventory	250,000	265,000
Total current assets	514,000	503,000
Plant assets		
Store equipment, net	400,000	350,000
Office equipment, net	45,000	50,000
Buildings, net	625,000	675,000
Land	100,000	100,000
Total plant assets	1,170,000	1,175,000
Total assets	$1,684,000	$1,678,000
Liabilities		
Current liabilities		
Accounts payable	$ 164,000	$ 190,000
Short-term notes payable	75,000	90,000
Taxes payable	26,000	12,000
Total current liabilities	265,000	292,000
Long-term liabilities		
Notes payable (secured by mortgage on buildings)	400,000	420,000
Total liabilities	665,000	712,000
Stockholders' Equity		
Common stock, $5 par value	475,000	475,000
Retained earnings	544,000	491,000
Total stockholders' equity	1,019,000	966,000
Total liabilities and equity	$1,684,000	$1,678,000

PRECISION COMPANY Comparative Income Statements For Years Ended December 31, 2009 and 2008	2009	2008
Sales	$2,486,000	$2,075,000
Cost of goods sold	1,523,000	1,222,000
Gross profit	963,000	853,000
Operating expenses		
Advertising expense	145,000	100,000
Sales salaries expense	240,000	280,000
Office salaries expense	165,000	200,000
Insurance expense	100,000	45,000
Supplies expense	26,000	35,000
Depreciation expense	85,000	75,000
Miscellaneous expenses	17,000	15,000
Total operating expenses	778,000	750,000
Operating income	185,000	103,000
Interest expense	44,000	46,000
Income before taxes	141,000	57,000
Income taxes	47,000	19,000
Net income	$ 94,000	$ 38,000
Earnings per share	$ 0.99	$ 0.40

Planning the Solution

- Set up a four-column income statement; enter the 2009 and 2008 amounts in the first two columns and then enter the dollar change in the third column and the percent change from 2008 in the fourth column.
- Set up a four-column balance sheet; enter the 2009 and 2008 year-end amounts in the first two columns and then compute and enter the amount of each item as a percent of total assets.
- Compute the required ratios using the data provided. Use the average of beginning and ending amounts when appropriate (see Exhibit 17.16 for definitions).

Solution to Demonstration Problem

1.

PRECISION COMPANY Comparative Income Statements For Years Ended December 31, 2009 and 2008			Increase (Decrease) in 2009	
	2009	2008	Amount	Percent
Sales	$2,486,000	$2,075,000	$411,000	19.8%
Cost of goods sold	1,523,000	1,222,000	301,000	24.6
Gross profit	963,000	853,000	110,000	12.9
Operating expenses				
Advertising expense	145,000	100,000	45,000	45.0
Sales salaries expense	240,000	280,000	(40,000)	(14.3)
Office salaries expense	165,000	200,000	(35,000)	(17.5)

[continued on next page]

[continued from previous page]

Insurance expense	100,000	45,000	55,000	122.2
Supplies expense	26,000	35,000	(9,000)	(25.7)
Depreciation expense	85,000	75,000	10,000	13.3
Miscellaneous expenses	17,000	15,000	2,000	13.3
Total operating expenses	778,000	750,000	28,000	3.7
Operating income	185,000	103,000	82,000	79.6
Interest expense	44,000	46,000	(2,000)	(4.3)
Income before taxes	141,000	57,000	84,000	147.4
Income taxes	47,000	19,000	28,000	147.4
Net income	$ 94,000	$ 38,000	$ 56,000	147.4
Earnings per share	$ 0.99	$ 0.40	$ 0.59	147.5

2.

PRECISION COMPANY
Common-Size Comparative Balance Sheets
December 31, 2009 and 2008

	December 31		Common-Size Percents	
	2009	2008	2009*	2008*
Assets				
Current assets				
Cash	$ 79,000	$ 42,000	4.7%	2.5%
Short-term investments	65,000	96,000	3.9	5.7
Accounts receivable, net	120,000	100,000	7.1	6.0
Merchandise inventory	250,000	265,000	14.8	15.8
Total current assets	514,000	503,000	30.5	30.0
Plant Assets				
Store equipment, net	400,000	350,000	23.8	20.9
Office equipment, net	45,000	50,000	2.7	3.0
Buildings, net	625,000	675,000	37.1	40.2
Land	100,000	100,000	5.9	6.0
Total plant assets	1,170,000	1,175,000	69.5	70.0
Total assets	$1,684,000	$1,678,000	100.0	100.0
Liabilities				
Current liabilities				
Accounts payable	$ 164,000	$ 190,000	9.7%	11.3%
Short-term notes payable	75,000	90,000	4.5	5.4
Taxes payable	26,000	12,000	1.5	0.7
Total current liabilities	265,000	292,000	15.7	17.4
Long-term liabilities				
Notes payable (secured by mortgage on buildings)	400,000	420,000	23.8	25.0
Total liabilities	665,000	712,000	39.5	42.4
Stockholders' Equity				
Common stock, $5 par value	475,000	475,000	28.2	28.3
Retained earnings	544,000	491,000	32.3	29.3
Total stockholders' equity	1,019,000	966,000	60.5	57.6
Total liabilities and equity	$1,684,000	$1,678,000	100.0	100.0

* Columns do not always exactly add to 100 due to rounding.

3. Ratios for 2009:

a. Current ratio: $514,000/$265,000 = 1.9:1 (liquidity and efficiency)

b. Acid-test ratio: ($79,000 + $65,000 + $120,000)/$265,000 = 1.0:1 (liquidity and efficiency)

c. Average receivables: ($120,000 + $100,000)/2 = $110,000
Accounts receivable turnover: $2,486,000/$110,000 = 22.6 times (liquidity and efficiency)

d. Days' sales uncollected: ($120,000/$2,486,000) × 365 = 17.6 days (liquidity and efficiency)

e. Average inventory: ($250,000 + $265,000)/2 = $257,500
Inventory turnover: $1,523,000/$257,500 = 5.9 times (liquidity and efficiency)

f. Debt ratio: \$665,000/\$1,684,000 = 39.5% (solvency)
g. Debt-to-equity ratio: \$665,000/\$1,019,000 = 0.65 (solvency)
h. Times interest earned: \$185,000/\$44,000 = 4.2 times (solvency)
i. Profit margin ratio: \$94,000/\$2,486,000 = 3.8% (profitability)
j. Average total assets: (\$1,684,000 + \$1,678,000)/2 = \$1,681,000
Total asset turnover: \$2,486,000/\$1,681,000 = 1.48 times (liquidity and efficiency)
k. Return on total assets: \$94,000/\$1,681,000 = 5.6% or 3.8% × 1.48 = 5.6% (profitability)
l. Average total common equity: (\$1,019,000 + \$966,000)/2 = \$992,500
Return on common stockholders' equity: \$94,000/\$992,500 = 9.5% (profitability)

APPENDIX

17A Sustainable Income

A2 Explain the form and assess the content of a complete income statement.

When a company's revenue and expense transactions are from normal, continuing operations, a simple income statement is usually adequate. When a company's activities include income-related events not part of its normal, continuing operations, it must disclose information to help users understand these events and predict future performance. To meet these objectives, companies separate the income statement into continuing operations, discontinued segments, extraordinary items, comprehensive income, and earnings per share. For illustration, Exhibit 17A.1 shows such an income statement for ComUS. These separate distinctions help us measure *sustainable income,* which is the income level most likely to continue into the future. Sustainable income is commonly used in PE ratios and other market-based measures of performance.

Continuing Operations

The first major section (①) shows the revenues, expenses, and income from continuing operations. Users especially rely on this information to predict future operations. Many users view this section as the most important. Earlier chapters explained the items comprising income from continuing operations.

Discontinued Segments

A **business segment** is a part of a company's operations that serves a particular line of business or class of customers. A segment has assets, liabilities, and financial results of operations that can be distinguished from those of other parts of the company. A company's gain or loss from selling or closing down a segment is separately reported. Section ② of Exhibit 17A.1 reports both (1) income from operating the discontinued segment for the current period prior to its disposal and (2) the loss from disposing of the segment's net assets. The income tax effects of each are reported separately from the income taxes expense in section ①.

Extraordinary Items

Section ③ reports **extraordinary gains and losses,** which are those that are *both unusual* and *infrequent.* An **unusual gain or loss** is abnormal or otherwise unrelated to the company's regular activities and environment. An **infrequent gain or loss** is not expected to recur given the company's operating environment. Reporting extraordinary items in a separate category helps users predict future performance, absent the effects of extraordinary items. Items usually considered extraordinary include (1) expropriation (taking away) of property by a foreign government, (2) condemning of property by a domestic government body, (3) prohibition against using an asset by a newly enacted law, and (4) losses and gains from an unusual and infrequent calamity ("act of God"). Items *not* considered extraordinary include (1) write-downs

EXHIBIT 17A.1

Income Statement (all-inclusive) for a Corporation

	ComUS Income Statement For Year Ended December 31, 2009		
	Net sales		$8,478,000
	Operating expenses		
	Cost of goods sold	$5,950,000	
	Depreciation expense	35,000	
	Other selling, general, and administrative expenses	515,000	
	Interest expense	20,000	
①	Total operating expenses		(6,520,000)
	Other gains (losses)		
	Loss on plant relocation		(45,000)
	Gain on sale of surplus land		72,000
	Income from continuing operations before taxes		1,985,000
	Income taxes expense		(595,500)
	Income from continuing operations		1,389,500
	Discontinued segment		
②	Income from operating Division A (net of $180,000 taxes)	420,000	
	Loss on disposal of Division A (net of $66,000 tax benefit)	(154,000)	266,000
	Income before extraordinary items		1,655,500
	Extraordinary items		
③	Gain on land expropriated by state (net of $85,200 taxes)	198,800	
	Loss from earthquake damage (net of $270,000 tax benefit)	(630,000)	(431,200)
	Net income		$1,224,300
	Earnings per common share (200,000 outstanding shares)		
	Income from continuing operations		$ 6.95
④	Discontinued operations		1.33
	Income before extraordinary items		8.28
	Extraordinary items		(2.16)
	Net income (basic earnings per share)		$ 6.12

of inventories and write-offs of receivables, (2) gains and losses from disposing of segments, and (3) financial effects of labor strikes.

Gains and losses that are neither unusual nor infrequent are reported as part of continuing operations. Gains and losses that are *either* unusual *or* infrequent, but *not* both, are reported as part of continuing operations *but* after the normal revenues and expenses.

Decision Maker

Small Business Owner You own an orange grove near Jacksonville, Florida. A bad frost destroys about one-half of your oranges. You are currently preparing an income statement for a bank loan. Can you claim the loss of oranges as extraordinary? [Answer—p. 706]

Earnings per Share

The final section ④ of the income statement in Exhibit 17A.1 reports earnings per share for each of the three subcategories of income (continuing operations, discontinued segments, and extraordinary items) when they exist. Earnings per share is discussed in Chapter 13.

Changes in Accounting Principles

Point: Changes in principles are sometimes required when new accounting standards are issued.

The *consistency concept* directs a company to apply the same accounting principles across periods. Yet a company can change from one acceptable accounting principle (such as FIFO, LIFO, or weighted-average) to another as long as the change improves the usefulness of information in its financial statements. A footnote would describe the accounting change and why it is an improvement.

Changes in accounting principles require retrospective application to prior periods' financial statements. *Retrospective application* involves applying a different accounting principle to prior periods as if that principle had always been used. Retrospective application enhances the consistency of financial information between periods, which improves the usefulness of information, especially with comparative analyses. (Prior to 2005, the cumulative effect of changes in accounting principles was recognized in net income in the period of the change.) Accounting standards also require that *a change in depreciation, amortization, or depletion method for long-term operating assets is accounted for as a change in accounting estimate*—that is, prospectively over current and future periods. This reflects the notion that an entity should change its depreciation, amortization, or depletion method only with changes in estimated asset benefits, the pattern of benefit usage, or information about those benefits.

Comprehensive Income

Comprehensive income is net income plus certain gains and losses that bypass the income statement. These items are recorded directly to equity. Specifically, comprehensive income equals the change in equity for the period, excluding investments from and distributions (dividends) to its stockholders. For **Best Buy**, it is computed as follows ($ millions):

Net income	$1,377
Accumulated other comprehensive income (loss)	(45)
Comprehensive income	$1,332

The most common items included in *accumulated other comprehensive income,* or *AOCI,* are unrealized gains and losses on available-for-sale securities and foreign currency translation adjustments. (Detailed computations for these items are in advanced courses.) Analysts disagree on how to treat these items. Some analysts believe that AOCI items should not be considered when predicting future performance, and some others believe AOCI items should be considered as they reflect on company and managerial performance. Whatever our position, we must be familiar with what AOCI items are as they are commonly reported in financial statements. Best Buy reports its comprehensive income in its statement of shareholders' equity (see Appendix A).

Quick Check

Answers—p. 706

13. Which of the following is an extraordinary item? (*a*) a settlement paid to a customer injured while using the company's product, (*b*) a loss to a plant from damages caused by a meteorite, or (*c*) a loss from selling old equipment.
14. Identify the four major sections of an income statement that are potentially reportable.
15. A company using FIFO for the past 15 years decides to switch to LIFO. The effect of this event on prior years' net income is (*a*) reported as if the new method had always been used; (*b*) ignored because it is a change in an accounting estimate; or (*c*) reported on the current year income statement.

Summary

C1 **Explain the purpose of analysis.** The purpose of financial statement analysis is to help users make better business decisions. Internal users want information to improve company efficiency and effectiveness in providing products and services. External users want information to make better and more informed decisions in pursuing their goals. The common goals of all users are to evaluate a company's (1) past and current performance, (2) current financial position, and (3) future performance and risk.

C2 **Identify the building blocks of analysis.** Financial statement analysis focuses on four "building blocks" of analysis: (1) liquidity and efficiency—ability to meet short-term obligations and efficiently generate revenues; (2) solvency—ability to generate future revenues and meet long-term obligations; (3) profitability—ability to provide financial rewards sufficient to attract and retain financing; and (4) market prospects—ability to generate positive market expectations.

C3 **Describe standards for comparisons in analysis.** Standards for comparisons include (1) intracompany—prior performance and relations between financial items for the company under analysis; (2) competitor—one or more direct competitors of the company; (3) industry—industry statistics; and (4) guidelines (rules of thumb)—general standards developed from past experiences and personal judgments.

C4 **Identify the tools of analysis.** The three most common tools of financial statement analysis are (1) horizontal analysis—comparing a company's financial condition and performance across time; (2) vertical analysis—comparing a company's financial condition and performance to a base amount such as revenues or total assets; and (3) ratio analysis—using and quantifying key relations among financial statement items.

A1 Summarize and report results of analysis. A financial statement analysis report is often organized around the building blocks of analysis. A good report separates interpretations and conclusions of analysis from the information underlying them. An analysis report often consists of six sections: (1) executive summary, (2) analysis overview, (3) evidential matter, (4) assumptions, (5) key factors, and (6) inferences.

A2[A] Explain the form and assess the content of a complete income statement. An income statement has four *potential* sections: (1) continuing operations, (2) discontinued segments, (3) extraordinary items, and (4) earnings per share.

P1 Explain and apply methods of horizontal analysis. Horizontal analysis is a tool to evaluate changes in data across time. Two important tools of horizontal analysis are comparative statements and trend analysis. Comparative statements show amounts for two or more successive periods, often with changes disclosed in both absolute and percent terms. Trend analysis is used to reveal important changes occurring from one period to the next.

P2 Describe and apply methods of vertical analysis. Vertical analysis is a tool to evaluate each financial statement item or group of items in terms of a base amount. Two tools of vertical analysis are common-size statements and graphical analyses. Each item in common-size statements is expressed as a percent of a base amount. For the balance sheet, the base amount is usually total assets, and for the income statement, it is usually sales.

P3 Define and apply ratio analysis. Ratio analysis provides clues to and symptoms of underlying conditions. Ratios, properly interpreted, identify areas requiring further investigation. A ratio expresses a mathematical relation between two quantities such as a percent, rate, or proportion. Ratios can be organized into the building blocks of analysis: (1) liquidity and efficiency, (2) solvency, (3) profitability, and (4) market prospects.

Guidance Answers to **Decision Maker**

Auditor The *joint relation* referred to is the combined increase in sales and the decrease in expenses yielding more than a 5% increase in income. Both *individual* accounts (sales and expenses) yield percent changes within the ±5% acceptable range. However, a joint analysis suggests a different picture. For example, consider a joint analysis using the profit margin ratio. The client's profit margin is 11.46% ($206,000 − $182,400/$206,000) for the current year compared with 5.0% ($200,000 − $190,000/$200,000) for the prior year—yielding a 129% increase in profit margin! This is what concerns the partner, and it suggests expanding audit tests to verify or refute the client's figures.

Banker Your decision on the loan application is positive for at least two reasons. First, the current ratio suggests a strong ability to meet short-term obligations. Second, current assets of $160,000 and a current ratio of 4:1 imply current liabilities of $40,000 (one-fourth of current assets) and a working capital excess of $120,000. This working capital excess is 60% of the loan amount. However, if the application is for a 10-year loan, our decision is less optimistic. The current ratio and working capital suggest a good safety margin, but indications of inefficiency in operations exist. In particular, a 4:1 current ratio is more than double its key competitors' ratio. This is characteristic of inefficient asset use.

Small Business Owner The frost loss is probably not extraordinary. Jacksonville experiences enough recurring frost damage to make it difficult to argue this event is both unusual and infrequent. Still, you want to highlight the frost loss and hope the bank views this uncommon event separately from continuing operations.

Guidance Answers to **Quick Checks**

1. General-purpose financial statements are intended for a variety of users interested in a company's financial condition and performance—users without the power to require specialized financial reports to meet their specific needs.

2. General-purpose financial statements include the income statement, balance sheet, statement of stockholders' (owner's) equity, and statement of cash flows plus the notes related to these statements.

3. *a*

4. Data from one or more direct competitors are usually preferred for comparative purposes.

5. *d*

6. Percents on comparative income statements show the increase or decrease in each item from one period to the next. On common-size comparative income statements, each item is shown as a percent of net sales for that period.

7. *c*

8. (*a*) ($820,000 + $240,000 + $470,000)/($350,000 + $180,000) = 2.9 to 1.
(*b*) ($820,000 + $240,000)/($350,000 + $180,000) = 2:1.

9. (*a*) $2,500,000/[($290,000 + $240,000)/2] = 9.43 times.
(*b*) ($290,000/$2,500,000) × 365 = 42 days.
(*c*) $750,000/[($530,000 + $470,000)/2] = 1.5 times.
(*d*) ($530,000/$750,000) × 365 = 258 days.

10. *c*

11. *b*

12. $$\text{Profit margin} \times \frac{\text{Total asset}}{\text{turnover}} = \frac{\text{Return on}}{\text{total assets}}$$

$$\frac{\$945{,}000}{\$8{,}500{,}000} \times 1.8 = 20\%$$

13. (*b*)

14. The four (potentially reportable) major sections are income from continuing operations, discontinued segments, extraordinary items, and earnings per share.

15. (*a*); known as retrospective application.

Key Terms

mhhe.com/wildFAP19e

Key Terms are available at the book's Website for learning and testing in an online Flashcard Format.

Business segment (p. 703)
Common-size financial statement (p. 687)
Comparative financial statements (p. 682)
Efficiency (p. 681)
Equity ratio (p. 695)
Extraordinary gains and losses (p. 703)
Financial reporting (p. 681)
Financial statement analysis (p. 680)
General-purpose financial statements (p. 681)
Horizontal analysis (p. 682)
Infrequent gain or loss (p. 703)
Liquidity (p. 681)
Market prospects (p. 681)
Profitability (p. 681)
Ratio analysis (p. 682)
Solvency (p. 681)
Unusual gain or loss (p. 703)
Vertical analysis (p. 682)
Working capital (p. 691)

Multiple Choice Quiz

Answers on p. 723

mhhe.com/wildFAP19e

Additional Quiz Questions are available at the book's Website.

Quiz17

1. A company's sales in 2008 were $300,000 and in 2009 were $351,000. Using 2008 as the base year, the sales trend percent for 2009 is:
a. 17%
b. 85%
c. 100%
d. 117%
e. 48%

Use the following information for questions 2 through 5.

GALLOWAY COMPANY
Balance Sheet
December 31, 2009

Assets	
Cash	$ 86,000
Accounts receivable	76,000
Merchandise inventory	122,000
Prepaid insurance	12,000
Long-term investments	98,000
Plant assets, net	436,000
Total assets	$830,000
Liabilities and Equity	
Current liabilities	$124,000
Long-term liabilities	90,000
Common stock	300,000
Retained earnings	316,000
Total liabilities and equity	$830,000

2. What is Galloway Company's current ratio?
a. 0.69
b. 1.31
c. 3.88
d. 6.69
e. 2.39

3. What is Galloway Company's acid-test ratio?
a. 2.39
b. 0.69
c. 1.31
d. 6.69
e. 3.88

4. What is Galloway Company's debt ratio?
a. 25.78%
b. 100.00%
c. 74.22%
d. 137.78%
e. 34.74%

5. What is Galloway Company's equity ratio?
a. 25.78%
b. 100.00%
c. 34.74%
d. 74.22%
e. 137.78%

Superscript letter A denotes assignments based on Appendix 17A.

Discussion Questions

1. What is the difference between comparative financial statements and common-size comparative statements?

2. Which items are usually assigned a 100% value on (*a*) a common-size balance sheet and (*b*) a common-size income statement?

3. Explain the difference between financial reporting and financial statements.

4. What three factors would influence your evaluation as to whether a company's current ratio is good or bad?

5. Suggest several reasons why a 2:1 current ratio might not be adequate for a particular company.
6. Why is working capital given special attention in the process of analyzing balance sheets?
7. What does the number of days' sales uncollected indicate?
8. What does a relatively high accounts receivable turnover indicate about a company's short-term liquidity?
9. Why is a company's capital structure, as measured by debt and equity ratios, important to financial statement analysts?
10. How does inventory turnover provide information about a company's short-term liquidity?
11. What ratios would you compute to evaluate management performance?
12. Why would a company's return on total assets be different from its return on common stockholders' equity?
13. Where on the income statement does a company report an unusual gain not expected to occur more often than once every two years or so?
14. Use Best Buy's financial statements in Appendix A to compute its return on total assets for the years ended March 3, 2007, and February 25, 2006. Total assets at February 26, 2005, were $10,294 (in millions).

15. Refer to Circuit City's financial statements in Appendix A to compute its equity ratio as of February 28, 2007, and February 28, 2006.

16. Refer to RadioShack's financial statements in Appendix A. Compute its debt ratio as of December 31, 2006, and December 31, 2005.

RadioShack.

17. Refer to Apple's financial statements in Appendix A. Compute its profit margin for the fiscal year ended September 30, 2006.

Denotes Discussion Questions that involve decision making.

Available with McGraw-Hill's Homework Manager — McGraw-Hill's HOMEWORK MANAGER®

QUICK STUDY

QS 17-1
Financial reporting C1

Which of the following items (1) through (9) are part of financial reporting but are *not* included as part of general-purpose financial statements? (1) stock price information and analysis, (2) statement of cash flows, (3) management discussion and analysis of financial performance, (4) income statement, (5) company news releases, (6) balance sheet, (7) financial statement notes, (8) statement of shareholders' equity, (9) prospectus.

QS 17-2
Standard of comparison C3

What are four possible standards of comparison used to analyze financial statement ratios? Which of these is generally considered to be the most useful? Which one is least likely to provide a good basis for comparison?

QS 17-3
Common-size and trend percents
P1 P2

Use the following information for Owens Corporation to determine (1) the 2008 and 2009 common-size percents for cost of goods sold using net sales as the base and (2) the 2008 and 2009 trend percents for net sales using 2008 as the base year.

($ thousands)	2009	2008
Net sales	$101,400	$58,100
Cost of goods sold	55,300	30,700

QS 17-4
Horizontal analysis
P1

Compute the annual dollar changes and percent changes for each of the following accounts.

	2009	2008
Short-term investments	$110,000	$80,000
Accounts receivable	22,000	25,000
Notes payable	30,000	0

QS 17-5
Building blocks of analysis
C2 C4 P3

Match the ratio to the building block of financial statement analysis to which it best relates.

A. Liquidity and efficiency
B. Solvency
C. Profitability
D. Market prospects

1. ______ Gross margin ratio
2. ______ Acid-test ratio
3. ______ Equity ratio
4. ______ Return on total assets
5. ______ Dividend yield
6. ______ Book value per common share
7. ______ Days' sales in inventory
8. ______ Accounts receivable turnover
9. ______ Debt-to-equity
10. ______ Times interest earned

QS 17-6
Identifying financial ratios
C4 P3

1. Which two short-term liquidity ratios measure how frequently a company collects its accounts?
2. What measure reflects the difference between current assets and current liabilities?
3. Which two ratios are key components in measuring a company's operating efficiency? Which ratio summarizes these two components?

QS 17-7
Ratio interpretation
P3

For each ratio listed, identify whether the change in ratio value from 2008 to 2009 is usually regarded as favorable or unfavorable.

Ratio	2009	2008	Ratio	2009	2008
1. Profit margin	10%	9%	5. Accounts receivable turnover	6.7	5.5
2. Debt ratio	43%	39%	6. Basic earnings per share	$1.25	$1.10
3. Gross margin	32%	44%	7. Inventory turnover	3.4	3.6
4. Acid-test ratio	1.20	1.05	8. Dividend yield	4%	3.2%

QS 17-8[A]
Error adjustments
A2

A review of the notes payable files discovers that three years ago the company reported the entire amount of a payment (principal and interest) on an installment note payable as interest expense. This mistake had a material effect on the amount of income in that year. How should the correction be reported in the current year financial statements?

McGraw-Hill's HOMEWORK MANAGER® Available with McGraw-Hill's Homework Manager

EXERCISES

Exercise 17-1
Computation and analysis of trend percents
P1

Compute trend percents for the following accounts, using 2007 as the base year. State whether the situation as revealed by the trends appears to be favorable or unfavorable for each account.

	2011	2010	2009	2008	2007
Sales	$282,700	$270,700	$252,500	$234,460	$150,000
Cost of goods sold	128,100	121,980	115,180	106,340	67,000
Accounts receivable	18,000	17,200	16,300	15,100	9,000

Exercise 17-2
Determination of income effects from common-size and trend percents
P1 P2

Common-size and trend percents for Danian Company's sales, cost of goods sold, and expenses follow. Determine whether net income increased, decreased, or remained unchanged in this three-year period.

	Common-Size Percents			Trend Percents		
	2010	2009	2008	2010	2009	2008
Sales	100.0%	100.0%	100.0%	104.9%	103.7%	100.0%
Cost of goods sold	67.7	61.2	58.4	102.5	108.6	100.0
Total expenses	14.4	13.9	14.2	106.5	101.5	100.0

Exercise 17-3
Common-size percent computation and interpretation
P2 

Express the following comparative income statements in common-size percents and assess whether or not this company's situation has improved in the most recent year.

MULAN CORPORATION Comparative Income Statements For Years Ended December 31, 2009 and 2008	2009	2008
Sales	$657,386	$488,400
Cost of goods sold	427,301	286,202
Gross profit	230,085	202,198
Operating expenses	138,051	94,750
Net income	$ 92,034	$107,448

Exercise 17-4
Analysis of short-term financial condition
A1 P3 

The following information is available for Orkay Company and Lowes Company, similar firms operating in the same industry. Write a half-page report comparing Orkay and Lowes using the available information. Your discussion should include their ability to meet current obligations and to use current assets efficiently.

Team Project: Assume that the two companies apply for a one-year loan from the team. Identify additional information the companies must provide before the team can make a loan decision.

	Orkay			Lowes		
	2010	2009	2008	2010	2009	2008
Current ratio	1.6	1.7	2.0	3.1	2.6	1.8
Acid-test ratio	0.9	1.0	1.1	2.7	2.4	1.5
Accounts receivable turnover	29.5	24.2	28.2	15.4	14.2	15.0
Merchandise inventory turnover	23.2	20.9	16.1	13.5	12.0	11.6
Working capital	$60,000	$48,000	$42,000	$121,000	$93,000	$68,000

Exercise 17-5
Analysis of efficiency and financial leverage
A1 P3 

Caren Company and Revlon Company are similar firms that operate in the same industry. Revlon began operations in 2009 and Caren in 2006. In 2011, both companies pay 7% interest on their debt to creditors. The following additional information is available.

	Caren Company			Revlon Company		
	2011	2010	2009	2011	2010	2009
Total asset turnover	3.0	2.7	2.9	1.6	1.4	1.1
Return on total assets	8.9%	9.5%	8.7%	5.8%	5.5%	5.2%
Profit margin ratio	2.3%	2.4%	2.2%	2.7%	2.9%	2.8%
Sales	$400,000	$370,000	$386,000	$200,000	$160,000	$100,000

Write a half-page report comparing Caren and Revlon using the available information. Your analysis should include their ability to use assets efficiently to produce profits. Also comment on their success in employing financial leverage in 2011.

Exercise 17-6
Common-size percents
P2 

Nabisco Company's year-end balance sheets follow. Express the balance sheets in common-size percents. Round amounts to the nearest one-tenth of a percent. Analyze and comment on the results.

At December 31	2010	2009	2008
Assets			
Cash	$ 36,229	$ 42,780	$ 44,562
Accounts receivable, net	106,073	76,377	57,087
Merchandise inventory	137,408	98,929	62,038
Prepaid expenses	11,548	11,003	4,903
Plant assets, net	335,317	311,062	272,710
Total assets	$626,575	$540,151	$441,300
Liabilities and Equity			
Accounts payable	$157,577	$ 94,024	$ 57,087
Long-term notes payable secured by mortgages on plant assets	116,618	127,962	99,478
Common stock, $10 par value	163,500	163,500	163,500
Retained earnings	188,880	154,665	121,235
Total liabilities and equity	$626,575	$540,151	$441,300

Exercise 17-7
Liquidity analysis
P3

Refer to Nabisco Company's balance sheets in Exercise 17-6. Analyze its year-end short-term liquidity position at the end of 2010, 2009, and 2008 by computing (1) the current ratio and (2) the acid-test ratio. Comment on the ratio results. (Round ratio amounts to two decimals.)

Exercise 17-8
Liquidity analysis and interpretation
P3

Refer to the Nabisco Company information in Exercise 17-6. The company's income statements for the years ended December 31, 2010 and 2009, follow. Assume that all sales are on credit and then compute: (1) days' sales uncollected, (2) accounts receivable turnover, (3) inventory turnover, and (4) days' sales in inventory. Comment on the changes in the ratios from 2009 to 2010. (Round amounts to one decimal.)

For Year Ended December 31	2010		2009	
Sales		$685,000		$557,000
Cost of goods sold	$417,850		$356,265	
Other operating expenses	207,282		141,971	
Interest expense	8,175		8,960	
Income taxes	12,900		12,450	
Total costs and expenses		646,207		519,646
Net income		$ 38,793		$ 37,354
Earnings per share		$ 2.37		$ 2.28

Exercise 17-9
Risk and capital structure analysis
P3

Refer to the Nabisco Company information in Exercises 17-6 and 17-8. Compare the company's long-term risk and capital structure positions at the end of 2010 and 2009 by computing these ratios: (1) debt and equity ratios, (2) debt-to-equity ratio, and (3) times interest earned. Comment on these ratio results.

Exercise 17-10
Efficiency and profitability analysis P3 

Refer to Nabisco Company's financial information in Exercises 17-6 and 17-8. Evaluate the company's efficiency and profitability by computing the following for 2010 and 2009: (1) profit margin ratio, (2) total asset turnover, and (3) return on total assets. Comment on these ratio results.

Exercise 17-11
Profitability analysis
P3

Refer to Nabisco Company's financial information in Exercises 17-6 and 17-8. Additional information about the company follows. To help evaluate the company's profitability, compute and interpret the following ratios for 2010 and 2009: (1) return on common stockholders' equity, (2) price-earnings ratio on December 31, and (3) dividend yield.

Common stock market price, December 31, 2010	$30.00
Common stock market price, December 31, 2009	28.00
Annual cash dividends per share in 2010	0.28
Annual cash dividends per share in 2009	0.24

Exercise 17-12[A]
Income statement categories
A2

In 2009, Simplon Merchandising, Inc., sold its interest in a chain of wholesale outlets, taking the company completely out of the wholesaling business. The company still operates its retail outlets. A listing of the major sections of an income statement follows:

A. Income (loss) from continuing operations

B. Income (loss) from operating, or gain (loss) from disposing, a discontinued segment

C. Extraordinary gain (loss)

Indicate where each of the following income-related items for this company appears on its 2009 income statement by writing the letter of the appropriate section in the blank beside each item.

Section	Item	Debit	Credit
______	1. Net sales		$3,000,000
______	2. Gain on state's condemnation of company property (net of tax)		330,000
______	3. Cost of goods sold	$1,580,000	
______	4. Income taxes expense	117,000	
______	5. Depreciation expense	332,500	
______	6. Gain on sale of wholesale business segment (net of tax)		875,000
______	7. Loss from operating wholesale business segment (net of tax)	544,000	
______	8. Salaries expense	740,000	

Exercise 17-13[A]
Income statement presentation
A2

Use the financial data for Simplon Merchandising, Inc., in Exercise 17-12 to prepare its income statement for calendar year 2009. (Ignore the earnings per share section.)

Available with McGraw-Hill's Homework Manager

McGraw-Hill's HOMEWORK MANAGER®

PROBLEM SET A

Problem 17-1A
Ratios, common-size statements, and trend percents
P1 P2 P3

mhhe.com/wildFAP19e

Selected comparative financial statements of Astalon Company follow.

ASTALON COMPANY Comparative Income Statements For Years Ended December 31, 2010, 2009, and 2008	2010	2009	2008
Sales	$526,304	$403,192	$279,800
Cost of goods sold	316,835	255,624	179,072
Gross profit	209,469	147,568	100,728
Selling expenses	74,735	55,640	36,934
Administrative expenses	47,367	35,481	23,223
Total expenses	122,102	91,121	60,157
Income before taxes	87,367	56,447	40,571
Income taxes	16,250	11,572	8,236
Net income	$ 71,117	$ 44,875	$ 32,335

ASTALON COMPANY Comparative Balance Sheets December 31, 2010, 2009, and 2008	2010	2009	2008
Assets			
Current assets	$ 48,242	$ 38,514	$ 51,484
Long-term investments	0	800	3,620
Plant assets, net	92,405	97,259	58,047
Total assets	$140,647	$136,573	$113,151
Liabilities and Equity			
Current liabilities	$ 20,534	$ 20,349	$ 19,801
Common stock	69,000	69,000	51,000
Other paid-in capital	8,625	8,625	5,667
Retained earnings	42,488	38,599	36,683
Total liabilities and equity	$140,647	$136,573	$113,151

Required

1. Compute each year's current ratio. (Round ratio amounts to one decimal.)

2. Express the income statement data in common-size percents. (Round percents to two decimals.)

3. Express the balance sheet data in trend percents with 2008 as the base year. (Round percents to two decimals.)

Check (3) 2010, Total assets trend, 124.30%

Analysis Component

4. Comment on any significant relations revealed by the ratios and percents computed.

Problem 17-2A
Calculation and analysis of trend percents
A1 P1

Selected comparative financial statements of Adobe Company follow.

ADOBE COMPANY
Comparative Income Statements
For Years Ended December 31, 2010–2004

($ thousands)	2010	2009	2008	2007	2006	2005	2004
Sales	$2,431	$2,129	$1,937	$1,776	$1,657	$1,541	$1,263
Cost of goods sold	1,747	1,421	1,223	1,070	994	930	741
Gross profit	684	708	714	706	663	611	522
Operating expenses	521	407	374	276	239	236	196
Net income	$ 163	$ 301	$ 340	$ 430	$ 424	$ 375	$ 326

ADOBE COMPANY
Comparative Balance Sheets
December 31, 2010–2004

($ thousands)	2010	2009	2008	2007	2006	2005	2004
Assets							
Cash	$ 163	$ 216	$ 224	$ 229	$ 238	$ 235	$ 242
Accounts receivable, net	1,173	1,232	1,115	855	753	714	503
Merchandise inventory	4,244	3,090	2,699	2,275	2,043	1,735	1,258
Other current assets	109	98	60	108	91	93	48
Long-term investments	0	0	0	334	334	334	334
Plant assets, net	5,192	5,172	4,526	2,553	2,639	2,345	2,015
Total assets	$10,881	$9,808	$8,624	$6,354	$6,098	$5,456	$4,400
Liabilities and Equity							
Current liabilities	$ 2,734	$2,299	$1,509	$1,255	$1,089	$1,030	$ 664
Long-term liabilities	2,924	2,547	2,478	1,151	1,176	1,273	955
Common stock	1,980	1,980	1,980	1,760	1,760	1,540	1,540
Other paid-in capital	495	495	495	440	440	385	385
Retained earnings	2,748	2,487	2,162	1,748	1,633	1,228	856
Total liabilities and equity	$10,881	$9,808	$8,624	$6,354	$6,098	$5,456	$4,400

Required

1. Compute trend percents for all components of both statements using 2004 as the base year. (Round percents to one decimal.)

Check (1) 2010, Total assets trend, 247.3%

Analysis Component

2. Analyze and comment on the financial statements and trend percents from part 1.

Problem 17-3A
Transactions, working capital, and liquidity ratios
P3

mhhe.com/wildFAP19e

Page Corporation began the month of May with $884,000 of current assets, a current ratio of 2.6:1, and an acid-test ratio of 1.5:1. During the month, it completed the following transactions (the company uses a perpetual inventory system).

May 2 Purchased $70,000 of merchandise inventory on credit.
8 Sold merchandise inventory that cost $60,000 for $130,000 cash.
10 Collected $30,000 cash on an account receivable.
15 Paid $31,000 cash to settle an account payable.

Check May 22: Current ratio, 2.23; Acid-test ratio, 1.37

May 29: Current ratio, 2.00; Working capital, $462,000

17 Wrote off a $5,000 bad debt against the Allowance for Doubtful Accounts account.
22 Declared a $1 per share cash dividend on its 67,000 shares of outstanding common stock.
26 Paid the dividend declared on May 22.
27 Borrowed $85,000 cash by giving the bank a 30-day, 10% note.
28 Borrowed $100,000 cash by signing a long-term secured note.
29 Used the $185,000 cash proceeds from the notes to buy new machinery.

Required

Prepare a table showing Page's (1) current ratio, (2) acid-test ratio, and (3) working capital, after each transaction. Round ratios to two decimals.

Problem 17-4A
Calculation of financial statement ratios
P3

mhhe.com/wildFAP19e

Selected year-end financial statements of Cadet Corporation follow. (All sales were on credit; selected balance sheet amounts at December 31, 2008, were inventory, $56,900; total assets, $219,400; common stock, $85,000; and retained earnings, $52,348.)

CADET CORPORATION
Income Statement
For Year Ended December 31, 2009

Sales	$456,600
Cost of goods sold	297,450
Gross profit	159,150
Operating expenses	99,400
Interest expense	3,900
Income before taxes	55,850
Income taxes	22,499
Net income	$ 33,351

CADET CORPORATION
Balance Sheet
December 31, 2009

Assets		Liabilities and Equity	
Cash	$ 20,000	Accounts payable	$ 21,500
Short-term investments	8,200	Accrued wages payable	4,400
Accounts receivable, net	29,400	Income taxes payable	3,700
Notes receivable (trade)*	7,000	Long-term note payable, secured by mortgage on plant assets	67,400
Merchandise inventory	34,150	Common stock	85,000
Prepaid expenses	2,700	Retained earnings	66,750
Plant assets, net	147,300		
Total assets	$248,750	Total liabilities and equity	$248,750

* These are short-term notes receivable arising from customer (trade) sales.

Required

Check Acid-test ratio, 2.2 to 1: Inventory turnover, 6.5

Compute the following: (1) current ratio, (2) acid-test ratio, (3) days' sales uncollected, (4) inventory turnover, (5) days' sales in inventory, (6) debt-to-equity ratio, (7) times interest earned, (8) profit margin ratio, (9) total asset turnover, (10) return on total assets, and (11) return on common stockholders' equity.

Problem 17-5A
Comparative ratio analysis A1 P3

Summary information from the financial statements of two companies competing in the same industry follows.

	Karto Company	Bryan Company
Data from the current year-end balance sheets		
Assets		
Cash	$ 19,500	$ 36,000
Accounts receivable, net	36,400	53,400
Current notes receivable (trade)	9,400	7,600
Merchandise inventory	84,740	134,500
Prepaid expenses	6,200	7,250
Plant assets, net	350,000	307,400
Total assets	$506,240	$546,150
Liabilities and Equity		
Current liabilities	$ 63,340	$ 73,819
Long-term notes payable	82,485	99,000
Common stock, $5 par value	190,000	196,000
Retained earnings	170,415	177,331
Total liabilities and equity	$506,240	$546,150

	Karto Company	Bryan Company
Data from the current year's income statement		
Sales	$790,000	$897,200
Cost of goods sold	588,100	634,500
Interest expense	7,600	19,000
Income tax expense	15,185	24,769
Net income	$179,115	$218,931
Basic earnings per share	$ 4.71	$ 5.58
Beginning-of-year balance sheet data		
Accounts receivable, net	$ 26,800	$ 51,200
Current notes receivable (trade)	0	0
Merchandise inventory	55,600	107,400
Total assets	408,000	422,500
Common stock, $5 par value	190,000	196,000
Retained earnings	124,300	95,600

Required

1. For both companies compute the (*a*) current ratio, (*b*) acid-test ratio, (*c*) accounts (including notes) receivable turnover, (*d*) inventory turnover, (*e*) days' sales in inventory, and (*f*) days' sales uncollected. Identify the company you consider to be the better short-term credit risk and explain why.

Check (1) Bryan: Accounts receivable turnover, 16.0; Inventory turnover, 5.2

2. For both companies compute the (*a*) profit margin ratio, (*b*) total asset turnover, (*c*) return on total assets, and (*d*) return on common stockholders' equity. Assuming that each company paid cash dividends of $3.50 per share and each company's stock can be purchased at $85 per share, compute their (*e*) price-earnings ratios and (*f*) dividend yields. Identify which company's stock you would recommend as the better investment and explain why.

(2) Karto: Profit margin, 22.7%; PE, 18.0

Problem 17-6A[A]
Income statement computations and format

A2 

Selected account balances from the adjusted trial balance for Lindo Corporation as of its calendar year-end December 31, 2009, follow.

	Debit	Credit
a. Interest revenue		$ 15,000
b. Depreciation expense—Equipment	$ 35,000	
c. Loss on sale of equipment	26,850	
d. Accounts payable		45,000
e. Other operating expenses	107,400	
f. Accumulated depreciation—Equipment		72,600
g. Gain from settlement of lawsuit		45,000
h. Accumulated depreciation—Buildings		175,500
i. Loss from operating a discontinued segment (pretax)	19,250	
j. Gain on insurance recovery of tornado damage (pretax and extraordinary)		30,120
k. Net sales		999,500
l. Depreciation expense—Buildings	53,000	
m. Correction of overstatement of prior year's sales (pretax)	17,000	
n. Gain on sale of discontinued segment's assets (pretax)		35,000
o. Loss from settlement of lawsuit	24,750	
p. Income taxes expense	?	
q. Cost of goods sold	483,500	

Required

Answer each of the following questions by providing supporting computations.

1. Assume that the company's income tax rate is 30% for all items. Identify the tax effects and after-tax amounts of the four items labeled pretax.
2. What is the amount of income from continuing operations before income taxes? What is the amount of the income taxes expense? What is the amount of income from continuing operations?
3. What is the total amount of after-tax income (loss) associated with the discontinued segment?
4. What is the amount of income (loss) before the extraordinary items?
5. What is the amount of net income for the year?

Check (3) $11,025
(4) $241,325
(5) $262,409

PROBLEM SET B

Problem 17-1B

Ratios, common-size statements, and trend percents

P1 P2 P3 

Selected comparative financial statement information of Danno Corporation follows.

DANNO CORPORATION
Comparative Income Statements
For Years Ended December 31, 2010, 2009, and 2008

	2010	2009	2008
Sales	$392,000	$300,304	$208,400
Cost of goods sold	235,984	190,092	133,376
Gross profit	156,016	110,212	75,024
Selling expenses	55,664	41,442	27,509
Administrative expenses	35,280	26,427	17,297
Total expenses	90,944	67,869	44,806
Income before taxes	65,072	42,343	30,218
Income taxes	12,103	8,680	6,134
Net income	$ 52,969	$ 33,663	$ 24,084

DANNO CORPORATION
Comparative Balance Sheets
December 31, 2010, 2009, and 2008

	2010	2009	2008
Assets			
Current assets	$ 53,776	$ 42,494	$ 55,118
Long-term investments	0	400	4,110
Plant assets, net	99,871	106,303	64,382
Total assets	$153,647	$149,197	$123,610
Liabilities and Equity			
Current liabilities	$ 22,432	$ 22,230	$ 21,632
Common stock	70,000	70,000	52,000
Other paid-in capital	8,750	8,750	5,778
Retained earnings	52,465	48,217	44,200
Total liabilities and equity	$153,647	$149,197	$123,610

Required

1. Compute each year's current ratio. (Round ratio amounts to one decimal.)
2. Express the income statement data in common-size percents. (Round percents to two decimals.)
3. Express the balance sheet data in trend percents with 2008 as the base year. (Round percents to two decimals.)

Check (3) 2010, Total assets trend, 124.30%

Analysis Component

4. Comment on any significant relations revealed by the ratios and percents computed.

Problem 17-2B
Calculation and analysis of trend percents
A1 P1

Selected comparative financial statements of Park Company follow.

PARK COMPANY Comparative Income Statements For Years Ended December 31, 2010–2004 ($ thousands)	2010	2009	2008	2007	2006	2005	2004
Sales	$570	$620	$640	$690	$750	$780	$870
Cost of goods sold	286	300	304	324	350	360	390
Gross profit	284	320	336	366	400	420	480
Operating expenses	94	114	122	136	150	154	160
Net income	$190	$206	$214	$230	$250	$266	$320

PARK COMPANY Comparative Balance Sheets December 31, 2010–2004 ($ thousands)	2010	2009	2008	2007	2006	2005	2004
Assets							
Cash	$ 54	$ 56	$ 62	$ 64	$ 70	$ 72	$ 78
Accounts receivable, net	140	146	150	154	160	164	170
Merchandise inventory	176	182	188	190	196	200	218
Other current assets	44	44	46	48	48	50	50
Long-term investments	46	40	36	120	120	120	120
Plant assets, net	520	524	530	422	430	438	464
Total assets	$980	$992	$1,012	$998	$1,024	$1,044	$1,100
Liabilities and Equity							
Current liabilities	$158	$166	$ 196	$200	$ 220	$ 270	$ 290
Long-term liabilities	102	130	152	158	204	224	270
Common stock	180	180	180	180	180	180	180
Other paid-in capital	80	80	80	80	80	80	80
Retained earnings	460	436	404	380	340	290	280
Total liabilities and equity	$980	$992	$1,012	$998	$1,024	$1,044	$1,100

Required

1. Compute trend percents for all components of both statements using 2004 as the base year. (Round percents to one decimal.)

Check (1) 2010, Total assets trend, 89.1%

Analysis Component

2. Analyze and comment on the financial statements and trend percents from part 1.

Problem 17-3B
Transactions, working capital, and liquidity ratios
P3

Check June 3: Current ratio, 2.88; Acid-test ratio, 2.40

June 30: Working capital, $(20,000); Current ratio, 0.97

Menardo Corporation began the month of June with $600,000 of current assets, a current ratio of 2.5:1, and an acid-test ratio of 1.4:1. During the month, it completed the following transactions (the company uses a perpetual inventory system).

June	1	Sold merchandise inventory that cost $150,000 for $240,000 cash.
	3	Collected $176,000 cash on an account receivable.
	5	Purchased $300,000 of merchandise inventory on credit.
	7	Borrowed $200,000 cash by giving the bank a 60-day, 8% note.
	10	Borrowed $240,000 cash by signing a long-term secured note.
	12	Purchased machinery for $550,000 cash.
	15	Declared a $1 per share cash dividend on its 160,000 shares of outstanding common stock.
	19	Wrote off a $10,000 bad debt against the Allowance for Doubtful Accounts account.
	22	Paid $24,000 cash to settle an account payable.
	30	Paid the dividend declared on June 15.

Required

Prepare a table showing the company's (1) current ratio, (2) acid-test ratio, and (3) working capital after each transaction. Round ratios to two decimals.

Problem 17-4B
Calculation of financial statement ratios
P3

Selected year-end financial statements of Steele Corporation follow. (All sales were on credit; selected balance sheet amounts at December 31, 2008, were inventory, $55,900; total assets, $249,400; common stock, $105,000; and retained earnings, $17,748.)

STEELE CORPORATION Income Statement For Year Ended December 31, 2009	
Sales	$447,600
Cost of goods sold	298,150
Gross profit	149,450
Operating expenses	98,500
Interest expense	4,600
Income before taxes	46,350
Income taxes	18,672
Net income	$ 27,678

STEELE CORPORATION Balance Sheet December 31, 2009			
Assets		**Liabilities and Equity**	
Cash	$ 8,000	Accounts payable	$ 25,500
Short-term investments	8,000	Accrued wages payable	3,000
Accounts receivable, net	28,800	Income taxes payable	4,000
Notes receivable (trade)*	8,000	Long-term note payable, secured by mortgage on plant assets	63,400
Merchandise inventory	34,150	Common stock, $5 par value	105,000
Prepaid expenses	2,750	Retained earnings	39,100
Plant assets, net	150,300		
Total assets	$240,000	Total liabilities and equity	$240,000

* These are short-term notes receivable arising from customer (trade) sales.

Required

Compute the following: (1) current ratio, (2) acid-test ratio, (3) days' sales uncollected, (4) inventory turnover, (5) days' sales in inventory, (6) debt-to-equity ratio, (7) times interest earned, (8) profit margin ratio, (9) total asset turnover, (10) return on total assets, and (11) return on common stockholders' equity.

Check Acid-test ratio, 1.6 to 1; Inventory turnover, 6.6

Problem 17-5B
Comparative ratio analysis A1 P3

Summary information from the financial statements of two companies competing in the same industry follows.

	Crisco Company	Silas Company
Data from the current year-end balance sheets		
Assets		
Cash	$ 21,000	$ 37,500
Accounts receivable, net	78,100	71,500
Current notes receivable (trade)	12,600	10,000
Merchandise inventory	87,800	83,000
Prepaid expenses	10,700	11,100
Plant assets, net	177,900	253,300
Total assets	$388,100	$466,400
Liabilities and Equity		
Current liabilities	$100,500	$ 98,000
Long-term notes payable	85,650	62,400
Common stock, $5 par value	150,000	170,000
Retained earnings	51,950	136,000
Total liabilities and equity	$388,100	$466,400

	Crisco Company	Silas Company
Data from the current year's income statement		
Sales	$394,600	$668,500
Cost of goods sold	291,600	481,000
Interest expense	6,900	13,300
Income tax expense	6,700	14,300
Net income	34,850	62,700
Basic earnings per share	1.16	1.84
Beginning-of-year balance sheet data		
Accounts receivable, net	$ 73,200	$ 74,300
Current notes receivable (trade)	0	0
Merchandise inventory	106,100	81,500
Total assets	384,400	444,000
Common stock, $5 par value	150,000	170,000
Retained earnings	50,100	110,700

Required

1. For both companies compute the (*a*) current ratio, (*b*) acid-test ratio, (*c*) accounts (including notes) receivable turnover, (*d*) inventory turnover, (*e*) days' sales in inventory, and (*f*) days' sales uncollected. Identify the company you consider to be the better short-term credit risk and explain why.

2. For both companies compute the (*a*) profit margin ratio, (*b*) total asset turnover, (*c*) return on total assets, and (*d*) return on common stockholders' equity. Assuming that each company paid cash dividends of $1.10 per share and each company's stock can be purchased at $25 per share, compute their (*e*) price-earnings ratios and (*f*) dividend yields. Identify which company's stock you would recommend as the better investment and explain why.

Check (1) Crisco: Accounts receivable turnover, 4.8; Inventory turnover, 3.0

(2) Silas: Profit margin, 9.4%; PE, 13.6

Problem 17-6B^A
Income statement computations and format

A2 

Selected account balances from the adjusted trial balance for Harton Corp. as of its calendar year-end December 31, 2009, follow.

	Debit	Credit
a. Accumulated depreciation—Buildings		$ 410,000
b. Interest revenue		30,000
c. Net sales		2,650,000
d. Income taxes expense	$?	
e. Loss on hurricane damage (pretax and extraordinary)	74,000	
f. Accumulated depreciation—Equipment		230,000
g. Other operating expenses	338,000	
h. Depreciation expense—Equipment	110,000	
i. Loss from settlement of lawsuit	46,000	
j. Gain from settlement of lawsuit		78,000
k. Loss on sale of equipment	34,000	
l. Loss from operating a discontinued segment (pretax)	130,000	
m. Depreciation expense—Buildings	166,000	
n. Correction of overstatement of prior year's expense (pretax)		58,000
o. Cost of goods sold	1,050,000	
p. Loss on sale of discontinued segment's assets (pretax)	190,000	
q. Accounts payable		142,000

Required

Answer each of the following questions by providing supporting computations.

1. Assume that the company's income tax rate is 25% for all items. Identify the tax effects and after-tax amounts of the four items labeled pretax.

2. What is the amount of income from continuing operations before income taxes? What is the amount of income taxes expense? What is the amount of income from continuing operations?

3. What is the total amount of after-tax income (loss) associated with the discontinued segment?

4. What is the amount of income (loss) before the extraordinary items?

5. What is the amount of net income for the year?

Check (3) $(240,000)
(4) $520,500
(5) $465,000

SERIAL PROBLEM

Success Systems

(This serial problem began in Chapter 1 and continues through most of the book. If previous chapter segments were not completed, the serial problem can begin at this point. It is helpful, but not necessary, to use the Working Papers that accompany the book.)

SP 17 Use the following selected data from Success Systems' income statement for the three months ended March 31, 2010, and from its March 31, 2010, balance sheet to complete the requirements below: computer services revenue, $25,160; net sales (of goods), $18,693; total sales and revenue, $43,853; cost of goods sold, $14,052; net income, $18,686; quick assets, $100,205; current assets, $105,209; total assets, $129,909; current liabilities, $875; total liabilities, $875; and total equity, $129,034.

Required

1. Compute the gross margin ratio (both with and without services revenue) and net profit margin ratio.
2. Compute the current ratio and acid-test ratio.
3. Compute the debt ratio and equity ratio.
4. What percent of its assets are current? What percent are long term?

BEYOND THE NUMBERS

REPORTING IN ACTION

A1 P1 P2

BTN 17-1 Refer to **Best Buy**'s financial statements in Appendix A to answer the following.

1. Using fiscal 2005 as the base year, compute trend percents for fiscal years 2005, 2006, and 2007 for revenues, cost of sales, selling general and administrative expenses, income taxes, and net income. (Round to the nearest whole percent.)
2. Compute common-size percents for fiscal years 2007 and 2006 for the following categories of assets: (*a*) total current assets, (*b*) property and equipment, net, and (*c*) intangible assets. (Round to the nearest tenth of a percent.)
3. Comment on any significant changes across the years for the income statement trends computed in part 1 and the balance sheet percents computed in part 2.

Fast Forward

4. Access Best Buy's financial statements for fiscal years ending after March 3, 2007, from Best Buy's Website (BestBuy.com) or the SEC database (www.SEC.gov). Update your work for parts 1, 2, and 3 using the new information accessed.

COMPARATIVE ANALYSIS

C3 P2

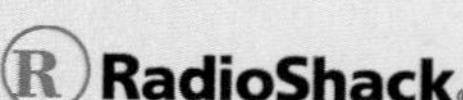

BTN 17-2 Key figures for **Best Buy**, **Circuit City**, and **RadioShack** follow.

($ millions)	Best Buy	Circuit City	RadioShack
Cash and equivalents	$ 1,205	$ 141	$ 472
Accounts receivable, net	548	383	248
Inventories	4,028	1,637	752
Retained earnings	5,507	1,336	1,781
Cost of sales	27,165	9,501	2,544
Revenues	35,934	12,430	4,778
Total assets	13,570	4,007	2,070

Required

1. Compute common-size percents for each of the companies using the data provided. (Round percents to one decimal.)
2. Which company retains a higher portion of cumulative net income in the company?
3. Which company has a higher gross margin ratio on sales?
4. Which company holds a higher percent of its total assets as inventory?

ETHICS CHALLENGE

A1

BTN 17-3 As Beacon Company controller, you are responsible for informing the board of directors about its financial activities. At the board meeting, you present the following information.

	2009	2008	2007
Sales trend percent	147.0%	135.0%	100.0%
Selling expenses to sales	10.1%	14.0%	15.6%
Sales to plant assets ratio	3.8 to 1	3.6 to 1	3.3 to 1
Current ratio	2.9 to 1	2.7 to 1	2.4 to 1
Acid-test ratio	1.1 to 1	1.4 to 1	1.5 to 1
Inventory turnover	7.8 times	9.0 times	10.2 times
Accounts receivable turnover	7.0 times	7.7 times	8.5 times
Total asset turnover	2.9 times	2.9 times	3.3 times
Return on total assets	10.4%	11.0%	13.2%
Return on stockholders' equity	10.7%	11.5%	14.1%
Profit margin ratio	3.6%	3.8%	4.0%

After the meeting, the company's CEO holds a press conference with analysts in which she mentions the following ratios.

	2009	2008	2007
Sales trend percent	147.0%	135.0%	100.0%
Selling expenses to sales	10.1%	14.0%	15.6%
Sales to plant assets ratio	3.8 to 1	3.6 to 1	3.3 to 1
Current ratio	2.9 to 1	2.7 to 1	2.4 to 1

Required

1. Why do you think the CEO decided to report 4 ratios instead of the 11 prepared?

2. Comment on the possible consequences of the CEO's reporting of the ratios selected.

COMMUNICATING IN PRACTICE

C2 A1 P3

BTN 17-4 Each team is to select a different industry, and each team member is to select a different company in that industry and acquire its financial statements. Use those statements to analyze the company, including at least one ratio from each of the four building blocks of analysis. When necessary, use the financial press to determine the market price of its stock. Communicate with teammates via a meeting, e-mail, or telephone to discuss how different companies compare to each other and to industry norms. The team is to prepare a single one-page memorandum reporting on its analysis and the conclusions reached.

TAKING IT TO THE NET

C4 P3

BTN 17-5 Access the February 23, 2007, filing of the 2006 10-K report of the **Hershey Foods Corporation** (ticker HSY) at www.SEC.gov and complete the following requirements.

Required

Compute or identify the following profitability ratios of Hershey for its years ending December 31, 2006, *and* December 31, 2005. Interpret its profitability using the results obtained for these two years.

1. Profit margin ratio.

2. Gross profit ratio.

3. Return on total assets. (Total assets in 2004 were $3,794,750,000.)

4. Return on common stockholders' equity. (Total shareholders' equity in 2004 was $1,137,103,000.)

5. Basic earnings per common share.

TEAMWORK IN ACTION

C2 P1 P2 P3

BTN 17-6 A team approach to learning financial statement analysis is often useful.

Required

1. Each team should write a description of horizontal and vertical analysis that all team members agree with and understand. Illustrate each description with an example.

2. *Each* member of the team is to select *one* of the following categories of ratio analysis. Explain what the ratios in that category measure. Choose one ratio from the category selected, present its formula, and explain what it measures.

a. Liquidity and efficiency
b. Solvency
c. Profitability
d. Market prospects

3. Each team member is to present his or her notes from part 2 to teammates. Team members are to confirm or correct other teammates' presentation.

Hint: Pairing within teams may be necessary for part 2. Use as an in-class activity or as an assignment. Consider presentations to the entire class using team rotation with transparencies.

ENTREPRENEURIAL DECISION

A1 P1 P2 P3 

BTN 17-7 Assume that David and Tom Gardner of **The Motley Fool** (Fool.com) have impressed you since you first heard of their rather improbable rise to prominence in financial circles. You learn of a staff opening at The Motley Fool and decide to apply for it. Your resume is successfully screened from the thousands received and you advance to the interview process. You learn that the interview consists of analyzing the following financial facts and answering analysis questions. (*Note:* The data are taken from a small merchandiser in outdoor recreational equipment.)

	2008	2007	2006
Sales trend percents	137.0%	125.0%	100.0%
Selling expenses to sales	9.8%	13.7%	15.3%
Sales to plant assets ratio	3.5 to 1	3.3 to 1	3.0 to 1
Current ratio	2.6 to 1	2.4 to 1	2.1 to 1
Acid-test ratio	0.8 to 1	1.1 to 1	1.2 to 1
Merchandise inventory turnover	7.5 times	8.7 times	9.9 times
Accounts receivable turnover	6.7 times	7.4 times	8.2 times
Total asset turnover	2.6 times	2.6 times	3.0 times
Return on total assets	8.8%	9.4%	11.1%
Return on equity	9.75%	11.50%	12.25%
Profit margin ratio	3.3%	3.5%	3.7%

Required

Use these data to answer each of the following questions with explanations.

1. Is it becoming easier for the company to meet its current liabilities on time and to take advantage of any available cash discounts? Explain.
2. Is the company collecting its accounts receivable more rapidly? Explain.
3. Is the company's investment in accounts receivable decreasing? Explain.
4. Is the company's investment in plant assets increasing? Explain.
5. Is the owner's investment becoming more profitable? Explain.
6. Did the dollar amount of selling expenses decrease during the three-year period? Explain.

HITTING THE ROAD

C1 P3

BTN 17-8 You are to devise an investment strategy to enable you to accumulate $1,000,000 by age 65. Start by making some assumptions about your salary. Next compute the percent of your salary that you will be able to save each year. If you will receive any lump-sum monies, include those amounts in your calculations. Historically, stocks have delivered average annual returns of 10–11%. Given this history, you should probably not assume that you will earn above 10% on the money you invest. It is not necessary to specify exactly what types of assets you will buy for your investments; just assume a rate you expect to earn. Use the future value tables in Appendix B to calculate how your savings will grow. Experiment a bit with your figures to see how much less you have to save if you start at, for example, age 25 versus age 35 or 40. (For this assignment, do not include inflation in your calculations.)

GLOBAL DECISION

A1

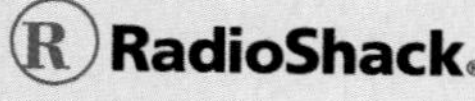

BTN 17-9 **DSG international plc** (www.DSGiplc.com), **Best Buy**, **Circuit City**, and **RadioShack** are competitors in the global marketplace. Key figures for DSG follow (in millions).

Cash and equivalents	£ 441
Accounts receivable, net	393
Inventories	1,031
Retained earnings	1,490
Cost of sales	7,285
Revenues	7,930
Total assets	3,977

Required

1. Compute common-sized percents for DSG using the data provided. (Round percents to one decimal.)

2. Compare the results with Best Buy, Circuit City, and RadioShack from BTN 17-2.

ANSWERS TO MULTIPLE CHOICE QUIZ

1. d; ($351,000/$300,000) × 100 = 117%

2. e; ($86,000 + $76,000 + $122,000 + $12,000)/$124,000 = 2.39

3. c; ($86,000 + $76,000)/$124,000 = 1.31

4. a; ($124,000 + $90,000)/$830,000 = 25.78%

5. d; ($300,000 + $316,000)/$830,000 = 74.22%

A Look Back

Chapter 17 described the analysis and interpretation of financial statement information. We applied horizontal, vertical, and ratio analyses to better understand company performance and financial condition.

A Look at This Chapter

We begin our study of managerial accounting by explaining its purpose and describing its major characteristics. We also discuss cost concepts and describe how they help managers gather and organize information for making decisions. The reporting of manufacturing activities is also discussed.

A Look Ahead

The remaining chapters discuss the types of decisions managers must make and how managerial accounting helps with those decisions. The first of these chapters, Chapter 19, considers how we measure costs assigned to certain types of projects.

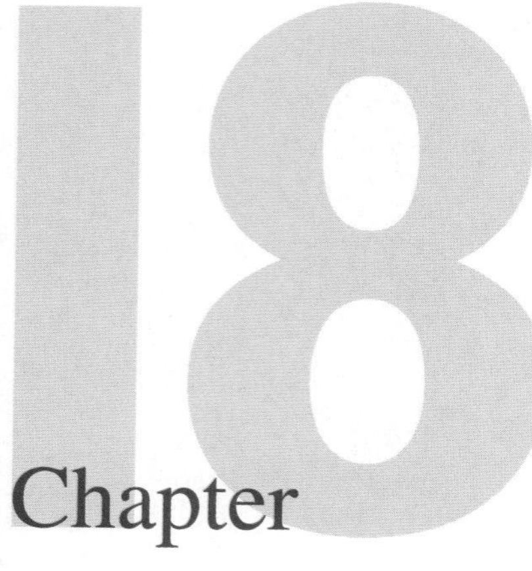

Chapter 18 Managerial Accounting Concepts and Principles

Learning Objectives

CAP

Conceptual

C1 Explain the purpose and nature of managerial accounting. *(p. 726)*

C2 Describe the lean business model. *(p. 729)*

C3 Describe fraud and the role of ethics in managerial accounting. *(p. 731)*

C4 Describe accounting concepts useful in classifying costs. *(p. 732)*

C5 Define product and period costs and explain how they impact financial statements. *(p. 733)*

C6 Explain how balance sheets and income statements for manufacturing and merchandising companies differ. *(p. 735)*

C7 Explain manufacturing activities and the flow of manufacturing costs. *(p. 739)*

Analytical

A1 Compute cycle time and cycle efficiency, and explain their importance to production management *(p. 742)*

Procedural

P1 Compute cost of goods sold for a manufacturer. *(p. 737)*

P2 Prepare a manufacturing statement and explain its purpose and links to financial statements. *(p. 740)*

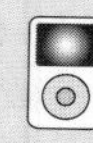

LP18

Decision Feature

No Naked Popcorn

"Find a niche and stay focused"—Brian Taylor

ELK GROVE VILLAGE, IL—As a hungry college student, Brian Taylor liked to eat popcorn. Lots of it. Bored with "naked popcorn," Brian began experimenting with seasonings such as nacho cheese, cajun, jalapeño, and apple cinnamon. After he shared his concoctions with friends, dorm mates, and others, the demand for Brian's seasonings ballooned. In less than two years, Brian had the number one shake-on popcorn seasoning in the market, **Kernel Season's (KernelSeasons.com).**

Brian launched Kernel Season's with $7,000 he earned from giving tennis lessons and selling knives. In the beginning, he gave away his popcorn seasonings to local theaters to build awareness. Just like his college friends, moviegoers loved the all-natural, low-calorie seasonings. Soon theaters across the country were asking for his seasonings, and Brian worked hard to meet demand. "I was the only employee," explains Brian. "I made sales and shipped orders. I was figuring it out as I went along."

Well, business is now popping. Fourteen varieties of Kernel Season's are available in over 14,000 movie theaters and 15,000 grocery stores. Annual sales now exceed $5 million, and Brian is on Inc.com's "30 under 30," a list of America's coolest young entrepreneurs.

Brian believes college is the best time to start a new business. "Risk is low, and banks understand young entrepreneurs are trying to get things going," explains Brian. But Brian emphasizes that understanding basic managerial principles, product and period costs, manufacturing statements, and cost flows is equally crucial. "[I was] dedicated to business classes," says Brian, including my "accounting class." Brian uses managerial accounting information from his production process to monitor and control costs and to assess new business opportunities, including Kernel Season's apparel. Brian further stresses that company success and growth require him to develop budgets, monitor product performance, and make quick decisions.

Brian believes entrepreneurs fill a void by creating a niche. However, financial success depends on monitoring and controlling operations to best meet customer needs. Brian cautions would-be entrepreneurs to "stay focused" because in the absence of applying managerial accounting principles and concepts, it's just naked popcorn.

[Sources: *Kernel Season's Website,* January 2009; *Lake County News Sun,* October 2003; *Female Entrepreneur,* July/August 2003; *Chicago Tonight* interview, August 2007; *StartupNation.com,* May 2007; *Inc.com Website,* May 2008]

Chapter Preview

Managerial accounting, like financial accounting, provides information to help users make better decisions. However, managerial accounting and financial accounting differ in important ways, which this chapter explains. This chapter also compares the accounting and reporting practices used by manufacturing and merchandising companies. A merchandising company sells products without changing their condition. A manufacturing company buys raw materials and turns them into finished products for sale to customers. A third type of company earns revenues by providing services rather than products. The skills, tools, and techniques developed for measuring a manufacturing company's activities apply to service companies as well. The chapter concludes by explaining the flow of manufacturing activities and preparing the manufacturing statement.

Managerial Accounting Concepts and Principles

Managerial Accounting Basics
- Purpose of managerial accounting
- Nature of managerial accounting
- Managerial decisions
- Managerial accounting in business
- Fraud and ethics in managerial accounting

Managerial Cost Concepts
- Types of cost classifications
- Identification of cost classifications
- Cost concepts for service companies

Reporting Manufacturing Activities
- Balance sheet
- Income statement
- Flow of activities
- Manufacturing statement

Managerial Accounting Basics

Video18.1

Managerial accounting is an activity that provides financial and nonfinancial information to an organization's managers and other internal decision makers. This section explains the purpose of managerial accounting (also called *management accounting*) and compares it with financial accounting. The main purpose of the financial accounting system is to prepare general-purpose financial statements. That information is incomplete for internal decision makers who manage organizations.

Purpose of Managerial Accounting

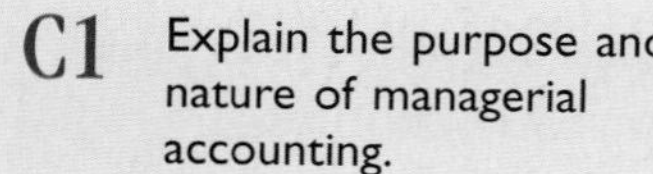

C1 Explain the purpose and nature of managerial accounting.

The purpose of both managerial accounting and financial accounting is providing useful information to decision makers. They do this by collecting, managing, and reporting information in demand by their users. Both areas of accounting also share the common practice of reporting monetary information, although managerial accounting includes the reporting of nonmonetary information. They even report some of the same information. For instance, a company's financial statements contain information useful for both its managers (insiders) and other persons interested in the company (outsiders).

The remainder of this book looks carefully at managerial accounting information, how to gather it, and how managers use it. We consider the concepts and procedures used to determine the costs of products and services as well as topics such as budgeting, break-even analysis, product costing, profit planning, and cost analysis. Information about the costs of products and services is important for many decisions that managers make. These decisions include predicting the future costs of a product or service. Predicted costs are used in product pricing, profitability analysis, and in deciding whether to make or buy a product or component. More generally, much of managerial accounting involves gathering information about costs for planning and control decisions.

Point: Nonfinancial information, also called nonmonetary information, includes customer and employee satisfaction data, the percentage of on-time deliveries, and product defect rates.

Point: Costs are important to managers because they impact both the financial position and profitability of a business. Managerial accounting assists in analysis, planning, and control of costs.

Planning is the process of setting goals and making plans to achieve them. Companies formulate long-term strategic plans that usually span a 5- to 10-year horizon and then refine them with medium-term and short-term plans. Strategic plans usually set a firm's long-term direction by developing a road map based on opportunities such as new products, new markets, and capital investments. A strategic plan's goals and objectives are broadly defined given its long-term orientation. Medium- and short-term plans are more operational in nature. They translate the strategic plan into actions. These plans are more concrete and consist of better defined objectives and goals. A short-term plan often covers a one-year period that, when translated in monetary terms, is known as a budget.

Control is the process of monitoring planning decisions and evaluating an organization's activities and employees. It includes the measurement and evaluation of actions, processes, and outcomes. Feedback provided by the control function allows managers to revise their plans. Measurement of actions and processes also allows managers to take corrective actions to avoid undesirable outcomes. For example, managers periodically compare actual results with planned results. Exhibit 18.1 portrays the important management functions of planning and control.

EXHIBIT 18.1

Planning and Control

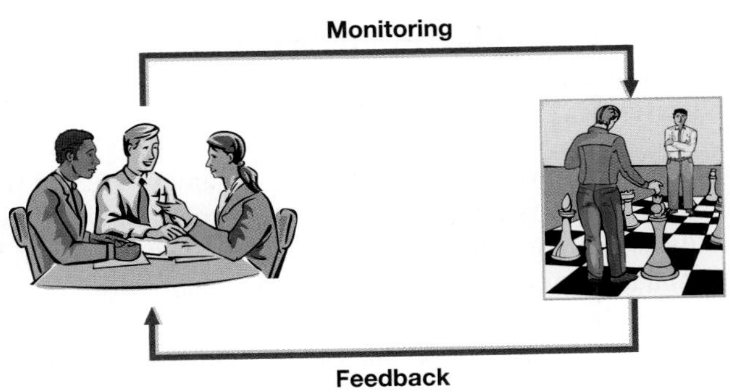

Planning
- Strategic aims
- Long- & short-term
- Annual budgets

Control
- Measurement
- Evaluation
- Oversight

Managers use information to plan and control business activities. In later chapters, we explain how managers also use this information to direct and improve business operations.

Nature of Managerial Accounting

Managerial accounting has its own special characteristics. To understand these characteristics, we compare managerial accounting to financial accounting; they differ in at least seven important ways. These differences are summarized in Exhibit 18.2. This section discusses each of these characteristics.

EXHIBIT 18.2

Key Differences between Managerial Accounting and Financial Accounting

	Financial Accounting	Managerial Accounting
1. Users and decision makers	Investors, creditors, and other users external to the organization	Managers, employees, and decision makers internal to the organization
2. Purpose of information	Assist external users in making investment, credit, and other decisions	Assist managers in making planning and control decisions
3. Flexibility of practice	Structured and often controlled by GAAP	Relatively flexible (no GAAP constraints)
4. Timeliness of information	Often available only after an audit is complete	Available quickly without the need to wait for an audit
5. Time dimension	Focus on historical information with some predictions	Many projections and estimates; historical information also presented
6. Focus of information	Emphasis on whole organization	Emphasis on an organization's projects, processes, and subdivisions
7. Nature of information	Monetary information	Mostly monetary; but also nonmonetary information

Users and Decision Makers Companies accumulate, process, and report financial accounting and managerial accounting information for different groups of decision makers. Financial accounting information is provided primarily to external users including investors, creditors, analysts, and regulators. External users rarely have a major role in managing a company's daily activities. Managerial accounting information is provided primarily to internal users who are responsible for making and implementing decisions about a company's business activities.

Point: It is desirable to accumulate information for management reports in a database separate from financial accounting records.

Purpose of Information Investors, creditors, and other external users of financial accounting information must often decide whether to invest in or lend to a company. If they have already done so, they must decide whether to continue owning the company or carrying the loan. Internal decision makers must plan a company's future. They seek to take advantage of opportunities or to overcome obstacles. They also try to control activities and ensure their effective and efficient implementation. Managerial accounting information helps these internal users make both planning and control decisions.

Flexibility of Practice External users compare companies by using financial reports and need protection against false or misleading information. Accordingly, financial accounting relies on accepted principles that are enforced through an extensive set of rules and guidelines, or GAAP. Internal users need managerial accounting information for planning and controlling their company's activities rather than for external comparisons. They require different types of information depending on the activity. This makes standardizing managerial accounting systems across companies difficult. Instead, managerial accounting systems are flexible. The design of a company's managerial accounting system depends largely on the nature of the business and the arrangement of its internal operations. Managers can decide for themselves what information they want and how they want it reported. Even within a single company, different managers often design their own systems to meet their special needs. The important question a manager must ask is whether the information being collected and reported is useful for planning, decision making, and control purposes.

Point: The *Institute of Management Accountants* issues statements that govern the practice of managerial accounting. Accountants who pass a qualifying exam are awarded the CMA.

Timeliness of Information Formal financial statements reporting past transactions and events are not immediately available to outside parties. Independent certified public accountants often must *audit* a company's financial statements before it provides them to external users. Thus, because audits often take several weeks to complete, financial reports to outsiders usually are not available until well after the period-end. However, managers can quickly obtain managerial accounting information. External auditors need not review it. Estimates and projections are acceptable. To get information quickly, managers often accept less precision in reports. As an example, an early internal report to management prepared right after the year-end could report net income for the year between $4.2 and $4.8 million. An audited income statement could later show net income for the year at $4.6 million. The internal report is not precise, but its information can be more useful because it is available earlier.

Internal auditing plays an important role in managerial accounting. Internal auditors evaluate the flow of information not only inside but also outside the company. Managers are responsible for preventing and detecting fraudulent activities in their companies.

Point: Financial statements are usually issued several weeks after the period-end. GAAP requires the reporting of important events that occur while the statements are being prepared. These events are called *subsequent events.*

Point: Independent auditors test the integrity of managerial accounting records when they are used in preparing financial statements.

Time Dimension To protect external users from false expectations, financial reports deal primarily with results of both past activities and current conditions. While some predictions such as service lives and salvage values of plant assets are necessary, financial accounting avoids predictions whenever possible. Managerial accounting regularly includes predictions of conditions and events. As an example, one important managerial accounting report is a budget, which predicts revenues, expenses, and other items. If managerial accounting reports were restricted to the past and present, managers would be less able to plan activities and less effective in managing and evaluating current activities.

Focus of Information Companies often organize into divisions and departments, but investors rarely can buy shares in one division or department. Nor do creditors lend money to a company's single division or department. Instead, they own shares in or make loans to the entire company. Financial accounting focuses primarily on a company as a whole as depicted in Exhibit 18.3.

EXHIBIT 18.3

Focus of External Reports

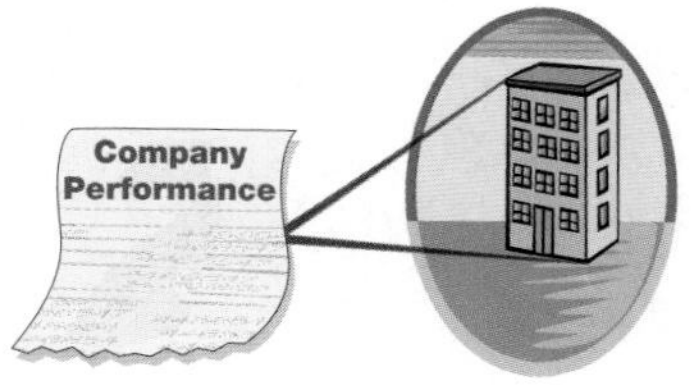

The focus of managerial accounting is different. While top-level managers are responsible for managing the whole company, most other managers are responsible for much smaller sets of activities. These middle-level and lower-level managers need managerial accounting reports dealing with specific activities, projects, and subdivisions for which they are responsible. For instance, division sales managers are directly responsible only for the results achieved in their divisions. Accordingly, division sales managers need information about results achieved in their own divisions to improve their performance. This information includes the level of success achieved by each individual, product, or department in each division as depicted in Exhibit 18.4.

EXHIBIT 18.4

Focus of Internal Reports

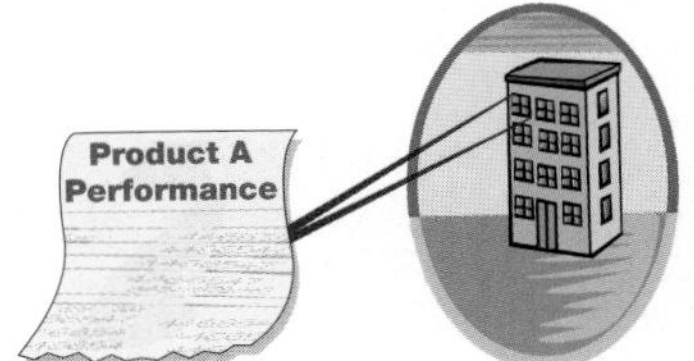

Nature of Information Both financial and managerial accounting systems report monetary information. Managerial accounting systems also report considerable nonmonetary information. Monetary information is an important part of managerial decisions, and nonmonetary information plays a crucial role, especially when monetary effects are difficult to measure. Common examples of nonmonetary information are the quality and delivery criteria of purchasing decisions.

Decision Ethics

Production Manager You invite three friends to a restaurant. When the dinner check arrives, David, a self-employed entrepreneur, picks it up saying, "Here, let me pay. I'll deduct it as a business expense on my tax return." Denise, a salesperson, takes the check from David's hand and says, "I'll put this on my company's credit card. It won't cost us anything." Derek, a factory manager for a company, laughs and says, "Neither of you understands. I'll put this on my company's credit card and call it overhead on a cost-plus contract my company has with a client." (*A cost-plus contract means the company receives its costs plus a percent of those costs.*) Adds Derek, "That way, my company pays for dinner *and* makes a profit." Who should pay the bill? Why? [Answer—p. 748]

Managerial Decision Making

The previous section emphasized differences between financial and managerial accounting, but they are not entirely separate. Similar information is useful to both external and internal users. For instance, information about costs of manufacturing products is useful to all users in making decisions. Also, both financial and managerial accounting affect peoples' actions. For example, Trek's design of a sales compensation plan affects the behavior of its salesforce. It also must estimate the dual effects of promotion and sales compensation plans on buying patterns of customers. These estimates impact the equipment purchase decisions for manufacturing and can affect the supplier selection criteria established by purchasing. Thus, financial and managerial accounting systems do more than measure; they also affect people's decisions and actions.

Managerial Accounting in Business

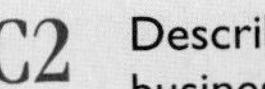

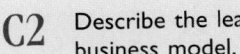

Describe the lean business model.

We have explained the importance of managerial accounting for internal decision making. Although the analytical tools and techniques of managerial accounting have always been useful, their relevance and importance continue to increase. This is so because of changes in the business environment. This section describes some of these changes and their impact on managerial accounting.

Lean Business Model Two important factors have encouraged companies to be more effective and efficient in running their operations. First, there is an increased emphasis on *customers* as the most important constituent of a business. Customers expect to derive a certain value for the money they spend to buy products and services. Specifically, they expect that their suppliers will offer them the right service (or product) at the right time and the right price. This implies that companies accept the notion of **customer orientation,** which means that employees

understand the changing needs and wants of their customers and align their management and operating practices accordingly.

Second, our *global economy* expands competitive boundaries, thereby providing customers more choices. The global economy also produces changes in business activities. One notable case that reflects these changes in customer demand and global competition is auto manufacturing. The top three Japanese auto manufacturers (**Honda**, **Nissan**, and **Toyota**) once controlled more than 40% of the U.S. auto market. Customers perceived that Japanese auto manufacturers provided value not available from other manufacturers. Many European and North American auto manufacturers responded to this challenge and regained much of the lost market share.

Companies must be alert to these and other factors. Many companies have responded by adopting the **lean business model,** whose goal is to *eliminate waste* while "satisfying the customer" and "providing a positive return" to the company.

Lean Practices **Continuous improvement** rejects the notions of "good enough" or "acceptable" and challenges employees and managers to continuously experiment with new and improved business practices. This has led companies to adopt practices such as total quality management (TQM) and just-in-time (JIT) manufacturing. The philosophy underlying both practices is continuous improvement; the difference is in the focus.

Point: Goals of a TQM process include reduced waste, better inventory control, fewer defects, and continuous improvement. Just-in-time concepts have similar goals.

Total quality management focuses on quality improvement and applies this standard to all aspects of business activities. In doing so, managers and employees seek to uncover waste in business activities including accounting activities such as payroll and disbursements. To encourage an emphasis on quality, the U.S. Congress established the Malcolm Baldrige National Quality Award (MBQNA). Entrants must conduct a thorough analysis and evaluation of their business using guidelines from the Baldrige committee. **Ritz Carlton Hotel** is a recipient of the Baldrige award in the service category. The company applies a core set of values, collectively called *The Gold Standards,* to improve customer service.

Point: The time between buying raw materials and selling finished goods is called *throughput time*.

Just-in-time manufacturing is a system that acquires inventory and produces only when needed. An important aspect of JIT is that companies manufacture products only after they receive an order (a *demand-pull* system) and then deliver the customer's requirements on time. This means that processes must be aligned to eliminate any delays and inefficiencies including inferior inputs and outputs. Companies must also establish good relations and communications with their suppliers. On the downside, JIT is more susceptible to disruption than traditional systems. As one example, several **General Motors** plants were temporarily shut down due to a strike at an assembly division; the plants supplied components *just in time* to the assembly division.

Decision Insight

Global Lean **Toyota Motor Corporation** pioneered lean manufacturing, and it has since spread to other manufacturers throughout the world. The goals include improvements in quality, reliability, inventory turnover, productivity, exports, and—above all—sales and income.

Video18.3

Implications for Managerial Accounting Adopting the lean business model can be challenging because to foster its implementation, all systems and procedures that a company follows must be realigned. Managerial accounting has an important role to play by providing accurate cost and performance information. Companies must understand the nature and sources of cost and must develop systems that capture costs accurately. Developing such a system is important to measuring the "value" provided to customers. The price that customers pay for acquiring goods and services is an important determinant of value. In turn, the costs a company incurs are key determinants of price. All else being equal, the better a company is at controlling its costs, the better its performance.

Decision Insight

Balanced Scorecard The *balanced scorecard* aids continuous improvement by augmenting financial measures with information on the "drivers" (indicators) of future financial performance along four dimensions: (1) *financial*—profitability and risk, (2) *customer*—value creation and product and service differentiation, (3) *internal business processes*—business activities that create customer and owner satisfaction, and (4) *learning and growth*—organizational change, innovation, and growth.

Fraud and Ethics in Managerial Accounting

C3 Describe fraud and the role of ethics in managerial accounting.

Fraud, and the role of ethics in reducing fraud, are important factors in running business operations. Fraud involves the use of one's job for personal gain through the deliberate misuse of the employer's assets. Examples include theft of the employer's cash or other assets, overstating reimbursable expenses, payroll schemes, and financial statement fraud. Fraud affects all business and it is costly: A 2006 *Report to the Nation* from the Association of Certified Fraud Examiners estimates the average U.S. business loses 5% of its annual revenues to fraud.

The most common type of fraud, where employees steal or misuse the employer's resources, results in an average loss of $150,000 per occurrence. For example, in a billing fraud, an employee sets up a bogus supplier. The employee then prepares bills from the supplier and pays these bills from the employer's checking account. The employee cashes the checks sent to the bogus supplier and uses them for his or her own personal benefit.

Although there are many types of fraud schemes, all fraud

- Is done to provide direct or indirect benefit to the employee.
- Violates the employee's duties to his employer.
- Costs the employer money.
- Is secret.

Implications for Managerial Accounting Fraud increases a business's costs. Left undetected, these inflated costs can result in poor pricing decisions, an improper product mix, and faulty performance evaluations. Management can develop accounting systems to closely track costs and identify deviations from expected amounts. In addition, managers rely on an **internal control system** to monitor and control business activities. An internal control system is the policies and procedures managers use to

- Urge adherence to company policies.
- Promote efficient operations.
- Ensure reliable accounting.
- Protect assets.

Combating fraud and other dilemmas requires ethics in accounting. **Ethics** are beliefs that distinguish right from wrong. They are accepted standards of good and bad behavior. Identifying the ethical path can be difficult. The preferred path is a course of action that avoids casting doubt on one's decisions.

Point: The IMA also issues the Certified Management Accountant (CMA) and the Certified Financial Manager (CFM) certifications. Employees with the CMA or CFM certifications typically earn higher salaries than those without.

The **Institute of Management Accountants** (IMA), the professional association for management accountants, has issued a code of ethics to help accountants involved in solving ethical dilemmas. The IMA's Statement of Ethical Professional Practice requires that management accountants be competent, maintain confidentiality, act with integrity, and communicate information in a fair and credible manner.

Point: The **Sarbanes-Oxley Act** requires each issuer of securities to disclose whether it has adopted a code of ethics for its senior officers and the content of that code.

The IMA provides a "road map" for resolving ethical conflicts. It suggests that an employee follow the company's policies on how to resolve such conflicts. If the conflict remains unresolved, an employee should contact the next level of management (such as the immediate supervisor) who is not involved in the ethical conflict.

Quick Check Answers—p. 749

1. Managerial accounting produces information (*a*) to meet internal users' needs, (*b*) to meet a user's specific needs, (*c*) often focusing on the future, or (*d*) all of these.
2. What is the difference between the intended users of financial and managerial accounting?
3. Do generally accepted accounting principles (GAAP) control and dictate managerial accounting?
4. What is the basic objective for a company practicing total quality management?

Managerial Cost Concepts

C4 Describe accounting concepts useful in classifying costs.

An organization incurs many different types of costs that are classified differently, depending on management needs (different costs for different purposes). We can classify costs on the basis of their (1) behavior, (2) traceability, (3) controllability, (4) relevance, and (5) function. This section explains each concept for assigning costs to products and services.

Types of Cost Classifications

Video18.2

Classification by Behavior At a basic level, a cost can be classified as fixed or variable. A **fixed cost** does not change with changes in the volume of activity (within a range of activity known as an activity's *relevant range*). For example, straight-line depreciation on equipment is a fixed cost. A **variable cost** changes in proportion to changes in the volume of activity. Sales commissions computed as a percent of sales revenue are variable costs. Additional examples of fixed and variable costs for a bike manufacturer are provided in Exhibit 18.5. When cost items are combined, total cost can be fixed, variable, or mixed. *Mixed* refers to a combination of fixed and variable costs. Equipment rental often includes a fixed cost for some minimum amount and a variable cost based on amount of usage. Classification of costs by behavior is helpful in cost-volume-profit analyses and short-term decision making. We discuss these in Chapters 22 and 25.

EXHIBIT 18.5

Fixed and Variable Costs

Fixed Cost: Rent for Rocky Mountain Bikes' building is $22,000, and it doesn't change with the number of bikes produced.

Variable Cost: Cost of bicycle tires is variable with the number of bikes produced—this cost is $15 per pair.

Classification by Traceability A cost is often traced to a **cost object,** which is a product, process, department, or customer to which costs are assigned. **Direct costs** are those traceable to a single cost object. For example, if a product is a cost object, its material and labor costs are usually directly traceable. **Indirect costs** are those that cannot be easily and cost–beneficially traced to a single cost object. An example of an indirect cost is a maintenance plan that benefits two or more departments. Exhibit 18.6 identifies examples of both direct and indirect costs for the maintenance department in a manufacturing plant. Thus, salaries of Rocky Mountain Bikes' maintenance department employees are considered indirect if the cost object is bicycles and direct if the cost object is the maintenance department. Classification of costs by traceability is useful for cost allocation. This is discussed in Chapter 21.

Decision Maker

Entrepreneur You wish to trace as many of your assembly department's direct costs as possible. You can trace 90% of them in an economical manner. To trace the other 10%, you need sophisticated and costly accounting software. Do you purchase this software? [Answer—p. 748]

EXHIBIT 18.6

Direct and Indirect Costs of a Maintenance Department

Direct Costs

- Salaries of maintenance department employees
- Equipment purchased by maintenance department
- Materials purchased by maintenance department
- Maintenance department equipment depreciation

Indirect Costs

- Factory accounting
- Factory administration
- Factory rent
- Factory managers' salary
- Factory light and heat
- Factory internal audit
- Factory intranet
- Insurance on factory

Classification by Controllability A cost can be defined as **controllable** or **not controllable.** Whether a cost is controllable or not depends on the employee's responsibilities, as shown in Exhibit 18.7. This is referred to as *hierarchical levels* in management, or *pecking order.* For example, investments in machinery are controllable by upper-level managers but not lower-level managers. Many daily operating expenses such as overtime often are controllable by lower-level managers. Classification of costs by controllability is especially useful for assigning responsibility to and evaluating managers.

EXHIBIT 18.7

Controllability of Costs

Senior Manager
Controls costs of investments in land, buildings, and equipment.

Supervisor
Controls daily expenses such as supplies, maintenance, and overtime.

Classification by Relevance A cost can be classified by relevance by identifying it as either a sunk cost or an out-of-pocket cost. A **sunk cost** has already been incurred and cannot be avoided or changed. It is irrelevant to future decisions. One example is the cost of a company's office equipment previously purchased. An **out-of-pocket cost** requires a future outlay of cash and is relevant for decision making. Future purchases of equipment involve out-of-pocket costs. A discussion of relevant costs must also consider opportunity costs. An **opportunity cost** is the potential benefit lost by choosing a specific action from two or more alternatives. One example is a student giving up wages from a job to attend evening classes. Consideration of opportunity cost is important when, for example, an insurance company must decide whether to outsource its payroll function or maintain it internally. This is discussed in Chapter 25.

Point: Opportunity costs are not recorded by the accounting system.

C5 Define product and period costs and explain how they impact financial statements.

Classification by Function Another cost classification (for manufacturers) is capitalization as inventory or to expense as incurred. Costs capitalized as inventory are called **product costs,** which refer to expenditures necessary and integral to finished products. They include direct materials, direct labor, and indirect manufacturing costs called *overhead costs*. Product costs pertain to activities carried out to manufacture the product. Costs expensed are called **period costs,** which refer to expenditures identified more with a time period than with finished products. They include selling and general administrative expenses. Period costs pertain to activities that are not part of the manufacturing process. A distinction between product and period costs is important because period costs are expensed in the income statement and product costs are assigned to inventory on the balance sheet until that inventory is sold. An ability to understand and identify product costs and period costs is crucial to using and interpreting a *manufacturing statement* described later in this chapter.

Exhibit 18.8 shows the different effects of product and period costs. Period costs flow directly to the current income statement as expenses. They are not reported as assets. Product costs are first assigned to inventory. Their final treatment depends on when inventory is sold or disposed of. Product costs assigned to finished goods that are sold in year 2009 are reported on the 2009 income statement as part of cost of goods sold. Product costs assigned to unsold inventory are carried forward on the balance sheet at the end of year 2009. If this inventory is sold in year 2010, product costs assigned to it are reported as part of cost of goods sold in that year's income statement.

Point: Only costs of production and purchases are classed as product costs.

EXHIBIT 18.8

Period and Product Costs in Financial Statements

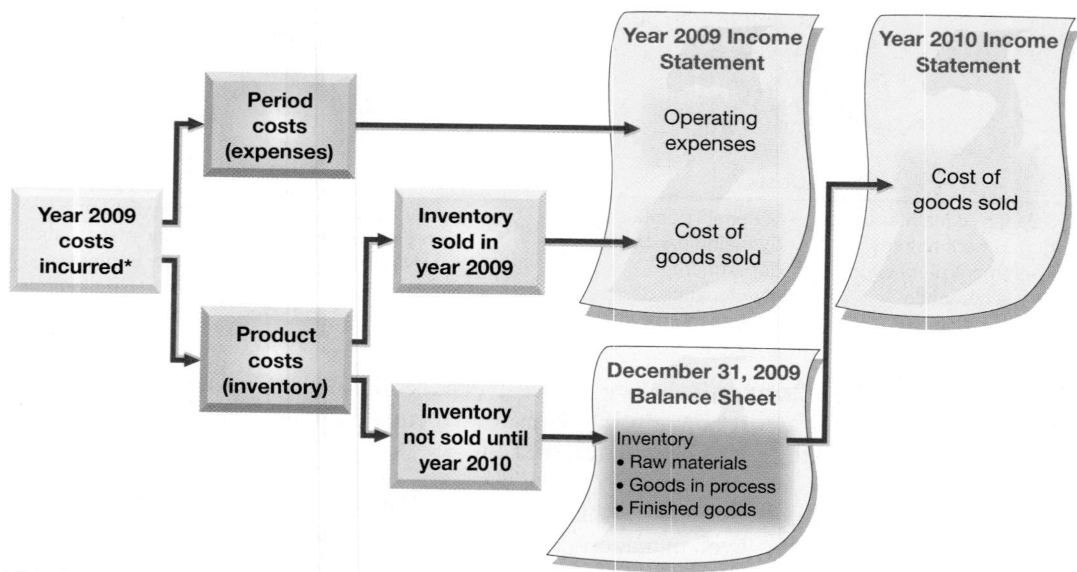

* This diagram excludes costs to acquire assets other than inventory.

Point: Product costs are either in the income statement as part of cost of goods sold or in the balance sheet as inventory. Period costs appear only on the income statement under operating expenses. See Exhibit 18.8.

Point: For a team approach to identifying period and product costs, see *Teamwork in Action* in the *Beyond the Numbers* section.

The difference between period and product costs explains why the year 2009 income statement does not report operating expenses related to either factory workers' wages or depreciation on factory buildings and equipment. Instead, both costs are combined with the cost of raw materials to compute the product cost of finished goods. A portion of these manufacturing costs (related to the goods sold) is reported in the year 2009 income statement as part of Cost of Goods Sold. The other portion is reported on the balance sheet at the end of that year as part of Inventory. The portion assigned to inventory could be included in any or all of raw materials, goods in process, or finished goods inventories.

Decision Maker

Purchase Manager You are evaluating two potential suppliers of seats for the manufacturing of motorcycles. One supplier (A) quotes a $145 price per seat and ensures 100% quality standards and on-time delivery. The second supplier (B) quotes a $115 price per seat but does not give any written assurances on quality or delivery. You decide to contract with the second supplier (B), saving $30 per seat. Does this decision have opportunity costs? [Answer—p. 749]

Identification of Cost Classifications

It is important to understand that a cost can be classified using any one (or combination) of the five different means described here. To do this we must understand costs and operations. Specifically, for the five classifications, we must be able to identify the *activity* for behavior, *cost object* for traceability, *management hierarchical level* for controllability, *opportunity cost* for relevance, and *benefit period* for function. Factory rent, for instance, can be classified as a product cost; it is fixed with respect to number of units produced, it is indirect with respect to the product, and it is not controllable by a production supervisor. Potential multiple classifications are shown in Exhibit 18.9 using different cost items incurred in manufacturing mountain bikes. The finished bike is the cost object. Proper allocation of these costs and the managerial decisions based on cost data depend on a correct cost classification.

Cost Concepts for Service Companies

Point: All expenses of service companies are period costs because these companies do not have inventory.

The cost concepts described are generally applicable to service organizations. For example, consider **Southwest Airlines**. Its cost of beverages for passengers is a variable cost based on number of passengers. The cost of leasing an aircraft is fixed with respect to number of passengers. We can also trace a flight crew's salary to a specific flight whereas we likely

EXHIBIT 18.9

Examples of Multiple Cost Classifications

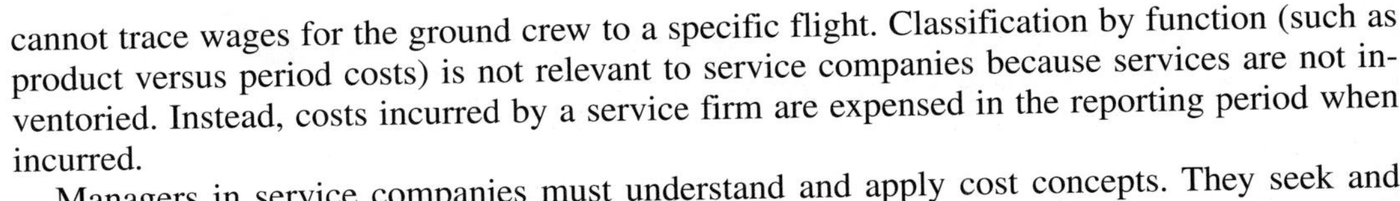

Cost Item	By Behavior	By Traceability	By Function
Bicycle tires	Variable	Direct	Product
Wages of assembly worker*	Variable	Direct	Product
Advertising	Fixed	Indirect	Period
Production manager's salary	Fixed	Indirect	Product
Office depreciation	Fixed	Indirect	Period

* Although an assembly worker's wages are classified as variable costs, their actual behavior depends on how workers are paid and whether their wages are based on a union contract (such as piece rate or monthly wages).

cannot trace wages for the ground crew to a specific flight. Classification by function (such as product versus period costs) is not relevant to service companies because services are not inventoried. Instead, costs incurred by a service firm are expensed in the reporting period when incurred.

Managers in service companies must understand and apply cost concepts. They seek and rely on accurate cost estimates for many decisions. For example, an airline manager must often decide between canceling or rerouting flights. The manager must also be able to estimate costs saved by canceling a flight versus rerouting. Knowledge of fixed costs is equally important. We explain more about the cost requirements for these and other managerial decisions in Chapter 25.

Service Costs
- Beverages and snacks
- Cleaning fees
- Pilot and copilot salaries
- Attendant salaries
- Fuel and oil costs
- Travel agent fees
- Ground crew salaries

Quick Check Answers—p. 749

5. Which type of cost behavior increases total costs when volume of activity increases?
6. How could traceability of costs improve managerial decisions?

Reporting Manufacturing Activities

Companies with manufacturing activities differ from both merchandising and service companies. The main difference between merchandising and manufacturing companies is that merchandisers buy goods ready for sale while manufacturers produce goods from materials and labor. Payless is an example of a merchandising company. It buys and sells shoes without physically changing them. Adidas is primarily a manufacturer of shoes, apparel, and accessories. It purchases materials such as leather, cloth, dye, plastic, rubber, glue, and laces and then uses employees' labor to convert these materials to products. Southwest Airlines is a service company that transports people and items.

Manufacturing activities differ from both selling merchandise and providing services. Also, the financial statements for manufacturing companies differ slightly. This section considers some of these differences and compares them to accounting for a merchandising company.

Manufacturer's Balance Sheet

C6 Explain how balance sheets and income statements for manufacturing and merchandising companies differ.

Manufacturers carry several unique assets and usually have three inventories instead of the single inventory that merchandisers carry. Exhibit 18.10 shows three different inventories in the current asset section of the balance sheet for Rocky Mountain Bikes, a manufacturer. The three inventories are raw materials, goods in process, and finished goods.

Raw Materials Inventory **Raw materials inventory** refers to the goods a company acquires to use in making products. It uses raw materials in two ways: directly and indirectly. Most raw materials physically become part of a product and are identified with specific units or batches of a product. Raw materials used directly in a product are called *direct materials*. Other materials used to support production processes are sometimes not as clearly identified with specific units or batches of product. These materials are called **indirect materials** because they are not clearly identified with specific product units or batches. Items used as indirect materials often appear on a

Point: Reducing the size of inventories saves storage costs and frees money for other uses.

EXHIBIT 18.10

Balance Sheet for a Manufacturer

ROCKY MOUNTAIN BIKES
Balance Sheet
December 31, 2009

Assets		**Liabilities and Equity**	
Current assets		Current liabilities	
Cash	$ 11,000	Accounts payable	$ 14,000
Accounts receivable, net	30,150	Wages payable	540
Raw materials inventory	**9,000**	Interest payable	2,000
Goods in process inventory	**7,500**	Income taxes payable	32,600
Finished goods inventory	**10,300**	Total current liabilities	49,140
Factory supplies	350	Long-term liabilities	
Prepaid insurance	300	Long-term notes payable	50,000
Total current assets	68,600	Total liabilities	99,140
Plant assets			
Small tools, net	1,100	Stockholders' equity	
Delivery equipment, net	5,000	Common stock, $1.2 par	24,000
Office equipment, net	1,300	Paid-in capital	76,000
Factory machinery, net	65,500	Retained earnings	49,760
Factory building, net	86,700	Total stockholders' equity	149,760
Land	9,500	Total liabilities and equity	$248,900
Total plant assets, net	169,100		
Intangible assets (patents), net	11,200		
Total assets	$248,900		

balance sheet as factory supplies or are included in raw materials. Some direct materials are classified as indirect materials when their costs are low (insignificant). Examples include screws and nuts used in assembling mountain bikes and staples and glue used in manufacturing shoes. Using the *materiality principle,* individually tracing the costs of each of these materials and classifying them separately as direct materials does not make much economic sense. For instance, keeping detailed records of the amount of glue used to manufacture one shoe is not cost beneficial.

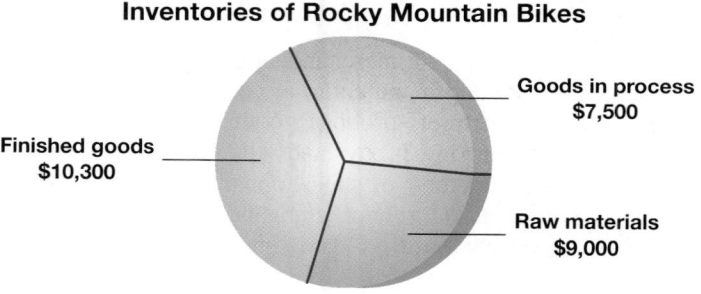

Inventories of Rocky Mountain Bikes

Goods in process	$7,500
Finished goods	$10,300
Raw materials	$9,000

Goods in Process Inventory Another inventory held by manufacturers is **goods in process inventory,** also called *work in process inventory.* It consists of products in the process of being manufactured but not yet complete. The amount of goods in process inventory depends on the type of production process. If the time required to produce a unit of product is short, the goods in process inventory is likely small; but if weeks or months are needed to produce a unit, the goods in process inventory is usually larger.

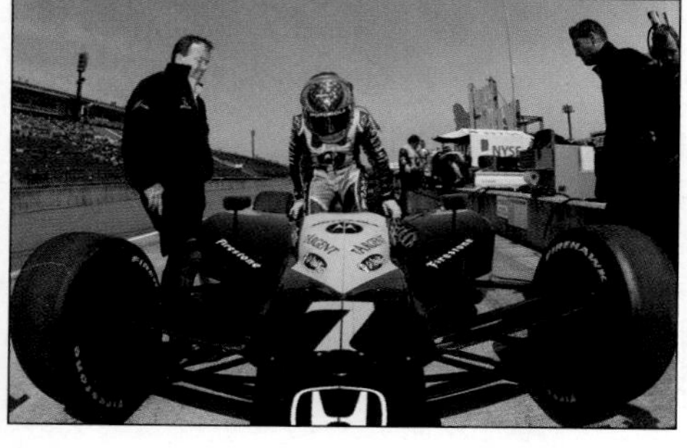

Finished Goods Inventory A third inventory owned by a manufacturer is **finished goods inventory,** which consists of completed products ready for sale. This inventory is similar to merchandise inventory owned by a merchandising company. Manufacturers also often own unique plant assets such as small tools, factory buildings, factory equipment, and patents to manufacture products. The balance sheet in Exhibit 18.10 shows that Rocky Mountain Bikes owns all of these assets. Some manufacturers invest millions or even billions of dollars in production facilities and patents. Briggs & Stratton's recent balance sheet shows about $1 billion net investment in land, buildings, machinery and equipment, much of which involves production facilities. It manufactures more racing engines than any other company in the world.

Manufacturer's Income Statement

P1 Compute cost of goods sold for a manufacturer.

The main difference between the income statement of a manufacturer and that of a merchandiser involves the items making up cost of goods sold. Exhibit 18.11 compares the components of cost of goods sold for a manufacturer and a merchandiser. A merchandiser adds cost of goods purchased to beginning merchandise inventory and then subtracts ending merchandise inventory to get cost of goods sold. A manufacturer adds cost of goods manufactured to beginning finished goods inventory and then subtracts ending finished goods inventory to get cost of goods sold.

EXHIBIT 18.11

Cost of Goods Sold Computation

Merchandiser	Manufacturer
Beginning merchandise inventory	Beginning finished goods inventory
+	+
Cost of goods purchased	Cost of goods manufactured
−	−
Ending merchandise inventory	Ending finished goods inventory
= Cost of goods sold	= Cost of goods sold

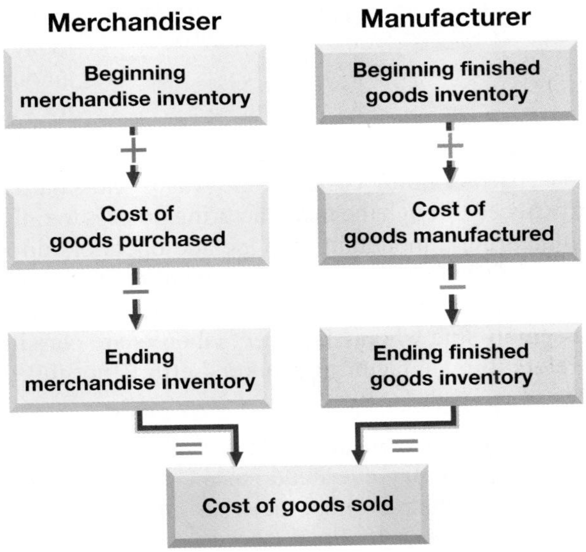

A merchandiser often uses the term *merchandise* inventory; a manufacturer often uses the term *finished goods* inventory. A manufacturer's inventories of raw materials and goods in process are not included in finished goods because they are not available for sale. A manufacturer also shows cost of goods *manufactured* instead of cost of goods *purchased.* This difference occurs because a manufacturer produces its goods instead of purchasing them ready for sale. We show later in this chapter how to derive cost of goods manufactured from the manufacturing statement.

The Cost of Goods Sold sections for both a merchandiser (Tele-Mart) and a manufacturer (Rocky Mountain Bikes) are shown in Exhibit 18.12 to highlight these differences. The remaining income statement sections are similar.

EXHIBIT 18.12

Cost of Goods Sold for a Merchandiser and Manufacturer

Merchandising (Tele-Mart) Company		Manufacturing (Rocky Mtn. Bikes) Company	
Cost of goods sold		Cost of goods sold	
Beginning *merchandise* inventory	$ 14,200	**Beginning *finished goods* inventory**	$ 11,200
Cost of merchandise *purchased*	234,150	**Cost of goods *manufactured****	170,500
Goods available for sale	248,350	Goods available for sale	181,700
Less ending *merchandise* inventory	12,100	**Less ending *finished goods* inventory**	10,300
Cost of goods sold	$236,250	Cost of goods sold	$171,400

* Cost of goods manufactured is reported in the income statement of Exhibit 18.14.

Although the cost of goods sold computations are similar, the numbers in these computations reflect different activities. A merchandiser's cost of goods purchased is the cost of buying products to be sold. A manufacturer's cost of goods manufactured is the sum of direct materials, direct labor, and factory overhead costs incurred in producing products. The remainder of this section further explains these three manufacturing costs and describes prime and conversion costs.

Direct Materials **Direct materials** are tangible components of a finished product. **Direct material costs** are the expenditures for direct materials that are separately and readily traced through the manufacturing process to finished goods. Examples of direct materials in manufacturing a mountain bike include its tires, seat, frame, pedals, brakes, cables, gears, and handlebars. The chart in the margin shows that direct materials generally make up about 45% of manufacturing costs in today's products, but this amount varies across industries and companies.

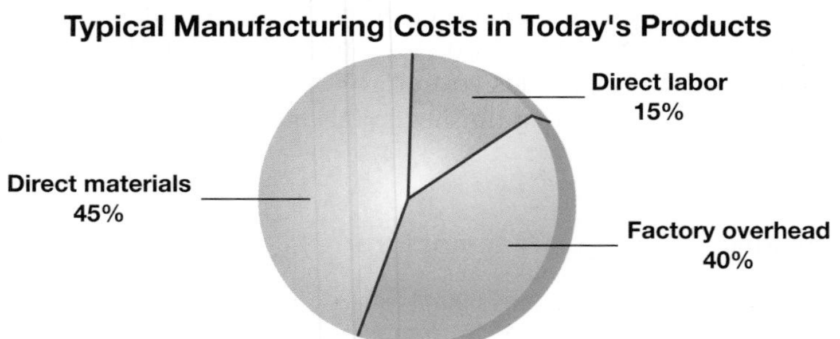

Direct Labor **Direct labor** refers to the efforts of employees who physically convert materials to finished product. **Direct labor costs** are the wages and salaries for direct labor that are separately and readily traced through the manufacturing process to finished goods. Examples of direct labor in manufacturing a mountain bike include operators directly involved in converting raw materials into finished products (welding, painting, forming) and assembly workers who attach materials such as tires, seats, pedals, and brakes to the bike frames. Costs of other workers on the assembly line who assist direct laborers are classified as **indirect labor costs. Indirect labor** refers to manufacturing workers' efforts not linked to specific units or batches of the product.

Point: Indirect labor costs are part of factory overhead.

Factory Overhead **Factory overhead** consists of all manufacturing costs that are not direct materials or direct labor. **Factory overhead costs** cannot be separately or readily traced to finished goods. These costs include indirect materials and indirect labor, costs not directly traceable to the product. Overtime paid to direct laborers is also included in overhead because overtime is due to delays, interruptions, or constraints not necessarily identifiable to a specific product or batches of product. Factory overhead costs also include maintenance of the mountain bike factory, supervision of its employees, repairing manufacturing equipment, factory utilities (water, gas, electricity), production manager's salary, factory rent, depreciation on factory buildings and equipment, factory insurance, property taxes on factory buildings and equipment, and factory accounting and legal services. Factory overhead does *not* include selling and administrative expenses because they are not incurred in manufacturing products. These expenses are called *period costs* and are recorded as expenses on the income statement when incurred.

Point: Factory overhead is also called *manufacturing overhead.*

EXHIBIT 18.13

Prime and Conversion Costs and Their Makeup

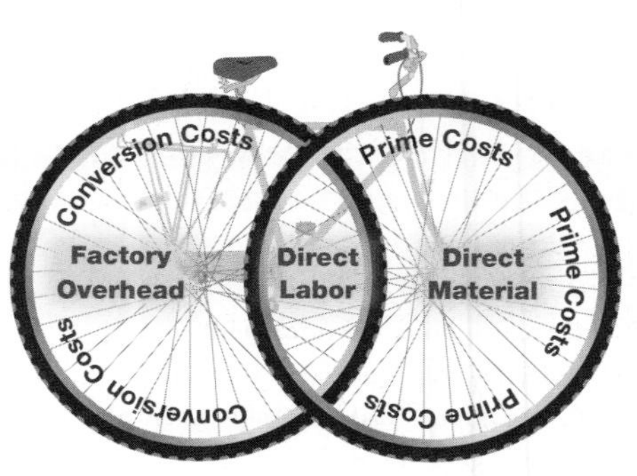

Prime and Conversion Costs Direct material costs and direct labor costs are also called **prime costs**—expenditures directly associated with the manufacture of finished goods. Direct labor costs and overhead costs are called **conversion costs**—expenditures incurred in the process of converting raw materials to finished goods. Direct labor costs are considered both prime costs and conversion costs. Exhibit 18.13 conveys the relation between prime and conversion costs and their components of direct material, direct labor, and factory overhead.

Point: Prime costs = Direct materials + Direct labor. Conversion costs = Direct labor + Factory overhead.

Reporting Performance Exhibit 18.14 shows the income statement for Rocky Mountain Bikes. Its operating expenses include sales salaries, office salaries, and depreciation of delivery and office equipment. Operating expenses do not include manufacturing costs such as factory workers' wages and depreciation of production equipment and the factory buildings. These manufacturing costs are reported as part of cost of goods manufactured and included in cost of goods sold. We explained why and how this is done in the section "Classification by Function."

Point: Manufacturers treat costs such as depreciation and rent as product costs if they are related to manufacturing.

EXHIBIT 18.14

Income Statement for a Manufacturer

ROCKY MOUNTAIN BIKES Income Statement For Year Ended December 31, 2009		
Sales		$310,000
Cost of goods sold		
Finished goods inventory, Dec. 31, 2008	$ 11,200	
Cost of goods manufactured	**170,500**	
Goods available for sale	181,700	
Less finished goods inventory, Dec. 31, 2009	10,300	
Cost of goods sold		171,400
Gross profit		138,600
Operating expenses		
Selling expenses		
Sales salaries expense	18,000	
Advertising expense	5,500	
Delivery wages expense	12,000	
Shipping supplies expense	250	
Insurance expense—Delivery equipment	300	
Depreciation expense—Delivery equipment	2,100	
Total selling expenses		38,150
General and administrative expenses		
Office salaries expense	15,700	
Miscellaneous expense	200	
Bad debts expense	1,550	
Office supplies expense	100	
Depreciation expense—Office equipment	200	
Interest expense	4,000	
Total general and administrative expenses		21,750
Total operating expenses		59,900
Income before income taxes		78,700
Income taxes expense		32,600
Net income		$ 46,100
Net income per common share (20,000 shares)		$ 2.31

Quick Check

Answers—p. 749

7. What are the three types of inventory on a manufacturing company's balance sheet?
8. How does cost of goods sold differ for merchandising versus manufacturing companies?

Flow of Manufacturing Activities

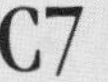
C7 Explain manufacturing activities and the flow of manufacturing costs.

To understand manufacturing and its reports, we must first understand the flow of manufacturing activities and costs. Exhibit 18.15 shows the flow of manufacturing activities for a manufacturer. This exhibit has three important sections: *materials activity, production activity,* and *sales activity.* We explain each activity in this section.

Materials Activity The far left side of Exhibit 18.15 shows the flow of raw materials. Manufacturers usually start a period with some beginning raw materials inventory carried over from the previous period. The company then acquires additional raw materials in the current period. Adding these purchases to beginning inventory gives total raw materials available for use in production. These raw materials are then either used in production in the current period or remain in inventory at the end of the period for use in future periods.

Point: Knowledge of managerial accounting provides us a means of measuring manufacturing costs and is a sound foundation for studying advanced business topics.

Production Activity The middle section of Exhibit 18.15 describes production activity. Four factors come together in production: beginning goods in process inventory, direct materials,

EXHIBIT 18.15

Activities and Cost Flows in Manufacturing

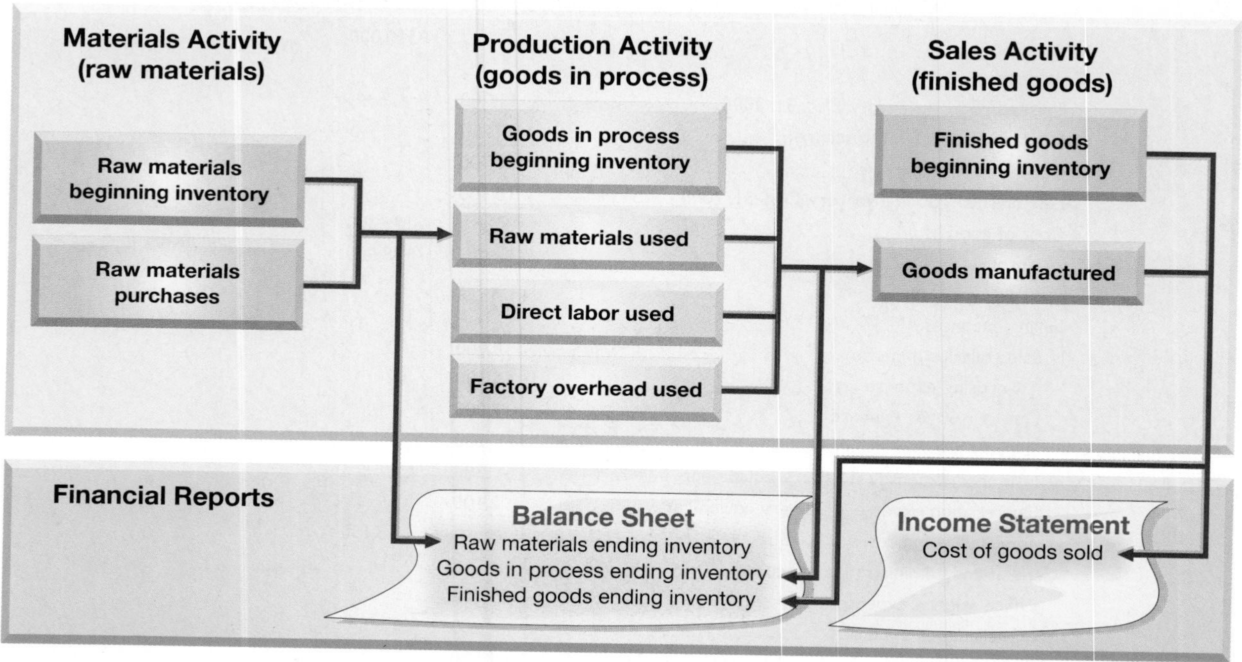

direct labor, and overhead. Beginning goods in process inventory consists of partly assembled products from the previous period. Production activity results in products that are either finished or remain unfinished. The cost of finished products makes up the cost of goods manufactured for the current period. Unfinished products are identified as ending goods in process inventory. The cost of unfinished products consists of direct materials, direct labor, and factory overhead, and is reported on the current period's balance sheet. The costs of both finished goods manufactured and goods in process are *product costs.*

Point: The series of activities that add value to a company's products or services is called a **value chain.**

Sales Activity The company's sales activity is portrayed in the far right side of Exhibit 18.15. Newly completed units are combined with beginning finished goods inventory to make up total finished goods available for sale in the current period. The cost of finished products sold is reported on the income statement as cost of goods sold. The cost of products not sold is reported on the current period's balance sheet as ending finished goods inventory.

Manufacturing Statement

P2 Prepare a manufacturing statement and explain its purpose and links to financial statements.

A company's manufacturing activities are described in a **manufacturing statement,** also called the *schedule of manufacturing activities* or the *schedule of cost of goods manufactured.* The manufacturing statement summarizes the types and amounts of costs incurred in a company's manufacturing process. Exhibit 18.16 shows the manufacturing statement for Rocky Mountain Bikes. The statement is divided into four parts: *direct materials, direct labor, overhead,* and *computation of cost of goods manufactured.* We describe each of these parts in this section.

① The manufacturing statement begins by computing direct materials used. We start by adding beginning raw materials inventory of $8,000 to the current period's purchases of $86,500. This yields $94,500 of total raw materials available for use. A physical count of inventory shows $9,000 of ending raw materials inventory. This implies a total cost of raw materials used during the period of $85,500 ($94,500 total raw materials available for use − $9,000 ending inventory). (*Note:* All raw materials are direct materials for Rocky Mountain Bikes.)

EXHIBIT 18.16

Manufacturing Statement

	ROCKY MOUNTAIN BIKES Manufacturing Statement For Year Ended December 31, 2009		
①	**Direct materials**		
	Raw materials inventory, Dec. 31, 2008	$ 8,000	
	Raw materials purchases	86,500	
	Raw materials available for use	94,500	
	Less raw materials inventory, Dec. 31, 2009	9,000	
	Direct materials used		$ 85,500
②	**Direct labor**		60,000
③	**Factory overhead**		
	Indirect labor	9,000	
	Factory supervision	6,000	
	Factory utilities	2,600	
	Repairs—Factory equipment	2,500	
	Property taxes—Factory building	1,900	
	Factory supplies used	600	
	Factory insurance expired	1,100	
	Depreciation expense—Small tools	200	
	Depreciation expense—Factory equipment	3,500	
	Depreciation expense—Factory building	1,800	
	Amortization expense—Patents	800	
	Total factory overhead		30,000
④	Total manufacturing costs		175,500
	Add goods in process inventory, Dec. 31, 2008		2,500
	Total cost of goods in process		178,000
	Less goods in process inventory, Dec. 31, 2009		7,500
	Cost of goods manufactured		$170,500

② The second part of the manufacturing statement reports direct labor costs. Rocky Mountain Bikes had total direct labor costs of $60,000 for the period. This amount includes payroll taxes and fringe benefits.

③ The third part of the manufacturing statement reports overhead costs. The statement lists each important factory overhead item and its cost. Total factory overhead cost for the period is $30,000. Some companies report only *total* factory overhead on the manufacturing statement and attach a separate schedule listing individual overhead costs.

④ The final section of the manufacturing statement computes and reports the *cost of goods manufactured.* (Total manufacturing costs for the period are $175,500 [$85,500 + $60,000 + $30,000], the sum of direct materials used and direct labor and overhead costs incurred.) This amount is first added to beginning goods in process inventory. This gives the total goods in process inventory of $178,000 ($175,500 + $2,500). We then compute the current period's cost of goods manufactured of $170,500 by taking the $178,000 total goods in process and subtracting the $7,500 cost of ending goods in process inventory that consists of direct materials, direct labor, and factory overhead. The cost of goods manufactured amount is also called *net cost of goods manufactured* or *cost of goods completed.* Exhibit 18.14 shows that this item and amount are listed in the Cost of Goods Sold section of Rocky Mountain Bikes' income statement and the balance sheet.

Point: Direct material and direct labor costs increase with increases in production volume and are called *variable costs.* Overhead can be both variable and fixed. When overhead costs vary with production, they are called *variable overhead.* When overhead costs don't vary with production, they are called *fixed overhead.*

Point: Manufacturers sometimes report variable and fixed overhead separately in the manufacturing statement to provide more information to managers about cost behavior.

A managerial accounting system records costs and reports them in various reports that eventually determine financial statements. Exhibit 18.17 shows how overhead costs flow through the system: from an initial listing of specific costs, to a section of the manufacturing statement, to the reporting on the income statement and the balance sheet.

"My boss wants us to appeal to a younger and hipper crowd. So, I'd like to get a tattoo that says-- 'Accounting rules!'"

EXHIBIT 18.17

Overhead Cost Flows across Accounting Reports

Rocky Mountain Bikes
Factory Overhead Costs
For Year Ended December 31, 2009

Indirect labor	$ 9,000
Supervision	6,000
Other overhead items*	15,000
Total overhead	**$30,000**

*Overhead items are listed in Exhibit 18.16.

Rocky Mountain Bikes
Manufacturing Statement
For Year Ended December 31, 2009

Direct materials	$ 85,500
Direct labor	60,000
Factory overhead	**30,000**
Total manuf. costs	175,500
Beg. goods in process	2,500
Total goods in process	178,000
End. goods in process	(7,500)
Cost of goods manuf.	**$170,500**

Rocky Mountain Bikes
Income Statement
For Year Ended December 31, 2009

Sales		$310,000
Cost of goods sold		
Beg. finished goods	11,200	
Cost of goods manuf.	**170,500**	
End. finished goods	(10,300)	
Cost of goods sold		171,400
Gross profit		138,600
Expenses		59,900
Income taxes		32,600
Net income		$ 46,100

Rocky Mountain Bikes
Balance Sheet–PARTIAL
December 31, 2009

Cash	$11,000
Accounts receivable, net	30,150
Raw materials inventory	**9,000**
Goods in process inventory	**7,500**
Finished goods inventory	**10,300**
Factory supplies	350
Prepaid insurance	300
Total current assets	$68,600

Management uses information in the manufacturing statement to plan and control the company's manufacturing activities. To provide timely information for decision making, the statement is often prepared monthly, weekly, or even daily. In anticipation of release of its much-hyped iPhone, **Apple** grew its inventory of Flash-based memory chips, a critical component, and its finished goods inventory. The manufacturing statement contains information useful to external users but is not a general-purpose financial statement. Companies rarely publish the manufacturing statement because managers view this information as proprietary and potentially harmful to them if released to competitors.

Quick Check

Answers—p. 749

9. A manufacturing statement (*a*) computes cost of goods manufactured for the period, (*b*) computes cost of goods sold for the period, or (*c*) reports operating expenses incurred for the period.

10. Are companies required to report a manufacturing statement?

11. How are both beginning and ending goods in process inventories reported on a manufacturing statement?

Decision Analysis

Cycle Time and Cycle Efficiency

A1 Compute cycle time and cycle efficiency, and explain their importance to production management.

As lean manufacturing practices help companies move toward just-in-time manufacturing, it is important for these companies to reduce the time to manufacture their products and to improve manufacturing efficiency. One metric that measures that time element is **cycle time (CT).** A definition of cycle time is in Exhibit 18.18.

EXHIBIT 18.18
Cycle Time

$$\textbf{Cycle time} = \textbf{Process time} + \textbf{Inspection time} + \textbf{Move time} + \textbf{Wait time}$$

Process time is the time spent producing the product. *Inspection time* is the time spent inspecting (1) raw materials when received, (2) goods in process while in production, and (3) finished goods prior to shipment. *Move time* is the time spent moving (1) raw materials from storage to production and (2) goods in process from factory location to another factory location. *Wait time* is the time that an order or job sits with no production applied to it; this can be due to order delays, bottlenecks in production, and poor scheduling.

Process time is considered **value-added time** because it is the only activity in cycle time that adds value to the product from the customer's perspective. The other three time activities are considered **non-value-added time** because they add no value to the customer.

Companies strive to reduce non-value-added time to improve **cycle efficiency (CE).** Cycle efficiency is the ratio of value-added time to total cycle time—see Exhibit 18.19.

EXHIBIT 18.19
Cycle Efficiency

$$\textbf{Cycle efficiency} = \frac{\textbf{Value-added time}}{\textbf{Cycle time}}$$

To illustrate, assume that Rocky Mountain Bikes receives and produces an order for 500 Tracker® mountain bikes. Assume that the following times were measured during production of this order.

Process time... 1.8 days

Inspection time... 0.5 days

Move time... 0.7 days

Wait time... 3.0 days

In this case, cycle time is 6.0 days, computed as 1.8 days + 0.5 days + 0.7 days + 3.0 days. Also, cycle efficiency is 0.3, or 30%, computed as 1.8 days divided by 6.0 days. This means that Rocky Mountain Bikes spends 30% of its time working on the product (value-added time). The other 70% is spent on non-value-added activities.

If a company has a CE of 1, it means that its time is spent entirely on value-added activities. If the CE is low, the company should evaluate its production process to see if it can identify ways to reduce non-value-added activities. The 30% CE for Rocky Mountain Bikes is low and its management should look for ways to reduce non-value-added activities.

Demonstration Problem 1: Cost Behavior and Classification

DP18

Understanding the classification and assignment of costs is important. Consider a company that manufactures computer chips. It incurs the following costs in manufacturing chips and in operating the company.

1. Plastic board used to mount the chip, $3.50 each.
2. Assembly worker pay of $15 per hour to attach chips to plastic board.
3. Salary for factory maintenance workers who maintain factory equipment.
4. Factory supervisor pay of $55,000 per year to supervise employees.
5. Real estate taxes paid on the factory, $14,500.
6. Real estate taxes paid on the company office, $6,000.
7. Depreciation costs on machinery used by workers, $30,000.
8. Salary paid to the chief financial officer, $95,000.
9. Advertising costs of $7,800 paid to promote products.
10. Salespersons' commissions of $0.50 for each assembled chip sold.
11. Management has the option to rent the manufacturing plant to six local hospitals to store medical records instead of producing and assembling chips.

Classify each cost in the following table according to the categories listed in the table header. A cost can be classified under more than one category. For example, the plastic board used to mount chips is classified as a direct material product cost and as a direct unit cost.

	Period Costs	Product Costs			Unit Cost Classification		Sunk Cost	Opportunity Cost
Cost	Selling and Administrative	Direct Material (Prime Cost)	Direct Labor (Prime and Conversion)	Factory Overhead (Conversion Cost)	Direct	Indirect		
1. Plastic board used to mount the chip, $3.50 each		✔			✔			

Solution to Demonstration Problem 1

	Period Costs	Product Costs			Unit Cost Classification		Sunk Cost	Opportunity Cost
Cost*	Selling and Administrative	Direct Material (Prime Cost)	Direct Labor (Prime and Conversion)	Factory Overhead (Conversion Cost)	Direct	Indirect		
1.		✔			✔			
2.			✔		✔			
3.				✔		✔		
4.				✔		✔		
5.				✔		✔		
6.	✔							
7.				✔		✔	✔	
8.	✔							
9.	✔							
10.	✔							
11.								✔

* Costs 1 through 11 refer to the 11 cost items described at the beginning of the problem.

Demonstration Problem 2: Reporting for Manufacturers

A manufacturing company's balance sheet and income statement differ from those for a merchandising or service company.

Required

1. Fill in the [BLANK] descriptors on the partial balance sheets for both the manufacturing company and the merchandising company. Explain why a different presentation is required.

Manufacturing Company

ADIDAS GROUP Partial Balance Sheet December 31, 2009	
Current assets	
Cash	$10,000
[BLANK]	8,000
[BLANK]	5,000
[BLANK]	7,000
Supplies	500
Prepaid insurance	500
Total current assets	$31,000

Merchandising Company

PAYLESS SHOE OUTLET Partial Balance Sheet December 31, 2009	
Current assets	
Cash	$ 5,000
[BLANK]	12,000
Supplies	500
Prepaid insurance	500
Total current assets	$18,000

2. Fill in the [BLANK] descriptors on the income statements for the manufacturing company and the merchandising company. Explain why a different presentation is required.

Manufacturing Company

ADIDAS GROUP Partial Income Statement For Year Ended December 31, 2009	
Sales	$200,000
Cost of goods sold	
Finished goods inventory, Dec. 31, 2008	10,000
[BLANK]	120,000
Goods available for sale	130,000
Finished goods inventory, Dec. 31, 2009	(7,000)
Cost of goods sold	123,000
Gross profit	$ 77,000

Merchandising Company

PAYLESS SHOE OUTLET Partial Income Statement For Year Ended December 31, 2009	
Sales	$190,000
Cost of goods sold	
Merchandise inventory, Dec. 31, 2008	8,000
[BLANK]	108,000
Goods available for sale	116,000
Merchandise inventory, Dec. 31, 2009	(12,000)
Cost of goods sold	104,000
Gross profit	$ 86,000

3. The manufacturer's cost of goods manufactured is the sum of (a) ______, (b) ______, and (c) ______ costs incurred in producing the product.

Solution to Demonstration Problem 2

1. Inventories for a manufacturer and for a merchandiser.

Manufacturing Company

ADIDAS GROUP Partial Balance Sheet December 31, 2009	
Current assets	
Cash	$10,000
Raw materials inventory	8,000
Goods in process inventory	5,000
Finished goods inventory	7,000
Supplies	500
Prepaid insurance	500
Total current assets	$31,000

Merchandising Company

PAYLESS SHOE OUTLET Partial Balance Sheet December 31, 2009	
Current assets	
Cash	$ 5,000
Merchandise inventory	12,000
Supplies	500
Prepaid insurance	500
Total current assets	$18,000

Explanation: A manufacturing company must control and measure three types of inventories: raw materials, goods in process, and finished goods. In the sequence of making a product, the raw materials move into production—called *goods in process inventory*—and then to finished goods. All raw materials and goods in process inventory at the end of each accounting period are considered current assets. All unsold finished inventory is considered a current asset at the end of each accounting period. The merchandising company must control and measure only one type of inventory, purchased goods.

2. Cost of goods sold for a manufacturer and for a merchandiser.

Manufacturing Company

ADIDAS GROUP Partial Income Statement For Year Ended December 31, 2009	
Sales	$200,000
Cost of goods sold	
Finished goods inventory, Dec. 31, 2008	10,000
Cost of goods manufactured	120,000
Goods available for sale	130,000
Finished goods inventory, Dec. 31, 2009	(7,000)
Cost of goods sold	123,000
Gross profit	$ 77,000

Merchandising Company

PAYLESS SHOE OUTLET Partial Income Statement For Year Ended December 31, 2009	
Sales	$190,000
Cost of goods sold	
Merchandise inventory, Dec. 31, 2008	8,000
Cost of purchases	108,000
Goods available for sale	116,000
Merchandise inventory, Dec. 31, 2009	(12,000)
Cost of goods sold	104,000
Gross profit	$ 86,000

Explanation: Manufacturing and merchandising companies use different reporting terms. In particular, the terms *finished goods* and *cost of goods manufactured* are used to reflect the production of goods, yet the concepts and techniques of reporting cost of goods sold for a manufacturing company and merchandising company are similar.

3. A manufacturer's cost of goods manufactured is the sum of (a) *direct material,* (b) *direct labor,* and (c) *factory overhead* costs incurred in producing the product.

Demonstration Problem 3: Manufacturing Statement

The following account balances and other information are from SUNN Corporation's accounting records for year-end December 31, 2009. Use this information to prepare (1) a table listing factory overhead costs, (2) a manufacturing statement (show only the total factory overhead cost), and (3) an income statement.

Advertising expense	$ 85,000	Goods in process inventory, Dec. 31, 2008	$ 8,000
Amortization expense—Factory Patents	16,000	Goods in process inventory, Dec. 31, 2009	9,000
Bad debts expense	28,000	Income taxes	53,400
Depreciation expense—Office equipment	37,000	Indirect labor	26,000
Depreciation expense—Factory building	133,000	Interest expense	25,000
Depreciation expense—Factory equipment	78,000	Miscellaneous expense	55,000
Direct labor	250,000	Property taxes on factory equipment	14,000
Factory insurance expired	62,000	Raw materials inventory, Dec. 31, 2008	60,000
Factory supervision	74,000	Raw materials inventory, Dec. 31, 2009	78,000
Factory supplies used	21,000	Raw materials purchases	313,000
Factory utilities	115,000	Repairs expense—Factory equipment	31,000
Finished goods inventory, Dec. 31, 2008	15,000	Salaries expense	150,000
Finished goods inventory, Dec. 31, 2009	12,500	Sales	1,630,000

Planning the Solution

- Analyze the account balances and select those that are part of factory overhead costs.
- Arrange these costs in a table that lists factory overhead costs for the year.
- Analyze the remaining costs and select those related to production activity for the year; selected costs should include the materials and goods in process inventories and direct labor.

- Prepare a manufacturing statement for the year showing the calculation of the cost of materials used in production, the cost of direct labor, and the total factory overhead cost. When presenting overhead cost on this statement, report only total overhead cost from the table of overhead costs for the year. Show the costs of beginning and ending goods in process inventory to determine cost of goods manufactured.
- Organize the remaining revenue and expense items into the income statement for the year. Combine cost of goods manufactured from the manufacturing statement with the finished goods inventory amounts to compute cost of goods sold for the year.

Solution to Demonstration Problem 3

SUNN CORPORATION
Factory Overhead Costs
For Year Ended December 31, 2009

Amortization expense—Factory patents	$ 16,000
Depreciation expense—Factory building	133,000
Depreciation expense—Factory equipment	78,000
Factory insurance expired	62,000
Factory supervision	74,000
Factory supplies used	21,000
Factory utilities	115,000
Indirect labor	26,000
Property taxes on factory equipment	14,000
Repairs expense—Factory equipment	31,000
Total factory overhead	$570,000

SUNN CORPORATION
Manufacturing Statement
For Year Ended December 31, 2009

Direct materials	
Raw materials inventory, Dec. 31, 2008	$ 60,000
Raw materials purchase	313,000
Raw materials available for use	373,000
Less raw materials inventory, Dec. 31, 2009	78,000
Direct materials used	295,000
Direct labor	250,000
Factory overhead	570,000
Total manufacturing costs	1,115,000
Goods in process inventory, Dec. 31, 2008	8,000
Total cost of goods in process	1,123,000
Less goods in process inventory, Dec. 31, 2009	9,000
Cost of goods manufactured	$1,114,000

SUNN CORPORATION
Income Statement
For Year Ended December 31, 2009

Sales		$1,630,000
Cost of goods sold		
Finished goods inventory, Dec. 31, 2008	$ 15,000	
Cost of goods manufactured	1,114,000	
Goods available for sale	1,129,000	
Less finished goods inventory, Dec. 31, 2009	12,500	
Cost of goods sold		1,116,500
Gross profit		513,500
Operating expenses		
Advertising expense	85,000	
Bad debts expense	28,000	
Depreciation expense—Office equipment	37,000	
Interest expense	25,000	
Miscellaneous expense	55,000	
Salaries expense	150,000	
Total operating expenses		380,000
Income before income taxes		133,500
Income taxes		53,400
Net income		$ 80,100

Summary

C1 Explain the purpose and nature of managerial accounting. The purpose of managerial accounting is to provide useful information to management and other internal decision makers. It does this by collecting, managing, and reporting both monetary and nonmonetary information in a manner useful to internal users. Major characteristics of managerial accounting include (1) focus on internal decision makers, (2) emphasis on planning and control, (3) flexibility, (4) timeliness, (5) reliance on forecasts and estimates, (6) focus on segments and projects, and (7) reporting both monetary and nonmonetary information.

C2 Describe the lean business model. The main purpose of the lean business model is the elimination of waste. Concepts such as total quality management and just-in-time production often aid in effective application of the model.

C3 Describe fraud and the role of ethics in managerial accounting. Fraud involves the use of one's job for personal gain through deliberate misuse of the employer's assets. All fraud is secret, violates the employee's job duties, provides financial benefits to the employee, and costs the employer money. A code of ethical beliefs can be used to resolve ethical conflicts.

C4 Describe accounting concepts useful in classifying costs. We can classify costs on the basis of their (1) behavior—fixed vs. variable, (2) traceability—direct vs. indirect, (3) controllability—controllable vs. uncontrollable, (4) relevance—sunk vs. out of pocket, and (5) function—product vs. period. A cost can be classified in more than one way, depending on the purpose for which the cost is being determined. These classifications help us understand cost patterns, analyze performance, and plan operations.

C5 Define product and period costs and explain how they impact financial statements. Costs that are capitalized because they are expected to have future value are called *product costs;* costs that are expensed are called *period costs.* This classification is important because it affects the amount of costs expensed in the income statement and the amount of costs assigned to inventory on the balance sheet. Product costs are commonly made up of direct materials, direct labor, and overhead. Period costs include selling and administrative expenses.

C6 Explain how balance sheets and income statements for manufacturing and merchandising companies differ. The main difference is that manufacturers usually carry three inventories on their balance sheets—raw materials, goods in process, and finished goods—instead of one inventory that merchandisers carry. The main difference between income statements of manufacturers and merchandisers is the items making up cost of goods sold. A merchandiser adds beginning merchandise inventory to cost of goods purchased and then subtracts ending merchandise inventory to get cost of goods sold. A manufacturer adds beginning finished goods inventory to cost of goods manufactured and then subtracts ending finished goods inventory to get cost of goods sold.

C7 Explain manufacturing activities and the flow of manufacturing costs. Manufacturing activities consist of materials, production, and sales activities. The materials activity consists of the purchase and issuance of materials to production. The production activity consists of converting materials into finished goods. At this stage in the process, the materials, labor, and overhead costs have been incurred and the manufacturing statement is prepared. The sales activity consists of selling some or all of finished goods available for sale. At this stage, the cost of goods sold is determined.

A1 Compute cycle time and cycle efficiency, and explain their importance to production management. It is important for companies to reduce the time to produce their products and to improve manufacturing efficiency. One measure of that time is cycle time (CT), defined as Process time + Inspection time + Move time + Wait time. Process time is value-added time; the others are non-value-added time. Cycle efficiency (CE) is the ratio of value-added time to total cycle time. If CE is low, management should evaluate its production process to see if it can reduce non-value-added activities.

P1 Compute cost of goods sold for a manufacturer. A manufacturer adds beginning finished goods inventory to cost of goods manufactured and then subtracts ending finished goods inventory to get cost of goods sold.

P2 Prepare a manufacturing statement and explain its purpose and links to financial statements. The manufacturing statement reports computation of cost of goods manufactured for the period. It begins by showing the period's costs for direct materials, direct labor, and overhead and then adjusts these numbers for the beginning and ending inventories of the goods in process to yield cost of goods manufactured.

Guidance Answers to **Decision Maker** and **Decision Ethics**

Production Manager It appears that all three friends want to pay the bill with someone else's money. David is using money belonging to the tax authorities, Denise is taking money from her company, and Derek is defrauding the client. To prevent such practices, companies have internal audit mechanisms. Many companies also adopt ethical codes of conduct to help guide employees. We must recognize that some entertainment expenses are justifiable and even encouraged. For example, the tax law allows certain deductions for entertainment that have a business purpose. Corporate policies also sometimes allow and encourage reimbursable spending for social activities, and contracts can include entertainment as allowable costs. Nevertheless, without further details, payment for this bill should be made from personal accounts.

Entrepreneur Tracing all costs directly to cost objects is always desirable, but you need to be able to do so in an economically feasible manner. In this case, you are able to trace 90% of the assembly department's direct costs. It may not be economical to spend more money on a new software to trace the final 10% of costs. You need to make a cost–benefit trade-off. If the software offers benefits beyond tracing the remaining 10% of the assembly department's costs, your decision should consider this.

Purchase Manager Opportunity costs relate to the potential quality and delivery benefits given up by not choosing supplier (A). Selecting supplier (B) might involve future costs of poor-quality seats (inspection, repairs, and returns). Also, potential delivery delays could interrupt work and increase manufacturing costs. Your company could also incur sales losses if the product quality of supplier (B) is low. As purchase manager, you are responsible for these costs and must consider them in making your decision.

Guidance Answers to **Quick Checks**

1. *d*
2. Financial accounting information is intended for users external to an organization such as investors, creditors, and government authorities. Managerial accounting focuses on providing information to managers, officers, and other decision makers within the organization.
3. No, GAAP do not control the practice of managerial accounting. Unlike external users, the internal users need managerial accounting information for planning and controlling business activities rather than for external comparison. Different types of information are required, depending on the activity. Therefore it is difficult to standardize managerial accounting.
4. Under TQM, all managers and employees should strive toward higher standards in their work and in the products and services they offer to customers.
5. Variable costs increase when volume of activity increases.
6. By being able to trace costs to cost objects (say, to products and departments), managers better understand the total costs associated with a cost object. This is useful when managers consider making changes to the cost object (such as when dropping the product or expanding the department).
7. Raw materials inventory, goods in process inventory, and finished goods inventory.
8. The cost of goods sold for merchandising companies includes all costs of acquiring the merchandise; the cost of goods sold for manufacturing companies includes the three costs of manufacturing: direct materials, direct labor, and overhead.
9. *a*
10. No; companies rarely report a manufacturing statement.
11. Beginning goods in process inventory is added to total manufacturing costs to yield total goods in process. Ending goods in process inventory is subtracted from total goods in process to yield cost of goods manufactured for the period.

Key Terms

mhhe.com/wildFAP19e

Key Terms are available at the book's Website for learning and testing in an online Flashcard Format.

Continuous improvement (p. 730)
Control (p. 727)
Controllable or not controllable cost (p. 733)
Conversion costs (p. 738)
Cost object (p. 732)
Customer orientation (p. 729)
Cycle efficiency (CE) (p. 743)
Cycle time (CT) (p. 742)
Direct costs (p. 732)
Direct labor (p. 738)
Direct labor costs (p. 738)
Direct material (p. 738)
Direct material costs (p. 738)
Ethics (p. 731)
Factory overhead (p. 738)
Factory overhead costs (p. 738)
Finished goods inventory (p. 736)
Fixed cost (p. 732)
Goods in process inventory (p. 736)
Indirect costs (p. 732)
Indirect labor (p. 738)
Indirect labor costs (p. 738)
Indirect material (p. 735)
Institute of Management Accountants (IMA) (p. 731)
Internal control system (p. 731)
Just-in-time (JIT) manufacturing (p. 730)
Lean business model (p. 730)
Managerial accounting (p. 726)
Manufacturing statement (p. 740)
Non-value-added time (p. 743)
Opportunity cost (p. 733)
Out-of-pocket cost (p. 733)
Period costs (p. 733)
Planning (p. 726)
Prime costs (p. 738)
Product costs (p. 733)
Raw materials inventory (p. 735)
Sunk cost (p. 733)
Total quality management (TQM) (p. 730)
Value-added time (p. 743)
Value chain (p. 740)
Variable cost (p. 732)

Multiple Choice Quiz

Answers on p. 767 mhhe.com/wildFAP19e

Additional Quiz Questions are available at the book's Website.

Quiz18

1. Continuous improvement
   a. Is used to reduce inventory levels.
   b. Is applicable only in service businesses.
   c. Rejects the notion of "good enough."
   d. Is used to reduce ordering costs.
   e. Is applicable only in manufacturing businesses.

2. A direct cost is one that is
   a. Variable with respect to the cost object.
   b. Traceable to the cost object.
   c. Fixed with respect to the cost object.
   d. Allocated to the cost object.
   e. A period cost.
3. Costs that are incurred as part of the manufacturing process, but are not clearly traceable to the specific unit of product or batches of product, are called
   a. Period costs.
   b. Factory overhead.
   c. Sunk costs.
   d. Opportunity costs.
   e. Fixed costs.
4. The three major cost components of manufacturing a product are
   a. Direct materials, direct labor, and factory overhead.
   b. Period costs, product costs, and sunk costs.
   c. Indirect labor, indirect materials, and fixed expenses.
   d. Variable costs, fixed costs, and period costs.
   e. Opportunity costs, sunk costs, and direct costs.
5. A company reports the following for the current year.

Finished goods inventory, beginning year	$6,000
Finished goods inventory, ending year	3,200
Cost of goods sold	7,500

   Its cost of goods manufactured for the current year is
   a. $1,500.
   b. $1,700.
   c. $7,500.
   d. $2,800.
   e. $4,700.

Discussion Questions

1. Describe the managerial accountant's role in business planning, control, and decision making.
2. Distinguish between managerial and financial accounting on
   a. Users and decision makers.
   b. Purpose of information.
   c. Flexibility of practice.
   d. Time dimension.
   e. Focus of information.
   f. Nature of information.
3. Identify the usual changes that a company must make when it adopts a customer orientation.
4. Distinguish between direct material and indirect material.
5. Distinguish between direct labor and indirect labor.
6. Distinguish between (*a*) factory overhead and (*b*) selling and administrative overhead.
7. What product cost is listed as both a prime cost and a conversion cost?
8. Assume that you tour Apple's factory where it makes its products. List three direct costs and three indirect costs that you are likely to see.

9. Should we evaluate a manager's performance on the basis of controllable or noncontrollable costs? Why?
10. Explain why knowledge of cost behavior is useful in product performance evaluation.
11. Explain why product costs are capitalized but period costs are expensed in the current accounting period.
12. Explain how business activities and inventories for a manufacturing company, a merchandising company, and a service company differ.
13. Why does managerial accounting often involve working with numerous predictions and estimates?
14. How do an income statement and a balance sheet for a manufacturing company and a merchandising company differ?
15. Besides inventories, what other assets often appear on manufacturers' balance sheets but not on merchandisers' balance sheets?
16. Why does a manufacturing company require three different inventory categories?
17. Manufacturing activities of a company are described in the _______. This statement summarizes the types and amounts of costs incurred in its manufacturing _______.
18. What are the three categories of manufacturing costs?
19. List several examples of factory overhead.
20. List the four components of a manufacturing statement and provide specific examples of each for Apple.

21. Prepare a proper title for the annual "manufacturing statement" of Apple. Does the date match the balance sheet or income statement? Why?
22. Describe the relations among the income statement, the manufacturing statement, and a detailed listing of factory overhead costs.
23. Define and describe *cycle time* and identify the components of cycle time.
24. Explain the difference between value-added time and non-value-added time.
25. Define and describe *cycle efficiency*.
26. Can management of a company such as Best Buy use cycle time and cycle efficiency as useful measures of performance? Explain.

27. Access Anheuser-Busch's 2006 annual report (10-K) for the fiscal year ended December 31, 2006, at the SEC's EDGAR database (SEC.gov) or its Website (Anheuser-Busch.com). From its financial statement notes, identify the titles and amounts of its inventory components.

Denotes Discussion Questions that involve decision making.

McGraw-Hill's HOMEWORK MANAGER® Available with McGraw-Hill's Homework Manager

QUICK STUDY

QS 18-1
Managerial accounting defined
C1

Managerial accounting (choose one)

1. Provides information that is widely available to all interested parties.
2. Is directed at reporting aggregate data on the company as a whole.
3. Must follow generally accepted accounting principles.
4. Provides information to aid management in planning and controlling business activities.

QS 18-2
Managerial accounting versus financial accounting
C1

Identify whether each description most likely applies to managerial or financial accounting.

1. _______ It is directed at external users in making investment, credit, and other decisions.
2. _______ Its information is often available only after an audit is complete.
3. _______ Its primary focus is on the organization as a whole.
4. _______ Its principles and practices are very flexible.
5. _______ Its primary users are company managers.

QS 18-3
Lean business concepts
C2

Match each lean business concept with its best description by entering its letter in the blank.

1. _______ Just-in-time manufacturing	**A.** Every manager and employee constantly looks for ways to improve company operations.
2. _______ Continuous improvements	**B.** Focuses on quality throughout the production process.
3. _______ Customer orientation	**C.** Inventory is acquired or produced only as needed.
4. _______ Total quality management	**D.** Flexible product designs can be modified to accommodate customer choices.

QS 18-4
Fixed and variable costs
C4

Which of these statements is true regarding fixed and variable costs?

1. Fixed costs increase and variable costs decrease in total as activity volume decreases.
2. Both fixed and variable costs stay the same in total as activity volume increases.
3. Both fixed and variable costs increase as activity volume increases.
4. Fixed costs stay the same and variable costs increase in total as activity volume increases.

QS 18-5
Direct and indirect costs
C4

Crosby Company produces sporting equipment, including footballs. Identify each of the following costs as direct or indirect if the cost object is a football produced by Crosby.

1. Depreciation on equipment used to produce footballs.
2. Salary of manager who supervises the entire plant.
3. Labor used on the football production line.
4. Electricity used in the production plant.
5. Materials used to produce footballs.

QS 18-6
Product and period costs
C5

Which of these statements is true regarding product and period costs?

1. Factory maintenance is a product cost and sales commission is a period cost.
2. Sales commission is a product cost and factory rent is a period cost.
3. Factory wages are a product cost and direct material is a period cost.
4. Sales commission is a product cost and depreciation on factory equipment is a product cost.

QS 18-7
Inventory reporting for manufacturers
C6

Three inventory categories are reported on a manufacturing company's balance sheet: (*a*) raw materials, (*b*) goods in process, and (*c*) finished goods. Identify the usual order in which these inventory items are reported on the balance sheet.

1. (*b*)(*c*)(*a*) **2.** (*c*)(*b*)(*a*) **3.** (*a*)(*b*)(*c*) **4.** (*b*)(*a*)(*c*)

QS 18-8
Cost of goods sold P1

A company has year-end cost of goods manufactured of $8,000, beginning finished goods inventory of $1,000, and ending finished goods inventory of $1,500. Its cost of goods sold is

1. $8,500 **2.** $8,000 **3.** $7,500 **4.** $7,800

QS 18-9
Manufacturing flows identified
C7

Identify the usual sequence of manufacturing activities by filling in the blank (with 1, 2, or 3) corresponding to its order: ______ Production activities; ______ sales activities; ______ materials activities.

QS 18-10
Cost of goods manufactured
P2

Prepare the 2009 manufacturing statement for Biron Company using the following information.

Direct materials	$381,000
Direct labor	126,300
Factory overhead costs	48,000
Goods in process, Dec. 31, 2008	315,200
Goods in process, Dec. 31, 2009	285,500

QS 18-11
Manufacturing cycle time and efficiency
A1

Compute and interpret (*a*) manufacturing cycle time and (*b*) manufacturing cycle efficiency using the following information from a manufacturing company.

Process time	7.5 hours
Inspection time	1.0 hours
Move time	3.2 hours
Wait time	18.3 hours

QS 18-12
Cost of goods sold
P1

Compute cost of goods sold for year 2009 using the following information.

Finished goods inventory, Dec. 31, 2008	$ 690,000
Goods in process inventory, Dec. 31, 2008	167,000
Goods in process inventory, Dec. 31, 2009	144,600
Cost of goods manufactured, year 2009	1,837,400
Finished goods inventory, Dec. 31, 2009	567,200

Available with McGraw-Hill's Homework Manager McGraw-Hill's HOMEWORK MANAGER®

EXERCISES

Exercise 18-1
Sources of accounting information
C1

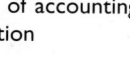

Both managerial accounting and financial accounting provide useful information to decision makers. Indicate in the following chart the most likely source of information for each business decision (a decision can require major input from both sources, in which case both can be marked).

Business Decision	Primary Information Source	
	Managerial	Financial
1. Determine amount of dividends to pay stockholders	___	___
2. Evaluate a purchasing department's performance	___	___
3. Report financial performance to board of directors	___	___
4. Estimate product cost for a new line of shoes	___	___
5. Plan the budget for next quarter	___	___
6. Measure profitability of all individual stores	___	___
7. Prepare financial reports according to GAAP	___	___
8. Determine location and size for a new plant	___	___

Exercise 18-2
Planning and control descriptions
C1

Complete the following statements by filling in the blanks.

1. _______ is the process of monitoring planning decisions and evaluating an organization's activities and employees.
2. _______ is the process of setting goals and making plans to achieve them.
3. _______ _______ usually covers a period of 5 to 10 years.
4. _______ _______ usually covers a period of one year.

Exercise 18-3
Characteristics of financial accounting and managerial accounting
C1

In the following chart, compare financial accounting and managerial accounting by describing how each differs for the items listed. Be specific in your responses.

	Financial Accounting	Managerial Accounting
1. Users and decision makers	_______	_______
2. Timeliness of information	_______	_______
3. Purpose of information	_______	_______
4. Nature of information	_______	_______
5. Flexibility of practice	_______	_______
6. Focus of information	_______	_______
7. Time dimension	_______	_______

Exercise 18-4
Customer orientation in practice
C2 

Customer orientation means that a company's managers and employees respond to customers' changing wants and needs. A manufacturer of plastic fasteners has created a customer satisfaction survey that it asks each of its customers to complete. The survey asks about the following factors: (A) lead time; (B) delivery; (C) price; (D) product performance. Each factor is to be rated as unsatisfactory, marginal, average, satisfactory, or very satisfied.

a. Match the competitive forces 1 through 4 to the factors on the survey. A factor can be matched to more than one competitive force.

Survey Factor	Competitive Force
A. Lead time	_______ **1.** Cost
B. Delivery	_______ **2.** Time
C. Price	_______ **3.** Quality
D. Product performance	_______ **4.** Flexibility of service

b. How can managers of this company use the information from this customer satisfaction survey to better meet competitive forces and satisfy their customers?

Exercise 18-5
Management concepts
C2

Following are three separate events affecting the managerial accounting systems for different companies. Match the management concept(s) that the company is likely to adopt for the event identified. There is some overlap in the meaning of customer orientation and total quality management and, therefore, some responses can include more than one concept.

Event	Management Concept
_______ 1. The company starts reporting measures on customer complaints and product returns from customers.	a. Total quality management (TQM)
_______ 2. The company starts reporting measures such as the percent of defective products and the number of units scrapped.	b. Continuous improvement (CI)
_______ 3. The company starts measuring inventory turnover and discontinues elaborate inventory records. Its new focus is to pull inventory through the system.	c. Customer orientation (CO)
	d. Just-in-time (JIT) system

Exercise 18-6
Cost analysis and identification
C4 C5

Georgia Pacific, a manufacturer, incurs the following costs. (1) Classify each cost as either a product or a period cost. If a product cost, identify it as a prime and/or conversion cost. (2) Classify each product cost as either a direct cost or an indirect cost using the product as the cost object.

Cost	Product Cost		Period Cost	Direct Cost	Indirect Cost
	Prime	Conversion			
1. Amortization of patents on factory machine	___	___	___	___	___
2. Payroll taxes for production supervisor	___	___	___	___	___
3. Accident insurance on factory workers	___	___	___	___	___
4. Depreciation—Factory building	___	___	___	___	___
5. State and federal income taxes	___	___	___	___	___
6. Wages to assembly workers	___	___	___	___	___
7. Direct materials used	___	___	___	___	___
8. Office supplies used	___	___	___	___	___
9. Bad debts expense	___	___	___	___	___
10. Small tools used	___	___	___	___	___
11. Factory utilities	___	___	___	___	___
12. Advertising	___	___	___	___	___

Exercise 18-7
Cost classifications C4

(1) Identify each of the five cost classifications discussed in the chapter. (2) List two purposes of identifying these separate cost classifications.

Exercise 18-8
Cost analysis and classification
C4

Listed here are product costs for the production of soccer balls. (1) Classify each cost (a) as either fixed or variable and (b) as either direct or indirect. (2) What pattern do you see regarding the relation between costs classified by behavior and costs classified by traceability?

Product Cost	Cost by Behavior		Cost by Traceability	
	Variable	Fixed	Direct	Indirect
1. Annual flat fee paid for office security	___	___	___	___
2. Leather covers for soccer balls	___	___	___	___
3. Lace to hold leather together	___	___	___	___
4. Wages of assembly workers	___	___	___	___
5. Coolants for machinery	___	___	___	___
6. Machinery depreciation	___	___	___	___
7. Taxes on factory	___	___	___	___

Exercise 18-9
Balance sheet identification and preparation
C6

Current assets for two different companies at calendar year-end 2009 are listed here. One is a manufacturer, Nordic Skis Mfg., and the other, Fresh Foods, is a grocery distribution company. (1) Identify which set of numbers relates to the manufacturer and which to the merchandiser. (2) Prepare the current asset section for each company from this information. Discuss why the current asset section for these two companies is different.

Account	Company 1	Company 2
Cash	$13,000	$11,000
Raw materials inventory	—	41,250
Merchandise inventory	44,250	—
Goods in process inventory	—	30,000
Finished goods inventory	—	50,000
Accounts receivable, net	62,000	81,000
Prepaid expenses	3,000	600

Exercise 18-10
Cost of goods sold computation
C6 P1

Compute cost of goods sold for each of these two companies for the year ended December 31, 2009.

		Computer Merchandising	Log Homes Manufacturing
1			
2			
3	Beginning inventory		
4	Merchandise	$301,000	
5	Finished goods		$602,000
6	Cost of purchases	580,000	
7	Cost of goods manufactured		790,000
8	Ending inventory		
9	Merchandise	201,000	
10	Finished goods		195,000

Check Computer Merchandising COGS, $680,000

Exercise 18-11
Cost of goods manufactured and cost of goods sold computation
P1 P2

Using the following data, compute (1) the cost of goods manufactured and (2) the cost of goods sold for both Jahmed Company and Kabiro Company.

	Jahmed Company	Kabiro Company
Beginning finished goods inventory	$15,000	$15,000
Beginning goods in process inventory	21,000	21,500
Beginning raw materials inventory	9,500	13,000
Rental cost on factory equipment	33,000	27,000
Direct labor	22,000	44,000
Ending finished goods inventory	19,500	12,000
Ending goods in process inventory	22,000	21,000
Ending raw materials inventory	10,500	9,400
Factory utilities	13,000	17,000
Factory supplies used	10,600	10,000
General and administrative expenses	22,000	54,000
Indirect labor	3,250	9,660
Repairs—Factory equipment	6,780	3,500
Raw materials purchases	24,000	47,000
Sales salaries	49,000	41,000

Check Jahmed COGS, $106,130

Exercise 18-12
Components of accounting reports
C7 P2

For each of the following account balances for a manufacturing company, place a ✔ in the appropriate column indicating that it appears on the balance sheet, the income statement, the manufacturing statement, and/or a detailed listing of factory overhead costs. Assume that the income statement shows the calculation of cost of goods sold and the manufacturing statement shows only the total amount of factory overhead. (An account balance can appear on more than one report.)

	Account	Balance Sheet	Income Statement	Manufacturing Statement	Overhead Report
3	Accounts receivable				
4	Computer supplies used in office				
5	Beginning finished goods inventory				
6	Beginning goods in process inventory				
7	Beginning raw materials inventory				
8	Cash				
9	Depreciation expense—Factory building				
10	Depreciation expense—Factory equipment				
11	Depreciation expense—Office building				
12	Depreciation expense—Office equipment				
13	Direct labor				
14	Ending finished goods inventory				
15	Ending goods in process inventory				
16	Ending raw materials inventory				
17	Factory maintenance wages				
18	Computer supplies used in factory				
19	Income taxes				
20	Insurance on factory building				
21	Rent cost on office building				
22	Office supplies used				
23	Property taxes on factory building				
24	Raw materials purchases				
25	Sales				

Exercise 18-13
Manufacturing statement preparation P2

Given the following selected account balances of Spalding Company, prepare its manufacturing statement for the year ended on December 31, 2009. Include a listing of the individual overhead account balances in this statement.

Sales	$1,363,000
Raw materials inventory, Dec. 31, 2008	40,000
Goods in process inventory, Dec. 31, 2008	53,600
Finished goods inventory, Dec. 31, 2008	60,400
Raw materials purchases	181,900
Direct labor	243,000
Factory computer supplies used	15,700
Indirect labor	54,000
Repairs—Factory equipment	7,250
Rent cost of factory building	56,000
Advertising expense	92,000
General and administrative expenses	140,000
Raw materials inventory, Dec. 31, 2009	44,000
Goods in process inventory, Dec. 31, 2009	41,200
Finished goods inventory, Dec. 31, 2009	66,200

Check Cost of goods manufactured, $566,250

Exercise 18-14
Income statement preparation P2

Use the information in Exercise 18-13 to prepare an income statement for Spalding Company (a manufacturer). Assume that its cost of goods manufactured is $566,250.

Exercise 18-15
Cost flows in manufacturing C7 P2

The following chart shows how costs flow through a business as a product is manufactured. Some boxes in the flowchart show cost amounts. Compute the cost amounts for the boxes that contain question marks.

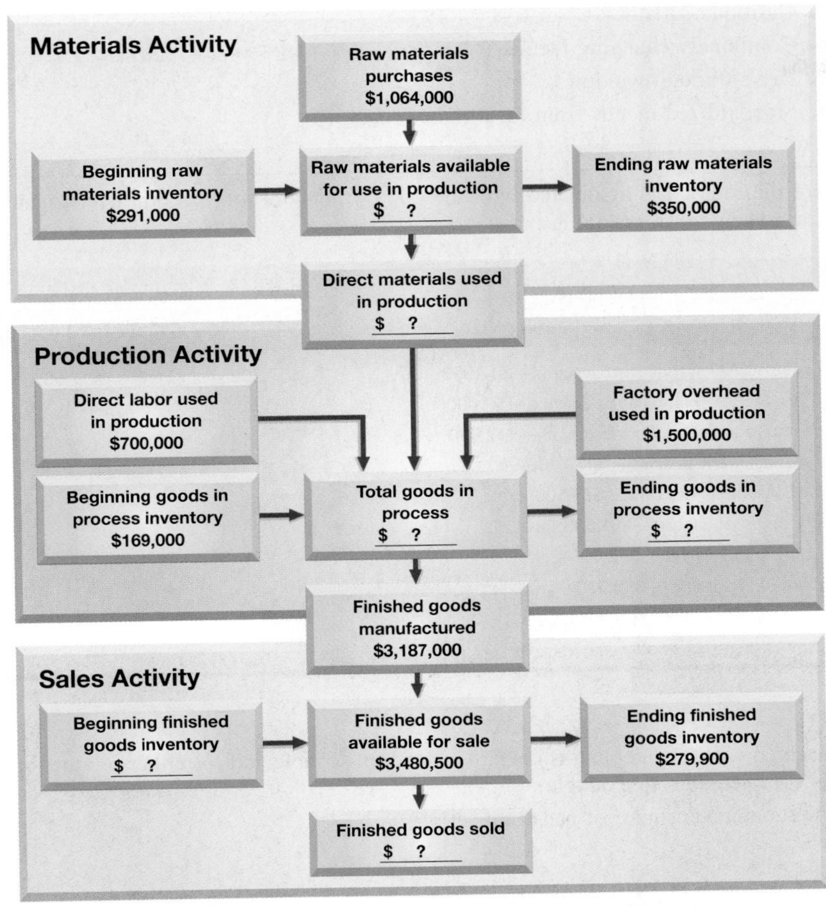

Exercise 18-16
C3

Fraud affects **Best Buy**. Refer to Best Buy's financial statements in Appendix A to answer the following:

1. Explain how inventory losses (such as theft) impact how Best Buy reports inventory on its balance sheet.

2. In what income statement account does Best Buy report inventory losses?

McGraw-Hill's HOMEWORK MANAGER® Available with McGraw-Hill's Homework Manager

PROBLEM SET A

Problem 18-1A
Managerial accounting role
C1 C2

This chapter explained the purpose of managerial accounting in the context of the current business environment. Review the *automobile* section of your local newspaper; the Sunday paper is often best. Review advertisements of sport-utility vehicles and identify the manufacturers that offer these products and the factors on which they compete.

Required

Discuss the potential contributions and responsibilities of the managerial accounting professional in helping an automobile manufacturer succeed. (*Hint:* Think about information and estimates that a managerial accountant might provide new entrants into the sport-utility market.)

Problem 18-2A
Lean business concepts
C2 

Many fast-food restaurants compete on lean business concepts. Match each of the following activities at a fast-food restaurant with the lean business concept it strives to achieve. Some activities might relate to more than one lean business concept.

_______ **1.** Courteous employees
_______ **2.** Food produced to order
_______ **3.** New product development
_______ **4.** Clean tables and floors
_______ **5.** Orders filled within three minutes
_______ **6.** Standardized food making processes

a. Just-in-time (JIT)
b. Continuous improvement (CI)
c. Total quality management (TQM)

[continued on next page]

_______ **7.** Customer satisfaction surveys
_______ **8.** Continually changing menus
_______ **9.** Drive-through windows
_______ **10.** Standardized menus from location to location

Problem 18-3A
Cost computation, classification, and analysis
C4

Listed here are the total costs associated with the 2009 production of 700 drum sets manufactured by Roland. The drum sets sell for $600 each.

Costs	Cost by Behavior		Cost by Function	
	Variable	Fixed	Product	Period
1. Drum stands (700 stands outsourced)—$17,500	$17,500		$17,500	
2. Annual flat fee for maintenance service—$7,000				
3. Rent cost of equipment for sales staff—$12,000				
4. Upper management salaries—$170,000				
5. Wages of assembly workers—$59,500				
6. Property taxes on factory—$3,500				
7. Accounting staff salaries—$42,000				
8. Machinery depreciation—$28,000				
9. Sales commissions—$20 per unit				
10. Plastic for casing—$12,600				

Required

Check (1) Total variable manufacturing cost, $89,600

1. Classify each cost and its amount as (*a*) either fixed or variable and (*b*) either product or period (the last cost is completed as an example).
2. Compute the manufacturing cost per drum set.

Analysis Component

3. Assume that 1,000 drum sets are produced in the next month. What do you predict will be the total cost of plastic for the casings and the per unit cost of the plastic for the casings? Explain.
4. Assume that 1,000 drum sets are produced in the next month. What do you predict will be the total cost of property taxes and the per unit cost of the property taxes? Explain.

Problem 18-4A
Cost classification and explanation
C4 C5

Assume that you must make a presentation to the marketing staff explaining the difference between product and period costs. Your supervisor tells you the marketing staff would also like clarification regarding prime and conversion costs and an explanation of how these terms fit with product and period cost. You are told that many on the staff are unable to classify costs in their merchandising activities.

Required

Prepare a one-page memorandum to your supervisor outlining your presentation to the marketing staff.

Problem 18-5A
Opportunity cost estimation and application
C1 C4 

Refer to *Decision Maker*, **Purchase Manager,** in this chapter. Assume that you are the motorcycle manufacturer's managerial accountant. The purchasing manager asks you about preparing an estimate of the related costs for buying motorcycle seats from supplier (B). She tells you this estimate is needed because unless dollar estimates are attached to nonfinancial factors, such as lost production time, her supervisor will not give it full attention. The manager also shows you the following information.

- Production output is 1,000 motorcycles per year based on 250 production days a year.
- Production time per day is 8 hours at a cost of $2,000 per hour to run the production line.
- Lost production time due to poor quality is 1%.
- Satisfied customers purchase, on average, three motorcycles during a lifetime.
- Satisfied customers recommend the product, on average, to five other people.
- Marketing predicts that using seat (B) will result in five lost customers per year from repeat business and referrals.
- Average contribution margin per motorcycle is $3,000.

Required

Estimate the costs (including opportunity costs) of buying motorcycle seats from supplier (B). This problem requires that you think creatively and make reasonable estimates; thus there could be more than one correct answer. (*Hint:* Reread the answer to *Decision Maker* and compare the cost savings for buying from supplier [B] to the sum of lost customer revenue from repeat business and referrals and the cost of lost production time.)

Check Estimated cost of lost production time, $40,000

Problem 18-6A
Ending inventory computation and evaluation
C2 C6

Laredo Boot Company makes specialty boots for the rodeo circuit. On December 31, 2008, the company had (*a*) 300 pairs of boots in finished goods inventory and (*b*) 1,400 heels at a cost of $16 each in raw materials inventory. During 2009, the company purchased 46,000 additional heels at $16 each and manufactured 16,800 pairs of boots.

Required

1. Determine the unit and dollar amounts of raw materials inventory in heels at December 31, 2009.

Check (1) Ending (heel) inventory, 13,800 units; $220, 800

Analysis Component

2. Write a one-half page memorandum to the production manager explaining why a just-in-time inventory system for heels should be considered. Include the amount of working capital that can be reduced at December 31, 2009, if the ending heel raw material inventory is cut by 75%.

Problem 18-7A
Inventory computation and reporting
C4 C6 P1

eXcel
mhhe.com/wildFAP19e

Shown here are annual financial data at December 31, 2009, taken from two different companies.

	Active Sports Retail	Sno-Board Manufacturing
Beginning inventory		
Merchandise	$145,000	
Finished goods		$340,000
Cost of purchases	240,000	
Cost of goods manufactured		582,000
Ending inventory		
Merchandise	110,000	
Finished goods		150,000

Required

1. Compute the cost of goods sold section of the income statement at December 31, 2009, for each company. Include the proper title and format in the solution.

2. Write a half-page memorandum to your instructor (*a*) identifying the inventory accounts and (*b*) describing where each is reported on the income statement and balance sheet for both companies.

Check (1) Sno-Board's cost of goods sold, $772,000

Problem 18-8A
Manufacturing and income statements; inventory analysis P2

The following calendar year-end information is taken from the December 31, 2009, adjusted trial balance and other records of Gucci Company.

Advertising expense	$ 26,600	Direct labor	680,400
Depreciation expense—Office equipment	11,500	Income taxes expense	291,500
Depreciation expense—Selling equipment	10,800	Indirect labor	58,800
Depreciation expense—Factory equipment	38,200	Miscellaneous production costs	9,800
Factory supervision	105,700	Office salaries expense	74,000
Factory supplies used	7,800	Raw materials purchases	965,000
Factory utilities	34,000	Rent expense—Office space	23,000
Inventories		Rent expense—Selling space	25,200
Raw materials, December 31, 2008	165,900	Rent expense—Factory building	81,600
Raw materials, December 31, 2009	187,000	Maintenance expense—Factory equipment	37,100
Goods in process, December 31, 2008	18,100	Sales	4,630,000
Goods in process, December 31, 2009	24,600	Sales discounts	63,600
Finished goods, December 31, 2008	164,100	Sales salaries expense	398,400
Finished goods, December 31, 2009	135,900		

Required

Check (1) Cost of goods manufactured, $1,990,800

1. Prepare the company's 2009 manufacturing statement.
2. Prepare the company's 2009 income statement that reports separate categories for (*a*) selling expenses and (*b*) general and administrative expenses.

Analysis Component

3. Compute the (*a*) inventory turnover, defined as cost of goods sold divided by average inventory, and (*b*) days' sales in inventory, defined as 365 times ending inventory divided by cost of goods sold, for both its raw materials inventory and its finished goods inventory. (To compute turnover and days' sales in inventory for raw materials, use raw materials used rather than cost of goods sold.) Discuss some possible reasons for differences between these ratios for the two types of inventories.

Problem 18-9A
Manufacturing cycle time and efficiency
A1 

Mission Oak Company produces oak bookcases to customer order. It received an order from a customer to produce 5,000 bookcases. The following information is available for the production of the bookcases.

Process time	18.0 days
Inspection time	2.0 days
Move time	4.4 days
Wait time	20.6 days

Required

1. Compute the company's manufacturing cycle time.
2. Compute the company's manufacturing cycle efficiency. Interpret your answer.

Check (2) Manufacturing cycle efficiency, 0.40

Analysis Component

3. Assume that Mission Oak wishes to increase its manufacturing cycle efficiency to 0.75. What are some ways that it can accomplish this?

PROBLEM SET B

Problem 18-1B
Managerial accounting role
C1 C2

This chapter described the purpose of managerial accounting in the context of the current business environment. Review the *home electronics* section of your local newspaper; the Sunday paper is often best. Review advertisements of home electronics and identify the manufacturers that offer these products and the factors on which they compete.

Required

Discuss the potential contributions and responsibilities of the managerial accounting professional in helping a home electronics manufacturer succeed. (*Hint:* Think about information and estimates that a managerial accountant might provide new entrants into the home electronics market.)

Problem 18-2B
Lean business concepts
C2

Eastman-Kodak manufactures digital cameras and must compete on lean manufacturing concepts. Match each of the following activities that it engages in with the lean manufacturing concept it strives to achieve. (Some activities might relate to more than one lean manufacturing concept.)

_______ 1. Lenses are received daily based on customer orders.
_______ 2. Customers receive a satisfaction survey with each camera purchased.
_______ 3. The manufacturing process is standardized and documented.
_______ 4. Cameras are produced in small lots, and only to customer order.
_______ 5. Manufacturing facilities are arranged to reduce move time and wait time.
_______ 6. Kodak conducts focus groups to determine new features that customers want in digital cameras.

a. Just-in-time (JIT)
b. Continuous improvement (CI)
c. Total quality management (TQM)

[continued on next page]

_______ **7.** Orders received are filled within two business days.

_______ **8.** Kodak works with suppliers to reduce inspection time of incoming materials.

_______ **9.** Kodak monitors the market to determine what features its competitors are offering on digital cameras.

_______ **10.** Kodak asks production workers for ideas to improve production.

Problem 18-3B
Cost computation, classification, and analysis
C4

Listed here are the total costs associated with the production of 10,000 Blu-ray Discs (BDs) manufactured by New Age. The BDs sell for $15 each.

Costs	Cost by Behavior		Cost by Function	
	Variable	Fixed	Product	Period
1. Annual fixed fee for cleaning service—$3,000		$3,000		$3,000
2. Cost of office equipment rent—$700				
3. Upper management salaries—$100,000				
4. Labeling (10,000 outsourced)—$2,500				
5. Wages of assembly workers—$20,000				
6. Sales commissions—$0.50 per BD				
7. Machinery depreciation—$15,000				
8. Systems staff salaries—$10,000				
9. Cost of factory rent—$4,500				
10. Plastic for BDs—$1,000				

Required

1. Classify each cost and its amount as (*a*) either fixed or variable and (*b*) either product or period.

2. Compute the manufacturing cost per BD.

Check (2) Total variable manufacturing cost, $23,500

Analysis Component

3. Assume that 12,000 BDs are produced in the next month. What do you predict will be the total cost of plastic for the BDs and the per unit cost of the plastic for the BDs? Explain.

4. Assume that 12,000 BDs are produced in the next month. What do you predict will be the total cost of factory rent and the per unit cost of the factory rent? Explain.

Problem 18-4B
Cost classification and explanation
C4 C5

Assume that you must make a presentation to a client explaining the difference between prime and conversion costs. The client makes and sells 200,000 cookies per week. The client tells you that her sales staff also would like a clarification regarding product and period costs. She tells you that most of the staff lack training in managerial accounting.

Required

Prepare a one-page memorandum to your client outlining your planned presentation to her sales staff.

Problem 18-5B
Opportunity cost estimation and application
C1 C4 

Refer to *Decision Maker,* **Purchase Manager,** in this chapter. Assume that you are the motorcycle manufacturer's managerial accountant. The purchasing manager asks you about preparing an estimate of the related costs for buying motorcycle seats from supplier (B). She tells you this estimate is needed because unless dollar estimates are attached to nonfinancial factors such as lost production time, her supervisor will not give it full attention. The manager also shows you the following information.

- Production output is 1,000 motorcycles per year based on 250 production days a year.
- Production time per day is 8 hours at a cost of $500 per hour to run the production line.
- Lost production time due to poor quality is 1%.
- Satisfied customers purchase, on average, three motorcycles during a lifetime.
- Satisfied customers recommend the product, on average, to four other people.
- Marketing predicts that using seat (B) will result in four lost customers per year from repeat business and referrals.
- Average contribution margin per motorcycle is $4,000.

Required

Check Cost of lost customer revenue, $16,000

Estimate the costs (including opportunity costs) of buying motorcycle seats from supplier (B). This problem requires that you think creatively and make reasonable estimates; thus there could be more than one correct answer. (*Hint:* Reread the answer to *Decision Maker,* and compare the cost savings for buying from supplier [B] to the sum of lost customer revenue from repeat business and referrals and the cost of lost production time.)

Problem 18-6B
Ending inventory computation and evaluation
C2 C6 

CCMD Company makes specialty skates for the ice skating circuit. On December 31, 2008, the company had (*a*) 1,500 skates in finished goods inventory and (*b*) 2,500 blades at a cost of $15 each in raw materials inventory. During 2009, CCMD purchased 45,000 additional blades at $15 each and manufactured 20,000 pairs of skates.

Required

Check (1) Ending (blade) inventory, 7,500 units; $112,500

1. Determine the unit and dollar amounts of raw materials inventory in blades at December 31, 2009.

Analysis Component

2. Write a one-half page memorandum to the production manager explaining why a just-in-time inventory system for blades should be considered. Include the amount of working capital that can be reduced at December 31, 2009, if the ending blade raw material inventory is cut in half.

Problem 18-7B
Inventory computation and reporting
C4 C6 P1

Shown here are annual financial data at December 31, 2009, taken from two different companies.

	AAA Imports (Retail)	Marina Boats (Manufacturing)
Beginning inventory		
Merchandise	$ 50,000	
Finished goods		$200,000
Cost of purchases	350,000	
Cost of goods manufactured		686,000
Ending inventory		
Merchandise	25,000	
Finished goods		300,000

Required

Check (1) AAA Imports cost of goods sold, $375,000

1. Compute the cost of goods sold section of the income statement at December 31, 2009, for each company. Include the proper title and format in the solution.

2. Write a half-page memorandum to your instructor (*a*) identifying the inventory accounts and (*b*) identifying where each is reported on the income statement and balance sheet for both companies.

Problem 18-8B
Manufacturing and income statements; analysis of inventories
P2

The following calendar year-end information is taken from the December 31, 2009, adjusted trial balance and other records of Homestyle Furniture.

Advertising expense	$ 22,250	Direct labor	564,500
Depreciation expense—Office equipment	10,440	Income taxes expense	138,700
Depreciation expense—Selling equipment	12,125	Indirect labor	61,000
Depreciation expense—Factory equipment	37,400	Miscellaneous production costs	10,440
Factory supervision	123,500	Office salaries expense	72,875
Factory supplies used	8,060	Raw materials purchases	896,375
Factory utilities	39,500	Rent expense—Office space	25,625
Inventories		Rent expense—Selling space	29,000
Raw materials, December 31, 2008	42,375	Rent expense—Factory building	95,500
Raw materials, December 31, 2009	72,430	Maintenance expense—Factory equipment	32,375
Goods in process, December 31, 2008	14,500	Sales	5,002,000
Goods in process, December 31, 2009	16,100	Sales discounts	59,375
Finished goods, December 31, 2008	179,200	Sales salaries expense	297,300
Finished goods, December 31, 2009	143,750		

Required

1. Prepare the company's 2009 manufacturing statement.

2. Prepare the company's 2009 income statement that reports separate categories for (*a*) selling expenses and (*b*) general and administrative expenses.

Check (1) Cost of goods manufactured, $1,836,995

Analysis Component

3. Compute the (*a*) inventory turnover, defined as cost of goods sold divided by average inventory, and (*b*) days' sales in inventory, defined as 365 times ending inventory divided by cost of goods sold, for both its raw materials inventory and its finished goods inventory. (To compute turnover and days' sales in inventory for raw materials, use raw materials used rather than cost of goods sold.) Discuss some possible reasons for differences between these ratios for the two types of inventories.

Problem 18-9B
Manufacturing cycle time and efficiency

A1 

Fast Ink produces ink-jet printers for personal computers. It received an order for 400 printers from a customer. The following information is available for this order.

Process time	8.0 hours
Inspection time	1.7 hours
Move time	4.5 hours
Wait time	10.8 hours

Required

1. Compute the company's manufacturing cycle time.

2. Compute the company's manufacturing cycle efficiency. Interpret your answer.

Analysis Component

3. Assume that Fast Ink wishes to increase its manufacturing cycle efficiency to 0.80. What are some ways that it can accomplish this?

SERIAL PROBLEM

Success Systems

(This serial problem begins in Chapter 1 and continues through most of the book. If previous chapter segments were not completed, the serial problem can begin at this point. It is helpful, but not necessary, to use the Working Papers that accompany the book.)

SP 18 Adriana Lopez, owner of Success Systems, decides to diversify her business by also manufacturing computer workstation furniture.

Required

1. Classify the following manufacturing costs of Success Systems by behavior and traceability.

Product Costs	Cost by Behavior		Cost by Traceability	
	Variable	Fixed	Direct	Indirect
1. Monthly flat fee to clean workshop	___	___	___	___
2. Laminate coverings for desktops	___	___	___	___
3. Taxes on assembly workshop	___	___	___	___
4. Glue to assemble workstation component parts	___	___	___	___
5. Wages of desk assembler	___	___	___	___
6. Electricity for workshop	___	___	___	___
7. Depreciation on tools	___	___	___	___

2. Prepare a manufacturing statement for Success Systems for the month ended January 31, 2010. Assume the following manufacturing costs:

Direct materials: $2,200

Factory overhead: $490

Direct labor: $900

Beginning goods in process: none (December 31, 2009)

Ending goods in process: $540 (January 31, 2010)

Beginning finished goods inventory: none (December 31, 2009)

Ending finished goods inventory: $350 (January 31, 2010)

Check (3) COGS, $2,700

3. Prepare the cost of goods sold section of a partial income statement for Success Systems for the month ended January 31, 2010.

BEYOND THE NUMBERS

REPORTING IN ACTION

C1 C2

BTN 18-1 Managerial accounting is more than recording, maintaining, and reporting financial results. Managerial accountants must provide managers with both financial and nonfinancial information including estimates, projections, and forecasts. There are many accounting estimates that management accountants must make, and **Best Buy** must notify shareholders of these estimates.

Required

1. Access and read Best Buy's "Critical Accounting Estimates" section (six pages), which is part of its *Management's Discussion and Analysis of Financial Condition and Results of Operations* section, from either its annual report or its 10-K for the year ended March 3, 2007 [BestBuy.com]. What are some of the accounting estimates that Best Buy made in preparing its financial statements? What are some of the effects if the actual results of Best Buy differ from its assumptions?

2. What is the management accountant's role in determining those estimates?

Fast Forward

3. Access **Best Buy**'s annual report for a fiscal year ending after March 3, 2007, from either its Website [BestBuy.com] or the SEC's EDGAR database [www.SEC.gov]. Answer the questions in parts (1) and (2) after reading the current MD&A section. Identify any major changes.

COMPARATIVE ANALYSIS

C1 C2

BTN 18-2 **Best Buy** and **RadioShack** are both merchandisers that rely on customer satisfaction. Access and read (1) Best Buy's "Business Strategy and Core Philosophies" section (one page) and (2) RadioShack's "Financial Impact of Turnaround Program" section (one page). Both sections are located in the respective company's *Management Discussion and Analysis of Financial Condition and Results of Operations* section from the annual report or 10-K. The Best Buy report is for the year ended March 3, 2007, and the RadioShack report is for the year ended December 31, 2006.

Required

1. Identify the strategic initiatives that each company put forward in its desire to better compete and succeed in the marketplace.

2. For each of these strategic initiatives for both companies, explain how it reflects (or does not reflect) a customer satisfaction focus.

ETHICS CHALLENGE

C3 C4 C5

BTN 18-3 Assume that you are the managerial accountant at Infostore, a manufacturer of hard drives, CDs, and diskettes. Its reporting year-end is December 31. The chief financial officer is concerned about having enough cash to pay the expected income tax bill because of poor cash flow management. On November 15, the purchasing department purchased excess inventory of CD raw materials in anticipation of rapid growth of this product beginning in January. To decrease the company's tax liability, the chief financial officer tells you to record the purchase of this inventory as part of supplies and expense it in the current year; this would decrease the company's tax liability by increasing expenses.

Required

1. In which account should the purchase of CD raw materials be recorded?

2. How should you respond to this request by the chief financial officer?

COMMUNICATING IN PRACTICE

BTN 18-4 Write a one-page memorandum to a prospective college student about salary expectations for graduates in business. Compare and contrast the expected salaries for accounting (including different subfields such as public, corporate, tax, audit, and so forth), marketing, management, and finance majors. Prepare a graph showing average starting salaries (and those for experienced professionals in those fields if available). To get this information, stop by your school's career services office; libraries also have this information. The Website JobStar.org (click on *Salary Info*) also can get you started.

TAKING IT TO THE NET

C1 C3

BTN 18-5 Managerial accounting professionals follow a code of ethics. As a member of the Institute of Management Accountants, the managerial accountant must comply with Standards of Ethical Conduct.

Required

1. Identify, print, and read the *Statement of Ethical Professional Practice* posted at www.IMAnet.org. (Search using "ethical professional practice.")

2. What four overarching ethical principles underlie the IMA's statement?

3. Describe the courses of action the IMA recommends in resolving ethical conflicts.

TEAMWORK IN ACTION

C7 P2

BTN 18-6 The following calendar-year information is taken from the December 31, 2009, adjusted trial balance and other records of Dahlia Company.

Advertising expense	$ 19,125	Direct labor	650,750
Depreciation expense—Office equipment	8,750	Indirect labor	60,000
Depreciation expense—Selling equipment	10,000	Miscellaneous production costs	8,500
Depreciation expense—Factory equipment	32,500	Office salaries expense	100,875
Factory supervision	122,500	Raw materials purchases	872,500
Factory supplies used	15,750	Rent expense—Office space	21,125
Factory utilities	36,250	Rent expense—Selling space	25,750
Inventories		Rent expense—Factory building	79,750
Raw materials, December 31, 2008	177,500	Maintenance expense—Factory equipment	27,875
Raw materials, December 31, 2009	168,125	Sales	3,275,000
Goods in process, December 31, 2008	15,875	Sales discounts	57,500
Goods in process, December 31, 2009	14,000	Sales salaries expense	286,250
Finished goods, December 31, 2008	164,375		
Finished goods, December 31, 2009	129,000		

Required

1. *Each* team member is to be responsible for computing **one** of the following amounts. You are not to duplicate your teammates' work. Get any necessary amounts from teammates. Each member is to explain the computation to the team in preparation for reporting to class.
   - **a.** Materials used.
   - **b.** Factory overhead.
   - **c.** Total manufacturing costs.
   - **d.** Total cost of goods in process.
   - **e.** Cost of goods manufactured.
2. Check your cost of goods manufactured with the instructor. If it is correct, proceed to part (3).
3. *Each* team member is to be responsible for computing **one** of the following amounts. You are not to duplicate your teammates' work. Get any necessary amounts from teammates. Each member is to explain the computation to the team in preparation for reporting to class.
   - **a.** Net sales.
   - **b.** Cost of goods sold.
   - **c.** Gross profit.
   - **d.** Total operating expenses.
   - **e.** Net income or loss before taxes.

Point: Provide teams with transparencies and markers for presentation purposes.

ENTREPRENEURIAL DECISION

C1 C4 

BTN 18-7 Brian Taylor of **Kernel Season's** must understand his manufacturing costs to effectively operate and succeed as a profitable and efficient company.

Required

1. What are the three main categories of manufacturing costs that Brian must monitor and control? Provide examples of each.
2. How can Brian make the Kernel Season's manufacturing process more cost-effective? Provide examples of two useful managerial measures of time and efficiency.
3. What are four goals of a total quality management process? How can Kernel Season's use TQM to improve its business activities?

HITTING THE ROAD

C1 C5

BTN 18-8 Visit your favorite fast-food restaurant. Observe its business operations.

Required

1. Describe all business activities from the time a customer arrives to the time that customer departs.
2. List all costs you can identify with the separate activities described in part 1.
3. Classify each cost from part 2 as fixed or variable, and explain your classification.

BTN 18-9 Access DSG's annual report for the year ended April 28, 2007 (www.DSGiplc.com). Read the section "Corporate Governance" dealing with the responsibilities of the board of directors.

GLOBAL DECISION

DSG

Required

1. Identify the responsibilities (see the "schedule of matters reserved for the board") of DSG's board of directors.
2. How would management accountants be involved in assisting the board of directors in carrying out their responsibilities? Explain.

ANSWERS TO MULTIPLE CHOICE QUIZ

1. c
2. b
3. b
4. a
5. Beginning finished goods + Cost of goods manufactured (COGM) − Ending finished goods = Cost of goods sold
   $6,000 + COGM − $3,200 = $7,500
   COGM = $4,700

A Look Back

Chapter 18 introduced managerial accounting and explained basic cost concepts. We also described the lean business model and the reporting of manufacturing activities, including the manufacturing statement.

A Look at This Chapter

We begin this chapter by describing a cost accounting system. We then explain the procedures used to determine costs using a job order costing system. We conclude with a discussion of over- and underapplied overhead.

A Look Ahead

Chapter 20 focuses on measuring costs in process production companies. We explain process production, describe how to assign costs to processes, and compute and analyze cost per equivalent unit.

Chapter 19 Job Order Cost Accounting

Learning Objectives

CAP

Conceptual

C1 Explain the cost accounting system. *(p. 770)*

C2 Describe important features of job order production. *(p. 770)*

C3 Explain job cost sheets and how they are used in job order cost accounting. *(p. 772)*

Analytical

A1 Apply job order costing in pricing services. *(p. 782)*

LP19

Procedural

P1 Describe and record the flow of materials costs in job order cost accounting. *(p. 773)*

P2 Describe and record the flow of labor costs in job order cost accounting. *(p. 775)*

P3 Describe and record the flow of overhead costs in job order cost accounting. *(p. 776)*

P4 Determine adjustments for overapplied and underapplied factory overhead. *(p. 781)*

Decision Feature

Working the Field

"Being successful is having a vision which you are excited to follow without the fear of failure"
—Hank Julicher

PHILADELPHIA, PA—One size fits all? Not when it comes to synthetic turf for athletic fields—this according to Hank Julicher, founder of **Sprinturf** **(Sprinturf.com).** "Not all fields are exactly alike, because no two owners have the same exact needs," insists Hank. "Many variables must be considered, including playing requirements, climate, and financial considerations." Designing, installing, and servicing synthetic turf systems are Sprinturf's mission.

"There is much more to a playing field than just the surface," explains Hank. "Many would argue that the base is the most important—it needs the strength to support athletes and vehicles, while still being able to drain over 20″ of rainfall per hour." For this, Sprinturf relies on its all-rubber infill system for its installations. Still, understanding customer needs is key. In extremely hot, arid climates, Sprinturf uses light-colored rubber infill to reduce the temperature of playing surfaces. In cold areas, Sprinturf offers solutions to reduce snow and ice buildup. Hank has put in fields from Utah State University to University of Montana to Long Beach City College. While a touchdown is worth 6 points on every Sprinturf field, each field is otherwise unique.

Manufacturers of custom products, such as that from Sprinturf, use state-of-the-art job order cost accounting to track costs. This includes tracking the cost of materials, labor and overhead, and managing those expenses. To help control costs and ensure product quality, Sprinturf does not outsource any part of the design or installation process. Controlling all aspects of the process enables it to better isolate costs and avoid the run-away costs often experienced by startups that fail to use costing techniques. Recruiting top-notch personnel and experienced supervisors also helps control labor costs. Reflecting the unique nature of each field, each installation is videotaped to ensure it is done exactly according to customer specifications.

Hank Julicher stresses cost control as vital to Sprinturf's success. "To take on two 800 pound gorillas in our industry, we had to be more creative, efficient, and cost-effective to win," explains Hank. "We just hung in there until the public recognized our quality and value." This winning formula has led to product growth that any team would envy.

[Sources: *Sprinturf Website,* January 2009; *Entrepreneur,* 2007; *PanStadia,* February and November 2005]

Chapter Preview

This chapter introduces a system for assigning costs to the flow of goods through a production process. We then describe the details of a *job order cost accounting system*. Job order costing is frequently used by manufacturers of custom products or providers of custom services. Manufacturers that use job order costing typically base it on a perpetual inventory system, which provides a continuous record of materials, goods in process, and finished goods inventories.

Job Order Cost Accounting

Job Order Cost Accounting
- Cost accounting system
- Job order manufacturing
- Events in job order costing
- Job cost sheet

Job Order Cost Flows and Reports
- Materials cost flows and documents
- Labor cost flows and documents
- Overhead cost flows and documents
- Summary of cost flows

Adjustment of Overapplied or Underapplied Overhead
- Underapplied overhead
- Overapplied overhead

Job Order Cost Accounting

This section describes a cost accounting system and job order production and costing.

Cost Accounting System

C1 Explain the cost accounting system.

Point: Cost accounting systems accumulate costs and then assign them to products and services.

An ever-increasing number of companies use a cost accounting system to generate timely and accurate inventory information. A **cost accounting system** records manufacturing activities using a *perpetual* inventory system, which continuously updates records for costs of materials, goods in process, and finished goods inventories. A cost accounting system also provides timely information about inventories and manufacturing costs per unit of product. This is especially helpful for managers' efforts to control costs and determine selling prices. (A **general accounting system** records manufacturing activities using a *periodic* inventory system. Some companies still use a general accounting system, but its use is declining as competitive forces and customer demands have increased pressures on companies to better manage inventories.)

The two basic types of cost accounting systems are *job order cost accounting* and *process cost accounting.* We describe job order cost accounting in this chapter. Process cost accounting is explained in the next chapter.

Job Order Production

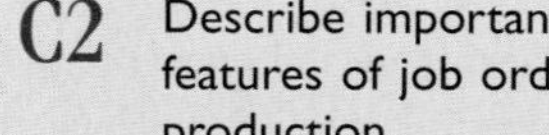

C2 Describe important features of job order production.

Many companies produce products individually designed to meet the needs of a specific customer. Each customized product is manufactured separately and its production is called **job order production,** or *job order manufacturing* (also called *customized production,* which is the production of products in response to special orders). Examples of such products include synthetic football fields, special-order machines, a factory building, custom jewelry, wedding invitations, and artwork.

The production activities for a customized product represent a **job.** The principle of customization is equally applicable to both manufacturing *and* service companies. Most service companies meet customers' needs by performing a custom service for a specific customer. Examples of such services include an accountant auditing a client's financial statements, an interior designer remodeling an office, a wedding consultant planning and supervising a reception, and a lawyer defending a client. Whether the setting is manufacturing or services, job order operations involve meeting the needs of customers by producing or performing custom jobs.

Boeing's aerospace division is one example of a job order production system. Its primary business is twofold: (1) design, develop, and integrate space carriers and (2) provide systems engineering and integration of Department of Defense (DoD) systems. Many of its orders are customized and produced through job order operations.

When a job involves producing more than one unit of a custom product, it is often called a **job lot.** Products produced as job lots could include benches for a church, imprinted T-shirts for a 10K race or company picnic, or advertising signs for a chain of stores. Although these orders involve more than one unit, the volume of production is typically low, such as 50 benches, 200 T-shirts, or 100 signs. Another feature of job order production is the diversity, often called *heterogeneity,* of the products produced. Namely, each customer order is likely to differ from another in some important respect. These variations can be minor or major.

Point: Many professional examinations including the CPA and CMA exams require knowledge of job order and process cost accounting.

Decision Insight

Custom Design Managers once saw companies as the center of a solar system orbited by suppliers and customers. Now the customer has become the center of the business universe. **Nike** allows custom orders over the Internet, enabling customers to select materials, colors, and to personalize their shoes with letters and numbers. Soon consumers may be able to personalize almost any product, from cellular phones to appliances to furniture.

Events in Job Order Costing

The initial event in a normal job order operation is the receipt of a customer order for a custom product. This causes the company to begin work on a job. A less common case occurs when management decides to begin work on a job before it has a signed contract. This is referred to as *jobs produced on speculation.*

Video19.1

The first step in both cases is to predict the cost to complete the job. This cost depends on the product design prepared by either the customer or the producer. The second step is to negotiate a sales price and decide whether to pursue the job. Other than for government or other cost-plus contracts, the selling price is determined by market factors. Producers evaluate the market price, compare it to cost, and determine whether the profit on the job is reasonable. If the profit is not reasonable, the producer would determine a desired **target cost.** The third step is for the producer to schedule production of the job to meet the customer's needs and to fit within its own production constraints. Preparation of this work schedule should consider workplace facilities including equipment, personnel, and supplies. Once this schedule is complete, the producer can place orders for raw materials. Production occurs as materials and labor are applied to the job.

Point: Some jobs are priced on a *cost-plus basis:* The customer pays the manufacturer for costs incurred on the job plus a negotiated amount or rate of profit.

An overview of job order production activity is shown in Exhibit 19.1. This exhibit shows the March production activity of Road Warriors, which manufactures security-equipped cars and trucks. The company converts any vehicle by giving it a diversity of security items such as alarms, reinforced exterior, bulletproof glass, and bomb detectors. The company began by catering to high-profile celebrities, but it now caters to anyone who desires added security in a vehicle.

Job order production for Road Warriors requires materials, labor, and overhead costs. Recall that direct materials are goods used in manufacturing that are clearly identified with a particular job. Similarly, direct labor is effort devoted to a particular job. Overhead costs support production of more than one job. Common overhead items are depreciation on factory buildings and equipment, factory supplies, supervision, maintenance, cleaning, and utilities.

Exhibit 19.1 shows that materials, labor, and overhead are added to Jobs B15, B16, B17, B18, and B19, which were started during March. Road Warriors completed Jobs B15, B16, and B17 in March and delivered Jobs B15 and B16 to customers. At the end of March, Jobs B18 and B19 remain in goods in process inventory and Job B17 is in finished goods inventory. Both labor and materials costs are also separated into their direct and indirect components. Their indirect amounts are added to overhead. Total overhead cost is then allocated to the various jobs.

Decision Insight

Target Costing Many producers determine a target cost for their jobs. Target cost is determined as follows: Expected selling price − Desired profit = Target cost. If the projected target cost of the job as determined by job costing is too high, the producer can apply *value engineering,* which is a method of determining ways to reduce job cost until the target cost is met.

EXHIBIT 19.1

Job Order Production Activities

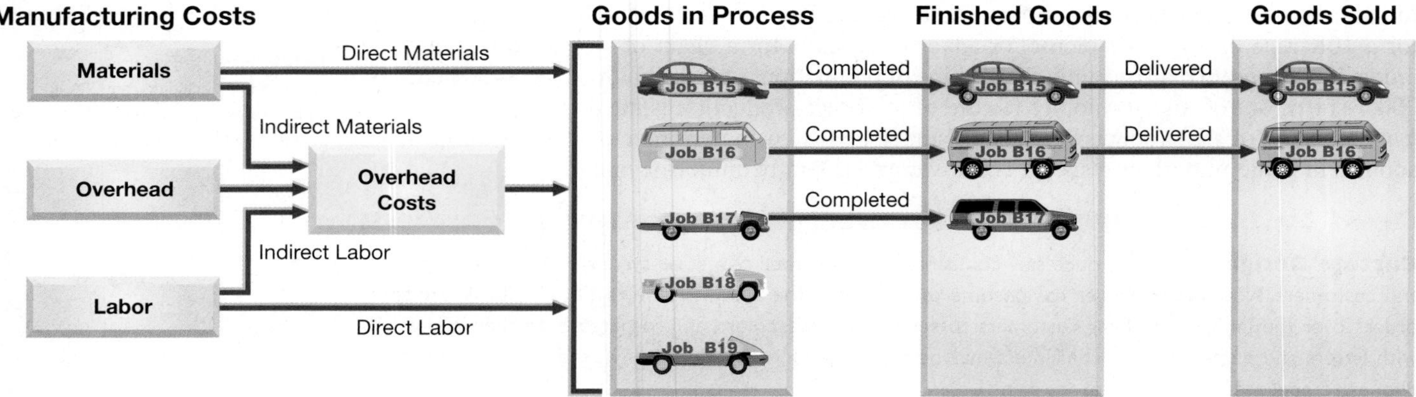

Job Cost Sheet

C3 Explain job cost sheets and how they are used in job order cost accounting.

General ledger accounts usually do not provide the accounting information that managers of job order cost operations need to plan and control production activities. This is so because the needed information often requires more detailed data. Such detailed data are usually stored in subsidiary records controlled by general ledger accounts. Subsidiary records store information about raw materials, overhead costs, jobs in process, finished goods, and other items. This section describes the use of these records.

A major aim of a **job order cost accounting system** is to determine the cost of producing each job or job lot. In the case of a job lot, the system also aims to compute the cost per unit. The accounting system must include separate records for each job to accomplish this, and it must capture information about costs incurred and charge these costs to each job.

A **job cost sheet** is a separate record maintained for each job. Exhibit 19.2 shows a job cost sheet for an alarm system that Road Warriors produced for a customer. This job cost sheet identifies the customer, the job number assigned, the product, and key dates. Costs incurred on the job are immediately recorded on this sheet. When each job is complete, the supervisor enters the date of completion, records any remarks, and signs the sheet. The job cost sheet in Exhibit 19.2 classifies costs as direct materials, direct labor, or overhead. It shows that a total of $600 in direct materials is added to Job B15 on four different dates. It also shows seven entries for direct labor costs that total $1,000. Road Warriors *allocates* (also termed *applies, assigns,* or *charges*) factory overhead costs of $1,600 to this job using an allocation rate of 160% of direct labor cost (160% × $1,000)—we discuss overhead allocation later in this chapter.

Point: Factory overhead consists of costs (other than direct materials and direct labor) that ensure the production activities are carried out.

While a job is being produced, its accumulated costs are kept in **Goods in Process Inventory.** The collection of job cost sheets for all jobs in process makes up a subsidiary ledger controlled by the Goods in Process Inventory account in the general ledger. Managers use job cost sheets to monitor costs incurred to date and to predict and control costs for each job.

Point: Documents (electronic and paper) are crucial in a job order system, and the job cost sheet is a cornerstone. Understanding it aids in grasping concepts of capitalizing product costs and product cost flow.

When a job is finished, its job cost sheet is completed and moved from the jobs in process file to the finished jobs file. This latter file acts as a subsidiary ledger controlled by the **Finished Goods Inventory** account. When a finished job is delivered to a customer, the job cost sheet is moved to a permanent file supporting the total cost of goods sold. This permanent file contains records from both current and prior periods.

Decision Maker

Management Consultant One of your tasks is to control and manage costs for a consulting company. At the end of a recent month, you find that three consulting jobs were completed and two are 60% complete. Each unfinished job is estimated to cost $10,000 and to earn a revenue of $12,000. You are unsure how to recognize goods in process inventory and record costs and revenues. Do you recognize any inventory? If so, how much? How much revenue is recorded for unfinished jobs this month? [Answer—p. 786]

EXHIBIT 19.2

Job Cost Sheet

Accounting System: Exhibit 19-2

File Edit Maintain Tasks Analysis Options Reports Window Help

Road Warriors, Los Angeles, California — **JOB COST SHEET**

Customer's Name Carroll Connor — **Job No.** B15

Address 1542 High Point Dr. — **City & State** Portland, Oregon

Job Description Level 1 Alarm System on Ford Expedition

Date promised March 15 — **Date started** March 3 — **Date completed** March 11

Direct Materials			Direct Labor			Overhead		
Date	Requisition	Cost	Date	Time Ticket	Cost	Date	Rate	Cost
3/3/2009	R-4698	100.00	3/3/2009	L-3393	120.00	3/11/2009	160% of Direct Labor Cost	1,600.00
3/7/2009	R-4705	225.00	3/4/2009	L-3422	150.00			
3/9/2009	R-4725	180.00	3/5/2009	L-3456	180.00			
3/10/2009	R-4777	95.00	3/8/2009	L-3479	60.00			
			3/9/2009	L-3501	90.00			
			3/10/2009	L-3535	240.00			
			3/11/2009	L-3559	160.00			
	Total	600.00		Total	1,000.00		Total	1,600.00

REMARKS: Completed job on March 11, and shipped to customer on March 15. Met all specifications and requirements.

SUMMARY:

Materials	600.00
Labor	1,000.00
Overhead	1,600.00
Total cost	3,200.00

Signed: *C. Luther, Supervisor*

Quick Check

Answers—p. 787

1. Which of these products is likely to involve job order production? (*a*) inexpensive watches, (*b*) racing bikes, (*c*) bottled soft drinks, or (*d*) athletic socks.
2. What is the difference between a job and a job lot?
3. Which of these statements is correct? (*a*) The collection of job cost sheets for unfinished jobs makes up a subsidiary ledger controlled by the Goods in Process Inventory account, (*b*) Job cost sheets are financial statements provided to investors, or (*c*) A separate job cost sheet is maintained in the general ledger for each job in process.
4. What three costs are normally accumulated on job cost sheets?

Job Order Cost Flows and Reports

Materials Cost Flows and Documents

P1 Describe and record the flow of materials costs in job order cost accounting.

Materials

This section focuses on the flow of materials costs and the related documents in a job order cost accounting system. We begin analysis of the flow of materials costs by examining Exhibit 19.3. When materials are first received from suppliers, the employees count and inspect them and record the items' quantity and cost on a receiving report. The receiving report serves as the *source document* for recording materials received in both a materials ledger card and in the general ledger. In nearly all job order cost systems, **materials ledger cards** (or files) are perpetual records that are updated each time units are purchased and each time units are issued for use in production.

Point: Some companies certify certain suppliers based on the quality of their materials. Goods received from these suppliers are not always inspected by the purchaser to save costs.

To illustrate the purchase of materials, Road Warriors acquired $450 of wiring and related materials on March 4, 2009. This purchase is recorded as follows.

Mar. 4	Raw Materials Inventory—M-347.	450	
	Accounts Payable		450
	To record purchase of materials for production.		

Assets = Liabilities + Equity
+450 +450

EXHIBIT 19.3

Materials Cost Flows through Subsidiary Records

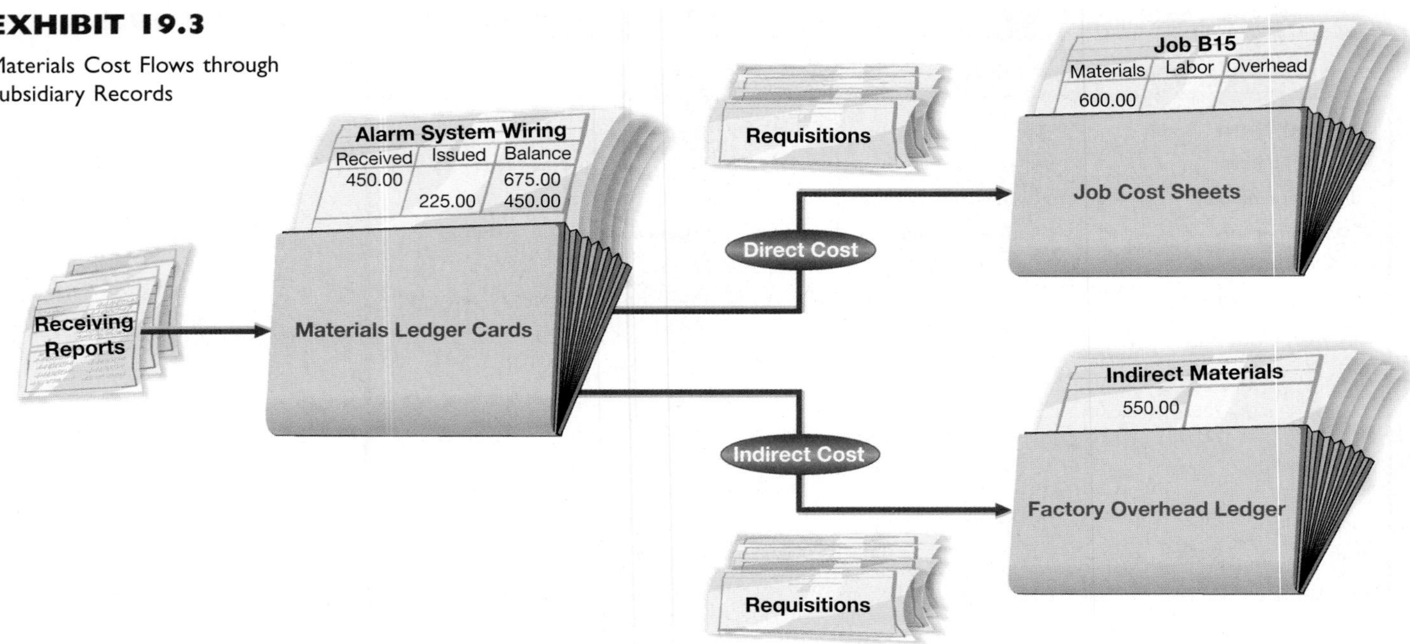

Exhibit 19.3 shows that materials can be requisitioned for use either on a specific job (direct materials) or as overhead (indirect materials). Cost of direct materials flows from the materials ledger card to the job cost sheet. The cost of indirect materials flows from the materials ledger card to the Indirect Materials account in the factory overhead ledger, which is a subsidiary ledger controlled by the Factory Overhead account in the general ledger.

Video19.1

Exhibit 19.4 shows a materials ledger card for material received and issued by Road Warriors. The card identifies the item as alarm system wiring and shows the item's stock number, its location in the storeroom, information about the maximum and minimum quantities that should be available, and the reorder quantity. For example, alarm system wiring is issued and recorded on March 7, 2009. The job cost sheet in Exhibit 19.2 showed that Job B15 used this wiring.

EXHIBIT 19.4

Materials Ledger Card

MATERIALS LEDGER CARD

Road Warriors
Los Angeles, California

Item	Alarm system wiring	Stock No.	M–347	Location in Storeroom	Bin 137
Maximum quantity	5 units	Minimum quantity	1 unit	Quantity to reorder	2 units

	Received				Issued				Balance		
Date	Receiving Report Number	Units	Unit Price	Total Price	Requisition Number	Units	Unit Price	Total Price	Units	Unit Price	Total Price
									1	225.00	225.00
3/ 4/2009	C-7117	2	225.00	450.00					3	225.00	675.00
3/ 7/2009					R–4705	1	225.00	225.00	2	225.00	450.00

When materials are needed in production, a production manager prepares a **materials requisition** and sends it to the materials manager. The requisition shows the job number, the type of material, the quantity needed, and the signature of the manager authorized to make the requisition. Exhibit 19.5 shows the materials requisition for alarm system wiring for Job B15. To see how this requisition ties to the flow of costs, compare the information on the requisition with the March 7, 2009, data in Exhibits 19.2 and 19.4.

Point: Requisitions are often accumulated and recorded in one entry. The frequency of entries depends on the job, the industry, and management procedures.

EXHIBIT 19.5

Materials Requisition

MATERIALS REQUISITION No. R–4705

Road Warriors
Los Angeles, California

Job No. B15
Date 3/7/2009
Material Stock No. M–347
Material Description Alarm system wiring
Quantity Requested 1
Requested By C. Luther

Quantity Provided 1
Date Provided 3/7/2009
Filled By M. Bateman
Material Received By C. Luther
Remarks

The use of alarm system wiring on Job B15 yields the following entry (locate this cost item in the job cost sheet shown in Exhibit 19.2).

Mar. 7	Goods in Process Inventory—Job B15.	225	
	Raw Materials Inventory—M-347.		225
	To record use of material on Job B15.		

Assets = Liabilities + Equity
+225
−225

This entry is posted both to its general ledger accounts and to subsidiary records. Posting to subsidiary records includes a debit to a job cost sheet and a credit to a materials ledger card. (*Note:* An entry to record use of indirect materials is the same as that for direct materials *except* the debit is to Factory Overhead. In the subsidiary factory overhead ledger, this entry is posted to Indirect Materials.)

Labor Cost Flows and Documents

P2 Describe and record the flow of labor costs in job order cost accounting.

Labor

Exhibit 19.6 shows the flow of labor costs from clock cards and the Factory Payroll account to subsidiary records of the job order cost accounting system. Recall that costs in subsidiary records give detailed information needed to manage and control operations.

EXHIBIT 19.6

Labor Cost Flows through Subsidiary Records

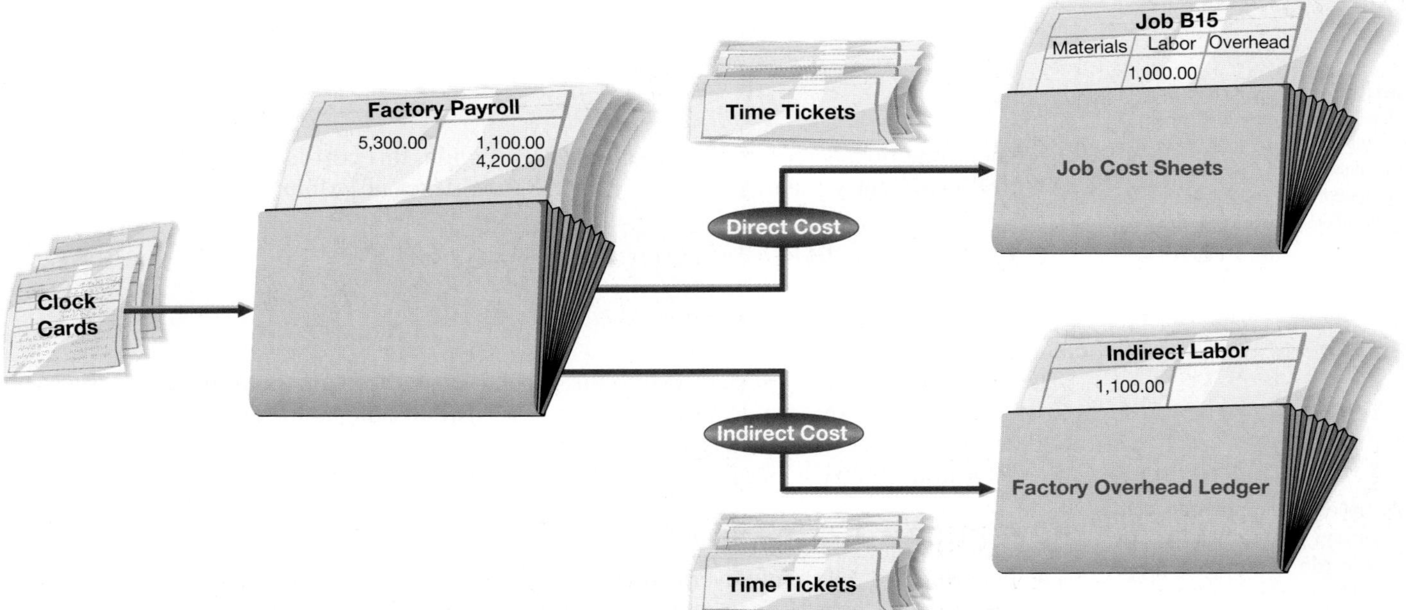

Point: Indirect materials are included in overhead on the job cost sheet. Assigning overhead costs to products is described in the next section.

Point: Many employee fraud schemes involve payroll, including overstated hours on clock cards.

The flow of costs in Exhibit 19.6 begins with **clock cards.** Employees commonly use these cards to record the number of hours worked, and they serve as source documents for entries to record labor costs. Clock card data on the number of hours worked is used at the end of each pay period to determine total labor cost. This amount is then debited to the Factory Payroll account, a temporary account containing the total payroll cost (both direct and indirect). Payroll cost is later allocated to both specific jobs and overhead.

According to clock card data, workers earned $1,500 for the week ended March 5. Illustrating the flow of labor costs, the accrual and payment of these wages are recorded as follows.

Assets = Liabilities + Equity
−1,500 −1,500

Mar. 6	Factory payroll	1,500	
	Cash		1,500
	To record the weekly payroll.		

"It's on Corporate Standard Time... It loses an hour of your pay every day."

To assign labor costs to specific jobs and to overhead, we must know how each employee's time is used and its costs. Source documents called **time tickets** usually capture these data. Employees regularly fill out time tickets to report how much time they spent on each job. An employee who works on several jobs during a day completes a separate time ticket for each job. Tickets are also prepared for time charged to overhead as indirect labor. A supervisor signs an employee's time ticket to confirm its accuracy.

Exhibit 19.7 shows a time ticket reporting the time a Road Warrior employee spent working on Job B15. The employee's supervisor signed the ticket to confirm its accuracy. The hourly rate and total labor cost are computed after the time ticket is turned in. To see the effect of this time ticket on the job cost sheet, look at the entry dated March 8, 2009, in Exhibit 19.2.

EXHIBIT 19.7

Time Ticket

ROAD WARRIORS
Road Warriors
Los Angeles, California

No. L–3479

TIME TICKET **Date** March 8 **20** 09

Employee Name	Employee Number	Job No.
T. Zeller	3969	B15

TIME AND RATE INFORMATION:

Start Time	Finish Time	Elapsed Time	Hourly Rate
9:00	12:00	3.0	$20.00
Approved By C. Luther		**Total Cost**	$60.00

Remarks

Point: In the accounting equation, we treat accounts such as Factory Overhead and Factory Payroll as temporary accounts, which hold various expenses until they are allocated to balance sheet or income statement accounts.

When time tickets report labor used on a specific job, this cost is recorded as direct labor. The following entry records the data from the time ticket in Exhibit 19.7.

Assets = Liabilities + Equity
+60 +60

Mar. 8	Goods in Process Inventory—Job B15	60	
	Factory Payroll		60
	To record direct labor used on Job B15.		

The debit in this entry is posted both to the general ledger account and to the appropriate job cost sheet. (*Note:* An entry to record indirect labor is the same as for direct labor *except* that it debits Factory Overhead and credits Factory Payroll. In the subsidiary factory overhead ledger, the debit in this entry is posted to the Indirect Labor account.)

P3 Describe and record the flow of overhead costs in job order cost accounting.

Overhead Cost Flows and Documents

Factory overhead (or simply overhead) cost flows are shown in Exhibit 19.8. Factory overhead includes all production costs other than direct materials and direct labor. Two sources of

EXHIBIT 19.8

Overhead Cost Flows through Subsidiary Records

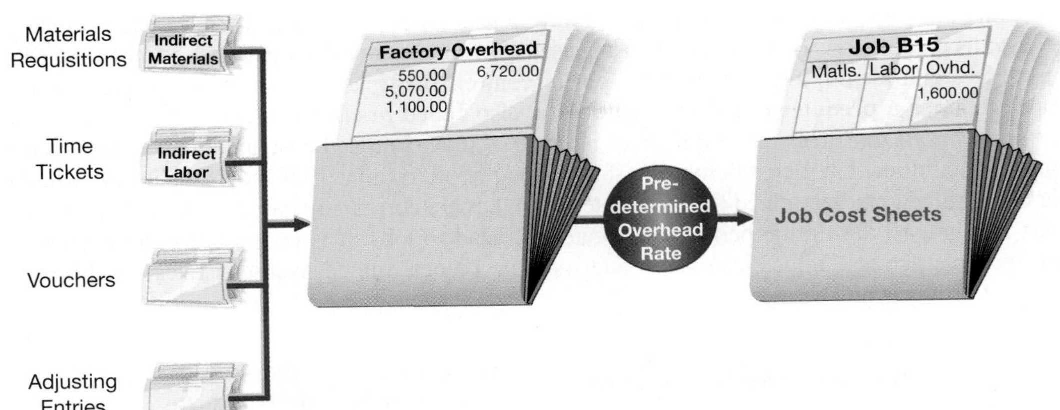

overhead costs are indirect materials and indirect labor. These costs are recorded from requisitions for indirect materials and time tickets for indirect labor. Two other sources of overhead are (1) vouchers authorizing payments for items such as supplies or utilities and (2) adjusting entries for costs such as depreciation on factory assets.

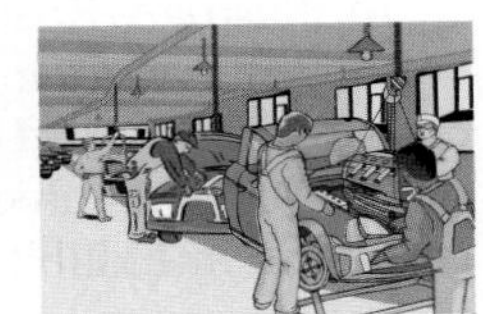
Overhead

Factory overhead usually includes many different costs and, thus, a separate account for each is often maintained in a subsidiary factory overhead ledger. This ledger is controlled by the Factory Overhead account in the general ledger. Factory Overhead is a temporary account that accumulates costs until they are allocated to jobs.

Recall that overhead costs are recorded with debits to the Factory Overhead account and with credits to other accounts such as Cash, Accounts Payable, and Accumulated Depreciation—Equipment. In the subsidiary factory overhead ledger, the debits are posted to their respective accounts such as Depreciation Expense—Equipment, Insurance Expense—Warehouse, or Amortization Expense—Patents.

To illustrate the recording of overhead, the following two entries reflect the depreciation of factory equipment and the accrual of utilities, respectively, for the week ended March 6.

Mar. 6	Factory Overhead	600	
	Accumulated Depreciation—Equipment		600
	To record depreciation on factory equipment.		
Mar. 6	Factory Overhead	250	
	Utilities Payable.		250
	To record the accrual of factory utilities.		

Assets	=	Liabilities	+	Equity
−600				−600

Assets	=	Liabilities	+	Equity
		+250		−250

Exhibit 19.8 shows that overhead costs flow from the Factory Overhead account to job cost sheets. Because overhead is made up of costs not directly associated with specific jobs or job lots, we cannot determine the dollar amount incurred on a specific job. We know, however, that overhead costs represent a necessary part of business activities. If a job cost is to include all costs needed to complete the job, some amount of overhead must be included. Given the difficulty in determining the overhead amount for a specific job, however, we allocate overhead to individual jobs in some reasonable manner.

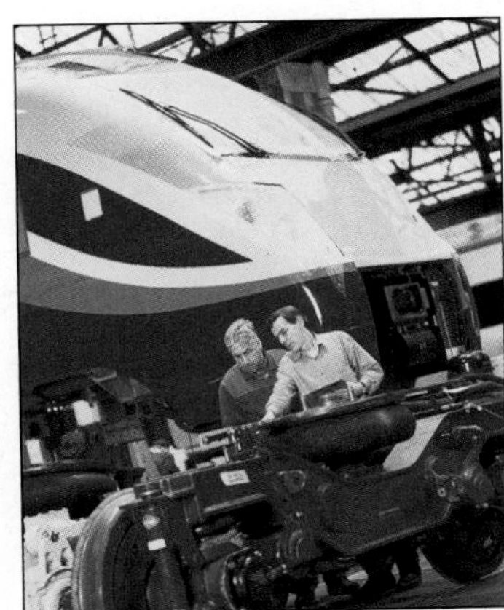

We generally allocate overhead by linking it to another factor used in production, such as direct labor or machine hours. The factor to which overhead costs are linked is known as the *allocation base.* A manager must think carefully about how many and which allocation bases to use. This managerial decision influences the accuracy with which overhead costs are allocated to individual jobs. In turn, the cost of individual jobs might impact a manager's decisions for pricing or performance evaluation. In Exhibit 19.2, overhead is expressed as 160% of direct labor. We then allocate overhead by multiplying 160% by the estimated amount of direct labor on the jobs.

We cannot wait until the end of a period to allocate overhead to jobs because perpetual inventory records are part of the job order costing system (demanding up-to-date costs). Instead, we

Point: The predetermined overhead rate is computed at the start of the period and is used throughout the period to allocate overhead to jobs.

Point: Predetermined overhead rates can be estimated using mathematical equations, statistical analysis, or professional experience.

must predict overhead in advance and assign it to jobs so that a job's total costs can be estimated prior to its completion. This estimated cost is useful for managers in many decisions including setting prices and identifying costs that are out of control. Being able to estimate overhead in advance requires a **predetermined overhead rate,** also called *predetermined overhead allocation* (or *application*) *rate.* This rate requires an estimate of total overhead cost and an allocation factor such as total direct labor cost before the start of the period. Exhibit 19.9 shows the usual formula for computing a predetermined overhead rate (estimates are commonly based on annual amounts). This rate is used during the period to allocate overhead to jobs. It is common for companies to use multiple activity (allocation) bases and multiple predetermined overhead rates for different types of products and services.

EXHIBIT 19.9

Predetermined Overhead Allocation Rate Formula

Predetermined overhead rate = Estimated overhead costs ÷ Estimated activity base

Example: If management predicts total direct labor costs of $100,000 and total overhead costs of $200,000, what is its predetermined overhead rate? *Answer:* 200% of direct labor cost.

To illustrate, Road Warriors allocates overhead by linking it to direct labor. At the start of the current period, management predicts total direct labor costs of $125,000 and total overhead costs of $200,000. Using these estimates, management computes its predetermined overhead rate as 160% of direct labor cost ($200,000 ÷ $125,000). Specifically, reviewing the job order cost sheet in Exhibit 19.2, we see that $1,000 of direct labor went into Job B15. We then use the predetermined overhead rate of 160% to allocate $1,600 (equal to $1,000 × 1.60) of overhead to this job. The entry to record this allocation is

Assets	= Liabilities	+ Equity
+1,600		+1,600

Mar. 11	Goods in Process Inventory—Job B15	1,600	
	Factory Overhead		1,600
	To assign overhead to Job B15.		

Since the allocation rate for overhead is estimated at the start of a period, the total amount assigned to jobs during a period rarely equals the amount actually incurred. We explain how this difference is treated later in this chapter.

Decision Ethics

Web Consultant You are working on seven client engagements. Two clients reimburse your firm for actual costs plus a 10% markup. The other five pay a fixed fee for services. Your firm's costs include overhead allocated at $47 per labor hour. The managing partner of your firm instructs you to record as many labor hours as possible to the two markup engagements by transferring labor hours from the other five. What do you do? [Answer—p. 786]

Summary of Cost Flows

Point: Study the flow of manufacturing costs through general ledger accounts and job cost sheets. Use Exhibit 19.11 as reinforcement.

We showed journal entries for charging Goods in Process Inventory (Job B15) with the cost of (1) direct materials requisitions, (2) direct labor time tickets, and (3) factory overhead. We made separate entries for each of these costs, but they are usually recorded in one entry. Specifically, materials requisitions are often collected for a day or a week and recorded with a single entry summarizing them. The same is done with labor time tickets. When summary entries are made, supporting schedules of the jobs charged and the types of materials used provide the basis for postings to subsidiary records.

To show all production cost flows for a period and their related entries, we again look at Road Warriors' activities. Exhibit 19.10 shows costs linked to all of Road Warriors' production activities for March. Road Warriors did not have any jobs in process at the beginning of March, but it did apply materials, labor, and overhead costs to five new jobs in March. Jobs B15 and B16 are completed and delivered to customers in March, Job B17 is completed but not delivered, and Jobs B18 and B19 are still in process. Exhibit 19.10 also shows purchases of raw materials for $2,750, labor costs incurred for $5,300, and overhead costs of $6,720.

The upper part of Exhibit 19.11 shows the flow of these costs through general ledger accounts and the end-of-month balances in key subsidiary records. Arrow lines are numbered

EXHIBIT 19.10

Job Order Costs of All Production Activities

ROAD WARRIORS
Job Order Manufacturing Costs
For Month Ended March 31, 2009

Explanation	Materials	Labor	Overhead Incurred	Overhead Allocated	Goods in Process	Finished Goods	Cost of Goods Sold
Job B15	$ 600	$1,000		$1,600			$3,200
Job B16	300	800		1,280			2,380
Job B17	500	1,100		1,760		$3,360	
Job B18	150	700		1,120	$1,970		
Job B19	250	600		960	1,810		
Total job costs	1,800	4,200		$6,720	$3,780	$3,360	$5,580
Indirect materials	550		$ 550				
Indirect labor		1,100	1,100				
Other overhead			5,070				
Total costs used in production	2,350	$5,300	$6,720				
Ending materials inventory	1,400						
Materials available	3,750						
Less beginning materials inventory	(1,000)						
Materials purchased	$2,750						

EXHIBIT 19.11

Job Order Cost Flows and Ending Job Cost Sheets

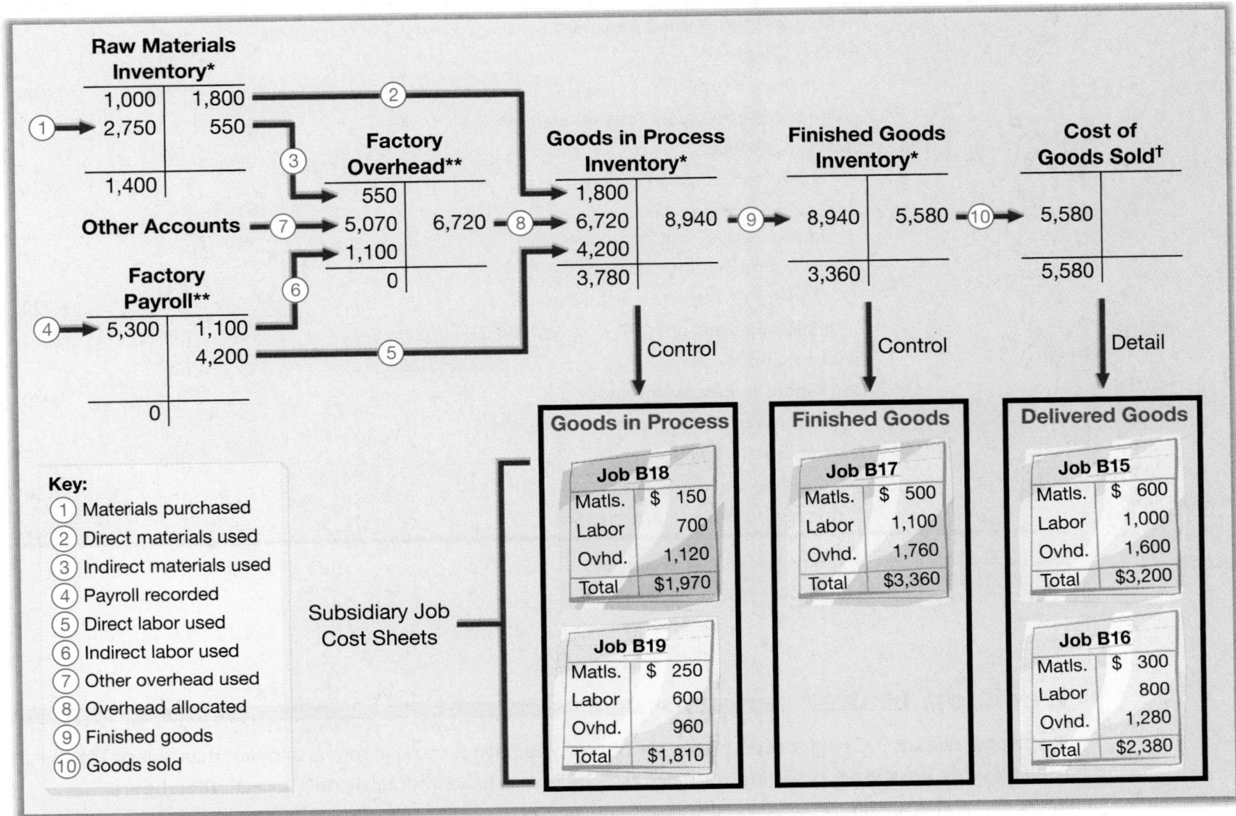

* The ending balances in the inventory accounts are carried to the balance sheet.

† The Cost of Goods Sold balance is carried to the income statement.

** Factory Payroll and Factory Overhead are considered temporary accounts; when these costs are allocated to jobs, the balances in these accounts are reduced.

to show the flows of costs for March. Each numbered cost flow reflects several entries made in March. The lower part of Exhibit 19.11 shows summarized job cost sheets and their status at the end of March. The sum of costs assigned to the jobs in process ($1,970 + $1,810) equals the $3,780 balance in Goods in Process Inventory shown in Exhibit 19.10. Also, costs assigned to Job B17 equal the $3,360 balance in Finished Goods Inventory. The sum of costs assigned to Jobs B15 and B16 ($3,200 + $2,380) equals the $5,580 balance in Cost of Goods Sold.

Exhibit 19.12 shows each cost flow with a single entry summarizing the actual individual entries made in March. Each entry is numbered to link with the arrow lines in Exhibit 19.11.

EXHIBIT 19.12

Entries for Job Order Production Costs*

		Debit	Credit
①	Raw Materials Inventory	2,750	
	Accounts Payable		2,750
	Acquired materials on credit for factory use.		
②	Goods in Process Inventory	1,800	
	Raw Materials Inventory		1,800
	To assign costs of direct materials used.		
③	Factory Overhead	550	
	Raw Materials Inventory		550
	To record use of indirect materials.		
④	Factory Payroll	5,300	
	Cash (and other accounts)		5,300
	To record salaries and wages of factory workers (including various payroll liabilities).		
⑤	Goods in Process Inventory	4,200	
	Factory Payroll		4,200
	To assign costs of direct labor used.		
⑥	Factory Overhead	1,100	
	Factory Payroll		1,100
	To record indirect labor costs as overhead.		
⑦	Factory Overhead	5,070	
	Cash (and other accounts)		5,070
	To record factory overhead costs such as insurance, utilities, rent, and depreciation.		
⑧	Goods in Process Inventory	6,720	
	Factory Overhead		6,720
	To apply overhead at 160% of direct labor.		
⑨	Finished Goods Inventory	8,940	
	Goods in Process Inventory		8,940
	To record completion of Jobs B15, B16, and B17.		
⑩	Cost of Goods Sold	5,580	
	Finished Goods Inventory		5,580
	To record sale of Jobs B15 and B16.		

* Transactions are numbered to be consistent with arrow lines in Exhibit 19.11.

Point: *Actual* overhead is debited to Factory Overhead. *Allocated* overhead is credited to Factory Overhead.

Decision Maker

Entrepreneur Competitors' prices on one of your product segments are lower than yours. Of the total product cost used in setting your prices, 53% is overhead allocated using direct labor hours. You believe that product costs are distorted and wonder whether there is a better way to allocate overhead and to set product price. What do you suggest? [Answer—p. 787]

Quick Check Answers—p. 787

5. In job order cost accounting, which account is debited in recording a raw materials requisition? (*a*) Raw Materials Inventory, (*b*) Raw Materials Purchases, (*c*) Goods in Process Inventory if for a job, or (*d*) Goods in Process Inventory if they are indirect materials.
6. What are four sources of information for recording costs in the Factory Overhead account?
7. Why does job order cost accounting require a predetermined overhead rate?
8. What events result in a debit to Factory Payroll? What events result in a credit?

Adjustment of Overapplied or Underapplied Overhead

Video19.1

Refer to the debits in the Factory Overhead account in Exhibit 19.11 (or Exhibit 19.12). The total cost of factory overhead incurred during March is $6,720 ($550 + $5,070 + $1,100). The $6,720 exactly equals the amount assigned to goods in process inventory (see arrow line ⑧). Therefore, the overhead incurred equals the overhead applied in March. The amount of overhead incurred rarely equals the amount of overhead applied, however, because a job order cost accounting system uses a predetermined overhead rate in applying factory overhead costs to jobs. This rate is determined using estimated amounts before the period begins, and estimates rarely equal the exact amounts actually incurred. This section explains what we do when too much or too little overhead is applied to jobs.

Underapplied Overhead

P4 Determine adjustments for overapplied and underapplied factory overhead.

When less overhead is applied than is actually incurred, the remaining debit balance in the Factory Overhead account at the end of the period is called **underapplied overhead.** To illustrate, assume that Road Warriors actually incurred *other overhead costs* of $5,550 instead of the $5,070 shown in Exhibit 19.11. This yields an actual total overhead cost of $7,200 in March. Since the amount of overhead applied was only $6,720, the Factory Overhead account is left with a $480 debit balance as shown in the ledger account in Exhibit 19.13.

EXHIBIT 19.13

Underapplied Overhead in the Factory Overhead Ledger Account

Factory Overhead				Acct. No. 540
Date	Explanation	Debit	Credit	Balance
Mar. 31	Indirect materials cost	550		550 Dr.
31	Indirect labor cost	1,100		1,650 Dr.
31	Other overhead cost	5,550		7,200 Dr.
31	Overhead costs applied to jobs		6,720	480 Dr.

The $480 debit balance reflects manufacturing costs not assigned to jobs. This means that the balances in Goods in Process Inventory, Finished Goods Inventory, and Cost of Goods Sold do not include all production costs incurred. When the underapplied overhead amount is immaterial, it is allocated (closed) to the Cost of Goods Sold account with the following adjusting entry.

Example: If we do not adjust for underapplied overhead, will net income be overstated or understated? *Answer:* Overstated.

Mar. 31	Cost of Goods Sold	480	
	Factory Overhead		480
	To adjust for underapplied overhead costs.		

Assets = Liabilities + Equity
−480
+480

The $480 debit (increase) to Cost of Goods Sold reduces income by $480. (When the underapplied (or overapplied) overhead is material, the amount is normally allocated to the Cost of Goods Sold, Finished Goods Inventory, and Goods in Process Inventory accounts. This process is covered in advanced courses.)

Overapplied Overhead

When the overhead applied in a period exceeds the overhead incurred, the resulting credit balance in the Factory Overhead account is called **overapplied overhead.** We treat overapplied overhead at the end of the period in the same way we treat underapplied overhead, except that we debit Factory Overhead and credit Cost of Good Sold for the amount.

Decision Insight

Job Order Education Many companies invest in their employees, and the demand for executive education is strong. Annual spending on training and education exceeds $20 billion. Annual revenues for providers of executive education continue to rise, with about 40% of revenues coming from custom programs designed for one or a select group of companies.

Quick Check

Answers—p. 787

9. In a job order cost accounting system, why does the Factory Overhead account usually have an overapplied or underapplied balance at period-end?
10. When the Factory Overhead account has a debit balance at period-end, does this reflect overapplied or underapplied overhead?

Decision Analysis — Pricing for Services

A1 Apply job order costing in pricing services.

The chapter described job order costing mainly using a manufacturing setting. However, these concepts and procedures are applicable to a service setting. Consider AdWorld, an advertising agency that develops Web-based ads for small firms. Each of its customers has unique requirements, so costs for each individual job must be tracked separately.

AdWorld uses two types of labor: Web designers ($65 per hour) and computer staff ($50 per hour). It also incurs overhead costs that it assigns using two different predetermined overhead allocation rates: $125 per designer hour and $96 per staff hour. For each job, AdWorld must estimate the number of designer and staff hours needed. Then total costs pertaining to each job are determined using the procedures in the chapter. (*Note:* Most service firms have neither the category of materials cost nor inventory.)

To illustrate, a manufacturer of golf balls requested a quote from AdWorld for an advertising engagement. AdWorld estimates that the job will require 43 designer hours and 61 staff hours, with the following total estimated cost for this job.

Direct Labor		
Designers (43 hours × $65)	$ 2,795	
Staff (61 hours × $50)	3,050	
Total direct labor		$ 5,845
Overhead		
Designer related (43 hours × $125)	5,375	
Staff related (61 hours × $96)	5,856	
Total overhead		11,231
Total estimated job cost		$17,076

AdWorld can use this cost information to help determine the price quote for the job (see *Decision Maker,* **Sales Manager,** scenario in this chapter).

Another source of information that AdWorld must consider is the market, that is, how much competitors will quote for this job. Competitor information is often unavailable; therefore, AdWorld's managers must use estimates based on their assessment of the competitive environment.

Decision Maker 

Sales Manager As AdWorld's sales manager, assume that you estimate costs pertaining to a proposed job as $17,076. Your normal pricing policy is to apply a markup of 18% from total costs. However, you learn that three other agencies are likely to bid for the same job, and that their quotes will range from $16,500 to $22,000. What price should you quote? What factors other than cost must you consider? [Answer—p. 787]

Demonstration Problem—Job Order Costing

DP19

The following information reflects Walczak Company's job order production activities for May.

Raw materials purchases	$16,000
Factory payroll cost	15,400
Overhead costs incurred	
Indirect materials	5,000
Indirect labor	3,500
Other factory overhead	9,500

Walczak's predetermined overhead rate is 150% of direct labor cost. Costs are allocated to the three jobs worked on during May as follows.

	Job 401	Job 402	Job 403
In-process balances on April 30			
Direct materials	$3,600		
Direct labor	1,700		
Applied overhead	2,550		
Costs during May			
Direct materials	3,550	$3,500	$1,400
Direct labor	5,100	6,000	800
Applied overhead	?	?	?
Status on May 31	**Finished (sold)**	**Finished (unsold)**	**In process**

Required

1. Determine the total cost of:

a. The April 30 inventory of jobs in process.

b. Materials used during May.

c. Labor used during May.

d. Factory overhead incurred and applied during May and the amount of any over- or underapplied overhead on May 31.

e. Each job as of May 31, the May 31 inventories of both goods in process and finished goods, and the goods sold during May.

2. Prepare summarized journal entries for the month to record:

a. Materials purchases (on credit), the factory payroll (paid with cash), indirect materials, indirect labor, and the other factory overhead (paid with cash).

b. Assignment of direct materials, direct labor, and overhead costs to the Goods in Process Inventory account. (Use separate debit entries for each job.)

c. Transfer of each completed job to the Finished Goods Inventory account.

d. Cost of goods sold.

e. Removal of any underapplied or overapplied overhead from the Factory Overhead account. (Assume the amount is not material.)

3. Prepare a manufacturing statement for May.

Planning the Solution

- Determine the cost of the April 30 goods in process inventory by totaling the materials, labor, and applied overhead costs for Job 401.

- Compute the cost of materials used and labor by totaling the amounts assigned to jobs and to overhead.
- Compute the total overhead incurred by summing the amounts for the three components. Compute the amount of applied overhead by multiplying the total direct labor cost by the predetermined overhead rate. Compute the underapplied or overapplied amount as the difference between the actual cost and the applied cost.
- Determine the total cost charged to each job by adding the costs incurred in April (if any) to the cost of materials, labor, and overhead applied during May.
- Group the costs of the jobs according to their completion status.
- Record the direct materials costs assigned to the three jobs, using a separate Goods in Process Inventory account for each job; do the same for the direct labor and the applied overhead.
- Transfer costs of Jobs 401 and 402 from Goods in Process Inventory to Finished Goods.
- Record the costs of Job 401 as cost of goods sold.
- Record the transfer of underapplied overhead from the Factory Overhead account to the Cost of Goods Sold account.
- On the manufacturing statement, remember to include the beginning and ending goods in process inventories and to deduct the underapplied overhead.

Solution to Demonstration Problem

1. Total cost of

a. April 30 inventory of jobs in process (Job 401).

Direct materials	$3,600
Direct labor	1,700
Applied overhead	2,550
Total cost	$7,850

b. Materials used during May.

Direct materials	
Job 401	$ 3,550
Job 402	3,500
Job 403	1,400
Total direct materials	8,450
Indirect materials	5,000
Total materials used	$13,450

c. Labor used during May.

Direct labor	
Job 401	$ 5,100
Job 402	6,000
Job 403	800
Total direct labor	11,900
Indirect labor	3,500
Total labor used	$15,400

d. Factory overhead incurred in May.

Actual overhead	
Indirect materials	$ 5,000
Indirect labor	3,500
Other factory overhead	9,500
Total actual overhead	18,000
Overhead applied (150% × $11,900)	17,850
Underapplied overhead	$ 150

e. Total cost of each job.

	401	402	403
In-process costs from April			
Direct materials	$ 3,600		
Direct labor	1,700		
Applied overhead*	2,550		
Cost incurred in May			
Direct materials	3,550	$ 3,500	$1,400
Direct labor	5,100	6,000	800
Applied overhead*	7,650	9,000	1,200
Total costs	$24,150	$18,500	$3,400

* Equals 150% of the direct labor cost.

Total cost of the May 31 inventory of goods in process (Job 403) = $3,400

Total cost of the May 31 inventory of finished goods (Job 402) = $18,500

Total cost of goods sold during May (Job 401) = $24,150

2. Journal entries.

a.

Account	Debit	Credit
Raw Materials Inventory	16,000	
Accounts Payable		16,000
To record materials purchases.		
Factory Payroll	15,400	
Cash		15,400
To record factory payroll.		
Factory Overhead	5,000	
Raw Materials Inventory		5,000
To record indirect materials.		
Factory Overhead	3,500	
Factory Payroll		3,500
To record indirect labor.		
Factory Overhead	9,500	
Cash		9,500
To record other factory overhead.		

b. Assignment of costs to Goods in Process Inventory.

Account	Debit	Credit
Goods in Process Inventory (Job 401)	3,550	
Goods in Process Inventory (Job 402)	3,500	
Goods in Process Inventory (Job 403)	1,400	
Raw Materials Inventory		8,450
To assign direct materials to jobs.		
Goods in Process Inventory (Job 401)	5,100	
Goods in Process Inventory (Job 402)	6,000	
Goods in Process Inventory (Job 403)	800	
Factory Payroll		11,900
To assign direct labor to jobs.		
Goods in Process Inventory (Job 401)	7,650	
Goods in Process Inventory (Job 402)	9,000	
Goods in Process Inventory (Job 403)	1,200	
Factory Overhead		17,850
To apply overhead to jobs.		

c. Transfer of completed jobs to Finished Goods Inventory.

Account	Debit	Credit
Finished Goods Inventory	42,650	
Goods in Process Inventory (Job 401)		24,150
Goods in Process Inventory (Job 402)		18,500
To record completion of jobs.		

d.

Account	Debit	Credit
Cost of Goods Sold	24,150	
Finished Goods Inventory		24,150
To record sale of Job 401.		

e.

Account	Debit	Credit
Cost of Goods Sold	150	
Factory Overhead		150
To assign underapplied overhead.		

3.

WALCZAK COMPANY Manufacturing Statement For Month Ended May 31		
Direct materials		$ 8,450
Direct labor		11,900
Factory overhead		
Indirect materials	$5,000	
Indirect labor	3,500	
Other factory overhead	9,500	18,000
Total production costs		38,350
Add goods in process, April 30		7,850
Total cost of goods in process		46,200
Less goods in process, May 31		3,400
Less underapplied overhead		150
Cost of goods manufactured		$42,650

Note how underapplied overhead is reported. Overapplied overhead is similarly reported, but is added.

Summary

C1 Explain the cost accounting system. A cost accounting system records production activities using a perpetual inventory system, which continuously updates records for transactions and events that affect inventory costs.

C2 Describe important features of job order production. Certain companies called *job order manufacturers* produce custom-made products for customers. These customized products are produced in response to a customer's orders. A job order manufacturer produces products that usually are different and, typically, produced in low volumes. The production systems of job order companies are flexible and are not highly standardized.

C3 Explain job cost sheets and how they are used in job order cost accounting. In a job order cost accounting system, the costs of producing each job are accumulated on a separate job cost sheet. Costs of direct materials, direct labor, and overhead are accumulated separately on the job cost sheet and then added to determine the total cost of a job. Job cost sheets for jobs in process, finished jobs, and jobs sold make up subsidiary records controlled by general ledger accounts.

A1 Apply job order costing in pricing services. Job order costing can usefully be applied to a service setting. The resulting job cost estimate can then be used to help determine a price for services.

P1 Describe and record the flow of materials costs in job order cost accounting. Costs of materials flow from receiving reports to materials ledger cards and then to either job cost sheets or the Indirect Materials account in the factory overhead ledger.

P2 Describe and record the flow of labor costs in job order cost accounting. Costs of labor flow from clock cards to the Factory Payroll account and then to either job cost sheets or the Indirect Labor account in the factory overhead ledger.

P3 Describe and record the flow of overhead costs in job order cost accounting. Overhead costs are accumulated in the Factory Overhead account that controls the subsidiary factory overhead ledger. Then, using a predetermined overhead rate, overhead costs are charged to jobs.

P4 Determine adjustments for overapplied and underapplied factory overhead. At the end of each period, the Factory Overhead account usually has a residual debit (underapplied overhead) or credit (overapplied overhead) balance. If the balance is not material, it is transferred to Cost of Goods Sold, but if it is material, it is allocated to Goods in Process Inventory, Finished Goods Inventory, and Cost of Goods Sold.

Guidance Answers to **Decision Maker** and **Decision Ethics**

Management Consultant Service companies (such as this consulting firm) do not recognize goods in process inventory or finished goods inventory—an important difference between service and manufacturing companies. For the two jobs that are 60% complete, you could recognize revenues and costs at 60% of the total expected amounts. This means you could recognize revenue of $7,200 (0.60 × $12,000) and costs of $6,000 (0.60 × $10,000), yielding net income of $1,200 from each job.

Web Consultant The partner has a monetary incentive to *manage* the numbers and assign more costs to the two cost-plus engagements. This also would reduce costs on the fixed-price engagements. To act in such a manner is unethical. As a professional and an honest person, it is your responsibility to engage in ethical behavior. You must not comply with the partner's instructions. If the partner insists you act in an unethical manner, you should report the matter to a higher authority in the organization.

Entrepreneur An inadequate cost system can distort product costs. You should review overhead costs in detail. Once you know the different cost elements in overhead, you can classify them into groups such as material related, labor related, or machine related. Other groups can also be formed (we discuss this in Chapter 21). Once you have classified overhead items into groups, you can better establish overhead allocation bases and use them to compute predetermined overhead rates. These multiple rates and bases can then be used to assign overhead costs to products. This will likely improve product pricing.

Sales Manager The price based on AdWorld's normal pricing policy is $20,150 ($17,076 × 1.18), which is within the price range offered by competitors. One option is to apply normal pricing policy and quote a price of $20,150. On the other hand, assessing the competition, particularly in terms of their service quality and other benefits they might offer, would be useful. Although price is an input customers use to select suppliers, factors such as quality and timeliness (responsiveness) of suppliers are important. Accordingly, your price can reflect such factors.

Guidance Answers to **Quick Checks**

1. *b*
2. A job is a special order for a custom product. A job lot consists of a quantity of identical, special-order items.
3. *a*
4. Three costs normally accumulated on a job cost sheet are direct materials, direct labor, and factory overhead.
5. *c*
6. Four sources of factory overhead are materials requisitions, time tickets, vouchers, and adjusting entries.
7. Since a job order cost accounting system uses perpetual inventory records, overhead costs must be assigned to jobs before the end of a period. This requires the use of a predetermined overhead rate.
8. Debits are recorded when wages and salaries of factory employees are paid or accrued. Credits are recorded when direct labor costs are assigned to jobs and when indirect labor costs are transferred to the Factory Overhead account.
9. Overapplied or underapplied overhead usually exists at the end of a period because application of overhead is based on estimates of overhead and another variable such as direct labor. Estimates rarely equal actual amounts incurred.
10. A debit balance reflects underapplied factory overhead.

Key Terms

mhhe.com/wildFAP19e

Key Terms are available at the book's Website for learning and testing in an online Flashcard Format.

Clock card (p. 776)
Cost accounting system (p. 770)
Finished Goods Inventory (p. 772)
General accounting system (p. 770)
Goods in Process Inventory (p. 772)
Job (p. 770)
Job cost sheet (p. 772)
Job lot (p. 771)
Job order cost accounting system (p. 772)
Job order production (p. 770)
Materials ledger card (p. 773)
Materials requisition (p. 774)
Overapplied overhead (p. 782)
Predetermined overhead rate (p. 778)
Target cost (p. 771)
Time ticket (p. 776)
Underapplied overhead (p. 781)

Multiple Choice Quiz

Answers on p. 805.

mhhe.com/wildFAP19e

Additional Quiz Questions are available at the book's Website.

Quiz19

1. A company's predetermined overhead allocation rate is 150% of its direct labor costs. How much overhead is applied to a job that requires total direct labor costs of $30,000?
   a. $15,000
   b. $30,000
   c. $45,000
   d. $60,000
   e. $75,000
2. A company's cost accounting system uses direct labor costs to apply overhead to goods in process and finished goods inventories. Its production costs for the period are: direct materials, $45,000; direct labor, $35,000; and overhead applied, $38,500. What is its predetermined overhead allocation rate?
   a. 10%
   b. 110%
   c. 86%
   d. 91%
   e. 117%
3. A company's ending inventory of finished goods has a total cost of $10,000 and consists of 500 units. If the overhead applied to these goods is $4,000, and the predetermined

overhead rate is 80% of direct labor costs, how much direct materials cost was incurred in producing these 500 units?
a. $10,000
b. $ 6,000
c. $ 4,000
d. $ 5,000
e. $ 1,000

4. A company's Goods in Process Inventory T-account follows.

Goods in Process Inventory			
Beginning balance	9,000		
Direct materials	94,200		
Direct labor	59,200	?	Finished goods
Overhead applied	31,600		
Ending balance	17,800		

The cost of units transferred to Finished Goods inventory is
a. $193,000
b. $211,800
c. $185,000
d. $144,600
e. $176,200

5. At the end of its current year, a company learned that its overhead was underapplied by $1,500 and that this amount is not considered material. Based on this information, the company should
a. Close the $1,500 to Finished Goods Inventory.
b. Close the $1,500 to Cost of Goods Sold.
c. Carry the $1,500 to the next period.
d. Do nothing about the $1,500 because it is not material and it is likely that overhead will be overapplied by the same amount next year.
e. Carry the $1,500 to the Income Statement as "Other Expense."

Discussion Questions

1. Why must a company estimate the amount of factory overhead assigned to individual jobs or job lots?

2. The chapter used a percent of labor cost to assign factory overhead to jobs. Identify another factor (or base) a company might reasonably use to assign overhead costs.

3. What information is recorded on a job cost sheet? How do management and employees use job cost sheets?

4. In a job order cost accounting system, what records serve as a subsidiary ledger for Goods in Process Inventory? For Finished Goods Inventory?

5. What journal entry is recorded when a materials manager receives a materials requisition and then issues materials (both direct and indirect) for use in the factory?

6. How does the materials requisition help safeguard a company's assets?

7. What is the difference between a clock card and a time ticket?

8. What events cause debits to be recorded in the Factory Overhead account? What events cause credits to be recorded in the Factory Overhead account?

9. What account(s) is(are) used to eliminate overapplied or underapplied overhead from the Factory Overhead account, assuming the amount is not material?

10. Assume that **Apple** produces a batch of 1,000 iPods. Does it account for this as 1,000 individual jobs or as a job lot? Explain (consider costs and benefits).

11. Why must a company prepare a predetermined overhead rate when using job order cost accounting?

12. How would a hospital apply job order costing? Explain.

13. **Harley-Davidson** manufactures 30 custom-made, luxury-model motorcycles. Does it account for these motorcycles as 30 individual jobs or as a job lot? Explain.

Harley-Davidson

14. **Best Buy**'s GeekSquad performs computer and home theater installation and service, for an upfront flat price. How can Best Buy use a job order costing system?

Denotes Discussion Questions that involve decision making.

Available with McGraw-Hill's Homework Manager

McGraw-Hill's HOMEWORK MANAGER®

QUICK STUDY

QS 19-1
Jobs and job lots
C2

Determine which products are most likely to be manufactured as a job and which as a job lot.

1. A custom-designed home.
2. Hats imprinted with company logo.
3. Little League trophies.
4. A hand-crafted table.
5. A 90-foot motor yacht.
6. Wedding dresses for a chain of stores.

QS 19-2
Job cost computation
C3

The following information is from the materials requisitions and time tickets for Job 9-1005 completed by Franklin Boats. The requisitions are identified by code numbers starting with the letter Q and the time tickets start with W. At the start of the year, management estimated that overhead cost would equal 110% of direct labor cost for each job. Determine the total cost on the job cost sheet for Job 9-1005.

Date	Document	Amount
7/1/2009	Q-4698	$2,500
7/1/2009	W-3393	1,200
7/5/2009	Q-4725	2,000
7/5/2009	W-3479	900
7/10/2009	W-3559	600

QS 19-3
Direct materials journal entries
P1

During the current month, a company that uses a job order cost accounting system purchases $25,000 in raw materials for cash. It then uses $6,000 of raw materials indirectly as factory supplies and uses $16,000 of raw materials as direct materials. Prepare entries to record these three transactions.

QS 19-4
Direct labor journal entries P2

During the current month, a company that uses a job order cost accounting system incurred a monthly factory payroll of $75,000, paid in cash. Of this amount, $29,000 is classified as indirect labor and the remainder as direct. Prepare entries to record these transactions.

QS 19-5
Factory overhead rates P3

A company incurred the following manufacturing costs this period: direct labor, $234,000; direct materials, $292,000; and factory overhead, $58,500. Compute its overhead cost as a percent of (1) direct labor and (2) direct materials.

QS 19-6
Factory overhead journal entries
P3

During the current month, a company that uses a job order cost accounting system incurred a monthly factory payroll of $350,000, paid in cash. Of this amount, $90,000 is classified as indirect labor and the remainder as direct for the production of Job 65A. Factory overhead is applied at 90% of direct labor. Prepare the entry to apply factory overhead to this job lot.

QS 19-7
Entry for over- or underapplied overhead P4

A company allocates overhead at a rate of 150% of direct labor cost. Actual overhead cost for the current period is $475,000, and direct labor cost is $300,000. Prepare the entry to close over- or underapplied overhead to cost of goods sold.

McGraw-Hill's HOMEWORK MANAGER® Available with McGraw-Hill's Homework Manager

EXERCISES

Exercise 19-1
Documents in job order cost accounting
C2 C3 P1 P2 P3

The left column lists the titles of documents and accounts used in job order cost accounting. The right column presents short descriptions of the purposes of the documents. Match each document in the left column to its numbered description in the right column.

A. Voucher
B. Materials requisition
C. Factory Overhead account
D. Clock card
E. Factory Payroll account
F. Materials ledger card
G. Time ticket

____ **1.** Shows amount of time an employee works on a job.
____ **2.** Temporarily accumulates incurred labor costs until they are assigned to specific jobs or to overhead.
____ **3.** Shows only total time an employee works each day.
____ **4.** Perpetual inventory record of raw materials received, used, and available for use.
____ **5.** Shows amount approved for payment of an overhead or other cost.
____ **6.** Temporarily accumulates the cost of incurred overhead until the cost is assigned to specific jobs.
____ **7.** Communicates the need for materials to complete a job.

Exercise 19-2
Analysis of cost flows
C2 P1 P2 P3

As of the end of June, the job cost sheets at Tracer Wheels, Inc., show the following total costs accumulated on three custom jobs.

	Job 102	Job 103	Job 104
Direct materials	$25,000	$59,000	$56,000
Direct labor	14,000	26,700	40,000
Overhead	7,000	13,350	20,000

Job 102 was started in production in May and the following costs were assigned to it in May: direct materials, $13,000; direct labor, $3,600; and overhead, $1,600. Jobs 103 and 104 are started in June. Overhead cost is applied with a predetermined rate based on direct labor cost. Jobs 102 and 103 are finished in June, and Job 104 is expected to be finished in July. No raw materials are used indirectly in June. Using this information, answer the following questions. (Assume this company's predetermined overhead rate did not change across these months).

1. What is the cost of the raw materials requisitioned in June for each of the three jobs?
2. How much direct labor cost is incurred during June for each of the three jobs?
3. What predetermined overhead rate is used during June?
4. How much total cost is transferred to finished goods during June?

Check (4) $145,050

Exercise 19-3
Overhead rate; costs assigned to jobs
P3

In December 2008, Matsushi Electronics' management establishes the year 2009 predetermined overhead rate based on direct labor cost. The information used in setting this rate includes estimates that the company will incur $750,000 of overhead costs and $500,000 of direct labor cost in year 2009. During March 2009, Matsushi began and completed Job No. 13-56.

1. What is the predetermined overhead rate for year 2009?
2. Use the information on the following job cost sheet to determine the total cost of the job.

Check (2) $23,450

JOB COST SHEET

Customer's Name: ESPN Co. **Job No.** 13-56

Job Description: 5 plasma monitors—150 inch

	Direct Materials		Direct Labor		Overhead Costs Applied	
Date	**Requisition No.**	**Amount**	**Time-Ticket No.**	**Amount**	**Rate**	**Amount**
Mar. 8	4-129	$4,000	T-306	$ 680		
Mar. 11	4-142	7,450	T-432	1,280		
Mar. 18	4-167	3,800	T-456	1,320		
Totals						

Exercise 19-4
Analysis of costs assigned to goods in process
P3

Wilson Company uses a job order cost accounting system that charges overhead to jobs on the basis of direct material cost. At year-end, the Goods in Process Inventory account shows the following.

Accounting System
File Edit Maintain Tasks Analysis Options Reports Window Help

Goods in Process Inventory — Acct. No. 121

Date	Explanation	Debit	Credit	Balance
2009				
Dec. 31	Direct materials cost	1,200,000		1,200,000
31	Direct labor cost	270,000		1,470,000
31	Overhead costs	480,000		1,950,000
31	To finished goods		1,860,000	90,000

Sales Purchases General Ledger Payroll Inventory Company Analysis

1. Determine the overhead rate used (based on direct material cost).
2. Only one job remained in the goods in process inventory at December 31, 2009. Its direct materials cost is $40,000. How much direct labor cost and overhead cost are assigned to it?

Check (2) Direct labor cost, $34,000

Exercise 19-5
Cost flows in a job order cost system
C3 P3

The following information is available for SafeLife Company, which produces special-order security products and uses a job order cost accounting system.

	April 30	May 31
Inventories		
Raw materials	$27,000	$ 41,000
Goods in process	9,000	20,600
Finished goods	70,000	33,000
Activities and information for May		
Raw materials purchases (paid with cash)		183,000
Factory payroll (paid with cash)		500,000
Factory overhead		
Indirect materials		6,000
Indirect labor		74,000
Other overhead costs		95,500
Sales (received in cash)		1,500,000
Predetermined overhead rate based on direct labor cost		55%

Compute the following amounts for the month of May.

1. Cost of direct materials used.
2. Cost of direct labor used.
3. Cost of goods manufactured.
4. Cost of goods sold.*
5. Gross profit.
6. Overapplied or underapplied overhead.

*Do not consider any underapplied or overapplied overhead.

Check (3) $811,700

Exercise 19-6
Journal entries for a job order cost accounting system
P1 P2 P3 P4

Use information in Exercise 19-5 to prepare journal entries for the following events in May.

1. Raw materials purchases for cash.
2. Direct materials usage.
3. Indirect materials usage.
4. Factory payroll costs in cash.
5. Direct labor usage.
6. Indirect labor usage.
7. Factory overhead excluding indirect materials and indirect labor (record credit to Other Accounts).
8. Application of overhead to goods in process.
9. Transfer of finished jobs to the finished goods inventory.
10. Sale and delivery of finished goods to customers for cash (record unadjusted cost of sales).
11. Allocation (closing) of overapplied or underapplied overhead to Cost of Goods Sold.

Exercise 19-7
Factory overhead computed, applied, and adjusted
P3 P4

In December 2008, Dreamvision established its predetermined overhead rate for movies produced during year 2009 by using the following cost predictions: overhead costs, $1,700,000, and direct labor costs, $500,000. At year end 2009, the company's records show that actual overhead costs for the year are $1,710,000. Actual direct labor cost had been assigned to jobs as follows.

Movies completed and released	$400,000
Movies still in production	90,000
Total actual direct labor cost	$490,000

1. Determine the predetermined overhead rate for year 2009.
2. Set up a T-account for overhead and enter the overhead costs incurred and the amounts applied to movies during the year using the predetermined overhead rate.
3. Determine whether overhead is overapplied or underapplied (and the amount) during the year.
4. Prepare the adjusting entry to allocate any over- or underapplied overhead to Cost of Goods Sold.

Check (3) $44,000 underapplied

Exercise 19-8
Factory overhead computed, applied, and adjusted
P3 P4

In December 2008, Jens Company established its predetermined overhead rate for jobs produced during year 2009 by using the following cost predictions: overhead costs, $1,500,000, and direct labor costs, $1,250,000. At year end 2009, the company's records show that actual overhead costs for the year are $1,660,000. Actual direct labor cost had been assigned to jobs as follows.

Jobs completed and sold	$1,027,500
Jobs in finished goods inventory	205,500
Jobs in goods in process inventory	137,000
Total actual direct labor cost	$1,370,000

1. Determine the predetermined overhead rate for year 2009.
2. Set up a T-account for Factory Overhead and enter the overhead costs incurred and the amounts applied to jobs during the year using the predetermined overhead rate.
3. Determine whether overhead is overapplied or underapplied (and the amount) during the year.
4. Prepare the adjusting entry to allocate any over- or underapplied overhead to Cost of Goods Sold.

Check (3) $16,000 underapplied

Exercise 19-9
Overhead rate calculation, allocation, and analysis P3

Campton Company applies factory overhead based on direct labor costs. The company incurred the following costs during 2009: direct materials costs, $635,500; direct labor costs, $2,000,000; and factory overhead costs applied, $1,200,000.

1. Determine the company's predetermined overhead rate for year 2009.
2. Assuming that the company's $54,000 ending Goods in Process Inventory account for year 2009 had $13,000 of direct labor costs, determine the inventory's direct materials costs.
3. Assuming that the company's $337,435 ending Finished Goods Inventory account for year 2009 had $137,435 of direct materials costs, determine the inventory's direct labor costs and its overhead costs.

Check (3) $75,000 overhead costs

Exercise 19-10
Costs allocated to ending inventories
P3

Santana Company's ending Goods in Process Inventory account consists of 10,000 units of partially completed product, and its Finished Goods Inventory account consists of 12,000 units of product. The factory manager determines that Goods in Process Inventory includes direct materials cost of $20 per unit and direct labor cost of $14 per unit. Finished goods are estimated to have $24 of direct materials cost per unit and $18 of direct labor cost per unit. The company established the predetermined overhead rate using the following predictions: estimated direct labor cost, $600,000, and estimated factory overhead, $750,000. The company allocates factory overhead to its goods in process and finished goods inventories based on direct labor cost. During the period, the company incurred these costs: direct materials, $1,070,000; direct labor, $580,000; and factory overhead applied, $725,000.

1. Determine the predetermined overhead rate.
2. Compute the total cost of the two ending inventories.
3. Compute cost of goods sold for the year (assume no beginning inventories and no underapplied or overapplied overhead).

Check (3) Cost of goods sold, $1,086,000

Exercise 19-11
Cost-based pricing
A1

Clemente Corporation has requested bids from several architects to design its new corporate headquarters. Troy Architects is one of the firms bidding on the job. Troy estimates that the job will require the following direct labor.

	Labor	Estimated Hours	Hourly Rate
2	Architects	300	$400
3	Staff	300	65
4	Clerical	600	20

Troy applies overhead to jobs at 160% of direct labor cost. Troy would like to earn at least $90,000 profit on the architectural job. Based on past experience and market research, it estimates that the competition will bid between $450,000 and $550,000 for the job.

1. What is Troy's estimated cost of the architectural job?

2. What bid would you suggest that Troy submit?

Check (1) $393,900

McGraw-Hill's HOMEWORK MANAGER® Available with McGraw-Hill's Homework Manager

PROBLEM SET A

Problem 19-1A
Production costs computed and recorded; reports prepared

C3 P1 P2 P3 P4 

Lemmon Co.'s March 31 inventory of raw materials is $170,000. Raw materials purchases in April are $310,000, and factory payroll cost in April is $224,000. Overhead costs incurred in April are: indirect materials, $25,000; indirect labor, $19,000; factory rent, $25,000; factory utilities, $13,000; and factory equipment depreciation, $41,000. The predetermined overhead rate is 65% of direct labor cost. Job 306 is sold for $400,000 cash in April. Costs of the three jobs worked on in April follow.

	Job 306	Job 307	Job 308
Balances on March 31			
Direct materials	$ 9,000	$ 17,000	
Direct labor	19,000	5,000	
Applied overhead	12,350	3,250	
Costs during April			
Direct materials	75,000	160,000	$ 65,000
Direct labor	31,000	74,000	100,000
Applied overhead	?	?	?
Status on April 30	Finished (sold)	Finished (unsold)	In process

Required

1. Determine the total of each production cost incurred for April (direct labor, direct materials, and applied overhead), and the total cost assigned to each job (including the balances from March 31).

2. Prepare journal entries for the month of April to record the following.

a. Materials purchases (on credit), factory payroll (paid in cash), and actual overhead costs including indirect materials and indirect labor. (Factory rent and utilities are paid in cash.)

b. Assignment of direct materials, direct labor, and applied overhead costs to the Goods in Process Inventory.

c. Transfer of Jobs 306 and 307 to the Finished Goods Inventory.

d. Cost of goods sold for Job 306.

e. Revenue from the sale of Job 306.

f. Assignment of any underapplied or overapplied overhead to the Cost of Goods Sold account. (The amount is not material.)

Check (2f) $10,250 overapplied

3. Prepare a manufacturing statement for April (use a single line presentation for direct materials and show the details of overhead cost).

(3) Cost of goods manufactured, $473,850

4. Compute gross profit for April. Show how to present the inventories on the April 30 balance sheet.

Analysis Component

5. The over- or underapplied overhead is closed to Cost of Goods Sold. Discuss how this adjustment impacts business decision making regarding individual jobs or batches of jobs.

Problem 19-2A
Source documents, journal entries, overhead, and financial reports

P1 P2 P3 P4 

Mead Bay's computer system generated the following trial balance on December 31, 2009. The company's manager knows something is wrong with the trial balance because it does not show any balance for Goods in Process Inventory but does show balances for the Factory Payroll and Factory Overhead accounts.

	Debit	Credit
Cash	$ 40,000	
Accounts receivable	34,000	
Raw materials inventory	22,000	

[continued on next page]

[continued from previous page]

Goods in process inventory	0	
Finished goods inventory	12,000	
Prepaid rent	4,000	
Accounts payable		$ 8,500
Notes payable		11,500
Common stock		40,000
Retained earnings		84,000
Sales		178,000
Cost of goods sold	112,000	
Factory payroll	18,000	
Factory overhead	26,000	
Operating expenses	54,000	
Totals	$322,000	$322,000

After examining various files, the manager identifies the following six source documents that need to be processed to bring the accounting records up to date.

Materials requisition 21-3010:	$4,100 direct materials to Job 402
Materials requisition 21-3011:	$7,100 direct materials to Job 404
Materials requisition 21-3012:	$2,400 indirect materials
Labor time ticket 6052:	$2,000 direct labor to Job 402
Labor time ticket 6053:	$15,000 direct labor to Job 404
Labor time ticket 6054:	$1,000 indirect labor

Jobs 402 and 404 are the only units in process at year-end. The predetermined overhead rate is 150% of direct labor cost.

Required

1. Use information on the six source documents to prepare journal entries to assign the following costs.

a. Direct materials costs to Goods in Process Inventory.

b. Direct labor costs to Goods in Process Inventory.

c. Overhead costs to Goods in Process Inventory.

d. Indirect materials costs to the Factory Overhead account.

e. Indirect labor costs to the Factory Overhead account.

Check (2) $3,900 underapplied overhead

2. Determine the revised balance of the Factory Overhead account after making the entries in part 1. Determine whether there is any under- or overapplied overhead for the year. Prepare the adjusting entry to allocate any over- or underapplied overhead to Cost of Goods Sold, assuming the amount is not material.

(3) T. B. totals, $322,000

3. Prepare a revised trial balance.

(4) Net income, $8,100

4. Prepare an income statement for year 2009 and a balance sheet as of December 31, 2009.

Analysis Component

5. Assume that the $2,400 on materials requisition 21-3012 should have been direct materials charged to Job 404. Without providing specific calculations, describe the impact of this error on the income statement for 2009 and the balance sheet at December 31, 2009.

Problem 19-3A
Source documents, journal entries, and accounts in job order cost accounting
P1 P2 P3

Challenger Watercraft's predetermined overhead rate for year 2009 is 200% of direct labor. Information on the company's production activities during May 2009 follows.

a. Purchased raw materials on credit, $200,000.

b. Paid $130,000 cash for factory wages.

c. Paid $16,000 cash to a computer consultant to reprogram factory equipment.

d. Materials requisitions record use of the following materials for the month.

Job 136	$ 50,000
Job 137	33,000
Job 138	19,800
Job 139	22,600
Job 140	6,800
Total direct materials	132,200
Indirect materials	20,000
Total materials used	$152,200

e. Time tickets record use of the following labor for the month.

Job 136	$ 12,100
Job 137	10,800
Job 138	37,500
Job 139	39,400
Job 140	3,200
Total direct labor	103,000
Indirect labor	27,000
Total	$130,000

f. Applied overhead to Jobs 136, 138, and 139.
g. Transferred Jobs 136, 138, and 139 to Finished Goods.
h. Sold Jobs 136 and 138 on credit at a total price of $550,000.
i. The company incurred the following overhead costs during the month (credit Prepaid Insurance for expired factory insurance).

Depreciation of factory building	$68,500
Depreciation of factory equipment	37,500
Expired factory insurance	11,000
Accrued property taxes payable	35,000

j. Applied overhead at month-end to the Goods in Process (Jobs 137 and 140) using the predetermined overhead rate of 200% of direct labor cost.

Required

1. Prepare a job cost sheet for each job worked on during the month. Use the following simplified form.

Job No. ________	
Materials	$ ________
Labor	________
Overhead	________
Total cost	$ ________

2. Prepare journal entries to record the events and transactions *a* through *j*.

Check (2f) Cr. Factory Overhead, $178,000

3. Set up T-accounts for each of the following general ledger accounts, each of which started the month with a zero balance: Raw Materials Inventory; Goods in Process Inventory; Finished Goods Inventory; Factory Payroll; Factory Overhead; Cost of Goods Sold. Then post the journal entries to these T-accounts and determine the balance of each account.

Check (3) Finished Goods Inventory, $140,800

4. Prepare a report showing the total cost of each job in process and prove that the sum of their costs equals the Goods in Process Inventory account balance. Prepare similar reports for Finished Goods Inventory and Cost of Goods Sold.

Problem 19-4A
Overhead allocation and adjustment using a predetermined overhead rate

C3 P3 P4

mhhe.com/wildFAP19e

In December 2008, Zander Company's manager estimated next year's total direct labor cost assuming 50 persons working an average of 2,000 hours each at an average wage rate of $30 per hour. The manager also estimated the following manufacturing overhead costs for year 2009.

Indirect labor	$ 339,200
Factory supervision	240,000
Rent on factory building	140,000
Factory utilities	318,000
Factory insurance expired	88,000
Depreciation—Factory equipment	480,000
Repairs expense—Factory equipment	60,000
Factory supplies used	88,800
Miscellaneous production costs	46,000
Total estimated overhead costs	$1,800,000

At the end of 2009, records show the company incurred $1,554,900 of actual overhead costs. It completed and sold five jobs with the following direct labor costs: Job 201, $604,000; Job 202, $573,000; Job 203, $318,000; Job 204, $726,000; and Job 205, $324,000. In addition, Job 206 is in process at the end of 2009 and had been charged $27,000 for direct labor. No jobs were in process at the end of 2008. The company's predetermined overhead rate is based on direct labor cost.

Required

1. Determine the following.

a. Predetermined overhead rate for year 2009.

b. Total overhead cost applied to each of the six jobs during year 2009.

c. Over- or underapplied overhead at year-end 2009.

2. Assuming that any over- or underapplied overhead is not material, prepare the adjusting entry to allocate any over- or underapplied overhead to Cost of Goods Sold at the end of year 2009.

Check (1c) $11,700 underapplied

(2) Cr. Factory Overhead $11,700

Problem 19-5A
Production transactions; subsidiary records; and source documents

P1 P2 P3 P4

If the working papers that accompany this book are unavailable, do not attempt to solve this problem.
Morton Company manufactures variations of its product, a technopress, in response to custom orders from its customers. On May 1, the company had no inventories of goods in process or finished goods but held the following raw materials.

Material M	200 units @ $125 =	$25,000
Material R	95 units @ 90 =	8,550
Paint	55 units @ 40 =	2,200
Total cost		$35,750

On May 4, the company began working on two technopresses: Job 102 for Global Company and Job 103 for Kaddo Company.

Required

Follow the instructions in this list of activities and complete the sheets provided in the working papers.

a. Purchased raw materials on credit and recorded the following information from receiving reports and invoices.

Receiving Report No. 426, Material M, 250 units at $125 each.
Receiving Report No. 427, Material R, 90 units at $90 each.

Instructions: Record these purchases with a single journal entry and post it to general ledger T-accounts, using the transaction letter *a* to identify the entry. Enter the receiving report information on the materials ledger cards.

b. Requisitioned the following raw materials for production.

Requisition No. 35, for Job 102, 135 units of Material M.
Requisition No. 36, for Job 102, 72 units of Material R.
Requisition No. 37, for Job 103, 70 units of Material M.
Requisition No. 38, for Job 103, 38 units of Material R.
Requisition No. 39, for 15 units of paint.

Instructions: Enter amounts for direct materials requisitions on the materials ledger cards and the job cost sheets. Enter the indirect material amount on the materials ledger card and record a debit to the Indirect Materials account in the subsidiary factory overhead ledger. Do not record a journal entry at this time.

c. Received the following employee time tickets for work in May.

Time tickets Nos. 1 to 10 for direct labor on Job 102, $45,000.
Time tickets Nos. 11 to 30 for direct labor on Job 103, $32,500.
Time tickets Nos. 31 to 36 for equipment repairs, $9,625.

Instructions: Record direct labor from the time tickets on the job cost sheets and then debit indirect labor to the Indirect Labor account in the subsidiary factory overhead ledger. Do not record a journal entry at this time.

d. Paid cash for the following items during the month: factory payroll, $87,125, and miscellaneous overhead items, $51,000.

Instructions: Record these payments with journal entries and then post them to the general ledger accounts. Also record a debit in the Miscellaneous Overhead account in the subsidiary factory overhead ledger.

e. Finished Job 102 and transferred it to the warehouse. The company assigns overhead to each job with a predetermined overhead rate equal to 80% of direct labor cost.

Instructions: Enter the allocated overhead on the cost sheet for Job 102, fill in the cost summary section of the cost sheet, and then mark the cost sheet "Finished." Prepare a journal entry to record the job's completion and its transfer to Finished Goods and then post it to the general ledger accounts.

f. Delivered Job 102 and accepted the customer's promise to pay $200,000 within 30 days.

Instructions: Prepare journal entries to record the sale of Job 102 and the cost of goods sold. Post them to the general ledger accounts.

g. Applied overhead to Job 103 based on the job's direct labor to date.

Instructions: Enter overhead on the job cost sheet but do not make a journal entry at this time.

h. Recorded the total direct and indirect materials costs as reported on all the requisitions for the month.

Instructions: Prepare a journal entry to record these costs and post it to general ledger accounts.

Check (h) Dr. Goods in Process Inventory, $35,525

i. Recorded the total direct and indirect labor costs as reported on all time tickets for the month.

Instructions: Prepare a journal entry to record these costs and post it to general ledger accounts.

j. Recorded the total overhead costs applied to jobs.

Instructions: Prepare a journal entry to record the allocation of these overhead costs and post it to general ledger accounts.

Check Balance in Factory Overhead, $775 Cr., overapplied

PROBLEM SET B

Problem 19-1B
Production costs computed and recorded; reports prepared
C3 P1 P2 P3 P4 

Grant Co.'s August 31 inventory of raw materials is $75,000. Raw materials purchases in September are $200,000, and factory payroll cost in September is $110,000. Overhead costs incurred in September are: indirect materials, $15,000; indirect labor, $7,000; factory rent, $10,000; factory utilities, $6,000; and factory equipment depreciation, $15,000. The predetermined overhead rate is 50% of direct labor cost. Job 114 is sold for $190,000 cash in September. Costs for the three jobs worked on in September follow.

	Job 114	Job 115	Job 116
Balances on August 31			
Direct materials	$ 7,000	$ 9,000	
Direct labor	9,000	8,000	
Applied overhead	4,500	4,000	

[continued on next page]

[continued from previous page]

Costs during September			
Direct materials	50,000	85,000	$40,000
Direct labor	15,000	34,000	60,000
Applied overhead	?	?	?
Status on September 30	Finished (sold)	Finished (unsold)	In process

Required

1. Determine the total of each production cost incurred for September (direct labor, direct materials, and applied overhead), and the total cost assigned to each job (including the balances from August 31).

2. Prepare journal entries for the month of September to record the following.

a. Materials purchases (on credit), factory payroll (paid in cash), and actual overhead costs including indirect materials and indirect labor. (Factory rent and utilities are paid in cash.)

b. Assignment of direct materials, direct labor, and applied overhead costs to Goods in Process Inventory.

c. Transfer of Jobs 114 and 115 to the Finished Goods Inventory.

d. Cost of Job 114 in the Cost of Goods Sold account.

e. Revenue from the sale of Job 114.

Check (2f) $1,500 overapplied

f. Assignment of any underapplied or overapplied overhead to the Cost of Goods Sold account. (The amount is not material.)

(3) Cost of goods manufactured, $250,000

3. Prepare a manufacturing statement for September (use a single line presentation for direct materials and show the details of overhead cost).

4. Compute gross profit for September. Show how to present the inventories on the September 30 balance sheet.

Analysis Component

5. The over- or underapplied overhead adjustment is closed to Cost of Goods Sold. Discuss how this adjustment impacts business decision making regarding individual jobs or batches of jobs.

Problem 19-2B
Source documents, journal entries, overhead, and financial reports
P1 P2 P3 P4 

Coleman Company's computer system generated the following trial balance on December 31, 2009. The company's manager knows that the trial balance is wrong because it does not show any balance for Goods in Process Inventory but does show balances for the Factory Payroll and Factory Overhead accounts.

	Debit	Credit
Cash	$ 96,000	
Accounts receivable	84,000	
Raw materials inventory	52,000	
Goods in process inventory	0	
Finished goods inventory	18,000	
Prepaid rent	6,000	
Accounts payable		$ 21,000
Notes payable		27,000
Common stock		60,000
Retained earnings		174,000
Sales		360,000
Cost of goods sold	210,000	
Factory payroll	32,000	
Factory overhead	54,000	
Operating expenses	90,000	
Totals	$642,000	$642,000

After examining various files, the manager identifies the following six source documents that need to be processed to bring the accounting records up to date.

Materials requisition 94-231:	$9,200 direct materials to Job 603
Materials requisition 94-232:	$15,200 direct materials to Job 604
Materials requisition 94-233:	$4,200 indirect materials
Labor time ticket 765:	$10,000 direct labor to Job 603
Labor time ticket 766:	$16,000 direct labor to Job 604
Labor time ticket 777:	$6,000 indirect labor

Jobs 603 and 604 are the only units in process at year-end. The predetermined overhead rate is 200% of direct labor cost.

Required

1. Use information on the six source documents to prepare journal entries to assign the following costs.

a. Direct materials costs to Goods in Process Inventory.

b. Direct labor costs to Goods in Process Inventory.

c. Overhead costs to Goods in Process Inventory.

d. Indirect materials costs to the Factory Overhead account.

e. Indirect labor costs to the Factory Overhead account.

2. Determine the revised balance of the Factory Overhead account after making the entries in part 1. Determine whether there is under- or overapplied overhead for the year. Prepare the adjusting entry to allocate any over- or underapplied overhead to Cost of Goods Sold, assuming the amount is not material.

Check (2) $12,200 underapplied overhead

3. Prepare a revised trial balance.

(3) T. B. totals, $642,000

4. Prepare an income statement for year 2009 and a balance sheet as of December 31, 2009.

(4) Net income, $47,800

Analysis Component

5. Assume that the $4,200 indirect materials on materials requisition 94-233 should have been direct materials charged to Job 604. Without providing specific calculations, describe the impact of this error on the income statement for 2009 and the balance sheet at December 31, 2009.

Problem 19-3B
Source documents, journal entries, and accounts in job order cost accounting
P1 P2 P3

Bradley Company's predetermined overhead rate is 200% of direct labor. Information on the company's production activities during September 2009 follows.

a. Purchased raw materials on credit, $250,000.

b. Paid $168,000 cash for factory wages.

c. Paid $22,000 cash for miscellaneous factory overhead costs.

d. Materials requisitions record use of the following materials for the month.

Job 487	$60,000
Job 488	40,000
Job 489	24,000
Job 490	28,000
Job 491	8,000
Total direct materials	160,000
Indirect materials	24,000
Total materials used	$184,000

e. Time tickets record use of the following labor for the month.

Job 487	$ 16,000
Job 488	14,000
Job 489	50,000
Job 490	52,000
Job 491	4,000
Total direct labor	136,000
Indirect labor	32,000
Total	$168,000

f. Allocated overhead to Jobs 487, 489, and 490.
g. Transferred Jobs 487, 489, and 490 to Finished Goods.
h. Sold Jobs 487 and 489 on credit for a total price of $680,000.
i. The company incurred the following overhead costs during the month (credit Prepaid Insurance for expired factory insurance).

Depreciation of factory building	$74,000
Depreciation of factory equipment	42,000
Expired factory insurance	14,000
Accrued property taxes payable	62,000

j. Applied overhead at month-end to the Goods in Process (Jobs 488 and 491) using the predetermined overhead rate of 200% of direct labor cost.

Required

1. Prepare a job cost sheet for each job worked on in the month. Use the following simplified form.

Job No. ________	
Materials	$ ________
Labor	________
Overhead	________
Total cost	$ ________

Check (2f) Cr. Factory Overhead, $236,000

(3) Finished Goods Inventory, $184,000

2. Prepare journal entries to record the events and transactions *a* through *j*.
3. Set up T-accounts for each of the following general ledger accounts, each of which started the month with a zero balance: Raw Materials Inventory, Goods in Process Inventory, Finished Goods Inventory, Factory Payroll, Factory Overhead, Cost of Goods Sold. Then post the journal entries to these T-accounts and determine the balance of each account.
4. Prepare a report showing the total cost of each job in process and prove that the sum of their costs equals the Goods in Process Inventory account balance. Prepare similar reports for Finished Goods Inventory and Cost of Goods Sold.

Problem 19-4B
Overhead allocation and adjustment using a predetermined overhead rate
C3 P3 P4

In December 2008, Bigby Company's manager estimated next year's total direct labor cost assuming 100 persons working an average of 2,000 hours each at an average wage rate of $15 per hour. The manager also estimated the following manufacturing overhead costs for year 2009.

Indirect labor	$ 319,200
Factory supervision	240,000
Rent on factory building	140,000
Factory utilities	88,000
Factory insurance expired	68,000
Depreciation—Factory equipment	480,000
Repairs expense—Factory equipment	60,000
Factory supplies used	68,800
Miscellaneous production costs	36,000
Total estimated overhead costs	$1,500,000

At the end of 2009, records show the company incurred $1,450,000 of actual overhead costs. It completed and sold five jobs with the following direct labor costs: Job 625, $708,000; Job 626, $660,000; Job 627, $350,000; Job 628, $840,000; and Job 629, $368,000. In addition, Job 630 is in process at the end of 2009 and had been charged $20,000 for direct labor. No jobs were in process at the end of 2008. The company's predetermined overhead rate is based on direct labor cost.

Required

1. Determine the change in DSG's inventories for the last two years. Then identify the impact on net resources generated by operating activities (increase or decrease) for changes in inventory levels (increase or decrease) for DSG for the last two years.
2. Would a move to a JIT system likely impact DSG more than it would Best Buy or Circuit City? Explain.

ANSWERS TO MULTIPLE CHOICE QUIZ

1. c; $30,000 × 150% = $45,000
2. b; $38,500/$35,000 = 110%
3. e; Direct materials + Direct labor + Overhead = Total cost;
   Direct materials + ($4,000/.80) + $4,000 = $10,000
   Direct materials = $1,000
4. e; $9,000 + $94,200 + $59,200 + $31,600 − Finished goods = $17,800
   Thus, finished goods = $176,200
5. b

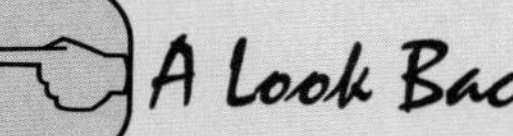

A Look Back

Chapter 18 introduced managerial accounting and described cost concepts and the reporting of manufacturing activities. Chapter 19 explained job order costing—an important cost accounting system for customized products and services.

A Look at This Chapter

This chapter focuses on how to measure and account for costs in process operations. We explain process production, describe how to assign costs to processes, and compute cost per equivalent unit for a process.

A Look Ahead

Chapter 21 explains how to allocate factory overhead costs to different products and introduces the activity-based costing method of overhead allocation. It also explains responsibility accounting and measures of departmental performance.

Chapter 20 Process Cost Accounting

Learning Objectives

CAP

Conceptual

C1 Explain process operations and the way they differ from job order operations. *(p. 808)*

C2 Define equivalent units and explain their use in process cost accounting. *(p. 815)*

C3 Explain the four steps in accounting for production activity in a period. *(p. 816)*

C4 Define a process cost summary and describe its purposes. *(p. 820)*

C5 *Appendix 20A*—Explain and illustrate the four steps in accounting for production activity using FIFO. *(p. 827)*

Analytical

A1 Compare process cost accounting and job order cost accounting. *(p. 809)*

A2 Explain and illustrate a hybrid costing system. *(p. 823)*

Procedural

P1 Record the flow of direct materials costs in process cost accounting. *(p. 812)*

P2 Record the flow of direct labor costs in process cost accounting. *(p. 813)*

P3 Record the flow of factory overhead costs in process cost accounting. *(p. 813)*

P4 Compute equivalent units produced in a period. *(p. 815)*

P5 Prepare a process cost summary. *(p. 820)*

P6 Record the transfer of completed goods to Finished Goods Inventory and Cost of Goods Sold. *(p. 821)*

LP20

Decision Feature

The Big Apple

"If we are willing to eat it, we're willing to squeeze it"
—David Ryan

HOOD RIVER, OR—After a few years of working in the family business of growing apples and making cider, David Ryan launched his own company, **Hood River Juice Company** [HRJCO.com], to focus on the processing stage of apple juice and cider. Like many entrepreneurs, David sought guidance from experienced mentors, in his case the Small Business Development Center located in the local community college. These mentors explained managerial accounting and the financial aspects of successful manufacturing.

Today, before an apple enters David's production process, it is inspected by his drivers when the apples are loaded from the field. A foreman then inspects the apples again when unloading them at his factory. David's factory employees then wash and hand select the best apples from those that survive the previous two inspections.

Apple quality is paramount. Explains David, "If we are willing to eat it, we're willing to squeeze it." From cutting apples into small pieces and squeezing those pieces into juice, through filtering the juice and packaging the finished product, David's production process is monitored and accounting reports are produced.

Entrepreneurs such as David are aided by process cost summaries that help them monitor and control the costs of material, labor, and overhead applied to production processes. For example, David tries to maintain regular full-time employees to better manage costs. Thus, he purchases and processes apples year-round as opposed to only seasonal production. David estimates this year-round process reduces his overhead costs by 40%. "Needless to say, every company has their own overhead they have to deal with," explains David. "If your total throughput is down by 35%, you must look elsewhere to get the margin to be sustainable. The only way to do that is to cut your overhead." Managerial accounting information aids in his decisions.

David's focus on cost management minimizes the risk of bad decisions, and his passion for quality control enables him to improve process operations. His overriding goal is customer satisfaction. That focus has led him to produce bulk apple juice for use in protein shakes and smoothies, and it has allowed his customers to select from over 50 varieties of apples for a custom-blended juice. Juice drinkers seem happy: From an initial investment of $36,000 in 2000, David's annual sales now exceed $14 million. Those are juicy numbers.

[Sources: *Hood River Juice Company Website*, January 2009; *Yakima-Herald.com*, March 2008; *Hood River News*, February 2006; *Entrepreneur*, April 2008]

Chapter Preview

The type of product or service a company offers determines its cost accounting system. Job order costing is used to account for custom products and services that meet the demands of a particular customer. Not all products are manufactured in this way; many carry standard designs so that one unit is no different than any other unit. Such a system often produces large numbers of units on a continuous basis, all of which pass through similar processes. This chapter describes how to use a process cost accounting system to account for these types of products. It also explains how costs are accumulated for each process and then assigned to units passing through those processes. This information helps us understand and estimate the cost of each process as well as find ways to reduce costs and improve processes.

Process Cost Accounting

Process Operations
- Comparing job order and process operations
- Organization of process operations
- GenX Company—an illustration

Process Cost Accounting
- Direct and indirect costs
- Accounting for materials costs
- Accounting for labor costs
- Accounting for factory overhead

Equivalent Units of Production (EUP)
- Accounting for goods in process
- Differences between EUP for materials, labor, and overhead

Process Costing Illustration
- Physical flow of units
- EUP
- Cost per EUP
- Cost reconciliation
- Process cost summary
- Transfers to finished goods and to cost of goods sold

Process Operations

C1 Explain process operations and the way they differ from job order operations.

Process operations, also called *process manufacturing* or *process production,* is the mass production of products in a continuous flow of steps. This means that products pass through a series of sequential processes. Petroleum refining is a common example of process operations. Crude oil passes through a series of steps before it is processed into different grades of petroleum. **Exxon Mobil**'s oil activities reflect a process operation. An important characteristic of process operations is the high level of standardization necessary if the system is to produce large volumes of products. Process operations also extend to services. Examples include mail sorting in large post offices and order processing in large mail-order firms such as **L.L. Bean**. The common feature in these service organizations is that operations are performed in a sequential manner using a series of standardized processes. Other companies using process operations include **Kellogg** (cereals), **Pfizer** (drugs), **Procter & Gamble** (household products), **Xerox** (copiers), **Coca-Cola** (soft drinks), **Heinz** (ketchup), **Penn** (tennis balls), and **Hershey** (chocolate). For a virtual tour of tennis ball manufacturing, see pennracquet.com/factory.html.

Each of these examples of products and services involves operations having a series of *processes,* or steps. Each process involves a different set of activities. A production operation that processes chemicals, for instance, might include the four steps shown in Exhibit 20.1. Understanding such processes for companies with process operations is crucial for measuring their costs. Increasingly, process operations use machines and automation to control product quality and reduce manufacturing costs.

EXHIBIT 20.1

Process Operations: Chemicals

Preparing the chemicals → Mixing the chemicals → Bottling the chemical mix → Packaging the bottles

Comparing Job Order and Process Operations

A1 Compare process cost accounting and job order cost accounting.

Job order and process operations can be considered as two ends of a continuum. Important features of both systems are shown in Exhibit 20.2. We often describe job order and process operations with manufacturing examples, but both also apply to service companies. In a job order costing system, the measurement focus is on the individual job or batch. In a process costing system, the measurement focus is on the process itself and the standardized units produced.

EXHIBIT 20.2

Comparing Job Order and Process Operations

Job Order Operations	Process Operations
• Custom orders	• Repetitive procedures
• Heterogeneous products and services	• Homogeneous products and services
• Low production volume	• High production volume
• High product flexibility	• Low product flexibility
• Low to medium standardization	• High standardization

Organization of Process Operations

In a process operation, each process is identified as a separate *production department, workstation,* or *work center.* With the exception of the first process or department, each receives the output from the prior department as a partially processed product. Depending on the nature of the process, a company applies direct labor, overhead, and, perhaps, additional direct materials to move the product toward completion. Only the final process or department in the series produces finished goods ready for sale to customers.

Tracking costs for several related departments can seem complex. Yet because process costing procedures are applied to the activity of each department or process separately, we need to consider only one process at a time. This simplifies the procedures.

When the output of one department becomes an input to another department, as is the case in sequential processing, we simply transfer the costs associated with those units from the first department into the next. We repeat these steps from department to department until the final process is complete. At that point the accumulated costs are transferred with the product from Goods in Process Inventory to Finished Goods Inventory. The next section illustrates a company with a single process, but the methods illustrated apply to a multiprocess scenario as each department's costs are handled separately for each department.

Decision Insight

Accounting for Health Many service companies use process departments to perform specific tasks for consumers. Hospitals, for instance, have radiology and physical therapy facilities with special equipment and trained employees. When patients need services, they are processed through departments to receive prescribed care. Service companies need process cost accounting information as much as manufacturers to estimate costs of services, to plan future operations, to control costs, and to determine customer charges.

GenX Company— An Illustration

The GenX Company illustrates process operations. It produces Profen®, an over-the-counter pain reliever for athletes. GenX sells Profen to wholesale distributors, who in turn sell it to retailers. Profen is produced by mixing its active ingredient, Profelene, with flavorings and preservatives, molding it into Profen tablets, and packaging the tablets. Exhibit 20.3 shows a summary floor plan of the GenX factory, which has five areas.

1. *Storeroom*—materials are received and then distributed when requisitioned.
2. *Production support offices*—used by administrative and maintenance employees who support manufacturing operations.
3. *Locker rooms*—workers change from street clothes into sanitized uniforms before working in the factory.
4. *Production floor*—area where the powder is processed into tablets.
5. *Warehouse*—finished products are stored before being shipped to wholesalers.

Point: Electronic monitoring of operations is common in factories.

EXHIBIT 20.3

Floor Plan of GenX's Factory

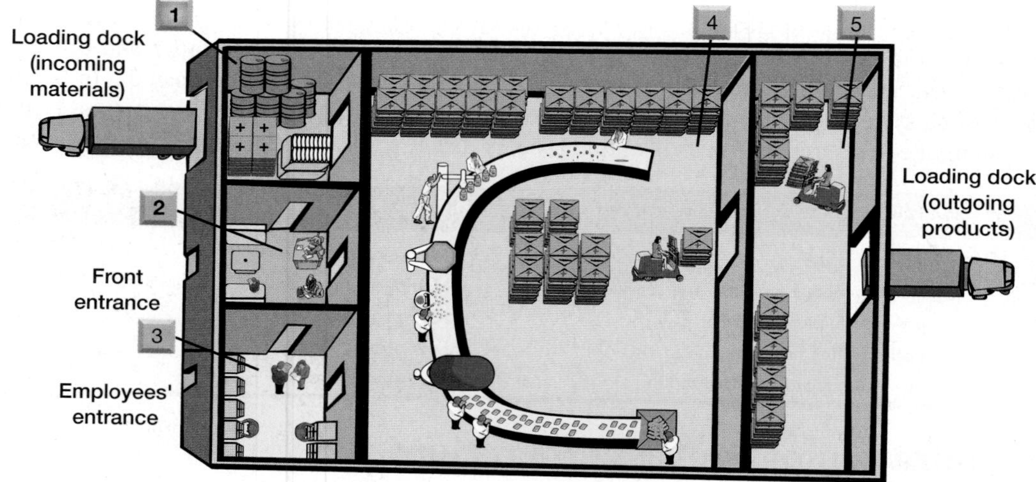

The first step in process manufacturing is to decide when to produce a product. Management determines the types and quantities of materials and labor needed and then schedules the work. Unlike a job order process, where production often begins only after receipt of a custom order, managers of companies with process operations often forecast the demand expected for their products. Based on these plans, production begins. The flowchart in Exhibit 20.4 shows the production steps for GenX. The following sections explain how GenX uses a process cost accounting system to compute these costs. Many of the explanations refer to this exhibit and its numbered cost flows ① through ⑩. (*Hint:* The amounts for the numbered cost flows in Exhibit 20.4 are summarized in Exhibit 20.21. Those amounts are explained in the following pages, but it can help to refer to Exhibit 20.21 as we proceed through the explanations.)

EXHIBIT 20.4

Process Operations and Costs: GenX

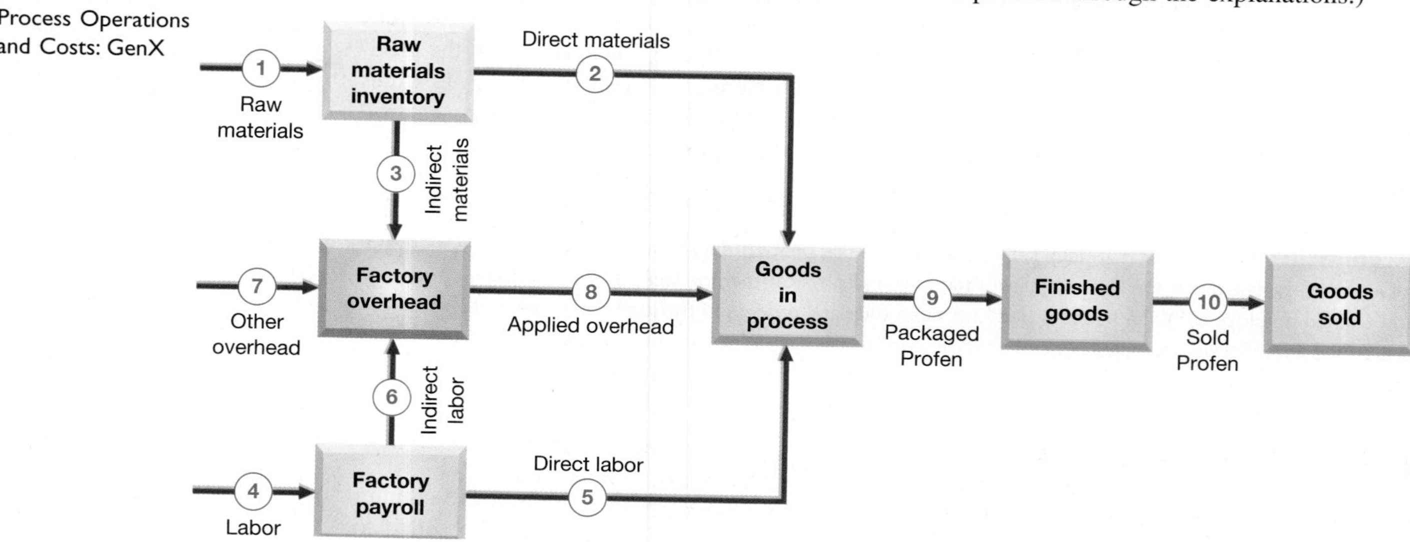

Process Cost Accounting

Video20.1

Process and job order operations are similar in that both combine materials, labor, and overhead in the process of producing products. They differ in how they are organized and managed. The measurement focus in a job order costing system is on the individual job or batch, whereas in a process costing system, it is on the individual process. Regardless of the measurement focus, we are ultimately interested in determining the cost per unit of product (or service) resulting from either system.

Specifically, the **job order cost accounting system** assigns direct materials, direct labor, and overhead to jobs. The total job cost is then divided by the number of units to compute a cost per unit for that job. The **process cost accounting system** assigns direct materials, direct labor, and overhead to specific processes (or departments). The total costs associated with each process are then divided by the number of units passing through that process to determine the cost per equivalent unit (defined later in the chapter) for that process. Differences in the way these two systems apply materials, labor, and overhead costs are highlighted in Exhibit 20.5.

Point: The cost object in a job order system is the specific job; the cost object in a process costing system is the process.

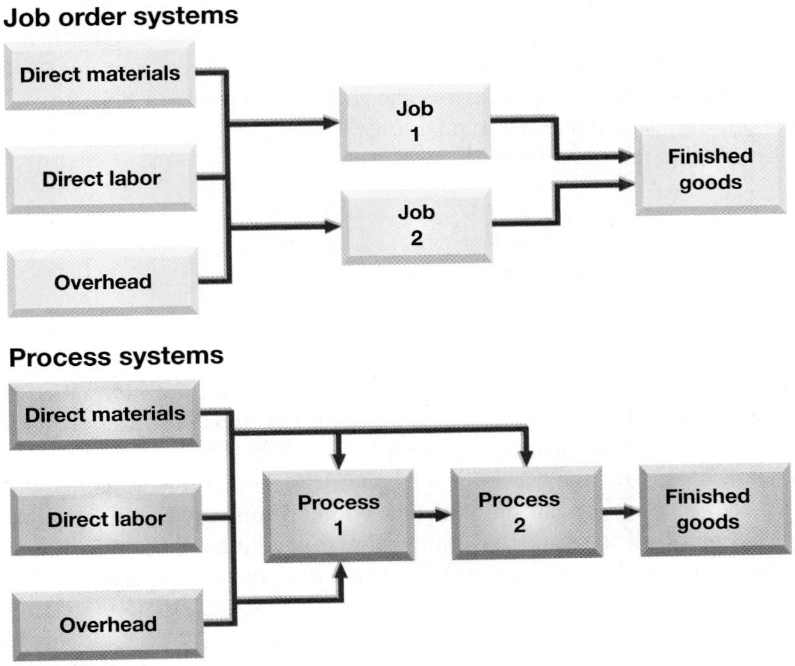

EXHIBIT 20.5

Comparing Job Order and Process Cost Accounting Systems

Direct and Indirect Costs

Like job order operations, process cost accounting systems use the concepts of direct and indirect costs. Materials and labor that can be traced to specific processes are assigned to those processes as direct costs. Materials and labor that cannot be traced to a specific process are indirect costs and are assigned to overhead. Some costs classified as overhead in a job order system may be classified as direct costs in process cost accounting. For example, depreciation of a machine used entirely by one process is a direct cost of that process.

Point: If a cost can be traced to the cost object, it is direct; if it cannot, it is indirect.

Decision Insight

JIT Boon to Process Operations Companies that adopt JIT manufacturing often organize their production system as a series of sequential processes. One survey found 60% of companies that converted to JIT used process operations; this compares to only 20% before converting to JIT.

P1 Record the flow of direct materials costs in process cost accounting.

Accounting for Materials Costs

In Exhibit 20.4, arrow line ① reflects the arrival of materials at GenX's factory. These materials include Profelene, flavorings, preservatives, and packaging. They also include supplies for the production support office. GenX uses a perpetual inventory system and makes all purchases on credit. The summary entry for receipts of raw materials in April follows (dates in journal entries numbered ① through ⑩ are omitted because they are summary entries, often reflecting two or more transactions or events).

Assets	= Liabilities	+ Equity
+11,095	+11,095	

		Debit	Credit
①	Raw Materials Inventory	11,095	
	Accounts Payable		11,095
	Acquired materials on credit for factory use.		

Arrow line ② in Exhibit 20.4 reflects the flow of direct materials to production, where they are used to produce Profen. Most direct materials are physically combined into the finished product; the remaining direct materials include those used and clearly linked with a specific process. The manager of a process usually obtains materials by submitting a *materials requisition* to the materials storeroom manager. In some situations, materials move continuously from raw materials inventory through the manufacturing process. **Pepsi Bottling**, for instance, uses a process in which inventory moves continuously through the system. In these cases, a **materials consumption report** summarizes the materials used by a department during a reporting period and replaces materials requisitions. The entry to record the use of direct materials by GenX's production department in April follows.

Assets	= Liabilities	+ Equity
+9,900		
−9,900		

		Debit	Credit
②	Goods in Process Inventory	9,900	
	Raw Materials Inventory		9,900
	To assign costs of direct materials used in production.		

This entry transfers costs from one asset account to another asset account. (When two or more production departments exist, a company uses two or more Goods in Process Inventory accounts to separately accumulate costs incurred by each.)

Example: What types of materials might the flow of arrow line ③ in Exhibit 20.4 reflect? *Answer:* Goggles, gloves, protective clothing, recordkeeping supplies, and cleaning supplies.

In Exhibit 20.4, the arrow line ③ reflects the flow of indirect materials from the storeroom to factory overhead. These materials are not clearly linked with any specific production process or department but are used to support overall production activity. The following entry records the cost of indirect materials used by GenX in April.

Assets	= Liabilities	+ Equity
−1,195		−1,195

		Debit	Credit
③	Factory Overhead	1,195	
	Raw Materials Inventory		1,195
	To record indirect materials used in April.		

After the entries for both direct and indirect materials are posted, the Raw Materials Inventory account appears as shown in Exhibit 20.6. The April 30 balance sheet reports the $4,000 Raw Materials Inventory account as a current asset.

EXHIBIT 20.6

Raw Materials Inventory

Raw Materials Inventory					Acct. No. 132
Date		Explanation	Debit	Credit	Balance
Mar.	31	Balance			4,000
Apr.	30	Materials purchases	11,095		15,095
	30	Direct materials usage		9,900	5,195
	30	Indirect materials usage		1,195	4,000

Accounting for Labor Costs

P2 Record the flow of direct labor costs in process cost accounting.

Exhibit 20.4 shows GenX factory payroll costs as reflected in arrow line ④. Total labor costs of $8,920 are paid in cash and are recorded in the Factory Payroll account.

④	Factory Payroll	8,920	
	Cash		8,920
	To record factory wages for April.		

Assets = Liabilities + Equity
−8,920 −8,920

Time reports from the production department and the production support office triggered this entry. (For simplicity, we do not separately identify withholdings and additional payroll taxes for employees.) In a process operation, the direct labor of a production department includes all labor used exclusively by that department. This is the case even if the labor is not applied to the product itself. If a production department in a process operation, for instance, has a full-time manager and a full-time maintenance worker, their salaries are direct labor costs of that process and are not factory overhead.

Arrow line ⑤ in Exhibit 20.4 shows GenX's use of direct labor in the production department. The following entry transfers April's direct labor costs from the Factory Payroll account to the Goods in Process Inventory account.

⑤	Goods in Process Inventory	5,700	
	Factory Payroll		5,700
	To assign costs of direct labor used in production.		

Assets = Liabilities + Equity
+5,700 +5,700

Arrow line ⑥ in Exhibit 20.4 reflects GenX's indirect labor costs. These employees provide clerical, maintenance, and other services that help produce Profen efficiently. For example, they order materials, deliver them to the factory floor, repair equipment, operate and program computers used in production, keep payroll and other production records, clean up, and move the finished goods to the warehouse. The following entry charges these indirect labor costs to factory overhead.

Point: A department's indirect labor cost might include an allocated portion of the salary of a manager who supervises two or more departments. Allocation of costs between departments is discussed in a later chapter.

⑥	Factory Overhead	3,220	
	Factory Payroll		3,220
	To record indirect labor as overhead.		

Assets = Liabilities + Equity
−3,220
+3,220

After these entries for both direct and indirect labor are posted, the Factory Payroll account appears as shown in Exhibit 20.7. The temporary Factory Payroll account is now closed to another temporary account, Factory Overhead, and is ready to receive entries for May. Next we show how to apply overhead to production and close the temporary Factory Overhead account.

EXHIBIT 20.7

Factory Payroll

Factory Payroll					Acct. No. 530
Date		**Explanation**	**Debit**	**Credit**	**Balance**
Mar.	31	Balance			0
Apr.	30	Total payroll for April	8,920		8,920
	30	Direct labor costs		5,700	3,220
	30	Indirect labor costs		3,220	0

Accounting for Factory Overhead

P3 Record the flow of factory overhead costs in process cost accounting.

Overhead costs other than indirect materials and indirect labor are reflected by arrow line ⑦ in Exhibit 20.4. These overhead items include the costs of insuring production assets, renting the factory building, using factory utilities, and depreciating equipment not directly related to a specific process. The following entry records overhead costs for April.

Assets = Liabilities + Equity
−180 +645 −2,425
−750
−850

		Debit	Credit
⑦	Factory Overhead	2,425	
	Prepaid Insurance		180
	Utilities Payable		645
	Cash		750
	Accumulated Depreciation—Factory Equipment		850
	To record overhead items incurred in April.		

After this entry is posted, the Factory Overhead account balance is $6,840, comprising indirect materials of $1,195, indirect labor of $3,220, and $2,425 of other overhead.

Arrow line ⑧ in Exhibit 20.4 reflects the application of factory overhead to production. Factory overhead is applied to processes by relating overhead cost to another variable such as direct labor hours or machine hours used. With increasing automation, companies with process operations are more likely to use machine hours to allocate overhead. In some situations, a single allocation basis such as direct labor hours (or a single rate for the entire plant) fails to provide useful allocations. As a result, management can use different rates for different production departments. Based on an analysis of its operations, GenX applies its April overhead at a rate of 120% of direct labor cost, as shown in Exhibit 20.8.

Point: The time it takes to process (cycle) products through a process is sometimes used to allocate costs.

EXHIBIT 20.8
Applying Factory Overhead

	Direct Labor Cost	Predetermined Rate	Overhead Applied
Production Department	$5,700	120%	$6,840

GenX records its applied overhead with the following entry.

Assets = Liabilities + Equity
+6,840 +6,840

		Debit	Credit
⑧	Goods in Process Inventory	6,840	
	Factory Overhead		6,840
	Allocated overhead costs to production at 120% of direct labor cost.		

After posting this entry, the Factory Overhead account appears as shown in Exhibit 20.9. For GenX, the amount of overhead applied equals the actual overhead incurred during April. In most cases, using a predetermined overhead rate leaves an overapplied or underapplied balance in the Factory Overhead account. At the end of the period, this overapplied or underapplied balance should be closed to the Cost of Goods Sold account, as described in the job order costing chapter.

EXHIBIT 20.9
Factory Overhead

Example: If applied overhead results in a $6,940 credit to the factory overhead account, does it yield an over- or underapplied overhead amount? *Answer:* $100 overapplied overhead

Factory Overhead					Acct. No. 540
Date		Explanation	Debit	Credit	Balance
Mar.	31	Balance			0
Apr.	30	Indirect materials usage	1,195		1,195
	30	Indirect labor costs	3,220		4,415
	30	Other overhead costs	2,425		6,840
	30	Applied to production departments		6,840	0

Decision Ethics

Budget Officer You are working to identify the direct and indirect costs of a new processing department that has several machines. This department's manager instructs you to classify a majority of the costs as indirect to take advantage of the direct labor-based overhead allocation method so it will be charged a lower amount of overhead (because of its small direct labor cost). This would penalize other departments with higher allocations. It also will cause the performance ratings of managers in these other departments to suffer. What action do you take? [Answer—p. 832]

Quick Check

Answers—p. 833

1. A process operation (*a*) is another name for a job order operation, (*b*) does not use the concepts of direct materials or direct labor, or (*c*) typically produces large quantities of homogeneous products or services.
2. Under what conditions is a process cost accounting system more suitable for measuring production costs than a job order cost accounting system?
3. When direct materials are assigned and used in production, the entry to record their use includes (*a*) a credit to Goods in Process Inventory, (*b*) a debit to Goods in Process Inventory, or (*c*) a debit to Raw Materials Inventory.
4. What are the three cost categories incurred by both job order and process operations?
5. How many Goods in Process Inventory accounts are needed in a process cost system?

Equivalent Units of Production

C2 Define equivalent units and explain their use in process cost accounting.

We explained how materials, labor, and overhead costs for a period are accumulated in the Goods in Process Inventory account, but we have not explained the arrow lines labeled ⑨ and ⑩ in Exhibit 20.4. These lines reflect the transfer of products from the production department to finished goods inventory, and from finished goods inventory to cost of goods sold. To determine the costs recorded for these flows, we must first determine the cost per unit of product and then apply this result to the number of units transferred.

Accounting for Goods in Process

If a process has *no beginning and no ending goods in process inventory,* the unit cost of goods transferred out of a process is computed as follows.

Video20.1

$$\frac{\textbf{Total cost assigned to the process (direct materials, direct labor, and overhead)}}{\textbf{Total number of units started and finished in the period}}$$

If a process has a beginning or ending inventory of partially processed units (or both), then the total cost assigned to the process must be allocated to all completed and incomplete units worked on during the period. Therefore, the denominator must measure the entire production activity of the process for the period, called **equivalent units of production** (or **EUP**), a phrase that refers to the number of units that could have been started *and* completed given the cost incurred during a period. This measure is then used to compute the cost per equivalent unit and to assign costs to finished goods and goods in process inventory.

To illustrate, assume that GenX adds (or introduces) 100 units into its process during a period. Suppose at the end of that period, the production supervisor determines that those 100 units are 60% of the way through the process. Therefore, equivalent units of production for that period total 60 EUP (100 units × 60%). This means that with the resources used to put 100 units 60% of the way through the process, GenX could have started and completed 60 whole units.

Point: For GenX, "units" might refer to individual Profen tablets. For a juice maker, units might refer to gallons.

Differences in Equivalent Units for Materials, Labor, and Overhead

P4 Compute equivalent units produced in a period.

In many processes, the equivalent units of production for direct materials are not the same with respect to direct labor and overhead. To illustrate, consider a five-step process operation shown in Exhibit 20.10.

EXHIBIT 20.10

An Illustrative Five-Step Process Operation

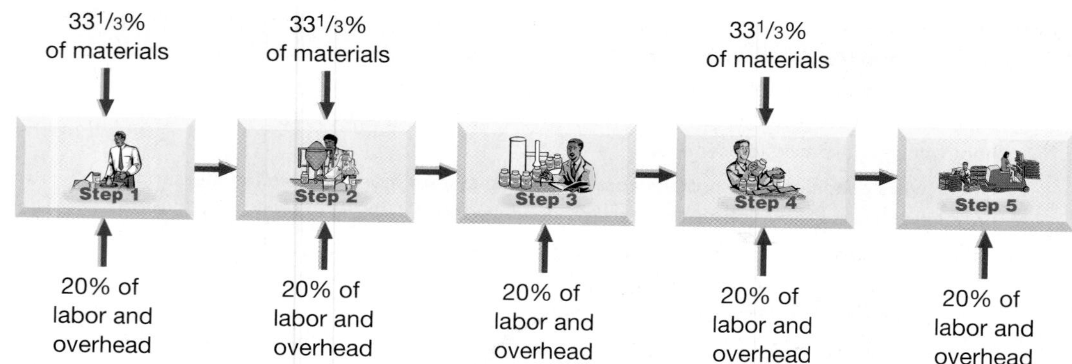

This exhibit shows that one-third of the direct material cost is added at each of three steps: 1, 2, and 4. One-fifth of the direct labor cost is added at each of the five steps. One-fifth of the overhead also is added at each step because overhead is applied as a percent of direct labor for this company.

When units finish step 1, they are one-third complete with respect to direct materials but only one-fifth complete with respect to direct labor and overhead. When they finish step 2, they are two-thirds complete with respect to direct materials but only two-fifths complete with respect to direct labor and overhead. When they finish step 3, they remain two-thirds complete with respect to materials but are now three-fifths complete with respect to labor and overhead. When they finish step 4, they are 100% complete with respect to materials (all direct materials have been added) but only four-fifths complete with respect to labor and overhead.

For example, if 300 units of product are started and processed through step 1 of Exhibit 20.10, they are said to be one-third complete *with respect to materials*. Expressed in terms of equivalent finished units, the processing of these 300 units is equal to finishing 100 EUP with respect to materials (300 units × 33⅓%). However, only one-fifth of direct labor and overhead has been applied to the 300 units at the end of step 1. This means that the equivalent units of production *with respect to labor and overhead* total 60 EUP (300 units × 20%).

Decision Insight

Process Services Customer interaction software is a hot item in customer service processes. Whether in insurance, delivery, or technology services, companies are finding that this software can turn their customer service process into an asset. How does it work? For starters, it cuts time spent on service calls because a customer describes a problem only once. It also yields a database of customer questions and complaints that gives insights into needed improvements. It recognizes incoming phone numbers and accesses previous dealings.

Process Costing Illustration

C3 Explain the four steps in accounting for production activity in a period.

This section applies process costing concepts and procedures to GenX. **This illustration uses the weighted-average method for inventory costs. The FIFO method is illustrated in Appendix 20A.** (Assume a weighted-average cost flow for all computations and assignments in this chapter unless explicitly stated differently. When using a just-in-time inventory system, different inventory methods yield similar results because inventories are immaterial.)

Exhibit 20.11 shows selected information from the production department for the month of April. Accounting for a department's activity for a period includes four steps involving analysis of (1) physical flow, (2) equivalent units, (3) cost per equivalent unit, and (4) cost assignment and reconciliation. The next sections describe each step.

EXHIBIT 20.11

Production Data

Beginning goods in process inventory (March 31)	
Units of product	30,000
Percentage of completion—Direct materials	100%
Percentage of completion—Direct labor	65%
Direct materials costs	$ 3,300
Direct labor costs	$ 600
Factory overhead costs applied (120% of direct labor)	$ 720
Activities during the current period (April)	
Units started this period	90,000
Units transferred out (completed)	100,000
Direct materials costs	$ 9,900
Direct labor costs	$ 5,700
Factory overhead costs applied (120% of direct labor)	$ 6,840
Ending goods in process inventory (April 30)	
Units of product	20,000
Percentage of completion—Direct materials	100%
Percentage of completion—Direct labor	25%

Step 1: Determine the Physical Flow of Units

Video20.1

A *physical flow reconciliation* is a report that reconciles (1) the physical units started in a period with (2) the physical units completed in that period. A physical flow reconciliation for GenX is shown in Exhibit 20.12 for April.

EXHIBIT 20.12

Physical Flow Reconciliation

Units to Account For		Units Accounted For	
Beginning goods in process inventory	30,000 units	Units completed and transferred out	100,000 units
Units started this period	90,000 units	Ending goods in process inventory	20,000 units
Total units to account for	**120,000 units**	Total units accounted for	**120,000 units**

↑ reconciled ↑

The weighted-average method does not require us to separately track the units in beginning work in process from those units started this period. Instead, the units are treated as part of a large pool with an average cost per unit.

Step 2: Compute Equivalent Units of Production

The second step is to compute *equivalent units of production* for direct materials, direct labor, and factory overhead for April. Overhead is applied using direct labor as the allocation base for GenX. This also implies that equivalent units are the same for both labor and overhead.

GenX used its direct materials, direct labor, and overhead to make finished units of Profen and to begin processing some units that are not yet complete. We must convert the physical units measure to equivalent units based on how each input has been used. Equivalent units are computed by multiplying the number of physical units by the percentage of completion for each input—see Exhibit 20.13.

EXHIBIT 20.13

Equivalent Units of Production—Weighted Average

Equivalent Units of Production	Direct Materials	Direct Labor	Factory Overhead
Equivalent units completed and transferred out (100,000 × 100%)	100,000 EUP	100,000 EUP	100,000 EUP
Equivalent units for ending goods in process			
Direct materials (20,000 × 100%)	20,000		
Direct labor (20,000 × 25%)		5,000	
Factory overhead (20,000 × 25%)			5,000
Equivalent units of production	120,000 EUP	105,000 EUP	105,000 EUP

The first row of Exhibit 20.13 reflects units transferred out in April. The production department entirely completed its work on the 100,000 units transferred out. These units have 100% of the materials, labor, and overhead required, or 100,000 equivalent units of each input (100,000 × 100%).

The second row references the ending goods in process, and rows three, four, and five break it down by materials, labor, and overhead. For direct materials, the units in ending goods in process inventory (20,000 physical units) include all materials required, so there are 20,000 equivalent units (20,000 × 100%) of materials in the unfinished physical units. Regarding labor, the units in ending goods in process inventory include 25% of the labor required, which implies 5,000 equivalent units of labor (20,000 × 25%). These units are only 25% complete and labor is used uniformly through the process. Overhead is applied on the basis of direct labor for GenX, so equivalent units for overhead are computed identically to labor (20,000 × 25%).

The final row reflects the whole units of product that could have been manufactured with the amount of inputs used to create some complete and some incomplete units. For GenX, the amount of inputs used to produce 100,000 complete units and to start 20,000 additional units is equivalent to the amount of direct materials in 120,000 whole units, the amount of direct labor in 105,000 whole units, and the amount of overhead in 105,000 whole units.

Step 3: Compute the Cost per Equivalent Unit

Equivalent units of production for each product (from step 2) is used to compute the average cost per equivalent unit. Under the **weighted-average method,** the computation of EUP does not separate the units in beginning inventory from those started this period; similarly, this method combines the costs of beginning goods in process inventory with the costs incurred in the current period. This process is illustrated in Exhibit 20.14.

EXHIBIT 20.14

Cost per Equivalent Unit of Production—Weighted Average

Cost per Equivalent Unit of Production	Direct Materials	Direct Labor	Factory Overhead
Costs of beginning goods in process inventory	$ 3,300	$ 600	$ 720
Costs incurred this period	9,900	5,700	6,840
Total costs	$13,200	$6,300	$7,560
÷ Equivalent units of production (from Step 2)	120,000 EUP	105,000 EUP	105,000 EUP
= Cost per equivalent unit of production	$0.11 per EUP*	$0.06 per EUP†	$0.072 per EUP‡

*$13,200 ÷ 120,000 EUP †$6,300 ÷ 105,000 EUP ‡$7,560 ÷ 105,000 EUP

For direct materials, the cost averages $0.11 per EUP, computed as the sum of direct materials cost from beginning goods in process inventory ($3,300) and the direct materials cost incurred in April ($9,900), and this sum ($13,200) is then divided by the 120,000 EUP for materials (from step 2). The costs per equivalent unit for labor and overhead are similarly computed. Specifically, direct labor cost averages $0.06 per EUP, computed as the sum of labor cost in beginning goods in process inventory ($600) and the labor costs incurred in April ($5,700), and this sum ($6,300) divided by 105,000 EUP for labor. Overhead costs averages $0.072 per EUP, computed as the sum of overhead cost in the beginning goods in process inventory ($720) and the overhead costs applied in April ($6,840), and this sum ($7,560) divided by 105,000 EUP for overhead.

Step 4: Assign and Reconcile Costs

The EUP from step 2 and the cost per EUP from step 3 are used in step 4 to assign costs to (a) units that production completed and transferred to finished goods and (b) units that remain in process. This is illustrated in Exhibit 20.15.

EXHIBIT 20.15

Report of Costs Accounted For—Weighted Average

Cost of units completed and transferred out		
Direct materials (100,000 EUP × $0.11 per EUP)	$11,000	
Direct labor (100,000 EUP × $0.06 per EUP)	6,000	
Factory overhead (100,000 EUP × $0.072 per EUP)	7,200	
Cost of units completed this period		$ 24,200
Cost of ending goods in process inventory		
Direct materials (20,000 EUP × $0.11 per EUP)	2,200	
Direct labor (5,000 EUP × $0.06 per EUP)	300	
Factory overhead (5,000 EUP × $0.072 per EUP)	360	
Cost of ending goods in process inventory		2,860
Total costs accounted for		$27,060

Cost of Units Completed and Transferred The 100,000 units completed and transferred to finished goods inventory required 100,000 EUP of direct materials. Thus, we assign $11,000 (100,000 EUP × $0.11 per EUP) of direct materials cost to those units. Similarly, those units had received 100,000 EUP of direct labor and 100,000 EUP of factory overhead (recall Exhibit 20.13). Thus, we assign $6,000 (100,000 EUP × $0.06 per EUP) of direct labor and $7,200 (100,000 EUP × $0.072 per EUP) of overhead to those units. The total cost of the 100,000 completed and transferred units is $24,200 ($11,000 + $6,000 + $7,200) and their average cost per unit is $0.242 ($24,200 ÷ 100,000 units).

Cost of Units for Ending Goods in Process There are 20,000 incomplete units in goods in process inventory at period-end. For direct materials, those units have 20,000 EUP of material (from step 2) at a cost of $0.11 per EUP (from step 3), which yields the materials cost of goods in process inventory of $2,200 (20,000 EUP × $0.11 per EUP). For direct labor, the in-process units have 25% of the required labor, or 5,000 EUP (from step 2). Using the $0.06 labor cost per EUP (from step 3) we obtain the labor cost of goods in process inventory of $300 (5,000 EUP × $0.06 per EUP). For overhead, the in-process units reflect 5,000 EUP (from step 2). Using the $0.072 overhead cost per EUP (from step 3) we obtain overhead costs with in-process inventory of $360 (5,000 EUP × $0.072 per EUP). Total cost of goods in process inventory at period-end is $2,860 ($2,200 + $300 + $360).

As a check, management verifies that total costs assigned to those units completed and transferred plus the costs of those in process (from Exhibit 20.15) equal the costs incurred by production. Exhibit 20.16 shows the costs incurred by production this period. We then reconcile the *costs accounted for* in Exhibit 20.15 with the *costs to account for* in Exhibit 20.16.

EXHIBIT 20.16

Report of Costs to Account For—Weighted Average

Cost of beginning goods in process inventory		
Direct materials	$3,300	
Direct labor	600	
Factory overhead	720	$ 4,620
Cost incurred this period		
Direct materials	9,900	
Direct labor	5,700	
Factory overhead	6,840	22,440
Total costs to account for		$27,060

At GenX, the production department manager is responsible for $27,060 in costs: $4,620 that is assigned to the goods in process at the start of the period plus $22,440 of materials, labor, and overhead incurred in the period. At period-end, that manager must show where these costs are assigned. The manager for GenX reports that $2,860 are assigned to units in process and $24,200 are assigned to units completed (per Exhibit 20.15). The sum of these amounts equals $27,060. Thus, the total *costs to account for* equal the total *costs accounted for* (minor differences can sometimes occur from rounding).

C4 Define a process cost summary and describe its purposes.

Point: Managers can examine changes in monthly costs per equivalent unit to help control the production process. When prices are set in a competitive market, managers can use process cost summary information to determine which costs should be cut to achieve a profit.

Process Cost Summary An important managerial accounting report for a process cost accounting system is the **process cost summary** (also called *production report*), which is prepared separately for each process or production department. Three reasons for the summary are to (1) help department managers control and monitor their departments, (2) help factory managers evaluate department managers' performances, and (3) provide cost information for financial statements. A process cost summary achieves these purposes by describing the costs charged to each department, reporting the equivalent units of production achieved by each department, and determining the costs assigned to each department's output. For our purposes, it is prepared using a combination of Exhibits 20.13, 20.14, 20.15, and 20.16.

P5 Prepare a process cost summary.

The process cost summary for GenX is shown in Exhibit 20.17. The report is divided into three sections. Section ① lists the total costs charged to the department, including direct materials, direct labor, and overhead costs incurred, as well as the cost of the beginning goods in process inventory. Section ② describes the equivalent units of production for the department. Equivalent units for materials, labor, and overhead are in separate columns. It also reports direct

EXHIBIT 20.17

Process Cost Summary

GenX COMPANY
Process Cost Summary
For Month Ended April 30, 2009

①

Costs Charged to Production		
Costs of beginning goods in process		
Direct materials	$3,300	
Direct labor	600	
Factory overhead	720	$ 4,620
Costs incurred this period		
Direct materials	9,900	
Direct labor	5,700	
Factory overhead	6,840	22,440
Total costs to account for		**$27,060**

②

Unit Cost Information			
Units to account for:		Units accounted for:	
Beginning goods in process	30,000	Completed and transferred out	100,000
Units started this period	90,000	Ending goods in process	20,000
Total units to account for	120,000	Total units accounted for	120,000

Equivalent Units of Production (EUP)	**Direct Materials**	**Direct Labor**	**Factory Overhead**
Units completed and transferred out	100,000 EUP	100,000 EUP	100,000 EUP
Units of ending goods in process			
Direct materials (20,000 × 100%)	20,000		
Direct labor (20,000 × 25%)		5,000	
Factory overhead (20,000 × 25%)			5,000
Equivalent units of production	120,000 EUP	105,000 EUP	105,000 EUP

Cost per EUP	**Direct Materials**	**Direct Labor**	**Factory Overhead**
Costs of beginning goods in process	$ 3,300	$ 600	$ 720
Costs incurred this period	9,900	5,700	6,840
Total costs	$13,200	$6,300	$7,560
÷EUP	120,000 EUP	105,000 EUP	105,000 EUP
Cost per EUP	$0.11 per EUP	$0.06 per EUP	$0.072 per EUP

③

Cost Assignment and Reconciliation		
Costs transferred out (cost of goods manufactured)		
Direct materials (100,000 EUP × $0.11 per EUP)	$11,000	
Direct labor (100,000 EUP × $0.06 per EUP)	6,000	
Factory overhead (100,000 EUP × $0.072 per EUP)	7,200	$ 24,200
Costs of ending goods in process		
Direct materials (20,000 EUP × $0.11 per EUP)	2,200	
Direct labor (5,000 EUP × $0.06 per EUP)	300	
Factory overhead (5,000 EUP × $0.072 per EUP)	360	2,860
Total costs accounted for		**$27,060**

reconciled

materials, direct labor, and overhead costs per equivalent unit. Section ③ allocates total costs among units worked on in the period. The $24,200 is the total cost of goods transferred out of the department, and the $2,860 is the cost of partially processed ending inventory units. The assigned costs are then added to show that the total $27,060 cost charged to the department in section ① is now assigned to the units in section ③.

Quick Check

Answers—p. 833

6. Equivalent units are (*a*) a measure of a production department's productivity in using direct materials, direct labor, or overhead; (*b*) units of a product produced by a foreign competitor that are similar to units produced by a domestic company; or (*c*) generic units of a product similar to brand name units of a product.
7. Interpret the meaning of a department's equivalent units with respect to direct labor.
8. A department began the period with 8,000 units that were one-fourth complete with respect to direct labor. It completed 58,000 units, and ended with 6,000 units that were one-third complete with respect to direct labor. What were its direct labor equivalent units for the period using the weighted-average method?
9. A process cost summary for a department has three sections. What information is presented in each of them?

Transfers to Finished Goods Inventory and Cost of Goods Sold

P6 Record the transfer of completed goods to Finished Goods Inventory and Cost of Goods Sold.

Arrow line ⑨ in Exhibit 20.4 reflects the transfer of completed products from production to finished goods inventory. The process cost summary shows that the 100,000 units of finished Profen are assigned a cost of $24,200. The entry to record this transfer follows.

⑨	Finished Goods Inventory	24,200	
	Goods in Process Inventory		24,200
	To record transfer of completed units.		

Assets	=	Liabilities	+	Equity
+24,200				
−24,200				

The credit to Goods in Process Inventory reduces that asset balance to reflect that 100,000 units are no longer in production. The cost of these units has been transferred to Finished Goods Inventory, which is recognized as a $24,200 increase in this asset. After this entry is posted, there remains a balance of $2,860 in the Goods in Process Inventory account, which is the amount computed in Step 4 previously. The cost of units transferred from Goods in Process Inventory to Finished Goods Inventory is called the **cost of goods manufactured.** Exhibit 20.18 reveals the activities in the Goods in Process Inventory account for this period. The ending balance of this account equals the cost assigned to the partially completed units in section ③ of Exhibit 20.17.

EXHIBIT 20.18

Goods in Process Inventory

Goods in Process Inventory					Acct. No. 134
Date		**Explanation**	**Debit**	**Credit**	**Balance**
Mar.	31	Balance			4,620
Apr.	30	Direct materials usage	9,900		14,520
	30	Direct labor costs incurred	5,700		20,220
	30	Factory overhead applied	6,840		27,060
	30	Transfer completed product to warehouse		24,200	2,860

Arrow line ⑩ in Exhibit 20.4 reflects the sale of finished goods. Assume that GenX sold 106,000 units of Profen this period, and that its beginning inventory of finished goods consisted of 26,000 units with a cost of $6,292. Also assume that its ending finished goods inventory consists of 20,000 units at a cost of $4,840. Using this information, we can compute its cost of goods sold for April as shown in Exhibit 20.19.

Point: We omit the journal entry for sales, but it totals the number of units sold times price per unit.

EXHIBIT 20.19
Cost of Goods Sold

Beginning finished goods inventory	$ 6,292
+ Cost of goods manufactured this period	24,200
= Cost of goods available for sale	$30,492
− Ending finished goods inventory	4,840
= Cost of goods sold	$25,652

The summary entry to record cost of goods sold for this period follows.

Assets	= Liabilities +	Equity
−25,652		−25,652

		Debit	Credit
(10)	Cost of Goods Sold	25,652	
	Finished Goods Inventory		25,652
	To record cost of goods sold for April.		

The Finished Goods Inventory account now appears as shown in Exhibit 20.20.

EXHIBIT 20.20
Finished Goods Inventory

Finished Goods Inventory — Acct. No. 135

Date		Explanation	Debit	Credit	Balance
Mar.	31	Balance			6,292
Apr.	30	Transfer in cost of goods manufactured	24,200		30,492
	30	Cost of goods sold		25,652	4,840

Summary of Cost Flows Exhibit 20.21 shows GenX's manufacturing cost flows for April. Each of these cost flows and the entries to record them have been explained. The flow of costs through the accounts reflects the flow of production activities and products.

EXHIBIT 20.21*
Cost Flows through GenX

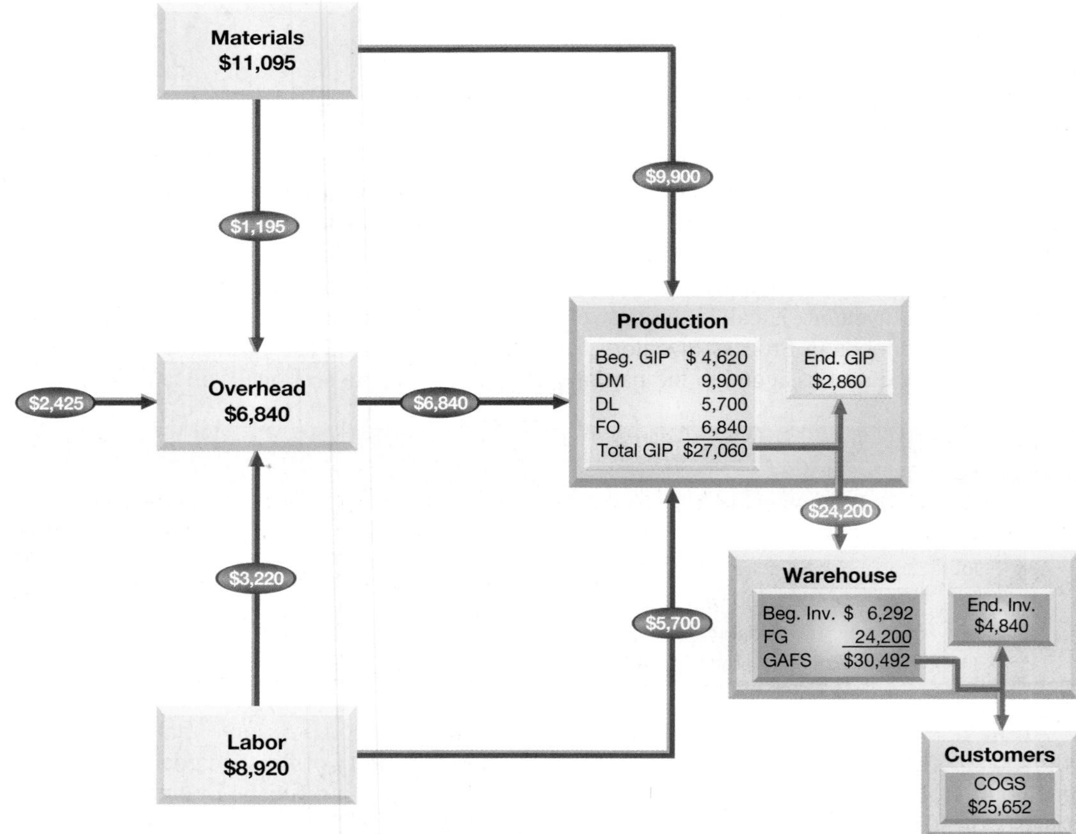

*Abbreviations: GIP (goods in process); DM (direct materials); DL (direct labor); FO (factory overhead); FG (finished goods); GAFS (goods available for sale); COGS (cost of goods sold).

Decision Insight

Best of Both Customer orientation demands both flexibility and standardization. Flexibility allows companies to supply products or services to a customer's specifications as in a job order setting, and standardization helps achieve efficiencies and lower costs as in a process operation.

Effect of the Lean Business Model on Process Operations

Adopting lean business practices often yields changes in process operations. Management concerns with throughput and just-in-time manufacturing, for instance, cause boundary lines between departments to blur. In some cases, higher quality and better efficiency are obtained by entirely reorganizing production processes. For example, instead of producing different types of computers in a series of departments, a separate work center for each computer can be established in one department. When such a rearrangement occurs, the process cost accounting system is changed to account for each work center's costs.

To illustrate, when a company adopts a just-in-time inventory system, its inventories can be minimal. If raw materials are not ordered or received until needed, a Raw Materials Inventory account may be unnecessary. Instead, materials cost is immediately debited to the Goods in Process Inventory account. Similarly, a Finished Goods Inventory account may not be needed. Instead, cost of finished goods may be immediately debited to the Cost of Goods Sold account.

Decision Insight

Lean Machine Attention to customer orientation has led to improved processes for companies. A manufacturer of control devices improved quality and reduced production time by forming teams to study processes and suggest improvements. Another company set up project groups to evaluate its production processes.

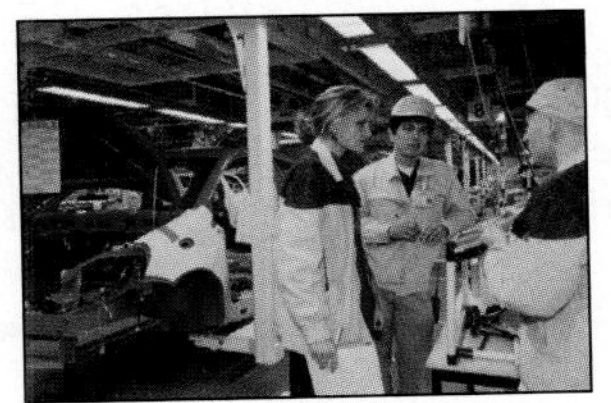

Decision Analysis

Hybrid Costing System

A2 Explain and illustrate a hybrid costing system.

This chapter explained the process costing system and contrasted it with the job order costing system. Many organizations use a *hybrid system* that contains features of both process and job order operations. A recent survey of manufacturers revealed that a majority use hybrid systems.

To illustrate, consider a car manufacturer's assembly line. On one hand, the line resembles a process operation in that the assembly steps for each car are nearly identical. On the other hand, the specifications of most cars have several important differences. At the **Ford** Mustang plant, each car assembled on a given day can be different from the previous car and the next car. This means that the costs of materials (subassemblies or components) for each car can differ. Accordingly, while the conversion costs (direct labor and overhead) can be accounted for using a process costing system, the component costs (direct materials) are accounted for using a job order system (separately for each car or type of car).

A hybrid system of processes requires a *hybrid costing system* to properly cost products or services. In the Ford plant, the assembly costs per car are readily determined using process costing. The costs of additional components can then be added to the assembly costs to determine each car's total cost (as in job order costing). To illustrate, consider the following information for a daily assembly process at Ford.

Assembly process costs	
Direct materials	$10,600,000
Direct labor	$5,800,000
Factory overhead	$6,200,000
Number of cars assembled	1,000
Costs of three different types of steering wheels	$240, $330, $480
Costs of three different types of seats	$620, $840, $1,360

The assembly process costs $22,600 per car. Depending on the type of steering wheel and seats the customer requests, the cost of a car can range from $23,460 to $24,440 (a $980 difference).

Today companies are increasingly trying to standardize processes while attempting to meet individual customer needs. To the extent that differences among individual customers' requests are large, understanding the costs to satisfy those requests is important. Thus, monitoring and controlling both process and job order costs are important.

Decision Ethics

Entrepreneur You operate a process production company making similar products for three different customers. One customer demands 100% quality inspection of products at your location before shipping. The added costs of that inspection are spread across all customers, not just the one demanding it. If you charge the added costs to that customer, you could lose that customer and experience a loss. Moreover, your other two customers have agreed to pay 110% of full costs. What actions (if any) do you take? [Answer—pp. 832–833]

Demonstration Problem

Pennsylvania Company produces a product that passes through a single production process. Then completed products are transferred to finished goods in its warehouse. Information related to its manufacturing activities for July follows.

Raw Materials	
Beginning inventory	$100,000
Raw materials purchased on credit	211,400
Direct materials used	(190,000)
Indirect materials used	(51,400)
Ending inventory	$ 70,000
Factory Payroll	
Direct labor incurred	$ 55,500
Indirect labor incurred	50,625
Total payroll (paid in cash)	$106,125
Factory Overhead	
Indirect materials used	$ 51,400
Indirect labor used	50,625
Other overhead costs	71,725
Total factory overhead incurred	$173,750
Factory Overhead Applied	
Overhead applied (200% of direct labor)	$111,000

Production Department	
Beginning goods in process inventory (units)	5,000
Percentage completed—Materials	100%
Percentage completed—Labor and overhead	60%
Beginning goods in process inventory (costs)	
Direct materials used	$ 20,000
Direct labor incurred	9,600
Overhead applied (200% of direct labor)	19,200
Total costs of beginning goods in process	$ 48,800
Units started this period	20,000
Units completed this period	17,000
Ending goods in process inventory (units)	8,000
Percentage completed—Materials	100%
Percentage completed—Labor and overhead	20%
Finished Goods Inventory	
Beginning finished goods inventory	$ 96,400
Cost transferred in from production	321,300
Cost of goods sold	(345,050)
Ending finished goods inventory	$ 72,650

DP20

Required

1. Prepare a physical flow reconciliation for July as illustrated in Exhibit 20.12.
2. Compute the equivalent units of production in July for direct materials, direct labor, and factory overhead.
3. Compute the costs per equivalent units of production in July for direct materials, direct labor, and factory overhead.
4. Prepare a report of costs accounted for and a report of costs to account for.

5. Prepare summary journal entries to record the transactions and events of July for (a) raw materials purchases, (b) direct materials usage, (c) indirect materials usage, (d) factory payroll costs, (e) direct labor usage, (f) indirect labor usage, (g) other overhead costs (credit Other Accounts), (h) application of overhead to production, (i) transfer of finished goods from production, and (j) the cost of goods sold.

Planning the Solution

- Track the physical flow to determine the number of units completed in July.
- Compute the equivalent unit of production for direct materials, direct labor, and factory overhead.
- Compute the costs per equivalent unit of production with respect to direct materials, direct labor, and overhead; and determine the cost per unit for each.
- Compute the total cost of the goods transferred to production by using the equivalent units and unit costs. Determine (a) the cost of the beginning in-process inventory, (b) the materials, labor, and overhead costs added to the beginning in-process inventory, and (c) the materials, labor, and overhead costs added to the units started and completed in the month.
- Determine the cost of goods sold using balances in finished goods and cost of units completed this period.
- Use the information to record the summary journal entries for July.

Solution to Demonstration Problem

1. Physical flow reconciliation.

Units to Account For		Units Accounted For	
Beginning goods in process inventory	5,000 units	Units completed and transferred out	17,000 units
Units started this period	20,000 units	Ending goods in process inventory	8,000 units
Total units to account for	**25,000 units**	Total units accounted for	**25,000 units**

reconciled

2. Equivalent units of production.

Equivalent Units of Production	Direct Materials	Direct Labor	Factory Overhead
Equivalent units completed and transferred out	17,000 EUP	17,000 EUP	17,000 EUP
Equivalent units in ending goods in process			
Direct materials (8,000 × 100%)	8,000		
Direct labor (8,000 × 20%)		1,600	
Factory overhead (8,000 × 20%)			1,600
Equivalent units of production	25,000 EUP	18,600 EUP	18,600 EUP

3. Costs per equivalent unit of production.

Costs per Equivalent Unit of Production	Direct Materials	Direct Labor	Factory Overhead
Costs of beginning goods in process	$ 20,000	$ 9,600	$ 19,200
Costs incurred this period	190,000	55,500	111,000**
Total costs	$210,000	$65,100	$130,200
÷ Equivalent units of production (from part 2)	25,000 EUP	18,600 EUP	18,600 EUP
= Costs per equivalent unit of production	$8.40 per EUP	$3.50 per EUP	$7.00 per EUP

**Factory overhead applied

4. Reports of costs accounted for and of costs to account for

Report of Costs Accounted For		
Cost of units transferred out (cost of goods manufactured)		
Direct materials ($8.40 per EUP × 17,000 EUP)	$142,800	
Direct labor ($3.50 per EUP × 17,000 EUP)	59,500	
Factory overhead ($7.00 per EUP × 17,000 EUP)	119,000	
Cost of units completed this period		$ 321,300
Cost of ending goods in process inventory		
Direct materials ($8.40 per EUP × 8,000 EUP)	67,200	
Direct labor ($3.50 per EUP × 1,600 EUP)	5,600	
Factory overhead ($7.00 per EUP × 1,600 EUP)	11,200	
Cost of ending goods in process inventory		84,000
Total costs accounted for		**$405,300**

Report of Costs to Account For		
Cost of beginning goods in process inventory		
Direct materials	$ 20,000	
Direct labor	9,600	
Factory overhead	19,200	$ 48,800
Cost incurred this period		
Direct materials	190,000	
Direct labor	55,500	
Factory overhead	111,000	356,500
Total costs to account for		**$405,300**

reconciled

5. Summary journal entries for the transactions and events in July.

		Debit	Credit
a.	Raw Materials Inventory	211,400	
	Accounts Payable		211,400
	To record raw materials purchases.		
b.	Goods in Process Inventory	190,000	
	Raw Materials Inventory		190,000
	To record direct materials usage.		
c.	Factory Overhead	51,400	
	Raw Materials Inventory		51,400
	To record indirect materials usage.		
d.	Factory Payroll	106,125	
	Cash		106,125
	To record factory payroll costs.		
e.	Goods in Process Inventory	55,500	
	Factory Payroll		55,500
	To record direct labor usage.		
f.	Factory Overhead	50,625	
	Factory Payroll		50,625
	To record indirect labor usage.		
g.	Factory Overhead	71,725	
	Other Accounts		71,725
	To record other overhead costs.		

[continued on next page]

[continued from previous page]

h.	Goods in Process Inventory	111,000	
	Factory Overhead		111,000
	To record application of overhead.		
i.	Finished Goods Inventory	321,300	
	Goods in Process Inventory		321,300
	To record transfer of finished goods from production.		
j.	Cost of Goods Sold	345,050	
	Finished Goods Inventory		345,050
	To record cost of goods sold.		

APPENDIX

FIFO Method of Process Costing

20A

C5 Explain and illustrate the four steps in accounting for production activity using FIFO.

The **FIFO method** of process costing assigns costs to units assuming a first-in, first-out flow of product. The objectives, concepts, and journal entries (not amounts) are the same as for the weighted-average method, but computation of equivalent units of production and cost assignment are slightly different.

Exhibit 20A.1 shows selected information from GenX's production department for the month of April. Accounting for a department's activity for a period includes four steps: (1) determine physical flow, (2) compute equivalent units, (3) compute cost per equivalent unit, and (4) determine cost assignment and reconciliation. This appendix describes each of these steps using the FIFO method for process costing.

EXHIBIT 20A.1

Production Data

Beginning goods in process inventory (March 31)	
Units of product	30,000
Percentage of completion—Direct materials	100%
Percentage of completion—Direct labor	65%
Direct materials costs	$ 3,300
Direct labor costs	$ 600
Factory overhead costs applied (120% of direct labor)	$ 720
Activities during the current period (April)	
Units started this period	90,000
Units transferred out (completed)	100,000
Direct materials costs	$ 9,900
Direct labor costs	$ 5,700
Factory overhead costs applied (120% of direct labor)	$ 6,840
Ending goods in process inventory (April 30)	
Units of product	20,000
Percentage of completion—Direct materials	100%
Percentage of completion—Direct labor	25%

Step 1: Determine Physical Flow of Units

A *physical flow reconciliation* is a report that reconciles (1) the physical units started in a period with (2) the physical units completed in that period. The physical flow reconciliation for GenX is shown in Exhibit 20A.2 for April.

EXHIBIT 20A.2

Physical Flow Reconciliation

Units to Account For		Units Accounted For	
Beginning goods in process inventory	30,000 units	Units completed and transferred out	100,000 units
Units started this period	90,000 units	Ending goods in process inventory ...	20,000 units
Total units to account for ...	**120,000 units**	Total units accounted for	**120,000 units**

reconciled

FIFO assumes that the 100,000 units transferred to finished goods during April include the 30,000 units from the beginning goods in process inventory. The remaining 70,000 units transferred out are from units started in April. Of the total 90,000 units started in April, 70,000 were completed, leaving 20,000 units unfinished at period-end.

Step 2: Compute Equivalent Units of Production—FIFO

GenX used its direct materials, direct labor, and overhead both to make complete units of Profen and to start some units that are not yet complete. We need to convert the physical measure of units to equivalent units based on how much of each input has been used. We do this by multiplying the number of physical units by the percentage of processing applied to those units in the current period; this is done for each input (materials, labor, and overhead). The FIFO method accounts for cost flow in a sequential manner—earliest costs are the first to flow out. (This is different from the weighted-average method, which combines prior period costs—those in beginning Goods in Process Inventory—with costs incurred in the current period.)

Three distinct groups of units must be considered in determining the equivalent units of production under the FIFO method: (a) units in beginning Goods in Process Inventory that were completed this period, (b) units started *and* completed this period, and (c) units in ending Goods in Process Inventory. We must determine how much material, labor, and overhead are used for each of these unit groups. These computations are shown in Exhibit 20A.3. The remainder of this section explains these computations.

EXHIBIT 20A.3

Equivalent Units of Production—FIFO

Equivalent Units of Production	Direct Materials	Direct Labor	Factory Overhead
(a) Equivalent units to complete beginning goods in process			
Direct materials (30,000 × 0%)	0 EUP		
Direct labor (30,000 × 35%)		10,500 EUP	
Factory overhead (30,000 × 35%)			10,500 EUP
(b) Equivalent units started and completed*	70,000	70,000	70,000
(c) Equivalent units in ending goods in process			
Direct materials (20,000 × 100%)	20,000		
Direct labor (20,000 × 25%)		5,000	
Factory overhead (20,000 × 25%)			5,000
Equivalent units of production	90,000 EUP	85,500 EUP	85,500 EUP

*Units completed this period	100,000 units
Less units in beginning goods in process	30,000
Units started and completed this period	70,000 units

(a) Beginning Goods in Process Under FIFO, we assume that production first completes any units started in the prior period. There were 30,000 physical units in beginning goods in process inventory. Those units were 100% complete with respect to direct materials as of the end of the prior period. This means that no materials (0%) are needed in April to complete those 30,000 units. So the equivalent units of *materials* to complete beginning goods in process are zero (30,000 × 0%)—see first row under row "(a)" in Exhibit 20A.3. The units in process as of April 1 had already been through 65% of production prior to this period and need only go through the remaining 35% of production. The equivalent units of *labor* to complete the beginning goods in process are 10,500 (30,000 × 35%)—

see the second row under row "(a)." This implies that the amount of labor required this period to complete the 30,000 units started in the prior period is the amount of labor needed to make 10,500 units, start-to-finish. Finally, overhead is applied based on direct labor costs, so GenX computes equivalent units for overhead as it would for direct labor.

(b) Units Started and Completed This Period After completing any beginning goods in process, FIFO assumes that production begins on newly started units. GenX began work on 90,000 new units this period. Of those units, 20,000 remain incomplete at period-end. This means that 70,000 of the units started in April were completed in April. These complete units have received 100% of materials, labor, and overhead. Exhibit 20A.3 reflects this by including 70,000 equivalent units (70,000 × 100%) of materials, labor, and overhead in its equivalent units of production—see row "(b)."

(c) Ending Goods in Process The 20,000 units started in April that GenX was not able to complete by period-end consumed materials, labor, and overhead. Specifically, those 20,000 units received 100% of materials and, therefore, the equivalent units of materials in ending goods in process inventory are 20,000 (20,000 × 100%)—see the first row under row "(c)." For labor and overhead, the units in ending goods in process were 25% complete in production. This means the equivalent units of labor and overhead for those units are 5,000 (20,000 × 25%) as GenX incurs labor and overhead costs uniformly throughout its production process. Finally, for each input (direct materials, direct labor, and factory overhead), the equivalent units for each of the unit groups (a), (b), and (c) are added to determine the total equivalent units of production with respect to each—see the final row in Exhibit 20A.3.

Step 3: Compute Cost per Equivalent Unit—FIFO

To compute cost per equivalent unit, we take the product costs (for each of direct materials, direct labor, and factory overhead from Exhibit 20A.1) added in April and divide by the equivalent units of production from step 2. Exhibit 20A.4 illustrates these computations.

EXHIBIT 20A.4

Cost per Equivalent Unit of Production—FIFO

Cost per Equivalent Unit of Production	Direct Materials	Direct Labor	Factory Overhead
Costs incurred this period	$9,900	$5,700	$6,840
÷ Equivalent units of production (from Step 2)	90,000 EUP	85,500 EUP	85,500 EUP
Cost per equivalent unit of production	$0.11 per EUP	$0.067 per EUP	$0.08 per EUP

It is essential to compute costs per equivalent unit for *each* input because production inputs are added at different times in the process. The FIFO method computes the cost per equivalent unit based solely on this period's EUP and costs (unlike the weighted-average method, which adds in the costs of the beginning goods in process inventory).

Step 4: Assign and Reconcile Costs

The equivalent units determined in step 2 and the cost per equivalent unit computed in step 3 are both used to assign costs (1) to units that the production department completed and transferred to finished goods and (2) to units that remain in process at period-end.

In Exhibit 20A.5, under the section for cost of units transferred out, we see that the cost of units completed in April includes the $4,620 cost carried over from March for work already applied to the 30,000 units that make up beginning Goods in Process Inventory, plus the $1,544 incurred in April to complete those units. This section also includes the $17,990 of cost assigned to the 70,000 units started and completed this period. Thus, the total cost of goods manufactured in April is $24,154 ($4,620 + $1,544 + $17,990). The average cost per unit for goods completed in April is $0.242 ($24,154 ÷ 100,000 completed units).

The computation for cost of ending goods in process inventory is in the lower part of Exhibit 20A.5. The cost of units in process includes materials, labor, and overhead costs corresponding to the percentage of these resources applied to those incomplete units in April. That cost of $2,935 ($2,200 + $335 + $400) also is the ending balance for the Goods in Process Inventory account.

EXHIBIT 20A.5

Report of Costs Accounted For—FIFO

Cost of units transferred out (cost of goods manufactured)		
Cost of beginning goods in process inventory		$ 4,620
Cost to complete beginning goods in process		
Direct materials ($0.11 per EUP × 0 EUP)	$ 0	
Direct labor ($0.067 per EUP × 10,500 EUP)	704	
Factory overhead ($0.08 per EUP × 10,500 EUP)	840	1,544
Cost of units started and completed this period		
Direct materials ($0.11 per EUP × 70,000 EUP)	7,700	
Direct labor ($0.067 per EUP × 70,000 EUP)	4,690	
Factory overhead ($0.08 per EUP × 70,000 EUP)	5,600	17,990
Total cost of units finished this period		24,154
Cost of ending goods in process inventory		
Direct materials ($0.11 per EUP × 20,000 EUP)	2,200	
Direct labor ($0.067 per EUP × 5,000 EUP)	335	
Factory overhead ($0.08 per EUP × 5,000 EUP)	400	
Total cost of ending goods in process inventory		2,935
Total costs accounted for		**$27,089**

Management verifies that the total costs assigned to units transferred out and units still in process equal the total costs incurred by production. We reconcile the costs accounted for (in Exhibit 20A.5) to the costs that production was charged for as shown in Exhibit 20A.6.

EXHIBIT 20A.6

Report of Costs to Account For—FIFO

Cost of beginning goods in process inventory		
Direct materials	$3,300	
Direct labor	600	
Factory overhead	720	$ 4,620
Costs incurred this period		
Direct materials	9,900	
Direct labor	5,700	
Factory overhead	6,840	22,440
Total costs to account for		**$27,060**

The production manager is responsible for $27,060 in costs: $4,620 that had been assigned to the department's Goods in Process Inventory as of April 1 plus $22,440 of materials, labor, and overhead costs the department incurred in April. At period-end, the manager must identify where those costs were assigned. The production manager can report that $24,154 of cost was assigned to units completed in April and $2,935 was assigned to units still in process at period-end. The sum of these amounts is $29 different from the $27,060 total costs incurred by production due to rounding in step 3—rounding errors are common and not a concern.

The final report is the process cost summary, which summarizes key information from Exhibits 20A.3, 20A.4, 20A.5, and 20A.6. Reasons for the summary are to (1) help managers control and monitor costs, (2) help upper management assess department manager performance, and (3) provide cost information for financial reporting. The process cost summary, using FIFO, for GenX is in Exhibit 20A.7. Section ① lists the total costs charged to the department, including direct materials, direct labor, and overhead costs incurred, as well as the cost of the beginning goods in process inventory. Section ② describes the equivalent units of production for the department. Equivalent units for materials, labor, and overhead are in separate columns. It also reports direct materials, direct labor, and overhead costs per equivalent unit. Section ③ allocates total costs among units worked on in the period.

Decision Maker

Cost Manager As cost manager for an electronics manufacturer, you apply a process costing system using FIFO. Your company plans to adopt a just-in-time system and eliminate inventories. What is the impact of the use of FIFO (versus the weighted-average method) given these plans? [Answer—p. 833]

EXHIBIT 20A.7
Process Cost Summary

GenX COMPANY
Process Cost Summary
For Month Ended April 30, 2009

Costs charged to production		
Costs of beginning goods in process inventory		
Direct materials	$3,300	
Direct labor	600	
Factory overhead	720	$ 4,620
Costs incurred this period		
Direct materials	9,900	
Direct labor	5,700	
Factory overhead	6,840	22,440
Total costs to account for		$27,060

Unit cost information

Units to account for		Units accounted for	
Beginning goods in process	30,000	Transferred out	100,000
Units started this period	90,000	Ending goods in process	20,000
Total units to account for	120,000	Total units accounted for	120,000

Equivalent units of production	**Direct Materials**	**Direct Labor**	**Factory Overhead**
Equivalent units to complete beginning goods in process			
Direct materials (30,000 × 0%)	0 EUP		
Direct labor (30,000 × 35%)		10,500 EUP	
Factory overhead (30,000 × 35%)			10,500 EUP
Equivalent units started and completed	70,000	70,000	70,000
Equivalent units in ending goods in process			
Direct materials (20,000 × 100%)	20,000		
Direct labor (20,000 × 25%)		5,000	
Factory overhead (20,000 × 25%)			5000
Equivalent units of production	90,000 EUP	85,500 EUP	85,500 EUP

Cost per equivalent unit of production	**Direct Materials**	**Direct Labor**	**Factory Overhead**
Costs incurred this period	$9,900	$5,700	$6,840
÷ Equivalent units of production	90,000 EUP	85,500 EUP	85,500 EUP
Cost per equivalent unit of production	$0.11 per EUP	$0.067 per EUP	$0.08 per EUP

Cost assignment and reconciliation (cost of units completed and transferred out)		
Cost of beginning goods in process		$ 4,620
Cost to complete beginning goods in process		
Direct materials ($0.11 per EUP × 0 EUP)	$ 0	
Direct labor ($0.067 per EUP × 10,500 EUP)	704	
Factory overhead ($0.08 per EUP × 10,500 EUP)	840	1,544
Cost of units started and completed this period		
Direct materials ($0.11 per EUP × 70,000 EUP)	7,700	
Direct labor ($0.067 per EUP × 70,000 EUP)	4,690	
Factory overhead ($0.08 per EUP × 70,000 EUP)	5,600	17,990
Total cost of units finished this period		24,154
Cost of ending goods in process		
Direct materials ($0.11 per EUP × 20,000 EUP)	2,200	
Direct labor ($0.067 per EUP × 5,000 EUP)	335	
Factory overhead ($0.08 per EUP × 5,000 EUP)	400	
Total cost of ending goods in process		2,935
Total costs accounted for		$27,089*

(1) Costs charged to production; (2) Unit cost information; (3) Cost assignment and reconciliation. Total costs to account for and total costs accounted for: reconciled.

*$29 difference due to rounding

Summary

C1 Explain process operations and the way they differ from job order operations. Process operations produce large quantities of similar products or services by passing them through a series of processes, or steps, in production. Like job order operations, they combine direct materials, direct labor, and overhead in the operations. Unlike job order operations that assign the responsibility for each job to a manager, process operations assign the responsibility for each *process* to a manager.

C2 Define equivalent units and explain their use in process cost accounting. Equivalent units of production measure the activity of a process as the number of units that would be completed in a period if all effort had been applied to units that were started and finished. This measure of production activity is used to compute the cost per equivalent unit and to assign costs to finished goods and goods in process inventory.

C3 Explain the four steps in accounting for production activity in a period. The four steps involved in accounting for production activity in a period are (1) recording the physical flow of units, (2) computing the equivalent units of production, (3) computing the cost per equivalent unit of production, and (4) reconciling costs. The last step involves assigning costs to finished goods and goods in process inventory for the period.

C4 Define a process cost summary and describe its purposes. A process cost summary reports on the activities of a production process or department for a period. It describes the costs charged to the department, the equivalent units of production for the department, and the costs assigned to the output. The report aims to (1) help managers control their departments, (2) help factory managers evaluate department managers' performances, and (3) provide cost information for financial statements.

C5 Explain and illustrate the four steps in accounting for production activity using FIFO. The FIFO method for process costing is applied and illustrated to (1) report the physical flow of units, (2) compute the equivalent units of production, (3) compute the cost per equivalent unit of production, and (4) assign and reconcile costs.

A1 Compare process cost accounting and job order cost accounting. Process and job order manufacturing operations are similar in that both combine materials, labor, and factory overhead to produce products or services. They differ in the way they are organized and managed. In job order operations, the job order cost accounting system assigns materials, labor, and overhead to specific jobs. In process operations, the process cost accounting system assigns materials, labor, and overhead to specific processes. The total costs associated with each process are then divided by the number of units passing through that process to get cost per equivalent unit. The costs per equivalent unit for all processes are added to determine the total cost per unit of a product or service.

A2 Explain and illustrate a hybrid costing system. A hybrid costing system contains features of both job order and process costing systems. Generally, certain direct materials are accounted for by individual products as in job order costing, but direct labor and overhead costs are accounted for similar to process costing.

P1 Record the flow of direct materials costs in process cost accounting. Materials purchased are debited to a Raw Materials Inventory account. As direct materials are issued to processes, they are separately accumulated in a Goods in Process Inventory account for that process.

P2 Record the flow of direct labor costs in process cost accounting. Direct labor costs are initially debited to the Factory Payroll account. The total amount in it is then assigned to the Goods in Process Inventory account pertaining to each process.

P3 Record the flow of factory overhead costs in process cost accounting. The different factory overhead items are first accumulated in the Factory Overhead account and are then allocated, using a predetermined overhead rate, to the different processes. The allocated amount is debited to the Goods in Process Inventory account pertaining to each process.

P4 Compute equivalent units produced in a period. To compute equivalent units, determine the number of units that would have been finished if all materials (or labor or overhead) had been used to produce units that were started and completed during the period. The costs incurred by a process are divided by its equivalent units to yield cost per unit.

P5 Prepare a process cost summary. A process cost summary includes the physical flow of units, equivalent units of production, costs per equivalent unit, and a cost reconciliation. It reports the units and costs to account for during the period and how they were accounted for during the period. In terms of units, the summary includes the beginning goods in process inventory and the units started during the month. These units are accounted for in terms of the goods completed and transferred out, and the ending goods in process inventory. With respect to costs, the summary includes materials, labor, and overhead costs assigned to the process during the period. It shows how these costs are assigned to goods completed and transferred out, and to ending goods in process inventory.

P6 Record the transfer of completed goods to Finished Goods Inventory and Cost of Goods Sold. As units complete the final process and are eventually sold, their accumulated cost is transferred to Finished Goods Inventory and finally to Cost of Goods Sold.

Guidance Answers to **Decision Maker** and **Decision Ethics**

Budget Officer By instructing you to classify a majority of costs as indirect, the manager is passing some of his department's costs to a common overhead pool that other departments will partially absorb. Since overhead costs are allocated on the basis of direct labor for this company and the new department has a relatively low direct labor cost, the new department will be assigned less overhead. Such action suggests unethical behavior by this manager. You must object to such reclassification. If this manager refuses to comply, you must inform someone in a more senior position.

Entrepreneur By spreading the added quality-related costs across three customers, the entrepreneur is probably trying to remain competitive with respect to the customer that demands the 100% quality inspection. Moreover, the entrepreneur is partly covering the added costs by recovering two-thirds of them from the other two customers who are paying 110% of total costs. This act likely breaches the trust placed by the two customers in this entrepreneur's application of its costing system. The costing system should be changed, and the entrepreneur should consider renegotiating the pricing and/or quality test agreement with this one customer (at the risk of losing this currently loss-producing customer).

Cost Manager Differences between the FIFO and weighted-average methods are greatest when large work in process inventories exist and when costs fluctuate. The method used if inventories are eliminated does not matter; both produce identical costs.

Guidance Answers to **Quick Checks**

1. *c*

2. When a company produces large quantities of similar products/services, a process cost system is often more suitable.

3. *b*

4. The costs are direct materials, direct labor, and overhead.

5. A goods in process inventory account is needed for *each* production department.

6. *a*

7. Equivalent units with respect to direct labor are the number of units that would have been produced if all labor had been used on units that were started and finished during the period.

8.

Units completed and transferred out	58,000 EUP
Units of ending goods in process	
Direct labor (6,000 × 1/3)	2,000 EUP
Units of production	60,000 EUP

9. The first section shows the costs charged to the department. The second section describes the equivalent units produced by the department. The third section shows the assignment of total costs to units worked on during the period.

Key Terms

mhhe.com/wildFAP19e

Key Terms are available at the book's Website for learning and testing in an online Flashcard Format.

Cost of goods manufactured (p. 821)
Equivalent units of production (EUP) (p. 815)
FIFO method (p. 827)
Job order cost accounting system (p. 811)
Materials consumption report (p. 812)
Process cost accounting system (p. 811)
Process cost summary (p. 820)
Process operations (p. 808)
Weighted-average method (p. 818)

Multiple Choice Quiz

Answers on p. 849

mhhe.com/wildFAP19e

Additional Quiz Questions are available at the book's Website.

Quiz20

1. Equivalent units of production are equal to
   a. Physical units that were completed this period from all effort being applied to them.
   b. The number of units introduced into the process this period.
   c. The number of finished units actually completed this period.
   d. The number of units that could have been started and completed given the cost incurred.
   e. The number of units in the process at the end of the period.

2. Recording the cost of raw materials purchased for use in a process costing system includes a
   a. Credit to Raw Materials Inventory.
   b. Debit to Goods in Process Inventory.
   c. Debit to Factory Overhead.
   d. Credit to Factory Overhead.
   e. Debit to Raw Materials Inventory.

3. The production department started the month with a beginning goods in process inventory of $20,000. During the month, it was assigned the following costs: direct materials, $152,000; direct labor, $45,000; overhead applied at the rate of 40% of direct labor cost. Inventory with a cost of $218,000 was transferred to finished goods. The ending balance of goods in process inventory is
   a. $330,000.
   b. $ 17,000.
   c. $220,000.
   d. $112,000.
   e. $118,000.

4. A company's beginning work in process inventory consists of 10,000 units that are 20% complete with respect to direct labor costs. A total of 40,000 units are completed this period. There are 15,000 units in goods in process, one-third complete for direct labor, at period-end. The equivalent units of production (EUP) with respect to direct labor at period-end, assuming the weighted average method, are

a. 45,000 EUP.
b. 40,000 EUP.
c. 5,000 EUP.
d. 37,000 EUP.
e. 43,000 EUP.

5. Assume the same information as in question 4. Also assume that beginning work in process had $6,000 in direct labor cost and that $84,000 in direct labor is added during this period. What is the cost per EUP for labor?

a. $0.50 per EUP
b. $1.87 per EUP
c. $2.00 per EUP
d. $2.10 per EUP
e. $2.25 per EUP

Assume the weighted-average inventory method is used for all assignments unless stated differently. Superscript letter [A] denotes assignments based on Appendix 20A.

Discussion Questions

1. Can services be delivered by means of process operations? Support your answer with an example.

2. What is the main factor for a company in choosing between the job order costing and process costing accounting systems? Give two likely applications of each system.

3. Identify the control document for materials flow when a materials requisition slip is not used.

4. The focus in a job order costing system is the job or batch. Identify the main focus in process costing.

5. Are the journal entries that match cost flows to product flows in process costing primarily the same or much different than those in job order costing? Explain.

6. Explain in simple terms the notion of equivalent units of production (EUP). Why is it necessary to use EUP in process costing?

7. What are the two main inventory methods used in process costing? What are the differences between these methods?

8. Why is it possible for direct labor in process operations to include the labor of employees who do not work directly on products or services?

9. Assume that a company produces a single product by processing it first through a single production department. Direct labor costs flow through what accounts in this company's process cost system?

10. After all labor costs for a period are allocated, what balance should remain in the Factory Payroll account?

11. Is it possible to have under- or overapplied overhead costs in a process cost accounting system? Explain.

12. Explain why equivalent units of production for both direct labor and overhead can be the same as, and why they can be different from, equivalent units for direct materials.

13. List the four steps in accounting for production activity in a reporting period (for process operations).

14. What purposes does a process cost summary serve?

15. Are there situations where **Best Buy** can use process costing? Identify at least one and explain it.

16. **Apple** produces iMacs with a multiple production line. Identify and list some of its production processing steps and departments.

Denotes Discussion Questions that involve decision making.

QUICK STUDY

QS 20-1
Matching of product to cost accounting system
C1

For each of the following products and services, indicate whether it is most likely produced in a process operation or in a job order operation.

1. Door hinges
2. Cut flower arrangements
3. House paints
4. Concrete swimming pools
5. Custom tailored suits
6. Grand pianos
7. Wall clocks
8. Sport shirts
9. Bolts and nuts
10. Folding chairs
11. Headphones
12. Designed boathouse

QS 20-2
Recording costs of direct materials
P1

Industrial Boxes makes cardboard shipping cartons in a single operation. This period, Industrial purchased $124,000 in raw materials. Its production department requisitioned $100,000 of those materials for use in producing cartons. Prepare journal entries to record its (1) purchase of raw materials and (2) requisition of direct materials.

QS 20-3
Recording costs of direct labor
P2

Refer to the information in QS 20-2. Industrial Boxes incurred $270,000 in factory payroll costs, of which $250,000 was direct labor. Prepare journal entries to record its (1) total factory payroll incurred and (2) direct labor used in production.

QS 20-4
Recording costs of factory overhead
P3

Refer to the information in QS 20-2 and QS 20-3. Industrial Boxes requisitioned $18,000 of indirect materials from its raw materials and used $20,000 of indirect labor in its production of boxes. Also, it incurred $312,000 of other factory overhead costs. It applies factory overhead at the rate of 135% of direct labor costs. Prepare journal entries to record its (1) indirect materials requisitioned, (2) indirect labor used in production, (3) other factory overhead costs incurred, and (4) application of overhead to production.

QS 20-5
Recording transfer of costs to finished goods P6

Refer to the information in QS 20-2, QS 20-3, and QS 20-4. Industrial Boxes completed 40,000 boxes costing $550,000 and transferred them to finished goods. Prepare its journal entry to record the transfer of the boxes from production to finished goods inventory.

QS 20-6
Computing equivalent units of production
P4

The following refers to units processed in Sunflower Printing's binding department in March. Compute the total equivalent units of production with respect to labor for March using the weighted-average inventory method.

	Units of Product	Percent of Labor Added
Beginning goods in process	75,000	85%
Goods started	155,000	100
Goods completed	170,000	100
Ending goods in process	60,000	25

QS 20-7
Computing EUP cost C4 P5

The cost of beginning inventory plus the costs added during the period should equal the cost of units ________________ plus the cost of ________________.

QS 20-8
Hybrid costing system A2

Explain a hybrid costing system. Identify a product or service operation that might well fit a hybrid costing system.

QS 20-9^A
Computing equivalent units—FIFO C2 C5 P4

Refer to QS 20-6 and compute the total equivalent units of production with respect to labor for March using the FIFO inventory method.

McGraw-Hill's HOMEWORK MANAGER® HM Available with McGraw-Hill's Homework Manager

EXERCISES

Exercise 20-1
Terminology in process cost accounting
C1 A1 P1 P2 P3

Match each of the following items A through G with the best numbered description of its purpose.

A. Raw Materials Inventory account
B. Materials requisition
C. Finished Goods Inventory account
D. Factory Overhead account
E. Process cost summary
F. Equivalent units of production
G. Goods in Process Inventory

_____ **1.** Notifies the materials manager to send materials to a production department.
_____ **2.** Holds costs of indirect materials, indirect labor, and similar costs until assigned to production.
_____ **3.** Holds costs of direct materials, direct labor, and applied overhead until products are transferred from production to finished goods (or another department).
_____ **4.** Standardizes partially completed units into equivalent completed units.
_____ **5.** Holds costs of finished products until sold to customers.
_____ **6.** Describes the activity and output of a production department for a period.
_____ **7.** Holds costs of materials until they are used in production or as factory overhead.

Exercise 20-2
Journal entries in process cost accounting
P1 P2 P3

Festive Toy Company manufactures toy trucks. Prepare journal entries to record its following production activities for January.

1. Purchased $40,000 of raw materials on credit.
2. Used $17,000 of direct materials in production.
3. Used $20,500 of indirect materials.

4. Incurred total labor cost of $77,000, which is paid in cash.
5. Used $58,000 of direct labor in production.
6. Used $19,000 of indirect labor.
7. Incurred overhead costs of $22,000 (paid in cash).
8. Applied overhead at 90% of direct labor costs.
9. Transferred completed products with a cost of $137,000 to finished goods inventory.
10. Sold $450,000 of products on credit. Their cost is $150,000.

Check (8) Cr. Factory Overhead, $52,200

Exercise 20-3
Recording cost flows in a process cost system
P1 P2 P3 P6

Seattle Lumber produces bagged bark for use in landscaping. Production involves packaging bark chips in plastic bags in a bagging department. The following information describes production operations for October.

	Bagging Department
Direct materials used	$ 460,000
Direct labor used	$ 76,000
Predetermined overhead rate (based on direct labor)	180%
Goods transferred from bagging to finished goods	$(407,000)

The company's revenue for the month totaled $900,000 from credit sales, and its cost of goods sold for the month is $500,000. Prepare summary journal entries dated October 31 to record its October production activities for (1) direct material usage, (2) direct labor usage, (3) overhead allocation, (4) goods transfer from production to finished goods, and (5) sales.

Check (3) Cr. Factory Overhead, $136,800

Exercise 20-4
Interpretation of journal entries in process cost accounting
P1 P2 P3 P6

The following journal entries are recorded in Lewis Co.'s process cost accounting system. Lewis produces apparel and accessories. Overhead is applied to production based on direct labor cost for the period. Prepare a brief explanation (including any overhead rates applied) for each journal entry *a* through *j*.

a.	Raw Materials Inventory	52,000	
	Accounts Payable		52,000
b.	Goods in Process Inventory	42,000	
	Raw Materials Inventory		42,000
c.	Goods in Process Inventory	26,000	
	Factory Payroll		26,000
d.	Factory Payroll	32,000	
	Cash		32,000
e.	Factory Overhead	10,000	
	Cash		10,000
f.	Factory Overhead	10,000	
	Raw Materials Inventory		10,000
g.	Factory Overhead	6,000	
	Factory Payroll		6,000
h.	Goods in Process Inventory	32,500	
	Factory Overhead		32,500
i.	Finished Goods Inventory	88,000	
	Goods in Process Inventory		88,000
j.	Accounts Receivable	250,000	
	Sales		250,000
	Cost of Goods Sold	100,000	
	Finished Goods Inventory		100,000

Exercise 20-5
Computing equivalent units of production—weighted average
C2 P4

During April, the production department of a process manufacturing system completed a number of units of a product and transferred them to finished goods. Of these transferred units, 30,000 were in process in the production department at the beginning of April and 120,000 were started and completed in April. April's beginning inventory units were 60% complete with respect to materials and 40% complete with respect to labor. At the end of April, 41,000 additional units were in process in the production department and were 80% complete with respect to materials and 30% complete with respect to labor.

1. Compute the number of units transferred to finished goods.

2. Compute the number of equivalent units with respect to both materials used and labor used in the production department for April using the weighted-average method.

Check (2) EUP for materials, 182,800

Exercise 20-6
Costs assigned to output and inventories—weighted average
C3 P4 P5 

The production department described in Exercise 20-5 had $425,184 of direct materials and $326,151 of direct labor cost charged to it during April. Also, its beginning inventory included $59,236 of direct materials cost and $22,794 of direct labor.

1. Compute the direct materials cost and the direct labor cost per equivalent unit for the department.

2. Using the weighted-average method, assign April's costs to the department's output—specifically, its units transferred to finished goods and its ending goods in process inventory.

Check (2) Costs accounted for, $833,365

Exercise 20-7^A
Computing equivalent units of production—FIFO
C5 P4

Refer to the information in Exercise 20-5 to compute the number of equivalent units with respect to both materials used and labor used in the production department for April using the FIFO method.

Exercise 20-8^A
Costs assigned to output—FIFO
C5 P4 P5

Refer to the information in Exercise 20-6 and complete its parts (1) and (2) using the FIFO method.

Exercise 20-9
Equivalent units computed—weighted average
C2 P4 P5 

The production department in a process manufacturing system completed 383,000 units of product and transferred them to finished goods during a recent period. Of these units, 63,000 were in process at the beginning of the period. The other 320,000 units were started and completed during the period. At period-end, 59,000 units were in process. Compute the department's equivalent units of production with respect to direct materials under each of three separate assumptions:

1. All direct materials are added to products when processing begins.

2. Direct materials are added to products evenly throughout the process. Beginning goods in process inventory was 40% complete, and ending goods in process inventory was 75% complete.

3. One-half of direct materials is added to products when the process begins and the other half is added when the process is 75% complete as to direct labor. Beginning goods in process inventory is 40% complete as to direct labor, and ending goods in process inventory is 60% complete as to direct labor.

Check (3) EUP for materials, 412,500

Exercise 20-10^A
Equivalent units computed—FIFO
C5 P4

Refer to the information in Exercise 20-9 and complete it for each of the three separate assumptions using the FIFO method for process costing.

Check (3) EUP for materials, 381,000

Exercise 20-11
Flowchart of costs for a process operation P1 P2 P3 P6

The following flowchart shows the August production activity of the Jez Company. Use the amounts shown on the flowchart to compute the missing four numbers identified by blanks.

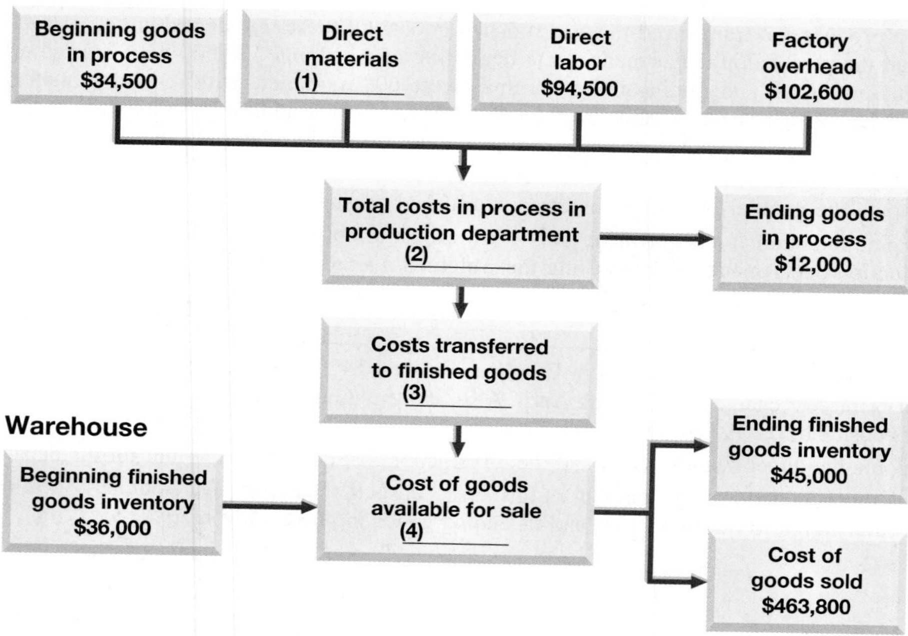

Exercise 20-12
Completing a process cost summary
P5

The following partially completed process cost summary describes the July production activities of Anton Company. Its production output is sent to its warehouse for shipping. Prepare its process cost summary using the weighted-average method.

Equivalent Units of Production	Direct Materials	Direct Labor	Factory Overhead
Units transferred out	64,000	64,000	64,000
Units of ending goods in process	5,000	3,000	3,000
Equivalent units of production	69,000	67,000	67,000
Costs per EUP	**Direct Materials**	**Direct Labor**	**Factory Overhead**
Costs of beginning goods in process	$ 37,100	$ 1,520	$ 3,040
Costs incurred this period	715,000	125,780	251,560
Total costs	$752,100	$127,300	$254,600
Units in beginning goods in process			4,000
Units started this period			65,000
Units completed and transferred out			64,000
Units in ending goods in process			5,000

Exercise 20-13
Process costing—weighted average
P1 P2 P6

Nu-Test Company uses the weighted-average method of process costing to assign production costs to its products. Information for September follows. Assume that all materials are added at the beginning of its production process, and that direct labor and factory overhead are added uniformly throughout the process.

Goods in process inventory, September 1 (4,000 units, 100% complete with respect to direct materials, 80% complete with respect to direct labor and overhead; includes $90,000 of direct material cost, $51,200 in direct labor cost, $61,440 overhead cost)	$202,640
Units started in September	56,000
Units completed and transferred to finished goods inventory	46,000
Goods in process inventory, September 30 (? units, 100% complete with respect to direct materials, 40% complete with respect to direct labor and overhead)	?

[continued on next page]

[continued from previous page]

Costs incurred in September	
Direct materials	$750,000
Direct labor	$310,000
Overhead applied at 120% of direct labor cost	?

Required

Fill in the blanks labeled *a* through *uu* in the following process cost summary.

NU-TEST COMPANY
Process Cost Summary
For Month Ended September 30

Costs Charged to Production

Costs of beginning goods in process		
Direct materials	$ 90,000	
Direct labor	51,200	
Factory overhead	61,440	$202,640
Costs incurred this period		
Direct materials	$750,000	
Direct labor	310,000	
Factory overhead	(a)____	(b)____
Total costs to account for		(c)____

Check (c) $1,634,640

Unit Cost Information

Units to account for		Units accounted for	
Beginning goods in process	4,000	Completed and transferred out	46,000
Units started this period	56,000	Ending goods in process	(d)____
Total units to account for	(e)____	Total units accounted for	(f)____

Equivalent Units of Production (EUP)			**Direct Materials**	**Direct Labor**	**Factory Overhead**
Units completed and transferred out			(g)____EUP	(h)____EUP	(i)____EUP
Units of ending goods in process					
Materials	(j)____	× 100%	(k)____EUP		
Direct labor	(l)____	× 40%		(m)____EUP	
Factory overhead	(n)____	× 40%			(o)____EUP
Equivalent units of production (EUP)			(p)____EUP	(q)____EUP	(r)____EUP

Cost per EUP	**Direct Materials**	**Direct Labor**	**Factory Overhead**
Costs of beginning goods in process	$ 90,000	$ 51,200	$61,440
Costs incurred this period	750,000	310,000	(s)____
Total costs	$840,000	$361,200	(t)____
÷ EUP	(u)____	(v)____	(w)____
Cost per EUP	(x)____	(y)____	(z)____

(z) $8.40 per EUP

Cost Assignment and Reconciliation

	Cost/EUP	×	EUP		
Costs transferred out					
Direct materials	(aa)____	×	(bb)____	(cc)____	
Direct labor	(dd)____	×	(ee)____	(ff)____	
Factory overhead	(gg)____	×	(hh)____	(ii)____	
Costs of goods completed and transferred out					(jj)____
Costs of ending goods in process					
Direct materials	(kk)____	×	(ll)____	(mm)____	
Direct labor	(nn)____	×	(oo)____	(pp)____	
Factory overhead	(qq)____	×	(rr)____	(ss)____	
Costs of ending goods in process					(tt)____
Total costs accounted for					(uu)____

Available with McGraw-Hill's Homework Manager

McGraw-Hill's HOMEWORK MANAGER®

PROBLEM SET A

Problem 20-1A

Production cost flow and measurement; journal entries

P1 P2 P3 P6

Harvey Company manufactures woven blankets and accounts for product costs using process costing. The following information is available regarding its May inventories.

	Beginning Inventory	Ending Inventory
Raw materials inventory	$ 56,000	$ 51,000
Goods in process inventory	441,500	504,000
Finished goods inventory	638,000	554,000

The following additional information describes the company's production activities for May.

Raw materials purchases (on credit)	$ 270,000
Factory payroll cost (paid in cash)	1,583,000
Other overhead cost (Other Accounts credited)	86,000
Materials used	
Direct	$ 187,000
Indirect	62,000
Labor used	
Direct	$ 704,000
Indirect	879,000
Overhead rate as a percent of direct labor	110%
Sales (on credit)	$3,000,000

Required

1. Compute the cost of (a) products transferred from production to finished goods, and (b) goods sold.

2. Prepare summary journal entries dated May 31 to record the following production activities during May: (a) raw materials purchases, (b) direct materials usage, (c) indirect materials usage, (d) payroll costs, (e) direct labor costs, (f) indirect labor costs, (g) other overhead costs, (h) overhead applied, (i) goods transferred from production to finished goods, and (j) sale of finished goods.

Check (1b) Cost of goods sold $1,686,900

Problem 20-2A

Cost per equivalent unit; costs assigned to products

P4 P5

mhhe.com/wildFAP19e

Carmen Company uses weighted-average process costing to account for its production costs. Direct labor is added evenly throughout the process. Direct materials are added at the beginning of the process. During November, the company transferred 735,000 units of product to finished goods. At the end of November, the goods in process inventory consists of 207,000 units that are 90% complete with respect to labor. Beginning inventory had $244,920 of direct materials and $69,098 of direct labor cost. The direct labor cost added in November is $1,312,852, and the direct materials cost added is $1,639,080.

Required

1. Determine the equivalent units of production with respect to (a) direct labor and (b) direct materials.

2. Compute both the direct labor cost and the direct materials cost per equivalent unit.

3. Compute both direct labor cost and direct materials cost assigned to (a) units completed and transferred out, and (b) ending goods in process inventory.

Check (2) Direct labor cost per equivalent unit, $1.50

(3b) $693,450

Analysis Component

4. The company sells and ships all units to customers as soon as they are completed. Assume that an error is made in determining the percentage of completion for units in ending inventory. Instead of being 90% complete with respect to labor, they are actually 75% complete. Write a one-page memo to the plant manager describing how this error affects its November financial statements.

Problem 20-3A
Journalizing in process costing; equivalent units and costs
P1 P2 P3 P4 P6

Crystal Company produces large quantities of a standardized product. The following information is available for its production activities for March.

Raw materials		**Factory overhead incurred**	
Beginning inventory	$ 26,000	Indirect materials used	$ 81,500
Raw materials purchased (on credit)	255,000	Indirect labor used	50,000
Direct materials used	(172,000)	Other overhead costs	159,308
Indirect materials used	(81,500)	Total factory overhead incurred	$290,808
Ending inventory	$ 27,500		
		Factory overhead applied (140% of direct labor cost)	
Factory payroll		Total factory overhead applied	$290,808
Direct labor used	$207,720		
Indirect labor used	50,000		
Total payroll cost (paid in cash)	$257,720		

Additional information about units and costs of production activities follows.

Units		**Costs**		
Beginning goods in process inventory	2,200	Beginning goods in process inventory		
Started	30,000	Direct materials	$3,500	
Ending goods in process inventory	5,900	Direct labor	3,225	
		Factory overhead	4,515	$ 11,240
Status of ending goods in process inventory		Direct materials added		172,000
Materials—Percent complete	50%	Direct labor added		207,720
Labor and overhead—Percent complete	65%	Overhead applied (140% of direct labor)		290,808
		Total costs		$681,768
		Ending goods in process inventory		$ 82,128

During March, 25,000 units of finished goods are sold for $85 cash each. Cost information regarding finished goods follows.

Beginning finished goods inventory	$155,000
Cost transferred in	599,640
Cost of goods sold	(612,500)
Ending finished goods inventory	$142,140

Required

1. Prepare journal entries dated March 31 to record the following March activities: (a) purchase of raw materials, (b) direct materials usage, (c) indirect materials usage, (d) factory payroll costs, (e) direct labor costs used in production, (f) indirect labor costs, (g) other overhead costs—credit Other Accounts, (h) overhead applied, (i) goods transferred to finished goods, and (j) sale of finished goods.

2. Prepare a process cost summary report for this company, showing costs charged to production, units cost information, equivalent units of production, cost per EUP, and its cost assignment and reconciliation.

Check (2) Cost per equivalent unit: materials, $6.00; labor, $7.00; overhead, $9.80

Analysis Component

3. The company provides incentives to its department managers by paying monthly bonuses based on their success in controlling costs per equivalent unit of production. Assume that the production department underestimates the percentage of completion for units in ending inventory with the result that its equivalent units of production in ending inventory for March are understated. What impact does this error have on the March bonuses paid to the production managers? What impact, if any, does this error have on April bonuses?

Problem 20-4A
Process cost summary; equivalent units
P4 P5 P6

mhhe.com/wildFAP19e

King Co. produces its product through a single processing department. Direct materials are added at the start of production, and direct labor and overhead are added evenly throughout the process. The company uses monthly reporting periods for its weighted-average process cost accounting system. Its Goods in Process Inventory account follows after entries for direct materials, direct labor, and overhead costs for October.

Goods in Process Inventory					Acct. No. 133
Date		Explanation	Debit	Credit	Balance
Oct.	1	Balance			348,638
	31	Direct materials	104,090		452,728
	31	Direct labor	416,360		869,088
	31	Applied overhead	244,920		1,114,008

Its beginning goods in process consisted of $60,830 of direct materials, $176,820 of direct labor, and $110,988 of factory overhead. During October, the company started 140,000 units and transferred 153,000 units to finished goods. At the end of the month, the goods in process inventory consisted of 20,600 units that were 80% complete with respect to direct labor and factory overhead.

Required

Check (1) Costs transferred to finished goods, $1,002,150

1. Prepare the company's process cost summary for October using the weighted-average method.
2. Prepare the journal entry dated October 31 to transfer the cost of the completed units to finished goods inventory.

Problem 20-5A
Process cost summary; equivalent units; cost estimates
P4 P5 

Cisneros Co. manufactures a single product in one department. All direct materials are added at the beginning of the manufacturing process. Direct labor and overhead are added evenly throughout the process. The company uses monthly reporting periods for its weighted-average process cost accounting. During May, the company completed and transferred 11,100 units of product to finished goods inventory. Its 1,500 units of beginning goods in process consisted of $9,900 of direct materials, $61,650 of direct labor, and $49,320 of factory overhead. It has 1,200 units (100% complete with respect to direct materials and 80% complete with respect to direct labor and overhead) in process at month-end. After entries to record direct materials, direct labor, and overhead for May, the company's Goods in Process Inventory account follows.

Goods in Process Inventory					Acct. No. 133
Date		Explanation	Debit	Credit	Balance
May	1	Balance			120,870
	31	Direct materials	248,400		369,270
	31	Direct labor	601,650		970,920
	31	Applied overhead	481,320		1,452,240

Required

Check (1) EUP for labor and overhead, 12,060 EUP

(2) Cost transferred to finished goods, $1,332,000

1. Prepare the company's process cost summary for May.
2. Prepare the journal entry dated May 31 to transfer the cost of completed units to finished goods inventory.

Analysis Components

3. The cost accounting process depends on numerous estimates.
   a. Identify two major estimates that determine the cost per equivalent unit.
   b. In what direction might you anticipate a bias from management for each estimate in part 3a (assume that management compensation is based on maintaining low inventory amounts)? Explain your answer.

Problem 20-6A[A]
Process cost summary; equivalent units; cost estimates—FIFO
C5 P5 P6

Refer to the data in Problem 20-5A. Assume that Cisneros uses the FIFO method to account for its process costing system. The following additional information is available:

- Beginning goods in process consisted of 1,500 units that were 100% complete with respect to direct materials and 40% complete with respect to direct labor and overhead.
- Of the 11,100 units completed, 1,500 were from beginning goods in process. The remaining 9,600 were units started and completed during May.

Required

1. Prepare the company's process cost summary for May using FIFO.

2. Prepare the journal entry dated May 31 to transfer the cost of completed units to finished goods inventory.

Check (1) EUP for labor and overhead, 11,460 EUP

(2) Cost transferred to finished goods, $1,333,920

PROBLEM SET B

Problem 20-1B
Production cost flow and measurement; journal entries

P1 P2 P3 P6

Select Toys Company manufactures video game consoles and accounts for product costs using process costing. The following information is available regarding its June inventories.

	Beginning Inventory	Ending Inventory
Raw materials inventory	$36,000	$ 55,000
Goods in process inventory	78,000	125,000
Finished goods inventory	80,000	99,000

The following additional information describes the company's production activities for June.

Raw materials purchases (on credit)	$100,000
Factory payroll cost (paid in cash)	200,000
Other overhead cost (Other Accounts credited)	85,250
Materials used	
Direct	$ 60,000
Indirect	21,000
Labor used	
Direct	$175,000
Indirect	25,000
Overhead rate as a percent of direct labor	75%
Sales (on credit)	$500,000

Required

1. Compute the cost of (a) products transferred from production to finished goods, and (b) goods sold.

2. Prepare journal entries dated June 30 to record the following production activities during June: (a) raw materials purchases, (b) direct materials usage, (c) indirect materials usage, (d) payroll costs, (e) direct labor costs, (f) indirect labor costs, (g) other overhead costs, (h) overhead applied, (i) goods transferred from production to finished goods, and (j) sale of finished goods.

Check (1b) Cost of goods sold, $300,250

Problem 20-2B
Cost per equivalent unit; costs assigned to products

P4 P5

Maximus Company uses process costing to account for its production costs. Direct labor is added evenly throughout the process. Direct materials are added at the beginning of the process. During September, the production department transferred 40,000 units of product to finished goods. Beginning goods in process had $116,000 of direct materials and $172,800 of direct labor cost. At the end of September, the goods in process inventory consists of 4,000 units that are 25% complete with respect to labor. The direct materials cost added in September is $1,424,000, and direct labor cost added is $3,960,000.

Required

1. Determine the equivalent units of production with respect to (a) direct labor and (b) direct materials.

2. Compute both the direct labor cost and the direct materials cost per equivalent unit.

3. Compute both direct labor cost and direct materials cost assigned to (a) units completed and transferred out, and (b) ending goods in process inventory.

Check (2) Direct labor cost per equivalent unit, $100.80

(3b) $240,800

Analysis Component

4. The company sells and ships all units to customers as soon as they are completed. Assume that an error is made in determining the percentage of completion for units in ending inventory. Instead of being 25% complete with respect to labor, they are actually 75% complete. Write a one-page memo to the plant manager describing how this error affects its September financial statements.

Problem 20-3B
Journalizing in process costing; equivalent units and costs
P1 P2 P3 P4 P6 

Fantasia Company produces large quantities of a standardized product. The following information is available for its production activities for May.

Raw materials		**Factory overhead incurred**	
Beginning inventory	$ 16,000	Indirect materials used	$20,280
Raw materials purchased (on credit)	110,560	Indirect labor used	18,160
Direct materials used	(98,560)	Other overhead costs	17,216
Indirect materials used	(20,280)	Total factory overhead incurred	$55,656
Ending inventory	$ 7,720	**Factory overhead applied (90% of direct labor cost)**	
Factory payroll			
Direct labor used	$ 61,840	Total factory overhead applied	$55,656
Indirect labor used	18,160		
Total payroll cost (paid in cash)	$ 80,000		

Additional information about units and costs of production activities follows.

Units		**Costs**		
Beginning goods in process inventory	8,000	Beginning goods in process inventory		
Started	24,000	Direct materials	$2,240	
Ending goods in process inventory	6,000	Direct labor	1,410	
		Factory overhead	1,269	$ 4,919
Status of ending goods in process inventory		Direct materials added		98,560
Materials—Percent complete	100%	Direct labor added		61,840
Labor and overhead—Percent complete	25%	Overhead applied (90% of direct labor)		55,656
		Total costs		$220,975
		Ending goods in process inventory		$ 25,455

During May, 30,000 units of finished goods are sold for $30 cash each. Cost information regarding finished goods follows.

Beginning finished goods inventory	$ 74,200
Cost transferred in from production	195,520
Cost of goods sold	(225,000)
Ending finished goods inventory	$ 44,720

Required

1. Prepare journal entries dated May 31 to record the following May activities: (a) purchase of raw materials, (b) direct materials usage, (c) indirect materials usage, (d) factory payroll costs, (e) direct labor costs used in production, (f) indirect labor costs, (g) other overhead costs—credit Other Accounts, (h) overhead applied, (i) goods transferred to finished goods, and (j) sale of finished goods.
2. Prepare a process cost summary report for this company, showing costs charged to production, unit cost information, equivalent units of production, cost per EUP, and its cost assignment and reconciliation.

Check (2) Cost per equivalent unit: materials, $3.15; labor, $2.30; overhead, $2.07

Analysis Component

3. This company provides incentives to its department managers by paying monthly bonuses based on their success in controlling costs per equivalent unit of production. Assume that production overestimates the percentage of completion for units in ending inventory with the result that its equivalent units of production in ending inventory for May are overstated. What impact does this error have on bonuses paid to the managers of the production department? What impact, if any, does this error have on these managers' June bonuses?

Problem 20-4B
Process cost summary; equivalent units
P4 P5 P6

Paloma Company produces its product through a single processing department. Direct materials are added at the beginning of the process. Direct labor and overhead are added to the product evenly throughout the process. The company uses monthly reporting periods for its weighted-average process cost accounting. Its Goods in Process Inventory account follows after entries for direct materials, direct labor, and overhead costs for November.

Goods in Process Inventory					Acct. No. 133
Date		Explanation	Debit	Credit	Balance
Nov.	1	Balance			10,650
	30	Direct materials	58,200		68,850
	30	Direct labor	213,400		282,250
	30	Applied overhead	320,100		602,350

The 3,750 units of beginning goods in process consisted of $3,400 of direct materials, $2,900 of direct labor, and $4,350 of factory overhead. During November, the company finished and transferred 50,000 units of its product to finished goods. At the end of the month, the goods in process inventory consisted of 6,000 units that were 100% complete with respect to direct materials and 25% complete with respect to direct labor and factory overhead.

Required

1. Prepare the company's process cost summary for November using the weighted-average method.

2. Prepare the journal entry dated November 30 to transfer the cost of the completed units to finished goods inventory.

Check (1) Cost transferred to finished goods, $580,000

Problem 20-5B
Process cost summary; equivalent units; cost estimates
P4 P5

Foster Co. manufactures a single product in one department. Direct labor and overhead are added evenly throughout the process. Direct materials are added as needed. The company uses monthly reporting periods for its weighted-average process cost accounting. During January, Foster completed and transferred 220,000 units of product to finished goods inventory. Its 10,000 units of beginning goods in process consisted of $8,400 of direct materials, $13,960 of direct labor, and $34,900 of factory overhead. 40,000 units (50% complete with respect to direct materials and 30% complete with respect to direct labor and overhead) are in process at month-end. After entries for direct materials, direct labor, and overhead for January, the company's Goods in Process Inventory account follows.

Goods in Process Inventory					Acct. No. 133
Date		Explanation	Debit	Credit	Balance
Jan.	1	Balance			57,260
	31	Direct materials	111,600		168,860
	31	Direct labor	176,280		345,140
	31	Applied overhead	440,700		785,840

Required

1. Prepare the company's process cost summary for January.

2. Prepare the journal entry dated January 31 to transfer the cost of completed units to finished goods inventory.

Check (1) EUP for labor and overhead, 232,000
(2) Cost transferred to finished goods, $741,400

Analysis Components

3. The cost accounting process depends on several estimates.

a. Identify two major estimates that affect the cost per equivalent unit.

b. In what direction might you anticipate a bias from management for each estimate in part 3a (assume that management compensation is based on maintaining low inventory amounts)? Explain your answer.

Problem 20-6B^A
Process cost summary; equivalent units; cost estimates—FIFO
C5 P5 P6

Refer to the information in Problem 20-5B. Assume that Foster uses the FIFO method to account for its process costing system. The following additional information is available.

- Beginning goods in process consists of 10,000 units that were 75% complete with respect to direct materials and 60% complete with respect to direct labor and overhead.
- Of the 220,000 units completed, 10,000 were from beginning goods in process; the remaining 210,000 were units started and completed during January.

Required

1. Prepare the company's process cost summary for January using FIFO. Round cost per EUP to one-tenth of a cent.

2. Prepare the journal entry dated January 31 to transfer the cost of completed units to finished goods inventory.

Check (1) Labor and overhead EUP, 226,000
(2) Cost transferred, $743,480

SERIAL PROBLEM

Success Systems
C1 A1

(This serial problem began in Chapter 1 and continues through most of the book. If previous chapter segments were not completed, the serial problem can begin at this point.)

SP 20 The computer workstation furniture manufacturing that Adriana Lopez started is progressing well. At this point, Adriana is using a job order costing system to account for the production costs of this product line. Adriana has heard about process costing and is wondering whether process costing might be a better method for her to keep track of and monitor her production costs.

Required

1. What are the features that distinguish job order costing from process costing?

2. Do you believe that Adriana should continue to use job order costing or switch to process costing for her workstation furniture manufacturing? Explain.

COMPREHENSIVE PROBLEM

Major League Bat Company
(Review of Chapters 2, 5, 18, 20)

CP 20 Major League Bat Company manufactures baseball bats. In addition to its goods in process inventories, the company maintains inventories of raw materials and finished goods. It uses raw materials as direct materials in production and as indirect materials. Its factory payroll costs include direct labor for production and indirect labor. All materials are added at the beginning of the process, and direct labor and factory overhead are applied uniformly throughout the production process.

Required

You are to maintain records and produce measures of inventories to reflect the July events of this company. Set up the following general ledger accounts and enter the June 30 balances: Raw Materials Inventory, $25,000; Goods in Process Inventory, $8,135 ($2,660 of direct materials, $3,650 of direct labor, and $1,825 of overhead); Finished Goods Inventory, $110,000; Sales, $0; Cost of Goods Sold, $0; Factory Payroll, $0; and Factory Overhead, $0.

1. Prepare journal entries to record the following July transactions and events.

a. Purchased raw materials for $125,000 cash (the company uses a perpetual inventory system).

b. Used raw materials as follows: direct materials, $52,440; and indirect materials, $10,000.

c. Incurred factory payroll cost of $227,250 paid in cash (ignore taxes).

d. Assigned factory payroll costs as follows: direct labor, $202,250; and indirect labor, $25,000.

e. Incurred additional factory overhead costs of $80,000 paid in cash.

f. Allocated factory overhead to production at 50% of direct labor costs.

2. Information about the July inventories follows. Use this information with that from part 1 to prepare a process cost summary, assuming the weighted-average method is used.

Check (1f) Cr. Factory Overhead, $101,125

Check (2) EUP for overhead, 14,200

Units	
Beginning inventory	5,000 units
Started	14,000 units
Ending inventory	8,000 units
Beginning inventory	
Materials—Percent complete	100%
Labor and overhead—Percent complete	75%
Ending inventory	
Materials—Percent complete	100%
Labor and overhead—Percent complete	40%

3. Using the results from part 2 and the available information, make computations and prepare journal entries to record the following:

a. Total costs transferred to finished goods for July (label this entry g). (3a) $271,150

b. Sale of finished goods costing $265,700 for $625,000 in cash (label this entry h).

4. Post entries from parts 1 and 3 to the ledger accounts set up at the beginning of the problem.

5. Compute the amount of gross profit from the sales in July. (*Note:* Add any underapplied overhead to, or deduct any overapplied overhead from, the cost of goods sold. Ignore the corresponding journal entry.)

BEYOND THE NUMBERS

REPORTING IN ACTION

C2 

BTN 20-1 **Best Buy** reports in notes to its financial statements that, in addition to its merchandise sold, it includes the following costs (among others) in cost of goods sold: freight expenses associated with moving inventories from vendors to distribution centers, costs of services provided, customer shipping and handling expenses, costs associated with operating its distribution network, and freight expenses associated with moving merchandise from distribution centers to retail stores.

Required

1. Why do you believe Best Buy includes these costs in its cost of goods sold?

2. What effect does this cost accounting policy for its cost of goods sold have on Best Buy's financial statements and any analysis of these statements? Explain.

Fast Forward

3. Access Best Buy's financial statements for the fiscal years after March 3, 2007, from its Website (BestBuy.com) or the SEC's EDGAR Website (sec.gov). Review its footnote relating to Cost of Goods Sold and Selling, General, and Administrative Expense. Has Best Buy changed its policy with respect to what costs are included in the cost of goods sold? Explain.

COMPARATIVE ANALYSIS

C1

BTN 20-2 Retailers such as **Best Buy, Circuit City,** and **RadioShack** usually work to maintain a high-quality and low-cost operation. One ratio routinely computed for this assessment is the cost of goods sold divided by total expenses. A decline in this ratio can mean that the company is spending too much on selling and administrative activities. An increase in this ratio beyond a reasonable level can mean that the company is not spending enough on selling activities. (Assume for this analysis that total expenses equal the cost of goods sold plus selling, general, and administrative expenses.)

Required

1. For Best Buy, Circuit City, and RadioShack refer to Appendix A and compute the ratios of cost of goods sold to total expenses for their two most recent fiscal years.

2. Comment on the similarities or differences in the ratio results across both years among the companies.

ETHICS CHALLENGE

C1 C3

BTN 20-3 Many accounting and accounting-related professionals are skilled in financial analysis, but most are not skilled in manufacturing. This is especially the case for process manufacturing environments (for example, a bottling plant or chemical factory). To provide professional accounting and financial services, one must understand the industry, product, and processes. We have an ethical responsibility to develop this understanding before offering services to clients in these areas.

Required

Write a one-page action plan, in memorandum format, discussing how you would obtain an understanding of key business processes of a company that hires you to provide financial services. The memorandum should specify an industry, a product, and one selected process and should draw on at least one reference, such as a professional journal or industry magazine.

COMMUNICATING IN PRACTICE

A1 C1 P1 P2

BTN 20-4 You hire a new assistant production manager whose prior experience is with a company that produced goods to order. Your company engages in continuous production of homogeneous products that go through various production processes. Your new assistant e-mails you questioning some cost classifications on an internal report—specifically why the costs of some materials that do not actually become part of the finished product, including some labor costs not directly associated with producing the product, are classified as direct costs. Respond to this concern via memorandum.

TAKING IT TO THE NET

C1 C3

BTN 20-5 Many companies acquire software to help them monitor and control their costs and as an aid to their accounting systems. One company that supplies such software is **proDacapo** (prodacapo.com). There are many other such vendors. Access proDacapo's Website, click on "Business Process Management," and review the information displayed.

Required

How is process management software helpful to businesses? Explain with reference to costs, efficiency, and examples, if possible.

TEAMWORK IN ACTION

C1 P1 P2 P3 P6

BTN 20-6 The purpose of this team activity is to ensure that each team member understands process operations and the related accounting entries. Find the activities and flows identified in Exhibit 20.4 with numbers ①–⑩. Pick a member of the team to start by describing activity number ① in this exhibit, then verbalizing the related journal entry, and describing how the amounts in the entry are computed. The other members of the team are to agree or disagree; discussion is to continue until all members express understanding. Rotate to the next numbered activity and next team member until all activities and entries have been discussed. If at any point a team member is uncertain about an answer, the team member may pass and get back in the rotation when he or she can contribute to the team's discussion.

ENTREPRENEURIAL DECISION

C4 A2

BTN 20-7 Read the chapter opener about **Hood River Juice Company**. David Ryan explained that purchasing apples year-round and processing them immediately reduces costs, and that his company blends juices to fit customer needs.

Required

1. How does not holding raw materials inventories (apples) reduce costs? If the items are not used in production, how can they affect profits? Explain.
2. Explain why Hood River Juice Company might use a hybrid costing system.

BTN 20-8 In process costing, the process is analyzed first and then a unit measure is computed in the form of equivalent units for direct materials, direct labor, overhead, and all three combined. The same analysis applies to both manufacturing and service processes.

HITTING THE ROAD

C3 

Point: The class can compare and discuss the different processes studied and the answers provided.

Required

Visit your local **U.S. Mail** center. Look into the back room, and you will see several ongoing processes. Select one process, such as sorting, and list the costs associated with this process. Your list should include materials, labor, and overhead; be specific. Classify each cost as fixed or variable. At the bottom of your list, outline how overhead should be assigned to your identified process. The following format (with an example) is suggested.

Cost Description	Direct Material	Direct Labor	Overhead	Variable Cost	Fixed Cost
Manual sorting		X		X	
⋮					
Overhead allocation suggestions:					

BTN 20-9 **DSG international plc**, **Best Buy**, **Circuit City**, and **RadioShack** are competitors in the global marketplace. Selected data for DSG follow.

GLOBAL DECISION

C1 

(millions of pounds)	Current Year	Prior Year
Cost of goods sold	£7,285	£6,369
General, selling, and administrative expenses	381	339
Total expenses	£7,666	£6,708

Required

1. Review the discussion of the importance of the cost of goods sold divided by total expenses ratio in BTN 20-2. Compute the cost of goods sold to total expenses ratio for DSG for the two years of data provided.
2. Comment on the similarities or differences in the ratio results calculated in part 1 and in BTN 20-2 across years and companies.

ANSWERS TO MULTIPLE CHOICE QUIZ

1. d
2. e
3. b; $20,000 + $152,000 + $45,000 + $18,000 − $218,000 = $17,000
4. a; 40,000 + (15,000 × 1/3) = 45,000 EUP
5. c; ($6,000 + $84,000) ÷ 45,000 EUP = $2 per EUP

A Look Back

Chapter 20 focused on how to measure and account for costs in process operations. It explained process production, described how to assign costs to processes, and computed cost per equivalent unit.

A Look at This Chapter

This chapter describes cost allocation and activity-based costing. It identifies managerial reports useful in directing a company's activities. It also describes responsibility accounting, measuring departmental performance, transfer pricing, and allocating common costs across departments.

A Look Ahead

Chapter 22 looks at cost behavior and explains how its identification is useful to managers in performing cost-volume-profit analyses. It also shows how to apply cost-volume-profit analysis for managerial decisions.

Chapter 21

Cost Allocation and Performance Measurement

Learning Objectives

CAP

Conceptual

C1 Explain departmentalization and the role of departmental accounting. *(p. 858)*

C2 Distinguish between direct and indirect expenses. *(p. 859)*

C3 Identify bases for allocating indirect expenses to departments. *(p. 860)*

C4 Explain controllable costs and responsibility accounting. *(p. 869)*

C5 *Appendix* 21A—Explain transfer pricing and methods to set transfer prices. *(p. 875)*

C6 *Appendix 21B*—Describe allocation of joint costs across products. *(p. 877)*

Analytical

A1 Analyze investment centers using return on assets, residual income, and balanced scorecard. *(p. 867)*

A2 Analyze investment centers using profit margin and investment turnover. *(p. 872)*

Procedural

P1 Assign overhead costs using two-stage cost allocation. *(p. 852)*

P2 Assign overhead costs using activity-based costing. *(p. 854)*

P3 Prepare departmental income statements. *(p. 861)*

P4 Prepare departmental contribution reports. *(p. 866)*

LP21

Decision Feature

On The Green

"The more clicks we can get, the better our future"
—Todd Rath

ROCHESTER, NY—Brothers Tom and Todd Rath paid their college tuition by diving for lost golf balls and then reselling them. Today, their company **RockBottomGolf.com** applies a similar strategy of buying leftover products and reselling them. "Some of our critics refer to us as the 'graveyard of golf,'" explains Tom. "Oftentimes, we may be selling the last 3,000 drivers a manufacturer has ever made. If anyone can find a home for it, we can." The company boasts over 500,000 customers, affectionately referred to as "Rock Heads."

RockBottom's warehouse sports signs with "Scratch," the company's cartoonish, red-bearded caveman mascot. Scratch is surrounded with slogans such as: "A Clean Cave Is a Happy Cave" and "A Happy Rock Head Stays a Rock Head." Though Scratch is goofy, the company is all business. Offering a wide inventory of well-known brands of golf clubs, bags, balls, apparel, and accessories, the company buys in large lots and strives to keep overhead low. For example, they located their distribution center in Virginia—enabling them to ship to over 60% of the U.S. population within two days. Also, they pack items in small, uniformly sized boxes to lower costs and offer free shipping on certain orders.

Many other cost management procedures are applied. For example, they analyze "checkout flow," providing details on the point at which potential customers drop out of the checkout process and how many drop out. "If I had a 50% checkout success rate one day and 23% the next day, this lets me see that," explains Todd. This mix of financial and nonfinancial information helps Todd steer more customers through the checkout process. He also tracks customer approval ratings, currently above 99%, as a performance measure.

The diversity of its product offerings requires additional cost management. Company managers monitor direct, indirect, and controllable costs, and allocate them to departments and products. Understanding how it's product lines—such as clubs, bags, apparel—are performing and their contribution margins helps them plan for expansion. As Todd emphasizes, "We use tools to measure our ROI (return on investment). We will only expand as long as there are customers to win."

Their expansion plans do not stop with golf. RockBottomGolf wants to become RockBottomSports, with many other sporting goods products available. This increased departmentalization will require them to monitor contribution margins, return on investment, checkout flow, and customer approval. With its fast-paced growth and position as the top golf retailer on the Internet, RockBottomGolf is "on the green."

[Sources: *RockBottomGolf.com Website,* January 2009; *Internet Retailer,* July 2007; *Inside Business-Hampton Roads,* October 2006.]

Chapter Preview

This chapter describes how to allocate costs shared by more than one product across those different products and how to allocate indirect costs of shared items such as utilities, advertising, and rent. The chapter also describes activity-based costing and how it traces the costs of individual activities. This knowledge helps managers better understand how to assign costs and assess company performance. The chapter also introduces additional managerial accounting reports useful in managing a company's activities and explains how and why management divides companies into departments.

Cost Allocation and Performance Measurement

Overhead Cost Allocation Methods
- Two-stage cost allocation
- Activity-based cost allocation
- Comparison of allocation methods

Departmental Accounting
- Motivation for departmentalization
- Departmental evaluation
- Departmental reporting and analysis

Departmental Expense Allocation
- Direct and indirect expenses
- Allocation of indirect expenses
- Departmental income statements
- Departmental contribution to overhead

Investment Centers
- Financial measures of performance
- Nonfinancial measures of performance
- Balanced scorecard

Responsibility Accounting
- Controllable versus direct costs
- Responsibility accounting system
- Transfer pricing

Section 1—Allocating Costs for Product Costing

Video21.1

This first of two sections in this chapter focuses on alternatives for allocation of costs to products and services. We explain and illustrate two basic methods: (1) traditional two-state cost allocation and (2) activity-based cost allocation. The second section describes and illustrates the allocation of costs for performance evaluation.

Overhead Cost Allocation Methods

P1 Assign overhead costs using two-stage cost allocation.

Point: Use of a single overhead allocation rate is known as using a *plantwide rate*.

We previously explained how to assign overhead costs to jobs (and processes) by using a predetermined overhead rate per unit of an allocation base such as direct labor cost. When a single overhead rate is used on a companywide basis, all overhead is lumped together, and a predetermined overhead rate per unit of an allocation base is computed and used to assign overhead to jobs (and processes). The use of a single predetermined overhead rate suggests that this allocation process is simple. In reality, it can be complicated. This chapter explains the traditional two-stage cost allocation procedure and then introduces the activity-based cost allocation procedure.

Two-Stage Cost Allocation

An organization incurs overhead costs in many activities. These activities can be identified with various departments, which can be broadly classified as either operating or service departments. *Operating departments* perform an organization's main functions. For example, an accounting firm's main functions usually include auditing, tax, and advisory services. Similarly, the production and selling departments of a manufacturing firm perform its main functions and serve as operating departments. *Service departments* provide support to an organization's operating departments. Examples of service departments are payroll, human resource management, accounting, and executive management. Service departments do not engage in activities that generate revenues, yet their support is crucial for the operating departments' success. In this section, we apply a two-stage cost allocation procedure to assign (1) service department costs to operating departments and (2) operating department costs, including those assigned from service departments, to the organization's output.

Illustration of Two-Stage Cost Allocation Exhibit 21.1 shows the two-stage cost allocation procedure. This exhibit uses data from AutoGrand, a custom automobile manufacturer. AutoGrand has five manufacturing-related departments: janitorial, maintenance, factory accounting, machining, and assembly. Expenses incurred by each of these departments are considered product costs. There are three service departments—janitorial, maintenance, and factory accounting; each incurs expenses of $10,000, $15,000 and $8,000, respectively. As shown in Exhibit 21.1, the first stage of the two-stage procedure involves allocating the costs of the three service departments to the two operating departments (machining and assembly). The two operating departments use the resources of these service departments.

EXHIBIT 21.1

Two-Stage Cost Allocation

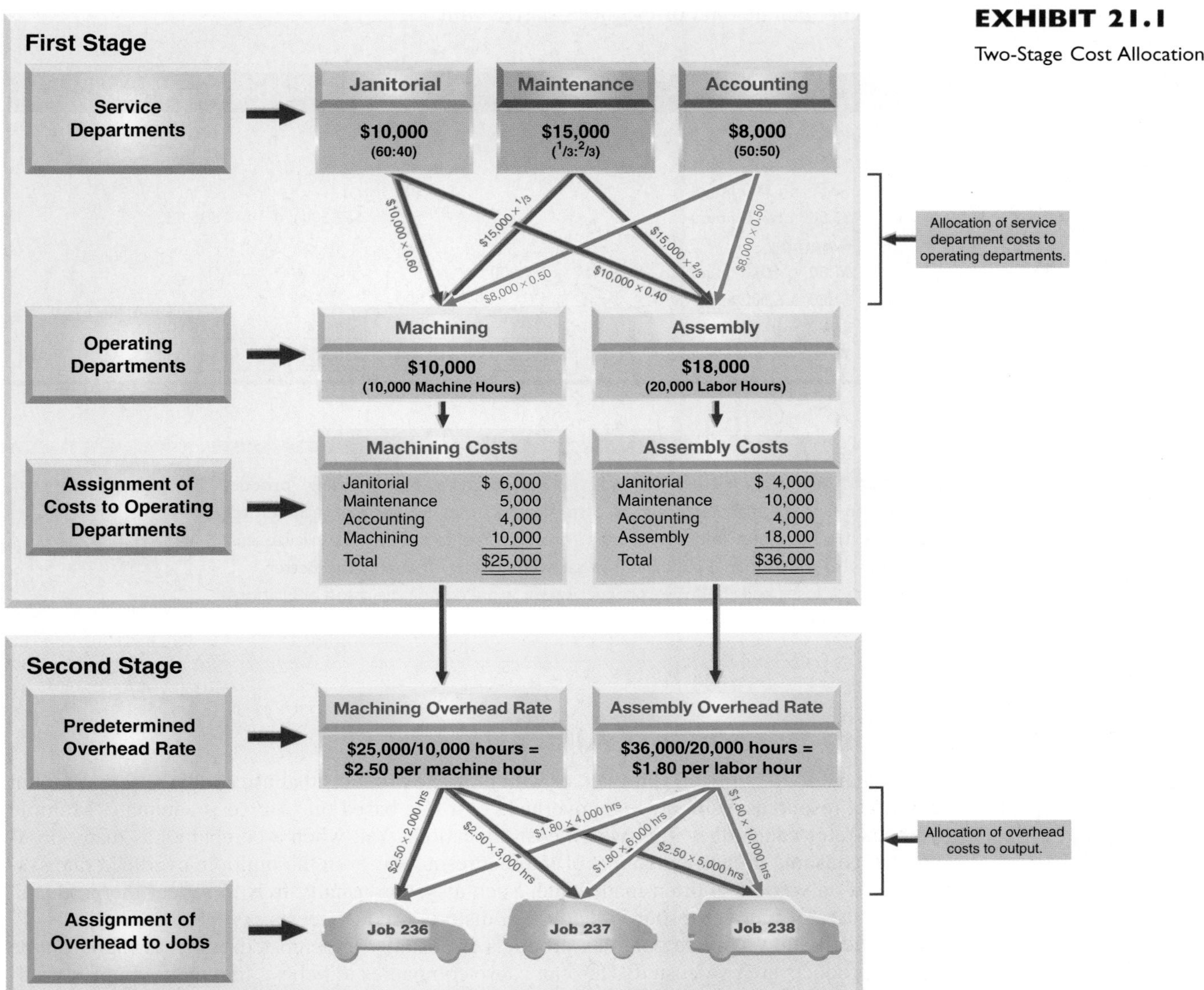

To illustrate the first stage of cost allocation, we use the janitorial department. Its costs are allocated to machining and assembly in the ratio 60 : 40. This means that 60%, or $6,000, of janitorial costs are assigned to the machining department and 40%, or $4,000, to the assembly department. The expenses incurred by the maintenance and factory accounting departments are similarly assigned to machining and assembly. We then add the expenses directly incurred by each operating department to these assigned costs to determine the total expenses for each operating department. This yields total costs of $25,000 for machining and $36,000 for assembly.

Point: Use of a separate overhead allocation rate for each department is known as using *departmental rates.*

In the second stage, predetermined overhead rates are computed for each operating department. The allocation base is machine hours for machining and labor hours for assembly. The predetermined overhead rate is $2.50 per machine hour for the machining department and $1.80 per labor hour for the assembly department. These predetermined overhead rates are then used to assign overhead to output.

To illustrate this second stage, assume that three jobs were started and finished in a recent month. These jobs consumed resources as follows: Job 236—2,000 machine hours in machining and 4,000 labor hours in assembly; Job 237—3,000 machine hours and 6,000 labor hours; Job 238—5,000 machine hours and 10,000 labor hours. The overhead assigned to these three jobs is shown with the arrow lines in the bottom row of Exhibit 21.1.

Exhibit 21.2 summarizes these allocations. Total overhead allocated to Jobs 236, 237, and 238, is $12,200, $18,300, and $30,500, respectively. These allocated costs sum to $61,000, which is the total amount of overhead started with.

EXHIBIT 21.2

Assignment of Overhead Costs to Output

	Job 236	Job 237	Job 238	Department Totals
Machining				
$2.50 × 2,000 hours	$ 5,000			
$2.50 × 3,000 hours		$ 7,500		
$2.50 × 5,000 hours			$12,500	$25,000
Assembly				
$1.80 × 4,000 hours	7,200			
$1.80 × 6,000 hours		10,800		
$1.80 × 10,000 hours			18,000	36,000
Total overhead assigned	$12,200	$18,300	$30,500	$61,000

Decision Insight

Overhead Misled Futura Computer outsourced a "money-losing" product to a Korean firm for manufacturing. Its own manufacturing facility was retooled to produce extra units of a "more profitable" product. Profits did not materialize, and losses grew to more than $20 million! What went wrong? It seems the better product was a loser and the losing product was a winner. Poor overhead allocations misled Futura's management.

Video21.2

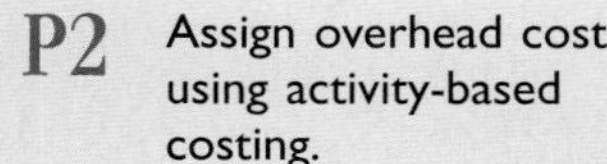

P2 Assign overhead costs using activity-based costing.

Activity-Based Cost Allocation

For companies with only one product, or with multiple products that use about the same amount of indirect resources, using a single overhead cost rate based on volume is adequate. Multiple overhead rates can further improve on cost allocations. Yet, when a company has many products that consume different amounts of indirect resources, even the multiple overhead rate system based on volume is often inadequate. Such a system usually fails to reflect the products' different uses of indirect resources and often distorts products costs.

Specifically, low-volume complex products are usually undercosted, whereas high-volume simpler products are overcosted. This can cause companies to believe that their complex products are more profitable than they really are, which can lead those companies to focus on them to the detriment of high-volume simpler products. This creates a demand for a better cost allocation system for these indirect (overhead) costs.

Point: A survey found that most respondents believe that activity-based costing is worth the investment because of improved management decisions.

Activity-based costing (ABC) attempts to better allocate costs to the proper users of overhead by focusing on *activities.* Costs are traced to individual activities and then allocated to cost objects. Exhibit 21.3 shows the (two-stage) activity-based cost allocation method. The first stage identifies the activities involved in processing Jobs 236, 237, and 238 and forms activity cost *pools* by combining those activities. The second stage involves computing predetermined overhead cost rates for each cost pool and then assigning costs to jobs.

We begin our explanation at the top of Exhibit 21.3. The first stage identifies individual activities, which are pooled in a logical manner into homogenous groups, or *cost pools.* A

EXHIBIT 21.3
Activity-Based Cost Allocation

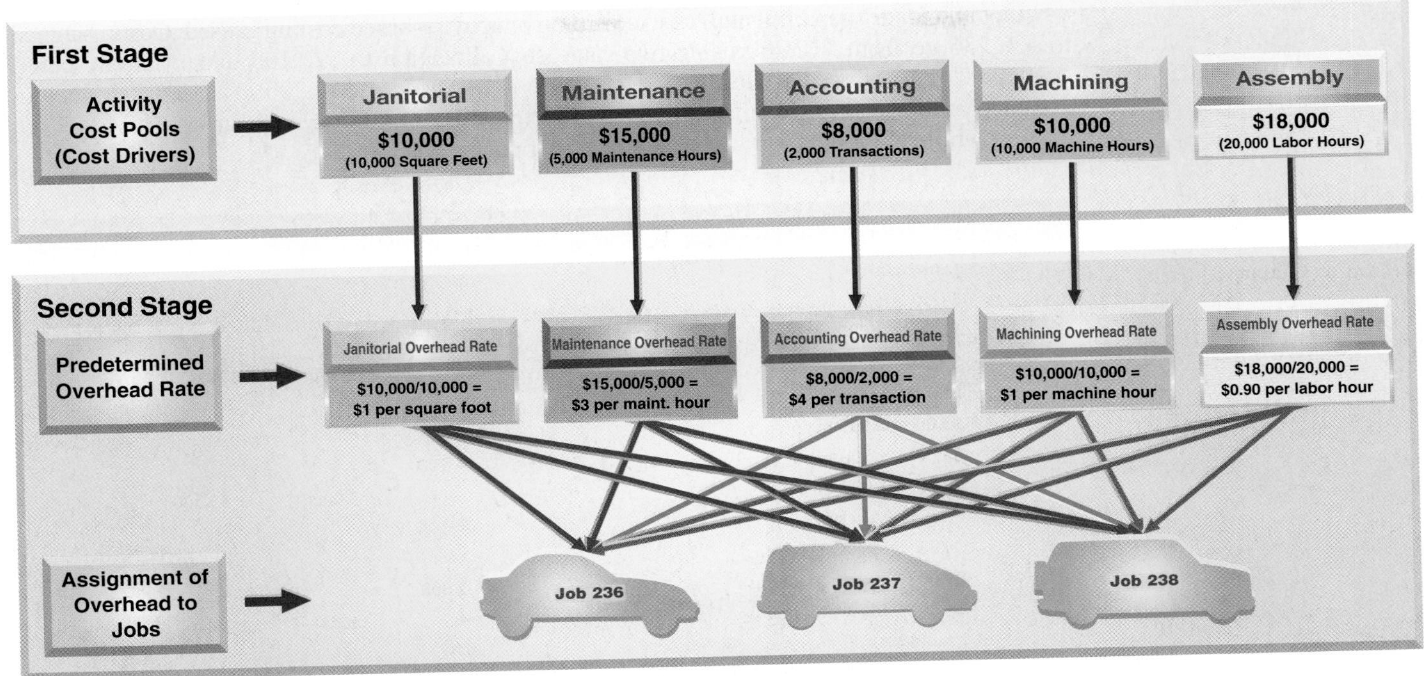

homogenous cost pool consists of activities that belong to the same process and/or are caused by the same cost driver. An **activity cost driver,** or simply *cost driver,* is a factor that causes the cost of an activity to go up or down. For example, preparing an invoice, checking it, and dispatching it are activities of the "invoicing" process and can therefore be grouped in a single cost pool. Moreover, the number of invoices processed likely drives the costs of these activities.

An **activity cost pool** is a temporary account accumulating the costs a company incurs to support an identified set of activities. Costs accumulated in an activity cost pool include the variable and fixed costs of the activities in the pool. Variable costs pertain to resources acquired as needed (such as materials); fixed costs pertain to resources acquired in advance (such as equipment). An activity cost pool account is handled like a factory overhead account.

In the second stage, after all activity costs are accumulated in an activity cost pool account, overhead rates are computed. Then, costs are allocated to cost objects (users) based on cost drivers (allocation bases).

Point: A cost driver is different from an allocation base. An allocation base is used as a basis for assigning overhead but need not have a cause-effect relation with the costs assigned. However, a cost driver has a cause-effect relation with the cost assigned.

Decision Insight

Measuring Health Activity-based costing is used in many settings. A study found that activity-based costing improves health care costing accuracy, enabling improved profitability analysis and decision making. However, identifying cost drivers in a health care setting is challenging.

Illustration of Activity-Based Costing To illustrate, let's return to AutoGrand's three jobs. Assume that resources used to complete Jobs 236, 237, and 238 are shown in Exhibit 21.4.

EXHIBIT 21.4
Activity Resource Use

Resources Used	Job 236	Job 237	Job 238
Square feet of space	5,000	3,000	2,000
Maintenance hours	2,500	1,500	1,000
Number of transactions	500	700	800
Machine hours	2,000	3,000	5,000
Direct labor hours	4,000	6,000	10,000

The $61,000 of total costs are assigned to these three jobs using activity-based costing as shown in Exhibit 21.5 (rates are taken from the second stage of Exhibit 21.3). Comparing Exhibits 21.2 and 21.5, we see that the costs assigned to the three jobs vary markedly depending on whether two-stage (departmental) cost allocation or activity-based costing is used. Costs assigned to Job 236 go from $12,200 using two-stage cost allocation to $20,100 under activity-based costing. Costs assigned to Job 238 decline from $30,500 to $22,200. These differences in assigned amounts result from more accurately tracing costs to each job using activity-based costing where the allocation bases reflect actual cost drivers.

EXHIBIT 21.5

Activity-Based Assignment of Overhead to Output

	Job 236	Job 237	Job 238	Activity Totals
Janitorial				
$1.00 × 5,000 sq. ft.	$ 5,000			
$1.00 × 3,000 sq. ft.		$ 3,000		
$1.00 × 2,000 sq. ft.			$ 2,000	$10,000
Maintenance				
$3.00 × 2,500 maint. hrs.	7,500			
$3.00 × 1,500 maint. hrs.		4,500		
$3.00 × 1,000 maint. hrs.			3,000	15,000
Factory Accounting				
$4.00 × 500 transactions	2,000			
$4.00 × 700 transactions		2,800		
$4.00 × 800 transactions			3,200	8,000
Machining				
$1.00 × 2,000 machine hrs.	2,000			
$1.00 × 3,000 machine hrs.		3,000		
$1.00 × 5,000 machine hrs.			5,000	10,000
Assembly				
$0.90 × 4,000 labor hrs.	3,600			
$0.90 × 6,000 labor hrs.		5,400		
$0.90 × 10,000 labor hrs.			9,000	18,000
Total overhead assigned	$20,100	$18,700	$22,200	$61,000

Decision Maker

Director of Operations Two department managers at your ad agency complain to you that overhead costs assigned to them are too high. Overhead is assigned on the basis of labor hours for designers. These managers argue that overhead depends not only on designers' hours but on many activities unrelated to these hours. What is your response? [Answer—p. 879]

Comparison of Two-Stage and Activity-Based Cost Allocation

Traditional cost systems capture overhead costs by individual department (or function) and accumulate these costs in one or more overhead accounts. Companies then assign these overhead costs using a single allocation base such as direct labor or multiple volume-based allocation bases. Unfortunately, traditional cost systems have tended to use allocation bases that are often not closely related to the way these costs are actually incurred.

In contrast, activity-based cost systems capture costs by individual activity. These activities and their costs are then accumulated into activity cost pools. A company selects a cost driver (allocation base) for each activity pool. It uses this cost driver to assign the accumulated activity costs to cost objects (such as jobs or products) benefiting from the activity.

An activity-based costing system commonly consists of more allocation bases as compared to a traditional cost system. For example, a Chicago-based manufacturer currently uses nearly

EXHIBIT 21.6

Cost Pools and Cost Drivers in Activity-Based Costing

Activity Cost Pool	Cost Driver
Materials purchasing	Number of purchase orders
Materials handling	Number of materials requisitions
Personnel processing	Number of employees hired or laid off
Equipment depreciation	Number of products produced or hours of use
Quality inspection	Number of units inspected
Indirect labor in setting up equipment	Number of setups required
Engineering costs for product modifications	Number of modifications (engineering change orders)

20 different activity cost drivers to assign overhead costs to its products. Exhibit 21.6 lists common examples of overhead cost pools and their usual cost drivers.

Activity-based costing is especially effective when the same department or departments produce many different types of products. For instance, more complex products often require more help from service departments such as engineering, maintenance, and materials handling. If the same amount of direct labor is applied to the complex and simple products, a traditional overhead allocation system assigns the same overhead cost to both. With activity-based costing, however, the complex products are assigned a larger portion of overhead. The difference in overhead assigned can affect product pricing, make-or-buy, and other managerial decisions.

Activity-based costing encourages managers to focus on *activities* as well as the use of those activities. For instance, assume AutoGrand can reduce the number of transactions processed in Factory Accounting to 1,500 (375 transactions for Job 236, 525 transactions for Job 237, and 600 transactions for Job 238) and that through continuous improvement it can reduce costs of processing those transactions to $4,500. The resulting rate to process a transaction is $3 per transaction ($4,500/1,500 transactions—down from $4 per Exhibit 21.3). The cost of transaction processing is reduced for all jobs (Job 236, $1,125; Job 237, $1,575; Job 238, $1,800). However, if those accounting costs were grouped in a single overhead cost pool, it is more difficult to identify cost savings and understand their effects on product costs.

Activity-based costing requires managers to look at each item and encourages them to manage each cost to increase the benefit from each dollar spent. It also encourages managers to cooperate because it shows how their efforts are interrelated. This results in *activity-based management.*

Decision Ethics

Accounting Officer Your company produces expensive garments, whose production involves many complex and specialized activities. Your general manager recently learned about activity-based costing (ABC) and asks your advice. However, your supervisor does not want to disturb the existing cost system and instructs you to prepare a report stating that "implementation of ABC is a complicated process involving too many steps and not worth the effort." You believe ABC will actually help the company identify sources of costs and control them. What action do you take? [Answer—p. 879]

Quick Check

Answers—p. 880

1. What is a cost driver?
2. When activity-based costing is used rather than traditional allocation methods, (*a*) managers must identify cost drivers for various items of overhead cost, (*b*) individual cost items in service departments are allocated directly to products or services, (*c*) managers can direct their attention to the activities that drive overhead cost, or (*d*) all of the above.

Section 2—Allocating Costs for Performance Evaluation

This second section of the chapter describes and illustrates allocation of costs for performance evaluation. We begin with departmental accounting and expense allocations and conclude with responsibility accounting.

Departmental Accounting

Video21.3

Companies are divided into *departments,* also called *subunits,* when they are too large to be managed effectively as a single unit. Managerial accounting for departments has two main goals. The first is to set up a **departmental accounting system** to provide information for managers to evaluate the profitability or cost effectiveness of each department's activities. The second goal is to set up a **responsibility accounting system** to control costs and expenses and evaluate managers' performances by assigning costs and expenses to the managers responsible for controlling them. Departmental and responsibility accounting systems are related and share much information.

Motivation for Departmentalization

C1 Explain departmentalization and the role of departmental accounting.

Many companies are so large and complex that they are broken into separate divisions for efficiency and/or effectiveness purposes. Divisions then are usually organized into separate departments. When a company is departmentalized, each department is often placed under the direction of a manager. As a company grows, management often divides departments into new departments so that responsibilities for a department's activities do not overwhelm the manager's ability to oversee and control them. A company also creates departments to take advantage of the skills of individual managers. Departments are broadly classified as either operating or service departments.

Departmental Evaluation

Point: To improve profitability, **Sears, Roebuck & Co.** eliminated several departments, including its catalog division.

When a company is divided into departments, managers need to know how each department is performing. The accounting system must supply information about resources used and outputs achieved by each department. This requires a system to measure and accumulate revenue and expense information for each department whenever possible.

Departmental information is rarely distributed publicly because of its potential usefulness to competitors. Information about departments is prepared for internal managers to help control operations, appraise performance, allocate resources, and plan strategy. If a department is highly profitable, management may decide to expand its operations, or if a department is performing poorly, information about revenues or expenses can suggest useful changes.

More companies are emphasizing customer satisfaction as a main responsibility of many departments. This has led to changes in the measures reported. Increasingly, financial measurements are being supplemented with quality and customer satisfaction indexes. **Motorola**, for instance, uses two key measures: the number of defective parts per million parts produced and the percent of orders delivered on time to customers. (Note that some departments have only "internal customers.")

Financial information used to evaluate a department depends on whether it is evaluated as a profit center, cost center, or investment center. A **profit center** incurs costs and generates revenues; selling departments are often evaluated as profit centers. A **cost center** incurs costs without directly generating revenues. An **investment center** incurs costs and generates revenues, and is responsible for effectively using center assets. The manufacturing departments of a manufacturer and its service departments such as accounting, advertising, and purchasing, are all cost centers.

Point: Selling departments are often treated as *revenue centers;* their managers are responsible for maximizing sales revenues.

Evaluating managers' performance depends on whether they are responsible for profit centers, cost centers, or investment centers. Profit center managers are judged on their abilities to generate revenues in excess of the department's costs. They are assumed to influence both revenue generation and cost incurrence. Cost center managers are judged on their abilities to control costs by keeping them within a satisfactory range under an assumption that only they influence costs. Investment center managers are evaluated on their use of center assets to generate income.

Decision Insight

Nonfinancial Measures A majority of companies now report nonfinancial performance measures to management. Common measures are cycle time, defect rate, on-time deliveries, inventory turnover, customer satisfaction, and safety. When nonfinancial measures are used with financial measures, the performance measurement system resembles a ***balanced scorecard.*** Many of these companies also use activity-based management as part of their performance measurement system.

Departmental Reporting and Analysis

Companies use various measures (financial and nonfinancial) and reporting formats to evaluate their departments. The type and form of information depend on management's focus and philosophy. Hewlett-Packard's statement of corporate objectives, for instance, indicates that its goal is to satisfy customer needs. Its challenge is to set up managerial accounting systems to provide relevant feedback for evaluating performance in terms of its stated objectives. Also, the means used to obtain information about departments depend on how extensively a company uses computer and information technology.

When accounts are not maintained separately in the general ledger by department, a company can create departmental information by using a *departmental spreadsheet analysis*. For example, after recording sales in its usual manner, a company can compute daily total sales by department and enter these totals on a sales spreadsheet. At period-end, column totals of the spreadsheet show sales by department. The combined total of all columns equals the balance of the Sales account. A merchandiser that uses a spreadsheet analysis of department sales often uses separate spreadsheets to accumulate sales, sales returns, purchases, and purchases returns by department. If each department keeps a count of its inventory, it can also compute its gross profit (assuming it's a profit center).

Point: Many retailers use a point-of-sales system capturing sales data and creating requests to release inventory from the warehouse and order more merchandise. **Wal-Mart**'s sales system not only collects data for internal use but also is used by **Procter & Gamble** to plan its production and product deliveries to **Wal-Mart.**

Point: Link Wood Products, a manufacturer of lawn and garden products, records each sale by department on a spreadsheet. Daily totals are accumulated in another spreadsheet to obtain monthly totals by department.

Quick Check

Answers—p. 880

3. What is the difference between a departmental accounting system and a responsibility accounting system?
4. Service departments (*a*) manufacture products, (*b*) make sales directly to customers, (*c*) produce revenues, (*d*) assist operating departments.
5. Explain the difference between a cost center and a profit center. Cite an example of each.

Departmental Expense Allocation

When a company computes departmental profits, it confronts some accounting challenges that involve allocating its expenses across its operating departments.

Direct and Indirect Expenses

Direct expenses are costs readily traced to a department because they are incurred for that department's sole benefit. They require no allocation across departments. For example, the salary of an employee who works in only one department is a direct expense of that one department.

C2 Distinguish between direct and indirect expenses.

Indirect expenses are costs that are incurred for the joint benefit of more than one department and cannot be readily traced to only one department. For example, if two or more departments share a single building, all enjoy the benefits of the expenses for rent, heat, and light. Indirect expenses are allocated across departments benefiting from them when we need information about departmental profits. Ideally, we allocate indirect expenses by using a cause-effect

Point: Utility expense has elements of both direct and indirect expenses.

relation. When we cannot identify cause-effect relations, we allocate each indirect expense on a basis approximating the relative benefit each department receives. Measuring the benefit for each department from an indirect expense can be difficult.

Illustration of Indirect Expense Allocation To illustrate how to allocate an indirect expense, we consider a retail store that purchases janitorial services from an outside company. Management allocates this cost across the store's three departments according to the floor space each occupies. Costs of janitorial services for a recent month are $300. Exhibit 21.7 shows the square feet of floor space each department occupies. The store computes the percent of total square feet allotted to each department and uses it to allocate the $300 cost.

EXHIBIT 21.7

Indirect Expense Allocation

Department	Square Feet	Percent of Total	Allocated Cost
Jewelry	2,400	60%	$180
Watch repair	600	15	45
China and silver	1,000	25	75
Totals	4,000	100%	$300

Specifically, because the jewelry department occupies 60% of the floor space, 60% of the total $300 cost is assigned to it. The same procedure is applied to the other departments. When the allocation process is complete, these and other allocated costs are deducted from the gross profit for each department to determine net income for each. One consideration in allocating costs is to motivate managers and employees to behave as desired. As a result, a cost incurred in one department might be best allocated to other departments when one of the other departments caused the cost.

Allocation of Indirect Expenses

C3 Identify bases for allocating indirect expenses to departments.

Point: Expense allocations cannot always avoid some arbitrariness.

This section describes how to identify the bases used to allocate indirect expenses across departments. No standard rule identifies the best basis because expense allocation involves several factors, and the relative importance of these factors varies across departments and organizations. Judgment is required, and people do not always agree. In our discussion, note the parallels between activity-based costing and the departmental expense allocation procedures described here.

Wages and Salaries Employee wages and salaries can be either direct or indirect expenses. If their time is spent entirely in one department, their wages are direct expenses of that department. However, if employees work for the benefit of more than one department, their wages are indirect expenses and must be allocated across the departments benefited. An employee's contribution to a department usually depends on the number of hours worked in contributing to that department. Thus, a reasonable basis for allocating employee wages and salaries is the *relative amount of time spent in each department.* In the case of a supervisor who manages more than one department, recording the time spent in each department may not always be practical. Instead, a company can allocate the supervisor's salary to departments on the basis of the number of employees in each department—a reasonable basis if a supervisor's main task is managing people. Another basis of allocation is on sales across departments, also a reasonable basis if a supervisor's job reflects on departmental sales.

Point: Some companies ask supervisors to estimate time spent supervising specific departments for purposes of expense allocation.

Rent and Related Expenses Rent expense for a building is reasonably allocated to a department on the basis of floor space it occupies. Location can often make some floor space more valuable than other space. Thus, the allocation method can charge departments that occupy more valuable space a higher expense per square foot. Ground floor retail space, for instance, is often more valuable than basement or upper-floor space because all customers pass departments near the entrance but fewer go beyond the first floor. When no precise measures of floor space values exist, basing allocations on data such as customer traffic and real estate assessments is helpful. When a company owns its building, its expenses for depreciation, taxes, insurance, and other related building expenses are allocated like rent expense.

Advertising Expenses Effective advertising of a department's products increases its sales and customer traffic. Moreover, advertising products for some departments usually helps other departments' sales because customers also often buy unadvertised products. Thus, many stores treat advertising as an indirect expense allocated on the basis of each department's proportion of total sales. For example, a department with 10% of a store's total sales is assigned 10% of advertising expense. Another method is to analyze each advertisement to compute the Web/newspaper space or TV/radio time devoted to the products of a department and charge that department for the proportional costs of advertisements. Management must consider whether this more detailed and costly method is justified.

Equipment and Machinery Depreciation Depreciation on equipment and machinery used only in one department is a direct expense of that department. Depreciation on equipment and machinery used by more than one department is an indirect expense to be allocated across departments. Accounting for each department's depreciation expense requires a company to keep records showing which departments use specific assets. The number of hours that a department uses equipment and machinery is a reasonable basis for allocating depreciation.

Point: Employee morale suffers when allocations are perceived as unfair. Thus, it is important to carefully design and explain the allocation of service department costs.

Utilities Expenses Utilities expenses such as heating and lighting are usually allocated on the basis of floor space occupied by departments. This practice assumes their use is uniform across departments. When this is not so, a more involved allocation can be necessary, although there is often a trade-off between the usefulness of more precise allocations and the effort to compute them.

Point: Manufacturers often allocate electricity cost to departments on the basis of the horsepower of equipment located in each department.

Service Department Expenses To generate revenues, operating departments require support services provided by departments such as personnel, payroll, advertising, and purchasing. Such service departments are typically evaluated as cost centers because they do not produce revenues. (Evaluating them as profit centers requires the use of a system that "charges" user departments a price that then serves as the "revenue" generated by service departments.) A departmental accounting system can accumulate and report costs incurred directly by each service department for this purpose. The system then allocates a service department's expenses to operating departments benefiting from them. This is often done, for example, using traditional two-stage cost allocation (see Exhibit 21.1). Exhibit 21.8 shows some commonly used bases for allocating service department expenses to operating departments.

Point: When a service department "charges" its user departments within a company, a *transfer pricing system* must be set up to determine the "revenue" from its services provided.

EXHIBIT 21.8

Bases for Allocating Service Department Expenses

Service Department	Common Allocation Bases
Office expenses	Number of employees or sales in each department
Personnel expenses	Number of employees in each department
Payroll expenses	Number of employees in each department
Advertising expenses	Sales or amount of advertising charged directly to each department
Purchasing costs	Dollar amounts of purchases or number of purchase orders processed
Cleaning expenses	Square feet of floor space occupied
Maintenance expenses	Square feet of floor space occupied

Departmental Income Statements

P3 Prepare departmental income statements.

An income statement can be prepared for each operating department once expenses have been assigned to it. Its expenses include both direct expenses and its share of indirect expenses. For this purpose, compiling all expenses incurred in service departments before assigning them to operating departments is useful. We illustrate the steps to prepare departmental income statements using A-1 Hardware and its five departments. Two of them (office and purchasing) are

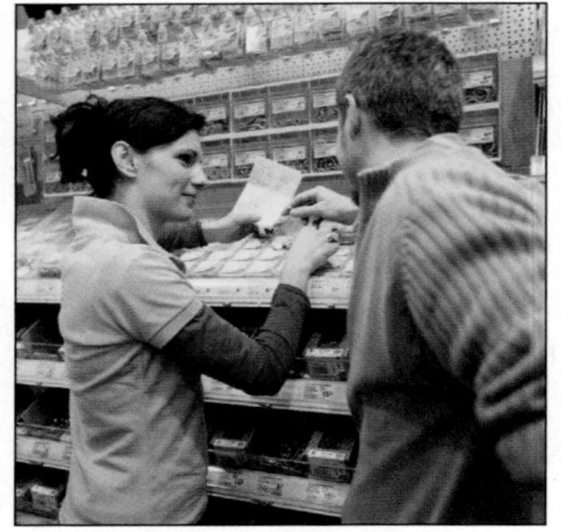

service departments and the other three (hardware, housewares, and appliances) are operating (selling) departments. Allocating costs to operating departments and preparing departmental income statements involves four steps. (1) Accumulating direct expenses by department. (2) Allocating indirect expenses across departments. (3) Allocating service department expenses to operating department. (4) Preparing departmental income statements.

Step 1 Step 1 accumulates direct expenses for each service and operating department as shown in Exhibit 21.9. Direct expenses include salaries, wages, and other expenses that each department incurs but does not share with any other department. This information is accumulated in departmental expense accounts.

EXHIBIT 21.9

Step 1: Direct Expense Accumulation

Direct Expenses → General office
Direct Expenses → Purchasing
Direct Expenses → Hardware
Direct Expenses → Housewares
Direct Expenses → Appliances

Point: We sometimes allocate service department costs across other service departments before allocating them to operating departments. This "step-wise" process is in advanced courses.

Step 2 Step 2 allocates indirect expenses across all departments as shown in Exhibit 21.10. Indirect expenses can include items such as depreciation, rent, advertising, and any other expenses that cannot be directly assigned to a department. Indirect expenses are recorded in company expense accounts, an allocation base is identified for each expense, and costs are allocated using a *departmental expense allocation spreadsheet* described in step 3.

EXHIBIT 21.10

Step 2: Indirect Expense Allocation

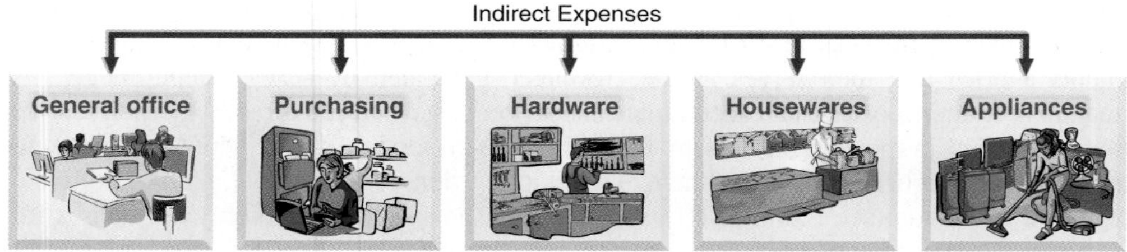

Step 3 Step 3 allocates expenses of the service departments (office and purchasing) to the operating departments. Service department costs are not allocated to other service departments. Exhibit 21.11 reflects the allocation of service department expenses using the allocation base(s). All of the direct and indirect expenses of service departments are allocated to operating departments.[1]

EXHIBIT 21.11

Step 3: Service Department Expense Allocation to Operating Departments

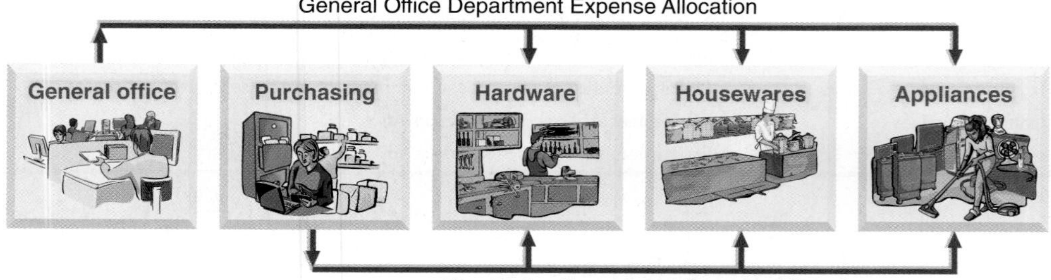

[1] In some cases we allocate a service department's expenses to other service departments when they use its services. For example, expenses of a payroll office benefit all service and operating departments and can be assigned to all departments. Nearly all examples and assignment materials in this book allocate service expenses only to operating departments for simplicity.

Computations for both steps 2 and 3 are commonly made using a departmental expense allocation spreadsheet as shown in Exhibit 21.12. The first two sections of this spreadsheet list direct expenses and indirect expenses by department. The third section lists the service department expenses and their allocations to operating departments. The allocation bases are identified in the second column, and total expense amounts are reported in the third column.

EXHIBIT 21.12

Departmental Expense Allocation Spreadsheet

A-1 HARDWARE
Departmental Expense Allocations
For Year Ended December 31, 2009

	Allocation Base	Expense Account Balance	Allocation of Expenses to Departments: General Office Dept.	Purchasing Dept.	Hardware Dept.	Housewares Dept.	Appliances Dept.
Direct expenses							
Salaries expense	Payroll records	$51,900	$13,300	$8,200	$15,600	$ 7,000	$ 7,800
Depreciation—Equipment	Depreciation records	1,500	500	300	400	100	200
Supplies expense	Requisitions	900	200	100	300	200	100
Indirect expenses							
Rent expense	Amount and value of space	12,000	600	600	4,860	3,240	2,700
Utilities expense	Floor space	2,400	300	300	810	540	450
Advertising expense	Sales	1,000			500	300	200
Insurance expense	Value of insured assets	2,500	400	200	900	600	400
Total department expenses		72,200	15,300	9,700	23,370	11,980	11,850
Service department expenses							
General office department	Sales		(15,300)		7,650	4,590	3,060
Purchasing department	Purchase orders			(9,700)	3,880	2,630	3,190
Total expenses allocated to operating departments		$72,200	$ 0	$ 0	$34,900	$19,200	$18,100

The departmental expense allocation spreadsheet is useful in implementing the first three steps. To illustrate, first (step 1) the three direct expenses of salaries, depreciation, and supplies are accumulated in each of the five departments.

Second (step 2), the four indirect expenses of rent, utilities, advertising, and insurance are allocated to all departments using the allocation bases identified. For example, consider rent allocation. Exhibit 21.13 lists the five departments' square footage of space occupied.

EXHIBIT 21.13

Departments' Allocation Bases

Department	Floor Space (Square Feet)	Value of Insured Assets ($)	Sales ($)	Number of Purchase Orders
General office	1,500	$ 38,000		—
Purchasing	1,500	19,000		—*
Hardware	4,050	85,500	$119,500	394
Housewares	2,700	57,000	71,700	267
Appliances	2,250	38,000	47,800	324
Total	12,000	$237,500	$239,000	985

* Purchasing department tracks purchase orders by department.

The two service departments (office and purchasing) occupy 25% of the total space (3,000 sq. feet/12,000 sq. feet). However, they are located near the back of the building, which is of lower value than space near the front that is occupied by operating departments. Management estimates that space near the back accounts for $1,200 of the total rent expense of $12,000. Exhibit 21.14 shows how we allocate the $1,200 rent expense between

EXHIBIT 21.14

Allocating Indirect (Rent) Expense to Service Departments

Department	Square Feet	Percent of Total	Allocated Cost
General office	1,500	50.0%	$ 600
Purchasing	1,500	50.0	600
Totals	3,000	100.0%	$1,200

these two service departments in proportion to their square footage. Exhibit 21.14 shows a simple rule for cost allocations: Allocated cost = Percentage of allocation base × Total cost. We then allocate the remaining $10,800 of rent expense to the three operating departments as shown in Exhibit 21.15. We continue step 2 by allocating the $2,400 of utilities expense to all departments based on the square footage occupied as shown in Exhibit 21.16.

EXHIBIT 21.15

Allocating Indirect (Rent) Expense to Operating Departments

Department	Square Feet	Percent of Total	Allocated Cost
Hardware	4,050	45.0%	$ 4,860
Housewares	2,700	30.0	3,240
Appliances	2,250	25.0	2,700
Totals	9,000	100.0%	$10,800

EXHIBIT 21.16

Allocating Indirect (Utilities) Expense to All Departments

Department	Square Feet	Percent of Total	Allocated Cost
General office	1,500	12.50%	$ 300
Purchasing	1,500	12.50	300
Hardware	4,050	33.75	810
Housewares	2,700	22.50	540
Appliances	2,250	18.75	450
Totals	12,000	100.00%	$2,400

Exhibit 21.17 shows the allocation of $1,000 of advertising expense to the three operating departments on the basis of sales dollars. We exclude service departments from this allocation because they do not generate sales.

EXHIBIT 21.17

Allocating Indirect (Advertising) Expense to Operating Departments

Department	Sales	Percent of Total	Allocated Cost
Hardware	$119,500	50.0%	$ 500
Housewares	71,700	30.0	300
Appliances	47,800	20.0	200
Totals	$239,000	100.0%	$1,000

To complete step 2 we allocate insurance expense to each service and operating department as shown in Exhibit 21.18.

EXHIBIT 21.18

Allocating Indirect (Insurance) Expense to All Departments

Department	Value of Insured Assets	Percent of Total	Allocated Cost
General Office	$ 38,000	16.0%	$ 400
Purchasing	19,000	8.0	200
Hardware	85,500	36.0	900
Housewares	57,000	24.0	600
Appliances	38,000	16.0	400
Total	$237,500	100.0%	$2,500

Third (step 3), total expenses of the two service departments are allocated to the three operating departments as shown in Exhibits 21.19 and 21.20.

EXHIBIT 21.19

Allocating Service Department (General Office) Expenses to Operating Departments

Department	Sales	Percent of Total	Allocated Cost
Hardware	$119,500	50.0%	$ 7,650
Housewares	71,700	30.0	4,590
Appliances	47,800	20.0	3,060
Total	$239,000	100.0%	$15,300

EXHIBIT 21.20

Allocating Service Department (Purchasing) Expenses to Operating Departments

Department	Number of Purchase Orders	Percent of Total	Allocated Cost
Hardware	394	40.00%	$3,880
Housewares	267	27.11	2,630
Appliances	324	32.89	3,190
Total	985	100.00%	$9,700

Step 4 The departmental expense allocation spreadsheet can now be used to prepare performance reports for the company's service and operating departments. The general office and purchasing departments are cost centers, and their managers will be evaluated on their control of costs. Actual amounts of service department expenses can be compared to budgeted amounts to help assess cost center manager performance.

Amounts in the operating department columns are used to prepare departmental income statements as shown in Exhibit 21.21. This exhibit uses the spreadsheet for its operating expenses; information on sales and cost of goods sold comes from departmental records.

Example: If the $15,300 general office expenses in Exhibit 21.12 are allocated equally across departments, what is net income for the hardware department and for the combined company? *Answer:* Hardware income, $13,350; combined income, $19,000.

EXHIBIT 21.21

Departmental Income Statements

A-1 HARDWARE
Departmental Income Statements
For Year Ended December 31, 2009

	Hardware Department	Housewares Department	Appliances Department	Combined
Sales	$119,500	$71,700	$47,800	$239,000
Cost of goods sold	73,800	43,800	30,200	147,800
Gross profit	45,700	27,900	17,600	91,200
Operating expenses				
Salaries expense	15,600	7,000	7,800	30,400
Depreciation expense—Equipment	400	100	200	700
Supplies expense	300	200	100	600
Rent expense	4,860	3,240	2,700	10,800
Utilities expense	810	540	450	1,800
Advertising expense	500	300	200	1,000
Insurance expense	900	600	400	1,900
Share of general office expenses	7,650	4,590	3,060	15,300
Share of purchasing expenses	3,880	2,630	3,190	9,700
Total operating expenses	34,900	19,200	18,100	72,200
Net income (loss)	**$ 10,800**	**$ 8,700**	**$ (500)**	**$ 19,000**

Departmental Contribution to Overhead

P4 Prepare departmental contribution reports.

Point: Net income is the same in Exhibits 21.21 and 21.22. The method of reporting indirect expenses in Exhibit 21.22 does not change total net income but does identify each department's contribution to overhead and net income.

Data from departmental income statements are not always best for evaluating each profit center's performance, especially when indirect expenses are a large portion of total expenses and when weaknesses in assumptions and decisions in allocating indirect expenses can markedly affect net income. In these and other cases, we might better evaluate profit center performance using the **departmental contribution to overhead,** which is a report of the amount of sales less *direct* expenses.[2] We can also examine cost center performance by focusing on control of direct expenses.

The upper half of Exhibit 21.22 shows a departmental (profit center) contribution to overhead as part of an expanded income statement. This format is common when reporting departmental contributions to overhead. Using the information in Exhibits 21.21 and 21.22, we can evaluate the profitability of the three profit centers. For instance, let's compare the performance of the appliances department as described in these two exhibits. Exhibit 21.21 shows a \$500 net loss resulting from this department's operations, but Exhibit 21.22 shows a \$9,500 positive contribution to overhead, which is 19.9% of the appliance department's sales. The contribution of the appliances department is not as large as that of the other selling departments, but a \$9,500 contribution to overhead is better than a \$500 loss. This tells us that the appliances department is not a money loser. On the contrary, it is contributing \$9,500 toward defraying total indirect expenses of \$40,500.

EXHIBIT 21.22

Departmental Contribution to Overhead

A-1 HARDWARE
Income Statement Showing Departmental Contribution to Overhead
For Year Ended December 31, 2009

	Hardware Department	Housewares Department	Appliances Department	Combined
Sales	$119,500	$ 71,700	$47,800	$239,000
Cost of goods sold	73,800	43,800	30,200	147,800
Gross profit	45,700	27,900	17,600	91,200
Direct expenses				
Salaries expense	15,600	7,000	7,800	30,400
Depreciation expense—Equipment	400	100	200	700
Supplies expense	300	200	100	600
Total direct expenses	16,300	7,300	8,100	31,700
Departmental contributions to overhead	**$ 29,400**	**$20,600**	**$ 9,500**	**$ 59,500**
Indirect expenses				
Rent expense				10,800
Utilities expense				1,800
Advertising expense				1,000
Insurance expense				1,900
General office department expense				15,300
Purchasing department expense				9,700
Total indirect expenses				40,500
Net income				$ 19,000
Contribution as percent of sales	24.6%	28.7%	19.9%	24.9%

[2] A department's contribution is said to be "to overhead" because of the practice of considering all indirect expenses as overhead. Thus, the excess of a department's sales over direct expenses is a contribution toward at least a portion of its total overhead.

Quick Check

Answers—p. 880

6. If a company has two operating (selling) departments (shoes and hats) and two service departments (payroll and advertising), which of the following statements is correct? (*a*) Wages incurred in the payroll department are direct expenses of the shoe department, (*b*) Wages incurred in the payroll department are indirect expenses of the operating departments, or (*c*) Advertising department expenses are allocated to the other three departments.
7. Which of the following bases can be used to allocate supervisors' salaries across operating departments? (*a*) Hours spent in each department, (*b*) number of employees in each department, (*c*) sales achieved in each department, or (*d*) any of the above, depending on which information is most relevant and accessible.
8. What three steps are used to allocate expenses to operating departments?
9. An income statement showing departmental contribution to overhead, (*a*) subtracts indirect expenses from each department's revenues, (*b*) subtracts only direct expenses from each department's revenues, or (*c*) shows net income for each department.

Evaluating Investment Center Performance

This section introduces both financial and nonfinancial measures of investment center performance.

Financial Performance Evaluation Measures

A1 Analyze investment centers using return on assets, residual income, and balanced scorecard.

Investment center managers are typically evaluated using performance measures that combine income and assets. Consider the following data for ZTel, a company which operates two divisions: LCD and S-Phone. The LCD division manufactures liquid crystal display (LCD) touch-screen monitors and sells them for use in computers, cellular phones, and other products. The S-Phone division sells smartphones, mobile phones that also function as personal computers, MP3 players, cameras, and global positioning satellite (GPS) systems. Exhibit 21.23 shows current year income and assets for those divisions.

EXHIBIT 21.23

Investment Center Income and Assets

	LCD	S-Phone
Net income	$ 526,500	$ 417,600
Average invested assets	2,500,000	1,850,000

Investment Center Return on Total Assets One measure to evaluate division performance is the **investment center return on total assets,** also called *return on investment* (ROI). This measure is computed as follows

$$\text{Return on investment} = \frac{\text{Investment center net income}}{\text{Investment center average invested assets}}$$

The return on investment for the LCD division is 21% (rounded), computed as $526,500/ $2,500,000. The S-Phone division's return on investment is 23% (rounded), computed as $417,600/$1,850,000. Though the LCD division earned more dollars of net income, it was less efficient in using its assets to generate income compared to the S-Phone division.

Investment Center Residual Income Another way to evaluate division performance is to compute **investment center residual income,** which is computed as follows

$$\text{Residual income} = \begin{matrix}\text{Investment center}\\ \text{net income}\end{matrix} - \begin{matrix}\text{Target investment center}\\ \text{net income}\end{matrix}$$

Assume ZTel's top management sets target net income at 8% of divisional assets. For an investment center, this **hurdle rate** is typically the cost of obtaining financing. Applying this hurdle rate using the data from Exhibit 21.23 yields the residual income for ZTel's divisions in Exhibit 21.24:

EXHIBIT 21.24

Investment Center Residual Income

	LCD	S-Phone
Net income	$526,500	$417,600
Less: Target net income		
$2,500,000 × 8%	200,000	
$1,850,000 × 8%		148,000
Investment center residual income	$326,500	$269,600

Unlike return on assets, residual income is expressed in dollars. The LCD division outperformed the S-Phone division on the basis of residual income. However, this result is due in part to the LCD division having a larger asset base than the S-Phone division.

Using residual income to evaluate division performance encourages division managers to accept all opportunities that return more than the target net income, thus increasing company value. For example, the S-Phone division might not want to accept a new customer that will provide a 15% return on investment, since that will reduce the S-Phone division's overall return on investment (23% as shown above). However, the S-Phone division should accept this opportunity because the new customer would increase residual income by providing net income above the target net income.

Point: Residual income is also called *economic value added* (EVA).

Nonfinancial Performance Evaluation Measures

Evaluating performance solely on financial measures such as return on investment or residual income has limitations. For example, some investment center managers might forgo profitable opportunities to keep their return on investment high. Also, residual income is less useful when comparing investment centers of different size. And, both return on investment and residual income can encourage managers to focus too heavily on short-term financial goals.

In response to these limitations, companies consider nonfinancial measures. For example, a delivery company such as FedEx might track the percentage of on-time deliveries. The percentage of defective tennis balls manufactured can be used to assess performance of Penn's production managers. Walmart's credit card screens commonly ask customers at check-out whether the cashier was friendly or the store was clean. This kind of information can help division managers run their divisions and help top management evaluate division manager performance.

Balanced Scorecard The **balanced scorecard** is a system of performance measures, including nonfinancial measures, used to assess company and division manager performance. The balanced scorecard requires managers to think of their company from four perspectives:

1. *Customer:* What do customers think of us?
2. *Internal processes:* Which of our operations are critical to meeting customer needs?
3. *Innovation and learning:* How can we improve?
4. *Financial:* What do our owners think of us?

Point: One survey indicates that nearly 60% of global companies use some form of balanced scorecard.

The balanced scorecard collects information on several key performance indicators within each of the four perspectives. These key indicators vary across companies. Exhibit 21.25 lists common performance measures.

After selecting key performance indicators, companies collect data on each indicator and compare actual amounts to expected amounts to assess performance. For example, a company might have a goal of filling 98% of customer orders within two hours. Balanced scorecard reports are often presented in graphs or tables that can be updated frequently. Such timely information aids division managers in their decisions, and can be used by top management to evaluate division manager performance.

EXHIBIT 21.25

Balanced Scorecard Performance Indicators

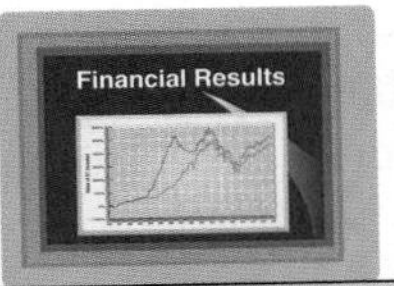

Customer	Internal Process	Innovation/Learning	Financial
• Customer satisfaction rating • # of new customers acquired • % of on-time deliveries • % of sales from new products • Time to fill orders % of sales returned	• Defect rates • Cycle time • Product costs • Labor hours per order • Production days without an accident	• Employee satisfaction • Employee turnover • $ spent on training • # of new products • # of patents • $ spent on research	• Net income • ROI • Sales growth • Cash flow • Residual income • Stock price

Exhibit 21.26 is an example of balanced scorecard reporting on the customer perspective for an Internet retailer. This scorecard reports for example that the retailer is getting 62% of its potential customers successfully through the checkout process, and that 2.2% of all orders are returned. The *color* of the arrows in the right-most column reveals whether the company is exceeding its goal (green), barely meeting the goal (yellow), or not meeting the goal (red). The *direction* of the arrows reveals any trend in performance: an upward arrow indicates improvement, a downward arrow indicates declining performance, and an arrow pointing sideways indicates no change. A review of these arrows' color and direction suggests the retailer is meeting or exceeding its goals on checkout success, orders returned, and customer satisfaction. Further, checkout success and customer satisfaction are improving. The red arrow shows the company has received more customer complaints than was hoped for; however, the number of customer complaints is declining. A manager would combine this information with similar information on the internal process, innovation and learning, and financial perspectives to get an overall view of division performance.

EXHIBIT 21.26

Balanced Scorecard Reporting: Internet Retailer

Customer Perspective	Actual	Goal
Checkout success	62%	↑
Orders returned	2.20%	↔
Customer satisfaction rating	9.5	↑
Number of customer complaints	142	↓

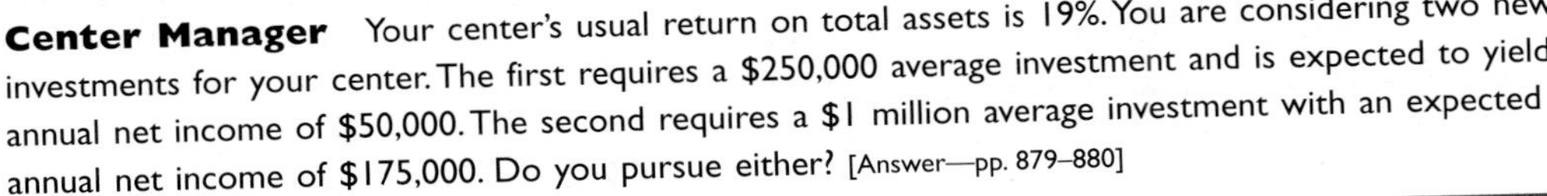

Decision Maker

Center Manager Your center's usual return on total assets is 19%. You are considering two new investments for your center. The first requires a $250,000 average investment and is expected to yield annual net income of $50,000. The second requires a $1 million average investment with an expected annual net income of $175,000. Do you pursue either? [Answer—pp. 879–880]

Responsibility Accounting

C4 Explain controllable costs and responsibility accounting.

Departmental accounting reports often provide data used to evaluate a department's performance, but are they useful in assessing how well a department *manager* performs? Neither departmental income nor its contribution to overhead may be useful because many expenses can be outside a manager's control. Instead, we often evaluate a manager's performance using responsibility accounting reports that describe a department's activities in terms of **controllable costs.**[3] A cost is controllable if a manager has the power to determine or at least significantly affect the amount incurred. **Uncontrollable costs** are not within the manager's control or influence.

Controllable versus Direct Costs

Controllable costs are not always the same as direct costs. Direct costs are readily traced to a department, but the department manager might or might not control their amounts. For example, department managers often have little or no control over depreciation expense because they cannot affect the amount of equipment assigned to their departments. Also, department managers rarely control their own salaries. However, they can control or influence items such as the cost of supplies used in their department. When evaluating managers' performances, we should use data reflecting their departments' outputs along with their controllable costs and expenses.

Distinguishing between controllable and uncontrollable costs depends on the particular manager and time period under analysis. For example, the cost of property insurance is usually not controllable at the department manager's level but by the executive responsible for obtaining the company's insurance coverage. Likewise, this executive might not control costs resulting from insurance policies already in force. However, when a policy expires, this executive can renegotiate a replacement policy and then controls these costs. Therefore, all costs are controllable at some management level if the time period is sufficiently long. We must use good judgment in identifying controllable costs.

Responsibility Accounting System

A *responsibility accounting system* uses the concept of controllable costs to assign managers the responsibility for costs and expenses under their control. Prior to each reporting period, a company prepares plans that identify costs and expenses under each manager's control. These plans are called **responsibility accounting budgets.** To ensure the cooperation of managers and the reasonableness of budgets, managers should be involved in preparing their budgets.

EXHIBIT 21.27

Organizational Responsibility Chart

A responsibility accounting system also involves performance reports. A **responsibility accounting performance report** accumulates and reports costs and expenses that a manager is responsible for and their budgeted amounts. Management's analysis of differences between budgeted amounts and actual costs and expenses often results in corrective or strategic managerial actions. Upper-level management uses performance reports to evaluate the effectiveness of lower-level managers in controlling costs and expenses and keeping them within budgeted amounts.

A responsibility accounting system recognizes that control over costs and expenses belongs to several levels of management. We illustrate this by considering the organization chart in Exhibit 21.27. The lines in this chart connecting the managerial positions reflect channels of authority. For example, the four department managers of this consulting firm (benchmarking, cost management, outsourcing, and service) are responsible for controllable costs and expenses incurred in their

[3] The terms *cost* and *expense* are often used interchangeably in managerial accounting, but they are not necessarily the same. *Cost* often refers to the monetary outlay to acquire some resource that can have present and future benefit. *Expense* usually refers to an expired cost. That is, as the benefit of a resource expires, a portion of its cost is written off as an expense.

departments, but these same costs are subject to the overall control of the vice president (VP) for operational consulting. Similarly, this VP's costs are subject to the control of the executive vice president (EVP) for operations, the president, and, ultimately, the board of directors.

At lower levels, managers have limited responsibility and relatively little control over costs and expenses. Performance reports for low-level management typically cover few controllable costs. Responsibility and control broaden for higher-level managers; therefore, their reports span a wider range of costs. However, reports to higher-level managers seldom contain the details reported to their subordinates but are summarized for two reasons: (1) lower-level managers are often responsible for these detailed costs and (2) detailed reports can obscure broader, more important issues facing a company.

Point: Responsibility accounting does not place blame. Instead, responsibility accounting is used to identify opportunities for improving performance.

Exhibit 21.28 shows summarized performance reports for the three management levels identified in Exhibit 21.27. Exhibit 21.28 shows that costs under the control of the benchmarking department manager are totaled and included among controllable costs of the VP for operational consulting. Also, costs under the control of the VP are totaled and included among controllable costs of the EVP for operations. In this way, a responsibility accounting system provides relevant information for each management level.

EXHIBIT 21.28

Responsibility Accounting Performance Reports

Executive Vice President, Operations

Controllable Costs	Budgeted Amount	Actual Amount	Over (Under) Budget
	For July		
Salaries, VPs	$ 80,000	$ 80,000	$ 0
Quality control costs	21,000	22,400	1,400
Office costs	29,500	28,800	(700)
Operational consulting	**276,700**	**279,500**	**2,800**
Strategic consulting	390,000	380,600	(9,400)
Totals	$ 797,200	$ 791,300	$ (5,900)

Vice President, Operational Consulting

Controllable Costs	Budgeted Amount	Actual Amount	Over (Under) Budget
	For July		
Salaries, department managers	$ 75,000	$ 78,000	$ 3,000
Depreciation	10,600	10,600	0
Insurance	6,800	6,300	(500)
Benchmarking department	**79,600**	**79,900**	**300**
Cost management department	61,500	60,200	(1,300)
Outsourcing department	24,300	24,700	400
Service department	18,900	19,800	900
Totals	**$276,700**	**$279,500**	**$2,800**

Manager, Benchmarking Department

Controllable Costs	Budgeted Amount	Actual Amount	Over (Under) Budget
	For July		
Salaries	$ 51,600	$ 52,500	$ 900
Supplies	8,000	7,800	(200)
Other controllable costs	20,000	19,600	(400)
Totals	**$ 79,600**	**$ 79,900**	**$ 300**

Technological advances increase our ability to produce vast amounts of information that often exceed our ability to use it. Good managers select relevant data for planning and controlling the areas under their responsibility. A good responsibility accounting system makes every effort to provide relevant information to the right person (the one who controls the cost) at the right time (before a cost is out of control).

Point: Responsibility accounting usually divides a company into subunits, or *responsibility centers*. A center manager is evaluated on how well the center performs, as reported in responsibility accounting reports.

Quick Check

Answers—p. 880

10. Are the reports of departmental net income and the departmental contribution to overhead useful in assessing a department manager's performance? Explain.
11. Performance reports to evaluate managers should (*a*) include data about controllable expenses, (*b*) compare actual results with budgeted levels, or (*c*) both (*a*) and (*b*).

Decision Analysis — Investment Center Profit Margin and Investment Turnover

A2 Analyze investment centers using profit margin and investment turnover.

We can further examine investment center (division) performance by splitting return on investment into **profit margin** and **investment turnover** as follows

$$\textbf{Return on investment} = \textbf{Profit margin} \times \textbf{Investment turnover}$$

$$\frac{\text{Investment center net income}}{\text{Investment center average assets}} = \frac{\text{Investment center net income}}{\text{Investment center sales}} \times \frac{\text{Investment center sales}}{\text{Investment center average assets}}$$

Profit margin measures the income earned per dollar of sales. **Investment turnover** measures how efficiently an investment center generates sales from its invested assets. Higher profit margin and higher investment turnover indicate better performance. To illustrate, consider **Best Buy** which reports in Exhibit 21.29 results for two divisions (segments): Domestic and International.

EXHIBIT 21.29

Best Buy Division Sales, Income, and Assets

($ millions)	Domestic	International
Sales	$24,616	$2,817
Net income	1,393	49
Average invested assets	8,372	1,922

Profit margin and investment turnover for its Domestic and International divisions are computed and shown in Exhibit 21.30:

EXHIBIT 21.30

Best Buy Division Profit Margin and Investment Turnover

($ millions)	Domestic	International
Profit Margin		
$1,393/$24,616	5.66%	
$49/$2,817		1.74%
Investment Turnover		
$24,616/$8,372	2.94	
$2,817/$1,922		1.47

Best Buy's Domestic division generates 5.66 cents of profit per $1 of sales, while its International division generates only 1.74 cents of profit per dollar of sales. Its Domestic division also uses its assets more efficiently; its investment turnover of 2.94 is twice that of its International division's 1.47. Top management can use profit margin and investment turnover to evaluate the performance of division managers. The measures can also aid management when considering further investment in its divisions.

Decision Maker

Division Manager You manage a division in a highly competitive industry. You will receive a cash bonus if your division achieves an ROI above 12%. Your division's profit margin is 7%, equal to the industry average, and your division's investment turnover is 1.5. What actions can you take to increase your chance of receiving the bonus? [Answer—p. 880]

Demonstration Problem

DP21

Management requests departmental income statements for Hacker's Haven, a computer store that has five departments. Three are operating departments (hardware, software, and repairs) and two are service departments (general office and purchasing).

	General Office	Purchasing	Hardware	Software	Repairs
Sales	—	—	$960,000	$600,000	$840,000
Cost of goods sold	—	—	500,000	300,000	200,000
Direct expenses					
Payroll	$60,000	$45,000	80,000	25,000	325,000
Depreciation	6,000	7,200	33,000	4,200	9,600
Supplies	15,000	10,000	10,000	2,000	25,000

The departments incur several indirect expenses. To prepare departmental income statements, the indirect expenses must be allocated across the five departments. Then the expenses of the two service departments must be allocated to the three operating departments. Total cost amounts and the allocation bases for each indirect expense follow.

Indirect Expense	Total Cost	Allocation Basis
Rent	$150,000	Square footage occupied
Utilities	50,000	Square footage occupied
Advertising	125,000	Dollars of sales
Insurance	30,000	Value of assets insured
Service departments		
General office	?	Number of employees
Purchasing	?	Dollars of cost of goods sold

The following additional information is needed for indirect expense allocations.

Department	Square Feet	Sales	Insured Assets	Employees	Cost of Goods Sold
General office	500		$ 60,000		
Purchasing	500		72,000		
Hardware	4,000	$ 960,000	330,000	5	$ 500,000
Software	3,000	600,000	42,000	5	300,000
Repairs	2,000	840,000	96,000	10	200,000
Totals	10,000	$2,400,000	$600,000	20	$1,000,000

Required

1. Prepare a departmental expense allocation spreadsheet for Hacker's Haven.

2. Prepare a departmental income statement reporting net income for each operating department and for all operating departments combined.

Planning the Solution

- Set up and complete four tables to allocate the indirect expenses—one each for rent, utilities, advertising, and insurance.
- Allocate the departments' indirect expenses using a spreadsheet like the one in Exhibit 21.12. Enter the given amounts of the direct expenses for each department. Then enter the allocated amounts of the indirect expenses that you computed.
- Complete two tables for allocating the general office and purchasing department costs to the three operating departments. Enter these amounts on the spreadsheet and determine the total expenses allocated to the three operating departments.
- Prepare departmental income statements like the one in Exhibit 21.17. Show sales, cost of goods sold, gross profit, individual expenses, and net income for each of the three operating departments and for the combined company.

Solution to Demonstration Problem

Allocations of the four indirect expenses across the five departments.

Rent	Square Feet	Percent of Total	Allocated Cost
General office	500	5.0%	$ 7,500
Purchasing	500	5.0	7,500
Hardware	4,000	40.0	60,000
Software	3,000	30.0	45,000
Repairs	2,000	20.0	30,000
Totals	10,000	100.0%	$150,000

Utilities	Square Feet	Percent of Total	Allocated Cost
General office	500	5.0%	$ 2,500
Purchasing	500	5.0	2,500
Hardware	4,000	40.0	20,000
Software	3,000	30.0	15,000
Repairs	2,000	20.0	10,000
Totals	10,000	100.0%	$50,000

Advertising	Sales Dollars	Percent of Total	Allocated Cost
Hardware	$ 960,000	40.0%	$ 50,000
Software	600,000	25.0	31,250
Repairs	840,000	35.0	43,750
Totals	$2,400,000	100.0%	$125,000

Insurance	Assets Insured	Percent of Total	Allocated Cost
General office	$ 60,000	10.0%	$ 3,000
Purchasing	72,000	12.0	3,600
Hardware	330,000	55.0	16,500
Software	42,000	7.0	2,100
Repairs	96,000	16.0	4,800
Totals	$600,000	100.0%	$30,000

1. Allocations of service department expenses to the three operating departments.

General Office Allocations to	Employees	Percent of Total	Allocated Cost
Hardware	5	25.0%	$23,500
Software	5	25.0	23,500
Repairs	10	50.0	47,000
Totals	20	100.0%	$94,000

Purchasing Allocations to	Cost of Goods Sold	Percent of Total	Allocated Cost
Hardware	$ 500,000	50.0%	$37,900
Software	300,000	30.0	22,740
Repairs	200,000	20.0	15,160
Totals	$1,000,000	100.0%	$75,800

HACKER'S HAVEN
Departmental Expense Allocations
For Year Ended December 31, 2009

	Allocation Base	Expense Account Balance	General Office Dept.	Purchasing Dept.	Hardware Dept.	Software Dept.	Repairs Dept.
Direct Expenses							
Payroll		$ 535,000	$ 60,000	$ 45,000	$ 80,000	$ 25,000	$ 325,000
Depreciation		60,000	6,000	7,200	33,000	4,200	9,600
Supplies		62,000	15,000	10,000	10,000	2,000	25,000
Indirect Expenses							
Rent	Square ft.	150,000	7,500	7,500	60,000	45,000	30,000
Utilities	Square ft.	50,000	2,500	2,500	20,000	15,000	10,000
Advertising	Sales	125,000	—	—	50,000	31,250	43,750
Insurance	Assets	30,000	3,000	3,600	16,500	2,100	4,800
Total expenses		1,012,000	94,000	75,800	269,500	124,550	448,150
Service Department Expenses							
General office	Employees		(94,000)		23,500	23,500	47,000
Purchasing	Goods sold			(75,800)	37,900	22,740	15,160
Total expenses allocated to operating departments		$1,012,000	$ 0	$ 0	$330,900	$170,790	$510,310

2. Departmental income statements for Hacker's Haven.

HACKER'S HAVEN Departmental Income Statements For Year Ended December 31, 2009	Hardware	Software	Repairs	Combined
Sales	$ 960,000	$ 600,000	$ 840,000	$2,400,000
Cost of goods sold	500,000	300,000	200,000	1,000,000
Gross profit	460,000	300,000	640,000	1,400,000
Expenses				
Payroll	80,000	25,000	325,000	430,000
Depreciation	33,000	4,200	9,600	46,800
Supplies	10,000	2,000	25,000	37,000
Rent	60,000	45,000	30,000	135,000
Utilities	20,000	15,000	10,000	45,000
Advertising	50,000	31,250	43,750	125,000
Insurance	16,500	2,100	4,800	23,400
Share of general office	23,500	23,500	47,000	94,000
Share of purchasing	37,900	22,740	15,160	75,800
Total expenses	330,900	170,790	510,310	1,012,000
Net income	**$129,100**	**$129,210**	**$129,690**	**$ 388,000**

APPENDIX

Transfer Pricing

21A

C5 Explain transfer pricing and methods to set transfer prices.

Divisions in decentralized companies sometimes do business with one another. For example, a separate division of **Harley-Davidson** manufactures its plastic and fiberglass parts used in the company's motorcycles. **Anheuser-Busch**'s metal container division makes cans and lids used in its brewing operations, and also sells cans and lids to soft-drink companies. A division of **Prince** produces strings used in tennis rackets made by **Prince** and other manufacturers.

Determining the price that should be used to record transfers between divisions in the same company is the focus of this appendix. Because these transactions are transfers within the same company, the price to record them is called the **transfer price.** In decentralized organizations, division managers have input on or decide those prices. Transfer prices can be used in cost, profit, and investment centers. Since these transfers are not with customers outside the company, the transfer price has no direct impact on the company's overall profits. However, transfer prices can impact performance evaluations and, if set incorrectly, lead to bad decisions.

Point: Transfer pricing can impact company profits when divisions are located in countries with different tax rates; this is covered in advanced courses.

Alternative Transfer Prices

Exhibit 21A.1 reports data on the LCD division of ZTel. LCD manufactures liquid crystal display (LCD) touch-screen monitors for use in ZTel's S-Phone division's smartphones, which sell for $400 each. The monitors can also be used in other products. So, LCD can sell its monitors to buyers other than S-Phone. Likewise, the S-Phone division can purchase monitors from suppliers other than LCD.

Exhibit 21A.1 reveals the range of transfer prices for transfers of monitors from LCD to S-Phone. The manager of LCD wants to report a division profit; thus, this manager will not accept a transfer price less than $40 (variable manufacturing cost per unit) because doing so would cause the division to lose

EXHIBIT 21A.1

LCD Division Manufacturing Information—Monitors

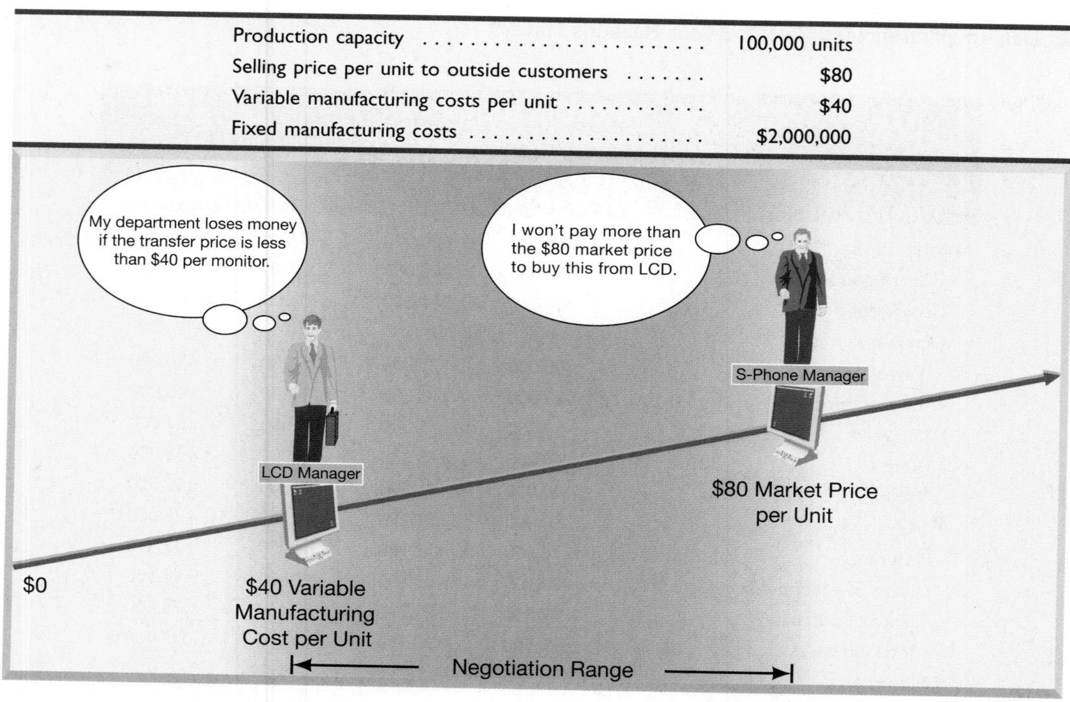

Production capacity	100,000 units
Selling price per unit to outside customers	$80
Variable manufacturing costs per unit	$40
Fixed manufacturing costs	$2,000,000

money on each monitor transferred. The LCD manager will only consider transfer prices of $40 or more. On the other hand, the S-Phone division manager also wants to report a division profit. Thus, this manager will not pay more than $80 per monitor because similar monitors can be bought from outside suppliers at that price. The S-Phone manager will only consider transfer prices of $80 or less. As any transfer price between $40 and $80 per monitor is possible, how does ZTel determine the transfer price? The answer depends in part on whether the LCD division has excess capacity to manufacture monitors.

No Excess Capacity Assume the LCD division can sell every monitor it produces, and thus is producing 100,000 units. In that case, a **market-based transfer price** of $80 per monitor is preferred. At that price, the LCD division manager is willing to either transfer monitors to S-Phone or sell to outside customers. The S-Phone manager cannot buy monitors for less than $80 from outside suppliers, so the $80 price is acceptable. Further, with a transfer price of $80 per monitor, top management of ZTel is indifferent to S-Phone buying from LCD or buying similar-quality monitors from outside suppliers.

With no excess capacity, the LCD manager will not accept a transfer price less than $80 per monitor. For example, suppose the S-Phone manager suggests a transfer price of $70 per monitor. At that price the LCD manager incurs an unnecessary *opportunity cost* of $10 per monitor (computed as $80 market price minus $70 transfer price). This would lower the LCD division's income and hurt its performance evaluation.

Excess Capacity Assume that the LCD division has excess capacity. For example, the LCD division might currently be producing only 80,000 units. Because LCD has $2,000,000 of fixed manufacturing costs, both LCD and the top management of ZTel prefer that S-Phone purchases its monitors from LCD. For example, if S-Phone purchases its monitors from an outside supplier at the market price of $80 each, LCD manufactures no units. Then, LCD reports a division loss equal to its fixed costs, and ZTel overall reports a lower net income as its costs are higher. Consequently, with excess capacity, LCD should accept any transfer price of $40 per unit or greater and S-Phone should purchase monitors from LCD. This will allow LCD to recover some (or all) of its fixed costs and increase ZTel's overall profits. For example, if a transfer price of $50 per monitor is used, the S-Phone manager is pleased to buy from LCD, since that price is below the market price of $80. For each monitor transferred from LCD to S-Phone at $50, the LCD division receives a *contribution margin* of $10 (computed as $50 transfer price less $40 variable cost) to contribute towards recovering its fixed costs. This form of transfer pricing is called **cost-based transfer pricing.** Under this approach the transfer price might be based on variable costs, total costs, or variable costs plus a markup. Determining the transfer price under excess capacity is complex and is covered in advanced courses.

Additional Issues in Transfer Pricing Several additional issues arise in determining transfer prices which include the following:

- **No market price exists.** Sometimes there is no market price for the product being transferred. The product might be a key component that requires additional conversion costs at the next stage and is not easily replicated by an outside company. For example, there is no market for a console for a **Nissan** Maxima and there is no substitute console **Nissan** can use in assembling a Maxima. In this case a market-based transfer price cannot be used.
- **Cost control.** To provide incentives for cost control, transfer prices might be based on standard, rather than actual costs. For example, if a transfer price of actual variable costs plus a markup of $20 per unit is used in the case above, LCD has no incentive to control its costs.
- **Division managers' negotiation.** With excess capacity, division managers will often negotiate a transfer price that lies between the variable cost per unit and the market price per unit. In this case, the **negotiated transfer price** and resulting departmental performance reports reflect, in part, the negotiating skills of the respective division managers. This might not be best for overall company performance.
- **Nonfinancial factors.** Factors such as quality control, reduced lead times, and impact on employee morale can be important factors in determining transfer prices.

Transfer Pricing Approaches Used by Companies

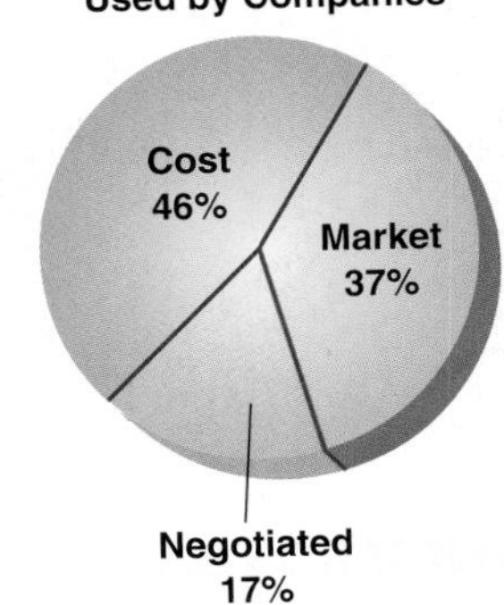

APPENDIX

Joint Costs and Their Allocation 21B

C6 Describe allocation of joint costs across products.

Most manufacturing processes involve **joint costs,** which refer to costs incurred to produce or purchase two or more products at the same time. A joint cost is like an indirect expense in the sense that more than one cost object share it. For example, a sawmill company incurs a joint cost when it buys logs that it cuts into lumber as shown in Exhibit 21B.1. The joint cost includes the logs (raw material) and its cutting (conversion) into boards classified as Clear, Select, No. 1 Common, No. 2 Common, No. 3 Common, and other types of lumber and by-products.

EXHIBIT 21B.1

Joint Products from Logs

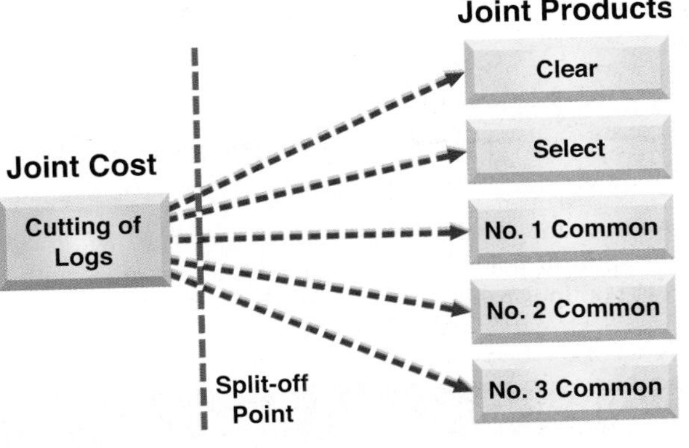

When a joint cost is incurred, a question arises as to whether to allocate it to different products resulting from it. The answer is that when management wishes to estimate the costs of individual products, joint costs are included and must be allocated to these joint products. However, when management needs information to help decide whether to sell a product at a certain point in the production process or to process it further, the joint costs are ignored.

Financial statements prepared according to GAAP must assign joint costs to products. To do this, management must decide how to allocate joint costs across products benefiting from these costs. If some products are sold and others remain in inventory, allocating joint costs involves assigning costs to both cost of goods sold and ending inventory.

The two usual methods to allocate joint costs are the (1) *physical basis* and (2) the *value basis.* The physical basis typically involves allocating joint cost using physical characteristics such as the ratio of pounds, cubic feet, or gallons of each joint product to the total pounds, cubic feet, or gallons of all joint products flowing from the cost. This method is not preferred because the resulting cost allocations do not reflect the relative market values the joint cost generates. The preferred approach is the value basis, which allocates joint cost in proportion to the sales value of the output produced by the process at the "split-off point"; see Exhibit 21B.1.

Physical Basis Allocation of Joint Cost To illustrate the physical basis of allocating a joint cost, we consider a sawmill that bought logs for $30,000. When cut, these logs produce 100,000 board feet of lumber in the grades and amounts shown in Exhibit 21B.2. The logs produce 20,000 board feet of No. 3 Common lumber, which is 20% of the total. With physical allocation, the No. 3 Common lumber is assigned 20% of the $30,000 cost of the logs, or $6,000 ($30,000 × 20%). Because this low-grade lumber sells for $4,000, this allocation gives a $2,000 loss from its production and sale. The physical basis for allocating joint costs does not reflect the extra value flowing into some products or the inferior value flowing into others. That is, the portion of a log that produces Clear and Select grade lumber is worth more than the portion used to produce the three grades of common lumber, but the physical basis fails to reflect this.

EXHIBIT 21B.2

Allocating Joint Costs on a Physical Basis

Grade of Lumber	Board Feet Produced	Percent of Total	Allocated Cost	Sales Value	Gross Profit
Clear and Select	10,000	10.0%	$ 3,000	$12,000	$ 9,000
No. 1 Common	30,000	30.0	9,000	18,000	9,000
No. 2 Common	40,000	40.0	12,000	16,000	4,000
No. 3 Common	20,000	20.0	6,000	4,000	(2,000)
Totals	100,000	100.0%	$30,000	$50,000	$20,000

Value Basis Allocation of Joint Cost Exhibit 21B.3 illustrates the value basis method of allocation. It determines the percents of the total costs allocated to each grade by the ratio of each grade's sales value to the total sales value of $50,000 (sales value is the unit selling price multiplied by the number of units produced). The Clear and Select lumber grades receive 24% of the total cost ($12,000/$50,000) instead of the 10% portion using a physical basis. The No. 3 Common lumber receives only 8% of the total cost, or $2,400, which is much less than the $6,000 assigned to it using the physical basis.

EXHIBIT 21B.3

Allocating Joint Costs on a Value Basis

Grade of Lumber	Sales Value	Percent of Total	Allocated Cost	Gross Profit
Clear and Select	$12,000	24.0%	$ 7,200	$ 4,800
No. 1 Common	18,000	36.0	10,800	7,200
No. 2 Common	16,000	32.0	9,600	6,400
No. 3 Common	4,000	8.0	2,400	1,600
Totals	$50,000	100.0%	$30,000	$20,000

Example: Refer to Exhibit 21B.3. If the sales value of Clear and Select lumber is changed to $10,000, what is the revised ratio of the market value of No. 1 Common to the total?
Answer: $18,000/$48,000 = 37.5%

An outcome of value basis allocation is that *each* grade produces exactly the same 40% gross profit at the split-off point. This 40% rate equals the gross profit rate from selling all the lumber made from the $30,000 logs for a combined price of $50,000.

Quick Check

Answers—p. 880

12. A company produces three products, B1, B2, and B3. The joint cost incurred for the current month for these products is $180,000. The following data relate to this month's production:

Product	Units Produced	Unit Sales Value
B1	96,000	$3.00
B2	64,000	6.00
B3	32,000	9.00

The amount of joint cost allocated to product B3 using the value basis allocation is (*a*) $30,000, (*b*) $54,000, or (*c*) $90,000.

Summary

C1 Explain departmentalization and the role of departmental accounting. Companies are divided into departments when they are too large to be effectively managed as a single unit. Operating departments carry out an organization's main functions. Service departments support the activities of operating departments. Departmental accounting systems provide information for evaluating departmental performance.

C2 Distinguish between direct and indirect expenses. Direct expenses are traced to a specific department and are incurred for the sole benefit of that department. Indirect expenses benefit more than one department. Indirect expenses are allocated to departments when computing departmental net income.

C3 Identify bases for allocating indirect expenses to departments. Ideally, we allocate indirect expenses by using a cause-effect relation for the allocation base. When a cause-effect relation is not identifiable, each indirect expense is allocated on a basis reflecting the relative benefit received by each department.

C4 Explain controllable costs and responsibility accounting. A controllable cost is one that is influenced by a specific management level. The total expenses of operating a department often include some items a department manager does not control. Responsibility accounting systems provide information for evaluating the performance of department managers. A responsibility accounting system's performance reports for evaluating department managers should include only the expenses (and revenues) that each manager controls.

C5 Explain transfer pricing and methods to set transfer prices. Transfer prices are used to record transfers of items between divisions of the same company. Transfer prices can be based on costs or market prices, or can be negotiated by division managers.

C6 Describe allocation of joint costs across products. A joint cost refers to costs incurred to produce or purchase two or more products at the same time. When income statements are prepared, joint costs are usually allocated to the resulting joint products using either a physical or value basis.

A1 Analyze investment centers using return on assets, residual income, and balanced scorecard. A financial measure often used to evaluate an investment center manager is the *investment center return on total assets,* also called *return on investment.* This measure is computed as the center's net income divided by the center's average total assets. Residual income, computed as investment center net income minus a target net income is an alternative financial measure of investment center performance. A balanced scorecard uses a combination of financial and non-financial measures to evaluate performance.

A2 Analyze investment centers using profit margin and investment turnover. Return on investment can also be computed as profit margin times investment turnover. Profit margin (equal to net income/sales) measures the income earned per dollar of sales and investment turnover (equal to sales/assets) measures how efficiently a division uses its assets.

P1 Assign overhead costs using two-stage cost allocation. In the traditional two-stage cost allocation procedure, service department costs are first assigned to operating departments. Then, in the second stage, a predetermined overhead allocation rate is computed for each operating department and is used to assign overhead to output.

P2 Assign overhead costs using activity-based costing. In activity-based costing, the costs of related activities are collected and then pooled in some logical manner into activity cost pools. After all activity costs have been accumulated in an activity cost pool account, users of the activity, termed *cost objects,* are assigned a portion of the total activity cost using a cost driver (allocation base).

P3 Prepare departmental income statements. Each profit center (department) is assigned its expenses to yield its own income statement. These costs include its direct expenses and its share of indirect expenses. The departmental income statement lists its revenues and costs of goods sold to determine gross profit. Its operating expenses (direct expenses and its indirect expenses allocated to the department) are deducted from gross profit to yield departmental net income.

P4 Prepare departmental contribution reports. The departmental contribution report is similar to the departmental income statement in terms of computing the gross profit for each department. Then the direct operating expenses for each department are deducted from gross profit to determine the contribution generated by each department. Indirect operating expenses are deducted *in total* from the company's combined contribution.

Guidance Answers to **Decision Maker** and **Decision Ethics**

Director of Operations You should collect details on overhead items and review them to see whether direct labor drives these costs. If it does not, overhead might be improperly assigned to departments. The situation also provides an opportunity to consider other overhead allocation bases, including use of activity-based costing.

Accounting Officer You should not author a report that you disagree with. You are responsible for ascertaining all the facts of ABC (implementation procedures, advantages and disadvantages, and costs). You should then approach your supervisor with these facts and suggest that you would like to modify the report to request, for example, a pilot test. The pilot test will allow you to further assess the suitability of ABC. Your suggestion might be rejected, at which time you may wish to speak with a more senior-level manager.

Center Manager We must first realize that the two investment opportunities are not comparable on the basis of absolute dollars of income or on assets. For instance, the second investment provides a higher income in absolute dollars but requires a higher investment. Accordingly, we need to compute return on total assets for each alternative: (1) $50,000 ÷ $250,000 = 20%, and (2) $175,000 ÷ $1 million = 17.5%. Alternative 1 has the higher return and is preferred over alternative 2. Do you pursue one, both, or neither? Because alternative 1's return is higher than the center's usual return of 19%, it should be pursued, assuming its risks are acceptable. Also, since alternative 1 requires a small investment, top management is likely to be more agreeable to pursuing it. Alternative 2's return is lower than the usual 19% and is not likely to be acceptable.

Division Manager Your division's ROI without further action is 10.5% (equal to 7% × 1.5). In a highly competitive industry, it is difficult to increase profit margins by raising prices. Your division might be better able to control its costs to increase its profit margin. In addition, you might engage in a marketing program to increase sales without increasing your division's invested assets. Investment turnover and thus ROI will increase if the marketing campaign attracts customers.

Guidance Answers to **Quick Checks**

1. Cost drivers are the factors that have a cause-effect relation with costs (or activities that pertain to costs).
2. *d*
3. A departmental accounting system provides information used to evaluate the performance of *departments.* A responsibility accounting system provides information used to evaluate the performance of *department managers.*
4. *d*
5. A cost center, such as a service department, incurs costs without directly generating revenues. A profit center, such as a product division, incurs costs but also generates revenues.
6. *b*
7. *d*
8. (1) Assign the direct expenses to each department. (2) Allocate indirect expenses to all departments. (3) Allocate the service department expenses to the operating departments.
9. *b*
10. No, because many expenses that enter into these calculations are beyond the manager's control, and managers should not be evaluated using costs they do not control.
11. *c*
12. *b*; $180,000 × ([32,000 × $9]/[96,000 × $3 + 64,000 × $6 + 32,000 × $9]) = $54,000.

Key Terms

mhhe.com/wildFAP19e

Key Terms are available at the book's Website for learning and testing in an online Flashcard Format.

Activity-based costing (ABC) (p. 854)
Activity cost driver (p. 855)
Activity cost pool (p. 855)
Balanced scorecard (p. 868)
Controllable costs (p. 870)
Cost-based transfer pricing (p. 876)
Cost center (p. 858)
Departmental accounting system (p. 858)
Departmental contribution to overhead (p. 866)
Direct expenses (p. 859)
Hurdle rate (p. 868)
Indirect expenses (p. 859)
Investment center (p. 858)
Investment center residual income (p. 867)
Investment center return on total assets (p. 867)
Investment turnover (p. 872)
Joint cost (p. 877)
Market-based transfer price (p. 876)
Negotiated transfer price (p. 877)
Profit center (p. 858)
Profit margin (p. 872)
Responsibility accounting budget (p. 870)
Responsibility accounting performance report (p. 870)
Responsibility accounting system (p. 858)
Transfer price (p. 875)
Uncontrollable costs (p. 870)

Multiple Choice Quiz

Answers on p. 899 mhhe.com/wildFAP19e

Additional Quiz Questions are available at the book's Website.

Quiz21

1. A retailer has three departments—housewares, appliances, and clothing—and buys advertising that benefits all departments. Advertising expense is $150,000 for the year, and departmental sales for the year follow: housewares, $356,250; appliances, $641,250; clothing, $427,500. How much advertising expense is allocated to appliances if allocation is based on departmental sales?
   - **a.** $37,500
   - **b.** $67,500
   - **c.** $45,000
   - **d.** $150,000
   - **e.** $641,250
2. An activity-based costing system
   - **a.** Does not require the level of detail that a traditional costing system requires.
   - **b.** Does not enable the calculation of unit cost data.
   - **c.** Allocates costs to products on the basis of activities performed on them.

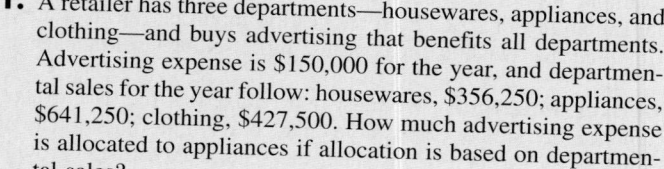

d. Cannot be used by a service company.
e. Allocates costs to products based on the number of direct labor hours used.

3. A company produces two products, Grey and Red. The following information is available relating to those two products. Assume that the company's total setup cost is $162,000. Using activity-based costing, how much setup cost is allocated to each unit of Grey?

	Grey	Red
Units produced	500	40,000
Number of setups	50	100
Direct labor hours per unit	15	15

a. $1,080
b. $ 72
c. $ 162
d. $2,000
e. $ 108

4. A company operates three retail departments as profit centers, and the following information is available for each. Which department has the largest dollar amount of departmental contribution to overhead and what is the dollar amount contributed?

Department	Sales	Cost of Goods Sold	Direct Expenses	Allocated Indirect Expenses
X	$500,000	$350,000	$50,000	$40,000
Y	200,000	75,000	20,000	50,000
Z	350,000	150,000	75,000	10,000

a. Department Y, $ 55,000
b. Department Z, $125,000
c. Department X, $500,000
d. Department Z, $200,000
e. Department X, $ 60,000

5. Using the data in question 4, Department X's contribution to overhead as a percentage of sales is
a. 20%
b. 30%
c. 12%
d. 48%
e. 32%

Superscript letter A(B) denotes assignments based on Appendix 21A (21B).

Discussion Questions

1. Why are many companies divided into departments?

2. Complete the following for a traditional two-stage allocation system: In the first stage, service department costs are assigned to ______ departments. In the second stage, a predetermined overhead rate is computed for each operating department and used to assign overhead to ______.

3. What is the difference between operating departments and service departments?

4. What is activity-based costing? What is its goal?

5. Identify at least four typical cost pools for activity-based costing in most organizations.

6. In activity-based costing, costs in a cost pool are allocated to ______ using predetermined overhead rates.

7. What company circumstances especially encourage use of activity-based costing?

8. What are two main goals in managerial accounting for reporting on and analyzing departments?

9. Is it possible to evaluate a cost center's profitability? Explain.

10. What is the difference between direct and indirect expenses?

11. Suggest a reasonable basis for allocating each of the following indirect expenses to departments: (a) salary of a supervisor who manages several departments, (b) rent, (c) heat, (d) electricity for lighting, (e) janitorial services, (f) advertising, (g) expired insurance on equipment, and (h) property taxes on equipment.

12. How is a department's contribution to overhead measured?

13. What are controllable costs?

14. Controllable and uncontrollable costs must be identified with a particular ______ and a definite ______ period.

15. Why should managers be closely involved in preparing their responsibility accounting budgets?

16. In responsibility accounting, who receives timely cost reports and specific cost information? Explain.

17.[A] What is a transfer price? Under what conditions is a market-based transfer price most likely to be used?

18.[B] What is a joint cost? How are joint costs usually allocated among the products produced from them?

19.[B] Give two examples of products with joint costs.

20. Each retail store of Best Buy has several departments. Why is it useful for its management to (a) collect accounting information about each department and (b) treat each department as a profit center?

BEST BUY

21. Apple delivers its products to locations around the world. List three controllable and three uncontrollable costs for its delivery department.

Denotes Discussion Questions that involve decision making.

QUICK STUDY

QS 21-1
Allocation and measurement terms
C1 C2 C3 C4 A1

In each blank next to the following terms, place the identifying letter of its best description.

1. _______ Cost center
2. _______ Investment center
3. _______ Departmental accounting system
4. _______ Operating department
5. _______ Profit center
6. _______ Responsibility accounting system
7. _______ Service department

A. Engages directly in manufacturing or in making sales directly to customers.
B. Does not directly manufacture products but contributes to profitability of the entire company.
C. Incurs costs and also generates revenues.
D. Provides information used to evaluate the performance of a department.
E. Incurs costs without directly yielding revenues.
F. Provides information used to evaluate the performance of a department manager.
G. Holds manager responsible for revenues, costs, and investments.

QS 21-2
Basis for cost allocation
C3 

For each of the following types of indirect expenses and service department expenses, identify one allocation basis that could be used to distribute it to the departments indicated.

1. Computer service expenses of production scheduling for operating departments.
2. General office department expenses of the operating departments.
3. Maintenance department expenses of the operating departments.
4. Electric utility expenses of all departments.

QS 21-3
Activity-based costing and overhead cost allocation
P2

The following is taken from Mortan Co.'s internal records of its factory with two operating departments. The cost driver for indirect labor and supplies is direct labor costs, and the cost driver for the remaining overhead items is number of hours of machine use. Compute the total amount of overhead cost allocated to Operating Department 1 using activity-based costing.

	Direct Labor	Machine Use Hours
Operating department 1	$18,800	2,000
Operating department 2	13,200	1,200
Totals	$32,000	3,200

Factory overhead costs	
Rent and utilities	$12,200
Indirect labor	5,400
General office expense	4,000
Depreciation—Equipment	3,000
Supplies	2,600
Total factory overhead	$27,200

Check Dept. 1 allocation, $16,700

QS 21-4
Departmental contribution to overhead
P4

Use the information in the following table to compute each department's contribution to overhead (both in dollars and as a percent). Which department contributes the largest dollar amount to total overhead? Which contributes the highest percent (as a percent of sales)?

	Dept. A	Dept. B	Dept. C
Sales	$106,000	$360,000	$168,000
Cost of goods sold	68,370	207,400	99,120
Gross profit	37,630	152,600	68,880
Total direct expenses	6,890	74,120	15,120
Contribution to overhead	$_____	$_____	$_____
Contribution percent	_____%	_____%	_____%

QS 21-5
Investment center analysis
A1

Compute return on assets for each of these **Best Buy** divisions (each is an investment center). Comment on the relative performance of each investment center.

Investment Center	Net Income	Average Assets	Return on Assets
Cameras and camcorders	$4,500,000	$20,000,000	______
Phones and communications	1,500,000	12,500,000	______
Computers and accessories	800,000	10,000,000	______

QS 21-6
Computing residual income
A1

Refer to information in QS 21-5. Assume a target income of 12% of average invested assets. Compute residual income for each of Best Buy's divisions.

QS 21-7
Computing performance measures
A1 A2

A company's shipping division (an investment center) has sales of $2,700,000, net income of $216,000, and average invested assets of $2,000,000. Compute the division's return on invested assets, profit margin, and investment turnover.

QS 21-8
Performance measures
A1 A2

Fill in the blanks in the schedule below for two separate investment centers A and B.

	Investment Center	
	A	B
Sales	$______	$3,200,000
Net income	$126,000	$______
Average invested assets	$700,000	______
Profit margin	6%	______%
Investment turnover	______	1.6
Return on assets	______%	10%

QS 21-9
Performance measures—balanced scorecard
A1

Classify each of the performance measures below into the most likely balanced scorecard perspective it relates to. Label your answers using C (customer), P (internal process), I (innovation and growth), or F (financial).

1. Change in market share ______
2. Employee training sessions attended ______
3. Number of days of employee absences ______
4. Customer wait time ______
5. Number of new products introduced ______
6. Length of time raw materials are in inventory ______
7. Profit margin ______
8. Customer satisfaction index ______

QS 21-10
Performance measures—balanced scorecard
A1

Walt Disney reports the following information for its two Parks and Resorts divisions.

	East Coast		West Coast	
	Current year	Prior year	Current year	Prior year
Hotel occupancy rates	89%	86%	92%	93%

Assume **Walt Disney** uses a balanced scorecard and sets a target of 90% occupancy in its resorts. Using Exhibit 21.26 as a guide, show how the company's performance on hotel occupancy would appear on a balanced scorecard report.

QS 21-11[A]
Determining transfer prices without excess capacity
C5

The Windshield division of Chee Cycles makes windshields for use in Chee's Assembly division. The Windshield division incurs variable costs of $175 per windshield and has capacity to make 50,000 windshields per year. The market price is $300 per windshield. The Windshield division incurs total fixed costs of $1,500,000 per year. If the Windshield division is operating at full capacity, what transfer price should be used on transfers between the Windshield and Assembly divisions? Explain.

QS 21-12[A]
Determining transfer prices with excess capacity
C5

Refer to information in QS 21-11. If the Windshield division has excess capacity, what is the range of possible transfer prices that could be used on transfers between the Windshield and Assembly divisions? Explain.

QS 21-13[B]
Joint cost allocation
C6

A company purchases a 10,020 square foot commercial building for $500,000 and spends an additional $50,000 to divide the space into two separate rental units and prepare it for rent. Unit A, which has the desirable location on the corner and contains 3,340 square feet, will be rented for $2.00 per square foot. Unit B contains 6,680 square feet and will be rented for $1.50 per square foot. How much of the joint cost should be assigned to Unit B using the value basis of allocation?

EXERCISES

Available with McGraw-Hill's Homework Manager McGraw-Hill's HOMEWORK MANAGER®

Exercise 21-1
Departmental expense allocations
P1 C3

Firefly Co. has four departments: materials, personnel, manufacturing, and packaging. In a recent month, the four departments incurred three shared indirect expenses. The amounts of these indirect expenses and the bases used to allocate them follow.

Indirect Expense	Cost	Allocation Base
Supervision	$ 80,000	Number of employees
Utilities	61,000	Square feet occupied
Insurance	16,700	Value of assets in use
Total	$157,700	

Departmental data for the company's recent reporting period follow.

Department	Employees	Square Feet	Asset Values
Materials	40	27,000	$ 60,000
Personnel	22	5,000	1,200
Manufacturing	104	45,000	42,000
Packaging	34	23,000	16,800
Total	200	100,000	$120,000

(1) Use this information to allocate each of the three indirect expenses across the four departments. (2) Prepare a summary table that reports the indirect expenses assigned to each of the four departments.

Check (2) Total of $40,820 assigned to Materials Dept.

Exercise 21-2
Activity-based costing of overhead
P2

Northwest Company produces two types of glass shelving, rounded edge and squared edge, on the same production line. For the current period, the company reports the following data.

	Rounded Edge	Squared Edge	Total
Direct materials	$19,000	$ 43,200	$ 62,200
Direct labor	12,200	23,800	36,000
Overhead (300% of direct labor cost)	36,600	71,400	108,000
Total cost	$67,800	$138,400	$206,200
Quantity produced	10,500 ft.	14,100 ft.	
Average cost per ft.	$ 6.46	$ 9.82	

Northwest's controller wishes to apply activity-based costing (ABC) to allocate the $108,000 of overhead costs incurred by the two product lines to see whether cost per foot would change markedly from that reported above. She has collected the following information.

Overhead Cost Category (Activity Cost Pool)	Cost
Supervision	$ 5,400
Depreciation of machinery	56,600
Assembly line preparation	46,000
Total overhead	$108,000

She has also collected the following information about the cost drivers for each category (cost pool) and the amount of each driver used by the two product lines.

Overhead Cost Category (Activity Cost Pool)	Driver	Usage		
		Rounded Edge	Squared Edge	Total
Supervision	Direct labor cost($)	$12,200	$23,800	$36,000
Depreciation of machinery	Machine hours	500 hours	1,500 hours	2,000 hours
Assembly line preparation	Setups (number)	40 times	210 times	250 times

Use this information to (1) assign these three overhead cost pools to each of the two products using ABC, (2) determine average cost per foot for each of the two products using ABC, and (3) compare the average cost per foot under ABC with the average cost per foot under the current method for each product. For part 3, explain why a difference between the two cost allocation methods exists.

Check (2) Rounded edge, $5.19; Squared edge, $10.76

Exercise 21-3
Rent expense allocated to departments
P1 C3

Expert Garage pays $128,000 rent each year for its two-story building. The space in this building is occupied by five departments as specified here.

Paint department	1,200 square feet of first-floor space
Engine department	3,600 square feet of first-floor space
Window department	1,920 square feet of second-floor space
Electrical department	1,056 square feet of second-floor space
Accessory department	1,824 square feet of second-floor space

The company allocates 65% of total rent expense to the first floor and 35% to the second floor, and then allocates rent expense for each floor to the departments occupying that floor on the basis of space occupied. Determine the rent expense to be allocated to each department. (Round percents to the nearest one-tenth and dollar amounts to the nearest whole dollar.)

Check Allocated to Paint Dept., $20,800

Exercise 21-4
Departmental expense allocation spreadsheet
C3 P1

Off-Road Cycle Shop has two service departments (advertising and administration) and two operating departments (cycles and clothing). During 2009, the departments had the following direct expenses and occupied the following amount of floor space.

Department	Direct Expenses	Square Feet
Advertising	$ 21,000	1,820
Administrative	15,000	1,540
Cycles	102,000	6,440
Clothing	12,000	4,200

The advertising department developed and distributed 100 advertisements during the year. Of these, 72 promoted cycles and 28 promoted clothing. The store sold $300,000 of merchandise during the year. Of this amount, $228,000 is from the cycles department, and $72,000 is from the clothing department. The utilities expense of $65,000 is an indirect expense to all departments. Prepare a departmental expense allocation spreadsheet for Off-Road Cycle Shop. The spreadsheet should assign (1) direct expenses to each of the four departments, (2) the $65,000 of utilities expense to the four departments on the basis of floor space occupied, (3) the advertising department's expenses to the two operating departments on the basis of the number of ads placed that promoted a department's products, and (4) the administrative department's expenses to the two operating departments based on the amount of sales. Provide supporting computations for the expense allocations.

Check Total expenses allocated to Cycles Dept., $169,938

Exercise 21-5
Service department expenses allocated to operating departments
P3

The following is a partially completed lower section of a departmental expense allocation spreadsheet for Haston Bookstore. It reports the total amounts of direct and indirect expenses allocated to its five departments. Complete the spreadsheet by allocating the expenses of the two service departments (advertising and purchasing) to the three operating departments.

		Allocation Base	Expense Account Balance	Advertising Dept.	Purchasing Dept.	Books Dept.	Magazines Dept.	Newspapers Dept.
1				Allocation of Expenses to Departments				
5	Total department expenses..........		$653,000	$23,000	$30,000	$426,000	$85,000	$89,000
6	**Service department expenses**							
7	Advertising department............	Sales		?		?	?	?
8	Purchasing department............	Purch. orders			?	?	?	?
9	Total expenses allocated to							
10	operating departments.............		?	$ 0	$ 0	?	?	?

Advertising and purchasing department expenses are allocated to operating departments on the basis of dollar sales and purchase orders, respectively. Information about the allocation bases for the three operating departments follows.

Department	Sales	Purchase Orders
Books	$440,000	400
Magazines	160,000	250
Newspapers	200,000	350
Total	$800,000	1,000

Check Total expenses allocated to Books Dept., $450,650

Exercise 21-6
Indirect payroll expense allocated to departments
C3

Jaria Stevens works in both the jewelry department and the hosiery department of a retail store. Stevens assists customers in both departments and arranges and stocks merchandise in both departments. The store allocates Stevens' $35,000 annual wages between the two departments based on a sample of the time worked in the two departments. The sample is obtained from a diary of hours worked that Stevens kept in a randomly chosen two-week period. The diary showed the following hours and activities spent in the two departments. Allocate Stevens' annual wages between the two departments.

Selling in jewelry department	41 hours
Arranging and stocking merchandise in jewelry department	4 hours
Selling in hosiery department	24 hours
Arranging and stocking merchandise in hosiery department	6 hours
Idle time spent waiting for a customer to enter one of the selling departments	5 hours

Check Assign $14,000 to Hosiery

Exercise 21-7
Managerial performance evaluation
C4 

Rex Stanton manages an auto dealership's service department. The recent month's income statement for his department follows. (1) Analyze the items on the income statement and identify those that definitely should be included on a performance report used to evaluate Stanton's performance. List them and explain why you chose them. (2) List and explain the items that should definitely be excluded. (3) List the items that are not definitely included or excluded and explain why they fall into that category.

Revenues		
Sales of parts	$ 72,000	
Sales of services	105,000	$177,000
Costs and expenses		
Cost of parts sold	30,000	
Building depreciation	9,300	
Income taxes allocated to department	8,700	
Interest on long-term debt	7,500	
Manager's salary	12,000	
Payroll taxes	8,100	
Supplies	15,900	
Utilities	4,400	
Wages (hourly)	16,000	
Total costs and expenses		111,900
Departmental net income		$ 65,100

Exercise 21-8
Investment center analysis
A1 

You must prepare a return on investment analysis for the regional manager of Veggie Burgers. This growing chain is trying to decide which outlet of two alternatives to open. The first location (A) requires a $500,000 investment and is expected to yield annual net income of $85,000. The second location (B) requires a $200,000 investment and is expected to yield annual net income of $42,000. Compute the return on investment for each Veggie Burgers alternative and then make your recommendation in a one-half page memorandum to the regional manager. (The chain currently generates an 18% return on total assets.)

Exercise 21-9
Computing performance measures
A1

ZMart, a retailer of consumer goods, provides the following information on two of its departments (each considered an investment center).

Investment Center	Sales	Net Income	Average Invested Assets
Electronics	$10,000,000	$750,000	$3,750,000
Sporting goods	8,000,000	800,000	5,000,000

(1) Compute return on investment for each department. Using return on investment, which department is most efficient at using assets to generate returns for the company? (2) Assume a target income level of 12% of average invested assets. Compute residual income for each department. Which department generated the most residual income for the company? (3) Assume the Electronics department is presented with a new investment opportunity that will yield a 15% return on assets. Should the new investment opportunity be accepted? Explain.

Exercise 21-10
Computing performance measures A2

Refer to information in Exercise 21-9. Compute profit margin and investment turnover for each department. Which department generates the most net income per dollar of sales? Which department is most efficient at generating sales from average invested assets?

Exercise 21-11
Performance measures—balanced scorecard
A1

MidCoast Airlines uses the following performance measures. Classify each of the performance measures below into the most likely balanced scorecard perspective it relates to. Label your answers using C (customer), P (internal process), I (innovation and growth), or F (financial).

1. Percentage of ground crew trained _______
2. On-time flight percentage _______
3. Percentage of on-time departures _______
4. Market value _______
5. Flight attendant training sessions attended _______
6. Revenue per seat _______
7. Customer complaints _______
8. Time airplane is on ground between flights _______
9. Number of reports of mishandled or lost baggage _______
10. Cash flow from operations _______
11. Accidents or safety incidents per mile flown _______
12. Airplane miles per gallon of fuel _______
13. Return on investment _______
14. Cost of leasing airplanes _______

Exercise 21-12[A]
Determining transfer prices
C5

The Trailer department of Sprint Bicycles makes bike trailers that attach to bicycles and can carry children or cargo. The trailers have a retail price of $100 each. Each trailer incurs $40 of variable manufacturing costs. The Trailer department has capacity for 20,000 trailers per year, and incurs fixed costs of $500,000 per year.

Required

1. Assume the Assembly division of Sprint Bicycles wants to buy 5,000 trailers per year from the Trailer division. If the Trailer division can sell all of the trailers it manufactures to outside customers, what price should be used on transfers between Sprint Bicycle's divisions? Explain.
2. Assume the Trailer division currently only sells 10,000 trailers to outside customers, and the Assembly division wants to buy 5,000 trailers per year from the Trailer division. What is the range of acceptable prices that could be used on transfers between Sprint Bicycle's divisions? Explain.
3. Assume transfer prices of either $40 per trailer or $70 per trailer are being considered. Comment on the preferred transfer prices from the perspectives of the Trailer division manager, the Assembly division manager, and the top management of Sprint Bicycles.

Exercise 21-13[B]
Joint real estate costs assigned
C6

Check Total Canyon cost, $2,700,000

Mountain Home Properties is developing a subdivision that includes 300 home lots. The 225 lots in the Canyon section are below a ridge and do not have views of the neighboring canyons and hills; the 75 lots in the Hilltop section offer unobstructed views. The expected selling price for each Canyon lot is $50,000 and for each Hilltop lot is $100,000. The developer acquired the land for $2,500,000 and spent another $2,000,000 on street and utilities improvements. Assign the joint land and improvement costs to the lots using the value basis of allocation and determine the average cost per lot.

Exercise 21-14[B]
Joint product costs assigned
C6

Ocean Seafood Company purchases lobsters and processes them into tails and flakes. It sells the lobster tails for $20 per pound and the flakes for $15 per pound. On average, 100 pounds of lobster are processed into 57 pounds of tails and 24 pounds of flakes, with 19 pounds of waste. Assume that the company purchased 3,000 pounds of lobster for $6.00 per pound and processed the lobsters with an additional labor cost of $1,800. No materials or labor costs are assigned to the waste. If 1,570 pounds of tails and 640 pounds of flakes are sold, what is (1) the allocated cost of the sold items and (2) the allocated cost of the ending inventory? The company allocates joint costs on a value basis. (Round the dollar cost per pound to the nearest thousandth.)

Check (2) Inventory cost, $1,760

McGraw-Hill's HOMEWORK MANAGER® Available with McGraw-Hill's Homework Manager

PROBLEM SET A

Problem 21-1A
Allocation of building occupancy costs to departments
C3 P1 

mhhe.com/wildFAP19e

Citizens Bank has several departments that occupy both floors of a two-story building. The departmental accounting system has a single account, Building Occupancy Cost, in its ledger. The types and amounts of occupancy costs recorded in this account for the current period follow.

Depreciation—Building	$ 31,500
Interest—Building mortgage	47,000
Taxes—Building and land	14,000
Gas (heating) expense	4,425
Lighting expense	5,250
Maintenance expense	9,625
Total occupancy cost	$111,800

The building has 5,000 square feet on each floor. In prior periods, the accounting manager merely divided the $111,800 occupancy cost by 10,000 square feet to find an average cost of $11.18 per square foot and then charged each department a building occupancy cost equal to this rate times the number of square feet that it occupied.

Helen Lanya manages a first-floor department that occupies 1,000 square feet, and Jose Jimez manages a second-floor department that occupies 1,700 square feet of floor space. In discussing the departmental reports, the second-floor manager questions whether using the same rate per square foot for all departments makes sense because the first-floor space is more valuable. This manager also references a recent real estate study of average local rental costs for similar space that shows first-floor space worth $40 per square foot and second-floor space worth $10 per square foot (excluding costs for heating, lighting, and maintenance).

Required

1. Allocate occupancy costs to the Lanya and Jimez departments using the current allocation method.
2. Allocate the depreciation, interest, and taxes occupancy costs to the Lanya and Jimez departments in proportion to the relative market values of the floor space. Allocate the heating, lighting, and maintenance costs to the Lanya and Jimez departments in proportion to the square feet occupied (ignoring floor space market values).

Check (1) Total allocated to Lanya and Jimez, $30,186 (2) Total occupancy cost to Lanya, $16,730

Analysis Component

3. Which allocation method would you prefer if you were a manager of a second-floor department? Explain.

Problem 21-2A
Activity-based costing
P2 

Health Co-op is an outpatient surgical clinic that was profitable for many years, but Medicare has cut its reimbursements by as much as 40%. As a result, the clinic wants to better understand its costs. It decides to prepare an activity-based cost analysis, including an estimate of the average cost of both general surgery and orthopedic surgery. The clinic's three cost centers and their cost drivers follow.

Cost Center	Cost	Cost Driver	Driver Quantity
Professional salaries	$1,600,000	Professional hours	10,000
Patient services and supplies	27,000	Number of patients	600
Building cost	150,000	Square feet	1,500

The two main surgical units and their related data follow.

Service	Hours	Square Feet*	Patients
General surgery	2,500	600	400
Orthopedic surgery	7,500	900	200

* Orthopedic surgery requires more space for patients, supplies, and equipment.

Required

Check (2) Average cost of general (orthopedic) surgery, $1,195 ($6,495) per patient

1. Compute the cost per cost driver for each of the three cost centers.
2. Use the results from part 1 to allocate costs from each of the three cost centers to both the general surgery and the orthopedic surgery units. Compute total cost and average cost per patient for both the general surgery and the orthopedic surgery units.

Analysis Component

3. Without providing computations, would the average cost of general surgery be higher or lower if all center costs were allocated based on the number of patients? Explain.

Problem 21-3A
Departmental income statements; forecasts

P3 

mhhe.com/wildFAP19e

Warton Company began operations in January 2009 with two operating (selling) departments and one service (office) department. Its departmental income statements follow.

WARTON COMPANY Departmental Income Statements For Year Ended December 31, 2009	Clock	Mirror	Combined
Sales	$170,000	$95,000	$265,000
Cost of goods sold	83,300	58,900	142,200
Gross profit	86,700	36,100	122,800
Direct expenses			
Sales salaries	21,000	7,100	28,100
Advertising	2,100	700	2,800
Store supplies used	550	350	900
Depreciation—Equipment	2,300	900	3,200
Total direct expenses	25,950	9,050	35,000
Allocated expenses			
Rent expense	7,040	3,780	10,820
Utilities expense	2,800	1,600	4,400
Share of office department expenses	13,500	6,500	20,000
Total allocated expenses	23,340	11,880	35,220
Total expenses	49,290	20,930	70,220
Net income	$ 37,410	$15,170	$ 52,580

Warton plans to open a third department in January 2010 that will sell paintings. Management predicts that the new department will generate $50,000 in sales with a 45% gross profit margin and will require the following direct expenses: sales salaries, $8,500; advertising, $1,100; store supplies, $400; and equipment depreciation, $1,000. It will fit the new department into the current rented space by taking some square footage from the other two departments. When opened the new painting department will fill one-fifth of the space presently used by the clock department and one-fourth used by the mirror department. Management does not predict any increase in utilities costs, which are allocated to the departments in proportion to occupied space (or rent expense). The company allocates office department expenses to the operating departments in proportion to their sales. It expects the painting department to increase total office department expenses by $8,000. Since the painting department will bring new customers into the store, management expects sales in both the clock and mirror departments to increase by 8%. No changes for those departments' gross profit percents or their direct expenses are expected except for store supplies used, which will increase in proportion to sales.

Required

Prepare departmental income statements that show the company's predicted results of operations for calendar year 2010 for the three operating (selling) departments and their combined totals. (Round percents to the nearest one-tenth and dollar amounts to the nearest whole dollar.)

Check 2010 forecasted combined net income (sales), $65,832 ($336,200)

Problem 21-4A
Responsibility accounting performance reports; controllable and budgeted costs
C4 P4

Billie Whitehorse, the plant manager of Travel Free's Ohio plant, is responsible for all of that plant's costs other than her own salary. The plant has two operating departments and one service department. The camper and trailer operating departments manufacture different products and have their own managers. The office department, which Whitehorse also manages, provides services equally to the two operating departments. A budget is prepared for each operating department and the office department. The company's responsibility accounting system must assemble information to present budgeted and actual costs in performance reports for each operating department manager and the plant manager. Each performance report includes only those costs that a particular operating department manager can control: raw materials, wages, supplies used, and equipment depreciation. The plant manager is responsible for the department managers' salaries, utilities, building rent, office salaries other than her own, and other office costs plus all costs controlled by the two operating department managers. The annual departmental budgets and actual costs for the two operating departments follow.

	Budget			Actual		
	Campers	Trailers	Combined	Campers	Trailers	Combined
Raw materials	$195,900	$276,200	$ 472,100	$194,800	$273,600	$ 468,400
Employee wages	104,200	205,200	309,400	107,200	208,000	315,200
Dept. manager salary	44,000	53,000	97,000	44,800	53,900	98,700
Supplies used	34,000	92,200	126,200	32,900	91,300	124,200
Depreciation—Equip.	63,000	127,000	190,000	63,000	127,000	190,000
Utilities	3,600	5,200	8,800	4,500	4,700	9,200
Building rent	5,700	10,000	15,700	6,200	9,300	15,500
Office department costs	67,750	67,750	135,500	68,550	68,550	137,100
Totals	$518,150	$836,550	$1,354,700	$521,950	$836,350	$1,358,300

The office department's annual budget and its actual costs follow.

	Budget	Actual
Plant manager salary	$100,000	$ 84,000
Other office salaries	46,500	30,100
Other office costs	22,000	21,000
Totals	$168,500	$135,100

Required

1. Prepare responsibility accounting performance reports like those in Exhibit 21.28 that list costs controlled by the following:

a. Manager of the camper department.

b. Manager of the trailer department.

c. Manager of the Ohio plant.

In each report, include the budgeted and actual costs and show the amount that each actual cost is over or under the budgeted amount.

Check (1a) $800 total over budget

(1c) Ohio plant controllable costs, $15,400 total under budget

Analysis Component

2. Did the plant manager or the operating department managers better manage costs? Explain.

Problem 21-5A[B]
Allocation of joint costs
C6

Florida Orchards produced a good crop of peaches this year. After preparing the following income statement, the company believes it should have given its No. 3 peaches to charity and saved its efforts.

FLORIDA ORCHARDS
Income Statement
For Year Ended December 31, 2009

	No. 1	No. 2	No. 3	Combined
Sales (by grade)				
No. 1: 300,000 lbs. @ $1.50/lb	$450,000			
No. 2: 250,000 lbs. @ $0.75/lb		$187,500		
No. 3: 600,000 lbs. @ $0.50/lb			$300,000	
Total sales				$937,500
Costs				
Tree pruning and care @ $0.40/lb	120,000	100,000	240,000	460,000
Picking, sorting, and grading @ $0.10/lb	30,000	25,000	60,000	115,000
Delivery costs	15,000	15,000	37,500	67,500
Total costs	165,000	140,000	337,500	642,500
Net income (loss)	$285,000	$ 47,500	$ (37,500)	$295,000

In preparing this statement, the company allocated joint costs among the grades on a physical basis as an equal amount per pound. The company's delivery cost records show that $30,000 of the $67,500 relates to crating the No. 1 and No. 2 peaches and hauling them to the buyer. The remaining $37,500 of delivery costs is for crating the No. 3 peaches and hauling them to the cannery.

Required

Check (1) $147,200 tree pruning and care costs allocated to No. 3

(2) Net income from No. 1 & No. 2 peaches, $152,820 & $63,680

1. Prepare reports showing cost allocations on a sales value basis to the three grades of peaches. Separate the delivery costs into the amounts directly identifiable with each grade. Then allocate any shared delivery costs on the basis of the relative sales value of each grade.
2. Using your answers to part 1, prepare an income statement using the joint costs allocated on a sales value basis.

Analysis Component

3. Do you think delivery costs fit the definition of a joint cost? Explain.

PROBLEM SET B

Problem 21-1B
Allocation of building occupancy costs to departments
C3 P1

Marshall's has several departments that occupy all floors of a two-story building that includes a basement floor. Marshall rented this building under a long-term lease negotiated when rental rates were low. The departmental accounting system has a single account, Building Occupancy Cost, in its ledger. The types and amounts of occupancy costs recorded in this account for the current period follow.

Building rent	$320,000
Lighting expense	20,000
Cleaning expense	32,000
Total occupancy cost	$372,000

The building has 7,500 square feet on each of the upper two floors but only 5,000 square feet in the basement. In prior periods, the accounting manager merely divided the $372,000 occupancy cost by 20,000 square feet to find an average cost of $18.60 per square foot and then charged each department a building occupancy cost equal to this rate times the number of square feet that it occupies.

Riley Miller manages a department that occupies 2,000 square feet of basement floor space. In discussing the departmental reports with other managers, she questions whether using the same rate per square foot for all departments makes sense because different floor space has different values. Miller checked a recent real estate report of average local rental costs for similar space that shows first-floor space worth $48 per square foot, second-floor space worth $24 per square foot, and basement space worth $12 per square foot (excluding costs for lighting and cleaning).

Required

1. Allocate occupancy costs to Miller's department using the current allocation method.

2. Allocate the building rent cost to Miller's department in proportion to the relative market value of the floor space. Allocate to Miller's department the lighting and heating costs in proportion to the square feet occupied (ignoring floor space market values). Then, compute the total occupancy cost allocated to Miller's department.

Check Total costs allocated to Miller's Dept., (1) $37,200; (2) $18,000

Analysis Component

3. Which allocation method would you prefer if you were a manager of a basement department?

Problem 21-2B
Activity-based costing
P2

Verdant Landscape Architects has enjoyed profits for many years, but new competition has cut service revenue by as much as 30%. As a result, the company wants to better understand its costs. It decides to prepare an activity-based cost analysis, including an estimate of the average cost of both general landscaping services and custom design landscaping services. The company's three cost centers and their cost drivers follow.

Cost Center	Cost	Cost Driver	Driver Quantity
Professional salaries	$900,000	Professional hours	15,000
Customer supplies	225,000	Number of customers	1,200
Building cost	360,000	Square feet	3,750

The two main landscaping units and their related data follow.

Service	Hours	Square Feet*	Customers
General landscaping	3,750	1,500	900
Custom design landscaping	11,250	2,250	300

* Custom design landscaping requires more space for equipment, supplies, and planning.

Required

1. Compute the cost per cost driver for each of the three cost centers.

2. Use the results from part 1 to allocate costs from each of the three cost centers to both the general landscaping and the custom design landscaping units. Compute total cost and average cost per customer for both the general landscaping and the custom design landscaping units.

Check (2) Average cost of general (custom) landscaping, $597.50 ($3,157.50) per customer

Analysis Component

3. Without providing computations, would the average cost of general landscaping be higher or lower if all center costs were allocated based on the number of customers? Explain.

Problem 21-3B
Departmental income statements; forecasts
P3

Collosal Entertainment began operations in January 2009 with two operating (selling) departments and one service (office) department. Its departmental income statements follow.

COLLOSAL ENTERTAINMENT
Departmental Income Statements
For Year Ended December 31, 2009

	Movies	Video Games	Combined
Sales	$900,000	$300,000	$1,200,000
Cost of goods sold	630,000	231,000	861,000
Gross profit	270,000	69,000	339,000
Direct expenses			
Sales salaries	55,500	22,500	78,000
Advertising	18,750	9,000	27,750
Store supplies used	6,000	1,500	7,500
Depreciation—Equipment	6,750	4,500	11,250
Total direct expenses	87,000	37,500	124,500

[continued on next page]

[continued from previous page]

Allocated expenses			
Rent expense	61,500	13,500	75,000
Utilities expense	11,070	2,430	13,500
Share of office department expenses	84,375	28,125	112,500
Total allocated expenses	156,945	44,055	201,000
Total expenses	243,945	81,555	325,500
Net income (loss)	$ 26,055	$ (12,555)	$ 13,500

The company plans to open a third department in January 2010 that will sell compact discs. Management predicts that the new department will generate $450,000 in sales with a 35% gross profit margin and will require the following direct expenses: sales salaries, $27,000; advertising, $15,000; store supplies, $3,000; and equipment depreciation, $1,800. The company will fit the new department into the current rented space by taking some square footage from the other two departments. When opened, the new compact disc department will fill one-fourth of the space presently used by the movie department and one-third of the space used by the video game department. Management does not predict any increase in utilities costs, which are allocated to the departments in proportion to occupied space (or rent expense). The company allocates office department expenses to the operating departments in proportion to their sales. It expects the compact disc department to increase total office department expenses by $15,000. Since the compact disc department will bring new customers into the store, management expects sales in both the movie and video game departments to increase by 8%. No changes for those departments' gross profit percents or for their direct expenses are expected, except for store supplies used, which will increase in proportion to sales.

Required

Check 2010 forecasted movies net income (sales), $78,674 ($972,000)

Prepare departmental income statements that show the company's predicted results of operations for calendar year 2010 for the three operating (selling) departments and their combined totals. (Round percents to the nearest one-tenth and dollar amounts to the nearest whole dollar.)

Problem 21-4B
Responsibility accounting performance reports; controllable and budgeted costs

C4 P4

Warren Brown, the plant manager of LMN Co.'s San Diego plant, is responsible for all of that plant's costs other than his own salary. The plant has two operating departments and one service department. The refrigerator and dishwasher operating departments manufacture different products and have their own managers. The office department, which Brown also manages, provides services equally to the two operating departments. A monthly budget is prepared for each operating department and the office department. The company's responsibility accounting system must assemble information to present budgeted and actual costs in performance reports for each operating department manager and the plant manager. Each performance report includes only those costs that a particular operating department manager can control: raw materials, wages, supplies used, and equipment depreciation. The plant manager is responsible for the department managers' salaries, utilities, building rent, office salaries other than his own, and other office costs plus all costs controlled by the two operating department managers. The April departmental budgets and actual costs for the two operating departments follow.

	Budget			Actual		
	Refrigerators	Dishwashers	Combined	Refrigerators	Dishwashers	Combined
Raw materials	$ 480,000	$240,000	$ 720,000	$ 462,000	$242,400	$ 704,400
Employee wages	204,000	96,000	300,000	209,640	97,800	307,440
Dept. manager salary	66,000	58,800	124,800	66,000	55,800	121,800
Supplies used	18,000	10,800	28,800	16,800	11,640	28,440
Depreciation—Equip.	63,600	44,400	108,000	63,600	44,400	108,000
Utilities	36,000	21,600	57,600	41,400	24,840	66,240
Building rent	75,600	20,400	96,000	78,960	19,800	98,760
Office department costs	84,600	84,600	169,200	90,000	90,000	180,000
Totals	$1,027,800	$576,600	$1,604,400	$1,028,400	$586,680	$1,615,080

The office department's budget and its actual costs for April follow.

	Budget	Actual
Plant manager salary	$ 96,000	$102,000
Other office salaries	48,000	42,240
Other office costs	25,200	35,760
Totals	$169,200	$180,000

Required

1. Prepare responsibility accounting performance reports like those in Exhibit 21.28 that list costs controlled by the following:

a. Manager of the refrigerator department.

b. Manager of the dishwasher department.

c. Manager of the San Diego plant.

In each report, include the budgeted and actual costs for the month and show the amount by which each actual cost is over or under the budgeted amount.

Check (1a) $13,560 total under budget

(1c) San Diego plant controllable costs, $4,680 total over budget

Analysis Component

2. Did the plant manager or the operating department managers better manage costs? Explain.

Problem 21-5B[B]

Allocation of joint costs

C6

Rita and Rick Redding own and operate a tomato grove. After preparing the following income statement, Rita believes they should have offered the No. 3 tomatoes to the public for free and saved themselves time and money.

RITA AND RICK REDDING
Income Statement
For Year Ended December 31, 2009

	No. 1	No. 2	No. 3	Combined
Sales (by grade)				
No. 1: 600,000 lbs. @ $1.80/lb	$1,080,000			
No. 2: 480,000 lbs. @ $1.25/lb		$600,000		
No. 3: 120,000 lbs. @ $0.40/lb			$ 48,000	
Total sales				$1,728,000
Costs				
Land preparation, seeding, and cultivating @ $0.70/lb	420,000	336,000	84,000	840,000
Harvesting, sorting, and grading @ $0.04/lb	24,000	19,200	4,800	48,000
Delivery costs	20,000	14,000	6,000	40,000
Total costs	464,000	369,200	94,800	928,000
Net income (loss)	$ 616,000	$230,800	$(46,800)	$ 800,000

In preparing this statement, Rita and Rick allocated joint costs among the grades on a physical basis as an equal amount per pound. Also, their delivery cost records show that $34,000 of the $40,000 relates to crating the No. 1 and No. 2 tomatoes and hauling them to the buyer. The remaining $6,000 of delivery costs is for crating the No. 3 tomatoes and hauling them to the cannery.

Required

1. Prepare reports showing cost allocations on a sales value basis to the three grades of tomatoes. Separate the delivery costs into the amounts directly identifiable with each grade. Then allocate any shared delivery costs on the basis of the relative sales value of each grade. (Round percents to the nearest one-tenth and dollar amounts to the nearest whole dollar.)

Check (1) $1,344 harvesting, sorting and grading costs allocated to No. 3

(2) Net income from No. 1 & No. 2 tomatoes, $503,138 & $279,726

2. Using your answers to part 1, prepare an income statement using the joint costs allocated on a sales value basis.

Analysis Component

3. Do you think delivery costs fit the definition of a joint cost? Explain.

BEYOND THE NUMBERS

REPORTING IN ACTION

C4

BTN 21-1 Review **Best Buy**'s income statement in Appendix A and identify its revenues for the years ended March 3, 2007, February 25, 2006, and February 26, 2005. For the year ended March 3, 2007, Best Buy reports the following product revenue mix. (Assume that its product revenue mix is the same for each of the three years reported when answering the requirements.)

Home Office	Entertainment Software	Consumer Electronics	Appliances
33%	12%	45%	10%

Required

1. Compute the amount of revenue from each of its product lines for the years ended March 3, 2007, February 25, 2006, and February 26, 2005.

2. If Best Buy wishes to evaluate each of its product lines, how can it allocate its operating expenses to each of them to determine each product line's profitability?

Fast Forward

3. Access Best Buy's annual report for a fiscal year ending after March 3, 2007, from its Website (BestBuy.com) or the SEC's EDGAR database (sec.gov). Compute its revenues for its product lines for the most recent year(s). Compare those results to those from part 1. How has its product mix changed?

COMPARATIVE ANALYSIS

P3

BTN 21-2 **Best Buy**, **Circuit City**, and **RadioShack** compete across the country in several markets. The most common competitive markets for these companies are by location.

Required

1. Design a three-tier responsibility accounting organizational chart assuming that you have available internal information for all three companies. Use Exhibit 21.19 as an example. The goal of this assignment is to design a reporting framework for the companies; numbers are not required. Limit your reporting framework to sales activity only.

2. Explain why it is important to have similar performance reports when comparing performance within a company (and across different companies). Be specific in your response.

ETHICS CHALLENGE

P3

BTN 21-3 Senior Security Co. offers a range of security services for senior citizens. Each type of service is considered within a separate department. Mary Pincus, the overall manager, is compensated partly on the basis of departmental performance by staying within the quarterly cost budget. She often revises operations to make sure departments stay within budget. Says Pincus, "I will not go over budget even if it means slightly compromising the level and quality of service. These are minor compromises that don't significantly affect my clients, at least in the short term."

Required

1. Is there an ethical concern in this situation? If so, which parties are affected? Explain.

2. Can Mary Pincus take action to eliminate or reduce any ethical concerns? Explain.

3. What is Senior Security's ethical responsibility in offering professional services?

COMMUNICATING IN PRACTICE

C4 C5 P3 

BTN 21-4 Home Station is a national home improvement chain with more than 100 stores throughout the country. The manager of each store receives a salary plus a bonus equal to a percent of the store's net income for the reporting period. The following net income calculation is on the Denver store manager's performance report for the recent monthly period.

Sales	$2,500,000
Cost of goods sold	800,000
Wages expense	500,000
Utilities expense	200,000
Home office expense	75,000
Net income	$925,000
Manager's bonus (0.5%)	$ 4,625

In previous periods, the bonus had also been 0.5%, but the performance report had not included any charges for the home office expense, which is now assigned to each store as a percent of its sales.

Required

Assume that you are the national office manager. Write a one-half page memorandum to your store managers explaining why home office expense is in the new performance report.

TAKING IT TO THE NET

A1 

BTN 21-5 This chapter described and used spreadsheets to prepare various managerial reports (see Exhibit 21-12). You can download from Websites various tutorials showing how spreadsheets are used in managerial accounting and other business applications.

Required

1. Link to the Website Lacher.com. Scroll down past "Microsoft Excel Examples" and select "Business Solutions." Identify and list three tutorials for review.

2. Describe in a one-half page memorandum to your instructor how the applications described in each tutorial are helpful in business and managerial decision making.

TEAMWORK IN ACTION

C1 C2

BTN 21-6 Activity-based costing (ABC) is increasingly popular as a useful managerial tool to (1) measure the cost of resources consumed and (2) assign cost to products and services. This managerial tool has been available to accounting and business decision makers for more than 25 years.

Required

Break into teams and identify at least three likely reasons that activity-based costing has gained popularity in recent years. Be prepared to present your answers in a class discussion. (*Hint:* What changes have occurred in products and services over the past 25 years?)

ENTREPRENEURIAL DECISION

P3

BTN 21-7 **RockBottomGolf** is an Internet retailer and the focus of this chapter's opener. It sells discounted golf merchandise through departments such as clubs, bags, apparel, and accessories. The company plans to expand to include many other types of sporting goods.

Required

1. How can RockBottomGolf use departmental income statements to assist in understanding and controlling operations?
2. Are departmental income statements always the best measure of a department's performance? Explain.
3. Provide examples of nonfinancial performace indicators RockBottomGolf might use as part of a balanced scorecard system of performance evaluation.

HITTING THE ROAD

P3

BTN 21-8 Visit a local movie theater and check out both its concession area and its showing areas. The manager of a theater must confront questions such as:

- How much return do we earn on concessions?
- What types of movies generate the greatest sales?
- What types of movies generate the greatest net income?

Required

Assume that you are the new accounting manager for a 16-screen movie theater. You are to set up a responsibility accounting reporting framework for the theater.

1. Recommend how to segment the different departments of a movie theater for responsibility reporting.
2. Propose an expense allocation system for heat, rent, insurance, and maintenance costs of the theater.

GLOBAL DECISION

DSG

BTN 21-9 Selected product data from **DSG international plc** (www.DSGiplc.com) follow.

Product Segment for Year Ended (£ millions)	Net Sales		Operating Income	
	April 28, 2007	April 29, 2006	April 28, 2007	April 29, 2006
Computing	£2,198	£2,040	£97	£107
Electrical	5,281	4,912	193	198
e-commerce	451	26	1	0

Required

1. Compute the percentage growth in net sales for each product line from fiscal year 2006 to 2007.
2. Which product line's net sales grew the fastest?
3. Which segment was the most profitable?
4. How can DSG's managers use this information?

ANSWERS TO MULTIPLE CHOICE QUIZ

1. b; [$641,250/($356,250 + $641,250 + $427,500)] × $150,000 = $67,500
2. c;
3. e; $162,000 × 50/150 setups = $54,000; $54,000/500 units = $108 per Grey unit. (Red is $2.70 per unit.)
4. b;

	Department X	Department Y	Department Z
Sales	$500,000	$200,000	$350,000
Cost of goods sold	350,000	75,000	150,000
Gross profit	150,000	125,000	200,000
Direct expenses	50,000	20,000	75,000
Departmental contribution	$100,000	$105,000	$125,000

5. a; $100,000/$500,000 = 20%

A Look Back

Chapter 21 focused on cost allocation, activity-based costing, and performance measurement. We identified ways to measure and analyze company activities, its departments, and its managers.

A Look at This Chapter

This chapter shows how information on both costs and sales behavior is useful to managers in performing cost-volume-profit analysis. This analysis is an important part of successful management and sound business decisions.

A Look Ahead

Chapter 23 introduces and describes the budgeting process and its importance to management. It also explains the master budget and its usefulness to the planning of future company activities.

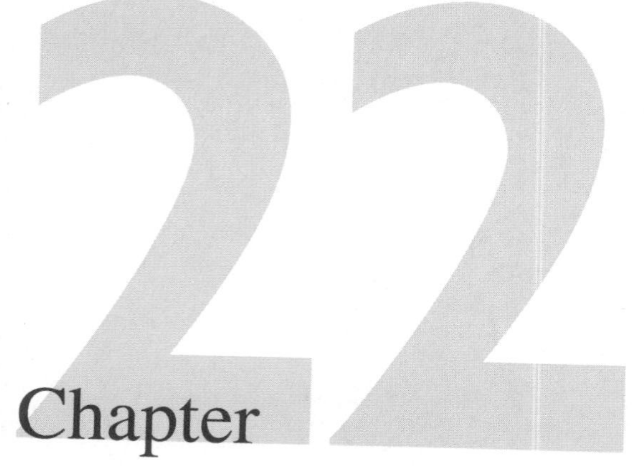

Chapter 22 Cost-Volume-Profit Analysis

Learning Objectives

CAP

Conceptual

C1 Describe different types of cost behavior in relation to production and sales volume. *(p. 902)*

C2 Identify assumptions in cost-volume-profit analysis and explain their impact. *(p. 911)*

C3 Describe several applications of cost-volume-profit analysis. *(p. 913)*

Analytical

A1 Compare the scatter diagram, high-low, and regression methods of estimating costs. *(p. 907)*

A2 Compute the contribution margin and describe what it reveals about a company's cost structure. *(p. 908)*

A3 Analyze changes in sales using the degree of operating leverage. *(p. 918)*

Procedural

P1 Determine cost estimates using three different methods. *(p. 905)*

P2 Compute the break-even point for a single product company. *(p. 909)*

P3 Graph costs and sales for a single product company. *(p. 910)*

P4 Compute the break-even point for a multiproduct company. *(p. 915)*

LP22

Decision Feature

Recipe for Growth

"Don't sit on the sidelines talking about your dream . . . get out and make it happen"—Martin Sprock

"Welcome to Moe's"! A chorus of welcomes greets each customer at **Moe's Southwest Grill (Moes.com),** a chain of quirky Tex-Mex restaurants, which is part of Raving Brands. The zaniness continues with menu items such as Art Vandalay, Joey Bag of Donuts, the Close Talker, and the Billy Barou. They play music from "dead rock stars" like the Beatles, Elvis Presley, and Jimi Hendrix because "Moe wanted to pay tribute to his heroes who have passed on and would never have a chance to taste his food."

Moe's founder Martin Sprock explains, "We make a point of having the happiest associates. You feel good visiting our stores, and that means something to me. I'd go so far as to say I'd actually be willing to take a date to them."

But there is more to Moe's than fun. Moe's features burritos, tacos, quesadillas, and salads. To appeal to health-conscious diners, Moe's does not use frozen ingredients or microwaves or cook with fat. This recipe has resulted in Moe's being one of the fastest-growing "fast casual" restaurants.

With such rapid growth, an understanding of cost behavior is critical. Identifying fixed and variable costs is key to understanding break-even points and maintaining the right mix of menu choices. Each Moe's manager earns a degree from "Moe's Training School," where the finer points of cost management are taught. Moe's online ordering and payment system is linked with its cash registers to enable managers to better determine which menu items are in demand. An understanding of how costs relate to sales volume and profits helps drive the menu options.

Martin Sprock's vision is to run a chain of restaurants that treats employees as well as they treat owners. This family-first mentality and service-oriented approach have spurred Moe's growth. Sprock, a former ski bum, encourages potential entrepreneurs to get out and make it happen. "I had no money when I started trying to fulfill my ambitions . . . I just did it."

[Sources: *Moe's Southwest Grill Website*, January 2009; *Go AirTran Airways* Magazine, 2005; *Atlanta Business Chronicle,* May 2008; *Pittsburgh Business Times,* March 2008.

Chapter Preview

This chapter describes different types of costs and shows how changes in a company's operating volume affect these costs. The chapter also analyzes a company's costs and sales to explain how different operating strategies affect profit or loss. Managers use this type of analysis to forecast what will happen if changes are made to costs, sales volume, selling prices, or product mix. They then use these forecasts to select the best business strategy for the company.

Cost-Volume-Profit Analysis

Identifying Cost Behavior
- Fixed costs
- Variable costs
- Mixed costs
- Step-wise costs
- Curvilinear costs

Measuring Cost Behavior
- Scatter diagrams
- High-low method
- Least-squares regression
- Comparison of cost estimation methods

Using Break-Even Analysis
- Computing contribution margin
- Computing break-even
- Preparing a cost-volume-profit chart
- Making assumptions in cost-volume-profit analysis

Applying Cost-Volume-Profit Analysis
- Computing income from sales and costs
- Computing sales for target income
- Computing margin of safety
- Using sensitivity analysis
- Computing multiproduct break-even

Identifying Cost Behavior

Video22.1

Point: *Profit* is another term for *income.*

Planning a company's future activities and events is a crucial phase in successful management. One of the first steps in planning is to predict the volume of activity, the costs to be incurred, sales to be made, and profit to be received. An important tool to help managers carry out this step is **cost-volume-profit (CVP) analysis,** which helps them predict how changes in costs and sales levels affect income. In its basic form, CVP analysis involves computing the sales level at which a company neither earns an income nor incurs a loss, called the *break-even point.* For this reason, this basic form of cost-volume-profit analysis is often called *break-even analysis.* Managers use variations of CVP analysis to answer questions such as these:

- What sales volume is needed to earn a target income?
- What is the change in income if selling prices decline and sales volume increases?
- How much does income increase if we install a new machine to reduce labor costs?
- What is the income effect if we change the sales mix of our products or services?

Consequently, cost-volume-profit analysis is useful in a wide range of business decisions.

Conventional cost-volume-profit analysis requires management to classify all costs as either *fixed* or *variable* with respect to production or sales volume. The remainder of this section discusses the concepts of fixed and variable cost behavior as they relate to CVP analysis.

Decision Insight

No Free Lunch Hardly a week goes by without a company advertising a free product with the purchase of another. Examples are a free printer with a digital camera purchase or a free monitor with a computer purchase. Can these companies break even, let alone earn profits? We are reminded of the *no-free-lunch* adage, meaning that companies expect profits from the companion or add-on purchase to make up for the free product.

C1 Describe different types of cost behavior in relation to production and sales volume.

Fixed Costs

A *fixed cost* remains unchanged in amount when the volume of activity varies from period to period within a relevant range. For example, $5,000 in monthly rent paid for a factory building remains the same whether the factory operates with a single eight-hour shift or around the clock with three shifts. This means that rent cost is the same each month at any level of output from zero to the plant's full productive capacity. Notice that while *total* fixed cost does not change as the level of production changes, the fixed cost *per unit* of output decreases as volume increases. For instance, if 20 units are produced when monthly rent is $5,000, the average rent cost per unit is $250 (computed as $5,000/20 units). When production increases to 100 units per month, the average cost per unit decreases to $50 (computed as $5,000/100 units). The average cost decreases to $10 per unit if production increases to 500 units per month. Common examples of fixed costs include depreciation, property taxes, office salaries, and many service department costs.

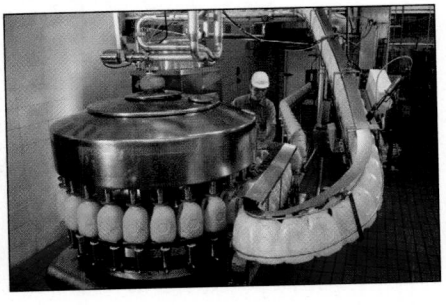

Point: Fixed costs do not change when volume changes, but the per unit cost declines as volume increases.

When production volume and costs are graphed, units of product are usually plotted on the *horizontal axis* and dollars of cost are plotted on the *vertical axis.* Fixed costs then are represented as a horizontal line because they remain constant at all levels of production. To illustrate, the graph in Exhibit 22.1 shows that fixed costs remain at $32,000 at all production levels up to the company's monthly capacity of 2,000 units of output. The *relevant range* for fixed costs in Exhibit 22.1 is 0 to 2,000 units. If the relevant range changes (that is, production capacity extends beyond this range), the amount of fixed costs will likely change.

Example: If the fixed cost line in Exhibit 22.1 is shifted upward, does the total cost line shift up, down, or remain in the same place? *Answer:* It shifts up by the same amount.

EXHIBIT 22.1

Relations of Fixed and Variable Costs to Volume

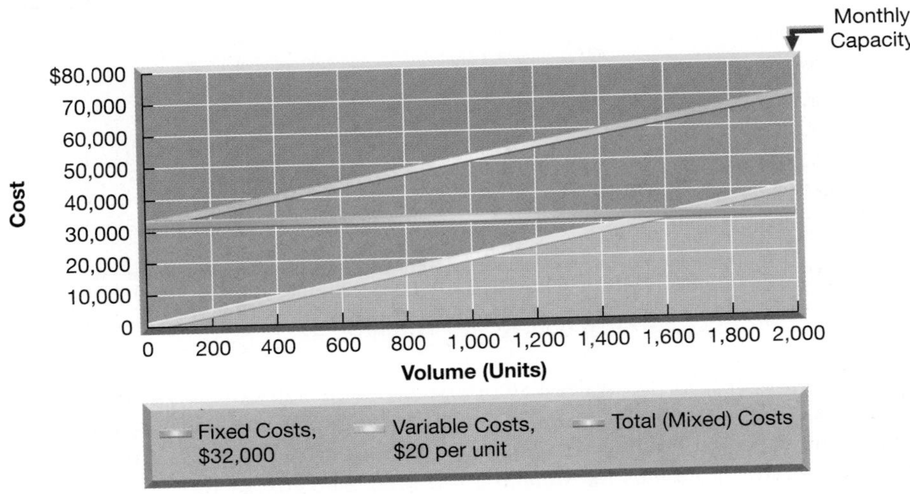

Example: If the level of fixed costs in Exhibit 22.1 changes, does the slope of the total cost line change? *Answer:* No, the slope doesn't change. The total cost line is simply shifted upward or downward.

Variable Costs

A *variable cost* changes in proportion to changes in volume of activity. The direct materials cost of a product is one example of a variable cost. If one unit of product requires materials costing $20, total materials costs are $200 when 10 units of product are manufactured, $400 for 20 units, $600 for 30 units, and so on. Notice that variable cost *per unit* remains constant but the *total* amount of variable cost changes with the level of production. In addition to direct materials, common variable costs include direct labor (if employees are paid per unit), sales commissions, shipping costs, and some overhead costs.

Point: Fixed costs are constant in total but vary (decline) per unit as more units are produced. Variable costs vary in total but are fixed per unit.

When variable costs are plotted on a graph of cost and volume, they appear as a straight line starting at the zero cost level. This straight line is upward (positive) sloping. The line rises as volume of activity increases. A variable cost line using a $20 per unit cost is graphed in Exhibit 22.1.

Mixed Costs

A **mixed cost** includes both fixed and variable cost components. For example, compensation for sales representatives often includes a fixed monthly salary and a variable commission based on sales. The total cost line in Exhibit 22.1 is a mixed cost. Like a fixed cost, it is greater than zero when volume is zero; but unlike a fixed cost, it increases steadily in proportion to increases in volume. The mixed cost line in Exhibit 22.1 starts on the vertical axis at the $32,000 fixed cost point. Thus, at the zero volume level, total cost equals the fixed costs. As the activity level increases, the mixed cost line increases at an amount equal to the variable cost per unit. This line is highest when volume of activity is at 2,000 units (the end point of the relevant range). In CVP analysis, mixed costs are often separated into fixed and variable components. The fixed component is added to other fixed costs, and the variable component is added to other variable costs.

Step-Wise Costs

A **step-wise cost** reflects a step pattern in costs. Salaries of production supervisors often behave in a step-wise manner in that their salaries are fixed within a *relevant range* of the current production volume. However, if production volume expands significantly (for example, with the addition of another shift), additional supervisors must be hired. This means that the total cost for supervisory salaries goes up by a lump-sum amount. Similarly, if volume takes another significant step up, supervisory salaries will increase by another lump sum. This behavior reflects a step-wise cost, also known as a *stair-step cost,* which is graphed in Exhibit 22.2. See how the step-wise cost line is flat within ranges (steps). Then, when volume significantly changes, it shifts to another level for that range (step).

EXHIBIT 22.2

Step-Wise and Curvilinear Costs

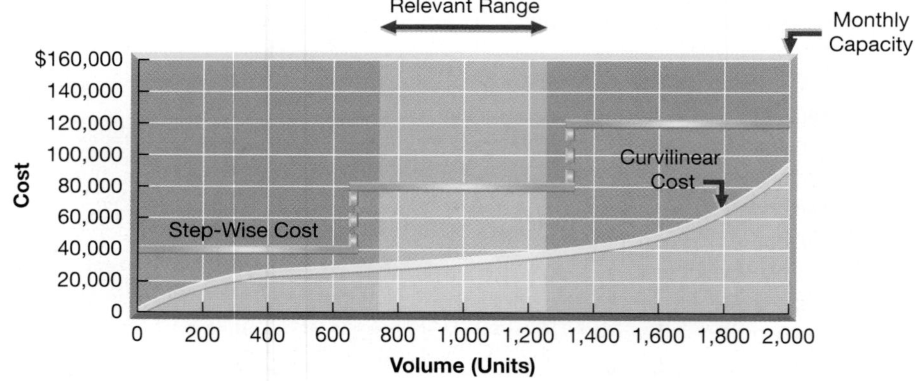

Point: Computer spreadsheets are important and effective tools for CVP analysis and for analyzing alternative "what-if" strategies.

In a conventional CVP analysis, a step-wise cost is usually treated as either a fixed cost or a variable cost. This treatment involves manager judgment and depends on the width of the range and the expected volume. To illustrate, suppose after the production of every 25 snowboards, an operator lubricates the finishing machine. The cost of this lubricant reflects a step-wise pattern. Also, suppose that after the production of every 1,000 units, the snowboard cutting tool is replaced. Again, this is a step-wise cost. Note that the range of 25 snowboards is much narrower than the range of 1,000 snowboards. Some managers might treat the lubricant cost as a variable cost and the cutting tool cost as a fixed cost.

Curvilinear Costs

A variable cost, as explained, is a *linear* cost; that is, it increases at a constant rate as volume of activity increases. A **curvilinear cost,** also called a *nonlinear cost,* increases at a nonconstant rate as volume increases. When graphed, curvilinear costs appear as a curved line. Exhibit 22.2 shows a curvilinear cost beginning at zero when production is zero and then increasing at different rates.

Point: Cost-volume-profit analysis helped Rod Canion, Jim Harris, and Bill Murto raise start-up capital of $20 million to launch **Compaq Computer.** They showed that break-even volumes were attainable within the first year.

An example of a curvilinear cost is total direct labor cost when workers are paid by the hour. At low to medium levels of production, adding more employees allows each of them to specialize by doing certain tasks repeatedly instead of doing several different tasks. This often yields additional units of output at lower costs. A point is eventually reached at which adding more employees creates inefficiencies. For instance, a large crew demands more time and effort in communicating and coordinating their efforts. While adding employees in this case increases output, the labor cost per unit increases, and the total labor cost goes up at a steeper slope. This pattern is seen in Exhibit 22.2 where the curvilinear cost curve starts at zero, rises, flattens out, and then increases at a faster rate as output nears the maximum.

Quick Check

Answers—p. 922

1. Which of the following statements is typically true? (*a*) Variable cost per unit increases as volume increases, (*b*) fixed cost per unit decreases as volume increases, or (*c*) a curvilinear cost includes both fixed and variable elements.
2. Describe the behavior of a fixed cost.
3. If cost per unit of activity remains constant (fixed), why is it called a variable cost?

Measuring Cost Behavior

P1 Determine cost estimates using three different methods.

Identifying and measuring cost behavior requires careful analysis and judgment. An important part of this process is to identify costs that can be classified as either fixed or variable, which often requires analysis of past cost behavior. Three methods are commonly used to analyze past costs: scatter diagrams, high-low method, and least-squares regression. Each method is discussed in this section using the unit and cost data shown in Exhibit 22.3, which are taken from a start-up company that uses units produced as the activity base in estimating cost behavior.

EXHIBIT 22.3

Data for Estimating Cost Behavior

Month	Units Produced	Total Cost
January	17,500	$20,500
February	27,500	21,500
March	25,000	25,000
April	35,000	21,500
May	47,500	25,500
June	22,500	18,500
July	30,000	23,500
August	52,500	28,500
September	37,500	26,000
October	57,500	26,000
November	62,500	31,000
December	67,500	29,000

Scatter Diagrams

Scatter diagrams display past cost and unit data in graphical form. In preparing a scatter diagram, units are plotted on the horizontal axis and cost is plotted on the vertical axis. Each individual point on a scatter diagram reflects the cost and number of units for a prior period. In Exhibit 22.4, the prior 12 months' costs and numbers of units are graphed. Each point reflects total costs incurred and units produced for one of those months. For instance, the point labeled March had units produced of 25,000 and costs of $25,000.

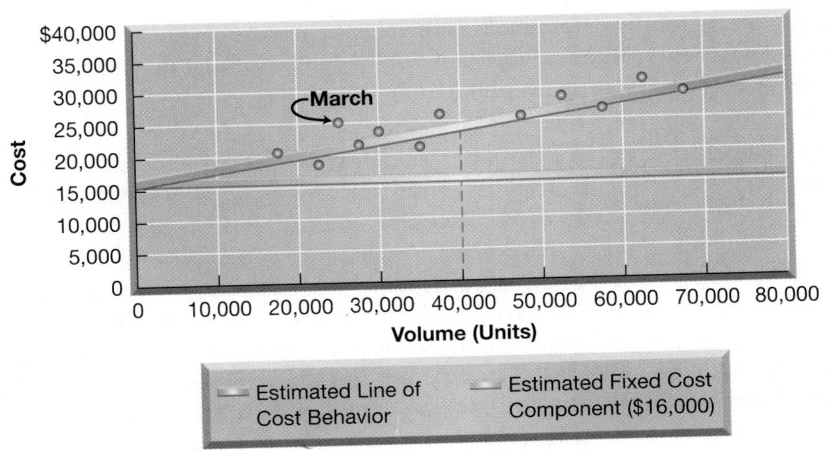

EXHIBIT 22.4

Scatter Diagram

The **estimated line of cost behavior** is drawn on a scatter diagram to reflect the relation between cost and unit volume. This line best visually "fits" the points in a scatter diagram. Fitting this line demands judgment. The line drawn in Exhibit 22.4 intersects the vertical axis at approximately $16,000, which reflects fixed cost. To compute variable cost per unit, or the slope, we perform three steps. First, we select any two points on the horizontal axis (units), say 0 and 40,000. Second, we draw a vertical line from each of these points to intersect the estimated line of cost behavior. The point on the vertical axis (cost) corresponding to the 40,000 units point that intersects the estimated line is roughly $24,000. Similarly, the cost corresponding to zero units is $16,000 (the fixed cost point). Third, we compute the slope of the line, or variable cost, as the change in cost divided by the change in units. Exhibit 22.5 shows this computation.

EXHIBIT 22.5

Variable Cost per Unit (Scatter Diagram)

$$\frac{\textbf{Change in cost}}{\textbf{Change in units}} = \frac{\$24{,}000 - \$16{,}000}{40{,}000 - 0} = \frac{\$8{,}000}{40{,}000} = \$0.20 \text{ per unit}$$

Example: In Exhibits 22.4 and 22.5, if units are projected at 30,000, what is the predicted cost? *Answer:* Approximately $22,000.

Variable cost is $0.20 per unit. Thus, the cost equation that management will use to estimate costs for different unit levels is **$16,000 plus $0.20 per unit**.

High-Low Method

The **high-low method** is a way to estimate the cost equation by graphically connecting the two cost amounts at the highest and lowest unit volumes. In our case, the lowest number of units is 17,500, and the highest is 67,500. The costs corresponding to these unit volumes are $20,500 and $29,000, respectively (see the data in Exhibit 22.3). The estimated line of cost behavior for the high-low method is then drawn by connecting these two points on the scatter diagram corresponding to the lowest and highest unit volumes as follows.

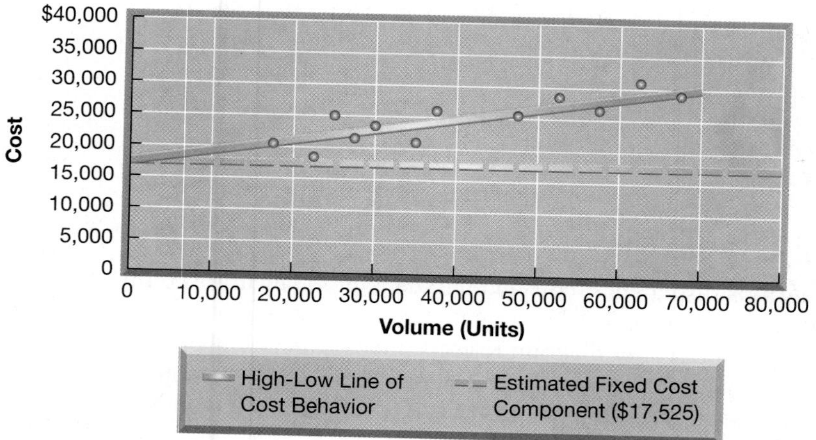

Point: Note that the high-low method identifies the high and low points of the volume (activity) base, and the costs linked with those extremes—which may not be the highest and lowest costs.

The variable cost per unit is determined as the change in cost divided by the change in units and uses the data from the high and low unit volumes. This results in a slope, or variable cost per unit, of $0.17 as computed in Exhibit 22.6.

EXHIBIT 22.6

Variable Cost per Unit (High-Low Method)

$$\frac{\textbf{Change in cost}}{\textbf{Change in units}} = \frac{\$29{,}000 - \$20{,}500}{67{,}500 - 17{,}500} = \frac{\$8{,}500}{50{,}000} = \$0.17 \text{ per unit}$$

To estimate the fixed cost for the high-low method, we use the knowledge that total cost equals fixed cost plus variable cost per unit times the number of units. Then we pick either the high or low point to determine the fixed cost. This computation is shown in Exhibit 22.7—where we use the high point (67,500 units) in determining the fixed cost of $17,525. Use of the low point (17,500 units) yields the same fixed cost estimate: $20,500 = Fixed cost + ($0.17 per unit × 17,500), or Fixed cost = $17,525.

EXHIBIT 22.7

Fixed Cost (High-Low Method)

Total cost	=	**Fixed cost + (Variable cost × Units)**
$29,000	=	Fixed cost + ($0.17 per unit × 67,500 units)
Then,		Fixed cost = $17,525

Thus, the cost equation used to estimate costs at different units is **$17,525 plus $0.17 per unit**. This cost equation differs slightly from that determined from the scatter diagram method. A deficiency of the high-low method is that it ignores all cost points except the highest and lowest. The result is less precision because the high-low method uses the most extreme points rather than the more usual conditions likely to recur.

Least-Squares Regression

Least-squares regression is a statistical method for identifying cost behavior. For our purposes, we use the cost equation estimated from this method but leave the computational details for more advanced courses. Such computations for least-squares regression are readily done using most spreadsheet programs or calculators. We illustrate this using Excel® in Appendix 22A.

The regression cost equation for the data presented in Exhibit 22.3 is **$16,947 plus $0.19 per unit**; that is, the fixed cost is estimated as $16,947 and the variable cost at $0.19 per unit. Both costs are reflected in the following graph.

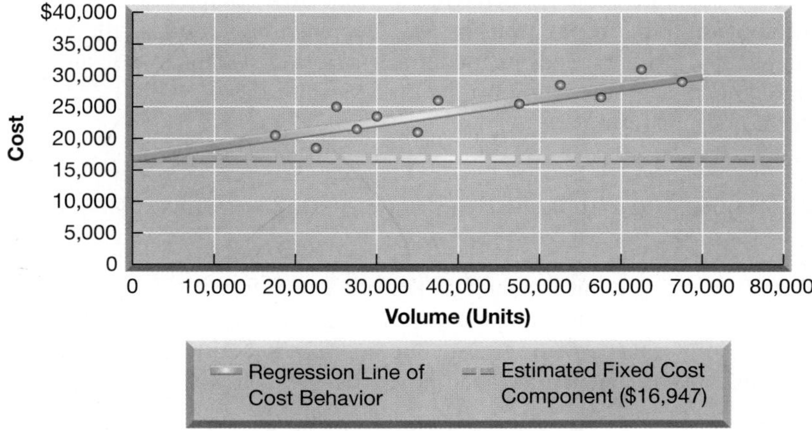

Comparison of Cost Estimation Methods

A1 Compare the scatter diagram, high-low, and regression methods of estimating costs.

The three cost estimation methods result in slightly different estimates of fixed and variable costs as summarized in Exhibit 22.8. Estimates from the scatter diagram are based on a visual fit of the cost line and are subject to interpretation. Estimates from the high-low method use only two sets of values corresponding to the lowest and highest unit volumes. Estimates from least-squares regression use a statistical technique and all available data points.

EXHIBIT 22.8

Comparison of Cost Estimation Methods

Estimation Method	Fixed Cost	Variable Cost
Scatter diagram	$16,000	$0.20 per unit
High-low method	17,525	0.17 per unit
Least-squares regression	16,947	0.19 per unit

We must remember that all three methods use *past data*. Thus, cost estimates resulting from these methods are only as good as the data used for estimation. Managers must establish that the data are reliable in deriving cost estimates for the future.

Quick Check Answers—p. 922

4. Which of the following methods is likely to yield the most precise estimated line of cost behavior? (*a*) High-low, (*b*) least-squares regression, or (*c*) scatter diagram.
5. What is the primary weakness of the high-low method?
6. Using conventional CVP analysis, a mixed cost should be (*a*) disregarded, (*b*) treated as a fixed cost, or (*c*) separated into fixed and variable components.

Using Break-Even Analysis

Video22.2

Break-even analysis is a special case of cost-volume-profit analysis. This section describes break-even analysis by computing the break-even point and preparing a CVP (or break-even) chart.

Contribution Margin and Its Measures

A2 Compute the contribution margin and describe what it reveals about a company's cost structure.

We explained how managers classify costs by behavior. This often refers to classifying costs as being fixed or variable with respect to volume of activity. In manufacturing companies, volume of activity usually refers to the number of units produced. We then classify a cost as either fixed or variable, depending on whether total cost changes as the number of units produced changes. Once we separate costs by behavior, we can then compute a product's contribution margin. **Contribution margin per unit,** or *unit contribution margin,* is the amount by which a product's unit selling price exceeds its total unit variable cost. This excess amount contributes to covering fixed costs and generating profits on a per unit basis. Exhibit 22.9 shows the contribution margin per unit formula.

EXHIBIT 22.9

Contribution Margin per Unit

Contribution margin per unit = Sales price per unit − Total variable cost per unit

The **contribution margin ratio,** which is the percent of a unit's selling price that exceeds total unit variable cost, is also useful for business decisions. It can be interpreted as the percent of each sales dollar that remains after deducting the total unit variable cost. Exhibit 22.10 shows the formula for the contribution margin ratio.

EXHIBIT 22.10

Contribution Margin Ratio

$$\textbf{Contribution margin ratio} = \frac{\textbf{Contribution margin per unit}}{\textbf{Sales price per unit}}$$

To illustrate the use of contribution margin, let's consider **Rydell,** which sells footballs for $100 per unit and incurs variable costs of $70 per unit sold. Its fixed costs are $24,000 per month with monthly capacity of 1,800 units (footballs). Rydell's contribution margin per unit is $30, which is computed as follows.

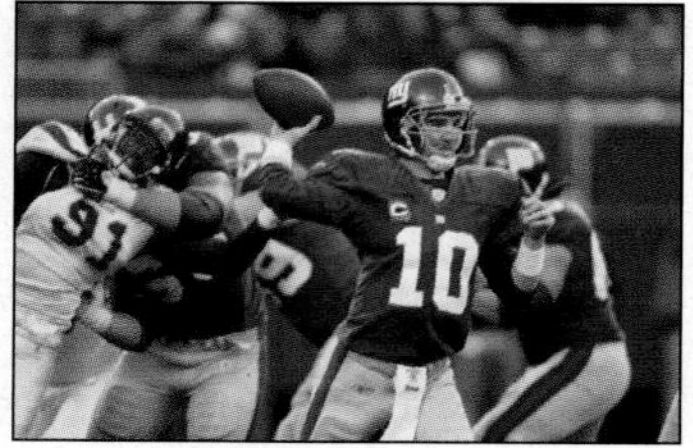

Selling price per unit	$100
Variable cost per unit	70
Contribution margin per unit	$ 30

Its contribution margin ratio is 30%, computed as $30/$100. This reveals that for each unit sold, Rydell has $30 that contributes to covering fixed cost and profit. If we consider sales in dollars, a contribution margin of 30% implies that for each $1 in sales, Rydell has $0.30 that contributes to fixed cost and profit.

Decision Maker

Sales Manager You are evaluating orders from two customers but can accept only one of the orders because of your company's limited capacity. The first order is for 100 units of a product with a contribution margin ratio of 60% and a selling price of $1,000. The second order is for 500 units of a product with a contribution margin ratio of 20% and a selling price of $800. The incremental fixed costs are the same for both orders. Which order do you accept? [Answer—p. 921]

Computing the Break-Even Point

P2 Compute the break-even point for a single product company.

The **break-even point** is the sales level at which a company neither earns a profit nor incurs a loss. The concept of break-even is applicable to nearly all organizations, activities, and events. One of the most important items of information when launching a project is whether it will break even—that is, whether sales will at least cover total costs. The break-even point can be expressed in either units or dollars of sales.

To illustrate the computation of break-even analysis, let's again look at Rydell, which sells footballs for $100 per unit and incurs $70 of variable costs per unit sold. Its fixed costs are $24,000 per month. Rydell breaks even for the month when it sells 800 footballs (sales volume of $80,000). We compute this break-even point using the formula in Exhibit 22.11. This formula uses the contribution margin per unit, which for Rydell is $30 ($100 − $70). From this we can compute the break-even sales volume as $24,000/$30, or 800 units per month.

EXHIBIT 22.11

Formula for Computing Break-Even Sales (in Units)

$$\textbf{Break-even point in units} = \frac{\textbf{Fixed costs}}{\textbf{Contribution margin per unit}}$$

At a price of $100 per unit, monthly sales of 800 units yield sales dollars of $80,000 (called *break-even sales dollars*). This $80,000 break-even sales can be computed directly using the formula in Exhibit 22.12.

Point: The break-even point is where total expenses equal total sales and the profit is zero.

EXHIBIT 22.12

Formula for Computing Break-Even Sales (in Dollars)

$$\textbf{Break-even point in dollars} = \frac{\textbf{Fixed costs}}{\textbf{Contribution margin ratio}}$$

Rydell's break-even point in dollars is computed as $24,000/0.30, or $80,000 of monthly sales. To verify that Rydell's break-even point equals $80,000 (or 800 units), we prepare a simplified income statement in Exhibit 22.13. It shows that the $80,000 revenue from sales of 800 units exactly equals the sum of variable and fixed costs.

Point: Even if a company operates at a level in excess of its break-even point, management may decide to stop operating because it is not earning a reasonable return on investment.

EXHIBIT 22.13

Contribution Margin Income Statement for Break-Even Sales

RYDELL COMPANY
Contribution Margin Income Statement (at Break-Even)
For Month Ended January 31, 2009

Sales (800 units at $100 each)	$80,000
Variable costs (800 units at $70 each)	56,000
Contribution margin	24,000
Fixed costs	24,000
Net income	$ 0

Point: A contribution margin income statement is also referred to as a ***variable costing income statement.*** This differs from the traditional ***absorption costing*** approach where all product costs are assigned to units sold and to units in ending inventory. Recall that variable costing expenses all fixed product costs. Thus, income for the two approaches differs depending on the level of finished goods inventory; the lower inventory is, the more similar the two approaches are.

The statement in Exhibit 22.13 is called a *contribution margin income statement.* It differs in format from a conventional income statement in two ways. First, it separately classifies costs and expenses as variable or fixed. Second, it reports contribution margin (Sales − Variable costs). The contribution margin income statement format is used in this chapter's assignment materials because of its usefulness in CVP analysis.

Preparing a Cost-Volume-Profit Chart

P3 Graph costs and sales for a single product company.

Exhibit 22.14 is a graph of Rydell's cost-volume-profit relations. This graph is called a **cost-volume-profit (CVP) chart,** or a *break-even chart* or *break-even graph.* The horizontal axis is the number of units produced and sold and the vertical axis is dollars of sales and costs. The lines in the chart depict both sales and costs at different output levels.

EXHIBIT 22.14

Cost-Volume-Profit Chart

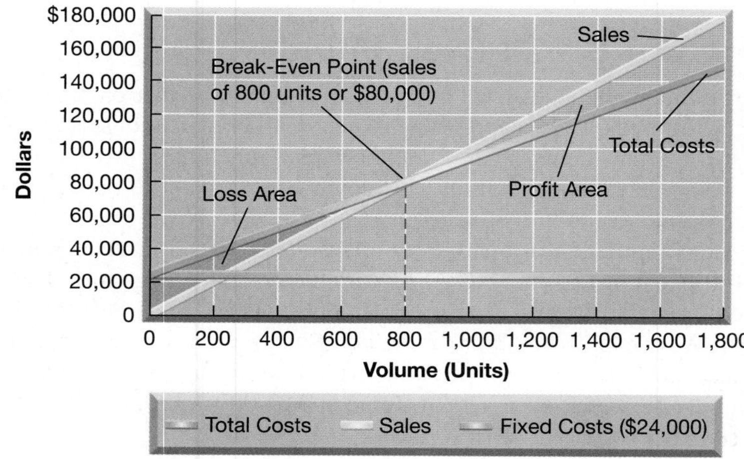

We follow three steps to prepare a CVP chart, which can also be drawn with computer programs that convert numeric data to graphs:

1. Plot fixed costs on the vertical axis ($24,000 for Rydell). Draw a horizontal line at this level to show that fixed costs remain unchanged regardless of output volume (drawing this fixed cost line is not essential to the chart).
2. Draw the total (variable plus fixed) costs line for a relevant range of volume levels. This line starts at the fixed costs level on the vertical axis because total costs equal fixed costs at zero volume. The slope of the total cost line equals the variable cost per unit ($70). To draw the line, compute the total costs for any volume level, and connect this point with the vertical axis intercept ($24,000). Do not draw this line beyond the productive capacity for the planning period (1,800 units for Rydell).
3. Draw the sales line. Start at the origin (zero units and zero dollars of sales) and make the slope of this line equal to the selling price per unit ($100). To sketch the line, compute dollar sales for any volume level and connect this point with the origin. Do not extend this line beyond the productive capacity. Total sales will be at the highest level at maximum capacity.

Example: In Exhibit 22.14, the sales line intersects the total cost line at 800 units. At what point would the two lines intersect if selling price is increased by 20% to $120 per unit? *Answer:* $24,000/($120 − $70) = 480 units

The total costs line and the sales line intersect at 800 units in Exhibit 22.14, which is the break-even point—the point where total dollar sales of $80,000 equals the sum of both fixed and variable costs ($80,000).

On either side of the break-even point, the vertical distance between the sales line and the total costs line at any specific volume reflects the profit or loss expected at that point. At volume levels to the left of the break-even point, this vertical distance is the amount of the expected loss because the total costs line is above the total sales line. At volume levels to the right of the break-even point, the vertical distance represents the expected profit because the total sales line is above the total costs line.

Decision Maker

Operations Manager As a start-up manufacturer, you wish to identify the behavior of manufacturing costs to develop a production cost budget. You know three methods can be used to identify cost behavior from past data, but past data are unavailable because this is a start-up. What do you do? [Answer—p. 921]

Making Assumptions in Cost-Volume-Profit Analysis

Cost-volume-profit analysis assumes that relations can normally be expressed as simple lines similar to those in Exhibits 22.4 and 22.14. Such assumptions allow users to answer several important questions, but the usefulness of the answers depends on the validity of three assumptions: (1) constant selling price per unit, (2) constant variable costs per unit, and (3) constant total fixed costs. These assumptions are not always realistic, but they do not necessarily limit the usefulness of CVP analysis as a way to better understand costs and sales. This section discusses these assumptions and other issues for CVP analysis.

C2 Identify assumptions in cost-volume-profit analysis and explain their impact.

Working with Assumptions The behavior of individual costs and sales often is not perfectly consistent with CVP assumptions. If the expected costs and sales behavior differ from the assumptions, the results of CVP analysis can be limited. Still, we can perform useful analyses in spite of limitations with these assumptions for several reasons.

Summing costs can offset individual deviations. Deviations from assumptions with individual costs are often minor when these costs are summed. That is, individual variable cost items may not be perfectly variable, but when we sum these variable costs, their individual deviations can offset each other. This means the assumption of variable cost behavior can be proper for total variable costs. Similarly, an assumption that total fixed costs are constant can be proper even when individual fixed cost items are not exactly constant.

Point: CVP analysis can be very useful for business decision making even when its assumptions are not strictly met.

CVP is applied to a relevant range of operations. Sales, variable costs, and fixed costs often are reasonably reflected in straight lines on a graph when the assumptions are applied over a relevant range. The **relevant range of operations** is the normal operating range for a business. Except for unusually difficult or prosperous times, management typically plans for operations within a range of volume neither close to zero nor at maximum capacity. The relevant range excludes extremely high and low operating levels that are unlikely to occur. The validity of assuming that a specific cost is fixed or variable is more acceptable when operations are within the relevant range. As shown in Exhibit 22.2, a curvilinear cost can be treated as variable and linear if the relevant range covers volumes where it has a nearly constant slope. If the normal range of activity changes, some costs might need reclassification.

Video22.2

CVP analysis yields estimates. CVP analysis yields approximate answers to questions about costs, volumes, and profits. These answers do not have to be precise because the analysis makes rough estimates about the future. As long as managers understand that CVP analysis gives estimates, it can be a useful tool for starting the planning process. Other qualitative factors also must be considered.

Working with Output Measures CVP analysis usually describes the level of activity in terms of *sales volume,* which can be expressed in terms of either units sold or dollar sales. However, other measures of output exist. For instance, a manufacturer can use the number of units produced as a measure of output. Also, to simplify analysis, we sometimes assume that the production level is the same as the sales level. That is, inventory levels do not change. This often is justified by arguing that CVP analysis provides only approximations.

Example: If the selling price declines, what happens to the break-even point? *Answer:* It increases.

Quick Check

Answers—p. 922

7. Fixed cost divided by the contribution margin ratio yields the (*a*) break-even point in dollars, (*b*) contribution margin per unit, or (*c*) break-even point in units.
8. A company sells a product for $90 per unit with variable costs of $54 per unit. What is the contribution margin ratio?
9. Refer to Quick Check (8). If fixed costs for the period are $90,000, what is the break-even point in dollars?
10. What three basic assumptions are used in CVP analysis?

Working with Changes in Estimates Because CVP analysis uses estimates, knowing how changes in those estimates impact breakeven is useful. For example, a manager might form three estimates for each of the components of breakeven: optimistic, most likely, and pessimistic. Then ranges of break-even points in units can be computed using the formula in Exhibit 22.11.

To illustrate, assume Rydell's managers provide the set of estimates in Exhibit 22.15.

EXHIBIT 22.15

Alternative Estimates for Break-Even Analysis

	Selling Price per Unit	Variable Cost per Unit	Total Fixed Costs
Optimistic	$105	$68	$21,000
Most likely	100	70	24,000
Pessimistic	95	72	27,000

If, for example, Rydell's managers believe they can raise the selling price of a football to $105, without any change in variable or fixed costs, then the revised contribution margin per football is $35, and the revised break-even in units follows in Exhibit 22.16.

EXHIBIT 22.16

Revised Break-Even in Units

$$\text{Revised break-even point in units} = \frac{\$24{,}000}{\$35} = 686 \text{ units}$$

EXHIBIT 22.17

Scatter Diagrams—Break-Even Points for Alternative Estimates

Repeating this calculation using each of the other eight separate estimates above, and graphing the results, yields the three scatter diagrams in Exhibit 22.17.

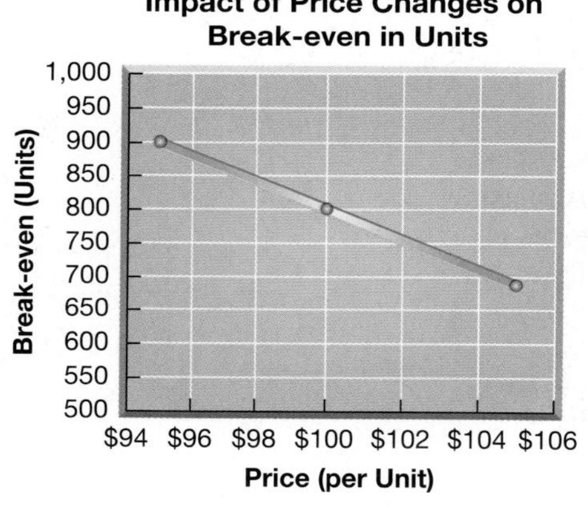

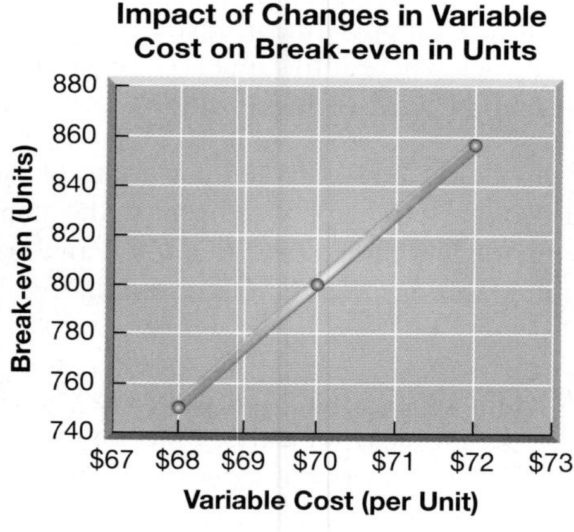

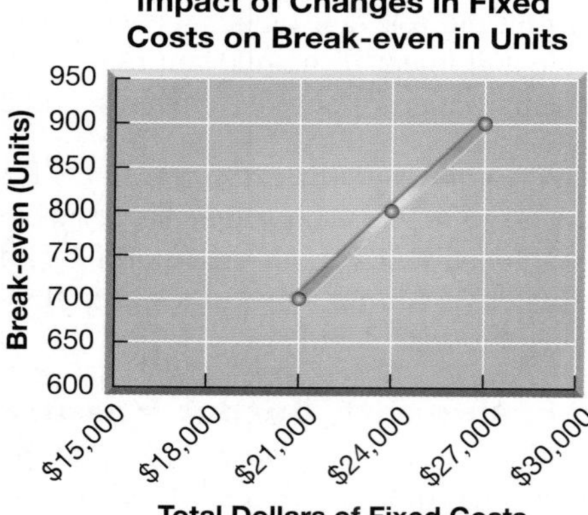

These scatter diagrams show how changes in selling prices, variable costs, and fixed costs impact break-even. When selling prices can be increased without impacting costs, break-even decreases. When competition drives selling prices down, and the company cannot reduce costs, break-even increases. Increases in either variable or fixed costs, if they cannot be passed on to customers via higher selling prices, will increase break-even. If costs can be reduced and selling prices held constant, the break-even decreases.

Point: This analysis changed only one estimate at a time; managers can examine how combinations of changes in estimates will impact break-even.

Applying Cost-Volume-Profit Analysis

Managers consider a variety of strategies in planning business operations. Cost-volume-profit analysis is useful in helping managers evaluate the likely effects of these strategies, which is the focus of this section.

Computing Income from Sales and Costs

C3 Describe several applications of cost-volume-profit analysis.

An important question managers often need an answer to is "What is the predicted income from a predicted level of sales?" To answer this, we look at four variables in CVP analysis. These variables and their relations to income (pretax) are shown in Exhibit 22.18. We use these relations to compute expected income from predicted sales and cost levels.

EXHIBIT 22.18

Income Relations in CVP Analysis

Sales
− Variable costs
Contribution margin
− Fixed costs
Income (pretax)

To illustrate, let's assume that Rydell's management expects to sell 1,500 units in January 2009. What is the amount of income if this sales level is achieved? Following Exhibit 22.18, we compute Rydell's expected income in Exhibit 22.19.

EXHIBIT 22.19

Computing Expected Pretax Income from Expected Sales

RYDELL COMPANY
Contribution Margin Income Statement
For Month Ended January 31, 2009

Sales (1,500 units at $100 each)	$150,000
Variable costs (1,500 units at $70 each)	105,000
Contribution margin	45,000
Fixed costs	24,000
Income (pretax)	$ 21,000

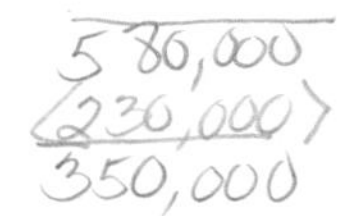

The $21,000 income is pretax. To find the amount of *after-tax* income from selling 1,500 units, management must apply the proper tax rate. Assume that the tax rate is 25%. Then we can prepare the after-tax income statement shown in Exhibit 22.20. We can also compute pretax income as after-tax income divided by (1 − tax rate); for Rydell, this is $15,750/(1 − 0.25), or $21,000.

EXHIBIT 22.20

Computing Expected After-Tax Income from Expected Sales

RYDELL COMPANY
Contribution Margin Income Statement
For Month Ended January 31, 2009

Sales (1,500 units at $100 each)	$150,000
Variable costs (1,500 units at $70 each)	105,000
Contribution margin	45,000
Fixed costs	24,000
Pretax income	21,000
Income taxes (25%)	5,250
Net income (after tax)	$ 15,750

Management then assesses whether this income is an adequate return on assets invested. Management should also consider whether sales and income can be increased by raising or lowering prices. CVP analysis is a good tool for addressing these kinds of "what-if" questions.

Computing Sales for a Target Income

"How many
units must I sell
to earn $50,000?"

Many companies' annual plans are based on certain income targets (sometimes called *budgets*). Rydell's income target for this year is to increase income by 10% over the prior year. When prior year income is known, Rydell easily computes its target income. CVP analysis helps to determine the sales level needed to achieve the target income. Computing this sales level is important because planning for the year is then based on this level. We use the formula shown in Exhibit 22.21 to compute sales for a target *after-tax* income.

EXHIBIT 22.21

Computing Sales (Dollars) for a Target After-Tax Income

$$\textbf{Dollar sales at target after-tax income} = \frac{\textbf{Fixed costs} + \textbf{Target pretax income}}{\textbf{Contribution margin ratio}}$$

To illustrate, Rydell has monthly fixed costs of $24,000 and a 30% contribution margin ratio. Assume that it sets a target monthly after-tax income of $9,000 when the tax rate is 25%. This means the pretax income is targeted at $12,000 [$9,000/(1 − 0.25)] with a tax expense of $3,000. Using the formula in Exhibit 22.21, we find that $120,000 of sales are needed to produce a $9,000 after-tax income as shown in Exhibit 22.22.

EXHIBIT 22.22

Rydell's Dollar Sales for a Target Income

$$\text{Dollar sales at target after-tax income} = \frac{\$24{,}000 + \$12{,}000}{30\%} = \$120{,}000$$

Point: Break-even is a special case of the formulas in Exhibits 22.21 and 22.23; simply set target pretax income to $0 and the formulas reduce to those in Exhibits 22.11 and 22.12.

We can alternatively compute *unit sales* instead of dollar sales. To do this, we substitute *contribution margin per unit* for the contribution margin ratio in the denominator. This gives the number of units to sell to reach the target after-tax income. Exhibit 22.23 illustrates this for Rydell. The two computations in Exhibits 22.22 and 22.23 are equivalent because sales of 1,200 units at $100 per unit equal $120,000 of sales.

EXHIBIT 22.23

Computing Sales (Units) for a Target After-Tax Income

$$\textbf{Unit sales at target after-tax income} = \frac{\textbf{Fixed costs} + \textbf{Target pretax income}}{\textbf{Contribution margin per unit}}$$

$$= \frac{\$24{,}000 + \$12{,}000}{\$30} = 1{,}200 \text{ units}$$

Computing the Margin of Safety

All companies wish to sell more than the break-even number of units. The excess of expected sales over the break-even sales level is called a company's **margin of safety,** the amount that sales can drop before the company incurs a loss. It can be expressed in units, dollars, or even as a percent of the predicted level of sales. To illustrate, if Rydell's expected sales are $100,000, the margin of safety is $20,000 above break-even sales of $80,000. As a percent, the margin of safety is 20% of expected sales as shown in Exhibit 22.24.

EXHIBIT 22.24

Computing Margin of Safety (in Percent)

$$\textbf{Margin of safety (in percent)} = \frac{\textbf{Expected sales} - \textbf{Break-even sales}}{\textbf{Expected sales}}$$

$$= \frac{\$100{,}000 - \$80{,}000}{\$100{,}000} = 20\%$$

Management must assess whether the margin of safety is adequate in light of factors such as sales variability, competition, consumer tastes, and economic conditions.

Decision Ethics

Supervisor Your team is conducting a cost-volume-profit analysis for a new product. Different sales projections have different incomes. One member suggests picking numbers yielding favorable income because any estimate is "as good as any other." Another member points to a scatter diagram of 20 months' production on a comparable product and suggests dropping unfavorable data points for cost estimation. What do you do? [Answer—p. 921]

Using Sensitivity Analysis

Earlier we showed how changing one of the estimates in a CVP analysis impacts breakeven. We can also examine strategies that impact several estimates in the CVP analysis. For instance, we might want to know what happens to income if we automate a currently manual process. We can use CVP analysis to predict income if we can describe how these changes affect a company's fixed costs, variable costs, selling price, and volume.

To illustrate, assume that Rydell Company is looking into buying a new machine that would increase monthly fixed costs from \$24,000 to \$30,000 but decrease variable costs from \$70 per unit to \$60 per unit. The machine is used to produce output whose selling price will remain unchanged at \$100. This results in increases in both the unit contribution margin and the contribution margin ratio. The revised contribution margin per unit is \$40 (\$100 − \$60), and the revised contribution margin ratio is 40% of selling price (\$40/\$100). Using CVP analysis, Rydell's revised break-even point in dollars would be \$75,000 as computed in Exhibit 22.25.

Example: If fixed costs decline, what happens to the break-even point? *Answer:* It decreases.

EXHIBIT 22.25

Revising Break-even When Changes Occur

$$\textbf{Revised break-even point in dollars} = \frac{\textbf{Revised fixed costs}}{\textbf{Revised contribution margin ratio}} = \frac{\$30{,}000}{40\%} = \$75{,}000$$

The revised fixed costs and the revised contribution margin ratio can be used to address other issues including computation of (1) expected income for a given sales level and (2) the sales level needed to earn a target income. Once again, we can use sensitivity analysis to generate different sets of revenue and cost estimates that are *optimistic, pessimistic,* and *most likely.* Different CVP analyses based on these estimates provide different scenarios that management can analyze and use in planning business strategy.

Point: Price competition led paging companies to give business to resellers—companies that lease services at a discount and then resell to subscribers. **Paging Network** charged some resellers under \$1 per month, less than a third of what was needed to break even. Its CEO now admits the low-price strategy was flawed.

Decision Insight

Eco-CVP Ford Escape, Toyota Prius, and Honda Insight are hybrids. Many promise to save owners \$1,000 or more a year in fuel costs relative to comparables, and they generate fewer greenhouse gases. Are these models economically feasible? Analysts estimate that **Ford** can break even with its Escape when a \$3,000 premium is paid over comparable gas-based models.

Quick Check

Answers—p. 922

11. A company has fixed costs of \$50,000 and a 25% contribution margin ratio. What dollar sales are necessary to achieve an after-tax net income of \$120,000 if the tax rate is 20%? (*a*) \$800,000, (*b*) \$680,000, or (*c*) \$600,000.

12. If a company's contribution margin ratio decreases from 50% to 25%, what can be said about the unit sales needed to achieve the same target income level?

13. What is a company's margin of safety?

Computing a Multiproduct Break-Even Point

P4 Compute the break-even point for a multiproduct company.

To this point, we have looked only at cases where the company sells a single product or service. This was to keep the basic CVP analysis simple. However, many companies sell multiple products or services, and we can modify the CVP analysis for use in these cases. An important assumption in a multiproduct setting is that the sales mix of different products is known and remains constant during the planning period. **Sales mix** is the ratio (proportion) of the sales volumes for the various products. For instance, if a company normally sells 10,000 footballs, 5,000 softballs, and 4,000 basketballs per month, its sales mix can be expressed as 10:5:4 for footballs, softballs, and basketballs.

To apply multiproduct CVP analysis, we can estimate the break-even point by using a **composite unit,** which consists of a specific number of units of each product in proportion to their expected sales mix. Multiproduct CVP analysis treats this composite unit as a single product. To illustrate, let's look at **Hair-Today,** a styling salon that offers three cuts: basic, ultra, and budget in the ratio of 4 basic units to 2 ultra units to 1 budget unit (expressed as 4:2:1). Management wants to estimate its break-even point for next year. Unit selling prices for these three cuts are basic, $20; ultra, $32; and budget, $16. Using the 4:2:1 sales mix, the selling price of a composite unit of the three products is computed as follows.

4 units of basic @ $20 per unit	$ 80
2 units of ultra @ $32 per unit	64
1 unit of budget @ $16 per unit	16
Selling price of a composite unit	$160

Point: Selling prices and variable costs are usually expressed in per unit amounts. Fixed costs are usually expressed in total amounts.

Hair-Today's fixed costs are $192,000 per year, and its variable costs of the three products are basic, $13; ultra, $18.00; and budget, $8.00. Variable costs for a composite unit of these products follow.

4 units of basic @ $13 per unit	$52
2 units of ultra @ $18 per unit	36
1 unit of budget @ $8 per unit	8
Variable costs of a composite unit	$96

Hair-Today's $64 contribution margin for a composite unit is computed by subtracting the variable costs of a composite unit ($96) from its selling price ($160). We then use the contribution margin to determine Hair-Today's break-even point in composite units in Exhibit 22.26.

EXHIBIT 22.26

Break-Even Point in Composite Units

$$\textbf{Break-even point in composite units} = \frac{\textbf{Fixed costs}}{\textbf{Contribution margin per composite unit}}$$

$$= \frac{\$192{,}000}{\$64} = 3{,}000 \text{ composite units}$$

Point: The break-even point in dollars for Exhibit 22.26 is $192,000/($64/$160) = $480,000.

This computation implies that Hair-Today breaks even when it sells 3,000 composite units. To determine how many units of each product it must sell to break even, we multiply the number of units of each product in the composite by 3,000 as follows.

Basic:	4 × 3,000	12,000 units
Ultra:	2 × 3,000	6,000 units
Budget:	1 × 3,000	3,000 units

Instead of computing contribution margin per composite unit, a company can compute a **weighted-average contribution margin.** Given the 4:2:1 product mix, basic cuts comprise 57.14% (computed as 4/7) of the company's haircuts, ultra makes up 14.29% of its business, and budget cuts comprise 28.57%. The weighted-average contribution margin follows in Exhibit 22.27.

EXHIBIT 22.27

Weighted-Average Contribution Margin

	Unit contribution margin	×	Percentage of sales mix	=	Weighted unit contribution margin
Basic	$ 7		57.14%		$4.000
Ultra	14		28.57		4.000
Budget	8		14.29		1.143
Weighted-average contribution margin					$9.143

The company's break-even point in units is computed as follows:

EXHIBIT 22.28

Break-Even in Units using Weighted-Average Contribution Margin

$$\textbf{Break-even point in units} = \frac{\textbf{Fixed costs}}{\textbf{Weighted-average contribution margin}}$$

$$= \frac{\$192{,}000}{\$9.143} = 21{,}000 \text{ units}$$

We see that the weighted-average contribution margin method yields 21,000 whole units as the break-even amount, the same total as the composite unit approach.

Exhibit 22.29 verifies the results for composite units by showing Hair-Today's sales and costs at this break-even point using a contribution margin income statement.

EXHIBIT 22.29

Multiproduct Break-Even Income Statement

HAIR-TODAY
Forecasted Contribution Margin Income Statement (at Breakeven)

	Basic	Ultra	Budget	Totals
Sales				
Basic (12,000 @ $20)	$240,000			
Ultra (6,000 @ $32)		$192,000		
Budget (3,000 @ $16)			$48,000	
Total sales				$480,000
Variable costs				
Basic (12,000 @ $13)	156,000			
Ultra (6,000 @ $18)		108,000		
Budget (3,000 @ $8)			24,000	
Total variable costs				288,000
Contribution margin	$ 84,000	$ 84,000	$24,000	192,000
Fixed costs				192,000
Net income				$ 0

A CVP analysis using composite units can be used to answer a variety of planning questions. Once a product mix is set, all answers are based on the assumption that the mix remains constant at all relevant sales levels as other factors in the analysis do. We also can vary the sales mix to see what happens under alternative strategies.

Decision Maker

Entrepreneur A CVP analysis indicates that your start-up, which markets electronic products, will break even with the current sales mix and price levels. You have a target income in mind. What analysis might you perform to assess the likelihood of achieving this income? [Answer—p. 921]

Quick Check

Answers—p. 922

14. The sales mix of a company's two products, X and Y, is 2:1. Unit variable costs for both products are $2, and unit sales prices are $5 for X and $4 for Y. What is the contribution margin per composite unit? (*a*) $5, (*b*) $10, or (*c*) $8.

15. What additional assumption about sales mix must be made in doing a conventional CVP analysis for a company that produces and sells more than one product?

Decision Analysis — Degree of Operating Leverage

A3 Analyze changes in sales using the degree of operating leverage.

CVP analysis is especially useful when management begins the planning process and wishes to predict outcomes of alternative strategies. These strategies can involve changes in selling prices, fixed costs, variable costs, sales volume, and product mix. Managers are interested in seeing the effects of changes in some or all of these factors.

One goal of all managers is to get maximum benefits from their fixed costs. Managers would like to use 100% of their output capacity so that fixed costs are spread over the largest number of units. This would decrease fixed cost per unit and increase income. The extent, or relative size, of fixed costs in the total cost structure is known as **operating leverage.** Companies having a higher proportion of fixed costs in their total cost structure are said to have higher operating leverage. An example of this is a company that chooses to automate its processes instead of using direct labor, increasing its fixed costs and lowering its variable costs. A useful managerial measure to help assess the effect of changes in the level of sales on income is the **degree of operating leverage (DOL)** defined in Exhibit 22.30.

EXHIBIT 22.30

Degree of Operating Leverage

DOL = Total contribution margin (in dollars)/Pretax income

To illustrate, let's return to Rydell Company. At a sales level of 1,200 units, Rydell's total contribution margin is \$36,000 (1,200 units × \$30 contribution margin per unit). Its pretax income, after subtracting fixed costs of \$24,000, is \$12,000 (\$36,000 − \$24,000). Rydell's degree of operating leverage at this sales level is 3.0, computed as contribution margin divided by pretax income (\$36,000/\$12,000). We then use DOL to measure the effect of changes in the level of sales on pretax income. For instance, suppose Rydell expects sales to increase by 10%. If this increase is within the relevant range of operations, we can expect this 10% increase in sales to result in a 30% increase in pretax income computed as DOL multiplied by the increase in sales (3.0 × 10%). Similar analyses can be done for expected decreases in sales.

Demonstration Problem

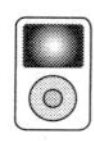

DP22

Sport Caps Co. manufactures and sells caps for different sporting events. The fixed costs of operating the company are \$150,000 per month, and the variable costs for caps are \$5 per unit. The caps are sold for \$8 per unit. The fixed costs provide a production capacity of up to 100,000 caps per month.

Required

1. Use the formulas in the chapter to compute the following:
   a. Contribution margin per cap.
   b. Break-even point in terms of the number of caps produced and sold.
   c. Amount of net income at 30,000 caps sold per month (ignore taxes).
   d. Amount of net income at 85,000 caps sold per month (ignore taxes).
   e. Number of caps to be produced and sold to provide \$45,000 of after-tax income, assuming an income tax rate of 25%.
2. Draw a CVP chart for the company, showing cap output on the horizontal axis. Identify (*a*) the break-even point and (*b*) the amount of pretax income when the level of cap production is 70,000. (Omit the fixed cost line.)
3. Use the formulas in the chapter to compute the
   a. Contribution margin ratio.
   b. Break-even point in terms of sales dollars.
   c. Amount of net income at \$250,000 of sales per month (ignore taxes).
   d. Amount of net income at \$600,000 of sales per month (ignore taxes).
   e. Dollars of sales needed to provide \$45,000 of after-tax income, assuming an income tax rate of 25%.

Planning the Solution

- Identify the formulas in the chapter for the required items expressed in units and solve them using the data given in the problem.

- Draw a CVP chart that reflects the facts in the problem. The horizontal axis should plot the volume in units up to 100,000, and the vertical axis should plot the total dollars up to $800,000. Plot the total cost line as upward sloping, starting at the fixed cost level ($150,000) on the vertical axis and increasing until it reaches $650,000 at the maximum volume of 100,000 units. Verify that the break-even point (where the two lines cross) equals the amount you computed in part 1.
- Identify the formulas in the chapter for the required items expressed in dollars and solve them using the data given in the problem.

Solution to Demonstration Problem

1. a. Contribution margin per cap = Selling price per unit − Variable cost per unit
= $8 − $5 = $3

b. Break-even point in caps $= \dfrac{\text{Fixed costs}}{\text{Contribution margin per cap}} = \dfrac{\$150{,}000}{\$3} = \underline{\underline{50{,}000 \text{ caps}}}$

c. Net income at 30,000 caps sold = (Units × Contribution margin per unit) − Fixed costs
= (30,000 × $3) − $150,000 = $(60,000) loss

d. Net income at 85,000 caps sold = (Units × Contribution margin per unit) − Fixed costs
= (85,000 × $3) − $150,000 = $105,000 profit

e. Pretax income = $45,000/(1 − 0.25) = $60,000
Income taxes = $60,000 × 25% = $15,000

Units needed for $45,000 income $= \dfrac{\text{Fixed costs + Target pretax income}}{\text{Contribution margin per cap}}$
$= \dfrac{\$150{,}000 + \$60{,}000}{\$3} = \underline{\underline{70{,}000 \text{ caps}}}$

2. CVP chart.

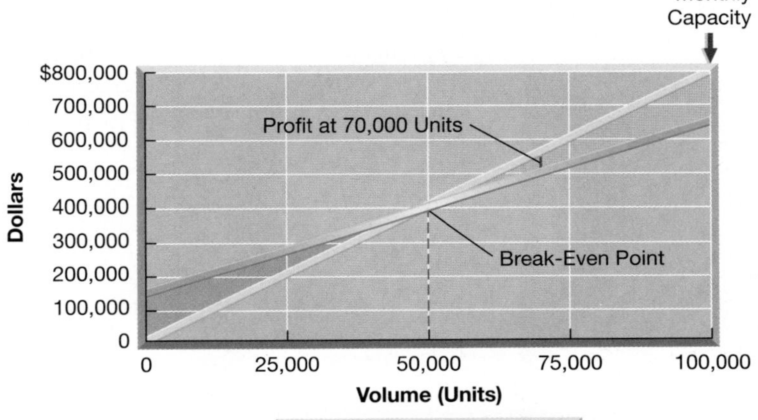

3. a. Contribution margin ratio $= \dfrac{\text{Contribution margin per unit}}{\text{Selling price per unit}} = \dfrac{\$3}{\$8} = \underline{\underline{0.375}}, \text{ or } \underline{\underline{37.5\%}}$

b. Break-even point in dollars $= \dfrac{\text{Fixed costs}}{\text{Contribution margin ratio}} = \dfrac{\$150{,}000}{37.5\%} = \underline{\underline{\$400{,}000}}$

c. Net income at sales of $250,000 = (Sales × Contribution margin ratio) − Fixed costs
= ($250,000 × 37.5%) − $150,000 = $(56,250) loss

d. Net income at sales of $600,000 = (Sales × Contribution margin ratio) − Fixed costs
= ($600,000 × 37.5%) − $150,000 = $75,000 income

e. Dollars of sales to yield $45,000 after-tax income $= \dfrac{\text{Fixed costs + Target pretax income}}{\text{Contribution margin ratio}}$
$= \dfrac{\$150{,}000 + \$60{,}000}{37.5\%} = \underline{\underline{\$560{,}000}}$

APPENDIX

22A Using Excel to Estimate Least-Squares Regression

Microsoft Excel® 2007 and other spreadsheet software can be used to perform least-squares regressions to identify cost behavior. In Excel®, the INTERCEPT and SLOPE functions are used. The following screen shot reports the data from Exhibit 22.3 in cells A1 through C13 and shows the cell contents to find the intercept (cell B16) and slope (cell B17). Cell B16 uses Excel® to find the intercept from a least-squares regression of total cost (shown as C2:C13 in cell B16) on units produced (shown as B2:B13 in cell B16). Spreadsheet software is useful in understanding cost behavior when many data points (such as monthly total costs and units produced) are available.

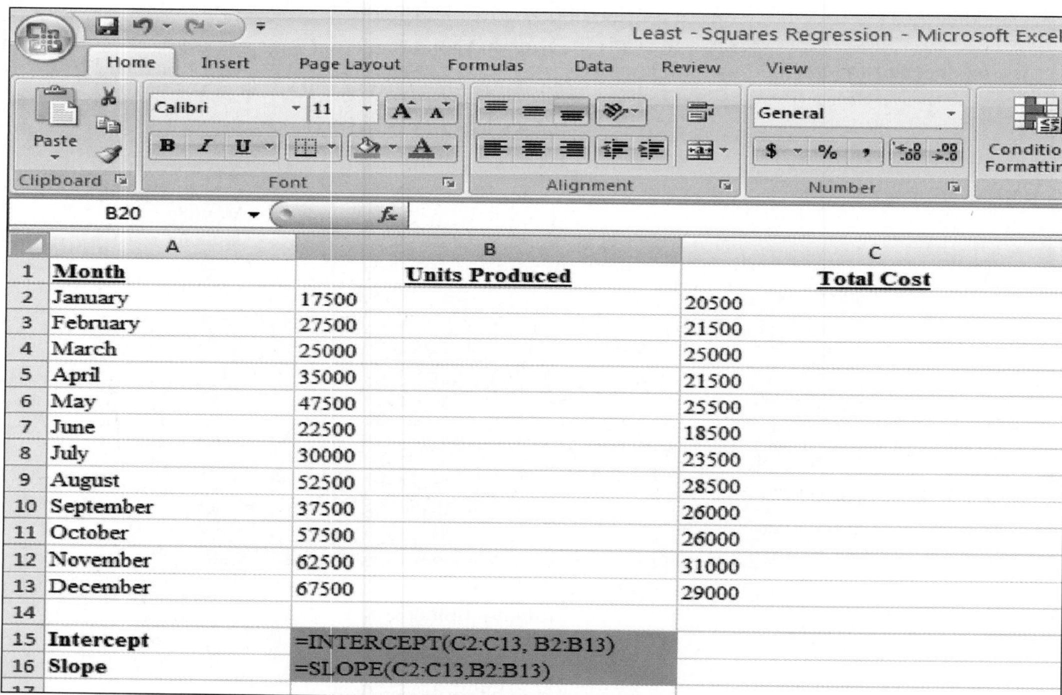

	A	B	C
1	**Month**	**Units Produced**	**Total Cost**
2	January	17500	20500
3	February	27500	21500
4	March	25000	25000
5	April	35000	21500
6	May	47500	25500
7	June	22500	18500
8	July	30000	23500
9	August	52500	28500
10	September	37500	26000
11	October	57500	26000
12	November	62500	31000
13	December	67500	29000
14			
15	**Intercept**	=INTERCEPT(C2:C13, B2:B13)	
16	**Slope**	=SLOPE(C2:C13,B2:B13)	

Excel® can also be used to create scatter diagrams such as that in Exhibit 22.4. In contrast to visually drawing a line that "fits" the data, Excel® more precisely fits the regression line. To draw a scatter diagram with a line of fit, follow these steps:

1. Highlight the data cells you wish to diagram; in this example, start from cell C13 and highlight through cell B2.
2. Then select "Insert" and "Scatter" from the drop-down menus. Selecting the chart type in the upper left corner of the choices under Scatter will produce a diagram that looks like that in Exhibit 22.4, without a line of fit.
3. To add a line of fit (also called trend line), select "Layout" and "Trendline" from the drop-down menus. Selecting "Linear Trendline" will produce a diagram that looks like that in Exhibit 22.4, including the line of fit.

Summary

C1 Describe different types of cost behavior in relation to production and sales volume. Cost behavior is described in terms of how its amount changes in relation to changes in volume of activity within a relevant range. Fixed costs remain constant to changes in volume. Total variable costs change in direct proportion to volume changes. Mixed costs display the effects of both fixed and variable components. Step-wise costs remain constant over a small volume range, then change by a lump sum and remain constant over another volume range, and so on. Curvilinear costs change in a nonlinear relation to volume changes.

C2 Identify assumptions in cost-volume-profit analysis and explain their impact. Conventional cost-volume-profit analysis is based on assumptions that the product's selling price remains constant and that variable and fixed costs behave in a manner consistent with their variable and fixed classifications.

C3 Describe several applications of cost-volume-profit analysis. Cost-volume-profit analysis can be used to predict what can happen under alternative strategies concerning sales volume, selling prices, variable costs, or fixed costs. Applications include "what-if" analysis, computing sales for a target income, and break-even analysis.

A1 Compare the scatter diagram, high-low, and regression methods of estimating costs. Cost estimates from a scatter diagram are based on a visual fit of the cost line. Estimates from the high-low method are based only on costs corresponding to the lowest and highest sales. The least-squares regression method is a statistical technique and uses all data points.

A2 Compute the contribution margin and describe what it reveals about a company's cost structure. Contribution margin per unit is a product's sales price less its total variable costs. Contribution margin ratio is a product's contribution margin per unit divided by its sales price. Unit contribution margin is the amount received from each sale that contributes to fixed costs and income. The contribution margin ratio reveals what portion of each sales dollar is available as contribution to fixed costs and income.

A3 Analyze changes in sales using the degree of operating leverage. The extent, or relative size, of fixed costs in a company's total cost structure is known as *operating leverage.* One tool useful in assessing the effect of changes in sales on income is the degree of operating leverage, or DOL. DOL is the ratio of the contribution margin divided by pretax income. This ratio can be used to determine the expected percent change in income given a percent change in sales.

P1 Determine cost estimates using three different methods. Three different methods used to estimate costs are the scatter diagram, the high-low method, and least-squares regression. All three methods use past data to estimate costs.

P2 Compute the break-even point for a single product company. A company's break-even point for a period is the sales volume at which total revenues equal total costs. To compute a break-even point in terms of sales units, we divide total fixed costs by the contribution margin per unit. To compute a break-even point in terms of sales dollars, divide total fixed costs by the contribution margin ratio.

P3 Graph costs and sales for a single product company. The costs and sales for a company can be graphically illustrated using a CVP chart. In this chart, the horizontal axis represents the number of units sold and the vertical axis represents dollars of sales or costs. Straight lines are used to depict both costs and sales on the CVP chart.

P4 Compute the break-even point for a multiproduct company. CVP analysis can be applied to a multiproduct company by expressing sales volume in terms of composite units. A composite unit consists of a specific number of units of each product in proportion to their expected sales mix. Multiproduct CVP analysis treats this composite unit as a single product.

Guidance Answers to **Decision Maker** and **Decision Ethics**

Sales Manager The contribution margin per unit for the first order is $600 (60% of $1,000); the contribution margin per unit for the second order is $160 (20% of $800). You are likely tempted to accept the first order based on its high contribution margin per unit, but you must compute the total contribution margin based on the number of units sold for each order. Total contribution margin is $60,000 ($600 per unit × 100 units) and $80,000 ($160 per unit × 500 units) for the two orders, respectively. The second order provides the largest return in absolute dollars and is the order you would accept. Another factor to consider in your selection is the potential for a long-term relationship with these customers including repeat sales and growth.

Operations Manager Without the availability of past data, none of the three methods described in the chapter can be used to measure cost behavior. Instead, the manager must investigate whether data from similar manufacturers can be accessed. This is likely difficult due to the sensitive nature of such data. In the absence of data, the manager should develop a list of the different production inputs and identify input-output relations. This provides guidance to the manager in measuring cost behavior. After several months, actual cost data will be available for analysis.

Supervisor Your dilemma is whether to go along with the suggestions to "manage" the numbers to make the project look like it will achieve sufficient profits. You should not succumb to these suggestions. Many people will likely be affected negatively if you manage the predicted numbers and the project eventually is unprofitable. Moreover, if it does fail, an investigation would likely reveal that data in the proposal were "fixed" to make it look good. Probably the only benefit from managing the numbers is the short-term payoff of pleasing those who proposed the product. One way to deal with this dilemma is to prepare several analyses showing results under different assumptions and then let senior management make the decision.

Entrepreneur You must first compute the level of sales required to achieve the desired net income. Then you must conduct sensitivity analysis by varying the price, sales mix, and cost estimates. Results from the sensitivity analysis provide information you can use to assess the possibility of reaching the target sales level. For instance, you might have to pursue aggressive marketing strategies to push the high-margin products, or you might have to cut prices to increase sales and profits, or another strategy might emerge.

Guidance Answers to **Quick Checks**

1. *b*
2. A fixed cost remains unchanged in total amount regardless of output levels. However, fixed *cost per unit* declines with increased output.
3. Such a cost is considered variable because the *total* cost changes in proportion to volume changes.
4. *b*
5. The high-low method ignores all costs and sales (activity base) volume data points except the costs corresponding to the highest and lowest (most extreme) sales (activity base) volume.
6. *c*
7. *a*
8. ($90 − $54)/$90 = 40%
9. $90,000/40% = $225,000
10. Three basic CVP assumptions are that (1) selling price per unit is constant, (2) variable costs per unit are constant, and (3) total fixed costs are constant.
11. a; Two steps are required for explanation:
    (1) Pretax income = $120,000/(1 − 0.20) = $150,000
    (2) $\frac{\$50{,}000 + \$150{,}000}{25\%} = \$800{,}000$
12. If the contribution margin ratio decreases from 50% to 25%, unit sales would have to double.
13. A company's margin of safety is the excess of the predicted sales level over its break-even sales level.
14. *c*; Selling price of a composite unit:

2 units of X @ $5 per unit	$10
1 unit of Y @ $4 per unit	4
Selling price of a composite unit	$14
Variable costs of a composite unit:	
2 units of X @ $2 per unit	$4
1 unit of Y @ $2 per unit	2
Variable costs of a composite unit	$6

    Therefore, the contribution margin per composite unit is $8.
15. It must be assumed that the sales mix remains unchanged at all sales levels in the relevant range.

Key Terms

mhhe.com/wildFAP19e

Key Terms are available at the book's Website for learning and testing in an online Flashcard Format.

Break-even point (p. 909)
Composite unit (p. 916)
Contribution margin per unit (p. 908)
Contribution margin ratio (p. 908)
Cost-volume-profit (CVP) analysis (p. 902)
Cost-volume-profit (CVP) chart (p. 910)
Curvilinear cost (p. 904)
Degree of operating leverage (DOL) (p. 918)
Estimated line of cost behavior (p. 906)
High-low method (p. 906)
Least-squares regression (p. 907)
Margin of safety (p. 914)
Mixed cost (p. 903)
Operating leverage (p. 918)
Relevant range of operations (p. 911)
Sales mix (p. 915)
Scatter diagram (p. 905)
Step-wise cost (p. 904)
Weighted-average contribution margin (p. 916)

Multiple Choice Quiz

Answers on p. 937

mhhe.com/wildFAP19e

Additional Quiz Questions are available at the book's Website.

Quiz22

1. A company's only product sells for $150 per unit. Its variable costs per unit are $100, and its fixed costs total $75,000. What is its contribution margin per unit?
   a. $50
   b. $250
   c. $100
   d. $150
   e. $25
2. Using information from question 1, what is the company's contribution margin ratio?
   a. 66⅔%
   b. 100%
   c. 50%
   d. 0%
   e. 33⅓%
3. Using information from question 1, what is the company's break-even point in units?
   a. 500 units
   b. 750 units
   c. 1,500 units
   d. 3,000 units
   e. 1,000 units
4. A company's forecasted sales are $300,000 and its sales at break-even are $180,000. Its margin of safety in dollars is
   a. $180,000.
   b. $120,000.

c. \$480,000.
d. \$60,000.
e. \$300,000.

5. A product sells for \$400 per unit and its variable costs per unit are \$260. The company's fixed costs are \$840,000. If the company desires \$70,000 pretax income, what is the required dollar sales?

a. \$2,400,000
b. \$200,000
c. \$2,600,000
d. \$2,275,000
e. \$1,400,000

Superscript letter [A] denotes assignments based on Appendix 22A.

Discussion Questions

1. How is cost-volume-profit analysis useful?

2. What is a variable cost? Identify two variable costs.

3. When output volume increases, do variable costs per unit increase, decrease, or stay the same within the relevant range of activity? Explain.

4. When output volume increases, do fixed costs per unit increase, decrease, or stay the same within the relevant range of activity? Explain.

5. How do step-wise costs and curvilinear costs differ?

6. Define and describe *contribution margin* per unit.

7. Define and explain the *contribution margin ratio.*

8. Describe the contribution margin ratio in layperson's terms.

9. In performing CVP analysis for a manufacturing company, what simplifying assumption is usually made about the volume of production and the volume of sales?

10. What two arguments tend to justify classifying all costs as either fixed or variable even though individual costs might not behave exactly as classified?

11. How does assuming that operating activity occurs within a relevant range affect cost-volume-profit analysis?

12. List three methods to measure cost behavior.

13. How is a scatter diagram used to identify and measure the behavior of a company's costs?

14. In cost-volume-profit analysis, what is the estimated profit at the break-even point?

15. Assume that a straight line on a CVP chart intersects the vertical axis at the level of fixed costs and has a positive slope that rises with each additional unit of volume by the amount of the variable costs per unit. What does this line represent?

16. Why are fixed costs depicted as a horizontal line on a CVP chart?

17. Each of two similar companies has sales of \$20,000 and total costs of \$15,000 for a month. Company A's total costs include \$10,000 of variable costs and \$5,000 of fixed costs. If Company B's total costs include \$4,000 of variable costs and \$11,000 of fixed costs, which company will enjoy more profit if sales double?

18. _______ of _______ reflects expected sales in excess of the level of break-even sales.

19. **Apple** produces iPods for sale. Identify some of the variable and fixed product costs associated with that production. [*Hint:* Limit costs to product costs.]

20. Should **Best Buy** use single product or multi-product break-even analysis? Explain.

21. **Apple** is thinking of expanding sales of its most popular Macintosh model by 65%. Do you expect its variable and fixed costs for this model to stay within the relevant range? Explain.

Denotes Discussion Questions that involve decision making.

McGraw-Hill's HOMEWORK MANAGER® Available with McGraw-Hill's Homework Manager

QUICK STUDY

QS 22-1
Cost behavior identification
C1

Determine whether each of the following is best described as a fixed, variable, or mixed cost with respect to product units.

1. Packaging expense.
2. Factory supervisor's salary.
3. Taxes on factory building.
4. Depreciation expense of warehouse.
5. Rubber used to manufacture athletic shoes.
6. Maintenance of factory machinery.
7. Wages of an assembly-line worker paid on the basis of acceptable units produced.

QS 22-2
Cost behavior identification
C1

Listed here are four series of separate costs measured at various volume levels. Examine each series and identify whether it is best described as a fixed, variable, step-wise, or curvilinear cost. (It can help to graph the cost series.)

Volume (Units)	Series 1	Series 2	Series 3	Series 4
0	$450	$ 0	$ 800	$100
100	450	800	800	105
200	450	1,600	800	120
300	450	2,400	1,600	145
400	450	3,200	1,600	190
500	450	4,000	2,400	250
600	450	4,800	2,400	320

QS 22-3
Cost behavior estimation
C1 P1

This scatter diagram reflects past maintenance hours and their corresponding maintenance costs.

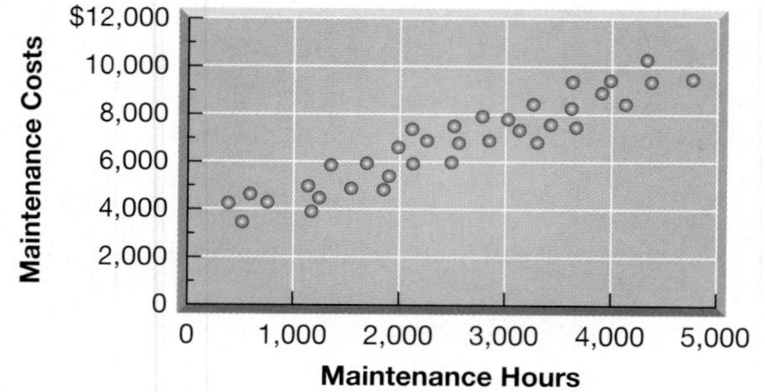

1. Draw an estimated line of cost behavior.
2. Estimate the fixed and variable components of maintenance costs.

QS 22-4
Cost behavior estimation—high-low method
C1 P1

The following information is available for a company's maintenance cost over the last seven months. Using the high-low method, estimate both the fixed and variable components of its maintenance cost.

Month	Maintenance Hours	Maintenance Cost
June	18	$5,450
July	36	6,900
August	24	5,100
September	30	6,000
October	42	6,900
November	48	8,100
December	12	3,600

QS 22-5
Contribution margin ratio
A2

Compute and interpret the contribution margin ratio using the following data: sales, $100,000; total variable cost, $60,000.

QS 22-6
Contribution margin per unit and break-even units
A2 P2

BSD Phone Company sells its cordless phone for $150 per unit. Fixed costs total $270,000, and variable costs are $60 per unit. Determine the (1) contribution margin per unit and (2) break-even point in units.

QS 22-7
Assumptions in CVP analysis
C2

Refer to the information from QS 22-6. How will the break-even point in units change in response to each of the following independent changes in selling price per unit, variable cost per unit, or total fixed costs? Use I for increase and D for decrease. (It is not necessary to compute new break-even points.)

Change	Breakeven in Units Will
1. Variable cost to $50 per unit	_______
2. Total fixed cost to $272,000	_______
3. Selling price per unit to $145	_______
4. Total fixed cost to $260,000	_______
5. Variable cost to $67 per unit	_______
6. Selling price per unit to $160	_______

QS 22-8
Contribution margin ratio and break-even dollars
P2

Refer to QS 22-6. Determine the (1) contribution margin ratio and (2) break-even point in dollars.

QS 22-9
CVP analysis and target income
C3 P2

Refer to QS 22-6. Assume that BSD Phone Co. is subject to a 30% income tax rate. Compute the units of product that must be sold to earn after-tax income of $252,000.

QS 22-10
CVP assumptions
C2

Which one of the following is an assumption that underlies cost-volume-profit analysis?

1. For costs classified as variable, the costs per unit of output must change constantly.
2. For costs classified as fixed, the costs per unit of output must remain constant.
3. All costs have approximately the same relevant range.
4. The selling price per unit must change in proportion to the number of units sold.

QS 22-11
Operating leverage analysis
A3

A high proportion of Company A's total costs are variable with respect to units sold; a high proportion of Company B's total costs are fixed with respect to units sold. Which company is likely to have a higher degree of operating leverage (DOL)? Explain.

QS 22-12
Multiproduct break-even
P4

Call Me Company manufactures and sells two products, green beepers and gold beepers, in the ratio of 5:3. Fixed costs are $66,500, and the contribution margin per composite unit is $95. What number of both green and gold beepers is sold at the break-even point?

McGraw-Hill's HOMEWORK MANAGER® Available with McGraw-Hill's Homework Manager

EXERCISES

Exercise 22-1
Measurement of cost behavior using a scatter diagram
P1

A company reports the following information about its sales and its cost of sales. Each unit of its product sells for $1,000. Use these data to prepare a scatter diagram. Draw an estimated line of cost behavior and determine whether the cost appears to be variable, fixed, or mixed.

Period	Sales	Cost of Sales
1	$45,000	$30,300
2	34,500	22,500
3	31,500	21,000
4	22,500	16,500
5	27,000	18,000
6	37,500	28,500

Exercise 22-2
Cost behavior in graphs
C1 

Following are five graphs representing various cost behaviors. (1) Identify whether the cost behavior in each graph is mixed, step-wise, fixed, variable, or curvilinear. (2) Identify the graph (by number) that best illustrates each cost behavior: (a) Factory policy requires one supervisor for every 30 factory workers; (b) real estate taxes on factory; (c) electricity charge that includes the standard monthly charge plus a charge for each kilowatt hour; (d) commissions to salespersons; and (e) costs of hourly paid workers

[continued on next page]

that provide substantial gains in efficiency when a few workers are added but gradually smaller gains in efficiency when more workers are added.

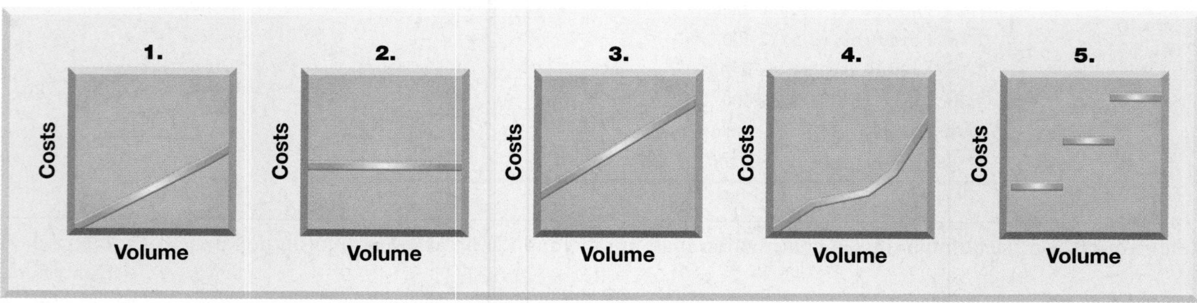

Exercise 22-3
Cost behavior defined
C1

The left column lists several cost classifications. The right column presents short definitions of those costs. In the blank space beside each of the numbers in the right column, write the letter of the cost best described by the definition.

A. Total cost
B. Variable cost
C. Fixed cost
D. Mixed cost
E. Curvilinear cost
F. Step-wise cost

_____ **1.** This cost is the combined amount of all the other costs.

_____ **2.** This cost remains constant over a limited range of volume; when it reaches the end of its limited range, it changes by a lump sum and remains at that level until it exceeds another limited range.

_____ **3.** This cost has a component that remains the same over all volume levels and another component that increases in direct proportion to increases in volume.

_____ **4.** This cost increases when volume increases, but the increase is not constant for each unit produced.

_____ **5.** This cost remains constant over all volume levels within the productive capacity for the planning period.

_____ **6.** This cost increases in direct proportion to increases in volume; its amount is constant for each unit produced.

Exercise 22-4
Cost behavior identification
C1

Following are five series of costs *A* through *E* measured at various volume levels. Examine each series and identify which is fixed, variable, mixed, step-wise, or curvilinear.

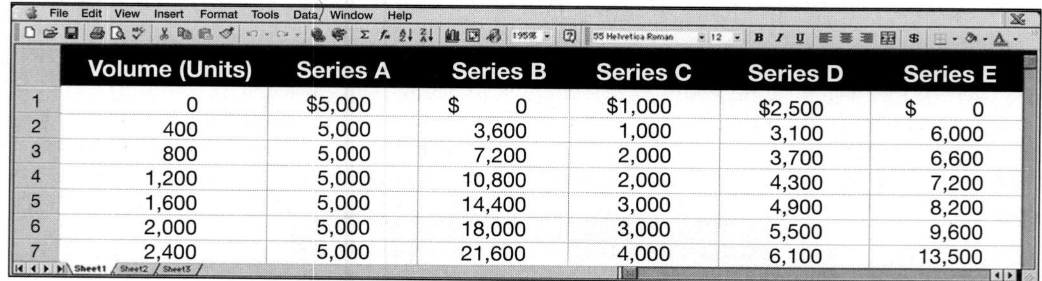

	Volume (Units)	Series A	Series B	Series C	Series D	Series E
1	0	$5,000	$ 0	$1,000	$2,500	$ 0
2	400	5,000	3,600	1,000	3,100	6,000
3	800	5,000	7,200	2,000	3,700	6,600
4	1,200	5,000	10,800	2,000	4,300	7,200
5	1,600	5,000	14,400	3,000	4,900	8,200
6	2,000	5,000	18,000	3,000	5,500	9,600
7	2,400	5,000	21,600	4,000	6,100	13,500

Exercise 22-5
Predicting sales and variable costs using contribution margin
C3

Stewart Company management predicts that it will incur fixed costs of $230,000 and earn pretax income of $350,000 in the next period. Its expected contribution margin ratio is 25%. Use this information to compute the amounts of (1) total dollar sales and (2) total variable costs.

Exercise 22-6
Scatter diagram and measurement of cost behavior
P1

Use the following information about sales and costs to prepare a scatter diagram. Draw a cost line that reflects the behavior displayed by this cost. Determine whether the cost is variable, step-wise, fixed, mixed, or curvilinear.

Period	Sales	Costs	Period	Sales	Costs
1	$1,520	$1,180	9	$1,160	$ 780
2	1,600	1,120	10	640	480
3	400	460	11	480	460
4	800	800	12	1,440	1,100
5	960	780	13	560	520
6	1,240	1,100	14	880	820
7	1,360	1,180	15	760	520
8	1,080	860			

Exercise 22-7
Cost behavior estimation—scatter diagram and high-low
P1

A company reports the following information about its sales and cost of sales. Draw an estimated line of cost behavior using a scatter diagram, and compute fixed costs and variable costs per unit sold. Then use the high-low method to estimate the fixed and variable components of the cost of sales.

Period	Units Sold	Cost of Sales	Period	Units Sold	Cost of Sales
1	0	$2,500	6	2,000	5,500
2	400	3,100	7	2,400	6,100
3	800	3,700	8	2,800	6,700
4	1,200	4,300	9	3,200	7,300
5	1,600	4,900	10	3,600	7,900

Exercise 22-8^A
Measurement of cost behavior using regression
P1

Refer to the information from Exercise 22-7. Use spreadsheet software to use ordinary least-squares regression to estimate the cost equation, including fixed and variable cost amounts.

Exercise 22-9
Contribution margin, break-even, and CVP chart
P2 P3 A2

Seton Company manufactures a single product that sells for $360 per unit and whose total variable costs are $270 per unit. The company's annual fixed costs are $1,125,000. (1) Use this information to compute the company's (a) contribution margin, (b) contribution margin ratio, (c) break-even point in units, and (d) break-even point in dollars of sales. (2) Draw a CVP chart for the company.

Exercise 22-10
Income reporting and break-even analysis
C3

Refer to Exercise 22-9. (1) Prepare a contribution margin income statement for Seton Company showing sales, variable costs, and fixed costs at the break-even point. (2) If the company's fixed costs increase by $270,000, what amount of sales (in dollars) is needed to break even? Explain.

Exercise 22-11
Computing sales to achieve target income
C3

Seton Company management (in Exercise 22-9) targets an annual after-tax income of $1,620,000. The company is subject to a 20% income tax rate. Assume that fixed costs remain at $1,125,000. Compute the (1) unit sales to earn the target after-tax net income and (2) dollar sales to earn the target after-tax net income.

Exercise 22-12
Forecasted income statement
C3

Seton Company sales manager (in Exercise 22-9) predicts that annual sales of the company's product will soon reach 80,000 units and its price will increase to $400 per unit. According to the production manager, the variable costs are expected to increase to $280 per unit but fixed costs will remain at $1,125,000. The income tax rate is 20%. What amounts of pretax and after-tax income can the company expect to earn from these predicted changes? (*Hint:* Prepare a forecasted contribution margin income statement as in Exhibit 22.20.)

Check Forecasted income, $6,780,000

Exercise 22-13
Predicting unit and dollar sales
C3

Maya Company management predicts $600,000 of variable costs, $700,000 of fixed costs, and a pretax income of $110,000 in the next period. Management also predicts that the contribution margin per unit will be $9. Use this information to compute the (1) total expected dollar sales for next period and (2) number of units expected to be sold next period.

Exercise 22-14
Computation of variable and fixed costs; CVP chart
P3

Corveau Company expects to sell 400,000 units of its product next year, which would generate total sales of $34 million. Management predicts that pretax net income for next year will be $2,500,000 and that the contribution margin per unit will be $50. (1) Use this information to compute next year's total expected (a) variable costs and (b) fixed costs. (2) Prepare a CVP chart from this information.

Exercise 22-15
CVP analysis using composite units P4

Check (3) 1,500 units

Modern Home sells windows and doors in the ratio of 9:1 (windows:doors). The selling price of each window is $90 and of each door is $250. The variable cost of a window is $60 and of a door is $220. Fixed costs are $450,000. Use this information to determine the (1) selling price per composite unit, (2) variable costs per composite unit, (3) break-even point in composite units, and (4) number of units of each product that will be sold at the break-even point.

Exercise 22-16
CVP analysis using weighted-average contribution margin
P4

Refer to the information from Exercise 22-15. Use the information to determine the (1) weighted-average contribution margin, (2) break-even point in units, and (3) number of units of each product that will be sold at the break-even point.

Exercise 22-17
CVP analysis using composite units
P4

Precision Tax Service offers tax and consulting services to individuals and small businesses. Data for fees and costs of three types of tax returns follow. Precision provides services in the ratio of 5:3:2 (easy, moderate, business). Fixed costs total $18,000 for the tax season. Use this information to determine the (1) selling price per composite unit, (2) variable costs per composite unit, (3) break-even point in composite units, and (4) number of units of each product that will be sold at the break-even point.

Type of Return	Fee Charged	Variable Cost per Return
Easy (form 1040EZ)	$ 50	$ 30
Moderate (form 1040)	125	75
Business	275	100

Exercise 22-18
CVP analysis using weighted-average contribution margin
P4

Refer to the information from Exercise 22-17. Use the information to determine the (1) weighted-average contribution margin, (2) break-even point in units, and (3) number of units of each product that will be sold at the break-even point.

Exercise 22-19
Operating leverage computed and applied
A3 

Company A is a manufacturer with current sales of $1,500,000 and a 60% contribution margin. Its fixed costs equal $650,000. Company B is a consulting firm with current service revenues of $1,500,000 and a 25% contribution margin. Its fixed costs equal $125,000. Compute the degree of operating leverage (DOL) for each company. Identify which company benefits more from a 20% increase in sales and explain why.

McGraw-Hill's HOMEWORK MANAGER® Available with McGraw-Hill's Homework Manager

PROBLEM SET A

Problem 22-1A
Contribution margin income statement and contribution margin ratio
A2

The following costs result from the production and sale of 2,000 drum sets manufactured by Harris Drum Company for the year ended December 31, 2009. The drum sets sell for $500 each. The company has a 25% income tax rate.

Variable production costs	
Plastic for casing	$ 34,000
Wages of assembly workers	164,000
Drum stands	52,000
Variable selling costs	
Sales commissions	30,000
Fixed manufacturing costs	
Taxes on factory	10,000
Factory maintenance	20,000
Factory machinery depreciation	80,000
Fixed selling and administrative costs	
Lease of equipment for sales staff	20,000
Accounting staff salaries	70,000
Administrative management salaries	250,000

Check (1) Net income, $202,500

Required

1. Prepare a contribution margin income statement for the company.
2. Compute its contribution margin per unit and its contribution margin ratio.

Analysis Component

3. Interpret the contribution margin and contribution margin ratio from part 2.

Problem 22-2A
CVP analysis and charting
P2 P3

mhhe.com/wildFAP19e

Extreme Equipment Co. manufactures and markets a number of rope products. Management is considering the future of Product HG, a special rope for hang gliding, that has not been as profitable as planned. Since Product HG is manufactured and marketed independently of the other products, its total costs can be precisely measured. Next year's plans call for a $200 selling price per 100 yards of HG rope. Its fixed costs for the year are expected to be $330,000, up to a maximum capacity of 20,000,000 yards of rope. Forecasted variable costs are $170 per 100 yards of HG rope.

Required

1. Estimate Product HG's break-even point in terms of (a) sales units and (b) sales dollars.
2. Prepare a CVP chart for Product HG like that in Exhibit 22.14. Use 20,000,000 yards as the maximum number of sales units on the horizontal axis of the graph, and $4,000,000 as the maximum dollar amount on the vertical axis.
3. Prepare a contribution margin income statement showing sales, variable costs, and fixed costs for Product HG at the break-even point.

Check (1) Break-even sales, 11,000 units or $2,200,000

Problem 22-3A
Scatter diagram and cost behavior estimation
P1

Alden Co.'s monthly sales and cost data for its operating activities of the past year follow. Management wants to use these data to predict future fixed and variable costs.

Period	Sales	Total Cost	Period	Sales	Total Cost
1	$325,000	$162,500	7	$355,000	$242,000
2	170,000	106,250	8	275,000	156,750
3	270,000	210,600	9	75,000	60,000
4	210,000	105,000	10	155,000	135,625
5	295,000	206,500	11	99,000	99,000
6	195,000	117,000	12	105,000	76,650

Required

1. Prepare a scatter diagram for these data with sales volume (in $) plotted on the horizontal axis and total cost plotted on the vertical axis.
2. Estimate both the variable costs per sales dollar and the total monthly fixed costs using the high-low method. Draw the total costs line on the scatter diagram in part 1.
3. Use the estimated line of cost behavior and results from part 2 to predict future total costs when sales volume is (a) $210,000 and (b) $300,000.

Check (2) Variable costs, $0.65 per sales dollar; fixed costs, $11,250

Problem 22-4A
Break-even analysis; income targeting and forecasting
C3 P2

Teller Co. sold 20,000 units of its only product and incurred a $70,000 loss (ignoring taxes) for the current year as shown here. During a planning session for year 2010's activities, the production manager notes that variable costs can be reduced 50% by installing a machine that automates several operations. To obtain these savings, the company must increase its annual fixed costs by $210,000. The maximum output capacity of the company is 40,000 units per year.

TELLER COMPANY Contribution Margin Income Statement For Year Ended December 31, 2009	
Sales	$1,000,000
Variable costs	800,000
Contribution margin	200,000
Fixed costs	270,000
Net loss	$ (70,000)

Required

1. Compute the break-even point in dollar sales for year 2009.
2. Compute the predicted break-even point in dollar sales for year 2010 assuming the machine is installed and there is no change in the unit sales price.
3. Prepare a forecasted contribution margin income statement for 2010 that shows the expected results with the machine installed. Assume that the unit sales price and the number of units sold will not change, and no income taxes will be due.
4. Compute the sales level required in both dollars and units to earn $210,000 of after-tax income in 2010 with the machine installed and no change in the unit sales price. Assume that the income tax rate is 30%. (*Hint:* Use the procedures in Exhibits 22.21 and 22.23.)
5. Prepare a forecasted contribution margin income statement that shows the results at the sales level computed in part 4. Assume an income tax rate of 30%.

Check (3) Net income, $120,000

(4) Required sales, $1,300,000 or 26,000 units

(5) Net income, $210,000

Problem 22-5A
Break-even analysis, different cost structures, and income calculations
C3

Shol Co. produces and sells two products, T and O. It manufactures these products in separate factories and markets them through different channels. They have no shared costs. This year, the company sold 51,000 units of each product. Sales and costs for each product follow.

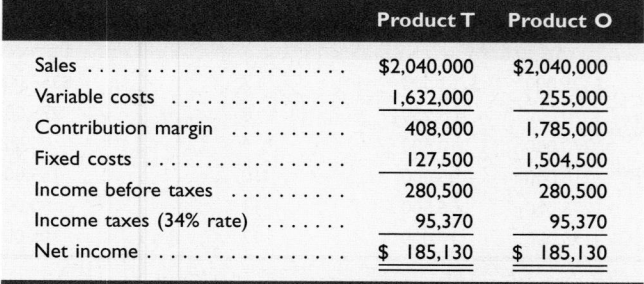

	Product T	Product O
Sales	$2,040,000	$2,040,000
Variable costs	1,632,000	255,000
Contribution margin	408,000	1,785,000
Fixed costs	127,500	1,504,500
Income before taxes	280,500	280,500
Income taxes (34% rate)	95,370	95,370
Net income	$ 185,130	$ 185,130

Required

1. Compute the break-even point in dollar sales for each product.

2. Assume that the company expects sales of each product to decline to 40,000 units next year with no change in unit sales price. Prepare forecasted financial results for next year following the format of the contribution margin income statement as just shown with columns for each of the two products (assume a 34% tax rate). Also, assume that any loss before taxes yields a 34% tax savings.

Check (2) After-tax income: T, $127,050; O, $(68,970)

3. Assume that the company expects sales of each product to increase to 65,000 units next year with no change in unit sales price. Prepare forecasted financial results for next year following the format of the contribution margin income statement shown with columns for each of the two products (assume a 34% tax rate).

(3) After-tax income: T, $259,050; O, $508,530

Analysis Component

4. If sales greatly decrease, which product would experience a greater loss? Explain.

5. Describe some factors that might have created the different cost structures for these two products.

Problem 22-6A
Analysis of price, cost, and volume changes for contribution margin and net income

C3 P2

excel

mhhe.com/wildFAP19e

This year Calypso Company sold 60,000 units of its only product for $20 per unit. Manufacturing and selling the product required $97,500 of fixed manufacturing costs and $157,500 of fixed selling and administrative costs. Its per unit variable costs follow.

Material	$8.00
Direct labor (paid on the basis of completed units)	5.00
Variable overhead costs	1.60
Variable selling and administrative costs	0.40

Next year the company will use new material, which will reduce material costs by 50% and direct labor costs by 60% and will not affect product quality or marketability. Management is considering an increase in the unit sales price to reduce the number of units sold because the factory's output is nearing its annual output capacity of 65,000 units. Two plans are being considered. Under plan 1, the company will keep the price at the current level and sell the same volume as last year. This plan will increase income because of the reduced costs from using the new material. Under plan 2, the company will increase price by 25%. This plan will decrease unit sales volume by 15%. Under both plans 1 and 2, the total fixed costs and the variable costs per unit for overhead and for selling and administrative costs will remain the same.

Required

1. Compute the break-even point in dollar sales for both (a) plan 1 and (b) plan 2.

Check (1) Breakeven: Plan 1, $425,000; Plan 2, $375,000

2. Prepare a forecasted contribution margin income statement with two columns showing the expected results of plan 1 and plan 2. The statements should report sales, total variable costs, contribution margin, total fixed costs, income before taxes, income taxes (30% rate), and net income.

(2) Net income: Plan 1, $325,500; Plan 2, $428,400

Problem 22-7A
Break-even analysis with composite units

P4 C3

Patriot Co. manufactures and sells three products: red, white, and blue. Their unit sales prices are red, $74; white, $108; and blue, $99. The per unit variable costs to manufacture and sell these products are red, $48; white, $75; and blue, $90. Their sales mix is reflected in a ratio of 5:4:2 (red:white:blue). Annual fixed costs shared by all three products are $179,200. One type of raw material has been used to manufacture all three products. The company has developed a new material of equal quality for less cost. The new material would reduce variable costs per unit as follows: red, by $10; white, by $16; and blue, by $13. However, the new material requires new equipment, which will increase annual fixed costs by $22,400. (Round answers to whole composite units.)

Required

1. If the company continues to use the old material, determine its break-even point in both sales units and sales dollars of each individual product.

Check (1) Old plan breakeven, 640 composite units

2. If the company uses the new material, determine its new break-even point in both sales units and sales dollars of each individual product.

(2) New plan breakeven, 480 composite units

Analysis Component

3. What insight does this analysis offer management for long-term planning?

PROBLEM SET B

Problem 22-1B
Contribution margin income statement and contribution margin ratio

A2

The following costs result from the production and sale of 240,000 CD sets manufactured by Jawan Company for the year ended December 31, 2009. The CD sets sell for $9 each. The company has a 25% income tax rate.

Variable manufacturing costs	
Plastic for CD sets	$ 21,600
Wages of assembly workers	300,000
Labeling	43,200
Variable selling costs	
Sales commissions	24,000
Fixed manufacturing costs	
Rent on factory	100,000
Factory cleaning service	75,000
Factory machinery depreciation	125,000
Fixed selling and administrative costs	
Lease of office equipment	120,000
Systems staff salaries	600,000
Administrative management salaries	300,000

Required

Check (1) Net income, $338,400

1. Prepare a contribution margin income statement for the company.

2. Compute its contribution margin per unit and its contribution margin ratio.

Analysis Component

3. Interpret the contribution margin and contribution margin ratio from part 2.

Problem 22-2B
CVP analysis and charting

P2 P3

Tip-Top Co. manufactures and markets several products. Management is considering the future of one product, electronic keyboards, that has not been as profitable as planned. Since this product is manufactured and marketed independently of the other products, its total costs can be precisely measured. Next year's plans call for a $175 selling price per unit. The fixed costs for the year are expected to be $420,000, up to a maximum capacity of 10,000 units. Forecasted variable costs are $105 per unit.

Required

Check (1) Break-even sales, 6,000 units or $1,050,000

1. Estimate the keyboards' break-even point in terms of (a) sales units and (b) sales dollars.

2. Prepare a CVP chart for keyboards like that in Exhibit 22.14. Use 10,000 keyboards as the maximum number of sales units on the horizontal axis of the graph, and $1,600,000 as the maximum dollar amount on the vertical axis.

3. Prepare a contribution margin income statement showing sales, variable costs, and fixed costs for keyboards at the break-even point.

Problem 22-3B
Scatter diagram and cost behavior estimation

P1

Merdam Co.'s monthly sales and costs data for its operating activities of the past year follow. Management wants to use these data to predict future fixed and variable costs.

Period	Sales	Total Cost	Period	Sales	Total Cost
1	$390	$194	7	$290	$186
2	250	174	8	370	210
3	210	146	9	270	170
4	310	178	10	170	116
5	190	162	11	350	190
6	430	220	12	230	158

Required

1. Prepare a scatter diagram for these data with sales volume (in $) plotted on the horizontal axis and total costs plotted on the vertical axis.

2. Estimate both the variable costs per sales dollar and the total monthly fixed costs using the high-low method. Draw the total costs line on the scatter diagram in part 1.

3. Use the estimated line of cost behavior and results from part 2 to predict future total costs when sales volume is (a) $200 and (b) $340.

Check (2) Variable costs, $0.40 per sales dollar; fixed costs, $48

Problem 22-4B
Break-even analysis; income targeting and forecasting
C3 P2

Noru Co. sold 30,000 units of its only product and incurred a $75,000 loss (ignoring taxes) for the current year as shown here. During a planning session for year 2010's activities, the production manager notes that variable costs can be reduced 40% by installing a machine that automates several operations. To obtain these savings, the company must increase its annual fixed costs by $220,000. The maximum output capacity of the company is 50,000 units per year.

NORU COMPANY Contribution Margin Income Statement For Year Ended December 31, 2009	
Sales	$1,125,000
Variable costs	900,000
Contribution margin	225,000
Fixed costs	300,000
Net loss	$ (75,000)

Required

1. Compute the break-even point in dollar sales for year 2009.

2. Compute the predicted break-even point in dollar sales for year 2010 assuming the machine is installed and no change occurs in the unit sales price. (Round the change in variable costs to a whole number.)

3. Prepare a forecasted contribution margin income statement for 2010 that shows the expected results with the machine installed. Assume that the unit sales price and the number of units sold will not change, and no income taxes will be due.

Check (3) Net income, $65,000

4. Compute the sales level required in both dollars and units to earn $104,000 of after-tax income in 2010 with the machine installed and no change in the unit sales price. Assume that the income tax rate is 20%. (*Hint:* Use the procedures in Exhibits 22.21 and 22.23.)

(4) Required sales, $1,250,000 or 33,334 units

5. Prepare a forecasted contribution margin income statement that shows the results at the sales level computed in part 4. Assume an income tax rate of 20%.

(5) Net income, $104,000 (rounded)

Problem 22-5B
Break-even analysis, different cost structures, and income calculations
C3 

Best Co. produces and sells two products, BB and TT. It manufactures these products in separate factories and markets them through different channels. They have no shared costs. This year, the company sold 100,000 units of each product. Sales and costs for each product follow.

	Product BB	Product TT
Sales	$1,600,000	$1,600,000
Variable costs	1,120,000	200,000
Contribution margin	480,000	1,400,000
Fixed costs	200,000	1,120,000
Income before taxes	280,000	280,000
Income taxes (32% rate)	89,600	89,600
Net income	$ 190,400	$ 190,400

Required

1. Compute the break-even point in dollar sales for each product.

2. Assume that the company expects sales of each product to decline to 67,000 units next year with no change in the unit sales price. Prepare forecasted financial results for next year following the format of the contribution margin income statement as shown here with columns for each of the two products (assume a 32% tax rate, and that any loss before taxes yields a 32% tax savings).

Check (2) After-tax income: BB, $82,688; TT, $(123,760)

3. Assume that the company expects sales of each product to increase to 125,000 units next year with no change in the unit sales prices. Prepare forecasted financial results for next year following the format of the contribution margin income statement as shown here with columns for each of the two products (assume a 32% tax rate).

(3) After-tax income: BB, $272,000; TT, $428,400

Analysis Component

4. If sales greatly increase, which product would experience a greater increase in profit? Explain.

5. Describe some factors that might have created the different cost structures for these two products.

Problem 22-6B
Analysis of price, cost, and volume changes for contribution margin and net income
C3 P2

This year Blanko Company earned a disappointing 3.85% after-tax return on sales (Net income/Sales) from marketing 50,000 units of its only product. The company buys its product in bulk and repackages it for resale at the price of $20 per unit. Blanko incurred the following costs this year.

Total variable unit costs	$400,000
Total variable packaging costs	50,000
Fixed costs	$495,000
Income tax rate	30%

The marketing manager claims that next year's results will be the same as this year's unless some changes are made. The manager predicts the company can increase the number of units sold by 60% if it reduces the selling price by 20% and upgrades the packaging. This change would increase variable packaging costs by 20%. Increased sales would allow the company to take advantage of a 25% quantity purchase discount on the cost of the bulk product. Neither the packaging change nor the volume discount would affect fixed costs, which provide an annual output capacity of 100,000 units.

Required

Check (1) Breakeven for new strategy, $900,000

(2) Net income: Existing strategy, $38,500; new strategy, $146,300

1. Compute the break-even point in dollar sales under the (a) existing business strategy and (b) new strategy that alters both unit sales price and variable costs.

2. Prepare a forecasted contribution margin income statement with two columns showing the expected results of (a) the existing strategy and (b) changing to the new strategy. The statements should report sales, total variable costs (unit and packaging), contribution margin, fixed costs, income before taxes, income taxes, and net income. Also determine the after-tax return on sales for these two strategies.

Problem 22-7B
Break-even analysis with composite units
P4 C3 

Milagro Co. manufactures and sells three products: product 1, product 2, and product 3. Their unit sales prices are product 1, $200; product 2, $150; and product 3, $100. The per unit variable costs to manufacture and sell these products are product 1, $150; product 2, $75; and product 3, $40. Their sales mix is reflected in a ratio of 6:4:2. Annual fixed costs shared by all three products are $5,400,000. One type of raw material has been used to manufacture products 1 and 2. The company has developed a new material of equal quality for less cost. The new material would reduce variable costs per unit as follows: product 1 by $50, and product 2, by $25. However, the new material requires new equipment, which will increase annual fixed costs by $200,000.

Required

Check (1) Old plan breakeven, 7,500 composite units

(2) New plan breakeven, 5,000 composite units

1. If the company continues to use the old material, determine its break-even point in both sales units and sales dollars of each individual product.

2. If the company uses the new material, determine its new break-even point in both sales units and sales dollars of each individual product.

Analysis Component

3. What insight does this analysis offer management for long-term planning?

SERIAL PROBLEM

Success Systems

(This serial problem began in Chapter 1 and continues through most of the book. If previous chapter segments were not completed, the serial problem can begin at this point. It is helpful, but not necessary, to use the working papers that accompany the book.)

SP 22 Success Systems sells upscale modular desk units and office chairs in the ratio of 3:2 (desk unit:chair). The selling prices are $1,250 per desk unit and $500 per chair. The variable costs are $750 per desk unit and $250 per chair. Fixed costs are $120,000.

Required

1. Compute the selling price per composite unit.
2. Compute the variable costs per composite unit.
3. Compute the break-even point in composite units.
4. Compute the number of units of each product that would be sold at the break-even point.

Check (3) 60 composite units

BEYOND THE NUMBERS

REPORTING IN ACTION

C1

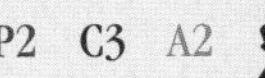

BTN 22-1 **Best Buy** offers services to customers that help them use products they purchase from Best Buy. One of these services is its Geek Squad, which is Best Buy's 24-hour computer support task force. As you complete the following requirements, assume that the Geek Squad uses many of Best Buy's existing resources such as its purchasing department and its buildings and equipment.

Required

1. Identify several of the variable, mixed, and fixed costs that the Geek Squad is likely to incur in carrying out its services.
2. Assume that Geek Squad revenues are expected to grow by 25% in the next year. How do you expect the costs identified in part 1 to change, if at all?
3. How is your answer to part 2 different from many of the examples discussed in the chapter? (*Hint:* Consider how the contribution margin ratio changes as volume—sales or customers served—increases.)

COMPARATIVE ANALYSIS

P2 C3 A2

BTN 22-2 Both **Best Buy** and **Circuit City** sell numerous consumer products, and each of these companies has a different product mix.

Required

1. Assume the following data are available for both companies. Compute each company's break-even point in unit sales. (Each company sells many products at many different selling prices, and each has its own variable costs. This assignment assumes an *average* selling price per unit and an *average* cost per item.)

	Best Buy	Circuit City
Average selling price per item sold	$90	$40
Average variable cost per item sold	$64	$30
Total fixed costs	$5,980 million	$2,570 million

2. If unit sales were to decline, which company would experience the larger decline in operating profit? Explain.

ETHICS CHALLENGE

C1

BTN 22-3 Labor costs of an auto repair mechanic are seldom based on actual hours worked. Instead, the amount paid a mechanic is based on an industry average of time estimated to complete a repair job. The repair shop bills the customer for the industry average amount of time at the repair center's billable cost per hour. This means a customer can pay, for example, $120 for two hours of work on a car when the actual time worked was only one hour. Many experienced mechanics can complete repair jobs faster than the industry average. The average data are compiled by engineering studies and surveys conducted in the auto repair business. Assume that you are asked to complete such a survey for a repair center. The survey calls for objective input, and many questions require detailed cost data and analysis. The mechanics and owners know you have the survey and encourage you to complete it in a way that increases the average billable hours for repair work.

Required

Write a one-page memorandum to the mechanics and owners that describes the direct labor analysis you will undertake in completing this survey.

COMMUNICATING IN PRACTICE

C2

BTN 22-4 Several important assumptions underlie CVP analysis. Assumptions often help simplify and focus our analysis of sales and costs. A common application of CVP analysis is as a tool to forecast sales, costs, and income.

Required

Assume that you are actively searching for a job. Prepare a one-half page report identifying (1) three assumptions relating to your expected revenue (salary) and (2) three assumptions relating to your expected costs for the first year of your new job. Be prepared to discuss your assumptions in class.

TAKING IT TO THE NET

C1 C3 

BTN 22-5 Access and review the entrepreneurial information at **Business Owner's Toolkit** [Toolkit.cch.com]. Access and review its *New Business Cash Needs Estimate* under the Business Tools/Business Finance menu bar or similar worksheets related to controls of cash and costs.

Required

Write a one-half page report that describes the information and resources available at the Business Owner's Toolkit to help the owner of a start-up business to control and monitor its costs.

TEAMWORK IN ACTION

C2

BTN 22-6 A local movie theater owner explains to you that ticket sales on weekends and evenings are strong, but attendance during the weekdays, Monday through Thursday, is poor. The owner proposes to offer a contract to the local grade school to show educational materials at the theater for a set charge per student during school hours. The owner asks your help to prepare a CVP analysis listing the cost and sales projections for the proposal. The owner must propose to the school's administration a charge per child. At a minimum, the charge per child needs to be sufficient for the theater to break even.

Required

Your team is to prepare two separate lists of questions that enable you to complete a reliable CVP analysis of this situation. One list is to be answered by the school's administration, the other by the owner of the movie theater.

ENTREPRENEURIAL DECISION

C1  

BTN 22-7 Martin Sprock is a diligent businessman. He continually searches for new menu items to further increase the profitability of **Moe's Southwest Grill**.

Required

1. What information should Sprock search for to help him decide whether to add new menu items or other products to existing Moe's product lines?
2. What managerial tools are available to Sprock to help make the decisions in part 1?

HITTING THE ROAD

P4 

BTN 22-8 Multiproduct break-even analysis is often viewed differently when actually applied in practice. You are to visit a local fast-food restaurant and count the number of items on the menu. To apply multiproduct break-even analysis to the restaurant, similar menu items must often be fit into groups. A reasonable approach is to classify menu items into approximately five groups. We then estimate average selling price and average variable cost to compute average contribution margin. (*Hint:* For fast-food restaurants, the highest contribution margin is with its beverages, at about 90%.)

Required

1. Prepare a one-year multiproduct break-even analysis for the restaurant you visit. Begin by establishing groups. Next, estimate each group's volume and contribution margin. These estimates are necessary to compute each group's contribution margin. Assume that annual fixed costs in total are \$500,000 per year. (*Hint:* You must develop your own estimates on volume and contribution margin for each group to obtain the break-even point and sales.)
2. Prepare a one-page report on the results of your analysis. Comment on the volume of sales necessary to break even at a fast-food restaurant.

BTN 22-9 Access and review DSG's Website (www.DSGiplc.com) to answer the following questions.

GLOBAL DECISION

C3

DSG

1. Do you believe that DSG's managers use single product CVP analysis or multiproduct break-even point analysis? Explain.
2. How does the addition of a new product line affect DSG's CVP analysis?
3. How does the addition of a new store affect DSG's CVP analysis?

ANSWERS TO MULTIPLE CHOICE QUIZ

1. a; \$150 − \$100 = \$50
2. e; (\$150 − \$100)/\$150 = 33⅓%
3. c; \$75,000/\$50 CM per unit = 1,500 units
4. b; \$300,000 − \$180,000 = \$120,000
5. c; Contribution margin ratio = (\$400 − \$260)/\$400 = 0.35
   Targeted sales = (\$840,000 + \$70,000)/0.35 = \$2,600,000

A Look Back

Chapter 22 looked at cost behavior and its use by managers in performing cost-volume-profit analysis. It also illustrated the application of cost-volume-profit analysis.

A Look at This Chapter

This chapter explains the importance of budgeting and describes the master budget and its preparation. It also discusses the value of the master budget to the planning of future business activities.

A Look Ahead

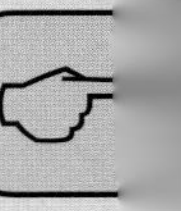

Chapter 24 focuses on flexible budgets, standard costs, and variance reporting. It explains the usefulness of these procedures and reports for business decisions.

Chapter 23 Master Budgets and Planning

Learning Objectives

CAP

Conceptual

C1 Describe the importance and benefits of budgeting. *(p. 940)*

C2 Explain the process of budget administration. *(p. 942)*

C3 Describe a master budget and the process of preparing it. *(p. 944)*

Analytical

A1 Analyze expense planning using activity-based budgeting. *(p. 953)*

LP23

Procedural

P1 Prepare each component of a master budget and link each to the budgeting process. *(p. 946)*

P2 Link both operating and capital expenditures budgets to budgeted financial statements. *(p. 950)*

P3 *Appendix 23A*—Prepare production and manufacturing budgets. *(p. 959)*

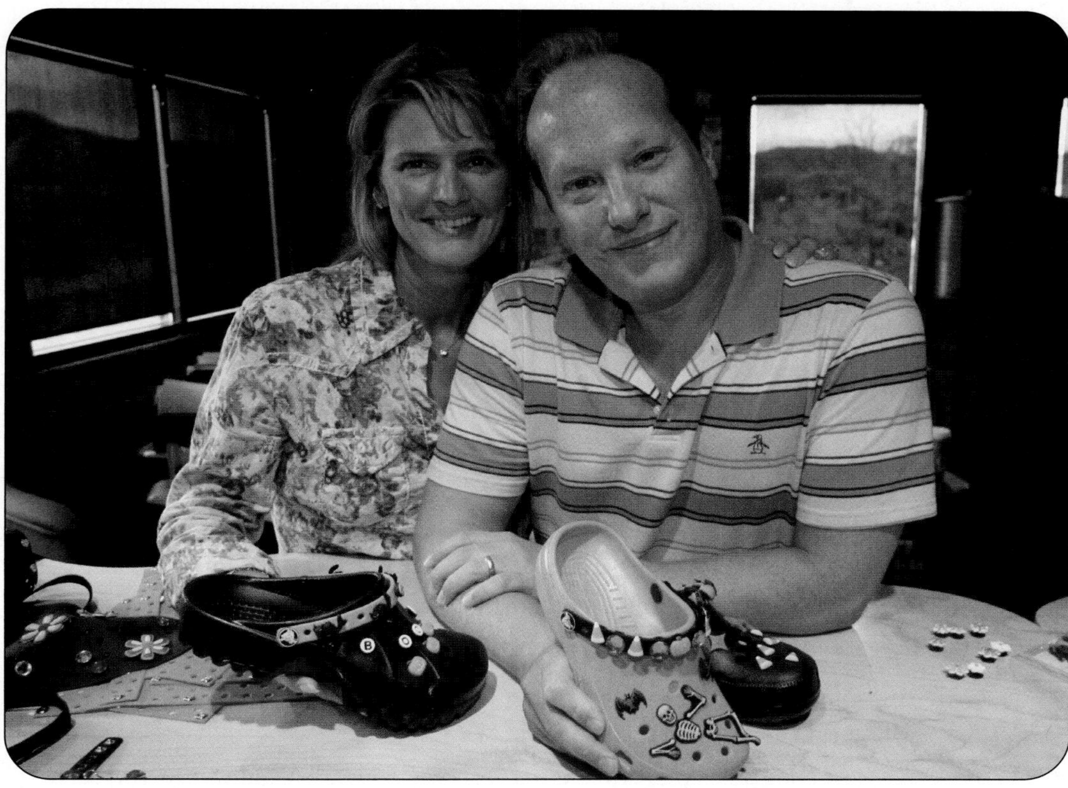

Decision Feature

Lucky Charms

"The Number One thing is you have got to take the chance"—Rich Schmelzer

BOULDER, CO—Each pair of Crocs **(Crocs.com)** shoes includes ventilation holes for breathability and to filter water out. Sheri Schmelzer and her kids thought it more fun to use clay and rhinestones to decorate the holes with fun charms. Sheri's husband Rich, an entrepreneur, immediately saw the profit potential—within 48 hours the Schmelzer's had filed patents for the design of Jibbitz **(Jibbitz.com),** which are small accessories made to fit in the holes of Crocs. Today, Jibbitz accessories come in various shapes and sizes, and include more than 1100 designs such as peace signs, flowers, musical notes, sports gear, and letters to spell out words.

Jibbitz started small, with an assembly line in the family's basement and a Website to process orders. Like many new businesses, Jibbitz began with few formal budgets or plans. "We didn't write a business plan" admits Sheri. Rich explains "We recalibrated our business every week depending on what we sold. We were very nimble." Soon, Jibbitz was processing hundreds of orders per day. "It turned from a very simple business to a very complex business," says Rich.

As business grew, master budgets and the budgeting process became more important. Budgets helped formalize business plans and goals, and helped direct employees—a team of staff designers and warehouse personnel in Boulder, and a manufacturing group in Asia. Realizing that a too-rapid sales growth could strain its capacity to meet customer expectations, Jibbitz avoids advertising and has turned down some large retailers' bids to carry its products. An understanding of sales budgets and their link to expense budgets was vital in making these decisions. Likewise, production and manufacturing budgets helped plan for use of materials, labor, and overhead.

Eventually, Rich and Sheri teamed up with Crocs. Now operating as a division within Crocs, budgeting remains important. If Jibbitz meets certain sales and income targets, Rich and Sheri will receive an additional payment from Crocs. Linking their budgeted data to budgeted income statements, and using that information to control costs, is key to that future payment. Still, both Sheri and Rich stress the importance of having fun and a passion for what they do as keys to success. "I'm having a blast," explains Sheri. "I don't want it to stop."

[Sources: *Jibbitz Website,* January 2009; *Crocs Website,* January 2009; *Crocs 2007 10-K report; Rocky Mountain News,* September 2007; *Ladies Who Launch Magazine,* March 2008; *Business 2.0,* November 2006; *Boulder Daily Camera,* August 2006; *Denverpost.com,* October 2006]

Chapter Preview

Management seeks to turn its strategies into action plans. These action plans include financial details that are compiled in a master budget. The budgeting process serves several purposes, including motivating employees and communicating with them. The budget process also helps coordinate a company's activities toward common goals and is useful in evaluating results and management performance. This chapter explains how to prepare a master budget and use it as a formal plan of a company's future activities. The ability to prepare this type of plan is of enormous help in starting and operating a company. Such planning gives managers a glimpse into the future, and it can help translate ideas into actions.

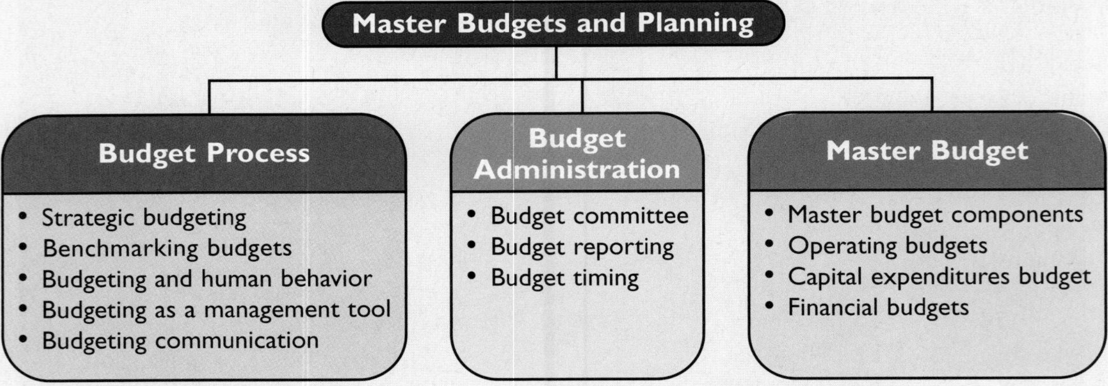

Budget Process

Strategic Budgeting

C1 Describe the importance and benefits of budgeting.

Most companies prepare long-term strategic plans spanning 5 to 10 years. They then fine-tune them in preparing medium-term and short-term plans. Strategic plans usually set a company's long-term direction. They provide a road map for the future about potential opportunities such as new products, markets, and investments. The strategic plan can be inexact, given its long-term focus. Medium- and short-term plans are more operational and translate strategic plans into actions. These action plans are fairly concrete and consist of defined objectives and goals.

Short-term financial plans are called *budgets* and typically cover a one-year period. A **budget** is a formal statement of a company's future plans. It is usually expressed in monetary terms because the economic or financial aspects of the business are the primary factors driving management's decisions. All managers should be involved in **budgeting,** the process of planning future business actions and expressing them as formal plans. Managers who plan carefully and formalize plans in a budgeting process increase the likelihood of both personal and company success. (Although most firms prepare annual budgets, it is not unusual for organizations to prepare three-year and five-year budgets that are revised at least annually.)

Companies Performing Annual Budgeting

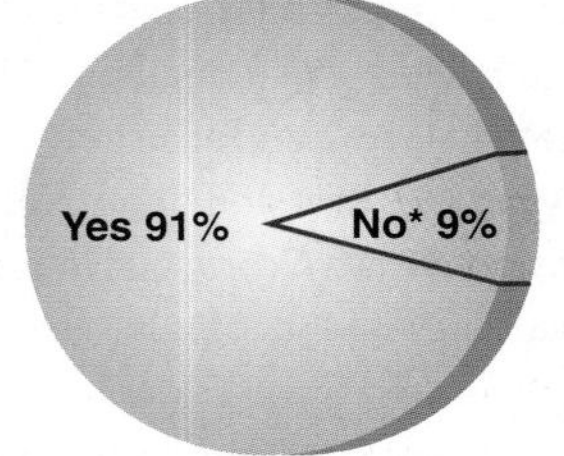

*Most of the 9% have eliminated annual budgeting in favor of rolling or continual budgeting.

The relevant focus of a budgetary analysis is the future. Management must focus on future transactions and events and the opportunities available. A focus on the future is important because the pressures of daily operating problems often divert management's attention and take precedence over planning. A good budgeting system counteracts this tendency by formalizing the planning process and demanding relevant input. Budgeting makes planning an explicit management responsibility.

Benchmarking Budgets

The control function requires management to evaluate (benchmark) business operations against some norm. Evaluation involves comparing actual results against one of two usual alternatives: (1) past performance or (2) expected performance.

An evaluation assists management in identifying problems and taking corrective actions if necessary. Evaluation using expected, or budgeted, performance is potentially superior to using past performance to decide whether actual results trigger a need for corrective actions. This is so because past performance fails to consider several changes that can affect current and future activities. Changes in economic conditions, shifts in competitive advantages within the industry, new product developments, increased or decreased advertising, and other factors reduce the usefulness of comparisons with past results. In hi-tech industries, for instance, increasing competition, technological advances, and other innovations often reduce the usefulness of performance comparisons across years.

Video23.1

Budgeted performance is computed after careful analysis and research that attempts to anticipate and adjust for changes in important company, industry, and economic factors. Therefore, budgets usually provide management an effective control and monitoring system.

Point: Managers can evaluate performance by preparing reports that compare actual results to budgeted plans.

Budgeting and Human Behavior

Budgeting provides standards for evaluating performance and can affect the attitudes of employees evaluated by them. It can be used to create a positive effect on employees' attitudes, but it can also create negative effects if not properly applied. Budgeted levels of performance, for instance, must be realistic to avoid discouraging employees. Personnel who will be evaluated should be consulted and involved in preparing the budget to increase their commitment to meeting it. Performance evaluations must allow the affected employees to explain the reasons for apparent performance deficiencies.

The budgeting process has three important guidelines: (1) Employees affected by a budget should be consulted when it is prepared (*participatory budgeting*), (2) goals reflected in a budget should be attainable, and (3) evaluations should be made carefully with opportunities to explain any failures. Budgeting can be a positive motivating force when these guidelines are followed. Budgeted performance levels can provide goals for employees to attain or even exceed as they carry out their responsibilities. This is especially important in organizations that consider the annual budget a "sacred" document.

Point: The practice of involving employees in the budgeting process is known as *participatory budgeting.*

Decision Insight

Budgets Exposed When companies go public and trade their securities on an organized exchange, management usually develops specific future plans and budgets. For this purpose, companies often develop detailed six- to twelve-month budgets and less-detailed budgets spanning 2 to 5 years.

Budgeting as a Management Tool

An important management objective in large companies is to ensure that activities of all departments contribute to meeting the company's overall goals. This requires coordination. Budgeting provides a way to achieve this coordination.

We describe later in this chapter that a company's budget, or operating plan, is based on its objectives. This operating plan starts with the sales budget, which drives all other budgets including production, materials, labor, and overhead. The budgeting process coordinates the activities of these various departments to meet the company's overall goals.

Budgeting Communication

Managers of small companies can adequately explain business plans directly to employees through conversations and other informal communications. However, conversations can create uncertainty and confusion if not supported by clear documentation of the plans. A written budget is preferred and can inform employees in all types of organizations about management's plans. The budget can also communicate management's specific action plans for the employees in the budget period.

Decision Ethics

Budget Staffer Your company's earnings for the current period will be far below the budgeted amount reported in the press. One of your superiors, who is aware of the upcoming earnings shortfall, has accepted a management position with a competitor. This superior is selling her shares of the company. What are your ethical concerns, if any? [Answer—p. 961]

Budget Administration

Budget Committee

C2 Explain the process of budget administration.

The task of preparing a budget should not be the sole responsibility of any one department. Similarly, the budget should not be simply handed down as top management's final word. Instead, budget figures and budget estimates developed through a *bottom-up* process usually are more useful. This includes, for instance, involving the sales department in preparing sales estimates. Likewise, the production department should have initial responsibility for preparing its own expense budget. Without active employee involvement in preparing budget figures, there is a risk these employees will feel that the numbers fail to reflect their special problems and needs.

Most budgets should be developed by a bottom-up process, but the budgeting system requires central guidance. This guidance is supplied by a budget committee of department heads and other executives responsible for seeing that budgeted amounts are realistic and coordinated. If a department submits initial budget figures not reflecting efficient performance, the budget committee should return them with explanatory comments on how to improve them. Then the originating department must either adjust its proposals or explain why they are acceptable. Communication between the originating department and the budget committee should continue as needed to ensure that both parties accept the budget as reasonable, attainable, and desirable.

Point: In a large company, developing a budget through a bottom-up process can involve hundreds of employees and take several weeks to finalize.

The concept of continuous improvement applies to budgeting as well as production. BP, one of the world's largest energy companies, streamlined its monthly budget report from a one-inch-thick stack of monthly control reports to a tidy, two-page flash report on monthly earnings and key production statistics. The key to this efficiency gain was the integration of new budgeting and cost allocation processes with its strategic planning process. BP's controller explained the new role of the finance department with respect to the budgetary control process as follows: "there's less of an attitude that finance's job is to control. People really have come to see that our job is to help attain business objectives."

Budget Reporting

The budget period usually coincides with the accounting period. Most companies prepare at least an annual budget, which reflects the objectives for the next year. To provide specific guidance, the annual budget usually is separated into quarterly or monthly budgets. These short-term budgets allow management to periodically evaluate performance and take needed corrective action.

Managers can compare actual results to budgeted amounts in a report such as that shown in Exhibit 23.1. This report shows actual amounts, budgeted amounts, and their differences. A difference is called a *variance*. Management examines variances to identify areas for improvement and corrective action.

Budget Timing

The time period required for the annual budgeting process can vary considerably. For example, budgeting for 2010 can begin as early as January 2009 or as late as December 2009. Large, complex organizations usually require a longer time to prepare their budgets than do smaller organizations. This is so because considerable effort is required to coordinate the different units (departments) within large organizations.

Companies Using Rolling Budgets

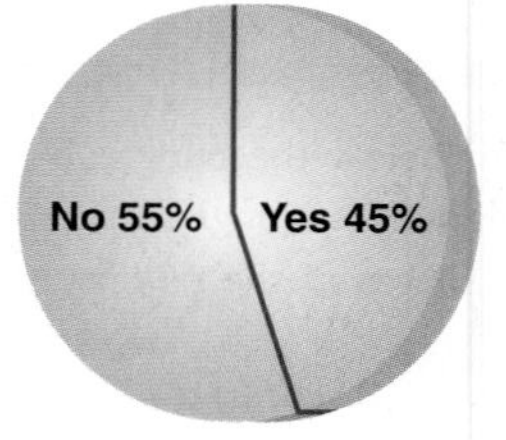

Many companies apply **continuous budgeting** by preparing **rolling budgets.** As each monthly or quarterly budget period goes by, these companies revise their entire set of budgets for the months or quarters remaining and add new monthly or quarterly budgets to replace the ones that have lapsed. At any point in time, monthly or quarterly budgets are available for the next

EXHIBIT 23.1

Comparing Actual Performance with Budgeted Performance

ECCENTRIC MUSIC Income Statement with Variations from Budget For Month Ended April 30, 2009	Actual	Budget	Variance
Net sales	$60,500	$57,150	$+3,350
Cost of goods sold	41,350	39,100	+2,250
Gross profit	19,150	18,050	+1,100
Operating expenses			
Selling expenses			
Sales salaries	6,250	6,000	+250
Advertising	900	800	+100
Store supplies	550	500	+50
Depreciation—Store equipment	1,600	1,600	
Total selling expenses	9,300	8,900	+400
General and administrative expenses			
Office salaries	2,000	2,000	
Office supplies used	165	150	+15
Rent	1,100	1,100	
Insurance	200	200	
Depreciation—Office equipment	100	100	
Total general and administrative expenses	3,565	3,550	+15
Total operating expenses	12,865	12,450	+415
Net income	$ 6,285	$ 5,600	$ +685

Example: Assume that you must explain variances to top management. Which variances in Exhibit 23.1 would you research and why? *Answer:* Sales and cost of goods sold—due to their large variances.

12 months or four quarters. Exhibit 23.2 shows rolling budgets prepared at the end of five consecutive periods. The first set (at top) is prepared in December 2008 and covers the four calendar quarters of 2009. In March 2009, the company prepares another rolling budget for the next four quarters through March 2010. This same process is repeated every three months. As a result, management is continuously planning ahead.

EXHIBIT 23.2

Rolling Budgets

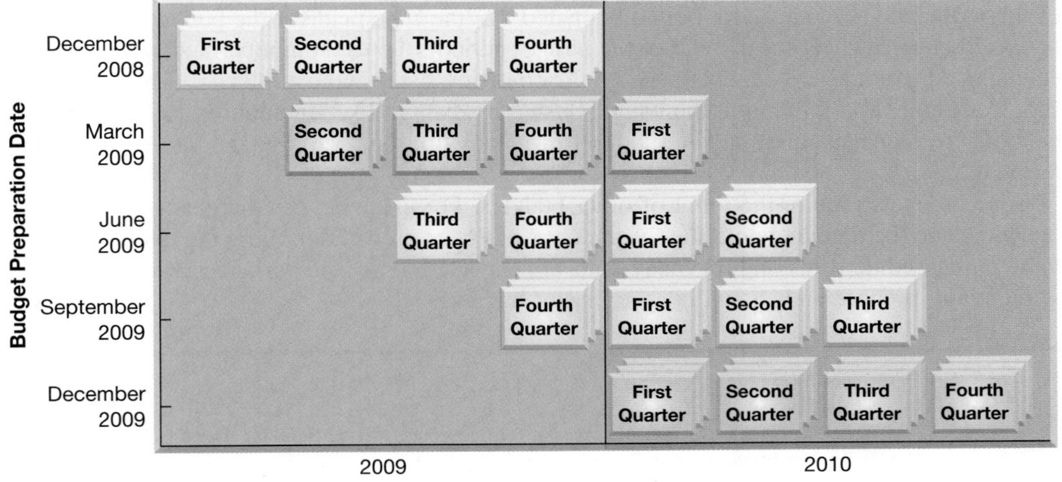

Exhibit 23.2 reflects an annual budget composed of four quarters prepared four times per year using the most recent information available. For example, the budget for the fourth quarter of 2009 is prepared in December 2008 and revised in March, June, and September of 2009. When continuous budgeting is not used, the fourth-quarter budget is nine months old and perhaps out of date when applied.

Decision Insight

Budget Calendar Many companies use long-range operating budgets. For large companies, three groups usually determine or influence the budgets: creditors, directors, and management. All three are interested in the companies' future cash flows and earnings. The annual budget process often begins six months or more before the budget is due to the board of directors. A typical budget calendar, shown here, provides insight into the budget process during a typical calendar year.

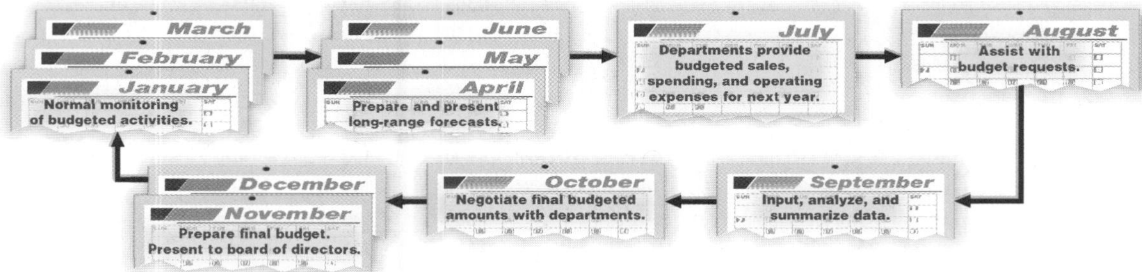

Quick Check

Answers—p. 961

1. What are the major benefits of budgeting?
2. What is the main responsibility of the budget committee?
3. What is the usual time period covered by a budget?
4. What are rolling budgets?

Master Budget

C3 Describe a master budget and the process of preparing it.

A **master budget** is a formal, comprehensive plan for a company's future. It contains several individual budgets that are linked with each other to form a coordinated plan.

Master Budget Components

The master budget typically includes individual budgets for sales, purchases, production, various expenses, capital expenditures, and cash. Managers often express the expected financial results of these planned activities with both a budgeted income statement for the budget period and a budgeted balance sheet for the end of the budget period. The usual number and types of budgets included in a master budget depend on the company's size and complexity. A master budget should include, at a minimum, the budgets listed in Exhibit 23.3. In addition to these individual budgets, managers often include supporting calculations and additional tables with the master budget.

Some budgets require the input of other budgets. For example, the merchandise purchases budget cannot be prepared until the sales budget has been prepared because the number of units to be purchased depends on how many units are expected to be sold. As a result, we often must sequentially prepare budgets within the master budget.

EXHIBIT 23.3

Basic Components of a Master Budget

Operating budgets
- *Sales budget*
- For merchandisers add: *Merchandise purchases budget* (units to be purchased)
- For manufacturers add: *Production budget* (units to be produced)
  Manufacturing budget (manufacturing costs)
- *Selling expense budget*
- *General and administrative expense budget*

Capital expenditures budget (expenditures for plant assets)

Financial budgets
- *Cash budget* (cash receipts and disbursements)
- *Budgeted income statement*
- *Budgeted balance sheet*

Decision Insight

Budgeting Targets Budgeting is a crucial part of any acquisition. Analysis begins by projecting annual sales volume and prices. It then estimates cost of sales, expenses, and income for the next several years. Using the present value of this projected income stream, buyers determine an offer price.

Video23.1

A typical sequence for a quarterly budget consists of the five steps in Exhibit 23.4. Any stage in this budgeting process might reveal undesirable outcomes, so changes often must be made to prior budgets by repeating the previous steps. For instance, an early version of the cash budget could show an insufficient amount of cash unless cash outlays are reduced. This could yield a reduction in planned equipment purchases. A preliminary budgeted balance sheet could also reveal too much debt from an ambitious capital expenditures budget. Findings such as these often result in revised plans and budgets.

EXHIBIT 23.4

Master Budget Sequence

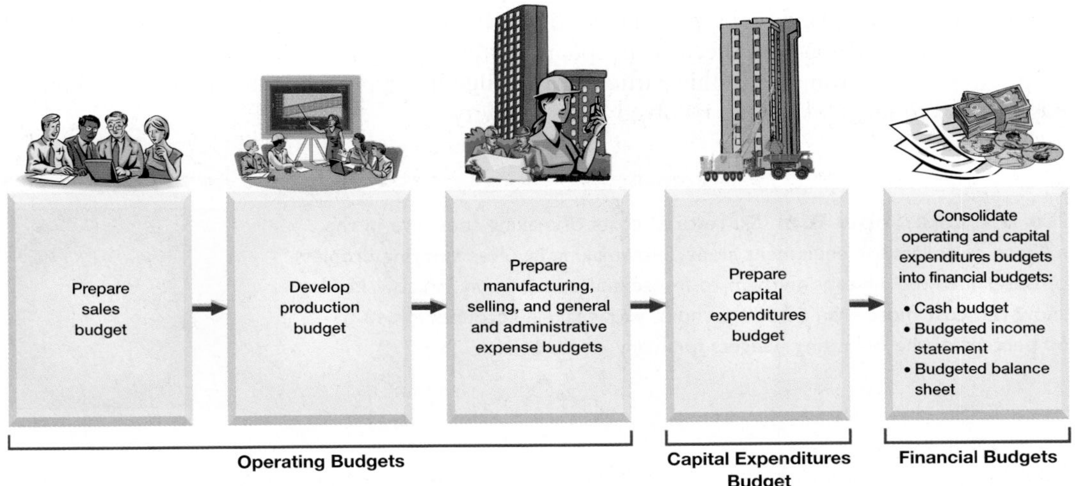

The remainder of this section explains how Hockey Den (HD), a retailer of youth hockey sticks, prepares its master budget. Its master budget includes operating, capital expenditures, and cash budgets for each month in each quarter. It also includes a budgeted income statement for each quarter and a budgeted balance sheet as of the last day of each quarter. We show how HD prepares budgets for October, November, and December 2009. Exhibit 23.5 presents HD's balance sheet at the start of this budgeting period, which we often refer to as we prepare the component budgets.

EXHIBIT 23.5

Balance Sheet Prior to the Budgeting Periods

HOCKEY DEN
Balance Sheet
September 30, 2009

Assets		
Cash		$ 20,000
Accounts receivable		42,000
Inventory (900 units @ $60)		54,000
Equipment*	$200,000	
Less accumulated depreciation	36,000	164,000
Total assets		$280,000
Liabilities and Equity		
Liabilities		
Accounts payable	$ 58,200	
Income taxes payable (due 10/31/2009)	20,000	
Note payable to bank	10,000	$ 88,200
Stockholders' equity		
Common stock	150,000	
Retained earnings	41,800	191,800
Total liabilities and equity		$280,000

* Equipment is depreciated on a straight-line basis over 10 years (salvage value is $20,000).

Operating Budgets

P1 Prepare each component of a master budget and link each to the budgeting process.

This section explains HD's preparation of operating budgets. Its operating budgets consist of the sales budget, merchandise purchases budget, selling expense budget, and general and administrative expense budget. HD does not prepare production and manufacturing budgets because it is a merchandiser. (The preparation of production budgets and manufacturing budgets is described in Appendix 23A.)

Sales Budget The first step in preparing the master budget is planning the **sales budget,** which shows the planned sales units and the expected dollars from these sales. The sales budget is the starting point in the budgeting process because plans for most departments are linked to sales.

The sales budget should emerge from a careful analysis of forecasted economic and market conditions, business capacity, proposed selling expenses (such as advertising), and predictions of unit sales. A company's sales personnel are usually asked to develop predictions of sales for each territory and department because people normally feel a greater commitment to goals they help set. Another advantage to this participatory budgeting approach is that it draws on knowledge and experience of people involved in the activity.

Decision Insight

No Biz Like Snow Biz Ski resorts' costs of making snow are in the millions of dollars for equipment alone. Snowmaking involves spraying droplets of water into the air, causing them to freeze and come down as snow. Making snow can cost more than $2,000 an hour. Snowmaking accounts for 40 to 50 percent of the operating budgets for many ski resorts.

Example: Assume a company's sales force receives a bonus when sales exceed the budgeted amount. How would this arrangement affect the bottom-up process of sales forecasts? *Answer:* Sales reps may understate their budgeted sales.

To illustrate, in September 2009, HD sold 700 hockey sticks at $100 per unit. After considering sales predictions and market conditions, HD prepares its sales budget for the next quarter (three months) plus one extra month (see Exhibit 23.6). The sales budget includes January 2010 because the purchasing department relies on estimated January sales to decide on December 2009 inventory purchases. The sales budget in Exhibit 23.6 includes forecasts of both unit sales and unit prices. Some sales budgets are expressed only in total sales dollars, but most are more detailed. Management finds it useful to know budgeted units and unit prices for many different products, regions, departments, and sales representatives.

EXHIBIT 23.6

Sales Budget for Planned Unit and Dollar Sales

HOCKEY DEN
Monthly Sales Budget
October 2009–January 2010

	Budgeted Unit Sales	Budgeted Unit Price	Budgeted Total Sales
September 2009 (actual)	700	$100	$ 70,000
October 2009	1,000	$100	$100,000
November 2009	800	100	80,000
December 2009	1,400	100	140,000
Totals for the quarter	3,200	100	$320,000
January 2010	900	100	$ 90,000

Decision Maker

Entrepreneur You run a start-up that manufactures designer clothes. Business is seasonal, and fashions and designs quickly change. How do you prepare reliable annual sales budgets? [Answer—p. 961]

Merchandise Purchases Budget Companies use various methods to help managers make inventory purchasing decisions. These methods recognize that the number of units added to inventory depends on budgeted sales volume. Whether a company manufactures or purchases the product it sells, budgeted future sales volume is the primary factor in most inventory management decisions. A company must also consider its inventory system and other factors that we discuss next.

Just-in-time inventory systems. Managers of *just-in-time* (JIT) inventory systems use sales budgets for short periods (often as few as one or two days) to order just enough merchandise or materials to satisfy the immediate sales demand. This keeps the amount of inventory to a minimum (or zero in an ideal situation). A JIT system minimizes the costs of maintaining inventory, but it is practical only if customers are content to order in advance or if managers can accurately determine short-term sales demand. Suppliers also must be able and willing to ship small quantities regularly and promptly.

Point: Accurate estimates of future sales are crucial in a JIT system.

Safety stock inventory systems. Market conditions and manufacturing processes for some products do not allow use of a just-in-time system. Companies in these cases maintain sufficient inventory to reduce the risk and cost of running short. This practice requires enough purchases to satisfy the budgeted sales amounts and to maintain a **safety stock,** a quantity of inventory that provides protection against lost sales caused by unfulfilled demands from customers or delays in shipments from suppliers.

Merchandise purchases budget preparation. A merchandiser usually expresses a **merchandise purchases budget** in both units and dollars. Exhibit 23.7 shows the general layout for this budget in equation form. If this formula is expressed in units and only one product is involved, we can compute the number of dollars of inventory to be purchased for the budget by multiplying the units to be purchased by the cost per unit.

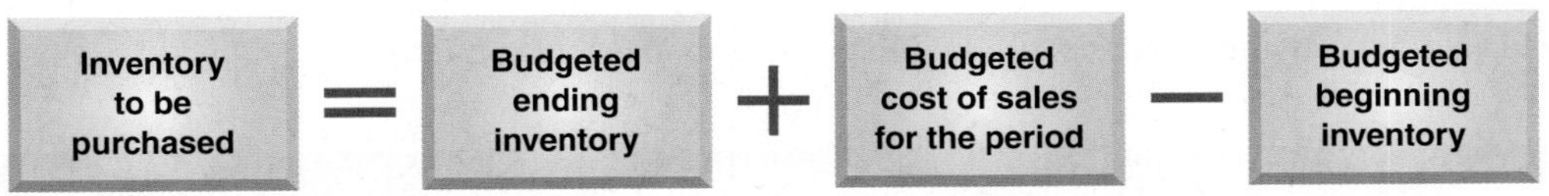

EXHIBIT 23.7

General Formula for a Merchandise Purchases Budget

To illustrate, after assessing the cost of keeping inventory along with the risk and cost of inventory shortages, HD decided that the number of units in its inventory at each month-end should equal 90% of next month's predicted sales. For example, inventory at the end of October should equal 90% of budgeted November sales, and the November ending inventory should equal 90% of budgeted December sales, and so on. Also, HD's suppliers expect the September 2009 per unit cost of $60 to remain unchanged through January 2010. This information along with knowledge of 900 units in inventory at September 30 (see Exhibit 23.5) allows the company to prepare the merchandise purchases budget shown in Exhibit 23.8.

Example: Assume Hockey Den adopts a JIT system in purchasing merchandise. How will its sales budget differ from its merchandise purchases budget? *Answer:* The two budgets will be similar because future inventory should be near zero.

EXHIBIT 23.8

Merchandise Purchases Budget

HOCKEY DEN
Merchandise Purchases Budget
October 2009–December 2009

	October	November	December
Next month's budgeted sales (units)	800	1,400	900
Ratio of inventory to future sales	× 90%	× 90%	× 90%
Budgeted ending inventory (units)	720	1,260	810
Add budgeted sales (units)	1,000	800	1,400
Required units of available merchandise	1,720	2,060	2,210
Deduct beginning inventory (units)	900	720	1,260
Units to be purchased	820	1,340	950
Budgeted cost per unit	$ 60	$ 60	$ 60
Budgeted cost of merchandise purchases	$49,200	$80,400	$57,000

Example: If ending inventory in Exhibit 23.8 is required to equal 80% of next month's predicted sales, how many units must be purchased each month? *Answer:* Budgeted ending inventory: Oct. = 640 units; Nov. = 1,120 units; Dec. = 720 units. Required purchases: Oct. = 740 units; Nov. = 1,280 units; Dec. = 1,000 units.

The first three lines of HD's merchandise purchases budget determine the required ending inventories (in units). Budgeted unit sales are then added to the desired ending inventory to give the required units of available merchandise. We then subtract beginning inventory to determine the budgeted number of units to be purchased. The last line is the budgeted cost of the purchases, computed by multiplying the number of units to be purchased by the predicted cost per unit.

We already indicated that some budgeting systems describe only the total dollars of budgeted sales. Likewise, a system can express a merchandise purchases budget only in terms of the total cost of merchandise to be purchased, omitting the number of units to be purchased. This method assumes a constant relation between sales and cost of goods sold. HD, for instance, might assume the expected cost of goods sold to be 60% of sales, computed from the budgeted unit cost of $60 and the budgeted sales price of $100. However, it still must consider the effects of changes in beginning and ending inventories in determining the amounts to be purchased.

Selling Expense Budget The **selling expense budget** is a plan listing the types and amounts of selling expenses expected during the budget period. Its initial responsibility usually rests with the vice president of marketing or an equivalent sales manager. The selling expense budget is normally created to provide sufficient selling expenses to meet sales goals reflected in the sales budget. Predicted selling expenses are based on both the sales budget and the experience of previous periods. After some or all of the master budget is prepared, management might decide that projected sales volume is inadequate. If so, subsequent adjustments in the sales budget can require corresponding adjustments in the selling expense budget.

Example: If sales commissions in Exhibit 23.9 are increased, which budgets are affected? *Answer:* Selling expenses budget, cash budget, and budgeted income statement.

To illustrate, HD's selling expense budget is in Exhibit 23.9. The firm's selling expenses consist of commissions paid to sales personnel and a $2,000 monthly salary paid to the sales manager. Sales commissions equal 10% of total sales and are paid in the month sales occur. Sales commissions are variable with respect to sales volume, but the sales manager's salary is fixed. No advertising expenses are budgeted for this particular quarter.

EXHIBIT 23.9

Selling Expense Budget

HOCKEY DEN
Selling Expense Budget
October 2009–December 2009

	October	November	December	Totals
Budgeted sales	$100,000	$80,000	$140,000	$320,000
Sales commission percent	× 10%	× 10%	× 10%	× 10%
Sales commissions	10,000	8,000	14,000	32,000
Salary for sales manager	2,000	2,000	2,000	6,000
Total selling expenses	$ 12,000	$10,000	$ 16,000	$ 38,000

General and Administrative Expense Budget The **general and administrative expense budget** plans the predicted operating expenses not included in the selling expenses budget. General and administrative expenses can be either variable or fixed with respect to sales volume. The office manager responsible for general administration often is responsible for preparing the initial general and administrative expense budget.

Interest expense and income tax expense are often classified as general and administrative expenses in published income statements, but normally cannot be planned at this stage of the budgeting process. The prediction of interest expense follows the preparation of the cash budget and the decisions regarding debt. The predicted income tax expense depends on the budgeted amount of pretax income. Both interest and income taxes are usually beyond the control of the office manager. As a result, they are not used in comparison to the budget to evaluate that person's performance.

Exhibit 23.10 shows HD's general and administrative expense budget. It includes salaries of $54,000 per year, or $4,500 per month (paid each month when they are earned). Using information in Exhibit 23.5, the depreciation on equipment is computed as $18,000 per year [($200,000 − $20,000)/10 years], or $1,500 per month ($18,000/12 months).

EXHIBIT 23.10

General and Administrative Expense Budget

HOCKEY DEN General and Administrative Expense Budget October 2009–December 2009	October	November	December	Totals
Administrative salaries	$4,500	$4,500	$4,500	$13,500
Depreciation of equipment	1,500	1,500	1,500	4,500
Total general and administrative expenses	$6,000	$6,000	$6,000	$18,000

Example: In Exhibit 23.10, how would a rental agreement of $5,000 per month plus 1% of sales affect the general and administrative expense budget? (Budgeted sales are in Exhibit 23.6.)
Answer: Rent expense: Oct. = $6,000; Nov. = $5,800; Dec. = $6,400; Total = $18,200; *Revised total general and administrative expenses:* Oct. = $12,000; Nov. = $11,800; Dec. = $12,400; Total = $36,200.

Quick Check

Answers—p. 961

5. What is a master budget?
6. A master budget (*a*) always includes a manufacturing budget specifying the units to be produced; (*b*) is prepared with a process starting with the operating budgets and continues with the capital expenditures budget and then financial budgets; or (*c*) is prepared with a process ending with the sales budget.
7. What are the three primary categories of budgets in the master budget?
8. In preparing monthly budgets for the third quarter, a company budgeted sales of 120 units for July and 140 units for August. Management wants each month's ending inventory to be 60% of next month's sales. The June 30 inventory consists of 50 units. How many units of product for July acquisition should the merchandise purchases budget specify for the third quarter? (*a*) 84, (*b*) 120, (*c*) 154, or (*d*) 204.
9. How do the operating budgets for merchandisers and manufacturers differ?
10. How does a just-in-time inventory system differ from a safety stock system?

Capital Expenditures Budget

The **capital expenditures budget** lists dollar amounts to be both received from plant asset disposals and spent to purchase additional plant assets to carry out the budgeted business activities. It is usually prepared after the operating budgets. Since a company's plant assets determine its productive capacity, this budget is usually affected by long-range plans for the business. Yet the process of preparing a sales or purchases budget can reveal that the company requires more (or less) capacity, which implies more (or less) plant assets.

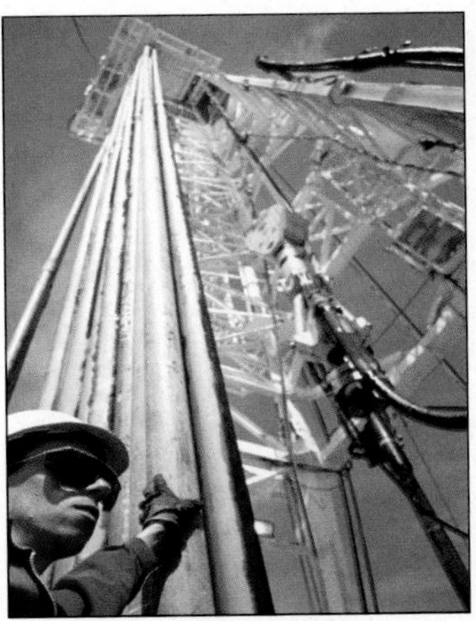

Capital budgeting is the process of evaluating and planning for capital (plant asset) expenditures. This is an important management task because these expenditures often involve long-run commitments of large amounts, affect predicted cash flows, and impact future debt and equity financing. This means that the capital expenditures budget is often linked with management's evaluation of the company's ability to take on more debt. We describe capital budgeting in Chapter 25.

Hockey Den does not anticipate disposal of any plant assets through December 2009, but it does plan to acquire additional equipment for $25,000 cash near the end of December 2009. This is the only budgeted capital expenditure from October 2009 through January 2010. Thus, no separate budget is shown. The cash budget in Exhibit 23.11 reflects this $25,000 planned expenditure.

Financial Budgets

After preparing its operating and capital expenditures budgets, a company uses information from these budgets to prepare at least three financial budgets: the cash budget, budgeted income statement, and budgeted balance sheet.

EXHIBIT 23.11

Cash Budget

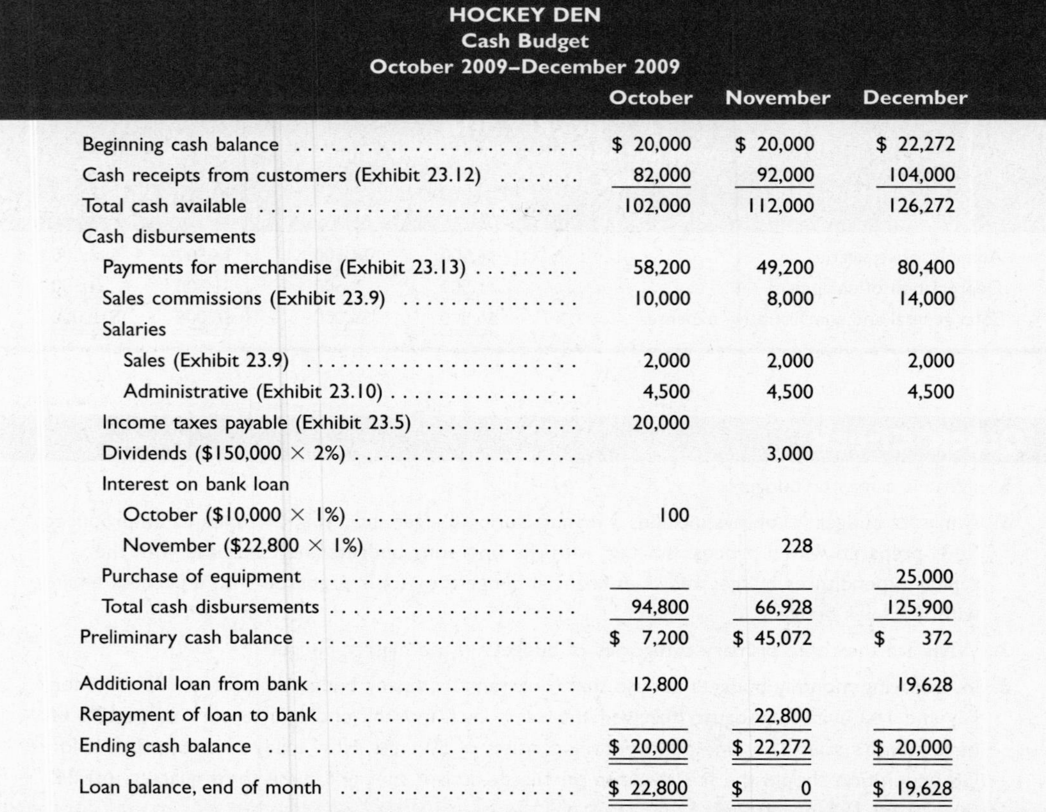

HOCKEY DEN Cash Budget October 2009–December 2009	October	November	December
Beginning cash balance	$ 20,000	$ 20,000	$ 22,272
Cash receipts from customers (Exhibit 23.12)	82,000	92,000	104,000
Total cash available	102,000	112,000	126,272
Cash disbursements			
Payments for merchandise (Exhibit 23.13)	58,200	49,200	80,400
Sales commissions (Exhibit 23.9)	10,000	8,000	14,000
Salaries			
Sales (Exhibit 23.9)	2,000	2,000	2,000
Administrative (Exhibit 23.10)	4,500	4,500	4,500
Income taxes payable (Exhibit 23.5)	20,000		
Dividends ($150,000 × 2%)		3,000	
Interest on bank loan			
October ($10,000 × 1%)	100		
November ($22,800 × 1%)		228	
Purchase of equipment			25,000
Total cash disbursements	94,800	66,928	125,900
Preliminary cash balance	$ 7,200	$ 45,072	$ 372
Additional loan from bank	12,800		19,628
Repayment of loan to bank		22,800	
Ending cash balance	$ 20,000	$ 22,272	$ 20,000
Loan balance, end of month	$ 22,800	$ 0	$ 19,628

Example: If the minimum ending cash balance in Exhibit 23.11 is changed to $25,000 for each month, what is the projected loan balance at Dec. 31, 2009?

Answer:

Loan balance, Oct. 31	$27,800
November interest	278
November payment	25,022
Loan balance, Nov. 30	2,778
December interest	28
Additional loan in Dec.	21,928
Loan balance, Dec. 31	$24,706

P2 Link both operating and capital expenditures budgets to budgeted financial statements.

Cash Budget After developing budgets for sales, merchandise purchases, expenses, and capital expenditures, the next step is to prepare the **cash budget,** which shows expected cash inflows and outflows during the budget period. It is especially important to maintain a cash balance necessary to meet ongoing obligations. By preparing a cash budget, management can prearrange loans to cover anticipated cash shortages before they are needed. A cash budget also helps management avoid a cash balance that is too large. Too much cash is undesirable because it earns a relatively low (if any) return.

When preparing a cash budget, we add expected cash receipts to the beginning cash balance and deduct expected cash disbursements. If the expected ending cash balance is inadequate, additional cash requirements appear in the budget as planned increases from short-term loans. If the expected ending cash balance exceeds the desired balance, the excess is used to repay loans or to acquire short-term investments. Information for preparing the cash budget is mainly taken from the operating and capital expenditures budgets.

To illustrate, Exhibit 23.11 presents HD's cash budget. The beginning cash balance for October is taken from the September 30, 2009, balance sheet in Exhibit 23.5. The remainder of this section describes the computations in the cash budget.

We begin with reference to HD's budgeted sales (Exhibit 23.6). Analysis of past sales indicates that 40% of the firm's sales are for cash. The remaining 60% are credit sales; these customers are expected to pay in full in the month following the sales. We now can compute the budgeted cash receipts from customers as shown in Exhibit 23.12. October's budgeted cash receipts consist of $40,000 from expected cash sales ($100,000 × 40%) plus the anticipated collection of $42,000 of accounts receivable from the end of September. Each month's cash receipts from customers are transferred to the second line of Exhibit 23.11.

Next, we see that HD's merchandise purchases are entirely on account. It makes full payment during the month following its purchases. Therefore, cash disbursements for

EXHIBIT 23.12

Computing Budgeted Cash Receipts

	September	October	November	December
Sales	$70,000	$100,000	$80,000	$140,000
Less ending accounts receivable (60%)	42,000	60,000	48,000	84,000
Cash receipts from				
Cash sales (40% of sales)		40,000	32,000	56,000
Collections of prior month's receivables		42,000	60,000	48,000
Total cash receipts		$ 82,000	$92,000	$104,000

purchases can be computed from the September 30, 2009, balance sheet (Exhibit 23.5) and the merchandise purchases budget (Exhibit 23.8). This computation is shown in Exhibit 23.13.

EXHIBIT 23.13

Computing Cash Disbursements for Purchases

October payments (September 30 balance)	$58,200
November payments (October purchases)	49,200
December payments (November purchases)	80,400

The monthly budgeted cash disbursements for sales commissions and salaries are taken from the selling expense budget (Exhibit 23.9) and the general and administrative expense budget (Exhibit 23.10). The cash budget is unaffected by depreciation as reported in the general and administrative expenses budget.

Income taxes are due and payable in October as shown in the September 30, 2009, balance sheet (Exhibit 23.5). The cash budget in Exhibit 23.11 shows this $20,000 expected payment in October. Predicted income tax expense for the quarter ending December 31 is 40% of net income and is due in January 2010. It is therefore not reported in the October–December 2009 cash budget but in the budgeted income statement as income tax expense and on the budgeted balance sheet as income tax liability.

Hockey Den also pays a cash dividend equal to 2% of the par value of common stock in the second month of each quarter. The cash budget in Exhibit 23.11 shows a November payment of $3,000 for this purpose (2% of $150,000; see Exhibit 23.5).

Hockey Den has an agreement with its bank that promises additional loans at each month-end, if necessary, to keep a minimum cash balance of $20,000. If the cash balance exceeds $20,000 at a month-end, HD uses the excess to repay loans. Interest is paid at each month-end at the rate of 1% of the beginning balance of these loans. For October, this payment is 1% of the $10,000 amount reported in the balance sheet of Exhibit 23.5. For November, HD expects to pay interest of $228, computed as 1% of the $22,800 expected loan balance at October 31. No interest is budgeted for December because the company expects to repay the loans in full at the end of November. Exhibit 23.11 shows that the October 31 cash balance declines to $7,200 (before any loan-related activity). This amount is less than the $20,000 minimum. Hockey Den will bring this balance up to the minimum by borrowing $12,800 with a short-term note. At the end of November, the budget shows an expected cash balance of $45,072 before any loan activity. This means that HD expects to repay $22,800 of debt. The equipment purchase budgeted for December reduces the expected cash balance to $372, far below the $20,000 minimum. The company expects to borrow $19,628 in that month to reach the minimum desired ending balance.

Example: Give one reason for maintaining a minimum cash balance when the budget shows extra cash is not needed. *Answer:* For unexpected events.

Decision Insight

Netting Cash The Hockey Company—whose brands include CCM, JOFA, and KOHO—reported net cash outflows for investing activities of $32 million. Much of this amount was a prepayment to the NHL for a 10-year license agreement.

Budgeted Income Statement One of the final steps in preparing the master budget is to summarize the income effects. The **budgeted income statement** is a managerial accounting report showing predicted amounts of sales and expenses for the budget period. Information needed for preparing a budgeted income statement is primarily taken from already prepared budgets. The volume of information summarized in the budgeted income statement is so large for some companies that they often use spreadsheets to accumulate the budgeted transactions and classify them by their effects on income. We condense HD's budgeted income statement and show it in Exhibit 23.14. All information in this exhibit is taken from earlier budgets. Also, we now can predict the amount of income tax expense for the quarter, computed as 40% of the budgeted pretax income. This amount is included in the cash budget and/or the budgeted balance sheet as necessary.

EXHIBIT 23.14

Budgeted Income Statement

HOCKEY DEN
Budgeted Income Statement
For Three Months Ended December 31, 2009

Sales (Exhibit 23.6, 3,200 units @ $100)		$320,000
Cost of goods sold (3,200 units @ $60)		192,000
Gross profit		128,000
Operating expenses		
Sales commissions (Exhibit 23.9)	$32,000	
Sales salaries (Exhibit 23.9)	6,000	
Administrative salaries (Exhibit 23.10)	13,500	
Depreciation on equipment (Exhibit 23.10)	4,500	
Interest expense (Exhibit 23.11)	328	56,328
Income before income taxes		71,672
Income tax expense ($71,672 × 40%)		28,669
Net income		$ 43,003

Budgeted Balance Sheet The final step in preparing the master budget is summarizing the company's financial position. The **budgeted balance sheet** shows predicted amounts for the company's assets, liabilities, and equity as of the end of the budget period. HD's budgeted balance sheet in Exhibit 23.15 is prepared using information from the other budgets. The sources of amounts are reported in the notes to the budgeted balance sheet.[1]

Point: Lending institutions often require potential borrowers to provide cash budgets, budgeted income statements, and budgeted balance sheets, as well as data on past performance.

Decision Insight

Plan Ahead Most companies allocate dollars based on budgets submitted by department managers. These managers verify the numbers and monitor the budget. Managers must remember, however, that a budget is judged by its success in helping achieve the company's mission. One analogy is that a hiker must know the route to properly plan a hike and monitor hiking progress.

[1] An eight-column spreadsheet, or work sheet, can be used to prepare a budgeted balance sheet (and income statement). The first two columns show the ending balance sheet amounts from the period prior to the budget period. The budgeted transactions and adjustments are entered in the third and fourth columns in the same manner as adjustments are entered on an ordinary work sheet. After all budgeted transactions and adjustments have been entered, the amounts in the first two columns are combined with the budget amounts in the third and fourth columns and sorted to the proper Income Statement (fifth and sixth columns) and Balance Sheet columns (seventh and eighth columns). Amounts in these columns are used to prepare the budgeted income statement and balance sheet.

EXHIBIT 23.15

Budgeted Balance Sheet

HOCKEY DEN Budgeted Balance Sheet December 31, 2009		
Assets		
Cash[a]		$ 20,000
Accounts receivable[b]		84,000
Inventory[c]		48,600
Equipment[d]	$225,000	
Less accumulated depreciation[e]	40,500	184,500
Total assets		$337,100
Liabilities and Equity		
Liabilities		
Accounts payable[f]	$ 57,000	
Income taxes payable[g]	28,669	
Bank loan payable[h]	19,628	$105,297
Stockholders' equity		
Common stock[i]	150,000	
Retained earnings[j]	81,803	231,803
Total liabilities and equity		$337,100

[a] Ending balance for December from the cash budget in Exhibit 23.11.

[b] 60% of $140,000 sales budgeted for December from the sales budget in Exhibit 23.6.

[c] 810 units in budgeted December ending inventory at the budgeted cost of $60 per unit (from the purchases budget in Exhibit 23.8).

[d] September 30 balance of $200,000 from the beginning balance sheet in Exhibit 23.5 plus $25,000 cost of new equipment from the cash budget in Exhibit 23.11.

[e] September 30 balance of $36,000 from the beginning balance sheet in Exhibit 23.5 plus $4,500 expense from the general and administrative expense budget in Exhibit 23.10.

[f] Budgeted cost of purchases for December from the purchases budget in Exhibit 23.8.

[g] Income tax expense from the budgeted income statement for the fourth quarter in Exhibit 23.14.

[h] Budgeted December 31 balance from the cash budget in Exhibit 23.11.

[i] Unchanged from the beginning balance sheet in Exhibit 23.5.

[j] September 30 balance of $41,800 from the beginning balance sheet in Exhibit 23.5 plus budgeted net income of $43,003 from the budgeted income statement in Exhibit 23.14 minus budgeted cash dividends of $3,000 from the cash budget in Exhibit 23.11.

Quick Check

Answers—p. 961

11. In preparing a budgeted balance sheet, (*a*) plant assets are determined by analyzing the capital expenditures budget and the balance sheet from the beginning of the budget period, (*b*) liabilities are determined by analyzing the general and administrative expense budget, or (*c*) retained earnings are determined from information contained in the cash budget and the balance sheet from the beginning of the budget period.
12. What sequence is followed in preparing the budgets that constitute the master budget?

Activity-Based Budgeting

Decision Analysis

A1 Analyze expense planning using activity-based budgeting.

Activity-based budgeting (ABB) is a budget system based on expected activities. Knowledge of expected activities and their levels for the budget period enables management to plan for resources required to perform the activities. To illustrate, we consider the budget of a company's accounting department. Traditional budgeting systems list items such as salaries, supplies, equipment, and utilities. Such an itemized budget informs management of the use of the funds budgeted (for example, salaries), but management cannot assess the basis for increases or decreases in budgeted amounts as compared to prior periods. Accordingly, management often makes across-the-board cuts or increases. In contrast, ABB requires management to list activities performed by, say, the accounting department such as auditing, tax reporting, financial reporting, and cost accounting. Exhibit 23.16 contrasts a traditional budget with an activity-based budget for a company's accounting department. An understanding of the resources required to perform the activities, the costs associated with these resources,

EXHIBIT 23.16

Activity-Based Budgeting versus Traditional Budgeting (for an accounting department)

Activity-Based Budget		Traditional Budget	
Auditing	$ 58,000	Salaries	$152,000
Tax reporting	71,000	Supplies	22,000
Financial reporting	63,000	Depreciation	36,000
Cost accounting	32,000	Utilities	14,000
Total	$224,000	Total	$224,000

and the way resource use changes with changes in activity levels allows management to better assess how expenses will change to accommodate changes in activity levels. Moreover, by knowing the relation between activities and costs, management can attempt to reduce costs by eliminating nonvalue-added activities.

Decision Maker

Environmental Manager You hold the new position of environmental control manager for a chemical company. You are asked to develop a budget for your job and identify job responsibilities. How do you proceed? [Answer—p. 961]

Demonstration Problem

DP23

Wild Wood Company's management asks you to prepare its master budget using the following information. The budget is to cover the months of April, May, and June of 2009.

WILD WOOD COMPANY
Balance Sheet
March 31, 2009

Assets		Liabilities and Equity	
Cash	$ 50,000	Accounts payable	$156,000
Accounts receivable	175,000	Short-term notes payable	12,000
Inventory	126,000	Total current liabilities	168,000
Total current assets	351,000	Long-term note payable	200,000
Equipment, gross	480,000	Total liabilities	368,000
Accumulated depreciation	(90,000)	Common stock	235,000
Equipment, net	390,000	Retained earnings	138,000
		Total stockholders' equity	373,000
Total assets	$741,000	Total liabilities and equity	$741,000

Additional Information

a. Sales for March total 10,000 units. Each month's sales are expected to exceed the prior month's results by 5%. The product's selling price is $25 per unit.

b. Company policy calls for a given month's ending inventory to equal 80% of the next month's expected unit sales. The March 31 inventory is 8,400 units, which complies with the policy. The purchase price is $15 per unit.

c. Sales representatives' commissions are 12.5% of sales and are paid in the month of the sales. The sales manager's monthly salary will be $3,500 in April and $4,000 per month thereafter.

d. Monthly general and administrative expenses include $8,000 administrative salaries, $5,000 depreciation, and 0.9% monthly interest on the long-term note payable.

e. The company expects 30% of sales to be for cash and the remaining 70% on credit. Receivables are collected in full in the month following the sale (none is collected in the month of the sale).

f. All merchandise purchases are on credit, and no payables arise from any other transactions. One month's purchases are fully paid in the next month.

g. The minimum ending cash balance for all months is $50,000. If necessary, the company borrows enough cash using a short-term note to reach the minimum. Short-term notes require an interest payment of 1% at each month-end (before any repayment). If the ending cash balance exceeds the minimum, the excess will be applied to repaying the short-term notes payable balance.

h. Dividends of $100,000 are to be declared and paid in May.

i. No cash payments for income taxes are to be made during the second calendar quarter. Income taxes will be assessed at 35% in the quarter.

j. Equipment purchases of $55,000 are scheduled for June.

Required

Prepare the following budgets and other financial information as required:

1. Sales budget, including budgeted sales for July.
2. Purchases budget, the budgeted cost of goods sold for each month and quarter, and the cost of the June 30 budgeted inventory.
3. Selling expense budget.
4. General and administrative expense budget.
5. Expected cash receipts from customers and the expected June 30 balance of accounts receivable.
6. Expected cash payments for purchases and the expected June 30 balance of accounts payable.
7. Cash budget.
8. Budgeted income statement.
9. Budgeted statement of retained earnings.
10. Budgeted balance sheet.

Planning the Solution

- The sales budget shows expected sales for each month in the quarter. Start by multiplying March sales by 105% and then do the same for the remaining months. July's sales are needed for the purchases budget. To complete the budget, multiply the expected unit sales by the selling price of $25 per unit.
- Use these results and the 80% inventory policy to budget the size of ending inventory for April, May, and June. Add the budgeted sales to these numbers and subtract the actual or expected beginning inventory for each month. The result is the number of units to be purchased each month. Multiply these numbers by the per unit cost of $15. Find the budgeted cost of goods sold by multiplying the unit sales in each month by the $15 cost per unit. Compute the cost of the June 30 ending inventory by multiplying the expected units available at that date by the $15 cost per unit.
- The selling expense budget has only two items. Find the amount of the sales representatives' commissions by multiplying the expected dollar sales in each month by the 12.5% commission rate. Then include the sales manager's salary of $3,500 in April and $4,000 in May and June.
- The general and administrative expense budget should show three items. Administrative salaries are fixed at $8,000 per month, and depreciation is $5,000 per month. Budget the monthly interest expense on the long-term note by multiplying its $200,000 balance by the 0.9% monthly interest rate.
- Determine the amounts of cash sales in each month by multiplying the budgeted sales by 30%. Add to this amount the credit sales of the prior month (computed as 70% of prior month's sales). April's cash receipts from collecting receivables equals the March 31 balance of $175,000. The expected June 30 accounts receivable balance equals 70% of June's total budgeted sales.
- Determine expected cash payments on accounts payable for each month by making them equal to the merchandise purchases in the prior month. The payments for April equal the March 31 balance of accounts payable shown on the beginning balance sheet. The June 30 balance of accounts payable equals merchandise purchases for June.
- Prepare the cash budget by combining the given information and the amounts of cash receipts and cash payments on account that you computed. Complete the cash budget for each month by either borrowing enough to raise the preliminary balance to the minimum or paying off short-term debt as much as the balance allows without falling below the minimum. Show the ending balance of the short-term note in the budget.
- Prepare the budgeted income statement by combining the budgeted items for all three months. Determine the income before income taxes and multiply it by the 35% rate to find the quarter's income tax expense.
- The budgeted statement of retained earnings should show the March 31 balance plus the quarter's net income minus the quarter's dividends.

- The budgeted balance sheet includes updated balances for all items that appear in the beginning balance sheet and an additional liability for unpaid income taxes. Amounts for all asset, liability, and equity accounts can be found either in the budgets, other calculations, or by adding amounts found there to the beginning balances.

Solution to Demonstration Problem

1. Sales budget

	April	May	June	July
Prior period's unit sales	10,000	10,500	11,025	11,576
Plus 5% growth	500	525	551	579
Projected unit sales	10,500	11,025	11,576	12,155

	April	May	June	Quarter
Projected unit sales	10,500	11,025	11,576	
Selling price per unit	× $25	× $25	× $25	
Projected sales	$262,500	$275,625	$289,400	$827,525

2. Purchases budget

	April	May	June	Quarter
Next period's unit sales (part 1)	11,025	11,576	12,155	
Ending inventory percent	× 80%	× 80%	× 80%	
Desired ending inventory	8,820	9,261	9,724	
Current period's unit sales (part 1)	10,500	11,025	11,576	
Units to be available	19,320	20,286	21,300	
Less beginning inventory	8,400	8,820	9,261	
Units to be purchased	10,920	11,466	12,039	
Budgeted cost per unit	× $15	× $15	× $15	
Projected purchases	$163,800	$171,990	$180,585	$516,375

Budgeted cost of goods sold

	April	May	June	Quarter
This period's unit sales (part 1)	10,500	11,025	11,576	
Budgeted cost per unit	× $15	× $15	× $15	
Projected cost of goods sold	$157,500	$165,375	$173,640	$496,515

Budgeted inventory for June 30

Units (part 2)	9,724
Cost per unit	× $15
Total	$145,860

3. Selling expense budget

	April	May	June	Quarter
Budgeted sales (part 1)	$262,500	$275,625	$289,400	$827,525
Commission percent	× 12.5%	× 12.5%	× 12.5%	× 12.5%
Sales commissions	32,813	34,453	36,175	103,441
Manager's salary	3,500	4,000	4,000	11,500
Projected selling expenses	$ 36,313	$ 38,453	$ 40,175	$114,941

4. General and administrative expense budget

	April	May	June	Quarter
Administrative salaries	$ 8,000	$ 8,000	$ 8,000	$24,000
Depreciation	5,000	5,000	5,000	15,000
Interest on long-term note payable (0.9% × $200,000)	1,800	1,800	1,800	5,400
Projected expenses	$14,800	$14,800	$14,800	$44,400

5. Expected cash receipts from customers

	April	May	June	Quarter
Budgeted sales (part 1)	$262,500	$275,625	$289,400	
Ending accounts receivable (70%)	$183,750	$192,938	$202,580	
Cash receipts				
Cash sales (30%)	$ 78,750	$ 82,687	$ 86,820	$248,257
Collections of prior period's receivables	175,000	183,750	192,938	551,688
Total cash to be collected	$253,750	$266,437	$279,758	$799,945

6. Expected cash payments to suppliers

	April	May	June	Quarter
Cash payments (equal to prior period's purchases)	$156,000	$163,800	$171,990	$491,790
Expected June 30 balance of accounts payable (June purchases)			$180,585	

7. Cash budget

	April	May	June
Beginning cash balance	$ 50,000	$ 89,517	$ 50,000
Cash receipts (part 5)	253,750	266,437	279,758
Total cash available	303,750	355,954	329,758
Cash payments			
Payments for merchandise (part 6)	156,000	163,800	171,990
Sales commissions (part 3)	32,813	34,453	36,175
Salaries			
Sales (part 3)	3,500	4,000	4,000
Administrative (part 4)	8,000	8,000	8,000
Interest on long-term note (part 4)	1,800	1,800	1,800
Dividends		100,000	
Equipment purchase			55,000
Interest on short-term notes			
April ($12,000 × 1.0%)	120		
June ($6,099 × 1.0%)			61
Total cash payments	202,233	312,053	277,026
Preliminary balance	101,517	43,901	52,732
Additional loan		6,099	
Loan repayment	(12,000)		(2,732)
Ending cash balance	$ 89,517	$ 50,000	$ 50,000
Ending short-term notes	$ 0	$ 6,099	$ 3,367

8.

WILD WOOD COMPANY Budgeted Income Statement For Quarter Ended June 30, 2009		
Sales (part 1)		$ 827,525
Cost of goods sold (part 2)		496,515
Gross profit		331,010
Operating expenses		
Sales commissions (part 3)	$103,441	
Sales salaries (part 3)	11,500	
Administrative salaries (part 4)	24,000	
Depreciation (part 4)	15,000	
Interest on long-term note (part 4)	5,400	
Interest on short-term notes (part 7)	181	
Total operating expenses		159,522
Income before income taxes		171,488
Income taxes (35%)		60,021
Net income		$ 111,467

9.

WILD WOOD COMPANY Budgeted Statement of Retained Earnings For Quarter Ended June 30, 2009	
Beginning retained earnings (given)	$138,000
Net income (part 8)	111,467
	249,467
Less cash dividends (given)	100,000
Ending retained earnings	$149,467

10.

WILD WOOD COMPANY Budgeted Balance Sheet June 30, 2009		
Assets		
Cash (part 7)		$ 50,000
Accounts receivable (part 5)		202,580
Inventory (part 2)		145,860
Total current assets		398,440
Equipment (given plus purchase)	$535,000	
Less accumulated depreciation (given plus expense)	105,000	430,000
Total assets		$828,440
Liabilities and Equity		
Accounts payable (part 6)		$180,585
Short-term notes payable (part 7)		3,367
Income taxes payable (part 8)		60,021
Total current liabilities		243,973
Long-term note payable (given)		200,000
Total liabilities		443,973
Common stock (given)		235,000
Retained earnings (part 9)		149,467
Total stockholders' equity		384,467
Total liabilities and equity		$828,440

APPENDIX

Production and Manufacturing Budgets

23A

P3 Prepare production and manufacturing budgets.

Unlike a merchandising company, a manufacturer must prepare a **production budget** instead of a merchandise purchases budget. A production budget, which shows the number of units to be produced each month, is similar to merchandise purchases budgets except that the number of units to be purchased each month (as shown in Exhibit 23.8) is replaced by the number of units to be manufactured each month. A production budget does not show costs; it is *always expressed in units of product*. Exhibit 23A.1 shows the production budget for **Toronto Sticks Company (TSC),** a manufacturer of hockey sticks. TSC is an exclusive supplier of hockey sticks to Hockey Den, meaning that TSC uses HD's budgeted sales figures (Exhibit 23.6) to determine its production and manufacturing budgets.

EXHIBIT 23A.1

Production Budget

TSC
Production Budget
October 2009–December 2009

	October	November	December
Next period's budgeted sales (units)	800	1,400	900
Ratio of inventory to future sales	× 90%	× 90%	× 90%
Budgeted ending inventory (units)	720	1,260	810
Add budgeted sales for the period (units)	1,000	800	1,400
Required units of available production	1,720	2,060	2,210
Deduct beginning inventory (units)	(900)	(720)	(1,260)
Units to be produced	820	1,340	950

A **manufacturing budget** shows the budgeted costs for direct materials, direct labor, and overhead. It is based on the budgeted production volume from the production budget. The manufacturing budget for most companies consists of three individual budgets: direct materials budget, direct labor budget, and overhead budget. Exhibits 23A.2–23A.4 show these three manufacturing budgets for TSC. These budgets yield the total expected cost of goods to be manufactured in the budget period.

The *direct materials budget* is driven by the budgeted materials needed to satisfy each month's production requirement. To this we must add the desired ending inventory requirements. The desired ending inventory of direct materials as shown in Exhibit 23A.2 is 50% of next month's budgeted materials requirements of wood. For instance, in October 2009, an ending inventory of 335 units of material is desired (50% of November's 670 units). The desired ending inventory for December 2009 is 225 units,

EXHIBIT 23A.2

Direct Materials Budget

TSC
Direct Materials Budget
October 2009–December 2009

	October	November	December
Budget production (units)	820	1,340	950
Materials requirements per unit	× 0.5	× 0.5	× 0.5
Materials needed for production (units)	410	670	475
Add budgeted ending inventory (units)	335	237.5	225
Total materials requirements (units)	745	907.5	700
Deduct beginning inventory (units)	(205)	(335)	(237.5)
Materials to be purchased (units)	540	572.5	462.5
Material price per unit	$ 20	$ 20	$ 20
Total cost of direct materials purchases	$10,800	$11,450	$9,250

computed from the direct material requirement of 450 units for a production level of 900 units in January 2010. The total materials requirements are computed by adding the desired ending inventory figures to that month's budgeted production material requirements. For October 2009, the total materials requirement is 745 units (335 + 410). From the total materials requirement, we then subtract the units of materials available in beginning inventory. For October 2009, the materials available from September 2009 are computed as 50% of October's materials requirements to satisfy production, or 205 units (50% of 410). Therefore, direct materials purchases in October 2009 are budgeted at 540 units (745 − 205). See Exhibit 23A.2.

TSC's *direct labor budget* is shown in Exhibit 23A.3. About 15 minutes of labor time is required to produce one unit. Labor is paid at the rate of $12 per hour. Budgeted labor hours are computed by multiplying the budgeted production level for each month by one-quarter (0.25) of an hour. Direct labor cost is then computed by multiplying budgeted labor hours by the labor rate of $12 per hour.

EXHIBIT 23A.3

Direct Labor Budget

TSC
Direct Labor Budget
October 2009–December 2009

	October	November	December
Budgeted production (units)	820	1,340	950
Labor requirements per unit (hours)	× 0.25	× 0.25	× 0.25
Total labor hours needed	205	335	237.5
Labor rate (per hour)	$ 12	$ 12	$ 12
Labor dollars	$2,460	$4,020	$2,850

TSC's *factory overhead budget* is shown in Exhibit 23A.4. The variable portion of overhead is assigned at the rate of $2.50 per unit of production. The fixed portion stays constant at $1,500 per month. The budget in Exhibit 23A.4 is in condensed form; most overhead budgets are more detailed, listing each overhead cost item.

EXHIBIT 23A.4

Factory Overhead Budget

TSC
Factory Overhead Budget
October 2009–December 2009

	October	November	December
Budgeted production (units)	820	1,340	950
Variable factory overhead rate	× $2.50	× $2.50	× $2.50
Budgeted variable overhead	2,050	3,350	2,375
Budgeted fixed overhead	1,500	1,500	1,500
Budgeted total overhead	$3,550	$4,850	$3,875

Summary

C1 Describe the importance and benefits of budgeting. Planning is a management responsibility of critical importance to business success. Budgeting is the process management uses to formalize its plans. Budgeting promotes management analysis and focuses its attention on the future. Budgeting also provides a basis for evaluating performance, serves as a source of motivation, is a means of coordinating activities, and communicates management's plans and instructions to employees.

C2 Explain the process of budget administration. Budgeting is a detailed activity that requires administration. At least three aspects are important: budget committee, budget reporting, and budget timing. A budget committee oversees the budget preparation. The budget period pertains to the time period for which the budget is prepared such as a year or month.

C3 Describe a master budget and the process of preparing it. A master budget is a formal overall plan for a company. It consists of plans for business operations and capital expenditures, plus the financial results of those activities. The budgeting process begins with a sales budget. Based on expected sales volume, companies can budget purchases, selling expenses, and administrative expenses. Next, the capital expenditures budget is prepared, followed by the cash budget and budgeted financial statements. Manufacturers also must budget production quantities, materials purchases, labor costs, and overhead.

A1 Analyze expense planning using activity-based budgeting. Activity-based budgeting requires management to identify activities performed by departments, plan necessary activity levels, identify resources required to perform these activities, and budget the resources.

P1 Prepare each component of a master budget and link each to the budgeting process. The term *master budget* refers to a collection of individual component budgets. Each component budget is designed to guide persons responsible for activities covered by that component. A master budget must reflect the components of a company and their interaction in pursuit of company goals.

P2 Link both operating and capital expenditures budgets to budgeted financial statements. The operating budgets, capital expenditures budget, and cash budget contain much of the information to prepare a budgeted income statement for the budget period and a budgeted balance sheet at the end of the budget period. Budgeted financial statements show the expected financial consequences of the planned activities described in the budgets.

P3 Prepare production and manufacturing budgets. A manufacturer must prepare a *production budget* instead of a purchases budget. A *manufacturing budget* shows the budgeted production costs for direct materials, direct labor, and overhead.

Guidance Answers to **Decision Maker** and **Decision Ethics**

Budget Staffer Your superior's actions appear unethical because she is using private information for personal gain. As a budget staffer, you are low in the company's hierarchical structure and probably unable to confront this superior directly. You should inform an individual with a position of authority within the organization about your concerns.

Entrepreneur You must deal with two issues. First, because fashions and designs frequently change, you cannot heavily rely on previous budgets. As a result, you must carefully analyze the market to understand what designs are in vogue. This will help you plan the product mix and estimate demand. The second issue is the budgeting period. An annual sales budget may be unreliable because tastes can quickly change. Your best bet might be to prepare monthly and quarterly sales budgets that you continuously monitor and revise.

Environmental Manager You are unlikely to have data on this new position to use in preparing your budget. In this situation, you can use activity-based budgeting. This requires developing a list of activities to conduct, the resources required to perform these activities, and the expenses associated with these resources. You should challenge yourself to be absolutely certain that the listed activities are necessary and that the listed resources are required.

Guidance Answers to **Quick Checks**

1. Major benefits include promoting a focus on the future; providing a basis for evaluating performance; providing a source of motivation; coordinating the departments of a business; and communicating plans and instructions.
2. The budget committee's responsibility is to provide guidance to ensure that budget figures are realistic and coordinated.
3. Budget periods usually coincide with accounting periods and therefore cover a month, quarter, or a year. Budgets can also be prepared for longer time periods, such as five years.
4. Rolling budgets are budgets that are periodically revised in the ongoing process of continuous budgeting.
5. A master budget is a comprehensive or overall plan for the company that is generally expressed in monetary terms.
6. *b*
7. The master budget includes operating budgets, the capital expenditures budget, and financial budgets.
8. *c*; Computed as $(60\% \times 140) + 120 - 50 = 154$.
9. Merchandisers prepare merchandise purchases budgets; manufacturers prepare production and manufacturing budgets.
10. A just-in-time system keeps the level of inventory to a minimum and orders merchandise or materials to meet immediate sales demand. A safety stock system maintains an inventory that is large enough to meet sales demands plus an amount to satisfy unexpected sales demands and an amount to cover delayed shipments from suppliers.
11. *a*
12. (a) Operating budgets (such as sales, selling expense, and administrative budgets), (b) capital expenditures budget, (c) financial budgets: cash budget, budgeted income statement, and budgeted balance sheet.

Key Terms

mhhe.com/wildFAP19e

Key Terms are available at the book's Website for learning and testing in an online Flashcard Format.

Activity-based budgeting (ABB) (p. 953)
Budget (p. 940)
Budgeted balance sheet (p. 952)
Budgeted income statement (p. 952)
Budgeting (p. 940)
Capital expenditures budget (p. 949)
Cash budget (p. 950)
Continuous budgeting (p. 942)
General and administrative expense budget (p. 948)
Manufacturing budget (p. 959)
Master budget (p. 944)
Merchandise purchases budget (p. 947)
Production budget (p. 959)
Rolling budgets (p. 942)
Safety stock (p. 947)
Sales budget (p. 946)
Selling expense budget (p. 948)

Multiple Choice Quiz

Answers on p. 977 mhhe.com/wildFAP19e

Additional Quiz Questions are available at the book's Website.

Quiz23

1. A plan that reports the units or costs of merchandise to be purchased by a merchandising company during the budget period is called a
   - a. Capital expenditures budget.
   - b. Cash budget.
   - c. Merchandise purchases budget.
   - d. Selling expenses budget.
   - e. Sales budget.
2. A hardware store has budgeted sales of $36,000 for its power tool department in July. Management wants to have $7,000 in power tool inventory at the end of July. Its beginning inventory of power tools is expected to be $6,000. What is the budgeted dollar amount of merchandise purchases?
   - a. $36,000
   - b. $43,000
   - c. $42,000
   - d. $35,000
   - e. $37,000
3. A store has the following budgeted sales for the next five months.

May	$210,000
June	186,000
July	180,000
August	220,000
September	240,000

   Cash sales are 25% of total sales and all credit sales are expected to be collected in the month following the sale. The total amount of cash expected to be received from customers in September is
   - a. $240,000
   - b. $225,000
   - c. $ 60,000
   - d. $165,000
   - e. $220,000
4. A plan that shows the expected cash inflows and cash outflows during the budget period, including receipts from loans needed to maintain a minimum cash balance and repayments of such loans, is called
   - a. A rolling budget.
   - b. An income statement.
   - c. A balance sheet.
   - d. A cash budget.
   - e. An operating budget.
5.[A] The following sales are predicted for a company's next four months.

	September	October	November	December
Unit sales	480	560	600	480

   Each month's ending inventory of finished goods should be 30% of the next month's sales. At September 1, the finished goods inventory is 140 units. The budgeted production of units for October is
   - a. 572 units.
   - b. 560 units.
   - c. 548 units.
   - d. 600 units.
   - e. 180 units.

Superscript letter [A] denotes assignments based on Appendix 23A.

Discussion Questions

1. Identify at least three roles that budgeting plays in helping managers control and monitor a business.
2. What two common benchmarks can be used to evaluate actual performance? Which of the two is generally more useful?
3. What is the benefit of continuous budgeting?
4. Identify three usual time horizons for short-term planning and budgets.
5. Why should each department participate in preparing its own budget?
6. How does budgeting help management coordinate and plan business activities?
7. Why is the sales budget so important to the budgeting process?
8. What is a selling expense budget? What is a capital expenditures budget?
9. Budgeting promotes good decision making by requiring managers to conduct ______ and by focusing their attention on the ______.
10. What is a cash budget? Why must operating budgets and the capital expenditures budget be prepared before the cash budget?
11.[A] What is the difference between a production budget and a manufacturing budget?
12. Would a manager of a **Best Buy** retail store participate more in budgeting than a manager at the corporate offices? Explain.
13. Does the manager of a local **Circuit City** retail store participate in long-term budgeting? Explain.
14. Assume that **Apple**'s iMac division is charged with preparing a master budget. Identify the participants—for example, the sales manager for the sales budget—and describe the information each person provides in preparing the master budget.

Denotes Discussion Questions that involve decision making.

McGraw-Hill's HOMEWORK MANAGER® Available with McGraw-Hill's Homework Manager

QUICK STUDY

QS 23-1
Components of a master budget
C3

Which one of the following sets of items are all necessary components of the master budget?

1. Prior sales reports, capital expenditures budget, and financial budgets.
2. Sales budget, operating budgets, and historical financial budgets.
3. Operating budgets, financial budgets, and capital expenditures budget.
4. Operating budgets, historical income statement, and budgeted balance sheet.

QS 23-2
Budget motivation C1

The motivation of employees is one goal of budgeting. Identify three guidelines that organizations should follow if budgeting is to serve effectively as a source of motivation for employees.

QS 23-3
Purchases budget P1

Brill Company's July sales budget calls for sales of $800,000. The store expects to begin July with $30,000 of inventory and to end the month with $35,000 of inventory. Gross margin is typically 40% of sales. Determine the budgeted cost of merchandise purchases for July.

QS 23-4
Budgeting process C2

Good management includes good budgeting. (1) Explain why the bottom-up approach to budgeting is considered a more successful management technique than a top-down approach. (2) Provide an example of implementation of the bottom-up approach to budgeting.

QS 23-5
Computing budgeted accounts receivable
P2

RedTop Company anticipates total sales for June and July of $540,000 and $472,000, respectively. Cash sales are normally 30% of total sales. Of the credit sales, 25% are collected in the same month as the sale, 70% are collected during the first month after the sale, and the remaining 5% are collected in the second month. Determine the amount of accounts receivable reported on the company's budgeted balance sheet as of July 31.

QS 23-6
Cash budget
P1 P2

Use the following information to prepare a cash budget for the month ended on March 31 for Grant Company. The budget should show expected cash receipts and cash disbursements for the month of March and the balance expected on March 31.

a. Beginning cash balance on March 1, $75,000.
b. Cash receipts from sales, $315,000.
c. Budgeted cash disbursements for purchases, $204,000.
d. Budgeted cash disbursements for salaries, $90,000.
e. Other budgeted cash expenses, $30,000.
f. Cash repayment of bank loan, $25,000.

QS 23-7
Activity-based budgeting
A1

Activity-based budgeting is a budget system based on *expected activities*. (1) Describe activity-based budgeting, and explain its preparation of budgets. (2) How does activity-based budgeting differ from traditional budgeting?

QS 23-8[A]
Production budget
P3

Luna Company manufactures watches and has a JIT policy that ending inventory must equal 8% of the next month's sales. It estimates that October's actual ending inventory will consist of 24,000 watches. November and December sales are estimated to be 300,000 and 250,000 watches, respectively. Compute the number of watches to be produced that would appear on the company's production budget for the month of November.

QS 23-9[A]
Factory overhead budget P3

Refer to information from QS 23-8[A]. Luna Company assigns variable overhead at the rate of $1.75 per unit of production. Fixed overhead equals $5,000,000 per month. Prepare a factory overhead budget for November.

QS 23-10
Sales budget P1

Tech-Cam sells miniature digital cameras for $800 each. 450 units were sold in May, and it forecasts 2% growth in unit sales each month. Determine (a) the number of camera sales and (b) the dollar amount of camera sales for the month of June.

QS 23-11
Selling expense budget P1

Refer to information from QS 23-10. Tech-Cam pays a sales manager a monthly salary of $3,000 and a commission of 7.5% of camera sales (in dollars). Prepare a selling expense budget for the month of June.

QS 23-12
Cash budget P1

Refer to information from QS 23-10. Assume 30% of Tech-Cam's sales are for cash. The remaining 70% are credit sales; these customers pay in the month following the sale. Compute the budgeted cash receipts for June.

QS 23-13
Budgeted financial statements P2

Following are selected accounts for a company. For each account, indicate whether it will appear on a budgeted income statement (BIS) or a budgeted balance sheet (BBS). If an item will not appear on either budgeted financial statement, label it NA.

Sales	______
Administrative salaries paid	______
Accumulated depreciation	______
Depreciation expense	______
Interest paid on bank loan	______
Cash dividends paid	______
Bank loan owed	______

Available with McGraw-Hill's Homework Manager McGraw-Hill's HOMEWORK MANAGER®

EXERCISES

Exercise 23-1
Preparation of merchandise purchases budgets (for three periods)
C3 P1

Troy Company prepares monthly budgets. The current budget plans for a September ending inventory of 38,000 units. Company policy is to end each month with merchandise inventory equal to a specified percent of budgeted sales for the following month. Budgeted sales and merchandise purchases for the three most recent months follow. (1) Prepare the merchandise purchases budget for the months of July, August, and September. (2) Compute the ratio of ending inventory to the next month's sales for each budget prepared in part 1. (3) How many units are budgeted for sale in October?

	Sales (Units)	Purchases (Units)
July	170,000	200,000
August	320,000	312,000
September	280,000	262,000

Check July budgeted ending inventory, 64,000

Exercise 23-2
Preparation of cash budgets (for three periods)
C3 P2

Franke Co. budgeted the following cash receipts and cash disbursements for the first three months of next year.

	Cash Receipts	Cash Disbursements
January	$525,000	$484,000
February	411,000	350,000
March	456,000	520,000

According to a credit agreement with the company's bank, Franke promises to have a minimum cash balance of $20,000 at each month-end. In return, the bank has agreed that the company can borrow up to $160,000 at an annual interest rate of 12%, paid on the last day of each month. The interest is computed based on the beginning balance of the loan for the month. The company has a cash balance of $20,000 and a loan balance of $40,000 at January 1. Prepare monthly cash budgets for each of the first three months of next year.

Check January ending cash balance, $20,600

Exercise 23-3
Preparation of a cash budget
C3 P2

Use the following information to prepare the July cash budget for Anker Co. It should show expected cash receipts and cash disbursements for the month and the cash balance expected on July 31.

a. Beginning cash balance on July 1: $63,000.

b. Cash receipts from sales: 30% is collected in the month of sale, 50% in the next month, and 20% in the second month after sale (uncollectible accounts are negligible and can be ignored). Sales amounts are: May (actual), $1,700,000; June (actual), $1,200,000; and July (budgeted), $1,400,000.

c. Payments on merchandise purchases: 90% in the month of purchase and 10% in the month following purchase. Purchases amounts are: June (actual), $620,000; and July (budgeted), $790,000.

d. Budgeted cash disbursements for salaries in July: $220,000.

e. Budgeted depreciation expense for July: $11,000.

f. Other cash expenses budgeted for July: $230,000.

g. Accrued income taxes due in July: $50,000.

h. Bank loan interest due in July: $7,000.

Check Ending cash balance, $143,000

Exercise 23-4
Preparing a budgeted income statement and balance sheet
C3 P2

Use the information in Exercise 23-3 and the following additional information to prepare a budgeted income statement for the month of July and a budgeted balance sheet for July 31.

a. Cost of goods sold is 60% of sales.

b. Inventory at the end of June is $80,000 and at the end of July is $30,000.

c. Salaries payable on June 30 are $50,000 and are expected to be $60,000 on July 31.

d. The equipment account balance is $1,600,000 on July 31. On June 30, the accumulated depreciation on equipment is $280,000.

e. The $7,000 cash payment of interest represents the 1% monthly expense on a bank loan of $700,000.

f. Income taxes payable on July 31 are $24,600, and the income tax rate applicable to the company is 30%.

g. The only other balance sheet accounts are: Common Stock, with a balance of $850,000 on June 30; and Retained Earnings, with a balance of $931,000 on June 30.

Check Net income, $57,400; Total assets, $2,702,000

Exercise 23-5
Computing budgeted cash payments for purchases
C3 P2

DeVon Company's cost of goods sold is consistently $30 per unit. The company plans to carry ending merchandise inventory for each month equal to 20% of the next month's budgeted unit sales; August beginning inventory is 2,000 units. All merchandise is purchased on credit, and 40% of the purchases made during a month is paid for in that month. Another 25% is paid for during the first month after purchase, and the remaining 35% is paid for during the second month after purchase. Expected unit sales are: August (actual), 10,000; September (actual), 9,500; October (estimated), 8,750; November (estimated), 8,250. Use this information to determine October's expected cash payments for purchases. (*Hint:* Use the layout of Exhibit 23.8, but revised for the facts given here.)

Check Budgeted purchases: August, $297,000; October, $259,500

Exercise 23-6
Computing budgeted purchases and costs of goods sold
C3 P1 P2

Dollar Value Company purchases all merchandise on credit. It recently budgeted the following month-end accounts payable balances and merchandise inventory balances. Cash payments on accounts payable during each month are expected to be: May, $1,500,000; June, $1,530,000; July, $1,350,000; and August, $1,495,000. Use the available information to compute the budgeted amounts of (1) merchandise purchases for June, July, and August, and (2) cost of goods sold for June, July, and August.

	Accounts Payable	Merchandise Inventory
May 31	$120,000	$250,000
June 30	170,000	200,000
July 31	300,000	250,000
August 31	150,000	350,000

Check June purchases, $1,580,000; June cost of goods sold, $1,630,000

Exercise 23-7
Computing budgeted accounts payable and purchases—sales forecast in dollars
P1 P2

E-Sound, a merchandising company specializing in home computer speakers, budgets its monthly cost of goods sold to equal 50% of sales. Its inventory policy calls for ending inventory in each month to equal 40% of the next month's budgeted cost of goods sold. All purchases are on credit, and 40% of the purchases in a month is paid for in the same month. Another 40% is paid for during the first month after purchase, and the remaining 20% is paid for in the second month after purchase. The following sales budgets are set: July, $200,000; August, $140,000; September, $170,000; October, $125,000; and

Check July purchases, $88,000; Sept. payments on accts. pay., $78,400

November, $115,000. Compute the following: (1) budgeted merchandise purchases for July, August, September, and October; (2) budgeted payments on accounts payable for September and October; and (3) budgeted ending balances of accounts payable for September and October. (*Hint:* For part 1, refer to Exhibits 23.7 and 23.8 for guidance, but note that budgeted sales are in dollars for this assignment.)

Exercise 23-8A
Preparing production budgets (for two periods) P3

Check Second quarter production, 381,300 units

Electro Company manufactures an innovative automobile transmission for electric cars. Management predicts that ending inventory for the first quarter will be 38,500 units. The following unit sales of the transmissions are expected during the rest of the year: second quarter, 221,000 units; third quarter, 497,000 units; and fourth quarter, 243,500 units. Company policy calls for the ending inventory of a quarter to equal 40% of the next quarter's budgeted sales. Prepare a production budget for both the second and third quarters that shows the number of transmissions to manufacture.

Exercise 23-9A
Direct materials budget P3

Refer to information from Exercise 23-8A. Electro Company reports direct materials requirements of 0.60 per unit. It also aims to end each quarter with an ending inventory of direct materials equal to 40% of next quarter's budgeted materials requirements. Direct materials cost $175 per unit. Prepare a direct materials budget for the second quarter.

Exercise 23-10A
Direct labor budget P3

Refer to information from Exercise 23-8A. Each transmission requires 2 direct labor hours, at a cost of $18 per hour. Prepare a direct labor budget for the second quarter.

Available with McGraw-Hill's Homework Manager McGraw-Hill's HOMEWORK MANAGER®

PROBLEM SET A

Problem 23-1A
Preparation and analysis of merchandise purchases budgets
C3 P1

mhhe.com/wildFAP19e

Herron Supply is a merchandiser of three different products. The company's February 28 inventories are footwear, 18,500 units; sports equipment, 80,000 units; and apparel, 50,000 units. Management believes that excessive inventories have accumulated for all three products. As a result, a new policy dictates that ending inventory in any month should equal 29% of the expected unit sales for the following month. Expected sales in units for March, April, May, and June follow.

	Budgeted Sales in Units			
	March	April	May	June
Footwear	15,000	26,500	31,500	35,000
Sports equipment	70,500	89,000	96,000	89,500
Apparel	40,000	38,000	34,000	23,000

Required

Check (1) March budgeted purchases Footwear, 4,185; Sports equip., 16,310; Apparel, 1,020

1. Prepare a merchandise purchases budget (in units) for each product for each of the months of March, April, and May.

Analysis Component

2. The purchases budgets in part 1 should reflect fewer purchases of all three products in March compared to those in April and May. What factor caused fewer purchases to be planned? Suggest business conditions that would cause this factor to both occur and impact the company in this way.

Problem 23-2A
Preparation of cash budgets (for three periods) C3 P2

mhhe.com/wildFAP19e

During the last week of August, Muir Company's owner approaches the bank for a $100,000 loan to be made on September 2 and repaid on November 30 with annual interest of 12%, for an interest cost of $3,000. The owner plans to increase the store's inventory by $80,000 during September and needs the loan to pay for inventory acquisitions. The bank's loan officer needs more information about Muir's ability to repay the loan and asks the owner to forecast the store's November 30 cash position. On September 1, Muir is expected to have a $4,000 cash balance, $152,000 of accounts receivable, and $115,000 of accounts payable. Its budgeted sales, merchandise purchases, and various cash disbursements for the next three months follow.

Budgeted Figures*	September	October	November
Sales	$350,000	$400,000	$425,000
Merchandise purchases	275,000	185,000	180,000
Cash disbursements			
Payroll	25,000	30,000	35,000
Rent	12,000	12,000	12,000
Other cash expenses	38,000	29,000	24,500
Repayment of bank loan			100,000
Interest on the bank loan			3,000

* Operations began in August; August sales were $200,000 and purchases were $115,000.

The budgeted September merchandise purchases include the inventory increase. All sales are on account. The company predicts that 24% of credit sales is collected in the month of the sale, 44% in the month following the sale, 21% in the second month, 8% in the third, and the remainder is uncollectible. Applying these percents to the August credit sales, for example, shows that $88,000 of the $200,000 will be collected in September, $42,000 in October, and $16,000 in November. All merchandise is purchased on credit; 85% of the balance is paid in the month following a purchase, and the remaining 15% is paid in the second month. For example, of the $115,000 August purchases, $97,750 will be paid in September and $17,250 in October.

Required

Prepare a cash budget for September, October, and November for Muir Company. Show supporting calculations as needed.

Check Budgeted cash balance: September, $103,250; October, $73,250; November, $67,750

Problem 23-3A
Preparation and analysis of cash budgets with supporting inventory and purchases budgets
C3 P2

Culver Company sells its product for $165 per unit. Its actual and projected sales follow.

	Units	Dollars
April (actual)	4,000	$ 660,000
May (actual)	2,200	363,000
June (budgeted)	5,000	825,000
July (budgeted)	6,500	1,072,500
August (budgeted)	3,700	610,500

All sales are on credit. Recent experience shows that 28% of credit sales is collected in the month of the sale, 42% in the month after the sale, 25% in the second month after the sale, and 5% proves to be uncollectible. The product's purchase price is $110 per unit. All purchases are payable within 10 days. Thus, 60% of purchases made in a month is paid in that month and the other 40% is paid in the next month. The company has a policy to maintain an ending monthly inventory of 19% of the next month's unit sales plus a safety stock of 135 units. The April 30 and May 31 actual inventory levels are consistent with this policy. Selling and administrative expenses for the year are $1,140,000 and are paid evenly throughout the year in cash. The company's minimum cash balance at month-end is $60,000. This minimum is maintained, if necessary, by borrowing cash from the bank. If the balance exceeds $60,000, the company repays as much of the loan as it can without going below the minimum. This type of loan carries an annual 12% interest rate. On May 31, the loan balance is $39,000, and the company's cash balance is $60,000.

Required

1. Prepare a table that shows the computation of cash collections of its credit sales (accounts receivable) in each of the months of June and July.
2. Prepare a table that shows the computation of budgeted ending inventories (in units) for April, May, June, and July.
3. Prepare the merchandise purchases budget for May, June, and July. Report calculations in units and then show the dollar amount of purchases for each month.

Check (1) Cash collections: June, $548,460; July, $737,550

(3) Budgeted purchases: May, $300,520; June, $581,350

(5) Budgeted ending loan balance: June, $54,948; July, $39,375

4. Prepare a table showing the computation of cash payments on product purchases for June and July.

5. Prepare a cash budget for June and July, including any loan activity and interest expense. Compute the loan balance at the end of each month.

Analysis Component

6. Refer to your answer to part 5. Culver's cash budget indicates the company will need to borrow more than $15,000 in June and will be able to pay most of it back in July. Suggest some reasons that knowing this information in May would be helpful to management.

Problem 23-4A

Preparation and analysis of budgeted income statements

C3 P2 

Poole, a one-product mail-order firm, buys its product for $75 per unit and sells it for $140 per unit. The sales staff receives a 10% commission on the sale of each unit. Its December income statement follows.

POOLE COMPANY
Income Statement
For Month Ended December 31, 2009

Sales	$1,400,000
Cost of goods sold	750,000
Gross profit	650,000
Expenses	
Sales commissions (10%)	140,000
Advertising	215,000
Store rent	26,000
Administrative salaries	42,000
Depreciation	52,000
Other expenses	13,000
Total expenses	488,000
Net income	$ 162,000

Management expects December's results to be repeated in January, February, and March of 2010 without any changes in strategy. Management, however, has an alternative plan. It believes that unit sales will increase at a rate of 10% *each* month for the next three months (beginning with January) if the item's selling price is reduced to $125 per unit and advertising expenses are increased by 15% and remain at that level for all three months. The cost of its product will remain at $75 per unit, the sales staff will continue to earn a 10% commission, and the remaining expenses will stay the same.

Required

Check (1) Budgeted net income: January, $32,250; February, $73,500; March, $118,875

1. Prepare budgeted income statements for each of the months of January, February, and March that show the expected results from implementing the proposed changes. Use a three-column format, with one column for each month.

Analysis Component

2. Use the budgeted income statements from part 1 to recommend whether management should implement the proposed changes. Explain.

Problem 23-5A

Preparation of a complete master budget

C2 C3 P1 P2

Near the end of 2009, the management of Nygaard Sports Co., a merchandising company, prepared the following estimated balance sheet for December 31, 2009.

NYGAARD SPORTS COMPANY
Estimated Balance Sheet
December 31, 2009

Assets		
Cash		$ 35,000
Accounts receivable		520,000
Inventory		142,500
Total current assets		697,500
Equipment	$540,000	
Less accumulated depreciation	67,500	472,500
Total assets		$1,170,000

[continued on next page]

[continued from previous page]

Liabilities and Equity		
Accounts payable	$345,000	
Bank loan payable	14,000	
Taxes payable (due 3/15/2010)	91,000	
Total liabilities		$ 450,000
Common stock	473,000	
Retained earnings	247,000	
Total stockholders' equity		720,000
Total liabilities and equity		$1,170,000

To prepare a master budget for January, February, and March of 2010, management gathers the following information.

a. Nygaard Sports' single product is purchased for $30 per unit and resold for $53 per unit. The expected inventory level of 4,750 units on December 31, 2009, is more than management's desired level for 2010, which is 20% of the next month's expected sales (in units). Expected sales are: January, 7,500 units; February, 9,250 units; March, 10,750 units; and April, 10,500 units.

b. Cash sales and credit sales represent 20% and 80%, respectively, of total sales. Of the credit sales, 57% is collected in the first month after the month of sale and 43% in the second month after the month of sale. For the December 31, 2009, accounts receivable balance, $130,000 is collected in January and the remaining $390,000 is collected in February.

c. Merchandise purchases are paid for as follows: 20% in the first month after the month of purchase and 80% in the second month after the month of purchase. For the December 31, 2009, accounts payable balance, $70,000 is paid in January and the remaining $275,000 is paid in February.

d. Sales commissions equal to 20% of sales are paid each month. Sales salaries (excluding commissions) are $72,000 per year.

e. General and administrative salaries are $156,000 per year. Maintenance expense equals $2,100 per month and is paid in cash.

f. Equipment reported in the December 31, 2009, balance sheet was purchased in January 2009. It is being depreciated over eight years under the straight-line method with no salvage value. The following amounts for new equipment purchases are planned in the coming quarter: January, $36,000; February, $96,000; and March, $28,800. This equipment will be depreciated under the straight-line method over eight years with no salvage value. A full month's depreciation is taken for the month in which equipment is purchased.

g. The company plans to acquire land at the end of March at a cost of $155,000, which will be paid with cash on the last day of the month.

h. Nygaard Sports has a working arrangement with its bank to obtain additional loans as needed. The interest rate is 12% per year, and interest is paid at each month-end based on the beginning balance. Partial or full payments on these loans can be made on the last day of the month. The company has agreed to maintain a minimum ending cash balance of $25,000 in each month.

i. The income tax rate for the company is 43%. Income taxes on the first quarter's income will not be paid until April 15.

Required

Prepare a master budget for each of the first three months of 2010; include the following component budgets (show supporting calculations as needed, and round amounts to the nearest dollar):

1. Monthly sales budgets (showing both budgeted unit sales and dollar sales).

2. Monthly merchandise purchases budgets.

3. Monthly selling expense budgets.

4. Monthly general and administrative expense budgets.

5. Monthly capital expenditures budgets.

6. Monthly cash budgets.

7. Budgeted income statement for the entire first quarter (not for each month).

8. Budgeted balance sheet as of March 31, 2010.

Check (2) Budgeted purchases: January, $138,000; February, $286,500
(3) Budgeted selling expenses: January, $85,500; February, $104,050

(6) Ending cash bal.: January, $25,000; February, $175,308
(8) Budgeted total assets at March 31, $1,527,448

Problem 23-6A[A]
Preparing production and direct materials budgets
C3 P3

Black Diamond Company produces snow skis. Each ski requires 2 pounds of carbon fiber. The company's management predicts that 4,800 skis and 6,100 pounds of carbon fiber will be in inventory on June 30 of the current year and that 152,000 skis will be sold during the next (third) quarter. Management wants to end the third quarter with 3,700 skis and 4,200 pounds of carbon fiber in inventory. Carbon fiber can be purchased for $15 per pound.

Check (1) Units manuf., 150,900; (2) Cost of carbon fiber purchases, $4,498,500

Required

1. Prepare the third-quarter production budget for skis.
2. Prepare the third-quarter direct materials (carbon fiber) budget; include the dollar cost of purchases.

PROBLEM SET B

Problem 23-1B
Preparation and analysis of merchandise purchases budgets
C3 P1 

Water Sports Corp. is a merchandiser of three different products. The company's March 31 inventories are water skis, 60,000 units; tow ropes, 45,000 units; and life jackets, 75,000 units. Management believes that excessive inventories have accumulated for all three products. As a result, a new policy dictates that ending inventory in any month should equal 10% of the expected unit sales for the following month. Expected sales in units for April, May, June, and July follow.

	Budgeted Sales in Units			
	April	May	June	July
Water skis	105,000	135,000	195,000	150,000
Tow ropes	50,000	45,000	55,000	50,000
Life jackets	80,000	95,000	100,000	60,000

Check (1) April budgeted purchases: Water skis, 58,500; Tow ropes, 9,500; Life jackets, 14,500

Required

1. Prepare a merchandise purchases budget (in units) for each product for each of the months of April, May, and June.

Analysis Component

2. The purchases budgets in part 1 should reflect fewer purchases of all three products in April compared to those in May and June. What factor caused fewer purchases to be planned? Suggest business conditions that would cause this factor to both occur and affect the company as it has.

Problem 23-2B
Preparation of cash budgets (for three periods)
C3 P2

During the last week of March, Harlan Stereo's owner approaches the bank for an $80,000 loan to be made on April 1 and repaid on June 30 with annual interest of 12%, for an interest cost of $2,400. The owner plans to increase the store's inventory by $120,000 in April and needs the loan to pay for inventory acquisitions. The bank's loan officer needs more information about Harlan Stereo's ability to repay the loan and asks the owner to forecast the store's June 30 cash position. On April 1, Harlan Stereo is expected to have a $6,000 cash balance, $270,000 of accounts receivable, and $200,000 of accounts payable. Its budgeted sales, merchandise purchases, and various cash disbursements for the next three months follow.

	Budgeted Figures*	April	May	June
2	Sales	$440,000	$600,000	$760,000
3	Merchandise purchases	420,000	360,000	440,000
4	Cash disbursements			
5	Payroll	32,000	34,000	36,000
6	Rent	12,000	12,000	12,000
7	Other cash expenses	128,000	16,000	14,000
8	Repayment of bank loan			80,000
9	Interest on the bank loan........			2,400

* Operations began in March; March sales were $360,000 and purchases were $200,000.

The budgeted April merchandise purchases include the inventory increase. All sales are on account. The company predicts that 25% of credit sales is collected in the month of the sale, 45% in the month following the sale, 20% in the second month, 9% in the third, and the remainder is uncollectible. Applying these percents to the March credit sales, for example, shows that $162,000 of the $360,000 will be collected in April, $72,000 in May, and $32,400 in June. All merchandise is purchased on credit; 80% of the balance is paid in the month following a purchase and the remaining 20% is paid in the second month. For example, of the $200,000 March purchases, $160,000 will be paid in April and $40,000 in May.

Required

Prepare a cash budget for April, May, and June for Harlan Stereo. Show supporting calculations as needed.

Check Budgeted cash balance: April, $26,000; May, $8,000; June, $72,000

Problem 23-3B
Preparation and analysis of cash budgets with supporting inventory and purchases budgets
C3 P2

Parador Company sells its product for $22 per unit. Its actual and projected sales follow.

	Units	Dollars
January (actual)	9,000	$198,000
February (actual)	11,250	247,500
March (budgeted)	9,500	209,000
April (budgeted)	9,375	206,250
May (budgeted)	10,500	231,000

All sales are on credit. Recent experience shows that 40% of credit sales is collected in the month of the sale, 35% in the month after the sale, 23% in the second month after the sale, and 2% proves to be uncollectible. The product's purchase price is $12 per unit. All purchases are payable within 21 days. Thus, 30% of purchases made in a month is paid in that month and the other 70% is paid in the next month. The company has a policy to maintain an ending monthly inventory of 20% of the next month's unit sales plus a safety stock of 100 units. The January 31 and February 28 actual inventory levels are consistent with this policy. Selling and administrative expenses for the year are $960,000 and are paid evenly throughout the year in cash. The company's minimum cash balance for month-end is $25,000. This minimum is maintained, if necessary, by borrowing cash from the bank. If the balance exceeds $25,000, the company repays as much of the loan as it can without going below the minimum. This type of loan carries an annual 12% interest rate. At February 28, the loan balance is $20,000, and the company's cash balance is $25,000.

Required

1. Prepare a table that shows the computation of cash collections of its credit sales (accounts receivable) in each of the months of March and April.
2. Prepare a table showing the computations of budgeted ending inventories (units) for January, February, March, and April.
3. Prepare the merchandise purchases budget for February, March, and April. Report calculations in units and then show the dollar amount of purchases for each month.
4. Prepare a table showing the computation of cash payments on product purchases for March and April.
5. Prepare a cash budget for March and April, including any loan activity and interest expense. Compute the loan balance at the end of each month.

Check (1) Cash collections: March, $215,765; April, $212,575

(3) Budgeted purchases: February, $130,800; March, $113,700

(5) Ending cash balance: March, $25,000, April, $33,219

Analysis Component

6. Refer to your answer to part 5. Parador's cash budget indicates whether the company must borrow additional funds at the end of March. Suggest some reasons that knowing the loan needs in advance would be helpful to management.

Problem 23-4B
Preparation and analysis of budgeted income statements
C3 P2

Tech-Media buys its product for $90 and sells it for $200 per unit. The sales staff receives a 12% commission on the sale of each unit. Its June income statement follows.

TECH-MEDIA COMPANY Income Statement For Month Ended June 30, 2009	
Sales	$2,000,000
Cost of goods sold	900,000
Gross profit	1,100,000
Expenses	
Sales commissions (12%)	240,000
Advertising	225,000
Store rent	32,000
Administrative salaries	75,000
Depreciation	80,000
Other expenses	25,000
Total expenses	677,000
Net income	$ 423,000

Management expects June's results to be repeated in July, August, and September without any changes in strategy. Management, however, has another plan. It believes that unit sales will increase at a rate of 10% *each* month for the next three months (beginning with July) if the item's selling price is reduced to $180 per unit and advertising expenses are increased by 20% and remain at that level for all three months. The cost of its product will remain at $90 per unit, the sales staff will continue to earn a 12% commission, and the remaining expenses will stay the same.

Check Budgeted net income: July, $270,400; August, $345,640; September, $428,404

Required

1. Prepare budgeted income statements for each of the months of July, August, and September that show the expected results from implementing the proposed changes. Use a three-column format, with one column for each month.

Analysis Component

2. Use the budgeted income statements from part 1 to recommend whether management should implement the proposed plan. Explain.

Problem 23-5B
Preparation of a complete master budget
C2 C3 P1 P2

Near the end of 2009, the management of Pak Corp., a merchandising company, prepared the following estimated balance sheet for December 31, 2009.

PAK CORPORATION Estimated Balance Sheet December 31, 2009		
Assets		
Cash		$ 36,000
Accounts receivable		470,000
Inventory		300,000
Total current assets		806,000
Equipment	$1,080,000	
Less accumulated depreciation	135,000	945,000
Total assets		$1,751,000
Liabilities and Equity		
Accounts payable	$395,000	
Bank loan payable	25,000	
Taxes payable (due 3/15/2010)	20,000	
Total liabilities		$ 440,000
Common stock	550,000	
Retained earnings	761,000	
Total stockholders' equity		1,311,000
Total liabilities and equity		$1,751,000

To prepare a master budget for January, February, and March of 2010, management gathers the following information.

a. Pak Corp.'s single product is purchased for $30 per unit and resold for $45 per unit. The expected inventory level of 10,000 units on December 31, 2009, is more than management's desired level for 2010, which is 25% of the next month's expected sales (in units). Expected sales are: January, 12,000 units; February, 16,000 units; March, 20,000 units; and April, 18,000 units.

b. Cash sales and credit sales represent 25% and 75%, respectively, of total sales. Of the credit sales, 60% is collected in the first month after the month of sale and 40% in the second month after the month of sale. For the $470,000 accounts receivable balance at December 31, 2009, $330,000 is collected in January 2010 and the remaining $140,000 is collected in February 2010.

c. Merchandise purchases are paid for as follows: 20% in the first month after the month of purchase and 80% in the second month after the month of purchase. For the $395,000 accounts payable balance at December 31, 2009, $207,000 is paid in January 2010 and the remaining $188,000 is paid in February 2010.

d. Sales commissions equal to 20% of sales are paid each month. Sales salaries (excluding commissions) are $180,000 per year.

e. General and administrative salaries are $540,000 per year. Maintenance expense equals $6,000 per month and is paid in cash.

f. Equipment reported in the December 31, 2009, balance sheet was purchased in January 2009. It is being depreciated over 8 years under the straight-line method with no salvage value. The following amounts for new equipment purchases are planned in the coming quarter: January, $72,000; February, $96,000; and March, $28,800. This equipment will be depreciated using the straight-line method over 8 years with no salvage value. A full month's depreciation is taken for the month in which equipment is purchased.

g. The company plans to acquire land at the end of March at a cost of $150,000, which will be paid with cash on the last day of the month.

h. Pak Corp. has a working arrangement with its bank to obtain additional loans as needed. The interest rate is 12% per year, and interest is paid at each month-end based on the beginning balance. Partial or full payments on these loans can be made on the last day of the month. Pak has agreed to maintain a minimum ending cash balance of $36,000 in each month.

i. The income tax rate for the company is 30%. Income taxes on the first quarter's income will not be paid until April 15.

Required

Prepare a master budget for each of the first three months of 2010; include the following component budgets (show supporting calculations as needed, and round amounts to the nearest dollar):

1. Monthly sales budgets (showing both budgeted unit sales and dollar sales).

2. Monthly merchandise purchases budgets.

3. Monthly selling expense budgets.

4. Monthly general and administrative expense budgets.

5. Monthly capital expenditures budgets.

6. Monthly cash budgets.

7. Budgeted income statement for the entire first quarter (not for each month).

8. Budgeted balance sheet as of March 31, 2010.

Check (2) Budgeted purchases: January, $180,000; February, $510,000; (3) Budgeted selling expenses: January, $123,000; February, $159,000

(6) Ending cash bal.: January, $36,000; February, $55,617

(8) Budgeted total assets at March 31, $2,355,317

Problem 23-6B^A
Preparing production and direct materials budgets
C3 P3

Thorpe Company produces baseball bats. Each bat requires 3 pounds of aluminum alloy. Management predicts that 4,000 bats and 7,500 pounds of aluminum alloy will be in inventory on March 31 of the current year and that 125,000 bats will be sold during this year's second quarter. Management wants to end the second quarter with 3,000 finished bats and 6,000 pounds of aluminum alloy in inventory. Aluminum alloy can be purchased for $4 per pound.

Required

1. Prepare the second-quarter production budget for bats.

2. Prepare the second-quarter direct materials (aluminum alloy) budget; include the dollar cost of purchases.

Check (1) Units manuf., 124,000; (2) Cost of aluminum purchases, $1,482,000

SERIAL PROBLEM

Success Systems

(This serial problem began in Chapter 1 and continues through most of the book. If previous chapter segments were not completed, the serial problem can begin at this point. It is helpful, but not necessary, to use the Working Papers that accompany the book.)

SP 23 Adriana Lopez expects second quarter 2010 sales of her new line of computer furniture to be the same as the first quarter's sales (reported below) without any changes in strategy. Monthly sales averaged 40 desk units (sales price of $1,250) and 20 chairs (sales price of $500).

SUCCESS SYSTEMS Segment Income Statement* For Quarter Ended March 31, 2010	
Sales†	$180,000
Cost of goods sold‡	115,000
Gross profit	65,000
Expenses	
Sales commissions (10%)	18,000
Advertising expenses	9,000
Other fixed expenses	18,000
Total expenses	45,000
Net income	$ 20,000

* Reflects revenue and expense activity only related to the computer furniture segment.

† Revenue: (120 desks × $1,250) + (60 chairs × $500) = $150,000 + $30,000 = $180,000

‡ Cost of goods sold: (120 desks × $750) + (60 chairs × $250) + $10,000 = $115,000

Lopez believes that sales will increase each month for the next three months (April, 48 desks, 32 chairs; May, 52 desks, 35 chairs; June, 56 desks, 38 chairs) *if* selling prices are reduced to $1,150 for desks and $450 for chairs, and advertising expenses are increased by 10% and remain at that level for all three months. The products' variable cost will remain at $750 for desks and $250 for chairs. The sales staff will continue to earn a 10% commission, the fixed manufacturing costs per month will remain at $10,000 and other fixed expenses will remain at $6,000 per month.

Required

Check (1) Budgeted income (loss): April, $(660); May, $945

1. Prepare budgeted income statements for each of the months of April, May, and June that show the expected results from implementing the proposed changes. Use a three-column format, with one column for each month.
2. Use the budgeted income statements from part 1 to recommend whether Lopez should implement the proposed changes. Explain.

BEYOND THE NUMBERS

REPORTING IN ACTION

P2 C2 C3 

BTN 23-1 Financial statements often serve as a starting point in formulating budgets. You are assigned to review **Best Buy**'s financial statements to determine its cash paid for dividends in the current year and the budgeted cash needed to pay its next year's dividend.

Required

1. Which financial statement(s) reports the amount of (a) cash dividends paid and (b) annual cash dividends declared? Explain where on the statement(s) this information is reported.
2. Indicate the amount of cash dividends (a) paid in the year ended March 3, 2007, and (b) to be paid (budgeted for) next year under the assumption that annual cash dividends equal 20% of the prior year's net income.

Fast Forward

3. Access Best Buy's financial statements for a fiscal year ending after March 3, 2007, from either its Website [BestBuy.com] or the SEC's EDGAR database [www.SEC.gov]. Compare your answer for part 2 with actual cash dividends paid for that fiscal year. Compute the error, if any, in your estimate. Speculate as to why dividends were higher or lower than budgeted.

COMPARATIVE ANALYSIS

P2 

BTN 23-2 One source of cash savings for a company is improved management of inventory. To illustrate, assume that **Best Buy** and **Circuit City** both have $300,000 per month in sales in the Virginia area, and both forecast this level of sales per month for the next 24 months. Also assume that both Best Buy and Circuit City have a 20% contribution margin and equal fixed costs, and that cost of goods sold is the only variable cost. Assume that the main difference between Best Buy and Circuit City is the distribution system. Best Buy uses a just-in-time system and requires ending inventory of only 10% of next month's sales in inventory at each month-end. However, Circuit City is building an improved distribution system and currently requires 40% of next month's sales in inventory at each month-end.

Required

1. Compute the amount by which Circuit City can reduce its inventory level if it can match Best Buy's system of maintaining an inventory equal to 10% of next month's sales. (*Hint:* Focus on the facts given and only on the Virginia area.)
2. Explain how the analysis in part 1 that shows ending inventory levels for both the 40% and 10% required inventory policies can help justify a just-in-time inventory system. You can assume a 15% interest cost for resources that are tied up in ending inventory.

ETHICS CHALLENGE

C1 C2

BTN 23-3 Both the budget process and budgets themselves can impact management actions, both positively and negatively. For instance, a common practice among not-for-profit organizations and government agencies is for management to spend any amounts remaining in a budget at the end of the budget period, a practice often called "use it or lose it." The view is that if a department manager does not spend the budgeted amount, top management will reduce next year's budget by the amount not spent. To avoid losing budget dollars, department managers often spend all budgeted amounts regardless of the value added to products or services. All of us pay for the costs associated with this budget system.

Required

Write a one-half page report to a local not-for-profit organization or government agency offering a solution to the "use it or lose it" budgeting problem.

COMMUNICATING IN PRACTICE

P1 

BTN 23-4 The sales budget is usually the first and most crucial of the component budgets in a master budget because all other budgets usually rely on it for planning purposes.

Required

Assume that your company's sales staff provides information on expected sales and selling prices for items making up the sales budget. Prepare a one-page memorandum to your supervisor outlining concerns with the sales staff's input in the sales budget when its compensation is at least partly tied to these budgets. More generally, explain the importance of assessing any potential bias in information provided to the budget process.

TAKING IT TO THE NET

C2 P1 P2

BTN 23-5 Access information on e-budgets through The Manage Mentor:
http://www.themanagementor.com/kuniverse/kmailers_universe/finance_kmailers/cfa/budgeting2.htm
Read the information provided.

Required

1. Assume the role of a senior manager in a large, multidivision company. What are the benefits of using e-budgets?
2. As a senior manager, what concerns do you have with the concept and application of e-budgets?

TEAMWORK IN ACTION

A1

BTN 23-6 Your team is to prepare a budget report outlining the costs of attending college (full-time) for the next two semesters (30 hours) or three quarters (45 hours). This budget's focus is solely on attending college; do not include personal items in the team's budget. Your budget must include tuition, books, supplies, club fees, food, housing, and all costs associated with travel to and from college. This budgeting exercise is similar to the initial phase in activity-based budgeting. Include a list of any assumptions you use in completing the budget. Be prepared to present your budget in class.

ENTREPRENEURIAL DECISION

C1

BTN 23-7 **Jibbitz** produces charms to fit in the holes of **Crocs** shoes. Assume Jibbitz is considering expanding its product line to include necklaces that hold the charms. They plan on meeting with a financial institution for potential funding and have asked by its loan officers for their business plan.

Required

1. What should Jibbitz's business plan include?
2. How can budgeting help the owners efficiently develop and operate their business?

HITTING THE ROAD

C3 P1

BTN 23-8 To help understand the factors impacting a sales budget, you are to visit three businesses with the same ownership or franchise membership. Record the selling prices of two identical products at each location, such as regular and premium gas sold at **Chevron** stations. You are likely to find a difference in prices for at least one of the three locations you visit.

Required

1. Identify at least three external factors that must be considered when setting the sales budget. (*Note:* There is a difference between internal and external factors that impact the sales budget.)
2. What factors might explain any differences identified in the prices of the businesses you visited?

GLOBAL DECISION

BTN 23-9 Access **DSG**'s income statement (www.DSGiplc.com) for the year ended April 28, 2007.

Required

1. Is DSG's administrative expense budget likely to be an important budget in its master budgeting process? Explain. (*Hint:* Review its Note 3.)
2. Identify three types of expenses that would be reported as administrative expenses on DSG's income statement.
3. Who likely has the initial responsibility for DSG's administrative expense budget? Explain.

ANSWERS TO MULTIPLE CHOICE QUIZ

1. c

2. e; Budgeted purchases = $36,000 + $7,000 − $6,000 = $37,000

3. b; Cash collected = 25% of September sales + 75% of August sales = (0.25 × $240,000) + (0.75 × $220,000) = $225,000

4. d

5. a; 560 units + (0.30 × 600 units) − (0.30 × 560 units) = 572 units

A Look Back

Chapter 23 explained the master budget and its component budgets as well as their usefulness for planning and monitoring company activities.

A Look at This Chapter

This chapter describes flexible budgets, variance analysis, and standard costs. It explains how each is used for purposes of better controlling and monitoring business activities.

A Look Ahead

Chapter 25 focuses on capital budgeting decisions. It also explains and illustrates several procedures used in evaluating short-term managerial decisions.

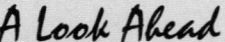

Chapter 24 Flexible Budgets and Standard Costs

Learning Objectives

CAP

Conceptual

C1 Define *standard costs* and explain their computation and uses. *(p. 985)*

C2 Describe variances and what they reveal about performance. *(p. 986)*

C3 Explain how standard cost information is useful for management by exception. *(p. 996)*

Analytical

A1 Compare fixed and flexible budgets. *(p. 982)*

A2 Analyze changes in sales from expected amounts. *(p. 998)*

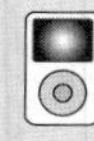

LP24

Procedural

P1 Prepare a flexible budget and interpret a flexible budget performance report. *(p. 982)*

P2 Compute materials and labor variances. *(p. 988)*

P3 Compute overhead variances. *(p. 992)*

P4 Prepare journal entries for standard costs and account for price and quantity variances. *(p. 996)*

Decision Feature

Good Vibrations

"Look at each part of the process and improve it"
—Chris Martin

NAZARETH, PA—Eric Clapton. Paul McCartney. Johnny Cash. Jimi Hendrix. What do these musical legends have in common? All played guitars manufactured by the **Martin Guitar Company** **(MartinGuitar.com).** Martin manufactures high-quality guitars and recently sold its millionth. This family-owned company, headed by Christian (Chris) F. Martin, has prospered by hurdling challenges facing all manufacturers—materials quality, product design, quality control, manufacturing methods, and new investment.

Chris' entrepreneurial spirit stimulated innovative product design and growth while adhering closely to product quality. Understanding cost analysis and variances, flexible and fixed budgets, and standard costs helps his company control its production process. Martin's "X" bracing system is a key part of the distinctive Martin guitar tone. The company also embraces continuous improvement. Recently it began a lean manufacturing project to improve production efficiency, work flow, and cycle time in one of its plants.

Martin Guitar adheres to tight standards variances. Vince Gentilcore, Martin's director of quality, classifies production problems into three types: materials, process, and employee. Developing managerial accounting systems to evaluate its performance on each of these dimensions is key. "[Defects] in wood affect yield, productivity, and costs of quality," explains Vince. "We have exacting specifications and controls in place to detect problems; we don't allow material to go into a guitar that doesn't satisfy our requirements." As for process, he closely monitors the company's computer-controlled machines to ensure excessive tool wear does not impair product quality. Another key to process control, explains Vince, is "the moisture content of the wood, which we track on a regular basis." Regarding employee costs, Chris Martin explains that "we have work quotas; we know how much labor costs and how long it takes."

Achieving high standards is the goal at Martin Guitar. "We're trying to make the best," proclaims Chris. "We are doing so much more volume today, even with all those competitors. [Our workers] hold the company to an extraordinarily high standard." With standards like these, Chris' company produces a pretty tune.

[Sources: *Martin Guitar Website,* January 2009; *Quality Digest,* November 2007; *Modern Guitars Magazine,* December and March 2005; For a virtual tour of Martin Guitars see MartinGuitar.com/visit/vtour.php]

Chapter Preview

Budgeting helps organize and formalize management's planning activities. This chapter extends the study of budgeting to look more closely at the use of budgets to evaluate performance. Evaluations are important for controlling and monitoring business activities. This chapter also describes and illustrates the use of standard costs and variance analyses. These managerial tools are useful for both evaluating and controlling organizations and for the planning of future activities.

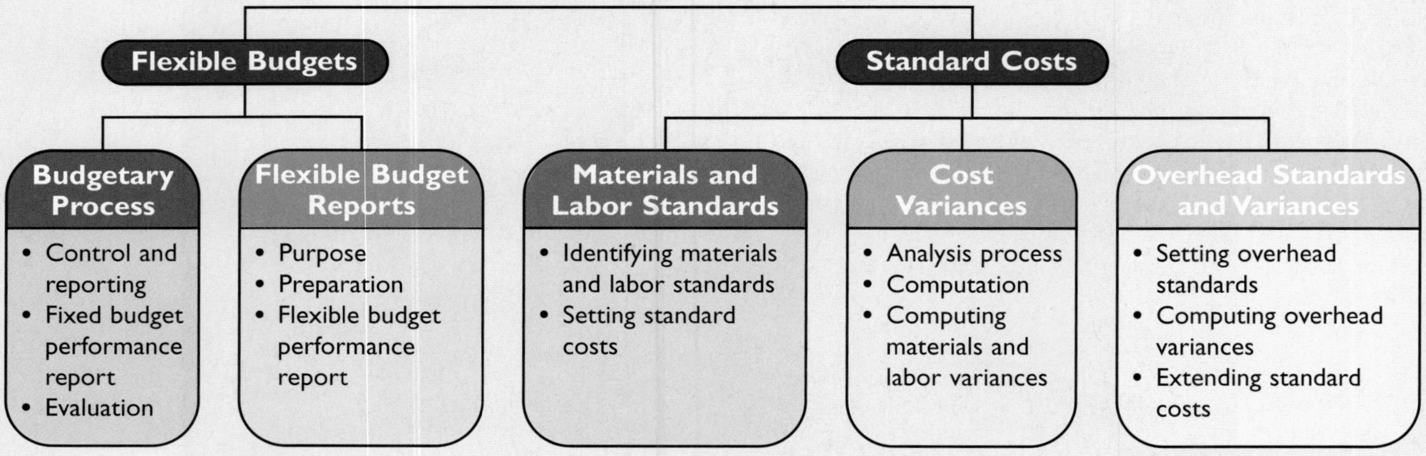

Section 1—Flexible Budgets

This section introduces fixed budgets and fixed budget performance reports. It then introduces flexible budgets and flexible budget performance reports and illustrates their advantages.

Budgetary Process

Video24.2

A master budget reflects management's planned objectives for a future period. The preparation of a master budget is based on a predicted level of activity such as sales volume for the budget period. This section discusses the effects on the usefulness of budget reports when the actual level of activity differs from the predicted level.

Budgetary Control and Reporting

Point: Budget reports are often used as a base to determine bonuses of managers.

Budgetary control refers to management's use of budgets to monitor and control a company's operations. This includes using budgets to see that planned objectives are met. **Budget reports** contain relevant information that compares actual results to planned activities. This comparison is motivated by a need to both monitor performance and control activities. Budget reports are sometimes viewed as progress reports, or *report cards,* on management's performance in achieving planned objectives. These reports can be prepared at any time and for any period. Three common periods for a budget report are a month, quarter, and year.

The budgetary control process involves at least four steps: (1) develop the budget from planned objectives, (2) compare actual results to budgeted amounts and analyze any differences, (3) take corrective and strategic actions, and (4) establish new planned objectives and prepare a new budget. Exhibit 24.1 shows this continual process of budgetary control. Budget

EXHIBIT 24.1

Process of Budgetary Control

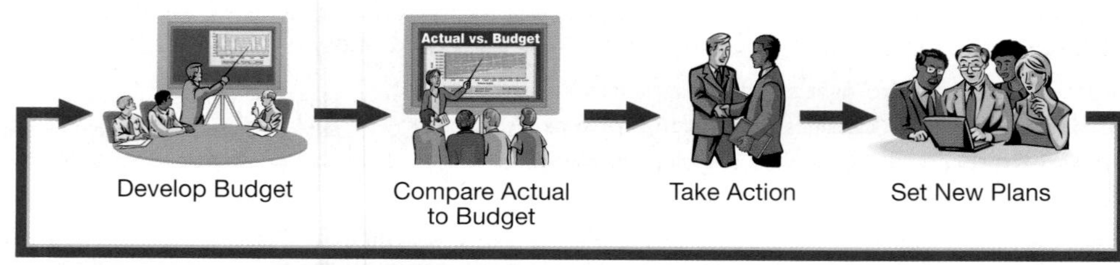

reports and related documents are effective tools for managers to obtain the greatest benefits from this budgetary process.

Fixed Budget Performance Report

In a fixed budgetary control system, the master budget is based on a single prediction for sales volume or other activity level. The budgeted amount for each cost essentially assumes that a specific (or *fixed*) amount of sales will occur. A **fixed budget,** also called a *static budget,* is based on a single predicted amount of sales or other measure of activity.

One benefit of a budget is its usefulness in comparing actual results with planned activities. Information useful for analysis is often presented for comparison in a performance report. As shown in Exhibit 24.2, a **fixed budget performance report** for **Optel** compares actual results for January 2009 with the results expected under its fixed budget that predicted 10,000 (composite) units of sales. Optel manufactures inexpensive eyeglasses, frames, contact lens, and related supplies. For this report, its production volume equals sales volume (its inventory level did not change).

EXHIBIT 24.2

Fixed Budget Performance Report

OPTEL
Fixed Budget Performance Report
For Month Ended January 31, 2009

	Fixed Budget	Actual Results	Variances*
Sales (in units)	10,000	12,000	
Sales (in dollars)	$100,000	$125,000	$25,000 F
Cost of goods sold			
Direct materials	10,000	13,000	3,000 U
Direct labor	15,000	20,000	5,000 U
Overhead			
Factory supplies	2,000	2,100	100 U
Utilities	3,000	4,000	1,000 U
Depreciation—machinery	8,000	8,000	0
Supervisory salaries	11,000	11,000	0
Selling expenses			
Sales commissions	9,000	10,800	1,800 U
Shipping expenses	4,000	4,300	300 U
General and administrative expenses			
Office supplies	5,000	5,200	200 U
Insurance expenses	1,000	1,200	200 U
Depreciation—office equipment	7,000	7,000	0
Administrative salaries	13,000	13,000	0
Total expenses	88,000	99,600	11,600 U
Income from operations	$ 12,000	$ 25,400	$13,400 F

* F = Favorable variance; U = Unfavorable variance.

This type of performance report designates differences between budgeted and actual results as variances. We see the letters *F* and *U* located beside the numbers in the third number column of this report. Their meanings are as follows:

F = **Favorable variance** When compared to budget, the actual cost or revenue contributes to a *higher* income. That is, actual revenue is higher than budgeted revenue, or actual cost is lower than budgeted cost.

U = **Unfavorable variance** When compared to budget, the actual cost or revenue contributes to a *lower* income; actual revenue is lower than budgeted revenue, or actual cost is higher than budgeted cost.

This convention is common in practice and is used throughout this chapter.

Example: How is it that the favorable sales variance in Exhibit 24.2 is linked with so many unfavorable cost and expense variances? *Answer:* Costs have increased with the increase in sales.

Budget Reports for Evaluation

A primary use of budget reports is as a tool for management to monitor and control operations. Evaluation by Optel management is likely to focus on a variety of questions that might include these:

- Why is actual income from operations $13,400 higher than budgeted?
- Are amounts paid for each expense item too high?
- Is manufacturing using too much direct material?
- Is manufacturing using too much direct labor?

The performance report in Exhibit 24.2 provides little help in answering these questions because actual sales volume is 2,000 units higher than budgeted. A manager does not know if this higher level of sales activity is the cause of variations in total dollar sales and expenses or if other factors have influenced these amounts. This inability of fixed budget reports to adjust for changes in activity levels is a major limitation of a fixed budget performance report. That is, it fails to show whether actual costs are out of line due to a change in actual sales volume or some other factor.

Decision Insight

Green Budget Budget reporting and evaluation are used at the **Environmental Protection Agency (EPA)**. It regularly prepares performance plans and budget requests that describe performance goals, measure outcomes, and analyze variances.

Flexible Budget Reports

Purpose of Flexible Budgets

A1 Compare fixed and flexible budgets.

To help address limitations with the fixed budget performance report, particularly from the effects of changes in sales volume, management can use a flexible budget. A **flexible budget,** also called a *variable budget,* is a report based on predicted amounts of revenues and expenses corresponding to the actual level of output. Flexible budgets are useful both before and after the period's activities are complete.

Video24.2

A flexible budget prepared before the period is often based on several levels of activity. Budgets for those different levels can provide a "what-if" look at operations. The different levels often include both a best case and worst case scenario. This allows management to make adjustments to avoid or lessen the effects of the worst case scenario.

A flexible budget prepared after the period helps management evaluate past performance. It is especially useful for such an evaluation because it reflects budgeted revenues and costs based on the actual level of activity. Thus, comparisons of actual results with budgeted performance are more likely to identify the causes of any differences. This can help managers focus attention on real problem areas and implement corrective actions. This is in contrast to a fixed budget, whose primary purpose is to assist managers in planning future activities and whose numbers are based on a single predicted amount of budgeted sales or production.

Preparation of Flexible Budgets

P1 Prepare a flexible budget and interpret a flexible budget performance report.

A flexible budget is designed to reveal the effects of volume of activity on revenues and costs. To prepare a flexible budget, management relies on the distinctions between fixed and variable costs. Recall that the cost per unit of activity remains constant for variable costs so that the total amount of a variable cost changes in direct proportion to a change in activity level. The total amount of fixed cost remains unchanged regardless of changes in the level of activity within a relevant (normal) operating range. (Assume that costs can be reasonably classified as variable or fixed within a relevant range.)

When we create the numbers constituting a flexible budget, we express each variable cost as either a constant amount per unit of sales or as a percent of a sales dollar. In the case of a fixed cost, we express its budgeted amount as the total amount expected to occur at any sales volume within the relevant range.

Exhibit 24.3 shows a set of flexible budgets for Optel in January 2009. Seven of its expenses are classified as variable costs. Its remaining five expenses are fixed costs. These classifications result from management's investigation of each expense. Variable and fixed expense categories are *not* the same for every company, and we must avoid drawing conclusions from specific cases. For example, depending on the nature of a company's operations, office supplies expense can be either fixed or variable with respect to sales.

Point: The usefulness of a flexible budget depends on valid classification of variable and fixed costs. Some costs are mixed and must be analyzed to determine their variable and fixed portions.

EXHIBIT 24.3

Flexible Budgets

OPTEL
Flexible Budgets
For Month Ended January 31, 2009

	Flexible Budget		Flexible Budget for Unit Sales of 10,000	Flexible Budget for Unit Sales of 12,000	Flexible Budget for Unit Sales of 14,000
	Variable Amount per Unit	Total Fixed Cost			
Sales	$10.00		$100,000	$120,000	$140,000
Variable costs					
Direct materials	1.00		10,000	12,000	14,000
Direct labor	1.50		15,000	18,000	21,000
Factory supplies	0.20		2,000	2,400	2,800
Utilities	0.30		3,000	3,600	4,200
Sales commissions	0.90		9,000	10,800	12,600
Shipping expenses	0.40		4,000	4,800	5,600
Office supplies	0.50		5,000	6,000	7,000
Total variable costs	4.80		48,000	57,600	67,200
Contribution margin	$ 5.20		$ 52,000	$ 62,400	$ 72,800
Fixed costs					
Depreciation—machinery		$ 8,000	8,000	8,000	8,000
Supervisory salaries		11,000	11,000	11,000	11,000
Insurance expense		1,000	1,000	1,000	1,000
Depreciation—office equipment		7,000	7,000	7,000	7,000
Administrative salaries		13,000	13,000	13,000	13,000
Total fixed costs		$40,000	40,000	40,000	40,000
Income from operations			$ 12,000	$ 22,400	$ 32,800

The layout for the flexible budgets in Exhibit 24.3 follows a *contribution margin format*—beginning with sales followed by variable costs and then fixed costs. Both the expected individual and total variable costs are reported and then subtracted from sales. The difference between sales and variable costs equals contribution margin. The expected amounts of fixed costs are listed next, followed by the expected income from operations before taxes.

Example: Using Exhibit 24.3, what is the budgeted income from operations for unit sales of (a) 11,000 and (b) 13,000? *Answers:* $17,200 for unit sales of 11,000; $27,600 for unit sales of 13,000.

The first and second number columns of Exhibit 24.3 show the flexible budget amounts for variable costs per unit and each fixed cost for any volume of sales in the relevant range. The third, fourth, and fifth columns show the flexible budget amounts computed for three different sales volumes. For instance, the third column's flexible budget is based on 10,000 units. These numbers are the same as those in the fixed budget of Exhibit 24.2 because the expected volumes are the same for these two budgets.

Recall that Optel's actual sales volume for January is 12,000 units. This sales volume is 2,000 units more than the 10,000 units originally predicted in the master budget. When differences between actual and predicted volume arise, the usefulness of a flexible budget is apparent. For instance, compare the flexible budget for 10,000 units in the third column (which is the same as the fixed budget in Exhibit 24.2) with the flexible budget for 12,000 units in the

Point: Flexible budgeting allows a budget to be prepared at the *actual* output level. Performance reports are then prepared comparing the flexible budget to actual revenues and costs.

Point: A flexible budget yields an "apples to apples" comparison because budgeted activity levels are the same as the actual.

fourth column. The higher levels for both sales and variable costs reflect nothing more than the increase in sales activity. Any budget analysis comparing actual with planned results that ignores this information is less useful to management.

To illustrate, when we evaluate Optel's performance, we need to prepare a flexible budget showing actual and budgeted values at 12,000 units. As part of a complete profitability analysis, managers could compare the actual income of $25,400 (from Exhibit 24.2) with the $22,400 income expected at the actual sales volume of 12,000 units (from Exhibit 24.3). This results in a total favorable income variance of $3,000 to be explained and interpreted. This variance is markedly lower from the $13,400 favorable variance identified in Exhibit 24.2 using a fixed budget, but still suggests good performance. After receiving the flexible budget based on January's actual volume, management must determine what caused this $3,000 difference. The next section describes a flexible budget performance report that provides guidance in this analysis.

Decision Maker

Entrepreneur The heads of both the strategic consulting and tax consulting divisions of your financial services firm complain to you about the unfavorable variances on their performance reports. "We worked on more consulting assignments than planned. It's not surprising our costs are higher than expected. To top it off, this report characterizes our work as *poor!*" How do you respond? [Answer—p. 1004]

Flexible Budget Performance Report

A **flexible budget performance report** lists differences between actual performance and budgeted performance based on actual sales volume or other activity level. This report helps direct management's attention to those costs or revenues that differ substantially from budgeted amounts. Exhibit 24.4 shows Optel's flexible budget performance report for January. We prepare this report after the actual volume is known to be 12,000 units. This report shows a $5,000 favorable variance in total dollar sales. Because actual and budgeted volumes are both 12,000 units, the $5,000 sales variance must have resulted from a higher than expected selling price. Further analysis of the facts surrounding this $5,000 sales variance reveals a favorable sales variance per unit of nearly $0.42 as shown here:

Actual average price per unit (rounded to cents)	$125,000/12,000 =	$10.42
Budgeted price per unit	$120,000/12,000 =	10.00
Favorable sales variance per unit	$5,000/12,000 =	$ 0.42

The other variances in Exhibit 24.4 also direct management's attention to areas where corrective actions can help control Optel's operations. Each expense variance is analyzed as the sales variance was. We can think of each expense as the joint result of using a given number of units of input and paying a specific price per unit of input. Optel's expense variances total $2,000 unfavorable, suggesting poor control of some costs, particularly direct materials and direct labor.

Each variance in Exhibit 24.4 is due in part to a difference between *actual price* per unit of input and *budgeted price* per unit of input. This is a **price variance.** Each variance also can be due in part to a difference between *actual quantity* of input used and *budgeted quantity* of input. This is a **quantity variance.** We explain more about this breakdown, known as **variance analysis,** later in the standard costs section.

Quick Check

Answers—p. 1004

1. A flexible budget (*a*) shows fixed costs as constant amounts of cost per unit of activity, (*b*) shows variable costs as constant amounts of cost per unit of activity, or (*c*) is prepared based on one expected amount of budgeted sales or production.
2. What is the initial step in preparing a flexible budget?
3. What is the main difference between a fixed and a flexible budget?
4. What is the contribution margin?

EXHIBIT 24.4

Flexible Budget Performance Report

OPTEL Flexible Budget Performance Report For Month Ended January 31, 2009	Flexible Budget	Actual Results	Variances*
Sales (12,000 units)	$120,000	$125,000	$5,000 F
Variable costs			
Direct materials	12,000	13,000	1,000 U
Direct labor	18,000	20,000	2,000 U
Factory supplies	2,400	2,100	300 F
Utilities	3,600	4,000	400 U
Sales commissions	10,800	10,800	0
Shipping expenses	4,800	4,300	500 F
Office supplies	6,000	5,200	800 F
Total variable costs	57,600	59,400	1,800 U
Contribution margin	62,400	65,600	3,200 F
Fixed costs			
Depreciation—machinery	8,000	8,000	0
Supervisory salaries	11,000	11,000	0
Insurance expense	1,000	1,200	200 U
Depreciation—office equipment	7,000	7,000	0
Administrative salaries	13,000	13,000	0
Total fixed costs	40,000	40,200	200 U
Income from operations	$ 22,400	$ 25,400	$3,000 F

* F = Favorable variance; U = Unfavorable variance.

Section 2—Standard Costs

C1 Define *standard costs* and explain their computation and uses.

Standard costs are preset costs for delivering a product or service under normal conditions. These costs are established by personnel, engineering, and accounting studies using past experiences and data. Management uses these costs to assess the reasonableness of actual costs incurred for producing the product or service. When actual costs vary from standard costs, management follows up to identify potential problems and take corrective actions.

Standard costs are often used in preparing budgets because they are the anticipated costs incurred under normal conditions. Terms such as *standard materials cost, standard labor cost,* and *standard overhead cost* are often used to refer to amounts budgeted for direct materials, direct labor, and overhead.

Point: Since standard costs are often budgeted costs, they can be used to prepare both fixed budgets and flexible budgets.

Materials and Labor Standards

This section explains how to set materials and labor standards and how to prepare a standard cost card.

Video24.1

Identifying Standard Costs

Managerial accountants, engineers, personnel administrators, and other managers combine their efforts to set standard costs. To identify standards for direct labor costs, we can conduct time and motion studies for each labor operation in the process of providing a product or service. From these studies, management can learn the best way to perform the operation and then set the standard labor time required for the operation under normal conditions. Similarly, standards for materials are set by studying the quantity, grade, and cost of each material used. Standards for overhead costs are explained later in the chapter.

Point: Business practice often uses the word *budget* when speaking of total amounts and *standard* when discussing per unit amounts.

Regardless of the care used in setting standard costs and in revising them as conditions change, actual costs frequently differ from standard costs, often as a result of one or more factors. For instance, the actual quantity of material used can differ from the standard, or the price paid per unit of material can differ from the standard. Quantity and price differences from

Example: What factors might be considered when deciding whether to revise standard costs? *Answer:* Changes in the processes and/or resources needed to carry out the processes.

standard amounts can also occur for labor. That is, the actual labor time and actual labor rate can vary from what was expected. The same analysis applies to overhead costs.

Decision Insight

Cruis'n Standards The Corvette consists of hundreds of parts for which engineers set standards. Various types of labor are also involved in its production, including machining, assembly, painting, and welding, and standards are set for each. Actual results are periodically compared with standards to assess performance.

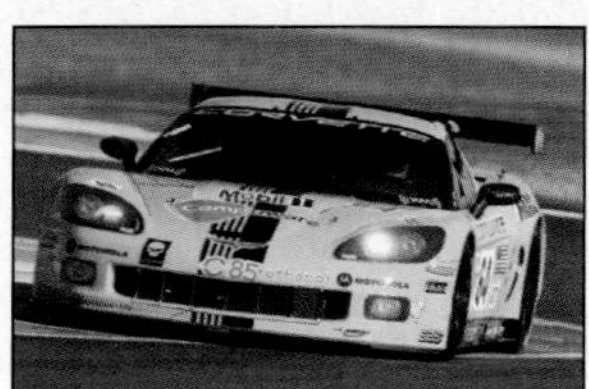

Setting Standard Costs

To illustrate the setting of a standard cost, we consider a professional league baseball bat manufactured by **ProBat.** Its engineers have determined that manufacturing one bat requires 0.90 kg. of high-grade wood. They also expect some loss of material as part of the process because of inefficiencies and waste. This results in adding an *allowance* of 0.10 kg., making the standard requirement 1.0 kg. of wood for each bat.

The 0.90 kg. portion is called an *ideal standard;* it is the quantity of material required if the process is 100% efficient without any loss or waste. Reality suggests that some loss of material usually occurs with any process. The standard of 1.0 kg. is known as the *practical standard,* the quantity of material required under normal application of the process.

Point: Companies promoting continuous improvement strive to achieve ideal standards by eliminating inefficiencies and waste.

High-grade wood can be purchased at a standard price of $25 per kg. The purchasing department sets this price as the expected price for the budget period. To determine this price, the purchasing department considers factors such as the quality of materials, future economic conditions, supply factors (shortages and excesses), and any available discounts. The engineers also decide that two hours of labor time (after including allowances) are required to manufacture a bat. The wage rate is $20 per hour (better than average skilled labor is required). ProBat assigns all overhead at the rate of $10 per labor hour. The standard costs of direct materials, direct labor, and overhead for one bat are shown in Exhibit 24.5 in what is called a *standard cost card.* These cost amounts are then used to prepare manufacturing budgets for a budgeted level of production.

EXHIBIT 24.5

Standard Cost Card

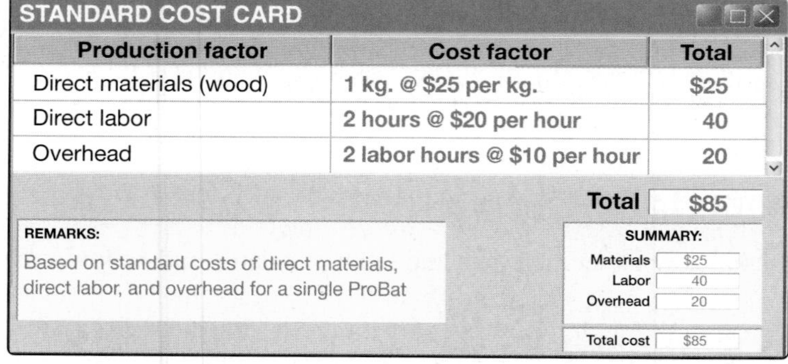

STANDARD COST CARD

Production factor	Cost factor	Total
Direct materials (wood)	1 kg. @ $25 per kg.	$25
Direct labor	2 hours @ $20 per hour	40
Overhead	2 labor hours @ $10 per hour	20
	Total	$85

REMARKS:
Based on standard costs of direct materials, direct labor, and overhead for a single ProBat

SUMMARY:

Materials	$25
Labor	40
Overhead	20
Total cost	$85

Cost Variances

C2 Describe variances and what they reveal about performance.

A **cost variance,** also simply called a *variance,* is the difference between actual and standard costs. A cost variance can be favorable or unfavorable. A variance from standard cost is considered favorable if actual cost is less than standard cost. It is considered unfavorable if actual cost is more than standard cost.[1] This section discusses variance analysis.

[1] Short-term favorable variances can sometimes lead to long-term unfavorable variances. For instance, if management spends less than the budgeted amount on maintenance or insurance, the performance report would show a favorable variance. Cutting these expenses can lead to major losses in the long run if machinery wears out prematurely or insurance coverage proves inadequate.

Cost Variance Analysis

Video24.1

Variances are usually identified in performance reports. When a variance occurs, management wants to determine the factors causing it. This often involves analysis, evaluation, and explanation. The results of these efforts should enable management to assign responsibility for the variance and then to take actions to correct the situation.

To illustrate, ProBat's standard materials cost for producing 500 bats is $12,500. Assume, that its actual materials cost for those 500 bats proved to be $13,000. The $500 unfavorable variance raises questions that call for answers that, in turn, can lead to changes to correct the situation and eliminate this variance in the next period. A performance report often identifies the existence of a problem, but we must follow up with further investigation to see what can be done to improve future performance.

Exhibit 24.6 shows the flow of events in the effective management of variance analysis. It shows four steps: (1) preparing a standard cost performance report, (2) computing and analyzing variances, (3) identifying questions and their explanations, and (4) taking corrective and strategic actions. These variance analysis steps are interrelated and are frequently applied in good organizations.

EXHIBIT 24.6

Variance Analysis

Cost Variance Computation

Management needs information about the factors causing a cost variance, but first it must properly compute the variance. In its most simple form, a cost variance (CV) is computed as the difference between actual cost (AC) and standard cost (SC) as shown in Exhibit 24.7.

EXHIBIT 24.7

Cost Variance Formulas

Cost Variance (CV) = **Actual Cost** (AC) − **Standard Cost** (SC)

where:

Actual Cost (AC) = **Actual Quantity** (AQ) × **Actual Price** (AP)

Standard Cost (SC) = **Standard Quantity** (SQ) × **Standard Price** (SP)

A cost variance is further defined by its components. Actual quantity (AQ) is the input (material or labor) used to manufacture the quantity of output. Standard quantity (SQ) is the expected input for the quantity of output. Actual price (AP) is the amount paid to acquire the input (material or labor), and standard price (SP) is the expected price.

Two main factors cause a cost variance: (1) the difference between actual price and standard price results in a *price* (or rate) *variance* and (2) the difference between actual quantity and standard quantity results in a *quantity* (or usage or efficiency) *variance*. To assess the impacts of these two factors in a cost variance, we use the formulas in Exhibit 24.8.

Point: Price and quantity variances for direct labor are nearly always referred to as *rate* and *efficiency variances*, respectively.

EXHIBIT 24.8

Price Variance and Quantity Variance Formulas

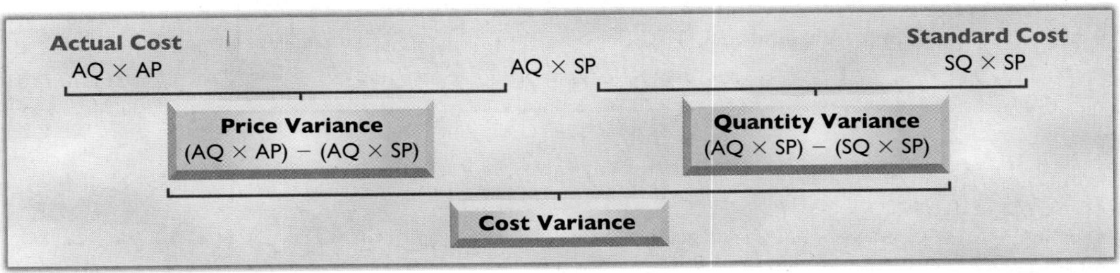

In computing a price variance, the quantity (actual) is held constant. In computing a quantity variance, the price (standard) is held constant. The cost variance, or total variance, is the sum of the price and quantity variances. These formulas identify the sources of the cost variance. Managers sometimes find it useful to apply an alternative (but equivalent) computation for the price and quantity variances as shown in Exhibit 24.9.

EXHIBIT 24.9

Alternative Price Variance and Quantity Variance Formulas

Price Variance (PV) = [**Actual Price** (AP) − **Standard Price** (SP)] × **Actual Quantity** (AQ)

Quantity Variance (QV) = [**Actual Quantity** (AQ) − **Standard Quantity** (SQ)] × **Standard Price** (SP)

The results from applying the formulas in Exhibits 24.8 and 24.9 are identical.

Computing Materials and Labor Variances

P2 Compute materials and labor variances.

We illustrate the computation of the materials and labor cost variances using data from **G-Max,** a company that makes specialty golf equipment and accessories for individual customers. This company has set the following standard quantities and costs for materials and labor per unit for one of its hand-crafted golf clubheads:

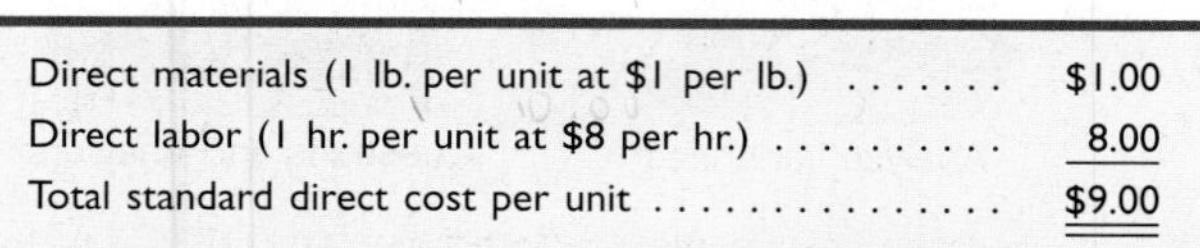

Direct materials (1 lb. per unit at $1 per lb.)	$1.00
Direct labor (1 hr. per unit at $8 per hr.)	8.00
Total standard direct cost per unit	$9.00

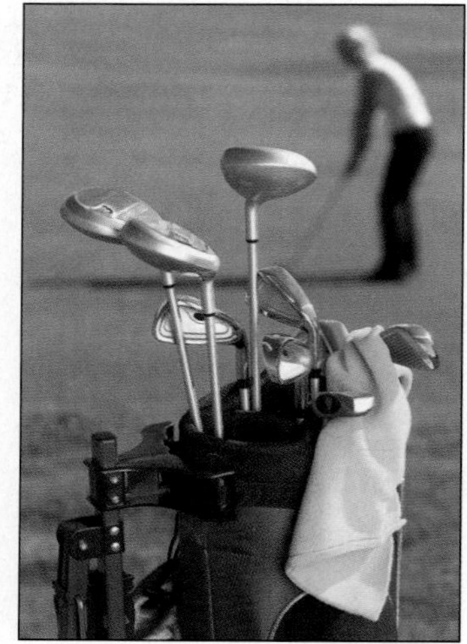

Materials Cost Variances During May 2009, G-Max budgeted to produce 4,000 clubheads (units). It actually produced only 3,500 units. It used 3,600 pounds of direct materials (titanium) costing $1.05 per pound, meaning its total materials cost was $3,780. This information allows us to compute both actual and standard direct materials costs for G-Max's 3,500 units and its direct materials cost variance as follows:

Actual cost	3,600 lbs. @ $1.05 per lb.	= $3,780
Standard cost	3,500 lbs. @ $1.00 per lb.	= 3,500
Direct materials cost variance (unfavorable)		= $ 280

To better isolate the causes of this $280 unfavorable total direct materials cost variance, the materials price and quantity variances for these G-Max clubheads are computed and shown in Exhibit 24.10.

EXHIBIT 24.10

Materials Price and Quantity Variances

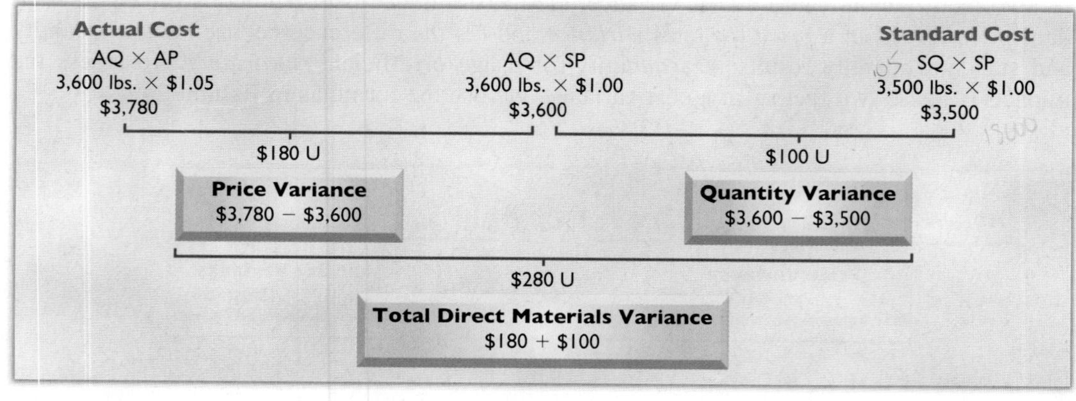

The $180 unfavorable price variance results from paying 5 cents more per unit than the standard price, computed as 3,600 lbs. × $0.05. The $100 unfavorable quantity variance is due to using 100 lbs. more materials than the standard quantity, computed as 100 lbs. × $1. The total direct materials variance is $280 and it is unfavorable. This information allows management to ask the responsible individuals for explanations and corrective actions.

Example: Identify at least two factors that might have caused the $100 unfavorable quantity variance and the $180 unfavorable price variance in Exhibit 24.10. *Answer:* Poor quality materials or untrained workers for the former; poor price negotiation or higher-quality materials for the latter.

The purchasing department is usually responsible for the price paid for materials. Responsibility for explaining the price variance in this case rests with the purchasing manager if a price higher than standard caused the variance. The production department is usually responsible for the amount of material used and in this case is responsible for explaining why the process used more than the standard amount of materials.

Variance analysis presents challenges. For instance, the production department could have used more than the standard amount of material because its quality did not meet specifications and led to excessive waste. In this case, the purchasing manager is responsible for explaining why inferior materials were acquired. However, the production manager is responsible for explaining what happened if analysis shows that waste was due to inefficiencies, not poor quality material.

In evaluating price variances, managers must recognize that a favorable price variance can indicate a problem with poor product quality. **Redhook Ale**, a micro brewery in the Pacific Northwest, can probably save 10% to 15% in material prices by buying six-row barley malt instead of the better two-row from Washington's Yakima valley. Attention to quality, however, has helped Redhook Ale become the first craft brewer to be kosher certified. Redhook's purchasing activities are judged on both the quality of the materials and the purchase price variance.

Labor Cost Variances Labor cost for a specific product or service depends on the number of hours worked (quantity) and the wage rate paid to employees (price). When actual amounts for a task differ from standard, the labor cost variance can be divided into a rate (price) variance and an efficiency (quantity) variance.

To illustrate, G-Max's direct labor standard for 3,500 units of its hand-crafted clubheads is one hour per unit, or 3,500 hours at $8 per hour. Since only 3,400 hours at $8.30 per hour were actually used to complete the units, the actual and standard labor costs are

Actual cost	3,400 hrs. @ $8.30 per hr.	= $28,220
Standard cost	3,500 hrs. @ $8.00 per hr.	= 28,000
Direct labor cost variance (unfavorable)		= $ 220

This analysis shows that actual cost is merely $220 over the standard and suggests no immediate concern. Computing both the labor rate and efficiency variances reveals a different picture, however, as shown in Exhibit 24.11.

EXHIBIT 24.11

Labor Rate and Efficiency Variances*

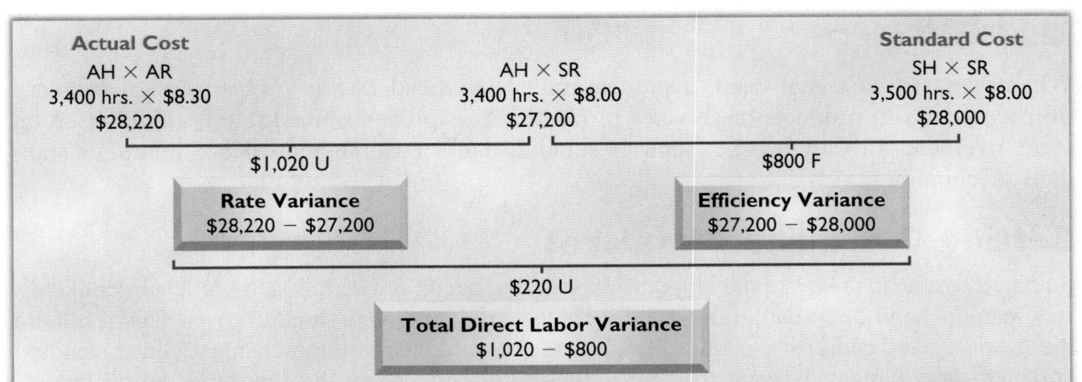

* AH is actual direct labor hours: AR is actual wage rate; SH is standard direct labor hours allowed for actual output; SR is standard wage rate.

Example: Compute the rate variance and the efficiency variance for Exhibit 24.11 if 3,700 actual hours are used at an actual price of $7.50 per hour. *Answer:* $1,850 favorable labor rate variance and $1,600 unfavorable labor efficiency variance.

The analysis in Exhibit 24.11 shows that an $800 favorable efficiency variance results from using 100 fewer direct labor hours than standard for the units produced, but this favorable variance is more than offset by a wage rate that is $0.30 per hour higher than standard. The personnel administrator or the production manager needs to explain why the wage rate is higher than expected. The production manager should also explain how the labor hours were reduced. If this experience can be repeated and transferred to other departments, more savings are possible.

One possible explanation of these labor rate and efficiency variances is the use of workers with different skill levels. If this is the reason, senior management must discuss the implications with the production manager who has the responsibility to assign workers to tasks with the appropriate skill level. In this case, an investigation might show that higher-skilled workers were used to produce 3,500 units of hand-crafted clubheads. As a result, fewer labor hours might be required for the work, but the wage rate paid these workers is higher than standard because of their greater skills. The effect of this strategy is a higher than standard total cost, which would require actions to remedy the situation or adjust the standard.

Decision Maker

Human Resource Manager You receive the manufacturing variance report for June and discover a large unfavorable labor efficiency (quantity) variance. What factors do you investigate to identify its possible causes? [Answer—p. 1004]

Quick Check

Answers—pp. 1004–1005

5. A standard cost (*a*) changes in direct proportion to changes in the level of activity, (*b*) is an amount incurred at the actual level of production for the period, or (*c*) is an amount incurred under normal conditions to provide a product or service.
6. What is a cost variance?
7. The following information is available for York Company.

Actual direct labor hours per unit	2.5 hours
Standard direct labor hours per unit	2.0 hours
Actual production (units)	2,500 units
Budgeted production (units)	3,000 units
Actual rate per hour	$3.10
Standard rate per hour	$3.00

The labor efficiency variance is (*a*) $3,750 U, (*b*) $3,750 F, or (*c*) $3,875 U.

8. Refer to Quick Check 7; the labor rate variance is (*a*) $625 F or (*b*) $625 U.
9. If a materials quantity variance is favorable and a materials price variance is unfavorable, can the total materials cost variance be favorable?

Overhead Standards and Variances

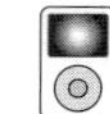

Video24.1&24.3

When standard costs are used, a predetermined overhead rate is used to assign standard overhead costs to products or services produced. This predetermined rate is often based on some overhead allocation base (such as standard labor cost, standard labor hours, or standard machine hours).

Setting Overhead Standards

Standard overhead costs are the amounts expected to occur at a certain activity level. Unlike direct materials and direct labor, overhead includes fixed costs and variable costs. This results in the average overhead cost per unit changing as the predicted volume changes. Since standard costs are also budgeted costs, they must be established before the reporting period begins. Standard overhead costs are therefore average per unit costs based on the predicted activity level.

To establish the standard overhead cost rate, management uses the same cost structure it used to construct a flexible budget at the end of a period. This cost structure identifies the different overhead cost components and classifies them as variable or fixed. To get the standard overhead rate, management selects a level of activity (volume) and predicts total overhead cost. It then divides this total by the allocation base to get the standard rate. Standard direct labor hours expected to be used to produce the predicted volume is a common allocation base and is used in this section.

Point: Managers consider the types of overhead costs when choosing the basis for assigning overhead costs to products.

Point: With increased automation, machine hours are frequently used in applying overhead instead of labor hours.

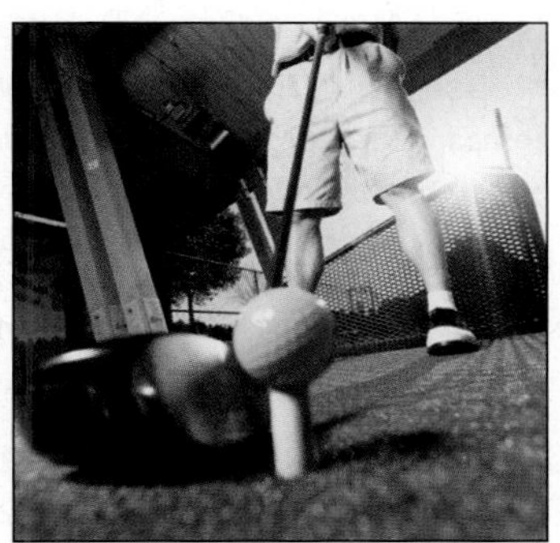

To illustrate, Exhibit 24.12 shows the overhead cost structure used to develop G-Max's flexible overhead budgets for May 2009. The predetermined standard overhead rate for May is set before the month begins. The first two number columns list the per unit amounts of variable costs and the monthly amounts of fixed costs. The four right-most columns show the costs expected to occur at four different levels of production activity. The predetermined overhead rate per labor hour is smaller as volume of activity increases because total fixed costs remain constant.

G-Max managers predicted an 80% activity level for May, or a production volume of 4,000 clubheads. At this volume, they budget $8,000 as the May total overhead. This choice implies a $2 per unit (labor hour) average overhead cost ($8,000/4,000 units). Since G-Max has a standard of one direct labor hour per unit, the predetermined standard overhead rate for May is $2 per standard direct labor hour. The variable overhead rate remains constant at $1 per direct labor hour regardless of the budgeted production level. The fixed overhead rate changes according to the budgeted production volume. For instance, for the predicted level of 4,000 units of production, the fixed rate is $1 per hour ($4,000 fixed costs/4,000 units). For a production level of 5,000 units, however, the fixed rate is $0.80 per hour ($4,000 fixed costs/5,000 units).

Point: Variable costs per unit remain constant, but fixed costs per unit decline with increases in volume. This means the average total overhead cost per unit declines with increases in volume.

When choosing the predicted activity level, management considers many factors. The level can be set as high as 100% of capacity, but this is rare. Factors causing the activity level to

EXHIBIT 24.12

Flexible Overhead Budgets

G-MAX
Flexible Overhead Budgets
For Month Ended May 31, 2009

	Flexible Budget					
	Variable Amount per Unit	Total Fixed Cost	Flexible Budget at 70% Capacity	Flexible Budget at 80% Capacity	Flexible Budget at 90% Capacity	Flexible Budget at 100% Capacity
Production (in units)	1 unit		3,500	**4,000**	4,500	5,000
Factory overhead						
Variable costs						
Indirect labor	$0.40/unit		$1,400	**$1,600**	$1,800	$2,000
Indirect materials	0.30/unit		1,050	**1,200**	1,350	1,500
Power and lights	0.20/unit		700	**800**	900	1,000
Maintenance	0.10/unit		350	**400**	450	500
Total variable overhead costs	$1.00/unit		3,500	**4,000**	4,500	5,000
Fixed costs (per month)						
Building rent		$1,000	1,000	**1,000**	1,000	1,000
Depreciation—machinery		1,200	1,200	**1,200**	1,200	1,200
Supervisory salaries		1,800	1,800	**1,800**	1,800	1,800
Total fixed overhead costs		$4,000	4,000	**4,000**	4,000	4,000
Total factory overhead			$7,500	**$8,000**	$8,500	$9,000
Standard direct labor hours 1 hr./unit			3,500 hrs.	**4,000 hrs.**	4,500 hrs.	5,000 hrs.
Predetermined overhead rate per standard direct labor hour			$ 2.14	**$ 2.00**	$ 1.89	$ 1.80

be less than full capacity include difficulties in scheduling work, equipment under repair or maintenance, and insufficient product demand. Good long-run management practices often call for some plant capacity in excess of current operating needs to allow for special opportunities and demand changes.

Decision Insight

Measuring Up In the spirit of continuous improvement, competitors compare their processes and performance standards against benchmarks established by industry leaders. Those that use **benchmarking** include Precision Lube, Jiffy Lube, All Tune and Lube, and Speedee Oil Change and Tune-Up.

Computing Overhead Cost Variances

When standard costs are used, the cost accounting system applies overhead to the good units produced using the predetermined standard overhead rate. At period-end, the difference between the total overhead cost applied to products and the total overhead cost actually incurred is called an **overhead cost variance** (total overhead variance), which is defined in Exhibit 24.13.

EXHIBIT 24.13

Overhead Cost Variance

Overhead cost variance (OCV) = Actual overhead incurred (AOI) − Standard overhead applied (SOA)

EXHIBIT 24.14

Framework for Understanding Total Overhead Variance

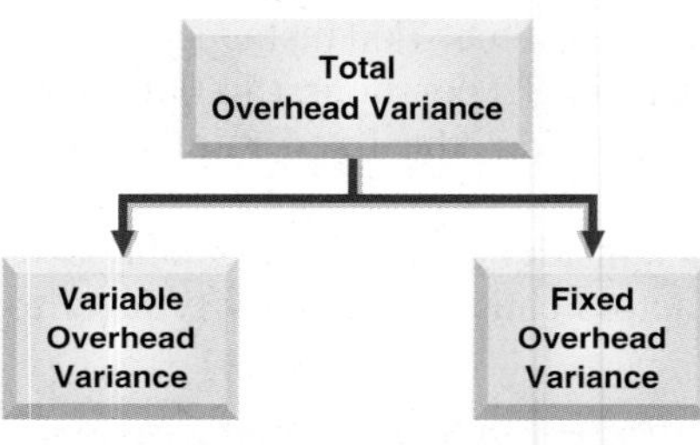

To help identify factors causing the overhead cost variance, managers analyze this variance separately for variable and fixed overhead, as illustrated in Exhibit 24.14. The results provide information useful for taking strategic actions to improve company performance.

P3 Compute overhead variances.

Computing Variable and Fixed Overhead Cost Variances To illustrate the computation of overhead cost variances, we return to the G-Max data. We know that G-Max produced 3,500 units when 4,000 units were budgeted. Additional data from cost reports show that the actual overhead cost incurred is $7,650 (the variable portion of $3,650 and the fixed portion of $4,000). Recall from Exhibit 24.12 that each unit requires 1 hour of direct labor, that variable overhead is applied at a rate of $1.00 per direct labor hour, and that the predetermined fixed overhead rate is $1.00 per direct labor hour. Using this information, we can compute overhead variances for both variable and fixed overhead as follows:

Actual variable overhead (given)	$3,650
Applied variable overhead (3,500 × $1.00)	3,500
Unfavorable variable overhead variance	$ 150

Actual fixed overhead (given)	$4,000
Applied fixed overhead (3,500 × $1.00)	3,500
Unfavorable fixed overhead variance	$ 500

"Well, according to the books, you've got too much overhead."

Management should seek to determine the causes of these unfavorable variances and take corrective action. To help better isolate the causes of these variances, more detailed overhead variances can be used, as shown in the next section.

Computing Controllable Overhead Variances and Volume Variances The total overhead variance for G-Max is $650 unfavorable, consisting of $150 unfavorable variable overhead variance and $500 unfavorable fixed overhead variance.

Similar to analysis of direct materials and direct labor, both the variable and fixed overhead variances can be separately analyzed. Exhibit 24.15 shows an expanded framework for understanding these component overhead variances. A **spending variance** occurs when management pays an amount different than the standard price to acquire an item. For instance, the actual wage rate paid to indirect labor might be higher than the standard rate. Similarly, actual supervisory salaries might be different than expected. Spending variances such as these cause management to investigate the reasons that the amount paid differs from the standard. Both variable and fixed overhead costs can yield their own spending variances. Analyzing variable overhead includes computing an **efficiency variance,** which occurs when standard direct labor hours (the allocation base) expected for actual production differ from the actual direct labor hours used. This efficiency variance reflects on the cost-effectiveness in using the overhead allocation base (such as direct labor).

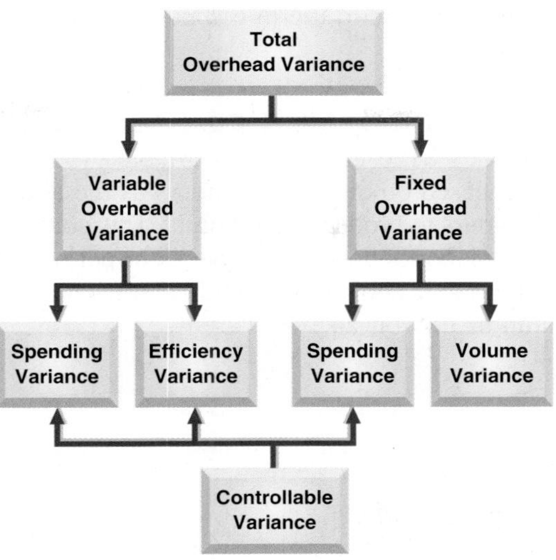

EXHIBIT 24.15

Expanded Framework for Total Overhead Variance

A **volume variance** occurs when a difference occurs between the actual volume of production and the standard volume of production. The budgeted fixed overhead amount is the same regardless of the volume of production (within the relevant range). This budgeted amount is computed based on the standard direct labor hours that the budgeted production volume allows. The applied overhead is based, however, on the standard direct labor hours allowed for the actual volume of production. A difference between budgeted and actual production volumes results in a difference in the standard direct labor hours allowed for these two production levels. This situation yields a volume variance different from zero.

Example: Does an unfavorable volume variance indicate poor management performance? *Answer.* No, it only indicates production volume was less than expected. This can be due to many factors, such as falling demand for company products, that are usually viewed outside a manager's control.

We can combine the variable overhead spending variance, the fixed overhead spending variance, and the variable overhead efficiency variance to get **controllable variance.** The controllable variance is so named because it refers to activities usually under management control. Exhibit 24.16

EXHIBIT 24.16

Variable and Fixed Overhead Variances

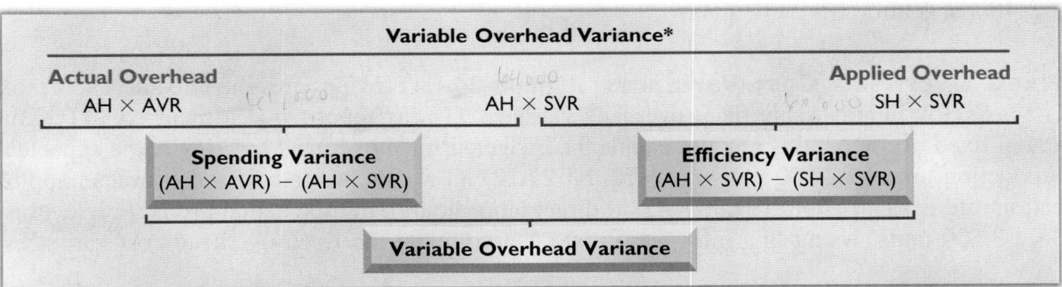

* AH = actual direct labor hours; AVR = actual variable overhead rate; SH = standard direct labor hours; SVR = standard variable overhead rate.

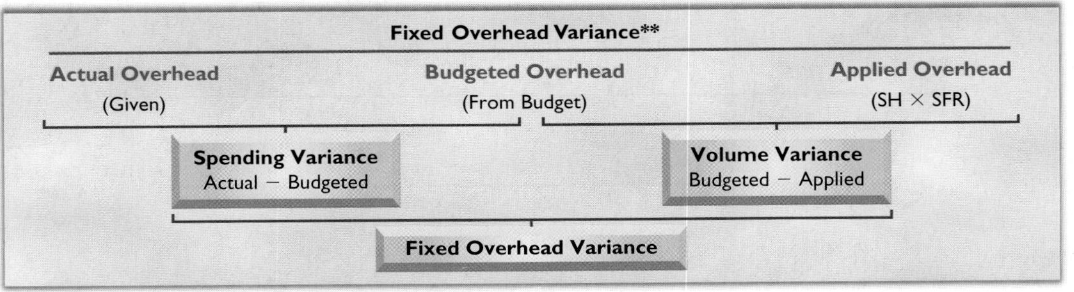

** SH = standard direct labor hours; SFR = standard fixed overhead rate.

shows formulas to use in computing detailed overhead variances that can better identify reasons for variances.

Variable Overhead Cost Variances Exhibit 24.17 offers insight into the causes of G-Max's $150 unfavorable variable overhead cost variance. Recall that G-Max applies overhead based on direct labor hours as the allocation base. We know that it used 3,400 direct labor hours to produce 3,500 units. This compares favorably to the standard requirement of 3,500 direct labor hours at one labor hour per unit. At a standard variable overhead rate of $1.00 per direct labor hour, this should have resulted in variable overhead costs of $3,400 (middle column of Exhibit 24.17).

EXHIBIT 24.17

Computing Variable Overhead Cost Variances

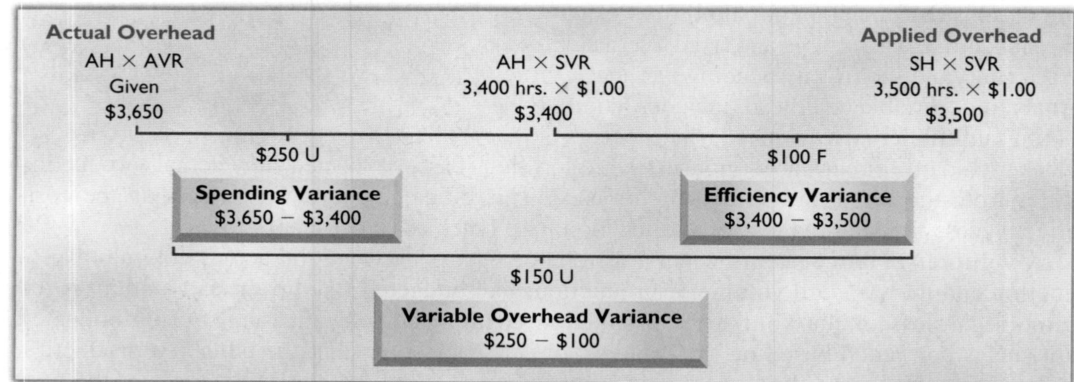

G-Max's cost records, however, report actual variable overhead of $3,650, or $250 higher than expected. This means G-Max has an unfavorable variable overhead spending variance of $250 ($3,650 − $3,400). On the other hand, G-Max used 100 fewer labor hours than expected to make 3,500 units, and its actual variable overhead is lower than its applied variable overhead. Thus, G-Max has a favorable variable overhead efficiency variance of $100 ($3,400 − $3,500).

Fixed Overhead Cost Variances Exhibit 24.18 provides insight into the causes of G-Max's $500 unfavorable fixed overhead variance. G-Max reports that it incurred $4,000 in actual fixed overhead; this amount equals the budgeted fixed overhead for May at the expected production level of 4,000 units (see Exhibit 24.12). G-Max's budgeted fixed overhead application rate is $1 per hour ($4,000/4,000 direct labor hours), but the actual production level is only 3,500 units. Using this information, we can compute the fixed overhead cost variances

EXHIBIT 24.18

Computing Fixed Overhead Cost Variances

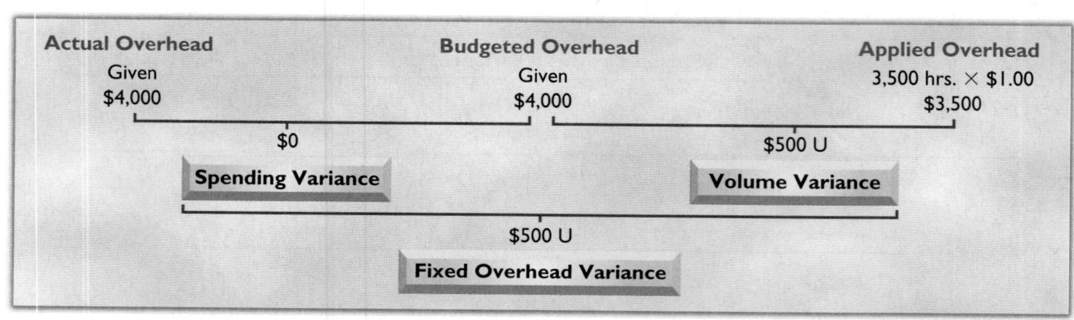

shown in Exhibit 24.18. The applied fixed overhead is computed by multiplying 3,500 standard hours allowed for the actual production by the $1 fixed overhead allocation rate. Exhibit 24.18 reveals that the fixed overhead spending variance is zero, suggesting good control of fixed overhead costs. The volume variance of $500 occurs because 500 fewer units are produced than budgeted; namely, 80% of the manufacturing capacity is budgeted but only 70% is used.

An unfavorable volume variance implies that the company did not reach its predicted operating level. Management needs to know why the actual level of performance differs from the expected level. The main purpose of the volume variance is to identify what portion of the total variance is caused by failing to meet the expected volume level. This information permits management to focus on the controllable variance.

Overhead Variance Reports Using the information from Exhibits 24.17 and 24.18, we compute the total controllable overhead variance as $150 unfavorable ($250 U + $100 F + $0). To help management isolate the reasons for this controllable variance, an *overhead variance report* can be prepared.

A complete overhead variance report provides managers information about specific overhead costs and how they differ from budgeted amounts. Exhibit 24.19 shows G-Max's overhead variance report for May. It reveals that (1) fixed costs and maintenance cost were incurred as expected, (2) costs for indirect labor and power and lights were higher than expected, and (3) indirect materials cost was less than expected.

The total controllable variance amount is also readily available from Exhibit 24.19. The overhead variance report shows the total volume variance as $500 unfavorable (shown at the top) and the $150 unfavorable controllable variance (reported at the bottom right). The sum of the controllable variance and the volume variance equals the total (fixed and variable) overhead variance of $650 unfavorable.

EXHIBIT 24.19

Overhead Variance Report

G-MAX
Overhead Variance Report
For Month Ended May 31, 2009

Volume Variance			
Expected production level	80% of capacity		
Production level achieved	70% of capacity		
Volume variance	**$500 (unfavorable)**		

Controllable Variance	**Flexible Budget**	**Actual Results**	**Variances***
Variable overhead costs			
Indirect labor	$1,400	$1,525	$125 U
Indirect materials	1,050	1,025	25 F
Power and lights	700	750	50 U
Maintenance	350	350	0
Total variable overhead costs	3,500	3,650	150 U†
Fixed overhead costs			
Building rent	1,000	1,000	0
Depreciation—machinery	1,200	1,200	0
Supervisory salaries	1,800	1,800	0
Total fixed overhead costs	4,000	4,000	0‡
Total overhead costs	$7,500	$7,650	$150 U

* F = Favorable variance; U = Unfavorable variance.

† Total variable overhead (spending and efficiency) variance.

‡ Fixed overhead spending variance.

Extensions of Standard Costs

This section extends the application of standard costs for control purposes, for service companies, and for accounting systems.

Standard Costs for Control

C3 Explain how standard cost information is useful for management by exception.

To control business activities, top management must be able to affect the actions of lower-level managers responsible for the company's revenues and costs. After preparing a budget and establishing standard costs, management should take actions to gain control when actual costs differ from standard or budgeted amounts.

Reports such as the ones illustrated in this chapter call management's attention to variances from business plans and other standards. When managers use these reports to focus on problem areas, the budgeting process contributes to the control function. In using budgeted performance reports, practice of management by exception is often useful. **Management by exception** means that managers focus attention on the most significant variances and give less attention to areas where performance is reasonably close to the standard. This practice leads management to concentrate on the exceptional or irregular situations. Management by exception is especially useful when directed at controllable items.

Decision Ethics

Internal Auditor You discover a manager who always spends exactly what is budgeted. About 30% of her budget is spent just before the period-end. She admits to spending what is budgeted, whether or not it is needed. She offers three reasons: (1) she doesn't want her budget cut, (2) "management by exception" focuses on budget deviations; and (3) she believes the money is budgeted to be spent. What action do you take? [Answer—p. 1004]

Standard Costs for Services

Many managers use standard costs and variance analysis to investigate manufacturing costs. Many managers also recognize that standard costs and variances can help them control *nonmanufacturing* costs. Companies providing services instead of products can benefit from the use of standard costs. Application of standard costs and variances can be readily adapted to nonmanufacturing situations. To illustrate, many service providers use standard costs to help control expenses. First, they use standard costs as a basis for budgeting all services. Second, they use periodic performance reports to compare actual results to standards. Third, they use these reports to identify significant variances within specific areas of responsibility. Fourth, they implement the appropriate control procedures.

Decision Insight

Health Budget Medical professionals continue to struggle with business realities. Quality medical service is paramount, but efficiency in providing that service also is important. The use of budgeting and standard costing is touted as an effective means to control and monitor medical costs, especially overhead.

Standard Cost Accounting System

P4 Prepare journal entries for standard costs and account for price and quantity variances.

We have shown how companies use standard costs in management reports. Most standard cost systems also record these costs and variances in accounts. This practice simplifies recordkeeping and helps in preparing reports. Although we do not need knowledge of standard cost accounting practices to understand standard costs and their use, we must know how to interpret the accounts in which standard costs and variances are recorded. The entries in this section briefly illustrate the important aspects of this process for G-Max's standard costs and variances for May.

The first of these entries records standard materials cost incurred in May in the Goods in Process Inventory account. This part of the entry is similar to the usual accounting entry, but the amount of the debit equals the standard cost ($3,500) instead of the actual cost ($3,780).

This entry credits Raw Materials Inventory for actual cost. The difference between standard and actual direct materials costs is recorded with debits to two separate materials variance accounts (recall Exhibit 21.10). Both the materials price and quantity variances are recorded as debits because they reflect additional costs higher than the standard cost (if actual costs were less than the standard, they are recorded as credits). This treatment (debit) reflects their unfavorable effect because they represent higher costs and lower income.

May 31	Goods in Process Inventory	3,500	
	Direct Materials Price Variance*	**180**	
	Direct Materials Quantity Variance	**100**	
	Raw Materials Inventory		3,780
	To charge production for standard quantity of materials used (3,500 lbs.) at the standard price ($1 per lb.), and to record material price and material quantity variances.		

Assets = Liabilities + Equity
+3,500 −100
−3,780 −180

* Many companies record the materials price variance when materials are purchased. For simplicity, we record both the materials price and quantity variances when materials are issued to production.

The second entry debits Goods in Process Inventory for the standard labor cost of the goods manufactured during May ($28,000). Actual labor cost ($28,220) is recorded with a credit to the Factory Payroll account. The difference between standard and actual labor costs is explained by two variances (see Exhibit 21.11). The direct labor rate variance is unfavorable and is debited to that account. The direct labor efficiency variance is favorable and that account is credited. The direct labor efficiency variance is favorable because it represents a lower cost and a higher net income.

May 31	Goods in Process Inventory	28,000	
	Direct Labor Rate Variance	**1,020**	
	Direct Labor Efficiency Variance		**800**
	Factory Payroll		28,220
	To charge production with 3,500 standard hours of direct labor at the standard $8 per hour rate, and to record the labor rate and efficiency variances.		

Assets = Liabilities + Equity
+28,000 +28,220
− 1,020
+ 800

The entry to assign standard predetermined overhead to the cost of goods manufactured must debit the $7,000 predetermined amount to the Goods in Process Inventory account. Actual overhead costs of $7,650 were debited to Factory Overhead during the period (entries not shown here). Thus, when Factory Overhead is applied to Goods in Process Inventory, the actual amount is credited to the Factory Overhead account. To account for the difference between actual and standard overhead costs, the entry includes a $250 debit to the Variable Overhead Spending Variance, a $100 credit to the Variable Overhead Efficiency Variance, and a $500 debit to the Volume Variance (recall Exhibits 21.17 and 21.18). An alternative (simpler) approach is to record the difference with a $150 debit to the Controllable Variance account and a $500 debit to the Volume Variance account (recall from Exhibit 21.15 that controllable variance is the sum of both variable overhead variances and the fixed overhead spending variance).

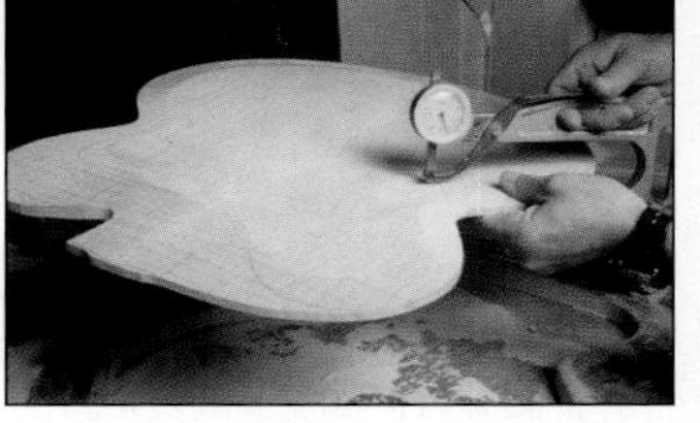

May 31	Goods in Process Inventory	7,000	
	Volume Variance	**500**	
	Variable Overhead Spending Variance	**250**	
	Variable Overhead Efficiency Variance		**100**
	Factory Overhead		7,650
	To apply overhead at the standard rate of $2 per standard direct labor hour (3,500 hours), and to record overhead variances.		

Assets = Liabilities + Equity
+7,000 +7,650
− 250
− 500
+ 100

The balances of these different variance accounts accumulate until the end of the accounting period. As a result, the unfavorable variances of some months can offset the favorable variances of other months.

These ending variance account balances, which reflect results of the period's various transactions and events, are closed at period-end. If the amounts are *immaterial,* they are added to or subtracted from the balance of the Cost of Goods Sold account. This process is similar to that shown in the job order costing chapter for eliminating an underapplied or overapplied balance in the Factory Overhead account. (*Note:* These variance balances, which represent differences between actual and standard costs, must be added to or subtracted from the materials, labor, and overhead costs recorded. In this way, the recorded costs equal the actual costs incurred in the period; a company must use actual costs in external financial statements prepared in accordance with generally accepted accounting principles.)

Point: If variances are material they can be allocated between Goods in Process Inventory, Finished Goods Inventory, and Cost of Goods Sold. This closing process is explained in advanced courses.

Quick Check

Answers—p. 1005

10. Under what conditions is an overhead volume variance considered favorable?

11. To use management by exception with standard costs, a company (*a*) must record standard costs in its accounting, (*b*) should compute variances from flexible budget amounts to allow management to focus its attention on significant differences between actual and budgeted results, or (*c*) should analyze only variances for direct materials and direct labor.

12. A company uses a standard cost accounting system. Prepare the journal entry to record these direct materials variances:

Direct materials cost actually incurred	$73,200
Direct materials quantity variance (favorable)	3,800
Direct materials price variance (unfavorable)	1,300

13. If standard costs are recorded in the manufacturing accounts, how are recorded variances treated at the end of an accounting period?

Decision Analysis — Sales Variances

A2 Analyze changes in sales from expected amounts.

This chapter explained the computation and analysis of cost variances. A similar variance analysis can be applied to sales. To illustrate, consider the following sales data from G-Max for two of its golf products, Excel golf balls and Big Bert® drivers.

	Budgeted	Actual
Sales of Excel golf balls (units)	1,000 units	1,100 units
Sales price per Excel golf ball	$10	$10.50
Sales of Big Bert® drivers (units)	150 units	140 units
Sales price per Big Bert® driver	$200	$190

Using this information, we compute both the *sales price variance* and the *sales volume variance* as shown in Exhibit 24.20. The total sales price variance is $850 unfavorable, and the total sales volume variance is $1,000 unfavorable. Neither variance implies anything positive about these two products. However, further analysis of these total sales variances reveals that both the sales price and sales volume variances for Excel golf balls are favorable, meaning that both the unfavorable total sales price variance and the unfavorable total sales volume variance are due to the Big Bert driver.

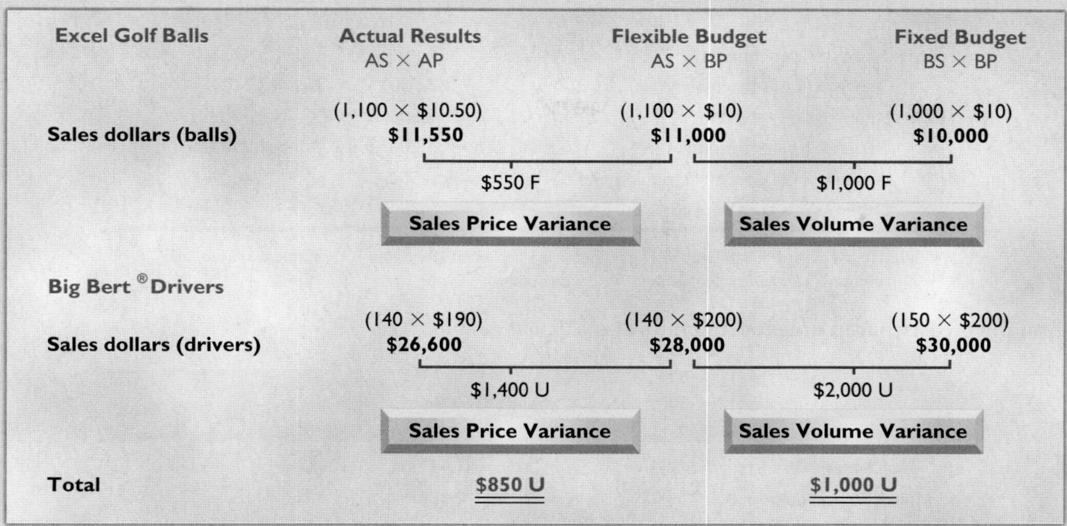

Excel Golf Balls
Actual Results
AS × AP
Flexible Budget
AS × BP
Fixed Budget
BS × BP
Sales dollars (balls)
(1,100 × $10.50)
$11,550
(1,100 × $10)
$11,000
(1,000 × $10)
$10,000
$550 F
Sales Price Variance
$1,000 F
Sales Volume Variance
Big Bert® Drivers
Sales dollars (drivers)
(140 × $190)
$26,600
(140 × $200)
$28,000
(150 × $200)
$30,000
$1,400 U
Sales Price Variance
$2,000 U
Sales Volume Variance
Total
$850 U
$1,000 U

EXHIBIT 24.20

Computing Sales Variances*

* AS = actual sales units; AP = actual sales price; BP = budgeted sales price; BS = budgeted sales units (fixed budget).

Managers use sales variances for planning and control purposes. The sales variance information is used to plan future actions to avoid unfavorable variances. G-Max sold 90 total combined units (both balls and drivers) more than planned, but these 90 units were not sold in the proportion budgeted. G-Max sold fewer than the budgeted quantity of the higher-priced driver, which contributed to the unfavorable total sales variances. Managers use such detail to question what caused the company to sell more golf balls and fewer drivers. Managers also use this information to evaluate and even reward their salespeople. Extra compensation is paid to salespeople who contribute to a higher profit margin. Finally, with multiple products, the sales volume variance can be separated into a *sales mix variance* and a *sales quantity variance*. The sales mix variance is the difference between the actual and budgeted sales mix of the products. The sales quantity variance is the difference between the total actual and total budgeted quantity of units sold.

Decision Maker

Sales Manager The current performance report reveals a large favorable sales volume variance but an unfavorable sales price variance. You did not expect to see a large increase in sales volume. What steps do you take to analyze this situation? [Answer—p. 1004]

Demonstration Problem

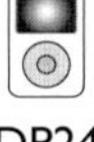

DP24

Pacific Company provides the following information about its budgeted and actual results for June 2009. Although the expected June volume was 25,000 units produced and sold, the company actually produced and sold 27,000 units as detailed here:

	Budget (25,000 units)	Actual (27,000 units)
Selling price	$5.00 per unit	$5.23 per unit
Variable costs (per unit)		
Direct materials	1.24 per unit	1.12 per unit
Direct labor	1.50 per unit	1.40 per unit
Factory supplies*	0.25 per unit	0.37 per unit
Utilities*	0.50 per unit	0.60 per unit
Selling costs	0.40 per unit	0.34 per unit

[continued on next page]

[continued from previous page]

Fixed costs (per month)		
Depreciation—machinery*	$3,750	$3,710
Depreciation—building*	2,500	2,500
General liability insurance	1,200	1,250
Property taxes on office equipment	500	485
Other administrative expense	750	900

* Indicates factory overhead item; $0.75 per unit or $3 per direct labor hour for variable overhead, and $0.25 per unit or $1 per direct labor hour for fixed overhead.

Standard costs based on expected output of 25,000 units

	Per Unit of Output	Quantity to Be Used	Total Cost
Direct materials, 4 oz. @ $0.31/oz.	$1.24/unit	100,000 oz.	$31,000
Direct labor, 0.25 hrs. @ $6.00/hr.	1.50/unit	6,250 hrs.	37,500
Overhead	1.00/unit		25,000

Actual costs incurred to produce 27,000 units

	Per Unit of Output	Quantity Used	Total Cost
Direct materials, 4 oz. @ $0.28/oz.	$1.12/unit	108,000 oz.	$30,240
Direct labor, 0.20 hrs. @ $7.00/hr.	1.40/unit	5,400 hrs.	37,800
Overhead	1.20/unit		32,400

Standard costs based on expected output of 27,000 units

	Per Unit of Output	Quantity to Be Used	Total Cost
Direct materials, 4 oz. @ $0.31/oz.	$1.24/unit	108,000 oz.	$33,480
Direct labor, 0.25 hrs. @ $6.00/hr.	1.50/unit	6,750 hrs.	40,500
Overhead			26,500

Required

1. Prepare June flexible budgets showing expected sales, costs, and net income assuming 20,000, 25,000, and 30,000 units of output produced and sold.
2. Prepare a flexible budget performance report that compares actual results with the amounts budgeted if the actual volume had been expected.
3. Apply variance analysis for direct materials, for direct labor, and for overhead.
4. Prepare journal entries to record standard costs, and price and quantity variances, for direct materials, direct labor, and factory overhead.

Planning the Solution

- Prepare a table showing the expected results at the three specified levels of output. Compute the variable costs by multiplying the per unit variable costs by the expected volumes. Include fixed costs at the given amounts. Combine the amounts in the table to show total variable costs, contribution margin, total fixed costs, and income from operations.
- Prepare a table showing the actual results and the amounts that should be incurred at 27,000 units. Show any differences in the third column and label them with an *F* for favorable if they increase income or a *U* for unfavorable if they decrease income.
- Using the chapter's format, compute these total variances and the individual variances requested:
  - Total materials variance (including the direct materials quantity variance and the direct materials price variance).

- Total direct labor variance (including the direct labor efficiency variance and rate variance).
- Total overhead variance (including both variable and fixed overhead variances and their component variances).

Solution to Demonstration Problem

1.

PACIFIC COMPANY
Flexible Budgets
For Month Ended June 30, 2009

	Flexible Budget: Variable Amount per Unit	Flexible Budget: Total Fixed Cost	Flexible Budget for Unit Sales of 20,000	Flexible Budget for Unit Sales of 25,000	Flexible Budget for Unit Sales of 30,000
Sales	$5.00		$100,000	$125,000	$150,000
Variable costs					
Direct materials	1.24		24,800	31,000	37,200
Direct labor	1.50		30,000	37,500	45,000
Factory supplies	0.25		5,000	6,250	7,500
Utilities	0.50		10,000	12,500	15,000
Selling costs	0.40		8,000	10,000	12,000
Total variable costs	3.89		77,800	97,250	116,700
Contribution margin	$1.11		22,200	27,750	33,300
Fixed costs					
Depreciation—machinery		$3,750	3,750	3,750	3,750
Depreciation—building		2,500	2,500	2,500	2,500
General liability insurance		1,200	1,200	1,200	1,200
Property taxes on office equipment		500	500	500	500
Other administrative expense		750	750	750	750
Total fixed costs		$8,700	8,700	8,700	8,700
Income from operations			$ 13,500	$ 19,050	$ 24,600

2.

PACIFIC COMPANY
Flexible Budget Performance Report
For Month Ended June 30, 2009

	Flexible Budget	Actual Results	Variance*
Sales (27,000 units)	$135,000	$141,210	$6,210 F
Variable costs			
Direct materials	33,480	30,240	3,240 F
Direct labor	40,500	37,800	2,700 F
Factory supplies	6,750	9,990	3,240 U
Utilities	13,500	16,200	2,700 U
Selling costs	10,800	9,180	1,620 F
Total variable costs	105,030	103,410	1,620 F
Contribution margin	29,970	37,800	7,830 F
Fixed costs			
Depreciation—machinery	3,750	3,710	40 F
Depreciation—building	2,500	2,500	0
General liability insurance	1,200	1,250	50 U
Property taxes on office equipment	500	485	15 F
Other administrative expense	750	900	150 U
Total fixed costs	8,700	8,845	145 U
Income from operations	$ 21,270	$ 28,955	$7,685 F

* F = Favorable variance; U = Unfavorable variance.

3. Variance analysis of materials, labor, and overhead costs.

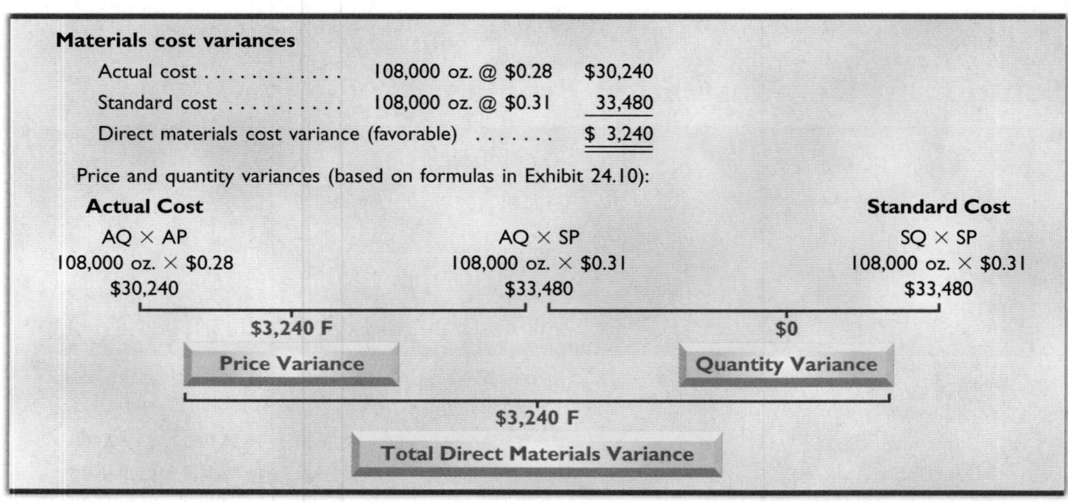
Materials cost variances
Actual cost . . . . 108,000 oz. @ $0.28 $30,240
Standard cost . . . . 108,000 oz. @ $0.31 33,480
Direct materials cost variance (favorable) . . . . $ 3,240
Price and quantity variances (based on formulas in Exhibit 24.10):
Actual Cost
AQ × AP
108,000 oz. × $0.28
$30,240
AQ × SP
108,000 oz. × $0.31
$33,480
Standard Cost
SQ × SP
108,000 oz. × $0.31
$33,480
$3,240 F
Price Variance
$0
Quantity Variance
$3,240 F
Total Direct Materials Variance

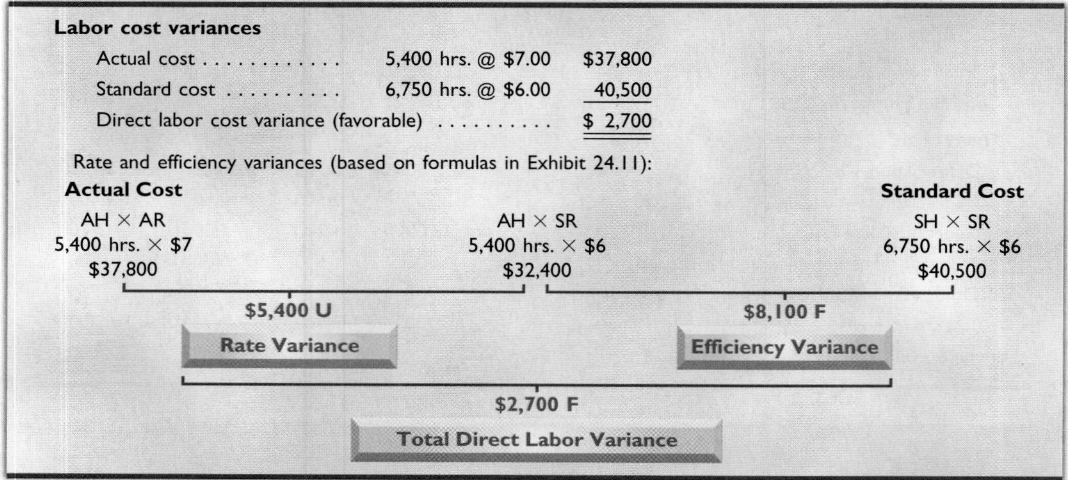
Labor cost variances
Actual cost . . . . 5,400 hrs. @ $7.00 $37,800
Standard cost . . . . 6,750 hrs. @ $6.00 40,500
Direct labor cost variance (favorable) . . . . $ 2,700
Rate and efficiency variances (based on formulas in Exhibit 24.11):
Actual Cost
AH × AR
5,400 hrs. × $7
$37,800
AH × SR
5,400 hrs. × $6
$32,400
Standard Cost
SH × SR
6,750 hrs. × $6
$40,500
$5,400 U
Rate Variance
$8,100 F
Efficiency Variance
$2,700 F
Total Direct Labor Variance

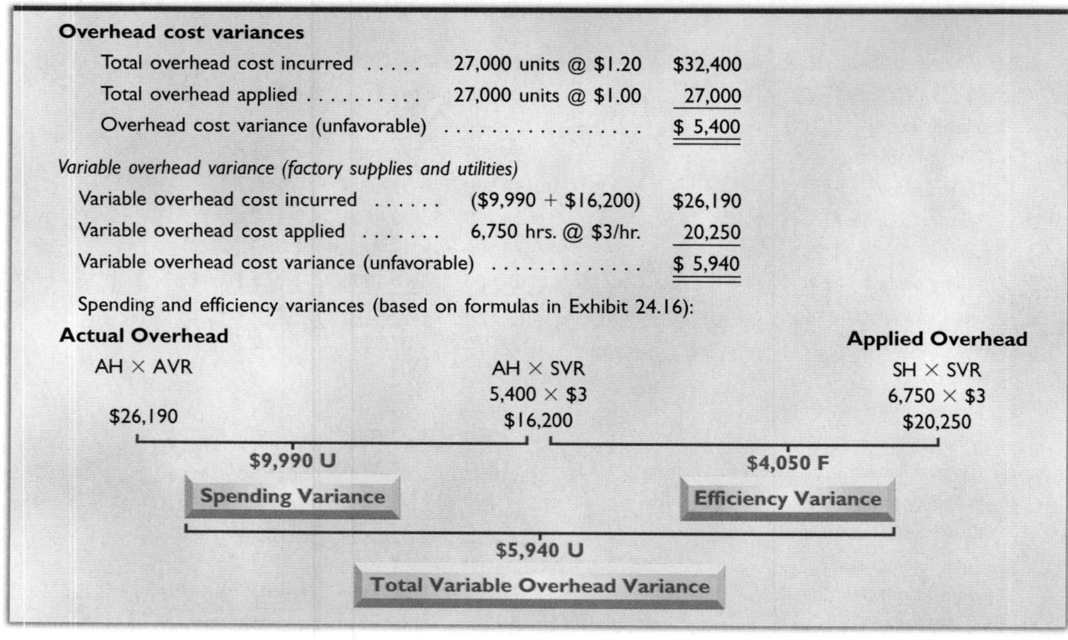
Overhead cost variances
Total overhead cost incurred . . . . . 27,000 units @ $1.20 $32,400
Total overhead applied . . . . 27,000 units @ $1.00 27,000
Overhead cost variance (unfavorable) . . . . $ 5,400
Variable overhead variance (factory supplies and utilities)
Variable overhead cost incurred . . . . . . ($9,990 + $16,200) $26,190
Variable overhead cost applied . . . . 6,750 hrs. @ $3/hr. 20,250
Variable overhead cost variance (unfavorable) . . . . $ 5,940
Spending and efficiency variances (based on formulas in Exhibit 24.16):
Actual Overhead
AH × AVR
$26,190
AH × SVR
5,400 × $3
$16,200
Applied Overhead
SH × SVR
6,750 × $3
$20,250
$9,990 U
Spending Variance
$4,050 F
Efficiency Variance
$5,940 U
Total Variable Overhead Variance

[continued on next page]

[continued from previous page]

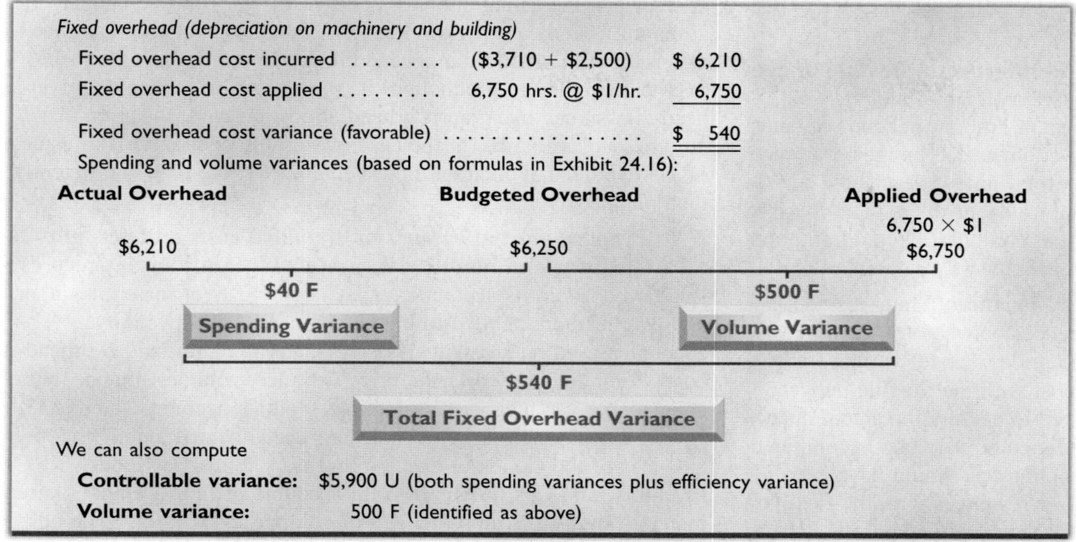

Fixed overhead (depreciation on machinery and building)

Fixed overhead cost incurred	($3,710 + $2,500)	$ 6,210
Fixed overhead cost applied	6,750 hrs. @ $1/hr.	6,750
Fixed overhead cost variance (favorable)		$ 540

Spending and volume variances (based on formulas in Exhibit 24.16):

We can also compute

Controllable variance: $5,900 U (both spending variances plus efficiency variance)

Volume variance: 500 F (identified as above)

4.

Goods in Process Inventory	33,480	
Direct Materials Price Variance		3,240
Raw Materials Inventory		30,240
Goods in Process Inventory	40,500	
Direct Labor Rate Variance	5,400	
Direct Labor Efficiency Variance		8,100
Factory Payroll		37,800
Goods in Process Inventory*	27,000	
Variable Overhead Spending Variance	9,990	
Variable Overhead Efficiency Variance		4,050
Fixed Overhead Spending Variance		40
Fixed Overhead Volume Variance		500
Factory Overhead**		32,400

* $20,250 + $6,750 **$26,190 + $6,210

Summary

C1 Define *standard costs* and explain their computation and uses. Standard costs are the normal costs that should be incurred to produce a product or perform a service. They should be based on a careful examination of the processes used to produce a product or perform a service as well as the quantities and prices that should be incurred in carrying out those processes. On a performance report, standard costs (which are flexible budget amounts) are compared to actual costs, and the differences are presented as variances.

C2 Describe variances and what they reveal about performance. Management can use variances to monitor and control activities. Total cost variances can be broken into price and quantity variances to direct management's attention to those responsible for quantities used and prices paid.

C3 Explain how standard cost information is useful for management by exception. Standard cost accounting provides management information about costs that differ from budgeted (expected) amounts. Performance reports disclose the costs or areas of operations that have significant variances from budgeted amounts. This allows managers to focus attention on the exceptions and less attention on areas proceeding normally.

A1 Compare fixed and flexible budgets. A fixed budget shows the revenues and costs expected to occur at a specified volume level. If actual volume is at some other level, the amounts in the fixed budget do not provide a reasonable basis for evaluating actual performance. A flexible budget expresses variable costs in per unit terms so that it can be used to develop budgeted amounts for any volume level within the relevant range. Thus, managers compute budgeted amounts for evaluation after a period for the volume that actually occurred.

A2 Analyze changes in sales from expected amounts. Actual sales can differ from budgeted sales, and managers can investigate this difference by computing both the sales price and sales volume variances. The *sales price variance* refers to that portion of total variance resulting from a difference between actual and budgeted selling prices. The *sales volume variance* refers to that portion of total variance resulting from a difference between actual and budgeted sales quantities.

P1 **Prepare a flexible budget and interpret a flexible budget performance report.** To prepare a flexible budget, we express each variable cost as a constant amount per unit of sales (or as a percent of sales dollars). In contrast, the budgeted amount of each fixed cost is expressed as a total amount expected to occur at any sales volume within the relevant range. The flexible budget is then determined using these computations and amounts for fixed and variable costs at the expected sales volume.

P2 **Compute materials and labor variances.** Materials and labor variances are due to differences between the actual costs incurred and the budgeted costs. The price (or rate) variance is computed by comparing the actual cost with the flexible budget amount that should have been incurred to acquire the actual quantity of resources. The quantity (or efficiency) variance is computed by comparing the flexible budget amount that should have been incurred to acquire the actual quantity of resources with the flexible budget amount that should have been incurred to acquire the standard quantity of resources.

P3 **Compute overhead variances.** Overhead variances are due to differences between the actual overhead costs incurred and the overhead applied to production. An overhead spending variance arises when the actual amount incurred differs from the budgeted amount of overhead. An overhead efficiency (or volume) variance arises when the flexible overhead budget amount differs from the overhead applied to production. It is important to realize that overhead is assigned using an overhead allocation base, meaning that an efficiency variance (in the case of variable overhead) is a result of the overhead application base being used more or less efficiently than planned.

P4 **Prepare journal entries for standard costs and account for price and quantity variances.** When a company records standard costs in its accounts, the standard costs of materials, labor, and overhead are debited to the Goods in Process Inventory account. Based on an analysis of the material, labor, and overhead costs, each quantity variance, price variance, volume variance, and controllable variance is recorded in a separate account. At period-end, if the variances are material, they are allocated among the balances of the Goods in Process Inventory, Finished Goods Inventory, and Cost of Goods Sold accounts. If they are not material, they are simply debited or credited to the Cost of Goods Sold account.

Guidance Answers to **Decision Maker** and **Decision Ethics**

Entrepreneur From the complaints, this performance report appears to compare actual results with a fixed budget. This comparison is useful in determining whether the amount of work actually performed was more or less than planned, but it is not useful in determining whether the divisions were more or less efficient than planned. If the two consulting divisions worked on more assignments than expected, some costs will certainly increase. Therefore, you should prepare a flexible budget using the actual number of consulting assignments and then compare actual performance to the flexible budget.

Human Resource Manager As HR manager, you should investigate the causes for any labor-related variances although you may not be responsible for them. An unfavorable labor efficiency variance occurs because more labor hours than standard were used during the period. There are at least three possible reasons for this: (1) materials quality could be poor, resulting in more labor consumption due to rework; (2) unplanned interruptions (strike, breakdowns, accidents) could have occurred during the period; and (3) the production manager could have used a different labor mix to expedite orders. This new labor mix could have consisted of a larger proportion of untrained labor, which resulted in more labor hours.

Internal Auditor Although the manager's actions might not be unethical, this action is undesirable. The internal auditor should report this behavior, possibly recommending that for the purchase of such discretionary items, the manager must provide budgetary requests using an activity-based budgeting process. The internal auditor would then be given full authority to verify this budget request.

Sales Manager The unfavorable sales price variance suggests that actual prices were lower than budgeted prices. As the sales manager, you want to know the reasons for a lower than expected price. Perhaps your salespeople lowered the price of certain products by offering quantity discounts. You then might want to know what prompted them to offer the quantity discounts (perhaps competitors were offering discounts). You want to break the sales volume variance into both the sales mix and sales quantity variances. You could find that although the sales quantity variance is favorable, the sales mix variance is not. Then you need to investigate why the actual sales mix differs from the budgeted sales mix.

Guidance Answers to **Quick Checks**

1. *b*
2. The first step is classifying each cost as variable or fixed.
3. A fixed budget is prepared using an expected volume of sales or production. A flexible budget is prepared using the actual volume of activity.
4. The contribution margin equals sales less variable costs.
5. *c*
6. It is the difference between actual cost and standard cost.

7. *a*; Total actual hours: 2,500 × 2.5 = 6,250
Total standard hours: 2,500 × 2.0 = 5,000
Efficiency variance = (6,250 − 5,000) × $3.00
= $3,750 U

8. *b*; Rate variance = ($3.10 − $3.00) × 6,250 = $625 U

9. Yes, this will occur when the materials quantity variance is more than the materials price variance.

10. The overhead volume variance is favorable when the actual operating level is higher than the expected level.

11. *b*

12.

Goods in Process Inventory	75,700	
Direct Materials Price Variance	1,300	
Direct Materials Quantity Variance		3,800
Raw Materials Inventory		73,200

13. If the variances are material, they should be prorated among the Goods in Process Inventory, Finished Goods Inventory, and Cost of Goods Sold accounts. If they are not material, they can be closed to Cost of Goods Sold.

Key Terms

mhhe.com/wildFAP19e

Key Terms are available at the book's Website for learning and testing in an online Flashcard Format.

Budgetary control (p. 980)
Budget report (p. 980)
Controllable variance (p. 993)
Cost variance (p. 986)
Efficiency variance (p. 993)
Favorable variance (p. 981)
Fixed budget (p. 981)
Fixed budget performance report (p. 981)
Flexible budget (p. 982)
Flexible budget performance report (p. 984)
Management by exception (p. 996)
Overhead cost variance (p. 992)
Price variance (p. 984)
Quantity variance (p. 984)
Spending variance (p. 993)
Standard costs (p. 985)
Unfavorable variance (p. 981)
Variance analysis (p. 984)
Volume variance (p. 993)

Multiple Choice Quiz

Answers on p. 1021

mhhe.com/wildFAP19e

Additional Quiz Questions are available at the book's Website.

Quiz24

1. A company predicts its production and sales will be 24,000 units. At that level of activity, its fixed costs are budgeted at $300,000, and its variable costs are budgeted at $246,000. If its activity level declines to 20,000 units, what will be its fixed costs and its variable costs?
a. Fixed, $300,000; variable, $246,000
b. Fixed, $250,000; variable, $205,000
c. Fixed, $300,000; variable, $205,000
d. Fixed, $250,000; variable, $246,000
e. Fixed, $300,000; variable, $300,000

2. Using the following information about a single product company, compute its total actual cost of direct materials used.
- Direct materials standard cost: 5 lbs. × $2 per lb. = $10.
- Total direct materials cost variance: $15,000 unfavorable.
- Actual direct materials used: 300,000 lbs.
- Actual units produced: 60,000 units.

a. $585,000
b. $600,000
c. $300,000
d. $315,000
e. $615,000

3. A company uses four hours of direct labor to produce a product unit. The standard direct labor cost is $20 per hour. This period the company produced 20,000 units and used 84,160 hours of direct labor at a total cost of $1,599,040. What is its labor rate variance for the period?
a. $83,200 F
b. $84,160 U
c. $84,160 F
d. $83,200 U
e. $ 960 F

4. A company's standard for a unit of its single product is $6 per unit in variable overhead (4 hours × $1.50 per hour). Actual data for the period show variable overhead costs of $150,000 and production of 24,000 units. Its total variable overhead cost variance is
a. $ 6,000 F.
b. $ 6,000 U.
c. $114,000 U.
d. $114,000 F.
e. $ 0.

5. A company's standard for a unit of its single product is $4 per unit in fixed overhead ($24,000 total/6,000 units budgeted). Actual data for the period show total actual fixed overhead of $24,100 and production of 4,800 units. Its volume variance is
a. $4,800 U.
b. $4,800 F.
c. $ 100 U.
d. $ 100 F.
e. $4,900 U.

Discussion Questions

1. What limits the usefulness to managers of fixed budget performance reports?
2. Identify the main purpose of a flexible budget for managers.
3. Prepare a flexible budget performance report title (in proper form) for Spalding Company for the calendar year 2009. Why is a proper title important for this or any report?
4. What type of analysis does a flexible budget performance report help management perform?
5. In what sense can a variable cost be considered constant?
6. What department is usually responsible for a direct labor rate variance? What department is usually responsible for a direct labor efficiency variance? Explain.
7. What is a price variance? What is a quantity variance?
8. What is the purpose of using standard costs?
9. In an analysis of fixed overhead cost variances, what is the volume variance?
10. What is the predetermined standard overhead rate? How is it computed?
11. In general, variance analysis is said to provide information about ________ and ________ variances.
12. In an analysis of overhead cost variances, what is the controllable variance and what causes it?
13. What are the relations among standard costs, flexible budgets, variance analysis, and management by exception?
14. How can the manager of a music department of a **Best Buy** retail store use flexible budgets to enhance performance?

15. Is it possible for a retail store such as **Circuit City** to use variances in analyzing its operating performance? Explain.

16. Assume that **Apple** is budgeted to operate at 80% of capacity but actually operates at 75% of capacity. What effect will the 5% deviation have on its controllable variance? Its volume variance?

Denotes Discussion Questions that involve decision making.

Available with McGraw-Hill's Homework Manager — McGraw-Hill's HOMEWORK MANAGER®

QUICK STUDY

QS 24-1
Flexible budget performance report
P1

Quail Company reports the following selected financial results for May. For the level of production achieved in May, the budgeted amounts would be sales, $650,000; variable costs, $375,000; and fixed costs, $150,000. Prepare a flexible budget performance report for May.

Sales (100,000 units)	$637,500
Variable costs	356,250
Fixed costs	150,000

QS 24-2
Labor cost variances
C2 P2

Martin Company's output for the current period results in a $10,000 unfavorable direct labor rate variance and a $5,000 unfavorable direct labor efficiency variance. Production for the current period was assigned a $200,000 standard direct labor cost. What is the actual total direct labor cost for the current period?

QS 24-3
Materials cost variances
C2 P2

Blanda Company's output for the current period was assigned a $300,000 standard direct materials cost. The direct materials variances included a $24,000 favorable price variance and a $4,000 favorable quantity variance. What is the actual total direct materials cost for the current period?

QS 24-4
Materials cost variances
C2 P2

For the current period, Roja Company's manufacturing operations yield an $8,000 unfavorable price variance on its direct materials usage. The actual price per pound of material is $156; the standard price is $154. How many pounds of material are used in the current period?

QS 24-5
Management by exception
C3

Managers use *management by exception* for control purposes. (1) Describe the concept of management by exception. (2) Explain how standard costs help managers apply this concept to monitor and control costs.

QS 24-6
Overhead cost variances P3

Gohan Company's output for the current period yields a $12,000 favorable overhead volume variance and a $21,500 unfavorable overhead controllable variance. Standard overhead charged to production for the period is $410,000. What is the actual total overhead cost incurred for the period?

QS 24-7
Preparing overhead entries P4

Refer to the information in QS 24-6. Gohan records standard costs in its accounts. Prepare the journal entry to charge overhead costs to the Goods in Process Inventory account and to record any variances.

QS 24-8
Computing sales price and volume variances
A2

Wills Company specializes in selling used trucks. During the first six months of 2009, the dealership sold 50 trucks at an average price of $18,000 each. The budget for the first six months of 2009 was to sell 45 trucks at an average price of $19,000 each. Compute the dealership's sales price variance and sales volume variance for the first six months of 2009.

QS 24-9
Overhead cost variances
P3

Harp Company applies overhead using machine hours and reports the following information. Compute the total variable overhead cost variance.

Actual machine hours used	4,950 hours
Standard machine hours	5,000 hours
Actual variable overhead rate per hour	$2.10
Standard variable overhead rate per hour	$2.00

QS 24-10
Overhead spending and efficiency variances P3

Refer to the information from QS 24-9. Compute the variable overhead spending variance and the variable overhead efficiency variance.

McGraw-Hill's HOMEWORK MANAGER® Available with McGraw-Hill's Homework Manager

EXERCISES

Exercise 24-1
Preparation of flexible budgets
P1

Tryon Company's fixed budget for the first quarter of calendar year 2009 reveals the following. Prepare flexible budgets following the format of Exhibit 24.3 that show variable costs per unit, fixed costs, and three different flexible budgets for sales volumes of 14,500, 15,000, and 15,500 units.

Sales (15,000 units)		$3,030,000
Cost of goods sold		
Direct materials	$345,000	
Direct labor	705,000	
Production supplies	405,000	
Plant manager salary	90,000	1,545,000
Gross profit		1,485,000
Selling expenses		
Sales commissions	150,000	
Packaging	240,000	
Advertising	100,000	490,000
Administrative expenses		
Administrative salaries	110,000	
Depreciation—office equip.	60,000	
Insurance	48,000	
Office rent	54,000	272,000
Income from operations		$ 723,000

Check Income (at 14,500 units), $683,500

Exercise 24-2
Classification of costs as fixed or variable
P1

RTEX Company manufactures and sells mountain bikes. It normally operates eight hours a day, five days a week. Using this information, classify each of the following costs as fixed or variable. If additional information would affect your decision, describe the information.

a. Management salaries
b. Incoming shipping expenses
c. Office supplies
d. Taxes on property
e. Gas used for heating
f. Direct labor
g. Repair expense for tools
h. Depreciation on tools
i. Pension cost
j. Bike frames
k. Screws for assembly

Exercise 24-3
Preparation of a flexible budget performance report
A1

Hall Company's fixed budget performance report for June follows. The $660,000 budgeted expenses include $450,000 variable expenses and $210,000 fixed expenses. Actual expenses include $200,000 fixed expenses. Prepare a flexible budget performance report that shows any variances between budgeted results and actual results. List fixed and variable expenses separately.

	Fixed Budget	Actual Results	Variances
Sales (in units)	9,000	7,900	
Sales (in dollars)	$720,000	$647,800	$72,200 U
Total expenses	660,000	606,850	53,150 F
Income from operations	$ 60,000	$ 40,950	$19,050 U

Check Income variance, $13,950 F

Exercise 24-4
Preparation of a flexible budget performance report
A1

Burton Company's fixed budget performance report for July follows. The $675,000 budgeted expenses include $634,500 variable expenses and $40,500 fixed expenses. Actual expenses include $52,500 fixed expenses. Prepare a flexible budget performance report showing any variances between budgeted and actual results. List fixed and variable expenses separately.

	Fixed Budget	Actual Results	Variances
Sales (in units)	9,000	11,400	
Sales (in dollars)	$900,000	$1,140,000	$240,000 F
Total expenses	675,000	810,000	135,000 U
Income from operations	$225,000	$ 330,000	$105,000 F

Check Income variance, $34,200 F

Exercise 24-5
Computation and interpretation of labor variances C2 P2

Check October rate variance, $14,880 F

After evaluating Pima Company's manufacturing process, management decides to establish standards of 1.4 hours of direct labor per unit of product and $15 per hour for the labor rate. During October, the company uses 3,720 hours of direct labor at a $40,920 total cost to produce 4,000 units of product. In November, the company uses 4,560 hours of direct labor at a $54,720 total cost to produce 3,500 units of product. (1) Compute the rate variance, the efficiency variance, and the total direct labor cost variance for each of these two months. (2) Interpret the October direct labor variances.

Exercise 24-6
Computation and interpretation of total variable and fixed overhead variances
C2 P3

Venture Company set the following standard costs for one unit of its product for 2009.

Direct material (20 lbs. @ $5.00 per lb.)	$100.00
Direct labor (10 hrs. @ $16.00 per hr.)	160.00
Factory variable overhead (10 hrs. @ $8.00 per hr.)	80.00
Factory fixed overhead (10 hrs. @ $3.20 per hr.)	32.00
Standard cost	$372.00

The $11.20 ($8.00 + $3.20) total overhead rate per direct labor hour is based on an expected operating level equal to 75% of the factory's capacity of 50,000 units per month. The following monthly flexible budget information is also available.

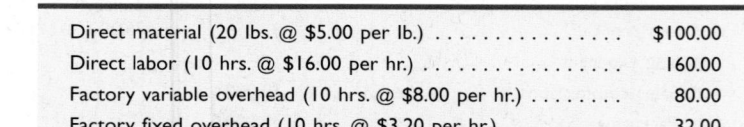

		Operating Levels (% of capacity)		
		70%	75%	80%
3	Budgeted output (units)	35,000	37,500	40,000
4	Budgeted labor (standard hours)	350,000	375,000	400,000
5	Budgeted overhead (dollars)			
6	Variable overhead	$2,800,000	$3,000,000	$3,200,000
7	Fixed overhead	1,200,000	1,200,000	1,200,000
8	Total overhead	$4,000,000	$4,200,000	$4,400,000

During the current month, the company operated at 70% of capacity, employees worked 340,000 hours, and the following actual overhead costs were incurred.

Variable overhead costs	$2,750,000
Fixed overhead costs	1,257,200
Total overhead costs	$4,007,200

(1) Show how the company computed its predetermined overhead application rate per hour for total overhead, variable overhead, and fixed overhead. (2) Compute the variable and fixed overhead variances.

Check (2) Variable overhead cost variance, $50,000 F

Exercise 24-7
Computation and interpretation of overhead spending, efficiency, and volume variances P3

Refer to the information from Exercise 24-6. Compute and interpret the following.

1. Variable overhead spending and efficiency variances.
2. Fixed overhead spending and volume variances.
3. Controllable variance.

Check (2) Variable overhead: Spending, $30,000 U; efficiency, $80,000 F

Exercise 24-8
Computation and interpretation of materials variances
C2 P2 

Listor Company made 3,800 bookshelves using 23,200 board feet of wood costing $290,000. The company's direct materials standards for one bookshelf are 8 board feet of wood at $12 per board foot. (1) Compute the direct materials variances incurred in manufacturing these bookshelves. (2) Interpret the direct materials variances.

Check Price variance, $11,600 U

Exercise 24-9
Materials variances recorded and closed
C3 P4

Refer to Exercise 24-8. Listor Company records standard costs in its accounts and its material variances in separate accounts when it assigns materials costs to the Goods in Process Inventory account. (1) Show the journal entry that both charges the direct materials costs to the Goods in Process Inventory account and records the materials variances in their proper accounts. (2) Assume that Listor's material variances are the only variances accumulated in the accounting period and that they are immaterial. Prepare the adjusting journal entry to close the variance accounts at period-end. (3) Identify the variance that should be investigated according to the management by exception concept. Explain.

Check (2) Cr. to cost of goods sold, $74,800

Exercise 24-10
Computation of total variable and fixed overhead variances
P3

Integra Company expects to operate at 80% of its productive capacity of 52,000 units per month. At this planned level, the company expects to use 26,000 standard hours of direct labor. Overhead is allocated to products using a predetermined standard rate based on direct labor hours. At the 80% capacity level, the total budgeted cost includes $57,200 fixed overhead cost and $280,800 variable overhead cost. In the current month, the company incurred $320,000 actual overhead and 23,000 actual labor hours while producing 37,000 units. (1) Compute its overhead application rate for total overhead, variable overhead, and fixed overhead. (2) Compute its total overhead variance.

Check (1) Variable overhead rate, $10.80 per hour

Exercise 24-11
Computation of volume and controllable overhead variances P3

Refer to the information from Exercise 24-10. Compute the (1) overhead volume variance and (2) overhead controllable variance.

Check (2) $13,050 U

Exercise 24-12
Computing and interpreting sales variances A2

Wiz Electronics sells computers. During May 2009, it sold 500 computers at a $1,000 average price each. The May 2009 fixed budget included sales of 550 computers at an average price of $950 each. (1) Compute the sales price variance and the sales volume variance for May 2009. (2) Interpret the findings.

McGraw-Hill's HOMEWORK MANAGER® Available with McGraw-Hill's Homework Manager

PROBLEM SET A

Problem 24-1A
Computation of materials, labor, and overhead variances
C2 P2 P3

Beck Company set the following standard unit costs for its single product.

Direct materials (26 lbs. @ $4 per lb.)	$104.00
Direct labor (8 hrs. @ $8 per hr.)	64.00
Factory overhead—variable (8 hrs. @ $5 per hr.)	40.00
Factory overhead—fixed (8 hrs. @ $7 per hr.)	56.00
Total standard cost	$264.00

mhhe.com/wildFAP19e

The predetermined overhead rate is based on a planned operating volume of 70% of the productive capacity of 50,000 units per quarter. The following flexible budget information is available.

	Operating Levels		
	60%	70%	80%
Production in units	30,000	35,000	40,000
Standard direct labor hours	240,000	280,000	320,000
Budgeted overhead			
Fixed factory overhead	$1,960,000	$1,960,000	$1,960,000
Variable factory overhead	$1,200,000	$1,400,000	$1,600,000

During the current quarter, the company operated at 80% of capacity and produced 40,000 units of product; actual direct labor totaled 178,600 hours. Units produced were assigned the following standard costs:

Direct materials (1,040,000 lbs. @ $4 per lb.)	$ 4,160,000
Direct labor (320,000 hrs. @ $8 per hr.)	2,560,000
Factory overhead (320,000 hrs. @ $12 per hr.)	3,840,000
Total standard cost	$10,560,000

Actual costs incurred during the current quarter follow:

Direct materials (1,035,000 lbs. @ $4.10)	$ 4,243,500
Direct labor (327,000 hrs. @ $7.75)	2,534,250
Fixed factory overhead costs	1,875,000
Variable factory overhead costs	1,482,717
Total actual costs	$10,135,467

Check (1) Materials variances: Price, $103,500 U; quantity, $20,000 F. (2) Labor variances: Rate, $81,750 F; efficiency, $56,000 U

Required

1. Compute the direct materials cost variance, including its price and quantity variances.
2. Compute the direct labor variance, including its rate and efficiency variances.
3. Compute the total variable overhead and total fixed overhead variances.
4. Compute these variances: (a) variable overhead spending and efficiency, (b) fixed overhead spending and volume, and (c) total overhead controllable.

Problem 24-2A
Preparation and analysis of a flexible budget
P1 A1

Major Company's 2009 master budget included the following fixed budget report. It is based on an expected production and sales volume of 15,000 units.

MAJOR COMPANY Fixed Budget Report For Year Ended December 31, 2009		
Sales		$3,300,000
Cost of goods sold		
Direct materials	$960,000	
Direct labor	240,000	
Machinery repairs (variable cost)	60,000	
Depreciation—plant equipment	300,000	
Utilities ($60,000 is variable)	180,000	
Plant management salaries	210,000	1,950,000
Gross profit		1,350,000
Selling expenses		
Packaging	75,000	
Shipping	105,000	
Sales salary (fixed annual amount)	235,000	415,000
General and administrative expenses		
Advertising expense	100,000	
Salaries	241,000	
Entertainment expense	85,000	426,000
Income from operations		$ 509,000

Required

1. Classify all items listed in the fixed budget as variable or fixed. Also determine their amounts per unit or their amounts for the year, as appropriate.

2. Prepare flexible budgets (see Exhibit 24.3) for the company at sales volumes of 14,000 and 16,000 units.

3. The company's business conditions are improving. One possible result is a sales volume of approximately 18,000 units. The company president is confident that this volume is within the relevant range of existing capacity. How much would operating income increase over the 2009 budgeted amount of $509,000 if this level is reached without increasing capacity?

4. An unfavorable change in business is remotely possible; in this case, production and sales volume for 2009 could fall to 12,000 units. How much income (or loss) from operations would occur if sales volume falls to this level?

Check (2) Budgeted income at 16,000 units, $629,000

(4) Potential operating income, $149,000

Problem 24-3A
Preparation and analysis of a flexible budget performance report

P1 A2

eXcel

mhhe.com/wildFAP19e

Refer to the information in Problem 24-2A. Major Company's actual income statement for 2009 follows.

MAJOR COMPANY Statement of Income from Operations For Year Ended December 31, 2009		
Sales (18,000 units)		$3,948,000
Cost of goods sold		
Direct materials	$1,160,000	
Direct labor	293,000	
Machinery repairs (variable cost)	63,000	
Depreciation—plant equipment	300,000	
Utilities (fixed cost is $147,500)	215,500	
Plant management salaries	220,000	2,251,500
Gross profit		1,696,500
Selling expenses		
Packaging	87,500	
Shipping	118,500	
Sales salary (annual)	253,000	459,000
General and administrative expenses		
Advertising expense	107,000	
Salaries	241,000	
Entertainment expense	88,500	436,500
Income from operations		$ 801,000

Required

1. Prepare a flexible budget performance report for 2009.

Check (1) Variances: Fixed costs, $66,000 U; income, $68,000 U

Analysis Component

2. Analyze and interpret both the (a) sales variance and (b) direct materials variance.

Problem 24-4A
Flexible budget preparation; computation of materials, labor, and overhead variances; and overhead variance report

P1 P2 P3 C2

Silver Company set the following standard costs for one unit of its product.

Direct materials (5 lbs. @ $6 per lb.)	$30.00
Direct labor (2 hrs. @ $12 per hr.)	24.00
Overhead (2 hrs. @ $16.65 per hr.)	33.30
Total standard cost	$87.30

The predetermined overhead rate ($16.65 per direct labor hour) is based on an expected volume of 75% of the factory's capacity of 20,000 units per month. Following are the company's budgeted overhead costs per month at the 75% level.

Overhead Budget (75% Capacity)		
Variable overhead costs		
Indirect materials	$ 21,000	
Indirect labor	96,000	
Power	22,500	
Repairs and maintenance	57,000	
Total variable overhead costs		$196,500
Fixed overhead costs		
Depreciation—building	23,000	
Depreciation—machinery	71,000	
Taxes and insurance	18,000	
Supervision	191,000	
Total fixed overhead costs		303,000
Total overhead costs		$499,500

The company incurred the following actual costs when it operated at 75% of capacity in October.

Direct materials (75,500 lbs. @ $6.10 per lb.)		$ 460,550
Direct labor (29,000 hrs. @ $12.20 per hr.)		353,800
Overhead costs		
Indirect materials	$ 22,500	
Indirect labor	88,800	
Power	21,500	
Repairs and maintenance	60,250	
Depreciation—building	23,000	
Depreciation—machinery	65,000	
Taxes and insurance	18,100	
Supervision	185,000	484,150
Total costs		$1,298,500

Check (2) Budgeted total overhead at 13,000 units, $473,300.

(3) Materials variances: Price, $7,550 U; quantity, $3,000 U

(4) Labor variances: Rate, $5,800 U; efficiency, $12,000 F

Required

1. Examine the monthly overhead budget to (a) determine the costs per unit for each variable overhead item and its total per unit costs, and (b) identify the total fixed costs per month.
2. Prepare flexible overhead budgets (as in Exhibit 24.12) for October showing the amounts of each variable and fixed cost at the 65%, 75%, and 85% capacity levels.
3. Compute the direct materials cost variance, including its price and quantity variances.
4. Compute the direct labor cost variance, including its rate and efficiency variances.
5. Compute the (a) variable overhead spending and efficiency variances, (b) fixed overhead spending and volume variances, and (c) total overhead controllable variance.
6. Prepare a detailed overhead variance report (as in Exhibit 24.19) that shows the variances for individual items of overhead.

Problem 24-5A
Materials, labor, and overhead variances; and overhead variance report
C2 P2 P3

Green Company has set the following standard costs per unit for the product it manufactures.

Direct materials (15 lbs. @ $3.90 per lb.)	$ 58.50
Direct labor (4 hrs. @ $18 per hr.)	72.00
Overhead (4 hrs. @ $4.20 per hr.)	16.80
Total standard cost	$147.30

The predetermined overhead rate is based on a planned operating volume of 80% of the productive capacity of 10,000 units per month. The following flexible budget information is available.

	Operating Levels		
	70%	80%	90%
Production in units	7,000	8,000	9,000
Standard direct labor hours	28,000	32,000	36,000
Budgeted overhead			
Variable overhead costs			
Indirect materials	$ 14,000	$ 16,000	$ 18,000
Indirect labor	20,300	23,200	26,100
Power	5,600	6,400	7,200
Maintenance	38,500	44,000	49,500
Total variable costs	78,400	89,600	100,800
Fixed overhead costs			
Rent of factory building	15,000	15,000	15,000
Depreciation—machinery	10,000	10,000	10,000
Supervisory salaries	19,800	19,800	19,800
Total fixed costs	44,800	44,800	44,800
Total overhead costs	$123,200	$134,400	$145,600

During May, the company operated at 90% of capacity and produced 9,000 units, incurring the following actual costs.

Direct materials (139,000 lbs. @ $3.80 per lb.)		$ 528,200
Direct labor (33,000 hrs. @ $18.50 per hr.)		610,500
Overhead costs		
Indirect materials	$16,000	
Indirect labor	27,500	
Power	7,200	
Maintenance	42,000	
Rent of factory building	15,000	
Depreciation—machinery	10,000	
Supervisory salaries	24,000	141,700
Total costs		$1,280,400

Required

1. Compute the direct materials variance, including its price and quantity variances.
2. Compute the direct labor variance, including its rate and efficiency variances.
3. Compute these variances: (a) variable overhead spending and efficiency, (b) fixed overhead spending and volume, and (c) total overhead controllable.
4. Prepare a detailed overhead variance report (as in Exhibit 24.19) that shows the variances for individual items of overhead.

Check (1) Materials variances: Price, $13,900 F; quantity, $15,600 U (2) Labor variances: Rate, $16,500 U; efficiency, $54,000 F

Problem 24-6A
Materials, labor, and overhead variances recorded and analyzed

C3 P4 

Brose Company's standard cost accounting system recorded this information from its December operations.

Standard direct materials cost	$104,000
Direct materials quantity variance (unfavorable)	3,000
Direct materials price variance (favorable)	550
Actual direct labor cost	90,000
Direct labor efficiency variance (favorable)	6,850
Direct labor rate variance (unfavorable)	1,200
Actual overhead cost	375,000
Volume variance (unfavorable)	13,000
Controllable variance (unfavorable)	9,000

Check (1) Dr. Goods in Process Inventory (for overhead), $353,000

Required

1. Prepare December 31 journal entries to record the company's costs and variances for the month. (Do not prepare the journal entry to close the variances.)

Analysis Component

2. Identify the areas that would attract the attention of a manager who uses management by exception. Explain what action(s) the manager should consider.

PROBLEM SET B

Problem 24-1B
Computation of materials, labor, and overhead variances
C2 P2 P3

Krug Company set the following standard unit costs for its single product.

Direct materials (5 lbs. @ $2 per lb.)	$10.00
Direct labor (0.3 hrs. @ $15 per hr.)	4.50
Factory overhead—variable (0.3 hrs. @ $10 per hr.)	3.00
Factory overhead—fixed (0.3 hrs. @ $14 per hr.)	4.20
Total standard cost	$21.70

The predetermined overhead rate is based on a planned operating volume of 80% of the productive capacity of 600,000 units per quarter. The following flexible budget information is available.

	Operating Levels		
	70%	80%	90%
Production in units	420,000	480,000	540,000
Standard direct labor hours	126,000	144,000	162,000
Budgeted overhead			
Fixed factory overhead	$2,016,000	$2,016,000	$2,016,000
Variable factory overhead	1,260,000	1,440,000	1,620,000

During the current quarter, the company operated at 70% of capacity and produced 420,000 units of product; direct labor hours worked were 125,000. Units produced were assigned the following standard costs:

Direct materials (2,100,000 lbs. @ $2 per lb.)	$4,200,000
Direct labor (126,000 hrs. @ $15 per hr.)	1,890,000
Factory overhead (126,000 hrs. @ $24 per hr.)	3,024,000
Total standard cost	$9,114,000

Actual costs incurred during the current quarter follow:

Direct materials (2,000,000 lbs. @ $2.15)	$4,300,000
Direct labor (125,000 hrs. @ $15.50)	1,937,500
Fixed factory overhead costs	1,960,000
Variable factory overhead costs	1,200,000
Total actual costs	$9,397,500

Check (1) Materials variances: Price, $300,000 U; quantity, $200,000 F
(2) Labor variances: Rate, $62,500 U; efficiency, $15,000 F

Required

1. Compute the direct materials cost variance, including its price and quantity variances.
2. Compute the direct labor variance, including its rate and efficiency variances.
3. Compute the total variable overhead and total fixed overhead variances.
4. Compute these variances: (a) variable overhead spending and efficiency, (b) fixed overhead spending and volume, and (c) total overhead controllable.

Problem 24-2B
Preparation and analysis of a flexible budget P1 A1

Toronto Company's 2009 master budget included the following fixed budget report. It is based on an expected production and sales volume of 10,000 units.

TORONTO COMPANY Fixed Budget Report For Year Ended December 31, 2009		
Sales		$1,500,000
Cost of goods sold		
Direct materials	$600,000	
Direct labor	130,000	
Machinery repairs (variable cost)	28,500	
Depreciation—machinery	125,000	
Utilities (25% is variable cost)	100,000	
Plant manager salaries	70,000	1,053,500
Gross profit		446,500
Selling expenses		
Packaging	40,000	
Shipping	58,000	
Sales salary (fixed annual amount)	80,000	178,000
General and administrative expenses		
Advertising	40,500	
Salaries	120,500	
Entertainment expense	45,000	206,000
Income from operations		$ 62,500

Required

1. Classify all items listed in the fixed budget as variable or fixed. Also determine their amounts per unit or their amounts for the year, as appropriate.

2. Prepare flexible budgets (see Exhibit 24.3) for the company at sales volumes of 9,500 and 10,500 units.

Check (2) Budgeted income at 10,500 units, $93,425

3. The company's business conditions are improving. One possible result is a sales volume of approximately 12,000 units. The company president is confident that this volume is within the relevant range of existing capacity. How much would operating income increase over the 2009 budgeted amount of $62,500 if this level is reached without increasing capacity?

4. An unfavorable change in business is remotely possible; in this case, production and sales volume for 2009 could fall to 8,000 units. How much income (or loss) from operations would occur if sales volume falls to this level?

(4) Potential operating loss, $(61,200)

Problem 24-3B
Preparation and analysis of a flexible budget performance report
P1 A2

Refer to the information in Problem 24-2B. Toronto Company's actual income statement for 2009 follows.

TORONTO COMPANY Statement of Income from Operations For Year Ended December 31, 2009		
Sales (10,500 units)		$1,596,000
Cost of goods sold		
Direct materials	$612,500	
Direct labor	157,500	
Machinery repairs (variable cost)	26,250	
Depreciation—machinery	125,000	
Utilities (variable cost, $28,000)	105,000	
Plant manager salaries	77,500	1,103,750
Gross profit		492,250
Selling expenses		
Packaging	39,375	
Shipping	54,250	
Sales salary (annual)	81,000	174,625
General and administrative expenses		
Advertising expense	52,000	
Salaries	116,000	
Entertainment expense	50,000	218,000
Income from operations		$ 99,625

Check (1) Variances: Fixed costs, $22,500 U; income, $6,200 F

Required

1. Prepare a flexible budget performance report for 2009.

Analysis Component

2. Analyze and interpret both the (a) sales variance and (b) direct materials variance.

Problem 24-4B
Flexible budget preparation; computation of materials, labor, and overhead variances; and overhead variance report

P1 P2 P3 C2

Stevens Company set the following standard costs for one unit of its product.

Direct materials (9 lb. @ $6 per lb.)	$ 54.00
Direct labor (3 hrs. @ $16 per hr.)	48.00
Overhead (3 hrs. @ $11.75 per hr.)	35.25
Total standard cost	137.25

The predetermined overhead rate ($11.75 per direct labor hour) is based on an expected volume of 75% of the factory's capacity of 20,000 units per month. Following are the company's budgeted overhead costs per month at the 75% level.

Overhead Budget (75% Capacity)		
Variable overhead costs		
Indirect materials	$ 33,750	
Indirect labor	135,000	
Power	22,500	
Repairs and maintenance	67,500	
Total variable overhead costs		$258,750
Fixed overhead costs		
Depreciation—building	36,000	
Depreciation—machinery	108,000	
Taxes and insurance	27,000	
Supervision	99,000	
Total fixed overhead costs		270,000
Total overhead costs		$528,750

The company incurred the following actual costs when it operated at 75% of capacity in December.

Direct materials (139,000 lbs. @ $6.10)		$ 847,900
Direct labor (43,500 hrs. @ $16.30)		709,050
Overhead costs		
Indirect materials	$ 31,600	
Indirect labor	133,400	
Power	23,500	
Repairs and maintenance	69,700	
Depreciation—building	36,000	
Depreciation—machinery	110,000	
Taxes and insurance	24,500	
Supervision	99,000	527,700
Total costs		$2,084,650

Required

1. Examine the monthly overhead budget to (a) determine the costs per unit for each variable overhead item and its total per unit costs, and (b) identify the total fixed costs per month.

Check (2) Budgeted total overhead at 17,000 units, $563,250

2. Prepare flexible overhead budgets (as in Exhibit 24.12) for December showing the amounts of each variable and fixed cost at the 65%, 75%, and 85% capacity levels.

(3) Materials variances: Price, $13,900 U; quantity, $24,000 U

3. Compute the direct materials cost variance, including its price and quantity variances.

4. Compute the direct labor cost variance, including its rate and efficiency variances.
5. Compute the (a) variable overhead spending and efficiency variances, (b) fixed overhead spending and volume variances, and (c) total overhead controllable variance.
6. Prepare a detailed overhead variance report (as in Exhibit 24.19) that shows the variances for individual items of overhead.

(4) Labor variances: Rate, $13,050 U; efficiency, $24,000 F

Problem 24-5B
Materials, labor, and overhead variances; and overhead variance report
C2 P2 P3

Harris Company has set the following standard costs per unit for the product it manufactures.

Direct materials (5 lbs. @ $3.00 per lb.)	$15
Direct labor (2 hr. @ $20 per hr.)	40
Overhead (2 hr. @ $10 per hr.)	20
Total standard cost	$75

The predetermined overhead rate is based on a planned operating volume of 80% of the productive capacity of 10,000 units per month. The following flexible budget information is available.

	Operating Levels		
	70%	80%	90%
Production in units	7,000	8,000	9,000
Standard direct labor hours	14,000	16,000	18,000
Budgeted overhead			
Variable overhead costs			
Indirect materials	$ 17,500	$ 20,000	$22,500
Indirect labor	28,000	32,000	36,000
Power	7,000	8,000	9,000
Maintenance	3,500	4,000	4,500
Total variable costs	56,000	64,000	72,000
Fixed overhead costs			
Rent of factory building	24,000	24,000	24,000
Depreciation—machinery	40,000	40,000	40,000
Taxes and insurance	4,800	4,800	4,800
Supervisory salaries	27,200	27,200	27,200
Total fixed costs	96,000	96,000	96,000
Total overhead costs	$152,000	$160,000	$168,000

During March, the company operated at 90% of capacity and produced 9,000 units, incurring the following actual costs.

Direct materials (46,000 lbs. @ $2.95 per lb.)		$ 135,700
Direct labor (18,800 hrs. @ $20.10 per hr.)		377,880
Overhead costs		
Indirect materials	$22,000	
Indirect labor	32,000	
Power	9,600	
Maintenance	4,750	
Rent of factory building	24,000	
Depreciation—machinery	39,400	
Taxes and insurance	5,200	
Supervisory salaries	28,000	164,950
Total costs		$678,530

Required

Check (1) Materials variances: Price, $2,300 F; quantity, $3,000 U
(2) Labor variances: Rate, $1,880 U; efficiency, $16,000 U

1. Compute the direct materials cost variance, including its price and quantity variances.
2. Compute the direct labor variance, including its rate and efficiency variances.
3. Compute these variances: (a) variable overhead spending and efficiency, (b) fixed overhead spending and volume, and (c) total overhead controllable.
4. Prepare a detailed overhead variance report (as in Exhibit 24.19) that shows the variances for individual items of overhead.

Problem 24-6B

Materials, labor, and overhead variances recorded and analyzed

C3 P4 

Del Company's standard cost accounting system recorded this information from its June operations.

Standard direct materials cost	$260,000
Direct materials quantity variance (favorable)	10,000
Direct materials price variance (favorable)	3,000
Actual direct labor cost	130,000
Direct labor efficiency variance (favorable)	6,000
Direct labor rate variance (unfavorable)	1,000
Actual overhead cost	500,000
Volume variance (unfavorable)	24,000
Controllable variance (unfavorable)	16,000

Required

Check (1) Dr. Goods in Process Inventory (for overhead), $460,000

1. Prepare journal entries dated June 30 to record the company's costs and variances for the month. (Do not prepare the journal entry to close the variances.)

Analysis Component

2. Identify the areas that would attract the attention of a manager who uses management by exception. Describe what action(s) the manager should consider.

SERIAL PROBLEM

Success Systems

(This serial problem began in Chapter 1 and continues through most of the book. If previous chapter segments were not completed, the serial problem can begin at this point. It is helpful, but not necessary, to use the working papers that accompany the book.)

SP 24 Success Systems' second quarter 2010 fixed budget performance report for its computer furniture operations follows. The $156,000 budgeted expenses include $108,000 in variable expenses for desks and $18,000 in variable expenses for chairs, as well as $30,000 fixed expenses. The actual expenses include $31,000 fixed expenses. Prepare a flexible budget performance report that shows any variances between budgeted results and actual results. List fixed and variable expenses separately.

	Fixed Budget	Actual Results	Variances
Desk sales (in units)	144	150	
Chair sales (in units)	72	80	
Desk sales (in dollars)	$180,000	$186,000	$6,000 F
Chair sales (in dollars)	$ 36,000	$ 41,200	$5,200 F
Total expenses	$156,000	$163,880	$7,880 U
Income from operations	$ 60,000	$ 63,320	$3,320 F

Check Variances: Fixed expenses, $1,000 U

BEYOND THE NUMBERS

REPORTING IN ACTION

C1 

BTN 24-1 Analysis of flexible budgets and standard costs emphasizes the importance of a similar unit of measure for meaningful comparisons and evaluations. When **Best Buy** compiles its financial reports in compliance with GAAP, it applies the same unit of measurement, U.S. dollars, for most measures of business operations. One issue for Best Buy is how best to adjust account values for its subsidiaries that compile financial reports in currencies other than the U.S. dollar.

Required

1. Read Best Buy's Note 1 in Appendix A and identify the financial statement where it reports the annual adjustment for foreign currency translation.
2. Record the annual amount of its foreign currency translation adjustment for the fiscal years 2005 through 2007.

Fast Forward

3. Access Best Buy's financial statements for a fiscal year ending after March 3, 2007, from either its Website [BestBuy.com] or the SEC's EDGAR database [www.SEC.gov]. (a) Identify its foreign currency translation adjustment. (b) Does this adjustment increase or decrease net income? Explain.

COMPARATIVE ANALYSIS

A2

BTN 24-2 The usefulness of budgets, variances, and related analyses often depends on the accuracy of management's estimates of future sales activity.

Required

1. Identify and record the prior three years' sales (in dollars) for both **Best Buy**, **Circuit City**, and **RadioShack** using their financial statements in Appendix A.
2. Using the data in part 1, predict all three companies' sales activity for the next two to three years. (If possible, compare your predictions to actual sales figures for these years.)

ETHICS CHALLENGE

C1

BTN 24-3 Setting materials, labor, and overhead standards is challenging. If standards are set too low, companies might purchase inferior products and employees might not work to their full potential. If standards are set too high, companies could be unable to offer a quality product at a profitable rate and employees could be overworked. The ethical challenge is to set a high but reasonable standard. Assume that as a manager, you are asked to set the standard materials price and quantity for the new 1,000 CKB Mega-Max chip, a technically advanced product. To properly set the price and quantity standards, you assemble a team of specialists to provide input.

Required

Identify four types of specialists that you would assemble to provide information to help set the materials price and quantity standards. Briefly explain why you chose each individual.

COMMUNICATING IN PRACTICE

P4 C2

BTN 24-4 The reason we use the words *favorable* and *unfavorable* when evaluating variances is made clear when we look at the closing of accounts. To see this, consider that (1) all variance accounts are closed at the end of each period (temporary accounts), (2) a favorable variance is always a credit balance, and (3) an unfavorable variance is always a debit balance. Write a one-half page memorandum to your instructor with three parts that answer the three following requirements. (Assume that variance accounts are closed to Cost of Goods Sold.)

Required

1. Does Cost of Goods Sold increase or decrease when closing a favorable variance? Does gross margin increase or decrease when a favorable variance is closed to Cost of Goods Sold? Explain.
2. Does Cost of Goods Sold increase or decrease when closing an unfavorable variance? Does gross margin increase or decrease when an unfavorable variance is closed to Cost of Goods Sold? Explain.
3. Explain the meaning of a favorable variance and an unfavorable variance.

TAKING IT TO THE NET

C1

BTN 24-5 Access iSixSigma's Website (iSixSigma.com) to search for and read information about *benchmarking* to complete the following requirements.

Required

1. Write a one-paragraph explanation (in layperson's terms) of benchmarking.

2. How does standard costing relate to benchmarking?

TEAMWORK IN ACTION

C2

BTN 24-6 Many service industries link labor rate and time (quantity) standards with their processes. One example is the standard time to board an aircraft. The reason time plays such an important role in the service industry is that it is viewed as a competitive advantage: best service in the shortest amount of time. Although the labor rate component is difficult to observe, the time component of a service delivery standard is often readily apparent—for example, "Lunch will be served in less than five minutes, or it is free."

Required

Break into teams and select two service industries for your analysis. Identify and describe all the time elements each industry uses to create a competitive advantage.

ENTREPRENEURIAL DECISION

C1 C2

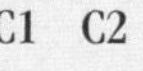

BTN 24-7 Entrepreneur Chris Martin of Martin Guitar Company (see Chapter opener) uses a costing system with standard costs for direct materials, direct labor, and overhead costs. Two comments frequently are mentioned in relation to standard costing and variance analysis: "Variances are not explanations" and "Management's goal is not to minimize variances."

Required

Write Chris Martin a short memo (no more than 1 page) interpreting these two comments.

HITTING THE ROAD

C1

BTN 24-8 Training employees to use standard amounts of materials in production is common. Typically large companies invest in this training but small organizations do not. One can observe these different practices in a trip to two different pizza businesses. Visit both a local pizza business and a national pizza chain business and then complete the following.

Required

1. Observe and record the number of raw material items used to make a typical cheese pizza. Also observe how the person making the pizza applies each item when preparing the pizza.

2. Record any differences in how items are applied between the two businesses.

3. Estimate which business is more profitable from your observations. Explain.

GLOBAL DECISION

BTN 24-9 Access the annual report of DSG (at www.DSGiplc.com) for the year ended April 28, 2007. The usefulness of its budgets, variances, and related analyses depends on the accuracy of management's estimates of future sales activity.

Required

1. Identify and record the prior two years' sales (in pounds) for DSG from its income statement.

2. Using the data in part 1, predict sales activity for DSG for the next two years. Explain your prediction process.

ANSWERS TO MULTIPLE CHOICE QUIZ

1. c; Fixed costs remain at $300,000; Variable costs = ($246,000/24,000 units) × 20,000 units = $205,000.
2. e; Budgeted direct materials + Unfavorable variance = Actual cost of direct materials used; or, 60,000 units × $10 per unit = $600,000 + $15,000 U = $615,000.
3. c; (AH × AR) − (AH × SR) = $1,599,040 – (84,160 hours × $20 per hour) = $84,160 F.
4. b; Actual variable overhead − Variable overhead applied to production = Variable overhead cost variance; or $150,000 − (96,000 hours × $1.50 per hour) = $6,000 U.
5. a; Budgeted fixed overhead − Fixed overhead applied to production = Volume variance; or $24,000 − (4,800 units × $4 per unit) = $4,800 U.

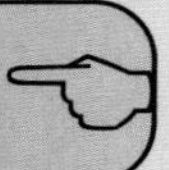

A Look Back

Chapter 24 discussed flexible budgets, variance analysis, and standard costs. It explained how management uses each to control and monitor business activities.

A Look at This Chapter

This chapter focuses on evaluating capital budgeting decisions. It also explains several tools and procedures used in making and evaluating short-term managerial decisions.

Chapter 25 Capital Budgeting and Managerial Decisions

Learning Objectives

CAP

Conceptual

C1 Explain the importance of capital budgeting. *(p. 1024)*

C2 Describe the selection of a hurdle rate for an investment. *(p. 1033)*

C3 Describe the importance of relevant costs for short-term decisions. *(p. 1035)*

Analytical

A1 Evaluate short-term managerial decisions using relevant costs. *(p. 1035)*

A2 Analyze a capital investment project using break-even time. *(p. 1043)*

LP25

Procedural

P1 Compute payback period and describe its use. *(p. 1025)*

P2 Compute accounting rate of return and explain its use. *(p. 1027)*

P3 Compute net present value and describe its use. *(p. 1029)*

P4 Compute internal rate of return and explain its use. *(p. 1031)*

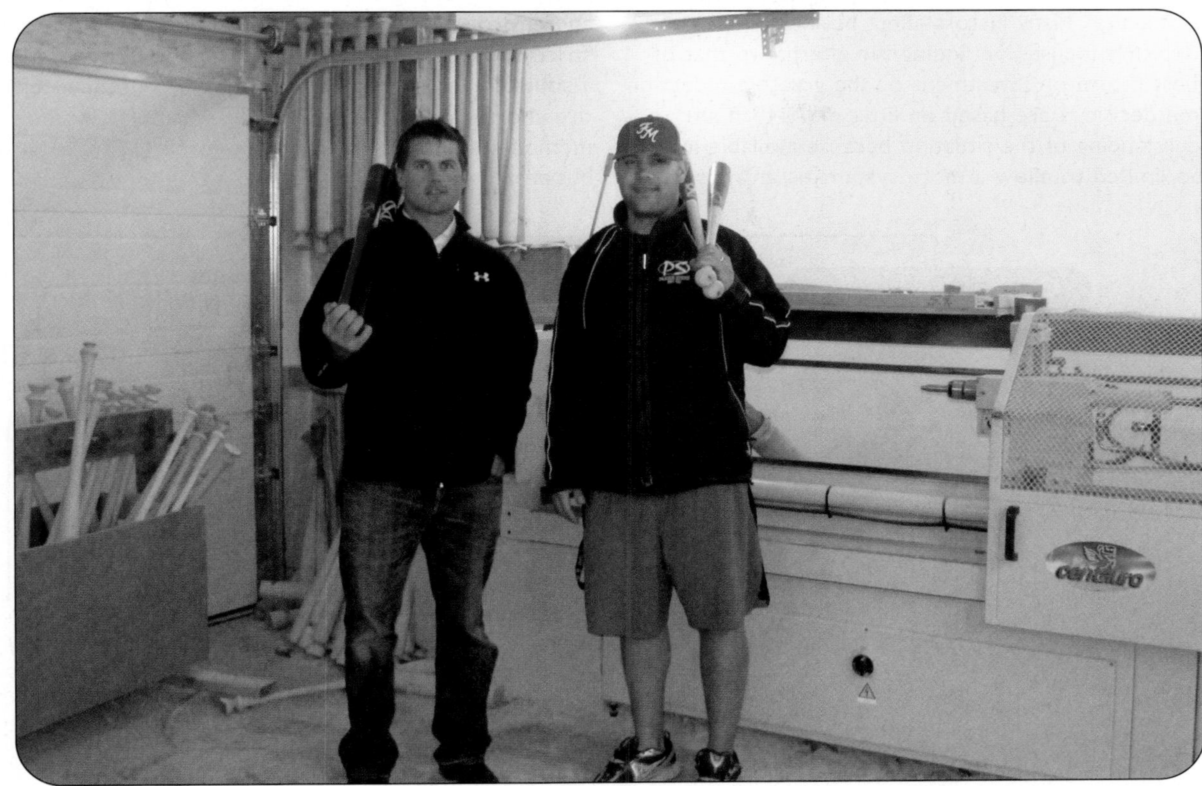

Decision Feature

Batter Up

"Now batting, a 34-ounce Prairie Sticks double-dipped black maple bat!"—PA Announcer

RED DEER, CANADA—Jared Greenberg, of the Red Deer Riggers, and Dan Zinger of the Red Deer Stags, dream to make it to the major leagues . . . not as players, but as makers of baseball bats. Their start-up company, **Prairie Sticks Bat Company (PrairieSticks.com),** started in Jared's workshop with a hand lathe and a piece of wood when local amateur players had trouble getting maple bats from manufacturers. Jared says he began producing bats for his teammates and friends "just like you would do in your middle school shop class."

Prairie Sticks' bats are made from four different types of wood, each with different prices (the company also makes fungo bats and training bats). Jared and Dan use product contribution margins in determining their best sales mix. This is especially important given their constraints on machine hours and labor—they have only one hydraulic tracing lathe and no other employees that make bats.

This past year they sold 1,500 bats. With production growth comes new business questions. Do we take a one-time deal with a buyer? Do we scrap or rework unacceptable inventory? Do we make or buy certain raw materials? These questions need answers. Jared and Dan focus on relevant costs and incremental revenues for insight into answering those questions. If a customer wants a bat in a color Prairie Sticks does not stock, the company charges a higher price to cover the incremental cost of the new color. The company makes novelty bats, unusable for play but fine for gifts and awards, out of inferior wood. These novelty bats sell at reduced prices, but enable the company to avoid costly rework and processing costs. They also sell apparel and hats, made by outside manufacturers.

Prairie Sticks now makes bats for big leaguers. It uses the same wood as the major batmakers; and $100,000 worth of equipment, including the hydraulic lathe, can turn out an unfinished bat in less than two minutes. Soon, they hope to step to the plate to accept additional business. Jared and Dan apply capital budgeting methods to help assess payback periods, rates of return, present values, and break-even points to their equipment and other expenditures. This aids them in decisions on what, and when, to buy.

A recent news release reported that a minor league player had been traded for "10 Prairie Sticks double-dipped maple bats, black," which led to major publicity and a surge in orders. "It's been crazy," says Jared. "[Since] this story has broken . . . we're on the verge of picking up our Major League vendor's license," explains Dan. That would be a tape-measure home run.

[Sources: *Prairie Sticks Bat Company Website,* January 2009; *AlbertaLocalNews.com,* May 2008; *Fox Sports on MSN.com,* May 2008; *Edmonton CityTV.com* interview, May 2008]

Chapter Preview

Making business decisions involves choosing between alternative courses of action. Many factors affect business decisions, yet analysis typically focuses on finding the alternative that offers the highest return on investment or the greatest reduction in costs. Some decisions are based on little more than an intuitive understanding of the situation because available information is too limited to allow a more systematic analysis. In other cases, intangible factors such as convenience, prestige, and environmental considerations are more important than strictly quantitative factors. In all situations, managers can reach a sounder decision if they identify the consequences of alternative choices in financial terms. This chapter explains several methods of analysis that can help managers make those business decisions.

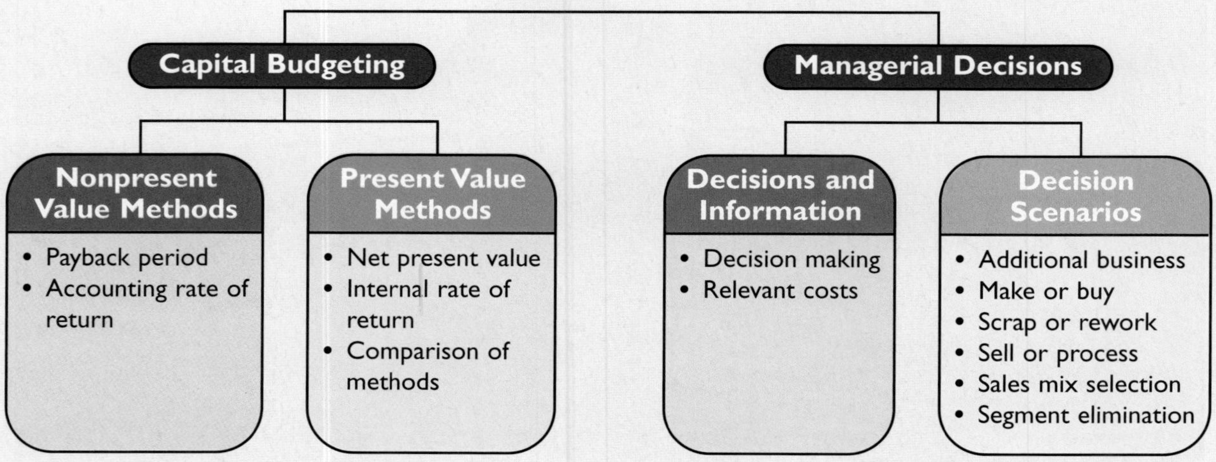

Section 1—Capital Budgeting

C1 Explain the importance of capital budgeting.

Video25.2

The capital expenditures budget is management's plan for acquiring and selling plant assets. **Capital budgeting** is the process of analyzing alternative long-term investments and deciding which assets to acquire or sell. These decisions can involve developing a new product or process, buying a new machine or a new building, or acquiring an entire company. An objective for these decisions is to earn a satisfactory return on investment.

Capital budgeting decisions require careful analysis because they are usually the most difficult and risky decisions that managers make. These decisions are difficult because they require predicting events that will not occur until well into the future. Many of these predictions are tentative and potentially unreliable. Specifically, a capital budgeting decision is risky because (1) the outcome is uncertain, (2) large amounts of money are usually involved, (3) the investment involves a long-term commitment, and (4) the decision could be difficult or impossible to reverse, no matter how poor it turns out to be. Risk is especially high for investments in technology due to innovations and uncertainty.

Managers use several methods to evaluate capital budgeting decisions. Nearly all of these methods involve predicting cash inflows and cash outflows of proposed investments, assessing the risk of and returns on those flows, and then choosing the investments to make. Management often restates future cash flows in terms of their present value. This approach applies the time value of money: A dollar today is worth more than a dollar tomorrow. Similarly, a dollar tomorrow is worth less than a dollar today. The process of restating future cash flows in terms of their present value is called *discounting*. The time value of money is important when evaluating capital investments, but managers sometimes apply evaluation methods that ignore present value. This section describes four methods for comparing alternative investments.

Point: The nature of capital spending has changed with the business environment. Budgets for information technology have increased from about 25% of corporate capital spending 20 years ago to an estimated 35% today.

Methods Not Using Time Value of Money

All investments, whether they involve the purchase of a machine or another long-term asset, are expected to produce net cash flows. *Net cash flow* is cash inflows minus cash outflows. Sometimes managers perform simple analyses of the financial feasibility of an investment's net cash flow without using the time value of money. This section explains two of the most common methods in this category: (1) payback period and (2) accounting rate of return.

Payback Period

P1 Compute payback period and describe its use.

An investment's **payback period (PBP)** is the expected time period to recover the initial investment amount. Managers prefer investing in assets with shorter payback periods to reduce the risk of an unprofitable investment over the long run. Acquiring assets with short payback periods reduces a company's risk from potentially inaccurate long-term predictions of future cash flows.

Computing Payback Period with Even Cash Flows To illustrate use of the payback period for an investment with even cash flows, we look at data from FasTrac, a manufacturer of exercise equipment and supplies. (*Even cash flows* are cash flows that are the same each and every year; *uneven cash flows* are cash flows that are not all equal in amount.) FasTrac is considering several different capital investments, one of which is to purchase a machine to use in manufacturing a new product. This machine costs $16,000 and is expected to have an eight-year life with no salvage value. Management predicts this machine will produce 1,000 units of product each year and that the new product will be sold for $30 per unit. Exhibit 25.1 shows the expected annual net cash flows for this asset over its life as well as the expected annual revenues and expenses (including depreciation and income taxes) from investing in the machine.

EXHIBIT 25.1

Cash Flow Analysis

FASTRAC
Cash Flow Analysis—Machinery Investment
January 15, 2009

	Expected Accrual Figures	Expected Net Cash Flows
Annual sales of new product	$30,000	$30,000
Deduct annual expenses		
Cost of materials, labor, and overhead (except depreciation)	15,500	15,500
Depreciation—Machinery	2,000	
Additional selling and administrative expenses	9,500	9,500
Annual pretax accrual income	3,000	
Income taxes (30%)	900	900
Annual net income	$ 2,100	
Annual net cash flow		**$ 4,100**

The amount of net cash flow from the machinery is computed by subtracting expected cash outflows from expected cash inflows. The cash flows column of Exhibit 25.1 excludes all noncash revenues and expenses. Depreciation is FasTrac's only noncash item. Alternatively, managers can adjust the projected net income for revenue and expense items that do not affect cash flows. For FasTrac, this means taking the $2,100 net income and adding back the $2,000 depreciation.

Point: Annual net cash flow in Exhibit 25.1 equals net income plus depreciation (a noncash expense).

The formula for computing the payback period of an investment that yields even net cash flows is in Exhibit 25.2.

EXHIBIT 25.2

Payback Period Formula with Even Cash Flows

$$\textbf{Payback period} = \frac{\textbf{Cost of investment}}{\textbf{Annual net cash flow}}$$

The payback period reflects the amount of time for the investment to generate enough net cash flow to return (or pay back) the cash initially invested to purchase it. FasTrac's payback period for this machine is just under four years:

$$\text{Payback period} = \frac{\$16{,}000}{\$4{,}100} = 3.9 \text{ years}$$

Example: If an alternative machine (with different technology) yields a payback period of 3.5 years, which one does a manager choose? Answer: The alternative (3.5 is less than 3.9).

The initial investment is fully recovered in 3.9 years, or just before reaching the halfway point of this machine's useful life of eight years.

Decision Insight

Payback Phones Profits of telecoms have declined as too much capital investment chased too little revenue. Telecom success depends on new technology, and communications gear is evolving at a dizzying rate. Consequently, managers of telecoms often demand short payback periods and large expected net cash flows to compensate for the investment risk.

Computing Payback Period with Uneven Cash Flows Computing the payback period in the prior section assumed even net cash flows. What happens if the net cash flows are uneven? In this case, the payback period is computed using the *cumulative total of net cash flows.* The word *cumulative* refers to the addition of each period's net cash flows as we progress through time. To illustrate, consider data for another investment that FasTrac is considering. This machine is predicted to generate uneven net cash flows over the next eight years. The relevant data and payback period computation are shown in Exhibit 25.3.

EXHIBIT 25.3

Payback Period Calculation with Uneven Cash Flows

Period*	Expected Net Cash Flows	Cumulative Net Cash Flows
Year 0	$(16,000)	$(16,000)
Year 1	3,000	(13,000)
Year 2	4,000	(9,000)
Year 3	4,000	(5,000)
Year 4	4,000	(1,000)
Year 5	5,000	4,000
Year 6	3,000	7,000
Year 7	2,000	9,000
Year 8	2,000	11,000
		Payback period = 4.2 years

* All cash inflows and outflows occur uniformly during the year.

Example: Find the payback period in Exhibit 25.3 if net cash flows for the first 4 years are:
Year 1 = $6,000; Year 2 = $5,000;
Year 3 = $4,000; Year 4 = $3,000.
Answer: 3.33 years

Year 0 refers to the period of initial investment in which the $16,000 cash outflow occurs at the end of year 0 to acquire the machinery. By the end of year 1, the cumulative net cash flow is reduced to $(13,000), computed as the $(16,000) initial cash outflow plus year 1's $3,000 cash inflow. This process continues throughout the asset's life. The cumulative net cash flow amount changes from negative to positive in year 5. Specifically, at the end of year 4, the cumulative net cash flow is $(1,000). As soon as FasTrac receives net cash inflow of $1,000 during the fifth year, it has fully recovered the investment. If we assume that cash flows are received uniformly *within* each year, receipt of the $1,000 occurs about one-fifth of the way through the year. This is computed as $1,000 divided by year 5's total net cash flow of $5,000, or 0.20. This yields a payback period of 4.2 years, computed as 4 years plus 0.20 of year 5.

Using the Payback Period Companies desire a short payback period to increase return and reduce risk. The more quickly a company receives cash, the sooner it is available for other uses and the less time it is at risk of loss. A shorter payback period also improves the company's ability to respond to unanticipated changes and lowers its risk of having to keep an unprofitable investment.

Payback period should never be the only consideration in evaluating investments. This is so because it ignores at least two important factors. First, it fails to reflect differences in the timing of net cash flows within the payback period. In Exhibit 25.3, FasTrac's net cash flows in the first five years were $3,000, $4,000, $4,000, $4,000, and $5,000. If another investment had predicted cash flows of $9,000, $3,000, $2,000, $1,800, and $1,000 in these five years, its payback period would also be 4.2 years, but this second alternative could be more desirable because it provides cash more quickly. The second important factor is that the payback period ignores *all* cash flows after the point where its costs are fully recovered. For example, one investment might pay back its cost in 3 years but stop producing cash after 4 years. A second investment might require 5 years to pay back its cost yet continue to produce net cash flows for another 15 years. A focus on only the payback period would mistakenly lead management to choose the first investment over the second.

"So what if I underestimated costs and overestimated revenues? It all averages out in the end."

Quick Check Answers—p. 1049

1. Capital budgeting is (*a*) concerned with analyzing alternative sources of capital, including debt and equity, (*b*) an important activity for companies when considering what assets to acquire or sell, or (*c*) best done by intuitive assessments of the value of assets and their usefulness.
2. Why are capital budgeting decisions often difficult?
3. A company is considering purchasing equipment costing $75,000. Future annual net cash flows from this equipment are $30,000, $25,000, $15,000, $10,000, and $5,000. The payback period is (*a*) 4 years, (*b*) 3.5 years, or (*c*) 3 years.
4. If depreciation is an expense, why is it added back to an investment's net income to compute the net cash flow from that investment?
5. If two investments have the same payback period, are they equally desirable? Explain.

Accounting Rate of Return

P2 Compute accounting rate of return and explain its use.

The **accounting rate of return,** also called *return on average investment,* is computed by dividing a project's after-tax net income by the average amount invested in it. To illustrate, we return to FasTrac's $16,000 machinery investment described in Exhibit 25.1. We first compute (1) the after-tax net income and (2) the average amount invested. The $2,100 after-tax net income is already available from Exhibit 25.1. To compute the average amount invested, we assume that net cash flows are received evenly throughout each year. Thus, the average investment for each year is computed as the average of its beginning and ending book values. If FasTrac's $16,000 machine is depreciated $2,000 each year, the average amount invested in the machine for each year is computed as shown in Exhibit 25.4. The average for any year is the average of the beginning and ending book values.

EXHIBIT 25.4

Computing Average Amount Invested

	Beginning Book Value	Annual Depreciation	Ending Book Value	Average Book Value
Year 1	$16,000	$2,000	$14,000	$15,000
Year 2	14,000	2,000	12,000	13,000
Year 3	12,000	2,000	10,000	11,000
Year 4	10,000	2,000	8,000	9,000
Year 5	8,000	2,000	6,000	7,000
Year 6	6,000	2,000	4,000	5,000
Year 7	4,000	2,000	2,000	3,000
Year 8	2,000	2,000	0	1,000
All years				$ 8,000

Next we need the average book value for the asset's entire life. This amount is computed by taking the average of the individual yearly averages. This average equals $8,000, computed as $64,000 (the sum of the individual years' averages) divided by eight years (see last column of Exhibit 25.4).

Point: General formula for *annual average investment* is the sum of individual years' average book values divided by the number of years of the planned investment.

If a company uses straight-line depreciation, we can find the average amount invested by using the formula in Exhibit 25.5. Because FasTrac uses straight-line depreciation, its average amount invested for the eight years equals the sum of the book value at the beginning of the asset's investment period and the book value at the end of its investment period, divided by 2, as shown in Exhibit 25.5.

EXHIBIT 25.5

Computing Average Amount Invested under Straight-Line Depreciation

$$\textbf{Annual average investment} = \frac{\textbf{Beginning book value + Ending book value}}{\textbf{2}}$$

(straight-line case only)

$$= \frac{\$16{,}000 + \$0}{2} = \$8{,}000$$

If an investment has a salvage value, the average amount invested when using straight-line depreciation is computed as (Beginning book value + Salvage value)/2.

Once we determine the after-tax net income and the average amount invested, the accounting rate of return on the investment can be computed from the annual after-tax net income divided by the average amount invested, as shown in Exhibit 25.6.

EXHIBIT 25.6

Accounting Rate of Return Formula

$$\textbf{Accounting rate of return} = \frac{\textbf{Annual after-tax net income}}{\textbf{Annual average investment}}$$

This yields an accounting rate of return of 26.25% ($2,100/$8,000). FasTrac management must decide whether a 26.25% accounting rate of return is satisfactory. To make this decision, we must factor in the investment's risk. For instance, we cannot say an investment with a 26.25% return is preferred over one with a lower return unless we recognize any differences in risk. Thus, an investment's return is satisfactory or unsatisfactory only when it is related to returns from other investments with similar lives and risk.

When accounting rate of return is used to choose among capital investments, the one with the least risk, the shortest payback period, and the highest return for the longest time period is often identified as the best. However, use of accounting rate of return to evaluate investment opportunities is limited because it bases the amount invested on book values (not predicted market values) in future periods. Accounting rate of return is also limited when an asset's net incomes are expected to vary from year to year. This requires computing the rate using *average* annual net incomes, yet this accounting rate of return fails to distinguish between two investments with the same average annual net income but different amounts of income in early years versus later years or different levels of income variability.

Quick Check

Answers—p. 1049

6. The following data relate to a company's decision on whether to purchase a machine:

Cost	$180,000
Salvage value	15,000
Annual after-tax net income	40,000

The machine's accounting rate of return, assuming the even receipt of its net cash flows during the year and use of straight-line depreciation, is (*a*) 22%, (*b*) 41%, or (*c*) 21%.

7. Is a 15% accounting rate of return for a machine a good rate?

Methods Using Time Value of Money

This section describes two methods that help managers with capital budgeting decisions and that use the time value of money: (1) net present value and (2) internal rate of return. *(To apply these methods, you need a basic understanding of the concept of present value. An expanded explanation of present value concepts is in Appendix B near the end of the book. You can use the present value tables at the end of Appendix B to solve many of this chapter's assignments that use the time value of money.)*

Net Present Value

P3 Compute net present value and describe its use.

Net present value analysis applies the time value of money to future cash inflows and cash outflows so management can evaluate a project's benefits and costs at one point in time. Specifically, **net present value (NPV)** is computed by discounting the future net cash flows from the investment at the project's required rate of return and then subtracting the initial amount invested. A company's required return, often called its hurdle rate, is typically its **cost of capital,** which is the rate the company must pay to its long-term creditors and shareholders.

To illustrate, let's return to FasTrac's proposed machinery purchase described in Exhibit 25.1. Does this machine provide a satisfactory return while recovering the amount invested? Recall that the machine requires a $16,000 investment and is expected to provide $4,100 annual net cash inflows for the next eight years. If we assume that net cash flows from this machine are received at each year-end and that FasTrac requires a 12% annual return, net present value can be computed as in Exhibit 25.7.

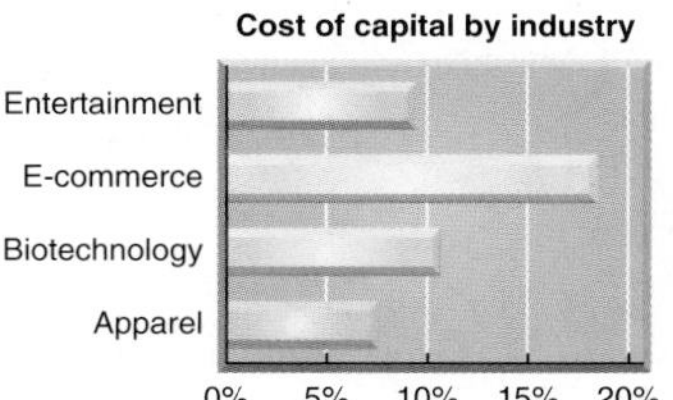

EXHIBIT 25.7

Net Present Value Calculation with Equal Cash Flows

	Net Cash Flows*	Present Value of 1 at 12%†	Present Value of Net Cash Flows
Year 1	$ 4,100	0.8929	$ 3,661
Year 2	4,100	0.7972	3,269
Year 3	4,100	0.7118	2,918
Year 4	4,100	0.6355	2,606
Year 5	4,100	0.5674	2,326
Year 6	4,100	0.5066	2,077
Year 7	4,100	0.4523	1,854
Year 8	4,100	0.4039	1,656
Totals	$32,800		$20,367
Amount invested			(16,000)
Net present value			$ 4,367

* Cash flows occur at the end of each year.

† Present value of 1 factors are taken from Table B.1 in Appendix B.

The first number column of Exhibit 25.7 shows the annual net cash flows. Present value of 1 factors, also called *discount factors,* are shown in the second column. Taken from Table B.1 in Appendix B, they assume that net cash flows are received at each year-end. *(To simplify present value computations and for assignment material at the end of this chapter, we assume that net cash flows are received at each year-end.)* Annual net cash flows from the first column of Exhibit 25.7 are multiplied by the discount factors in the second column to give present values shown in the third column. The last three lines of this exhibit show the final NPV computations. The asset's $16,000 initial cost is deducted from the $20,367 total present value of all future net cash flows to give this asset's NPV of $4,367. The machine is thus expected to (1) recover its cost, (2) provide a 12% compounded return, and (3) generate $4,367 above cost. We summarize this analysis by saying the present value of this machine's future net cash flows to FasTrac exceeds the $16,000 investment by $4,367.

Point: The assumption of end-of-year cash flows simplifies computations and is common in practice.

Point: The amount invested includes all costs that must be incurred to get the asset in its proper location and ready for use.

Example: What is the net present value in Exhibit 25.7 if a 10% return is applied? *Answer:* $5,873

Net Present Value Decision Rule The decision rule in applying NPV is as follows: When an asset's expected cash flows are discounted at the required rate and yield a *positive* net present value, the asset should be acquired. This decision rule is reflected in the graphic below. When comparing several investment opportunities of about the same cost and same risk, we prefer the one with the highest positive net present value.

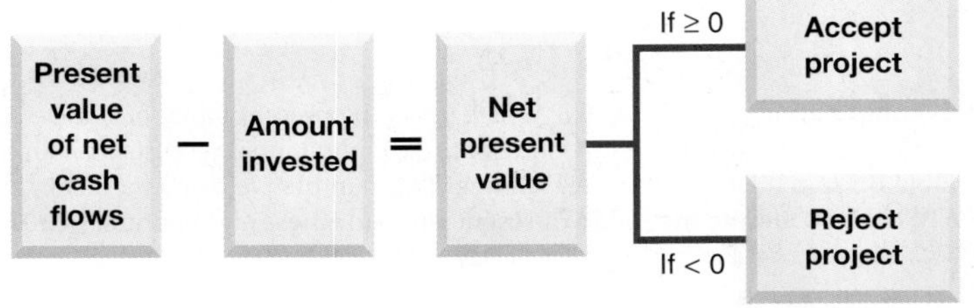

Simplifying Computations The computations in Exhibit 25.7 use separate present value of 1 factors for each of the eight years. Each year's net cash flow is multiplied by its present value of 1 factor to determine its present value. The individual present values for each of the eight net cash flows are added to give the asset's total present value. This computation can be simplified in two ways if annual net cash flows are equal in amount. One way is to add the eight annual present value of 1 factors for a total of 4.9676 and multiply this amount by the annual $4,100 net cash flow to get the $20,367 total present value of net cash flows.[1] A second simplification is to use a calculator with compound interest functions or a spreadsheet program. We show how to use Excel functions to compute net present value in this chapter's Appendix. Whatever procedure you use, it is important to understand the concepts behind these computations.

Example: Why does the net present value of an investment increase when a lower discount rate is used? *Answer:* The present value of net cash flows increases.

Decision Ethics

Systems Manager Top management adopts a policy requiring purchases in excess of $5,000 to be submitted with cash flow projections to the cost analyst for capital budget approval. As systems manager, you want to upgrade your computers at a $25,000 cost. You consider submitting several orders all under $5,000 to avoid the approval process. You believe the computers will increase profits and wish to avoid a delay. What do you do? [Answer—p. 1048]

Uneven Cash Flows Net present value analysis can also be applied when net cash flows are uneven (unequal). To illustrate, assume that FasTrac can choose only one capital investment from among projects A, B, and C. Each project requires the same $12,000 initial investment. Future net cash flows for each project are shown in the first three number columns of Exhibit 25.8.

EXHIBIT 25.8

Net Present Value Calculation with Uneven Cash Flows

	Net Cash Flows			Present Value of 1 at 10%	Present Value of Net Cash Flows		
	A	B	C		A	B	C
Year 1	$ 5,000	$ 8,000	$ 1,000	0.9091	$ 4,546	$ 7,273	$ 909
Year 2	5,000	5,000	5,000	0.8264	4,132	4,132	4,132
Year 3	5,000	2,000	9,000	0.7513	3,757	1,503	6,762
Totals	$15,000	$15,000	$15,000		12,435	12,908	11,803
Amount invested					(12,000)	(12,000)	(12,000)
Net present value					$ 435	$ 908	$ (197)

Example: If 12% is the required return in Exhibit 25.8, which project is preferred? *Answer:* Project B. Net present values are: A = $10; B = $553; C = $(715).

Example: Will the rankings of Projects A, B, and C change with the use of different discount rates, assuming the same rate is used for all projects? *Answer:* No; only the NPV amounts will change.

The three projects in Exhibit 25.8 have the same expected total net cash flows of $15,000. Project A is expected to produce equal amounts of $5,000 each year. Project B is expected to produce a larger amount in the first year. Project C is expected to produce a larger amount in the third year. The fourth column of Exhibit 25.8 shows the present value of 1 factors from Table B.1 assuming 10% required return.

Computations in the right-most columns show that Project A has a $435 positive NPV. Project B has the largest NPV of $908 because it brings in cash more quickly. Project C has a $(197) *negative* NPV because its larger cash inflows are delayed. If FasTrac requires a 10% return, it should reject Project C because its NPV implies a return *under* 10%. If only one project can be accepted, project B appears best because it yields the highest NPV.

[1] We can simplify this computation using Table B.3, which gives the present value of 1 to be received periodically for a number of periods. To determine the present value of these eight annual receipts discounted at 12%, go down the 12% column of Table B.3 to the factor on the eighth line. This cumulative discount factor, also known as an *annuity* factor, is 4.9676. We then compute the $20,367 present value for these eight annual $4,100 receipts, computed as 4.9676 × $4,100.

Salvage Value and Accelerated Depreciation FasTrac predicted the $16,000 machine to have zero salvage value at the end of its useful life (recall Exhibit 25.1). In many cases, assets are expected to have salvage values. If so, this amount is an additional net cash inflow received at the end of the final year of the asset's life. All other computations remain the same.

Depreciation computations also affect net present value analysis. FasTrac computes depreciation using the straight-line method. Accelerated depreciation is also commonly used, especially for income tax reports. Accelerated depreciation produces larger depreciation deductions in the early years of an asset's life and smaller deductions in later years. This pattern results in smaller income tax payments in early years and larger payments in later years. Accelerated depreciation does not change the basics of a present value analysis, but it can change the result. Using accelerated depreciation for tax reporting affects the NPV of an asset's cash flows because it produces larger net cash inflows in the early years of the asset's life and smaller ones in later years. Being able to use accelerated depreciation for tax reporting always makes an investment more desirable because early cash flows are more valuable than later ones.

Point: Projects with higher cash flows in earlier years generally yield higher net present values.

Example: When is it appropriate to use different discount rates for different projects? *Answer:* When risk levels are different.

Point: Tax savings from depreciation is called: **depreciation tax shield.**

Use of Net Present Value In deciding whether to proceed with a capital investment project, we approve the proposal if the NPV is positive but reject it if the NPV is negative. When considering several projects of similar investment amounts and risk levels, we can compare the different projects' NPVs and rank them on the basis of their NPVs. However, if the amount invested differs substantially across projects, the NPV is of limited value for comparison purposes. One means to compare projects, especially when a company cannot fund all positive net present value projects, is to use the **profitability index,** which is computed as:

$$\textbf{Profitability index} = \frac{\textbf{Net present value of cash flows}}{\textbf{Investment}}$$

A higher profitability index suggests a more desirable project. To illustrate, suppose that Project X requires a $1 million investment and provides a $100,000 NPV. Project Y requires an investment of only $100,000 and returns a $75,000 NPV. Ranking on the basis of NPV puts Project X ahead of Y, yet X's profitability index is only 0.10 ($100,000/$1,000,000) whereas Y's profitability index is 0.75. We must also remember that when reviewing projects with different risks, we computed the NPV of individual projects using different discount rates. The higher the risk, the higher the discount rate.

Inflation Large price-level increases should be considered in NPV analyses. Hurdle rates already include investor's inflation forecasts. Net cash flows can be adjusted for inflation by using *future value* computations. For example, if the expected net cash inflow in year 1 is $4,100 and 5% inflation is expected, then the expected net cash inflow in year 2 is $4,305, computed as $4,100 × 1.05 (1.05 is the future value of $1 (Table B.2) for 1 period with a 5% rate).

Internal Rate of Return

P4 Compute internal rate of return and explain its use.

Another means to evaluate capital investments is to use the **internal rate of return (IRR),** which equals the rate that yields an NPV of zero for an investment. This means that if we compute the total present value of a project's net cash flows using the IRR as the discount rate and then subtract the initial investment from this total present value, we get a zero NPV.

To illustrate, we use the data for FasTrac's Project A from Exhibit 25.8 to compute its IRR. Exhibit 25.9 shows the two-step process in computing IRR.

EXHIBIT 25.9

Computing Internal Rate of Return (with even cash flows)

Step 1: Compute the present value factor for the investment project.

$$\textbf{Present value factor} = \frac{\textbf{Amount invested}}{\textbf{Net cash flows}} = \frac{\$12,000}{\$5,000} = 2.4000$$

Step 2: Identify the discount rate (IRR) yielding the present value factor

Search Table B.3 for a present value factor of 2.4000 in the three-year row (equaling the 3-year project duration). The 12% discount rate yields a present value factor of 2.4018. This implies that the IRR is approximately 12%.*

* Since the present value factor of 2.4000 is not exactly equal to the 12% factor of 2.4018, we can more precisely estimate the IRR as follows:

Discount rate	Present Value Factor from Table B.3
12%	2.4018
15%	2.2832
	0.1186 = difference

$$\text{Then, IRR} = 12\% + \left[(15\% - 12\%) \times \frac{2.4018 - 2.4000}{0.1186}\right] = \underline{\underline{12.05\%}}$$

When cash flows are equal, as with Project A, we compute the present value factor (as shown in Exhibit 25.9) by dividing the initial investment by its annual net cash flows. We then use an annuity table to determine the discount rate equal to this present value factor. For FasTrac's Project A, we look across the three-period row of Table B.3 and find that the discount rate corresponding to the present value factor of 2.4000 roughly equals the 2.4018 value for the 12% rate. This row is reproduced here:

Present Value of an Annuity of 1 for Three Periods

	Discount Rate				
Periods	1%	5%	10%	12%	15%
3	2.9410	2.7232	2.4869	2.4018	2.2832

The 12% rate is the Project's IRR. A more precise IRR estimate can be computed following the procedure shown in the note to Exhibit 25.9. Spreadsheet software and calculators can also compute this IRR. We show how to use an Excel function to compute IRR in this chapter's Appendix.

Uneven Cash Flows If net cash flows are uneven, we must use trial and error to compute the IRR. We do this by selecting any reasonable discount rate and computing the NPV. If the amount is positive (negative), we recompute the NPV using a higher (lower) discount rate. We continue these steps until we reach a point where two consecutive computations result in NPVs having different signs (positive and negative). Because the NPV is zero using IRR, we know that the IRR lies between these two discount rates. We can then estimate its value. Spreadsheet programs and calculators can do these computations for us.

Decision Insight

Fun-IRR Many theme parks use both financial and nonfinancial criteria to evaluate their investments in new rides and activities. The use of IRR is a major part of this evaluation. This requires good estimates of future cash inflows and outflows. It also requires risk assessments of the uncertainty of the future cash flows.

Use of Internal Rate of Return When we use the IRR to evaluate a project, we compare it to a predetermined **hurdle rate,** which is a minimum acceptable rate of return and is applied as follows.

C2 Describe the selection of a hurdle rate for an investment.

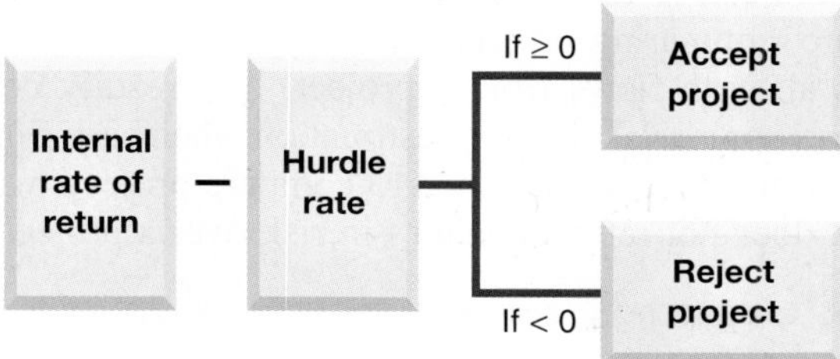

Top management selects the hurdle rate to use in evaluating capital investments. Financial formulas aid in this selection, but the choice of a minimum rate is subjective and left to management. For projects financed from borrowed funds, the hurdle rate must exceed the interest rate paid on these funds. The return on an investment must cover its interest and provide an additional profit to reward the company for its risk. For instance, if money is borrowed at 10%, an average risk investment often requires an after-tax return of 15% (or 5% above the borrowing rate). Remember that lower-risk investments require a lower rate of return compared with higher-risk investments.

If the project is internally financed, the hurdle rate is often based on actual returns from comparable projects. If the IRR is higher than the hurdle rate, the project is accepted. Multiple projects are often ranked by the extent to which their IRR exceeds the hurdle rate. The hurdle rate for individual projects is often different, depending on the risk involved. IRR is not subject to the limitations of NPV when comparing projects with different amounts invested because the IRR is expressed as a percent rather than as an absolute dollar value in NPV.

Example: How can management evaluate the risk of an investment? *Answer:* It must assess the uncertainty of future cash flows.

Point: A survey reports that 41% of top managers would reject a project with an internal rate of return *above* the cost of capital, *if* the project would cause the firm to miss its earnings forecast. The roles of benchmarks and manager compensation plans must be considered in capital budgeting decisions.

Decision Maker

Entrepreneur You are developing a new product and you use a 12% discount rate to compute its NPV. Your banker, from whom you hope to obtain a loan, expresses concern that your discount rate is too low. How do you respond? [Answer—p. 1048]

Comparison of Capital Budgeting Methods

We explained four methods that managers use to evaluate capital investment projects. How do these methods compare with each other? Exhibit 25.10 addresses that question. Neither the payback period nor the accounting rate of return considers the time value of money. On the other hand, both the net present value and the internal rate of return do.

EXHIBIT 25.10
Comparing Capital Budgeting Methods

	Payback Period	Accounting Rate of Return	Net Present Value	Internal Rate of Return
Measurement basis	■ Cash flows	■ Accrual income	■ Cash flows ■ Profitability	■ Cash flows ■ Profitability
Measurement unit	■ Years	■ Percent	■ Dollars	■ Percent
Strengths	■ Easy to understand ■ Allows comparison of projects	■ Easy to understand ■ Allows comparison of projects	■ Reflects time value of money ■ Reflects varying risks over project's life	■ Reflects time value of money ■ Allows comparisons of dissimilar projects
Limitations	■ Ignores time value of money ■ Ignores cash flows after payback period	■ Ignores time value of money ■ Ignores annual rates over life of project	■ Difficult to compare dissimilar projects	■ Ignores varying risks over life of project

The payback period is probably the simplest method. It gives managers an estimate of how soon they will recover their initial investment. Managers sometimes use this method when they have limited cash to invest and a number of projects to choose from. The accounting rate of return yields a percent measure computed using accrual income instead of cash flows. The accounting rate of return is an average rate for the entire investment period. Net present value considers all estimated net cash flows for the project's expected life. It can be applied to even and uneven cash flows and can reflect changes in the level of risk over a project's life. Since it yields a dollar measure, comparing projects of unequal sizes is more difficult. The internal rate of return considers all cash flows from a project. It is readily computed when the cash flows are even but requires some trial and error estimation when cash flows are uneven. Because the IRR is a percent measure, it is readily used to compare projects with different investment amounts. However, IRR does not reflect changes in risk over a project's life.

Decision Insight

And the Winner Is . . . How do we choose among the methods for evaluating capital investments? Management surveys consistently show the internal rate of return (IRR) as the most popular method followed by the payback period and net present value (NPV). Few companies use the accounting rate of return (ARR), but nearly all use more than one method.

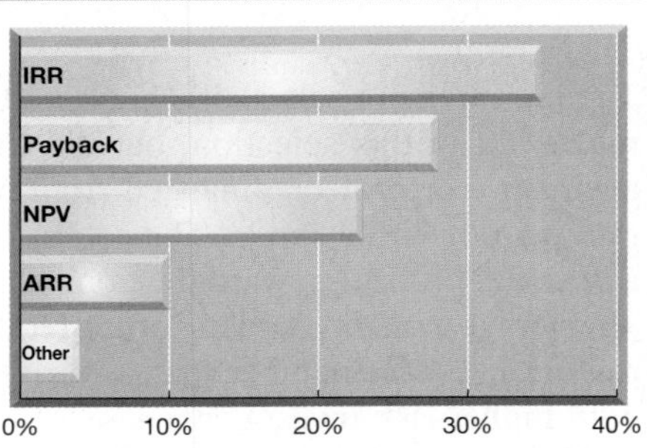

Quick Check

Answers—p. 1049

8. A company can invest in only one of two projects, A or B. Each project requires a $20,000 investment and is expected to generate end-of-period, annual cash flows as follows:

	Year 1	Year 2	Year 3	Total
Project A	$12,000	$8,500	$4,000	$24,500
Project B	4,500	8,500	13,000	26,000

Assuming a discount rate of 10%, which project has the higher net present value?

9. Two investment alternatives are expected to generate annual cash flows with the same net present value (assuming the same discount rate applied to each). Using this information, can you conclude that the two alternatives are equally desirable?

10. When two investment alternatives have the same total expected cash flows but differ in the timing of those flows, which method of evaluating those investments is superior, (*a*) accounting rate of return or (*b*) net present value?

Section 2—Managerial Decisions

This section focuses on methods that use accounting information to make several important managerial decisions. Most of these involve short-term decisions. This differs from methods used for longer-term managerial decisions that are described in the first section of this chapter and in several other chapters of this book.

Decisions and Information

Video25.1

This section explains how managers make decisions and the information relevant to those decisions.

Decision Making

Managerial decision making involves five steps: (1) define the decision task, (2) identify alternative courses of action, (3) collect relevant information and evaluate each alternative,

(4) select the preferred course of action, and (5) analyze and assess decisions made. These five steps are illustrated in Exhibit 25.11.

EXHIBIT 25.11

Managerial Decision Making

Both managerial and financial accounting information play an important role in most management decisions. The accounting system is expected to provide primarily *financial* information such as performance reports and budget analyses for decision making. *Nonfinancial* information is also relevant, however; it includes information on environmental effects, political sensitivities, and social responsibility.

Relevant Costs

C3 Describe the importance of relevant costs for short-term decisions.

Most financial measures of revenues and costs from accounting systems are based on historical costs. Although historical costs are important and useful for many tasks such as product pricing and the control and monitoring of business activities, we sometimes find that an analysis of *relevant costs,* or *avoidable costs,* is especially useful. Three types of costs are pertinent to our discussion of relevant costs: sunk costs, out-of-pocket costs, and opportunity costs.

A *sunk cost* arises from a past decision and cannot be avoided or changed; it is irrelevant to future decisions. An example is the cost of computer equipment previously purchased by a company. Most of a company's allocated costs, including fixed overhead items such as depreciation and administrative expenses, are sunk costs.

An *out-of-pocket cost* requires a future outlay of cash and is relevant for current and future decision making. These costs are usually the direct result of management's decisions. For instance, future purchases of computer equipment involve out-of-pocket costs.

Example: Depreciation and amortization are allocations of the original cost of plant and intangible assets. Are they out-of-pocket costs? *Answer:* No; they are sunk costs.

An *opportunity cost* is the potential benefit lost by taking a specific action when two or more alternative choices are available. An example is a student giving up wages from a job to attend summer school. Companies continually must choose from alternative courses of action. For instance, a company making standardized products might be approached by a customer to supply a special (nonstandard) product. A decision to accept or reject the special order must consider not only the profit to be made from the special order but also the profit given up by devoting time and resources to this order instead of pursuing an alternative project. The profit given up is an opportunity cost. Consideration of opportunity costs is important. The implications extend to internal resource allocation decisions. For instance, a computer manufacturer must decide between internally manufacturing a chip versus buying it externally. In another case, management of a multidivisional company must decide whether to continue operating or close a particular division.

Point: Opportunity costs are not entered in accounting records. This does not reduce their relevance for managerial decisions.

Besides relevant costs, management must also consider the relevant benefits associated with a decision. **Relevant benefits** refer to the additional or *incremental* revenue generated by selecting a particular course of action over another. For instance, a student must decide the relevant benefits of taking one course over another. In sum, both relevant costs and relevant benefits are crucial to managerial decision making.

Managerial Decision Scenarios

A1 Evaluate short-term managerial decisions using relevant costs.

Managers experience many different scenarios that require analyzing alternative actions and making a decision. We describe several different types of decision scenarios in this section. We set these tasks in the context of FasTrac, an exercise supplies and equipment manufacturer introduced earlier. *We treat each of these decision tasks as separate from each other.*

Video25.1

Additional Business

FasTrac is operating at its normal level of 80% of full capacity. At this level, it produces and sells approximately 100,000 units of product annually. Its per unit and annual total costs are shown in Exhibit 25.12.

EXHIBIT 25.12

Selected Operating Income Data

	Per Unit	Annual Total
Sales (100,000 units)	$10.00	$1,000,000
Direct materials	(3.50)	(350,000)
Direct labor	(2.20)	(220,000)
Overhead	(1.10)	(110,000)
Selling expenses	(1.40)	(140,000)
Administrative expenses	(0.80)	(80,000)
Total costs and expenses	(9.00)	(900,000)
Operating income	$ 1.00	$ 100,000

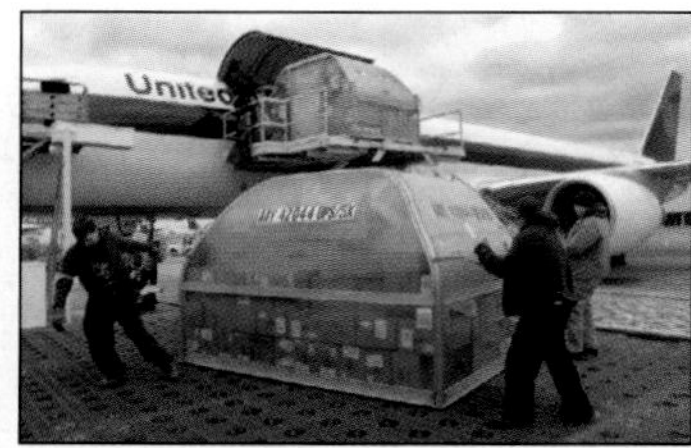

A current buyer of FasTrac's products wants to purchase additional units of its product and export them to another country. This buyer offers to buy 10,000 units of the product at $8.50 per unit, or $1.50 less than the current price. The offer price is low, but FasTrac is considering the proposal because this sale would be several times larger than any single previous sale and it would use idle capacity. Also, the units will be exported, so this new business will not affect current sales.

To determine whether to accept or reject this order, management needs to know whether accepting the offer will increase net income. The analysis in Exhibit 25.13 shows that if management relies on per unit historical costs, it would reject the sale because it yields a loss. However, historical costs are *not* relevant to this decision. Instead, the relevant costs are the additional costs, called **incremental costs.** These costs, also called *differential costs,* are the additional costs incurred if a company pursues a certain course of action. FasTrac's incremental costs are those related to the added volume that this new order would bring.

EXHIBIT 25.13

Analysis of Additional Business Using Historical Costs

	Per Unit	Total
Sales (10,000 additional units)	$ 8.50	$ 85,000
Direct materials	(3.50)	(35,000)
Direct labor	(2.20)	(22,000)
Overhead	(1.10)	(11,000)
Selling expenses	(1.40)	(14,000)
Administrative expenses	(0.80)	(8,000)
Total costs and expenses	(9.00)	(90,000)
Operating loss	$(0.50)	$ (5,000)

To make its decision, FasTrac must analyze the costs of this new business in a different manner. The following information regarding the order is available:

- Manufacturing 10,000 additional units requires direct materials of $3.50 per unit and direct labor of $2.20 per unit (same as for all other units).
- Manufacturing 10,000 additional units adds $5,000 of incremental overhead costs for power, packaging, and indirect labor (all variable costs).
- Incremental commissions and selling expenses from this sale of 10,000 additional units would be $2,000 (all variable costs).
- Incremental administrative expenses of $1,000 for clerical efforts are needed (all fixed costs) with the sale of 10,000 additional units.

We use this information, as shown in Exhibit 25.14, to assess how accepting this new business will affect FasTrac's income.

EXHIBIT 25.14

Analysis of Additional Business Using Relevant Costs

	Current Business	Additional Business	Combined
Sales	$1,000,000	$ 85,000	$1,085,000
Direct materials	(350,000)	(35,000)	(385,000)
Direct labor	(220,000)	(22,000)	(242,000)
Overhead	(110,000)	(5,000)	(115,000)
Selling expenses	(140,000)	(2,000)	(142,000)
Administrative expense	(80,000)	(1,000)	(81,000)
Total costs and expenses	(900,000)	(65,000)	(965,000)
Operating income	$ 100,000	$ 20,000	$ 120,000

The analysis of relevant costs in Exhibit 25.14 suggests that the additional business be accepted. It would provide $85,000 of added revenue while incurring only $65,000 of added costs. This would yield $20,000 of additional pretax income, or a pretax profit margin of 23.5%. More generally, FasTrac would increase its income with any price that exceeded $6.50 per unit ($65,000 incremental cost/10,000 additional units).

An analysis of the incremental costs pertaining to the additional volume is always relevant for this type of decision. We must proceed cautiously, however, when the additional volume approaches or exceeds the factory's existing available capacity. If the additional volume requires the company to expand its capacity by obtaining more equipment, more space, or more personnel, the incremental costs could quickly exceed the incremental revenue. Another cautionary note is the effect on existing sales. All new units of the extra business will be sold outside FasTrac's normal domestic sales channels. If accepting additional business would cause existing sales to decline, this information must be included in our analysis. The contribution margin lost from a decline in sales is an opportunity cost. If future cash flows over several time periods are affected, their net present value also must be computed and used in this analysis.

Example: Exhibit 25.14 uses quantitative information. Suggest some qualitative factors to be considered when deciding whether to accept this project. *Answer:* (1) Impact on relationships with other customers and (2) Improved relationship with customer buying additional units.

The key point is that *management must not blindly use historical costs, especially allocated overhead costs.* Instead, the accounting system needs to provide information about the incremental costs to be incurred if the additional business is accepted.

Decision Maker

Partner You are a partner in a small accounting firm that specializes in keeping the books and preparing taxes for clients. A local restaurant is interested in obtaining these services from your firm. Identify factors that are relevant in deciding whether to accept the engagement. [Answer—p. 1048]

Make or Buy

The managerial decision to make or buy a component for one of its current products is commonplace and depends on incremental costs. To illustrate, FasTrac has excess productive capacity it can use to manufacture Part 417, a component of the main product it sells. The part is currently purchased and delivered to the plant at a cost of $1.20 per unit. FasTrac estimates that making Part 417 would cost $0.45 for direct materials, $0.50 for direct labor, and an undetermined amount for overhead. The task is to determine how much overhead to add to these costs so we can decide whether to make or buy Part 417. If FasTrac's normal predetermined overhead application rate is 100% of direct labor cost, we might be tempted to conclude that overhead cost is $0.50 per unit, computed as 100% of the $0.50 direct labor cost. We would then mistakenly conclude that total cost is $1.45 ($0.45 of materials + $0.50 of labor + $0.50 of overhead). A wrong decision in this case would be to conclude that the company is better off buying the part at $1.20 each than making it for $1.45 each.

Instead, as we explained earlier, only incremental overhead costs are relevant in this situation. Thus, we must compute an *incremental overhead rate.* Incremental overhead costs might include, for example, additional power for operating machines, extra supplies, added cleanup costs, materials handling, and quality control. We can prepare a per unit analysis in this case as shown in Exhibit 25.15.

EXHIBIT 25.15

Make or Buy Analysis

	Make	Buy
Direct materials	$0.45	—
Direct labor	0.50	—
Overhead costs	[?]	—
Purchase price	—	$ 1.20
Total incremental costs	**$0.95 + [?]**	**$1.20**

We can see that if incremental overhead costs are less than $0.25 per unit, the total cost of making the component is less than the purchase price of $1.20 and FasTrac should make the part. FasTrac's decision rule in this case is that any amount of overhead less than $0.25 per unit yields a total cost for Part 417 that is less than the $1.20 purchase price. FasTrac must consider several nonfinancial factors in the make or buy decision, including product quality, timeliness of delivery (especially in a just-in-time setting), reactions of customers and suppliers, and other intangibles such as employee morale and workload. It must also consider whether making the part requires incremental fixed costs to expand plant capacity. When these added factors are considered, small cost differences may not matter.

Point: Managers must consider nonfinancial factors when making decisions.

Decision Insight

Make or Buy Services Companies apply make or buy decisions to their services. Many now outsource their payroll activities to a payroll service provider. It is argued that the prices paid for such services are close to what it costs them to do it, and without the headaches.

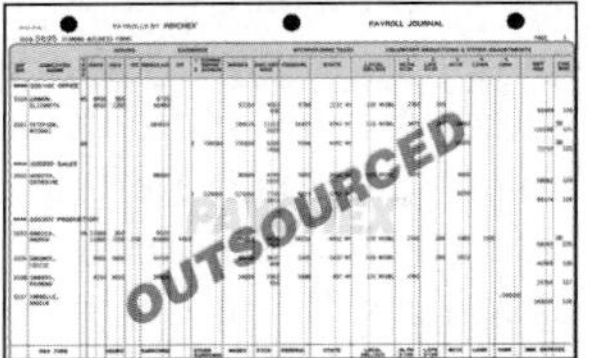

Scrap or Rework

Managers often must make a decision on whether to scrap or rework products in process. Remember that costs already incurred in manufacturing the units of a product that do not meet quality standards are sunk costs that have been incurred and cannot be changed. Sunk costs are irrelevant in any decision on whether to sell the substandard units as scrap or to rework them to meet quality standards.

To illustrate, assume that FasTrac has 10,000 defective units of a product that have already cost $1 per unit to manufacture. These units can be sold as is (as scrap) for $0.40 each, or they can be reworked for $0.80 per unit and then sold for their full price of $1.50 each. Should FasTrac sell the units as scrap or rework them?

To make this decision, management must recognize that the already incurred manufacturing costs of $1 per unit are sunk (unavoidable). These costs are *entirely irrelevant* to the decision. In addition, we must be certain that all costs of reworking defects, including interfering with normal operations, are accounted for in our analysis. For instance, reworking the defects means that FasTrac is unable to manufacture 10,000 *new* units with an incremental cost of $1 per unit and a selling price of $1.50 per unit, meaning it incurs an opportunity cost equal to the lost $5,000 net return from making and selling 10,000 new units. This opportunity cost is the difference between the $15,000 revenue (10,000 units × $1.50) from selling these new units and their $10,000 manufacturing costs (10,000 units × $1). Our analysis is reflected in Exhibit 25.16.

EXHIBIT 25.16

Scrap or Rework Analysis

	Scrap	Rework
Sale of scrapped/reworked units	$ 4,000	$ 15,000
Less costs to rework defects		(8,000)
Less opportunity cost of not making new units		**(5,000)**
Incremental net income	**$4,000**	**$ 2,000**

The analysis yields a $2,000 difference in favor of scrapping the defects, yielding a total incremental net income of $4,000. If we had failed to include the opportunity costs of $5,000, the rework option would have shown an income of $7,000 instead of $2,000, mistakenly making the reworking appear more favorable than scrapping.

Quick Check Answers—p. 1049

11. A company receives a special order for 200 units that requires stamping the buyer's name on each unit, yielding an additional fixed cost of $400 to its normal costs. Without the order, the company is operating at 75% of capacity and produces 7,500 units of product at the following costs:

Direct materials	$37,500
Direct labor	60,000
Overhead (30% variable)	20,000
Selling expenses (60% variable)	25,000

The special order will not affect normal unit sales and will not increase fixed overhead and selling expenses. Variable selling expenses on the special order are reduced to one-half the normal amount. The price per unit necessary to earn $1,000 on this order is (*a*) $14.80, (*b*) $15.80, (*c*) $19.80, (*d*) $20.80, or (*e*) $21.80.

12. What are the incremental costs of accepting additional business?

Sell or Process

The managerial decision to sell partially completed products as is or to process them further for sale depends significantly on relevant costs. To illustrate, suppose that FasTrac has 40,000 units of partially finished Product Q. It has already spent $0.75 per unit to manufacture these 40,000 units at a $30,000 total cost. FasTrac can sell the 40,000 units to another manufacturer as raw material for $50,000. Alternatively, it can process them further and produce finished products X, Y, and Z at an incremental cost of $2 per unit. The added processing yields the products and revenues shown in Exhibit 25.17. FasTrac must decide whether the added revenues from selling finished products X, Y, and Z exceed the costs of finishing them.

EXHIBIT 25.17

Revenues from Processing Further

Product	Price	Units	Revenues
Product X	$4.00	10,000	$ 40,000
Product Y	6.00	22,000	132,000
Product Z	8.00	6,000	48,000
Spoilage	—	2,000	0
Totals		40,000	$220,000

Exhibit 25.18 shows the two-step analysis for this decision. First, FasTrac computes its incremental revenue from further processing Q into products X, Y, and Z. This amount is the difference between the $220,000 revenue from the further processed products and the $50,000 FasTrac will give up by not selling Q as is (a $50,000 opportunity cost). Second, FasTrac computes its incremental costs from further processing Q into X, Y, and Z. This amount is $80,000 (40,000 units × $2 incremental cost). The analysis shows that FasTrac can earn incremental net income of $90,000 from a decision to further process Q. (Notice that the earlier incurred $30,000 manufacturing cost for the 40,000 units of Product Q does not appear in Exhibit 25.18 because it is a sunk cost and as such is irrelevant to the decision.)

Example: Does the decision change if incremental costs in Exhibit 25.18 increase to $4 per unit and the opportunity cost increases to $95,000? *Answer:* Yes. There is now an incremental net loss of $35,000.

EXHIBIT 25.18

Sell or Process Analysis

Revenue if processed	$220,000
Revenue if sold as is	(50,000)
Incremental revenue	170,000
Cost to process	(80,000)
Incremental net income	**$ 90,000**

Quick Check

Answers—p. 1049

13. A company has already incurred a $1,000 cost in partially producing its four products. Their selling prices when partially and fully processed follow with additional costs necessary to finish these partially processed units:

Product	Unfinished Selling Price	Finished Selling Price	Further Processing Costs
Alpha	$300	$600	$150
Beta	450	900	300
Gamma	275	425	125
Delta	150	210	75

Which product(s) should *not* be processed further, (*a*) Alpha, (*b*) Beta, (*c*) Gamma, or (*d*) Delta?

14. Under what conditions is a sunk cost relevant to decision making?

Sales Mix Selection

Point: A method called *linear programming* is useful for finding the optimal sales mix for several products subject to many market and production constraints. This method is described in advanced courses.

When a company sells a mix of products, some are likely to be more profitable than others. Management is often wise to concentrate sales efforts on more profitable products. If production facilities or other factors are limited, an increase in the production and sale of one product usually requires reducing the production and sale of others. In this case, management must identify the most profitable combination, or *sales mix* of products. To identify the best sales mix, management must know the contribution margin of each product, the facilities required to produce each product, any constraints on these facilities, and its markets.

To illustrate, assume that FasTrac makes and sells two products, A and B. The same machines are used to produce both products. A and B have the following selling prices and variable costs per unit:

	Product A	Product B
Selling price per unit	$5.00	$7.50
Variable costs per unit	3.50	5.50
Contribution margin per unit	$1.50	$2.00

The variable costs are included in the analysis because they are the incremental costs of producing these products within the existing capacity of 100,000 machine hours per month. We consider three separate cases.

Case 1: Assume that (1) each product requires 1 machine hour per unit for production and (2) the markets for these products are unlimited. Under these conditions, FasTrac should produce as much of Product B as it can because of its larger contribution margin of $2 per unit. At full capacity, FasTrac would produce $200,000 of total contribution margin per month, computed as $2 per unit times 100,000 machine hours.

Case 2: Assume that (1) Product A requires 1 machine hour per unit, (2) Product B requires 2 machine hours per unit, and (3) the markets for these products are unlimited. Under these conditions, FasTrac should produce as much of Product A as it can because it has a contribution margin of $1.50 per machine hour compared with only $1 per machine hour for Product B. Exhibit 25.19 shows the relevant analysis.

EXHIBIT 25.19

Sales Mix Analysis

	Product A	Product B
Selling price per unit	$ 5.00	$ 7.50
Variable costs per unit	3.50	5.50
Contribution margin per unit	$ 1.50	$ 2.00
Machine hours per unit	1.0	2.0
Contribution margin per machine hour	**$1.50**	**$1.00**

At its full capacity of 100,000 machine hours, FasTrac would produce 100,000 units of Product A, yielding $150,000 of total contribution margin per month. In contrast, if it uses all 100,000 hours to produce Product B, only 50,000 units would be produced yielding a contribution margin of $100,000. These results suggest that when a company faces excess demand and limited capacity, only the most profitable product per input should be manufactured.

Example: For Case 2, if Product B's variable costs per unit increase to $6, Product A's variable costs per unit decrease to $3, and the same machine hours per unit are used, which product should FasTrac produce? *Answer:* Product A. Its contribution margin of $2 per machine hour is higher than B's $.75 per machine hour.

Case 3: The need for a mix of different products arises when market demand is not sufficient to allow a company to sell all that it produces. For instance, assume that (1) Product A requires 1 machine hour per unit, (2) Product B requires 2 machine hours per unit, and (3) the market for Product A is limited to 80,000 units. Under these conditions, FasTrac should produce no more than 80,000 units of Product A. This would leave another 20,000 machine hours of capacity for making Product B. FasTrac should use this spare capacity to produce 10,000 units of Product B. This sales mix would maximize FasTrac's total contribution margin per month at an amount of $140,000.

Decision Insight

Companies such as **Gap, Abercrombie & Fitch,** and **American Eagle** must continuously monitor and manage the sales mix of their product lists. Selling their products in hundreds of countries and territories further complicates their decision process. The contribution margin of each product is crucial to their product mix strategies.

Segment Elimination

When a segment such as a department or division is performing poorly, management must consider eliminating it. Segment information on either net income (loss) or its contribution to overhead is not sufficient for this decision. Instead, we must look at the segment's avoidable expenses and unavoidable expenses. **Avoidable expenses,** also called *escapable expenses,* are amounts the company would not incur if it eliminated the segment. **Unavoidable expenses,** also called *inescapable expenses,* are amounts that would continue even if the segment is eliminated.

Point: FasTrac might consider buying another machine to reduce the constraint on production. A strategy designed to reduce the impact of constraints or bottlenecks, on production, is called the *theory of constraints.*

To illustrate, FasTrac considers eliminating its treadmill division because its $48,300 total expenses are higher than its $47,800 sales. Classification of this division's operating expenses into avoidable or unavoidable expenses is shown in Exhibit 25.20.

EXHIBIT 25.20

Classification of Segment Operating Expenses for Analysis

	Total	Avoidable Expenses	Unavoidable Expenses
Cost of goods sold	$ 30,000	$ 30,000	—
Direct expenses			
Salaries expense	7,900	7,900	—
Depreciation expense—Equipment	200	—	$ 200
Indirect expenses			
Rent and utilities expense	3,150	—	3,150
Advertising expense	400	400	—
Insurance expense	400	300	100
Service department costs			
Share of office department expenses	3,060	2,200	860
Share of purchasing expenses	3,190	1,000	2,190
Total	**$48,300**	**$41,800**	**$6,500**

Example: How can insurance be classified as either avoidable or unavoidable? *Answer:* Depends on whether the assets insured can be removed and the premiums canceled.

FasTrac's analysis shows that it can avoid $41,800 expenses if it eliminates the treadmill division. Because this division's sales are $47,800, eliminating it will cause FasTrac to lose $6,000 of income. *Our decision rule is that a segment is a candidate for elimination if its revenues are less than its avoidable expenses.* Avoidable expenses can be viewed as the costs to generate this segment's revenues.

When considering elimination of a segment, we must assess its impact on other segments. A segment could be unprofitable on its own, but it might still contribute to other segments' revenues and profits. It is possible then to continue a segment even when its revenues are less than its avoidable expenses. Similarly, a profitable segment might be discontinued if its space, assets, or staff can be more profitably used by expanding existing segments or by creating new ones. Our decision to keep or eliminate a segment requires a more complex analysis than simply looking at a segment's performance report. Such reports provide useful information, but they do not provide all the information necessary for this decision.

Example: Give an example of a segment that a company might profitably use to attract customers even though it might incur a loss. *Answer:* Warranty and post-sales services.

Qualitative Decision Factors

Managers must consider qualitative factors in making managerial decisions. Consider a decision on whether to buy a component from an outside supplier or continue to make it. Several qualitative decision factors must be considered. For example, the quality, delivery, and reputation of the proposed supplier are important. The effects from deciding not to make the component can include potential layoffs and impaired worker morale. Consider another situation in which a company is considering a one-time sale to a new customer at a special low price. Qualitative factors to consider in this situation include the effects of a low price on the company's image and the threat that regular customers might demand a similar price. The company must also consider whether this customer is really a one-time customer. If not, can it continue to offer this low price in the long run? Clearly, management cannot rely solely on financial data to make such decisions.

Quick Check Answers—p. 1049

15. What is the difference between avoidable and unavoidable expenses?

16. A segment is a candidate for elimination if (*a*) its revenues are less than its avoidable expenses, (*b*) it has a net loss, (*c*) its unavoidable expenses are higher than its revenues.

Break-Even Time

Decision Analysis

A2 Analyze a capital investment project using break-even time.

The first section of this chapter explained several methods to evaluate capital investments. Break-even time of an investment project is a variation of the payback period method that overcomes the limitation of not using the time value of money. **Break-even time (BET)** is a time-based measure used to evaluate a capital investment's acceptability. Its computation yields a measure of expected time, reflecting the time period until the *present value* of the net cash flows from an investment equals the initial cost of the investment. In basic terms, break-even time is computed by restating future cash flows in terms of present values and then determining the payback period using these present values.

To illustrate, we return to the FasTrac case described in Exhibit 25.1 involving a $16,000 investment in machinery. The annual net cash flows from this investment are projected at $4,100 for eight years. Exhibit 25.21 shows the computation of break-even time for this investment decision.

EXHIBIT 25.21

Break-Even Time Analysis*

Year	Cash Flows	Present Value of 1 at 10%	Present Value of Cash Flows	Cumulative Present Value of Cash Flows
0	$(16,000)	1.0000	$(16,000)	$(16,000)
1	4,100	0.9091	3,727	(12,273)
2	4,100	0.8264	3,388	(8,885)
3	4,100	0.7513	3,080	(5,805)
4	4,100	0.6830	2,800	(3,005)
5	4,100	0.6209	2,546	**(459)**
6	4,100	0.5645	2,314	**1,855**
7	4,100	0.5132	2,104	3,959
8	4,100	0.4665	1,913	5,872

* The time of analysis is the start of year 1 (same as end of year 0). All cash flows occur at the end of each year.

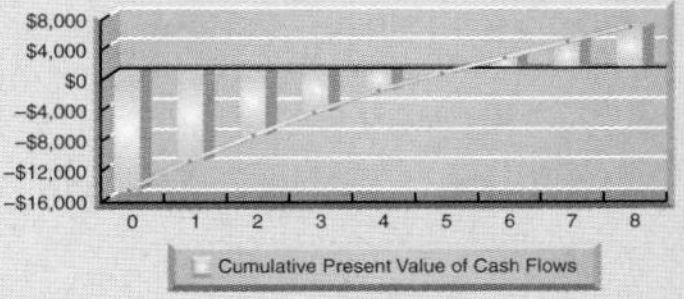

The right-most column of this exhibit shows that break-even time is between 5 and 6 years, or about 5.2 years—also see margin graph (where the line crosses the zero point). This is the time the project takes to break even after considering the time value of money (recall that the payback period computed without considering the time value of money was 3.9 years). We interpret this as cash flows earned after 5.2 years contribute to a positive net present value that, in this case, eventually amounts to $5,872.

Break-even time is a useful measure for managers because it identifies the point in time when they can expect the cash flows to begin to yield net positive returns. Managers expect a positive net present value from an investment if break-even time is less than the investment's estimated life. The method allows managers to compare and rank alternative investments, giving the project with the shortest break-even time the highest rank.

Decision Maker

Investment Manager Management asks you, the investment manager, to evaluate three alternative investments. Investment recovery time is crucial because cash is scarce. The time value of money is also important. Which capital budgeting method(s) do you use to assess the investments? [Answer—p. 1048]

Demonstration Problem

DP25

Determine the appropriate action in each of the following managerial decision situations.

1. Packer Company is operating at 80% of its manufacturing capacity of 100,000 product units per year. A chain store has offered to buy an additional 10,000 units at $22 each and sell them to customers so as not to compete with Packer Company. The following data are available.

Costs at 80% Capacity	Per Unit	Total
Direct materials	$ 8.00	$ 640,000
Direct labor	7.00	560,000
Overhead (fixed and variable)	12.50	1,000,000
Totals	$27.50	$2,200,000

In producing 10,000 additional units, fixed overhead costs would remain at their current level but incremental variable overhead costs of $3 per unit would be incurred. Should the company accept or reject this order?

2. Green Company uses Part JR3 in manufacturing its products. It has always purchased this part from a supplier for $40 each. It recently upgraded its own manufacturing capabilities and has enough excess capacity (including trained workers) to begin manufacturing Part JR3 instead of buying it. The company prepares the following cost projections of making the part, assuming that overhead is allocated to the part at the normal predetermined rate of 200% of direct labor cost.

Direct materials	$11
Direct labor	15
Overhead (fixed and variable) (200% of direct labor)	30
Total	$56

The required volume of output to produce the part will not require any incremental fixed overhead. Incremental variable overhead cost will be $17 per unit. Should the company make or buy this part?

3. Gold Company's manufacturing process causes a relatively large number of defective parts to be produced. The defective parts can be (a) sold for scrap, (b) melted to recover the recycled metal for reuse, or (c) reworked to be good units. Reworking defective parts reduces the output of other good units because no excess capacity exists. Each unit reworked means that one new unit cannot be produced. The following information reflects 500 defective parts currently available.

Proceeds of selling as scrap	$2,500
Additional cost of melting down defective parts	400
Cost of purchases avoided by using recycled metal from defects	4,800
Cost to rework 500 defective parts	
Direct materials	0
Direct labor	1,500
Incremental overhead	1,750
Cost to produce 500 new parts	
Direct materials	6,000
Direct labor	5,000
Incremental overhead	3,200
Selling price per good unit	40

Should the company melt the parts, sell them as scrap, or rework them?

4. White Company can invest in one of two projects, TD1 or TD2. Each project requires an initial investment of $100,000 and produces the year-end cash inflows shown in the following table. Use net present values to determine which project, if any, should be chosen. Assume that the company requires a 10% return from its investments.

	Net Cash Flows	
	TD1	TD2
Year 1	$ 20,000	$ 40,000
Year 2	30,000	40,000
Year 3	70,000	40,000
Totals	$120,000	$120,000

Planning the Solution

- Determine whether Packer Company should accept the additional business by finding the incremental costs of materials, labor, and overhead that will be incurred if the order is accepted. Omit fixed costs that the order will not increase. If the incremental revenue exceeds the incremental cost, accept the order.
- Determine whether Green Company should make or buy the component by finding the incremental cost of making each unit. If the incremental cost exceeds the purchase price, the component should be purchased. If the incremental cost is less than the purchase price, make the component.
- Determine whether Gold Company should sell the defective parts, melt them down and recycle the metal, or rework them. To compare the three choices, examine all costs incurred and benefits received from the alternatives in working with the 500 defective units versus the production of 500 new units. For the scrapping alternative, include the costs of producing 500 new units and subtract the $2,500 proceeds from selling the old ones. For the melting alternative, include the costs of melting the defective units, add the net cost of new materials in excess over those obtained from recycling, and add the direct labor and overhead costs. For the reworking alternative, add the costs of direct labor and incremental overhead. Select the alternative that has the lowest cost. The cost assigned to the 500 defective units is sunk and not relevant in choosing among the three alternatives.
- Compute White Company's net present value of each investment using a 10% discount rate.

Solution to Demonstration Problem

1. This decision involves accepting additional business. Since current unit costs are $27.50, it appears initially as if the offer to sell for $22 should be rejected, but the $27.50 cost includes fixed costs. When the analysis includes only *incremental* costs, the per unit cost is as shown in the following table. The offer should be accepted because it will produce $4 of additional profit per unit (computed as $22 price less $18 incremental cost), which yields a total profit of $40,000 for the 10,000 additional units.

Direct materials	$ 8.00
Direct labor	7.00
Variable overhead (given)	3.00
Total incremental cost	$18.00

2. For this make or buy decision, the analysis must not include the $13 nonincremental overhead per unit ($30 − $17). When only the $17 incremental overhead is included, the relevant unit cost of manufacturing the part is shown in the following table. It would be better to continue buying the part for $40 instead of making it for $43.

Direct materials	$11.00
Direct labor	15.00
Variable overhead	17.00
Total incremental cost	$43.00

3. The goal of this scrap or rework decision is to identify the alternative that produces the greatest net benefit to the company. To compare the alternatives, we determine the net cost of obtaining 500 marketable units as follows:

Incremental Cost to Produce 500 Marketable Units	Sell as Is	Melt and Recycle	Rework Units
Direct materials			
New materials	$ 6,000	$6,000	
Recycled metal materials		(4,800)	
Net materials cost		1,200	
Melting costs		400	
Total direct materials cost	6,000	1,600	
Direct labor	5,000	5,000	$1,500
Incremental overhead	3,200	3,200	1,750
Cost to produce 500 marketable units	14,200	9,800	3,250
Less proceeds of selling defects as scrap	(2,500)		
Opportunity costs*			5,800
Net cost	$11,700	$9,800	$9,050

* The $5,800 opportunity cost is the lost contribution margin from not being able to produce and sell 500 units because of reworking, computed as ($40 − [$14,200/500 units]) × 500 units.

The incremental cost of 500 marketable parts is smallest if the defects are reworked.

4. TD1:

	Net Cash Flows	Present Value of 1 at 10%	Present Value of Net Cash Flows
Year 1	$ 20,000	0.9091	$ 18,182
Year 2	30,000	0.8264	24,792
Year 3	70,000	0.7513	52,591
Totals	$120,000		95,565
Amount invested			(100,000)
Net present value			**$ (4,435)**

TD2:

	Net Cash Flows	Present Value of 1 at 10%	Present Value of Net Cash Flows
Year 1	$ 40,000	0.9091	$ 36,364
Year 2	40,000	0.8264	33,056
Year 3	40,000	0.7513	30,052
Totals	$120,000		99,472
Amount invested			(100,000)
Net present value			**$ (528)**

White Company should not invest in either project. Both are expected to yield a negative net present value, and it should invest only in positive net present value projects.

APPENDIX

Using Excel to Compute Net Present Value and Internal Rate of Return

25A

Computing present values and internal rates of return for projects with uneven cash flows is tedious and error prone. These calculations can be performed simply and accurately by using functions built into Excel. Many calculators and other types of spreadsheet software can perform them too. To illustrate, consider Fastrac, a company that is considering investing in a new machine with the expected cash flows shown in the following spreadsheet. Cash outflows are entered as negative numbers, and cash inflows are entered as positive numbers. Assume Fastrac requires a 12% annual return, entered as 0.12 in cell C1.

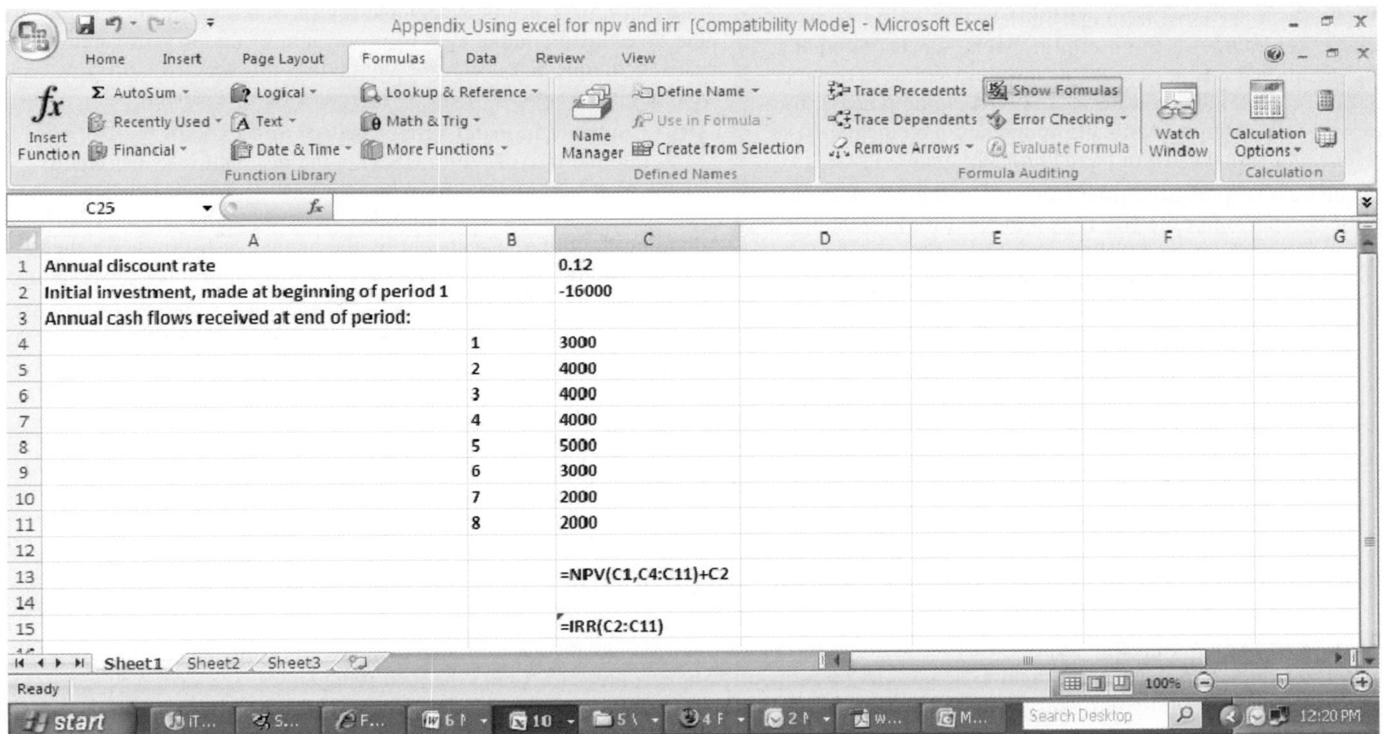

	A	B	C
1	Annual discount rate		0.12
2	Initial investment, made at beginning of period 1		-16000
3	Annual cash flows received at end of period:		
4		1	3000
5		2	4000
6		3	4000
7		4	4000
8		5	5000
9		6	3000
10		7	2000
11		8	2000
12			
13			=NPV(C1,C4:C11)+C2
14			
15			=IRR(C2:C11)

To compute the net present value of this project, the following is entered into cell C13:

=NPV(C1,C4:C11)+C2.

This instructs Excel to use its NPV function to compute the present value of the cash flows in cells C4 through C11, using the discount rate in cell C1, and then add the amount of the (negative) initial investment. For this stream of cash flows and a discount rate of 12%, the net present value is $1,326.03.

To compute the internal rate of return for this project, the following is entered into cell C15:

=IRR(C2:C11).

This instructs Excel to use its IRR function to compute the internal rate of return of the cash flows in cells C2 through C11. By default, Excel starts with a guess of 10%, and then uses trial and error to find the IRR. The IRR equals 14% for this project.

Summary

C1 **Explain the importance of capital budgeting.** Capital budgeting is the process of analyzing alternative investments and deciding which assets to acquire or sell. It involves predicting the cash flows to be received from the alternatives, evaluating their merits, and then choosing which ones to pursue.

C2 **Describe the selection of a hurdle rate for an investment.** Top management should select the hurdle (discount) rate to use in evaluating capital investments. The required hurdle rate should be at least higher than the interest rate on money borrowed because the return on an investment must cover the interest and provide an additional profit to reward the company for risk.

C3 **Describe the importance of relevant costs for short-term decisions.** A company must rely on relevant costs pertaining to alternative courses of action rather than historical costs. Out-of-pocket expenses and opportunity costs are relevant because these are avoidable; sunk costs are irrelevant because they result from past decisions and are therefore unavoidable. Managers must also consider the relevant benefits associated with alternative decisions.

A1 **Evaluate short-term managerial decisions using relevant costs.** Relevant costs are useful in making decisions such as to accept additional business, make or buy, and sell as is or process further. For example, the relevant factors in deciding whether to produce and sell additional units of product are incremental costs and incremental revenues from the additional volume.

A2 **Analyze a capital investment project using break-even time.** Break-even time (BET) is a method for evaluating capital investments by restating future cash flows in terms of their present values (discounting the cash flows) and then calculating the payback period using these present values of cash flows.

P1 **Compute payback period and describe its use.** One way to compare potential investments is to compute and compare their payback periods. The payback period is an estimate of the expected time before the cumulative net cash inflow from the investment equals its initial cost. A payback period analysis fails to reflect risk of the cash flows, differences in the timing of cash flows within the payback period, and cash flows that occur after the payback period.

P2 **Compute accounting rate of return and explain its use.** A project's accounting rate of return is computed by dividing the expected annual after-tax net income by the average amount of investment in the project. When the net cash flows are received evenly throughout each period and straight-line depreciation is used, the average investment is computed as the average of the investment's initial book value and its salvage value.

P3 **Compute net present value and describe its use.** An investment's net present value is determined by predicting the future cash flows it is expected to generate, discounting them at a rate that represents an acceptable return, and then by subtracting the investment's initial cost from the sum of the present values. This technique can deal with any pattern of expected cash flows and applies a superior concept of return on investment.

P4 **Compute internal rate of return and explain its use.** The internal rate of return (IRR) is the discount rate that results in a zero net present value. When the cash flows are equal, we can compute the present value factor corresponding to the IRR by dividing the initial investment by the annual cash flows. We then use the annuity tables to determine the discount rate corresponding to this present value factor.

Guidance Answers to **Decision Maker** and **Decision Ethics**

Systems Manager Your dilemma is whether to abide by rules designed to prevent abuse or to bend them to acquire an investment that you believe will benefit the firm. You should not pursue the latter action because breaking up the order into small components is dishonest and there are consequences of being caught at a later stage. Develop a proposal for the entire package and then do all you can to expedite its processing, particularly by pointing out its benefits. When faced with controls that are not working, there is rarely a reason to overcome its shortcomings by dishonesty. A direct assault on those limitations is more sensible and ethical.

Entrepreneur The banker is probably concerned because new products are risky and should therefore be evaluated using a higher rate of return. You should conduct a thorough technical analysis and obtain detailed market data and information about any similar products available in the market. These factors might provide sufficient information to support the use of a lower return. You must convince yourself that the risk level is consistent with the discount rate used. You should also be confident that your company has the capacity and the resources to handle the new product.

Partner You should identify the differences between existing clients and this potential client. A key difference is that the restaurant business has additional inventory components (groceries, vegetables, meats, etc.) and is likely to have a higher proportion of depreciable assets. These differences imply that the partner must spend more hours auditing the records and understanding the business, regulations, and standards that pertain to the restaurant business. Such differences suggest that the partner must use a different "formula" for quoting a price to this potential client vis-à-vis current clients.

Investment Manager You should probably focus on either the payback period or break-even time because both the time value of money and recovery time are important. Break-even time method is superior because it accounts for the time value of money, which is an important consideration in this decision.

Guidance Answers to **Quick Checks**

1. *b*
2. A capital budgeting decision is difficult because (1) the outcome is uncertain, (2) large amounts of money are usually involved, (3) a long-term commitment is required, and (4) the decision could be difficult or impossible to reverse.
3. *b*
4. Depreciation expense is subtracted from revenues in computing net income but does not use cash and should be added back to net income to compute net cash flows.
5. Not necessarily. One investment can continue to generate cash flows beyond the payback period for a longer time period than the other. The timing of their cash flows within the payback period also can differ.
6. *b*; Annual average investment = ($180,000 + $15,000)/2 = $97,500
   Accounting rate of return = $40,000/$97,500 = 41%
7. For this determination, we need to compare it to the returns expected from alternative investments with similar risk.
8. Project A has the higher net present value as follows:

		Project A		Project B	
Year	Present Value of 1 at 10%	Net Cash Flows	Present Value of Net Cash Flows	Net Cash Flows	Present Value of Net Cash Flows
1	0.9091	$12,000	$10,909	$ 4,500	$ 4,091
2	0.8264	8,500	7,024	8,500	7,024
3	0.7513	4,000	3,005	13,000	9,767
Totals		$24,500	$20,938	$26,000	$20,882
Amount invested			(20,000)		(20,000)
Net present value			$ 938		$ 882

9. No, the information is too limited to draw that conclusion. For example, one investment could be riskier than the other, or one could require a substantially larger initial investment.
10. *b*
11. *e*; Variable costs per unit for this order of 200 units follow:

Direct materials ($37,500/7,500)	$ 5.00
Direct labor ($60,000/7,500)	8.00
Variable overhead [(0.30 × $20,000)/7,500]	0.80
Variable selling expenses [(0.60 × $25,000 × 0.5)/7,500]	1.00
Total variable costs per unit	$14.80

Cost to produce special order: (200 × $14.80) + $400 = $3,360.

Price per unit to earn $1,000: ($3,360 + $1,000)/200 = 21.80.

12. They are the additional (new) costs of accepting new business.
13. *d*;

	Incremental benefits		Incremental costs
Alpha	$300 ($600 − $300)	>	$150 (given)
Beta	$450 ($900 − $450)	>	$300 (given)
Gamma	$150 ($425 − $275)	>	$125 (given)
Delta	$ 60 ($210 − $150)	<	$ 75 (given)

14. A sunk cost is *never* relevant because it results from a past decision and is already incurred.
15. Avoidable expenses are ones a company will not incur by eliminating a segment; unavoidable expenses will continue even after a segment is eliminated.
16. *a*

Key Terms

mhhe.com/wildFAP19e

Key Terms are available at the book's Website for learning and testing in an online Flashcard Format.

Accounting rate of return (p. 1027)
Avoidable expense (p. 1041)
Break-even time (BET) (p. 1043)
Capital budgeting (p. 1024)
Cost of capital (p. 1029)
Hurdle rate (p. 1033)
Incremental cost (p. 1036)
Internal rate of return (IRR) (p. 1031)
Net present value (NPV) (p. 1029)
Payback period (PBP) (p. 1025)
Profitability index (p. 1031)
Relevant benefits (p. 1035)
Unavoidable expense (p. 1041)

Multiple Choice Quiz

Answers on p. 1064 mhhe.com/wildFAP19e

Additional Quiz Questions are available at the book's Website.

Quiz25

1. A company inadvertently produced 3,000 defective MP3 players. The players cost $12 each to produce. A recycler offers to purchase the defective players as they are for $8 each. The production manager reports that the defects can be corrected for $10 each, enabling them to be sold at their regular market price of $19 each. The company should:
   a. Correct the defect and sell them at the regular price.
   b. Sell the players to the recycler for $8 each.
   c. Sell 2,000 to the recycler and repair the rest.
   d. Sell 1,000 to the recycler and repair the rest.
   e. Throw the players away.

2. A company's productive capacity is limited to 480,000 machine hours. Product X requires 10 machine hours to produce; and Product Y requires 2 machine hours to produce. Product X sells for $32 per unit and has variable costs of $12 per unit; Product Y sells for $24 per unit and has variable costs of $10 per unit. Assuming that the company can sell as many of either product as it produces, it should:
   a. Produce X and Y in the ratio of 57% and 43%.
   b. Produce X and Y in the ratio of 83% X and 17% Y.
   c. Produce equal amounts of Product X and Product Y.
   d. Produce only Product X.
   e. Produce only Product Y.
3. A company receives a special one-time order for 3,000 units of its product at $15 per unit. The company has excess capacity and it currently produces and sells the units at $20 each to its regular customers. Production costs are $13.50 per unit, which includes $9 of variable costs. To produce the special order, the company must incur additional fixed costs of $5,000. Should the company accept the special order?
   a. Yes, because incremental revenue exceeds incremental costs.
   b. No, because incremental costs exceed incremental revenue.
   c. No, because the units are being sold for $5 less than the regular price.
   d. Yes, because incremental costs exceed incremental revenue.
   e. No, because incremental cost exceeds $15 per unit when total costs are considered.
4. A company is considering the purchase of equipment for $270,000. Projected annual cash inflow from this equipment is $61,200 per year. The payback period is:
   a. 0.2 years
   b. 5.0 years
   c. 4.4 years
   d. 2.3 years
   e. 3.9 years
5. A company buys a machine for $180,000 that has an expected life of nine years and no salvage value. The company expects an annual net income (after taxes of 30%) of $8,550. What is the accounting rate of return?
   a. 4.75%
   b. 42.75%
   c. 2.85%
   d. 9.50%
   e. 6.65%

Discussion Questions

1. What is capital budgeting?
2. Identify four reasons that capital budgeting decisions by managers are risky.
3. Capital budgeting decisions require careful analysis because they are generally the ________ ________ and ________ decisions that management faces.
4. Identify two disadvantages of using the payback period for comparing investments.
5. Why is an investment more attractive to management if it has a shorter payback period?
6. What is the average amount invested in a machine during its predicted five-year life if it costs $200,000 and has a $20,000 salvage value? Assume that net income is received evenly throughout each year and straight-line depreciation is used.
7. If the present value of the expected net cash flows from a machine, discounted at 10%, exceeds the amount to be invested, what can you say about the investment's expected rate of return? What can you say about the expected rate of return if the present value of the net cash flows, discounted at 10%, is less than the investment amount?
8. Why is the present value of $100 that you expect to receive one year from today worth less than $100 received today? What is the present value of $100 that you expect to receive one year from today, discounted at 12%?
9. Why should managers set the required rate of return higher than the rate at which money can be borrowed when making a typical capital budgeting decision?
10. Why does the use of the accelerated depreciation method (instead of straight line) for income tax reporting increase an investment's value?
11. What is an out-of-pocket cost? What is an opportunity cost? Are opportunity costs recorded in the accounting records?
12. Why are sunk costs irrelevant in deciding whether to sell a product in its present condition or to make it into a new product through additional processing?
13. Identify the incremental costs incurred by **Best Buy** for shipping one additional iPod from a warehouse to a retail store along with the store's normal order of 75 iPods.

14. **Circuit City** is considering expanding a store. Identify three methods management can use to evaluate whether to expand.

15. Assume that **Apple** manufactures and sells 500,000 units of a product at $30 per unit in domestic markets. It costs $20 per unit to manufacture ($13 variable cost per unit, $7 fixed cost per unit). Can you describe a situation under which the company is willing to sell an additional 25,000 units of the product in an international market at $15 per unit?

Denotes Discussion Questions that involve decision making.

McGraw-Hill's HOMEWORK MANAGER® Available with McGraw-Hill's Homework Manager

QUICK STUDY

QS 25-1
Analyzing payback periods P1

Trek Company is considering two alternative investments. The payback period is 2.5 years for Investment A and 3 years for Investment B. (1) If management relies on the payback period, which investment is preferred? (2) Why might Trek's analysis of these two alternatives lead to the selection of B over A?

QS 25-2
Payback period P1

Foster Company is considering an investment that requires immediate payment of $360,000 and provides expected cash inflows of $120,000 annually for four years. What is the investment's payback period?

QS 25-3
Computation of net present value P3

If Kimball Company invests $100,000 today, it can expect to receive $20,000 at the end of each year for the next seven years plus an extra $12,000 at the end of the seventh year. What is the net present value of this investment assuming a required 8% return on investments?

QS 25-4
Computation of accounting rate of return P2

Camino Company is considering an investment expected to generate an average net income after taxes of $3,825 for three years. The investment costs $90,000 and has an estimated $12,000 salvage value. Compute the accounting rate of return for this investment; assume the company uses straight-line depreciation. Hint: Use the formula in Exhibit 25.5 when computing the average annual investment.

QS 25-5
Selection of sales mix
C3 A1

Flash Memory Company can sell all units of computer memory X and Y that it can produce, but it has limited production capacity. It can produce four units of X per hour *or* six units of Y per hour, and it has 16,000 production hours available. Contribution margin is $10 for Product X and $8 for Product Y. What is the most profitable sales mix for this company?

QS 25-6
Analysis of incremental costs
C3 A1

Falcon Company incurs a $18 per unit cost for Product A, which it currently manufactures and sells for $27 per unit. Instead of manufacturing and selling this product, the company can purchase Product B for $10 per unit and sell it for $24 per unit. If it does so, unit sales would remain unchanged and $10 of the $18 per unit costs assigned to Product A would be eliminated. Should the company continue to manufacture Product A or purchase Product B for resale?

QS 25-7
Computation of break-even time
A2

Fast Feet, a shoe manufacturer, is evaluating the costs and benefits of new equipment that would custom fit each pair of athletic shoes. The customer would have his or her foot scanned by digital computer equipment; this information would be used to cut the raw materials to provide the customer a perfect fit. The new equipment costs $300,000 and is expected to generate an additional $105,000 in cash flows for five years. A bank will make a $300,000 loan to the company at a 8% interest rate for this equipment's purchase. Use the following table to determine the break-even time for this equipment. (Round the present value of cash flows to the nearest dollar.)

Year	Cash Flows*	Present Value of 1 at 8%	Present Value of Cash Flows	Cumulative Present Value of Cash Flows
0	$(300,000)	1.0000		
1	105,000	0.9259		
2	105,000	0.8573		
3	105,000	0.7938		
4	105,000	0.7350		
5	105,000	0.6806		

* All cash flows occur at year-end.

QS 25-8
Profitability index
P3

Jemak Company is considering two alternative projects. Project 1 requires an initial investment of $800,000 and has a net present value of cash flows of $1,600,000. Project 2 requires an initial investment of $4,000,000 and has a net present value of cash flows of $2,000,000. Compute the profitability index for each project. Based on the profitability index, which project should the company prefer? Explain.

EXERCISES

Exercise 25-1
Payback period computation; even cash flows
P1

Compute the payback period for each of these two separate investments (round the payback period to two decimals):

a. A new operating system for an existing machine is expected to cost $250,000 and have a useful life of four years. The system yields an incremental after-tax income of $72,000 each year after deducting its straight-line depreciation. The predicted salvage value of the system is $10,000.

b. A machine costs $180,000, has a $12,000 salvage value, is expected to last eight years, and will generate an after-tax income of $39,000 per year after straight-line depreciation.

Exercise 25-2
Payback period computation; uneven cash flows
P1

Walker Company is considering the purchase of an asset for $90,000. It is expected to produce the following net cash flows. The cash flows occur evenly throughout each year. Compute the payback period for this investment.

	Year 1	Year 2	Year 3	Year 4	Year 5	Total
Net cash flows	$40,000	$30,000	$40,000	$70,000	$29,000	$209,000

Check 2.5 years

Exercise 25-3
Payback period computation; declining-balance depreciation
P1

A machine can be purchased for $600,000 and used for 5 years, yielding the following net incomes. In projecting net incomes, double-declining balance depreciation is applied, using a 5-year life and a zero salvage value. Compute the machine's payback period (ignore taxes). (Round the payback period to two decimals.)

	Year 1	Year 2	Year 3	Year 4	Year 5
Net incomes	$40,000	$100,000	$200,000	$150,000	$400,000

Check 2.27 years

Exercise 25-4
Accounting rate of return P2

A machine costs $200,000 and is expected to yield an after-tax net income of $5,040 each year. Management predicts this machine has a 12-year service life and a $40,000 salvage value, and it uses straight-line depreciation. Compute this machine's accounting rate of return.

Exercise 25-5
Payback period and accounting rate of return on investment
P1 P2

MLM Co. is considering the purchase of equipment that would allow the company to add a new product to its line. The equipment is expected to cost $324,000 with a 12-year life and no salvage value. It will be depreciated on a straight-line basis. The company expects to sell 128,000 units of the equipment's product each year. The expected annual income related to this equipment follows. Compute the (1) payback period and (2) accounting rate of return for this equipment.

Sales	$200,000
Costs	
Materials, labor, and overhead (except depreciation)	107,000
Depreciation on new equipment	27,000
Selling and administrative expenses	20,000
Total costs and expenses	154,000
Pretax income	46,000
Income taxes (30%)	13,800
Net income	$ 32,200

Check (1) 5.47 years (2) 19.88%

Exercise 25-6
Computing net present value P3

After evaluating the risk of the investment described in Exercise 25-5, MLM Co. concludes that it must earn at least a 10% return on this investment. Compute the net present value of this investment. (Round the net present value to the nearest dollar.)

Exercise 25-7
Computation and interpretation of net present value and internal rate of return
P3 P4

Cerritos Company can invest in each of three cheese-making projects: C1, C2, and C3. Each project requires an initial investment of $438,374 and would yield the following annual cash flows.

	C1	C2	C3
Year 1	$ 24,000	$192,000	$360,000
Year 2	216,000	192,000	120,000
Year 3	336,000	192,000	96,000
Totals	$576,000	$576,000	$576,000

(1) Assuming that the company requires a 12% return from its investments, use net present value to determine which projects, if any, should be acquired. (2) Using the answer from part 1, explain whether the internal rate of return is higher or lower than 12% for project C2. (3) Compute the internal rate of return for project C2.

Check (3) IRR = 15%

Exercise 25-8
NPV and profitability index
P3

Following is information on two alternative investments being considered by Jakem Company. The company requires a 10% return from its investments.

	Project A	Project B
Initial investment	$(180,325)	$(150,960)
Expected net cash flows in year:		
1	45,000	35,000
2	50,000	52,000
3	82,295	58,000
4	86,400	75,000
5	64,000	29,000

For each alternative project compute the (a) net present value, and (b) profitability index. If the company can only select one project, which should it choose? Explain.

Exercise 25-9[A]
Using Excel to compute IRR
P4

Refer to the information in Exercise 25-8. Create an Excel spreadsheet to compute the internal rate of return for each of the projects. Round the percentage return to two decimals.

Exercise 25-10
Decision to accept additional business or not
C3 A1

Harlan Co. expects to sell 300,000 units of its product in the next period with the following results.

Sales (300,000 units)	$4,500,000
Costs and expenses	
Direct materials	600,000
Direct labor	1,200,000
Overhead	300,000
Selling expenses	450,000
Administrative expenses	771,000
Total costs and expenses	3,321,000
Net income	$1,179,000

The company has an opportunity to sell 30,000 additional units at $13 per unit. The additional sales would not affect its current expected sales. Direct materials and labor costs per unit would be the same for the additional units as they are for the regular units. However, the additional volume would create the following incremental costs: (1) total overhead would increase by 16% and (2) administrative expenses would increase by $129,000. Prepare an analysis to determine whether the company should accept or reject the offer to sell additional units at the reduced price of $13 per unit.

Check Income increase, $33,000

Exercise 25-11
Make or buy decision
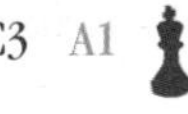
C3 A1

Check $1,600 increased costs to make

Simons Company currently manufactures one of its crucial parts at a cost of $2.72 per unit. This cost is based on a normal production rate of 40,000 units per year. Variable costs are $1.20 per unit, fixed costs related to making this part are $40,000 per year, and allocated fixed costs are $50,000 per year. Allocated fixed costs are unavoidable whether the company makes or buys the part. Simons is considering buying the part from a supplier for a quoted price of $2.16 per unit guaranteed for a three-year period. Should the company continue to manufacture the part, or should it buy the part from the outside supplier? Support your answer with analyses.

Exercise 25-12
Sell or process decision
C3 A1

Starr Company has already manufactured 50,000 units of Product A at a cost of $50 per unit. The 50,000 units can be sold at this stage for $1,250,000. Alternatively, it can be further processed at a $750,000 total additional cost and be converted into 10,000 units of Product B and 20,000 units of Product C. Per unit selling price for Product B is $75 and for Product C is $50. Prepare an analysis that shows whether the 50,000 units of Product A should be processed further or not.

Exercise 25-13
Analysis of income effects from eliminating departments
C3 A1

Johns Co. expects its five departments to yield the following income for next year.

		Dept. M	Dept. N	Dept. O	Dept. P	Dept. T
2	Sales	$34,000	$23,500	$33,000	$27,500	$ 10,500
3	Expenses					
4	Avoidable	4,700	18,900	15,800	8,000	14,900
5	Unavoidable	20,000	5,100	2,900	15,000	5,900
6	Total expenses	24,700	24,000	18,700	23,000	20,800
7	Net income (loss)	$ 9,300	$ (500)	$14,300	$ 4,500	$(10,300)

Check Total income (2) $17,100, (3) $21,700

Recompute and prepare the departmental income statements (including a combined total column) for the company under each of the following separate scenarios: Management (1) does not eliminate any department, (2) eliminates departments with expected net losses, and (3) eliminates departments with sales dollars that are less than avoidable expenses. Explain your answers to parts 2 and 3.

Exercise 25-14
Sales mix determination and analysis
C3 A1

Jersey Company owns a machine that can produce two specialized products. Production time for Product TLX is two units per hour and for Product MTV is five units per hour. The machine's capacity is 2,200 hours per year. Both products are sold to a single customer who has agreed to buy all of the company's output up to a maximum of 3,740 units of Product TLX and 2,090 units of Product MTV. Selling prices and variable costs per unit to produce the products follow. Determine (1) the company's most profitable sales mix and (2) the contribution margin that results from that sales mix.

	Product TLX	Product MTV
Selling price per unit	$11.50	$6.90
Variable costs per unit	3.45	4.14

Check (2) $34,661

Exercise 25-15
Comparison of payback and BET
P1 A2

This chapter explained two methods to evaluate investments using recovery time, the payback period and break-even time (BET). Refer to QS 25-7 and (1) compute the recovery time for both the payback period and break-even time, (2) discuss the advantage(s) of break-even time over the payback period, and (3) list two conditions under which payback period and break-even time are similar.

McGraw-Hill's HOMEWORK MANAGER® Available with McGraw-Hill's Homework Manager

PROBLEM SET A

Problem 25-1A
Computation of payback period, accounting rate of return, and net present value
P1 P2 P3

mhhe.com/wildFAP19e

Burtle Company is planning to add a new product to its line. To manufacture this product, the company needs to buy a new machine at a $488,000 cost with an expected four-year life and a $15,200 salvage value. All sales are for cash, and all costs are out of pocket except for depreciation on the new machine. Additional information includes the following.

Expected annual sales of new product	$1,870,000
Expected annual costs of new product	
Direct materials	465,000
Direct labor	680,000
Overhead excluding straight-line depreciation on new machine	335,000
Selling and administrative expenses	158,000
Income taxes	40%

Required

1. Compute straight-line depreciation for each year of this new machine's life. (Round depreciation amounts to the nearest dollar.)

2. Determine expected net income and net cash flow for each year of this machine's life. (Round answers to the nearest dollar.)

3. Compute this machine's payback period, assuming that cash flows occur evenly throughout each year. (Round the payback period to two decimals.)

4. Compute this machine's accounting rate of return, assuming that income is earned evenly throughout each year. (Round the percentage return to two decimals.)

5. Compute the net present value for this machine using a discount rate of 8% and assuming that cash flows occur at each year-end. (*Hint:* Salvage value is a cash inflow at the end of the asset's life. Round the net present value to the nearest dollar.)

Check (4) 27.14%

(5) $140,794

Problem 25-2A
Analysis and computation of payback period, accounting rate of return, and net present value
P1 P2 P3 

Jackson Company has an opportunity to invest in one of two new projects. Project Y requires a $360,000 investment for new machinery with a four-year life and no salvage value. Project Z requires a $360,000 investment for new machinery with a three-year life and no salvage value. The two projects yield the following predicted annual results. The company uses straight-line depreciation, and cash flows occur evenly throughout each year.

	Project Y	Project Z
Sales	$355,000	$265,000
Expenses		
Direct materials	49,700	30,125
Direct labor	71,000	36,750
Overhead including depreciation	127,800	129,250
Selling and administrative expenses	25,000	20,000
Total expenses	273,500	216,125
Pretax income	81,500	48,875
Income taxes (30%)	24,450	14,663
Net income	$ 57,050	$ 34,212

Required

1. Compute each project's annual expected net cash flows. (Round the net cash flows to the nearest dollar.)

2. Determine each project's payback period. (Round the payback period to two decimals.)

3. Compute each project's accounting rate of return. (Round the percentage return to one decimal.)

4. Determine each project's net present value using 6% as the discount rate. For part 4 only, assume that cash flows occur at each year-end. (Round the net present value to the nearest dollar.)

Check For Project Y: (2) 2.45 years, (3) 31.7%, (4) $149,543

Analysis Component

5. Identify the project you would recommend to management and explain your choice.

Problem 25-3A
Computation of cash flows and net present values with alternative depreciation methods

P3

Deandra Corporation is considering a new project requiring a $97,500 investment in test equipment with no salvage value. The project would produce $71,000 of pretax income before depreciation at the end of each of the next six years. The company's income tax rate is 32%. In compiling its tax return and computing its income tax payments, the company can choose between the two alternative depreciation schedules shown in the table.

	Straight-Line Depreciation	MACRS Depreciation*
Year 1	$ 9,750	$19,500
Year 2	19,500	31,200
Year 3	19,500	18,720
Year 4	19,500	11,232
Year 5	19,500	11,232
Year 6	9,750	5,616
Totals	$97,500	$97,500

* The modified accelerated cost recovery system (MACRS) for depreciation is discussed in Chapter 10.

Required

1. Prepare a five-column table that reports amounts (assuming use of straight-line depreciation) for each of the following for each of the six years: (a) pretax income before depreciation, (b) straight-line depreciation expense, (c) taxable income, (d) income taxes, and (e) net cash flow. Net cash flow equals the amount of income before depreciation minus the income taxes. (Round answers to the nearest dollar.)
2. Prepare a five-column table that reports amounts (assuming use of MACRS depreciation) for each of the following for each of the six years: (a) pretax income before depreciation, (b) MACRS depreciation expense, (c) taxable income, (d) income taxes, and (e) net cash flow. Net cash flow equals the income amount before depreciation minus the income taxes. (Round answers to the nearest dollar.)
3. Compute the net present value of the investment if straight-line depreciation is used. Use 10% as the discount rate. (Round the net present value to the nearest dollar.)
4. Compute the net present value of the investment if MACRS depreciation is used. Use 10% as the discount rate. (Round the net present value to the nearest dollar.)

Check Net present value: (3) $135,347, (4) $136,893

Analysis Component

5. Explain why the MACRS depreciation method increases this project's net present value.

Problem 25-4A
Analysis of income effects of additional business

C3 A1

mhhe.com/wildFAP19e

Ingraham Products manufactures and sells to wholesalers approximately 200,000 packages per year of underwater markers at $4 per package. Annual costs for the production and sale of this quantity are shown in the table.

Direct materials	$256,000
Direct labor	64,000
Overhead	192,000
Selling expenses	80,000
Administrative expenses	53,000
Total costs and expenses	$645,000

A new wholesaler has offered to buy 33,000 packages for $3.44 each. These markers would be marketed under the wholesaler's name and would not affect Ingraham Products' sales through its normal channels. A study of the costs of this additional business reveals the following:

- Direct materials costs are 100% variable.
- Per unit direct labor costs for the additional units would be 50% higher than normal because their production would require overtime pay at one-and-one-half times the usual labor rate.
- 35% of the normal annual overhead costs are fixed at any production level from 150,000 to 300,000 units. The remaining 65% of the annual overhead cost is variable with volume.

- Accepting the new business would involve no additional selling expenses.
- Accepting the new business would increase administrative expenses by a $5,000 fixed amount.

Required

Prepare a three-column comparative income statement that shows the following:

1. Annual operating income without the special order (column 1).
2. Annual operating income received from the new business only (column 2).
3. Combined annual operating income from normal business and the new business (column 3).

Check Operating income: (1) $155,000, (2) $29,848

Problem 25-5A
Analysis of sales mix strategies
C3 A1

Virginia Company is able to produce two products, G and B, with the same machine in its factory. The following information is available.

	Product G	Product B
Selling price per unit	$280	$240
Variable costs per unit	130	60
Contribution margin per unit	$150	$180
Machine hours to produce 1 unit	0.2 hours	2.0 hours
Maximum unit sales per month	1,200 units	200 units

The company presently operates the machine for a single eight-hour shift for 22 working days each month. Management is thinking about operating the machine for two shifts, which will increase its productivity by another eight hours per day for 22 days per month. This change would require $63,000 additional fixed costs per month.

Required

1. Determine the contribution margin per machine hour that each product generates.
2. How many units of Product G and Product B should the company produce if it continues to operate with only one shift? How much total contribution margin does this mix produce each month?
3. If the company adds another shift, how many units of Product G and Product B should it produce? How much total contribution margin would this mix produce each month? Should the company add the new shift? Explain.
4. Suppose that the company determines that it can increase Product G's maximum sales to 1,400 units per month by spending $24,000 per month in marketing efforts. Should the company pursue this strategy and the double shift? Explain.

Check Units of Product G: (2) 880, (3) 1,200, (4) 1,400

Problem 25-6A
Analysis of possible elimination of a department
C3 A1

Eclectic Decor Company's management is trying to decide whether to eliminate Department 200, which has produced losses or low profits for several years. The company's 2009 departmental income statement shows the following.

ECLECTIC DECOR COMPANY Departmental Income Statements For Year Ended December 31, 2009	Dept. 100	Dept. 200	Combined
Sales	$437,000	$280,000	$717,000
Cost of goods sold	263,000	207,000	470,000
Gross profit	174,000	73,000	247,000
Operating expenses			
Direct expenses			
Advertising	17,500	13,500	31,000
Store supplies used	5,000	4,600	9,600
Depreciation—Store equipment	4,200	3,000	7,200
Total direct expenses	26,700	21,100	47,800

[continued on next page]

[continued from previous page]

Allocated expenses			
Sales salaries	52,000	31,200	83,200
Rent expense	9,500	4,750	14,250
Bad debts expense	9,500	7,400	16,900
Office salary	15,600	10,400	26,000
Insurance expense	1,900	1,000	2,900
Miscellaneous office expenses	2,500	1,700	4,200
Total allocated expenses	91,000	56,450	147,450
Total expenses	117,700	77,550	195,250
Net income (loss)	$ 56,300	$ (4,550)	$ 51,750

In analyzing whether to eliminate Department 200, management considers the following:

a. The company has one office worker who earns $500 per week, or $26,000 per year, and four salesclerks who each earn $400 per week, or $20,800 per year.

b. The full salaries of two salesclerks are charged to Department 100. The full salary of one sales clerk is charged to Department 200. The salary of the fourth clerk, who works half-time in both departments, is divided evenly between the two departments.

c. Eliminating Department 200 would avoid the sales salaries and the office salary currently allocated to it. However, management prefers another plan. Two salesclerks have indicated that they will be quitting soon. Management believes that their work can be done by the other two clerks if the one office worker works in sales half-time. Eliminating Department 200 will allow this shift of duties. If this change is implemented, half the office worker's salary would be reported as sales salaries and half would be reported as office salary.

d. The store building is rented under a long-term lease that cannot be changed. Therefore, Department 100 will use the space and equipment currently used by Department 200.

e. Closing Department 200 will eliminate its expenses for advertising, bad debts, and store supplies; 70% of the insurance expense allocated to it to cover its merchandise inventory; and 25% of the miscellaneous office expenses presently allocated to it.

Required

Check (1) Total expenses: (a) $665,250, (b) $275,225

1. Prepare a three-column report that lists items and amounts for (a) the company's total expenses (including cost of goods sold)—in column 1, (b) the expenses that would be eliminated by closing Department 200—in column 2, and (c) the expenses that will continue—in column 3.

(2) Forecasted net income without Department 200, $46,975

2. Prepare a forecasted annual income statement for the company reflecting the elimination of Department 200 assuming that it will not affect Department 100's sales and gross profit. The statement should reflect the reassignment of the office worker to one-half time as a salesclerk.

Analysis Component

3. Reconcile the company's combined net income with the forecasted net income assuming that Department 200 is eliminated (list both items and amounts). Analyze the reconciliation and explain why you think the department should or should not be eliminated.

PROBLEM SET B

Problem 25-1B

Computation of payback period, accounting rate of return, and net present value

P1 P2 P3

Sorbo Company is planning to add a new product to its line. To manufacture this product, the company needs to buy a new machine at a $600,000 cost with an expected four-year life and a $20,000 salvage value. All sales are for cash and all costs are out of pocket, except for depreciation on the new machine. Additional information includes the following.

Expected annual sales of new product	$2,300,000
Expected annual costs of new product	
Direct materials	600,000
Direct labor	840,000
Overhead excluding straight-line depreciation on new machine	420,000
Selling and administrative expenses	200,000
Income taxes	30%

Required

1. Compute straight-line depreciation for each year of this new machine's life. (Round depreciation amounts to the nearest dollar.)
2. Determine expected net income and net cash flow for each year of this machine's life. (Round answers to the nearest dollar.)
3. Compute this machine's payback period, assuming that cash flows occur evenly throughout each year. (Round the payback period to two decimals.)
4. Compute this machine's accounting rate of return, assuming that income is earned evenly throughout each year. (Round the percentage return to two decimals.)
5. Compute the net present value for this machine using a discount rate of 7% and assuming that cash flows occur at each year-end. (*Hint:* Salvage value is a cash inflow at the end of the asset's life.)

Check (4) 21.45%

(5) $131,650

Problem 25-2B
Analysis and computation of payback period, accounting rate of return, and net present value

P1 P2 P3

Morris Company has an opportunity to invest in one of two projects. Project A requires a $480,000 investment for new machinery with a four-year life and no salvage value. Project B also requires a $480,000 investment for new machinery with a three-year life and no salvage value. The two projects yield the following predicted annual results. The company uses straight-line depreciation, and cash flows occur evenly throughout each year.

	Project A	Project B
Sales	$500,000	$400,000
Expenses		
Direct materials	70,000	50,000
Direct labor	100,000	60,000
Overhead including depreciation	180,000	180,000
Selling and administrative expenses	36,000	36,000
Total expenses	386,000	326,000
Pretax income	114,000	74,000
Income taxes (30%)	34,200	22,200
Net income	$ 79,800	$ 51,800

Required

1. Compute each project's annual expected net cash flows. (Round net cash flows to the nearest dollar.)
2. Determine each project's payback period. (Round the payback period to two decimals.)
3. Compute each project's accounting rate of return. (Round the percentage return to one decimal.)
4. Determine each project's net present value using 8% as the discount rate. For part 4 only, assume that cash flows occur at each year-end. (Round net present values to the nearest dollar.)

Check For Project A: (2) 2.4 years, (3) 33.3%, (4) $181,758

Analysis Component

5. Identify the project you would recommend to management and explain your choice.

Problem 25-3B
Computation of cash flows and net present values with alternative depreciation methods

P3  

Lee Corporation is considering a new project requiring a $300,000 investment in an asset having no salvage value. The project would produce $125,000 of pretax income before depreciation at the end of each of the next six years. The company's income tax rate is 35%. In compiling its tax return and computing its income tax payments, the company can choose between two alternative depreciation schedules as shown in the table.

	Straight-Line Depreciation	MACRS Depreciation*
Year 1	$ 30,000	$ 60,000
Year 2	60,000	96,000
Year 3	60,000	57,600
Year 4	60,000	34,560
Year 5	60,000	34,560
Year 6	30,000	17,280
Totals	$300,000	$300,000

* The modified accelerated cost recovery system (MACRS) for depreciation is discussed in Chapter 10.

Required

1. Prepare a five-column table that reports amounts (assuming use of straight-line depreciation) for each of the following items for each of the six years: (a) pretax income before depreciation, (b) straight-line depreciation expense, (c) taxable income, (d) income taxes, and (e) net cash flow. Net cash flow equals the amount of income before depreciation minus the income taxes. (Round answers to the nearest dollar.)

2. Prepare a five-column table that reports amounts (assuming use of MACRS depreciation) for each of the following items for each of the six years: (a) income before depreciation, (b) MACRS depreciation expense, (c) taxable income, (d) income taxes, and (e) net cash flow. Net cash flow equals the amount of income before depreciation minus the income taxes. (Round answers to the nearest dollar.)

Check Net present value: (3) $129,846, (4) $135,050

3. Compute the net present value of the investment if straight-line depreciation is used. Use 10% as the discount rate. (Round the net present value to the nearest dollar.)

4. Compute the net present value of the investment if MACRS depreciation is used. Use 10% as the discount rate. (Round the net present value to the nearest dollar.)

Analysis Component

5. Explain why the MACRS depreciation method increases the net present value of this project.

Problem 25-4B
Analysis of income effects of additional business

C3 A1

Wyn Company manufactures and sells to local wholesalers approximately 150,000 units per month at a sales price of $4 per unit. Monthly costs for the production and sale of this quantity follow.

Direct materials	$192,000
Direct labor	48,000
Overhead	144,000
Selling expenses	60,000
Administrative expenses	40,000
Total costs and expenses	$484,000

A new out-of-state distributor has offered to buy 25,000 units next month for $3.44 each. These units would be marketed in other states and would not affect Wyn's sales through its normal channels. A study of the costs of this new business reveals the following:

- Direct materials costs are 100% variable.
- Per unit direct labor costs for the additional units would be 50% higher than normal because their production would require time-and-a-half overtime pay to meet the distributor's deadline.
- Twenty-five percent of the normal annual overhead costs are fixed at any production level from 125,000 to 200,000 units. The remaining 75% is variable with volume.
- Accepting the new business would involve no additional selling expenses.
- Accepting the new business would increase administrative expenses by a $2,000 fixed amount.

Required

Prepare a three-column comparative income statement that shows the following:

Check Operating income: (1) $116,000, (2) $22,000

1. Monthly operating income without the special order (column 1).

2. Monthly operating income received from the new business only (column 2).

3. Combined monthly operating income from normal business and the new business (column 3).

Problem 25-5B
Analysis of sales mix strategies

C3 A1

Verto Company is able to produce two products, R and T, with the same machine in its factory. The following information is available.

	Product R	Product T
Selling price per unit	$ 120	$160
Variable costs per unit	65	90
Contribution margin per unit	$ 55	$ 70
Machine hours to produce 1 unit	0.2 hours	0.5 hours
Maximum unit sales per month	1,100 units	350 units

The company presently operates the machine for a single eight-hour shift for 22 working days each month. Management is thinking about operating the machine for two shifts, which will increase its productivity by another eight hours per day for 22 days per month. This change would require $30,000 additional fixed costs per month.

Required

1. Determine the contribution margin per machine hour that each product generates.

2. How many units of Product R and Product T should the company produce if it continues to operate with only one shift? How much total contribution margin does this mix produce each month?

3. If the company adds another shift, how many units of Product R and Product T should it produce? How much total contribution margin would this mix produce each month? Should the company add the new shift? Explain.

Check Units of Product R: (2) 880, (3) 1,100, (4) 1,350

4. Suppose that the company determines that it can increase Product R's maximum sales to 1,350 units per month by spending $9,000 per month in marketing efforts. Should the company pursue this strategy and the double shift? Explain.

Problem 25-6B
Analysis of possible elimination of a department
C3 A1 

Kumar Company's management is trying to decide whether to eliminate Department Z, which has produced low profits or losses for several years. The company's 2009 departmental income statement shows the following.

KUMAR COMPANY
Departmental Income Statements
For Year Ended December 31, 2009

	Dept. A	Dept. Z	Combined
Sales	$1,050,000	$262,500	$1,312,500
Cost of goods sold	691,950	187,650	879,600
Gross profit	358,050	74,850	432,900
Operating expenses			
Direct expenses			
Advertising	40,500	4,500	45,000
Store supplies used	8,400	2,100	10,500
Depreciation—Store equipment	21,000	10,500	31,500
Total direct expenses	69,900	17,100	87,000
Allocated expenses			
Sales salaries	105,300	35,100	140,400
Rent expense	33,120	8,280	41,400
Bad debts expense	31,500	6,000	37,500
Office salary	31,200	7,800	39,000
Insurance expense	6,300	2,100	8,400
Miscellaneous office expenses	2,550	3,750	6,300
Total allocated expenses	209,970	63,030	273,000
Total expenses	279,870	80,130	360,000
Net income (loss)	$ 78,180	$ (5,280)	$ 72,900

In analyzing whether to eliminate Department Z, management considers the following items:

a. The company has one office worker who earns $750 per week or $39,000 per year and four salesclerks who each earn $675 per week or $35,100 per year.

b. The full salaries of three salesclerks are charged to Department A. The full salary of one salesclerk is charged to Department Z.

c. Eliminating Department Z would avoid the sales salaries and the office salary currently allocated to it. However, management prefers another plan. Two salesclerks have indicated that they will be quitting soon. Management believes that their work can be done by the two remaining clerks if the one office worker works in sales half time. Eliminating Department Z will allow this shift of duties. If this change is implemented, half the office worker's salary would be reported as sales salaries and half would be reported as office salary.

d. The store building is rented under a long-term lease that cannot be changed. Therefore, Department A will use the space and equipment currently used by Department Z.

e. Closing Department Z will eliminate its expenses for advertising, bad debts, and store supplies; 65% of the insurance expense allocated to it to cover its merchandise inventory; and 30% of the miscellaneous office expenses presently allocated to it.

Required

Check (1) Total expenses: (a) $1,239,600, (b) $272,940

1. Prepare a three-column report that lists items and amounts for (a) the company's total expenses (including cost of goods sold)—in column 1, (b) the expenses that would be eliminated by closing Department Z—in column 2, and (c) the expenses that will continue—in column 3.

(2) Forecasted net income without Department Z, $83,340

2. Prepare a forecasted annual income statement for the company reflecting the elimination of Department Z assuming that it will not affect Department A's sales and gross profit. The statement should reflect the reassignment of the office worker to one-half time as a salesclerk.

Analysis Component

3. Reconcile the company's combined net income with the forecasted net income assuming that Department Z is eliminated (list both items and amounts). Analyze the reconciliation and explain why you think the department should or should not be eliminated.

SERIAL PROBLEM

Success Systems

(This serial problem began in Chapter 1 and continues through most of the book. If previous chapter segments were not completed, the serial problem can begin at this point. It is helpful, but not necessary, to use the Working Papers that accompany the book.)

SP 25 Adriana Lopez is considering the purchase of equipment for Success Systems that would allow the company to add a new product to its computer furniture line. The equipment is expected to cost $300,000 and to have a six-year life and no salvage value. It will be depreciated on a straight-line basis. Success Systems expects to sell 100 units of the equipment's product each year. The expected annual income related to this equipment follows.

Sales	$375,000
Costs	
Materials, labor, and overhead (except depreciation)	200,000
Depreciation on new equipment	50,000
Selling and administrative expenses	37,500
Total costs and expenses	287,500
Pretax income	87,500
Income taxes (30%)	26,250
Net income	$ 61,250

Required

Compute the (1) payback period and (2) accounting rate of return for this equipment.

BEYOND THE NUMBERS

REPORTING IN ACTION

C1 A1 P3 

BTN 25-1 In fiscal 2007, **Best Buy** invested $251 million in store-related projects that included store remodels, relocations, expansions, and various merchandising projects. Assume that these projects have a seven-year life, and that Best Buy requires a 12% internal rate of return on these projects.

Required

1. What is the amount of annual cash flows that Best Buy must earn from these projects to have a 12% internal rate of return? (*Hint:* Identify the seven-period, 12% factor from the present value of an annuity table, and then divide $251 million by this factor to get the annual cash flows necessary.)

Fast Forward

2. Access Best Buy's financial statements for fiscal years ended after March 3, 2007, from its Website (BestBuy.com) or the SEC's Website (SEC.gov).

a. Determine the amount that Best Buy invested in similar store-related projects for the most recent year.

b. Assume a seven-year life and a 12% internal rate of return. What is the amount of cash flows that Best Buy must earn on these new projects?

COMPARATIVE ANALYSIS

C3

BTN 25-2 Best Buy, Circuit City, and RadioShack sell several different products; most are profitable but some are not. Teams of employees in each company make advertising, investment, and product mix decisions. A certain portion of advertising for both companies is on a local basis to a target audience.

Required

1. Find one major advertisement of a product or group of products for each company in your local newspaper. Contact the newspaper and ask the approximate cost of this ad space (for example, cost of one page or one-half page of advertising).

2. Estimate how many products this advertisement must sell to justify its cost. Begin by taking the product's sales price advertised for each company and assume a 20% contribution margin.

3. Prepare a one-half page memorandum explaining the importance of effective advertising when making a product mix decision. Be prepared to present your ideas in class.

ETHICS CHALLENGE

P3

BTN 25-3 A consultant commented that "too often the numbers look good but feel bad." This comment often stems from estimation error common to capital budgeting proposals that relate to future cash flows. Three reasons for this error often exist. First, reliably predicting cash flows several years into the future is very difficult. Second, the present value of cash flows many years into the future (say, beyond 10 years) is often very small. Third, it is difficult for personal biases and expectations not to unduly influence present value computations.

Required

1. Compute the present value of $100 to be received in 10 years assuming a 12% discount rate.

2. Why is understanding the three reasons mentioned for estimation errors important when evaluating investment projects? Link this response to your answer for part 1.

COMMUNICATING IN PRACTICE

P1 P2 P3 P4

BTN 25-4 Payback period, accounting rate of return, net present value, and internal rate of return are common methods to evaluate capital investment opportunities. Assume that your manager asks you to identify the type of measurement basis and unit that each method offers and to list the advantages and disadvantages of each. Present your response in memorandum format of less than one page.

TAKING IT TO THE NET

A1

BTN 25-5 Many companies must determine whether to internally produce their component parts or to outsource them. Further, some companies now outsource key components or business processes to international providers. Access the Website BizBrim.com and review the available information on outsourcing—especially as it relates to both the advantages and the negative effects of outsourcing.

Required

1. What does Bizbrim identify as the major advantages and the major disadvantages of outsourcing?

2. Does it seem that Bizbrim is generally in favor of or opposed to outsourcing? Explain.

TEAMWORK IN ACTION

P1 P3

BTN 25-6 Break into teams and identify four reasons that an international airline such as Southwest, Northwest, or American would invest in a project when its direct analysis using both payback period and net present value indicate it to be a poor investment. (*Hint:* Think about qualitative factors.) Provide an example of an investment project supporting your answer.

ENTREPRENEURIAL DECISION

A1   

BTN 25-7 Jared Greenberg and Dan Zinger of **Prairie Sticks Bat Company** make baseball bats. They must decide on the best sales mix. Assume their company has a capacity of 80 hours of lathe/processing time available each month and it makes two types of bats, Deluxe and Premium. Information on these bats follows.

	Deluxe	Premium
Selling price per bat	$70	$90
Variable costs per bat	$40	$50
Lathe/processing minutes per bat	6 minutes	12 minutes

Required

1. Assume the markets for both models of bats are unlimited. How many Deluxe bats and how many Premium bats should the company make each month? Explain. How much total contribution margin does this mix produce each month?

2. Assume the market for Deluxe bats is limited to 600 bats per month, with no market limit for Premium bats. How many Deluxe bats and how many Premium bats should the company make each month? Explain. How much total contribution margin does this mix produce each month?

HITTING THE ROAD

C1 P3

BTN 25-8 Visit or call a local auto dealership and inquire about leasing a car. Ask about the down payment and the required monthly payments. You will likely find the salesperson does not discuss the cost to purchase this car but focuses on the affordability of the monthly payments. This chapter gives you the tools to compute the cost of this car using the lease payment schedule in present dollars and to estimate the profit from leasing for an auto dealership.

Required

1. Compare the cost of leasing the car to buying it in present dollars using the information from the dealership you contact. (Assume you will make a final payment at the end of the lease and then own the car.)

2. Is it more costly to lease or buy the car? Support your answer with computations.

GLOBAL DECISION

C1 

DSG

BTN 25-9 Access **DSG**'s 2006 annual report dated April 29, 2006, from its Website www.DSGiplc.com. Identify its report on corporate responsibility.

Required

Dixons reports that it recycled 25,607 tons of waste. Efforts such as these can be costly to a company. Why would a company like DSG pursue these costly efforts?

ANSWERS TO MULTIPLE CHOICE QUIZ

1. a; Reworking provides incremental revenue of $11 per unit ($19 − $8); and, it costs $10 to rework them. The company is better off by $1 per unit when it reworks these products and sells them at the regular price.

2. e; Product X has a $2 contribution margin per machine hour [($32 − $12)/10 MH]; Product Y has a $7 contribution margin per machine hour [($24 − $10)/2 MH]. It should produce as much of Product Y as possible.

3. a; Total revenue from the special order = 3,000 units × $15 per unit = $45,000; and, Total costs for the special order = (3,000 units × $9 per unit) + $5,000 = $32,000. Net income from the special order = $45,000 − $32,000 = $13,000. Thus, yes, it should accept the order.

4. c; Payback = $270,000/$61,200 per year = 4.4 years.

5. d; Accounting rate of return = $8,550/[($180,000 + $0)/2] = 9.5%.

A Financial Statement Information

This appendix includes financial information for (1) **Best Buy**, (2) **Circuit City**, (3) **RadioShack**, and (4) **Apple**. This information is taken from their annual 10-K reports filed with the SEC. An **annual report** is a summary of a company's financial results for the year along with its current financial condition and future plans. This report is directed to external users of financial information, but it also affects the actions and decisions of internal users.

A company uses an annual report to showcase itself and its products. Many annual reports include attractive photos, diagrams, and illustrations related to the company. The primary objective of annual reports, however, is the *financial section,* which communicates much information about a company, with most data drawn from the accounting information system. The layout of an annual report's financial section is fairly established and typically includes the following:

- Letter to Shareholders
- Financial History and Highlights
- Management Discussion and Analysis
- Management's Report on Financial Statements and on Internal Controls
- Report of Independent Accountants (Auditor's Report) and on Internal Controls
- Financial Statements
- Notes to Financial Statements
- List of Directors and Officers

This appendix provides the financial statements for Best Buy (plus selected notes), Circuit City, RadioShack, and Apple. The appendix is organized as follows:

Many assignments at the end of each chapter refer to information in this appendix. We encourage readers to spend time with these assignments; they are especially useful in showing the relevance and diversity of financial accounting and reporting.

Special note: The SEC maintains the EDGAR (**E**lectronic **D**ata **G**athering, **A**nalysis, and **R**etrieval) database at www.sec.gov. The **Form 10-K** is the annual report form for most companies. It provides electronically accessible information. The **Form 10-KSB** is the annual report form filed by small businesses. It requires slightly less information than the Form 10-K. One of these forms must be filed within 90 days after the company's fiscal year-end. (Forms 10-K405, 10-KT, 10-KT405, and 10-KSB405 are slight variations of the usual form due to certain regulations or rules.)

BEST BUY

Financial Report

Selected Financial Data

The following table presents our selected financial data. In fiscal 2004, we sold our interest in Musicland. All fiscal years presented reflect the classification of Musicland's financial results as discontinued operations.

Five-Year Financial Highlights

$ in millions, except per share amounts

Fiscal Year	2007[1]	2006	2005	2004	2003
Consolidated Statements of Earnings Data					
Revenue	$35,934	$30,848	$27,433	$24,548	$20,943
Operating income	1,999	1,644	1,442	1,304	1,010
Earnings from continuing operations	1,377	1,140	934	800	622
Loss from discontinued operations, net of tax	—	—	—	(29)	(441)
Gain (loss) on disposal of discontinued operations, net of tax	—	—	50	(66)	—
Cumulative effect of change in accounting principles, net of tax	—	—	—	—	(82)
Net earnings	1,377	1,140	984	705	99
Per Share Data					
Continuing operations	$ 2.79	$ 2.27	$ 1.86	$ 1.61	$ 1.27
Discontinued operations	—	—	—	(0.06)	(0.89)
Gain (loss) on disposal of discontinued operations	—	—	0.10	(0.13)	—
Cumulative effect of accounting changes	—	—	—	—	(0.16)
Net earnings	2.79	2.27	1.96	1.42	0.20
Cash dividends declared and paid	0.36	0.31	0.28	0.27	—
Common stock price:					
High	59.50	56.00	41.47	41.80	35.83
Low	43.51	31.93	29.25	17.03	11.33
Operating Statistics					
Comparable store sales gain	5.0%	4.9%	4.3%	7.1%	2.4%
Gross profit rate	24.4%	25.0%	23.7%	23.9%	23.6%
Selling, general and administrative expenses rate	18.8%	19.7%	18.4%	18.6%	18.8%
Operating income rate	5.6%	5.3%	5.3%	5.3%	4.8%
Year-End Data					
Current ratio	1.4	1.3	1.4	1.3	1.3
Total assets	$13,570	$11,864	$10,294	$ 8,652	$ 7,694
Debt, including current portion	650	596	600	850	834
Total shareholders' equity	6,201	5,257	4,449	3,422	2,730
Number of stores					
Domestic	868	774	694	631	567
International	304	167	144	127	112
Total	1,172	941	838	758	679
Retail square footage (000s)					
Domestic	33,959	30,826	28,465	26,640	24,432
International	7,926	3,564	3,139	2,800	2,375
Total	41,885	34,390	31,604	29,440	26,807

(1) Fiscal 2007 included 53 weeks. All other periods presented included 52 weeks.

Consolidated Balance Sheets
$ in millions, except per share amounts

	March 3, 2007	February 25, 2006
Assets		
Current Assets		
Cash and cash equivalents	$ 1,205	$ 748
Short-term investments	2,588	3,041
Receivables	548	449
Merchandise inventories	4,028	3,338
Other current assets	712	409
Total current assets	9,081	7,985
Property and Equipment		
Land and buildings	705	580
Leasehold improvements	1,540	1,325
Fixtures and equipment	2,627	2,898
Property under capital lease	32	33
	4,904	4,836
Less accumulated depreciation	1,966	2,124
Net property and equipment	2,938	2,712
Goodwill	919	557
Tradenames	81	44
Long-Term Investments	318	218
Other Assets	233	348
Total Assets	$13,570	$11,864
Liabilities and Shareholders' Equity		
Current Liabilities		
Accounts payable	$ 3,934	$ 3,234
Unredeemed gift card liabilities	496	469
Accrued compensation and related expenses	332	354
Accrued liabilities	990	878
Accrued income taxes	489	703
Short-term debt	41	—
Current portion of long-term debt	19	418
Total current liabilities	6,301	6,056
Long-Term Liabilities	443	373
Long-Term Debt	590	178
Minority Interests	35	—
Shareholders' Equity		
Preferred stock, $1.00 par value: Authorized — 400,000 shares; Issued and outstanding — none	—	—
Common stock, $.10 par value: Authorized — 1 billion shares; Issued and outstanding — 480,655,000 and 485,098,000 shares, respectively	48	49
Additional paid-in capital	430	643
Retained earnings	5,507	4,304
Accumulated other comprehensive income	216	261
Total shareholders' equity	6,201	5,257
Total Liabilities and Shareholders' Equity	$13,570	$11,864

Consolidated Statements of Earnings
$ in millions, except per share amounts

Fiscal Years Ended	March 3, 2007	February 25, 2006	February 26, 2005
Revenue	$35,934	$30,848	$27,433
Cost of goods sold	27,165	23,122	20,938
Gross profit	8,769	7,726	6,495
Selling, general and administrative expenses	6,770	6,082	5,053
Operating income	1,999	1,644	1,442
Net interest income	111	77	1
Gain on investments	20	—	—
Earnings from continuing operations before income tax expense	2,130	1,721	1,443
Income tax expense	752	581	509
Minority interest in earnings	1	—	—
Earnings from continuing operations	1,377	1,140	934
Gain on disposal of discontinued operations, net of tax	—	—	50
Net earnings	$ 1,377	$ 1,140	$ 984
Basic earnings per share:			
Continuing operations	$ 2.86	$ 2.33	$ 1.91
Gain on disposal of discontinued operations	—	—	0.10
Basic earnings per share	$ 2.86	$ 2.33	$ 2.01
Diluted earnings per share:			
Continuing operations	$ 2.79	$ 2.27	$ 1.86
Gain on disposal of discontinued operations	—	—	0.10
Diluted earnings per share	$ 2.79	$ 2.27	$ 1.96
Basic weighted-average common shares outstanding (in millions)	482.1	490.3	488.9
Diluted weighted-average common shares outstanding (in millions)	496.2	504.8	505.0

Consolidated Statements of Changes in Shareholders' Equity
$ and shares in millions

	Common Shares	Common Stock	Additional Paid-In Capital	Retained Earnings	Accumulated Other Comprehensive Income	Total
Balances at February 28, 2004	**487**	**$49**	**$819**	**$ 2,468**	**$ 86**	**$3,422**
Net earnings	—	—	—	984	—	984
Other comprehensive income, net of tax:						
Foreign currency translation adjustments	—	—	—	—	59	59
Other	—	—	—	—	4	4
Total comprehensive income						1,047
Stock options exercised	10	1	219	—	—	220
Tax benefit from stock options exercised and employee stock purchase plan	—	—	60	—	—	60
Issuance of common stock under employee stock purchase plan	2	—	36	—	—	36
Vesting of restricted stock awards	—	—	1	—	—	1
Common stock dividends, $0.28 per share	—	—	—	(137)	—	(137)
Repurchase of common stock	(6)	(1)	(199)	—	—	(200)
Balances at February 26, 2005	**493**	**49**	**936**	**3,315**	**149**	**4,449**
Net earnings	—	—	—	1,140	—	1,140
Other comprehensive income, net of tax:						
Foreign currency translation adjustments	—	—	—	—	101	101
Other	—	—	—	—	11	11
Total comprehensive income						1,252
Stock options exercised	9	1	256	—	—	257
Tax benefit from stock options exercised and employee stock purchase plan	—	—	55	—	—	55
Issuance of common stock under employee stock purchase plan	1	—	35	—	—	35
Stock-based compensation	—	—	132	—	—	132
Common stock dividends, $0.31 per share	—	—	—	(151)	—	(151)
Repurchase of common stock	(18)	(1)	(771)	—	—	(772)
Balances at February 25, 2006	**485**	**49**	**643**	**4,304**	**261**	**5,257**
Net earnings	—	—	—	1,377	—	1,377
Other comprehensive loss, net of tax:						
Foreign currency translation adjustments	—	—	—	—	(33)	(33)
Other	—	—	—	—	(12)	(12)
Total comprehensive income						1,332
Stock options exercised	7	1	167	—	—	168
Tax benefit from stock options exercised and employee stock purchase plan	—	—	47	—	—	47
Issuance of common stock under employee stock purchase plan	1	—	49	—	—	49
Stock-based compensation	—	—	121	—	—	121
Common stock dividends, $0.36 per share	—	—	—	(174)	—	(174)
Repurchase of common stock	(12)	(2)	(597)	—	—	(599)
Balances at March 3, 2007	**481**	**$48**	**$430**	**$5,507**	**$216**	**$6,201**

Consolidated Statements of Cash Flows
$ in millions

Fiscal Years Ended	March 3, 2007	February 25, 2006	February 26, 2005
Operating Activities			
Net earnings	$1,377	$1,140	$ 984
Gain from disposal of discontinued operations, net of tax	—	—	(50)
Earnings from continuing operations	1,377	1,140	934
Adjustments to reconcile earnings from continuing operations to total cash provided by operating activities from continuing operations:			
Depreciation	509	456	459
Asset impairment charges	32	4	22
Stock-based compensation	121	132	(1)
Deferred income taxes	82	(151)	(28)
Excess tax benefits from stock-based compensation	(50)	(55)	—
Other, net	(11)	(3)	24
Changes in operating assets and liabilities, net of acquired assets and liabilities:			
Receivables	(70)	(43)	(30)
Merchandise inventories	(550)	(457)	(240)
Other assets	(47)	(11)	(50)
Accounts payable	320	385	347
Other liabilities	185	165	243
Accrued income taxes	(136)	178	301
Total cash provided by operating activities from continuing operations	1,762	1,740	1,981
Investing Activities			
Additions to property and equipment, net of $75 and $117 noncash capital expenditures in fiscal 2006 and 2005, respectively	(733)	(648)	(502)
Purchases of available-for-sale securities	(4,541)	(4,319)	(8,517)
Sales of available-for-sale securities	4,886	4,187	7,730
Acquisitions of businesses, net of cash acquired	(421)	—	—
Proceeds from disposition of investments	24	—	—
Change in restricted assets	—	(20)	(140)
Other, net	5	46	7
Total cash used in investing activities from continuing operations	(780)	(754)	(1,422)
Financing Activities			
Repurchase of common stock	(599)	(772)	(200)
Issuance of common stock under employee stock purchase plan and for the exercise of stock options	217	292	256
Dividends paid	(174)	(151)	(137)
Repayments of debt	(84)	(69)	(371)
Proceeds from issuance of debt	96	36	—
Excess tax benefits from stock-based compensation	50	55	—
Other, net	(19)	(10)	(7)
Total cash used in financing activities from continuing operations	(513)	(619)	(459)
Effect of Exchange Rate Changes on Cash	(12)	27	9
Increase in Cash and Cash Equivalents	457	394	109
Cash and Cash Equivalents at Beginning of Year	748	354	245
Cash and Cash Equivalents at End of Year	$1,205	$ 748	$ 354
Supplemental Disclosure of Cash Flow Information			
Income taxes paid	$ 804	$ 547	$ 241
Interest paid	14	16	35

SELECTED Notes to Consolidated Financial Statements

$ in millions, except per share amounts

1. Summary of Significant Accounting Policies

Description of Business

Best Buy Co., Inc. is a specialty retailer of consumer electronics, home-office products, entertainment software, appliances and related services, with fiscal 2007 revenue from continuing operations of $35.9 billion.

We operate two reportable segments: Domestic and International. The Domestic segment is comprised of all U.S. store and online operations of Best Buy, Geek Squad, Magnolia Audio Video and Pacific Sales Kitchen and Bath Centers, Inc. ("Pacific Sales"). We acquired Pacific Sales on March 7, 2006. U.S. Best Buy stores offer a wide variety of consumer electronics, home-office products, entertainment software, appliances and related services through 822 stores at the end of fiscal 2007. Geek Squad provides residential and commercial computer repair, support and installation services in all U.S. Best Buy stores and at 12 stand-alone stores at the end of fiscal 2007. Magnolia Audio Video stores offer high-end audio and video products and related services through 20 stores at the end of fiscal 2007. Pacific Sales stores offer high-end home-improvement products, appliances and related services through 14 stores at the end of fiscal 2007.

Fiscal Year

Our fiscal year ends on the Saturday nearest the end of February. Fiscal 2007 included 53 weeks and fiscal 2006 and 2005 each included 52 weeks.

Cash and Cash Equivalents

Cash primarily consists of cash on hand and bank deposits. Cash equivalents primarily consist of money market accounts and other highly liquid investments with an original maturity of three months or less when purchased. We carry these investments at cost, which approximates market value. The amounts of cash equivalents at March 3, 2007, and February 25, 2006, were $695 and $350, respectively, and the weighted-average interest rates were 4.8% and 3.3%, respectively.

Outstanding checks in excess of funds on deposit ("book overdrafts") totaled $183 and $230 at March 3, 2007, and February 25, 2006, respectively, and are reflected as current liabilities in our consolidated balance sheets.

Merchandise Inventories

Merchandise inventories are recorded at the lower of average cost or market. In-bound freight-related costs from our vendors are included as part of the net cost of merchandise inventories. Also included in the cost of inventory are certain vendor allowances that are not a reimbursement of specific, incremental and identifiable costs to promote a vendor's products. Other costs associated with acquiring, storing and transporting merchandise inventories to our retail stores are expensed as incurred and included in cost of goods sold.

Our inventory loss reserve represents anticipated physical inventory losses (e.g., theft) that have occurred since the last physical inventory date. Independent physical inventory counts are taken on a regular basis to ensure that the inventory reported in our consolidated financial statements is properly stated. During the interim period between physical inventory counts, we reserve for anticipated physical inventory losses on a location-by-location basis.

Property and Equipment

Property and equipment are recorded at cost. We compute depreciation using the straight-line method over the estimated useful lives of the assets. Leasehold improvements are depreciated over the shorter of their estimated useful lives or the period from the date the assets are placed in service to the end of the initial lease term. Leasehold improvements made significantly after the initial lease term are depreciated over the shorter of their estimated useful lives or the remaining lease term, including renewal periods, if reasonably assured.

$ in millions, except per share amounts

Accelerated depreciation methods are generally used for income tax purposes.

When property is fully depreciated, retired or otherwise disposed of, the cost and accumulated depreciation are removed from the accounts and any resulting gain or loss is reflected in the consolidated statement of earnings.

Repairs and maintenance costs are charged directly to expense as incurred. Major renewals or replacements that substantially extend the useful life of an asset are capitalized and depreciated.

Estimated useful lives by major asset category are as follows:

Asset	Life (in years)
Buildings	30–40
Leasehold improvements	3–25
Fixtures and equipment	3–20
Property under capital lease	3–20

Impairment of Long-Lived Assets

We account for the impairment or disposal of long-lived assets in accordance with SFAS No. 144, *Accounting for the Impairment* or *Disposal of Long-Lived Assets,* which requires long-lived assets, such as property and equipment, to be evaluated for impairment whenever events or changes in circumstances indicate the carrying value of an asset may not be recoverable. Factors considered important that could result in an impairment review include, but are not limited to, significant underperformance relative to historical or planned operating results, significant changes in the manner of use of the assets or significant changes in our business strategies. An impairment loss is recognized when the estimated undiscounted cash flows expected to result from the use of the asset plus net proceeds expected from disposition of the asset (if any) are less than the carrying value of the asset. When an impairment loss is recognized, the carrying amount of the asset is reduced to its estimated fair value based on quoted market prices or other valuation techniques.

Leases

We conduct the majority of our retail and distribution operations from leased locations. The leases require payment of real estate taxes, insurance and common area maintenance, in addition to rent. The terms of our lease agreements generally range from 10 to 20 years. Most of the leases contain renewal options and escalation clauses, and certain store leases require contingent rents based on factors such as specified percentages of revenue or the consumer price index. Other leases contain covenants related to the maintenance of financial ratios.

Goodwill and Intangible Assets

Goodwill

Goodwill is the excess of the purchase price over the fair value of identifiable net assets acquired in business combinations accounted for under the purchase method. We do not amortize goodwill but test it for impairment annually, or when indications of potential impairment exist, utilizing a fair value approach at the reporting unit level. A reporting unit is the operating segment, or a business unit one level below that operating segment, for which discrete financial information is prepared and regularly reviewed by segment management.

Tradenames

We have an indefinite-lived intangible asset related to our Pacific Sales tradename which is included in the Domestic segment. We also have indefinite-lived intangible assets related to our Future Shop and Five Star tradenames which are included in the International segment.

We determine fair values utilizing widely accepted valuation techniques, including discounted cash flows and market multiple analyses. During the fourth quarter of fiscal 2007, we completed our annual impairment testing of our goodwill and tradenames, using the valuation techniques as described above, and determined there was no impairment.

Lease Rights

Lease rights represent costs incurred to acquire the lease of a specific commercial property. Lease rights are recorded at cost and are amortized to rent expense over the remaining lease term, including renewal periods, if reasonably assured. Amortization periods range up to 16 years, beginning with the date we take possession of the property.

$ in millions, except per share amounts

Investments

Short-term and long-term investments are comprised of municipal and United States government debt securities as well as auction-rate securities and variable-rate demand notes. In accordance with SFAS No. 115, *Accounting for Certain Investments in Debt and Equity Securities,* and based on our ability to market and sell these instruments, we classify auction-rate securities, variable-rate demand notes and other investments in debt securities as available-for-sale and carry them at amortized cost, which approximates fair value. Auction-rate securities and variable-rate demand notes are similar to short-term debt instruments because their interest rates are reset periodically. Investments in these securities can be sold for cash on the auction date. We classify auction-rate securities and variable-rate demand notes as short-term or long-term investments based on the reset dates.

We also hold investments in marketable equity securities and classify them as available-for-sale. Investments in marketable equity securities are included in other assets in our consolidated balance sheets. Investments in marketable equity securities are reported at fair value, based on quoted market prices when available. All unrealized holding gains or losses are reflected net of tax in accumulated other comprehensive income in shareholders' equity.

We review the key characteristics of our debt and marketable equity securities portfolio and their classification in accordance with GAAP on an annual basis, or when indications of potential impairment exist. If a decline in the fair value of a security is deemed by management to be other than temporary, the cost basis of the investment is written down to fair value, and the amount of the write-down is included in the determination of net earnings.

Income Taxes

We account for income taxes under the liability method. Under this method, deferred tax assets and liabilities are recognized for the estimated future tax consequences attributable to differences between the financial statement carrying amounts of existing assets and liabilities and their respective tax bases, and operating loss and tax credit carryforwards. Deferred tax assets and liabilities are measured using enacted income tax rates in effect for the year in which those temporary differences are expected to be recovered or settled. The effect on deferred tax assets and liabilities of a change in income tax rates is recognized in our consolidated statement of earnings in the period that includes the enactment date. A valuation allowance is recorded to reduce the carrying amounts of deferred tax assets if it is more likely than not that such assets will not be realized.

Long-Term Liabilities

The major components of long-term liabilities at March 3, 2007, and February 25, 2006, included long-term rent-related liabilities, deferred compensation plan liabilities, self-insurance reserves and advances received under vendor alliance programs.

Foreign Currency

Foreign currency denominated assets and liabilities are translated into U.S. dollars using the exchange rates in effect at our consolidated balance sheet date. Results of operations and cash flows are translated using the average exchange rates throughout the period. The effect of exchange rate fluctuations on translation of assets and liabilities is included as a component of shareholders' equity in accumulated other comprehensive income. Gains and losses from foreign currency transactions, which are included in SG&A, have not been significant.

Revenue Recognition

We recognize revenue when the sales price is fixed or determinable, collectibility is reasonably assured and the customer takes possession of the merchandise, or in the case of services, at the time the service is provided.

$ in millions, except per share amounts

Amounts billed to customers for shipping and handling are included in revenue. Revenue is reported net of estimated sales returns and excludes sales taxes.

We estimate our sales returns reserve based on historical return rates. We initially established our sales returns reserve in the fourth quarter of fiscal 2005. Our sales returns reserve was $104 and $78, at March 3, 2007, and February 25, 2006, respectively.

We sell extended service contracts on behalf of an unrelated third party. In jurisdictions where we are not deemed to be the obligor on the contract, commissions are recognized in revenue at the time of sale. In jurisdictions where we are deemed to be the obligor on the contract, commissions are recognized in revenue ratably over the term of the service contract. Commissions represented 2.2%, 2.5% and 2.6% of revenues in fiscal 2007, 2006 and 2005, respectively.

For revenue transactions that involve multiple deliverables, we defer the revenue associated with any undelivered elements. The amount of revenue deferred in connection with the undelivered elements is determined using the relative fair value of each element, which is generally based on each element's relative retail price. See additional information regarding our customer loyalty program in *Sales Incentives* below.

Gift Cards

We sell gift cards to our customers in our retail stores, through our Web sites, and through selected third parties. We do not charge administrative fees on unused gift cards and our gift cards do not have an expiration date. We recognize income from gift cards when: (i) the gift card is redeemed by the customer; or (ii) the likelihood of the gift card being redeemed by the customer is remote ("gift card breakage") and we determine that we do not have a legal obligation to remit the value of unredeemed gift cards to the relevant jurisdictions. We determine our gift card breakage rate based upon historical redemption patterns. Based on our historical information, the likelihood of a gift card remaining unredeemed can be determined 24 months after the gift card is issued. At that time, we recognize breakage income for those cards for which the likelihood of redemption is deemed remote and we do not have a legal obligation to remit the value of such unredeemed gift cards to the relevant jurisdictions. Gift card breakage income is included in revenue in our consolidated statements of earnings.

We began recognizing gift card breakage income during the third quarter of fiscal 2006. Gift card breakage income was as follows in fiscal 2007, 2006 and 2005:

	2007[1]	2006[1]	2005
Gift card breakage income	$46	$43	$ —

(1) Due to the resolution of certain legal matters associated with gift card liabilities, we recognized $19 and $27 of gift card breakage income in fiscal 2007 and 2006, respectively, that related to prior fiscal years.

Sales Incentives

We frequently offer sales incentives that entitle our customers to receive a reduction in the price of a product or service. Sales incentives include discounts, coupons and other offers that entitle a customer to receive a reduction in the price of a product or service by submitting a claim for a refund or rebate. For sales incentives issued to a customer in conjunction with a sale of merchandise or services, for which we are the obligor, the reduction in revenue is recognized at the time of sale, based on the retail value of the incentive expected to be redeemed.

Customer Loyalty Program

We have a customer loyalty program which allows members to earn points for each qualifying purchase. Points earned enable members to receive a certificate that may be redeemed on future purchases at U.S. Best Buy stores.

BEST BUY

$ in millions, except per share amounts

Cost of Goods Sold and Selling, General and Administrative Expenses

The following table illustrates the primary costs classified in each major expense category:

Cost of Goods Sold	SG&A
• Total cost of products sold including: —Freight expenses associated with moving merchandise inventories from our vendors to our distribution centers; —Vendor allowances that are not a reimbursement of specific, incremental and identifiable costs to promote a vendor's products; and —Cash discounts on payments to vendors; • Cost of services provided including: —Payroll and benefits costs for services employees; and —Cost of replacement parts and related freight expenses; • Physical inventory losses; • Markdowns; • Customer shipping and handling expenses; • Costs associated with operating our distribution network, including payroll and benefit costs, occupancy costs, and depreciation; • Freight expenses associated with moving merchandise inventories from our distribution centers to our retail stores; and • Promotional financing costs.	• Payroll and benefit costs for retail and corporate employees; • Occupancy costs of retail, services and corporate facilities; • Depreciation related to retail, services and corporate assets; • Advertising; • Vendor allowances that are a reimbursement of specific, incremental and identifiable costs to promote a vendor's products; • Charitable contributions; • Outside service fees; • Long-lived asset impairment charges; and • Other administrative costs, such as credit card service fees, supplies, and travel and lodging.

Advertising Costs

Advertising costs, which are included in SG&A, are expensed the first time the advertisement runs. Advertising costs consist primarily of print and television advertisements as well as promotional events. Net advertising expenses were $692, $644 and $597 in fiscal 2007, 2006 and 2005, respectively. Allowances received from vendors for advertising of $140, $123 and $115, in fiscal 2007, 2006 and 2005, respectively, were classified as reductions of advertising expenses.

$ in millions, except per share amounts

4. Investments

Short-Term and Long-Term Investments

The following table presents the amortized principal amounts, related weighted-average interest rates, maturities and major security types for our investments:

	March 3, 2007		Feb. 25, 2006	
	Amortized Principal Amount	Weighted-Average Interest Rate	Amortized Principal Amount	Weighted-Average Interest Rate
Short-term investments (less than one year)	$2,588	5.68%	$3,041	4.76%
Long-term investments (one to three years)	318	5.68%	218	4.95%
Total	$2,906		$3,259	
Municipal debt securities	$2,840		$3,155	
Auction-rate and asset-backed securities	66		97	
Debt securities issued by U.S. Treasury and other U.S. government entities	—		7	
Total	$2,906		$3,259	

The carrying value of our investments approximated fair value at March 3, 2007, and February 25, 2006, due to the rapid turnover of our portfolio and the highly liquid nature of these investments. Therefore, there were no significant realized or unrealized gains or losses.

Marketable Equity Securities

The carrying values of our investments in marketable equity securities at March 3, 2007, and February 25, 2006, were $4 and $28, respectively. Net unrealized (loss)/gain, net of tax, included in accumulated other comprehensive income was ($1) and $12 at March 3, 2007, and February 25, 2006, respectively.

$ in millions, except per share amounts

5. Debt

Short-term debt consisted of the following:

	March 3, 2007	Feb. 25, 2006
Notes payable to banks, secured, interest rates ranging from 3.5% to 6.7%	$ 21	$ —
Revolving credit facility, secured, variable interest rate of 5.6% at March 3, 2007	20	—
Total short-term debt	$ 41	$ —
Weighted-average interest rate	5.3%	—

Long-term debt consisted of the following:

	March 3, 2007	Feb. 25, 2006
Convertible subordinated debentures, unsecured, due 2022, interest rate 2.25%	$402	$ 402
Financing lease obligations, due 2009 to 2023, interest rates ranging from 3.0% to 6.5%	171	157
Capital lease obligations, due 2008 to 2026, interest rates ranging from 1.8% to 8.0%	24	27
Other debt, due 2010, interest rate 8.8%	12	10
Total debt	609	596
Less: current portion[1]	(19)	(418)
Total long-term debt	$590	$ 178

(1) Since holders of our debentures due in 2022 could have required us to purchase all or a portion of their debentures on January 15, 2007, we classified our debentures in the current portion of long-term debt at February 25, 2006. However, no holders of our debentures exercised this put option on January 15, 2007. The next time the holders of our debentures could require us to purchase all or a portion of their debentures is January 15, 2012. Therefore, we classified our debentures as long-term debt at March 3, 2007.

Certain debt is secured by property and equipment with a net book value of $80 and $41 at March 3, 2007, and February 25, 2006, respectively.

Convertible Debentures

In January 2002, we sold convertible subordinated debentures having an aggregate principal amount of $402. The proceeds from the offering, net of $6 in offering expenses, were $396. The debentures mature in 2022 and are callable at par, at our option, for cash on or after January 15, 2007.

Holders may require us to purchase all or a portion of their debentures on January 15, 2012, and January 15, 2017, at a purchase price equal to 100% of the principal amount of the debentures plus accrued and unpaid interest up to but not including the date of purchase. We have the option to settle the purchase price in cash, stock, or a combination of cash and stock.

$ in millions, except per share amounts

Other

The fair value of debt approximated $683 and $693 at March 3, 2007, and February 25, 2006, respectively, based on the ask prices quoted from external sources, compared with carrying values of $650 and $596, respectively.

At March 3, 2007, the future maturities of long-term debt, including capitalized leases, consisted of the following:

Fiscal Year	
2008	$ 19
2009	18
2010	27
2011	18
2012	420
Thereafter	107
	$609

Earnings per Share

Our basic earnings per share calculation is computed based on the weighted-average number of common shares outstanding. Our diluted earnings per share calculation is computed based on the weighted-average number of common shares outstanding adjusted by the number of additional shares that would have been outstanding had the potentially dilutive common shares been issued. Potentially dilutive shares of common stock include stock options, nonvested share awards and shares issuable under our ESPP, as well as common shares that would have resulted from the assumed conversion of our convertible debentures. Since the potentially dilutive shares related to the convertible debentures are included in the calculation, the related interest expense, net of tax, is added back to earnings from continuing operations, as the interest would not have been paid if the convertible debentures had been converted to common stock. Nonvested market-based share awards and nonvested performance-based share awards are included in the average diluted shares outstanding each period if established market or performance criteria have been met at the end of the respective periods.

The following table presents a reconciliation of the numerators and denominators of basic and diluted earnings per share from continuing operations in fiscal 2007, 2006 and 2005:

	2007	2006	2005
Numerator:			
Earnings from continuing operations, basic	$1,377	$1,140	$ 934
Adjustment for assumed dilution:			
Interest on convertible debentures due in 2022, net of tax	7	7	7
Earnings from continuing operations, diluted	$1,384	$1,147	$ 941
Denominator (in millions):			
Weighted-average common shares outstanding	482.1	490.3	488.9
Effect of potentially dilutive securities:			
Shares from assumed conversion of convertible debentures	8.8	8.8	8.8
Stock options and other	5.3	5.7	7.3
Weighted-average common shares outstanding, assuming dilution	496.2	504.8	505.0
Basic earnings per share — continuing operations	$ 2.86	$ 2.33	$ 1.91
Diluted earnings per share — continuing operations	$ 2.79	$ 2.27	$ 1.86

$ in millions, except per share amounts

Comprehensive Income

Comprehensive income is computed as net earnings plus certain other items that are recorded directly to shareholders' equity. In addition to net earnings, the significant components of comprehensive income include foreign currency translation adjustments and unrealized gains and losses, net of tax, on available-for-sale marketable equity securities. Foreign currency translation adjustments do not include a provision for income tax expense when earnings from foreign operations are considered to be indefinitely reinvested outside the United States. Comprehensive income was $1,332, $1,252 and $1,047 in fiscal 2007, 2006 and 2005, respectively.

7. Net Interest Income

Net interest income was comprised of the following in fiscal 2007, 2006 and 2005:

	2007	2006	2005
Interest income	$142	$103	$ 45
Interest expense	(31)	(30)	(44)
Dividend income	—	4	—
Net interest income	$111	$ 77	$ 1

8. Leases

The composition of net rent expense for all operating leases, including leases of property and equipment, was as follows in fiscal 2007, 2006 and 2005:

	2007	2006	2005
Minimum rentals	$679	$569	$516
Contingent rentals	1	1	1
Total rent expense	680	570	517
Less: sublease income	(20)	(18)	(16)
Net rent expense	$660	$552	$501

$ in millions, except per share amounts

The future minimum lease payments under our capital, financing and operating leases by fiscal year (not including contingent rentals) at March 3, 2007, were as follows:

Fiscal Year	Capital Leases	Financing Leases	Operating Leases
2008	$ 6	$ 23	$ 741
2009	4	23	715
2010	4	23	672
2011	3	23	632
2012	1	23	592
Thereafter	17	112	3,316
Subtotal	35	227	$6,668
Less: imputed interest	(11)	(56)	
Present value of lease obligations	$24	$171	

Total minimum lease payments have not been reduced by minimum sublease rent income of approximately $119 due under future noncancelable subleases.

10. Income Taxes

The following is a reconciliation of the federal statutory income tax rate to income tax expense from continuing operations in fiscal 2007, 2006 and 2005:

	2007	2006	2005
Federal income tax at the statutory rate	$ 747	$ 603	$ 505
State income taxes, net of federal benefit	38	34	29
Benefit from foreign operations	(36)	(37)	(7)
Non-taxable interest income	(34)	(28)	(22)
Other	37	9	4
Income tax expense	$ 752	$ 581	$ 509
Effective income tax rate	35.3%	33.7%	35.3%

Income tax expense was comprised of the following in fiscal 2007, 2006 and 2005:

	2007	2006	2005
Current:			
Federal	$609	$640	$502
State	45	78	36
Foreign	16	14	(1)
	670	732	537
Deferred:			
Federal	51	(131)	(4)
State	19	(14)	(20)
Foreign	12	(6)	(4)
	82	(151)	(28)
Income tax expense	$752	$581	$509

Deferred taxes are the result of differences between the bases of assets and liabilities for financial reporting and income tax purposes.

BEST BUY

$ in millions, except per share amounts

11. Segment and Geographic Information

Segment Information

We operate two reportable segments: Domestic and International. The Domestic segment is comprised of U.S. store and online operations, including Best Buy, Geek Squad, Magnolia Audio Video and Pacific Sales. The International segment is comprised of all Canada store and online operations, including Best Buy, Future Shop and Geek Squad, as well as our Five Star and Best Buy retail and online operations in China.

The following tables present our business segment information for continuing operations in fiscal 2007, 2006 and 2005:

	2007	2006	2005
Revenue			
Domestic	$31,031	$27,380	$24,616
International	4,903	3,468	2,817
Total revenue	$35,934	$30,848	$27,433
Operating Income			
Domestic	$ 1,889	$ 1,588	$ 1,393
International	110	56	49
Total operating income	1,999	1,644	1,442
Net interest income	111	77	1
Gain on investments	20	—	—
Earnings from continuing operations before income tax expense	$ 2,130	$ 1,721	$ 1,443
Assets			
Domestic	$10,614	$ 9,722	$ 8,372
International	2,956	2,142	1,922
Total assets	$13,570	$11,864	$10,294

12. Contingencies and Commitments

Contingencies

On December 8, 2005, a purported class action lawsuit captioned, *Jasmen Holloway, et cl. v. Best Buy Co., Inc.*, was filed in the U.S. District Court for the Northern District of California alleging we discriminate against women and minority individuals on the basis of gender, race, color and/or national origin with respect to our employment policies and practices. The action seeks an end to discriminatory policies and practices, an award of back and front pay, punitive damages and injunctive relief, including rightful place relief for all class members. As of March 3, 2007, no accrual had been established as it was not possible to estimate the possible loss or range of loss because this matter had not advanced to a stage where we could make any such estimate. We believe the allegations are without merit and intend to defend this action vigorously.

We are involved in various other legal proceedings arising in the normal course of conducting business. We believe the amounts provided in our consolidated financial statements, as prescribed by GAAP, are adequate in light of the probable and estimable liabilities. The resolution of those other proceedings is not expected to have a material impact on our results of operations or financial condition.

Commitments

We engage Accenture LLP ("Accenture") to assist us with improving our operational capabilities and reducing our costs in the information systems, procurement and human resources areas. Our future contractual obligations to Accenture are expected to range from $76 to $334 per year through 2012, the end of the contract period. Prior to our engagement of Accenture, a significant portion of these costs were incurred as part of normal operations.

We had outstanding letters of credit for purchase obligations with a fair value of $85 at March 3, 2007.

At March 3, 2007, we had commitments for the purchase and construction of facilities valued at approximately $69. Also, at March 3, 2007, we had entered into lease commitments for land and buildings for 115 future locations. These lease commitments with real estate developers provide for minimum rentals ranging from seven to 20 years, which if consummated based on current cost estimates, will approximate $84 annually over the initial lease terms. These minimum rentals have been included in the future minimum lease payments included in Note 8, Leases.

Financial Reports

CIRCUIT CITY STORES, INC.

CIRCUIT CITY

Circuit City Stores, Inc.
CONSOLIDATED BALANCE SHEETS

(Amounts in thousands except share data)	At February 28 2007	2006
ASSETS		
CURRENT ASSETS:		
Cash and cash equivalents	**$ 141,141**	$ 315,970
Short-term investments	**598,341**	521,992
Accounts receivable, net of allowance for doubtful accounts	**382,555**	220,869
Merchandise inventory	**1,636,507**	1,698,026
Deferred income taxes	**34,868**	29,598
Income tax receivable	**42,722**	5,571
Prepaid expenses and other current assets	**47,378**	41,315
TOTAL CURRENT ASSETS	**2,883,512**	2,833,341
Property and equipment, net of accumulated depreciation	**921,027**	839,356
Deferred income taxes	**31,910**	97,889
Goodwill	**121,774**	223,999
Other intangible assets, net of accumulated amortization	**19,285**	30,372
Other assets	**29,775**	44,087
TOTAL ASSETS	**$4,007,283**	$4,069,044
LIABILITIES AND STOCKHOLDERS' EQUITY		
CURRENT LIABILITIES:		
Merchandise payable	**$ 922,205**	$ 850,359
Expenses payable	**281,709**	202,300
Accrued expenses and other current liabilities	**404,444**	379,768
Accrued compensation	**98,509**	84,743
Accrued income taxes	**–**	75,909
Short-term debt	**–**	22,003
Current installments of long-term debt	**7,162**	7,248
TOTAL CURRENT LIABILITIES	**1,714,029**	1,622,330
Long-term debt, excluding current installments	**50,487**	51,985
Accrued straight-line rent and deferred rent credits	**277,636**	256,120
Accrued lease termination costs	**76,326**	79,091
Other liabilities	**97,561**	104,885
TOTAL LIABILITIES	**2,216,039**	2,114,411
Commitments and contingent liabilities		
STOCKHOLDERS' EQUITY:		
Common stock, $0.50 par value; 525,000,000 shares authorized; 170,689,406 shares issued and outstanding (174,789,390 in 2006)	**85,345**	87,395
Additional paid-in capital	**344,144**	458,211
Retained earnings	**1,336,317**	1,364,740
Accumulated other comprehensive income	**25,438**	44,287
TOTAL STOCKHOLDERS' EQUITY	**1,791,244**	1,954,633
TOTAL LIABILITIES AND STOCKHOLDERS' EQUITY	**$4,007,283**	$4,069,044

Circuit City Stores, Inc.
CONSOLIDATED STATEMENTS OF OPERATIONS

(Amounts in thousands except per share data)	Years Ended February 28 2007	%	2006	%	2005	%
NET SALES	**$12,429,754**	100.0	$11,514,151	100.0	$10,413,524	100.0
Cost of sales, buying and warehousing	**9,501,438**	76.4	8,703,683	75.6	7,861,364	75.5
GROSS PROFIT	**2,928,316**	23.6	2,810,468	24.4	2,552,160	24.5
Selling, general and administrative expenses	**2,841,619**	22.9	2,595,706	22.5	2,470,712	23.7
Impairment of goodwill	**92,000**	0.7	–	–	–	–
Finance income	**–**	**–**	–	–	5,564	0.1
OPERATING (LOSS) INCOME	**(5,303)**	–	214,762	1.9	87,012	0.8
Interest income	**27,150**	0.2	21,826	0.2	14,404	0.1
Interest expense	**1,519**	–	3,143	–	4,451	–
Earnings from continuing operations before income taxes	**20,328**	0.2	233,445	2.0	96,965	0.9
Income tax expense	**30,510**	0.2	85,996	0.7	36,396	0.3
NET (LOSS) EARNINGS FROM CONTINUING OPERATIONS	**(10,182)**	(0.1)	147,449	1.3	60,569	0.6
EARNINGS (LOSS) FROM DISCONTINUED OPERATIONS, NET OF TAX	**128**	**–**	(5,350)	–	1,089	–
CUMULATIVE EFFECT OF CHANGE IN ACCOUNTING PRINCIPLES, NET OF TAX	**1,773**	–	(2,353)	–	–	–
NET (LOSS) EARNINGS	**$ (8,281)**	(0.1)	$ 139,746	1.2	$ 61,658	0.6

	2007	2006	2005
Weighted average common shares:			
Basic	**170,448**	177,456	193,466
Diluted	**170,448**	180,653	196,227
(LOSS) EARNINGS PER SHARE:			
Basic:			
Continuing operations	**$ (0.06)**	$ 0.83	$ 0.31
Discontinued operations	**$ –**	$ (0.03)	$ 0.01
Cumulative effect of change in accounting principles	**$ 0.01**	$ (0.01)	$ –
Basic (loss) earnings per share	**$ (0.05)**	$ 0.79	$ 0.32
Diluted:			
Continuing operations	**$ (0.06)**	$ 0.82	$ 0.31
Discontinued operations	**$ –**	$ (0.03)	$ 0.01
Cumulative effect of change in accounting principles	**$ 0.01**	$ (0.01)	$ –
Diluted (loss) earnings per share	**$ (0.05)**	$ 0.77	$ 0.31

Circuit City Stores, Inc.

CONSOLIDATED STATEMENTS OF STOCKHOLDERS' EQUITY AND COMPREHENSIVE INCOME

(Amounts in thousands except per share data)	Common Stock Shares	Common Stock Amount	Additional Paid-in Capital	Retained Earnings	Accumulated Other Comprehensive Income	Total
BALANCE AT FEBRUARY 29, 2004	203,899	$101,950	$922,600	$1,191,904	$ –	$2,216,454
Comprehensive income:						
Net earnings	–	–	–	61,658	–	61,658
Other comprehensive income, net of taxes:						
Foreign currency translation adjustment (net of deferred taxes of $13,707)	–	–	–	–	25,100	25,100
Comprehensive income						86,758
Repurchases of common stock	(19,163)	(9,582)	(250,250)	–	–	(259,832)
Compensation for stock awards	–	–	18,305	–	–	18,305
Exercise of common stock options	3,489	1,745	26,761	–	–	28,506
Shares issued under stock-based incentive plans, net of cancellations, and other	(75)	(38)	(1,312)	–	–	(1,350)
Tax effect from stock issued	–	–	(1,564)	–	–	(1,564)
Shares issued in acquisition of InterTAN, Inc.	–	–	6,498	–	–	6,498
Dividends – common stock ($0.07 per share)	–	–	–	(13,848)	–	(13,848)
BALANCE AT FEBRUARY 28, 2005	188,150	94,075	721,038	1,239,714	25,100	2,079,927
Comprehensive income:						
Net earnings	–	–	–	139,746	–	139,746
Other comprehensive income (loss), net of taxes:						
Foreign currency translation adjustment (net of deferred taxes of $11,316)	–	–	–	–	19,500	19,500
Minimum pension liability adjustment (net of deferred taxes of $182)	–	–	–	–	(313)	(313)
Comprehensive income						158,933
Repurchases of common stock	(19,396)	(9,698)	(328,778)	–	–	(338,476)
Compensation for stock awards	–	–	24,386	–	–	24,386
Exercise of common stock options	3,830	1,915	36,752	–	–	38,667
Shares issued under stock-based incentive plans, net of cancellations, and other	2,205	1,103	(2,160)	–	–	(1,057)
Tax effect from stock issued	–	–	6,973	–	–	6,973
Redemption of preferred share purchase rights	–	–	–	(1,876)	–	(1,876)
Dividends – common stock ($0.07 per share)	–	–	–	(12,844)	–	(12,844)
BALANCE AT FEBRUARY 28, 2006	174,789	87,395	458,211	1,364,740	44,287	1,954,633
Comprehensive loss:						
Net loss	–	–	–	(8,281)	–	(8,281)
Other comprehensive (loss) income, net of taxes:						
Foreign currency translation adjustment (net of deferred taxes of $3,630)	–	–	–	–	(7,793)	(7,793)
Unrealized gain on available-for-sale securities (net of deferred taxes of $219)	–	–	–	–	377	377
Minimum pension liability adjustment (net of deferred taxes of $136)	–	–	–	–	(229)	(229)
Comprehensive loss						(15,926)
Adjustment to initially apply SFAS No. 158 (net of deferred taxes of $6,628)	–	–	–	–	(11,204)	(11,204)
Repurchases of common stock	(10,032)	(5,016)	(232,187)	–	–	(237,203)
Compensation for stock awards	–	–	26,727	–	–	26,727
Adjustment to initially apply SFAS No. 123(R)	–	–	(2,370)	–	–	(2,370)
Exercise of common stock options, net	5,767	2,883	86,228	–	–	89,111
Shares issued under stock-based incentive plans, net of cancellations, and other	165	83	(1,027)	–	–	(944)
Tax effect from stock issued	–	–	8,562	–	–	8,562
Dividends – common stock ($0.115 per share)	–	–	–	(20,142)	–	(20,142)
BALANCE AT FEBRUARY 28, 2007	170,689	$85,345	$344,144	$1,336,317	$25,438	$1,791,244

Circuit City Stores, Inc.

CONSOLIDATED STATEMENTS OF CASH FLOWS

(Amounts in thousands)	Years Ended February 28 **2007**	2006	2005[a]
OPERATING ACTIVITIES:			
Net (loss) earnings	$ **(8,281)**	$ 139,746	$ 61,658
Adjustments to reconcile net (loss) earnings to net cash provided by operating activities of continuing operations:			
Net (earnings) loss from discontinued operations	**(128)**	5,350	(1,089)
Depreciation expense	**177,828**	160,608	151,597
Amortization expense	**3,645**	2,618	1,851
Impairment of goodwill	**92,000**	–	–
Stock-based compensation expense	**26,727**	24,386	18,305
(Gain) loss on dispositions of property and equipment	**(1,439)**	2,370	(206)
Provision for deferred income taxes	**72,717**	(14,252)	(116,300)
Cumulative effect of change in accounting principles	**(1,773)**	2,353	–
Other	**1,689**	(1,726)	–
Changes in operating assets and liabilities:			
Accounts receivable, net	**(133,152)**	16,552	(58,738)
Retained interests in securitized receivables	**–**	–	32,867
Merchandise inventory	**49,352**	(231,114)	160,037
Prepaid expenses and other current assets	**(9,580)**	(17,341)	7,207
Other assets	**535**	(3,061)	3,816
Merchandise payable	**73,317**	211,362	28,199
Expenses payable	**55,722**	40,921	(17,372)
Accrued expenses and other current liabilities, and accrued income taxes	**(81,364)**	43,202	54,021
Other long-term liabilities	**(1,474)**	(17,032)	63,494
NET CASH PROVIDED BY OPERATING ACTIVITIES OF CONTINUING OPERATIONS	**316,341**	364,942	389,347
INVESTING ACTIVITIES:			
Purchases of property and equipment	**(285,725)**	(254,451)	(261,461)
Proceeds from sales of property and equipment	**38,620**	55,421	106,369
Purchases of investment securities	**(2,002,123)**	(1,409,760)	(125,325)
Sales and maturities of investment securities	**1,926,086**	1,014,910	–
Other investing activities	**(11,567)**	–	–
Proceeds from the sale of the private-label finance operation	**–**	–	475,857
Acquisitions, net of cash acquired of $30,615	**–**	–	(262,320)
NET CASH USED IN INVESTING ACTIVITIES OF CONTINUING OPERATIONS	**(334,709)**	(593,880)	(66,880)
FINANCING ACTIVITIES:			
Proceeds from short-term borrowings	**35,657**	73,954	12,329
Principal payments on short-term borrowings	**(56,912)**	(53,893)	(13,458)
Proceeds from long-term debt	**1,216**	1,032	–
Principal payments on long-term debt	**(6,724)**	(1,829)	(28,008)
Changes in overdraft balances	**19,347**	(22,540)	36,329
Repurchases of common stock	**(237,203)**	(338,476)	(259,832)
Issuances of common stock	**89,662**	38,038	27,156
Dividends paid	**(20,126)**	(12,844)	(13,848)
Excess tax benefit from stock-based payments	**15,729**	–	–
Redemption of preferred share purchase rights	**–**	(1,876)	–
Other financing activities	**(1,424)**	–	–
NET CASH USED IN FINANCING ACTIVITIES OF CONTINUING OPERATIONS	**(160,778)**	(318,434)	(239,332)
DISCONTINUED OPERATIONS:			
Operating cash flows	**3,310**	(9,884)	(7,193)
Investing cash flows	**2,958**	(8,089)	(6,615)
Financing cash flows	**(592)**	–	(724)
NET CASH PROVIDED BY (USED IN) DISCONTINUED OPERATIONS	**5,676**	(17,973)	(14,532)
EFFECT OF EXCHANGE RATE CHANGES ON CASH	**(1,359)**	1,655	2,016
(Decrease) increase in cash and cash equivalents	**(174,829)**	(563,690)	70,619
Cash and cash equivalents at beginning of year	**315,970**	879,660	809,041
CASH AND CASH EQUIVALENTS AT END OF YEAR	$ **141,141**	$ 315,970	$879,660

CIRCUIT CITY

Alabama Albertville, Alexander City, Andalusia, Arab, Ardmore, Athens, Atmore, Attalla, Bay Minette, Bayou La Batre, Bessemer, Birmingham, Butler, Calera, Camden, Center Point, Centre, Childersburg, Clant
Daphne, Decatur, Demopolis, Dothan, Enterprise, Fairfield, Fairhope, Florence, Foley, Fort Payne, Gadsden, Gardendale, Gulf Shores, Guntersville, Haleyville, Hamilton, Hartselle, Hoover, Huntsville, Jackson, Ja
Linden, Luverne, Madison, Marion, Mobile, Montgomery, Moulton, Northport, Opelika, Opp, Oxford, Pelham, Pell City, Phenix City, Piedmont, Prattville, Robertsdale, Rogersville, Russellville, Saraland, Scotts
Sumiton, Sylacauga, Tallassee, Thomasville, Troy, Tuscaloosa *Alaska* Anchorage, Bethel, Cordova, Craig, Eagle River, Fairbanks, Glennallen, Haines, Homer, Juneau, Kenai, Ketchikan, Kodiak, Petersburg, Se
Skagway, Soldotna, Valdez, Wasilla *Arizona* Ajo, Apache Junction, Avondale, Benson, Bullhead City, Camp Verde, Casa Grande, Chandler, Chino Valley, Colorado City, Coolidge, Cottonwood, Douglas, Flagsta
Fort Mohave, Fountain Hills, Gilbert, Glendale, Greenvalley, Heber, Holbrook, Kayenta, Kingman, Lake Havasu, Lakeside, Maricopa, Mesa, Miami, Morenci, New River, Nogales, Oro Valley, Parker, Payson, Peo
Prescott, Prescott Valley, Quartzsite, Safford, San Manuel, Scottsdale, Sedona, Show Low, Sierra Vista, Springerville, St. Johns, Sun City, Surprise, Taylor, Tempe, Thatcher, Tuba City, Tucson, Wickenburg, W
Arkansas Arkadelphia, Ash Flat, Batesville, Beebe, Benton, Bentonville, Berryville, Brinkley, Bryant, Cabot, Camden, Cave City, Clarksville, Clinton, Conway, Danville, De Queen, De Witt, Dumas, El Dorado, Fayette
Forrest City, Fort Smith, Glenwood, Harrison, Heber Springs, Hope, Hot Springs, Jacksonville, Jasper, Jonesboro, Little Rock, Magnolia, Malvern, Mammoth Springs, Marshall, Melbourne, Mena, Mountain Hom
View, North Little Rock, Nashville, Newport, Paragould, Paris, Pine Bluff, Prescott, Rogers, Russellville, Salem, Searcy, Sheridan, Siloam Springs, Springdale, Star City, Stuttgart, Van Buren, West Helena, Wes
Wynne *California* Agoura, Alameda, Albany, Alhambra, Alta Loma, Alturas, American Canyon, Anaheim, Anaheim Hills, Anderson, Angels Camp, Antioch, Apple Valley, Arcadia, Arcata, Arnold, Arroyo Grande,
Atwater, Auburn, Avalon, Azusa, Bakersfield, Baldwin Park, Barstow, Beaumont, Bell, Belmont, Benicia, Berkeley, Beverly Hills, Big Bear Lake, Bishop, Blue Jay, Blythe, Brawley, Brea, Buellton, Buena Par
Burlingame, Calexico, California City, Camarillo, Canoga Park, Canyon Country, Capitola, Carlsbad, Carmichael, Carpinteria, Carson, Castro Valley, Cathedral City, Cerritos, Chatsworth, Chico, Chino, Chino Hills,
Citrus Heights, City of Industry, Clearlake, Cloverdale, Clovis, Coachella, Coalinga, Colton, Colusa, Compton, Concord, Corcoran, Corning, Corona, Corte Madera, Costa Mesa, Covina, Crescent City, Crestline,
Cupertino, Cypress, Daly City, Dana Point, Danville, Davis, Del Mar, Delano, Desert Hot Springs, Diamond Bar, Dinuba, Downey, Duarte, Dublin, E Los Angeles, El Cajon, El Centro, El Cerrito, El Monte, Elk Grove,
Encinitas, Encino, Escondido, Eureka, Fairfield, Fall River Mills, Fallbrook, Folsom, Fontana, Foothill Ranch, Fortuna, Foster City, Fountain Valley, Freedom, Fremont, Fresno, Fort Bragg, Fullerton, Garberville, Ga
Gardena, Gilroy, Glendale, Glendora, Goleta, Gonzales, Granada Hills, Grass Valley, Greenfield, Grover Beach, Hanford, Harbor City, Hawthorne, Hayward, Hemet, Hercules, Hesperia, Highland, Hollister,
Huntington Beach, Huntington Park, Indio, Inglewood, Irvine, Jackson, King City, La Habra, La Jolla, La Mesa, La Mirada, La Puente, La Quinta, La Verne, Lafayette, Laguna Hills, Laguna Niguel, Lake Elsinore, La
Lakeport, Lakewood, Lancaster, Lawndale, Lemoore, Lincoln Heights, Livermore, Lodi, Lompoc, Long Beach, Los Alamitos, Los Angeles, Los Banos, Los Gatos, Los Osos, Lynwood, Madera, Malibu, Mamm
Manhattan Beach, Manteca, Marina Del Rey, Martinez, Marysville, Maywood, Merced, Milpitas, Mission Hills, Modesto, Mojave, Monrovia, Montclair, Montebello, Monterey, Monterey Park, Montrose, Moorpa
Valley, Morgan Hill, Morro Bay, Mountain View, Mount Shasta, Murrieta, Napa, National City, Newbury Park, Newhall, Newport Beach, North Highlands, North Hollywood, Northridge, Norwalk, Novato, Oakdale
Oakland, Oakley, Oceanside, Ojai, Ontario, Orange, Orangevale, Orland, Oroville, Oxnard, Pacifica, Palm Desert, Palm Springs, Palmdale, Palo Alto, Panorama City, Paradise, Paramount, Pasadena, Paso Robles,
Perris, Petaluma, Phelan, Pico Rivera, Pinole, Pittsburg, Placentia, Placerville, Pleasant Hill, Pleasanton, Pollock Pines, Pomona, Porterville, Poway, Quincy, Ramona, Rancho Cordova, Rancho Cucamonga, Ran
Margarita, Red Bluff, Redding, Redlands, Redondo Beach, Redwood City, Reedley, Rialto, Ridgecrest, Rio Vista, Riverbank, Riverside, Rocklin, Rohnert Park, Rolling Hills, Rosamond, Rosemead, Roseville, Rowlan
Sacramento, Salinas, San Bernardino, San Bruno, San Clemente, San Diego, San Dimas, San Francisco, San Jose, San Leandro, San Luis Obispo, San Marcos, San Mateo, San Pablo, San Pedro, San Rafael, Sa
Sanger, Santa Ana, Santa Barbara, Santa Clara, Santa Cruz, Santa Maria, Santa Monica, Santa Paula, Santa Rosa, Santee, Saugus, Scotts Valley, Seal Beach, Seaside, Sebastopol, Selma, Sherman Oaks, Signal
San Juan Capistrano, Soledad, Sonoma, Sonora, South Gate, South Lake Tahoe, South Pasadena, South San Francisco, Spring Valley, Stockton, Studio City, Sun Valley, Sunnyvale, Susanville, Sylmar, Taft,
Temecula, Temple City, Thousand Oaks, Torrance, Tracy, Truckee, Tujunga, Tulare, Turlock, Tustin, Twentynine Palms, Ukiah, Union City, Upland, Vacaville, Valencia, Vallejo, Valley Springs, Van Nuys, Venice
Victorville, Visalia, Vista, Walnut Creek, Wasco, Watsonville, Weaverville, West Covina, West Hollywood, West Los Angeles, West Sacramento, Westchester, Westminster, Whittier, Willits, Willows, Wilmington,
Woodland, Woodland Hills, Yorba Linda, Yreka, Yuba City, Yucaipa, Yucca Valley *Colorado* Alamosa, Arvada, Aspen, Aurora, Avon, Bayfield, Bennett, Boulder, Brighton, Broomfield, Buena Vista, Burlington, Canon C
Rock, Castle Rock, Centennial, Center, Colorado Springs, Conifer, Cortez, Craig, Crested Butte, Denver, Durango, Elizabeth, Englewood, Estes Park, Evergreen, Flagler, Fort Collins, Fountain, Fraser, Frisco, Glenwo
Golden, Grand Junction, Greeley, Greenwood Village, Gunnison, Highlands Ranch, Holyoke, Idaho Springs, La Junta, Lafayette, Lakewood, Lamar, Limon, Littleton, Longmont, Loveland, Meeker, Monte Vista,
Monument, Northglenn, Pagosa Springs, Paonia, Parachute, Parker, Pueblo, Rifle, Salida, Springfield, Steamboat Springs, Sterling, Thornton, Westminster, Woodland Park, Wray, Yuma *Connecticut* Avon, Bark
Bloomfield, Branford, Bridgeport, Bristol, Canaan, Cheshire, Clinton, Cos Cob, Cromwell, Danbury, Derby, East Haven, Enfield, Fairfield, Farmington, Glastonbury, Groton, Guilford, Hamden, Hartford, Manchester,
Middletown, Milford, Naugatuck, New Britain, New Canaan, New Haven, New London, New Milford, Newington, Newtown, North Haven, Norwalk, Norwich, Old Saybrook, Orange, Plainfield, Putnam, Ridgefield,
Southbury, Southington, Stamford, Torrington, Trumbull, Vernon, Wallingford, Waterbury, Waterford, Watertown, West Hartford, Westport, Wethersfield, Willimantic, Wilton, Windsor, *D.C.* Washington *Delaw*
Claymont, Dover, Georgetown, Middletown, Milford, New Castle, Newark, Rehoboth Beach, Seaford, Smyrna, Wilmington *Florida* Alachua, Altamonte, Altamonte Springs, Apopka, Arcadia, Atlantic Beach, Auburnd
Park, Bartow, Bayonet Point, Belle Glade, Belleview, Big Pine Key, Boca Raton, Bonita Springs, Boynton Beach, Bradenton, Brandon, Branford, Brooksville, Callaway, Cape Coral, Casselberry, Century, Chiefland
Clearwater, Clermont, Clewiston, Cocoa, Cocoa Beach, Cooper City, Coral Gables, Coral Springs, Crawfordville, Crestview, Crystal River, Davie, Daytona Beach, Deerfield, Deerfield Beach, Defuniak Springs, Delan
Beach, Deltona, Destin, Dunnellon, Englewood, Fernandina Beach, Florida City, Fort Lauderdale, Fort Myers, Fort Pierce, Fort Walton Beach, Gainesville, Greenacres, Gulf Breeze, Haines City, Hialeah, Hilliard,
Hollywood, Homestead, Homosassa, Immokalee, Indiantown, Inverness, Jacksonville, Jensen Beach, Jupiter, Key Largo, Key West, Keystone Heights, Kissimmee, Lady Lake, Lake City, Lake Mary, Lake Placid, Lak
Lake Worth, Lakeland, Lantana, Largo, Lauderdale Lakes, Lauderhill, Leesburg, Lehigh Acres, Live Oak, Longwood, Lutz, Macclenny, Madison, Marathon, Marco Island, Margate, Marianna, Mary Esther, Melbourne
Island, Miami, Miami Beach, Milton, Miramar, Monticello, Mount Dora, North Fort Myers, North Miami Beach, Naples, Navarre, New Port Richey, New Smyrna Beach, Niceville, Oakland Park, Ocala, Ocoee, Oke
Orange City, Orange Park, Orlando, Ormond Beach, Oviedo, Palatka, Palm Bay, Palm Beach Garden, Palm Coast, Palm Harbor, Panama City, Pembroke Pines, Pensacola, Perry, Plant City, Plantation, Pompano Be
Charlotte, Port Orange, Port Richey, Port St. Joe, Port St. Lucie, Punta Gorda, Riverview, Royal Palm Beach, Ruskin, Sanford, Santa Rosa Beach, Sarasota, Satellite Beach, Sebastian, Sebring, Seffner, Seminol
Daytona, Spring Hill, St. Augustine, St. Cloud, St. Petersburg, Starke, Stuart, Sunrise, Tallahassee, Tampa, Tarpon Springs, Temple Terrace, Tequesta, Titusville, Venice, Vero Beach, Wauchula, Wellington, West Palr
Weston, Wildwood, Wilton Manors, Winter Haven, Winter Park, Winter Springs, Zephyrhills *Georgia* Adel, Albany, Alpharetta, Americus, Athens, Atlanta, Augusta, Austell, Bainbridge, Barnesville, Baxley, Blairsville,
Blue Ridge, Brunswick, Buford, Cairo, Calhoun, Canton, Carrollton, Cartersville, Cedartown, Centerville, Chamblee, Chatsworth, Clayton, Cleveland, Columbus, Commerce, Conyers, Cordele, Cornelia, Covington, Cu
Cuthbert, Dahlonega, Dalton, Dawson, Dawsonville, Decatur, Donalsonville, Douglas, Douglasville, Dublin, Duluth, East Ellijay, Elberton, Fayetteville, Fitzgerald, Folkston, Forest Park, Forsyth, Fort Gaines, Fort Ogl
Fort Valley, Gainesville, Griffin, Hampton, Hartwell, Hazlehurst, Hiawassee, Hinesville, Hiram, Homerville, Jackson, Jasper, Jesup, Kennesaw, Lafayette, Lagrange, Lawrenceville, Lilburn, Lincolnton, Lithonia,
Madison, Marietta, Martinez, Mc Rae, McDonough, Metter, Milledgeville, Monroe, Monticello, Morrow, Moultrie, Nashville, Newnan, Norcross, Oakwood, Peachtree City, Perry, Quitman, Richmond Hill, Riverdale, Ro
Rome, Roswell, Royston, Savannah, Smyrna, Snellville, St. Marys, St. Simons Island, Statesboro, Stockbridge, Stone Mountain, Summerville, Suwanee, Sylvania, Sylvester, Thomaston, Thomasville, Thomson, Tifton,
Trenton, Union City, Valdosta, Vidalia, Villa Rica, Warner Robins, Washington, Waycross, Winder, Woodbury, Woodstock *Hawaii* Aiea, Ewa Beach, Haleiwa, Hilo, Honolulu, Kahului, Kailua, Kailua-Kona, Kamuela, K
Kapolei, Kihei, Lahaina, Lihue, Mililani, Wahiawa, Waianae, Waipahu *Idaho* American Falls, Blackfoot, Boise, Bonners Ferry, Buhl, Burley, Caldwell, Chubbuck, Coeur d'Alene, Cottonwood, Driggs, Emmett, Grangeville,
Idaho Falls, Lewiston, McCall, Meridian, Montpelier, Moscow, Mountain Home, Nampa, Orofino, Pocatello, Post Falls, Rexburg, Rigby, Salmon, Sandpoint, Twin Falls, Wendell *Illinois* Aledo, Alton, Anna, Antioch,
Arlington Heights, Arthur, Aurora, Bartlett, Batavia, Belleville, Belvidere, Bensenville, Benton, Berwyn, Bloomingdale, Bloomington, Blue Island, Bolingbrook, Bourbonnais, Burbank, Calumet City, Canton, Carb
Carlinville, Carmi, Centralia, Champaign, Channahon, Chester, Chicago, Chicago Heights, Cicero, Collinsville, Crystal Lake, Danville, Decatur, Des Plaines, Dixon, Dolton, Downers Grove, Du Quoin, Dwight, East Peor
St Louis, Effingham, El Paso, Elgin, Elk Grove Village, Eureka, Evanston, Fairbury, Fairfield, Fairview Heights, Flora, Fox Lake, Frankfort, Freeport, Galesburg, Geneseo, Gibson City, Glen Carbon, Glen Ellyn, Glencoe, Gl
Granite City, Greenville, Gurnee, Harrisburg, Havana, Highland, Highland Park, Hoffman Estates, Homer Glen, Homewood, Hoopeston, Jacksonville, Jerseyville, Joliet, Kankakee, Kewanee, La Grange, Lake Zurich, L
Lemont, Lincoln, Litchfield, Lake in the Hills, Lombard, Machesney Park, Macomb, Marengo, Marion, Markham, Mascoutah, Matteson, Mattoon, McHenry, Melrose Park, Mendota, Midlothian, Moline, Montgomery,
Mount Vernon, Mundelein, Naperville, Nashville, Niles, Norridge, North Riverside, Oak Lawn, Oak Park, Olney, Ottawa, Palatine, Palos Heights, Paris, Pekin, Peoria, Peru, Petersburg, Pontiac, Princeton, Quincy, Ro
Rochelle, Rockford, Round Lake Beach, Salem, Sandwich, Savanna, Savoy, Schaumburg, Seneca, Shiloh, Skokie, South Elgin, South Holland, Sparta, Springfield, St. Charles, Staunton, Sterling, Streator, Sullivan, Syc
Tinley Park, Tuscola, Urbana, Vernon Hills, Villa Park, Virden, Waterloo, Watseka, Waukegan, West Dundee, Wheaton, Wheeling, Willowbrook, Wilmington, Wood River, Yorkville, Zion *Indiana* Anderson, Angola,
Auburn, Aurora, Avon, Batesville, Bedford, Berne, Bicknell, Bloomington, Bluffton, Brazil, Bremen, Brook, Brookville, Brownsburg, Brownstown, Cannelton, Carmel, Clarksville, Columbia City, Columbus, Corydon, Cov
Crawfordsville, Crown Point, Decatur, Demotte, Elkhart, Elwood, Evansville, Fishers, Fort Wayne, Fowler, Frankfort, Franklin, Gary, Goshen, Greencastle, Greenfield, Greensburg, Greenwood, Griffith, Hammond, H
Huntington, Indianapolis, Jasper, Kendallville, Knox, Kokomo, La Porte, Lafayette, Lagrange, Lebanon, Ligonier, Linton, Madison, Marion, Martinsville, Merrillville, Michigan City, Mishawaka, Monticello, Mooresville, M
Munster, Nappanee, New Albany, New Carlisle, New Castle, New Haven, Noblesville, North Manchester, North Vernon, Paoli, Peru, Petersburg, Plainfield, Plymouth, Portage, Portland, Princeton, Rensselaer, Rich
Rising Sun, Rochester, Rockport, Rockville, Rushville, Schererville, Seymour, Shelbyville, South Bend, Syracuse, Terre Haute, Tipton, Valparaiso, Vincennes, W Lafayette, Wabash, Warsaw, Washington, Winamac, Winc
Iowa Adel, Altoona, Ames, Ankeny, Atlantic, Belle Plaine, Boone, Carroll, Cedar Falls, Cedar Rapids, Chariton, Charles City, Cherokee, Clarinda, Clinton, Coralville, Council Bluffs, Cresco, Creston, Davenport, De
Denison, Des Moines, Dubuque, Dyersville, Eagle Grove, Estherville, Fairfield, Fort Dodge, Fort Madison, Garner, Glenwood, Greenfield, Grinnell, Hampton, Harlan, Humboldt, Independence, Iowa City, Iowa Falls, Jeff
Keokuk, Knoxville, Le Mars, Logan, Manchester, Maquoketa, Marengo, Marshalltown, Mason City, Mount Pleasant, Muscatine, New Hampton, Newton, Orange City, Osage, Osceola, Ottumwa, Pella, Perry, Pocahonta
Oak, Rock Valley, Sac City, Sheldon, Sioux Center, Sioux City, Spencer, Spirit Lake, Stuart, Vinton, Washington, Waterloo, Webster City, West Burlington, West Des Moines, West Union, Winterset *Kansas* Abilene, An
Arkansas City, Atchison, Atwood, Bonner Springs, Burlington, Chanute, Clay Center, Colby, Columbus, Concordia, Derby, Dodge City, El Dorado, Ellsworth, Emporia, Fort Scott, Garden City, Garnett, Girard, Goodland,
Bend, Hays, Hillsboro, Horton, Hutchinson, Independence, Iola, Junction City, Kansas City, Lawrence ... Lenexa, Liberal, Manhattan, McPherson, Mission, Newton, Oakley, Olathe, Osage City, Osawa
Ottawa, Overland Park, Parsons, Pittsburg, Pratt, Salina, Scott City, Seneca, Shawnee Mission ... Wellington, Wichita, Winfield *Kentucky* Alexandria, Ashland, Barbourville, Bardstown, Bar
Beaver Dam, Berea, Bowling Green, Brandenburg, Cadiz, Campbellsville, Campton, Carrollt... City, Columbia, ... Danville, Dry Ridge, Elizabethtown, Erlanger, Falmouth, Flemingsburg, Florence, Fra
Franklin, Georgetown, Glasgow, Grayson, Hazard, Henderson, Hopkinsville, Jackson, ... La Grange, Latonia, Leba... exington, London, Louisville, Madisonville, Mayfield, Maysville, Middlesboro, Mont
Morehead, Morgantown, Mount Sterling, Mount Vernon, Murray, Newport, Nichol... Owensboro, Paducah, Paris, Pike... Pineville, Prestonsburg, Princeton, Radcliff, Richmond, Russell Springs, Russe
Salyersville, Scottsville, Shelbyville, Somerset, South Williamson, Stanton, Taylorsvil... arsaw, West Liberty, Whitley City, Williams... Winchester *Louisiana* Abbeville, Alexandria, Bastrop, Baton Rouge, Bogalusa, Bo
City, Boutte, Crowley, Cut Off, Denham Springs, Deridder, Eunice, Franklinton, G... ies, Hammond, Harahan, Harvey, Houma, Jea... te, Jena, Jennings, Kenner, Kentwood, La Place, Lafayette, Lake Charles, Lees
Mandeville, Mansfield, Many, Metairie, Minden, Monroe, Morgan City, Natchit... s, New Iberia, New Orleans, New Roads, Oakdale... elousas, Pineville, Plaquemine, Rayne, Ruston, Shreveport, Slidell, Springhi
Francisville, Sulphur, Thibodaux, Ville Platte, West Monroe, Westwego, Winfiel... innsboro, Zachary *Maine* Auburn, Augusta, Bangor, B... arbor, Belfast, Biddeford, Boothbay Harbor, Brunswick, Bucksport, Damarisc
Dover-Foxcroft, Ellsworth, Falmouth, Farmington, Fort Kent, Lewiston, Mac... s, Madawaska, Mexico, Millinocket, Oxford, Portland, P... ue Isle, Rockland, Sanford, Skowhegan, South Portland, Standish, Tops
Waterville, Wells, Windham *Maryland* Aberdeen, Annapolis, Baltimore, Bel ... Beltsville. Bethesda. Bowie. Burtonsville, Cambridge, Cator... le, Charlotte Hall, Chestertown, Clinton, Cockeysville, College Park, Colur
Denton, Derwood, Dunkirk, Easton, Edgewood, Eldersburg, Elkton, Ellicott... y, F... Frederick, Gaithersburg, Gan... lls, Germantown, Glen Burnie, Greenbelt, Hagerstown, Hampstead, Han
Hyattsville, Kensington, La Plata, La Vale, Largo, Laurel, Leonardtown, Lexi... on Park, M... ights, M... Mount Airy, Oakland, Ocea... ity, Odenton, Olney, Owings Mills, Oxon Hill, Oxon Hill, Pasadena, Pocor
City, Potomac, Prince Fredrick, Randallstown, Reisterstown, Rockville, S... bury, Seat... , Severna... er Spring, Stevensville, ... oma Park, Towson, Waldorf, Westminster, Wheaton *Massachusetts* A
Andover, Ashland, Athol, Auburn, Bedford, Beverly, Billerica, Boston, Bra... ee, Bridge... ckton, Br... rlington, Cambridge, Che... sford, Chicopee, Danvers, Dedham, Dorchester, East Boston, East Wal
East Wareham, Fairhaven, Fall River, Falmouth, Fitchburg, Foxboro, Fra... , Gardner, ... r, Greenfi... Barrington, Hadley, Hano... Haverhill, Holyoke, Hyannis, Kingston, Lanesborough, Lenox, Leomin
Lowell, Lynn, Malden, Marlborough, Marshfield, Medford, Milford, Nan... ket, Natick, ... ford, New... Newton, North Adams, N... Attleboro, North Dartmouth, Northampton, Orleans, Peabody, Pitts
Plymouth, Quincy, Raynham, Revere, Roslindale, Saugus, South Attle... o, South B... uth Denni... Easton, South Lawrence, ... th Yarmouth, Southbridge, Springfield, Stoneham, Stoughton, Sudb
Swampscott, Swansea, Taunton, Vineyard Haven, Waltham, Watertow... Webster, We... field, We... n, Westfield, Westford, Whi... sville, Wilmington, Woburn, Worcester *Michigan* Adrian, Albion, Alle
Alpena, Ann Arbor, Auburn Hills, Bad Axe, Battle Creek, Bay City, Bellaire ... lleville, Ben... Big Rapids, Birmingham, Bloomfie... Boyne City, Brighton, Brooklyn, Brown City, Burton, Byron Center, Cadi
Canton, Caro, Carson City, Cass City, Center Line, Charlevoix, Cheboygan ... esaning, C... n Township, Clio, Coldwater, Co... erce, Davison, Dearborn, Dearborn Heights, Detroit, Dowagiac, Eastpo
Eaton Rapids, Escanaba, Evart, Farmington Hills, Farmington, Fenton, Fe... lale, Flint, F... t, Fra... Fremont, Gaylord, Grand Bla... Grand Haven, Grand Rapids, Grayling, Greenville, Grosse Pointe, Hasti
Hemlock, Highland Park, Holland, Houghton Lake, Howell, Imlay City, Ion... ron Mount... ood, Is... ackson, Jenison, Jonesville ... lamazoo, Kalkaska, Kentwood, Lake Orion, L'Anse, Lansing, Lapeer, Lin
Park, Livonia, Ludington, Madison Heights, Manistee, Manistique, Marin... ty, Marqu... hall, Mi... ord, Monroe, Mount Pleas... , Munising, Muskegon, Newberry, Niles, Novi, Oak Park, Okemos, Osc
Owosso, Petoskey, Pinconning, Plainwell, Pontiac, Port Huron, Portage, Re... d, Reed C... ond, Ro... s, Rogers City, Roseville, ... al Oak, Saginaw, Sandusky, Sault St. Marie, Shelby, South Haven, Southfi
Southgate, St. Ignace, St. Johns, Standish, Stanton, Sturgis, Suttons Bay, ... as City, ... ee Oaks, ... rs, Traverse City, Troy, ... a, Vassar, Washington Township, Waterford, Wayne, Westland, White Clo
White Pigeon, Whitehall, Woodhaven, Wyoming, Ypsilanti *Minnesota* Ada, ... n, Alba... Lea, Alex... ole Valley, Austin, Ba... e, Baxter, Bemidji, Benson, Blaine, Bloomington, Brooklyn Center, Burnsv
Cambridge, Chanhassen, Coon Rapids, Cottage Grove, Crystal, Detroit Lakes, ... uth, D... gan, Eden ... na, Elk River, Erskine ... irmont, Faribault, Fergus Falls, Forest Lake, Golden Valley, Grand Marais, Gra
Rapids, Hibbing, Hilltop, Hutchinson, International Falls, Jackson, Lake City, L... ueur ... Little Fall... airie, Mankato, M... Grove, Marshall, Minneapolis, Minnetonka, Montevideo, Monticello, Moorhe
Moose Lake, Mora, Morris, New Ulm, North Branch, Ortonville, Owatonna, Pa... pids, Pi... eton, Red W... Redwood Falls, Richfield, Rochester, Roseau, Roseville, Saint Cloud, Saint Pa
Savage, Shakopee, Sleepy Eye, St. Cloud, St. James, St. Louis Park, St. Paul, S... ter, Stillwater, Thief River Falls, Vadnais Height... rginia, Walker, Warroad, Waseca, Wayzata, Willmar, Windom, Winona, Woodbu
Worthington, Young America *Mississippi* Amory, Batesville, Biloxi, Booneville, Bro... ven, Canton, Carthage, Clarksdale, Clevel... Clinton, Columbia, Columbus, Corinth, Crystal Springs, D'Iberville, Flora, Greenvi
Greenwood, Grenada, Gulfport, Hattiesburg, Houston, Jackson, Laurel, Lucedale, Mag... McComb, Mendenhall, Meridian, Mont... , Morton, Natchez, New Albany, Ocean Springs, Olive Branch, Oxford, Pascagoula, Pe
Philadelphia, Picayune, Pontotoc, Poplarville, Prentiss, Purvis, Quitman, Ridgeland, Se... , Southaven, Starkville, Tupel... rtown, Vicksburg, Waynesboro, West Point, Wiggins, Yazoo City *Missouri* Alton, Arno

RadioShack.

RadioShack Corporation | Financial Reports

RADIOSHACK

CONSOLIDATED BALANCE SHEETS
RadioShack Corporation and Subsidiaries

(In millions, except for share amounts)	December 31, 2006	December 31, 2005
Assets		
Current assets:		
Cash and cash equivalents	$ 472.0	$ 224.0
Accounts and notes receivable, net	247.9	309.4
Inventories	752.1	964.9
Other current assets	127.6	129.0
Total current assets	1,599.6	1,627.3
Property, plant and equipment, net	386.3	476.2
Other assets, net	84.1	101.6
Total assets	$ 2,070.0	$ 2,205.1
Liabilities and Stockholders' Equity		
Current liabilities:		
Short-term debt, including current maturities of long-term debt	$ 194.9	$ 40.9
Accounts payable	254.5	490.9
Accrued expenses and other current liabilities	442.2	379.5
Income taxes payable	92.6	75.0
Total current liabilities	984.2	986.3
Long-term debt, excluding current maturities	345.8	494.9
Other non-current liabilities	86.2	135.1
Total liabilities	1,416.2	1,616.3
Commitments and contingent liabilities		
Stockholders' equity:		
Preferred stock, no par value, 1,000,000 shares authorized:		
Series A junior participating, 300,000 shares designated and none issued	—	—
Common stock, $1 par value, 650,000,000 shares authorized; 191,033,000 shares issued	191.0	191.0
Additional paid-in capital	92.6	87.7
Retained earnings	1,780.9	1,741.4
Treasury stock, at cost; 55,196,000 and 56,071,000 shares, respectively	(1,409.1)	(1,431.6)
Accumulated other comprehensive (loss) income	(1.6)	0.3
Total stockholders' equity	653.8	588.8
Total liabilities and stockholders' equity	$ 2,070.0	$ 2,205.1

RADIOSHACK

CONSOLIDATED STATEMENTS OF INCOME
RadioShack Corporation and Subsidiaries

	Year Ended December 31,					
	2006		2005		2004	
(In millions, except per share amounts)	Dollars	% of Revenues	Dollars	% of Revenues	Dollars	% of Revenues
Net sales and operating revenues	$ 4,777.5	100.0%	$ 5,081.7	100.0%	$ 4,841.2	100.0%
Cost of products sold	2,544.4	53.3	2,706.3	53.3	2,406.7	49.7
Gross profit	2,233.1	46.7	2,375.4	46.7	2,434.5	50.3
Operating expenses:						
Selling, general and administrative	1,903.7	39.8	1,901.7	37.4	1,774.8	36.7
Depreciation and amortization	128.2	2.7	123.8	2.4	101.4	2.1
Impairment of long-lived assets and other charges	44.3	0.9	—	—	—	—
Total operating expenses	2,076.2	43.4	2,025.5	39.8	1,876.2	38.8
Operating income	156.9	3.3	349.9	6.9	558.3	11.5
Interest income	7.4	0.1	5.9	0.1	11.4	0.2
Interest expense	(44.3)	(0.9)	(44.5)	(0.8)	(29.6)	(0.5)
Other (loss) income	(8.6)	(0.2)	10.2	0.2	2.0	—
Income before income taxes	111.4	2.3	321.5	6.4	542.1	11.2
Income tax provision	38.0	0.8	51.6	1.0	204.9	4.2
Income before cumulative effect of change in accounting principle	73.4	1.5	269.9	5.4	337.2	7.0
Cumulative effect of change in accounting principle, net of $1.8 million tax benefit in 2005	—	—	(2.9)	(0.1)	—	—
Net income	$ 73.4	1.5%	$ 267.0	5.3%	$ 337.2	7.0%
Net income per share						
Basic:						
Income before cumulative effect of change in accounting principle	$ 0.54		$ 1.82		$ 2.09	
Cumulative effect of change in accounting principle, net of taxes	—		(0.02)		—	
Basic income per share	$ 0.54		$ 1.80		$ 2.09	
Assuming dilution:						
Income before cumulative effect of change in accounting principle	$ 0.54		$ 1.81		$ 2.08	
Cumulative effect of change in accounting principle, net of taxes	—		(0.02)		—	
Diluted income per share	$ 0.54		$ 1.79		$ 2.08	
Shares used in computing income per share:						
Basic	136.2		148.1		161.0	
Diluted	136.2		148.8		162.5	

CONSOLIDATED STATEMENTS OF STOCKHOLDERS' EQUITY AND COMPREHENSIVE INCOME
RadioShack Corporation and Subsidiaries

	Shares at December 31,			Dollars at December 31,		
(In millions)	2006	2005	2004	2006	2005	2004
Common stock						
Beginning and end of year	191.0	191.0	191.0	$ 191.0	$ 191.0	$ 191.0
Treasury stock						
Beginning of year	(56.0)	(32.8)	(28.5)	$ (1,431.6)	$ (859.4)	$ (707.2)
Purchase of treasury stock	—	(25.3)	(8.0)	—	(625.8)	(246.9)
Issuance of common stock	0.6	1.2	1.3	18.6	31.8	33.8
Exercise of stock options and grant of stock awards	0.2	0.9	2.4	3.9	21.8	60.9
End of year	(55.2)	(56.0)	(32.8)	$ (1,409.1)	$ (1,431.6)	$ (859.4)
Additional paid-in capital						
Beginning of year				$ 87.7	$ 82.7	$ 75.2
Issuance of common stock				(5.7)	3.5	5.7
Exercise of stock options and grant of stock awards				(1.7)	(5.0)	(9.5)
Stock option compensation				12.0	—	—
Stock option income tax benefits				0.3	6.5	11.3
End of year				$ 92.6	$ 87.7	$ 82.7
Retained earnings						
Beginning of year				$ 1,741.4	$ 1,508.1	$ 1,210.6
Net income				73.4	267.0	337.2
Common stock cash dividends declared				(33.9)	(33.7)	(39.7)
End of year				$ 1,780.9	$ 1,741.4	$ 1,508.1
Accumulated other comprehensive (loss) income						
Beginning of year				$ 0.3	$ (0.3)	$ (0.3)
Pension adjustments, net of tax				(1.0)	—	—
Other comprehensive (loss) income				(0.9)	0.6	—
End of year				$ (1.6)	$ 0.3	$ (0.3)
Total stockholders' equity				$ 653.8	$ 588.8	$ 922.1
Comprehensive income						
Net income				$ 73.4	$ 267.0	$ 337.2
Other comprehensive income, net of tax:						
Foreign currency translation adjustments				0.3	(0.4)	0.1
Amortization of gain on cash flow hedge				(0.1)	(0.1)	(0.1)
Unrealized (loss) gain on securities				(1.1)	1.1	—
Other comprehensive (loss) income				(0.9)	0.6	—
Comprehensive income				$ 72.5	$ 267.6	$ 337.2

RADIOSHACK

CONSOLIDATED STATEMENTS OF CASH FLOWS
RadioShack Corporation and Subsidiaries

(In millions)	Year Ended December 31, 2006	2005	2004
Cash flows from operating activities:			
Net income	$ 73.4	$ 267.0	$ 337.2
Adjustments to reconcile net income to net cash provided by operating activities:			
Depreciation and amortization	128.2	123.8	101.4
Cumulative effect of change in accounting principle	—	4.7	—
Impairment of long-lived assets and other charges	44.3	—	—
Stock option compensation	12.0	—	—
Deferred income taxes and other items	(27.6)	(76.9)	50.2
Provision for credit losses and bad debts	0.4	0.1	(0.3)
Changes in operating assets and liabilities, excluding acquisitions:			
Accounts and notes receivable	61.8	(68.2)	(53.0)
Inventories	212.8	38.8	(234.2)
Other current assets	2.5	28.5	(7.5)
Accounts payable, accrued expenses, income taxes payable and other	(193.0)	45.1	158.7
Net cash provided by operating activities	314.8	362.9	352.5
Cash flows from investing activities:			
Additions to property, plant and equipment	(91.0)	(170.7)	(229.4)
Proceeds from sale of property, plant and equipment	11.1	226.0	2.5
Purchase of kiosk business	—	—	(59.1)
Other investing activities	0.6	(16.0)	(4.2)
Net cash (used in) provided by investing activities	(79.3)	39.3	(290.2)
Cash flows from financing activities:			
Purchases of treasury stock	—	(625.8)	(251.1)
Sale of treasury stock to employee benefit plans	10.5	30.1	35.4
Proceeds from exercise of stock options	1.7	17.4	50.4
Payments of dividends	(33.9)	(33.7)	(39.7)
Changes in short-term borrowings and outstanding checks in excess of cash balances, net	42.2	(4.0)	(14.0)
Reductions of long-term borrowings	(8.0)	(0.1)	(40.1)
Net cash provided by (used in) financing activities	12.5	(616.1)	(259.1)
Net increase (decrease) in cash and cash equivalents	248.0	(213.9)	(196.8)
Cash and cash equivalents, beginning of period	224.0	437.9	634.7
Cash and cash equivalents, end of period	$ 472.0	$ 224.0	$ 437.9
Supplemental cash flow information:			
Interest paid	$ 44.0	$ 43.4	$ 29.3
Income taxes paid	52.9	158.5	182.7

Apple Financial Report

CONSOLIDATED BALANCE SHEETS
(In millions, except share amounts)

	September 30, 2006	September 24, 2005
ASSETS		
Current assets:		
Cash and cash equivalents	$ 6,392	$ 3,491
Short-term investments	3,718	4,770
Accounts receivable, less allowances of $52 and $46, respectively	1,252	895
Inventories	270	165
Deferred tax assets	607	331
Other current assets	2,270	648
Total current assets	14,509	10,300
Property, plant, and equipment, net	1,281	817
Goodwill	38	69
Acquired intangible assets, net	139	27
Other assets	1,238	303
Total assets	$17,205	$11,516
LIABILITIES AND SHAREHOLDERS' EQUITY		
Current liabilities:		
Accounts payable	$ 3,390	$ 1,779
Accrued expenses	3,081	1,708
Total current liabilities	6,471	3,487
Noncurrent liabilities	750	601
Total liabilities	7,221	4,088
Commitments and contingencies		
Shareholders' equity:		
Common stock, no par value; 1,800,000,000 shares authorized; 855,262,568 and 835,019,364 shares issued and outstanding, respectively	4,355	3,564
Deferred stock compensation	—	(61)
Retained earnings	5,607	3,925
Accumulated other comprehensive income	22	—
Total shareholders' equity	9,984	7,428
Total liabilities and shareholders' equity	$17,205	$11,516

APPLE

CONSOLIDATED STATEMENTS OF OPERATIONS
(In millions, except share and per share amounts)

Three fiscal years ended September 30, 2006	2006	2005	2004
Net sales	$ 19,315	$ 13,931	$ 8,279
Cost of sales	13,717	9,889	6,022
Gross margin	5,598	4,042	2,257
Operating expenses:			
Research and development	712	535	491
Selling, general, and administrative	2,433	1,864	1,430
Restructuring costs	—	—	23
Total operating expenses	3,145	2,399	1,944
Operating income	2,453	1,643	313
Other income and expense	365	165	57
Income before provision for income taxes	2,818	1,808	370
Provision for income taxes	829	480	104
Net income	$ 1,989	$ 1,328	$ 266
Earnings per common share:			
Basic	$ 2.36	$ 1.64	$ 0.36
Diluted	$ 2.27	$ 1.55	$ 0.34
Shares used in computing earnings per share (in thousands):			
Basic	844,058	808,439	743,180
Diluted	877,526	856,878	774,776

APPLE

CONSOLIDATED STATEMENTS OF SHAREHOLDERS' EQUITY
(In millions, except share amounts which are in thousands)

	Common Stock		Deferred Stock Compensation	Retained Earnings	Accumulated Other Comprehensive Income (Loss)	Total Shareholders' Equity
	Shares	Amount				
Balances as of September 27, 2003 as previously reported	733,454	$1,926	$ (62)	$2,394	$(35)	$4,223
Adjustments to opening shareholders' equity	—	85	(22)	(63)	—	—
Balance as of September 27, 2003 as restated	733,454	$2,011	$ (84)	$2,331	$(35)	$4,223
Components of comprehensive income:						
Net income	—	—	—	266	—	266
Change in foreign currency translation	—	—	—	—	13	13
Change in unrealized gain on available-for-sale securities, net of tax	—	—	—	—	(5)	(5)
Change in unrealized loss on derivative investments, net of tax	—	—	—	—	12	12
Total comprehensive income						286
Issuance of stock-based compensation awards	—	63	(63)	—	—	—
Adjustment to common stock related to a prior year acquisition	(159)	(2)	—	—	—	(2)
Stock-based compensation	—	—	46	—	—	46
Common stock issued under stock plans	49,592	427	—	—	—	427
Tax benefit related to stock options	—	83	—	—	—	83
Balances as of September 25, 2004	782,887	$2,582	$(101)	$2,597	$(15)	$5,063
Components of comprehensive income:						
Net income	—	—	—	1,328	—	1,328
Change in foreign currency translation	—	—	—	—	7	7
Change in unrealized gain on derivative investments, net of tax	—	—	—	—	8	8
Total comprehensive income						1,343
Issuance of stock-based compensation awards	—	7	(7)	—	—	—
Stock-based compensation	—	—	47	—	—	47
Common stock issued under stock plans	52,132	547	—	—	—	547
Tax benefit related to stock options	—	428	—	—	—	428
Balances as of September 24, 2005	835,019	$3,564	$ (61)	$3,925	$ —	$7,428
Components of comprehensive income:						
Net income	—	—	—	1,989	—	1,989
Change in foreign currency translation	—	—	—	—	19	19
Change in unrealized gain on available-for-sale securities, net of tax	—	—	—	—	4	4
Change in unrealized loss on derivative investments, net of tax	—	—	—	—	(1)	(1)
Total comprehensive income						2,011
Common stock repurchased	(4,574)	(48)	—	(307)	—	(355)
Stock-based compensation	—	163	—	—	—	163
Deferred compensation	—	(61)	61	—	—	—
Common stock issued under stock plans	24,818	318	—	—	—	318
Tax benefit related to stock-based compensation	—	419	—	—	—	419
Balances as of September 30, 2006	855,263	$4,355	$ —	$5,607	$ 22	$9,984

CONSOLIDATED STATEMENTS OF CASH FLOWS
(In millions)

Three fiscal years ended September 30, 2006	2006	2005	2004
Cash and cash equivalents, beginning of the year	$ 3,491	$ 2,969	$ 3,396
Operating Activities:			
Net income	1,989	1,328	266
Adjustments to reconcile net income to cash generated by operating activities:			
Depreciation, amortization and accretion	225	179	150
Stock-based compensation expense	163	49	46
Provision for deferred income taxes	53	50	19
Excess tax benefits from stock options	—	428	83
Gain on sale of PowerSchool net assets	(4)	—	—
Loss on disposition of property, plant, and equipment	15	9	7
Gains on sales of investments, net	—	—	(5)
Changes in operating assets and liabilities:			
Accounts receivable	(357)	(121)	(8)
Inventories	(105)	(64)	(45)
Other current assets	(1,626)	(150)	(176)
Other assets	(1,040)	(35)	(25)
Accounts payable	1,611	328	297
Other liabilities	1,296	534	325
Cash generated by operating activities	2,220	2,535	934
Investing Activities:			
Purchases of short-term investments	(7,255)	(11,470)	(3,270)
Proceeds from maturities of short-term investments	7,226	8,609	1,141
Proceeds from sales of investments	1,086	586	806
Purchases of long-term investments	(25)	—	—
Proceeds from sale of PowerSchool net assets	40	—	—
Purchases of property, plant, and equipment	(657)	(260)	(176)
Other	(58)	(21)	11
Cash generated by (used for) investing activities	357	(2,556)	(1,488)
Financing Activities:			
Payment of long-term debt	—	—	(300)
Proceeds from issuance of common stock	318	543	427
Excess tax benefits from stock-based compensation	361	—	—
Repurchases of common stock	(355)	—	—
Cash generated by financing activities	324	543	127
Increase (decrease) in cash and cash equivalents	2,901	522	(427)
Cash and cash equivalents, end of the year	$ 6,392	$ 3,491	$ 2,969
Supplemental cash flow disclosures:			
Cash paid during the year for interest	$ —	$ —	$ 10
Cash paid (received) for income taxes, net	$ 194	$ 17	$ (7)

APPLE

B Time Value of Money

Learning Objectives

CAP

Conceptual

C1 Describe the earning of interest and the concepts of present and future values. *(p. B-1)*

Procedural

P1 Apply present value concepts to a single amount by using interest tables. *(p. B-3)*

P2 Apply future value concepts to a single amount by using interest tables. *(p. B-4)*

P3 Apply present value concepts to an annuity by using interest tables. *(p. B-5)*

P4 Apply future value concepts to an annuity by using interest tables. *(p. B-6)*

Appendix Preview

The concepts of present and future values are important to modern business, including the preparation and analysis of financial statements. The purpose of this appendix is to explain, illustrate, and compute present and future values. This appendix applies these concepts with reference to both business and everyday activities.

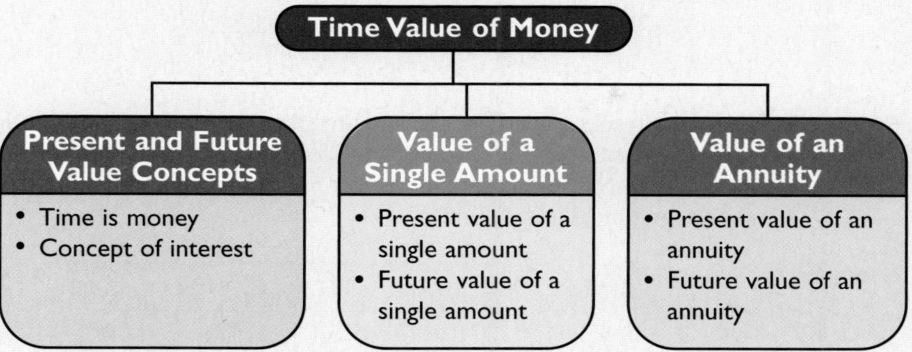

Present and Future Value Concepts

C1 Describe the earning of interest and the concepts of present and future values.

The old saying "Time is money" reflects the notion that as time passes, the values of our assets and liabilities change. This change is due to *interest,* which is a borrower's payment to the owner of an asset for its use. The most common example of interest is a savings account asset. As we keep a balance of cash in the account, it earns interest that the financial institution pays us. An example of a liability is a car loan. As we carry the balance of the loan, we accumulate interest costs on it. We must ultimately repay this loan with interest.

Present and future value computations enable us to measure or estimate the interest component of holding assets or liabilities over time. The present value computation is important when we want to know the value of future-day assets *today.* The future value computation is important when we want to know the value of present-day assets *at a future date.* The first section focuses on the present value of a single amount. The second section focuses on the future value of a single amount. Then both the present and future values of a series of amounts (called an *annuity*) are defined and explained.

Decision Insight

Keep That Job Lottery winners often never work again. Kenny Dukes, a recent Georgia lottery winner, doesn't have that option. He is serving parole for burglary charges, and Georgia requires its parolees to be employed (or in school). For his lottery winnings, Dukes had to choose between $31 million in 30 annual payments or $16 million in one lump sum ($10.6 million after-tax); he chose the latter.

Present Value of a Single Amount

We graphically express the present value, called p, of a single future amount, called f, that is received or paid at a future date in Exhibit B.1.

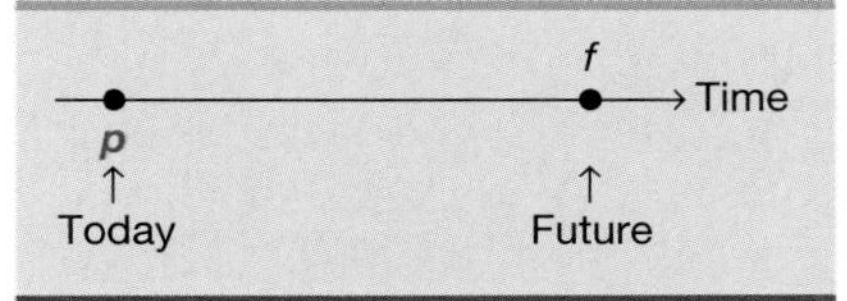

EXHIBIT B.1

Present Value of a Single Amount Diagram

The formula to compute the present value of a single amount is shown in Exhibit B.2, where p = present value; f = future value; i = rate of interest per period; and n = number of periods. (Interest is also called the *discount,* and an interest rate is also called the *discount rate.*)

EXHIBIT B.2

Present Value of a Single Amount Formula

$$p = \frac{f}{(1 + i)^n}$$

To illustrate present value concepts, assume that we need $220 one period from today. We want to know how much we must invest now, for one period, at an interest rate of 10% to provide for this $220. For this illustration, the p, or present value, is the unknown amount—the specifics are shown graphically as follows:

p = ?	(i = 0.10)	f = $220

Conceptually, we know p must be less than $220. This is obvious from the answer to this question: Would we rather have $220 today or $220 at some future date? If we had $220 today, we could invest it and see it grow to something more than $220 in the future. Therefore, we would prefer the $220 today. This means that if we were promised $220 in the future, we would take less than $220 today. But how much less? To answer that question, we compute an estimate of the present value of the $220 to be received one period from now using the formula in Exhibit B.2 as follows:

$$p = \frac{f}{(1 + i)^n} = \frac{\$220}{(1 + 0.10)^1} = \$200$$

We interpret this result to say that given an interest rate of 10%, we are indifferent between $200 today or $220 at the end of one period.

We can also use this formula to compute the present value for *any number of periods.* To illustrate, consider a payment of $242 at the end of two periods at 10% interest. The present value of this $242 to be received two periods from now is computed as follows:

$$p = \frac{f}{(1 + i)^n} = \frac{\$242}{(1 + 0.10)^2} = \$200$$

I will pay your allowance at the end of the month. Do you want to wait or receive its present value today?

Together, these results tell us we are indifferent between $200 today, or $220 one period from today, or $242 two periods from today given a 10% interest rate per period.

The number of periods (n) in the present value formula does not have to be expressed in years. Any period of time such as a day, a month, a quarter, or a year can be used. Whatever period is used, the interest rate (i) must be compounded for the same period. This means that if a situation expresses n in months and i equals 12% per year, then i is transformed into interest earned per month (or 1%). In this case, interest is said to be *compounded monthly.*

A present value table helps us with present value computations. It gives us present values (factors) for a variety of both interest rates (i) and periods (n). Each present value in a present value table assumes that the future value (f) equals 1. When the future value (f) is different from 1, we simply multiply the present value (p) from the table by that future value to give us the estimate. The formula used to construct a table of present values for a single future amount of 1 is shown in Exhibit B.3.

EXHIBIT B.3

Present Value of 1 Formula

$$p = \frac{1}{(1 + i)^n}$$

This formula is identical to that in Exhibit B.2 except that f equals 1. Table B.1 at the end of this appendix is such a present value table. It is often called a **present value of 1 table**. A present value table involves three factors: p, i, and n. Knowing two of these three factors allows us to compute the third. (A fourth is f, but as already explained, we need only multiply the 1 used in the formula by f.) To illustrate the use of a present value table, consider three cases.

P1 Apply present value concepts to a single amount by using interest tables.

Case 1 (solve for p when knowing i and n). To show how we use a present value table, let's look again at how we estimate the present value of \$220 (the f value) at the end of one period ($n = 1$) where the interest rate (i) is 10%. To solve this case, we go to the present value table (Table B.1) and look in the row for 1 period and in the column for 10% interest. Here we find a present value (p) of 0.9091 based on a future value of 1. This means, for instance, that \$1 to be received one period from today at 10% interest is worth \$0.9091 today. Since the future value in this case is not \$1 but \$220, we multiply the 0.9091 by \$220 to get an answer of \$200.

Case 2 (solve for n when knowing p and i). To illustrate, assume a \$100,000 future value (f) that is worth \$13,000 today (p) using an interest rate of 12% (i) but where n is unknown. In particular, we want to know how many periods (n) there are between the present value and the future value. To put this in context, it would fit a situation in which we want to retire with \$100,000 but currently have only \$13,000 that is earning a 12% return and we will be unable to save any additional money. How long will it be before we can retire? To answer this, we go to Table B.1 and look in the 12% interest column. Here we find a column of present values (p) based on a future value of 1. To use the present value table for this solution, we must divide \$13,000 (p) by \$100,000 (f), which equals 0.1300. This is necessary because *a present value table defines* f *equal to 1, and* p *as a fraction of 1.* We look for a value nearest to 0.1300 (p), which we find in the row for 18 periods (n). This means that the present value of \$100,000 at the end of 18 periods at 12% interest is \$13,000; alternatively stated, we must work 18 more years.

Case 3 (solve for i when knowing p and n). In this case, we have, say, a \$120,000 future value (f) worth \$60,000 today (p) when there are nine periods (n) between the present and future values, but the interest rate is unknown. As an example, suppose we want to retire with \$120,000, but we have only \$60,000 and we will be unable to save any additional money, yet we hope to retire in nine years. What interest rate must we earn to retire with \$120,000 in nine years? To answer this, we go to the present value table (Table B.1) and look in the row for nine periods. To use the present value table, we must divide \$60,000 (p) by \$120,000 (f), which equals 0.5000. Recall that this step is necessary because a present value table defines f equal to 1 and p as a fraction of 1. We look for a value in the row for nine periods that is nearest to 0.5000 (p), which we find in the column for 8% interest (i). This means that the present value of \$120,000 at the end of nine periods at 8% interest is \$60,000 or, in our example, we must earn 8% annual interest to retire in nine years.

Quick Check Answer—p. B-7

1. A company is considering an investment expected to yield \$70,000 after six years. If this company demands an 8% return, how much is it willing to pay for this investment?

Future Value of a Single Amount

We must modify the formula for the present value of a single amount to obtain the formula for the future value of a single amount. In particular, we multiply both sides of the equation in Exhibit B.2 by $(1 + i)^n$ to get the result shown in Exhibit B.4.

EXHIBIT B.4

Future Value of a Single Amount Formula

$$f = p \times (1 + i)^n$$

The future value (f) is defined in terms of p, i, and n. We can use this formula to determine that \$200 (p) invested for 1 (n) period at an interest rate of 10% (i) yields a future value of

\$220 as follows:

$$f = p \times (1 + i)^n$$
$$= \$200 \times (1 + 0.10)^1$$
$$= \$220$$

P2 Apply future value concepts to a single amount by using interest tables.

This formula can also be used to compute the future value of an amount for *any number of periods* into the future. To illustrate, assume that \$200 is invested for three periods at 10%. The future value of this \$200 is \$266.20, computed as follows:

$$f = p \times (1 + i)^n$$
$$= \$200 \times (1 + 0.10)^3$$
$$= \$266.20$$

A future value table makes it easier for us to compute future values (f) for many different combinations of interest rates (i) and time periods (n). Each future value in a future value table assumes the present value (p) is 1. As with a present value table, if the future amount is something other than 1, we simply multiply our answer by that amount. The formula used to construct a table of future values (factors) for a single amount of 1 is in Exhibit B.5.

EXHIBIT B.5

Future Value of 1 Formula

$$f = (1 + i)^n$$

Table B.2 at the end of this appendix shows a table of future values for a current amount of 1. This type of table is called a **future value of 1 table**.

There are some important relations between Tables B.1 and B.2. In Table B.2, for the row where $n = 0$, the future value is 1 for each interest rate. This is so because no interest is earned when time does not pass. We also see that Tables B.1 and B.2 report the same information but in a different manner. In particular, one table is simply the *inverse* of the other. To illustrate this inverse relation, let's say we invest \$100 for a period of five years at 12% per year. How much do we expect to have after five years? We can answer this question using Table B.2 by finding the future value (f) of 1, for five periods from now, compounded at 12%. From that table we find $f = 1.7623$. If we start with \$100, the amount it accumulates to after five years is \$176.23 (\$100 × 1.7623). We can alternatively use Table B.1. Here we find that the present value (p) of 1, discounted five periods at 12%, is 0.5674. Recall the inverse relation between present value and future value. This means that $p = 1/f$ (or equivalently, $f = 1/p$). We can compute the future value of \$100 invested for five periods at 12% as follows: $f = \$100 \times (1/0.5674) = \$176.24$ (which equals the \$176.23 just computed, except for a 1 cent rounding difference).

A future value table involves three factors: f, i, and n. Knowing two of these three factors allows us to compute the third. To illustrate, consider these three possible cases.

Case 1 (solve for f when knowing i and n). Our preceding example fits this case. We found that \$100 invested for five periods at 12% interest accumulates to \$176.24.

Case 2 (solve for n when knowing f and i). In this case, we have, say, \$2,000 (p) and we want to know how many periods (n) it will take to accumulate to \$3,000 (f) at 7% (i) interest. To answer this, we go to the future value table (Table B.2) and look in the 7% interest column. Here we find a column of future values (f) based on a present value of 1. To use a future value table, we must divide \$3,000 (f) by \$2,000 (p), which equals 1.500. This is necessary because *a future value table defines* p *equal to 1, and* f *as a multiple of 1.* We look for a value nearest to 1.50 (f), which we find in the row for six periods (n). This means that \$2,000 invested for six periods at 7% interest accumulates to \$3,000.

Case 3 (solve for i when knowing f and n). In this case, we have, say, \$2,001 (p), and in nine years (n) we want to have \$4,000 (f). What rate of interest must we earn to accomplish this? To answer that, we go to Table B.2 and search in the row for nine periods. To use a future value table, we must divide \$4,000 (f) by \$2,001 (p), which equals 1.9990. Recall that this is necessary because a future value table defines p equal to 1 and f as a multiple of 1. We look for a value nearest to 1.9990 (f), which we find in the column for 8% interest (i). This means that \$2,001 invested for nine periods at 8% interest accumulates to \$4,000.

Quick Check Answer—p. B-7

2. Assume that you win a $150,000 cash sweepstakes. You decide to deposit this cash in an account earning 8% annual interest, and you plan to quit your job when the account equals $555,000. How many years will it be before you can quit working?

Present Value of an Annuity

An *annuity* is a series of equal payments occurring at equal intervals. One example is a series of three annual payments of $100 each. An *ordinary annuity* is defined as equal end-of-period payments at equal intervals. An ordinary annuity of $100 for three periods and its present value (p) are illustrated in Exhibit B.6.

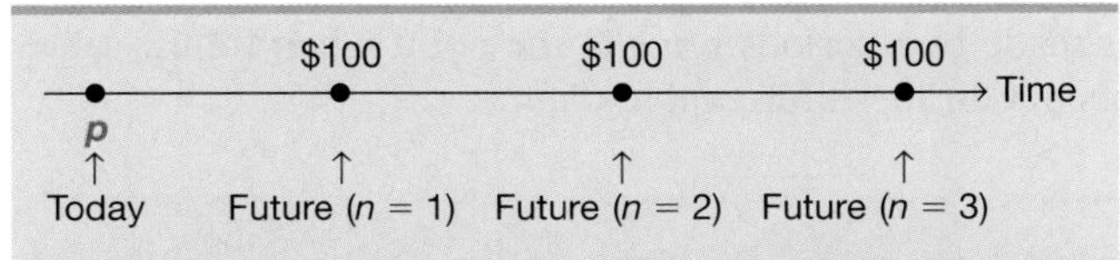

EXHIBIT B.6

Present Value of an Ordinary Annuity Diagram

P3 Apply present value concepts to an annuity by using interest tables.

One way to compute the present value of an ordinary annuity is to find the present value of each payment using our present value formula from Exhibit B.3. We then add each of the three present values. To illustrate, let's look at three $100 payments at the end of each of the next three periods with an interest rate of 15%. Our present value computations are

$$p = \frac{\$100}{(1 + 0.15)^1} + \frac{\$100}{(1 + 0.15)^2} + \frac{\$100}{(1 + 0.15)^3} = \$228.32$$

This computation is identical to computing the present value of each payment (from Table B.1) and taking their sum or, alternatively, adding the values from Table B.1 for each of the three payments and multiplying their sum by the $100 annuity payment.

A more direct way is to use a present value of annuity table. Table B.3 at the end of this appendix is one such table. This table is called a **present value of an annuity of 1 table.** If we look at Table B.3 where $n = 3$ and $i = 15\%$, we see the present value is 2.2832. This means that the present value of an annuity of 1 for three periods, with a 15% interest rate, equals 2.2832.

A present value of an annuity formula is used to construct Table B.3. It can also be constructed by adding the amounts in a present value of 1 table. To illustrate, we use Tables B.1 and B.3 to confirm this relation for the prior example:

From Table B.1		From Table B.3	
$i = 15\%, n = 1$	0.8696		
$i = 15\%, n = 2$	0.7561		
$i = 15\%, n = 3$	0.6575		
Total	2.2832	$i = 15\%, n = 3$	2.2832

We can also use business calculators or spreadsheet programs to find the present value of an annuity.

Decision Insight

Better Lucky Than Good "I don't have good luck—I'm blessed," proclaimed Andrew "Jack" Whittaker, 55, a sewage treatment contractor, after winning the largest ever undivided jackpot in a U.S. lottery. Whittaker had to choose between $315 million in 30 annual installments or $170 million in one lump sum ($112 million after-tax).

Quick Check Answer—p. B-7

3. A company is considering an investment paying $10,000 every six months for three years. The first payment would be received in six months. If this company requires an 8% annual return, what is the maximum amount it is willing to pay for this investment?

Future Value of an Annuity

The future value of an *ordinary annuity* is the accumulated value of each annuity payment with interest as of the date of the final payment. To illustrate, let's consider the earlier annuity of three annual payments of $100. Exhibit B.7 shows the point in time for the future value (f). The first payment is made two periods prior to the point when future value is determined, and the final payment occurs on the future value date.

EXHIBIT B.7

Future Value of an Ordinary Annuity Diagram

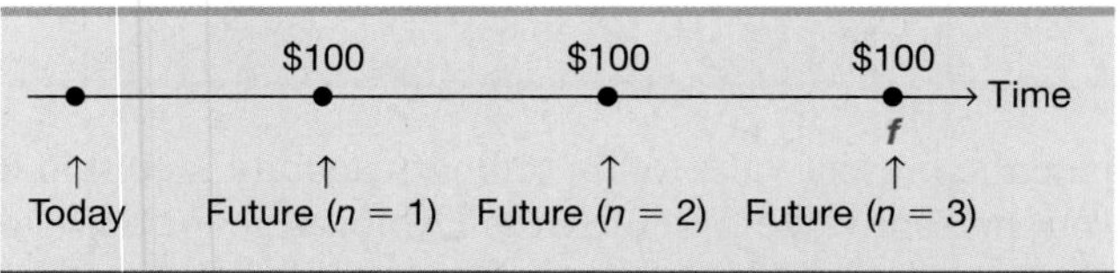

One way to compute the future value of an annuity is to use the formula to find the future value of *each* payment and add them. If we assume an interest rate of 15%, our calculation is

$$f = \$100 \times (1 + 0.15)^2 + \$100 \times (1 + 0.15)^1 + \$100 \times (1 + 0.15)^0 = \$347.25$$

This is identical to using Table B.2 and summing the future values of each payment, or adding the future values of the three payments of 1 and multiplying the sum by $100.

P4 Apply future value concepts to an annuity by using interest tables.

A more direct way is to use a table showing future values of annuities. Such a table is called a **future value of an annuity of 1 table**. Table B.4 at the end of this appendix is one such table. Note that in Table B.4 when $n = 1$, the future values equal 1 ($f = 1$) for all rates of interest. This is so because such an annuity consists of only one payment and the future value is determined on the date of that payment—no time passes between the payment and its future value. The future value of an annuity formula is used to construct Table B.4. We can also construct it by adding the amounts from a future value of 1 table. To illustrate, we use Tables B.2 and B.4 to confirm this relation for the prior example:

From Table B.2		From Table B.4	
$i = 15\%, n = 0$	1.0000		
$i = 15\%, n = 1$	1.1500		
$i = 15\%, n = 2$	1.3225		
Total	3.4725	$i = 15\%, n = 3$	3.4725

Note that the future value in Table B.2 is 1.0000 when $n = 0$, but the future value in Table B.4 is 1.0000 when $n = 1$. Is this a contradiction? No. When $n = 0$ in Table B.2, the future value is determined on the date when a single payment occurs. This means that no interest is earned because no time has passed, and the future value equals the payment. Table B.4 describes annuities with equal payments occurring at the end of each period. When $n = 1$, the annuity has one payment, and its future value equals 1 on the date of its final and only payment. Again, no time passes between the payment and its future value date.

Quick Check

Answer—p. B-7

4. A company invests $45,000 per year for five years at 12% annual interest. Compute the value of this annuity investment at the end of five years.

Summary

C1 **Describe the earning of interest and the concepts of present and future values.** Interest is payment by a borrower to the owner of an asset for its use. Present and future value computations are a way for us to estimate the interest component of holding assets or liabilities over a period of time.

P1 **Apply present value concepts to a single amount by using interest tables.** The present value of a single amount received at a future date is the amount that can be invested now at the specified interest rate to yield that future value.

P2 **Apply future value concepts to a single amount by using interest tables.** The future value of a single amount invested at a specified rate of interest is the amount that would accumulate by the future date.

P3 **Apply present value concepts to an annuity by using interest tables.** The present value of an annuity is the amount that can be invested now at the specified interest rate to yield that series of equal periodic payments.

P4 **Apply future value concepts to an annuity by using interest tables.** The future value of an annuity invested at a specific rate of interest is the amount that would accumulate by the date of the final payment.

Guidance Answers to Quick Checks

1. $70,000 × 0.6302 = $44,114 (use Table B.1, i = 8%, n = 6).
2. $555,000/$150,000 = 3.7000; Table B.2 shows this value is not achieved until after 17 years at 8% interest.
3. $10,000 × 5.2421 = $52,421 (use Table B.3, i = 4%, n = 6).
4. $45,000 × 6.3528 = $285,876 (use Table B.4, i = 12%, n = 5).

McGraw-Hill's HOMEWORK MANAGER® Available with McGraw-Hill's Homework Manager

QUICK STUDY

QS B-1 Identifying interest rates in tables C1

Assume that you must make future value estimates using the *future value of 1 table* (Table B.2). Which interest rate column do you use when working with the following rates?

1. 8% compounded quarterly
2. 12% compounded annually
3. 6% compounded semiannually
4. 12% compounded monthly

QS B-2 Interest rate on an investment P1

Ken Francis is offered the possibility of investing $2,745 today and in return to receive $10,000 after 15 years. What is the annual rate of interest for this investment? (Use Table B.1.)

QS B-3 Number of periods of an investment P1

Megan Brink is offered the possibility of investing $6,651 today at 6% interest per year in a desire to accumulate $10,000. How many years must Brink wait to accumulate $10,000? (Use Table B.1.)

QS B-4 Present value of an amount P1

Flaherty is considering an investment that, if paid for immediately, is expected to return $140,000 five years from now. If Flaherty demands a 9% return, how much is she willing to pay for this investment?

QS B-5 Future value of an amount P2

CII, Inc., invests $630,000 in a project expected to earn a 12% annual rate of return. The earnings will be reinvested in the project each year until the entire investment is liquidated 10 years later. What will the cash proceeds be when the project is liquidated?

QS B-6
Present value of an annuity P3

Beene Distributing is considering a project that will return $150,000 annually at the end of each year for six years. If Beene demands an annual return of 7% and pays for the project immediately, how much is it willing to pay for the project?

QS B-7
Future value of an annuity P4

Claire Fitch is planning to begin an individual retirement program in which she will invest $1,500 at the end of each year. Fitch plans to retire after making 30 annual investments in the program earning a return of 10%. What is the value of the program on the date of the last payment?

EXERCISES

Exercise B-1
Number of periods of an investment P2

Bill Thompson expects to invest $10,000 at 12% and, at the end of a certain period, receive $96,463. How many years will it be before Thompson receives the payment? (Use Table B.2.)

Exercise B-2
Interest rate on an investment P2

Ed Summers expects to invest $10,000 for 25 years, after which he wants to receive $108,347. What rate of interest must Summers earn? (Use Table B.2.)

Exercise B-3
Interest rate on an investment P3

Jones expects an immediate investment of $57,466 to return $10,000 annually for eight years, with the first payment to be received one year from now. What rate of interest must Jones earn? (Use Table B.3.)

Exercise B-4
Number of periods of an investment P3

Keith Riggins expects an investment of $82,014 to return $10,000 annually for several years. If Riggins earns a return of 10%, how many annual payments will he receive? (Use Table B.3.)

Exercise B-5
Interest rate on an investment P4

Algoe expects to invest $1,000 annually for 40 years to yield an accumulated value of $154,762 on the date of the last investment. For this to occur, what rate of interest must Algoe earn? (Use Table B.4.)

Exercise B-6
Number of periods of an investment P4

Kate Beckwith expects to invest $10,000 annually that will earn 8%. How many annual investments must Beckwith make to accumulate $303,243 on the date of the last investment? (Use Table B.4.)

Exercise B-7
Present value of an annuity P3

Sam Weber finances a new automobile by paying $6,500 cash and agreeing to make 40 monthly payments of $500 each, the first payment to be made one month after the purchase. The loan bears interest at an annual rate of 12%. What is the cost of the automobile?

Exercise B-8
Present value of bonds P1 P3

Spiller Corp. plans to issue 10%, 15-year, $500,000 par value bonds payable that pay interest semiannually on June 30 and December 31. The bonds are dated December 31, 2008, and are issued on that date. If the market rate of interest for the bonds is 8% on the date of issue, what will be the total cash proceeds from the bond issue?

Exercise B-9
Present value of an amount P1

McAdams Company expects to earn 10% per year on an investment that will pay $606,773 six years from now. Use Table B.1 to compute the present value of this investment. (Round the amount to the nearest dollar.)

Exercise B-10
Present value of an amount and of an annuity P1 P3

Compute the amount that can be borrowed under each of the following circumstances:

1. A promise to repay $90,000 seven years from now at an interest rate of 6%.
2. An agreement made on February 1, 2008, to make three separate payments of $20,000 on February 1 of 2009, 2010, and 2011. The annual interest rate is 10%.

Exercise B-11
Present value of an amount P1

On January 1, 2008, a company agrees to pay $20,000 in three years. If the annual interest rate is 10%, determine how much cash the company can borrow with this agreement.

Exercise B-12
Present value of an amount P1

Find the amount of money that can be borrowed today with each of the following separate debt agreements *a* through *f*. (Round amounts to the nearest dollar.)

Case	Single Future Payment	Number of Periods	Interest Rate
a.	$40,000	3	4%
b.	75,000	7	8
c.	52,000	9	10
d.	18,000	2	4
e.	63,000	8	6
f.	89,000	5	2

Exercise B-13
Present values of annuities
P3

C&H Ski Club recently borrowed money and agrees to pay it back with a series of six annual payments of $5,000 each. C&H subsequently borrows more money and agrees to pay it back with a series of four annual payments of $7,500 each. The annual interest rate for both loans is 6%.

1. Use Table B.1 to find the present value of these two separate annuities. (Round amounts to the nearest dollar.)

2. Use Table B.3 to find the present value of these two separate annuities. (Round amounts to the nearest dollar.)

Exercise B-14
Present value with semiannual compounding
C1 P3

Otto Co. borrows money on April 30, 2008, by promising to make four payments of $13,000 each on November 1, 2008; May 1, 2009; November 1, 2009; and May 1, 2010.

1. How much money is Otto able to borrow if the interest rate is 8%, compounded semiannually?

2. How much money is Otto able to borrow if the interest rate is 12%, compounded semiannually?

3. How much money is Otto able to borrow if the interest rate is 16%, compounded semiannually?

Exercise B-15
Future value of an amount P2

Mark Welsch deposits $7,200 in an account that earns interest at an annual rate of 8%, compounded quarterly. The $7,200 plus earned interest must remain in the account 10 years before it can be withdrawn. How much money will be in the account at the end of 10 years?

Exercise B-16
Future value of an annuity P4

Kelly Malone plans to have $50 withheld from her monthly paycheck and deposited in a savings account that earns 12% annually, compounded monthly. If Malone continues with her plan for two and one-half years, how much will be accumulated in the account on the date of the last deposit?

Exercise B-17
Future value of an amount plus an annuity P2 P4

Starr Company decides to establish a fund that it will use 10 years from now to replace an aging production facility. The company will make a $100,000 initial contribution to the fund and plans to make quarterly contributions of $50,000 beginning in three months. The fund earns 12%, compounded quarterly. What will be the value of the fund 10 years from now?

Exercise B-18
Future value of an amount P2

Catten, Inc., invests $163,170 today earning 7% per year for nine years. Use Table B.2 to compute the future value of the investment nine years from now. (Round the amount to the nearest dollar.)

Exercise B-19
Using present and future value tables
C1 P1 P2 P3 P4

For each of the following situations, identify (1) the case as either (*a*) a present or a future value and (*b*) a single amount or an annuity, (2) the table you would use in your computations (but do not solve the problem), and (3) the interest rate and time periods you would use.

a. You need to accumulate $10,000 for a trip you wish to take in four years. You are able to earn 8% compounded semiannually on your savings. You plan to make only one deposit and let the money accumulate for four years. How would you determine the amount of the one-time deposit?

b. Assume the same facts as in part (*a*) except that you will make semiannual deposits to your savings account.

c. You want to retire after working 40 years with savings in excess of $1,000,000. You expect to save $4,000 a year for 40 years and earn an annual rate of interest of 8%. Will you be able to retire with more than $1,000,000 in 40 years? Explain.

d. A sweepstakes agency names you a grand prize winner. You can take $225,000 immediately or elect to receive annual installments of $30,000 for 20 years. You can earn 10% annually on any investments you make. Which prize do you choose to receive?

TABLE B.1

Present Value of 1

$$p = 1/(1 + i)^n$$

	Rate											
Periods	**1%**	**2%**	**3%**	**4%**	**5%**	**6%**	**7%**	**8%**	**9%**	**10%**	**12%**	**15%**
1	0.9901	0.9804	0.9709	0.9615	0.9524	0.9434	0.9346	0.9259	0.9174	0.9091	0.8929	0.8696
2	0.9803	0.9612	0.9426	0.9246	0.9070	0.8900	0.8734	0.8573	0.8417	0.8264	0.7972	0.7561
3	0.9706	0.9423	0.9151	0.8890	0.8638	0.8396	0.8163	0.7938	0.7722	0.7513	0.7118	0.6575
4	0.9610	0.9238	0.8885	0.8548	0.8227	0.7921	0.7629	0.7350	0.7084	0.6830	0.6355	0.5718
5	0.9515	0.9057	0.8626	0.8219	0.7835	0.7473	0.7130	0.6806	0.6499	0.6209	0.5674	0.4972
6	0.9420	0.8880	0.8375	0.7903	0.7462	0.7050	0.6663	0.6302	0.5963	0.5645	0.5066	0.4323
7	0.9327	0.8706	0.8131	0.7599	0.7107	0.6651	0.6227	0.5835	0.5470	0.5132	0.4523	0.3759
8	0.9235	0.8535	0.7894	0.7307	0.6768	0.6274	0.5820	0.5403	0.5019	0.4665	0.4039	0.3269
9	0.9143	0.8368	0.7664	0.7026	0.6446	0.5919	0.5439	0.5002	0.4604	0.4241	0.3606	0.2843
10	0.9053	0.8203	0.7441	0.6756	0.6139	0.5584	0.5083	0.4632	0.4224	0.3855	0.3220	0.2472
11	0.8963	0.8043	0.7224	0.6496	0.5847	0.5268	0.4751	0.4289	0.3875	0.3505	0.2875	0.2149
12	0.8874	0.7885	0.7014	0.6246	0.5568	0.4970	0.4440	0.3971	0.3555	0.3186	0.2567	0.1869
13	0.8787	0.7730	0.6810	0.6006	0.5303	0.4688	0.4150	0.3677	0.3262	0.2897	0.2292	0.1625
14	0.8700	0.7579	0.6611	0.5775	0.5051	0.4423	0.3878	0.3405	0.2992	0.2633	0.2046	0.1413
15	0.8613	0.7430	0.6419	0.5553	0.4810	0.4173	0.3624	0.3152	0.2745	0.2394	0.1827	0.1229
16	0.8528	0.7284	0.6232	0.5339	0.4581	0.3936	0.3387	0.2919	0.2519	0.2176	0.1631	0.1069
17	0.8444	0.7142	0.6050	0.5134	0.4363	0.3714	0.3166	0.2703	0.2311	0.1978	0.1456	0.0929
18	0.8360	0.7002	0.5874	0.4936	0.4155	0.3503	0.2959	0.2502	0.2120	0.1799	0.1300	0.0808
19	0.8277	0.6864	0.5703	0.4746	0.3957	0.3305	0.2765	0.2317	0.1945	0.1635	0.1161	0.0703
20	0.8195	0.6730	0.5537	0.4564	0.3769	0.3118	0.2584	0.2145	0.1784	0.1486	0.1037	0.0611
25	0.7798	0.6095	0.4776	0.3751	0.2953	0.2330	0.1842	0.1460	0.1160	0.0923	0.0588	0.0304
30	0.7419	0.5521	0.4120	0.3083	0.2314	0.1741	0.1314	0.0994	0.0754	0.0573	0.0334	0.0151
35	0.7059	0.5000	0.3554	0.2534	0.1813	0.1301	0.0937	0.0676	0.0490	0.0356	0.0189	0.0075
40	0.6717	0.4529	0.3066	0.2083	0.1420	0.0972	0.0668	0.0460	0.0318	0.0221	0.0107	0.0037

TABLE B.2

Future Value of 1

$$f = (1 + i)^n$$

	Rate											
Periods	**1%**	**2%**	**3%**	**4%**	**5%**	**6%**	**7%**	**8%**	**9%**	**10%**	**12%**	**15%**
0	1.0000	1.0000	1.0000	1.0000	1.0000	1.0000	1.0000	1.0000	1.0000	1.0000	1.0000	1.0000
1	1.0100	1.0200	1.0300	1.0400	1.0500	1.0600	1.0700	1.0800	1.0900	1.1000	1.1200	1.1500
2	1.0201	1.0404	1.0609	1.0816	1.1025	1.1236	1.1449	1.1664	1.1881	1.2100	1.2544	1.3225
3	1.0303	1.0612	1.0927	1.1249	1.1576	1.1910	1.2250	1.2597	1.2950	1.3310	1.4049	1.5209
4	1.0406	1.0824	1.1255	1.1699	1.2155	1.2625	1.3108	1.3605	1.4116	1.4641	1.5735	1.7490
5	1.0510	1.1041	1.1593	1.2167	1.2763	1.3382	1.4026	1.4693	1.5386	1.6105	1.7623	2.0114
6	1.0615	1.1262	1.1941	1.2653	1.3401	1.4185	1.5007	1.5869	1.6771	1.7716	1.9738	2.3131
7	1.0721	1.1487	1.2299	1.3159	1.4071	1.5036	1.6058	1.7138	1.8280	1.9487	2.2107	2.6600
8	1.0829	1.1717	1.2668	1.3686	1.4775	1.5938	1.7182	1.8509	1.9926	2.1436	2.4760	3.0590
9	1.0937	1.1951	1.3048	1.4233	1.5513	1.6895	1.8385	1.9990	2.1719	2.3579	2.7731	3.5179
10	1.1046	1.2190	1.3439	1.4802	1.6289	1.7908	1.9672	2.1589	2.3674	2.5937	3.1058	4.0456
11	1.1157	1.2434	1.3842	1.5395	1.7103	1.8983	2.1049	2.3316	2.5804	2.8531	3.4785	4.6524
12	1.1268	1.2682	1.4258	1.6010	1.7959	2.0122	2.2522	2.5182	2.8127	3.1384	3.8960	5.3503
13	1.1381	1.2936	1.4685	1.6651	1.8856	2.1329	2.4098	2.7196	3.0658	3.4523	4.3635	6.1528
14	1.1495	1.3195	1.5126	1.7317	1.9799	2.2609	2.5785	2.9372	3.3417	3.7975	4.8871	7.0757
15	1.1610	1.3459	1.5580	1.8009	2.0789	2.3966	2.7590	3.1722	3.6425	4.1772	5.4736	8.1371
16	1.1726	1.3728	1.6047	1.8730	2.1829	2.5404	2.9522	3.4259	3.9703	4.5950	6.1304	9.3576
17	1.1843	1.4002	1.6528	1.9479	2.2920	2.6928	3.1588	3.7000	4.3276	5.0545	6.8660	10.7613
18	1.1961	1.4282	1.7024	2.0258	2.4066	2.8543	3.3799	3.9960	4.7171	5.5599	7.6900	12.3755
19	1.2081	1.4568	1.7535	2.1068	2.5270	3.0256	3.6165	4.3157	5.1417	6.1159	8.6128	14.2318
20	1.2202	1.4859	1.8061	2.1911	2.6533	3.2071	3.8697	4.6610	5.6044	6.7275	9.6463	16.3665
25	1.2824	1.6406	2.0938	2.6658	3.3864	4.2919	5.4274	6.8485	8.6231	10.8347	17.0001	32.9190
30	1.3478	1.8114	2.4273	3.2434	4.3219	5.7435	7.6123	10.0627	13.2677	17.4494	29.9599	66.2118
35	1.4166	1.9999	2.8139	3.9461	5.5160	7.6861	10.6766	14.7853	20.4140	28.1024	52.7996	133.1755
40	1.4889	2.2080	3.2620	4.8010	7.0400	10.2857	14.9745	21.7245	31.4094	45.2593	93.0510	267.8635

$$p = \left[1 - \frac{1}{(1+i)^n}\right]/i$$

TABLE B.3

Present Value of an Annuity of 1

Periods	Rate 1%	2%	3%	4%	5%	6%	7%	8%	9%	10%	12%	15%
1	0.9901	0.9804	0.9709	0.9615	0.9524	0.9434	0.9346	0.9259	0.9174	0.9091	0.8929	0.8696
2	1.9704	1.9416	1.9135	1.8861	1.8594	1.8334	1.8080	1.7833	1.7591	1.7355	1.6901	1.6257
3	2.9410	2.8839	2.8286	2.7751	2.7232	2.6730	2.6243	2.5771	2.5313	2.4869	2.4018	2.2832
4	3.9020	3.8077	3.7171	3.6299	3.5460	3.4651	3.3872	3.3121	3.2397	3.1699	3.0373	2.8550
5	4.8534	4.7135	4.5797	4.4518	4.3295	4.2124	4.1002	3.9927	3.8897	3.7908	3.6048	3.3522
6	5.7955	5.6014	5.4172	5.2421	5.0757	4.9173	4.7665	4.6229	4.4859	4.3553	4.1114	3.7845
7	6.7282	6.4720	6.2303	6.0021	5.7864	5.5824	5.3893	5.2064	5.0330	4.8684	4.5638	4.1604
8	7.6517	7.3255	7.0197	6.7327	6.4632	6.2098	5.9713	5.7466	5.5348	5.3349	4.9676	4.4873
9	8.5660	8.1622	7.7861	7.4353	7.1078	6.8017	6.5152	6.2469	5.9952	5.7590	5.3282	4.7716
10	9.4713	8.9826	8.5302	8.1109	7.7217	7.3601	7.0236	6.7101	6.4177	6.1446	5.6502	5.0188
11	10.3676	9.7868	9.2526	8.7605	8.3064	7.8869	7.4987	7.1390	6.8052	6.4951	5.9377	5.2337
12	11.2551	10.5753	9.9540	9.3851	8.8633	8.3838	7.9427	7.5361	7.1607	6.8137	6.1944	5.4206
13	12.1337	11.3484	10.6350	9.9856	9.3936	8.8527	8.3577	7.9038	7.4869	7.1034	6.4235	5.5831
14	13.0037	12.1062	11.2961	10.5631	9.8986	9.2950	8.7455	8.2442	7.7862	7.3667	6.6282	5.7245
15	13.8651	12.8493	11.9379	11.1184	10.3797	9.7122	9.1079	8.5595	8.0607	7.6061	6.8109	5.8474
16	14.7179	13.5777	12.5611	11.6523	10.8378	10.1059	9.4466	8.8514	8.3126	7.8237	6.9740	5.9542
17	15.5623	14.2919	13.1661	12.1657	11.2741	10.4773	9.7632	9.1216	8.5436	8.0216	7.1196	6.0472
18	16.3983	14.9920	13.7535	12.6593	11.6896	10.8276	10.0591	9.3719	8.7556	8.2014	7.2497	6.1280
19	17.2260	15.6785	14.3238	13.1339	12.0853	11.1581	10.3356	9.6036	8.9501	8.3649	7.3658	6.1982
20	18.0456	16.3514	14.8775	13.5903	12.4622	11.4699	10.5940	9.8181	9.1285	8.5136	7.4694	6.2593
25	22.0232	19.5235	17.4131	15.6221	14.0939	12.7834	11.6536	10.6748	9.8226	9.0770	7.8431	6.4641
30	25.8077	22.3965	19.6004	17.2920	15.3725	13.7648	12.4090	11.2578	10.2737	9.4269	8.0552	6.5660
35	29.4086	24.9986	21.4872	18.6646	16.3742	14.4982	12.9477	11.6546	10.5668	9.6442	8.1755	6.6166
40	32.8347	27.3555	23.1148	19.7928	17.1591	15.0463	13.3317	11.9246	10.7574	9.7791	8.2438	6.6418

$$f = [(1+i)^n - 1]/i$$

TABLE B.4

Future Value of an Annuity of 1

Periods	Rate 1%	2%	3%	4%	5%	6%	7%	8%	9%	10%	12%	15%
1	1.0000	1.0000	1.0000	1.0000	1.0000	1.0000	1.0000	1.0000	1.0000	1.0000	1.0000	1.0000
2	2.0100	2.0200	2.0300	2.0400	2.0500	2.0600	2.0700	2.0800	2.0900	2.1000	2.1200	2.1500
3	3.0301	3.0604	3.0909	3.1216	3.1525	3.1836	3.2149	3.2464	3.2781	3.3100	3.3744	3.4725
4	4.0604	4.1216	4.1836	4.2465	4.3101	4.3746	4.4399	4.5061	4.5731	4.6410	4.7793	4.9934
5	5.1010	5.2040	5.3091	5.4163	5.5256	5.6371	5.7507	5.8666	5.9847	6.1051	6.3528	6.7424
6	6.1520	6.3081	6.4684	6.6330	6.8019	6.9753	7.1533	7.3359	7.5233	7.7156	8.1152	8.7537
7	7.2135	7.4343	7.6625	7.8983	8.1420	8.3938	8.6540	8.9228	9.2004	9.4872	10.0890	11.0668
8	8.2857	8.5830	8.8923	9.2142	9.5491	9.8975	10.2598	10.6366	11.0285	11.4359	12.2997	13.7268
9	9.3685	9.7546	10.1591	10.5828	11.0266	11.4913	11.9780	12.4876	13.0210	13.5795	14.7757	16.7858
10	10.4622	10.9497	11.4639	12.0061	12.5779	13.1808	13.8164	14.4866	15.1929	15.9374	17.5487	20.3037
11	11.5668	12.1687	12.8078	13.4864	14.2068	14.9716	15.7836	16.6455	17.5603	18.5312	20.6546	24.3493
12	12.6825	13.4121	14.1920	15.0258	15.9171	16.8699	17.8885	18.9771	20.1407	21.3843	24.1331	29.0017
13	13.8093	14.6803	15.6178	16.6268	17.7130	18.8821	20.1406	21.4953	22.9534	24.5227	28.0291	34.3519
14	14.9474	15.9739	17.0863	18.2919	19.5986	21.0151	22.5505	24.2149	26.0192	27.9750	32.3926	40.5047
15	16.0969	17.2934	18.5989	20.0236	21.5786	23.2760	25.1290	27.1521	29.3609	31.7725	37.2797	47.5804
16	17.2579	18.6393	20.1569	21.8245	23.6575	25.6725	27.8881	30.3243	33.0034	35.9497	42.7533	55.7175
17	18.4304	20.0121	21.7616	23.6975	25.8404	28.2129	30.8402	33.7502	36.9737	40.5447	48.8837	65.0751
18	19.6147	21.4123	23.4144	25.6454	28.1324	30.9057	33.9990	37.4502	41.3013	45.5992	55.7497	75.8364
19	20.8109	22.8406	25.1169	27.6712	30.5390	33.7600	37.3790	41.4463	46.0185	51.1591	63.4397	88.2118
20	22.0190	24.2974	26.8704	29.7781	33.0660	36.7856	40.9955	45.7620	51.1601	57.2750	72.0524	102.4436
25	28.2432	32.0303	36.4593	41.6459	47.7271	54.8645	63.2490	73.1059	84.7009	98.3471	133.3339	212.7930
30	34.7849	40.5681	47.5754	56.0849	66.4388	79.0582	94.4608	113.2832	136.3075	164.4940	241.3327	434.7451
35	41.6603	49.9945	60.4621	73.6522	90.3203	111.4348	138.2369	172.3168	215.7108	271.0244	431.6635	881.1702
40	48.8864	60.4020	75.4013	95.0255	120.7998	154.7620	199.6351	259.0565	337.8824	442.5926	767.0914	1,779.0903

Glossary

Absorption costing Costing method that assigns both variable and fixed costs to products.

Accelerated depreciation method Method that produces larger depreciation charges in the early years of an asset's life and smaller charges in its later years. *(p. 398)*

Account Record within an accounting system in which increases and decreases are entered and stored in a specific asset, liability, equity, revenue, or expense. *(p. 49)*

Account balance Difference between total debits and total credits (including the beginning balance) for an account. *(p. 53)*

Account form balance sheet Balance sheet that lists assets on the left side and liabilities and equity on the right. *(p. 18)*

Account payable Liability created by buying goods or services on credit; backed by the buyer's general credit standing. *(p. 50)*

Accounting Information and measurement system that identifies, records, and communicates relevant information about a company's business activities. *(p. 4)*

Accounting cycle Recurring steps performed each accounting period, starting with analyzing transactions and continuing through the post-closing trial balance (or reversing entries). *(p. 144)*

Accounting equation Equality involving a company's assets, liabilities, and equity; Assets = Liabilities + Equity; also called *balance sheet equation*. *(p. 12)*

Accounting information system People, records, and methods that collect and process data from transactions and events, organize them in useful forms, and communicate results to decision makers. *(p. 268)*

Accounting period Length of time covered by financial statements; also called *reporting period*. *(p. 92)*

Accounting rate of return Rate used to evaluate the acceptability of an investment; equals the after-tax periodic income from a project divided by the average investment in the asset; also called *rate of return on average investment*. *(p. 1027)*

Accounts payable ledger Subsidiary ledger listing individual creditor (supplier) accounts. *(p. 273)*

Accounts receivable Amounts due from customers for credit sales; backed by the customer's general credit standing. *(p. 358)*

Accounts receivable ledger Subsidiary ledger listing individual customer accounts. *(p. 273)*

Accounts receivable turnover Measure of both the quality and liquidity of accounts receivable; indicates how often receivables are received and collected during the period; computed by dividing net sales by average accounts receivable. *(p. 372)*

Accrual basis accounting Accounting system that recognizes revenues when earned and expenses when incurred; the basis for GAAP. *(p. 93)*

Accrued expenses Costs incurred in a period that are both unpaid and unrecorded; adjusting entries for recording accrued expenses involve increasing expenses and increasing liabilities. *(p. 99)*

Accrued revenues Revenues earned in a period that are both unrecorded and not yet received in cash (or other assets); adjusting entries for recording accrued revenues involve increasing assets and increasing revenues. *(p. 101)*

Accumulated depreciation Cumulative sum of all depreciation expense recorded for an asset. *(p. 97)*

Acid-test ratio Ratio used to assess a company's ability to settle its current debts with its most liquid assets; defined as quick assets (cash, short-term investments, and current receivables) divided by current liabilities. *(p. 193)*

Activity-based budgeting (ABB) Budget system based on expected activities. *(p. 953)*

Activity-based costing (ABC) Cost allocation method that focuses on activities performed; traces costs to activities and then assigns them to cost objects. *(p. 854)*

Activity cost driver Variable that causes an activity's cost to go up or down; a causal factor. *(p. 855)*

Activity cost pool Temporary account that accumulates costs a company incurs to support an activity. *(p. 855)*

Adjusted trial balance List of accounts and balances prepared after period-end adjustments are recorded and posted. *(p. 104)*

Adjusting entry Journal entry at the end of an accounting period to bring an asset or liability account to its proper amount and update the related expense or revenue account. *(p. 94)*

Aging of accounts receivable Process of classifying accounts receivable by how long they are past due for purposes of estimating uncollectible accounts. *(p. 366)*

Allowance for Doubtful Accounts Contra asset account with a balance approximating uncollectible accounts receivable; also called *Allowance for Uncollectible Accounts*. *(p. 363)*

Allowance method Procedure that (a) estimates and matches bad debts expense with its sales for the period and/or (b) reports accounts receivable at estimated realizable value. *(p. 362)*

Amortization Process of allocating the cost of an intangible asset to expense over its estimated useful life. *(p. 407)*

Annual financial statements Financial statements covering a one-year period; often based on a calendar year, but any consecutive 12-month (or 52-week) period is acceptable. *(p. 92)*

Annual report Summary of a company's financial results for the year with its current financial condition and future plans; directed to external users of financial information. *(p. A-1)*

Annuity Series of equal payments at equal intervals. *(p. 568)*

Appropriated retained earnings Retained earnings separately reported to inform stockholders of funding needs. *(p. 523)*

Asset book value (See *book value.*)

Assets Resources a business owns or controls that are expected to provide current and future benefits to the business. *(p. 13)*

Audit Analysis and report of an organization's accounting system, its records, and its reports using various tests. *(p. 11)*

Auditors Individuals hired to review financial reports and information systems. *Internal auditors* of a company are employed to assess and evaluate its system of internal controls, including the resulting reports. *External auditors* are independent of a company and are hired to assess and evaluate the "fairness" of financial statements (or to perform other contracted financial services) *(p. 11).*

Authorized stock Total amount of stock that a corporation's charter authorizes it to issue. *(p. 509)*

Available-for-sale (AFS) securities Investments in debt and equity securities that are not classified as trading securities or held-to-maturity securities. *(p. 596)*

Average cost See *weighted average. (p. 230)*

Avoidable expense Expense (or cost) that is relevant for decision making; expense that is not incurred if a department, product, or service is eliminated. *(p. 1041)*

Bad debts Accounts of customers who do not pay what they have promised to pay; an expense of selling on credit; also called *uncollectible accounts. (p. 361)*

Balance column account Account with debit and credit columns for recording entries and another column for showing the balance of the account after each entry. *(p. 56)*

Balance sheet Financial statement that lists types and dollar amounts of assets, liabilities, and equity at a specific date. *(p. 18)*

Balance sheet equation (See *accounting equation.*)

Bank reconciliation Report that explains the difference between the book (company) balance of cash and the cash balance reported on the bank statement. *(p. 329)*

Bank statement Bank report on the depositor's beginning and ending cash balances, and a listing of its changes, for a period. *(p. 327)*

Basic earnings per share Net income less any preferred dividends and then divided by weighted-average common shares outstanding. *(p. 524)*

Batch processing Accumulating source documents for a period of time and then processing them all at once such as once a day, week, or month. *(p. 282)*

Bearer bonds Bonds made payable to whoever holds them (the *bearer*); also called *unregistered bonds. (p. 563)*

Benchmarking Practice of comparing and analyzing company financial performance or position with other companies or standards.

Betterments Expenditures to make a plant asset more efficient or productive; also called *improvements. (p. 403)*

Bond Written promise to pay the bond's par (or face) value and interest at a stated contract rate; often issued in denominations of $1,000. *(p. 550)*

Bond certificate Document containing bond specifics such as issuer's name, bond par value, contract interest rate, and maturity date. *(p. 552)*

Bond indenture Contract between the bond issuer and the bondholders; identifies the parties' rights and obligations. *(p. 552)*

Book value Asset's acquisition costs less its accumulated depreciation (or depletion, or amortization); also sometimes used synonymously as the *carrying value* of an account. *(p. 98)*

Book value per common share Recorded amount of equity applicable to common shares divided by the number of common shares outstanding. *(p. 526)*

Book value per preferred share Equity applicable to preferred shares (equals its call price [or par value if it is not callable] plus any cumulative dividends in arrears) divided by the number of preferred shares outstanding. *(p. 526)*

Bookkeeping (See *recordkeeping.*)

Break-even point Output level at which sales equals fixed plus variable costs; where income equals zero. *(p. 909)*

Break-even time (BET) Time-based measurement used to evaluate the acceptability of an investment; equals the time expected to pass before the present value of the net cash flows from an investment equals its initial cost. *(p. 1043)*

Budget Formal statement of future plans, usually expressed in monetary terms. *(p. 940)*

Budget report Report comparing actual results to planned objectives; sometimes used as a progress report. *(p. 980)*

Budgetary control Management use of budgets to monitor and control company operations. *(p. 980)*

Budgeted balance sheet Accounting report that presents predicted amounts of the company's assets, liabilities, and equity balances as of the end of the budget period. *(p. 952)*

Budgeted income statement Accounting report that presents predicted amounts of the company's revenues and expenses for the budget period. *(p. 952)*

Budgeting Process of planning future business actions and expressing them as formal plans. *(p. 940)*

Business An organization of one or more individuals selling products and/or services for profit. *(p. 10)*

Business entity assumption Principle that requires a business to be accounted for separately from its owner(s) and from any other entity. *(p. 10)*

Business segment Part of a company that can be separately identified by the products or services that it provides or by the geographic markets that it serves; also called *segment. (p. 703)*

C corporation Corporation that does not qualify for nor elect to be treated as a proprietorship or partnership for income tax purposes and therefore is subject to income taxes; also called *C corp. (p. 480)*

Call price Amount that must be paid to call and retire a callable preferred stock or a callable bond. *(p. 519)*

Callable bonds Bonds that give the issuer the option to retire them at a stated amount prior to maturity. *(p. 563)*

Callable preferred stock Preferred stock that the issuing corporation, at its option, may retire by paying the call price plus any dividends in arrears. *(p. 519)*

Canceled checks Checks that the bank has paid and deducted from the depositor's account. *(p. 328)*

Capital budgeting Process of analyzing alternative investments and deciding which assets to acquire or sell. *(p. 1024)*

Capital expenditures Additional costs of plant assets that provide material benefits extending beyond the current period; also called *balance sheet expenditures. (p. 402)*

Capital expenditures budget Plan that lists dollar amounts to be both received from disposal of plant assets and spent to purchase plant assets. *(p. 949)*

Capital leases Long-term leases in which the lessor transfers substantially all risk and rewards of ownership to the lessee. *(p. 574)*

Capital stock General term referring to a corporation's stock used in obtaining capital (owner financing). *(p. 509)*

Capitalize Record the cost as part of a permanent account and allocate it over later periods. *(p. 402)*

Carrying (book) value of bonds Net amount at which bonds are reported on the balance sheet; equals the par value of the bonds less any unamortized discount or plus any unamortized premium; also called *carrying amount* or *book value. (p. 554)*

Cash Includes currency, coins, and amounts on deposit in bank checking or savings accounts. *(p. 319)*

Cash basis accounting Accounting system that recognizes revenues when cash is received and records expenses when cash is paid. *(p. 93)*

Cash budget Plan that shows expected cash inflows and outflows during the budget period, including receipts from loans needed to maintain a minimum cash balance and repayments of such loans. *(p. 950)*

Cash disbursements journal Special journal normally used to record all payments of cash; also called *cash payments journal. (p. 280)*

Cash discount Reduction in the price of merchandise granted by a seller to a buyer when payment is made within the discount period. *(p. 181)*

Cash equivalents Short-term, investment assets that are readily convertible to a known cash amount or sufficiently close to their maturity date (usually within 90 days) so that market value is not sensitive to interest rate changes. *(p. 319)*

Cash flow on total assets Ratio of operating cash flows to average total assets; not sensitive to income recognition and measurement; partly reflects earnings quality. *(p. 646)*

Cash Over and Short Income statement account used to record cash overages and cash shortages arising from errors in cash receipts or payments. *(p. 321)*

Cash receipts journal Special journal normally used to record all receipts of cash. *(p. 277)*

Change in an accounting estimate Change in an accounting estimate that results from new information, subsequent developments, or improved judgment that impacts current and future periods. *(pp. 401 & 523)*

Chart of accounts List of accounts used by a company; includes an identification number for each account. *(p. 52)*

Check Document signed by a depositor instructing the bank to pay a specified amount to a designated recipient. *(p. 326)*

Check register Another name for a cash disbursements journal when the journal has a column for check numbers. *(pp. 280 & 337)*

Classified balance sheet Balance sheet that presents assets and liabilities in relevant subgroups, including current and noncurrent classifications. *(p. 145)*

Clock card Source document used to record the number of hours an employee works and to determine the total labor cost for each pay period. *(p. 776)*

Closing entries Entries recorded at the end of each accounting period to transfer end-of-period balances in revenue, gain, expense, loss, and withdrawal (dividend for a corporation) accounts to the capital account (to retained earnings for a corporation). *(p. 141)*

Closing process Necessary end-of-period steps to prepare the accounts for recording the transactions of the next period. *(p. 140)*

Columnar journal Journal with more than one column. *(p. 274)*

Common stock Corporation's basic ownership share; also generically called *capital stock. (pp. 11 & 508)*

Common-size financial statement Statement that expresses each amount as a percent of a base amount. In the balance sheet, total assets is usually the base and is expressed as 100%. In the income statement, net sales is usually the base. *(p. 687)*

Comparative financial statement Statement with data for two or more successive periods placed in side-by-side columns, often with changes shown in dollar amounts and percents. *(p. 682)*

Compatibility principle Information system principle that prescribes an accounting system to conform with a company's activities, personnel, and structure. *(p. 269)*

Complex capital structure Capital structure that includes outstanding rights or options to purchase common stock, or securities that are convertible into common stock. *(p. 524)*

Components of accounting systems Five basic components of accounting systems are source documents, input devices, information processors, information storage, and output devices. *(p. 269)*

Composite unit Generic unit consisting of a specific number of units of each product; unit comprised in proportion to the expected sales mix of its products. *(p. 916)*

Compound journal entry Journal entry that affects at least three accounts. *(p. 61)*

Comprehensive income Net change in equity for a period, excluding owner investments and distributions. *(p. 600)*

Computer hardware Physical equipment in a computerized accounting information system.

Computer network Linkage giving different users and different computers access to common databases and programs. *(p. 283)*

Computer software Programs that direct operations of computer hardware.

Conservatism constraint Principle that prescribes the less optimistic estimate when two estimates are about equally likely. *(p. 234)*

Consignee Receiver of goods owned by another who holds them for purposes of selling them for the owner. *(p. 224)*

Consignor Owner of goods who ships them to another party who will sell them for the owner. *(p. 224)*

Consistency concept Principle that prescribes use of the same accounting method(s) over time so that financial statements are comparable across periods. *(p. 233)*

Consolidated financial statements Financial statements that show all (combined) activities under the parent's control, including those of any subsidiaries. *(p. 599)*

Contingent liability Obligation to make a future payment if, and only if, an uncertain future event occurs. *(p. 445)*

Continuous budgeting Practice of preparing budgets for a selected number of future periods and revising those budgets as each period is completed. *(p. 942)*

Continuous improvement Concept requiring every manager and employee continually to look to improve operations. *(p. 730)*

Contra account Account linked with another account and having an opposite normal balance; reported as a subtraction from the other account's balance. *(p. 97)*

Contract rate Interest rate specified in a bond indenture (or note); multiplied by the par value to determine the interest paid each period; also called *coupon rate, stated rate,* or *nominal rate. (p. 553)*

Contributed capital Total amount of cash and other assets received from stockholders in exchange for stock; also called *paid-in capital. (p. 13)*

Contributed capital in excess of par value Difference between the par value of stock and its issue price when issued at a price above par.

Contribution margin Sales revenue less total variable costs.

Contribution margin income statement Income statement that separates variable and fixed costs; highlights the contribution margin, which is sales less variable expenses.

Contribution margin per unit Amount that the sale of one unit contributes toward recovering fixed costs and earning profit; defined as sales price per unit minus variable expense per unit. *(p. 908)*

Contribution margin ratio Product's contribution margin divided by its sale price. *(p. 908)*

Control Process of monitoring planning decisions and evaluating the organization's activities and employees. *(p. 727)*

Control principle Information system principle that prescribes an accounting system to aid managers in controlling and monitoring business activities. *(p. 268)*

Controllable costs Costs that a manager has the power to control or at least strongly influence. *(pp. 733 & 870)*

Controllable variance Combination of both overhead spending variances (variable and fixed) and the variable overhead efficiency variance. *(p. 993)*

Controlling account General ledger account, the balance of which (after posting) equals the sum of the balances in its related subsidiary ledger. *(p. 273)*

Conversion costs Expenditures incurred in converting raw materials to finished goods; includes direct labor costs and overhead costs. *(p. 738)*

Convertible bonds Bonds that bondholders can exchange for a set number of the issuer's shares. *(p. 563)*

Convertible preferred stock Preferred stock with an option to exchange it for common stock at a specified rate. *(p. 518)*

Copyright Right giving the owner the exclusive privilege to publish and sell musical, literary, or artistic work during the creator's life plus 70 years. *(p. 408)*

Corporation Business that is a separate legal entity under state or federal laws with owners called *shareholders* or *stockholders. (pp. 11 & 506)*

Cost All normal and reasonable expenditures necessary to get an asset in place and ready for its intended use. *(p. 393)*

Cost accounting system Accounting system for manufacturing activities based on the perpetual inventory system. *(p. 770)*

Cost-benefit principle Information system principle that prescribes the benefits from an activity in an accounting system to outweigh the costs of that activity. *(p. 269)*

Cost center Department that incurs costs but generates no revenues; common example is the accounting or legal department. *(p. 858)*

Cost object Product, process, department, or customer to which costs are assigned. *(p. 732)*

Cost of goods available for sale Consists of beginning inventory plus net purchases of a period.

Cost of goods manufactured Total manufacturing costs (direct materials, direct labor, and factory overhead) for the period plus beginning goods in process less ending goods in process; also called *net cost of goods manufactured* and *cost of goods completed. (p. 821)*

Cost of goods sold Cost of inventory sold to customers during a period; also called *cost of sales. (p. 178)*

Cost principle Accounting principle that prescribes financial statement information to be based on actual costs incurred in business transactions. *(p. 9)*

Cost variance Difference between the actual incurred cost and the standard cost. *(p. 986)*

Cost-volume-profit (CVP) analysis Planning method that includes predicting the volume of activity, the costs incurred, sales earned, and profits received. *(p. 902)*

Cost-volume-profit (CVP) chart Graphic representation of cost-volume-profit relations. *(p. 910)*

Coupon bonds Bonds with interest coupons attached to their certificates; bondholders detach coupons when they mature and present them to a bank or broker for collection. *(p. 563)*

Credit Recorded on the right side; an entry that decreases asset and expense accounts, and increases liability, revenue, and most equity accounts; abbreviated Cr. *(p. 53)*

Credit memorandum Notification that the sender has credited the recipient's account in the sender's records. *(p. 187)*

Credit period Time period that can pass before a customer's payment is due. *(p. 181)*

Credit terms Description of the amounts and timing of payments that a buyer (debtor) agrees to make in the future. *(p. 181)*

Creditors Individuals or organizations entitled to receive payments. *(p. 50)*

Cumulative preferred stock Preferred stock on which undeclared dividends accumulate until paid; common stockholders cannot receive dividends until cumulative dividends are paid. *(p. 517)*

Current assets Cash and other assets expected to be sold, collected, or used within one year or the company's operating cycle, whichever is longer. *(p. 146)*

Current liabilities Obligations due to be paid or settled within one year or the company's operating cycle, whichever is longer. *(pp. 147 & 435)*

Current portion of long-term debt Portion of long-term debt due within one year or the operating cycle, whichever is longer; reported under current liabilities. *(p. 442)*

Current ratio Ratio used to evaluate a company's ability to pay its short-term obligations, calculated by dividing current assets by current liabilities. *(p. 147)*

Curvilinear cost Cost that changes with volume but not at a constant rate. *(p. 904)*

Customer orientation Company position that its managers and employees be in tune with the changing wants and needs of consumers. *(p. 729)*

Cycle efficiency (CE) A measure of production efficiency, which is defined as value-added (process) time divided by total cycle time. *(p. 743)*

Cycle time (CT) A measure of the time to produce a product or service, which is the sum of process time, inspection time, move time, and wait time; also called *throughput time. (p. 742)*

Date of declaration Date the directors vote to pay a dividend. *(p. 513)*

Date of payment Date the corporation makes the dividend payment. *(p. 513)*

Date of record Date directors specify for identifying stockholders to receive dividends. *(p. 513)*

Days' sales in inventory Estimate of number of days needed to convert inventory into receivables or cash; equals ending inventory divided by cost of goods sold and then multiplied by 365; also called *days' stock on hand. (p. 237)*

Days' sales uncollected Measure of the liquidity of receivables computed by dividing the current balance of receivables by the annual credit (or net) sales and then multiplying by 365; also called *days' sales in receivables. (p. 332)*

Debit Recorded on the left side; an entry that increases asset and expense accounts, and decreases liability, revenue, and most equity accounts; abbreviated Dr. *(p. 53)*

Debit memorandum Notification that the sender has debited the recipient's account in the sender's records. *(p. 182)*

Debt ratio Ratio of total liabilities to total assets; used to reflect risk associated with a company's debts. *(p. 67)*

Debt-to-equity ratio Defined as total liabilities divided by total equity; shows the proportion of a company financed by non-owners (creditors) in comparison with that financed by owners. *(p. 564)*

Debtors Individuals or organizations that owe money. *(p. 49)*

Declining-balance method Method that determines depreciation charge for the period by multiplying a depreciation rate (often twice the straight-line rate) by the asset's beginning-period book value. *(p. 398)*

Deferred income tax liability Corporation income taxes that are deferred until future years because of temporary differences between GAAP and tax rules. *(p. 457)*

Degree of operating leverage (DOL) Ratio of contribution margin divided by pretax income; used to assess the effect on income of changes in sales. *(p. 918)*

Departmental accounting system Accounting system that provides information useful in evaluating the profitability or cost effectiveness of a department. *(p. 858)*

Departmental contribution to overhead Amount by which a department's revenues exceed its direct expenses. *(p. 866)*

Depletion Process of allocating the cost of natural resources to periods when they are consumed and sold. *(p. 406)*

Deposit ticket Lists items such as currency, coins, and checks deposited and their corresponding dollar amounts. *(p. 326)*

Deposits in transit Deposits recorded by the company but not yet recorded by its bank. *(p. 329)*

Depreciable cost Cost of a plant asset less its salvage value.

Depreciation Expense created by allocating the cost of plant and equipment to periods in which they are used; represents the expense of using the asset. *(pp. 97 & 395)*

Diluted earnings per share Earnings per share calculation that requires dilutive securities be added to the denominator of the basic EPS calculation. *(p. 524)*

Dilutive securities Securities having the potential to increase common shares outstanding; examples are options, rights, convertible bonds, and convertible preferred stock. *(p. 524)*

Direct costs Costs incurred for the benefit of one specific cost object. *(p. 732)*

Direct expenses Expenses traced to a specific department (object) that are incurred for the sole benefit of that department. *(p. 859)*

Direct labor Efforts of employees who physically convert materials to finished product. *(p. 738)*

Direct labor costs Wages and salaries for direct labor that are separately and readily traced through the production process to finished goods. *(p. 738)*

Direct material Raw material that physically becomes part of the product and is clearly identified with specific products or batches of product. *(p. 738)*

Direct material costs Expenditures for direct material that are separately and readily traced through the production process to finished goods. *(p. 738)*

Direct method Presentation of net cash from operating activities for the statement of cash flows that lists major operating cash receipts less major operating cash payments. *(p. 634)*

Direct write-off method Method that records the loss from an uncollectible account receivable at the time it is determined to be uncollectible; no attempt is made to estimate bad debts. *(p. 361)*

Discount on bonds payable Difference between a bond's par value and its lower issue price or carrying value; occurs when the contract rate is less than the market rate. *(p. 553)*

Discount on note payable Difference between the face value of a note payable and the (lesser) amount borrowed; reflects the added interest to be paid on the note over its life.

Discount on stock Difference between the par value of stock and its issue price when issued at a price below par value. *(p. 511)*

Discount period Time period in which a cash discount is available and the buyer can make a reduced payment. *(p. 181)*

Discount rate Expected rate of return on investments; also called *cost of capital, hurdle rate,* or *required rate of return. (p. B-2)*

Discounts lost Expenses resulting from not taking advantage of cash discounts on purchases. *(p. 338)*

Dividend in arrears Unpaid dividend on cumulative preferred stock; must be paid before any regular dividends on preferred stock and before any dividends on common stock. *(p. 517)*

Dividend yield Ratio of the annual amount of cash dividends distributed to common shareholders relative to the common stock's market value (price). *(p. 525)*

Dividends Corporation's distributions of assets to its owners.

Double-declining-balance (DDB) depreciation Depreciation equals beginning book value multiplied by 2 times the straight-line rate.

Double-entry accounting Accounting system in which each transaction affects at least two accounts and has at least one debit and one credit. *(p. 53)*

Double taxation Corporate income is taxed and then its later distribution through dividends is normally taxed again for shareholders. *(p. 11)*

Earnings (See *net income.*)

Earnings per share (EPS) Amount of income earned by each share of a company's outstanding common stock; also called *net income per share. (p. 524)*

Effective interest method Allocates interest expense over the bond life to yield a constant rate of interest; interest expense for a period is found by multiplying the balance of the liability at the beginning of the period by the bond market rate at issuance; also called *interest method. (p. 569)*

Efficiency Company's productivity in using its assets; usually measured relative to how much revenue a certain level of assets generates. *(p. 681)*

Efficiency variance Difference between the actual quantity of an input and the standard quantity of that input. *(p. 993)*

Electronic funds transfer (EFT) Use of electronic communication to transfer cash from one party to another. *(p. 327)*

Employee benefits Additional compensation paid to or on behalf of employees, such as premiums for medical, dental, life, and disability insurance, and contributions to pension plans. *(p. 443)*

Employee earnings report Record of an employee's net pay, gross pay, deductions, and year-to-date payroll information. *(p. 454)*

Enterprise resource planning (ERP) software Programs that manage a company's vital operations, which range from order taking to production to accounting. *(p. 283)*

Entity Organization that, for accounting purposes, is separate from other organizations and individuals. *(p. 10)*

EOM Abbreviation for *end of month;* used to describe credit terms for credit transactions. *(p. 181)*

Equity Owner's claim on the assets of a business; equals the residual interest in an entity's assets after deducting liabilities; also called *net assets. (p. 13)*

Equity method Accounting method used for long-term investments when the investor has "significant influence" over the investee. *(p. 598)*

Equity ratio Portion of total assets provided by equity, computed as total equity divided by total assets. *(p. 695)*

Equity securities with controlling influence Long-term investment when the investor is able to exert controlling influence over the investee; investors owning 50% or more of voting stock are presumed to exert controlling influence. *(p. 599)*

Equity securities with significant influence Long-term investment when the investor is able to exert significant influence over the investee; investors owning 20 percent or more (but less than 50 percent) of voting stock are presumed to exert significant influence. *(p. 598)*

Equivalent units of production (EUP) Number of units that would be completed if all effort during a period had been applied to units that were started and finished. *(p. 815)*

Estimated liability Obligation of an uncertain amount that can be reasonably estimated. *(p. 443)*

Estimated line of cost behavior Line drawn on a graph to visually fit the relation between cost and sales. *(p. 906)*

Ethics Codes of conduct by which actions are judged as right or wrong, fair or unfair, honest or dishonest. *(pp. 8, 731)*

Events Happenings that both affect an organization's financial position and can be reliably measured. *(p. 14)*

Expanded accounting equation Assets = Liabilities + Equity; Equity equals [Owner capital − Owner withdrawals + Revenues − Expenses] for a noncorporation; Equity equals [Contributed capital + Retained earnings + Revenues − Expenses] for a corporation where dividends are subtracted from retained earnings. *(p. 13)*

Expenses Outflows or using up of assets as part of operations of a business to generate sales. *(p. 13)*

External transactions Exchanges of economic value between one entity and another entity. *(p. 13)*

External users Persons using accounting information who are not directly involved in running the organization. *(p. 5)*

Extraordinary gains or losses Gains or losses reported separately from continuing operations because they are both unusual and infrequent. *(p. 703)*

Extraordinary repairs Major repairs that extend the useful life of a plant asset beyond prior expectations; treated as a capital expenditure. *(p. 403)*

Factory overhead Factory activities supporting the production process that are not direct material or direct labor; also called *overhead* and *manufacturing overhead. (p. 738)*

Factory overhead costs Expenditures for factory overhead that cannot be separately or readily traced to finished goods; also called *overhead costs. (p. 738)*

Favorable variance Difference in actual revenues or expenses from the budgeted amount that contributes to a higher income. *(p. 981)*

Federal depository bank Bank authorized to accept deposits of amounts payable to the federal government. *(p. 452)*

Federal Insurance Contributions Act (FICA) Taxes Taxes assessed on both employers and employees; for Social Security and Medicare programs. *(p. 440)*

Federal Unemployment Taxes (FUTA) Payroll taxes on employers assessed by the federal government to support its unemployment insurance program. *(p. 442)*

FIFO method (See *first-in, first-out.*)

Financial accounting Area of accounting mainly aimed at serving external users. *(p. 5)*

Financial Accounting Standards Board (FASB) Independent group of full-time members responsible for setting accounting rules. *(p. 9)*

Financial leverage Earning a higher return on equity by paying dividends on preferred stock or interest on debt at a rate lower than the return earned with the assets from issuing preferred stock or debt; also called *trading on the equity. (p. 519)*

Financial reporting Process of communicating information relevant to investors, creditors, and others in making investment, credit, and business decisions. *(p. 681)*

Financial statement analysis Application of analytical tools to general-purpose financial statements and related data for making business decisions. *(p. 680)*

Financial statements Includes the balance sheet, income statement, statement of owner's (or stockholders') equity, and statement of cash flows. *(p. 17)*

Financing activities Transactions with owners and creditors that include obtaining cash from issuing debt, repaying amounts borrowed, and obtaining cash from or distributing cash to owners. *(p. 630)*

Finished goods inventory Account that controls the finished goods files, which acts as a subsidiary ledger (of the Inventory account) in which the costs of finished goods that are ready for sale are recorded. *(pp. 736 & 772)*

First-in, first-out (FIFO) Method to assign cost to inventory that assumes items are sold in the order acquired; earliest items purchased are the first sold. *(pp. 229, 827)*

Fiscal year Consecutive 12-month (or 52-week) period chosen as the organization's annual accounting period. *(p. 93)*

Fixed budget Planning budget based on a single predicted amount of volume; unsuitable for evaluations if the actual volume differs from predicted volume. *(p. 981)*

Fixed budget performance report Report that compares actual revenues and costs with fixed budgeted amounts and identifies the differences as favorable or unfavorable variances. *(p. 981)*

Fixed cost Cost that does not change with changes in the volume of activity. *(p. 732)*

Flexibility principle Information system principle that prescribes an accounting system be able to adapt to changes in the company, its operations, and needs of decision makers. *(p. 269)*

Flexible budget Budget prepared (using actual volume) once a period is complete that helps managers evaluate past performance; uses fixed and variable costs in determining total costs. *(p. 982)*

Flexible budget performance report Report that compares actual revenues and costs with their variable budgeted amounts based on actual sales volume (or other level of activity) and identifies the differences as variances. *(p. 958)*

FOB Abbreviation for *free on board;* the point when ownership of goods passes to the buyer; *FOB shipping point* (or *factory*) means the buyer pays shipping costs and accepts ownership of goods when the seller transfers goods to carrier; *FOB destination* means the seller pays shipping costs and buyer accepts ownership of goods at the buyer's place of business. *(p. 183)*

Foreign exchange rate Price of one currency stated in terms of another currency. *(p. 605)*

Form 940 IRS form used to report an employer's federal unemployment taxes (FUTA) on an annual filing basis. *(p. 452)*

Form 941 IRS form filed to report FICA taxes owed and remitted. *(p. 450)*

Form 10-K (or 10-KSB) Annual report form filed with SEC by businesses (small businesses) with publicly traded securities. *(p. A-1)*

Form W-2 Annual report by an employer to each employee showing the employee's wages subject to FICA and federal income taxes along with amounts withheld. *(p. 452)*

Form W-4 Withholding allowance certificate, filed with the employer, identifying the number of withholding allowances claimed. *(p. 454)*

Franchises Privileges granted by a company or government to sell a product or service under specified conditions. *(p. 408)*

Full disclosure principle Principle that prescribes financial statements (including notes) to report all relevant information about an entity's operations and financial condition. *(p. 10)*

GAAP (See *generally accepted accounting principles.*)

General accounting system Accounting system for manufacturing activities based on the *periodic* inventory system. *(p. 770)*

General and administrative expenses Expenses that support the operating activities of a business. *(p. 191)*

General and administrative expense budget Plan that shows predicted operating expenses not included in the selling expenses budget. *(p. 948)*

General journal All-purpose journal for recording the debits and credits of transactions and events. *(pp. 54 & 272)*

General ledger (See *ledger.*)

General partner Partner who assumes unlimited liability for the debts of the partnership; responsible for partnership management. *(p. 479)*

General partnership Partnership in which all partners have mutual agency and unlimited liability for partnership debts. *(p. 479)*

Generally accepted accounting principles (GAAP) Rules that specify acceptable accounting practices. *(p. 8)*

Generally accepted auditing standards (GAAS) Rules that specify acceptable auditing practices.

General-purpose financial statements Statements published periodically for use by a variety of interested parties; includes the income statement, balance sheet, statement of owner's equity (or statement of retained earnings for a corporation), statement of cash flows, and notes to these statements. *(p. 681)*

Going-concern assumption Principle that prescribes financial statements to reflect the assumption that the business will continue operating. *(p. 10)*

Goods in process inventory Account in which costs are accumulated for products that are in the process of being produced but are not yet complete; also called *work in process inventory. (pp. 736 & 772)*

Goodwill Amount by which a company's (or a segment's) value exceeds the value of its individual assets less its liabilities. *(p. 409)*

Gross margin (See *gross profit.*)

Gross margin ratio Gross margin (net sales minus cost of goods sold) divided by net sales; also called *gross profit ratio. (p. 193)*

Gross method Method of recording purchases at the full invoice price without deducting any cash discounts. *(p. 338)*

Gross pay Total compensation earned by an employee. *(p. 440)*

Gross profit Net sales minus cost of goods sold; also called *gross margin. (p. 178)*

Gross profit method Procedure to estimate inventory when the past gross profit rate is used to estimate cost of goods sold, which is then subtracted from the cost of goods available for sale. *(p. 248)*

Held-to-maturity (HTM) securities Debt securities that a company has the intent and ability to hold until they mature. *(p. 596)*

High-low method Procedure that yields an estimated line of cost behavior by graphically connecting costs associated with the highest and lowest sales volume. *(p. 906)*

Horizontal analysis Comparison of a company's financial condition and performance across time. *(p. 682)*

Hurdle rate Minimum acceptable rate of return (set by management) for an investment. *(pp. 868 & 1033)*

Impairment Diminishment of an asset value. *(pp. 402 & 407)*

Imprest system Method to account for petty cash; maintains a constant balance in the fund, which equals cash plus petty cash receipts.

Inadequacy Condition in which the capacity of plant assets is too small to meet the company's production demands. *(p. 395)*

Income (See *net income.*)

Income statement Financial statement that subtracts expenses from revenues to yield a net income or loss over a specified period of time; also includes any gains or losses. *(p. 17)*

Income Summary Temporary account used only in the closing process to which the balances of revenue and expense accounts (including any gains or losses) are transferred; its balance is transferred to the capital account (or retained earnings for a corporation). *(p. 141)*

Incremental cost Additional cost incurred only if a company pursues a specific course of action. *(p. 1036)*

Indefinite life Asset life that is not limited by legal, regulatory, contractual, competitive, economic, or other factors. *(p. 407)*

Indirect costs Costs incurred for the benefit of more than one cost object. *(p. 732)*

Indirect expenses Expenses incurred for the joint benefit of more than one department (or cost object). *(p. 859)*

Indirect labor Efforts of production employees who do not work specifically on converting direct materials into finished products and who are not clearly identified with specific units or batches of product. *(p. 738)*

Indirect labor costs Labor costs that cannot be physically traced to production of a product or service; included as part of overhead. *(p. 738)*

Indirect material Material used to support the production process but not clearly identified with products or batches of product. *(p. 735)*

Indirect method Presentation that reports net income and then adjusts it by adding and subtracting items to yield net cash from operating activities on the statement of cash flows. *(p. 634)*

Information processor Component of an accounting system that interprets, transforms, and summarizes information for use in analysis and reporting. *(p. 270)*

Information storage Component of an accounting system that keeps data in a form accessible to information processors. *(p. 270)*

Infrequent gain or loss Gain or loss not expected to recur given the operating environment of the business. *(p. 703)*

Input device Means of capturing information from source documents that enables its transfer to information processors. *(p. 270)*

Installment note Liability requiring a series of periodic payments to the lender. *(p. 560)*

Institute of Management Accountants (IMA) A professional association of management accountants. *(p. 731)*

Intangible assets Long-term assets (resources) used to produce or sell products or services; usually lack physical form and have uncertain benefits. *(pp. 147 & 407)*

Interest Charge for using money (or other assets) loaned from one entity to another. *(p. 368)*

Interim financial statements Financial statements covering periods of less than one year; usually based on one-, three-, or six-month periods. *(pp. 92 & 247)*

Internal controls or **Internal control system** All policies and procedures used to protect assets, ensure reliable accounting, promote efficient operations, and urge adherence to company policies. *(pp. 268 & 314)*

Internal rate of return (IRR) Rate used to evaluate the acceptability of an investment; equals the rate that yields a net present value of zero for an investment. *(p. 1031)*

Internal transactions Activities within an organization that can affect the accounting equation. *(p. 13)*

Internal users Persons using accounting information who are directly involved in managing the organization. *(p. 6)*

International Accounting Standards Board (IASB) Group that identifies preferred accounting practices and encourages global acceptance; issues International Financial Reporting Standards (IFRS). *(p. 9)*

Inventory Goods a company owns and expects to sell in its normal operations. *(p. 179)*

Inventory turnover Number of times a company's average inventory is sold during a period; computed by dividing cost of goods sold by average inventory; also called *merchandise turnover. (p. 236)*

Investing activities Transactions that involve purchasing and selling of long-term assets, includes making and collecting notes receivable and investments in other than cash equivalents. *(p. 630)*

Investment center Center of which a manager is responsible for revenues, costs, and asset investments. *(p. 858)*

Investment center residual income The net income an investment center earns above a target return on average invested assets. *(p. 867)*

Investment center return on total assets Center net income divided by average total assets for the center. *(p. 867)*

Investment turnover The efficiency with which a company generates sales from its available assets; computed as sales divided by average invested assets. *(p. 872)*

Invoice Itemized record of goods prepared by the vendor that lists the customer's name, items sold, sales prices, and terms of sale. *(p. 335)*

Invoice approval Document containing a checklist of steps necessary for approving the recording and payment of an invoice; also called *check authorization. (p. 336)*

Job Production of a customized product or service. *(p. 770)*

Job cost sheet Separate record maintained for each job. *(p. 772)*

Job lot Production of more than one unit of a customized product or service. *(p. 771)*

Job order cost accounting system Cost accounting system to determine the cost of producing each job or job lot. *(pp. 772 & 811)*

Job order production Production of special-order products; also called *customized production. (p. 770)*

Joint cost Cost incurred to produce or purchase two or more products at the same time. *(p. 877)*

Journal Record in which transactions are entered before they are posted to ledger accounts; also called *book of original entry. (p. 54)*

Journalizing Process of recording transactions in a journal. *(p. 54)*

Just-in-time (JIT) manufacturing Process of acquiring or producing inventory only when needed. *(p. 730)*

Known liabilities Obligations of a company with little uncertainty; set by agreements, contracts, or laws; also called *definitely determinable liabilities. (p. 436)*

Land improvements Assets that increase the benefits of land, have a limited useful life, and are depreciated. *(p. 394)*

Large stock dividend Stock dividend that is more than 25% of the previously outstanding shares. *(p. 514)*

Last-in, first-out (LIFO) Method to assign cost to inventory that assumes costs for the most recent items purchased are sold first and charged to cost of goods sold. *(p. 229)*

Lean business model Practice of eliminating waste while meeting customer needs and yielding positive company returns. *(p. 730)*

Lease Contract specifying the rental of property. *(pp. 409 & 573)*

Leasehold Rights the lessor grants to the lessee under the terms of a lease. *(p. 409)*

Leasehold improvements Alterations or improvements to leased property such as partitions and storefronts. *(p. 409)*

Least-squares regression Statistical method for deriving an estimated line of cost behavior that is more precise than the high-low method and the scatter diagram. *(p. 907)*

Ledger Record containing all accounts (with amounts) for a business; also called *general ledger. (p. 49)*

Lessee Party to a lease who secures the right to possess and use the property from another party (the lessor). *(p. 409)*

Lessor Party to a lease who grants another party (the lessee) the right to possess and use its property. *(p. 409)*

Liabilities Creditors' claims on an organization's assets; involves a probable future payment of assets, products, or services that a company is obligated to make due to past transactions or events. *(p. 12)*

Licenses (See *franchises.*) *(p. 408)*

Limited liability Owner can lose no more than the amount invested. *(p. 11)*

Limited liability company Organization form that combines select features of a corporation and a limited partnership; provides limited liability to its members (owners), is free of business tax, and allows members to actively participate in management. *(p. 480)*

Limited liability partnership Partnership in which a partner is not personally liable for malpractice or negligence unless that partner is responsible for providing the service that resulted in the claim. *(p. 479)*

Limited life (See *useful life.*)

Limited partners Partners who have no personal liability for partnership debts beyond the amounts they invested in the partnership. *(p. 479)*

Limited partnership Partnership that has two classes of partners, limited partners and general partners. *(p. 479)*

Liquid assets Resources such as cash that are easily converted into other assets or used to pay for goods, services, or liabilities. *(p. 319)*

Liquidating cash dividend Distribution of assets that returns part of the original investment to stockholders; deducted from contributed capital accounts. *(p. 514)*

Liquidation Process of going out of business; involves selling assets, paying liabilities, and distributing remainder to owners.

Liquidity Availability of resources to meet short-term cash requirements. *(pp. 319 & 681)*

List price Catalog (full) price of an item before any trade discount is deducted. *(p. 180)*

Long-term investments Long-term assets not used in operating activities such as notes receivable and investments in stocks and bonds. *(pp. 147 & 592)*

Long-term liabilities Obligations not due to be paid within one year or the operating cycle, whichever is longer. *(pp. 147 & 435)*

Lower of cost or market (LCM) Required method to report inventory at market replacement cost when that market cost is lower than recorded cost. *(p. 233)*

Maker of the note Entity who signs a note and promises to pay it at maturity. *(p. 368)*

Management by exception Management process to focus on significant variances and give less attention to areas where performance is close to the standard. *(p. 996)*

Managerial accounting Area of accounting mainly aimed at serving the decision-making needs of internal users; also called *management accounting. (pp. 6 & 726)*

Manufacturer Company that uses labor and operating assets to convert raw materials to finished goods. *(p. 13)*

Manufacturing budget Plan that shows the predicted costs for direct materials, direct labor, and overhead to be incurred in manufacturing units in the production budget. *(p. 959)*

Manufacturing statement Report that summarizes the types and amounts of costs incurred in a company's production process for a period; also called *cost of goods manufacturing statement. (p. 740)*

Margin of safety Excess of expected sales over the level of break-even sales. *(p. 914)*

Market prospects Expectations (both good and bad) about a company's future performance as assessed by users and other interested parties. *(p. 681)*

Market rate Interest rate that borrowers are willing to pay and lenders are willing to accept for a specific lending agreement given the borrowers' risk level. *(p. 553)*

Market value per share Price at which stock is bought or sold. *(p. 509)*

Master budget Comprehensive business plan that includes specific plans for expected sales, product units to be produced, merchandise (or materials) to be purchased, expenses to be incurred, plant assets to be purchased, and amounts of cash to be borrowed or loans to be repaid, as well as a budgeted income statement and balance sheet. *(p. 944)*

Matching principle Prescribes expenses to be reported in the same period as the revenues that were earned as a result of the expenses. *(pp. 10 & 362)*

Materiality constraint Prescribes that accounting for items that significantly impact financial statement and any inferences from them adhere strictly to GAAP. *(p. 362)*

Materials consumption report Document that summarizes the materials a department uses during a reporting period; replaces materials requisitions. *(p. 812)*

Materials ledger card Perpetual record updated each time units are purchased or issued for production use. *(p. 773)*

Materials requisition Source document production managers use to request materials for production; used to assign materials costs to specific jobs or overhead. *(p. 774)*

Maturity date of a note Date when a note's principal and interest are due. *(p. 368)*

Merchandise (See *merchandise inventory.*)

Merchandise inventory Goods that a company owns and expects to sell to customers; also called *merchandise* or *inventory. (p. 179)*

Merchandise purchases budget Plan that shows the units or costs of merchandise to be purchased by a merchandising company during the budget period. *(p. 947)*

Merchandiser Entity that earns net income by buying and selling merchandise. *(p. 178)*

Merit rating Rating assigned to an employer by a state based on the employer's record of employment. *(p. 442)*

Minimum legal capital Amount of assets defined by law that stockholders must (potentially) invest in a corporation; usually defined as par value of the stock; intended to protect creditors. *(p. 509)*

Mixed cost Cost that behaves like a combination of fixed and variable costs. *(p. 903)*

Modified Accelerated Cost Recovery System (MACRS) Depreciation system required by federal income tax law. *(p. 400)*

Monetary unit assumption Principle that assumes transactions and events can be expressed in money units. *(p. 10)*

Mortgage Legal loan agreement that protects a lender by giving the lender the right to be paid from the cash proceeds from the sale of a borrower's assets identified in the mortgage. *(p. 562)*

Multinational Company that operates in several countries. *(p. 605)*

Multiple-step income statement Income statement format that shows subtotals between sales and net income, categorizes expenses, and often reports the details of net sales and expenses. *(p. 191)*

Mutual agency Legal relationship among partners whereby each partner is an agent of the partnership and is able to bind the partnership to contracts within the scope of the partnership's business. *(p. 478)*

Natural business year Twelve-month period that ends when a company's sales activities are at their lowest point. *(p. 93)*

Natural resources Assets physically consumed when used; examples are timber, mineral deposits, and oil and gas fields; also called *wasting assets. (p. 406)*

Net assets (See *equity.*)

Net income Amount earned after subtracting all expenses necessary for and matched with sales for a period; also called *income, profit,* or *earnings. (p. 13)*

Net loss Excess of expenses over revenues for a period. *(p. 18)*

Net method Method of recording purchases at the full invoice price less any cash discounts. *(p. 338)*

Net pay Gross pay less all deductions; also called *take-home pay. (p. 440)*

Net present value (NPV) Dollar estimate of an asset's value that is used to evaluate the acceptability of an investment; computed by discounting future cash flows from the investment at a satisfactory rate and then subtracting the initial cost of the investment. *(p. 1029)*

Net realizable value Expected selling price (value) of an item minus the cost of making the sale. *(p. 224)*

Noncumulative preferred stock Preferred stock on which the right to receive dividends is lost for any period when dividends are not declared. *(p. 517)*

Noninterest-bearing note Note with no stated (contract) rate of interest; interest is implicitly included in the note's face value.

Nonparticipating preferred stock Preferred stock on which dividends are limited to a maximum amount each year. *(p. 518)*

No-par value stock Stock class that has not been assigned a par (or stated) value by the corporate charter. *(p. 509)*

Nonsufficient funds (NSF) check Maker's bank account has insufficient money to pay the check; also called *hot check.*

Non-value-added time The portion of cycle time that is not directed at producing a product or service; equals the sum of inspection time, move time, and wait time. *(p. 743)*

Not controllable costs Costs that a manager does not have the power to control or strongly influence. *(p. 733)*

Note (See promissory note.)

Note payable Liability expressed by a written promise to pay a definite sum of money on demand or on a specific future date(s).

Note receivable Asset consisting of a written promise to receive a definite sum of money on demand or on a specific future date(s).

Objectivity principle Principle that prescribes independent, unbiased evidence to support financial statement information. *(p. 9)*

Obsolescence Condition in which, because of new inventions and improvements, a plant asset can no longer be used to produce goods or services with a competitive advantage. *(p. 395)*

Off-balance-sheet financing Acquisition of assets by agreeing to liabilities not reported on the balance sheet. *(p. 574)*

Online processing Approach to inputting data from source documents as soon as the information is available. *(p. 282)*

Operating activities Activities that involve the production or purchase of merchandise and the sale of goods or services to customers, including expenditures related to administering the business. *(p. 629)*

Operating cycle Normal time between paying cash for merchandise or employee services and receiving cash from customers. *(p. 145)*

Operating leases Short-term (or cancelable) leases in which the lessor retains risks and rewards of ownership. *(p. 573)*

Operating leverage Extent, or relative size, of fixed costs in the total cost structure. *(p. 918)*

Opportunity cost Potential benefit lost by choosing a specific action from two or more alternatives. *(p. 733)*

Ordinary repairs Repairs to keep a plant asset in normal, good operating condition; treated as a revenue expenditure and immediately expensed. *(p. 402)*

Organization expenses (costs) Costs such as legal fees and promoter fees to bring an entity into existence. *(pp. 507 & 512)*

Out-of-pocket cost Cost incurred or avoided as a result of management's decisions. *(p. 733)*

Output devices Means by which information is taken out of the accounting system and made available for use. *(p. 271)*

Outsourcing Manager decision to buy a product or service from another entity; part of a *make-or-buy* decision; also called *make or buy.*

Outstanding checks Checks written and recorded by the depositor but not yet paid by the bank at the bank statement date. *(p. 329)*

Outstanding stock Corporation's stock held by its shareholders.

Overapplied overhead Amount by which the overhead applied to production in a period using the predetermined overhead rate exceeds the actual overhead incurred in a period. *(p. 782)*

Overhead cost variance Difference between the total overhead cost applied to products and the total overhead cost actually incurred. *(p. 992)*

Owner, Capital Account showing the owner's claim on company assets; equals owner investments plus net income (or less net losses) minus owner withdrawals since the company's inception; also referred to as *equity. (p. 13)*

Owner investment Assets put into the business by the owner. *(p. 13)*

Owner's equity (See *equity.*)

Owner, Withdrawals Account used to record asset distributions to the owner. (See also *withdrawals.*) *(pp. 13 & 51)*

Paid-in capital (See *contributed capital.*) *(p. 510)*

Paid-in capital in excess of par value Amount received from issuance of stock that is in excess of the stock's par value. *(p. 511)*

Par value Value assigned a share of stock by the corporate charter when the stock is authorized. *(p. 509)*

Par value of a bond Amount the bond issuer agrees to pay at maturity and the amount on which cash interest payments are based; also called *face amount* or *face value* of a bond. *(p. 550)*

Par value stock Class of stock assigned a par value by the corporate charter. *(p. 509)*

Parent Company that owns a controlling interest in a corporation (requires more than 50% of voting stock). *(p. 599)*

Participating preferred stock Preferred stock that shares with common stockholders any dividends paid in excess of the percent stated on preferred stock. *(p. 518)*

Partner return on equity Partner net income divided by average partner equity for the period. *(p. 490)*

Partnership Unincorporated association of two or more persons to pursue a business for profit as co-owners. *(pp. 10 & 478)*

Partnership contract Agreement among partners that sets terms under which the affairs of the partnership are conducted; also called *articles of partnership. (p. 478)*

Partnership liquidation Dissolution of a partnership by (1) selling noncash assets and allocating any gain or loss according to partners' income-and-loss ratio, (2) paying liabilities, and (3) distributing any remaining cash according to partners' capital balances. *(p. 488)*

Patent Exclusive right granted to its owner to produce and sell an item or to use a process for 17 years. *(p. 408)*

Payback period (PBP) Time-based measurement used to evaluate the acceptability of an investment; equals the time expected to pass before an investment's net cash flows equal its initial cost. *(p. 1025)*

Payee of the note Entity to whom a note is made payable. *(p. 368)*

Payroll bank account Bank account used solely for paying employees; each pay period an amount equal to the total employees' net pay is deposited in it and the payroll checks are drawn on it. *(p. 454)*

Payroll deductions Amounts withheld from an employee's gross pay; also called *withholdings. (p. 440)*

Payroll register Record for a pay period that shows the pay period dates, regular and overtime hours worked, gross pay, net pay, and deductions. *(p. 452)*

Pension plan Contractual agreement between an employer and its employees for the employer to provide benefits to employees after they retire; expensed when incurred. *(p. 575)*

Period costs Expenditures identified more with a time period than with finished products costs; includes selling and general administrative expenses. *(p. 733)*

Periodic inventory system Method that records the cost of inventory purchased but does not continuously track the quantity available or sold to customers; records are updated at the end of each period to reflect the physical count and costs of goods available. *(p. 180)*

Permanent accounts Accounts that reflect activities related to one or more future periods; balance sheet accounts whose balances are not closed; also called *real accounts. (p. 140)*

Perpetual inventory system Method that maintains continuous records of the cost of inventory available and the cost of goods sold. *(p. 180)*

Petty cash Small amount of cash in a fund to pay minor expenses; accounted for using an imprest system. *(p. 323)*

Planning Process of setting goals and preparing to achieve them. *(p. 726)*

Plant assets Tangible long-lived assets used to produce or sell products and services; also called *property, plant and equipment (PP&E)* or *fixed assets. (p. 403)*

Pledged assets to secured liabilities Ratio of the book value of a company's pledged assets to the book value of its secured liabilities.

Post-closing trial balance List of permanent accounts and their balances from the ledger after all closing entries are journalized and posted. *(p. 144)*

Posting Process of transferring journal entry information to the ledger; computerized systems automate this process. *(p. 54)*

Posting reference (PR) column A column in journals in which individual ledger account numbers are entered when entries are posted to those ledger accounts. *(p. 56)*

Predetermined overhead rate Rate established prior to the beginning of a period that relates estimated overhead to another variable, such as estimated direct labor, and is used to assign overhead cost to production. *(p. 778)*

Preemptive right Stockholders' right to maintain their proportionate interest in a corporation with any additional shares issued. *(p. 508)*

Preferred stock Stock with a priority status over common stockholders in one or more ways, such as paying dividends or distributing assets. *(p. 516)*

Premium on bonds Difference between a bond's par value and its higher carrying value; occurs when the contract rate is higher than the market rate; also called *bond premium. (p. 556)*

Premium on stock (See *contributed capital in excess of par value.*) *(p. 511)*

Prepaid expenses Items paid for in advance of receiving their benefits; classified as assets. *(p. 95)*

Price-earnings (PE) ratio Ratio of a company's current market value per share to its earnings per share; also called *price-to-earnings. (p. 525)*

Price variance Difference between actual and budgeted revenue or cost caused by the difference between the actual price per unit and the budgeted price per unit. *(p. 984)*

Prime costs Expenditures directly identified with the production of finished goods; include direct materials costs and direct labor costs. *(p. 738)*

Principal of a note Amount that the signer of a note agrees to pay back when it matures, not including interest. *(p. 368)*

Principles of internal control Principles prescribing management to establish responsibility, maintain records, insure assets, separate recordkeeping from custody of assets, divide responsibility for related transactions, apply technological controls, and perform reviews. *(p. 315)*

Prior period adjustment Correction of an error in a prior year that is reported in the statement of retained earnings (or statement of stockholders' equity) net of any income tax effects. *(p. 523)*

Pro forma financial statements Statements that show the effects of proposed transactions and events as if they had occurred. *(p. 140)*

Process cost accounting system System of assigning direct materials, direct labor, and overhead to specific processes; total costs associated with each process are then divided by the number of units passing through that process to determine the cost per equivalent unit. *(p. 811)*

Process cost summary Report of costs charged to a department, its equivalent units of production achieved, and the costs assigned to its output. *(p. 820)*

Process operations Processing of products in a continuous (sequential) flow of steps; also called *process manufacturing* or *process production. (p. 808)*

Product costs Costs that are capitalized as inventory because they produce benefits expected to have future value; include direct materials, direct labor, and overhead. *(p. 733)*

Production budget Plan that shows the units to be produced each period. *(p. 959)*

Profit (See *net income.*)

Profit center Business unit that incurs costs and generates revenues. *(p. 858)*

Profit margin Ratio of a company's net income to its net sales; the percent of income in each dollar of revenue; also called *net profit margin. (pp. 106 & 872)*

Profitability Company's ability to generate an adequate return on invested capital. *(p. 681)*

Profitability index A measure of the relation between the expected benefits of a project and its investment, computed as the present value of expected future cash flows from the investment divided by the cost of the investment; a higher value indicates a more desirable investment, and a value below 1 indicates an unacceptable project. *(p. 1031)*

Promissory note (or **note**) Written promise to pay a specified amount either on demand or at a definite future date; is a *note receivable* for the lender but a *note payable* for the lendee. *(p. 368)*

Proprietorship (See *sole proprietorship.*)

Proxy Legal document giving a stockholder's agent the power to exercise the stockholder's voting rights. *(p. 507)*

Purchase discount Term used by a purchaser to describe a cash discount granted to the purchaser for paying within the discount period. *(p. 181)*

Purchase order Document used by the purchasing department to place an order with a seller (vendor). *(p. 335)*

Purchase requisition Document listing merchandise needed by a department and requesting it be purchased. *(p. 335)*

Purchases journal Journal normally used to record all purchases on credit. *(p. 279)*

Quantity variance Difference between actual and budgeted revenue or cost caused by the difference between the actual number of units and the budgeted number of units. *(p. 984)*

Ratio analysis Determination of key relations between financial statement items as reflected in numerical measures. *(p. 682)*

Raw materials inventory Goods a company acquires to use in making products. *(p. 735)*

Realizable value Expected proceeds from converting an asset into cash. *(p. 363)*

Receiving report Form used to report that ordered goods are received and to describe their quantity and condition. *(p. 336)*

Recordkeeping Part of accounting that involves recording transactions and events, either manually or electronically; also called *bookkeeping*. *(p. 4)*

Registered bonds Bonds owned by investors whose names and addresses are recorded by the issuer; interest payments are made to the registered owners. *(p. 563)*

Relevance principle Information system principle prescribing that its reports be useful, understandable, timely, and pertinent for decision making. *(p. 268)*

Relevant benefits Additional or incremental revenue generated by selecting a particular course of action over another. *(p. 1035)*

Relevant range of operations Company's normal operating range; excludes extremely high and low volumes not likely to occur. *(p. 911)*

Report form balance sheet Balance sheet that lists accounts vertically in the order of assets, liabilities, and equity. *(p. 18)*

Responsibility accounting budget Report of expected costs and expenses under a manager's control. *(p. 870)*

Responsibility accounting performance report Responsibility report that compares actual costs and expenses for a department with budgeted amounts. *(p. 870)*

Responsibility accounting system System that provides information that management can use to evaluate the performance of a department's manager. *(p. 858)*

Restricted retained earnings Retained earnings not available for dividends because of legal or contractual limitations. *(p. 510)*

Retail inventory method Method to estimate ending inventory based on the ratio of the amount of goods for sale at cost to the amount of goods for sale at retail. *(p. 247)*

Retailer Intermediary that buys products from manufacturers or wholesalers and sells them to consumers. *(p. 178)*

Retained earnings Cumulative income less cumulative losses and dividends. *(p. 510)*

Retained earnings deficit Debit (abnormal) balance in Retained Earnings; occurs when cumulative losses and dividends exceed cumulative income; also called *accumulated deficit*. *(p. 513)*

Return Monies received from an investment; often in percent form. *(p. 23)*

Return on assets (See *return on total assets*) *(p. 20)*

Return on equity Ratio of net income to average equity for the period.

Return on total assets Ratio reflecting operating efficiency; defined as net income divided by average total assets for the period; also called *return on assets* or *return on investment*. *(p. 600)*

Revenue expenditures Expenditures reported on the current income statement as an expense because they do not provide benefits in future periods. *(p. 402)*

Revenue recognition principle The principle prescribing that revenue is recognized when earned. *(p. 10)*

Revenues Gross increase in equity from a company's business activities that earn income; also called *sales*. *(p. 13)*

Reverse stock split Occurs when a corporation calls in its stock and replaces each share with less than one new share; increases both market value per share and any par or stated value per share. *(p. 516)*

Reversing entries Optional entries recorded at the beginning of a period that prepare the accounts for the usual journal entries as if adjusting entries had not occurred in the prior period. *(p. 151)*

Risk Uncertainty about an expected return. *(p. 24)*

Rolling budget New set of budgets a firm adds for the next period (with revisions) to replace the ones that have lapsed. *(p. 942)*

S corporation Corporation that meets special tax qualifications so as to be treated like a partnership for income tax purposes. *(p. 480)*

Safety stock Quantity of inventory or materials over the minimum needed to satisfy budgeted demand. *(p. 947)*

Sales (See *revenues*.)

Sales budget Plan showing the units of goods to be sold or services to be provided; the starting point in the budgeting process for most departments. *(p. 946)*

Sales discount Term used by a seller to describe a cash discount granted to buyers who pay within the discount period. *(p. 181)*

Sales journal Journal normally used to record sales of goods on credit. *(p. 274)*

Sales mix Ratio of sales volumes for the various products sold by a company. *(p. 915)*

Salvage value Estimate of amount to be recovered at the end of an asset's useful life; also called *residual value* or *scrap value*. *(p. 395)*

Sarbanes-Oxley Act (SOX) Created the Public *Company Accounting Oversight Board*, regulates analyst conflicts, imposes corporate governance requirements, enhances accounting and control disclosures, impacts insider transactions and executive loans, establishes new types of criminal conduct, and expands penalties for violations of federal securities laws. *(pp. 11 & 314)*

Scatter diagram Graph used to display data about past cost behavior and sales as points on a diagram. *(p. 905)*

Schedule of accounts payable List of the balances of all accounts in the accounts payable ledger and their total. *(p. 280)*

Schedule of accounts receivable List of the balances for all accounts in the accounts receivable ledger and their total. *(p. 275)*

Secured bonds Bonds that have specific assets of the issuer pledged as collateral. *(p. 563)*

Securities and Exchange Commission (SEC) Federal agency Congress has charged to set reporting rules for organizations that sell ownership shares to the public. *(p. 9)*

Segment return on assets Segment operating income divided by segment average (identifiable) assets for the period. *(p. 284)*

Selling expense budget Plan that lists the types and amounts of selling expenses expected in the budget period. *(p. 948)*

Selling expenses Expenses of promoting sales, such as displaying and advertising merchandise, making sales, and delivering goods to customers. *(p. 191)*

Serial bonds Bonds consisting of separate amounts that mature at different dates. *(p. 563)*

Service company Organization that provides services instead of tangible products.

Shareholders Owners of a corporation; also called *stockholders*. *(p. 11)*

Shares Equity of a corporation divided into ownership units; also called *stock*. *(p. 11)*

Short-term investments Debt and equity securities that management expects to convert to cash within the next 3 to 12 months (or the operating cycle if longer); also called *temporary investments* or *marketable securities*. *(p. 592)*

Short-term note payable Current obligation in the form of a written promissory note. *(p. 437)*

Shrinkage Inventory losses that occur as a result of theft or deterioration. *(p. 188)*

Signature card Includes the signatures of each person authorized to sign checks on the bank account. *(p. 326)*

Simple capital structure Capital structure that consists of only common stock and nonconvertible preferred stock; consists of no dilutive securities. *(p. 524)*

Single-step income statement Income statement format that includes cost of goods sold as an expense and shows only one subtotal for total expenses. *(p. 192)*

Sinking fund bonds Bonds that require the issuer to make deposits to a separate account; bondholders are repaid at maturity from that account. *(p. 563)*

Small stock dividend Stock dividend that is 25% or less of a corporation's previously outstanding shares. *(p. 514)*

Social responsibility Being accountable for the impact that one's actions might have on society. *(p. 8)*

Sole proprietorship Business owned by one person that is not organized as a corporation; also called *proprietorship*. *(p. 10)*

Solvency Company's long-run financial viability and its ability to cover long-term obligations. *(p. 681)*

Source documents Source of information for accounting entries that can be in either paper or electronic form; also called *business papers*. *(p. 49)*

Special journal Any journal used for recording and posting transactions of a similar type. *(p. 272)*

Specific identification Method to assign cost to inventory when the purchase cost of each item in inventory is identified and used to compute cost of inventory. *(p. 227)*

Spending variance Difference between the actual price of an item and its standard price. *(p. 993)*

Spreadsheet Computer program that organizes data by means of formulas and format; also called *electronic work sheet*.

Standard costs Costs that should be incurred under normal conditions to produce a product or component or to perform a service. *(p. 985)*

State Unemployment Taxes (SUTA) State payroll taxes on employers to support its unemployment programs. *(p. 442)*

Stated value stock No-par stock assigned a stated value per share; this amount is recorded in the stock account when the stock is issued. *(p. 510)*

Statement of cash flows A financial statement that lists cash inflows (receipts) and cash outflows (payments) during a period; arranged by operating, investing, and financing. *(p. 628)*

Statement of owner's equity Report of changes in equity over a period; adjusted for increases (owner investment and net income) and for decreases (withdrawals and net loss). *(p. 17)*

Statement of partners' equity Financial statement that shows total capital balances at the beginning of the period, any additional investment by partners, the income or loss of the period, the partners' withdrawals, and the partners' ending capital balances; also called *statement of partners' capital*. *(p. 483)*

Statement of retained earnings Report of changes in retained earnings over a period; adjusted for increases (net income), for decreases (dividends and net loss), and for any prior period adjustment. *(p. 7)*

Statement of stockholders' equity Financial statement that lists the beginning and ending balances of each major equity account and describes all changes in those accounts. *(p. 523)*

Statements of Financial Accounting Standards (SFAS) FASB publications that establish U.S. GAAP. *(p. 9)*

Step-wise cost Cost that remains fixed over limited ranges of volumes but changes by a lump sum when volume changes occur outside these limited ranges. *(p. 904)*.

Stock (See *shares*.)

Stock dividend Corporation's distribution of its own stock to its stockholders without the receipt of any payment. *(p. 514)*

Stock options Rights to purchase common stock at a fixed price over a specified period of time. *(p. 523)*

Stock split Occurs when a corporation calls in its stock and replaces each share with more than one new share; decreases both the market value per share and any par or stated value per share. *(p. 516)*

Stock subscription Investor's contractual commitment to purchase unissued shares at future dates and prices.

Stockholders (See *shareholders.*) *(p. 11)*

Stockholders' equity A corporation's equity; also called *shareholders' equity* or *corporate capital*. *(p. 510)*

Straight-line depreciation Method that allocates an equal portion of the depreciable cost of plant asset (cost minus salvage) to each accounting period in its useful life. *(pp. 97 & 396)*

Straight-line bond amortization Method allocating an equal amount of bond interest expense to each period of the bond life. *(p. 554)*

Subsidiary Entity controlled by another entity (parent) in which the parent owns more than 50% of the subsidiary's voting stock. *(p. 599)*

Subsidiary ledger List of individual sub-accounts and amounts with a common characteristic; linked to a controlling account in the general ledger. *(p. 272)*

Sunk cost Cost already incurred and cannot be avoided or changed. *(p. 733)*

Supplementary records Information outside the usual accounting records; also called *supplemental records*. *(p. 184)*

Supply chain Linkages of services or goods extending from suppliers, to the company itself, and on to customers.

T-account Tool used to show the effects of transactions and events on individual accounts. *(p. 53)*

Target cost Maximum allowable cost for a product or service; defined as expected selling price less the desired profit. *(p. 771)*

Temporary accounts Accounts used to record revenues, expenses, and withdrawals (dividends for a corporation); they are closed at the end of each period; also called *nominal accounts*. *(p. 140)*

Term bonds Bonds scheduled for payment (maturity) at a single specified date. *(p. 563)*

Throughput time (See *cycle time.*)

Time period assumption Assumption that an organization's activities can be divided into specific time periods such as months, quarters, or years. *(p. 92)*

Time ticket Source document used to report the time an employee spent working on a job or on overhead activities and then to determine the amount of direct labor to charge to the job or the amount of indirect labor to charge to overhead. *(p. 776)*

Times interest earned Ratio of income before interest expense (and any income taxes) divided by interest expense; reflects risk of covering interest commitments when income varies. *(p. 447)*

Total asset turnover Measure of a company's ability to use its assets to generate sales; computed by dividing net sales by average total assets. *(p. 410)*

Total quality management (TQM) Concept calling for all managers and employees at all stages of operations to strive toward higher standards and reduce number of defects. *(p. 730)*

Trade discount Reduction from a list or catalog price that can vary for wholesalers, retailers, and consumers. *(p. 180)*

Trademark or **Trade (Brand) name** Symbol, name, phrase, or jingle identified with a company, product, or service. *(p. 408)*

Trading on the equity (See *financial leverage.*)

Trading securities Investments in debt and equity securities that the company intends to actively trade for profit. *(p. 595)*

Transaction Exchange of economic consideration affecting an entity's financial position that can be reliably measured. *(p. 13)*

Treasury stock Corporation's own stock that it reacquired and still holds. *(p. 520)*

Trial balance List of accounts and their balances at a point in time; total debit balances equal total credit balances. *(p. 63)*

Unadjusted trial balance List of accounts and balances prepared before accounting adjustments are recorded and posted. *(p. 104)*

Unavoidable expense Expense (or cost) that is not relevant for business decisions; an expense that would continue even if a department, product, or service is eliminated. *(p. 1041)*

Unclassified balance sheet Balance sheet that broadly groups assets, liabilities, and equity accounts. *(p. 145)*

Uncontrollable costs Costs that a manager does not have the power to determine or strongly influence. *(p. 870)*

Underapplied overhead Amount by which overhead incurred in a period exceeds the overhead applied to that period's production using the predetermined overhead rate. *(p. 781)*

Unearned revenue Liability created when customers pay in advance for products or services; earned when the products or services are later delivered. *(pp. 50 & 98)*

Unfavorable variance Difference in revenues or costs, when the actual amount is compared to the budgeted amount, that contributes to a lower income. *(p. 981)*

Unit contribution margin Amount a product's unit selling price exceeds its total unit variable cost.

Units-of-production depreciation Method that charges a varying amount to depreciation expense for each period of an asset's useful life depending on its usage. *(p. 397)*

Unlimited liability Legal relationship among general partners that makes each of them responsible for partnership debts if the other partners are unable to pay their shares. *(p. 479)*

Unrealized gain (loss) Gain (loss) not yet realized by an actual transaction or event such as a sale. *(p. 595)*

Unsecured bonds Bonds backed only by the issuer's credit standing; almost always riskier than secured bonds; also called *debentures*. *(p. 563)*

Unusual gain or loss Gain or loss that is abnormal or unrelated to the company's ordinary activities and environment. *(p. 703)*

Useful life Length of time an asset will be productively used in the operations of a business; also called *service life* or *limited life*. *(p. 395)*

Value-added time The portion of cycle time that is directed at producing a product or service; equals process time. *(p. 743)*

Value chain Sequential activities that add value to an entity's products or services; includes design, production, marketing, distribution, and service. *(p. 740)*

Variable cost Cost that changes in proportion to changes in the activity output volume. *(p. 732)*

Variance analysis Process of examining differences between actual and budgeted revenues or costs and describing them in terms of price and quantity differences. *(p. 984)*

Vendee Buyer of goods or services. *(p. 335)*

Vendor Seller of goods or services. *(p. 335)*

Vertical analysis Evaluation of each financial statement item or group of items in terms of a specific base amount. *(p. 682)*

Volume variance Difference between two dollar amounts of fixed overhead cost; one amount is the total budgeted overhead cost, and the other is the overhead cost allocated to products using the predetermined fixed overhead rate. *(p. 993)*

Voucher Internal file used to store documents and information to control cash disbursements and to ensure that a transaction is properly authorized and recorded. *(p. 322)*

Voucher register Journal (referred to as *book of original entry*) in which all vouchers are recorded after they have been approved. *(p. 337)*

Voucher system Procedures and approvals designed to control cash disbursements and acceptance of obligations. *(p. 322)*

Wage bracket withholding table Table of the amounts of income tax withheld from employees' wages. *(p. 454)*

Warranty Agreement that obligates the seller to correct or replace a product or service when it fails to perform properly within a specified period. *(p. 444)*

Weighted average Method to assign inventory cost to sales; the cost of available-for-sale units is divided by the number of units available to determine per unit cost prior to each sale that is then multiplied by the units sold to yield the cost of that sale. *(pp. 230, 245 & 818)*

Weighted-average method (See *weighted average*.)

Wholesaler Intermediary that buys products from manufacturers or other wholesalers and sells them to retailers or other wholesalers. *(p. 178)*

Withdrawals Payment of cash or other assets from a proprietorship or partnership to its owner or owners. *(p. 13)*

Work sheet Spreadsheet used to draft an unadjusted trial balance, adjusting entries, adjusted trial balance, and financial statements. *(p. 136)*

Working capital Current assets minus current liabilities at a point in time. *(p. 691)*

Working papers Analyses and other informal reports prepared by accountants and managers when organizing information for formal reports and financial statements. *(p. 136)*

Credits

Chapter 12
Page 477 Courtesy of Samantashoes.com
Page 479 © David R. Frazier Photolibrary, Inc./Alamy
Page 481 © Erik Freeland/Corbis
Page 484 © Bill Bachmann/Alamy
Page 487 © James Doberman/Getty Images/Iconica

Chapter 13
Page 505 Courtesy of Inogen, Inc.
Page 508 Courtesy of Green Bay Packers, Inc.

Chapter 14
Page 549 © James Wasserman
Page 552 Courtesy of Dow Chemicals

Chapter 15
Page 591 Courtesy of Tibi.com
Page 593 Courtesy of Scripophily.com
Page 595 AP Images/Richard Drew

Chapter 16
Page 627 Courtesy of Jungle Jim's International Market
Page 628 AP Images/Brian Kersey
Page 634 © Corbis Super RF/Alamy

Chapter 17
Page 679 © Dirck Halstead/Liaison/Getty Images
Page 693 AP Images/Ben Margot
Page 698 AP Images/Chuck Burton

Chapter 18
Page 725 Courtesy of Kernel Seasons
Page 729 AP Images/KEYSTONE/Alessandro Della Bella
Page 735 © Jeff Greenberg/The Image Works
Page 736 © Darrell Ingham/Getty Images
Page 742 © Gabriel Bouys/AFP/Getty Images

Chapter 19
Page 769 Courtesy of Specialty Surfaces International, Inc. d/b/a Sprinturf
Page 770 Peter Newcomb/Bloomberg News/Landov
Page 777 © Photodisc/Alamy
Page 782 image100/Punchstock

Chapter 20
Page 807 Courtesy of Hood River Juice Company
Page 807 © Grant V. Faint/Getty Images/Iconica
Page 808 © INGO WAGNER/dpa/Landov
Page 812 © Tom Tracy Photography/Alamy
Page 818 © Lester Lefkowitz/Getty Images/Stone
Page 823 © Frederic Pitchal/Sygma/Corbis

Chapter 21
Page 851 Courtesy of RockBottomGolf.com
Page 852 © ACE STOCK LIMITED/Alamy
Page 854 © Royalty-Free/Corbis
Page 862 © Christian Hoehn/Getty Images/Stone

Chapter 22
Page 901 Courtesy of Moe's Southwest Grill
Page 903 © Royalty Free/Corbis
Page 909 © Rob Tringali/Sportschrome/Getty Images
Page 915 © Jonathan Fickies/Getty Images
Page 916 © Nick Onken/Getty Images/UpperCut Images

Chapter 23
Page 939 AP Images/David Zalubowski
Page 942 Courtesy © B.P., pl.l.c
Page 946 © Royalty Free/CORBIS
Page 950 © Jeff Vinnick/Getty Images
Page 951 © Jim McIsaac/Getty Images
Page 952 © Teo Lannie/Getty Images/PhotoAlto Agency RF Collections

Chapter 24
Page 979 Courtesy of Martin Guitar Co.
Page 982 © Ken Samuelsen/PhotoDisc/Getty Images
Page 984 © Royalty-Free/Corbis
Page 986 AP Images/David Vincent
Page 988 © Kristjan Maack/Getty Images/Nordic Photos
Page 989 © ColorBlind Images/Corbis
Page 991 © Patrik Giardino/Photolibrary
Page 992 © Nick Daly/Getty Images/Digital Vision
Page 997 © Photodisc/Alamy

Chapter 25
Page 1023 Courtesy of Danielle Greenberg/Prairie Sticks Bat Company
Page 1026 AP Images/Katsumi Kasahara
Page 1032 © Philip Lee Harvey/Getty Images/Taxi
Page 1036 © JOHN SOMMERS/Reuters/Corbis
Page 1041 © Dimas Ardian/Getty Images
Page 1042 © Louie Psihoyos/Corbis

Index

Note: Page numbers followed by *n* indicate material in footnotes.

Chart of Accounts

Following is a typical chart of accounts. Each company has its own unique accounts and numbering system.

Assets

Current Assets

101 Cash
102 Petty cash
103 Cash equivalents
104 Short-term investments
105 Market adjustment, _______ securities (S-T)
106 Accounts receivable
107 Allowance for doubtful accounts
108 Legal fees receivable
109 Interest receivable
110 Rent receivable
111 Notes receivable
119 Merchandise inventory
120 _________ inventory
121 _________ inventory
124 Office supplies
125 Store supplies
126 _______ supplies
128 Prepaid insurance
129 Prepaid interest
131 Prepaid rent
132 Raw materials inventory
133 Goods in process inventory, _______
134 Goods in process inventory, _______
135 Finished goods inventory

Long-Term Investments

141 Long-term investments
142 Market adjustment, _______ securities (L-T)
144 Investment in _______
145 Bond sinking fund

Plant Assets

151 Automobiles
152 Accumulated depreciation—Automobiles
153 Trucks
154 Accumulated depreciation—Trucks
155 Boats
156 Accumulated depreciation—Boats
157 Professional library
158 Accumulated depreciation—Professional library
159 Law library
160 Accumulated depreciation—Law library
161 Furniture
162 Accumulated depreciation—Furniture
163 Office equipment
164 Accumulated depreciation—Office equipment
165 Store equipment
166 Accumulated depreciation—Store equipment
167 _______ equipment
168 Accumulated depreciation—_______ equipment
169 Machinery
170 Accumulated depreciation—Machinery
173 Building _______
174 Accumulated depreciation—Building _______
175 Building _______
176 Accumulated depreciation—Building _______
179 Land improvements _______
180 Accumulated depreciation—Land improvements _______
181 Land improvements _______
182 Accumulated depreciation—Land improvements _______
183 Land

Natural Resources

185 Mineral deposit
186 Accumulated depletion—Mineral deposit

Intangible Assets

191 Patents
192 Leasehold
193 Franchise
194 Copyrights
195 Leasehold improvements
196 Licenses
197 Accumulated amortization—_______

Liabilities

Current Liabilities

201 Accounts payable
202 Insurance payable
203 Interest payable
204 Legal fees payable
207 Office salaries payable
208 Rent payable
209 Salaries payable
210 Wages payable
211 Accrued payroll payable
214 Estimated warranty liability
215 Income taxes payable
216 Common dividend payable
217 Preferred dividend payable
218 State unemployment taxes payable
219 Employee federal income taxes payable
221 Employee medical insurance payable
222 Employee retirement program payable
223 Employee union dues payable
224 Federal unemployment taxes payable
225 FICA taxes payable
226 Estimated vacation pay liability

Unearned Revenues

230 Unearned consulting fees
231 Unearned legal fees
232 Unearned property management fees
233 Unearned _______ fees
234 Unearned _______ fees
235 Unearned janitorial revenue
236 Unearned _______ revenue
238 Unearned rent

Notes Payable

240 Short-term notes payable
241 Discount on short-term notes payable
245 Notes payable
251 Long-term notes payable
252 Discount on long-term notes payable

Long-Term Liabilities

253 Long-term lease liability
255 Bonds payable
256 Discount on bonds payable
257 Premium on bonds payable
258 Deferred income tax liability

Equity

Owner's Equity

301 _____________, Capital
302 _____________, Withdrawals
303 _____________, Capital
304 _____________, Withdrawals
305 _____________, Capital
306 _____________, Withdrawals

Paid-In Capital

307 Common stock, $ _______ par value
308 Common stock, no-par value
309 Common stock, $ _______ stated value
310 Common stock dividend distributable
311 Paid-in capital in excess of par value, Common stock
312 Paid-in capital in excess of stated value, No-par common stock
313 Paid-in capital from retirement of common stock
314 Paid-in capital, Treasury stock
315 Preferred stock
316 Paid-in capital in excess of par value, Preferred stock

Retained Earnings

318 Retained earnings
319 Cash dividends (or Dividends)
320 Stock dividends

Other Equity Accounts

321 Treasury stock, Common
322 Unrealized gain—Equity
323 Unrealized loss—Equity

Revenues

401 ______________ fees earned
402 ______________ fees earned
403 ______________ services revenue
404 ______________ services revenue
405 Commissions earned
406 Rent revenue (or Rent earned)
407 Dividends revenue (or Dividend earned)
408 Earnings from investment in _______
409 Interest revenue (or Interest earned)
410 Sinking fund earnings
413 Sales
414 Sales returns and allowances
415 Sales discounts

Cost of Sales

Cost of Goods Sold

502 Cost of goods sold
505 Purchases
506 Purchases returns and allowances
507 Purchases discounts
508 Transportation-in

Manufacturing

520 Raw materials purchases
521 Freight-in on raw materials
530 Factory payroll
531 Direct labor
540 Factory overhead
541 Indirect materials
542 Indirect labor
543 Factory insurance expired
544 Factory supervision
545 Factory supplies used
546 Factory utilities
547 Miscellaneous production costs
548 Property taxes on factory building
549 Property taxes on factory equipment
550 Rent on factory building
551 Repairs, factory equipment
552 Small tools written off
560 Depreciation of factory equipment
561 Depreciation of factory building

Standard Cost Variance

580 Direct material quantity variance
581 Direct material price variance
582 Direct labor quantity variance
583 Direct labor price variance
584 Factory overhead volume variance
585 Factory overhead controllable variance

Expenses

Amortization, Depletion, and Depreciation

601 Amortization expense—_______
602 Amortization expense—_______
603 Depletion expense—_______
604 Depreciation expense—Boats
605 Depreciation expense—Automobiles
606 Depreciation expense—Building _______
607 Depreciation expense—Building _______
608 Depreciation expense—Land improvements _______
609 Depreciation expense—Land improvements _______
610 Depreciation expense—Law library
611 Depreciation expense—Trucks
612 Depreciation expense—_______ equipment
613 Depreciation expense—_______ equipment
614 Depreciation expense—_______
615 Depreciation expense—_______

Employee-Related Expenses

620 Office salaries expense
621 Sales salaries expense
622 Salaries expense
623 _______ wages expense
624 Employees' benefits expense
625 Payroll taxes expense

Financial Expenses

630 Cash over and short
631 Discounts lost
632 Factoring fee expense
633 Interest expense

Insurance Expenses

635 Insurance expense—Delivery equipment
636 Insurance expense—Office equipment
637 Insurance expense—_______

Rental Expenses

640 Rent expense
641 Rent expense—Office space
642 Rent expense—Selling space
643 Press rental expense
644 Truck rental expense
645 _______ rental expense

Supplies Expenses

650 Office supplies expense
651 Store supplies expense
652 _______ supplies expense
653 _______ supplies expense

Miscellaneous Expenses

655 Advertising expense
656 Bad debts expense
657 Blueprinting expense
658 Boat expense
659 Collection expense
661 Concessions expense
662 Credit card expense
663 Delivery expense
664 Dumping expense
667 Equipment expense
668 Food and drinks expense
671 Gas and oil expense
672 General and administrative expense
673 Janitorial expense
674 Legal fees expense
676 Mileage expense
677 Miscellaneous expenses
678 Mower and tools expense
679 Operating expense
680 Organization expense
681 Permits expense
682 Postage expense
683 Property taxes expense
684 Repairs expense—_______
685 Repairs expense—_______
687 Selling expense
688 Telephone expense
689 Travel and entertainment expense
690 Utilities expense
691 Warranty expense
695 Income taxes expense

Gains and Losses

701 Gain on retirement of bonds
702 Gain on sale of machinery
703 Gain on sale of investments
704 Gain on sale of trucks
705 Gain on _______
706 Foreign exchange gain or loss
801 Loss on disposal of machinery
802 Loss on exchange of equipment
803 Loss on exchange of _______
804 Loss on sale of notes
805 Loss on retirement of bonds
806 Loss on sale of investments
807 Loss on sale of machinery
808 Loss on _______
809 Unrealized gain—Income
810 Unrealized loss—Income

Clearing Accounts

901 Income summary
902 Manufacturing summary

A Rose by Any Other Name

The same financial statement sometimes receives different titles. Following are some of the more common aliases.*

Balance Sheet	Statement of Financial Position Statement of Financial Condition
Income Statement	Statement of Income Operating Statement Statement of Operations Statement of Operating Activity Earnings Statement Statement of Earnings Profit and Loss (P&L) Statement
Statement of Cash Flows	Statement of Cash Flow Cash Flows Statement Statement of Changes in Cash Position Statement of Changes in Financial Position
Statement of Owner's Equity	Statement of Changes in Owner's Equity Statement of Changes in Owner's Capital Statement of Shareholders' Equity† Statement of Changes in Shareholders' Equity† Statement of Stockholders' Equity and Comprehensive Income† Statement of Changes in Capital Accounts†

* The term **Consolidated** often precedes or follows these statement titles to reflect the combination of different entities, such as a parent company and its subsidiaries.
† Corporation only.

We thank Dr. Louella Moore from Arkansas State University for suggesting this listing.

Working Papers

for use with

Fundamental Accounting Principles

CHAPTERS 12-25

Nineteenth Edition

John J. Wild
University of Wisconsin – Madison

Ken W. Shaw
University of Missouri – Columbia

Barbara Chiappetta
Nassau Community College

Prepared By
John J. Wild
University of Wisconsin – Madison

Boston Burr Ridge, IL Dubuque, IA New York San Francisco St. Louis
Bangkok Bogotá Caracas Kuala Lumpur Lisbon London Madrid Mexico City
Milan Montreal New Delhi Santiago Seoul Singapore Sydney Taipei Toronto

The McGraw-Hill Companies

Working Papers for use with
FUNDAMENTAL ACCOUNTING PRINCIPLES, CHAPTERS 12-25
John J. Wild, Ken W. Shaw, and Barbara Chiappetta

Published by McGraw-Hill/Irwin, an imprint of The McGraw-Hill Companies, Inc., 1221 Avenue of the Americas, New York, NY 10020.

1 2 3 4 5 6 7 8 9 0 DOW/DOW 0 9 8

ISBN: 978-0-07-336636-4
MHID: 0-07-336636-6

www.mhhe.com

TABLE OF CONTENTS

Chapter

Chapter 12 Quick Study 12-1 *Name* ____________

(a)

(b)

Quick Study 12-2

	Share to Stolton	*Share to Bright*	*Total*
Net income			
Salary allowance:			
Stolton			
Bright			
Total salary allowances			
Balance of income			
Balance allocated:			
Stolton			
Bright			
Total allocated			
Balance of income			
Shares of the partners			

Quick Study 12-3

Quick Study 12-4

Chapter 12 Quick Study 12-5 *Name* ______________________________

GENERAL JOURNAL

Date		Account Titles and Explanation	PR	Debit	Credit

Quick Study 12-6

GENERAL JOURNAL

Date		Account Titles and Explanation	PR	Debit	Credit

Quick Study 12-7

Chapter 12 Exercise 12-1 *Name* ______________________

Characteristic		*General Partnerships*
1.	Life	
2.	Owners' liability	
3.	Legal status	
4.	Tax status of income	
5.	Owners' authority	
6.	Ease of formation	
7.	Transferability of ownership	
8.	Ability to raise large amounts of capital	

Exercise 12-2

Part a

Recommended Organization:

Taxation Effects:

Advantages:

Chapter 12 Exercise 12-2 (Continued) *Name* ______________________

Part b

Recommended Organization:

Taxation Effects:

Advantages:

Part c

Recommended Organization:

Taxation Effects:

Advantages:

Chapter 12 Exercise 12-10 *Name* ______________________

(a) Loss computation from selling assets:

(b) Loss allocation

	Brewster	Conway	Ogden	Total
Capital balance before loss liquidation......................				
Allocation of loss:				
Capital balances after loss............				

(c) Liability to be paid:

Chapter 12 Exercise 12-11 *Name* ______________________

(a) Loss computation from selling assets:

(b) Loss and deficit allocation:

	Brewster	*Conway*	*Ogden*	*Total*
Capital balance before loss.........				
Allocation of loss:				
Capital balances after loss...........				
Allocation of ________ deficit to:				
Cash paid by each partner...........				

(c) Liability to be paid:

Exercise 12-12

Chapter 12 Problem 12-2A or 12-2B *Name* ______
(Continued)

Inc./Loss Sharing Plan	YEAR 3		
	Calculations	*Partner:*	*Partner:*
(a)			
(b)			
(c)			
(d)			

Supporting Work Space:

Chapter 12 Problem 12-3A or 12-3B *Name* ______________________

Part 1

Inc./Loss Sharing Plan	Calculations	Partner: ________	Partner: ________	Partner: ________	Total for all Partners
(a)					
(b)					
(c)					

Chapter 12 Problem 12-3A or 12-3B (Continued) *Name* ____________________

Part 2

____________ PARTNERSHIP Statement of Partners' Equity For Year Ended December 31	Partner: ______	Partner: ______	Partner: ______	*Partners' Total*
Beg. capital balances				
Plus:				
Owner investments				
Net Income:				
Salary allowances				
Interest allowances				
Balance allocated				
Total net income				
Total				
Less partners' withdrawals				
End. capital balances				

Part 3

GENERAL JOURNAL

Date		Account Titles and Explanation	PR	Debit	Credit

Chapter 12 Problem 12-4A or 12-4B *Name* ____________________

Part 1

GENERAL JOURNAL

Date		Account Titles and Explanation	PR	Debit	Credit
(a)					
(b)					
(c)					
(d)					
(e)					

Chapter 12 Problem 12-4A or 12-4B (Continued) *Name* ____________________

Part 2

GENERAL JOURNAL

Date		Account Titles and Explanation	PR	Debit	Credit
(a)					
(b)					
(c)					

Chapter 12 **Problem 12-5A or 12-5B** *Name* ______________________

(1)

GENERAL JOURNAL

Date	Account Titles and Explanation	PR	Debit	Credit

Chapter 12 Problem 12-5A or 12-5B *Name* ________________________
(Continued)

(2)

GENERAL JOURNAL

Date		Account Titles and Explanation	PR	Debit	Credit

(3)

GENERAL JOURNAL

Date		Account Titles and Explanation	PR	Debit	Credit

(4)

GENERAL JOURNAL

Date		Account Titles and Explanation	PR	Debit	Credit

Chapter 12 Serial Problem, SP 12 *Name* ____________

Success Systems

(1)

(2) GENERAL JOURNAL

Date		Account Titles and Explanation	PR	Debit	Credit

(3) GENERAL JOURNAL

Date		Account Titles and Explanation	PR	Debit	Credit

(4)

Chapter 12 Reporting in Action—BTN 12-1 *Name* ______________________

(1)

(2)

(3)

Comparative Analysis—BTN 12-2

(1)

(2)

(3)

(4)

Chapter 12 Ethics Challenge—BTN 12-3 *Name* ____________________

(1) Income allocation per original agreement:

	Maben	Orlando	Clark	Total
Salary allowance				
Per patient charges				
Totals				

(2) Income allocation per Clark's proposal:

	Maben	Orlando	Clark	Total
Per patient charges				

(3)

Chapter 12 Communicating in Practice *Name* ______________________
BTN 12-4

STUDY NOTES
Organizations with Partnership Characteristics

Chapter 12 Taking It to the Net *Name* ______________________
BTN 12-5

(1)

(2)

(3)

Chapter 12 Teamwork in Action *Name* ______________________
BTN 12-6

(1)

Income/Loss Sharing Plan	Calculations	Baker	Warner	Rice	Total
(a)					
(b)					
(c)					
(d)					

(2) Team members share solutions

(3)

Chapter 12 ***Entrepreneurial Decision*** ***Name*** ______________________
BTN 12-7

(1) ______________________

(2) ______________________

(3) ______________________

Global Decision—BTN 12-8

(1) ______________________

(2) ______________________

(3) ______________________

Chapter 13 Quick Study 13-1 *Name* ____________________

True Statements:

Quick Study 13-2

GENERAL JOURNAL

Date		Account Titles and Explanation	PR	Debit	Credit

Quick Study 13-3

GENERAL JOURNAL

Date		Account Titles and Explanation	PR	Debit	Credit

Chapter 13 Quick Study 13-4 *Name* ____________

GENERAL JOURNAL

Date		Account Titles and Explanation	PR	Debit	Credit

Quick Study 13-5

GENERAL JOURNAL

Date		Account Titles and Explanation	PR	Debit	Credit

Quick Study 13-6

(1) GENERAL JOURNAL

Date		Account Titles and Explanation	PR	Debit	Credit

(2)

Chapter 13 Quick Study 13-7 *Name* ______________________

GENERAL JOURNAL

Date		Account Titles and Explanation	PR	Debit	Credit

Quick Study 13-8

Atari Company
Stockholders' Equity
April 2 (after stock dividend)

Quick Study 13-9

Cash Dividend to Common Shareholders

Chapter 13 Quick Study 13-10 *Name* ______________________

GENERAL JOURNAL

Date		Account Titles and Explanation	PR	Debit	Credit

Quick Study 13-11

(1)

(2)

Quick Study 13-12

Basic Earnings Per Share

Quick Study 13-13

Basic Earnings Per Share

Chapter 13 Problem 13-4A or 13-4B *Name* ______

Part 1

Outstanding Common Shares

Part 2

Cash Dividend Amounts:

Part 3

Capitalization of Retained Earnings:

Part 4

Cost Per Share of Treasury Stock:

Part 5

Net Income Computation:

Chapter 13 Problem 13-5A or 13-5B *Name* ______

(1) Market Price Per Share:

(2) Computation of Stock Par Values:

(3) Book Value Per Preferred Share:

Book Value Per Common Share:

(4) Book Value Per Preferred Share:

Book Value Per Common Share:

Chapter 13 Problem 13-5A or 13-5B *Name* ______________________
(Continued)

(5) Book Value Per Preferred Share:

Book Value Per Common Share:

(6)

(7)

Chapter 13 Serial Problem, SP 13 *Name* ______________________

Success Systems

(1a) GENERAL JOURNAL

Date		Account Titles and Explanation	PR	Debit	Credit

(1b) GENERAL JOURNAL

Date		Account Titles and Explanation	PR	Debit	Credit

(1c) GENERAL JOURNAL

Date		Account Titles and Explanation	PR	Debit	Credit

(2) (a)

(b)

(c)

(3)

Chapter 13 **Reporting in Action** ***Name***
BTN 13-1

(1)

(2)

(3)

(4)

(5)

(6) Fast Forward:

Chapter 13 Comparative Analysis BTN 13-2 *Name* ______________________

(1)
Best Buy Book Value Per Common Share:

Circuit City Book Value Per Common Share:

RadioShack Book Value Per Common Share:

(2)
Best Buy Earnings Per Share:

Circuit City Earnings per Share:

RadioShack Earnings per Share:

(3)
Best Buy Dividend Yield:

Circuit City Dividend Yield:

RadioShack Dividend Yield:

Analysis:

 Name ______________________

(4)

Best Buy Price-Earnings Ratio:

Circuit City Price-Earnings Ratio:

RadioShack Price-Earnings Ratio:

Analysis & Interpretation:

Chapter 13 Ethics Challenge **Name** ______
BTN 13-3

MEMORANDUM

TO:
FROM:
DATE:
SUBJECT:

Company	Earnings Per Share	Market Price of Stock	Price-Earnings Ratio

Industry Norm:

Meaning of Price-Earnings Ratio:

Comparison Across Companies:

Concluding Analysis:

Chapter 13 Taking It to the Net BTN 13-5 *Name* ______________________

Part 1

Part 2

Part 3

Part 4

Teamwork in Action—BTN 13-6

Part 1

(a) Impact on Financial Position due to Stock Buyback:

(b) Reasons for Stock Buyback:

Chapter 13 Teamwork in Action BTN 13-6 (Continued) *Name* ____________________

Part 2

GENERAL JOURNAL

Date		Account Titles and Explanation	PR	Debit	Credit
Reacquisition entry					
(a)					
(b)					
(c)					
(d)					
(e)					

Part 3

Similarities:

Differences:

Chapter 13 Entrepreneurial Decision *Name* ____________________
BTN 13-7

Part 1

	Plan A	Plan B

Part 2

	Plan A	Plan B

Part 3

Global Decision—BTN 13-9

(1) Book Value per Common Share

(2) Earnings per Share

(3) Analysis

Chapter 14 Quick Study 14-1 ***Name*** ______________________

(1) Cash Proceeds:

(2) Total Bond Interest Expense:

(3) Bond Interest Expense on 1st Payment Date:

Quick Study 14-2B

(1) Cash Proceeds:

(2) Total Bond Interest Expense:

(3) Bond Interest Expense on 1st Payment Date:

 Name ____________________

GENERAL JOURNAL

Date		Account Titles and Explanation	PR	Debit	Credit

Quick Study 14-4

(a)

(b)

 Name ______________________

Date		Account Titles and Explanation	PR	Debit	Credit
(a)					
(b)					
(c)					

Chapter 14 Quick Study 14-6 *Name* ____________________

GENERAL JOURNAL

Date		Account Titles and Explanation	PR	Debit	Credit

Quick Study 14-7

GENERAL JOURNAL

Date		Account Titles and Explanation	PR	Debit	Credit

Chapter 14 Quick Study 14-8 *Name* ____________________

(a)

(b)

(c)

Quick Study 14-9

1. ________	Convertible bond	5. ________	Registered bond
2 ________	Bond indenture	6. ________	Serial bond
3. ________	Sinking fund bond	7. ________	Secured bond
4. ________	Debenture	8. ________	Bearer bond

Quick Study 14-10

Ratio Computations:

Analysis and Interpretation:

Chapter 14 Exercise 14-9 *Name* ______________________

(1) Semiannual Cash Interest Payment:

(2) Number of Payments:

(3)

(4) Market Price Computation:

(5)

GENERAL JOURNAL

Date		Account Titles and Explanation	PR	Debit	Credit

Chapter 14 Exercise 14-10 *Name* ______________

(1) Semiannual Cash Interest Payment:

(2) Number of Payments:

(3)

(4) Market Price Computation:

(5)

GENERAL JOURNAL

Date		Account Titles and Explanation	PR	Debit	Credit

Chapter 14 Exercise 14-13 *Name* ______________________

(1) Straight-Line Amortization Table

Semiannual Period-End	Unamortized Discount	Carrying Value
6/01/2009		
11/30/2009		
5/31/2010		
11/30/2010		
5/31/2011		
11/30/2011		
5/31/2012		
11/30/2012		
5/31/2013		

Supporting computations:

Chapter 14 Exercise 14-13 **Name** ______________________

(Continued)

(2) **GENERAL JOURNAL**

Date		Account Titles and Explanation	PR	Debit	Credit

Chapter 14 Exercise 14-14 ***Name*** ______________________

(1) Amount of Each Payment:

(2)

		Payments			
	(A)	(B) Debit	(C) Debit	(D) Credit	(E)
Period Ending Date	Beginning Balance [Prior (E)]	Interest Expense [5% x (A)] +	Notes Payable [(D) – (B)] =	Cash [computed]	Ending Balance [(A) – (C)]
2009					
2010					
2011					
2012					

Chapter 14 Exercise 14-15 ***Name*** ______________________

GENERAL JOURNAL

Date		Account Titles and Explanation	PR	Debit	Credit

Chapter 14 Exercise 14-16 *Name* ____________________

(1)(a)

(b)

(2)

Exercise 14-17[D]

(1)

(2)

(3)

Chapter 14 Exercise 14-18[D] *Name* ______________________

GENERAL JOURNAL

Date		Account Titles and Explanation	PR	Debit	Credit
(1)					
(2)					

Exercise 14-19[D]

Chapter 14 Problem 14-3A or 14-3B (Continued) *Name* ____________________

Part 3

GENERAL JOURNAL

Date		Account Titles and Explanation	PR	Debit	Credit

Chapter 14 Problem 14-4A[B] or 14-4B[B] *Name* ______________________

Part 1

Total Bond Interest Expense:

Part 2 Effective Interest Amortization Table

Semiannual Interest Period-End	(A) Cash Interest Paid [__% x $___]	(B) Bond Interest Expense [__% x Prior (E)]	(C) Premium Amortization [(A) – (B)]	(D) Unamortized Premium [Prior (D) – (C)]	(E) Carrying Value [$____ + (D)]
1/01/2009					
6/30/2009					
12/31/2009					
6/30/2010					
12/31/2010					
6/30/2011					
12/31/2011					
6/30/2012					
12/31/2012					
6/30/2013					
12/31/2013					

Chapter 14 Problem 14-4A[B] or 14-4B[B] *Name* ______________________________
(Continued)

Part 3

GENERAL JOURNAL

Date			PR	Debit	Credit

Part 4

Cash Flow	PV Table Value	Amount	Present Value

Comparison to Part 2 Table:

Chapter 14 Problem 14-5A or 14-5B *Name* ______________________

Part 1

GENERAL JOURNAL

Date		Account Titles and Explanation	PR	Debit	Credit

Part 2

Total Bond Interest Expense:

Part 3 Straight-Line Amortization Table

Semiannual Interest Period-End	Unamortized Discount	Carrying Value
1/01/2009		
6/30/2009		
12/31/2009		
6/30/2010		
12/31/2010		

Chapter 14 Problem 14-5A or 14-5B (Continued) *Name* ______________________

Part 4

GENERAL JOURNAL

Date		Account Titles and Explanation	PR	Debit	Credit

Part 5 (for Problem 14-5A only)

Chapter 14 Problem 14-6A[B] or 14-6B[B] *Name* ______________________

Part 1

GENERAL JOURNAL

Date		Account Titles and Explanation	PR	Debit	Credit

Part 2

Total Bond Interest Expense:

Part 3 Effective Interest Amortization Table

Semiannual Interest Period-End	(A) Cash Interest Paid [__% x $___]	(B) Bond Interest Expense [__% x Prior (E)]	(C) Discount Amortization [(B) - (A)]	(D) Unamortized Discount [Prior (D) – (C)]	(E) Carrying Value [$______ – (D)]
1/01/2009					
6/30/2009					
12/31/2009					
6/30/2010					
12/31/2010					

Chapter 14 Problem 14-6A[B] or 14-6B[B] **Name** ____________________
(Continued)

Part 4

GENERAL JOURNAL

Date		Account Titles and Explanation	PR	Debit	Credit

Chapter 14 Problem 14-7A[B] or 14-7B[B] *Name* ____________________

Part 1

GENERAL JOURNAL

Date		Account Titles and Explanation	PR	Debit	Credit

Part 2

Total Bond Interest Expense:

Part 3 Effective Interest Amortization Table

Semiannual Interest Period-End	(A) Cash Interest Paid [__% x $___]	(B) Bond Interest Expense [__% x Prior (E)]	(C) Premium Amortization [(A) – (B)]	(D) Unamortized Premium [Prior (D) – (C)]	(E) Carrying Value [$______ + (D)]
1/01/2009					
6/30/2009					
12/31/2009					
6/30/2010					
12/31/2010					

Chapter 14 Problem 14-7A^B or 14-7B^B *Name* ____________________
(Continued)

Part 4

GENERAL JOURNAL

Date		Account Titles and Explanation	PR	Debit	Credit

Part 5

GENERAL JOURNAL

Date		Account Titles and Explanation	PR	Debit	Credit

Part 6

Chapter 14 Problem 14-8A or 14-8B *Name* ____________________

Part 1

Amount of Each Payment:

Part 2

		Payments			
	(A)	(B)	(C)	(D)	(E)
		Debit	Debit	Credit	
Period	Beginning	Interest	Notes		Ending
Ending	Balance	Expense +	Payable =	Cash	Balance
Date	[Prior (E)]	[___% x (A)]	[(D) − (B)]	[computed]	[(A) − (C)]

Part 3

GENERAL JOURNAL

Date		Account Titles and Explanation	PR	Debit	Credit

Problem 14-9A or 14-9B

Part 1

____________ **Company Ratio:**

____________ **Company Ratio:**

Part 2

Analysis and Interpretation:

Chapter 14 Problem 14-10A[D] or 14-10B[D] *Name* ____________________

Part 1

Present Value of the Lease Payments:

Part 2

GENERAL JOURNAL

Date		Account Titles and Explanation	PR	Debit	Credit

Part 3

Capital Lease Liability Payment (Amortization) Schedule:

Period Ending Date	Beginning Balance of Lease Liability	Interest on Lease Liability (__%)	Reduction of Lease Liability	Cash Lease Payment	Ending Balance of Lease Liability
Year 1					
Year 2					
Year 3					
Year 4					
Year 5					

Part 4

GENERAL JOURNAL

Date		Account Titles and Explanation	PR	Debit	Credit

Chapter 14 Serial Problem, SP 14 *Name* ____________

Success Systems

Part 1

Maximum Loan Allowed:

Part 2

(a) Percent of Assets Financed by Debt

(b) Percent of Assets Financed by Equity

Part 3

Chapter 14 Reporting in Action *Name* ________________
BTN 14-1

(1)

(2)

(3)

(4) Fast Forward:

Chapter 14 Comparative Analysis *Name* ____________________
BTN 14-2

(1) Best Buy

Current Year:

Prior Year:

Circuit City

Current Year:

Prior Year:

RadioShack

Current Year:

Prior Year:

(2)

Chapter 14 **Ethics Challenge** *Name* ____________

BTN 14-3

(1)

(2)

MEMORANDUM

TO:
FROM:
DATE:
SUBJECT:

Chapter 14 Taking It to the Net *Name* ____________________

BTN 14-5

(1) Long Term Liabilities:

(2a)

(2b)

Chapter 14 **Teamwork in Action** *Name* ____________

BTN 14-6

Parts 1 and 2

Part 3

Part 4

Name ____________________

Part 5

Similarities	Differences

Chapter 14 **Entrepreneurial Decision** *Name* ____________________
BTN 14-7

Part 1

	Current	Alternative Notes for Expansion				
		10% Note	15% Note	16% Note	17% Note	20% Note
Income before interest.............						
Interest expense.						
Net income.........						
Equity...............						
Return on equity.						

Work Space:

Part 2

Chapter 14 Hitting the Road BTN 14-8 **Name** ____________

Global Decision—BTN 14-9

(1) Current Year Ratio:

Prior Year Ratio:

(2)

Chapter 15 Quick Study 15-1 *Name* ______________________

GENERAL JOURNAL

Date		Account Titles and Explanation	PR	Debit	Credit

Quick Study 15-2

(1)

GENERAL JOURNAL

Date		Account Titles and Explanation	PR	Debit	Credit

(2) ______________________

(3)

GENERAL JOURNAL

Date		Account Titles and Explanation	PR	Debit	Credit

Chapter 15 Quick Study 15-3 *Name* ______________________

GENERAL JOURNAL

Date		Account Titles and Explanation	PR	Debit	Credit

Quick Study 15-4

GENERAL JOURNAL

Date		Account Titles and Explanation	PR	Debit	Credit

Chapter 15 Quick Study 15-5 *Name* ______________________

True:

Quick Study 15-6

(1) ______________________ (4) ______________________
(2) ______________________ (5) ______________________
(3) ______________________

Quick Study 15-7

GENERAL JOURNAL

Date		Account Titles and Explanation	PR	Debit	Credit

Quick Study 15-8

GENERAL JOURNAL

Date		Account Titles and Explanation	PR	Debit	Credit

Chapter 15 Quick Study 15-9 *Name* ______________________

GENERAL JOURNAL

Date		Account Titles and Explanation	PR	Debit	Credit

Quick Study 15-10

(1)

GENERAL JOURNAL

Date		Account Titles and Explanation	PR	Debit	Credit

(2)

Chapter 15 Quick Study 15-11 *Name* ____________________

Return on Total Assets:

Quick Study 15-12

Return on Total Assets—Component Analysis

Chapter 15 Quick Study 15-13[A] *Name* ______________________

GENERAL JOURNAL

Date		Account Titles and Explanation	PR	Debit	Credit
		Date of Sale:			
		Date of Payment:			

Quick Study 15-14[A]

GENERAL JOURNAL

Date		Account Titles and Explanation	PR	Debit	Credit

Chapter 15 Exercise 15-1 *Name* ____________________

GENERAL JOURNAL

Date	Account Titles and Explanation	PR	Debit	Credit
(a)				
(b)				
(c)				
(d)				
(e)				
(f)				
(g)				

Chapter 15 Exercise 15-2 *Name* ______________________

(1) GENERAL JOURNAL

Date		Account Titles and Explanation	PR	Debit	Credit

(2)

____

____

____

____

(3) GENERAL JOURNAL

Date		Account Titles and Explanation	PR	Debit	Credit

Exercise 15-3

Available-for-Sale Portfolio	Cost	Market	Unrealized Gain (Loss)

GENERAL JOURNAL

Date		Account Titles and Explanation	PR	Debit	Credit

Chapter 15 Exercise 15-4 *Name* ______________________

GENERAL JOURNAL

Date		Account Titles and Explanation	PR	Debit	Credit
(a)					
(b)					
(c)					
(d)					
(e)					
(f)					
(g)					

Chapter 15 Exercise 15-5 *Name* ____________________

GENERAL JOURNAL

Date		Account Titles and Explanation	PR	Debit	Credit

Computation of Market Adjustment:

Securities	Cost	Market	Unrealized Gain (Loss)

Exercise 15-6

GENERAL JOURNAL

Date		Account Titles and Explanation	PR	Debit	Credit

Computation of Market Adjustment:

	12/31/2008	12/31/2009
Cost		
Market		
Gain (Loss)		
Adjustments:		

Chapter 15 Exercise 15-7 *Name* ____________________

GENERAL JOURNAL

Date		Account Titles and Explanation	PR	Debit	Credit
2007:					
2008:					
2009:					
2010:					

Supporting Computations:

Chapter 15 Exercise 15-8 *Name* ____________________

(1) Classification of Investments

(a)

(b)

(c)

(d)

(e)

(2) GENERAL JOURNAL

Date		Account Titles and Explanation	PR	Debit	Credit

Computation of Market Adjustment:

Long-Term AFS Securities	Cost	Market

Chapter 15 Exercise 15-9 *Name* ____________________

GENERAL JOURNAL

Date		Account Titles and Explanation	PR	Debit	Credit
2009:					
2010:					

Chapter 15 Exercise 15-10 *Name* ______________________

2009 Return on Total Assets:

2010 Return on Total Assets:

Analysis and Interpretation:

Chapter 15 Exercise 15-11[A] *Name* ______________________

GENERAL JOURNAL

Date		Account Titles and Explanation	PR	Debit	Credit
2009:					
2010:					

Chapter 15 Exercise 15-12[A] *Name* ____________________

Reported on Quarterly Statement Ended June 30, 2009:

Reported on Quarterly Statement Ended September 30, 2009:

Reported on Quarterly Statement Ended December 31, 2009:

Reported on Quarterly Statement Ended March 31, 2010:

Chapter 15 Problem 15-1A or 15-1B *Name* ____________

GENERAL JOURNAL

Date		Account Titles and Explanation	PR	Debit	Credit
2009:					
2010:					

Chapter 15 Problem 15-1A or 15-1B (Continued) *Name* ____________

Part 1

GENERAL JOURNAL

Date		Account Titles and Explanation	PR	Debit	Credit
2011:					

Part 2

Date		Account Titles and Explanation	PR	Debit	Credit

Chapter 15 Problem 15-2A or 15-2B *Name* ______________________

Part 1

GENERAL JOURNAL

Date		Account Titles and Explanation	PR	Debit	Credit

Chapter 15 Problem 15-2A or 15-2B (Continued) *Name* ____________

Part 2

Comparison of Cost and Market Values for AFS Portfolio				
Security	Computations	Cost	Market	Unrealized Gain (Loss)

Part 3

GENERAL JOURNAL

Date		Account Titles and Explanation	PR	Debit	Credit

Part 4

Part 5

Income Statement:

Balance Sheet (Equity Section Only):

Chapter 15 Problem 15-3A or 15-3B ***Name*** ____________________

Part 1

GENERAL JOURNAL

Date		Account Titles and Explanation	PR	Debit	Credit
2009:					

Supporting work:

Chapter 15 Problem 15-3A or 15-3B *Name* ______________________

Part 1 (Continued)

GENERAL JOURNAL

Date		Account Titles and Explanation	PR	Debit	Credit
2010:					

Supporting work:

Chapter 15 Problem 15-3A or 15-3B *Name* ____________________

Part 1 (Continued)

GENERAL JOURNAL

Date		Account Titles and Explanation	PR	Debit	Credit
2011:					

Supporting work:

Chapter 15 Problem 15-3A or 15-3B (Continued) *Name* ____________

Part 2

	12/31/2009	12/31/2010	12/31/2011
Long-Term AFS Securities (cost)			
Market Adjustment			
Long-Term AFS Securities (market)			

Part 3

	2009	2010	2011
Realized Gains (Losses)			
Unrealized Gains (Losses) at year-end			

Problem 15-4A or 15-4B

Part 1

Balance sheet disclosure:

Supporting work:

AFS Securities on Dec. 31, 2009	Cost	Market

Chapter 15 Problem 15-4A or 15-4B (Continued) *Name* ____________

Part 2

GENERAL JOURNAL

Date		Account Titles and Explanation	PR	Debit	Credit

Supporting Computations:

AFS Securities	Cost	Market

Part 3

Disclosures:

Stock Sold	Cost	Sale Value	Realized Gain (Loss)

Chapter 15 Problem 15-5A or 15-5B ***Name*** ______________________

Part 1

(1)

GENERAL JOURNAL

Date		Account Titles and Explanation	PR	Debit	Credit
2009:					
2010:					
2011:					

Chapter 15 Problem 15-5A or 15-5B *Name* ____________

Part 1 (Continued)

(2) Carrying Value Per Share:

(3) Change in Equity:

Chapter 15 Problem 15-5A or 15-5B (Continued) *Name* ____________________

Part 2

(1)

GENERAL JOURNAL

Date		Account Titles and Explanation	PR	Debit	Credit
2009:					
2010:					
2011:					

Chapter 15 Problem 15-5A or 15-5B *Name* ______________________

Part 2 (Continued)

(2) Investment Cost Per Share:

(3) Change in Equity:

Chapter 15 Problem 15-6A[A] or 15-6B[A] *Name* ____________________

Part 1

GENERAL JOURNAL

Date		Account Titles and Explanation	PR	Debit	Credit
2009:					

Chapter 15 Problem 15-6A[A] or 15-6B[A] *Name* ______________________

Part 1 (Continued)

GENERAL JOURNAL

Date		Account Titles and Explanation	PR	Debit	Credit
2010:					

Part 2

Foreign Exchange Gain (Loss) Reported:

Part 3

Chapter 15 Serial Problem SP 15 *Name* ______________________
Success Systems

Part 1

GENERAL JOURNAL

Date		Account Titles and Explanation	PR	Debit	Credit

Part 2

GENERAL JOURNAL

Date		Account Titles and Explanation	PR	Debit	Credit

Chapter 15 Reporting in Action *Name* ____________________

BTN 15-1

(1)

(2)

(3)

(4)

(5) Fast Forward:

Chapter 15 Comparative Analysis Name ____________
BTN 15-2

(1) Best Buy's Return on Total Assets:

Current Year

Prior Year

Circuit City's Return on Total Assets:

Current Year

Prior Year

RadioShack's Return on Total Assets:

Current Year

Prior Year

(2) Best Buy's Component Analysis of Return on Total Assets:

Current Year

Prior Year

Circuit City's Component Analysis of Return on Total Assets:

Current Year

Prior Year

Chapter 15 Comparative Analysis BTN 15-2 (Continued) *Name* ______________________

(2 cont.)

RadioShack's Component Analysis of Return on Total Assets:

Current Year

Prior Year

(3) Current Year Analysis:

Prior Year Analysis:

Chapter 15 Ethics Challenge ***Name*** ______________________

BTN 15-3

(1)

(2)

(3)

 Name ______________________

BTN 15-4

MEMORANDUM

TO:
FROM:
DATE:
SUBJECT:

(1)

(2)

(3)

(4)

Chapter 15 Teamwork in Action *Name* ____________
BTN 15-6

Chapter 15 *Entrepreneurial Decision* BTN 15-7 *Name* ______________________

(1)

GENERAL JOURNAL

Date		Account Titles and Explanation	PR	Debit	Credit

(2)

GENERAL JOURNAL

Date		Account Titles and Explanation	PR	Debit	Credit

(3)

Chapter 15 Hitting the Road—BTN 15-8[A] *Name* ______________________

(1) ______________________

(2) ______________________

(3) ______________________

Global Decision—BTN 15-9

(1) Return on Total Assets:

Current Year

Prior Year

Component Analysis of Return on Total Assets:

Current Year

Prior Year

(2) Current Year Analysis:

Prior Year Analysis:

Overall:

Chapter 16 Quick Study 16-1 *Name* ____________

(1)

(2)

(3)

(4)

Quick Study 16-2

(1) (6)
(2) (7)
(3) (8)
(4) (9)
(5) (10)

Quick Study 16-3

Cash Flows from Operating Activities

Chapter 16 Quick Study 16-4 *Name* ______________________

Quick Study 16-5

(1)

(2)

Quick Study 16-6

Cash Flow from Operating Activities

Chapter 16 Quick Study 16-7 *Name* ______

Cash Inflow from Asset Sale:

Quick Study 16-8

(1) Cash Paid for Dividends

(2) Cash Payments toward Notes:

Quick Study 16-9B

(1) Cash Received from Customer:

(2) Net Increase or Decrease in Cash:

Chapter 16 Quick Study 16-10[B] *Name* ____________________

(1) Cash Paid for Merchandise:

(2) Cash Paid for Operating Expenses:

Quick Study 16-11[B]

Cash Flow from Operating Activities

Quick Study 16-12

(1)

(2)

Chapter 16 Quick Study 16-13A *Name* ______________________

Quick Study 16-14

Cash Flows from Operating Activities	Case A	Case B	Case C

Chapter 16 Quick Study 16-15 *Name* ____________________

Investing Activities

Quick Study 16-16

Financing Activities

Exercise 16-1

Cash Flow from Operating Activities

Chapter 16 Exercise 16-2 *Name* ______________

	Statement of Cash Flows			Noncash	Not Reported
	Operating Activities	*Investing Activities*	*Financing Activities*	*Investing & Financing Activities*	*on Statement or in Note*
a. Paid cash to purchase inventory.					
b. Purchased land by issuing stock.					
c. Accounts receivable decreased this year.					
d. Sold equipment for cash, yielding a loss.					
e. Recorded depreciation expense.					
f. Income taxes payable increased this year.					
g. Declared and paid a cash dividend.					
h. Accounts payable decreased this year.					
i. Paid cash to settle notes payable.					
j. Prepaid expenses increased this year.					

Chapter 16 Exercise 16-6 *Name* ______________________

Cash Flows from Operating Activities

Supporting computations:

Exercise 16-7[B]

Cash Flows from Operating Activities

Supporting computations:

Chapter 16 Exercise 16-8 *Name* ______________________

Cash Flows from Investing Activities

Exercise 16-9

Cash Flows for Financing Activities

Chapter 16 Exercise 16-10 *Name* ____________________

Boulware, Inc.
Statement of Cash Flows (Indirect Method)
For Year Ended June 30, 2009

Supporting Computations for:

(1) Cash received from sale of equipment:

Cash paid for new equipment:

Chapter 16 Exercise 16-10 (Continued) *Name* ______________

Part 1

Supporting computations continued.

(2) Cash received from stock issuance:

(3) Cash paid for dividends:

Part 2

Cash Flow on Total Assets Ratio:

Interpretation:

Chapter 16 Exercise 16-14 *Name* ______________________

Cash Flows from Operating Activities

Exercise 16-15

(1) Cash Flows from Operating Activities

(2)

(3)

Chapter 16 Problem 16-1A or 16-1B *Name* ____________________

Part 1

Statement of Cash Flows
For Year Ended December 31, 2009

Statement Footnotes:

Supporting calculations:

Chapter 16 Problem 16-1A or 16-1B (Continued) *Name* ____________________

Part 2

Chapter 16 Problem 16-2A[A] or 16-2B[A] Name ____________________

Spreadsheet for Statement of Cash Flows
For Year Ended December 31, 2009

	Dec. 31, 2008	Analysis of changes Debit	Analysis of changes Credit	Dec. 31, 2009
Balance sheet-debits:				
Cash..				
Accounts receivable.....................				
Merchandise inventory..................				
Prepaid expenses........................				
Equipment..................................				
Balance sheet-credits:				
Accum. depreciation-Equip.......				
Accounts payable.....................				
Short-term notes payable.........				
Long-term notes payable..........				
Common Stock, $___par value...				
Paid-in capital in excess of par value, common stock.......				
Retained earnings..................				
Statement of cash flows:				
Operating activities				
Net income..............................				
________ in accts. receivable...				
________ in merch. inventory...				
________ in prepaid expenses...				
________ in accounts payable...				
Depreciation expense..............				
________ on sale of equipment..				
Investing activities				
Receipt from sale of equipment...				
Payment to purchase equipment..				
Financing activities				
Borrowed on short-term note....				
Payment on long-term note......				
Issued common stock for cash..				
Payments of cash dividends.....				
Noncash investing and financing activities				
Purchase of equip. financed by long-term note payable.....				

Chapter 16 Problem 16-2A or 16-2B (Continued) *Name* ______

Statement of Cash Flows
For Year Ended December 31, 2009

Statement Footnotes:

Supporting calculations:

Chapter 16 Problem 16-3A[B] or 16-3B[B] *Name*

Statement of Cash Flows
For Year Ended December 31, 2009

Statement Footnotes:

Supporting calculations:

Chapter 16 Problem 16-4A or 16-4B *Name* ____________________

Statement of Cash Flows
For Year Ended December 31, 2009

Supporting calculations:

 Name ____________________

Spreadsheet for Statement of Cash Flows
For Year Ended December 31, 2009

	Dec. 31, 2008	Analysis of changes *Debit*	*Credit*	*Dec. 31, 2009*
Balance sheet-debits:				
Cash				
Accounts receivable				
Merchandise inventory				
Equipment				
Balance sheet-credits:				
Accum. depreciation-Equip				
Accounts payable				
Income taxes payable				
Common stock, $___par value				
Paid-in capital in excess of par value, common stock				
Retained earnings				
Statement of cash flows:				
Operating activities				
Net income				
________ in accts. receivable				
________ in merch. inventory				
________ in accounts payable				
________ in income taxes payable				
Depreciation expense				
Investing activities				
Payment for equipment				
Financing activities				
Issued common stock for cash				
Paid cash dividends				

Chapter 16 Problem 16-7A or 16-7B *Name* ______

Cash Flows from Operating Activities—Indirect Method

Problem 16-8A[B] or 16-8B[B]

Cash Flows from Operating Activities—Direct Method

Chapter 16 Serial Problem, SP 16 *Name* ________________

Success Systems

SUCCESS SYSTEMS
Statement of Cash Flows
For Three Months Ended March 31, 2010

Supporting calculations:

Chapter 16 Reporting in Action *Name* ________________

BTN 16-1

(1)

(2)

(3)

(4)

(5) Fast Forward:

Chapter 16 Comparative Analysis *Name* ____________

BTN 16-2

(1) Best Buy's Cash Flow on Total Assets Ratio:

Current Year

Prior Year

Circuit City's Cash Flow on Total Assets Ratio:

Current Year

Prior Year

RadioShack's Cash Flow on Total Assets Ratio:

Current Year

Prior Year

(2)

(3)

(4)

Chapter 16 Ethics Challenge *Name* ______________________
BTN 16-3

(1) (a)

(b)

(2)

 Name ____________________

MEMORANDUM

TO:
FROM:
DATE:
SUBJECT:

Chapter 16 Taking It to the Net **Name** ____________________
BTN 16-5

(1)

(2)

(3)	2007	2006	2005
Net income (net loss)			
Cash flow from operations			

Analysis:

(4)

(5)

(6)

Teamwork in Action—BTN 16-6

Part 1

(a)

Name ____________________

Part 1 **(Continued)**

(b)

Similarities	Differences

(c)

(d)

Part 2

Adjusting Net Income to Cash Flow from Operating Activities	
Items to Add	**Items to Subtract**
a.	
b.	
c.	
d.	

Chapter 16 Teamwork in Action Name ____________
BTN 16-6 (Continued)

Part 3

(a)

(b)

(c)

(d)

Chapter 16 Entrepreneurial Decision **Name** ______________
BTN 16-7

(1)

(2)

MEMORANDUM

TO:
FROM:
DATE:
SUBJECT:

Chapter 16 Hitting the Road
BTN 16-9

Name ____________________

(1)

(2)

(3)

Global Decision—BTN 16-10

(1) Cash Flow on Total Assets Ratio

Current Year:

Prior Year:

(2) Comparative Analysis:

Chapter 17 Quick Study 17-1 *Name* ______________________

Not part of General-Purpose Statements:

Quick Study 17-2

Quick Study 17-3

(1) Common-Size Percents

2009

2008

(2) Trend Percents

2009

2008

Chapter 17 Quick Study 17-4 *Name* ______________________

Account	2009	2008	Dollar Change	Percent Change

Quick Study 17-5

(1)	(6)
(2)	(7)
(3)	(8)
(4)	(9)
(5)	(10)

Quick Study 17-6

(1) ______________________

(2) ______________________

(3) ______________________

Quick Study 17-7

Ratio	2009	2008	Change
1. Profit Margin Ratio	10%	9%	
2. Debt Ratio	43%	39%	
3. Gross Margin Ratio	32%	44%	
4. Acid-Test Ratio	1.20	1.05	
5. Accounts Receivable Turnover	6.7	5.5	
6. Basic Earnings Per Share	$1.25	$1.10	
7. Inventory Turnover	3.4	3.6	
8. Dividend Yield	4.0%	3.2%	

Quick Study 17-8[A]

Chapter 17 Exercise 17-1 *Name* ______________________

Account	2011	2010	2009	2008	2007

Analysis:

Exercise 17-2

Answer:

Supporting Work:

Chapter 17 Exercise 17-3 *Name* ______________________

Account	2009	2008

Analysis:

Exercise 17-4

COMPARATIVE ANALYSIS REPORT

Chapter 17 Exercise 17-5 *Name* ______________________

COMPARATIVE ANALYSIS REPORT

Chapter 17 Exercise 17-6 *Name* ____________________

Nabisco Company Common-Size Comparative Balance Sheets December 31, 2008–2010	2010	2009	2008

Analysis and interpretation:

Chapter 17 Exercise 17-7 *Name* ____________________

(1) Current Ratio:

2010:

2009:

2008:

(2) Acid-test ratio

2010:

2009:

2008:

Analysis and interpretation:

Chapter 17 Exercise 17-8 *Name* ______________________

1. Days' sales uncollected:

2010:

2009:

2. Accounts receivable turnover:

2010:

2009:

3. Inventory turnover:

2010:

2009:

4. Days' sales in inventory:

2010:

2009:

Analysis and interpretation:

Chapter 17 Exercise 17-9 *Name* ______________________

(1)

Debt Ratio and Equity Ratio	2010	2009

(2) Debt-to-Equity Ratio

(3) Times Interest Earned

Analysis and interpretation:

Chapter 17 Exercise 17-10 *Name* ____________________

(1) Profit margin:

2010:

2009:

(2) Total asset turnover:

2010:

2009:

(3) Return on total assets:

2010:

2009:

Analysis and interpretation:

Chapter 17 Exercise 17-11 *Name* ______________________

(1) Return on common stockholders' equity:

2010:

2009:

(2) Price-earnings ratio, December 31:

2010:

2009:

(3) Dividend yield:

2010:

2009:

Analysis and interpretation:

Chapter 17 Exercise 17-12[A] *Name* ____________

(1)	(5)
(2)	(6)
(3)	(7)
(4)	(8)

Exercise 17-13

Simplon Merchandising
Income Statement
For Year Ended December 31, 2009

Chapter 17 Problem 17-1A or 17-1B *Name* ______________________

Part 1

Current Ratio
2010:

2009:

2008:

Part 2

Common-Size Comparative Income Statements For Years Ended December 31, 2010, 2009, and 2008	2010	2009	2008

Chapter 17 Problem 17-1A or 17-1B (Continued) *Name* ____________________

Part 3

Balance Sheet Data in Trend Percents December 31, 2010, 2009, and 2008	2010	2009	2008

Part 4

Significant relations revealed:

Chapter 17 Problem 17-2A or 17-2B *Name* ______________________

Part 1

Income Statement Trends For Years Ended December 31, 2010–2004	*2010*	*2009*	*2008*	*2007*	*2006*	*2005*	*2004*

Balance Sheet Trends December 31, 2010–2004	*2010*	*2009*	*2008*	*2007*	*2006*	*2005*	*2004*

Chapter 17 Problem 17-2A or 17-2B (Continued) *Name* ______

Part 2

Analysis and interpretation:

Chapter 17 Problem 17-3A or 17-3B ***Name*** ______________________

Transaction	***Current Assets***	***Quick Assets***	***Current Liabilities***	***Current Ratio***	***Acid-Test Ratio***	***Working Capital***
Beg. Bal.						
End. Bal.						

Supporting computations:

Chapter 17 Problem 17-4A or 17-4B *Name* ____________________

(1) Current ratio:

(2) Acid-test ratio:

(3) Days' sales uncollected:

(4) Inventory turnover:

(5) Days' sales in inventory:

(6) Debt-to-equity ratio:

(7) Times interest earned:

(8) Profit margin ratio:

Chapter 17 Problem 17-4A or 17-4B (Continued) *Name* ____________________

(9) Total asset turnover:

(10) Return on total assets:

(11) Return on common stockholders' equity:

Part 1

	________ *Company*	________ *Company*
a. Current ratio:		
b. Acid-test ratio:		
c. Accounts (incl. notes) receivable turnover:		
d. Inventory turnover:		
e. Days' sales in inventory:		
f. Days' sales uncollected:		

Short-term credit risk analysis:

Chapter 17 Problem 17-5A or 17-5B (Continued) *Name* ____________________

Part 2

	________ Company	________ Company
a. Profit margin ratio:		
b. Total asset turnover:		
c. Return on total assets:		
d. Return on common stockholders' equity:		
e. Price-earnings ratio:		
f. Dividend yield:		

Investment analysis:

Chapter 17 Problem 17-6A[A] or 17-6B[A] *Name* ____________________

Part 1

Effect of Income Taxes:

Items	PreTax	___% Tax Effect	After-Tax

Part 2

Income from Continuing Operations and its Components:

Chapter 17 Problem 17-6A[A] or 17-6B[A] *Name* ____________
(Continued)

Part 3

Income from Discontinued Segment:

Part 4

Income before Extraordinary Items:

Part 5

Net Income:

Chapter 17 Serial Problem, SP 17 Success Systems *Name* ______________

(1) Gross Margin Ratio (with services revenue):

Gross Margin Ratio (without services revenue):

Profit Margin Ratio:

(2) Current Ratio:

Acid-Test Ratio:

(3) Debt Ratio:

Equity Ratio:

(4) Current Assets as % of Total Assets:

Long-Term Assets as % of Total Assets:

Chapter 17 Reporting in Action *Name* ____________________
BTN 17-1

(1) Trend Percents for selected income statement accounts:

	2007	2006	2005
Revenues			
Cost of Goods Sold			
Selling general and admin. expenses			
Income taxes			
Net income			

(2) Common-size percents for asset categories and accounts:

	2007	2006
Total current assets		
Property and equipment, net		
Intangible assets		

(3) Analysis and Interpretation:

(4) Fast Forward

Chapter 17 **Comparative Analysis** *Name* ____________
BTN 17-2

(1)

Key figures	Best Buy	Circuit City	RadioShack
Cash and cash equivalents			
Accounts receivable, net			
Inventories			
Retained earnings			
Cost of Goods Sold*			
Revenues			
Total Assets			

*Circuit City's cost of goods sold is titled cost of sales.

(2)

(3)

(4)

Chapter 17 Ethics Challenge **Name** ____________________

BTN 17-3

(1)

(2)

 Name ____________

BTN 17-4

MEMORANDUM

TO:

FROM:

DATE:

SUBJECT:

Chapter 17 Taking It to the Net Name ____________________
BTN 17-5

	2006	2005

1. Profit margin ratio

2. Gross profit ratio

3. Return on total assets

4. Return on common stockholders' equity

5. Basic earnings per share

Analysis and Interpretation:

Chapter 17 **Teamwork in Action** *Name* ____________

BTN 17-6

Part 1

Part 2

Part 3

Chapter 17 **Entrepreneurial Decision** ***Name*** ______________________

BTN 17-7

(1)

(2)

(3)

(4)

(5)

(6)

Hitting the Road—BTN 17-8

(1)

Key Figures	Percent	Amount
Cash and equivalents..........................		
Accounts receivable, net......................		
Inventories..		
Retained earnings..............................		
Cost of Sales......................................		
Revenues...		
Total assets..		

(2) Comparisons and comments

Chapter 18 Quick Study 18-1 *Name* ____________________

Answer: ____________________

____

Quick Study 18-2

(1) ____________________ (4) ____________________

(2) ____________________ (5) ____________________

(3) ____________________

Quick Study 18-3

(1) ____________________ (3) ____________________

(2) ____________________ (4) ____________________

Quick Study 18-4

Answer: ____________________

____

Quick Study 18-5

(1) ____________________ (4) ____________________

(2) ____________________ (5) ____________________

(3) ____________________

Quick Study 18-6

Answer: ____________________

____

Quick Study 18-7

Usual Sequence: ____________________

____

____

Chapter 18 Quick Study 18-8

Name ______________________

Quick Study 18-9

Quick Study 18-10

Biron Company
Manufacturing Statement
For Year Ended December 31, 2009

Chapter 18 Exercise 18-3 *Name* ____________________

	Financial Accounting	Managerial Accounting
1. Users and decision makers		
2. Timeliness of information		
3. Purpose of information		
4. Nature of information		
5. Flexibility of practice		
6. Focus of information		
7. Time dimension		

Chapter 18 Exercise 18-4 *Name* ______________________

(a)

(1) (3)

(2) (4)

(b)

Exercise 18-5

(1)

(2)

(3)

Exercise 18-6

	Product Cost		Period Cost	Direct Cost	Indirect Cost
	Prime	Conversion			
Amortization of patents on factory machine......................					
Payroll taxes for production supervisor..............................					
Accident insurance on factory workers..................................					
Depreciation—Factory building....					
State and federal income taxes					
Wages to assembly workers.......					
Direct materials used...............					
Office supplies used.................					
Bad debts expense..................					
Small tools used......................					
Factory utilities........................					
Advertising.............................					

Chapter 18 Problem 18-3A or 18-3B *Name* ____________________

Part 1

Costs	*Cost by Behavior*		*Cost by Function*	
	Variable	*Fixed*	*Product*	*Period*
1.				
2.				
3.				
4.				
5.				
6.				
7.				
8.				
9.				
10.				

Part 2

____________________ Computation of Manufacturing Cost per ____________ For Year Ended December 31, 2009	Total Cost	Per Unit Cost
Variable costs		
Fixed Costs		

Part 3

____

____

____

____

Part 4

____

____

____

____

MEMORANDUM

TO:
FROM:
DATE:
SUBJECT: Cost classification and explanation

Chapter 18 Problem 18-5A or 18-5B *Name* ______________________

Cost Estimation (including opportunity costs):

Chapter 18 Problem 18-6A or 18-6B *Name* ______________________

Part 1

Units and Dollar Amounts for Raw Materials Inventory

Part 2

MEMORANDUM

TO:
FROM:
DATE:
SUBJECT: Consideration of JIT inventory system

Chapter 18 Problem 18-7A or 18-7B *Name* ______________________

Part 1

Merchandising Business
____
Partial Income Statement
For Year Ended December 31, 2009

Manufacturing Business
____
Partial Income Statement
For Year Ended December 31, 2009

Part 2

MEMORANDUM

TO:
FROM:
DATE:
SUBJECT: Identifying and reporting inventory accounts

Chapter 18 Problem 18-8A or 18-8B *Name* ______________________

Part 1

____

Manufacturing Statement
For Year Ended December 31, 2009

Part 2

____________________ Income Statement For Year Ended December 31, 2009

Chapter 18 Problem 18-8A or 18-8B (Continued) *Name* ____________________

Part 3

Amounts and Inventory Ratios	Raw Materials	Finished Goods

Analysis and discussion:

Chapter 18 Problem 18-9A or 18-9B *Name* ______________________

Part 1

Part 2

Part 3

Chapter 18 **Serial Problem, SP 18** ***Name*** ______________________

Success System

(1)

	Cost by Behavior		Cost by Traceability	
Product Costs	**Variable**	**Fixed**	**Direct**	**Indirect**
Monthly flat fee to clean workshop.				
Laminate coverings for desktops....				
Taxes on assembly workshop........				
Glue to assemble workstation component parts.....................				
Wages of desk assembler.............				
Electricity for workshop................				
Depreciation on tools..................				

(2)

Success Systems
Manufacturing Statement
For Month Ended January 31, 2010

(3)

Success Systems
Partial Income Statement
For Month Ended January 31, 2010

Cost of goods sold

Chapter 18 Reporting in Action Name ____________
BTN 18-1

(1)

Estimate	Effects if Actual Results differ from Assumptions

(2)

(3) Fast Forward:

Chapter 18 **Comparative Analysis** ***Name*** ____________________
BTN 18-2

(1)

Best Buy

RadioShack

(2)

Chapter 18 Ethics Challenge—BTN 18-3 *Name* ____________________

(1) Account Identification

(2) CFO Response

 Name ________________

MEMORANDUM

TO:
FROM:
DATE:
SUBJECT: Business student salary expectations

Chapter 18 Taking It to the Net *Name* ______________________

BTN 18-5

(1) Personal Notes from "Statement of Ethical Professional Practice":

(2) Overarching Ethical Principles:

(3)

Attach printout of IMA Ethical Standards

Chapter 18 **Teamwork in Action**
BTN 18-6

Name ______________________

Chapter 18 Entrepreneurial Decision **Name** ______________________
BTN 18-7

(1) Manufacturing Cost Categories

(a)

(b)

(c)

(2) Managerial Measures

(3) Total Quality Management

Chapter 18 Hitting the Road—BTN 18-8 ***Name*** ____________________

(1) Customer Business Activities (from arrival through departure)

(2) Costs of Customer Business Activities from Part 1

(3) Cost Classification and Explanation

Chapter 18 Global Decision—BTN 18-9 *Name* ____________________

(1) Responsibilities

(2) Involvement

Chapter 19 Quick Study 19-1 *Name* ______________________

Job: ______________________

Job lot: ______________________

Quick Study 19-2

Job Cost Sheet

Quick Study 19-3

GENERAL JOURNAL

Date		Account Titles and Explanation	PR	Debit	Credit

GENERAL JOURNAL

Date		Account Titles and Explanation	PR	Debit	Credit

Quick Study 19-5

(1) Overhead as Percent of Direct Labor

(2) Overhead as Percent of Direct Materials

Quick Study 19-6

GENERAL JOURNAL

Date		Account Titles and Explanation	PR	Debit	Credit

Chapter 19 Exercise 19-10 *Name* ____________________

(1) Predetermined Overhead Rate

(2)

	Goods in Process			*Finished Goods*		
	Cost per Unit	*Units*	*Total Cost*	*Cost per Unit*	*Units*	*Total Cost*
Direct materials						
Direct labor						
Overhead						
Total						

(3)

Chapter 19 Exercise 19-11 *Name* ____________________

(1) Estimated Cost of the Architectural Job

(2) Suggested Bid Price

Chapter 19 Problem 19-1A or 19-1B ***Name*** ______________________

Part 1

Total Manufacturing Costs and Costs Assigned to Each Job

Costs	*Job*________	*Job*________	*Job*________	*Total for Month*

Chapter 19 Problem 19-1A or 19-1B **Name** ____________________
(Continued)

Part 2

GENERAL JOURNAL

Date		Account Titles and Explanation	PR	Debit	Credit
(a)					
(b)					

Chapter 19 Problem 19-1A or 19-1B *Name* ______________________

Part 2 (Continued)

GENERAL JOURNAL

Date		Account Titles and Explanation	PR	Debit	Credit
(c)					
(d)					
(e)					
(f)					

Chapter 19 Problem 19-1A or 19-1B *Name* ______________________
(Continued)

Part 3

______________________ Manufacturing Statement For Month Ended __________

Part 4

Gross Profit Computation

Presentation of Inventories on Balance Sheet

Part 5

Impacts of Over- or Underapplied Overhead

Chapter 19 Problem 19-2A or 19-2B *Name* ____________________

Part 1

GENERAL JOURNAL

Date		Account Titles and Explanation	PR	Debit	Credit
(a)					
(b)					
(c)					
(d)					
(e)					

Chapter 19 Problem 19-2A or 19-2B (Continued) *Name* ______________________

Part 2

GENERAL JOURNAL

Date		Account Titles and Explanation	PR	Debit	Credit

Overhead computations:

Part 3

____

Trial Balance

December 31, 2009

	Debit	Credit

Chapter 19 Problem 19-2A or 19-2B *Name* ____________________
(Continued)

Part 4

Income Statement For Year Ended December 31, 2009

Balance Sheet December 31, 2009

Part 5

Error Analysis for Financial Statements

Chapter 19 Problem 19-3A or 19-3B *Name* ______________________

Part 1

JOB COST SHEETS

Job No. ______	
Materials..........	
Labor...............	
Overhead.........	
Total Cost.........	

Job No. ______	
Materials.........	
Labor...............	
Overhead.........	
Total Cost.........	

Job No. ______	
Materials.........	
Labor...............	
Overhead.........	
Total Cost.........	

Job No. ______	
Materials.........	
Labor...............	
Overhead.........	
Total Cost.........	

Job No. ______	
Materials.........	
Labor..............	
Overhead.........	
Total Cost.........	

Chapter 19 Problem 19-3A or 19-3B (Continued) *Name* ____________________

Part 2

GENERAL JOURNAL

Date		Account Titles and Explanation	PR	Debit	Credit
(a)					
(b)					
(c)					
(d)					
(e)					
(f)					
(g)					

Chapter 19 Problem 19-3A or 19-3B *Name* ____________

Part 2 (Continued)

GENERAL JOURNAL

Date		Account Titles and Explanation	PR	Debit	Credit
(h)					
(i)					
(j)					

Part 3

GENERAL LEDGER ACCOUNTS

Raw Materials Inventory

Factory Payroll

Goods in Process Inventory

Factory Overhead

Finished Goods Inventory

Cost of Goods Sold

Chapter 19 Problem 19-3A or 19-3B *Name* ____________________
(Continued)

Part 4

Reports of Job Costs
Goods in Process Inventory:
Finished Goods Inventory:
Cost of Goods Sold:

Chapter 19 Problem 19-4A or 19-4B *Name* ______________________

Part 1

(a) Predetermined Overhead Rate

(b) Overhead Costs Applied to Jobs

Job No.	*Direct Labor*	*Applied Overhead*
....		
....		
....		
....		
....		
....		
Totals..................		

(c) Overapplied or Underapplied Overhead

Part 2

GENERAL JOURNAL

Date		Account Titles and Explanation	PR	Debit	Credit

JOB COST SHEET

Customer's Name __________ Company ____________________ Job No. ________

Direct Materials			Direct Labor			Overhead Costs Applied		
Date	Requisition Number	Amount	Date	Time Ticket Number	Amount	Date	Rate	Amount
						SUMMARY OF COSTS		
						Dir. Materials..		
						Dir. Labor……		
						Overhead……		
Total			Total			Total Cost of		
						the Job………		

JOB COST SHEET

Customer's Name __________ Company ____________________ Job No. ________

Direct Materials			Direct Labor			Overhead Costs Applied		
Date	Requisition Number	Amount	Date	Time Ticket Number	Amount	Date	Rate	Amount
						SUMMARY OF COSTS		
						Dir. Materials..		
						Dir. Labor……		
						Overhead……		
Total			Total			Total Cost of		
						the Job………		

 Name ____________________

MATERIALS LEDGER CARD

Item ____

Received					Issued				Balance		
Date	Receiving Report	Units	Unit Price	Total Price	Requi-sition	Units	Unit Price	Total Price	Units	Unit Price	Total Price

MATERIALS LEDGER CARD

Item ____

Received					Issued				Balance		
Date	Receiving Report	Units	Unit Price	Total Price	Requi-sition	Units	Unit Price	Total Price	Units	Unit Price	Total Price

MATERIALS LEDGER CARD

Item ____

Received					Issued				Balance		
Date	Receiving Report	Units	Unit Price	Total Price	Requi-sition	Units	Unit Price	Total Price	Units	Unit Price	Total Price

GENERAL JOURNAL

Date		Account Titles and Explanation	PR	Debit	Credit

 Name ____________________

GENERAL LEDGER

Cash

Accounts Receivable

Sales

Cost of Goods Sold

Finished Goods Inventory

Accounts Payable

Raw Materials Inventory

Goods in Process Inventory

Factory Overhead

Factory Payroll

FACTORY OVERHEAD SUBSIDIARY LEDGER

Indirect Materials

Indirect Labor

Miscellaneous Overhead

Chapter 19 Serial Problem, SP 19 *Name* ____
Success Systems

(1) Cost of Direct Materials Used in Period for each Job and its Total

(2) Cost of Direct Labor Incurred in Period

(3) Predetermined Overhead Rate for Period

(4) Cost Transferred to Finished Goods Inventory in Period

Chapter 19 Reporting in Action ***Name*** ____________________

BTN 19-1

(1) Costs that will Predictably Increase as a Percent of Sales

(2) Explanation and Performance Assessment of the Costs in Part 1

(3) Fast Forward:

Chapter 19 Comparative Analysis *Name* ____________________
BTN 19-2

Part 1

Best Buy	Current Year	One Year Prior	Two Years Prior
Inventory change………..			
Operating cash flow effect from inventory change….			

Circuit City	Current Year	One Year Prior	Two Years Prior
Inventory change………..			
Operating cash flow effect from inventory change….			

Part 2

Impacts of JIT Inventory System

Part 3

Operating Cash Flow Impacts of JIT Inventory System

Name ______________________

MEMORANDUM

TO:
FROM:
DATE:
SUBJECT: Review of Overhead Allocations

Chapter 19 Communicating in Practice *Name* ____________________
BTN 19-4

(1) Cost Accounting System Recommendation and Explanation

(2) Document Description for Proposed Cost Accounting System

(3) Document Facilitation of Cost Accounting System

Name ______________________

MEMORANDUM

TO:
FROM:
DATE:
SUBJECT: Explanation and recommendation of job order costing software

Chapter 19 Teamwork in Action *Name* ______
BTN 19-6

(1) Appropriateness of Job Order Cost Accounting System

(2) Factors Indicative of Job Order System

Chapter 19 **Entrepreneurial Decision** ***Name*** ____________________
BTN 19-7

(1)

(2)

 Name ______________________

(1)

JOB COST SHEET								
Customer's Name ________ **Company** ________ **Job No.** ________								
	Direct Materials			**Direct Labor**		**Overhead Costs Applied**		
Date	**Requisition Number**	**Amount**	**Date**	**Time Ticket Number**	**Amount**	**Date**	**Rate**	**Amount**
						SUMMARY OF COSTS		
						Dir. Materials		______
						Dir. Labor.....		______
						Overhead.....		______
Total			**Total**			**Total Cost of**		
						the Job........		______

Explanation for Overhead Applied: ____

____

____

____

(2) Report Actual Job Cost Sheet and Compare to Your Own in Part 1

Chapter 19 Global Decision—BTN 19-9 *Name* ____________________

(1) (in pounds million)	Current Year	One Year Prior
Inventory change..		
Increase or decrease..................................		
Operating cash flow effect from inventory change..		

(2) Implications of JIT Inventory Systems

Best Buy	Current Year	One Year Prior	Two Years Prior
Inventory change...........			
Operating cash flow effect from inventory change..			

Circuit City	Current Year	One Year Prior	Two Years Prior
Inventory change...........			
Operating cash flow effect from inventory change..			

Chapter 20 Quick Study 20-1 *Name* ______________

(1)	(7)
(2)	(8)
(3)	(9)
(4)	(10)
(5)	(11)
(6)	(12)

Quick Study 20-2

GENERAL JOURNAL

Date		Account Titles and Explanation	PR	Debit	Credit

Quick Study 20-3

GENERAL JOURNAL

Date		Account Titles and Explanation	PR	Debit	Credit

Chapter 20 Quick Study 20-4 *Name* ______________________

GENERAL JOURNAL

Date		Account Titles and Explanation	PR	Debit	Credit

Quick Study 20-5

GENERAL JOURNAL

Date		Account Titles and Explanation	PR	Debit	Credit

Quick Study 20-6

EUP for Labor	*Equivalent* *Units*

Chapter 20 Quick Study 20-7 *Name* ____________________

The cost of beginning inventory plus the costs added during the period should equal the cost of units____________________plus the cost of ____________________

Quick Study 20-8

Explanation of Hybrid Costing System

Product or Service Identification for Hybrid Costing System

Quick Study 20-9[A]

EUP for Labor	*Equivalent* *Units*

Chapter 20 Exercise 20-3 *Name* ____________________

GENERAL JOURNAL

Date		Account Titles and Explanation	PR	Debit	Credit
1.					
2.					
3.					
4.					
5.					

Chapter 20   Exercise 20-4   *Name* ______________________

(a)

(b)

(c)

(d)

(e)

(f)

(g)

(h)

(i)

(j)

Chapter 20 Exercise 20-5 *Name* ____________________

(1) Units Transferred to Finished Goods

(2)

Equivalent units of production	*Direct Materials*	*Direct Labor*

Chapter 20 Exercise 20-6 *Name* ______________________

1.

Cost per equivalent unit	*Direct Materials*	*Direct Labor*

2. Cost Assignment and Reconciliation

(3)

EUP for Materials

Exercise 20-10[A]

(1)

EUP for Materials

(2)

EUP for Materials

(3)

EUP for Materials

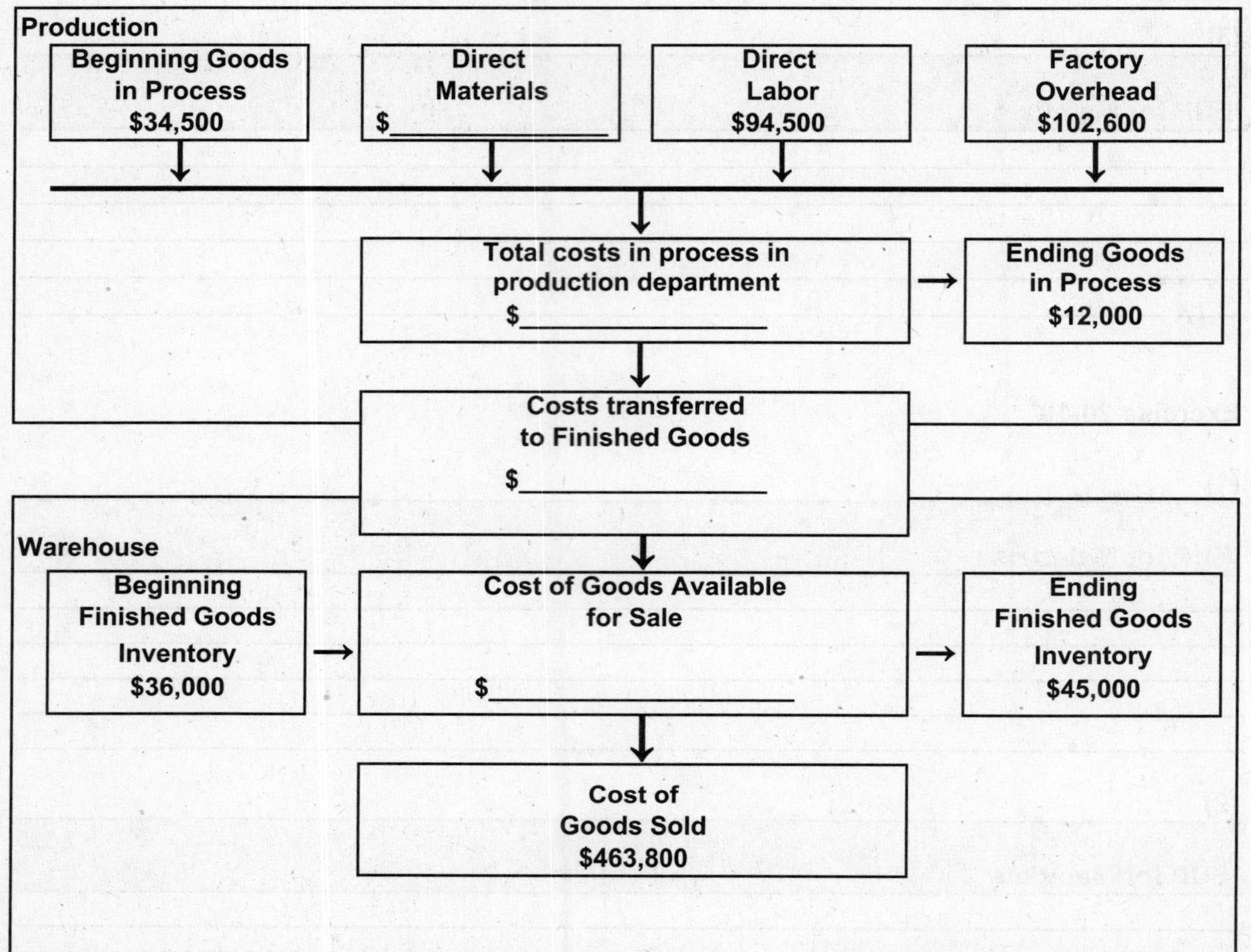
Production
Beginning Goods in Process $34,500
Direct Materials $________
Direct Labor $94,500
Factory Overhead $102,600
Total costs in process in production department $________
Ending Goods in Process $12,000
Costs transferred to Finished Goods $________
Warehouse
Beginning Finished Goods Inventory $36,000
Cost of Goods Available for Sale $________
Ending Finished Goods Inventory $45,000
Cost of Goods Sold $463,800

 Name ______________

ANTON COMPANY
Process Cost Summary
For Month Ended July 31

Costs Charged to Production

Unit Cost Information

Units to Account For	Units Accounted For

Equivalent Units of Production (EUP)	Direct Materials	Direct Labor	Factory Overhead

Cost Per EUP	Direct Materials	Direct Labor	Factory Overhead

Cost Assignment and Reconciliation

 Name ____________________

NU-TEST COMPANY
Process Cost Summary
For Month Ended September 30

Costs Charged to Production		
Costs of Beginning work in process		
Direct materials	$ 90,000	
Direct Labor	51,200	
Factory Overhead	61,440	$202,640
Costs incurred this period		
Direct materials	750,000	
Direct Labor	310,000	
Factory Overhead ($155,000 × 120%)	(a) ______	(b) ______
Total costs to account for		(c) ______

Unit Cost Information

Units to Account For		Units Accounted For	
Beginning goods in process	4,000	Completed & transferred out	46,000
Units started this period	56,000	Ending goods in process	(d) ______
Total units to account for (e)	______	Total units accounted for	(f) ______

Equivalent Units of Production (EUP)	Direct Materials	Direct Labor	Factory Overhead
Units completed and transferred out	(g)______ EUP	(h)______ EUP	(i)______ EUP
Units of ending goods in process			
Direct materials [(j)_____ × 100%]	(k)______ EUP		
Direct labor [(l)_____ × 40%]		(m)______ EUP	
Factory overhead [(n)_____ × 40%]			(o) EUP
Equivalent units of production	(p) EUP	(q) EUP	(r) EUP

Cost per EUP	Direct Materials	Direct Labor	Factory Overhead
Costs of beginning goods in process	$ 90,000	$ 51,200	$61,440
Costs incurred this period	750,000	310,000	(s) ______
Total costs	$840,000	$361,200	(t) ______
÷ Equivalent units of production	(u) ______	(v) ______	(w) ______
Cost per equivalent unit of production	(x) $____/EUP	(y) $____/EUP	(z) ____/EUP

(continued on next page)

 Name ______________________

Cost Assignment and Reconciliation

Costs transferred out

Direct materials [(aa)$_____ × (bb)______].....................	(cc) $__________	
Direct labor [(dd)$____ × (ee)______].............................	(ff) __________	
Factory overhead [(gg)$____ × (hh)______]...................	(ii) __________	
Total transferred out..		(jj) $______

Cost of ending good in process

Direct materials [(kk)$_____ × (ll)______].........................	(mm) __________	
Direct labor [(nn)$____ × (oo)______]..............................	(pp) __________	
Factory overhead [(qq)$____ × (rr)_____].......................	(ss) __________	
Total ending goods in process..		(tt) ______
Total costs accounted for..		(uu) $______

Chapter 20 Problem 20-1A or 20-1B *Name* ______________________

Part 1

Cost of goods transferred and cost of goods sold

Part 2

GENERAL JOURNAL

Date	Account Titles and Explanation	PR	Debit	Credit
a.				
b.				
c.				
d.				

Chapter 20 Problem 20-1A or 20-1B *Name* ______________________

Part 2 (Continued)

GENERAL JOURNAL

Date		Account Titles and Explanation	PR	Debit	Credit
e.					
f.					
g.					
h.					
i.					
j.					

Chapter 20 Problem 20-2A or 20 -2B *Name* ____________________

Part 1

(a and b)

Equivalent units of production	Direct Materials	Direct Labor

Part 2

Costs per equivalent unit	Direct Materials	Direct Labor

Assignment of product costs to units

 Name ______________________

Part 4

MEMORANDUM

TO:
FROM:
DATE:
SUBJECT: Percentage of completion error analysis

Chapter 20 Problem 20-3A or 20-3B *Name* ______________________________

Part 1

GENERAL JOURNAL

Date		Account Titles and Explanation	PR	Debit	Credit
a.					
b.					
c.					
d.					
e.					
f.					
g.					
h.					
i.					
j.					

Chapter 20 Problem 20-3A or 20-3B (Continued) *Name* ______________________________

Part 2

Process Cost Summary For Month Ended _____

Costs Charged to Production

Unit Cost Information

Units to Account For **Units Accounted For**

Equivalent Units of Production (EUP)	Direct Materials	Direct Labor	Factory Overhead

Cost per EUP	Direct Materials	Direct Labor	Factory Overhead

Cost Assignment and Reconciliation

Chapter 20 Problem 20-3A or 20-3B (Continued) *Name* ____________________

Part 3

Impacts of under- or overestimation of the percentage of completion for units in inventory:

 Name ____________________

Part 1

______

Process Cost Summary
For Month Ended _____

Costs Charged to Production

Unit Cost Information

Units to Account For | **Units Accounted For**

Equivalent Units of Production (EUP)	Direct Materials	Direct Labor	Factory Overhead

Cost per EUP	Direct Materials	Direct Labor	Factory Overhead

Cost Assignment and Reconciliation

 Name ____________________

Part 2

GENERAL JOURNAL

Date		Account Titles and Explanation	PR	Debit	Credit

 Name ______________________

Part 1

____

Process Cost Summary
For Month Ended _____

Costs Charged to Production

Unit Cost Information

Units to Account For

Units Accounted For

Equivalent Units of Production (EUP)	Direct Materials	Direct Labor	Factory Overhead

Cost per EUP	Direct Materials	Direct Labor	Factory Overhead

Process cost summary continued on next page.

Chapter 20 Problem 20-5A or 20-5B *Name* ____________________
(Continued)

Cost Assignment and Reconciliation

Part 2

GENERAL JOURNAL

Date		Account Titles and Explanation	PR	Debit	Credit

Part 3

(a)

(b)

 Name ______________________

Part 1

____
Process Cost Summary
For Month Ended _____

Costs Charged to Production

Unit Cost Information

Units to Account For

Units Accounted For

Equivalent Units of Production (EUP)	Direct Materials	Direct Labor	Factory Overhead

Cost per EUP	Direct Materials	Direct Labor	Factory Overhead

Process cost summary continued on next page.

Chapter 20 Problem 20-6A or 20-6B (Continued) *Name* ______________________

Cost Assignment and Reconciliation

Part 2

GENERAL JOURNAL

Date		Account Titles and Explanation	PR	Debit	Credit

Chapter 20 Serial Problem, SP 20 *Name* ____________________

Part 1

Job Order Costing	Process Costing

Part 2

Chapter 20 Comprehensive Problem *Name* ______________________

Part 1

[Note: General Ledger accounts shown in Part 4.]

GENERAL JOURNAL

Date		Account Titles and Explanation	PR	Debit	Credit
(a)					
(b)					
(c)					
(d)					
(e)					
(f)					

Chapter 20 Comprehensive Problem (Continued) *Name* ____________________

Part 2

Process Cost Summary
For Month Ended _____

Costs Charged to Production

Unit Cost Information

Units to Account For

Units Accounted For

Equivalent Units of Production (EUP)	Direct Materials	Direct Labor	Factory Overhead

Cost per EUP	Direct Materials	Direct Labor	Factory Overhead

Process cost summary continued on next page.

Chapter 20 Comprehensive Problem *Name* ____________________

Part 2 (Continued)

Cost Assignment and Reconciliation

Part 3

GENERAL JOURNAL

Date		Account Titles and Explanation	PR	Debit	Credit
(g)					
(h)					

Chapter 20 Comprehensive Problem (Continued) *Name* ____________________

Part 4

General Ledger accounts:

Raw Materials Inventory ACCOUNT NO. 132

Date	Explanation	PR	DEBIT	CREDIT	BALANCE
June 30	Balance				25,000

Goods in Process Inventory ACCOUNT NO. 133

Date	Explanation	PR	DEBIT	CREDIT	BALANCE
June 30	Balance				8,135

Finished Goods Inventory ACCOUNT NO. 135

Date	Explanation	PR	DEBIT	CREDIT	BALANCE
June 30	Balance				110,000

Sales ACCOUNT NO. 413

Date	Explanation	PR	DEBIT	CREDIT	BALANCE

Part 4 (Continued)

Cost of Goods Sold ACCOUNT NO. 502

Date	Explanation	PR	DEBIT	CREDIT	BALANCE

Factory Payroll ACCOUNT NO. 530

Date	Explanation	PR	DEBIT	CREDIT	BALANCE

Factory Overhead ACCOUNT NO. 540

Date	Explanation	PR	DEBIT	CREDIT	BALANCE

Part 5

Computation of gross profit for July:

Chapter 20 Reporting in Action **Name** ______________________

BTN 20-1

Part 1

Part 2

Part 3

Fast Forward:

Chapter 20 Comparative Analysis
BTN 20-2

Name ______________________

Part 1

	Best Buy		Circuit City		RadioShack	
	Current Year	Prior Year	Current Year	Prior Year	Current Year	Prior Year
COGS/ Total expenses						

Part 2

Analysis and Comparison of Cost Structures:

 Name ____________________

MEMORANDUM

TO:
FROM:
DATE:
SUBJECT: Action plan to understand business processes

 Name ________________________

MEMORANDUM

TO:
FROM:
DATE:
SUBJECT: Explanation of cost classifications

Chapter 20 Taking It to the Net **Name** ____________________

BTN 20-5

Chapter 20 Teamwork in Action
BTN 20-6

Name ____________________

GENERAL JOURNAL

Date		Account Titles and Explanation	PR	Debit	Credit

Chapter 20 *Entrepreneurial Decision* **Name** ______________________

BTN 20-7

(1)

(2)

BTN 20-8

Name ____________________

Cost description	Direct Materials	Direct Labor	Overhead	Variable cost	Fixed cost

Overhead allocation suggestions:

Chapter 20 Global Decision—BTN 20-9 *Name* ____________________

1. Ratio of Cost of Goods Sold to Total Expenses

	Current Year	Prior Year
DSG		

	Current Year	Prior Year
Best Buy..........................		

	Current Year	Prior Year
Circuit City.......................		

	Current Year	Prior Year
RadioShack......................		

2. Similarities or Differences Across Years and Companies:

Chapter 21 Quick Study 21-1 *Name* ____________

(1) ____________ (5) ____________
(2) ____________ (6) ____________
(3) ____________ (7) ____________
(4) ____________

Quick Study 21-2

(1) ____________

(2) ____________

(3) ____________

(4) ____________

Quick Study 21-3

Total Overhead Allocated to Operating Department 1: ____________

Chapter 21 Quick Study 21-4 *Name* ______________________

Contribution to Overhead (dollars):

Dept. A

Dept. B

Dept. C

Contribution to Overhead (percent of sales):

Dept. A

Dept. B

Dept. C

Highest Contribution (Dollar & Percent)

Quick Study 21-5

Center	Net Income	Average Assets	Return on Assets
Cameras & Camcorders	$ 4,500,000	$ 20,000,000	
Phones & Communications	1,500,000	12,500,000	
Computers & Accessories	800,000	10,000,000	

Center Performance Evaluation:

Quick Study 21-6

	Cameras & Camcorders	Phones & Communications	Computers & Accessories

 Name ____________________

Return on assets:

Profit Margin:

Investment Turnover:

Quick Study 21-8

INVESTMENT CENTER A

Return on assets:

Profit Margin:

Investment Turnover:

INVESTMENT CENTER B

Return on assets:

Profit Margin:

Investment Turnover:

Chapter 21 Quick Study 21-9 *Name* ______________________

1.	5.
2.	6
3.	7.
4.	8.

Quick Study 21-10

Quick Study 21-11[A]

Transfer Price Determination:

Chapter 21 Quick Study 21-12[A] *Name* ________________________

Range of Transfer Prices:

Quick Study 21-13[B]

Joint Cost Assigned to Unit B Using the Value Basis of Allocation

Chapter 21 Exercise 21-1 *Name* ______________________

(1) Allocation of Indirect Expenses to Operating Departments
Supervision:

	Employees	*% of Total*	*Cost*
Materials			
Personnel			
Manufacturing			
Packaging			
Totals			

Utilities:

	Square Feet	*% of Total*	*Cost*
Materials			
Personnel			
Manufacturing			
Packaging			
Totals			

Insurance:

	Asset Value	*% of Total*	*Cost*
Materials			
Personnel			
Manufacturing			
Packaging			
Totals			

(2) Total indirect expenses assigned to operating departments:

	Supervision	*Utilities*	*Insurance*	*Totals*
Materials				
Personnel				
Manufacturing				
Packaging				
Totals				

Chapter 21 Exercise 21-2 *Name* ____________________

Preliminary Computations (predetermined overhead rates)

Overhead Cost Pool	Total Cost	Amount of Cost Driver	Predetermined Overhead Rate
Supervision			
Depreciation			
Line Preparation			

(1) Assignment of overhead costs to the two products using ABC

Rounded edge:

	Cost Driver	*Cost per Driver Unit*	*Allocated Cost*
Supervision			
Machinery depreciation			
Line preparation			
Total overhead assigned			

Squared edge:

	Cost Driver	Cost per *Driver Unit*	Allocated Cost
Supervision			
Machinery depreciation			
Line preparation			
Total overhead assigned			

(2) Average cost per foot of the two products

	Rounded Edge	*Squared Edge*
Direct materials		
Direct labor		
Overhead (using ABC)		
Total Cost		
Quantity produced		
Average cost per foot		

Chapter 21 Exercise 21-2 (Continued) *Name* ____________________

(3) Comparison of Cost Allocation Methods

Exercise 21-3

Step 1: Allocate total rent expense between the floors.

	Amount Allocated	*% of Total*	*Cost*
First floor			
Second floor			
Totals			

Step 2: Allocate the floors' rent expense to the separate departments.

First Floor	*Sq. Feet*	*% of Total*	*Cost*
Paint Dept.			
Engine Dept.			
Totals			

Second Floor	*Sq. Feet*	*% of Total*	*Cost*
Window Dept.			
Electrical Dept.			
Accessory Dept.			
Totals			

Chapter 21 Exercise 21-4 Name ____________________

OFF-ROAD CYCLE SHOP Department Expense Allocation Spreadsheet For Year Ended December 31, 2009						
			Allocation of Expenses to Departments			
	Allocation Base	*Account Balance*	*Adver-tising*	*Admin-istrative*	*Cycles*	*Clothing*
Direct expenses						
Indirect utilities expense						
Total dept. expense						
Service dept. expenses:						
Advertising						
Administrative						
Total expenses allocated to operating depts.						

Supplemental expense allocation calculations:

Utilities expense:

	Square Feet	*% of Total*	*Cost*
Advertising			
Administrative			
Cycles			
Clothing			
Total			

Advertising expense:

	Ads Placed	*% of Total*	*Cost*
Cycles			
Clothing			
Total			

Administrative expense:

	Sales	*% of Total*	*Cost*
Cycles			
Clothing			
Total			

Chapter 21 Exercise 21-5 *Name* ____________________

HASTON BOOKSTORE Departmental Expense Allocation Spreadsheet For Period Ended __________			Allocation of Expenses to Departments				
	Allocation Base	*Expense Account Balance*	*Advertising Dept.*	*Purchasing Dept.*	*Books Dept.*	*Magazine Dept.*	*Newspaper Dept.*
Total dept. expenses.........							
Service dept. expenses:							
Advertising........	**Sales**						
Purchasing......	**Purchase Orders**						
Total expenses allocated to operating depts................							

Allocations of service department costs to operating departments

Advertising: ________

	Sales	*% of Total*	*Cost*
Books Dept.			
Magazines Dept.			
Newspapers Dept.			
Totals			

Purchasing: ________

	Purchase Orders	*% of Total*	*Cost*
Books Dept.			
Magazines Dept.			
Newspapers Dept.			
Totals			

Chapter 21 Exercise 21-6 *Name* ______________________

Allocation of annual wages between two departments

	*Hours Worked**	*% of Total*	*Cost*
Jewelry Dept.			
Hosiery Dept.			
Totals			

*Computation of hours worked in the two selling departments:

Jewelry department:

Selling................................

Arranging and stocking..........

Hosiery department:

Selling................................

Arranging and stocking..........

Total hours..............................

Chapter 21 Exercise 21-7 *Name* ______________________

Definitely Included:

Definitely Excluded:

Neither Definitely Included nor Definitely Excluded:

Chapter 21 Exercise 21-8 *Name* ______________________

(1)

Location	Net Income	Average Assets	Return on Assets
Location A			
Location B			

(2)

MEMORANDUM

TO:
FROM:
DATE:
SUBJECT: Investment analysis and recommendation

Chapter 21 Exercise 21-9 *Name* ______________________

(1)

Investment Center	Net Income	Average Assets	Return on Assets
Electronics			
Sporting Goods			

Comments: ______________________

(2)

Investment Center	Electronics	Sporting Goods
Net Income		
Target Net Income		
Residual Income		

Exercise 21-10

Investment Center	Net Income	Sales	Profit Margin
Electronics			
Sporting Goods			

Investment Center	Sales	Average Assets	Investment Turnover
Electronics			
Sporting Goods			

Comments: ______________________

Chapter 21 Exercise 21-11 *Name* ______________________

1.	8.
2.	9.
3.	10.
4.	11.
5.	12.
6.	13.
7.	14.

Exercise 21-12[A]

(1)

(2)

(3)

Chapter 21 Exercise 21-13A Name ____________________

Preliminary calculations

Land Cost......................

Improvements................

Total cost of lots............

Lots	Quantity	Price	Total
Canyon			
Hilltop			
Total Market value			

Allocated cost—value basis of allocation: __________

	Market Value	% of Total	Allocated Cost	Average Lot Cost
Canyon section				
Hilltop section				
Totals				

Chapter 21 Exercise 21-14[A] *Name* ______________________

Preliminary calculations

Parts	*Quantity*	*Price*	*Total*
Lobster Tails			
Lobster Flakes			
Total market value			

____

____

____

Allocated cost (value basis allocation): _______

Parts	*Market Value*	*% of Total*	*Allocated Cost*	*Cost per lb.*
Lobster Tails				
Lobster Flakes				
Total				

(1) Cost of goods sold

Parts	*Quantity*	*Cost*	*Total*
Lobster Tails			
Lobster Flakes			
Total cost of goods sold			

(2) Cost of ending inventory

Parts	*Quantity*	*Cost*	*Total*
Lobster Tails			
Lobster Flakes			
Total inventory cost			

Chapter 21 Problem 21-1A or 21-1B *Name* ____________________

Part 1

Average occupancy cost = ________________

These costs are assigned to departments as follows:

Department	*Square Footage*	*Rate*	*Total*
__________ Dept.			
__________ Dept. (for 1A)			

Part 2

VALUE-BASED costs are allocated to departments in two steps:

(i) Compute market value for each floor space.

Floor	*Square Footage*	*Value per Sq. Ft.*	*Total*
__________ floor			
__________ floor			
__________ floor (for 1B)			
Total market value			

(ii) Allocate $_________ to each floor based on its percent of market value.

	Market Value	*% of Total*	*Allocated Cost*	*Cost per Sq. Ft.*
__________ floor				
__________ floor				
__________ floor (for 1B)				
Totals				

USAGE-BASED costs allocation rate = _____________

(i) Compute total allocation rates for the floors.

Floor	*Value*	*Usage*	*Total*
__________ floor			
__________ floor			
__________ floor (for 1B)			

 Name ____________________

Part 2 (Continued)

(ii) Rates are applied to allocate occupancy costs to department(s).

Department	*Square Footage*	*Rate*	*Total*
__________ Depart.			
__________ Depart. (for 1A)			

Part 3

Preferred Allocation Method

Chapter 21 Problem 21-2A or 21-2B *Name* ______________________

Part 1

Cost Center	Cost	Driver	Cost per Driver
Professional salaries			
Patient services and supplies*			
Building cost			

*Patient Services and Supplies will be Customer Supplies for P21-2B

Part 2

______________Service

Activity	Cost Driver	Cost per Driver Unit	Allocated Cost
Professional salaries	Hours		
Patient services and supplies*			
Building cost	Sq. ft.		
Total			
Average cost per patient (or customer for 21-2B)			

*Patient Services and Supplies will be Customer Supplies for P21-2B

______________Service

Activity	Cost Driver	Cost per Driver Unit	Allocated Cost
Professional salaries	Hours		
Patient services and supplies*			
Building cost	Sq. ft.		
Total			
Average cost per patient (or customer for 21-2B)			

*Patient Services and Supplies will be Customer Supplies for P21-2B

 Name ____________________

Part 3

Analysis of Alternative Cost Allocation

Problem 21-3A or 21-3B

Forecasted Departmental Income Statements
For Year Ended December 31, 2010

				Combined

Chapter 21 Problem 21-3A or 21-3B (Continued) *Name* ______________________

Supporting computations:

 Name ____________________

Part 1

(a)

RESPONSIBILITY ACCOUNTING PERFORMANCE REPORT Manager, ____________ Department For the ____________			
	Budgeted Amount	Actual Amount	Over (Under) Budget
CONTROLLABLE COSTS			
Raw materials			
Employee wages			
Supplies used			
Depreciation—Equipment			
Totals			

(b)

RESPONSIBILITY ACCOUNTING PERFORMANCE REPORT Manager, ____________ Department For the ____________			
	Budgeted Amount	Actual Amount	Over (Under) Budget
CONTROLLABLE COSTS			
Raw materials			
Employee wages			
Supplies used			
Depreciation—Equipment			
Totals			

(c)

RESPONSIBILITY ACCOUNTING PERFORMANCE REPORT Manager, ____________ Plant For the ____________			
	Budgeted Amount	Actual Amount	Over (Under) Budget
CONTROLLABLE COSTS			
Dept. manager salaries			
Utilities			
Building rent			
Other office salaries			
Other office costs			
____________ department			
____________ department			
Totals			

Chapter 21 Problem 21-4A or 21-4B (Continued) *Name* ____________

Part 2

Comparative Analysis of Manager Performance

Problem 21-5A[B] or 21-5B[B]

Part 1

Allocation of joint costs on the basis of sales value

Cost Activity: ____________

Grade	*Sales Value*	*Percent of Total*	*Allocated Cost*
No. 1			
No. 2			
No. 3			
Total			

Cost Activity: ____________

Grade	*Sales Value*	*Percent of Total*	*Allocated Cost*
No. 1			
No. 2			
No. 3			
Total			

Cost Activity: ____________

Grade	*Sales Value*	*Percent of Total*	*Allocated Cost*
No. 1			
No. 2			
No. 3			
Total			

Chapter 21 Problem 21-5A[B] or 21-5B[B] *Name* ____________________
(Continued)

Part 2

Income Statement For Year Ended December 31, 2009				
	No. 1	**No. 2**	**No. 3**	**Combined**

Part 3

Analysis of Joint Cost

Chapter 21 **Reporting in Action** ***Name*** ____________________
BTN 21-1

Part 1

($ millions)	Fiscal 2007	Fiscal 2006	Fiscal 2005
Total Revenue			
Home Office			
Entertainment Software			
Consumer Electronics			
Appliances			

Part 2

____
____
____
____
____
____
____

Part 3

Fast Forward

Total Revenue		
Home Office		
Entertainment Software		
Consumer Electronics		
Appliances		

Chapter 21 Comparative Analysis *Name* ____________________
BTN 21-2

Part 1

Part 2

Importance of Comparable Responsibility Accounting Reports

Chapter 21 Ethics Challenge—BTN 21-3 *Name* ______________________

(1) Identification of any Ethical Concern(s)

(2) Action Plan to Eliminate or Reduce any Ethical Concern(s)

(3) Identification of Senior Security's Ethical Responsibility(ies)

Chapter 22 Problem 22-2A or 22-2B *Name* ____________________

Part 1

(a) Break-even point in unit sales:

(b) Break-even point in dollar sales:

Part 2

Graph for P22-2A

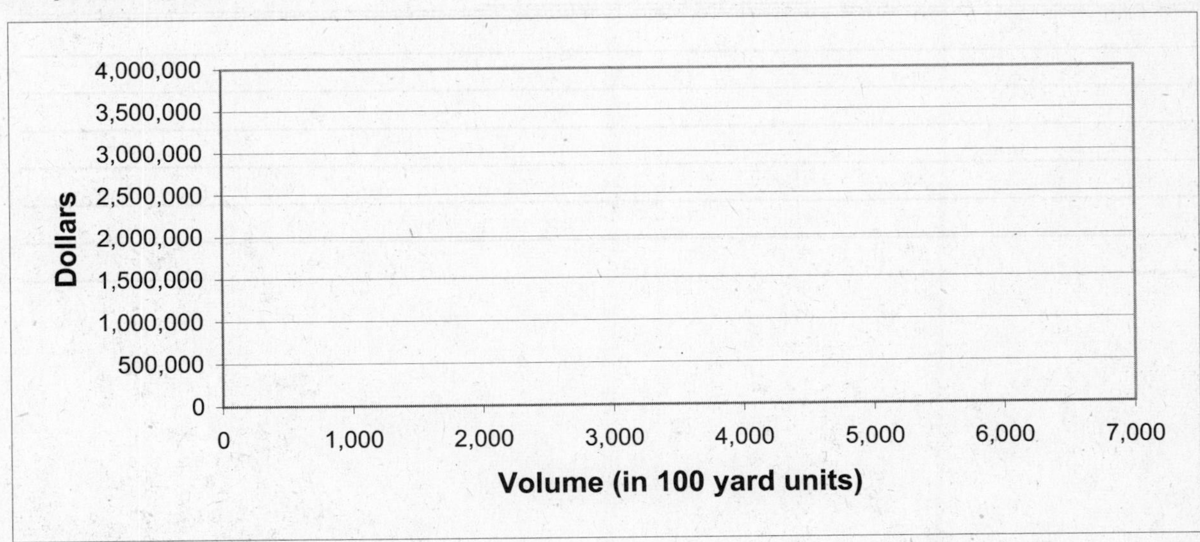

Chapter 22 Problem 22-2A or 22-2B *Name* ____________________

Part 2 (Continued)

Graph for P22-2B

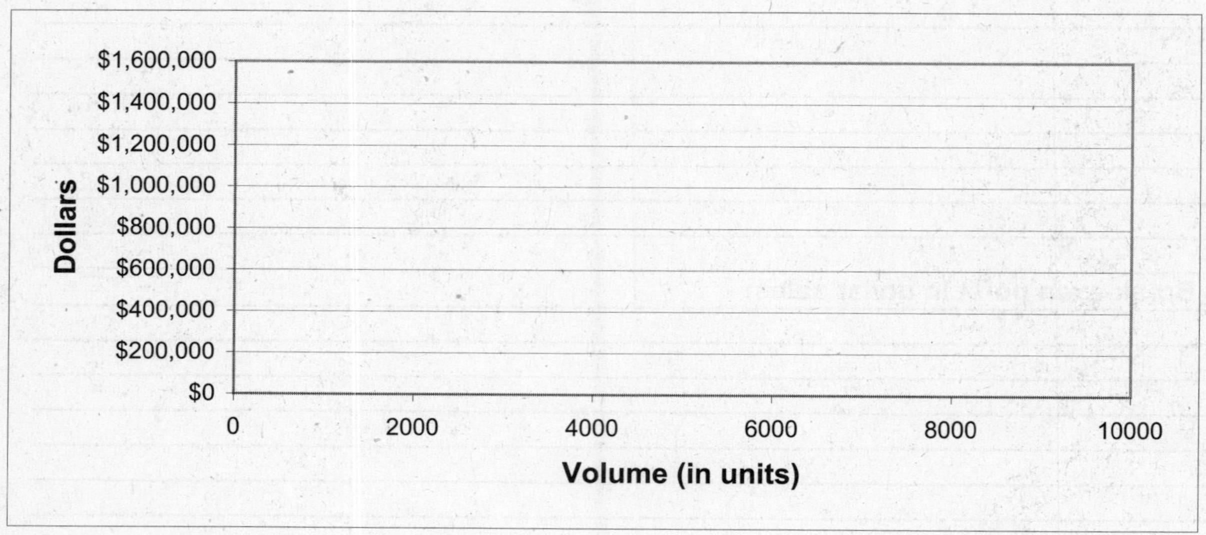

Part 3

Contribution Margin Income Statement (at Break-Even)

Product__________________

Chapter 22 Problem 22-3A or 22-3B *Name* ______________________________

Parts 1 and 2

Graph for P22-3A

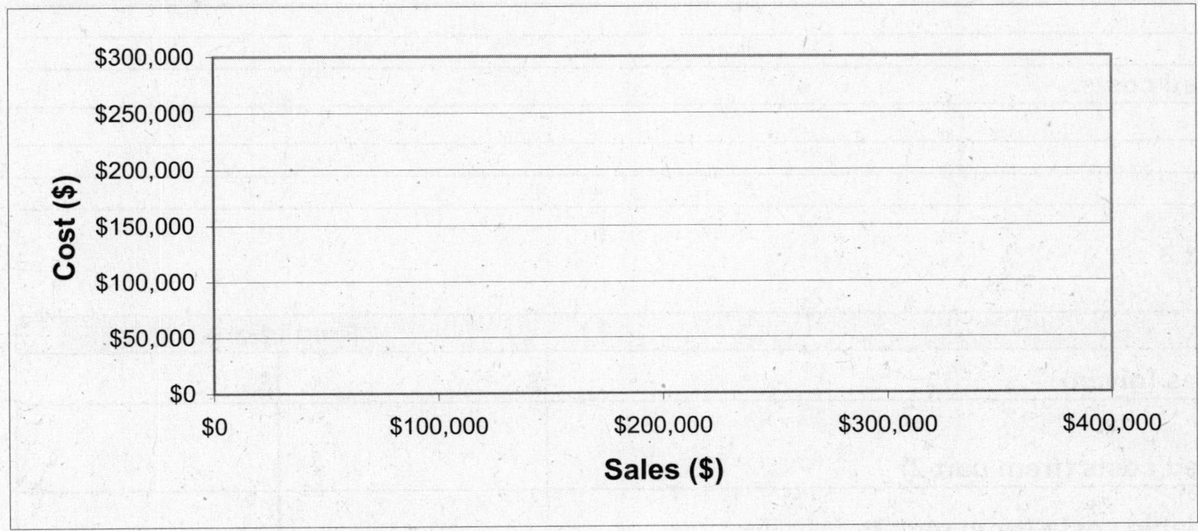

Graph for P22-3B

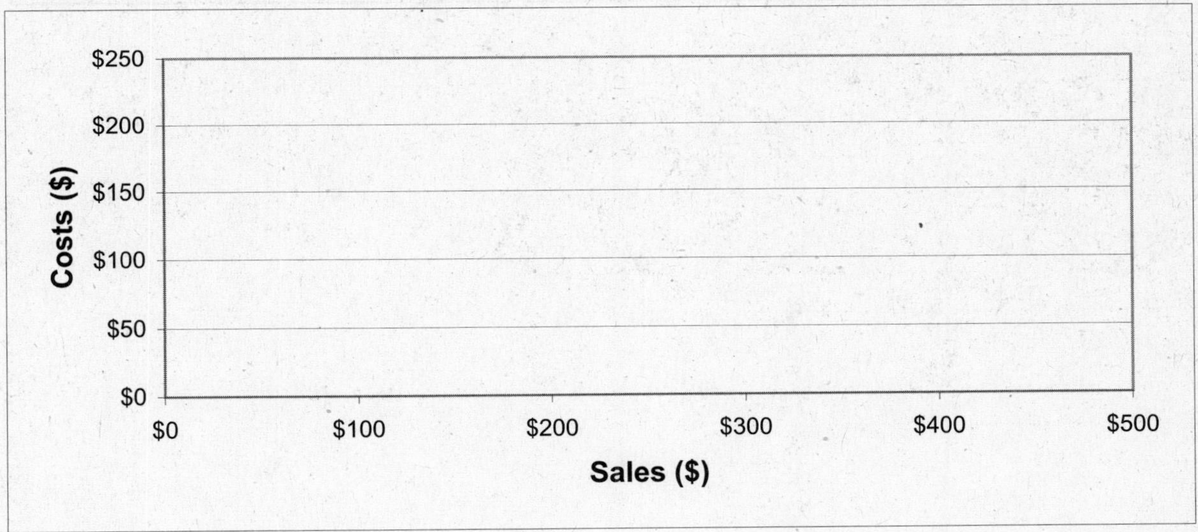

Chapter 22 Problem 22-3A or 22-3B *Name* ____________________

Part 2 (Continued)

Variable costs per sales dollar:

Fixed costs:

Part 3

	Predictions	
Sales (given)	$	$
Fixed costs (from part 2)		
Variable costs (from part 2)		
Total costs		

Chapter 22 Problem 22-4A or 22-4B *Name* ______________________

Part 1

Year 2009 break-even in dollar sales:

Part 2

Year 2010 break-even in dollar sales:

Part 3

Forecasted Contribution Margin Income Statement
For Year Ended December 31, 2010

Chapter 22 Problem 22-4A or 22-4B (Continued) *Name* ____________

Part 4

Required sales in dollars:

Required sales in units:

Part 5

Forecasted Contribution Margin Income Statement
For Year Ended December 31, 2010

Chapter 22 Problem 22-5A or 22-5B *Name* ____________________

Part 1

Break-even in dollar sales:

Product_____:

Product_____:

Part 2

________________COMPANY Forecasted Contribution Margin Income Statement	*Product* ______	*Product* ______

Chapter 22 Problem 22-5A or 22-5B (Continued) *Name* ______________________

Part 3

____________________COMPANY Forecasted Contribution Margin Income Statement	*Product* ______	*Product* ______

Part 4

Identification and Explanation of Greatest Change in Product Income (Loss)

Part 5

Description of Potential Factors Yielding Different Product Cost Structures

Chapter 22 Problem 22-6A or 22-6B ***Name*** ____________________

Part 1

(a) Plan 1's (Existing Strategy for 22-6B) break-even in dollar sales:

(b) Plan 2's (New Strategy for 22-6B) break-even in dollar sales:

Part 2

____________ COMPANY Forecasted Contribution Margin Income Statement	*Plan 1 (Existing Strategy)*	*Plan 2 (New Strategy)*

Chapter 22 Problem 22-7A or 22-7B *Name* ____________________

Part 1

Break-even analysis assuming use of <u>same</u> materials:

Step 1: Compute break-even in composite units

Step 2: Compute break-even in individual product units sales

Step 3: Compute break-even in individual product dollar sales

Chapter 22 Problem 22-7A or 22-7B *Name* ____________________
(Continued)

Part 2

Break-even analysis assuming use of new materials:

Step 1: Compute break-even in composite units

Step 2: Compute break-even in individual product unit sales

Step 3: Compute break-even in individual product dollar sales

Part 3

Management Insight for Long-Term Planning

Chapter 22 Serial Problem, SP 22 Success Systems

Name ____________________

1. Selling price per composite unit

2. Variable costs per composite unit

3. Break-even point in composite units

4. Unit sales of desk units and chairs at break-even point

Chapter 22 Reporting in Action *Name* ____________________

BTN 22-1

(1) Identification of Costs

(2)

(3)

Chapter 22 **Comparative Analysis** *Name* ______________________________
BTN 22-2

(1)

	Best Buy	Circuit City

(2)

MEMORANDUM

To: "Mechanics" and "Owners"
From:
Re: Analysis of labor costs from survey data
Date:

REPORT ON REVENUE & COST ASSUMPTIONS

Revenue Assumptions:

Cost Assumptions:

Chapter 22 Taking It to the Net *Name* ____________________
BTN 22-5

Information and Resources Available for Entrepreneurs

Name ________________________

Questions for Completion of CVP Analysis

For School Administration:

For Business Owner:

Chapter 22 Entrepreneurial Decision BTN 22-7 *Name* ______________________

(1) Types of information needed:

(2) Useful tool(s) for analysis:

Chapter 22 Hitting the Road—BTN 22-8 *Name* ____________________

(1) Potential Framework for Analysis

Product	Estimated Selling Price per unit	Estimated CM ratio	Estimated CM per unit	Estimated Sales Mix	Estimated CM for each component in composite unit
Total contribution margin (CM) per composite unit..................					

Estimated fixed costs per year: **$________**

Break-even point in composite unit sales: $________/$CM per composite unit =

Unit sales of individual products per year required to break-even:

Chapter 22 Hitting the Road—BTN 22-8 *Name* ______________________
(Continued)

(2) Report on Results of Analysis from Part 1 (including break-even analysis)

Name ______________________

(1) Single or Multi-Product CVP Analysis

(2) Products Impact for CVP Analysis

(3) Store Impact for CVP Analysis

Chapter 23 Quick Study 23-1 *Name* ______________

Necessary Component of Master Budget:

Quick Study 23-2

(1)

(2)

(3)

Quick Study 23-3

________ Company
Computation of Budgeted Cost of Purchases
For Month Ended July 31

Quick Study 23-4

(1) Comparative Analysis of Budgeting Approaches:

(2) Examples of Bottom-Up Budgeting:

Chapter 23 Quick Study 23-5 *Name* ______________________

Computation of Budgeted Accounts Receivable Balance:

Quick Study 23-6

_______ Company
Cash Budget
For Month Ended March 31

Quick Study 23-7

(1) Description of Activity-Based Budgeting and Explanation of Budget Preparation

(2) Explanation of Differences between Activity-Based and Traditional Budgeting

Chapter 23 Quick Study 23-8[A] *Name* ______________________

_________ Company
Production Budget
For Month Ended November 30

Quick Study 23-9[A]

_________ Company
Factory Overhead Budget
For Month Ended November 30

Quick Study 23-10

_________ Company
Sales Budget
For Month Ended June 30

Chapter 23 Quick Study 23-11 *Name* ____________________

__________ Company
Selling Expense Budget
For Month Ended June 30

Quick Study 23-12

__________ Company
Budgeted Cash Receipts
For Month Ended June 30

Quick Study 23-13

Chapter 23 Exercise 23-1 *Name* ____________________

(1)

________ Company			
Merchandise Purchases Budget			
For July, August and September			
	July	August	September

Supporting calculations:

(2) Ratio of Ending Inventory to Next Month's Sales for Each Budget Period

(3) Units Budgeted for Sale in October

Chapter 23 Exercise 23-2 *Name* ____________________

_____ Company			
Cash Budget			
For January, February, and March			
	January	February	March

Chapter 23 Exercise 23-3 *Name* ______________________

______ Company
Cash Budget
For Month Ended July 31

Supporting calculations:

Chapter 23 Exercise 23-4 *Name* ______________________

_______ Company
Budgeted Income Statement
For Month Ended July 31

Supporting calculations:

Name ____________________

_______ Company
Budgeted Balance Sheet
July 31

Chapter 23 Exercise 23-5 *Name* ____________________

Merchandise purchases budgets

	August	September	October

Cash payments for purchases (on accounts) in October

	Dollars	Percent	Paid

Chapter 23 Exercise 23-6 *Name* ____________________

(1) Budgeted merchandise purchases:

	June	July	August

(2) Budgeted cost of goods sold:

	June	July	August

Exercise 23-7

(1) Budgeted merchandise purchases:

	July	August	September	October

Supporting calculations:

Chapter 23 Exercise 23-7 (Continued) *Name* ____________________

(2) Budgeted payments on accounts payable in September:

	Purchases	Percent Paid	Dollars Paid

Budgeted payments on accounts payable in October:

	Purchases	Percent Paid	Dollars Paid

(3) Budgeted balance of accounts payable at the end of September:

	Purchases	Percent Unpaid	Dollars Unpaid

Budgeted balance of accounts payable at the end of October:

	Purchases	Percent Unpaid	Dollars Unpaid

Chapter 23 Exercise 23-8[A] *Name* ______________________

______ Company		
Production Budget		
Second and Third Quarters		
	Second Quarter	Third Quarter

Exercise 23-9[A]

______ Company
Direct Materials Budget
Second Quarter

Chapter 23 Exercise 23-10[A] *Name* ____________

______ Company
Direct Labor Budget
Second Quarter

Chapter 23 Problem 23-1A or 23-1B *Name* ____________________

Part 1

Merchandise Purchases Budgets (in Units) For Months of ____________	Month of __________	Month of __________	Month of __________
Product: ____________			
Product: ____________			
Product: ____________			

Chapter 23 Problem 23-1A or 23-1B (Continued) *Name* ____________

Part 2

Identification and Explanation of Factors Yielding Fewer Purchases

Chapter 23 Problem 23-2A or 23-2B *Name* ______________________

______________________ Cash Budgets For Months of ______________________	Month of __________	Month of __________	Month of __________

Supporting computations:

Chapter 23 Problem 23-3A or 23-3B *Name* ______________________

Part 1

Cash collections of credit sales (accounts receivable)

From sales in month of:	*Total*	*% Collected*	*Month of* ________	*Month of* ________

Part 2

Budgeted ending inventories (in units)

	Month of ________	Month of ________	Month of ________	Month of ________

Chapter 23 Problem 23-3A or 23-3B (Continued) *Name* ____________________

Part 3

______________Company Merchandise Purchases Budgets For Months of ______________	Month of ________	Month of ________	Month of ________

Part 4

Cash payments on product purchases

From purchases in month of:	*Total*	*% Paid*	Month of ________	Month of ________

Chapter 23 Problem 23-3A or 23-3B *Name* ____________
(Continued)

Part 5

____________ Cash Budgets For Months of____________	Month of ________	Month of ________

Part 6

Benefits to Management from Accurate Cash Budget Numbers

Chapter 23 Problem 23-4A or 23-4B *Name* ______________________________

Part 1

Budgeted Income Statements For Months of ____________________	Month of __________	Month of __________	Month of __________

Part 2

Recommendation on Implementation of Proposed Changes

Chapter 23 Problem 23-5A or 23-5B *Name* ____________________

Part 1

	Sales Budgets		
Month	Budgeted Units	Budgeted Unit Price	Budgeted Total Dollars

Part 2

	Merchandise Purchases Budgets			
	Month of ________	Month of ________	Month of ________	Total

Part 3

	Selling Expense Budgets			
	Month of ________	Month of ________	Month of ________	Total

Chapter 23 **Problem 23-5A or 23-5B** *Name* ______________________
(Continued)

Part 4

General and Administrative Expense Budgets				
	Month of	Month of	Month of	Total

Supporting calculations:

Part 5

Capital Expenditures Budgets			
	Month of	Month of	Month of

Chapter 23 Problem 23-5A or 23-5B (Continued) *Name* ____________________

Part 6

Cash Budgets			
	Month of	Month of	Month of

Part 7

______________________ Budgeted Income Statement For Three Months Ended______________

Chapter 23 Problem 23-5A or 23-5B *Name* ____________________
(Continued)

Part 8

Budgeted Balance Sheet

Chapter 23 Problem 23-6A[A] or 23-6B[A] *Name* ____________________

Part 1

____________________ Production Budget (in units) ____________Quarter

Part 2

____________________ Direct Materials Budget (in lbs., except where noted) ____________Quarter

Chapter 23 Serial Problem, SP 23 *Name* ____________________

Part 1 Success Systems

SUCCESS SYSTEMS Budgeted Income Statements For Months of April, May and June	April	May	June

Part 2

Recommendation on Implementation of Proposed Changes

Chapter 23 Reporting in Action BTN 23-1 *Name* ________________

Part 1

(a)

(b)

Part 2

(a)

(b)

Part 3

Fast Forward:

Chapter 23 Comparative Analysis BTN 23-2 *Name* ____________________

Part 1

Computation of inventory reduction under new distribution system	
Amount of ending inventory required at the 40% rule....	$
Amount of ending inventory required at the 10% rule....	________
Difference (inventory reduction)................................	$

Implication of Distribution System for Inventory Level:

Part 2

Explanation and Justification of JIT Inventory System

 Name ____________________

Report on "Use It or Lose It" Budgeting

 Name ______________________

MEMORANDUM

TO: ______________________
FROM: ______________________
DATE: ______________________
SUBJECT: Concerns with sales staff input for the sales budget

Chapter 23 Taking It to the Net
BTN 23-5

Name ______________________

Part 1

Benefits of Using e-Budgets

Part 2

Concerns with the Concept and Application of e-Budgets

Chapter 23 Teamwork in Action Name ____________________
BTN 23-6

College Costs Budget

Chapter 23 *Entrepreneurial Decision* Name ____________________
BTN 23-7

Part 1

Business Plan Elements

Part 2

Benefits of Budgeting

Hitting the Road—BTN 23-8

Part 1

Identification of External Factors When Setting Budgets

Part 2

Identification of Potential Factors Explaining Price Differences

Chapter 23 Global Decision—BTN 23-9 *Name* ______________________

Part 1

Importance of Administrative Expense Budget in Its Master Budgeting Process

Part 2

Identification of Administrative Expenses

Part 3

Identification and Explanation of Person Responsible for Administrative Expense Budge

Chapter 24 Quick Study 24-1 *Name* ______________________________

_______ Company Flexible Budget Performance Report For Month Ended May 31	*Flexible Budget*	*Actual Results*	*Variances*

Quick Study 24-2

Actual Total Direct Labor Cost

Quick Study 24-3

Actual Total Direct Materials Cost

Chapter 24 Quick Study 24-4 *Name* ____________

Actual Pounds of Materials Used

Quick Study 24-5

(1) Description of Management by Exception Concept

(2) Explanation of How Standard Costs Aid Management by Exception

Quick Study 24-6

Actual Total Overhead Cost

Chapter 24 Quick Study 24-7 *Name* ______________________

GENERAL JOURNAL

Date		Account Titles and Explanation	PR	Debit	Credit

Quick Study 24-8

Sales	Actual	Flexible Budget	Fixed Budget
Units			
Price per unit			
Total dollars			

Chapter 24 Quick Study 24-9 *Name* ______________________

Total Variable Overhead Cost Variance:

Quick Study 24-10

Variable Overhead Spending and Efficiency Variances:

Chapter 24 Exercise 24-11 *Name* ______________________

Preliminary Computations of Total Overhead Variances:

Part 1

Computation of Overhead Volume Variance

Chapter 24 Exercise 24-11 (Continued) *Name* ____________________

Part 2

Computation of Overhead Controllable Variance

Chapter 24 Problem 24-5A or 24-5B *Name* ____________________

Part 3 (Continued)

(b) Fixed Overhead Spending and Volume Variances

(c) Total Overhead Controllable Variance

Chapter 24 Problem 24-5A or 24-5B (Continued) *Name* ____________________

Part 4

____________Company Overhead Variance Report For Month Ended __________			
Volume Variance			
Controllable Variance	**Flexible Budget**	**Actual Results**	**Variances**

Chapter 24 Problem 24-6A or 24-6B *Name* ____________

Part 1

GENERAL JOURNAL

Date		Account Titles and Explanation	PR	Debit	Credit

Part 2

Identification of Areas and Actions when Applying Management by Exception

Chapter 24 Serial Problem, SP 24 *Name* ______________________
Success Systems

SUCCESS SYSTEMS Flexible Budget Performance Report For Quarter Ended June 30	Flexible Budget	Actual Results	Variances
Desk Sales...........................			
Chair Sales...........................			
Variable expenses..................			
Contribution margin...............			
Fixed expenses.....................			
Income from operations.........			

Supporting computations:

Chapter 24 Reporting in Action *Name* ____________
BTN 24-1

Part 1

Identification of Foreign Currency Translation (FTC) Information

Part 2

Fiscal Year	F.C.T. Adjustment
February 26, 2005	
February 25, 2006	
March 3, 2007	

Part 3

Fast Forward

(a)

(b)

Chapter 24 **Comparative Analysis** *Name* ____________________

BTN 24-2

Part 1

	2 Years Prior	*1 Year Prior*	*Current year*	*1 Year Ahead*	*2 Years Ahead*
Best Buy					
Circuit City					
RadioShack					

Part 2

Explanation of Sales Predictions

____

____

____

____

Ethics Challenge—BTN 24-3

Specialty	*Information Input and Explanation*

 Name ____________________

MEMORANDUM

TO: ____________________

FROM: ____________________

DATE: ____________________

SUBJECT: Explanation and Implications of Favorable and Unfavorable Variances

Chapter 24 Taking It to the Net Name ______________________
BTN 24-5

Part 1

Explanation of Benchmarking

Part 2

Relation between Standard Costing and Benchmarking

Chapter 24 Teamwork in Action
BTN 24-6

Name ______________________________

Identification and Description of Time Elements Used for Competitive Advantage

MEMORANDUM

TO: ____________
FROM: ____________
DATE: ____________
SUBJECT: Explanation of Standard Costing and Variance Comments

Chapter 24 Hitting the Road—BTN 24-8 *Name* ____________________

(1) Observe and Record the Number and Application of Raw Materials to Pizza

(2) Identify and Record Differences Across the Two Businesses in Part 1

(3) Estimate and Explain which Business is More Profitable

Global Decision—BTN 24-9

(1)

(in pounds million)	One Year Prior	Current Year	One Year Ahead	Two Years Ahead
Sales				

(2) Estimation and Explanation of Sales Predictions

Chapter 25 Quick Study 25-1 *Name* ____________________

(1) Identification of Preferred Investment

(2) Explanation of Why Investment B might be Preferred to Investment A

Quick Study 25-2

Payback Period

Quick Study 25-3

Net Present Value

Chapter 25 Quick Study 25-4 *Name* ____________________

Accounting Rate of Return

Quick Study 25-5

Most Profitable Sales Mix

Quick Study 25-6

Incremental Cost Analysis

Chapter 25 Quick Study 25-7 *Name* ____________________

Year	*Cash Flows*	*Present Value of 1 at ___%*	*Present value of cash flows*	*Cumulative present value of cash flows*
0				
1				
2				
3				
4				
5				

Break-Even Time

Quick Study 25-8

Profitability Index:

Project A:

Project B:

Interpretation:

Chapter 25 Exercise 25-14 *Name* ______________

(1) Sales Mix Computations and Recommendation:

(2) Contribution Margin from the Recommended Sales Mix:

Chapter 25 Exercise 25-15 *Name* ____________________

(1) Recovery time for:

Payback Period

Break-even Time

(2) Advantages of Break-Even time

(3) Conditions Yielding Similar Results for Payback Period and Break-Even Time

Chapter 25 Problem 25-1A or 25-1B *Name* ______

Part 1

Annual Straight-Line Depreciation

Part 2

	Net Income	Net Cash Flow
Expected annual sales of new product		
Expected annual costs of new product		
Direct materials		
Direct labor		
Overhead excluding depr. on new asset		
Depreciation on new asset		
Selling and administrative expenses		
Income before taxes		
Income taxes		
Net income		
Net cash flow		

Computations:

Part 3

Payback period

Part 4

Accounting rate of return

Part 5

	Net Cash Flows	Present Value of 1 at ____%	Present Value of Net Cash Flows
Year 1			
Year 2			
Year 3			
Year 4*			
Totals			
Amount invested			
Net present value			

*Includes the salvage value impact.

Chapter 25 Problem 25-2A or 25-2B *Name* ____________________

Part 1

Project ________ Net Cash Flow

Project ________ Net Cash Flow

Part 2

Project ________ Payback Period

Project ________ Payback Period

Chapter 25 Problem 25-2A or 25-2B (Continued) *Name* ____________________

Part 3

Project ________ Accounting Rate of Return

Project ________ Accounting Rate of Return

Part 4

Project _____ Present Value of Net Cash Flows

	Net Cash Flows	Present Value of Annuity of 1 at ____%	Present Value of Net Cash Flows

Project _____ Present Value of Net Cash Flows

	Net Cash Flows	Present Value of Annuity of 1 at ____%	Present Value of Net Cash Flows

Part 5

Management Recommendation:

Problem 25-3A or 25-3B

Part 1

Results Using Straight-Line

	(a) *Income Before Deprec.*	(b) *Straight-Line Deprec.*	(c) *Taxable Income (a) – (b)*	(d) *__% Income Taxes*	(e) *Net Cash Flows (a) – (d)*
Year 1					
Year 2					
Year 3					
Year 4					
Year 5					
Year 6					

Part 2

Results Using MACRS

	(a) *Income Before Deprec.*	(b) *MACRS Deprec.*	(c) *Taxable Income (a) – (b)*	(d) *__% Income Taxes*	(e) *Net Cash Flows (a) – (d)*
Year 1					
Year 2					
Year 3					
Year 4					
Year 5					
Year 6					

Chapter 25 Problem 25-3A or 25-3B (Continued) *Name* ______________________

Part 3

NPV Using Straight-Line

	Net Cash Flows	*Present Value of 1 at ___%*	*Present Value of Net Cash Flows*
Year 1			
Year 2			
Year 3			
Year 4			
Year 5			
Year 6			
Totals			
Amount invested			
Net present value			

Part 4

NPV Using MACRS

	Net Cash Flows	*Present Value of 1 at ___%*	*Present Value of Net Cash Flows*
Year 1			
Year 2			
Year 3			
Year 4			
Year 5			
Year 6			
Totals			
Amount invested			
Net present value			

Part 5

Explanation of MACRS Implications for NPV

Chapter 25 Problem 25-4A or 25-4B *Name* ____________________

____________ Company Comparative Income Statements	(1) *Normal* *Volume*	(2) *New* *Business*	(3) *Combined*
Sales			
Costs and expenses			
Direct materials			
Direct labor			
Overhead			
Selling expenses			
Administrative expenses			
Total costs & expenses			
Operating income			

Supporting calculations:

Chapter 25 Problem 25-5A or 25-5B *Name* ______________________

Part 1

	Product____	*Product ____*
Selling price per unit		
Variable costs per unit		
Contribution margin per unit		
Machine hours to produce 1 unit		
Contribution per machine hour (or Contribution/[Hours per unit])		

Part 2

Sales Mix Recommendation:

Contribution Margin at Recommended Sales Mix:

 Name ______________________

Part 3

Sales Mix Recommendation with Second Shift:

Contribution Margin at Recommended Sales Mix:

Management Decision:

Chapter 25 Problem 25-5A or 25-5B (Continued) *Name* ______________________

Part 4

Sales Mix Recommendation:

Contribution Margin at Recommended Sales Mix:

Management Decision:

Chapter 25 Problem 25-6A or 25-6B *Name* ____________________

Part 1

____________________ *Company* *Analysis of Expenses under Elimination of Department*__________			
	Total Expenses	*Eliminated Expenses*	*Continuing Expenses*
Cost of goods sold			
Direct expenses			
Advertising expense			
Store supplies used			
Depreciation of store equipment			
Allocated expenses			
Sales salaries			
Rent expense			
Bad debts expense			
Office salary expense			
Insurance expense			
Miscellaneous office expense			
Total expenses			

Supporting Computations:

 Name ____________________

Part 2

____________________Company
Forecasted Annual Income Statement
Under Plan to Eliminate Department________

Part 3

____________________Company
Reconciliation of Combined Income with Forecasted Income

Combined net income	$
Forecasted net income	$

Analysis and Recommendation:

Chapter 25 Serial Problem, SP 25 *Name* ____________________

Success Systems

COMPUTING NET CASH FLOWS FROM NET INCOME

	Net income	Cash flows
Sales	$ 375,000	$
Materials, labor, & overhead	(200,000)	
Depreciation	(50,000)	
Selling and administrative	(37,500)	
Pretax income	87,500	
Income taxes (30%)	(26,250)	
Net income	$ 61,250	
Net cash flows		$

1. Payback period

2. Accounting rate of return

Chapter 25 Reporting in Action
BTN 25-1

Name ____________________

Part 1

Part 2

Fast Forward

Chapter 25 Comparative Analysis *Name* ____________________
BTN 25-2

Part 1

Identification and Cost of Advertising Space

Part 2

Estimation of Additional Product Sales to Cover Advertising Cost

Part 3

MEMORANDUM

TO:
FROM:
SUBJECT: Effective Advertising for Product Mix Decisions
DATE:

Chapter 25 Ethics Challenge Name ______________________
BTN 25-3

Part 1

Present Value Computation

Part 2

Estimation Errors and Investment Project Evaluation

MEMORANDUM

TO:
FROM:
DATE:
SUBJECT: Evaluating Capital Investment Opportunities

Chapter 25 **Taking it to the Net** *Name* ____________________

BTN 25-5

Part 1

Part 2

Chapter 25 **Teamwork in Action** *Name* ____________
BTN 25-6

Project Identification

Qualitative Factors in Management's Decision

Chapter 25 Entrepreneurial Decision *Name* ____________________
BTN 25-7

Part 1

Preliminary Computations	Deluxe	Premium
Selling price per unit..		
Variable costs per unit..		
Contribution margin per unit..............................		
Lathe/processing hours to produce 1 unit............		
Contribution per lathe/Processing hours (Contribution margin per unit/[Hours per unit])..		

Sales Mix Recommendation

Contribution Margin at Recommended Sales Mix

Part 2

Sales Mix Recommendation with Sales Constraint

Contribution Margin with Sales Constraint

	Units	Contr./Unit	Total
From Deluxe bats..........................			
From Premium bats........................			
Total contribution margin..			